W9-AUR-382

GO!

Technology in Action

Sixth Edition

Alan Evans • Kendall Martin
Mary Anne Poatsy

Prentice Hall
Upper Saddle River New Jersey
Columbus Ohio

Library of Congress Cataloging-in-Publication Data

Evans, Alan.
  Technology in action / Alan Evans, Kendall Martin, Mary Anne Poatsy. -- Complete, 6th ed.
    p. cm.
  At head of title: Go!
  ISBN-13: 978-0-13-504624-1
  ISBN-10: 0-13-504624-6
  1. Microcomputers. I. Martin, Kendall. II. Poatsy, Mary Anne. III. Title. IV. Title: Go!
  QA76.5.E9195 2009
  004.16--dc22

                                                2008046493

VP/Editorial Director: Natalie E. Anderson
Editor in Chief: Michael Payne
Associate VP/Executive Acquisitions Editor, Print:
  Stephanie Wall
Director, Product Development: Pamela Hersperger
Product Development Manager: Eileen Bien Calabro
Editorial Project Manager: Laura Burgess
Development Editor: Jennifer Lynn
AVP/Director of Online Programs: Richard Keaveny
AVP/Director of Product Development: Lisa Strite
Editorial Media Project Manager: Alana Coles
Production Media Project Manager: Lorena Cerisano
  and John Cassar
Marketing Manager: Tori Olson Alves
Marketing Assistant: Angela Frey
Senior Managing Editor: Cynthia Zonneveld
Associate Managing Editor: Camille Trentacoste
Production Project Manager: Mike Lackey
Manager of Rights & Permissions: Charles Morris

Senior Operations Specialist: Nick Sklitsis
Operations Specialist: Natacha Moore
Senior Art Director: Jonathan Boylan
Art Director: Anthony Gemmellaro
AV Project Manager: Rhonda Aversa
Cover Design: Anthony Gemmellaro
Cover Photo: Shutterstock
Director, Image Resource Center: Melinda Patelli
Manager, Rights and Permissions: Zina Arabia
Manager, Visual Research: Beth Brenzel
Manager, Cover Visual Research and Permissions:
  Karen Sanatar
Image Permission Coordinator: Richard Rodrigues and
  Cynthia Vincenti
Photo Researcher: David Tietz
Composition: Macmillan Publishing Solutions
Printer/Binder: Quebecor World Color/Versailles
Cover Printer: Lehigh-Phoenix Color/Hagerstown
Typeface: 10/12 Palatino

Credits and acknowledgments borrowed from other sources and reproduced, with permission, in this textbook appear on appropriate page within text or in the illustration credits section.

Microsoft, Windows, Word, PowerPoint, Outlook, FrontPage, Visual Basic, MSN, The Microsoft Network, and/or other Microsoft products referenced herein are either trademarks or registered trademarks of the Microsoft Corporation in the U.S.A. and other countries. Screen shots and icons reprinted with permission from the Microsoft Corporation. This book is not sponsored or endorsed by or affiliated with the Microsoft Corporation.

Copyright © 2010, 2009, 2008, 2007, 2006, 2005 by Pearson Education, Inc., Upper Saddle River, New Jersey, 07458.
Pearson Prentice Hall. All rights reserved. Printed in the United States of America. This publication is protected by Copyright and permission should be obtained from the publisher prior to any prohibited reproduction, storage in a retrieval system, or transmission in any form or by any means, electronic, mechanical, photocopying, recording, or likewise. For information regarding permission(s), write to: Rights and Permissions Department.

Pearson Prentice Hall™ is a trademark of Pearson Education, Inc.
Pearson® is a registered trademark of Pearson plc
Prentice Hall® is a registered trademark of Pearson Education, Inc.

Pearson Education Ltd., London
Pearson Education Singapore, Pte. Ltd.
Pearson Education, Canada, Inc.
Pearson Education–Japan
Pearson Education Australia PTY, Limited

Pearson Education North Asia Ltd., Hong Kong
Pearson Educación de Mexico, S.A. de C.V.
Pearson Education Malaysia, Pte. Ltd.
Pearson Education, Upper Saddle River, New Jersey

Prentice Hall
is an imprint of

www.pearsonhighered.com

10 9 8 7 6 5 4 3 2 1

ISBN 13: 978-0-13-504625-8
ISBN 10: 0-13-504625-4

Contents at a Glance

Contents

CHAPTER 1

CHAPTER 2

CHAPTER 3

Using the Internet:
Making the Most of the Web's Resources

TECHNOLOGY IN FOCUS

CHAPTER 4

Application Software:
Programs That Let You Work and Play

CHAPTER 5

Using System Software: The Operating System, Utility Programs, and File Management

TECHNOLOGY IN FOCUS

Computing Alternatives

CHAPTER 6

Understanding and Assessing Hardware: Evaluating Your System

CHAPTER 7

Networking and Security: Connecting Computers and Keeping Them Safe from Hackers and Viruses

CHAPTER 9

TECHNOLOGY IN FOCUS

CHAPTER 10

CHAPTER 11

Behind the Scenes:
Databases and Information Systems

CHAPTER 12

Dedication

For my wife Patricia, whose patience, understanding, and support continue to make this work possible … especially when I stay up past midnight writing! And to my parents, Jackie and Dean, who taught me the best way to achieve your goals is to constantly strive to improve yourself through education.

Alan Evans

For all the teachers, mentors, and gurus who have popped in and out of my life.

Kendall Martin

For my husband Ted, who unselfishly continues to take on more than his fair share to support me throughout this process; and for my children, Laura, Carolyn, and Teddy, whose encouragement and love have been inspiring.

Mary Anne Poatsy

Alan Evans, MS, CPA

aevans@mc3.edu

Alan is currently a faculty member at Manor College and Montgomery County Community College teaching a variety of computer science and business courses. He holds a B.S. in accounting from Rider University and an M.S. in information systems from Drexel University, and he is a certified public accountant. After a successful career in business, Alan finally realized his true calling was education. He has been teaching at the college level since 2000. Alan enjoys giving presentations at technical conferences and meets regularly with computer science faculty and administrators from other colleges to discuss curriculum development and new methods of engaging students.

Kendall Martin, PhD

kmartin@mc3.edu

Kendall has been teaching since 1988 at a number of institutions, including Villanova University, DeSales University, Arcadia University, Ursinus College, County College of Morris, and Montgomery County Community College, at both the undergraduate and graduate level.

Kendall's education includes a B.S. in electrical engineering from the University of Rochester and an M.S. and a Ph.D. in engineering from the University of Pennsylvania. She has industrial experience in research and development environments (AT&T Bell Laboratories) as well as experience with several start-up technology firms.

At Ursinus College, Kendall developed a successful faculty training program for distance education instructors. She makes conference presentations throughout the year.

Mary Anne Poatsy, MBA, CFP

mpoatsy@mc3.edu

Mary Anne is a senior faculty member at Montgomery County Community College, teaching various computer application and concepts courses in face-to-face and online environments. She enjoys speaking at various professional conferences about innovative classroom strategies. She holds a B.A. in psychology and education from Mount Holyoke College and an MBA in finance from Northwestern University's Kellogg Graduate School of Management.

Mary Anne has more than 12 years of educational experience, ranging from elementary and secondary education to Montgomery County Community College, Muhlenberg College, and Bucks County Community College, as well as training in the professional environment. Before teaching, she was a vice president at Shearson Lehman Hutton in the Municipal Bond Investment Banking Department.

 **Sixth Edition**

Acknowledgments

First, we would like to thank our students. We constantly learn from them while teaching, and they are a continual source of inspiration and new ideas.

We could not have written this book without the loving support of our families. Our spouses and children made sacrifices (mostly in time not spent with us) to permit us to make this dream into a reality.

Although working with the entire team at Prentice Hall has been a truly enjoyable experience, a few individuals deserve special mention. The constant support and encouragement we receive from Stephanie Wall, Associate Vice President/Executive Editor, continually makes this book grow and change. Our heartfelt thanks go to Jennifer Lynn, our developmental editor. Jennifer has had a positive impact on the book, and we have benefited greatly from her creative ideas and efficient time management skills. In addition, Laura Burgess, our project manager, has done a fantastic job of coordinating all details of the project and always keeping the entire project on track. As Media Development Manager, Alana Coles works tirelessly to ensure that the media accompanying the text is produced professionally and is delivered in a timely fashion. Despite the inevitable problems that crop up when producing multimedia, she handles all challenges with a smile. And we can't forget Natalie Anderson, VP/Editorial Director. Natalie has a wonderful sense of humor, which helps smooth over the inevitable bumps in the road encountered on a project of this magnitude. We also would like to extend our appreciation to Mike Lackey, our Production Project Manager, who works tirelessly to ensure that our book is published on time and looks fabulous. The timelines are always short, the art is complex, and there are many people with whom he has to coordinate tasks. This edition involved converting to new tracking systems, and he made sure the transition was made accurately and smoothly.

There are many people whom we do not meet in person at Prentice Hall and elsewhere who make significant contributions by designing the book, illustrating, composing the pages, producing multimedia, and securing permissions. We thank them all. We would also like to thank the supplement authors for this edition: Linda Arnold, Penny Cypert, Lynn Bowen, Tony Nowakowski, Sue Birtwell, Chris Burns, Trina Maurer, Dawn Wood, Susan Fry, and Stacy Gee.

And finally, we would like to thank the reviewers and the many others who contribute their time, ideas, and talents to this project. We appreciate their time and energy, as their comments help us turn out a better product each edition.

Reviewers

Prentice Hall and the authors would like to thank the following people for their help and time in making this book what it is. We couldn't publish this book without their contributions.

Nazih Abdallah	University of Central Florida
Allen Alexander	Delaware Technical & Community College
Joan Alexander	Valencia Community College—West
Beverly Amer	Northern Arizona University
Wilma Andrews	Virginia Commonwealth University
LaDonna Bachand	Santa Rosa Junior College
LeeAnn Bates	
Linda Belton	Springfield Technical Community College
Kim Binstead, Ph.D	University of Hawaii at Manoa
Susan Birtwell	Kwantlen University College
Henry Bojack	Farmingdale State University of New York
Julie Boyles	
Gerald U. Brown Jr.	Tarrant County College
Jeff Burton	Daytona Beach Community College
Kristen Callahan	Mercer County Community College
Judy Cameron	Spokane Community College
Heather Cannon	Blinn College
Judy Cestaro	California State University—San Bernardino
Deborah Chapman	University of Southern Alabama
Gerianne Chapman	Johnson & Wales University
John P. Cicero, Ph.D	Shasta College—Redding, CA
Mark Connell	SUNY Cortland
Gail Cope	Sinclair Community College
Françoise Corey	California State University, Long Beach
Thad Crews	Western Kentucky University
Doug Cross	Clackamas Community College
Becky Cunningham	Arkansas Tech University
John Cusaac	Fullerton College
Ronald G. Deardorff	Shasta Community College
Joseph DeLibero	Arizona State University
K. Kay Delk	Seminole Community College
Charles DeSassure	Tarrant County College
Susan N. Dozier	Tidewater Community College
Annette Duvall	Albuquerque Technical Vocational Institute
Laurie Eakins	East Carolina University

James Fabrey	West Chester University
Catherine L. Ferguson	University of Oklahoma
Judy Firmin	Tarrant County College
Beverly Fite	Amarillo Colle
Howard Flomberg	The Metropolitan State College of Denver
Richard A. Flores	Citrus College
Alicen Flosi	Lamar University
Linda Foster-Turpen	Central New Mexico Community College
Ernest Gines	Tarrant County College
Tim Gottleber	North Lake College
Sherry Green	Purdue University—Calumet Campus
Debra Gross	The Ohio State University
Vivian Haddad	Nova Southeastern University
Terry Hanks	San Jacinto College—South Campus
Susan Hanson	Albuquerque Technical Vocational Institute
Marie Hartlein	Montgomery County Community College
Jim Hendricks	Pierce College
Catherine Hines	Albuquerque Technical Vocational Institute
Norm Hollingsworth	Georgia Perimeter College
Mary Carole Hollingsworth	Georgia Perimeter College
Sherry Hopkins	Anne Arundel Community College
Judy Irvine	Seneca College
Glen Johansson	Spokane Community College
Stephanie Jones	South Plains College
Kathy Johnson	DeVry Chicago
Robert R. Kendi	Lehigh University
David Kight	Brewton-Parker College
Frank Kuehn	Pikes Peak Community College
Jackie Lamoureux	Albuquerque Technical Vocational Institute
Yvonne Leonard	Coastal Carolina University
Judith Limkilde	Seneca College—King Campus
Richard Linge	Arizona Western College
Joelene Mack	Golden West College
Lisa Macon	Valencia Community College
Donna Madsen	Kirkwood Community College
Daniela Marghitu	Auburn University
Norma Marler	Catawba Valley Community College
Toni Marucco	Lincoln Land Community College
Evelynn McCain	Boise State University

Dana McCann	Central Michigan University
Lee McClain	West Washington University
Sue McCrory	Missouri State University
Helen McFadyen	Mass Bay Community College—Framingham
Laura Melella	Fullerton College
Josephine Mendoza	California State University, San Bernardino
Mike Michaelson	Palomar College
Gina Bowers Miller	Harrisburg Area Community College
Johnette Moody	Arkansas Tech University
Dona Mularkey	Southern Methodist University
Rebecca A. Mundy	University of Southern California
Linda Mushet	Golden West College
Lisa Nademlynsky	Johnson & Wales University
Maguerite Nedreberg	Youngstown State University
Omar Nooraldeen	Cape Fear Community College
Judy Ogden	Johnson County Community College
Connie O'Neill	Sinclair Community College
Claudia Orr	Northern Michigan University
Brenda Parker	Middle Tennessee State University
Woody Pekoske	North Carolina State University
Paul Quan	Albuquerque Technical Vocational Institute
Patricia Rahmlow	Montgomery County Community College
Russell Sabadosa	Manchester Community College
Peg Saragina	Santa Rosa Junior College
Judith Scheeren	Westmoreland County Community College
Samuel Scott	Pierce College
Vicky Seehusen	The Metropolitan State College of Denver
Ralph Shafer	Truckee Meadows Community College—Reno, NV
Mirella Shannon	Columbia College
Laurie Evin Shteir	Temple University
Steven Singer	Kapi'olani Community College
Robert Smolenski	Delaware County Community College
Kriss Stauber	El Camino College
Neal Stenlund	Northern Virginia Community College
Song Su	East Los Angeles College
John Taylor	Hillsborough Community College—Brandon Campus
Dennie Templeton	Radford University
Joyce Thompson	Lehigh Carbon Community College
Janine Tiffany	Reading Area Community College

Janet Towle	New Hampshire Community Technical College— Nashua
Goran Trajkovski	Towson University
Deborah Tyler	Tarrant County College
Bill VanderClock	Bentley Business University
Glenna Vanderhoof	Missouri State University
Catherine Werst	Cuesta College
Steven H. White	Anne Arundel Community College
Barbara Yancy	Community College of Baltimore County—Essex Camp
Thomas Yip	Passaic County Community College
Mary Zajac	Montgomery County Community College
Mary T. Zegarski	Northampton Community College
Mary Ann Zlotow	College of DuPage

Letter from the Authors

Why We Wrote This Book

Our combined 40 years of teaching computer concepts have coincided with sweeping innovations in computing technology that have affected every facet of society. From iPhones to Web 2.0, computers are more than ever a fixture of our daily lives—and the lives of our students. But although today's students have a greater comfort level with their digital environment than previous generations, their knowledge of the machines they use every day is still limited.

We wrote *Technology in Action* to focus on what matters most to today's student. Instead of a history lesson on the microchip, we focus on what tasks students can accomplish with their PCs and what skills they can apply immediately in the workplace, the classroom, and at home. We strive to be as current as the publishing timelines will allow us, constantly looking for the next technology trend or gadget. The result is a book that sparks student interest by focusing on the material they want to learn (such as how to set up a home network) while teaching the material they need to learn (such as how networks work). The sequence of topics is carefully set up to mirror the typical student learning experience.

As they read through this text, your students will progress through stages of increasing difficulty:

1. Examining why it's important to be computer fluent and how computers impact our society
2. Examining the basic components of the computer
3. Connecting to the Internet
4. Exploring software
5. Learning the operating system and personalizing the computer
6. Evaluating and upgrading the PC
7. Exploring home networking and keeping the computer safe from hackers
8. Going mobile with PDA/smartphones, Tablet PCs, and laptops
9. Going behind the scenes, looking at technology in more detail

We have written the book in a "spiraling" manner, intentionally introducing on a basic level in the earlier chapters those concepts that students have trouble with and then later expanding on those concepts in more detail when students have become more comfortable with them. Thus, the focus of the early chapters is on practical uses for the computer, with real-world examples to help the students place computing in a familiar context. For example, we introduce basic hardware components in Chapter 2, and then we go into increasingly greater detail on some hardware components in Chapters 6, 8, and 9.

The Behind the Scenes chapters venture deeper into the realm of computing through in-depth explanations of how elements of the system unit (CPU, motherboard, RAM) work. They are specifically designed to keep more experienced students engaged and to challenge them with interesting research assignments.

We have also developed a comprehensive multimedia program to reinforce the material taught in the text and to support both classroom lectures and distance learning. The Helpdesk training content, created specifically for *Technology in Action*, enables students to take on the role of a helpdesk operator and work through common questions asked by computer users. Exciting Sound Byte multimedia—fully integrated with the text—accelerates student mastery of complex topics.

Now that the computer has become a ubiquitous tool in our lives, a new approach to computer concepts is warranted. This book is designed to reach the students of the twenty-first century and prepare them for the challenges they will face in the new global economy.

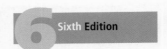
TOPIC SEQUENCE

Concepts are covered in a spiraling manner between chapters to mirror the typical student learning experience.

CHAPTER 2

CHAPTER 6

CHAPTER 9

Hardware Taught in More Depth in Additional Chapters
In later chapters, students are taught hardware in greater depth because they are more experienced and comfortable working with their computer.

Hardware First Introduced
Chapter 2 is the first time students read about introductory hardware. It is covered at the beginning level because this is their experience level at this point of the book.

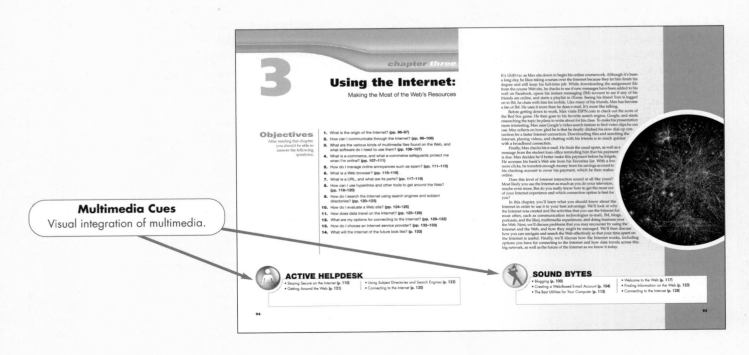

Multimedia Cues
Visual integration of multimedia.

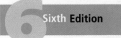

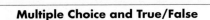

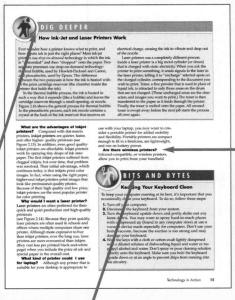

NEW

Ethics in IT boxes examine the ethical dilemmas caused by technology.

Trends in IT boxes explore newer topics involved in computing.

Dig Deeper boxes cover technical topics in depth to challenge advanced students.

Bits and Bytes teach good habits for safe computing.

Question/Answer Format
Written in an engaging and easy-to-read format.

Multiple Choice and True/False

Technology in Focus
Six special features that teach key uses of technology today.

Student CD
The launch pad to the multimedia.

© 2010 by Pearson Education, Inc., Upper Saddle River, NJ 07458

Companion Website
Includes an interactive study guide,
online end-of-chapter material,
additional Internet exercises,
and much more.

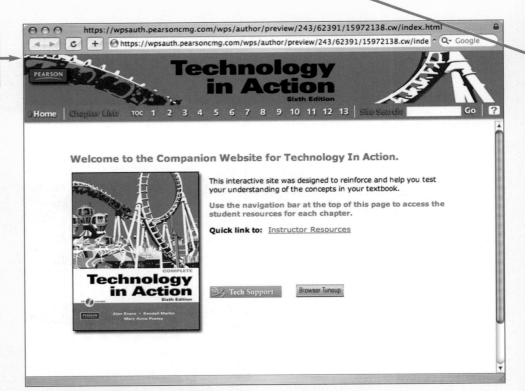

www.prenhall.com/techinaction

Active Helpdesk
Interactive training that puts the student in the role of a helpdesk staffer fielding questions from callers.

Supervisor available to assist students.

Assessment at the end of each call.

Textbook page references within each call.

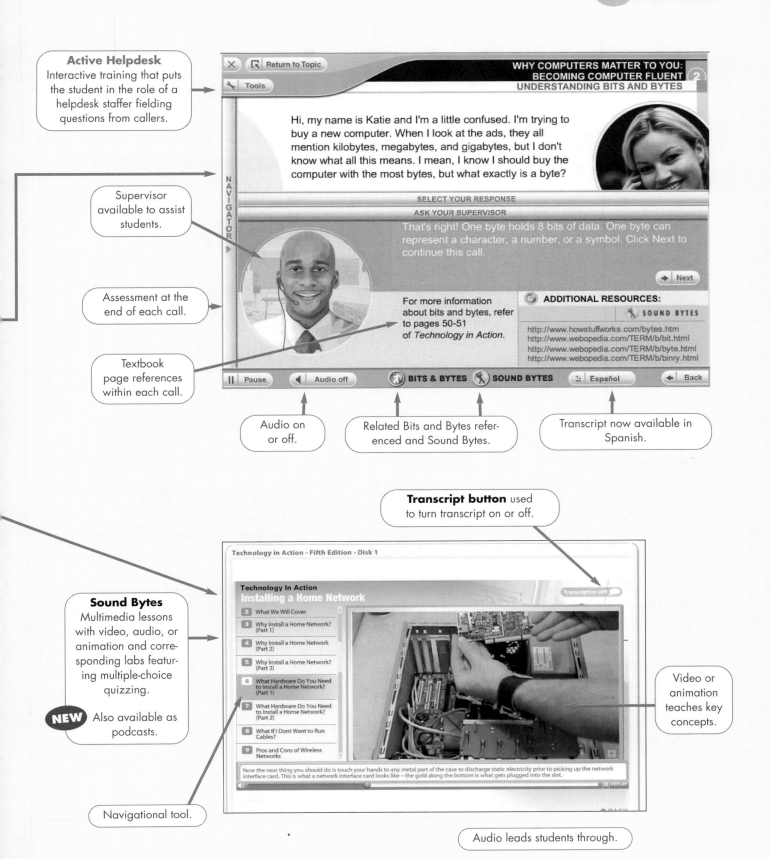

WHY COMPUTERS MATTER TO YOU:
BECOMING COMPUTER FLUENT
UNDERSTANDING BITS AND BYTES

Return to Topic

Tools

Hi, my name is Katie and I'm a little confused. I'm trying to buy a new computer. When I look at the ads, they all mention kilobytes, megabytes, and gigabytes, but I don't know what all this means. I mean, I know I should buy the computer with the most bytes, but what exactly is a byte?

SELECT YOUR RESPONSE
ASK YOUR SUPERVISOR

That's right! One byte holds 8 bits of data. One byte can represent a character, a number, or a symbol. Click Next to continue this call.

Next

For more information about bits and bytes, refer to pages 50-51 of *Technology in Action*.

ADDITIONAL RESOURCES:
SOUND BYTES

http://www.howstuffworks.com/bytes.htm
http://www.webopedia.com/TERM/b/bit.html
http://www.webopedia.com/TERM/b/byte.html
http://www.webopedia.com/TERM/b/binry.html

Pause   Audio off   BITS & BYTES   SOUND BYTES   Español   Back

Audio on or off.

Related Bits and Bytes referenced and Sound Bytes.

Transcript now available in Spanish.

Transcript button used to turn transcript on or off.

Technology in Action - Fifth Edition - Disk 1

Technology In Action
Installing a Home Network   Transcription OFF

2 What We Will Cover
3 Why Install a Home Network? (Part 1)
4 Why Install a Home Network? (Part 2)
5 Why Install a Home Network? (Part 3)
6 What Hardware Do You Need to Install a Home Network? (Part 1)
7 What Hardware Do You Need to Install a Home Network? (Part 2)
8 What If I Dont Want to Run Cables?
9 Pros and Cons of Wireless Networks

Now the next thing you should do is touch your hands to any metal part of the case to discharge static electricity prior to picking up the network interface card. This is what a network interface card looks like – the gold along the bottom is what gets plugged into the slot.

REPLAY

Sound Bytes
Multimedia lessons with video, audio, or animation and corresponding labs featuring multiple-choice quizzing.

NEW Also available as podcasts.

Video or animation teaches key concepts.

Navigational tool.

Audio leads students through.

Annotated Instructor Edition

Provided with each chapter are two divider pages like the ones outlined below.

FRONT OF CHAPTER TAB

On the front side of each chapter tab, you will find the following categories:

IN THE CLASSROOM: Activities you can use in a classroom or in online classes.

- **PowerPoint Presentations**
- **Discussion Exercises**
- **Active Helpdesk Calls**
- **Sound Bytes**

HOMEWORK: Activities used out of class for assessment or preparation for the next chapter, including:

- **Web Resource Project**
- **Active Helpdesk Calls**
- **Sound Byte Labs**
- **Online Study Guides**

ASSESSMENT:

- **Blackboard**
- **WebCT**
- **TestGen**
- **myitlab**

The backside of each Ethics tab includes the relevant Sound Bytes for that chapter.

FRONT OF ETHICS TAB

On the front of the Ethics tab, you will find the following:

OPPOSING VIEWPOINTS TABLE: Outlines debatable ethics topics that you can use in the classroom.

KEYWORDS: Provides you with additional words to search the Internet for more information related to the ethics topic.

For a list of the resources available for every chapter and where they are located, see the back of this tab.

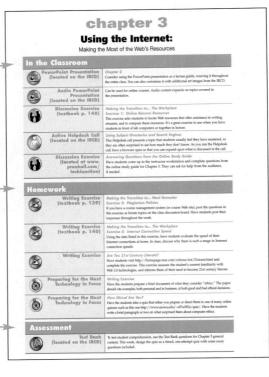

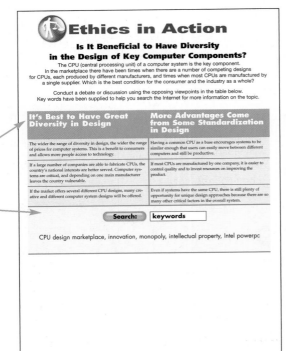

Instructor Resource CD

GREATLY ENHANCED

Instructor Resource CD

- **NEW! Interactive Course Builder** to help you integrate all the instructor resources.
- **NEW! Recommended chapter lectures** written by the authors that you can customize.
- All resources included with the *Technology in Action* Instructional System.

Technology in Action 6E - Complete - Instructor Resource CD - Disk 2

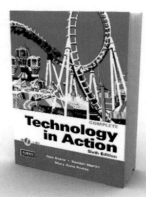

- View Active Helpdesks
- Download Instructor Materials
- Exit

© 2010 by Pearson Education, Inc., Upper Saddle River, NJ 07458

Contact your local Prentice Hall sales rep to learn more about the
Technology in Action instructional system.

GO!

Technology in Action

Sixth Edition

Why Computers Matter to You:

Becoming Computer Literate

Objectives

After reading this chapter, you should be able to answer the following questions:

1. What does it mean to be "computer literate"? **(p. 3)**
2. How does being computer literate make you a savvy computer user and consumer? **(pp. 4–5)**
3. How can becoming computer literate help you in a career? **(pp. 5–21)**
4. How can becoming computer literate help you understand and take advantage of newly emerging careers? **(pp. 21–23)**
5. How does becoming computer literate help you deal with the challenges associated with technology? **(pp. 23–24)**

ACTIVE HELPDESK

This chapter has no Active Helpdesks.

Why Should You Become Computer Literate?

It's safe to say that computers are nearly everywhere in our society. You find them in schools, cars, airports, shopping centers, toys, medical devices, homes, and in many people's pockets. You interact with computers almost every day, sometimes without even knowing it. Whenever you buy something with a credit card, you interact with a computer. And, of course, most of us can't imagine our lives without e-mail. Even if you don't yet have a home computer and don't feel comfortable using one, you still feel the impact of technology: Countless ads for computers, cell phones, digital cameras, and an assortment of Web sites surround us each day. We're constantly reminded of the ways in which computers, the Internet, and technology are integral parts of our lives.

So, just by being a member of our society, you already know quite a bit about computers. But why is it important to learn more about computers, becoming what is called *computer literate?* Being **computer literate** means being familiar enough with computers that you understand their capabilities and limitations, and you know how to use them. Being computer literate means more than just knowing about the parts of your computer. The following are some other benefits:

- As a computer-literate individual, you can use your computer more wisely and be a more knowledgeable consumer.

- Computer-literate employees are sought after in almost every vocation.

- Becoming computer literate will help you better understand and take advantage of future technologies.

In addition, understanding computers and their ethical, legal, and societal implications will make you a more active and aware participant in society.

Anyone can become computer literate—no matter what your degree of technical expertise. Being computer literate doesn't mean you need to know enough to program a computer or build one yourself. Just as with a car, you should know enough about it to take care of it and to use it effectively, but that doesn't mean you have to know how to build one. You should try to achieve the same familiarity with computers. In this chapter, we'll look at the ways in which computers can affect your life, now and in the future.

SOUND BYTES

- Questions to Ask Before You Buy a Computer **(p. 4)**
- The History of the Personal Computer **(p. 23)**

SOUND BYTE

Questions to Ask Before You Buy a Computer

This Sound Byte will help you consider some important questions you need to ask when you buy a computer, such as whether you should get a notebook or a desktop, or whether you should purchase a new computer or a used or refurbished one.

Becoming a Savvy Computer User and Consumer

One of the benefits of becoming computer literate is being a savvy computer user and consumer. What does this mean? The following are just a few examples of what it may mean to you:

- **Avoiding hackers and viruses.** Do you know what hackers and viruses are? Both can threaten a computer's security. Being aware of how hackers and viruses operate and knowing the damage they can do to your computer can help you avoid falling prey to them.

- **Protecting your privacy.** You've probably heard of identity theft—you see and hear news stories all the time about people whose "identities" are stolen and whose credit ratings are ruined by "identity thieves." But do you know how to protect yourself from identity theft when you're online?

- **Understanding the *real* risks.** Part of being computer literate means being able to separate the *real* privacy and security risks from things you don't have to worry about. For example, do you know what a *cookie* is? Do you know whether it poses a privacy risk for you when you're on the Internet? What about a *firewall*? Do you know what one is? Do you really need one to protect your computer?

- **Using the Internet wisely.** Anyone who has ever searched the Web can attest that finding information and *good* information are two different things. People who are computer literate make the Internet a powerful tool and know how to find the information they want effectively. How familiar with the Web are you, and how effective are your searches?

- **Avoiding online annoyances.** If you have an e-mail account, then chances are you've received electronic junk mail or **spam** (see Figure 1.1). How can you avoid being overwhelmed by spam? What about *adware* and *spyware*—do you know what they are? Do you know what **software** (the programs or instructions that tell the computer what to do) you should install on your computer to avoid online annoyances?

- **Being able to maintain, upgrade, and troubleshoot your computer.** Learning how to care for and maintain your computer and knowing how to diagnose and fix certain problems can save you a lot of time and hassle. Do you know how to upgrade your computer if you want more memory, for example? Do you know which software and computer settings can help you keep your computer in top shape?

- **Making good purchasing decisions.** Everywhere you go, you see ads like the one in Figure 1.2 for computers and other devices: notebooks (laptops), printers, monitors, cell phones, digital cameras, and personal digital assistants (PDAs). Do you know what all the words in the ads mean? What is *RAM?* What is a *CPU?* What are *MB, GB, GHz,* and *cache?* How fast do you need your computer to be, and how much memory should you have? Understanding computer buzzwords and keeping current with technology will help you better determine which computers and devices match your needs.

- **Knowing how to integrate the latest technology with your equipment.** Finally, becoming computer literate means knowing which technologies are on the horizon and how to integrate them

FIGURE 1.1

Understanding how to use e-mail effectively is just one example of what it means to be computer literate.

"That's funny — the computer said we had mail..."

www.CartoonStock.com

Processor:	Intel® Core 2™ Extreme Quad-Core Processor, 8 MB L2 Cache, 1066 FSB
RAM:	4 GB Dual Channel Corsair DDR2 (800 MHz)
Video:	NVIDIA GeForce 8800 GTX with DirectX 10 GPU
Audio:	Creative Labs X-Fi Elite Pro; HDA 7.1 surround channel sound
Network:	Native Gigabit Ethernet
Optical Drive:	Blu-ray drive, 16x DVD+/-RW drive
Storage Drive:	1 TB Serial ATA hard drive with support for up to 3 additional drives with RAID options
Ports:	10 USB 2 DVI and 1 S-Video 2 IEEE 1394 1 S/PDIF out
Physics Accelerator:	Ageia PhysX Card
Cooling:	Two-stage liquid cooling system
Portable Storage:	Bluetooth wireless 19-in 1-media hub with VoIP stereo headset
Operating System:	Windows Vista Ultimate with digital cable support

NEW!

FIGURE 1.2

Do you know what all the words in a computer ad mean? Can you tell whether the ad includes all the information necessary to make a purchasing decision?

into your home setup when possible (see Figure 1.3). Can you connect your notebook to a wireless network? What is *Bluetooth,* and does your computer "have" it? Can a device with a USB 2.0 connector be plugged into an old USB 1.0 port? (For that matter, what *is* a USB port?) How much memory should your cell phone have? Knowing the answers to these and other questions will help you make better purchasing decisions.

The benefits of being computer literate will help you in your career and in running your personal life. You'll be able to save money, time, and endless frustration by having a strong background in the basics of how computers and computer systems operate.

Being Prepared for Your Career

Computer careers are on the rise. Regardless of which profession you pursue, if computers are not already in use in that career, they most likely will be soon. **Information technology (IT)** is the set of techniques used in information handling

FIGURE 1.3

Can you identify all of these devices? Do you know how to get them all to work well together?

and retrieval of information automatically. IT includes computers, telecommunications, and software deployment. IT careers are on the rise, and the seven fastest-growing occupations are computer related. Even if you are interested in some other career path, by 2010, 70 percent of the U.S. workforce will be using computers at work. For more information about computers in the workplace, see the Technology in Focus section "Careers in IT."

Becoming truly computer literate—understanding the capabilities and limitations of computers and what you can do with them—will undoubtedly help you perform your job more effectively. It also will make you more desirable as an employee and more likely to earn more and grow your career. So, let's begin with a look at how computer systems are used in a wide range of careers. Whether you will become an employee in one of these industries or a user of their services, you will have a great advantage if you understand computer systems.

Computers in Today's Careers

We all are used to seeing computers at the checkout in stores, at the check-in at an airport, and so on, but there are many ways that computers are being used that you probably weren't aware of. Before we begin looking at a computer's parts and how it operates, let's take a look at a whole range of industries and examine how computers are a part of getting work done. Whether you are planning on a career in these fields or will just be a user of these products and services, your life will be affected by the use of computers in such fields as:

- business
- arts
- education
- legal system
- agriculture
- sciences

RETAIL: WORKING IN A DATA MINE

Businesses accumulate a lot of data, but just how do they manage to make sense of all of

it? How do they separate the anomalies from the trends? They use a process known as **data mining**, the process of searching huge amounts of data with the hope of finding a pattern. For example, large retailers often study the data gathered from register terminals to determine which products are selling on a given day and in a specific location. This helps managers figure out how much merchandise they need to order to replace stock that is sold. Managers also use mined data to determine that for a certain product to sell well, they must lower its price—especially if they cut the price at one store and see sales increase, for example. Data mining thus allows retailers to respond to consumer buying patterns.

Did you ever wonder how Amazon.com or Netflix can suggest items that fit your taste? Or how such Web sites automatically display lists of items people bought after they ordered the camera you just picked out? Data mining can keep track of the purchases customers are making along with their geographic data, past buying history, and lists of items they examined but did not purchase. This can be translated into extremely specific marketing, immediate and customized to your shopping experience. This is the motivation behind all of the "discount cards" that grocery stores and drugstores offer. In exchange for tracking your personal buying habits, they offer you some kind of special pricing. How much is your private information worth?

BUSINESS: DATA ON THE GO

Did you know that United Parcel Service (UPS) handles more than 15 million packages *per day*? Just how does the "brown" company ensure that all its customers' packages get from points A to B without ending up forever at point C? The company uses a sophisticated database and a highly efficient package tracking system that follows the packages as they move around the world.

For UPS, package tracking starts when the sender drops off a package and the company creates a "smart label" for the package (see Figure 1.4a). In addition to the standard postal bar code and a bar code showing UPS customer numbers, this smart label contains something called a *MaxiCode*. The MaxiCode is a specially designed scannable sticker that

FIGURE 1.4

(a) Package tracking starts at the point of sending by the generation of a smart label for the package. (b) Portable handheld devices allow warehouse and delivery personnel to scan packages for accurate transfer of information. (c) Devices carried by delivery personnel are used to direct them to customers with GPS systems, electronically capture customer signatures, and transfer information via wireless networks.

resembles an inkblot and contains all the important information about the package (class of service, destination, etc.). When the package is handled in processing centers, UPS workers scan the MaxiCode using portable handheld devices (see Figure 1.4b). These devices use **Bluetooth technology** (a type of wireless communication) to transmit the scanned data through radio waves to a terminal. This terminal then sends the data across a wireless network, where it is recorded in the UPS database.

To track package delivery, UPS carriers use delivery acquisition devices (see Figure 1.4c) that feature wireless networking capability, infrared scanners (to scan the smart labels and transmit the information back to the UPS database), and an electronic pad to capture customer signatures. By capturing all of this data and making it available on its Internet database, UPS enables its customers to track their packages. UPS is also able to make informed decisions about staffing and deploying equipment (trucks, airplanes, etc.) based on the volume and type of packages in the system at any given time.

ARTS: SHALL WE DANCE?

Some art students think that because they're studying art, there is no reason for them to

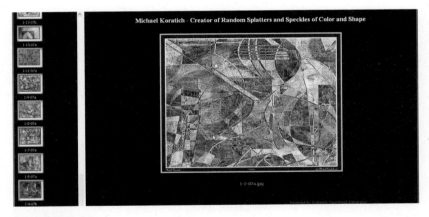

Michael Koratich - Creator of Random Splatters and Speckles of Color and Shape

FIGURE 1.5

Artists like Michael Koratich display and sell their creations by using custom Web galleries such as this one (**www.michaelkoratich.com**).

study computers. However, unless you plan on being a "starving artist," you'll probably want to sell your work. To do so, you'll need to advertise to the public and contact art galleries to convince them to purchase or display your work. Wouldn't it be helpful if you knew how to create a Web site like the one shown in Figure 1.5?

But using computers in the arts and entertainment fields goes way beyond using the Internet. The Atlanta Ballet, in conjunction with the Georgia Institute of Technology, is using computers to create virtual dancers

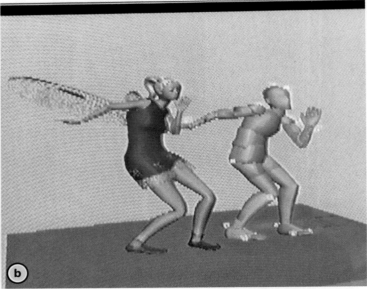

FIGURE 1.6

(a) A dancer is wired with sensors to capture his movements for digitization on a computer. (b) Computer-generated dancers can be integrated with live performances by projecting them on the stage.

FIGURE 1.7

Computers even figure directly into the development of artwork. Artist Camille Utterback develops interactive art that changes with the presence and movement of viewers in the gallery.

and new performances for audiences. As shown in Figure 1.6, live dancers are wired with sensors that are connected to a computer that captures the dancers' movements. Based on the data it collects, the computer generates a virtual dancer on a screen. The computer operator can easily manipulate this virtual dancer as well as change the dancer's costume with a click of a mouse. This allows artists to create new experiences for the audience.

Of course, not all artwork is created using traditional materials such as paint and canvas. Many artists today work exclusively with computers. Mastery of software programs such as Adobe Illustrator, Adobe Photoshop, and Adobe Flash are essential to creating digital art.

Other artists are pushing the envelope of creating art with computers even further. For example, through her series *External Measures,* artist Camille Utterback uses a computer to create a work of art that reacts to the presence—and the absence—of movement of the viewers in the gallery (see Figure 1.7). When no one is near the art piece, the image paints a small series of dots. However, as onlookers in the gallery move closer to the work, a camera mounted on the ceiling of the art gallery captures the movements and dimensions of the onlookers in the gallery. A computer with specialized software then uses this captured data to create smears of color and patterns of lines that reflect their movements. Because the image itself is created from the current and past movements and sizes of the gallery patrons, the work looks different to each person.

VIDEO GAME DEVELOPMENT: A LONG WAY FROM PAC-MAN

Revenues from video game sales in the United States are now larger than the movie industry's box office. Computer gaming is a $10 billion industry in the United States alone and is projected to continue its rapid growth over the next decade. If you're a gamer, you know games must be creative to grab their audience. Large-scale games are impossible to create on your own—you must be part of a team. The good news is that because computer games are best developed for a local market by people native to that market, game development will most likely stay in the United States instead of being **offshored**, or sent to other countries, as many other types of programming jobs have been.

You'll need an in-depth knowledge of computers to pursue a career in game programming or as a gaming artist. Mastering software animation tools such as 3ds Max will enable you to create compelling new worlds and new characters like the underwater world of BioShock (see Figure 1.8).

EDUCATION: TEACHING AND LEARNING

Today's teachers need to be at least as computer savvy as their students. Computers are part of most schools, even preschools. And at many colleges, students are required to have their own computers. Courses are designed to use management software such as Blackboard or Moodle so that students can communicate outside of class, take quizzes online, and find their class materials easily. Teachers must therefore have a working knowledge of computers to integrate computer technology effectively into the classroom.

The Internet has obvious advantages in the classroom as a research tool for

FIGURE 1.8

Using powerful tools such as 3ds Max from Autodesk, game developers can create complex worlds and characters to satisfy even the most demanding gamer.

students, and effective use of the Internet allows teachers to expose students to places students otherwise could not access. There are simulations and instructional software on the Web that are incredible learning tools. Teachers can employ these to give students a taste of running a global business (see Figure 1.9) or provide the experience of dissecting a human cadaver.

FIGURE 1.9

Internet applications have become sophisticated learning resources. IndustryPlayer.com allows students to compete online for domination of a global market while giving instructors the chance to introduce many business concepts.

What Can You Do with a Digital Home?

You're probably already using your computer in many different ways to fit your lifestyle. Perhaps you're ripping your CD collection to MP3 files so that you can transfer them from your computer to your iPod. Maybe you're burning a CD of all your favorite songs for a party you're having. But wouldn't it be great if you could manage the music for your party from the iTunes software straight from your computer? And what about that video of your friend's birthday party you shot last week? You've already imported it to your computer, edited it, and added a music track. But when your friends come over for the party this weekend, wouldn't it be fun to be able to show them the video on the TV in the living room instead of having them crowd around your computer monitor?

So when in the future will you do all this? Right now if you set up a digital home. Setting up a **digital home** means having an appropriate computer and digital devices that are all connected to a home network. Let's look at the key components you need to have to have a digital home, some of which are shown in Figure 1.10.

1. **A media computer:** A computer is the nerve center of any digital home, allowing you to interface with all the different digital devices you have connected to the network. For a Windows-based computer (see Figure 1.11), you should opt for a computer running the current version of Microsoft Windows Vista or at least Windows XP Media Center Edition

(MCE) as its operating system. (We'll discuss operating systems in more detail in Chapter 5.) A typical Media PC includes the following components:

a. **A TV tuner:** A TV tuner allows your computer to receive television channels from a cable connection and display them on your computer monitor. In fact, you can install more than one TV tuner in your computer, which allows you to receive multiple television channels at the same time.

b. **A radio tuner:** A radio tuner allows you to tune into Internet radio stations and record their broadcasts as digital files on your computer.

c. **Media software:** In addition to a computer and tuners, you'll also need software. Windows Vista includes software called Media Player, which functions as a digital video recorder (DVR), a video player, and a music player that you can use to view and organize the digital audio and video files on your computer. In combination with a TV tuner, digital video recorder software that is included as part of Windows Media Center allows you to turn your computer into a DVR such as TiVo. Digital video recorders record TV programs like VCRs, but they use your computer's hard drive to store the video. If you have multiple TV

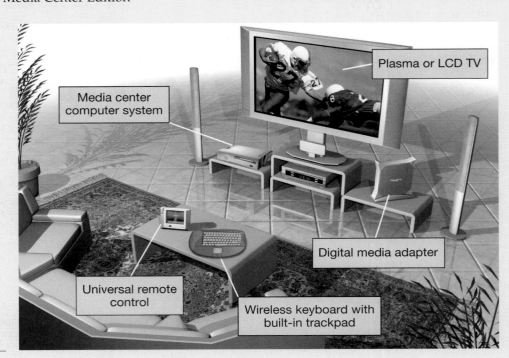

FIGURE 1.10

You can create a digital home with only a few devices.

Plasma or LCD TV

Media center computer system

Digital media adapter

Universal remote control

Wireless keyboard with built-in trackpad

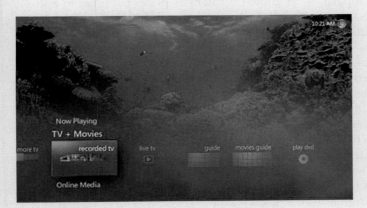

FIGURE 1.11

Microsoft Windows Vista Home Premium is an operating system that allows you to manage all your media entertainment from your computer.

tuners installed in your computer, you can record several programs onto your computer's hard drive at the same time.

d. **Blu-ray, DVD, and CD players and recorders:** To make it easy to transfer your audio or video files from one device to another, high-definition recorders and DVD and CD players and recorders allow you to record files onto high-definition media (such as Blu-ray discs) or onto standard resolution DVDs and CDs instead of your hard drive.

e. **A network adapter:** A network adapter is a special device that is installed in your computer and allows it to communicate with other devices on a network. (You'll learn more about network adapters in Chapter 7.) For digital devices to communicate with each other, they need to be connected to a network.

2. **A network:** Unless you're going to view digital and audio files only on your computer, then you will need a network to transfer such files easily to other devices (such as televisions) in your home. A wireless network has the advantage over a wired network in that it is easier to relocate devices. For example, suppose you rearrange your living room and need to move your TV to the opposite end of the room. If your TV was connected to a wired network, you might have to run a new cable or relocate the existing one. With a wireless network, you'd just

move the TV and be done with it. (You'll learn all about wired and wireless networks in Chapter 7.)

3. **A digital television:** Newer plasma and liquid crystal display (LCD) televisions (see inset, Figure 1.10) or high-definition TVs (HDTVs) are an important part of any digital home because they enable you to best show off all your digital entertainment (digital photos and so on). Note that even if you don't have a plasma or LCD television, as long as you bought your TV within the last five years or so, you can probably use it to display digital content as well. However, televisions are not usually ready to be integrated into a network right out of the box. For this you need a digital media adapter.

4. **A digital media adapter:** A digital media adapter (see inset, Figure 1.10) allows you to transfer media (such as videos, digital photos, or MP3s) from your computer to your other media devices (such as your plasma TV). These devices are also known as *media center extenders.* Essentially, a digital media adapter allows you to integrate your TV into your home network. This device connects to your computer network (either wired or wirelessly) and then to your TV through specially designed audiovisual connectors.

5. **A universal remote:** A universal remote is a single remote control that works with any infrared-controlled device (such as your computer, digital media adapters, amplifiers, or receivers) and allows you to access media (such as MP3 files) no matter where in the house it is stored. Universal remotes such as the iPronto from Philips (see inset, Figure 1.10) come with software that allows you to program your own custom interface for the remote. You can even program macros that perform multiple commands with the press of a button.

With these devices installed, you can get the maximum benefit from your computer and all your digital entertainment devices. When you're in your living room, you can play digital music files stored on your computer (in the den) for the party you're throwing. You can also display the video of your friend's birthday party (downloaded to your computer) on the TV for your friends to see. And when you're in your room, you can watch the latest episode of *CSI* that you recorded on your computer's hard drive, while your sister is simultaneously listening to MP3 files stored on your computer on the TV in the living room.

Many museums have virtual tours on their Web sites that allow students to examine objects in the museum collections. Often, these virtual tours include three-dimensional photos that can be viewed from all angles. So, even if you teach in Topeka, Kansas, you can take your students on a virtual tour of the Smithsonian Institution in Washington, D.C.

But what about when you actually want to take your students to visit museums firsthand? Today, technology is often used to enhance visitors' experiences at museums. New York's Museum of Modern Art, for example, offers PDA tours that provide visitors with additional information about the art they're viewing. By using a **personal digital assistant**, or **PDA** (a small device that enables users to carry digital information), you can listen to music that the artist listened to when he or she was creating the work or look at other works that reflect similar techniques or themes to the one you're viewing (see Figure 1.12). For more modern artists, you can watch interviews with the artist explaining his or her motivation for the work. You can even use the PDA to contact other members of your group and direct

them to specific works you want them to see. Knowing how to use a PDA effectively may help make a museum tour even more memorable.

Computers in the classroom will become more prevalent as prices continue to fall and parents demand that their children be provided with the necessary computer skills they will need to be successful in the workplace. Therefore, as an educator, being computer literate will help you plan constructive computerized lessons for your students and use technology to interact with them.

LAW ENFORCEMENT: PUT DOWN THAT MOUSE—YOU'RE UNDER ARREST!

Today, wearing out shoe leather to solve crimes is far from the only method available to investigators trying to catch criminals. Computers are being used in police cars and crime labs to solve an increasing number of crimes. For example, facial reconstruction systems like the one shown in Figure 1.13 can turn a skull into a finished digital image of a face, allowing investigators to proceed far more quickly with identification.

One technique used by modern detectives to solve crimes is to employ computers to search the vast number of databases on the Internet. Proprietary law enforcement databases such as the National Center for the Analysis of Violent Crime database enable detectives to track a wealth of information about similarities between crimes, trying to detect patterns that may reveal serial crimes. Detectives are also using their knowledge of wireless networking to intercept and read a criminal suspect's e-mail messages and chat sessions when he or she is online, all from the comfort of a car parked outside the suspect's home (where legally permissible).

As detective work goes more high tech, so, too, does crime. To fight such high-tech crime, a law enforcement specialty called **computer forensics** is growing. This specialty applies computer systems and techniques to gather potential legal evidence. The ability to recover and read deleted or damaged files from a criminal's computer is already providing evidence for trials.

Sara Krulwich/The New York Times

FIGURE 1.12

Multimedia tours using PDAs and wireless technology are now commonplace in museums and galleries. Aside from providing additional contextual material to visitors (such as displaying similar works by other artists), such multimedia tours enable patrons to participate in opinion polls and to send messages to other museum visitors.

Every day, businesses across the world use complicated forecasting models to make predictions about their sales and inventory levels. Thanks to recent technological advancements, law enforcement officials might soon have access to specialized software that can forecast criminal activity, helping police officers take preventive measures to stop crime.

Don't believe it? Criminologists Jacqueline Cohen and Wilpen Gorr and computer scientist Andreas Olligschlaeger received funding from the U.S. Department of Justice to study police reports from Rochester, New York, and Pittsburgh, Pennsylvania. After entering the data about criminal offenses, precinct staffing, and patrol routes, the two researchers used trend-spotting programs to analyze the data. As a result, the program was able to predict criminal activity before it happened an astounding 80 percent of the time. The key to the analysis was identifying and studying leading indicators that trigger crime sprees. Whereas consumer researchers may look at consumer spending patterns and levels of disposable income, criminologists study soft crime statistics such as disorderly conduct and trespassing. Increases in these types of crimes indicate that serious crimes may soon be on the rise. When a trend is identified, patrols in the area can be stepped up to try to head off crimes before they occur. Building, analyzing, and fine-tuning the models will keep law enforcement officials busy for years.

Even something as simple as parking enforcement uses computers today. Smart meters, such as the one shown in Figure 1.14, are being installed in major cities and can manage as many as 10 parking spaces each. When you park in a space, you go to the meter and pay with cash, by credit card, or over your cell phone. The meter can even send a text message to your cell phone when your time is almost up so you can pay for more. The meter reports revenue and any malfunctions to the parking authority's central computer on a regular basis. Parking officials can access the meter remotely and change parking rates in response to usage patterns, scheduling of special events, or time of day. Parking enforcement officers have special PDAs that communicate wirelessly with the meters to

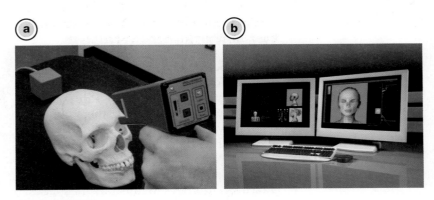

FIGURE 1.13

(a) The FastScan wand lets forensics teams quickly grab three-dimensional images of skulls and build wire three-dimensional frameworks. (b) Tissue-rendering programs then add layers of muscles, fat, and skin to create faces that can be used to identify victims.

determine when parked cars are in violation. The meters send information (such as the time, date, and location of the violation) to the PDAs, which makes generating tickets quicker and more accurate.

FIGURE 1.14

(a) Smart parking meters, such as the one shown here, let you pay with cash, by credit card, or over your cell phone and can send a text message to your phone when your time is almost up.
(b) Handheld devices help parking enforcement officers issue tickets faster and record the data from them more accurately.

LEGAL SYSTEM: WELCOME TO THE VIRTUAL COURTROOM

In courtrooms today, videos of crimes in progress (often captured by cameras at convenience stores or gas stations) are sometimes shown to juries to help them understand how crimes unfolded. But what happens if no surveillance camera recorded a crime? Paper diagrams, models, and still photos of a crime scene used to be the only choice for attorneys to illustrate their cases. Now there is a much more exciting and lively alternative: computer forensics animations.

Computer forensics animations are extremely detailed and often lifelike re-creations that have been generated with computers based on forensic evidence, depositions of witnesses, and the opinions of experts. Using sophisticated animation programs, similar to the ones used to create movies such as *Cars* and *Ratatouille*, forensic animators can depict one side's version of how events occurred, allowing the jury to watch it unfold.

Of course, being able to view sophisticated multimedia, televise trials, or record witness testimony for archiving requires modern courtrooms to be wired. Those such as Florida's Ninth Judicial Circuit Court (see Figure 1.15) are on the cutting edge, complete with robot-controlled video cameras that pivot to record whoever is speaking on the microphone at the time. Video images can be streamed directly to a Web site for immediate viewing or stored for archival purposes. Meanwhile, the judge has a touch-screen terminal to control the action in the courtroom, including turning on real-time

FIGURE 1.15

Courtrooms such as Florida's Ninth Judicial Circuit Court are on the cutting edge.

Touch-screens allow judges, lawyers, and witnesses to examine and mark up digital images during trials.

Digital recording devices capture all audio for immediate playback by the judge (if necessary) and for later transcribing by court reporters.

Video cameras can record whoever is speaking on the microphone.

Attorneys use wireless touch-screen handhelds to manipulate the multimedia systems in the courtroom to display evidence such as crime scene photos.

closed-captioning by linking in the court reporter's transcription terminal. Lawyers have access to wireless touch-screen hand-held devices that allow them to access and display evidence they have stored on the courtroom's multimedia systems. Attorneys can also connect their own notebooks to the system, and audio recordings of all proceedings are captured and available for immediate playback.

Outside the courtroom, lawyers and other legal professionals use vast online legal libraries and databases, such as LexisNexis, to research cases and prepare for court.

AGRICULTURE: HIGH-TECH DOWN ON THE FARM

You might think that ranching and farming are low-tech operations that have little use for computers and software. After all, the growing season can't be changed by any computer program! Even so, new technologies are changing life on farms and ranches in many ways.

Ranchers have many challenges in modern meat production. For example, they must watch for and prevent diseases such as hoof and mouth and mad cow and even an *E. coli* outbreak. The meat you purchase can be introduced to these dangers at many different places in the processing chain—from the ranch to the supermarket.

Fortunately, outbreaks can be managed and minimized with the use of **radio frequency identification tags (RFID tags)**. These RFID tags are small versions of the roadway electronic toll systems used in many states to automate paying tolls as you pass through the toll station. Each tag looks like a tiny button and is attached to the cow's ear. It contains a microchip that holds a unique sequence of numbers used to identify that animal. When the cow walks past a panel reader, its location is automatically recorded and tracked in a database.

If a cow is identified as having disease, then all of its recorded movements can be checked in the database that stores the RFID information. It is then simple to identify exactly which food lots that and other animals ate. Using RFID tags, potential crises can be averted or at least better controlled.

In cranberry bogs, computer technology is being used in some interesting ways. For example, cranberry crops easily can be destroyed by frost. In the past, growers had to race to protect the bogs of berries on cold nights by turning on pumps to force out water to surround the berries and keep them from freezing. Today, growers use a Web-based system that can automatically control the pumps. It analyzes information about the time, the temperature measured near the berries, watering schedules, rainfall, and wind conditions and then automatically turns the pumps around the bog fields on and off as needed.

AUTOMOTIVE TECHNOLOGY: SENSORS AND CPUS

An automotive technician is required to have knowledge of a range of tools—impact hammers, wrenches, pneumatic tools, lathes, and welding and flame-cutting equipment. But to consider a career in automotive repair today requires a sophisticated level of computer literacy as well (see Figure 1.16). Environmental trends and governmental regulation are driving auto manufacturers to develop vehicles that produce lower emissions, and the push for more efficient cars and higher gas mileage continues.

These changes have led to a greater number of sensors and computer CPU (central processing unit) systems needed in a typical vehicle. The fuel-injection and engine-management systems possible now go far beyond what a simple carburetor can

FIGURE 1.16

Automotive technicians need to know their way not only around a wrench but also around a computer to be current in their field.

do. Several sensors measure everything from air pressure to air temperature, engine temperature, and throttle position, for example. The data from these sensors is then used to compute the precise amount of fuel to spray into the cylinders, resulting in less fuel waste and reduced pollution. The braking, transmission, and steering systems also are primarily controlled by computers and electronic components.

As consumers come to expect digital music systems, airbags, voice-controlled phones, and GPS navigation screens in their cars as well, the number of computer subsystems will continue to grow. In addition to these driver-friendly features, the computers in today's cars even alert drivers when it's time to take the car in for maintenance or repair.

As a result, automotive technicians must be able to maintain current updates to documentation through the Internet, use computer databases to learn about common problems and solutions, and use computer systems to interface and run diagnostics on all the different automotive computer systems. The days of working on a car in the driveway with some screwdrivers and a socket wrench are long gone.

MEDICINE: FACT OR FICTION?

In movies set in the distant future, humans can sometimes interface with computers just by thinking and looking at a screen or monitor. Until recently, such scenes took place only in movies. But since 2006, companies such as Cyberkinetics have been working to understand the human neural interface system. In testing the company's software known as BrainGate, a man suffering from amyotrophic lateral sclerosis (ALS, which is also known as Lou Gehrig's disease), who no longer had any control of muscle movement, is able to control the movement of a robotic arm. The BrainGate software translates his thoughts into commands to the robotic limb. The patient has a tiny array of microelectrodes implanted in his brain (see Figure 1.17). The computer equipment receiving data from his neural activity identifies the impulses that the brain associates with physical movement (of his arm, for example) and then translates the instructions into commands to the robot. Patient Stephen Heywood explained, "After being paralyzed for so long, it is almost impossible to describe the magical feeling of imagining a motion and having it occur."

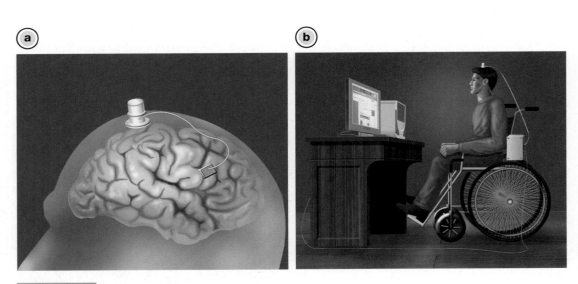

a **b**

FIGURE 1.17

(a) The BrainGate Neural Interface is implanted in the patient's body. A silicon chip studded with microelectrodes is embedded in the brain and connected to a signal converter that is, in turn, connected to a computer. (b) The converter sees how neurons fire when the patient thinks certain thoughts and begins to recognize patterns, which are then translated into commands to a robotic arm.

In addition to being an integral part of many medical research projects, computers are helping doctors and nurses learn their trades. Training for physicians and nurses can be difficult at best. Often, the best way for medical students to learn is to experience a real emergency situation. The problem is that students are then confined to watching as the emergency unfolds and already trained personnel actually care for patients. Students rarely get to train in real-life situations; when they do, a certain level of risk is involved.

Medical students are now getting access to better training opportunities thanks to a computer technology called a **patient simulator** (shown in Figure 1.18). Patient simulators are life-sized, computer-controlled mannequins that can speak, breathe, and blink (their eyes respond to external stimuli). They have a pulse and a heartbeat, and they respond just like humans to procedures such as the administration of intravenous drugs.

Medical students can train on patient simulators and experience firsthand how a human would react to their treatments. The best thing about these "patients" is that if they "die," students can restart the computer simulation and try again. Even the U.S. military is using patient simulators to train medics to respond to terrorist attacks that employ chemical and biological agents.

Even more exciting than patient simulators is the work being done on modeling complete human biological systems. The Physiome Project began as the brainchild of the Bioengineering Institute in Auckland, New Zealand. It now is a global **public domain** effort (not covered by copyright) in which bioengineers are creating realistic computer simulations of all systems and features of the human anatomy. They recently completed a digital re-creation of the human heart and lungs (shown in Figure 1.19).

Although the current system models a *theoretical* human's lungs, researchers hope to one day use computers to simulate a *specific* person's anatomical systems. With such a system, imaging scans (CTs, MRIs, etc.) of your body and a sample of your DNA would be fed into a computer, which would create an *exact* computer model of your body. This would allow doctors to experiment with different therapies to see how you would react to specific treatments.

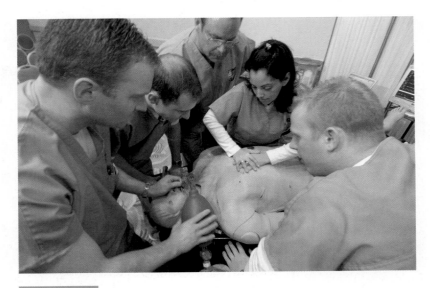

FIGURE 1.18

Patient simulators allow health care students to practice medical procedures without risk of injury or death to real patients.

A great deal of work is still to be done before this treatment becomes a reality, but computer-literate medical professionals will be needed to make it happen.

Surgeons are even using computer-guided robots to perform surgery. Surgeons are often limited by their manual dexterity and can have trouble making small, precise incisions. So how can robots help? Robotic surgery devices can exercise much finer control when making delicate incisions than can a human guiding a scalpel. To use the robots, doctors look into a surgery

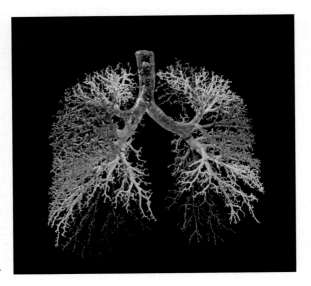

FIGURE 1.19

A working computer model of the human lungs, including 300 million air sacs.

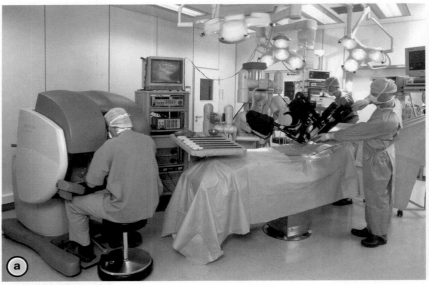

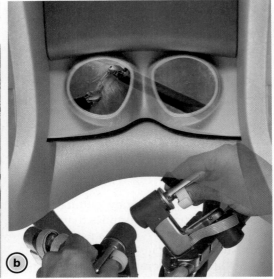

FIGURE 1.20

Surgeons use computer-guided robots, such as the da Vinci Surgical System from Intuitive Surgical, to perform surgery. (a) Here a doctor looks into the control device and manipulates controls that move the robotic devices hovering over the patient. (b) This is what surgeons see as they operate on the patient.

control device where they manipulate controls that move robotic devices hovering over the patient (see Figure 1.20). One robot control arm contains a slender imaging rod that allows the doctor to see inside the patient when the rod is inserted into the patient. Doctors can now perform a coronary bypass by making two small incisions in the patient and inserting the imaging rod in one incision and another robotic device with a scalpel into the other. The ability to make small incisions instead of the large ones required by conventional surgery means less trauma and blood loss for the patient. Theoretically, surgeons do not even have to be in the same room as the patient, although this remote method has not yet been attempted. They could be thousands of miles away, controlling the movements of the robotic devices from a control station.

MEDICINE: THE CHIP WITHIN

When you mention implanting technology into the human body, some people conjure up images of the Terminator, a futuristic cybernetic life form from the movie of the same name that looks human but is mostly machine. The goal of modern-day biomedical chip research is to provide technological solutions to physical problems and to provide a means for positively identifying individuals (see Figure 1.21).

One potential application of biomedical chip implants is to provide sight to the blind. Macular degeneration and retinitis pigmentosa are two diseases that account for the majority of blindness in developing nations. Both diseases result in damage to the photoreceptors contained in the retina of the eye. (Photoreceptors convert light energy into electrical energy that is transmitted to the brain, allowing us to see.) Researchers are experimenting with chips that contain microscopic solar cells and are implanted in the damaged retina of patients. The idea is to have the chip take over for the damaged photoreceptors and transmit electrical images to the brain. Although these chips have been tested in patients, they have not yet restored anyone's sight. But uses of biomedical chips such as these illustrate the type of medical devices you may "see" in the future.

One type of chip is already being implanted in humans as a means of verifying a person's identity. Called the VeriChip, this "personal ID chip" is about the size of a grain of rice and is implanted under the skin. When exposed to radio waves from a scanning device, the chip emits a signal that transmits its unique serial number to the scanner. The scanner then connects to a database that contains the name, address, and medical conditions of the person in whom the chip has been implanted.

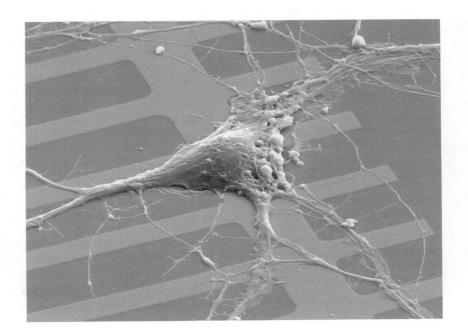

FIGURE 1.21

Researchers are experimenting with implantable chips such as this one. Here, we see a nerve cell on a silicon chip. The cell was cultured on the chip until it formed a network with nearby cells. The chip contains a transistor that stimulates the cell above it, which in turn passes the signal to neighboring neurons. Chips such as these could be used to repair nerve damage and restore movement or sensation to parts of the body.

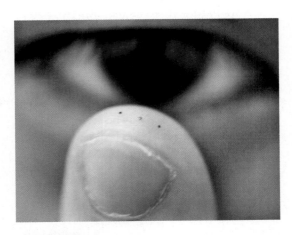

FIGURE 1.22

No bigger than the period at the end of this sentence, the Hitachi μ-chip can hold digital information, which can then be read when it passes a detector. A triumph of technology or a cause for concern?

Hitachi has a similar device, called the μ-chip (mu-chip), which is smaller than the period at the end of this sentence (see Figure 1.22). The μ-chip could be easily attached to, or ingested by, a person without his or her knowledge.

The creators of the VeriChip envision it speeding up airport security and being used together with other devices (such as electronic ID cards) to provide tamperproof security measures. If someone stole your credit card, that person couldn't use it if a salesclerk had to verify your identity by scanning a chip in your arm before authorizing a transaction.

Currently, nonimplant versions of identity chips are used in hospitals. When chips are attached with bands to newborn infants, the hospital staff can monitor the location of any baby instantly. Elevators and doors are designed to allow only certain people to enter with a specific baby, even if the hospital power is interrupted. Although the use of these tags is becoming more commonplace, it remains to be seen whether the general public will decide that the advantages of having personal identity and medical data quickly available justifies having chips implanted into their bodies.

SCIENCE: THE SIMS IS JUST THE BEGINNING

Thanks to a partnership between the National Severe Storms Lab and the National Center for Supercomputing Applications, tornado forecasting may be getting more accurate. Scientists have been able to create a model so detailed that it takes *nine days* for a supercomputer to generate, even though the computer is executing four billion operations *each second*. Simulations also can model the structure of solar magnetic flares, which can interfere with broadcasts on Earth (see Figure 1.23).

FIGURE 1.23

A simulation from the University of Michigan shows the structure of the magnetic fields around the sun and how they change in time.

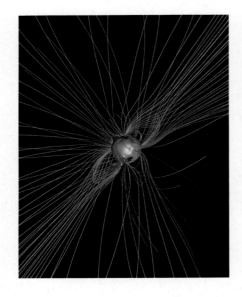

By studying the data produced by these simulations, forecasters hope to improve their predictions about weather phenomena.

Other technological applications in the sciences are being used on some of the oldest sites on Earth. The ancient site of Pompeii has been under the intense scrutiny of tourists and archaeologists for decades. Sadly, all the foot traffic and exposure to the elements is eroding portions of the ruins. Today scientists are using three-dimensional scanners and imaging software to capture a detailed record of the current condition

of the ruins (see Figure 1.24). The virtual re-creation of the ruins is so lifelike that archaeologists can study the ruins on-screen instead of at the actual site. Using the scans as well as satellite imagery, aerial photography, and other data, scientists will eventually be able to re-create missing portions of the ruins in a virtual model. And scientists won't stop at Pompeii. This method will soon be used to make records of other decaying sites.

SPORTS SCIENCE: COMPUTE YOUR WAY TO A BETTER GAME

Want to be a world-class swimmer or baseball player? Getting an Olympic-caliber coach and training for hours every day are no longer enough. To get that competitive edge, you really need to use a computer.

That's right, computers are now being used to help athletes analyze their performance and improve their game. How does this work? First, video recordings are made of the athlete in action. The video is then transferred into special motion-analysis software on a computer. This software measures the exact angles of the athlete's body parts as they progress through ranges of motion, such as the angle of a baseball player's left arm relative to his body as he swings the bat. Minor adjustments can be made on the

BITS AND BYTES

NASA Wants You . . . to Learn

As you read this chapter, hundreds of satellites are orbiting the globe and taking wonderfully detailed pictures of Earth. Until recently, these photos weren't available to the general public. However, thanks to NASA (and U.S. taxpayer dollars) and some savvy software developers, an application called World Wind is now making some 10 trillion bytes of imagery available to you. Need a picture of Mount Fuji for your science project or an aerial picture of your house for your PowerPoint presentation? Just download the software from **http://learn.arc.nasa.gov**, and you're ready to go. You'll find several terrific learning applications here as well. "Virtual Lab" lets you pretend you have your own scanning electron microscope, and "What's the Difference" takes you on a tour of the planets, complete with information about their composition and atmosphere and fly-throughs. With a few clicks you can have these interactive learning resources that open the world to you.

FIGURE 1.24

A digital re-creation of the ruins of Pompeii allows archaeologists to study the ruins without even being there, as well as recreate Pompei as it looked before the devastation.

computer regarding positioning of body parts and the force used in performing various movements. This helps baseball players, for example, enhance their performance by determining what adjustments they should make to hit the ball harder and farther.

The U.S. Olympic Training Center in Colorado makes extensive use of computers in training athletes such as swimmers. The major objective in training swimmers to swim faster is to reduce drag from the water and minimize turbulence (which also can slow down a swimmer). Software has been developed that simulates the way water flows around the parts of a swimmer's body when in motion. Coaches can use the software to experiment with small changes in the position of a swimmer's arms or legs to determine whether turbulence and drag are reduced. The coaches can then train the swimmers to use the new techniques to improve their strokes and speed.

Aren't planning on competing in the next Olympics or playing in the major leagues? How about improving your weekend golf game? Employees in golf shops are now using sophisticated motion-capture equipment to improve golfers' swings. To have your golf swing analyzed, golf shop personnel hook you up into shoulder, leg, and hip harnesses containing motion sensors (see Figure 1.25). As you swing away at a variety of shots (drives, chips, and so on), computers capture information about the motion of your swing, comparing it to a database of the ideal positions of pro golfers. Trainers then suggest adjustments you can make so that your swing more closely emulates that of successful golfers. Even weekend warriors can benefit from high-tech analysis.

The equipment athletes use is also getting a technology boost. Even in a sport such as soccer, where not much equipment is involved, technology is making an impact. Adidas is developing a new soccer ball that contains an integrated circuit chip. When the company's Smartball crosses the goal line, it sends a radio signal to the referee's watch. The ball is not yet approved for World Cup play, but you can expect to see Smartballs showing up in professional soccer matches soon.

NANOTECHNOLOGY: CAREERS YET TO COME

Have you ever heard of nanoscience? Developments in computing based on

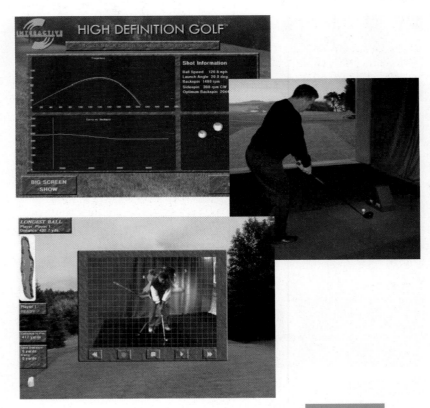

FIGURE 1.25

High-Definition Golf uses high-speed cameras to capture your swing and then identify swing problems. The software is also able to compare your swing with the swings of professional golfers.

the principles of nanoscience are being touted as the next big wave in computing. Ironically, this realm of science focuses on incredibly small objects. In fact, **nanoscience** involves the study of molecules and structures (called *nanostructures*) that range in size from 1 to 100 nanometers. It will provide numerous career paths and high-tech positions over the next several decades.

The prefix *nano* stands for one-billionth. Therefore, a nanometer is one-billionth of a meter. To put this in perspective, a human hair is approximately 50,000 nanometers wide. Put side by side, 10 hydrogen atoms (the simplest atom) would measure approximately 1 nanometer. Anything smaller than a nanometer is just a stray atom or particle floating around in space. Therefore, nanostructures represent the smallest human-made structures that can be built.

Nanotechnology is the science revolving around the use of nanostructures to build devices on an extremely small scale (see Figure 1.26). Right now, nanoscience is limited to improving existing products such as enhancing fibers used in clothing with coatings so that they repel stains, resist odors, or stop wrinkles. However, someday scientists hope to use nanostructures to build computing devices that will be too small to

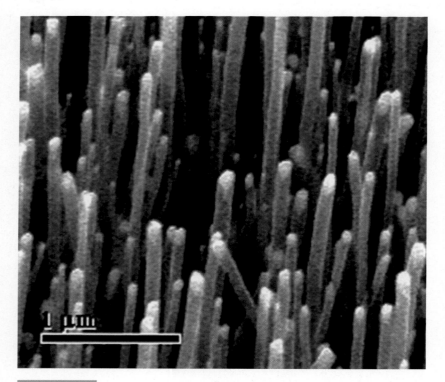

FIGURE 1.26

Nanostructures, each about one-hundredth of the size of a human hair, are shown here growing in a "nanoforest." Many nanostructures have special qualities, such as being extremely water repellent, that make them useful for material coatings.

FIGURE 1.27

This nanocar was constructed from a single molecule by a team at Rice University. The car can be used to deliver drugs or carry information within computer chips.

be seen by the naked eye. Nanowires, which are extremely small conductors, could be used to create extremely small pathways in computer chips. Developments such as this could lead to computers the size of a pencil eraser that will be far more powerful than today's desktop computers.

If you've ever watched *Star Trek,* then you know that *nanoprobes* (tiny machines that can be injected into the bloodstream) have already been envisioned. Nanotechnology researchers are now beginning to use carbon nanotubes to create devices that deliver medicine and information (see the nanocar in Figure 1.27). We are still a long way from developing nanoscale machines, and some scientists don't think this will ever be possible. However, researchers are investigating the use of nanostructures to deliver precise doses of drugs on a molecule-by-molecule basis within the human bloodstream. Universities and government laboratories are investing billions of dollars in nanotechnology research every year. If you have the background and interest in computing technology and science, then this is the time to pursue an education in nanoscience.

PSYCHOLOGY: YOU SHOULD SMILE... NOW

Science fiction shows and movies such as *Star Wars* have always been populated with robots that emulate humans, seemingly effortlessly. So, when will we have C-3PO, R2-D2, or the Terminator laughing at our jokes or bringing us our favorite snack when they recognize we're sad? It is a question that pushes us to explore the nature of being human and the nature of machines.

Research is jointly being conducted now between psychologists and computer scientists to develop computer systems that respond to human affect and emotional expression and to enable computer systems to develop social and emotional skills. **Affective computing** is computing that relates to emotion or deliberately tries to influence emotion. Most computers with which you are familiar can perform calculations and the tasks for which they are programmed much faster than humans, but they fail miserably in telling a good joke or modifying their behavior based on your frustration. This wide gap in the computing abilities of computers versus their emotional abilities is the target of research in affective computing.

One project to emerge is the emotional social prosthesis (ESP) device that has been developed by a group at the MIT Media Lab. The ESP system is targeted at helping people who have autism. Autistic individuals can have especially high intelligence but do not easily sense nonverbal cues such as facial expressions and tone of voice. ESP is a wearable system that isolates the movements and facial expressions of people, interprets what their mood and intention probably are, and communicates this information back to the user. Another project is the creation of computers that can analyze a person's movements, watch their use of the mouse, and interpret the pressure patterns on the chair in which the person is seated. That data is then used to determine the individual's level of attention. The computer could then interrupt the individual who is beginning to lose concentration and refocus him or her on a certain task.

While engineers work to create computers that can understand us emotionally, psychologists and computer scientists are also working to evolve systems toward a more human appearance (see Figure 1.28). Teams at the University of Michigan, Ohio State University, and the French Institute of Computer Science Research are working on robots that move in a more human fashion. Their biped (two-legged) robot named Rabbit is able to walk, run, and climb stairs, and it may lead to industrial robots that can tackle new tasks for us.

Understanding the Challenges Facing a Digital Society

Part of becoming computer literate is also being able to understand and form knowledgeable opinions on the challenges that face a digital society. Although computers offer us a world of opportunities, they also

FIGURE 1.28

Robots with articulated joints that mimic human limbs are stable enough to ride a bicycle! By creating robots that can walk, hop, and maintain their balance, scientists are pushing into new areas of automation.

pose ethical, legal, and moral challenges and questions. For example, how do you feel about the following?

- Since the tragic events of September 11, 2001, various nationwide surveillance programs have been proposed. Some programs include installing surveillance cameras in public places that could be considered attractive areas to stage terrorist activities. These cameras would be monitored via the Internet, possibly by volunteers. Should the government be allowed to monitor your activities in public places à la George Orwell's famous book *1984* to help keep the country secure?

- Advances in technology in surveillance devices (see Figure 1.29) are allowing these devices to become smaller and less noticeable. In certain jurisdictions, courts have upheld the rights of employers to install surveillance devices in the workplace (sometimes without needing to notify employees) to cut down on theft and prevent industrial espionage. Do you know if your employer is watching you? Do you think your employer should have this right?

- Many employees don't know that employers have the right to monitor e-mail and network traffic on the systems they use at work, because those

SOUND BYTE

The History of the Personal Computer

In this Sound Byte, you will explore the history of the personal computer, including the events that led to the development of today's computers and the people who made them possible.

FIGURE 1.29

With cameras becoming smaller, you could be under surveillance at any time and not even know it. Should the government be allowed to install cameras to monitor sensitive sites for criminal or terrorist activity— or should your privacy be respected?

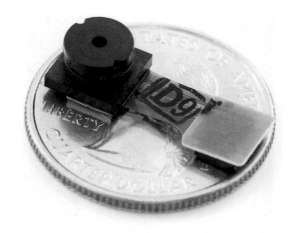

systems are provided at the employer's expense for the sole purpose of allowing employees to do their jobs. Have you visited Web sites that you don't want your employer to know about (such as employment sites as part of a new job search)? Have you sent personal e-mail through your company e-mail system? Does your employer know about these activities? Should employers have the right to know?

These are just a few examples of the kind of questions active participants in today's digital society need to be able to think about, discuss, and, at times, take action on. Being computer literate enables you to form

educated opinions on these issues and to take stands based on accurate information rather than media hype and misinformation. Here are a few other questions that you, as a member of our digital society, may be expected to think about and discuss:

- What privacy risks do biomedical chips such as the VeriChip pose? Do the privacy risks of such chips outweigh the potential benefits?

- Should companies be allowed to collect personal data from visitors to their Web sites without their permission?

- Should spam be illegal? If so, what penalties should be levied on people who send spam?

- Is it ethical to download music off the Web without paying for it (see Figure 1.30)? What about copying a friend's software onto your computer?

- What are the risks involved in humans attempting to create computers that can learn and become more human?

- Should we rely solely on computers to provide security for sensitive areas such as nuclear power plants?

As a computer user, you must consider these and other questions to define the boundaries of the digital society in which you live.

FIGURE 1.30

Does downloading music without paying for it hurt anyone? Or is it merely a cost absorbed by huge record companies? How will your choices create the future music market you experience?

Ethics: Knowledge Is Power—Bridging the Digital Divide

What would your life be like if you had never touched a computer because you simply couldn't afford one? What if there were no computers in your town? If you're like most people in the United States, access to computers is a given. But for many people, access to the opportunities and knowledge computers and the Internet offer is impossible. The discrepancy between the "haves" and "have-nots" with regards to computer technology is commonly referred to as the **digital divide**.

This discrepancy is a growing problem. People with access to computers and the Internet (that is, those who can afford it) are poised to take advantage of the many new developments technology offers, whereas poorer individuals, communities, and school systems that can't afford computer systems and Internet access are being left behind.

For example, in the United States, more teachers are using the Internet to communicate with parents than ever before. E-mail updates on student progress, Web sites with homework postings that allow parents to keep tabs on assignments, and even online parent–teacher conferences are becoming popular. Unwired parents and students are left out of the loop. In the United States, children who do not have access to the Internet and computers won't be prepared for future employment, contributing to the continuing cycle of poverty.

But the digital divide isn't always caused by low income. Terrain can be a factor that inhibits connectivity (see Figure 1.31). In Nepal's mountainous terrain, for example, even though a village might only be a few miles away "as the crow flies," it might take two days to hike there because of the lack of roads. Volunteers, funded by a generous donor, have installed 12 outdoor access points complete with directional antennas to connect a series of villages to the Internet via a wireless network. The last access point in the connectivity chain connects to an

FIGURE 1.31

Terrain (such as mountains) and remote locations (the Sahara Desert, for example) can present barriers to conquering the digital divide.

Internet service provider 22 miles away. The villagers are now able to hold meetings, school classes, and access the Internet without trekking across miles of mountainous terrain. Unfortunately, this solution isn't available throughout all of Nepal . . . or even throughout some areas of the United States.

So the United States must be the most wired country in the world with the smallest gap in the digital divide, right? Guess again. According to a 2007 Pew Center report, although 47 percent of adult Americans have a broadband connection at home (either cable or DSL), more than 80 percent of South Korean households have high-speed connections. This widespread connectivity is changing the face of Korean society. Government agencies, once known for long lines and mind-numbing paperwork, have installed efficient Web sites to streamline processes. Although we're still in the test-marketing phase of video-on-demand in a few markets in the United States, South Koreans routinely download movies and watch them whenever they want.

What is being done to bridge the digital divide in rural and poor areas of the world? Some organizations are attempting to increase local and global Internet and computer access, whereas community organizations such as libraries and recreation centers are providing free Internet access to the public. Meanwhile, others are sponsoring referendums that increase Internet capacity in schools or are e-mailing their local and state representatives, urging them to back legislation to provide funding for computer equipment in struggling school systems. Others suggest computer users donate their old computers to a charity that refurbishes and distributes them to needy families. To help bridge the digital divide, you can start by supporting such programs and institutions (such as your local library) in your area that are attempting to increase Internet and computer access.

1. What does it mean to be "computer literate"?

Computer literacy goes way beyond knowing how to use a mouse and send e-mail. If you are computer literate, you understand the capabilities and limitations of computers and know how to use them wisely. Being computer literate also enables you to make informed purchasing decisions, use computers in your career, and understand the many ethical, legal, and societal implications of technology today. Anyone can become computer literate.

2. How does being computer literate make you a savvy computer user and consumer?

By understanding how a computer is constructed and how its various parts function, you'll be able to get the most out of your computer. Among other things, you'll be able to avoid hackers, viruses, and Internet headaches; protect your privacy; and separate the real risks of privacy and security from those you don't have to worry about. You'll also be better able to maintain, upgrade, and troubleshoot your computer; make good purchasing decisions; and incorporate the latest technologies into your existing equipment.

3. How can becoming computer literate help you in a career?

As computers become more a part of our daily lives, it is difficult to imagine any career that does not use computers in some fashion. Understanding how to use computers effectively will help you be a more productive and valuable employee, no matter which profession you choose.

4. How can becoming computer literate help you understand and take advantage of newly emerging careers?

The world is changing every day, and many changes are a result of new computer technologies. Understanding how today's computers function should help you utilize technology effectively now. And by understanding computers and how they work today, you can contribute to such technologies of tomorrow as nanoscience and new medical technologies.

5. How does becoming computer literate help you deal with the challenges associated with technology?

Although computers offer us a world of opportunities, they also pose ethical, legal, and moral challenges and questions. Being computer literate enables you to form *educated* opinions on these issues and to take stands based on accurate information rather than media hype and misinformation.

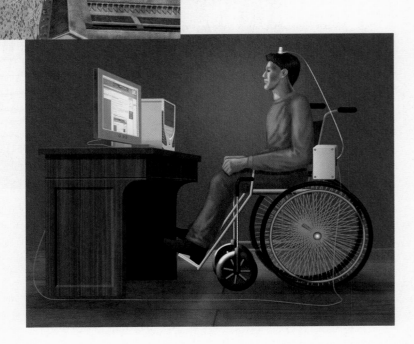

Buzzwords

Word Bank

- affective computing
- Bluetooth
- computer forensics
- computer literate
- data mining
- digital divide
- digital home
- information technology (IT)
- nanotechnology
- offshoring
- patient simulator
- personal digital assistant (PDA)
- public domain
- radio frequency identification tags (RFID tags)
- spam

Instructions: Fill in the blanks using the words from the Word Bank above.

Because of the integration of computers into business and society, many fields of study are available now that were unheard of a few years ago. (1) _____, the study of incredibly small computing devices built at the molecular level, will provide major advances in the miniaturization of computing. (2) _____ is already taking criminologists beyond what they could accomplish with conventional investigation techniques. And as the science of (3) _____ advances, computers will perform more and more like human beings in emotion and social cueing.

There are many reasons to know more about computing, or to become (4) _____. It can help you in eliminating unwanted e-mails or (5) _____. You will know how to upgrade your system to the latest standards, like the wireless communication technology (6) _____. More and more aspects of how our homes are run are being coordinated through computers, giving rise to the term (7) _____. You may even find you enjoy computers so much you want to explore careers in (8) _____.

People who fail to keep up with the knowledge of how to use and maintain computer systems will fall to one side of the gap known as the (9) _____. As an entire country begins to lose computer expertise, jobs leave and are relocated in other, more tech-savvy countries. This shift of work is known as (10) _____.

Becoming Computer Literate

Using the key terms and ideas you learned in this chapter, write a one- or two-paragraph summary for your school advisor so that he or she can use it to explain to students the importance of being computer literate in today's job market. Using the Internet, find examples of careers most people would not expect to use computers and add this to your document to further support this advice.

Self-Test

Instructions: Answer the multiple-choice and true–false questions below for more practice with key terms and concepts from this chapter.

MULTIPLE CHOICE

1. Which of the following is NOT a use of computers in the legal environment?
   a. Creating animations that simulate the crime for use in the courtroom
   b. Tracking criminal behavior patterns
   c. Predicting criminal behavior patterns
   d. Conducting interviews with suspects

2. Art interfaces with technology by
   a. using a computer to generate images that respond to the environment.
   b. having computers suggest appropriate solutions to a dispute.
   c. using software that completes the plot of a story.
   d. having Web sites that search for prospective clients for artists.

3. Affective computing is the science of relating computers and
   a. effective organizational skills.
   b. results-oriented outcomes.
   c. emotional and social skills.
   d. the calculation of interest rates.

4. Computer systems CANNOT be trained to understand
   a. the U.S. tax code. b. human emotion.
   c. a good joke.   d. the perfect golf swing.

5. Automotive technology requires an understanding of computers to
   a. properly bill customers.
   b. control computerized pneumatic tools.
   c. keep carburetor settings at the optimal positions.
   d. be able to run sensor and CPU diagnostics for the many computerized subsystems.

6. A device that tracks movement is
   a. a PSS.   b. an RFID tag.
   c. a PDA.   d. a patient simulator.

7. Which of the following is NOT a good reason to learn more about computers?
   a. To keep your home system secure
   b. To increase your career options
   c. To get attention from your friends when their systems break down
   d. To make informed purchasing decisions

8. Infrared scanners CANNOT
   a. scan packages and detect unusual objects.
   b. be worn on the wrist.
   c. translate a bar code into a computer data file.
   d. be used by shipping companies to track packages.

9. Computer forensics
   a. uses computer technology to gather potential legal evidence.
   b. helps identify the remains of bodies.
   c. investigates a suspect's home computer for evidence.
   d. All of the above

10. Robotic surgery devices help physicians because
    a. they make more accurate incisions.
    b. the doctor does not have to be involved in the actual surgery.
    c. they monitor and make suggestions to the surgeon during the procedure.
    d. if the operation runs into complications, they can suggest creative alternatives.

TRUE–FALSE

___ 1. Computer simulations are used for gaming purposes, but they are not yet accurate enough for criminal investigations.

___ 2. Affective computing is the science that attempts to produce machines that make people comfortable because they look human in form.

___ 3. Artists use computers for the business side of their work—for example, advertising or record keeping—but computers are not useful artistic tools.

___ 4. Ranchers tag their cattle and use computer systems to track and record their movements.

___ 5. In many hospitals, infants are "chipped," or injected with a small, computerized tracking device, so that nurses can monitor their location and keep them safe.

Making the Transition to...
Next Semester

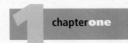

1. Computer Literacy

In your college career, you'll be spending time understanding the requirements of the degree program you choose. At many schools, computer literacy requirements exist either as incoming requirements (skills students must have before they are admitted) or outgoing requirements (skills students must prove they have before graduating). Does your program require specific computer skills? Which skills are these? Should they be required? How can students efficiently prove that they have these skills? How often does the set of skills need to be reviewed and updated?

2. Computing and Education

Think about the schedule of courses you will be taking next semester. How many courses will require you to produce papers in electronic format? How many will require you to use course management software, such as Blackboard or Moodle? Will any course require you to use some specialty software product such as a nutrition monitoring program or a statistics training application? Do any require specialized hardware such as a scanner for your computer? How many require the use of collaborative meeting software?

3. Old Technologies Holding On

What courses and careers have not been impacted by computer technology? Think of three courses that are taught effectively with no use of technology. Think of three careers that do not use computers in a significant way. Research and find the average salary and the rate of growth in these careers.

4. Using Biomedical Implants

If having such a chip implanted meant you would never need to carry cash or a credit card to the bookstore with you because your financial information was encoded on the chip, would you want one? If it could help instructors take attendance automatically in your class by reading your personal information, would that be an acceptable use? Would you consider using such a chip if it could be disabled whenever you wanted it to be or if only individuals you authorized had access to the information?

5. Campus Policing

In this chapter, the use of trend-spotting programs to predict criminal activity was discussed. If existing criminal statistics are used to help identify trouble spots (such as wild parties) on your campus and the potential for serious criminal activity, then is this the same as profiling? Does your campus police force have the right to take proactive steps to prevent crime based solely on developing trends? Should someone be held accountable if such information is not acted upon and a crime occurs?

Making the Transition to...
the Workplace

1. **Computer-Free Workplaces?**

   In this chapter, we listed several careers that require computer skills. How are computers used in the profession you are in or plan to enter? Can you think of any careers in which people do not use computers? Can you imagine computers being used in these careers in the future? If so, how? Are there benefits to having a "computer-free" zone in some aspects of some careers? How do computers impact creativity?

2. **Medical Computing Applications**

   In their training and work, doctors and nurses rely on computers. What about patients? Does having access to a computer and computer skills help a patient create better health care options? Does having access to a computer help when filing an insurance claim? Does it help with finding the best doctor or hospital for a specific procedure? Explain your answers.

3. **Preparing for a Job**

   An office is looking for help and needs an employee able to manipulate data on Excel spreadsheets, coordinate the computer file management for the office, and conduct backups of critical data. How could you prove to the interviewer that you have the skills to handle the job? How could you prove you have the ability to learn the job?

4. **Career Outlook**

   Which career fields are growing the fastest? (Suggestion: Try searching at **www.ask.com**.) Which fields are growing fastest in the state where you live? What computer skills and knowledge do the top 10 career paths demand? What kinds of continuing training in technology can you imagine would be required as you progress in these careers?

5. **IT Careers**

   Information technology (IT) careers are suited to a wide range of people at different points in their lives. The Technology in Focus piece on page 472 details more about IT careers. Review that section and then answer the following questions:
   a. Would an IT career have advantages for a single parent? How?
   b. How might an IT career be able to help someone pursue a later career in a nontechnical field?
   c. How might an IT career assist someone in completing a college degree?

6. **Job Skills Assessment**

   Frequently, job seekers are asked about their computer literacy when applying for a job.
   a. How do you think computer skill levels are determined by employers? How should they be determined?
   b. If your interpretation of "expert" doesn't match your prospective employer's definition, does that make you wrong?

Critical Thinking Questions

Instructions: Albert Einstein used *Gedanken experiments*, or critical thinking questions, to develop his theory of relativity. Some ideas are best understood by experimenting with them in our own minds. The following critical thinking questions are designed to demand your full attention but require only a comfortable chair—no technology.

1. Rating Your Computer Literacy

This chapter lists many ways in which knowing about computers (or becoming computer literate) will help you. How much do you know about computers? What else would you like to know? How do you think learning more about computers will help you in the future?

2. Data Mining

This chapter briefly discusses data mining, a technique companies use to study sales data and gather information from it. Have you heard of data mining before? How might companies like Wal-Mart or Target use data mining to better run their business? Can you think of any privacy risks data mining might pose?

3. Nanotechnology

As you learned in the chapter, nanotechnology is the science revolving around the use of nanostructures to build devices on an extremely small scale. What applications of tiny computers can you think of? How might nanotechnology impact your life?

4. Biomedical Chips

This chapter discusses various uses of biomedical chips. Many biomedical chip implants that will be developed in the future will most likely be aimed at correcting vision loss, hearing loss, or other physical impediments. But chips could also be developed to improve physical or mental capabilities of healthy individuals. For example, chips could be implanted in athletes to make their muscles work better together, thereby allowing them to run faster. Or your memory could be enhanced by providing additional storage capacity for your brain.

a. Should biomedical implant devices that increase athletic performance be permitted in the Olympics?
b. What about devices that repair a problem (such as blindness in one eye) but then increase the level of visual acuity in the affected eye so that it is better than normal vision?
c. Would you be willing to have a chip implanted in your brain to improve your memory?
d. Would you be willing to have a VeriChip implanted under your skin?

5. Affective Computing

Affective computing is the science that attempts to produce machines that understand and can respond to human emotions and social mores. Do you think humans will ever create a machine that cannot be distinguished from a human being? In your opinion, what are the ethical and moral implications associated with that development?

6. The World Stage

How might access to (or denial of) electronic information improve the education of a country's citizens? Could that affect who the world's next technology power will be? Could it eliminate third world status?

Problem:

People are often overwhelmed by the relentless march of technology. Accessibility of information is changing the way we work, play, and interact with our friends, family, and co-workers. In this Team Time, we consider the future and reflect on how the advent of new technologies will affect our daily lives 10 years in the future.

Task:

Your group has just returned from a trip in a time machine 10 years into the future. Amazing changes have taken place in just a short time. To a large extent, consumer acceptance of technology makes or breaks a new technology. Your mission is to develop a creative marketing strategy to promote the technological changes you observed in the future and accelerate their acceptance.

Process:

Divide the class into three or more teams.

1. With the other members of your team, use the Internet to research up-and-coming technologies (**www.howstuffworks.com** is a good starting point). Prepare a list of innovations that you believe will occur in the next 10 years. Determine how they will be integrated into society and the effect they will have on our culture.

2. Present your group's findings to the class for debate and discussion. Note specifically how the rest of the class reacts to your reports on the innovations. Are they excited? Skeptical? Incredulous? Do they laugh off your ideas, or do they become wildly enthusiastic?

3. Write a marketing-strategy paper that details how you would promote the technological changes that you envision for the future. Also note some barriers for acceptance the technology may have to overcome, as well as any legal or ethical challenges or questions you see the new technology posing.

Conclusion:

The future path of technology is determined by dreamers. If not for innovators such as Thomas Edison, Alexander Graham Bell, and Albert Einstein, we would not be as advanced a society as we are today. Innovators come from all walks of life, and our creative energies must be exercised to keep them in tune. Don't be afraid to suggest technological advancements that seem outrageous today. In 1966, when the original *Star Trek* series was on television, handheld communicators seemed astounding and beyond our reach. Yet the dreamers who created those communication devices for a science fiction series helped to inspire a multibillion-dollar cell phone industry in the 21st century. The next technological wave may be started in your imagination!

Multimedia

In addition to the review materials presented here, you'll find additional materials featured with the book's multimedia, including the *Technology in Action* Student Resource CD and the Companion Website (**www.prenhall.com/techinaction**), which will help reinforce your understanding of the chapter content. These materials include the following:

ACTIVE HELPDESK

In Active Helpdesk calls, you'll assume the role of helpdesk operator, taking calls about the concepts you've learned in this chapter. You'll apply what you've learned and receive feedback from a supervisor to review and reinforce those concepts. The Active Helpdesk call for this chapter is listed below and can be found on your Student Resource CD:

- This chapter has no Active Helpdesks.

SOUND BYTES

Sound Bytes are dynamic multimedia tutorials that help demystify even the most complex topics. You'll view video clips and animations that illustrate computer concepts and then apply what you've learned by reviewing with the Sound Byte Labs, which include quizzes and activities specifically tailored to each Sound Byte. The Sound Bytes for this chapter are listed below and can be found on your Student Resource CD:

- Questions to Ask Before You Buy a Computer
- The History of the Personal Computer

COMPANION WEBSITE

The *Technology in Action* Companion Website includes a variety of additional materials to help you review and learn more about the topics in this chapter. The resources available at **www.prenhall.com/techinaction** include:

- **Online Study Guide.** Each chapter features an online true–false and multiple-choice quiz. You can take these quizzes, automatically check the results, and e-mail the results to your instructor.
- **Web Research Projects.** Each chapter features several Web research projects that ask you to search the Web for information on computer-related careers, milestones in computer history, important people and companies, emerging technologies, and the applications and implications of different technologies.

The History
of THE PC

Do you ever wonder how big the first personal computer was, or how much the first portable computer weighed? Computers are such an integral part of our lives that we don't often stop to think about how far they've come or where they got their start. But in just 30 years, computers have evolved from expensive, huge machines that only corporations owned to small, powerful devices found in millions of homes. In this Technology in Focus feature, we look at the history of the computer. Along the way, we discuss some developments that helped make the computer powerful and portable, as well as the people who contributed to its development. But first, we start with the story of the personal computer and how it grew to be as integral to our lives as the automobile.

The First Personal Computer: The Altair

Our journey through the history of the personal computer starts in 1975. At that time, most people were unfamiliar with the mainframes and supercomputers that large corporations and the government owned. With price tags exceeding the cost of buildings, and with few if any practical home uses, these monster machines were not appealing or attainable to the vast majority of Americans. But that began to change when the January 1975 cover of *Popular Electronics* announced the debut of the **Altair 8800**, touted as the first personal computer (see Figure 1). For just $395 for a do-it-yourself kit or $498 for a fully assembled unit (about $1,000 in today's dollars), the price was reasonable enough so that computer fanatics could finally own their own computers.

The Altair was a very primitive computer, with just 256 bytes (not *kilo*bytes, just bytes) of memory. It didn't come with a keyboard, nor did it include a monitor or printer. Switches on the front of the machine were used to enter data in unfriendly machine code (strings of 1s and 0s). Flashing lights on the front indicated the results of a program. User-friendly it was not—at least not by today's standards.

Despite its limitations, computer "hackers" (as computer enthusiasts were called then) flocked to the machine. Many who bought the Altair had been taught to program, but until that point had access only to big, clumsy computers. They were often hired by corporations to program "boring" financial, statistical, or engineering programs in a workplace environment. The Altair offered these enthusiasts the opportunity to create their own programs. Within three months, Micro Instrumentation and Telemetry Systems (MITS), the company behind the Altair, received more than 4,000 orders for the machine.

The release of the Altair marked the start of the personal computer (PC) boom. In fact,

FIGURE 1

In 1975, the Altair was touted as the "world's first minicomputer" in the January issue of *Popular Electronics*.

two men who would play large roles in the development of the PC were among the first Altair owners. Recent high school grads Bill Gates and Paul Allen were so enamored by this "minicomputer," as these personal computers were called at the time, that they wrote a compiling program (a program that translates user commands into those that the computer can understand) for the Altair. The two friends later convinced its developer, Ed Roberts, to buy their program. This marked the start of a small company called Microsoft. But we'll get to that story later. First, let's see what their future archrivals were up to.

Why Was It Called the "Altair"?

For lack of a better name, the Altair's developers originally called the computer the PE-8, short for Popular Electronics 8-bit. However, Les Soloman, the *Popular Electronics* writer who introduced the Altair, wanted the machine to have a catchier name. The author's daughter, who was watching *Star Trek* at the time, suggested the name Altair (that's where the *Star Trek* crew was traveling that week). The first star of the PC industry was born.

The Apple I and II

Around the time the Altair was released, **Steve Wozniak**, an employee at Hewlett-Packard, was becoming fascinated with the burgeoning personal computer industry and was dabbling with his own computer design. He would bring his computer prototypes to meetings of the Homebrew Computing Club, a group of young computer fans who met to discuss computer ideas in Palo Alto, California. **Steve Jobs**, who was working for computer game manufacturer Atari at the time, liked Wozniak's prototypes and made a few suggestions. Together, the two built a personal computer, later known as the **Apple I**, in Wozniak's garage (see Figures 2 and 3). In that same year, on April 1, 1976, Jobs and Wozniak officially formed the **Apple Computer Company**.

No sooner had the Apple I hit the market than Wozniak was working to improve it. A year later, in 1977, the **Apple II** was born (see Figure 4). The Apple II included a color monitor, sound, and game paddles. Priced around $1,300 (quite a bit of money in those days), it included 4 kilobytes (KB) of random access memory (RAM) as well as an optional floppy disk drive that enabled users to run additional programs. Most of these programs were games. However, for many users, there was a special appeal to the Apple II: the program that made the computer function when the power was first turned on was stored in read-only memory (ROM).

Previously, such routine-task programs had to be rewritten every time the computer was turned on. This automation made it possible for the least technical computer enthusiast to write programs.

An instant success, the Apple II would be the most successful in the company's line, outshining even its successor, the **Apple III**, released in 1980. Eventually, the Apple II included a spreadsheet program, word processing, and desktop publishing software. These programs gave personal computers like the Apple functions beyond just gaming and special programming, leading to their increased popularity. We talk more about these advances later. For now, other players were entering the market.

FIGURE 2

Steve Jobs (a) and Steve Wozniak (b) were two computer hobbyists who worked together to form the Apple Computer Company.

FIGURE 3

The first Apple computer, the Apple I, looked like a typewriter in a box. It was one of the first computers to incorporate a keyboard.

FIGURE 4

The Apple II came with the addition of a monitor and an external floppy disk drive.

Why Is It Called "Apple"?

Steve Jobs wanted Apple Computer to be the "perfect" computer company. Having recently worked at an apple orchard, Jobs thought of the apple as the "perfect" fruit—it was high in nutrients, came in a nice package, and was not easily damaged. Thus, he and Wozniak decided to name their new computer company Apple.

Enter the Competition

Around the time Apple was experiencing success with its computers, a number of competitors entered the market. The largest among them were Commodore, RadioShack, and IBM. As Figure 5 shows, just years after the introduction of the Altair, the market was filled with personal computers from a variety of manufacturers.

The Commodore PET and TRS-80

Among Apple's strongest competitors were the **Commodore PET 2001**, shown in Figure 6, and Tandy RadioShack's **TRS-80**, shown in Figure 7. Commodore introduced the PET in January 1977. It was featured on the cover of *Popular Science* in October 1977 as the "new $595 home computer." Tandy RadioShack's home computer also garnered immediate popularity. Just one month after its release in 1977, the TRS-80 Model 1 sold approximately 10,000 units. Priced at $599.95, the easy-to-use machine included a monochrome display and 4 KB of memory. Many other manufacturers followed suit over the next decade, launching new desktop products, but none were as successful as the TRS-80 and the Commodore.

FIGURE 5
Personal Computer Development

YEAR	APPLE	IBM	OTHERS
1975			MITS Altair
1976	Apple I		
1977	Apple II		Tandy RadioShack's TRS-80 Commodore PET
1980	Apple III		
1981		IBM PC	Osborne
1983	Lisa		
1984	Macintosh	286-AT	IBM PC clones

FIGURE 6
The Commodore PET was well received because of its all-in-one design.

FIGURE 7
The TRS-80 hid its circuitry under the keyboard. The computer was nicknamed "trash-80," which was more a play on its initials than a reflection of its capabilities.

The Osborne

The Osborne Company introduced the **Osborne** in April 1981 as the industry's first portable computer (see Figure 8). Although portable, the computer weighed 24.5 pounds, and its screen was just 5 inches wide. In addition to its hefty weight, it came with a hefty price tag of $1,795. Still, the Osborne included 64 KB of memory, two floppy disk drives, and preinstalled software programs (such as word processing and spreadsheet software). The Osborne was an overnight success, with sales quickly reaching 10,000 units per month. However, despite the Osborne's popularity, the release of a successor machine, called the **Executive**, reduced sales of the Osborne significantly, and the Osborne Company eventually closed. Compaq bought the Osborne design and later produced its first portable in 1983.

IBM PCs

By 1980, IBM recognized it needed to get its feet wet in the personal computer market. Up until that point, the company had been a player in the computer industry, but primarily with mainframe computers, which it sold only to large corporations. It had not taken the smaller, personal computer seriously. In August 1981, however, IBM released its first personal computer, appropriately named the **IBM PC**. Because many companies were already familiar with IBM mainframes, they readily adopted the IBM PC. The term *PC* soon became the term used to describe all personal computers.

The IBM PC came with 64 KB of memory, expandable to 256 KB, and started at $1,565. IBM marketed its PC through retail outlets such as Sears and Computerland in order to reach the home market, and it quickly dominated the playing field. In January 1983, *Time* magazine, playing on its annual "man of the year" issue, named the computer "1982 machine of the year" (see Figure 9).

FIGURE 8

The Osborne was introduced as the first portable personal computer. It weighed a whopping 24.5 pounds and contained just 64 KB of memory.

FIGURE 9

The IBM PC was the first (and only) nonhuman object chosen as "man of the year" (actually, "machine of the year") by *Time* magazine in its January 1983 issue. This designation indicated the impact the PC was having on the general public.

Other Important Advancements

It was not just the *hardware* of the personal computer that was developing during the 1970s and 1980s. At the same time, advances in programming languages and operating systems and the influx of application software were leading to more useful and powerful machines.

The Importance of BASIC

The software industry began in the 1950s with the development of programming languages such as FORTRAN, ALGOL, and COBOL. These languages were used mainly by businesses to create financial, statistical, and engineering programs for corporate enterprises. But the 1964 introduction of **Beginners All-Purpose Symbolic Instruction Code (BASIC)** revolutionized the software industry. BASIC was a programming language that the beginning programming student could easily learn. It thus became enormously popular—and the key language of the PC. In fact, **Bill Gates** and **Paul Allen** (see Figure 10) used BASIC to write the program for the Altair. As we noted earlier, this program led to the creation of **Microsoft**, a company that produced software for the microcomputer.

The Advent of Operating Systems

Because data on the earliest personal computers was stored on audiocassettes (not floppies), many programs were not saved or reused. Rather, programs were rewritten as needed. Then Steve Wozniak developed a floppy disk drive called the **Disk II**, which he introduced in July 1978. With the introduction of the floppy drive, programs could be saved with more efficiency, and operating systems (OSs) developed.

OSs were (and still are) written to coordinate with the specific processor chip that controlled the computer. Apples ran exclusively on a Motorola chip, while PCs (IBMs and so on) ran exclusively on an Intel chip. **Disk Operating System (DOS)**, developed by Wozniak and introduced in December 1977, was the OS that controlled the first Apple computers. The **Control Program for Microcomputers (CP/M)**, developed by Gary Kildall, was the first OS designed for the Intel

FIGURE 10

Bill Gates and Paul Allen are the founders of Microsoft.

8080 chip (the processor for PCs). Intel hired Kildall to write a compiling program for the 8080 chip, but Kildall quickly saw the need for a program that could store computer operating instructions on a floppy disk rather than on a cassette. Intel wasn't interested in buying the CP/M program, but Kildall saw a future for the program and thus founded his own company, Digital Research.

In 1980, when IBM was considering entering the personal computer market, it approached Bill Gates at Microsoft to write an OS program for the IBM PC. Although Gates had written versions of BASIC for different computer systems, he had never written an OS. He therefore recommended IBM investigate the CP/M OS, but no one from Digital Research returned IBM's call. Microsoft reconsidered the opportunity and developed **MS-DOS** for IBM computers. (This was one phone call Digital Research certainly regrets not returning!)

MS-DOS was based on an OS called **Quick and Dirty Operating System (QDOS)** developed by Seattle Computer Products. Microsoft bought the nonexclusive rights to QDOS and distributed it to IBM. Eventually, virtually all personal computers running on the Intel chip used MS-DOS as their OS. Microsoft's reign as one of the dominant players in the PC landscape had begun. Meanwhile, many other software programs were being developed, taking personal computers to the next level of user acceptance.

The Software Application Explosion: VisiCalc and Beyond

Inclusion of floppy disk drives in personal computers not only facilitated the storage of operating systems, but also set off a software application explosion, because the floppy disk was a convenient way to distribute software. Around that same time, in 1978, Harvard Business School student Dan Bricklin recognized the potential for a spreadsheet program that could be used on PCs. He and his friend Bob Frankston (see Figure 11) thus created the program **VisiCalc**. VisiCalc not only became an instant success, it was also one of the main reasons for the rapid increase in PC sales. Finally, ordinary home users could see how owning a personal computer could benefit their lives. More than 100,000 copies of VisiCalc were sold in its first year.

After VisiCalc, other electronic spreadsheet programs entered the market. **Lotus 1-2-3** came on the market in 1982, and **Microsoft Excel** entered the scene in 1985. These two products became so popular that they eventually put VisiCalc out of business.

Meanwhile, word processing software was gaining a foothold in the PC industry. Up to this point, there were separate, dedicated word-processing machines, and the thought hadn't occurred to anyone to enable the personal computer to do word processing. Personal computers, it was believed, were for computation and data management. However, once **WordStar**, the first word processing application, came out in disk form in 1979 and was available on personal computers, word processing became another important use for the PC. In fact, word processing is now one of the most common PC applications. Competitors such as **Word for MS-DOS** (the precursor to Microsoft Word) and **WordPerfect** soon entered the market. Figure 12 lists some of the important dates in software application development.

FIGURE 11

Dan Bricklin and Bob Frankston created VisiCalc, the first business application developed for the personal computer.

FIGURE 12
Software Application Development

YEAR	APPLICATION
1978	**VisiCalc:** First electronic spreadsheet application. **WordStar:** First word processing application.
1980	**WordPerfect:** Thought to be the best word processing software for the PC. WordPerfect was eventually sold to Novell, then later acquired by Corel.
1982	**Lotus 1-2-3:** Added integrated charting, plotting, and database capabilities to spreadsheet software.
1983	**Word for MS-DOS:** Introduced in *PC World* magazine with the first magazine-inserted demo disk.
1985	**Excel:** One of the first spreadsheets to use a graphical user interface. **PageMaker:** First desktop publishing software.

The Graphical User Interface

Another important advancement in personal computers was the introduction of the **graphical user interface (GUI)**, which allowed users to interact with the computer more easily. Until that time, users had to use complicated command- or menu-driven interfaces to interact with the computer. Apple was the first company to take full commercial advantage of the GUI, but competitors were fast on its heels, and soon the GUI became synonymous with personal computers. But who developed the idea of the GUI? You'll probably be surprised to learn that a company known for its photocopiers was the real innovator.

Xerox

In 1972, a few years before Apple had launched its first PC, photocopier manufacturer **Xerox** was hard at work in its Palo Alto Research Center (PARC) designing a personal computer of its own. Named the **Alto** (shown in Figure 13), the computer included a word processor, based on the What You See Is What You Get (WYSIWYG) principle, that was a file management system with directories and folders. It also had a mouse and could connect to a network. None of the other personal computers of the time had any of these features. Still, for a variety of reasons, Xerox never sold the Alto commercially. Several years later, it developed the Star Office System, which was based on the Alto. Despite its convenient features, the Star never became popular, because no one was willing to pay the $17,000 asking price.

The Lisa and the Macintosh

Xerox's ideas were ahead of its time, but many of the ideas of the Alto and Star would soon catch on. In 1983, Apple introduced the **Lisa**, shown in Figure 14. Named after Apple founder Steve Jobs's daughter, the Lisa was the first successful PC brought to market to use a GUI. Legend has it that Jobs had seen the Alto during a visit to PARC in 1979 and was influenced by its GUI. He therefore incorporated a similar user interface into the Lisa, providing features such as windows, drop-down menus, icons, a hierarchical file system with folders and files, and a point-and-click device called a mouse. The only problem with the Lisa was its price. At $9,995 ($20,000 in today's dollars), few buyers were willing to take the plunge.

A year later, in 1984, Apple introduced the **Macintosh**, shown in Figure 15. The Macintosh was everything the Lisa was and then some, and at about a third of the cost. The Macintosh was also the first personal computer to introduce 3.5-inch floppy disks with a hard cover, which were smaller and sturdier than the previous 5.25-inch floppies.

The Internet Boom

The GUI made it easier for users to work on the computer. The Internet provided another reason for consumers to buy computers. Now they could conduct research and communicate with each other in a new and convenient way. In 1993, the Web browser **Mosaic** was introduced. This browser allowed users to view multimedia on the

FIGURE 13
The Alto was the first computer to use a graphical user interface, and it provided the basis for the GUI that Apple used. However, because of marketing problems, the Alto never was sold.

FIGURE 14
The Lisa was the first computer to introduce a GUI to the market. Priced too high, it never gained the popularity it deserved.

FIGURE 15
The Macintosh became one of Apple's best-selling computers, incorporating a graphical user interface along with other innovations such as the 3.5-inch floppy disk drive.

Web, causing Internet traffic to increase by nearly 350 percent.

Meanwhile, companies discovered the Internet as a means to do business, and computer sales took off. IBM-compatible PCs became the personal computer system of choice when, in 1995, Microsoft (the predominant software provider to PCs) introduced Internet Explorer, a Web browser that integrated Web functionality into Microsoft Office applications, and **Windows 95**, the first Microsoft OS designed to be principally a GUI OS, although it still was based on the DOS kernel.

About a year earlier, in mid-1994, Jim Clark, founder of the computer company Silicon Graphics Inc., Marc Andreessen, and others from the Mosaic development team developed the commercial Web browser Netscape. Netscape's popularity grew quickly, and it soon became a predominant player in browser software. However, pressures from Microsoft became too strong. In the beginning of 1998, Netscape announced it was moving to the open source market, no longer charging for the product and making the code available to the public.

Making the PC Possible: Early Computers

Since the first Altair was introduced in the 1970s, more than a billion personal computers have been distributed around the globe. Because of the declining prices of computers and the growth of the Internet, it's estimated that a billion more computers will be sold within the next decade. But what made all this possible? The computer is a compilation of parts, all of which are the result of individual inventions. From the earliest days of humankind, we have been looking for a more systematic way to count and calculate. Thus, the evolution of counting machines has led to the development of the computer we know today.

The Pascalene Calculator and the Jacquard Loom

The **Pascalene** was the first accurate mechanical calculator. This machine, created by the French mathematician **Blaise Pascal** in 1642, used revolutions of gears to count by tens, similar to odometers in cars. The Pascalene could be used to add, subtract, multiply, and divide. The basic design of the Pascalene was so sound that it lived on in mechanical calculators for more than 300 years.

Nearly 200 years later, **Joseph Jacquard** revolutionized the fabric industry by creating a machine that automated the weaving of complex patterns. Although not a counting or calculating machine, the **Jacquard Loom** (shown in Figure 16) was significant because it relied on stiff cards with punched holes to automate the process. Much later this process would be adopted as a means to record and read data by using punch cards in computers.

Babbage's Engines

Decades later, in 1834, **Charles Babbage** designed the first automatic calculator, called the **Analytical Engine** (see Figure 17). The machine was actually based on another

FIGURE 16

The Jacquard Loom used holes punched in stiff cards to make complex designs. This technique would later be used in the form of punch cards to control the input and output of data in computers.

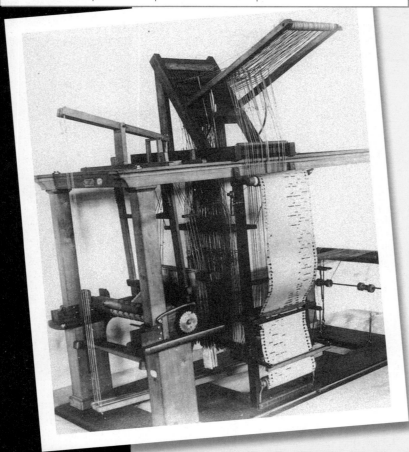

machine called the **Difference Engine**, which was a huge steam-powered mechanical calculator Babbage designed to print astronomical tables. Babbage stopped working on the Difference Engine to build the Analytical Engine. Although it was never developed, Babbage's detailed drawings and descriptions of the machine include components similar to those found in today's computers, including the store (RAM) and the mill (central processing unit), as well as input and output devices. This invention gave Charles Babbage the title of "father of computing."

Meanwhile, Ada Lovelace, the daughter of poet Lord Byron and a student of mathematics (which was unusual for women of that time), was fascinated with Babbage's Engine. She translated an Italian paper on Babbage's machine, and at the request of Babbage added her own extensive notes. Her efforts are thought of as the best description of Babbage's Engines.

The Hollerith Tabulating Machine

In 1890, **Herman Hollerith**, while working for the U.S. Census Bureau, was the first to take Jacquard's punch card concept and apply it to computing. Hollerith developed a machine called the **Hollerith Tabulating Machine** that used punch cards to tabulate census data. Up until that time, census data had been tabulated in a long, laborious process. Hollerith's tabulating machine automatically read data that had been punched onto small punch cards, speeding up the tabulation process. Hollerith's machine became so successful that he left the Census Bureau in 1896 to start the Tabulating Machine Company. His company later changed its name to International Business Machines, or IBM.

The Z1 and Atanasoff-Berry Computer

German inventor **Konrad Zuse** is credited with a number of computing inventions. His first, in 1936, was a mechanical calculator called the **Z1**. The Z1 is thought to be the first computer to include features that are integral to today's systems, including a control unit and separate memory functions, noted as important breakthroughs for future computer design.

FIGURE 17
The Analytical Engine, designed by Charles Babbage, was never fully developed, but included components similar to those found in today's computers.

In late 1939, John Atanasoff, a professor at Iowa State University, and his student Clifford Berry, built the first electrically powered digital computer, called the **Atanasoff-Berry Computer (ABC)**, shown in Figure 18. The computer was the first to use vacuum tubes to store data instead of the mechanical switches used in older computers. Although revolutionary at its time, the machine weighed 700 pounds, contained a mile of wire, and took about 15 seconds for each calculation. (In comparison, today's personal computers can calculate more than 300 billion operations in 15 seconds.) Most

FIGURE 18
The Atanasoff-Berry Computer laid the design groundwork for many computers to come.

important, the ABC was the first to use the binary system. It was also the first to have memory that repowered itself upon booting. The design of the ABC would end up being central to that of future computers.

The Harvard Mark I

From the late 1930s to the early 1950s, **Howard Aiken** and **Grace Hopper** designed the Mark series of computers at Harvard University. The U.S. Navy used these computers for ballistic and gunnery calculations. Aiken, an electrical engineer and physicist, designed the computer, while Hopper did the programming. The **Harvard Mark I**, finished in 1944, could perform all four arithmetic operations (addition, subtraction, multiplication, and division).

However, many believe Hopper's greatest contribution to computing was the invention of the **compiler**, a program that translates English language instructions into computer language. The team was also responsible for a common computer-related expression. Hopper was the first to "debug" a computer when she removed a moth that had flown into the Harvard Mark I. The moth caused the computer to break down. After that, problems that caused the computer to not run were called "bugs."

The Turing Machine

Meanwhile, in 1936, the British mathematician **Alan Turing** created an abstract computer model that could perform logical operations. The **Turing Machine** was not a real machine but rather a hypothetical model that mathematically defined a mechanical procedure (or algorithm). Additionally, Turing's concept described a process by which the machine could read, write, or erase symbols written on squares of an infinite paper tape. This concept of an infinite tape that could be read, written to, and erased was the precursor to today's RAM.

The ENIAC

The **Electronic Numerical Integrator and Computer (ENIAC)**, shown in Figure 20, was another U.S. government-sponsored machine developed to calculate the settings used for weapons. Created by **John W. Mauchly** and **J. Presper Eckert** at the University of Pennsylvania, it was placed in operation in June 1944. Although the ENIAC is generally thought of as the first successful high-speed electronic digital computer, it was big and clumsy. The ENIAC used nearly 18,000 vacuum tubes and filled approximately 1,800 square feet of floor space. Although inconvenient, the ENIAC served its purpose and remained in use until 1955.

FIGURE 19

Grace Hopper coined the term *computer bug*, referring to a moth that had flown into the Harvard Mark I, causing it to break down.

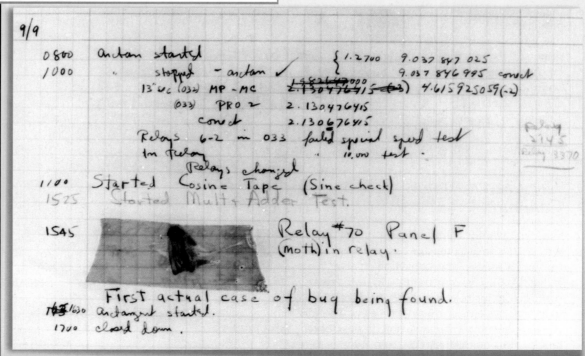

The UNIVAC

The **Universal Automatic Computer**, or **UNIVAC**, was the first commercially successful electronic digital computer. Completed in June 1951 and owned by the company Remington Rand, the UNIVAC operated on magnetic tape (as opposed to its competitors, which ran on punch cards). The UNIVAC gained notoriety when, in a 1951 publicity stunt, it was used to predict the outcome of the Stevenson-Eisenhower presidential race. By analyzing only 5 percent of the popular vote, the UNIVAC correctly identified Dwight D. Eisenhower as the victor. After that, the UNIVAC soon became a household name. The UNIVAC and computers like it were considered **first-generation computers** and were the last to use vacuum tubes to store data.

FIGURE 20

The ENIAC took up an entire room and required several people to manipulate it.

Transistors and Beyond

Only a year after the ENIAC was completed, scientists at the Bell Telephone Laboratories in New Jersey invented the **transistor** as a means to store data. The transistor replaced the bulky vacuum tubes of earlier computers and was smaller and more powerful. It was used in almost everything, from radios to phones. Computers that used transistors were referred to as **second-generation computers**. Still, transistors were limited as to how small they could be made.

A few years later, in 1958, **Jack Kilby**, while working at Texas Instruments, invented the world's first **integrated circuit**, a small chip capable of containing thousands of transistors. This consolidation in design enabled computers to become smaller and lighter. The computers in this early integrated circuit generation were considered **third-generation computers**.

Other innovations in the computer industry further refined the computer's speed, accuracy, and efficiency. However, none were as significant as the 1971 introduction by the Intel Corporation of the **microprocessor chip**, a small chip containing millions of transistors. The microprocessor functions as the central processing unit (CPU), or brains, of the computer. Computers that used a microprocessor chip were called **fourth-generation computers**. Over time, Intel and Motorola became the leading manufacturers of microprocessors. Today, the Intel Itanium 2 chip, shown in Figure 21, is one of Intel's most powerful processors.

As you can see, personal computers have come a long way since the Altair and have a number of inventions and people to thank for their amazing popularity. What will the future bring? If current trends continue, computers will be smaller, lighter, and more powerful. The advancement of wireless technology will also certainly play a big role in the development of the personal computer.

FIGURE 21

The Intel Itanium is one of Intel's most powerful processors.

2

Looking at Computers:

Understanding the Parts

Objectives

After reading this chapter, you should be able to answer the following questions:

1. What exactly is a computer, and what are its four main functions? **(p. 50)**

2. What is the difference between data and information? **(p. 50)**

3. What are bits and bytes, and how are they measured? **(pp. 50–51)**

4. What devices do you use to get data into the computer? **(pp. 52–62)**

5. What devices do you use to get information out of the computer? **(pp. 62–69)**

6. What's on the front of your system unit? **(pp. 70–74)**

7. What's on the back of your system unit? **(pp. 74–76)**

8. What's inside your system unit? **(pp. 76–78)**

9. How do you set up your computer to avoid strain and injury? **(pp. 79–81)**

ACTIVE HELPDESK

- Understanding Bits and Bytes **(p. 51)**
- Using Input Devices **(p. 57)**
- Using Output Devices **(p. 64)**

Setting Up Your System

Jillian has just bought a new computer and is setting it up. She spent more than she had planned on a wide-screen, flat-panel monitor, which she places on her small desk. It takes up far less room than her old monitor, which was big and bulky. Next she pulls out her system unit, which she knows is the component to which she'll connect all the other pieces of her system. Although she was tempted to buy the most powerful computer on the market, she bought one that best met her needs and was slightly less expensive. Still, it came with a combination CD-RW/DVD player, a 250-GB hard drive, and what the computer salesperson said was enough memory and power to do almost anything. She sets it on the floor next to her desk and attaches the monitor to it.

Next she pulls out her keyboard. She looked into buying a wireless keyboard, but because her budget was tight, she bought a standard, wired keyboard instead. The box tells her it is a USB keyboard, so she finds what looks to be the right port on the back of her system unit and plugs it in. Her mouse also needs a USB port. Finding another USB port, she attaches the mouse there. She's glad that her system has plenty of USB ports and sees there are even several on the front of the system unit. She sets up her speakers next. Although the salesperson told her she'd probably want to upgrade them, she decided to wait until she could afford it. She arranges them on her desk and inserts the speakers into the "speaker out" port on the back of her tower. Last is her printer. She debated over which type of printer to buy but decided to buy an inkjet because she prints a lot of color copies and photos. She finds another USB port on her system unit and connects it. She then plugs the power cables of the monitor, speakers, printer, and system unit into the surge protector, which the salesperson told her would protect her devices from power surges. All that's left is to make sure her setup is comfortable, and she's ready to go.

What kind of computer setup do you have? Do you know all the options available and what the different components of your system do? In this chapter, we'll take a look at your computer's basic parts. You'll learn about input devices (such as the mouse and keyboard), output devices (such as monitors and printers), and storage devices (such as the hard drive and flash drives), as well as components inside the computer (CPU and RAM) that help it to function. Finally, you'll learn how to set up your computer so that it's comfortable to work on.

SOUND BYTES

- Port Tour: How Do I Hook It Up? **(p. 76)**
- Virtual Computer Tour **(p. 77)**
- Healthy Computing **(p. 79)**

Understanding Your Computer

After reading Chapter 1, you can see why becoming computer literate is so important. But where do you start? You've no doubt gleaned some knowledge about computers just from being a member of our society. However, although you certainly know what a computer is, do you really understand how it works, what all its parts are, and what these parts do? In this section, we'll discuss what a computer does to make it such a useful machine.

COMPUTERS ARE DATA-PROCESSING DEVICES

Strictly defined, a **computer** is a data-processing device that performs four major functions:

1. It *gathers* data, or allows users to input data.
2. It *processes* that data into information.
3. It *outputs* data or information.
4. It *stores* data and information.

What is the difference between data and information? People often use the terms *data* and *information* interchangeably. Although they may mean the same thing in a simple conversation, the actual distinction between data and information is an important one.

In computer terms, **data** is a representation of a fact, figure, or idea. Data can be a number, a word, a picture, or even a recording of sound. For example, the number 6125553297 and the names Derek and Washington are pieces of data. Alone, these pieces of data probably mean little to you. **Information** is data that has been organized or presented in a meaningful fashion. When your computer provides you with a contact listing that indicates Derek Washington can be reached by phone at (612) 555-3297, then the previous data suddenly becomes useful—that is, it becomes information.

How do computers interact with data and information? Computers are excellent at **processing** (manipulating or organizing) data into information. When you first arrived on campus, you probably were directed to a place where you could get an ID card. You most likely provided a clerk with personal data (such as your name and address) that was entered into a computer. The clerk then took your picture with a digital camera (collecting more data). This information was then processed appropriately so that it could be printed on your ID card (see Figure 2.1). This organized output of data on your ID card is useful information. Finally, the information was probably stored as digital data on the computer for later use.

BITS AND BYTES: THE LANGUAGE OF COMPUTERS

How do computers process data into information? Unlike humans, computers work exclusively with numbers (not words). To process data into information, computers need to work in a language they understand. This language, called **binary language**, consists of just two digits: 0 and 1. Everything a computer does, such as process data or print a report, is broken down into a series of 0s and 1s. Each 0 and 1 is a **binary digit**, or **bit** for short. Eight binary digits (or bits) combine to create one **byte**. In computers, each letter of the alphabet, each

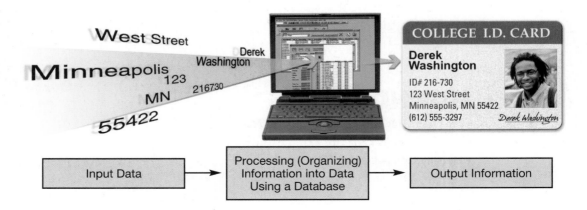

FIGURE 2.1

Computers process data into information.

West Street
Minneapolis 123
MN 216730
55422
Derek Washington

COLLEGE I.D. CARD
Derek Washington
ID# 216-730
123 West Street
Minneapolis, MN 55422
(612) 555-3297
Derek Washington

Input Data → Processing (Organizing) Information into Data Using a Database → Output Information

number, and each special character (such as the @ sign) consists of a unique combination of eight bits, or a string of eight 0s and 1s. So, for example, in binary (computer) language, the letter K is represented as 01001011. This equals eight bits, or one byte. (We'll discuss binary language in more detail in Chapter 9.)

What else can bits and bytes be used for? You've probably heard the terms *kilobyte (kB), megabyte (MB),* and *gigabyte (GB).* Bits and bytes not only are used as the language that tells the computer what to do, but also are what the computer uses to represent the data and information that it inputs and outputs. Word-processing files, digital pictures, and even software programs are all represented inside a computer as a series of bits and bytes. These files and applications can be quite large, containing many thousands and millions of bytes.

To make it easier to measure the size of these files, we need units of measure larger than a byte. Kilobytes, megabytes, and gigabytes are therefore simply amounts of bytes. As shown in Figure 2.2, a **kilobyte (kB)** is approximately 1,000 bytes, a **megabyte (MB)** is about 1 million bytes, and a **gigabyte (GB)** is around 1 billion bytes. As our information-processing needs have grown, so too have our storage needs. Today, many business computers can store up to a petabyte of data, and the Google search engine processes more than 20 petabytes of data per day—that's a lot of bytes!

How does your computer process bits and bytes? Your computer uses a combination of hardware and software to process data into information and enable you to complete tasks such as writing a letter or playing a game. An anonymous person once said that hardware is any part of a computer that you can kick when it doesn't work properly. A more formal definition of **hardware** is any part of the computer you can physically touch. However, a computer needs more than just hardware to work: It also needs some form of software (computer programs). Think of a book without words or a CD without music. Without words or music, these two common items are just shells that hold nothing.

ACTIVE HELPDESK

Understanding Bits and Bytes

In this Active Helpdesk call, you'll play the role of a helpdesk staffer, fielding calls about the difference between data and information and what bits and bytes are and how they are measured.

FIGURE 2.2 How Much Is a Byte?

Name	Abbreviation	Number of Bytes	Relative Size
Byte	B	1 byte	Can hold one character of data.
Kilobyte	kB	1,024 bytes (2^{10} bytes)	Can hold 1,024 characters or about half of a double-spaced typewritten page.
Megabyte	MB	1,048,576 bytes (2^{20} bytes)	Can hold approximately 768 pages of typed text.
Gigabyte	GB	1,073,741,824 bytes (2^{30} bytes)	Approximately 786,432 pages of text; 500 sheets of paper is approximately 2 inches, so this represents a stack of paper 262 feet high.
Terabyte	TB	1,099,511,627,776 bytes (2^{40} bytes)	This represents a stack of typewritten pages almost 51 miles high.
Petabyte	PB	1,125,899,906,842,624 bytes (2^{50} bytes)	The stack of pages is now 52,000 miles high, or approximately one-fourth the distance from the Earth to the moon.
Exabyte	EB	1,152,921,504,606,846,976 bytes (2^{60} bytes)	The stack of pages is now 52 million miles high, or just about twice the distance between the Earth and Venus.
Zettabyte	ZB	1,180,591,620,717,411,303,424 bytes (2^{70} bytes)	The stack of pages is now 52 billion miles high, some 20 times the distance between the Earth and Pluto.

Similarly, a computer without software is a shell full of hardware components that can't do anything. **Software** is the set of computer programs that enables the hardware to perform different tasks. There are two broad categories of software: application software and system software.

When you think of software, you are most likely thinking of application software. **Application software** is the set of programs you use on a computer to help you carry out tasks such as writing a research paper. If you've ever typed a document, created a spreadsheet, or edited a digital photo, for example, then you've used a form of application software.

System software is the set of programs that enables your computer's hardware devices and application software to work together. The most common type of system software is the **operating system (OS)**, or the program that controls the way in which your computer system functions. It manages the hardware of the computer system, such

as the monitor and the printer. The operating system also provides a means by which users can interact with the computer. We'll cover software in greater depth in Chapters 4 and 5. For the rest of this chapter, we'll explore hardware.

Your Computer's Hardware

Considering the amount of amazing things computers can do, they are really quite simple machines. You learned in the previous section that a basic computer system is made up of software and hardware. In the following sections, we look more closely at your computer's hardware, the parts you can actually touch (see Figure 2.3). Hardware components of a computer consist of the system unit (the box that contains the central electronic components of the computer), and **peripheral devices**, those

FIGURE 2.3

Each part of the computer serves a special function.

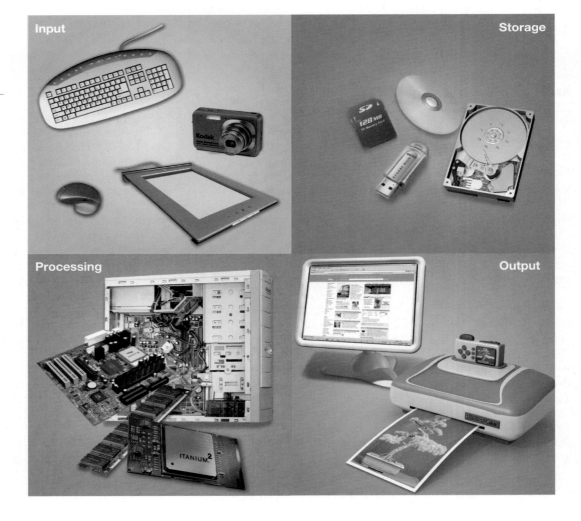

devices such as monitors and printers that are connected to the computer. In the case of a notebook computer, the system unit is combined with other input and output devices, such as the keyboard and monitor.

Other devices, such as routers, help a computer communicate with other computers to facilitate the sharing of documents and other resources. Together the system unit and peripheral devices perform four main functions: They enable the computer to (1) input data, (2) process that data into information, (3) output the data and information, and (4) store them. We begin our exploration of hardware by taking a look at your computer's input devices.

Input Devices

An **input device** enables you to enter data (text, images, and sounds) and instructions (user responses and commands) into the computer. The most common input devices are the **keyboard** and the **mouse**. Keyboards are used to enter typed data and commands, whereas the mouse is used to enter user responses and commands.

There are other input devices as well: Microphones input sounds, whereas scanners and digital cameras input nondigital text and digital images, respectively. Styluses (devices that look like skinny pens but have no ink) and electronic pens are also becoming quite popular and are often used in conjunction with graphics tablets that can translate a user's handwriting into digital input.

KEYBOARDS

Aren't all keyboards the same? Most desktop and notebook computers come with a standard **QWERTY keyboard** (see Figure 2.4a). This keyboard layout gets its name from the first six letters in the top-left row of alphabetic keys on the keyboard and is the standard English-language keyboard layout. Over the years, there has been some debate over what is the best keyboard layout. The QWERTY layout

was originally designed for typewriters and was meant to slow typists enough to keep typewriter keys from jamming. Today, though, the QWERTY layout is considered inefficient because it slows typing speeds. Now that technology can keep up with faster typing, other keyboard layouts are being considered.

The **Dvorak keyboard** is the leading alternative keyboard layout, although it is not nearly as common as the QWERTY. The Dvorak keyboard puts the most commonly used letters in the English language on "home keys," or the keys in the middle row of the keyboard (see Figure 2.4b). The Dvorak keyboard's design reduces the distance your fingers travel for most keystrokes, increasing typing speed.

Although alternative layout keyboards have not caught on with most users, they are popular with gamers. Keyboards such as the DX1 from Ergodex (see Figure 2.4c) allow placement of the keys in any position on the keyboard pad, and the keys can be programmed to individual keystrokes or with macros (a series of tasks) to perform specific tasks. This makes it easy for gamers to configure a keyboard in the most desirable way for each game they play.

FIGURE 2.4

(a) The first six keys in the top-left row of alphabetic keys give the QWERTY keyboard its name. (b) With a Dvorak keyboard, you can type most of the more commonly used words in the English language with the letters found on "home keys," or the keys in the middle row. (c) The Ergodex DX1 allows keys to be placed anywhere on the pad, and they can be relocated and reprogrammed easily, making the keyboard popular with gamers.

FIGURE 2.5

Light and portable, the virtual laser keyboard is a small device that projects the image of a QWERTY keyboard on any surface. Sensors detect the typing motions of a user's fingers, and data is transmitted to a computing device via Bluetooth technology.

Because users are demanding more portability out of their computing devices, recent development efforts have focused on reducing the size and weight of keyboards. The virtual laser keyboard (see Figure 2.5) is a device that is about the size of a cellular phone. It projects the image of a keyboard on any surface, and sensors detect the motion of your fingers as you "type" on a

desk or other flat surface. Data is transmitted via **Bluetooth technology**, which is a wireless transmission standard that facilitates the connection among electronic computing devices such as cell phones, PDAs, and computers to peripheral devices such as keyboards and headsets. We'll discuss Bluetooth in further detail in Chapter 8.

How can I use my keyboard most efficiently? All keyboards have the standard set of alpha and numeric keys that you regularly use when typing. As shown in Figure 2.6, the keyboard has additional keys that are used to perform special functions. Knowing how to use these special keys will help you improve your efficiency:

- The **numeric keypad** allows you to enter numbers quickly.

- **Function keys** act as shortcut keys you press to perform special tasks. They are sometimes referred to as the "F" keys because they start with the letter F followed by a number. Each software application has its own set of tasks assigned to the function keys, although some are more universal. For example, the F1 key is the Help key in most software applications. However, the F2 key, for example, moves text or graphics in Microsoft Word but allows editing of the active cell in Microsoft Excel.

- The **Control (Ctrl) key** is used in combination with other keys to perform short-

FIGURE 2.6

Desktop keyboards have a variety of keys that help you work more efficiently.

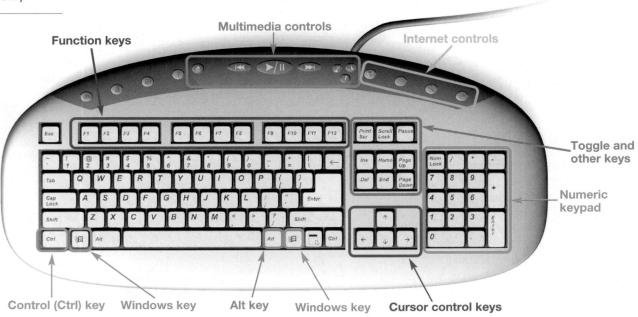

cuts and special tasks. For example, holding down the Control (Ctrl) key while pressing the B key adds bold formatting to selected text. Similarly, you use the **Alt key** with other keys for additional shortcuts and special tasks. (On Macs, the Control or Ctrl key is the Apple key or Command key, whereas the Alt key is the Option key.)

- The **Windows key** is specific to the Windows operating system. Used alone, it opens the Start menu, although it's used most often in combination with other keys to perform shortcuts, which can produce different results in different versions of Windows. For example, pressing the Windows key plus the M key minimizes all windows in Windows Vista and XP.

Some keyboards (such as the one shown in Figure 2.6) also include multimedia and Internet keys or buttons that enable you to open a Web browser, view e-mail, access Help features, or control your CD/DVD player. Unlike the other keys on a standard keyboard, these buttons are not always in the same position on every keyboard, but the symbols on top of the buttons generally help you determine their function.

For hard-core gamers, gaming companies are now selling **gaming keyboards** that are optimized for playing specific video games. These keyboards contain special keys that perform special functions (such as changing the weapon being used by a character) so that with one key press, game play speeds up, allowing players to react quicker to difficult challenges within the game.

Another set of controls on standard keyboards are the **cursor control keys** that move your **cursor** (the flashing I symbol on the monitor that indicates where the next character will be inserted). The cursor control keys also are known as *arrow keys* because they are represented by arrows on standard keyboards. The arrow keys move the cursor one space at a time in a document, either up, down, left, or right.

Above the arrow keys, usually you'll find keys that move the cursor up or down one full page or to the beginning (Home) or end (End) of a line of text. The Delete (Del) key allows you to delete characters, whereas the Insert key allows you to insert or overwrite characters within a document. The Insert key is a **toggle key** because its function changes between one of two options each time you press it: When toggled on, the Insert key inserts new text within a line of

BITS AND BYTES

Keystroke Shortcuts

Did you know that you can combine certain keystrokes to take shortcuts within the Windows operating system? The following are a few of the most helpful shortcuts to make more efficient use of your time. For more shortcuts for Windows-based PCs, visit **http://support. microsoft.com**. For a list of shortcuts for Macs, see **www.apple.com/support**.

Text Formatting	File Management	Cut/Copy/Paste	Windows Controls
CTRL+B Applies (or removes) **bold** formatting to selected text	**CTRL+O** Opens the Open dialog box	**CTRL+X** Cuts (removes) selected text from document	**Alt+F4** Closes the current window
CTRL+I Applies (or removes) *italic* formatting to selected text	**CTRL+N** Opens a new document	**CTRL+C** Copies selected text	**Ctrl+Esc** Opens the Start menu
	CTRL+S Saves a document	**CTRL+V** Pastes selected text (previously cut or copied)	**Windows Key + F1** Opens Windows Help
CTRL+U Applies (or removes) underlining to selected text	**CTRL+P** Opens the Print dialog box		**Windows Key + F** Opens the Search (Find Files) dialog box

existing text. When toggled off, the Insert key replaces (or overwrites) existing characters with new characters as you type. Other toggle keys include the Num Lock key and the Caps Lock key, which toggle between an on/off state.

Are keyboards different on notebooks? Notebook computers (or **laptop computers**) are portable computers that are powered by batteries (or a handy electrical outlet) and have keyboards, monitors, and other devices integrated into a single compact case. To save space and weight, notebook keyboards are more compact than standard keyboards and therefore have fewer keys. Still, a lot of the notebook keys have alternate functions so that you can get the same capabilities from the limited keys as you do from the special keys on standard keyboards. For example, many notebook keyboards do not have separate numeric keys. Instead, the letter keys function as number keys when they are pressed in combination with another key (every notebook will be different). The keys you use as numeric keys on notebooks have number notations on them so you can tell which keys to use (see Figure 2.7).

FIGURE 2.8

The stylus is the Tablet PC's primary input device. You use it by tapping or writing on the tablet's touch-sensitive screen.

If you don't care for the keyboard on your notebook computer, you can always buy a keyboard you like and connect it to your notebook via a universal serial bus (USB) port. Notebook users often do this if they will be using their computer in one place for long periods of time or if they find the built-in keyboard too small for comfortable typing.

What about keyboards for PDAs and Tablet PCs? Generally, you enter data and commands into a personal digital assistant (PDA) by using a **stylus**, a pen-shaped device that you use by tapping or writing on the PDA's touch-sensitive screen. As shown in Figure 2.8, **Tablet PCs** are similar to notebook PCs but also feature a touch-sensitive screen and handwriting-recognition software. Tablet PCs also allow user input via a stylus. However, all tablets and some PDAs have built-in keyboards that allow you to type text just as you would with a normal keyboard. If your PDA doesn't include a built-in keyboard, then you can buy a keyboard that attaches to the PDA or use a virtual laser keyboard. We'll discuss keyboards for mobile devices in more detail in Chapter 8.

Are all conventional keyboards connected to the computer via wires? Although most desktop PCs ship with wired keyboards, wireless keyboards are available. These keyboards are powered by batteries and send data to the computer

FIGURE 2.7

Notebook keyboards are more compact than traditional desktop keyboards and usually don't include extra keys such as the numeric keypad. However, on many notebooks, certain letter keys can function as number keys.

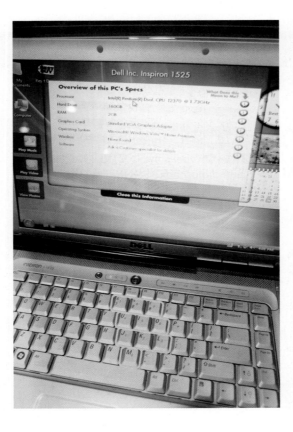

using a form of wireless technology. Infrared wireless keyboards communicate with the computer using infrared light waves (similar to how a remote control communicates with a TV). The computer receives the infrared light signals through a special infrared port. The disadvantage of infrared keyboards is that you need to point the keyboard directly at the infrared port on the computer for it to work. Other wireless keyboards use radio frequency signals to transmit data, and many adhere to the Bluetooth standard.

What are the best wireless keyboards? The best wireless keyboards send data to the computer using radio frequency (RF). These keyboards contain a radio transmitter that sends out radio wave signals. These signals are received in two ways. In one, a small receiving device sits on your desk and is plugged into the back of the computer where the keyboard would normally plug in. Or, in the case of Bluetooth-compatible computers, a receiving device is contained in the system unit. Unlike infrared technology, RF technology doesn't require that you point the keyboard at the receiver for it to work. RF keyboards used on home computers can be placed as far as 6 feet to 30 feet from the computer, depending on their quality. (Bluetooth devices have a much shorter range.) RF keyboards that are used in business conference rooms or auditoriums can be placed as far as 100 feet away from the computer, but they are far more expensive than traditional wired keyboards.

MICE AND OTHER POINTING DEVICES

What kinds of mice are there? The mouse you're probably most familiar with is the **optical mouse** (see Figure 2.9a). An optical mouse uses an internal sensor or laser to detect the mouse's movement. The sensor sends signals to the computer, telling it where to move the pointer on the screen.

ACTIVE HELPDESK

Using Input Devices

In this Active Helpdesk call, you'll play the role of a helpdesk staffer, fielding calls about different input devices, such as the different mice and keyboards on the market, what wireless input options are available, and how to best use these devices.

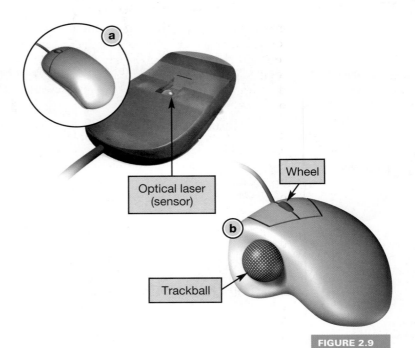

Optical laser (sensor)

Wheel

Trackball

FIGURE 2.9

(a) An optical mouse has an optical laser (or sensor) on the bottom that detects its movement. (b) A trackball mouse turns the traditional mouse on its back, allowing you to control the rollerball with your fingers.

Optical mice are often preferable to other types of mice because they have few moving parts, which lessens the chances that dirt will interfere with the mechanisms or that parts will break down. Although optical mice are most common now, you may still use a mouse at home or in school that has a rollerball on the bottom, which moves when you drag the mouse across a mouse pad. The movement of the rollerball controls the movement of your cursor that appears on the screen.

Mice also have two or three buttons that enable you to execute commands and open shortcut menus. (Mice for Macs sometimes have only one button.) Most new mice have additional programmable buttons and wheels that let you quickly scroll through documents or Web pages.

Do mice still need mouse pads? Optical mice will work on any surface without a mouse pad, but some people still use a pad to protect their furniture from being marred as the mouse moves. Trackball mice also don't require mouse pads. A **trackball mouse** (see Figure 2.9b) is basically a traditional mouse that has been turned on its back. The rollerball sits on top or on the side of the mouse, and you move the ball with your fingers, allowing the mouse to remain stationary. A trackball mouse doesn't demand much wrist motion, so it's considered better for the wrist than an optical mouse.

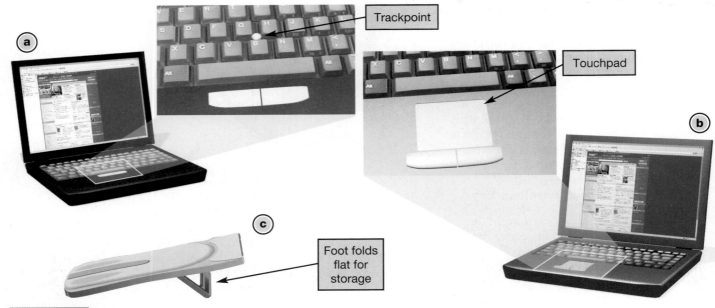

Trackpoint

Touchpad

Foot folds flat for storage

FIGURE 2.10

(a) This keyboard incorporates a track-point device that takes the place of a mouse. (b) With a touchpad, you control the cursor by moving your finger across the pad. (c) The MoGo Mouse is sleek, compact, and battery powered, making it a perfect companion on a business trip when a conventional mouse is desired.

Are there wireless mice? Just as there are wireless keyboards, there are wireless mice, both optical and trackball. Wireless mice are similar to wireless keyboards in that they use batteries and send data to the computer by radio or light waves. If you also have an RF wireless keyboard, then your RF wireless mouse and keyboard usually can share the same RF receiver.

What about mice for notebooks? Most notebooks do not come with mice. Instead, they have integrated pointing devices such as a **touchpad**, a small, touch-sensitive area at the base of the keyboard. To use the touchpad, you simply move your finger across the pad. Some touch pads are also sensitive to taps, interpreting them as mouse clicks while others have buttons beneath the pads to record mouse

Window provides magnified view

FIGURE 2.11

The magnifier is a new mouse feature that provides access to a window that can be dragged around the screen to provide instant magnification of images or text.

>To start magnifier, click **Start**, click **All Programs**, and then click the **Accessories** folder. Click the **Ease of Access** folder and then click **Magnifier** to launch the application.

clicks. Other notebooks incorporate a **trackpoint device**, a small, joystick-like nub that allows you to move the cursor with the tip of your finger. Figures 2.10a and 2.10b show some of the mouse options you'll find in notebooks.

Many people still prefer to use a traditional external mouse with their notebooks. Small, compact devices like the MoGo Mouse (see Figure 2.10c) are designed for portability. The MoGo Mouse fits into a peripheral slot on the side of a notebook; this slot serves to store the mouse, protect it, and charge its batteries all at the same time. The MoGo Mouse is wireless and uses Bluetooth technology to transmit data to the notebook.

What else can I do with my mouse? Manufacturers of mice are constantly releasing new models that allow you to perform ever more useful tasks with a few clicks of the mouse. For example, on new mouse models, Microsoft and Logitech now provide features such as the following:

- **Instant Viewer:** Shrinks all windows currently open to thumbnail-sized images so that you can see everything open on your desktop at a glance.

- **Magnifier:** Pulls up a magnification box that you can drag around the screen to enhance viewing of hard-to-read images (see Figure 2.11). This feature is often used by people with visual disabilities.

- **Customizable buttons:** Provides extra buttons on the mouse that can be programmed to perform the functions that you use most often to help you speed through tasks.

- **Web Search:** Allows you to quickly highlight a word or phrase and then press the search button on the mouse to start a Web search.

Be sure to check out the features of new mice as they come on the market to see if you can benefit from the purchase of a new mouse.

Are game controls considered mice? Game controls such as joysticks, game pads, and steering wheels are not mice per se, but they are considered input devices because they send data to the computer. Game pads, which are similar to the devices used on gaming consoles (such as the Xbox 360 and the PlayStation), are also available for computers. They have buttons and miniature pointing devices that provide input to the computer. Force-feedback joysticks and steering wheels deliver data in both directions. They translate your movements to the computer and translate its responses as forces on your hands, creating a richer simulated experience. If you like to move around a lot while you play games, you can purchase wireless game controllers at most computer stores. Portable gaming devices such as the Nintendo DS feature touch-sensitive screens that use a stylus (or finger) for input.

What other types of input devices are available? Tablet PCs were developed primarily because many people find it easier to write than type input into a computer. But Tablet PCs are expensive compared to conventional notebooks. An alternative is a digital pen like the EPOS Digital Pen (see Figure 2.12). This pen works in conjunction with a flash drive (a portable electronic storage device that connects to a port on a computer). You can write with the pen on any conventional paper, and your writing is captured and then wirelessly transmitted and stored in the flash drive. When the flash drive is connected to a computer, you can use software to translate your writing into digital text.

IMAGE INPUT

How can I input digital images into my computer? Digital cameras, camcorders, and webcams are the most common devices for capturing pictures and video, and all of them are considered input devices. Digital cameras and camcorders are usually used in remote settings (away from the computer) to capture images for later downloading to the computer. These devices are either connected to the computer by a data cable or transmit data wirelessly. Windows automatically recognizes these devices when they are connected to the computer and makes the input of the digital data to the computer simple and easy.

Webcams (see Figure 2.13) are small cameras that usually sit on top of your computer monitor (connected to the computer by a cable) or are built into your notebook computer. Although some webcams are able to capture still images, they are used mostly for transferring live video directly to your computer. Webcams make it possible to transmit live video over the Web and are often used to facilitate videoconferencing or calls made with video phones. Videoconferencing technology allows a person sitting at a computer equipped with a personal video camera (a webcam) and a microphone to transmit video and audio across the Internet.

SOUND INPUT

Why would I want to input sound to my computer? Equipping your computer to accept sound input opens up a variety of possibilities. You can conduct audio conferences with work colleagues, chat with friends or family over the Internet instead of using a phone, record podcasts, and more. Inputting sound to your computer requires equipping it with a **microphone** or **mic**, a device that allows you to capture sound waves (such as your voice) and transfer them to digital format on your computer. Many notebook computers come with built-in microphones, and some desktop computers come with inexpensive microphones. If you don't have a microphone or you aren't getting the quality you need from your existing microphone, then you will probably need to shop for one.

What types of microphones are available for my computer? Most microphones that are sold for use with computers are **magnetically shielded microphones**, also known as *computer microphones*. The microphone plugs into a port on the sound card in your computer, so make sure you select a microphone that has the correct connector to fit your available sound input port.

FIGURE 2.12

The EPOS Digital Pen captures writing and stores it in a flash drive for later transfer to a computer. No typing required!

FIGURE 2.13

A webcam is usually placed on top of a monitor, enabling you to stream live video into and out of your computer to facilitate video chats or conferences with your friends or co-workers.

Microphones come in two basic types, depending on how they are configured to pick up sound. **Unidirectional microphones** pick up sound from only one direction. These are best used for recording podcasts with a single voice or making phone calls over the Internet with only one person on your end of the call. **Omnidirectional microphones** pick up sounds from all directions at once. These mics are best for recording more than one voice, such as during a conference call when you need to pick up the voices of multiple speakers.

What's the best microphone to have? This answer depends on what you are using the microphone to do. Close-talk microphones, which are usually attached to a headset, are useful in situations such as using speech-recognition software, video-conferencing, or making telephone calls. With a microphone attached to a headset, your hands are free to perform other tasks while you speak (such as making notes or referring to paper documents), and the headset allows you to listen as well (such as when making Internet phone calls). All computers participating in a videoconference need to have a microphone and speakers installed so that participants can speak to and hear one another.

In **speech-recognition systems**, you operate your computer through a microphone, telling it to perform specific commands (such as to open a file) or to translate your spoken words into data input. Speech recognition has yet to truly catch on, but its popularity is growing. In fact, it's now included in the Windows Vista operating system. We discuss speech-recognition software in more detail in Chapter 4.

Desktop microphones, which have an attached base that allows them to sit on a flat surface (see Figure 2.14), are convenient for recording podcasts or in other situations where you might need your hands to be free. Clip-on (or lavaliere) microphones are useful in situations where you are presenting at a meeting and need to keep your hands free for other activities (such as writing on a white board) or move around the room. Many of these microphones are wireless.

Are expensive microphones worth the money? Microphone quality varies widely. For personal use, an inexpensive microphone is probably sufficient. However, if you plan to create professional products and sell them to others, you'll most likely need a more expensive professional recording studio microphone. Music stores and other stores that sell equipment for outfitting recording studios are usually good places to obtain advice on high-quality microphones.

FIGURE 2.14

Professional-quality microphones such as the Snowball are essential for producing quality podcasts.

INPUT DEVICES FOR PHYSICALLY CHALLENGED INDIVIDUALS

What input devices are available for people with disabilities? People who have physical challenges often use computers but sometimes need special input devices to access them. For visually impaired users, voice recognition is an obvious option. For those users whose visual limitations are less severe, keyboards with larger keys are available. On-screen keyboards also can make input easier for some individuals. These keyboards are displayed as graphics on the computer screen and represent a standard keyboard layout. Keys are pressed with the use of a pointing device or by using a touch-screen monitor.

People with motor control issues may have difficulty with pointing devices. To aid such users, special trackballs are available

ETHICS IN IT

Ethics: What Is Ethical Computing?

If you were asked to cite an example of unethical behavior while using a computer, you probably could easily provide an answer. You've probably heard news stories about people using computers to commit such crimes as unleashing viruses or committing identity theft. You may have read about students who were prosecuted at a neighboring university for illegally sharing copyrighted material such as videos. All of these are examples of unethical behavior while using a computer. But if you were asked what constitutes *ethical* behavior while using a computer, could you provide an answer just as quickly?

Loosely defined, ethics is a system of moral principles, rules, and accepted standards of conduct. So what are the accepted standards of conduct when using computers (see Figure 2.15)? The Computer Ethics Institute developed the Ten Commandments of Computer Ethics, which is widely cited as a benchmark for companies that are developing computer usage and compliance policies for employees. Our ethical computing guidelines listed below are based on the Computer Ethics Institute's work.

Ethical Computing Guidelines

1. Avoid causing harm to others when using computers.

2. Do not interfere with other people's efforts at accomplishing work with computers.

3. Resist the temptation to snoop in other people's computer files.

4. Do not use computers to commit theft.

5. Agree not to use computers to promote lies.

6. Do not use software (or make illegal copies for others) without paying the creator for it.

7. Avoid using other people's computer resources without appropriate authorization or proper compensation.

8. Do not claim other people's intellectual output as your own.

9. Consider the social consequences of the products of your computer labor.

10. Only use computers in ways that show consideration and respect for others.

The United States has enacted laws that support some of these guidelines such as Guideline 6, the breaking of which would violate copyright laws, and Guideline 4, which is covered by numerous federal and state larceny laws. Other guidelines, however, require more subtle interpretation as to their unethical nature because there are no laws designed to enforce them.

Consider Guideline 7, which recommends against using unauthorized resources, for example. The college you attend probably provides computer resources for you to complete coursework. However, just because you are provided with a computer and access to the Internet doesn't necessarily mean it is ethical for you to run a business on eBay in between classes or on the weekends in the college library. Although it might not be technically illegal, you are tying up computer resources that could be used by other students for the intended purpose of learning and completing coursework (which, of course, also violates Guidelines 2 and 10).

Throughout the chapters in this book, we'll touch on many topics related to these guidelines. So keep them in mind as you study, and think about how they relate to the actions you take as you use computers in your life.

FIGURE 2.15

Make sure the work you claim as your intellectual output is the product of your intellect alone.

that are manipulated easily with one finger and can be attached to almost any surface, including wheelchairs. When arm motion is severely restrained, head-mounted pointing devices can be used. Generally, these involve a camera mounted on the computer monitor and a device attached to the head (often installed in a hat). When the user moves his or her head, the camera detects the movement that controls the cursor on the screen. In this case, mouse clicks are controlled by a switch that can be manipulated by the user's hands or feet or even by using an instrument that fits into the mouth and senses the user blowing into it.

Output Devices

Output devices enable you to send processed data out of your computer in the form of text, pictures (graphics), sounds (audio), and video. One common output device is a **monitor** (sometimes referred to as a **display screen**), which displays text, graphics, and video as soft copies (copies you can see only on-screen). Another common output device is the **printer**, which creates tangible or hard copies (copies you can touch) of text and graphics. Speakers and earphones (or ear buds) are obviously the output devices for sound.

MONITORS

What are the different types of monitors? There are two basic types of monitors: CRTs and LCDs. If your monitor looks like a traditional television set, then it has a

picture-tube device called a **cathode ray tube (CRT)** such as the one shown in Figure 2.16a. If your monitor is flat like that typically found on a notebook, it's using **liquid crystal display (LCD)** technology (see Figure 2.16b), which is similar to that used in digital watches. LCD monitors, also called **flat-panel monitors**, are lighter and more energy efficient than CRT monitors, making them perfect for portable computers such as notebooks. The sleek style of LCD monitors also makes them a favorite for users with small workspaces.

Which monitor type is most popular? By far, LCD monitors are the most popular. In fact, CRT monitors can be difficult to find even if you want to buy one because they are fast becoming **legacy technology**, or computing devices or peripherals that use techniques, parts, and methods from an earlier time that are no longer popular. Although legacy technology may still be functional, it is quickly being replaced by newer technological advances. This doesn't mean that if you have a CRT monitor that is functioning well you should throw it away and buy an LCD monitor. But when your CRT monitor fails, you will most likely only be able to replace it with an LCD monitor.

Why did LCD monitors become so much more popular than CRT monitors? LCD monitors are much smaller than CRT monitors and therefore take up far less space on a desktop. They are also generally brighter than CRT monitors and use different refresh methods for their pixels (tiny dots of color), which causes less eyestrain. Another advantage is that LCD monitors use significantly less energy and emit less electromagnetic radiation, making them more environmentally friendly. Finally, LCD monitors weigh less, making them the obvious choice for mobile devices.

Key Monitor Features

How do monitors work? Monitor screens are grids made up of millions of **pixels**, or tiny dots (see Figure 2.17). Simply put, illuminated pixels are what create the images you see on your monitor. Each pixel actually comprises three subpixels of the colors red, blue, and green. LCD monitors are made of two (or more) sheets of material filled with a liquid crystal solution. A fluorescent panel at the back of the LCD monitor

FIGURE 2.16

(a) CRT monitors are big and bulky and look like traditional television sets. (b) LCDs (flat-panel monitors) save precious desktop space and weigh considerably less than CRT monitors.

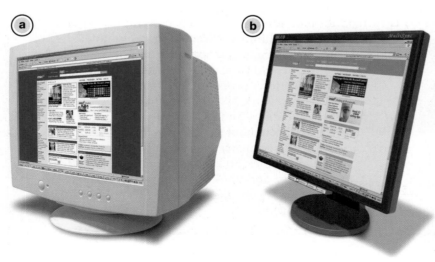

generates light waves. When electric current passes through the liquid crystal solution, the crystals move around and either block the fluorescent light or let the light shine through. This blocking or passing of light by the crystals causes images to form on the screen. The various combinations of red, blue, and green make up the components of color we see on our monitors.

What factors affect the quality of an LCD monitor? The most important factor to consider when choosing an LCD monitor is its **resolution**, or the clearness or sharpness of the image. Resolution is controlled by the number of pixels displayed on the screen. The higher the resolution, the sharper and clearer the image will be. Monitor resolution is listed as a number of pixels. A high-end monitor may have a native (or maximum) resolution of 1,600 × 1,200, meaning it contains 1,600 vertical columns with 1,200 pixels in each column. Note that you can adjust a monitor's resolution either to make the screen display larger (reducing the resolution) or to fit more on your screen (increasing the resolution). You cannot increase the resolution of an LCD monitor beyond its native (maximum) resolution. Generally, you should select a monitor with the highest resolution available for the screen size (measured in inches).

You'll generally find two types of LCD monitors on the market: passive-matrix displays and active-matrix displays. Less expensive LCD monitors use **passive-matrix displays**, whereas more expensive monitors use **active-matrix displays**. Passive-matrix technology passes an electrical current through the liquid crystal solution to charge groups of pixels, either in a row or a column. This causes the screen to brighten with each pass of electrical current and subsequently fade. With active-matrix displays, each pixel is charged individually as needed. The result is that an active-matrix display produces a clearer, brighter image with better viewing angles as noted below. As the price of active-matrix displays continues to drop, passive-matrix displays will soon become a thing of the past.

Factors to consider when judging the quality of an LCD monitor include the following:

- **Viewing angle:** An LCD's viewing angle, which is measured in degrees, tells how far you can move to the side of (or above or below) the monitor

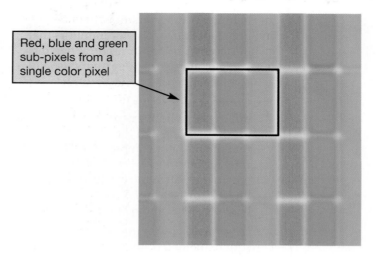

Red, blue and green sub-pixels from a single color pixel

Close-Up of an
LCD panel display

FIGURE 2.17

Short for *picture element*, a pixel is one dot on the screen. LCD pixels are rectangular and laid out in a matrix. Each pixel is made up of three subpixels: red, blue, and green. Millions of pixels make up an image, and color is created by various shades and combinations of these pixels.

BITS AND BYTES

Cleaning Your Monitor

Have you ever noticed how quickly your monitor attracts dust? It's important to keep your monitor clean because dust buildup can act like insulation, keeping heat in and causing the electronic components to wear out much faster. To clean your LCD monitor, follow these steps:

1. Turn off the monitor (or your notebook computer) and make sure it is unplugged from the electrical power outlet.
2. Never spray anything directly onto the monitor. (Check your monitor's user manual to see if there are cleaning products you should avoid using.) Use a 50/50 solution of rubbing alcohol and water on a soft cloth and wipe the screen surface gently.
3. In addition to the screen, wipe away the dust from around the case.

Also, don't place anything on top of the monitor or closely packed around it. This may block air from cooling it. Finally, avoid placing magnets (including your speaker system's subwoofer) anywhere near the monitor because they can interfere with the mechanisms inside the monitor.

before the image quality degrades to unacceptable levels. For monitors that measure 17 inches or more, a viewing angle of at least 150 degrees is usually recommended.

- **Contrast ratio:** This is a measure of the difference in light intensity between the brightest white and the darkest black that the monitor can produce. If the contrast ratio is too low, colors tend to fade when you adjust the brightness to a high or low setting. A contrast ratio of between 400:1 and 600:1 is preferable.

- **Brightness:** Measured as candelas per square meter (cd/m^2) or nits, brightness is a measure of the greatest amount of light showing when the monitor is displaying pure white. A brightness level of $250cd/m^2$ or greater is recommended.

- **Response time:** This is the measurement (in milliseconds) of the time it takes for a pixel to change color. The lower the response time, the smoother moving images will appear on the monitor. A response time lower than 15 milliseconds is important when using a monitor to play a game or display full-motion video such as movies or television.

What features of monitors can help physically challenged individuals? If a monitor (or display in a notebook or PDA) accepts input from a user touching the screen, then the monitor also doubles as an input device. These monitors,

FIGURE 2.18

Inexpensive projectors are showing up more frequently in the home to provide large images for movie viewing and gaming.

ACTIVE HELPDESK
Using Output Devices

In this Active Helpdesk call, you'll play the role of a helpdesk staffer, fielding calls about different output devices, including the differences between LCD and CRT monitor technologies and between inkjet and laser printers and the advantages and disadvantages of each.

known as **touch-screen monitors**, are available for home computers and are becoming more common. People with limited motor control that prevents them from typing quickly and accurately are often greatly assisted by touch-screen monitors. In fact, a person with significant paralysis often uses a stylus (sometimes held in the mouth) in conjunction with a touch-screen monitor to virtually eliminate the need for a keyboard.

Individuals with impaired vision can reduce the resolution of a monitor, which causes the images on the screen (like icons and text) to appear larger. Windows and many other software applications have magnification features that can further enhance viewing.

How do I show output to a large group of people? Crowding large groups of people around your computer just isn't practical. However, it is possible to do so with a **data projector**, a device that can project images from your computer onto a wall or viewing screen (see Figure 2.18). Data projectors are commonly used in business and education in conference rooms and classrooms. These projectors are becoming smaller and lighter, making them ideal for businesspeople who have to make presentations at client locations. The price of these projectors has been falling significantly in recent years, making them a good option for use in the home for displaying digital slideshows or games in a large format. Projectors such as the Zoombox Entertainment Projector from Hasbro not only can project a 60-inch image on a screen or wall but also play CDs and DVDs with the built-in DVD combo drive and speakers—all for less than $250.

PRINTERS

What are the different types of printers? There are two primary categories of printers: impact and nonimpact. **Impact printers** have tiny hammer-like keys that strike the paper through an inked ribbon, thus making a mark on the paper. The most common impact printer is the dot-matrix printer. In contrast, **nonimpact printers** spray ink or use laser beams to transfer marks onto the paper. The most common nonimpact printers are inkjet printers and laser printers. Such nonimpact printers have replaced dot-matrix printers almost entirely. They tend to be less expensive, quieter, and faster, and they offer better print quality. The only place you may still see a dot-matrix printer is at a company (like a car rental agency) that still uses them to print multi-part forms. Dot-matrix printers are truly legacy technology.

What are the advantages of inkjet printers? Compared with dot-matrix printers, **inkjet printers** (see Figure 2.19) are quieter, faster, and offer higher-quality print-outs. In addition, even high-quality printers are affordable. Inkjet printers work by spray-ing tiny drops of ink onto paper. The key advantage is that inkjets print acceptable quality color images cost effectively. In fact, when using the right paper, higher-end inkjet printers can print images that look like professional-quality photos. Because of their high quality and low price, inkjet printers are the most popular printer for color printing.

Why would I want a laser printer? **Laser printers** are often preferred because of their quick and quiet production and high-quality printouts (see Figure 2.20). Laser printers use laser beams and static electricity to deliver toner (similar to ink) onto the

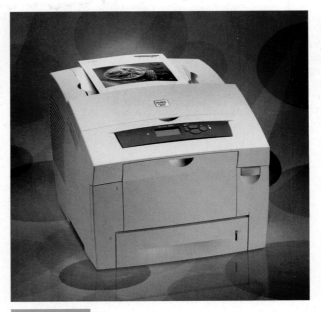

FIGURE 2.20

Laser printers print quickly and offer high-quality printouts. Models that print color at prices afford-able enough for personal use or a small business are becoming more common.

correct areas of the page. Heat is used to fuse the toner to the page, making the image permanent. Because they print quickly, laser printers are often used in schools and offices where multiple computers share one printer. Although more expensive to buy than inkjet printers, over the long run laser print-ers are more economical for high-volume printing than inkjets (they cost less per printed black-and-white page) when you include the price of ink and paper in the overall cost. Recently, the prices of color laser printers have fallen dramatically, making them highly price competitive with high-end inkjet printers.

What kind of printer could I use for my notebook? Although any printer that is suitable for your desktop computer is appropriate to use with your notebook, you may want to consider a portable printer for added mobility and flexibility (see Figure 2.21). Portable printers (including many inkjet printers) often are compact enough to fit in a briefcase, are lightweight, and sometimes run on battery power instead of AC current.

Are there wireless printers? Infrared-compatible or wireless printers allow you to print from your handheld

FIGURE 2.19

Inkjet printers are popular among home users, espe-cially with the rise of digital photography. Many inkjet printers are optimized for printing photos from digital cameras.

FIGURE 2.21

Paper exits here

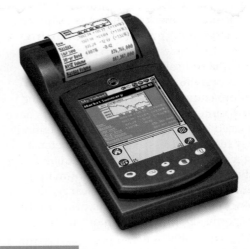

FIGURE 2.23

Thermal printers are ideal for mobile computing because they are compact, are lightweight, and require no ink cartridges. Here you see a PDA set into a thermal printer.

device, notebook, camera, or even your desktop computer. Most of these printers work using Bluetooth technology.

Are there any other types of specialty printers? A multifunction printer, or an **all-in-one printer**, is a device that combines the functions of a printer, scanner, copier, and fax into one machine. Popular for their space-saving convenience, all-in-one printers can be either inkjet or laser printers. **Plotters** are large printers used to produce oversize pictures that require the drawing of precise and continuous lines such as those required for maps, detailed images (see Figure 2.22), and architectural plans. Plotters use a computer-controlled pen that provides a greater level of precision than the series of dots that laser or inkjet printers are capable of making.

FIGURE 2.22

Plotters are large printers used to print oversize images, maps, and architectural plans.

Thermal printers, such as the one shown in Figure 2.23, are another kind of specialty printer. These printers work either by melting wax-based ink onto ordinary paper (in a process called *thermal wax transfer printing*) or by burning dots onto specially coated paper (in a process called *direct thermal printing*). They are used in stores to print receipts and in airports for electronic ticketing, among other places. Thermal printers are also emerging as a popular technology for mobile and portable printing, for example, in conjunction with PDAs and similar devices. These are the printers that car rental agencies use to give you an instant receipt when you drop off your rental car. Many models feature wireless infrared technology for complete portability.

Choosing a Printer

How do I select the best printer?

Hewlett-Packard's Web site (**www.hp.com**) has an excellent section called the HP Printer Buying Guide that provides excellent objective tips on selecting a printer appropriate for your needs. You should conduct research before buying a printer and be sure to consider these factors when making your choice:

- **Speed:** A printer's speed determines how many pages it can print per minute (called *pages per minute* or *ppm*). The speed of inkjet printers has improved over the years so that many inkjet printers now print as fast as laser printers. Printing speeds vary by model and range from 8 ppm to 30 ppm for both laser and inkjet printers. Text documents printed in black and white print faster than documents printed in color.

- **Resolution:** A printer's resolution (or printed image clarity) is measured in dots per inch (dpi), or the number of dots of ink in a one-inch line. The higher the dpi, the greater the level of detail and quality of the image. You'll sometimes see dpi represented as a horizontal number multiplied by a vertical number, such as 600×600, but you may also see the same resolution simply stated as 600 dpi. For general-purpose printing, 300 dpi is sufficient. For printing photos, 1,200 dpi is better. The dpi for professional photo-quality printers is twice that.

- **Color output:** If you're using an inkjet printer to print color images, buy a four-color (cyan, magenta, yellow, and black) or six-color printer (four-color plus light cyan and light magenta) for the highest-quality output. Some printers come with a single ink cartridge for all colors; others have two ink cartridges, one for black and one for color. The best setup is to have individual ink cartridges for each color so you can replace only the specific color cartridge that is empty. Color laser printers have four separate toner cartridges (black, cyan, magenta, and yellow), and the toner is blended in various quantities to produce the entire color printer spectrum.

- **Memory:** Printers need memory to print. Inkjet printers run slowly if they don't have enough memory. If you plan to print small text-only documents on an inkjet printer, then 1 MB to 2 MB of memory should be enough. You need approximately 4 MB of memory if you expect to print large text-only documents and 8 MB if you print graphics-heavy files. Unlike inkjet printers, laser printers won't print at all without sufficient memory. To ensure your laser printer meets your printing needs, buy one with at least 16 MB of memory. Some printers allow you to add more memory later.

- **Use and cost of the printer:** If you will be printing mostly black-and-white,

BITS AND BYTES

Does It Matter What Paper I Print On?

The quality of your printer is only part of what controls the quality of a printed image. The paper you use and the printer settings that control the amount of ink used are equally important. If you're printing text-only documents for personal use, then using low-cost paper is fine. You also may want to consider selecting "Draft" mode in your printer setting to conserve ink. However, if you're printing more formal documents such as résumés, then you may want to adjust your print settings to "Normal" or "Best" and choose a higher-quality paper. Paper quality is determined by the paper's weight, whiteness, and brightness.

The weight of paper is measured in pounds, with 20 pounds being standard. A heavier paper may be best for projects such as brochures, but be sure to check that your printer can handle the added thickness. It is a matter of personal preference as to the degree of paper whiteness. Generally, the whiter the paper, the brighter colors appear. However, in some more formal printings such as résumés, you may want to use a creamier color. The brightness of paper usually varies from 85 to 94. The higher the number, the brighter the paper and the easier it is to read printed text. Opacity is especially important if you're printing on both sides of the paper because it determines the amount of ink that shows through or is concealed from the opposite side of the paper.

If you're printing photos, then paper quality can have a big impact on the results. Photo paper is more expensive than regular paper and comes in a variety of textures ranging from matte to high gloss. For a photo-lab look, high-gloss paper is the best choice. Semigloss (often referred to as *satin*) is good for portraits, while a matte surface is often used for black-and-white printing.

text-based documents or will be sharing your printer with others, then a black-and-white laser printer is best because of its printing speed and overall economies for volume printing. If you're planning to print color photos and graphics, then an inkjet printer or color laser printer is a must, even though the cost per page will be higher.

- **Cost of consumables:** You should carefully investigate the cost of consumables (such as printer cartridges and paper) for any printer you are considering purchasing because the cost of inkjet cartridges often can exceed the cost of the actual printer when purchased on sale. Check reviews in consumer magazines such as *PC Magazine* and *Consumer Reports* to help you evaluate the overall cost of producing documents with a particular printer.

How Inkjet and Laser Printers Work

Ever wonder how a printer knows what to print and how it puts ink in just the right places? Most inkjet printers use drop-on-demand technology in which the ink is "demanded" and then "dropped" onto the paper. Two separate processes use drop-on-demand technology: thermal bubble is used by Hewlett-Packard and Canon, and piezoelectric is used by Epson. The difference between the two processes is how the ink is heated within the print cartridge reservoir (the chamber inside the printer that holds the ink).

In the thermal bubble process, the ink is heated in such a way that it expands (like a bubble) and leaves the cartridge reservoir through a small opening, or nozzle. Figure 2.24 shows the general process for thermal bubble.

In the piezoelectric process, each ink nozzle contains a crystal at the back of the ink reservoir that receives an electrical charge, causing the ink to vibrate and drop out of the nozzle.

Laser printers use a completely different process. Inside a laser printer is a big metal cylinder (or drum) that is charged with static electricity. When asked to print something, the printer sends signals to the laser in the laser printer, telling it to "uncharge" selected spots on the charged cylinder, corresponding to the document you wish to print. Toner, a fine powder that is used in place of liquid ink, is only attracted to those areas on the drum that are not charged, the areas where the desired characters and images are to be printed. The toner is then transferred to the paper as it feeds through the printer. Finally, the toner is melted onto the paper. All unused toner is swept away before the next job starts the process all over again.

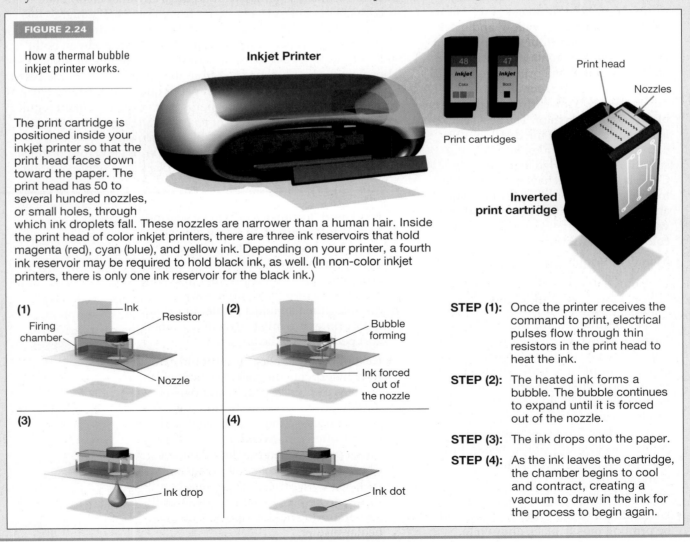

FIGURE 2.24

How a thermal bubble inkjet printer works.

Inkjet Printer

Print cartridges

Print head

Nozzles

Inverted print cartridge

The print cartridge is positioned inside your inkjet printer so that the print head faces down toward the paper. The print head has 50 to several hundred nozzles, or small holes, through which ink droplets fall. These nozzles are narrower than a human hair. Inside the print head of color inkjet printers, there are three ink reservoirs that hold magenta (red), cyan (blue), and yellow ink. Depending on your printer, a fourth ink reservoir may be required to hold black ink, as well. (In non-color inkjet printers, there is only one ink reservoir for the black ink.)

(1)
Ink
Resistor
Firing chamber
Nozzle

(2)
Bubble forming
Ink forced out of the nozzle

(3)
Ink drop

(4)
Ink dot

STEP (1): Once the printer receives the command to print, electrical pulses flow through thin resistors in the print head to heat the ink.

STEP (2): The heated ink forms a bubble. The bubble continues to expand until it is forced out of the nozzle.

STEP (3): The ink drops onto the paper.

STEP (4): As the ink leaves the cartridge, the chamber begins to cool and contract, creating a vacuum to draw in the ink for the process to begin again.

The Future of Printing

What will printers be like in the future? Technologies such as the Memjet printing technology (**www.memjet.com**) developed by Silverbrook Research should provide you with faster color printing at a lower cost (see Figure 2.25). Memjet technology employs printheads that are as wide as the width of a printed page instead of a small profile printhead that travels back and forth across a page like those in today's inkjet printers. The printhead in a Memjet printer has some 70,400 nozzles, as compared to the 6,100 nozzles in a conventional inkjet printer, and delivers 900 million drops of ink per second onto the paper. The combination of more nozzles and wider printhead allows printing at 30 pages per minute even for high-quality photos. Although potentially expensive when introduced to the consumer market in 2009 or 2010, this technology could rapidly become affordable and replace the inkjet and laserjet printers in your home.

FIGURE 2.25

Technologies utilized by modern high-speed printers will allow printing of high-quality photo images at 30 pages per minute.

SOUND OUTPUT

What are the output devices for sound? As noted earlier, most computers include inexpensive **speakers** as an output device for sound. These speakers are sufficient to play the standard audio clips you find on the Web and usually enable you to participate in videoconferencing or phone calls made over the Internet. However, if you plan to digitally edit audio files or are particular about how your music sounds, then you may want to upgrade to a more sophisticated speaker system, such as one that includes **subwoofers** (special speakers that produce only low bass sounds) and **surround-sound speakers** (speaker systems designed in such a way that you feel surrounded by sound). And wireless speaker systems are available now to help you avoid cluttering up your rooms with speaker wire! We discuss how to evaluate and upgrade your speaker system in more detail in Chapter 6.

If you work in close proximity to other employees or are traveling with a notebook, then you may need to use headphones or ear buds for your sound output to avoid distracting other people. Both devices will plug into the same jack on the computer that speakers are connected to, so using them

BITS AND BYTES

Maintaining Your Printer

In general, printers require minimal maintenance. Occasionally, it's a good idea to wipe the case of the printer with a damp cloth to free it from accumulated dust. However, do not wipe away any ink residue that has accumulated inside the printer. If you are experiencing streaking or blank areas on your printed paper, then your print head nozzles may be clogged. To fix this, run the printer's cleaning cycle. (Check your printer's manual for instructions, because every printer is different.) If this doesn't work, you may want to use a cleaning sheet to brush the print head clean. These sheets often come with printers or with reams of photo paper. If you still have a problem, try a cleaning cartridge. Cleaning cartridges contain a special fluid that scrubs the print head. Such cartridges can be found where most ink cartridges are sold. As with ink cartridges, just make sure you buy one that is compatible with your printer.

with a computer is easy. Studies of users of MP3 players have shown that hearing might be damaged by excessive volume, especially when using ear buds because they fit into the ear canals. Therefore, you should exercise caution when using these devices.

The System Unit

We just looked at the components of your computer that you use to input and output data. But where does the processing take place and where is the data stored? The **system unit** is the metal or plastic case that contains the central electronic components of the computer, including the computer's processor (its brain), its memory, and the many circuit boards that help the computer function. You'll also find the power source and all the storage devices (CD/DVD drive and hard drive) here. With a notebook computer, the system unit is combined with the monitor and the keyboard into a single package.

Which is the best system unit style? Most system units on desktop computers are tower configurations, which typically stand vertically (see Figure 2.26a). **All-in-one computers** such as the Apple iMac (see Figure 2.26b), the Dell XPS One, and the Gateway One house not just the computer's processor and memory but also its monitor. Although the all-in-ones take up less desktop space, tower configurations make it easier for you to expand your computer. This is because most tower configurations have more empty areas that allow you to install such additional devices as a second or even third DVD or CD drive.

ON THE FRONT PANEL

What's on the front panel of my computer? No matter whether you choose a tower or all-in-one design, the front panel (or possibly the sides of an all-in-one) of your computer provides you with access to power controls and the storage devices on your computer. Figure 2.27 shows the front panel of a typical system. Although your system might be slightly different, chances are it includes many of the same features.

Power Controls

What's the best way to turn my computer on and off? Your system has a power-on button on the front panel. (You may also find power-on buttons on some keyboards.) Although you use this button to turn on your system, you don't want to use it to turn off, or power off, your system. Modern operating systems want control over the shutdown procedure, so you turn off the power by clicking on a shutdown icon on the desktop, not by pushing the main power button. In fact, pushing the power button might actually just make your computer go into hibernation or sleep mode with many operating systems.

If you do shut off the power using the main power button without shutting down your operating system first, nothing on your system will be permanently damaged. However, some files and applications may not close properly, so the operating system may need to do extra work the next time you start your computer.

Should I turn off my computer every time I'm done using it? Some people say you should leave your computer on at all times. They argue that turning your computer on and off throughout the day subjects its components to stress as the heating and cooling process forces the components to expand and contract repeatedly. Other people say you should shut down

FIGURE 2.26

System units come in several different designs. (a) A standard tower configuration takes up more room than (b) the Apple iMac. However, the closed iMac cannot be easily upgraded.

your computer when you're not using it. They claim that you'll end up wasting money on electricity to keep the computer running all the time. However, modern operating systems include power management settings that allow the most power-hungry components of the system (the hard drive and monitor) to shut down after a short idle period.

If you use the computer sporadically throughout the day, then it may be best to keep it on when you're apt to use it and power it down when you're sure you won't be using it for long periods. However, if you use your computer only for a little while each day, you'll be paying electricity charges during long periods of nonuse. If you're truly concerned about the stresses incurred from powering on and off your computer, then you may want to buy a warranty with the computer.

Can I "rest" my computer without turning it off completely? As mentioned earlier, your computer has power management settings that help it conserve energy. In Windows Vista, the two main methods of power management are Sleep and Hibernate. When your computer enters **Sleep mode**, all of the documents, applications, and data you were using remain in RAM (memory), where they are quickly accessible when restarting your computer (in Windows XP this was called Stand By).

Hibernation mode is another power-saving mode that stores your data in memory and saves it to your computer's hard drive. In either mode, the computer then enters a state of greatly reduced power consumption to save energy. But a big advantage to using Hibernate is that if there is a power failure while your computer is conserving power, your information is protected from loss, because it is saved on the hard drive. To put your computer into Sleep (or Hibernate), open the Start menu and click the power button. To wake up your computer, tap a key on the keyboard or move the mouse; in a few seconds, the computer resumes with exactly the same programs running and documents displayed as when you put the computer to sleep.

In Windows Vista, you can change what happens when you press the power button on the Start menu. By accessing the Power Options screen (see Figure 2.28), you can

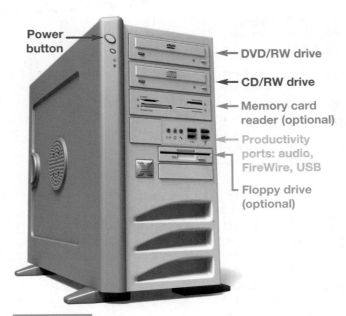

Power button — DVD/RW drive
← CD/RW drive
← Memory card reader (optional)
← Productivity ports: audio, FireWire, USB
← Floppy drive (optional)

FIGURE 2.27

The front panel of your computer provides access to both power controls and the storage devices on your computer.

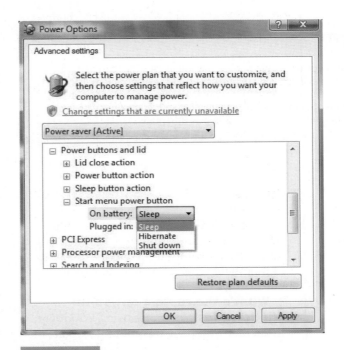

FIGURE 2.28

Using the Sleep and Hibernation settings is good not only for the environment but also for your wallet. Windows Vista allows you to control the Sleep and Hibernation settings for a variety of operations.

>To open Power Options, left-click the **Start** button, click **Control Panel**, and then click **Power Options**. On the **Select a power plan page**, click **Change plan settings under the selected plan**. On the **Change settings for the plan page**, click **Change advanced power settings**. On the **Advanced settings tab**, expand **Power buttons and lid**, expand **Start menu power button**, click **On battery** or **Plugged in** (or both), click the arrow, and then click **Sleep**, **Hibernate**, or **Shut down**.

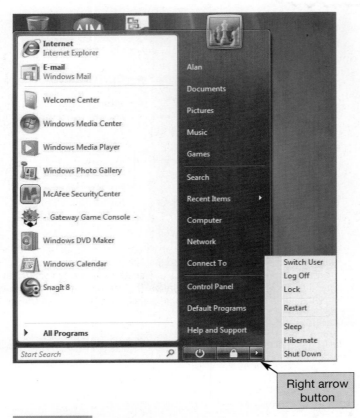

Right arrow button

FIGURE 2.29

When you select the right arrow button from the Start menu in Windows Vista, you are presented with several options. For a warm boot, choose **Restart**. To power down the computer completely, choose **Shut Down**. You can also put your computer into a lower power mode by selecting **Sleep** or **Hibernate**.

>To access Power Options, click the **Start** menu button in the taskbar and then click the right arrow button.

decide if you want your computer to sleep or hibernate when you click the power button.

What's the restart option in Windows for? If you're using Windows Vista, then you have the option to restart the computer when you click the right arrow button next to the lock button on the Start menu (see Figure 2.29). Restarting the system while it's powered on is called a **warm boot**. You might need to perform a warm boot if the operating system or other software application stops responding or if you have installed new programs. It takes less time to perform a warm boot than to power down completely and then restart all of your hardware.

Starting your computer when it has been completely powered down, such as first thing in the morning, is a **cold boot**. With the power management options of Windows Vista, however, you really need to shut down your computer completely only when you need to repair or install hardware in the system unit or move the system unit to another location.

Drive Bays: Your Access to Storage Devices
What else is on the front panel? Besides the power button, the other features that can be seen at the front of your system unit (or on the sides of notebooks and all-in-ones) are **drive bays**. These bays are special shelves reserved for storage devices—that is, those devices that hold your data and applications when the power is shut off. There are two kinds of drive bays:

1. Internal drive bays cannot be seen or accessed from outside the system unit. Generally, internal drive bays are reserved for **internal hard drives**. An internal hard drive usually holds all permanently stored programs and data.

2. External drive bays can be seen and accessed from outside the system unit. External drive bays house CD and DVD drives, for example. Empty external drive bays are covered by a faceplate.

By looking at the front panel of your system unit, you can tell which devices have been installed and often how many bays remain available for expansion.

What kind of data is saved on the internal hard drive? The **hard drive** is your computer's primary device for permanent storage of software and documents. The hard drive is a **nonvolatile storage** device, meaning it holds the data and instructions your computer needs permanently, even after the computer is turned off. Today's internal hard drives, with capacities of as much as 1 **terabyte (TB)**, can hold more data than would fit in the books in your neighborhood library.

Originally, all hard drives were installed inside the system unit with all the other drive bays (see Figure 2.30a). However, unlike the other drive bays, you can't access an internal hard drive from the outside of the system unit, making it a form of non-portable permanent storage. Today, external hard drives are readily available. **External hard drives** (see Figure 2.30b) are essentially internal hard drives that have been made portable by enclosing them in a protective case, enabling them to easily connect to computers via cables, and by making them small and lightweight. External hard drives are usually connected to your computer with a data transfer cable. They are often used to back up (make a copy of) data that is contained on the internal hard drive in case a problem develops with the internal hard drive and data needs to be recovered.

What kinds of external drive bays do most PCs have? On the front panel, you'll see one or two bays for other storage devices such as CD drives. **CD-ROM drives** read CDs, whereas **CD-RW drives** can both read from and write (record) data to CDs. Some computers may also come with a separate **DVD drive**, which allows them to play DVDs and CDs, or a **DVD±RW drive**, which allows them to both read and write DVDs. DVDs are the same size and shape as CDs but can hold more than 25 times as much data. DVD-RW drives are especially useful if you're creating digital movies. Today, most computers (especially notebook computers) come with a DVD drive that can read and write both CDs and DVDs.

Blu-ray is the latest incarnation of optical storage to hit the market. Although a dual-layered DVD can store approximately 9.8 GB of information, this isn't enough to hold movies in the high-definition (HD) digital format that has become so popular. Blu-ray discs, which are similar in size and shape to DVDs, can hold as much as 50 GB of data. This is enough to hold approximately 4.5 hours of high-definition video.

You may occasionally see a PC that still has a bay for a **floppy disk drive**, which reads and writes to easily transportable floppy disks that hold a limited amount of data. Some computers also feature a **Zip disk**, which resembles a floppy disk drive but has a slightly wider opening. Zip disks work just like standard floppies but can carry much more data. These storage devices are fast becoming legacy technologies and are no longer found on new computers.

Flash drives, sometimes referred to as *jump drives*, *USB drives*, or *thumb drives*, are

FIGURE 2.30

(a) Internal hard drives usually hold all the data and instructions that the computer needs, even after the power is turned off. Although this photo shows an open internal hard drive, the drives are actually enclosed within the system unit in a sealed protective case to prevent contamination. (b) External hard drives reside outside the system unit and are connected via cables, usually through a USB or FireWire port.

FIGURE 2.31

Flash drives are about the size of your thumb and can hold up to 16 GB of data, or more.

the new alternative to storing portable data (see Figure 2.31). These devices originally were more or less the size of a thumb, but now they vary in size and can hold as much as 16 GB of data. Flash drives conveniently plug into USB ports.

Several manufacturers now also include slots on the front of the system unit (or sides of notebooks) in which you can insert portable **flash memory cards** such as Memory Sticks and CompactFlash cards. Many notebooks also include slots for flash memory cards. Flash memory cards let you transfer digital data between your computer and devices such as digital

FIGURE 2.32 **Storage Media Capacities**

STORAGE MEDIUM	CAPABILITIES	STORAGE CAPACITY
Hard Drive	Read and write	External: as much as 2 terabytes (TB) Internal: as much as 750 GB
CD CD-RW CD+RW	Read only Read and write	700 MB
DVD DVD-RW DVD+RW	Read only Read and write	4.7 GB (for single-side, single-layer DVDs) 9.4 GB (for single-side, dual-layer DVDs)
Blu-ray (BD)	Read and write	27 GB (for single-layer discs) 50 GB (for dual-layer discs)
Flash memory cards	Read and write	16 GB or more
Flash drive	Read and write	16 GB or more

cameras, PDA/smartphones, video cameras, and printers. Although incredibly small—some are just the size of a postage stamp—these memory cards have capacities that exceed the capacity of a DVD. We discuss flash memory in more detail in Chapter 8.

Figure 2.32 shows the storage capacities of the various portable storage media used in your computer's drive bays. As you learned earlier in this chapter, storage capacity is measured in bytes.

Ports

What are the ports on the front of my computer for? Ports are the places on the system unit where peripheral devices attach to the computer so that data can be exchanged between them and the operating system. Traditionally, ports were located on the back of the system unit. However, in many new computer models, some commonly used ports are placed on the front of the computer (or sides of notebooks and all-in-ones) for easier access when connecting portable devices such as digital cameras, MP3 players, and PDAs to the computer.

On The Back

Are there still ports on the back of my system unit? Yes, even more ports are located on the back of your system unit, and often they duplicate ports that are provided on the front. Peripheral devices such as monitors, printers, keyboards, and mice connect to the system unit through ports. Because peripheral devices exchange data with the computer in various ways, many different types of ports have been created to accommodate these devices on the back of desktop systems (see Figure 2.33).

Notebooks have a similar selection of ports (see Figure 2.34). The ports on the back of the system unit are usually used for devices that stay attached to the computer at all times (such as a printer), while ports on the front are used for convenient connection of portable devices (such as a digital camera). Serial ports and parallel ports have long been used to connect input and output devices to the computer but are now legacy technology.

Traditional **serial ports** sent data one bit (or piece of data) at a time and were often used to connect modems (devices used to transmit data over telecommunications lines) to the computer. Sending data one bit at a time was a slow way to communicate. **Parallel ports** sent data between devices in groups of bits at speeds of 500 Kbps and were much faster than traditional serial ports. Parallel ports were often used to connect printers to computers. The speed advantage offered by USB ports made serial and parallel ports obsolete.

Universal serial bus (USB) ports are now the most popular ports used to connect input and output devices to the computer. This is mainly because of their ability to transfer data quickly. **USB 2.0 ports** transfer data at 480 megabits per second (Mbps) and are approximately 40 times faster than the original USB port. USB ports can connect a wide variety of peripherals to the computer, including keyboards, printers, mice, PDA/ smartphones, flash drives, and digital cameras. Because most peripheral devices today offer USB connectivity, given two equal computers, you should consider purchasing the computer with the greater number of USB ports.

Which ports help me connect with other computers and the Internet? Another set of ports on your computer helps you communicate with other computers. Called **connectivity ports**, these ports give you access to networks

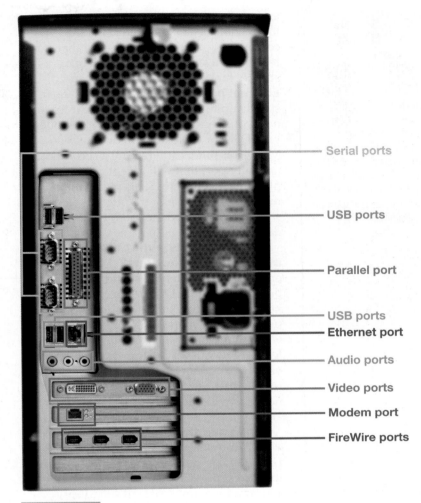

Serial ports
USB ports
Parallel port
USB ports
Ethernet port
Audio ports
Video ports
Modem port
FireWire ports

FIGURE 2.33

The back of your computer probably has many or all of these ports, although they may not be in the same places. There are several different ports because many devices exchange data with the computer in various ways. Color coding helps identify the correct device to connect to each port.

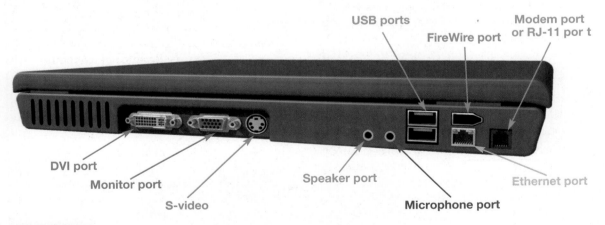

USB ports
FireWire port
Modem port or RJ-11 port
DVI port
Monitor port
S-video
Speaker port
Microphone port
Ethernet port

FIGURE 2.34

Notebooks have many of the ports you find on desktop computers.

SOUND BYTE

Port Tour: How Do I Hook It Up?

In this Sound Byte, you'll take a tour of both a desktop system and a notebook system to compare the number and variety of available ports. You'll also learn about the different types of ports and compare their speed and expandability.

and the Internet and enable your computer to function as a fax machine. To find connectivity ports, look for a port that resembles a standard phone jack but is slightly larger. This port is called an **Ethernet port**. This port transfers data at speeds up to 1,000 Mbps. You use it to connect your computer to a digital subscriber line (DSL) or cable modem or a network. Many computers still feature a second connectivity port that will accept a standard phone-line connector. This jack is the **modem port**. It uses a traditional telephone signal to connect to the Internet over a standard phone line.

Besides ports, what else can help me make connections? Many computers (especially notebooks) and other devices such as smartphones, printers, and keyboards feature built-in wireless connectivity devices. If your computer is equipped with technologies such as Bluetooth or wireless Ethernet (a way of transmitting Internet or network connection data), you can connect to other devices that have these technologies without using traditional ports and cables.

What are the fastest ports available? Interfaces such as **FireWire 400** (or **IEEE 1394**) and the latest **FireWire 800** are the fastest ports available. The FireWire 400 interface moves data at 400 Mbps,

while the newer FireWire 800 doubles the rate to 800 Mbps. Devices such as external hard drives, digital video cameras, MP3 players, and digital media players all benefit from the speedy data transfer of FireWire. Currently under development is the USB 3.0 standard. When this standard is ratified, it should provide transfer speeds of 4.8 Gbps, which is 10 times the speed of USB 2.0. USB 3.0 should quickly become the de facto port of choice.

What are the other ports on the back? Other ports on the back of the computer include the audio and video ports. The video graphics array (VGA) monitor port is the standard port to which monitors connect. The super video (S-video) and digital visual interface (DVI) ports facilitate connecting your computer to multimedia devices such as televisions, DVD players, external monitors, and projectors. Audio ports are where you connect headphones, microphones, and speakers to the computer. We'll explore all the ports on your system unit in more detail in Chapter 6.

INSIDE THE SYSTEM UNIT

What's inside the system unit? Figure 2.35 shows the layout that is common to many system units. As you can see, the **power supply** is housed inside the system

FIGURE 2.35

Inside the System Unit

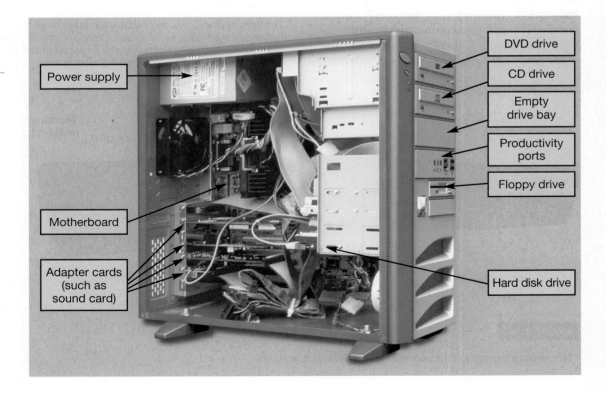

unit to regulate the wall voltage to the voltages required by computer chips. Inside the system unit, you'll also find many printed circuit boards, which are flat, thin boards made of material that won't conduct electricity. On top of this material, thin copper lines are traced, allowing designers to connect a set of computer chips.

The various circuit boards have specific functions that augment the computer's basic functions. Some provide connections to other devices, so these are usually referred to as **expansion cards** (or **adapter cards**). Typical expansion cards found in the system unit are the sound and video cards. A **sound card** provides a connection for the speakers and microphone, whereas a **video card** provides a connection for the monitor. Other expansion cards provide a means for network and Internet connections such as the **modem card**, which provides the computer with a connection to the Internet via a traditional phone line, and a **network interface card (NIC)**, which enables your computer to connect with other computers or to a cable modem to facilitate a high-speed Internet connection.

On the bottom or side of the system unit, you'll find the largest printed circuit board, called the **motherboard**. The motherboard is so named because all of the other boards (video cards, sound cards, and so on) connect to it to receive power and to communicate—therefore, it's the "mother" of all boards.

What's on the motherboard? The motherboard contains the set of chips that powers the system, including the central processing unit (CPU). The motherboard also houses the chips that provide the short-term memory for the computer and a set of slots available for expansion cards (see Figure 2.36). Many low-end computer models have video and sound capabilities integrated into their motherboards. High-end models still use expansion cards to provide video and sound capabilities.

What is the CPU? The **central processing unit (CPU**, or **processor**) is the largest and most important chip in the computer. It is sometimes referred to as the "brains" of the computer because it controls all the functions performed by the computer's other components and processes all the commands issued to it by software instructions. Modern CPUs (found in home and small business computers) can perform as many as 6 billion tasks a second without error, making them extremely powerful components.

What exactly is RAM? Because the CPU processes data so rapidly, there needs to be a way to store data and commands nearby so that they can be rapidly fed to the CPU. **Random access memory (RAM)** is that

SOUND BYTE

Virtual Computer Tour

In this Sound Byte, you'll take a video tour of the inside of a system unit. From opening the cover to locating the power supply, CPU, and memory, you'll become more familiar with what's inside your computer.

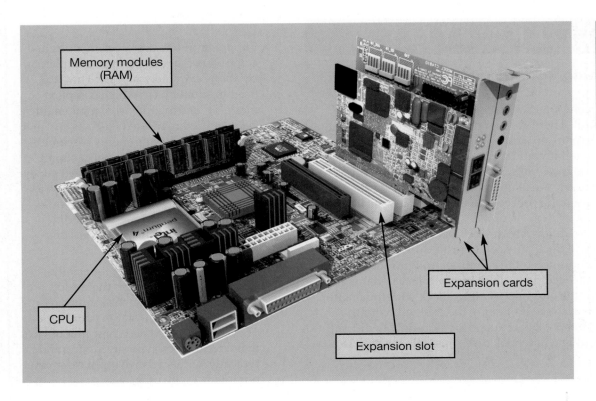

Memory modules (RAM)

CPU

Expansion cards

Expansion slot

FIGURE 2.36

A motherboard contains the CPU, the memory (RAM) modules, and slots available for expansion cards.

storage space. If you look at a motherboard, you'll see RAM as a series of small cards (called *memory cards* or *memory modules*) plugged into slots on the motherboard. The CPU can request the RAM's contents, which can be located, opened, and delivered to the CPU for processing in a few billionths of a second (or nanoseconds).

Sometimes RAM is referred to as *primary storage*, but it should not be confused with other types of permanent storage devices. Because the entire contents of RAM are erased when you turn off the computer, RAM is the temporary or **volatile storage** location for the computer. To save data permanently, you need to save it to the hard drive or to another permanent storage device such as a CD or flash drive. A more complete discussion of the CPU and RAM is in Chapter 6.

Does the system unit contain any other kinds of memory besides RAM? In addition to RAM, the motherboard also contains a form of memory called **read-only memory (ROM)**. ROM holds all the instructions the computer needs to start up. Unlike data stored in RAM, which is volatile storage, the instructions stored in ROM are permanent, making ROM a non-volatile storage location. As is the case with the hard drive, this means the data does not get erased when the power is turned off.

BITS AND BYTES

Opening Your System Unit

Many people use a computer for years without ever needing to open their system unit. There are two main reasons to do so: (1) to replace a defective expansion card or other device and (2) to upgrade your computer. If your hard drive or CD-ROM drive fails, with a bit of guidance you can open the system unit and replace the drive yourself. Adding more memory and adding a DVD-RW drive are upgrade procedures that you can do safely at home.

Be sure, however, to follow the device's specific installation instructions, which will detail any safety procedures you'll need to observe, such as unplugging the computer and grounding yourself to avoid static electricity discharge, which can damage internal components. It's also important to check with the manufacturer of your system to see if opening the case will void the system's warranty. Notebook computers are notoriously difficult to work on, and opening a notebook case is usually best left to a professional.

Does my computer need anything else to function? If you have other digital devices in your house (such as computers, a TiVo, or gaming consoles) that need to be connected to the Internet, then you probably need to set up a home computer network. A network is a combination of hardware and software that facilitates the sharing of information between computing devices. Your computer thus may require additional networking hardware such as a router, cables, and wireless hardware. A more complete discussion of computer networking is found in Chapter 7.

SPECIALTY COMPUTERS

Are there other types of computers besides desktop and notebook computers? Desktop and notebook computers are the computers that you will most likely encounter. Although you may never come into direct contact with the following types of computers, they are still important to our society:

- **Mainframes** are large, expensive computers that support hundreds of users simultaneously. They are often used in insurance companies, for example, where many people are working on similar operations (such as processing claims) all at once. Mainframes excel at executing many different computer programs at the same time.

- **Supercomputers** are specially designed computers that can perform complex calculations extremely rapidly. They are used in situations in which complex models requiring intensive mathematical calculations are needed (such as weather forecasting or atomic energy research). The main difference between a super-computer and a mainframe is that super-computers are designed to execute a few programs as quickly as possible while mainframes are designed to handle many programs running at the same time but at a slower pace.

- **Embedded computers** are specially designed computer chips that reside inside other devices such as your car or the electronic thermostat in your home. They are self-contained computer devices that have their own programming and typically neither receive input from you nor interact with other systems.

Setting It All Up

It's important that you understand not only your computer's components and how they work together but also how to set up these components safely. *Merriam-Webster's Dictionary* defines **ergonomics** as "an applied science concerned with designing and arranging things people use so that the people and things interact most efficiently and safely." In terms of computing, ergonomics refers to how you set up your computer and other equipment to minimize your risk of injury or discomfort.

Why is ergonomics important? Workplace injuries related to musculo-skeletal disorders occur frequently in the United States. More than 357,000 workers experienced such disorders in 2006 (the latest year for which data is available), and these disorders required an average of nine days off from work as reported by the U.S. Department of Labor's Bureau of Labor Statistics (**http://www.bls.gov/news.release/osh2.nr0.htm**). Affected businesses incurred billions of dollars of direct costs (sick pay, medical costs) and even more in indirect costs (lost productivity, overtime, value of employee time involved in the accident, cost of record keeping and investigation, etc.).

SOUND BYTE
Healthy Computing

In this Sound Byte, you'll see how to set up your workspace in an ergonomically correct way. You'll learn the proper location of the monitor, keyboard, and mouse, as well as ergonomic features to look for when choosing the most appropriate chair.

Avoiding workplace injuries is not only good for employees but also financially beneficial for businesses.

How can I avoid injuries when I'm working at my computer? As Figure 2.37 illustrates, it is important to arrange your monitor, chair, body, and keyboard in ways that will help you avoid injury, discomfort, and eyestrain as you work on your computer. The following additional guidelines can help keep you comfortable and productive:

- **Position your monitor correctly.** Studies suggest it's best to place your monitor at least 25 inches from your eyes. You may need to decrease the screen resolution to make text and images more readable at that distance. Also, experts recommend the monitor

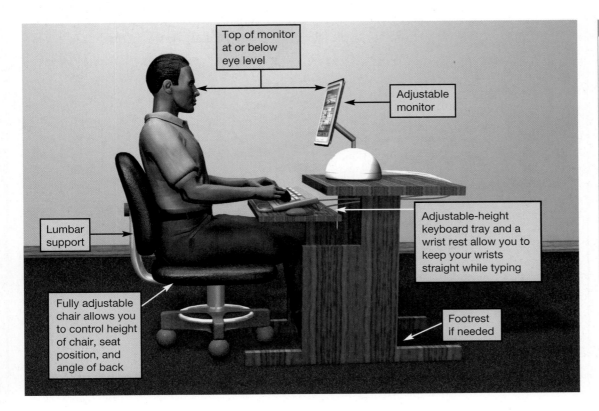

Top of monitor at or below eye level

Adjustable monitor

Lumbar support

Adjustable-height keyboard tray and a wrist rest allow you to keep your wrists straight while typing

Fully adjustable chair allows you to control height of chair, seat position, and angle of back

Footrest if needed

FIGURE 2.37

Achieving comfort and a proper typing position is the way to avoid repetitive strain injuries while working at a computer. Buy equipment that boasts as many adjustments as possible; these allow individuals to tailor their own workspaces. Ergonomically designed peripheral devices such as keyboards, wrist rests, and antiglare screens provide additional comfort.

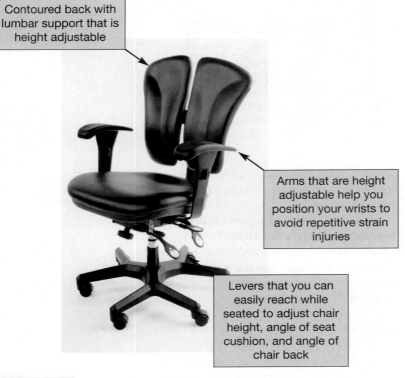

Contoured back with lumbar support that is height adjustable

Arms that are height adjustable help you position your wrists to avoid repetitive strain injuries

Levers that you can easily reach while seated to adjust chair height, angle of seat cushion, and angle of chair back

FIGURE 2.38

Look for these key features when selecting an ergonomic chair.

be positioned either at eye level or so that it is at an angle 15 to 20 degrees below your line of sight.

- **Purchase an adjustable chair.** Adjust the height of your chair (see Figure 2.38) so that your feet touch the floor. (You may need to use a footrest to get the right position.) Back support needs to be adjustable so that you can position it to support your lumbar (lower back) region. You should also be able to move the seat or adjust the back so that you can sit without exerting pressure on your knees. If your chair doesn't adjust, placing a pillow behind your back can provide the same support.

- **Assume a proper position while typing.** A repetitive strain injury (RSI) is a painful condition caused by repetitive or awkward movements of a part of the body. Improperly positioned keyboards are one of the leading causes of RSIs in computer users. Your wrists should be flat (unbent) with respect to the keyboard and your forearms parallel to the floor. You can either adjust the height of your chair or install a height-adjustable keyboard tray to ensure a proper position. Specially designed ergonomic keyboards such as the one shown in Figure 2.39 can help you achieve the proper position of your wrists.

FIGURE 2.39

(a) Ergonomic keyboards that curve and contain built-in wrist rests help maintain proper hand position and minimize strain on your wrists.
(b) Ergonomic pointing devices replace conventional mice to reduce stress on the wrist and fingers.

a

b

- **Take breaks from computer tasks.**
Remaining in the same position for long periods of time increases stress on your body. Shift your position in your chair and stretch your hands and fingers periodically. Likewise, staring at the screen for long periods of time can lead to eyestrain, so rest your eyes by periodically taking them off the screen and focusing them on an object at least 20 feet away.

- **Ensure the lighting is adequate.**
Ensuring proper lighting in your work area is a good way to minimize eyestrain. To do so, eliminate any sources of direct glare (light shining directly into your eyes) or reflected glare (light shining off the computer screen) and ensure there is enough light to read comfortably. If you still can't eliminate glare

from your computer screen, you can purchase an antiglare screen to place over your monitor. Look for ones that are polarized or have a purplish optical coating for the greatest relief.

Is ergonomics important when using mobile devices? Working with mobile computing devices also presents interesting challenges when it comes to injury prevention. For example, many users work with notebooks resting on their laps, placing the monitor outside of the optimal line of sight and thereby increasing neck strain. The table in Figure 2.40 provides guidelines on preventing injuries when on the go.

So whether you're computing at your desk or on the road, consider the ergonomics of your work environment. Doing so will help you avoid injury and discomfort.

	PDA/Smartphone RSIs	PMP Hearing Damage	Small-Screen Vision Issues	Lap Injuries	Back, Neck and Shoulder Injuries
Malady	Repetitive strain injuries (such as DeQuervain's tendonitis) from constant typing of instant messages.	Hearing loss from high decibel sound levels in ear buds or headphones.	Blurriness and dryness caused by squinting to view tiny screens on mobile devices.	Burns on legs from heat generated by laptop.	Pain caused from carrying laptop (messenger) bag hung over your shoulder.
Preventative measures	Restrict length and frequency of messages, take breaks often, perform other motions with your thumbs and fingers during breaks to relieve tension.	Turn down volume (you should be able to hear external noises such as people talking), use software programs that limit sound levels (not over 60 decibels), use external, over-ear style headphones instead of ear buds.	Blink frequently or use eye drops to maintain moisture level in eyes, after 10 minutes take a break and focus your eyes on something at least 8 feet away for 5 minutes, use an adequate amount of light, increase the size of fonts.	Place a book, magazine, or laptop cooling pad between your legs and your laptop.	Use a conventional backpack with two shoulder straps, lighten the load by only carrying essential equipment, consider buying a lightweight laptop.

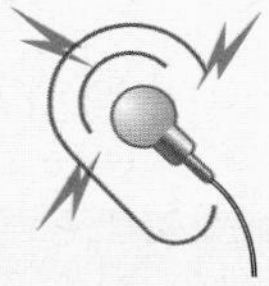

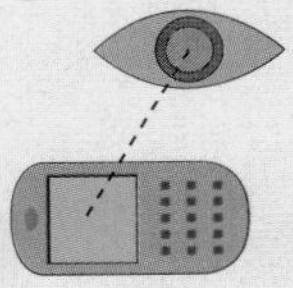

FIGURE 2.40

Preventing Injuries While On the Go

Emerging Technologies: Tomorrow's Display—You Can Take It with You!

Today, LCD monitors dominate the desktop PC and notebook markets. Lighter and less bulky than previous monitors, they can be easily moved and take up less space on a desk. LCD technology has improved significantly over the past several years, and now monitors are sporting increased viewing angles, higher resolutions, and faster pixel response time, which makes full-motion video (critical for gamers) appear extremely smooth.

Despite these advances, LCDs can still be improved and are expected to continue to be the dominant display device in the next few years. Here are a few technologies that sources such as *PC Magazine* feel will take LCD displays to the next level.

Flexible Screens

The most promising displays currently under development are organic light-emitting displays (OLEDs). These displays, currently used in digital cameras, use organic compounds that produce light when exposed to an electric current. OLEDs tend to use less power than other flat-screen technologies, making them ideal for portable battery-operated devices. However, most research is being geared toward flexible OLEDs (FOLEDs). Unlike LCDs, which use rigid surfaces such as glass, FOLED screens would be designed on lightweight, inexpensive, flexible material such as transparent plastics or metal foils. As shown in Figure 2.41, the computer screen of the future might roll up into an easily transported cylinder the size of a pen!

FOLEDs would allow advertising to progress to a new dimension. Screens could be hung where posters are hung now (such as on billboards). And wireless transmission of data to these screens would allow advertisers to display easily updatable full-motion images. Combining transparency and flexibility would also allow these displays to be mounted on windshields or eyeglasses.

FIGURE 2.41

With FOLED technology, you'll be able to unroll a computer screen wherever you need it from a container the size of a pen. The prototype shown is currently being developed by Universal Display Corporation (**www.universaldisplay.com**) and should be available within a few years.

Transparent thin-film transistors (TFTs) present another promising new technology. These transistors contain a mixture of zinc and tin oxides, instead of the traditional silicon. The coolest thing about them is that they are transparent, flexible, and extremely heat resistant! Imagine a computer chip crammed with transistors but totally clear. Because they are clear, TFTs could eventually find their way into heads-up displays on car windshields or in stores as advertising on plate-glass windows.

Obstacles remain to be overcome before these types of screens will be widely available. In OLEDs and FOLEDs, the compounds that create blue hues age faster than the ones that produce reds and greens. This makes it difficult to maintain balanced colors over time. And the compounds used to form the OLEDs can be contaminated by exposure to water vapor or oxygen. The TFT technology is so new that it will probably be at least a decade before this technology appears in the consumer market. Although flexible screens have been produced as prototypes using OLEDs by companies such as Sony, reducing costs to make them available in the consumer market remains a challenge. However, because of ongoing research, you can be sure that flexible displays will be popping up everywhere in your lifetime.

Wearable Screens

Who needs a screen when you can just wear one? With the rise of the iPod and other portable devices that play digital video, users are demanding larger viewing areas. Although a larger screen is often incompatible with the main design features of portable devices (lightweight and long battery life), wearable virtual displays offer a solution. Personal media viewer displays such as the myvu, shown in Figure 2.42, are available now (**www. myvu.com**). Eventually, when the technology advances sufficiently, you might be able to purchase conventional eyeglasses with displays built right in. Wearable displays might eventually replace heavier screens on notebooks, desktops, and even PDAs.

"Bistable" Screens

Your computer screen constantly changes its images when you are surfing the Internet or playing a game. Because PDA and cell phone screens don't necessarily change that often, something called a "bistable" display, which is currently used in retail stores for pricing signs and in Sony's Reader Digital Book (E-Reader), may one day be used in these devices. A bistable display has the ability to retain its image even when the power is turned off. In addition, bistable displays are lighter than LCD displays and reduce overall power consumption, resulting in longer battery life—perhaps as much as 600 times longer life, according to Motorola. As the market for portable devices such as smartphones continues to explode, you can expect to see bistable technologies emerging in mobile computer screens.

FIGURE 2.42

Personal media viewers allow you to have a big-screen experience from your mobile devices. The display is projected right in front of your eyes for that "in the action" experience.

Summary

1. What exactly is a computer, and what are its four main functions?

Computers are devices that process data. They help organize, sort, and categorize data to turn it into information. The computer's four major functions are: (1) to gather data (or allow users to input data), (2) to process that data (perform calculations or some other manipulation of the data), (3) to output data or information (display information in a form suitable for the user), and (4) to store data and information for later use.

2. What is the difference between data and information?

Data is a representation of a fact or idea. The number 3 and the words *televisions* and *Sony* are pieces of data. Information is data that has been organized or presented in a meaningful fashion. An inventory list that indicates that "3 Sony televisions" are in stock is processed information. It allows a retail clerk to answer a customer query about the availability of merchandise. Information is more powerful than raw data.

3. What are bits and bytes, and how are they measured?

To process data into information, computers need to work in a language they understand. This language, called *binary language,* consists of two numbers: 0 and 1. Each 0 and 1 is a binary digit, or bit. Eight bits create one byte. In computers, each letter of the alphabet, each number, and each special character consists of a unique combination of eight bits (one byte), or a string of eight 0s and 1s. For describing large amounts of storage capacity, the terms *megabyte* (approximately 1 million bytes), *gigabyte* (approximately 1 billion bytes), and *terabyte* (approximately 1 trillion bytes) are used.

4. What devices do you use to get data into the computer?

An input device enables you to enter data (text, images, and sounds) and instructions (user responses and commands) into a computer. You use keyboards to enter typed data and commands, whereas you use the mouse to enter user responses and commands. Keyboards are distinguished by the layout of the keys as well as the special keys found on the keyboard. The most common keyboard is the QWERTY keyboard. The Dvorak keyboard is a leader in alternative keyboards. The Dvorak keyboard puts the most commonly used letters in the English language on "home keys"—the keys in the middle row of the keyboard. Keyboards that feature keys that can be rearranged and reprogrammed are popular with gamers.

Notebook keyboards are more compact and have fewer keys than standard keyboards. Still, many notebook keys have alternate functions so that you can get the same capabilities from the limited number of keys as you do from the special keys on standard keyboards. Most PDAs use a stylus instead of a keyboard.

Most computers come with wired optical mice, but other options include trackball mice and wireless mice. An optical mouse uses an internal sensor or laser to control the mouse's movement. In a trackball mouse, a rollerball sits on top or on the side of the mouse so that you can move the ball with your fingers. Wireless mice use batteries and send data to the computer via radio or light waves.

Notebooks incorporate the mouse into the keyboard area. Notebook mice include trackpoints and touch pads. Microphones are the devices used to input sounds, whereas scanners and digital cameras input nondigital text and images.

5. What devices do you use to get information out of the computer?

Output devices enable you to send processed data out of your computer. This can take the form of text, pictures, sounds, and video. Monitors display soft copies of text, graphics, and video, while printers create hard copies of text and graphics. LCDs are the most popular type of monitor. Also called *flat-panel monitors,* they take up less space and are lighter and more energy efficient than older CRT monitors (which look like TV sets), making them

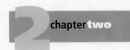

perfect for portable computers. Today's LCD monitors support high-screen resolutions, have wider viewing angles, and feature faster pixel response times so that full-motion video appears smooth.

There are two primary categories of printers: impact and nonimpact. Impact printers have hammer-like keys that strike the paper through an inked ribbon. Nonimpact printers spray ink or use laser beams to transfer marks on the paper. The most common nonimpact printers are inkjet printers and laser printers. Specialty printers are also available. These include multifunction printers, plotters, and thermal printers. When choosing a printer, you should be aware of factors such as speed, resolution, color output, memory, and cost.

Speakers are the output devices for sound. Most computers include speakers. However, you may want to upgrade to a more sophisticated speaker system, such as one that includes subwoofers and surround sound.

6. What's on the front of your system unit?

The system unit is a box that contains the central electronic components of a computer. On the front of the system unit, you'll find the power source as well as access to the storage devices in your computer. Most PCs include one or two bays for storage devices such as CD, DVD, and Blu-ray drives. Most computers include access to USB and other ports on the front panel, and some manufacturers now also include slots on the front of the system unit into which you can insert portable flash memory cards such as Memory Sticks and CompactFlash cards.

7. What's on the back of your system unit?

On the back of the system unit or notebook, you'll find a wide variety of ports that allow you to hook up peripheral devices (such as your monitor and keyboard) to your system. The most common ports found on the back of the system unit are USB and connectivity (networking) ports. Serial ports and parallel ports are legacy technology now. The most popular port for connecting devices is the USB port.

USB 2.0 ports transfer data at 480 Mbps, which is much faster than the parallel and serial ports they displaced. FireWire 800 ports provide even faster data transfer at approximately 800 Mbps. USB 3.0, when available, will increase throughput to 4.8 Gbps.

Connectivity ports give you access to networks and the Internet and enable your computer to function as a fax machine. Connectivity ports include Ethernet ports and modem ports.

8. What's inside your system unit?

The system unit contains the main electronic components of the computer. The motherboard, the main circuit board of the system, contains a computer's central processing unit (CPU), which coordinates the functions of all other devices on the computer. RAM, the computer's volatile memory, is also located on the motherboard. RAM is where all the data and instructions are held while the computer is running. ROM, a permanent type of memory, is responsible for housing instructions to help start up a computer. The hard drive (the permanent storage location) and other storage devices (CD and DVD drives) are also located inside the system unit, as are expansion cards (such as sound, video, modem, and network interface cards) that help a computer perform special functions.

9. How do you set up your computer to avoid strain and injury?

Ergonomics refers to how you arrange your computer and equipment to minimize your risk of injury or discomfort. This includes positioning your monitor correctly, buying an adjustable chair that ensures you have good posture while using the computer, assuming a proper position while typing, making sure the lighting is adequate, and avoiding looking only at the screen for long periods of time. Other good practices include taking frequent breaks as well as using other specially designed equipment such as ergonomic keyboards. Ergonomics is also important to consider when using mobile devices.

Buzzwords

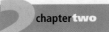

Word Bank

- CPU
- CRT
- Dvorak
- ergonomics
- FireWire
- inkjet printer
- laser printer
- LCD
- microphone
- monitor
- mouse
- optical
- QWERTY
- RAM
- ROM
- speakers
- system unit
- USB

Instructions: Fill in the blanks using the words from the Word Bank above.

Austin had been getting a sore back and stiff arms when he sat at his desk, so he redesigned the (1) _____ of his computer setup. He placed the (2) _____ so that it was 25 inches from his eyes, and he bought an adjustable chair. He also decided to improve his equipment in other ways. His (3) _____ was old, so he replaced it with a(n) (4) _____ mouse that didn't need a mouse pad. To plug in the mouse, he used a(n) (5) _____ port on the back of his (6) _____. He considered buying an alternative keyboard to replace the (7) _____ keyboard he got with his computer, but he didn't know much about alternative keyboards like the (8) _____ keyboard, so he decided to wait.

Because he often printed flyers for his band, Austin decided to buy a printer that could print text-based pages quickly. Although he decided to keep his (9) _____ to print photos, he decided to buy a new (10) _____ to print his flyers faster. While looking at printers, Austin also noticed widescreen (11) _____ monitors that would take up less space on his desk than the ancient (12) _____ monitor he had, so he bought one because it was on sale for $200. He also decided to buy new (13) _____ because the ones that came with his computer didn't have subwoofers. He also bought a professional (14) _____ awhile back for use with his band. Finally, knowing his system could use more memory, Austin checked out prices for additional (15) _____.

Becoming Computer Literate

Your parents live a day's drive from your school and have just called asking you for help in setting up their new computer.

Instructions: Because you can't help them in person, prepare a setup guide for your parents as either a Word document or a PowerPoint presentation. Your setup guide should have all the components of a computer system illustrated and defined. In addition, you should describe with illustrations and words the various ports your parents will need to use to attach various peripheral devices to the system unit. You may use the Internet for information, device pictures, and illustrations, but remember to credit all sources at the end of your guide.

Self-Test

Instructions: Answer the multiple-choice and true–false questions below for more practice with key terms and concepts from this chapter.

MULTIPLE CHOICE

1. Which of the following devices are considered output devices?
   a. Keyboard and mouse
   b. Monitor and printer
   c. Hard drive and speakers
   d. Microphone and CD-ROM drive

2. Which of the following is NOT one of the four major functions of a computer?
   a. Computation   b. Storage
   c. Processing   d. Input

3. Which of the following is NOT an output device?
   a. Mouse   b. Monitor
   c. Printer   d. Speakers

4. The resolution of a monitor is governed by the
   a. size of the screen.
   b. cost of the monitor.
   c. number of pixels on the screen.
   d. contrast of the pixels on the screen.

5. All of the following are important to consider when buying an LCD monitor EXCEPT
   a. brightness.
   b. pixel swap rate.
   c. viewing angle.
   d. resolution.

6. Restarting the system while the computer is running is called
   a. a warm boot.
   b. a Stand By start.
   c. hibernation.
   d. a cold boot.

7. An Ethernet port is used for connecting your computer to a
   a. network.
   b. printer.
   c. monitor.
   d. digital camera.

8. Which of the following devices is considered the "brains" of the computer?
   a. ROM   b. Motherboard
   c. RAM   d. CPU

9. Which of the following statements about hard drives is FALSE?
   a. Hard drives are not always installed inside the system unit of a computer.
   b. Hard drives are considered volatile storage devices.
   c. External hard drives are often used for backups.
   d. Hard drives are considered nonvolatile storage devices.

10. Why is an ergonomically correct setup for your computer system essential?
   a. Reduces eyestrain
   b. Prevents repetitive strain injuries
   c. Complies with federal laws
   d. a & b
   e. b & c
   f. All of the above

TRUE–FALSE

____ 1. The terms *data* and *information* can be used interchangeably.

____ 2. RAM is volatile storage that is located on the motherboard.

____ 3. The CPU is located on the ROM board.

____ 4. FireWire ports are the most popular port used for connecting peripherals to a computer.

____ 5. Keeping your wrists flat while typing at a computer will help prevent repetitive strain injuries.

Making the Transition to... Next Semester

1. **Choosing the Best Keyboard**

   Once you become more familiar with software products such as Microsoft Office, you may want to migrate to a customized keyboard design. Although keyboards have similar setups, some keyboards provide special keys and buttons to support different users. For example, some keyboards are designed specifically for multimedia use, Internet use, and gaming use. Which one is best for you?

   a. Examine the various keyboard setups at the Microsoft Web site (**www.microsoft.com/ hardware/mouseandkeyboard/default.mspx**). Which keyboard would best suit your needs and why? What features would be most useful to you? How would you evaluate the additional costs versus the benefits?

   b. When would you need a keyboard for your portable computing devices (such as a PDA/smartphone)? What is the current price for a portable folding keyboard? Would the virtual keyboard described in the chapter be a better choice for you? Explain your answers.

2. **Choosing the Best Mouse**

   On the Web, research the different kinds of mice available and list their special features, functions, and costs. Of these mice, which do you think would be most useful to you? Why?

3. **Pricing Computer Upgrades**

   On the Web, investigate the following:

   a. How much would it cost to add a Blu-ray drive to your computer? Does your system have an extra drive bay to install such a device? Could you install this type of drive in a notebook?

   b. How much would it cost to buy a new 21-inch LCD monitor? What kind of monitor would be best to play games, view DVDs, or play back recorded TV shows?

   c. How much do various computer speaker systems cost? What speakers would be best to listen to CDs? What speakers would be useful when playing games?

4. **Exploring Scanners**

   One input device we did not explore in the text is a scanner. Conduct the following research on the Web to find out about scanners:

   a. What are the different kinds of scanners on the market?

   b. What qualities do good scanners have?

   c. How much do scanners cost?

   Create a table comparing all the specifications listed earlier for several different scanners. Highlight the scanner you would be most interested in purchasing.

5. **Green Computing**

   Reducing energy consumption and promoting the recycling of computer components are key aspects of "green" (environmentally friendly) initiatives by businesses. Using the Web, research the following:

   a. What are the key attributes of the Energy Star and EPEAT Gold green PC certifications? Does your PC have these certifications?

   b. What toxic components are contained in computers and monitors? Where can you recycle computers and monitors in your area?

   c. Check out **www.goodcleantech.com** and find out which companies are currently working toward better green technology. If your school had to replace computers in a lab, which environmentally friendly company would you recommend? Why?

Making the Transition to... the Workplace

1. Desktop Versus Notebook

There are two main types of computers in the workplace: desktop computers with separate system units and monitors, and notebook computers that are portable and have the monitors, keyboards, and the system unit all contained within a single case. If you were being interviewed for a job, what types of questions would you need to ask your prospective boss about the job to determine whether you needed a desktop or a notebook computer?

2. What System Will You Use?

When you arrive at a new position for a company, you'll most likely be provided with a computer. Based on the career you are in now or are planning to pursue, answer the following questions:

a. What kind of computer system would you most like to use (PC, Mac, desktop configuration, notebook, PDA, and so on)?
b. If you were required to use a type of computer you had never used before (say a Mac instead of a PC), how would you go about learning to use the new computer?
c. What kind of keyboard, mouse, monitor, and printer would you like to have?
d. Would you need any additional input or output devices to perform your job?

3. What Hardware Will You Use?

What types of computer hardware would make your work life more efficient? What adjustments would you need to make on your current system to accommodate those hardware devices? (For example, does your computer have the right kind of port or enough ports to support additional hardware devices?)

4. Choosing the Best Printer

You are looking for a new printer for your home business. You have always had an inkjet printer, but now that the costs for color laser printers are dropping, you're considering buying a color laser printer. However, you're still unsure because they're more expensive than inkjet printers, although you've heard that there is an overall cost savings with laser printers when the cost of toner or ink and paper is taken into consideration.

a. Using the Web, investigate the merits of different inkjet and color laser printers. Narrow in on one printer in each category and note the initial cost of each.
b. Research the cost of ink or toner for each printer. Calculate the cost of ink or toner supplies for each printer, assuming you will print 5,000 color pages per year. How much will it cost per page of printing, not including the initial cost of the printer itself?
c. Investigate the multipurpose printers that also have faxing, scanning, and copying capabilities. How much more expensive are they than a traditional inkjet or laser printer? Are there any drawbacks to these multipurpose machines? Do they perform each function as well as their stand-alone counterparts? Can you print in color on these machines?
d. Based on your research, which printer would be the most economical?

5. Office Ergonomics

Your boss has designated you as the "ergonomics coordinator" for the department. She has asked you to design a flyer to be posted around the office informing your co-workers of the proper computer setup as well as the potential risks if such precautions are avoided. Create an ergonomics flyer, making sure it fits on an 8.5 × 11 piece of paper.

Critical Thinking Questions

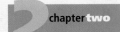

Instructions: Albert Einstein used *Gedanken experiments,* or critical thinking questions, to develop his theory of relativity. Some ideas are best understood by experimenting with them in our own minds. The following critical thinking questions are designed to demand your full attention but require only a comfortable chair—no technology.

1. **Keyboard of the Future**

   What do you think the keyboard of the future will look like? What capabilities will it have that keyboards currently don't have? Will it have ports? cables? special communications capabilities?

2. **Mouse of the Future**

   What do you think the mouse (or other pointing device) of the future will look like? What sorts of improvements on the traditional mouse can you imagine? Do you think there will ever be a day when we won't need mice and keyboards to use our computers?

3. **Storage Devices of the Future**

   How do you think storage devices will change in the future? Will increased storage capacity and decreased size affect the ways in which we use computers? Will we need storage devices in the future, or will we access all of our data via the Internet?

4. **Computers Decreasing Productivity?**

   Can you think of any situations in which computers actually decrease productivity? Why? Should we always expect computers to increase our productivity? What do you think the impact of using computers would be:
   a. in a third-grade classroom?
   b. in a manager's office for a large chain supermarket?
   c. for a retired couple who purchase their first computer?

5. **"Smart" Homes**

   The Smart Medical Home project of the University of Rochester's Center for Future Health is researching how to use technology to monitor many aspects of your health. The Smart Medical Home is the creation of a cross-disciplinary group of scientists and engineers from the college, the medical center, and the university's Center for Future Health. This particular "smart home" includes a sophisticated computer system that helps keep track of items such as eyeglasses or keys, and the kitchen is equipped with a new kind of packaging to signal the presence of dangerous bacteria in food. Spaces between ordinary walls are stuffed with gadgetry, including banks of powerful computers.
   a. What abilities should a smart home have to safeguard and improve the quality of your life?
   b. Could there be potential hazards related to a smart home?

6. **Toy or Computer?**

   When do you think a toy becomes a computer? The Microsoft Xbox 360 has a hard drive, a processor with three cores, internal RAM, and wireless capability. Apple iPods also have hard drives (or flash memory and a processor). Are these devices computers or toys? What capabilities do you think next-generation gaming consoles and iPods should have?

Problem:

There are two major classes of computer systems in the marketplace today: PCs and Apple computers. Many people have chosen one camp with an almost religious fervor. In this exercise, each team will explore the trade-offs between a PC and an Apple computer and defend their allegiance to one system or the other.

Task:

Split your class into two teams:

Team A is a group of PC diehards who believe these computers perform as well as Apple systems and cost less, thus providing better value.

Team B is a group of hard-working, Apple-loving users who believe there are no systems as user-friendly and reliable as those made by Apple.

Look at the following list of settings where these computers could be used. Each team should decide why its particular system would be the best choice in each of these settings.

1. An elementary school considering incorporating more technology into the classroom

2. A small accounting firm expanding into new offices

3. A video production company considering producing digital video

4. A computer system for a home office for an aspiring entrepreneur

Process:

1. Form the two teams. Think about what your goals are and what information and resources you need to tackle this project.

2. Research and then discuss the components of each system you are recommending. Are any components better suited for each particular need? Consider all the input, output, processing, and storage devices. Are any special devices or peripherals required?

3. Write a summary position paper. For each of the four settings, support your system recommendation for

Team A—a PC computer system

Team B—an Apple system

Conclusion:

There are many competing designs for computer systems. Being aware of the options in the marketplace and knowing how to analyze the trade-offs in different designs allows you to become a better consumer as well as a better computer user.

Multimedia

In addition to the review materials presented here, you'll find more materials featured with the book's multimedia, including the *Technology in Action* Student Resource CD and the Companion Website (**www.prenhall.com/techinaction**), which will help reinforce your understanding of the chapter content. These materials include the following:

ACTIVE HELPDESK

In Active Helpdesk calls, you'll assume the role of helpdesk operator, taking calls about the concepts you've learned in this chapter. You'll apply what you've learned and receive feedback from a supervisor to review and reinforce those concepts. The Active Helpdesk calls for this chapter are listed below and can be found on your Student Resource CD:

- Understanding Bits and Bytes
- Using Input Devices
- Using Output Devices

SOUND BYTES

Sound Bytes are dynamic multimedia tutorials that help demystify even the most complex topics. You'll view video clips and animations that illustrate computer concepts and then apply what you've learned by reviewing with the Sound Byte Labs, which include quizzes and activities specifically tailored to each Sound Byte. The Sound Bytes for this chapter are listed below and can be found on your Student Resource CD:

- Port Tour: How Do I Hook It Up?
- Virtual Computer Tour
- Healthy Computing

COMPANION WEBSITE

The *Technology in Action* Companion Website includes a variety of additional materials to help you review and learn more about the topics in this chapter. The resources available at **www.prenhall.com/techinaction** include:

- **Online Study Guide.** Each chapter features an online true–false and multiple-choice quiz. You can take these quizzes, automatically check the results, and e-mail the results to your instructor.
- **Web Research Projects.** Each chapter features several Web research projects that ask you to search the Web for information on computer-related careers, milestones in computer history, important people and companies, emerging technologies, and the applications and implications of different technologies.

3

Using the Internet:

Making the Most of the Web's Resources

Objectives

After reading this chapter,
you should be able to
answer the following
questions:

1. What is the origin of the Internet? **(pp. 96–97)**

2. How can I communicate through the Internet? **(pp. 98–106)**

3. What are the various kinds of multimedia files found on the Web, and what software do I need to use them? **(pp. 106–107)**

4. What is e-commerce, and what e-commerce safeguards protect me when I'm online? **(pp. 107–111)**

5. How do I manage online annoyances such as spam? **(pp. 111–115)**

6. What is a Web browser? **(pp. 115–116)**

7. What is a URL, and what are its parts? **(pp. 117–118)**

8. How can I use hyperlinks and other tools to get around the Web? **(pp. 118–120)**

9. How do I search the Internet using search engines and subject directories? **(pp. 120–123)**

10. How do I evaluate a Web site? **(pp. 124–125)**

11. How does data travel on the Internet? **(pp. 125–128)**

12. What are my options for connecting to the Internet? **(pp. 128–132)**

13. How do I choose an Internet service provider? **(pp. 132–133)**

14. What will the Internet of the future look like? **(p. 133)**

ACTIVE HELPDESK

- Staying Secure on the Internet **(p. 110)**
- Getting Around the Web **(p. 121)**

- Using Subject Directories and Search Engines **(p. 123)**
- Connecting to the Internet **(p. 130)**

It's 10:00 P.M. as Max sits down to begin his online coursework. Although it's been a long day, he likes taking courses over the Internet because they let him finish his degree and still keep his full-time job. While downloading the assignment file from the course Web site, he checks to see if new messages have been added to his wall on Facebook, opens his instant messaging (IM) account to see if any of his friends are online, and starts a playlist in iTunes. Seeing his friend Tom is logged on to IM, he chats with him for awhile. Like many of his friends, Max has become a fan of IM. He uses it more than he does e-mail. It's more like talking.

Before getting down to work, Max visits ESPN.com to check out the score of the Red Sox game. He then goes to his favorite search engine, Google, and starts researching the topic he plans to write about for his class. To make his presentation more interesting, Max uses Google's video search feature to find video clips he can use. Max reflects on how glad he is that he finally ditched his slow dial-up connection for a faster Internet connection. Downloading files and searching the Internet, playing videos, and chatting with his friends is so much quicker with a broadband connection.

Finally, Max checks his e-mail. He finds the usual spam, as well as a message from the student loan office reminding him that his payment is due. Max decides he'd better make this payment before he forgets. He accesses his bank's Web site from his Favorites list. With a few more clicks, he transfers enough money from his savings account to his checking account to cover his payment, which he then makes online.

Does this level of Internet interaction sound at all like yours? Most likely you use the Internet as much as you do your television, maybe even more. But do you really know how to get the most out of your Internet experience and which connection option is best for you?

In this chapter, you'll learn what you should know about the Internet in order to use it to your best advantage. We'll look at why the Internet was created and the activities that you use the Internet for most often, such as communication technologies (e-mail, IM, blogs, podcasts, and the like), multimedia experiences, and doing business over the Web. Next, we'll discuss problems that you may encounter by using the Internet and the Web, and how they might be managed. We'll then discuss how you can navigate and search the Web effectively so that your time spent on the Internet is useful. Finally, we'll discuss how the Internet works, including options you have for connecting to the Internet and how data travels across this big network, as well as the future of the Internet as we know it today.

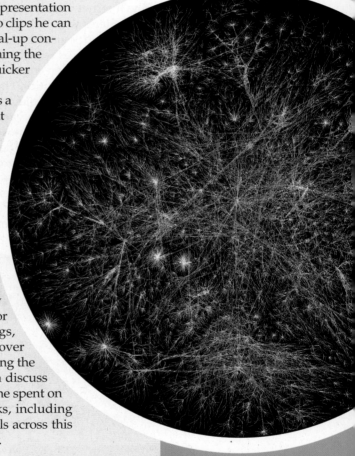

SOUND BYTES

- Blogging **(p. 100)**
- Creating a Web-Based E-mail Account **(p. 104)**
- The Best Utilities for Your Computer **(p. 115)**

- Welcome to the Web **(p. 117)**
- Finding Information on the Web **(p. 123)**
- Connecting to the Internet **(p. 128)**

The Internet

It's hard to imagine life without the Internet. We use it to shop, communicate, research, find places and get directions, and entertain ourselves (see Figure 3.1). It's accessible from our computers, cell phones, and portable music players, and we can get to it while at home, at work, at school—even at Starbucks. But what exactly is the Internet, and how did it begin?

Why was the Internet created? The **Internet**, or "Net" as it is sometimes called, is the largest computer network in the world—actually, a network of networks—that connects billions of computer users. The concept of the Internet was developed while the United States was in the midst of the Cold War with the Soviet Union. At that time, the U.S. armed forces were becoming increasingly dependent on computers to coordinate and plan their activities. They needed a computer system that would operate efficiently, one that was located in various parts of the country so that it could not be disrupted easily in the event of an attack.

At the same time, researchers also hoped the Internet would address the problems involved with getting different computers to communicate with each other. Although computers had been networked since the early 1960s, there was no reliable way to connect computers from different manufacturers because they used different proprietary designs and methods of communication. What was lacking was a common communications method that all computers could use. The Internet was created to respond to these two concerns: to establish a secure form of military communications and to create a means by which all computers could communicate.

Who invented the Internet? The modern Internet evolved from an early U.S. government-funded "internetworking" project called the Advanced Research Projects Agency Network (ARPANET). ARPANET began as a four-node network involving UCLA, Stanford Research Institute, the University of California at Santa Barbara, and the University of Utah in Salt Lake City. The first real communication occurred in late 1969 between the computer at Stanford and the computer at UCLA. Although the system crashed after the third letter was transmitted, it was the beginning of a revolution. Many people participated in the creation of the ARPANET, but two men who worked on the project, Vinton Cerf and Robert Kahn, are generally acknowledged as the "fathers" of the Internet. They earned this honor because they were primarily

FIGURE 3.1

From buying guitars on eBay to getting directions on your cell phone to checking e-mail or the latest snow stats, the Internet makes it all possible.

responsible for developing the communications protocols (or standards) in the 1970s that are still in use on the Internet today.

So are the Web and the Internet the same thing? Because the **World Wide Web** (**WWW** or the **Web**) is what we use the most, we sometimes think of the "Net" and the "Web" as being interchangeable. However, the Web is the means we use to access information over the Internet. What distinguishes the Web from the rest of the Internet is its use of

- common communication protocols that enable different computers to talk to each other and display information in compatible formats, and
- special links (called *hyperlinks*) that enable users to jump from one place to another on the Web.

Did the same people who invented the Internet invent the Web? The Web was invented many years after the original Internet. In 1989, Tim Berners-Lee, a physicist at the European Organization for Nuclear Research (CERN), wanted a method for linking his research documents so that other researchers could access them. In conjunction with Robert Cailliau, Berners-Lee developed the basic architecture of the Web and created the first Web browser, a software application that enables a user to display and interact with text and other media on the Web. The original browser could handle only text and was usable only on computers running the NeXT operating system (a commercially unsuccessful operating system, or OS), which limited its usage. So Berners-Lee put out a call to the Internet community to assist with development of browsers for other platforms.

In 1993, the National Center for Supercomputing Applications released its Mosaic browser for use on the Macintosh and Windows operating systems. Mosaic could display graphics as well as text. The once popular Netscape Navigator browser evolved from Mosaic and heralded the beginning of the Web's monumental growth.

How much has the Internet grown? There was explosive growth of the Internet in the early to mid-1990s. By 1997, nearly the entire world had access to an Internet connection.

Because of such global Internet availability and access, as well as the increasing capabilities of hardware and software, the number of Web sites (locations on the Internet) grew exponentially as shown in Figure 3.2. In December 1990, the first Web site was hosted on the Web. Four years later, approximately 10,000 sites were online; by June 1996, a whopping 252,000 Web sites were hosted.

The Web experienced the greatest amount of growth in the year 2000—more than 160 percent in a single year. The growth of the Web has since begun to slow down, but the growth is by no means complete. In December 2007, more than 150 million Web sites were online, representing an increase of 48 percent from the previous year. The Web's growth is expected to continue, reaching more than 200 million Web sites by 2010.

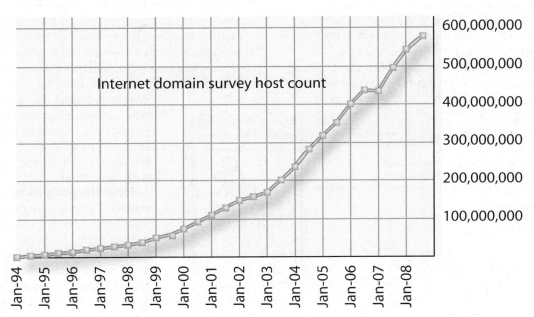

Internet domain survey host count

FIGURE 3.2

The growth of the number of Web sites on the Internet has been explosive since the first Web site was hosted in 1990. More than 150 million Web sites are hosted on the Web today.

Source: **http://www. carolina-advertising. com/free-advertising/ internet-growth.gif**

Why do people use the Internet?

Communication is the primary reason people use the Internet, but when Internet users are not communicating, they also spend the majority of their online time shopping, searching for information, and just browsing the Internet for fun. In the next section, we will explore these uses in more detail.

Communicating Through the Internet: E-Mail and Other Technologies

E-mail is fast becoming the main form of communication in the 21st century, and it is the primary use of the Web. However, e-mail is not the only type of Internet-based communication. You use instant messaging, blogs, podcasts, chat rooms, newsgroups, and more for communicating via the Internet. You can even talk over the phone through the Internet. Like any other means of communication, you need to know how to use these tools efficiently to get the most out of them.

INSTANT MESSAGING

How does instant messaging work?
Instant messaging (IM) services are programs that enable you to communicate in real time with others who are online (see Figure 3.3). Although IM is most often used for casual conversations between friends, many businesses use IM as a means of quick and instant communication between co-workers. AOL's AIM is one of the most popular instant messaging services. ICQ, Yahoo!, Google, and Windows Live Messenger also host popular instant messaging services. Even though these services are proprietary—meaning you can only chat with those who share the same IM service—ZangoMessenger and Messenger City are other IM services that allow users of all the popular IMs to talk to each other regardless of the service they are using.

How do I keep track of my IM contacts?
When you use IM, you set up a list of contacts, often called a **buddy list**. To communicate with someone from your buddy list, that person must be online at the same time as you are. When someone is trying to communicate with you when you're online, you are notified and can then accept or reject the communication. Some programs such as Yahoo! and AOL's AIM offer stealth settings so that you can appear offline to certain buddies.

If you want to chat (or communicate) with more than one person, you can hold simultaneous individual conversations, or if you all want to talk together, you can create custom IM chat rooms. Many IM services such as AOL AIM and Windows Live Messenger offer chat services so you can talk to your buddies if you have a microphone and speakers. A video camera will allow you to see them as you chat.

PODCASTS AND WEBCASTS

What is a podcast?
A **podcast** is a clip of audio or video content that is broadcast over the Internet using compressed files—MP3s, for example. This content might include radio shows, audio books, magazines, and even educational programs (see Figure 3.4). Typically, you must subscribe to be able to access the most current version of the online content, which is delivered to your computer automatically so that you can listen to the content when you want. You can use a media player such as iTunes, RealPlayer, or Windows Media Player on your computer, or you can transfer the content from your computer to a portable media device such as an iPod.

How do podcasts work?
Podcasts are possible because of **RSS technology**. RSS 2.0 (Really Simple Syndication) is an XML-based format that allows frequent updates of content on the World Wide

FIGURE 3.3

Instant messaging services such as AOL Instant Messenger enable you to have real-time online conversations with friends and family.

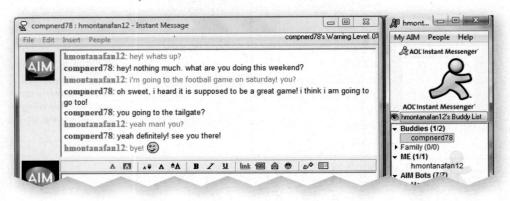

Web. Web content can be formatted in such a way that **aggregators** (programs that search for new Web content) can find them and download only the new content to your computer. Some aggregators work with Atom, another specification, to distribute new Web content.

Where can I find podcasts? Podcasts can be found all over the Web. Most newspapers, TV news organizations, and radio sites offer podcasts of their programs. But the content doesn't have to be news-related. The television network ABC, for example, offers podcasts of some of its most popular TV shows such as *Grey's Anatomy* and *Lost*. Many schools are beginning to recognize this format as a means to supply students with course content updates, and instructors are creating podcasts of their lectures.

Sites such as iTunes (**www.itunes.com**), Podcast Alley (**www.podcastalley.com**), and Podcast.net (**www.podcast.net**) are great directories of podcasts, organized by genre, to help you easily locate podcasts of most interest to you. If there is a particular topic for which you'd like to hear a podcast, Podscope (**www.podscope.com**) and Podzinger (**www.podzinger.com**) are podcast-specific search engines that search podcasts for specific words or phrases and then display the results with audio clips. YouTube (**www.youtube.com**) is also becoming a popular source of RSS feeds.

Do I need anything special to get and listen to podcasts? In addition to a computer and an Internet connection, you need to install an aggregator and have a media player. As noted earlier, aggregators are software programs that go out and grab the latest update of Web material according to your specifications. They are available for all major operating systems and some mobile devices such as PDA/smartphones. Podcast directories, such as iTunes and Podcast Alley, are also aggregators that work with both Windows and Macintosh platforms. To listen to a podcast on your computer, you'll need a media player such as iTunes, RealPlayer, or Windows Media Player. To listen to your podcasts while on the go, you'll need a mobile device such as an MP3 player, portable media player (PMP), or PDA/smartphone that plays MP3 files. If you want to enjoy a video podcast, you will need to make sure your mobile device can play video files as well.

FIGURE 3.4

Podcasts are available in a wide variety of topics and content. Web sites such as **www.podcast.net** allow you to add your own podcast to their directories.

Can I create my own podcast? The ability to create audio content that can be delivered to the Web and then listened to by people all over the world is simple, turning the average person into a radio broadcaster overnight. Although high-end equipment always will produce more sophisticated output, you really need only the most basic equipment to make your own podcast.

To record the content, at the minimum you need a computer with a microphone. If you want to make a video podcast, you also need a Web camera (webcam) or video camera. Additional software may be needed to edit the digital audio and video content. After the podcast content has been recorded and edited, it needs to be exported to MP3 format. Sound editing software, such as the freeware program Audacity, can be used to record and edit audio files and then export to MP3 format. The last step involves creating an RSS feed and then uploading the content to the Web.

What's a webcast? A webcast is the broadcast of audio or video content over the Internet. Most webcasts are not updated automatically, but some such as Microsoft's On-Demand Webcasts are RSS feeds. Webcasts use a special kind of media technology that continuously feeds the multimedia content to facilitate the viewing and downloading process of large audio and video files. Webcasts can include such non-interactive content as simulcasts of radio or TV broadcasts, but webcasts have more recently initiated interactive responses from

FIGURE 3.5

Blogs like the one shown here from **www.gizmodo.com** can be set up as online reviews organized by category or as personal journals that contain a record of the blogger's thoughts, viewpoints, and feelings.

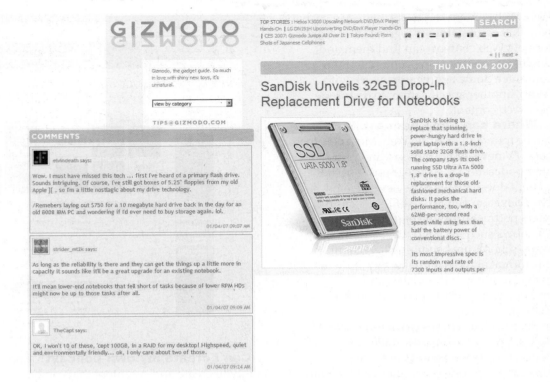

SOUND BYTE

Blogging

In this Sound Byte, you'll see why blogs are one of today's most popular publishing mediums. You'll also learn how to create and publish your own blog.

the viewing or listening audience. For example, ABC News held webcasts of many of the 2008 Democratic party debates between presidential candidates Barack Obama and Hillary Clinton. These webcasts gave potential voters the ability to ask questions as the debates happened. Webcasts also are used in the corporate world to broadcast annual meetings and in the educational arena to transmit seminars.

BLOGS (WEBLOGS) AND VIDEO LOGS (VLOGS)

What is a blog? Weblogs (or **blogs**) are personal logs, or journal entries, that are posted on the Web. The beauty of blogs is that they are simple to create, manage, and read; because of this, nearly 120,000 new blogs are created every day (translating to 1.4 blogs being created every second of every day). Although different types of blogs exist, there are some basic similarities. First, blogs are arranged as a listing of entries on a single page, with the most recent blog (entry) appearing on the top of the list. Second, blogs are searchable, making them user-friendly.

What do people write in blogs? Many people use blogs as a sort of personal scrapbook. Whenever the urge strikes, they just write a stream-of-consciousness flow of thoughts or a report of their daily activities. Many blogs, however, focus on a particular topic. For example, **www.rottentomatoes.com** is a blog site that contains reviews and opinions about movies, and **www.gizmodo.com** is a blog site that devotes itself to discussing techno-gadgets (see Figure 3.5). Blogcatalog (**www.blogcatalog.com**) and Bloghub (**www. bloghub.com**) are two of many blog directories to help you find blogs that best fit your interests.

How do I create a blog? It is easy to write and maintain a blog, and you'll find many Web sites that provide the necessary tools for you to create your own. Two sites that offer free blog hosting are **www.blogger .com** and **www.livejournal.com**. You can add other features to your blog such as pictures or subpages. Another alternative is to host your blog yourself. Hosting your own blog requires that you have your own Web site and a URL such as **www.pandoblog.com** so that people can access it.

Are there problems with blogs? The popularity of blogs has brought about a consequential problem—spam blogs (or splogs), which are artificially created blog sites filled with fake articles or stolen text (known as *blog scraping*). Spam blogs contain links to other sites associated with the splog's creator, with the intention of either increasing traffic to or increasing search engine rankings for their usually disreputable or useless Web sites. Although not terribly bad, splogs are another unwanted form of content that continues to grow like weeds on the Web.

What is a video blog? The traditional form of blogs are primarily text-based but may also include images and audio. **Video logs** (**vlogs** or **video blogs**) are personal journals that use video as the primary content in addition to text, images, and audio. Vlogs quickly are becoming a highly popular means of personal expression. Software such as Vlog It! (**www.adobe.com/motion**) makes adding video content to your blog easy. Video logs have become so popular that Google has added a video search engine to its list of features (see Figure 3.6).

WIKIS

What are wikis? Unlike traditional Web content, which the viewer of the site cannot change, a **wiki** is a type of Web site that allows users to change its content by adding, removing, or editing the content (see Figure 3.7). Although there are some Web-based document products such as Google Docs (**http://docs.google.com**) that allow for online collaboration, wikis add the extra benefit of tracking revisions so that past versions can be easily accessed at any time by any reader. The popular collaborative online encyclopedia Wikipedia (**www.wikipedia.org**) uses wiki technology so that the content can be updated continually and

kept accurate by the many expert eyes that view the content.

How accurate is Web content that anyone can change? In late 2005, Wikipedia content was measured for accuracy in its scientific content and was found to be as accurate as the *Encyclopedia Britannica*. Nonetheless, free and easy access to edit pages also can lead to improper manipulation, which results in tighter access controls. To thwart malicious editing of the wiki content, for example, users who want editing privileges are required to register. Citizendium (**www.citizendium.org**), another

BITS AND BYTES

Can Blogging Get You in Trouble?

The news is full of stories about bloggers getting fired from their jobs and, in some instances, even imprisoned because of the content of their blogs. Generally, the content may include negative discussion about the blogger's job, employer, or colleagues, or perhaps inappropriate content about the blogger. Because they are on the Internet, blogs can be found and read by anyone, including bosses, college administrators, potential employers, friends, relatives, neighbors, and colleagues. Therefore, illegal and socially unacceptable content should not be included in blogs. Bloggers who post negative or inappropriate content should be prepared for potential consequences.

FIGURE 3.6

Video logs use video in addition to text, images, and audio. Google has added a video search engine to its list of features to help you sift through the increasing number of vlogs.

FIGURE 3.7

Rather than collaborating by exchanging e-mails and attachments—and potentially losing track of the most recent version of a document—different users can collaborate on a wiki page. Wikis allow multiple collaborators to read and modify a single document.

Elijah provides initial text
(in black)

Stephanie inserts extra detail
(in blue)

Jordan includes
additional text
(in green)

Mackenzie-Jordan Law Associates has a significant number of celebrity clients. One of the most important aspects of our legal counsel to these individuals is to help protect the use of their images and likenesses.
Sometimes this is referred to as the right of publicity. This right is a valuable asset because there are endless licensing opportunities that can be quite lucrative. Some states have a publicity law that protects a celebrity's image and likeness for 100 years, but as yet that law has not been enacted in the state of Texas.
The merchandising of celebrity images has become a huge source of income for many celebrities as well as others.
In recent years, legal disputes have resulted from artists and illustrators manipulating celebrity images.
In the past, courts have typically protected the First Amendment rights of artists in these cases. But recently there have been a few cases where celebrities have been allowed to sue creators of fictional works for the violation of the right of publicity.
The right of publicity is intended to prevent others from capitalizing on a celebrity's fame. Many people in the entertainment industry are fearful that unauthorized biographies, docudramas, and celebrity spoofs and satires will no longer be protected. Many entertainment lawyers say a celebrity's right to publicity is intended solely for ads and merchandise, not for literary works.

open wiki encyclopedia, requires contributors to provide real names and sign an ethics pledge, and all postings are monitored.

These same collaborative efforts also extend to user manuals. wikiHow (**www.wikihow.org**) is an online project that is using both wikis and the collaborative process to build a large, online how-to manual. Blender (**www.blender.org**), an open source software application for 3D modeling, uses mediawiki, a more feature-rich wiki implementation product, to provide users with documentation, help with game development and 3D modeling, and tutorials for Blender software.

Are wikis used for anything other than encyclopedias and manuals? Wikis provide an excellent source for collaborative writing, both in and out of the classroom. Wiki technology is currently incorporated in Blackboard, a popular online course management software application, to encourage collaborative learning in online courses. Wikis are also becoming popular tools for business collaboration. Rather than passing documents back and forth via e-mail and losing track of the most updated version, wikis allow all who have access to the page to post their ideas and modify content already posted. A history of all changes is kept, so users can revert to earlier versions if desired.

Like blogs, wikis also can be used to express thoughts and opinions about certain topics. Unlike blogs, however, wikis can be edited and therefore maintain a more "common" opinion rather than the direct expressed opinion of the initial individual writer.

VOICE OVER INTERNET PROTOCOL (VoIP)

How is VoIP different from regular telephone service? Voice over Internet Protocol (VoIP) is a form of voice-based Internet communication that turns a standard Internet connection into a means to place phone calls, including long-distance calls. Traditional telephone communications use analog voice data and telephone connections. In contrast, VoIP uses technology similar to that used in e-mail to send your voice data digitally over the Internet.

What do I need to use VoIP? For the simplest and least costly VoIP service, you need speakers, a microphone, an Internet connection, and a VoIP provider (see Figure 3.8). Depending on the provider you choose, you also may need to install software or a special adapter. For example, Skype (**www.skype.com**) requires that both callers and receivers have the company's free software installed on their computers. An alternative VoIP service such as Vonage (**www.vonage.com**) lets you use your own telephone by connecting your phone to a special adapter that the company provides. A third alternative is to buy a special IP phone that connects to your broadband Internet connection (cable or DSL) or a USB port on your computer. New to join the market are WiFi (wireless Internet) IP phones, which will allow you to place calls from any WiFi hot spot location.

What are the advantages and disadvantages of VoIP? For people who make many long-distance phone calls, the advantage of VoIP is its free or low cost. Portability is another advantage because all you need is an Internet connection. With Internet accessibility so abundant, you can keep in touch with friends and family no matter where you are. Just plug in your headset or IP phone, sign onto your VoIP service, and make your call.

Although VoIP is affordable and convenient, it does have drawbacks. Some people regard sound quality and reliability issues as VoIP's primary disadvantages. Another drawback is the loss of service if power is interrupted. Although traditional phone service does not depend on electricity, your Internet connection and IP phone do. One serious drawback when VoIP service was first offered to the public was the inability for 911 calls to be traced back to the caller, unlike with a traditional phone. However, the FCC now requires all VoIP providers to automatically provide 911 service.

Another issue with VoIP is security. Security risks include those similar to those for e-mail (such as spam) and fraud (where a hacker breaks into a VoIP system to make unauthorized calls); these are real risks but avoidable with proper precautions. In addition, encryption services that convert data into a form that is not easily understood by unauthorized people (similar to those used with e-mail) are being deployed to help protect the very nature of calls made over the Internet. Despite these concerns, VoIP continues to enjoy explosive growth, and undoubtedly the technology will continue to improve.

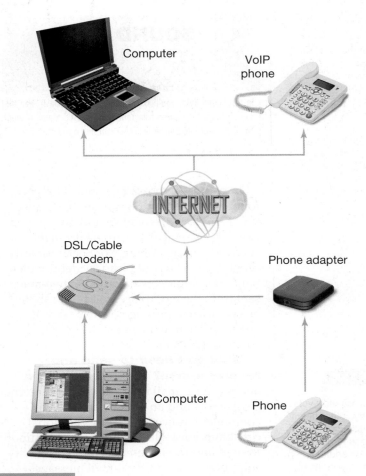

FIGURE 3.8

This is one way VoIP works. Depending on your VoIP service, you can hold conversations through a computer, a special VoIP telephone, or a regular telephone with an adapter. Those who receive your call do not need any special equipment or service.

E-MAIL

Why did e-mail catch on so quickly?

E-mail (short for **electronic mail**) is a written message that is sent and received over electronic communication systems. The messages can be formatted and enhanced with graphics as well as include other files as attachments. E-mail has quickly caught on as the primary method of electronic communication because it's fast and convenient and reduces the costs of postage and long-distance phone calls. In addition, with e-mail, the sender and receiver don't have to be available at the same time in order to communicate. Because of these and other reasons, approximately 80 percent of Americans who access the Internet claim that their main online activity is sending and receiving e-mail.

SOUND BYTE

Creating a Web-Based E-mail Account

In this Sound Byte, you'll see a step-by-step demonstration that explains how to create a free Yahoo! Web-based e-mail account. You'll also learn the options available with such accounts.

Is e-mail private? E-mail is not meant for every type of communication. Because it is not encrypted, e-mail should not be used to send personal or sensitive information such as banking numbers or Social Security numbers, which could lead to identity theft. Similarly, employers have access to e-mail sent from the workplace, so caution should be taken when putting negative or controversial content in an e-mail. It could just come back to haunt you.

What do I need to send and receive e-mail? All you need to send and receive e-mail is a computer, an Internet connection, and an e-mail account. Each component, however, entails additional considerations. Although it's most common to send and receive e-mail from your computer, today many e-mail messages are exchanged between cell phones, PDAs, and wireless notebooks. An Internet connection can be wired or wireless, and

an e-mail account may or may not be Web-based.

What is the difference between e-mail accounts? To read, send, and organize your e-mail, you use an e-mail client. **E-mail clients** such as Microsoft Outlook are software programs running on your computer that access your Internet service provider's (ISP's) server. However, with these e-mail clients, you are able to view your e-mail only from the computer on which the client program is installed, which can be less than convenient if you travel or want to view your e-mail when you're away from that computer.

Today, many ISPs offer the services of a Web-based e-mail client so that users can look at their e-mail directly from the Web. Web-based e-mail uses the Internet as the client; therefore, you can access a Web-based e-mail account from any computer that has access to the Web—no special client software is needed. Free e-mail accounts such as Yahoo!, Hotmail, or Gmail use Web-based e-mail clients. If you use a broadband connection such as cable or DSL, then your broadband provider will provide you with a Web-based e-mail account. Some e-mail clients—AOL, for example—offer both client and Web access to e-mail.

What are the advantages of a Web-based e-mail account? Unlike client-based e-mail, which is accessible only from

FIGURE 3.9

You can organize your e-mail by color coding it and assigning messages to specific folders. In addition, you can automatically filter out unwanted e-mail and sort the remaining e-mail into topic-specific folders.

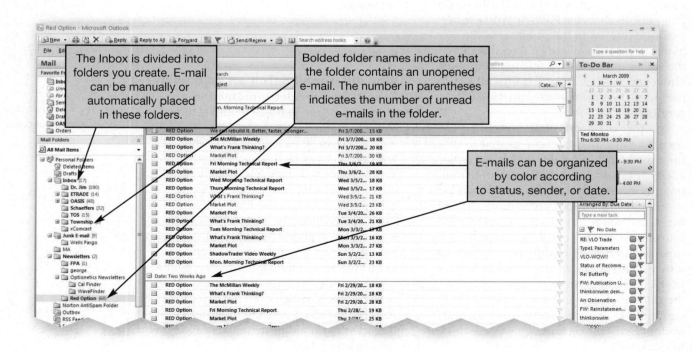

The Inbox is divided into folders you create. E-mail can be manually or automatically placed in these folders.

Bolded folder names indicate that the folder contains an unopened e-mail. The number in parentheses indicates the number of unread e-mails in the folder.

E-mails can be organized by color according to status, sender, or date.

the computer on which it is installed, if you have a Web-based e-mail account, then your e-mail is accessible from any computer as long as you have access to the Internet. A secondary Web-based e-mail account also provides you with a more permanent e-mail address. Your other e-mail accounts and addresses may change when you switch ISPs or change employers, so having a permanent e-mail address is important.

Why would I need a client-based e-mail program? Many people have more than one e-mail account. You may have a personal account, a work account, and an account you use when filling out forms on the Internet. One of the benefits of using a client-based e-mail program such as Microsoft Outlook is that you can download your e-mail from many different e-mail accounts so that it all can be accessed in one location. In addition, client e-mail programs offer several features to help you manage and organize your e-mail and coordinate e-mail with your calendar, tasks, and contact lists. As you can see in Figure 3.9, you can organize your e-mail by task, sender, or priority by using color codes, or you can distribute your messages to designated folders within your inbox.

GROUP COMMUNICATION

What kinds of online group communication exist? You can interact with a wide variety of people online in many ways. Some forms are in real time, or synchronous; others are asynchronous. Figure 3.10 describes the various ways in which you can communicate and interact with a group of people online.

Do dangers exist in group communications? When you use group communications, you generally need to register and sign in with a username and password. It's best not to disclose your identity but rather to "hide" behind a username, thus protecting your privacy. On the other hand, the people you are chatting with are also hiding their identities. Some chatters use this veil of privacy to cover dishonest intentions. Undoubtedly, you have heard stories of individuals, especially young teenagers, being deceived (and sometimes harmed) by someone they've met in a chat room. Several Web sites such as **www.chatdanger.com** try to protect vulnerable people, especially children, from malicious online users (see Figure 3.11).

Are there special ways to behave with group communication? General rules of etiquette (often referred to as

FIGURE 3.10 Ways to Communicate Online with Groups	
Internet Social Networking Sites **www.myspace.com** **www.facebook.com** **www.linkedin.com**	**Social networking sites** are online personal networks where individuals are invited or allowed to join. Social networks allow a group of individuals to create personal profiles, exchange information, and find others with similar interests. Some social networking sites such as LinkedIn are aimed at the business and professional community.
Multiplayer Online Game Services **www.xbox.com/live** **www.worldofwarcraft.com** **www.guildwars.com**	There are many **multiplayer online games** in which play occurs among hundreds or thousands of other players over the Internet in a persistent or always-on game environment. In some games, you can interact with other players around the world in a meaningful context by trading, chatting, or playing cooperative or combative minigames.
Chat Rooms **www.icq.com/icqchat**	**Chat rooms** are a form of synchronous communication in which online conversations occur in real time and are visible to everyone in the chat room. Usually, chat rooms are organized around a specific theme or topic.
Newsgroups **www.groups.google.com** **www.tile.net/news**	A **newsgroup** is similar to a discussion group or forum in which people create *threads*, or conversations. In a thread, a newsgroup member will post messages and read and reply to messages from other members of the newsgroup.
Listserv **www.tile.net/lists**	**Listservs** are electronic mailing lists of e-mail addresses of people who are interested in a certain topic or an area of interest. Information and updates on shared topics of interest are exchanged between members through e-mail.

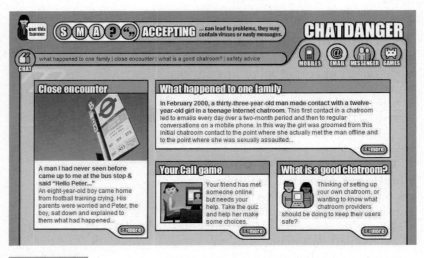

FIGURE 3.11

The site **www.chatdanger.com** is produced by Childnet International, a nonprofit organization working to help make the Internet safe for children. It provides a lot of good safety advice for using chat rooms, mobile phones, e-mail, instant messaging programs, and games.

netiquette) exist across chat rooms and other online forums, including obvious standards of behavior such as introducing yourself when you enter the room and specifically addressing the person to whom you are talking. Chat room users also are expected to refrain from swearing, name-calling, and using explicit or prejudiced language, and they are not allowed to harass other participants. In addition, chat room users cannot post the same text repeatedly with the intent to disrupt the chat, a behavior called *flooding*. Similarly, as in e-mail, users shouldn't type in all capital letters, because this is interpreted as shouting.

Web Entertainment: Multimedia and Beyond

Internet radio, MP3 music files, streaming video, and interactive gaming are all part of a growing entertainment world available over the Internet. What makes the Web appealing to many people is its enriched multimedia content. **Multimedia** is anything that involves one or more forms of media in addition to text.

Many types of multimedia are used on the Web. Graphics (drawings, charts, and photos) are the most basic form of multimedia on the Web. Audio files are what give sound to the Web—the clips of music you hear when you visit certain Web sites, MP3 files that you download, or live broadcasts you can listen to through Internet radio. Video files on the Web range from the simple (such as short video clips) to the complex (such as hour-long live concerts). In addition to movies, you can watch live or prerecorded television broadcasts, movie trailers, and sporting events. In early 2006, the Walt Disney Company, owner of the American Broadcasting Company (ABC), began putting prime-time television shows on the Internet to be viewed for free.

What is streaming audio and video? Because of the large file sizes of media content, watching video files such as movies or TV shows or listening to live audio broadcasting is possible because of streaming media. **Streaming audio** continuously feeds an audio file to your browser so you avoid having to wait for the entire file to download completely before listening to it. Likewise, **streaming video** continuously feeds a video file to your browser so that you can watch large files as they download instead of first having to download the files completely.

Do I need anything besides a browser to view or hear multimedia on the Web? Without any additional software, most graphics on the Web will appear in your browser when you visit a site. However, to view and hear some multimedia files—for example, podcasts, videos on YouTube, and MP3 files—you might need a special software program called a **plug-in** (or **player**). Figure 3.12 lists the most popular plug-ins.

If you've purchased your computer within the past several years, you'll find plug-ins already installed with your browser. For those plug-ins you don't have, the Web site requiring the plug-in usually displays a message on the screen that includes links to a site where you can download the plug-in free of charge. For example, to use streaming audio on a Web site, your browser might send you to **www. adobe.com**, where you can download Shockwave Player.

FIGURE 3.12 Popular Plug-Ins and Players and Their Uses

	Plug-In or Player Name	Where You Can Get the Plug-In or Player	What the Plug-In or Player Does
	Adobe Reader	www.adobe.com	Views and prints portable document format (PDF) files
	Authorware Player	www.adobe.com	Helps view animations
	Flash Player	www.adobe.com	Plays animation and other graphics files
	QuickTime Player	www.apple.com	Plays MP3 animation, music, musical instrument digital interface (MIDI), audio, and video files
	RealPlayer	www.real.com	Plays streaming audio, video, animations, and multimedia presentations
	Shockwave Player	www.adobe.com	Plays interactive games, multimedia, graphics, and streaming audio and video on the Web
	Windows Media Player	www.microsoft.com	Plays MP3 and WAV files, music files and live audio, and views movies and live video broadcasts on the Web

Do I need to update players and plug-ins? Like most technological resources, improvements and upgrades are available for players and plug-ins, and most will alert you to check for and download upgrades when they are available. It is best to keep the players and plug-ins as current as possible so that you get the full effects of the multimedia running with these players.

Are there any risks with using plug-ins? When a browser requires a plug-in to display particular Web content, it usually automatically accesses the plug-in, generally without asking you for consent to start the plug-in. This automatic access can present security risks. To minimize such risks, update your plug-ins and browser software frequently so that you will have the most up-to-date remedies against identified security flaws.

Is there any way to get multimedia Web content to load faster? When you're on the Internet, your browser keeps track of the Web sites you've visited so that it can load them faster the next time you visit them. This cache (or temporary storage

BITS AND BYTES

Travel Without the Cost

If you can't afford the time or money to get to visit places like the Colosseum in Rome or the Louvre in Paris, check out **www.fullscreenqtvr.com**. Full-screen QTVR is a collaborative effort that uses the QuickTime plug-in, panoramic photography, and virtual reality technology to display high-quality, full-screen photographic virtual reality exploration on the Internet.

place) of the HTML text pages, images, and video files from recently visited Web sites can make your Internet surfing more efficient, but it also can congest your hard drive. To keep your system running efficiently, delete your temporary Internet cache periodically. All popular Web browsers have an option to clear the Internet cache manually, and most have a setting to allow you to automatically clear the cache every time you exit the browser.

Social Networking

Networking has long been a means of creating links between you and your friends—and their friends and acquaintances. Traditionally, networking has been helpful in the business community for the purposes of finding and filling open job positions. The Internet, with its speedy connections and instantaneous means of communications, is facilitating such networking. For example, the site LinkedIn (**www.linkedin.com**) is a professional online network through which members can find potential clients, business opportunities, jobs, or job candidates. Like a true business network, LinkedIn helps you meet other professionals through the people you know.

The Internet also is promoting a different kind of networking among the younger, nonprofessional population. Social networking Web sites such as Facebook, MySpace, and Friendster (see Figure 3.13) have gained in popularity among high school and college students. They are becoming increasingly popular among

preteens as well. The growth has been explosive. MySpace membership, for example, has topped 200 million members. Facebook is quickly gaining popularity, with more than 60 million members and an average of 250,000 new members joining daily.

What's the attraction? Social networking sites such as MySpace and Facebook are easy places for members to hang out, meet new people, and share common interests. They also provide ways for members to communicate with their friends by voice, chat, instant message, videoconference, and blogs so that members don't need separate communication accounts.

Facebook, for example, is simple to set up and free of charge. Members quickly can create personalized profiles in which they include their own photographs and personal information and create a circle of friends by linking to friends' profiles or by inviting others to join their network.

FIGURE 3.13

Social networking sites are popular places for people to keep up with friends and learn more about the people they meet.

Conducting Business over the Internet: E-Commerce

E-commerce, or **electronic commerce**, is the process of conducting business online such as through advertising and selling products. A good example of an e-commerce business (or e-business) is **www.dell.com**. The company's online presence offers customers a convenient way to shop for computer systems. Its success is the result of creative marketing, an expanding product line, and reliable customer service and product

delivery—all hallmarks of traditional businesses as well.

Traditional stores that have an online presence are referred to as *click-and-brick* businesses. These stores, such as Best Buy (**www.bestbuy.com**) and Target (**www.target. com**), are able to provide a variety of services on Web sites. Customers can visit their sites to check the availability of items or to get store locations and directions. Some click and bricks allow online purchases and in-store pickup and returns.

A significant portion of e-commerce consists of **business-to-consumer (B2C)** transactions—exchanges that take place

Although most members congregate on these sites without a problem, the sites are susceptible to attacks by nefarious individuals, so users should take precautions to avoid interactions with cyberbullies, con artists, and other predators. Cyberbullies are just like real-life bullies. They pick on the weak or vulnerable just as in real life, only they use the Internet to do it. This type of behavior tends to occur more frequently among children or young adults.

Another risk associated with social networking sites occurs when users reveal too much personal information. In an effort to find other members with similar interests, members of social networking sites often include information such as age, school, and club affiliations (and sometimes home addresses, banking information, or even Social Security numbers) that make it easy to steal a person's identity or track down someone in an "offline" environment. Identity thieves constantly are searching social networking sites for new victims. Or, under the guise of a member with similar interests, con artists may ply people with phishing, e-mail messages, or bogus product offers in an attempt to defraud them.

Sexual predators who also operate online are a problem, especially if users of social networking sites reveal information that can help pinpoint their location in the "real world." Accounts of predators targeting minors through these sites create concern among parents, educators, and public officials. In response, some of the more popular social networking sites have instituted tighter security measures to protect their members from strangers. MySpace, for example, has hired a former federal prosecutor as its first chief security officer. His security initiatives include efforts to have MySpace staff members view all photos uploaded to the site to catch any occurrences of pornography and the introduction of technology security measures that allow children 14 to 16 years of age to shield their information from strangers. In early 2008, MySpace pledged to work with state attorneys general on a set of principles to combat harmful material on its site.

Although these initiatives are a good step, the question is whether these are enough to protect today's youth from the unfortunate perils of online communication. Ultimately, parents are the first line of defense in the battle of Internet safety. Most experts agree that parents must get involved in their children's online activities. This might be easier said than done, however, because many students have access to computers outside the home; despite the best efforts of any parent, a child might do something he or she knows is not right simply out of curiosity or peer pressure. The other defense is to make the security measures strong enough to keep predators away, but not so restrictive as to drive away the users to a less restrictive Web site where the predators will follow. Therefore, all the major players (Web site administrators, school officials, and parents) must actively participate in promoting and employing Internet safety measures. Web sites such as WiredSafety (**www.wiredsafety.org**) provide help and education to Internet and mobile device users of all ages. These sites are a good place to start for more information on protecting children and adults in online activities.

between businesses and consumers—such as the purchases that consumers make at online stores. There is also a **business-to-business (B2B)** portion of e-commerce; this consists of businesses buying and selling goods and services to other businesses such as Omaha Paper Company (**www.omahapaper.com**), which distributes paper products to other companies. Finally, the **consumer-to-consumer (C2C)** portion of e-commerce consists of consumers selling to each other through online auction sites such as eBay.

What are the most popular e-commerce activities? Approximately $100 billion each year is spent on goods purchased over the Internet. At a growth rate of 25 percent a year, some experts predict that Internet sales will make up 25 percent to 30 percent of all retail sales by 2012. So what is everyone buying online? Consumers buy books, music and videos, movie and event tickets, and toys and games more often online than in retail stores. Travel items such as plane tickets, hotel reservations, and rental car reservations are also frequently made online. With more lenient return policies, online retail sales of clothing and shoes also have increased. Auction sites such as eBay, together with payment exchange services such as PayPal, are

ACTIVE HELPDESK

Staying Secure on the Internet

In this Active Helpdesk call, you'll learn about e-commerce and what e-commerce safeguards protect you when you're online as well as what cookies are and what risks they pose.

becoming the online equivalent to the weekend yard sale and have dramatically increased in popularity.

But e-commerce encompasses more than just shopping opportunities. Today, anything you can do inside your bank you can do online, and more than 25 percent of U.S. households do some form of online banking. Many people use online services to check their account balances, and checking stock and mutual fund performances is also popular. Credit card companies allow you to view, schedule, and pay your credit card bill; brokerage houses allow you to conduct investment activities online; and banks allow you to pay your bills online.

E-COMMERCE SAFEGUARDS

Just how safe are online transactions? When you buy something over the Web, you most likely use a credit card; therefore, the exchange of money is done directly between you and a bank. Because online shopping eliminates a salesclerk or other human intermediary from the transaction, it can actually be safer than traditional retail shopping. Still, because users are told to be wary of online transactions and because the integrity of online transactions is the backbone of e-commerce,

businesses must have some form of security certification to give their customers a level of comfort. Businesses hire security companies such as VeriSign to certify that their online transactions are secure. Thus, if the Web site displays the VeriSign seal, you can usually trust that the information you submit to the site is protected.

Another indication that a Web site is secure is the appearance of a small icon of a closed padlock (in both Microsoft's Internet Explorer and Mozilla's Firefox) or the VeriSign seal on the status bar at the bottom of the browser screen as shown in Figure 3.14. In addition, the beginning of the URL of the site will change from "http://" to "https://," with the "s" standing for *secure*.

How else can I shop safely online? To ensure that your online shopping experience is a safe one, follow these guidelines:

- **Shop at well-known, reputable sites.** If you aren't familiar with a site, then investigate it with the Better Business Bureau (**www.bbb.org**) or at **www.bizrate.com** or **www.webassured.com**. When you place an order, print a copy of the order and make sure you receive a confirmation number. Make sure the company has a phone number and street address in addition to a Web site.

FIGURE 3.14

The VeriSign seal, a closed padlock icon in the browser status bar, and "https" in the URL are indications that the site is secure.

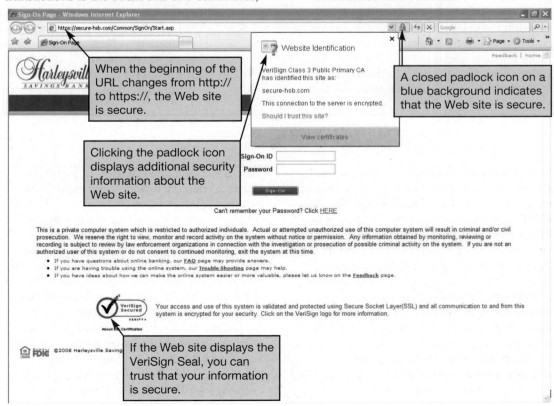

When the beginning of the URL changes from http:// to https://, the Web site is secure.

A closed padlock icon on a blue background indicates that the Web site is secure.

Clicking the padlock icon displays additional security information about the Web site.

If the Web site displays the VeriSign Seal, you can trust that your information is secure.

- **Pay by credit card, not debit card.** The U.S. federal consumer credit card protection laws protect credit card purchases, but debit cards do not have the same level of protection. If possible, reserve one credit card for Internet purchases only or, even better, use a prepaid credit card that has a small credit limit.
- **Check the return policy.** Print a copy and save it. If the site disappears overnight, this information may help you in filing a dispute or reporting a problem to a site such as the Better Business Bureau.

Managing Online Annoyances

Surfing the Web, sending and receiving e-mail, and chatting online have become a common part of most of our lives. Unfortunately, the Web has become fertile ground for people who want to advertise their products, track our Web browsing behaviors, or even con people to reveal personal information. In this section, we'll look at ways in which you can manage, if not avoid, these and other online headaches.

SPAM

How can I best avoid spam?
Companies that send out **spam**—unwanted or junk e-mail—find your e-mail address either from a list they purchase or with software that looks for e-mail addresses on the Internet. (Unsolicited instant messages are also known as spam.) If you've used your e-mail address to purchase anything online, open an online account, or participate in a newsgroup or a chat room, then your e-mail address eventually will appear on one of the lists that spammers get.

One way to avoid spam in your primary account is to create a free Web-based e-mail address that you use only when you fill out forms or purchase items on the Web. For example, both Hotmail and Yahoo! allow you to set up free e-mail accounts. If your free Web-based e-mail account is saturated with spam, then you can abandon that account with little inconvenience. It's much less convenient to abandon your primary e-mail address.

Another way to avoid spam is to filter it. A **spam filter** is an option you can select in your e-mail account that places known or suspected spam messages into a folder other than your inbox. Most Web-based e-mail services such as Hotmail and Yahoo! offer spam filters (see Figure 3.15). Since the release of Outlook 2003, Outlook has featured a spam filter, but if you still are using a previous version of Outlook to manage your e-mail, then you need to obtain special spam filtering software and install it on your computer. Programs that provide some control over spam include MailWasher Pro and Cactus Spam Filter, both of which can be obtained at **www.download. com**.

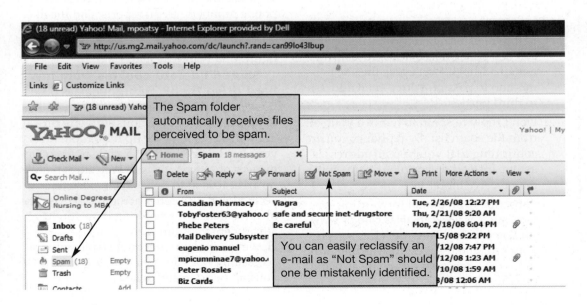

The Spam folder automatically receives files perceived to be spam.

You can easily reclassify an e-mail as "Not Spam" should one be mistakenly identified.

FIGURE 3.15

In Yahoo! Mail, turning on the SpamGuard feature alerts the Yahoo! Mail server to screen your incoming mail for obvious or suspected spam. This mail is then directed into a folder called "Spam" where you can review the mail (to ensure it is really spam) and delete it.

Configure a Firewall Before Going Online

As soon as you connect to the Internet, you are susceptible to unwanted communications to and from your PC. You may wish to install a firewall to help filter traffic entering or leaving your PC. Routers used to share Internet connections in a home network can act as a firewall, but some users prefer additional protection from dedicated firewall software applications. Individual software programs such as McAfee Firewall Plus or Norton Personal Firewall offer specific protection, or you can find firewall protection included in Internet security and utility suites such as McAfee Internet Security Suite and Norton Internet Security. However, the Windows firewall included with Windows Vista provides adequate protection from the majority of problems. When you use Vista's Connection Wizard to create a new Internet connection or enter the Security Center from the Control Panel, you have the opportunity to enable the Windows Firewall.

How do spam filters work? Spam filters and filtering software can catch as much as 95 percent of spam by checking incoming e-mail subject headers and sending addresses against databases of known spam. Spam filters also check your e-mail for frequently used spam patterns and keywords (such as "for free" and "over 21"). E-mail that the filter identifies as spam does not go into your inbox but rather to a folder set up for spam. Because spam filters aren't perfect, you should check the spam folder before deleting its contents because legitimate e-mail might end up there by mistake.

How else can I prevent spam? There are several additional ways you can prevent spam:

1. Before registering on a Web site, read its privacy policy to see how it uses your e-mail address. Don't give the site permission to pass on your e-mail address to third parties.

2. Don't reply to spam to remove yourself from the spam list. By replying, you are confirming that your e-mail address is active. Instead of stopping spam, you may receive more.

3. Subscribe to an e-mail forwarding service, such as **www.emailias.com** or **www. sneakemail.com**. These services screen your e-mail messages, forwarding only those messages you designate as being okay to accept.

COOKIES

What are cookies? Cookies are small text files that some Web sites automatically store on your computer's hard drive when you visit the site. When you log on to a Web site that uses cookies, a cookie file assigns an ID number to your computer. The unique ID is intended to make your return visit to a Web site more efficient and better geared to your interests. The next time you log on to that site, the site marks your visit and keeps track of it in its database.

What do Web sites do with cookie information? Cookies provide Web sites with information about your browsing habits, such as the ads you've opened, the products you've looked at, and the time and duration of your visits. Companies use this information to determine the traffic flowing through their Web site and the effectiveness of their marketing strategy and placement on Web sites. By tracking such information, cookies enable companies to identify different users' preferences.

Can companies get my personal information when I visit their sites? Cookies do not go through your hard drive in search of personal information such as passwords or financial data. The only personal information a cookie obtains is the information you supply when you fill out forms online.

Do privacy risks exist with cookies? Some sites sell the personal information their cookies collect to Web advertisers who are building huge databases of consumer preferences and habits, collecting personal and business information such as phone numbers, credit reports, and the like. The ultimate concern is that advertisers will use this information indiscriminately, thus infiltrating your privacy.

Should I delete cookies from my hard drive then? Because cookies pose no security threat (it is virtually impossible to hide a virus or malicious software program in a cookie), take up little room on your hard drive, and offer you small conveniences on return visits to Web sites, there is no great reason to delete them. Deleting your cookie files could actually cost you the inconvenience of reentering data you have already entered into Web site forms. However, if you're uncomfortable with the accessibility of your personal information, you can periodically delete cookies or

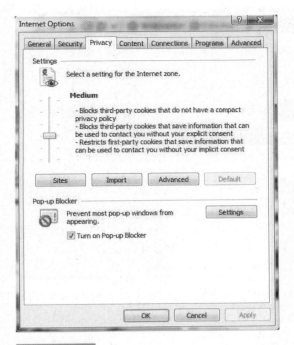

FIGURE 3.16

Tools are available, either through your browser or as a separate software application, to sort between cookies you want to keep and cookies you don't want on your system.

>To access the Internet Options dialog box, on the Internet Explorer menu toolbar, click **Tools**, and then click **Internet Options**. The cookie settings are on the **Privacy** tab.

configure your browser to block certain types of cookies, as shown in Figure 3.16. Software programs such as Cookie Pal (**www.kburra.com**) also exist to help monitor cookies for you.

MALWARE, ADWARE, AND SPYWARE

What is malware? Malware is software that has a malicious intent (hence the prefix *mal*). There are three primary forms of malware: adware, spyware, and viruses and worms. Viruses and worms are small programs that can be destructive and cause serious damage to a computer system. More information about viruses and worms can be found in Chapter 7.

Many of the initial instances of malware were forms of Internet pranks, but some had a more serious impact such as the Melissa worm virus that quickly spread infected e-mails throughout the Internet and eventually shut down many e-mail systems. Other malware programs known as *Trojan horses* disguise themselves as benign programs such as a game, but they really contain harmful code that is installed when the benign program is used.

Adware and spyware are not destructive like viruses and worms are. Known collectively as **grayware**, they are primarily intrusive, annoying, or objectionable online programs that are downloaded to your computer when you install or use other online content such as a freeware program, game, or utility.

What is adware? Adware is software that displays sponsored advertisements in a section of your browser window or as a pop-up ad box and is considered a legitimate (though sometimes annoying) means of generating revenue for those developers who do not charge for their software or information. **Pop-up windows** have been referred to as the billboards of the Internet because they pop up when you install freeware programs or enter certain Web sites and display advertisements or other promotional information. These pop-up windows, at one point, were so frequent that they were incredibly irritating and annoying.

Some pop-ups, however, are legitimate and increase the functionality of the originating site. For example, your account balance may pop up at your bank's Web site. Fortunately, because Web browsers such as Firefox, Safari, and Internet Explorer 7 have pop-up blockers built into their browsers (see Figure 3.17), the occurrence of annoying pop-ups has been greatly reduced. Whenever a pop-up is blocked, the browser displays an information bar at the top of the browser window to alert you. If you feel the pop-up is legitimate, then you can choose to accept it.

What is spyware? Some adware programs are more intrusive. Without your knowledge, they transmit information about you, such as your Internet surfing habits, to the owner of the adware program so that the information can be used for marketing purposes. In these instances, such adware becomes more malicious in intent and can be considered spyware. **Spyware** is an unwanted piggyback program that downloads with the software you want to install from the Internet and runs in the

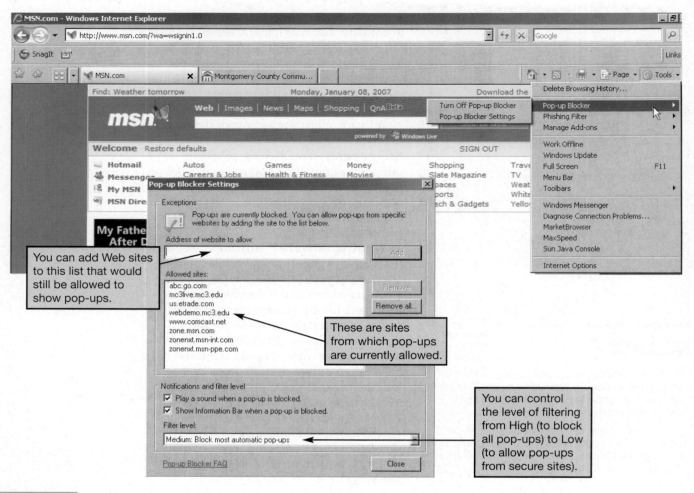

FIGURE 3.17

Internet Explorer 7 has pop-up controls built into the browser. You can toggle the blocker on and off, as well as selectively control specific sites by adding them to the Allowed sites box in the Pop-up Blocker Settings box.

>Pop-up Blocker is found in the **Tools** menu on the Internet Explorer 7 toolbar.

background of your system. Many spyware programs use tracking cookies to collect information, whereas others are disguised as benign programs that are really malicious programs (Trojan horses). Some spyware programs (known as *keystroke loggers*) monitor keystrokes with the intent of stealing passwords, login IDs, or credit card information.

Can I prevent spyware? Most antivirus software doesn't detect spyware or prevent spyware cookies from being placed on your hard drive. However, you can obtain spyware removal software and run it on your computer to delete unwanted spyware. Because new spyware is created all the time, you should update and run your spyware removal software regularly. Windows Vista comes with a program called Windows Defender, which scans your system for spyware and other potentially unwanted software. Ad-Aware and Spybot–Search & Destroy (both available for free at **www. download.com**) and eTrust PestPatrol (available at **www.pestpatrol.com**) are programs

that are easy to install and update. Figure 3.18 shows an example of Ad-Aware and Spybot in action.

PHISHING AND INTERNET HOAXES

What is phishing? One scam involving the Internet is **phishing** (pronounced "fishing"). Phishing lures Internet users to reveal personal information such as credit card numbers, Social Security numbers, or other sensitive information that could lead to identity theft. The scammers send e-mail messages that look like they are from a legitimate business such as an online bank. The e-mail states that the recipient needs to update or confirm his or her account information; when clicked, a provided link sends the recipient to a Web site. The site looks like a legitimate site but is really a fraudulent copy the scammer has created. Once the e-mail recipient confirms his or her personal

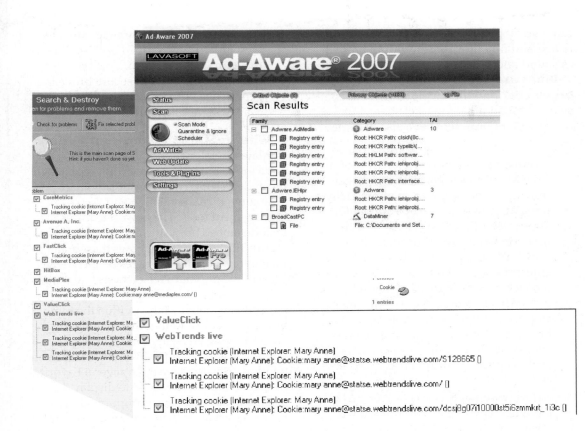

FIGURE 3.18

After performing a routine scan of a computer, Ad-Aware and Spybot each return a log of problems found on the system. Each program allows you to easily detect and delete unwanted "pests" from your computer.

information, the scammers capture it and can begin using it.

How can I avoid being caught by phishing scams? The following suggestions will help you to avoid falling for phishing scams:

- Do not reply directly to any e-mail asking you for personal information.

- Do not click on a link in an e-mail to go to a Web site. Instead, type the Web site address in the browser. Check with the company asking for the information and only give the information if you are certain it is needed.

- Never give personal information over the Internet unless you know the site is secure. Look for the closed padlock, https, or a certification seal such as VeriSign to indicate that the site is secure. Firefox 2 and Internet Explorer 7 have phishing filters built in, so each time you access a Web site, the phishing filter checks for the site's legitimacy and warns you of possible Web forgeries.

What is an Internet hoax? Internet **hoaxes** contain information that is untrue. Hoax e-mail messages may request that you send money to cover medical costs for an impoverished and sick child or ask you to pass on bogus information such as how to avoid a virus. Chain e-mail letters also are considered a form of Internet hoax.

Why are hoaxes so bad? The sheer number of e-mail messages generated by hoaxes can cost millions in lost opportunity costs caused by time spent reading, discarding, or resending the message, and they can clog up the Internet system. If you receive an e-mail you think might be a hoax, don't pass it on. First, determine whether it is a hoax by visiting a hoax-debunking site such as **www.snopes.com**.

Accessing the Web: Web Browsers

None of the activities for which we use the Web could happen without an important software application: a Web browser. A **Web browser**, or **browser**, is software installed on your computer system that allows you to locate, view, and navigate the Web. The most common browsers in use today are Microsoft's **Internet Explorer (IE)** and Mozilla's Firefox. Most browsers being used today are graphical browsers, meaning they

SOUND BYTE

The Best Utilities for Your Computer

In this Sound Byte, you'll explore various utilities that you can use to avoid Internet annoyances. You'll learn how to install and use specific programs and find out where to download some of them for free.

can display pictures (graphics) in addition to text and other forms of multimedia such as sound and video.

What are some common Web browsers? Internet Explorer (IE) has enjoyed predominant market share, but recently other browsers have also become popular.

- **Firefox**, a popular open source browser from Mozilla (**www.mozilla.org**), began from a version of the first commercially popular browser, Netscape Navigator. Supported by AOL, Netscape was the first popular browser that helped to transform the Web into the commercial enterprise it is today. Over time, Netscape fell victim to the increasing market share of Internet Explorer, and AOL formally stopped supporting the Netscape browser in January 2008. Firefox, however, continues to enjoy increasing popularity, capturing approximately 16 percent of the U.S. browser market.
- **Safari (www.apple.com)** is a Web browser developed by Apple. Although it was created as the default browser for Macs and is included with the Mac OS, a Window's-based version is also available. Safari has quickly gained public acceptance, and it now has nearly a 5 percent share of the U.S. browser market.
- **Opera (www.opera.com)** is a browser that has a small but dedicated following. Opera's advantage, similar to Firefox, is that it can preserve your surf sessions. When you launch Opera, it loads and opens all the Web sites you had open when you last used it.

- **Camino (www.caminobrowser.org)** is a new browser developed by Mozilla for the Mac OS X platform. This browser offers an efficient and secure browsing experience with the look and feel of a Mac OS X application.

What features do browsers offer? The latest version of Internet Explorer 7 (IE7), has a much more streamlined approach than its predecessors. The browser's toolbars provide convenient navigation and Web page management tools. The newest features include tabbed browsing and quick tabs (see Figure 3.19). Quick tabs shows thumbnail images of all open Web pages in open tabs. Most of the popular Web browsers, including IE7, have tabbed browsing in which Web pages are loaded in "tabs" within the same browser window. Rather than having to switch among Web pages in several open windows, you can flip between the tabs in one window. You can even open several Favorites from one folder and choose to display them as tabs. You may also save groups of tabs as a Favorites group, if there are always several you like to open together at the same time.

Other handy features found in Firefox are spell-checking for e-mail, blogs, and other Web postings; Session Restore, which brings back all your active Web pages if the system shuts down unexpectedly; and Live Titles, which fits nicely on the toolbar and provides updated summaries of the most important information on a Web page.

Most browsers also include a built-in search box in which you can designate your preferred default search engine and tools for printing, page formatting, and security settings.

FIGURE 3.19

Internet Explorer 7 (IE7) includes tabbed browsing and quick tabs. IE7 has also abbreviated the display of the navigation tools to a simple toolbar and built a Google search engine right into the browser.

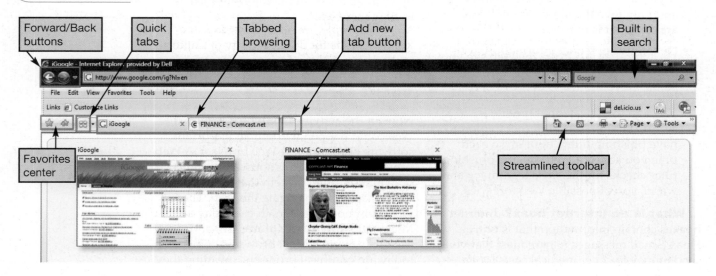

Forward/Back buttons | Quick tabs | Tabbed browsing | Add new tab button | Built in search

Favorites center

Streamlined toolbar

Getting Around the Web: URLs, Hyperlinks, and Other Tools

You gain initial access to a particular **Web site**, or location on the Web, by typing its unique address, or **Uniform Resource Locator** (**URL**, pronounced "you-are-ell"), in your browser. For example, the URL of the Web site for *Popular Science* magazine is **http://www.popsci.com**. By typing this URL for *Popular Science* magazine, you connect to the **home page**, or main page, of the Web site. Once you are in the home page, you can move all around the site by clicking specially formatted pieces of text called *hyperlinks*. Let's look at these and other navigation tools in more detail.

URLs

What do all the parts of the URL mean? As noted above, a URL is a Web site's address. Like a regular street address, a URL is composed of several parts that help identify the Web document for which it stands (see Figure 3.20). The first part of the URL indicates the set of rules, or **protocol**, used to retrieve the specified document. The protocol is generally followed by a colon, two forward slashes, *www* (indicating World Wide Web), and then the **domain name**. (Sometimes the domain name is also thought to include the *www*.) The domain name is also referred to as the *host name*.

What's the protocol? For the most part, URLs begin with http, which is short for the **hypertext transfer protocol (HTTP)**. The protocol allows files to be transferred from a computer that hosts the Web site you are requesting (known as a *Web server*) so that you can see the Web site on your computer by using a browser.

Another common protocol used to transfer files over the Internet is **file transfer protocol (FTP)**. FTP is used to upload and download files from one computer to another. FTP files use an FTP file server, whereas HTTP files use a Web server. To connect to most FTP servers, you need a user ID and a password. FTP addresses, like e-mail or URLs, identify one location on the Web. They can have several formats

BITS AND BYTES

Why Should You Run the Latest Version of Browser Software?

As new file formats are developed for the Web, browsers need new plug-ins to display them properly. Constantly downloading and installing plug-ins can be a tedious process. Although many Web sites provide links to sites that enable you to download plug-ins, not all do, resulting in frustration when you can't display the content you want. When new versions of browsers are released, they normally include the latest versions of popular plug-ins. Corrections of security breaches are typically included in these versions of browser software as well. Therefore, upgrading to the latest version of your browser software provides for safer, more convenient Web surfing. Fortunately, most updates are free, and you can set most of the popular Web browsers to notify you when updates are available or to download the updates automatically.

FIGURE 3.20

The parts of a URL.

such as **ftp://ftp.frognet.net** or **ftp://ourcompany.com**. To upload and download files from FTP sites, you can use a Web browser (such as Internet Explorer) or file transfer software such as WS_FTP, Fetch, or CuteFTP.

What's in a domain name? The domain name identifies who the site's **host** is. For example, **www.berkeley.edu** is the domain name for the University of California at Berkeley. Although using *www* is conventional, it is not necessary. The suffix in the domain name after the dot (such as .com or .edu) is called the **top-level domain (TLD)**.

SOUND BYTE

Welcome to the Web

In this Sound Byte, you'll visit the Web in a series of guided tours of useful Web sites. This tour serves as an introductory guide for Web newcomers and is a great resource for more experienced users.

FIGURE 3.21 Current Top-Level Domains and Their Authorized Users

Domain Name	Who Can Use the Domain Name
Unsponsored Top-Level Domains	
.biz	Businesses
.com	Originally for commercial sites but can be used by anyone now
.edu	Degree-granting institutions
.gov	United States government
.info	Information service providers
.int	Limited to organizations, offices, and programs that are sanctioned by a treaty between two or more nations
.mil	United States military
.name	Individuals
.net	Originally for networking organizations but no longer restricted
.org	Organizations (often nonprofits)
Sponsored Top-Level Domains	
.aero	Members of the air transport industry
.asia	For companies, organizations, and individuals based in Asia, Australia, and the Pacific
.cat	For Web sites in the Catalan language
.coop	Cooperative associations
.jobs	Posting and recruiting job opportunities
.mobi	Compatible for use with mobile devices
.museum	Museums
.pro	Credentialed professionals
.tel	Internet communication services
.travel	Travel-related services
Infrastructure Top-Level Domains	
.arpa	Address and Routing Parameter Area (an Internet infrastructure TLD)

FIGURE 3.22 Examples of Country Codes

Country Code	Country
.au	Australia
.ca	Canada
.uk	United Kingdom
.us	United States
.za	South Africa

Note: For a full listing of country codes, refer to **www.norid.no/domenenavnbaser/domreg.html**.

This suffix indicates the kind of organization to which the host belongs. Figure 3.21 lists the top-level domains that are currently approved and in use, broken down by those that were established by the Internet Corporation for Assigned Names and Numbers (ICAAN), the nonprofit corporation responsible for IP address allocation, and those that are sponsored by a narrower community that is most affected by the top-level domain.

Each country in the world has its own TLD. These are two-letter designations such as .za for South Africa and .us for the United States. A sampling of country codes is shown in Figure 3.22. Within a country-specific domain, further subdivisions can be made for regions or states. For instance, the .us domain contains subdomains for each state, using the two-letter abbreviation of the state. For example, the URL for Pennsylvania's Web site is **www.state.pa.us**.

What's the information after the domain name that I sometimes see? When the URL is only the domain name (such as **www.nytimes.com**), you are requesting a site's home page. However, sometimes a forward slash and additional text follow the domain name such as **www.nytimes.com/pages/cartoons**. The information after the slash indicates a particular file or **path** (or **subdirectory**) within the Web site. In this example, you would connect to the cartoon pages in the *New York Times* site.

HYPERLINKS AND BEYOND

What's the best way to get around in a Web site? Unlike text in a book or a Microsoft Word document, which is linear

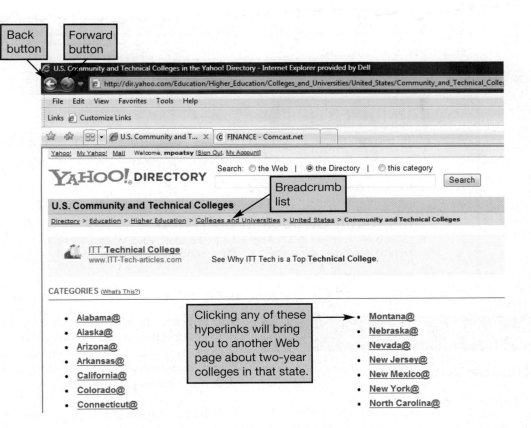

FIGURE 3.23

When you click on a hyperlink, you jump from one location in a Web site to another. When you click on the links in a breadcrumb list, you can navigate your way back through a Web site.

(meaning you read it from top to bottom, left to right, one page after another), the Web is anything but linear. As its name implies, the Web is a series of connected paths, or links, that connect you to different Web sites. You can jump from one location, or Web page, to another within the same Web site or to another Web site altogether by clicking on specially coded text called **hyperlinks**, which are shown in Figure 3.23. Generally, text that operates as a hyperlink appears in a different color (often blue) and is underlined. Sometimes images also act as hyperlinks. When you pass your cursor over a hyperlinked image, for example, a cursor may change to a hand with a finger pointing upward. To access the hyperlink, you simply click the image.

How do I return to a Web page I've already visited? To retrace your steps, some sites also provide a **breadcrumb list**—a list of pages within a Web site you've visited that usually appears at the top of a page. Figure 3.23 shows an example of a breadcrumb list. Breadcrumbs get their name from the Hansel and Gretel fairy tale in which the children dropped breadcrumbs on the trail to find their way out of the forest. By clicking on earlier links in a breadcrumb list, you can retrace your steps back to the page on which you first started.

To get back to your original location or visit a Web page you viewed previously, you use the browser's Back and Forward buttons (see Figure 3.23). To back up more than one page, click the down arrow next to the Back button to access a list of most recently visited Web sites. By selecting any one of these sites in the list, you can return to that page without having to navigate through other Web sites and Web pages you've visited.

The **History list** on your browser's toolbar is also a handy feature. The History list shows all the Web sites and pages that you've visited over a certain period of time. These Web sites are organized according to date and can go back as far as three weeks. To access the history list on IE7, click the down arrow next to the navigation arrows. On the Firefox toolbar, the history button is the alarm clock icon.

FAVORITES, LIVE BOOKMARKS, AND TAGGING

What's the best way to mark a site so I can return to it later? If you want an easy way to return to a specific Web page

FIGURE 3.24

Tagging tools are incorporated into Web browsers and in some Web pages for easy access.

BITS AND BYTES

The TV Domain Name

Two-letter domains are reserved for countries worldwide. The domain .tv is the domain for the little Pacific island country of Tuvalu. The domain name is popular as well as economically valuable because it is an abbreviation of the word "television." In the late 1990s, Tuvalu began selling the right to use the ".tv" Internet domain name as a means of generating revenue for the country. The domain is currently operated by The .tv Corporation, a VeriSign company.

without always having to remember to type in the address, you can use your browser's **Favorites** or **Bookmarks** feature. Internet Explorer and Safari call this feature Favorites; Firefox calls the same feature a Bookmark. This feature places a marker of the site's URL in an easily retrievable list in your browser's toolbar. To organize the sites into categories, most browsers offer tools to create folders. Most browsers also provide features to export the list of bookmarks to another computer or another browser.

What are live bookmarks? Found in the Firefox browser, **live bookmarks** add the technology of RSS feeds to bookmarking. Because the Web is constantly changing, the site you bookmarked last week may subsequently change and add new content. Traditionally, you would notice the change only the next time you visited the site. With live bookmarks, the content comes to you. Instead of constantly checking your favorite

Web pages for new content, a live bookmark delivers updates to you as soon as they become available. Live bookmarks are useful if you are interested in the most up-to-date news stories, sports scores, or stock prices.

What is tagging? Favorites and Bookmarks are great for quickly locating those sites you use the most, but they are only accessible to you when you are on your own computer. One way to access your Bookmarks and Favorites anywhere from any computer is to use MyBookmarks (**www.mybookmarks.com**), a free Internet service that stores your Bookmarks and Favorites online. You can also try **del.icio.us** and **digg.com**. In addition to letting you put your bookmarks on the Web, these sites allow you to provide your own keywords, called **tags**, so that you can categorize your favorite Web sites for easy use later on. You can also see how many other Web users tagged the same site. Del.icio.us and Digg offer convenient toolbars for your browsers, and many Web sites incorporate tagging icons for ease of use as shown in Figure 3.24.

Searching the Web: Search Engines and Subject Directories

With its billions of Web pages, the Internet offers visitors access to masses of information on virtually any topic. To narrow down the massive quantity of Web information to

FIGURE 3.25 **Popular Search Engines and Subject Directories**

Search Tools on the Internet		
AltaVista	**www.altavista.com**	Keyword search engine
Clusty	**www.clusty.com**	Keyword search engine that groups similar results into clusters
ChaCha	**www.chacha.com**	Don't like your search results? This site lets you chat with a real live professional guide who helps you search, and it's free of charge.
Complete-Planet	**www.completeplanet.com**	Deep Web directory that searches databases not normally searched by typical search engines
Dogpile	**www.dogpile.com**	Metasearch engine that searches Google, Yahoo!, MSN Search, and Ask
Excite	**www.excite.com**	Portal with keyword search capabilities
InfoMine	**http://infomine.ucr.edu**	Subject directory of academic resources with keyword search engine capabilities
Rollyo	**www.rollyo.com**	Short for Roll Your Own Search Engine. Basically, this site lets you create your own search engine (searchroll) that searches just the sites you want it to search.
Open Directory Project	**www.dmoz.org**	Subject directory with keyword search capabilities
Stumbleupon	**www.stumbleupon.com**	Lets you rate pages thumbs up or thumbs down. As it learns your preferences, your search results improve.
Technorati	**www.technorati.com**	Aside from Google Blog, the best search engine for blog content

Note: For a complete list of search engines, go to **www.searchengineguide.com**.

something more useful, there are several search tools you can use to find just the right information. The first tool is a **search engine**, which is a set of programs that searches the Web for specific words, or **keywords**, you wish to query (or look for) and then returns a list of the Web sites on which those keywords are found. Popular search engines include Google, Yahoo!, and Ask.com. Second, you also can search the Web using a **subject directory**, which is a structured outline of Web sites organized by topics and subtopics. Librarians' Internet Index (**www.lii.org**) is a subject directory, and popular search engines such as Google and Yahoo! also feature directories. If you can't decide which search engine is best, you may want to try a **metasearch engine**, such as Dogpile. Metasearch engines search other search engines rather than

individual Web sites. Figure 3.25 lists search engines and subject directories that are alternatives to Google, Yahoo!, and Ask.com.

SEARCH ENGINES

How do search engines work? Search engines have three parts. The first part is a program called a **spider**. The spider constantly collects data on the Web, following links in Web sites and reading Web pages. Spiders get their name because they crawl over the Web using multiple "legs" to visit many sites simultaneously. As the spider collects data, the second part of the search engine, an indexer program, organizes the data into a large database. When you use a search engine, you interact with the third part: the search engine software. This software

ACTIVE HELPDESK

Getting Around the Web

In this Active Helpdesk call, you'll play the role of a helpdesk staffer, fielding calls about Web browsers, URLs, and how to use hyperlinks and other tools to get around the Web.

Searching the Web: Search Engines and Subject Directories **121**

Ethics: What Can You Borrow from the Internet?

You've no doubt heard of plagiarism—claiming another person's words as your own. And you've probably heard the term *copyright violation*, especially if you've been following the music industry's battle to keep "free" music off the Web. But what constitutes plagiarism, and what constitutes copyright violation? And what can you borrow from the Web? Consider these scenarios:

1. You find a political cartoon that would be terrific in a PowerPoint presentation you're creating for your civics class. You copy it into your presentation.
2. Your hobby is cooking. You design a Web site that includes videos of you preparing recipes, as well as the recipes themselves. Some of these recipes you take from your favorite cookbooks; others you get from friends. You don't cite your sources, nor do you obtain permission from the originators of the recipes you post to your Web site.
3. You're pressed for time and need to do research for a paper due tomorrow. You find information on an obscure Web site and copy it into your paper without documenting the source.
4. You download a song from the Internet and incorporate it into a PowerPoint presentation for a school project. Because you figure everyone knows the song, you don't credit it in your sources.

Which of the preceding scenarios represent copyright violations? Which represent plagiarism? The distinctions between these scenarios are narrow in some cases, but it's important to understand the differences.

As noted earlier, plagiarism occurs when you use someone else's ideas or words and represent them as your own. In today's computer society, it's easy to copy information from the Internet and paste it into a Word document, change a few words, and call it your own. To avoid plagiarism, use quotation marks around all words you borrow directly and credit your sources for any ideas you paraphrase or borrow. Avoiding plagiarism means properly crediting all information you obtain from the Internet, including words, ideas, graphics, data, and audio and video clips.

Web sites such as **www.turnitin.com** help teachers, students, and other interested parties to check for plagiarism violations. Turnitin.com will scan a document and, within a few minutes, determine the percentage of the document that has exact wording from Web sites, highlight those areas of the document that have exactly the same wording as a Web site, and provide you with the Web site in question. Although some common phrasing may be truly coincidental, more purposeful plagiarism is reasonably easy to identify. Students can use Turnitin.com before submitting an assignment to ensure their paper is their own work.

Copyright violation is more serious because it is punishable by law. Copyright law assumes that *all* original work—including text, graphics, software, multimedia, audio and video clips, and even ideas—is copyrighted even if the work does not display the copyright symbol (©). Copyright violation occurs when you use another person's material for your own personal economic benefit, or when you take away from the economic benefit of the originator. Don't assume that by citing a source you're abiding by copyright laws. In most cases, you need to seek and receive written permission from the copyright holder. There are exceptions to this rule. For example, there is no copyright on government documents, so you can download and reproduce material from NASA, for example, without violating copyright laws. The British Broadcasting Corporation (BBC) is also beginning to digitize and make available its archives of material to the public without copyright restrictions.

Teachers and students receive special consideration regarding copyright violations. This special consideration falls under a provision called *academic fair use*. As long as the material is being used for educational purposes only, limited copying and distribution is allowed. For example, an instructor can make copies of a newspaper article and distribute it to her class, or a student can include a cartoon in a PowerPoint presentation without seeking permission from the artist. However, to avoid plagiarism in these situations, you still must credit your sources of information. So, do you now know which of the four scenarios above are plagiarism or copyright violations?

1. You are not in violation because the use of the cartoon is for educational purposes and falls under the academic fair use provision. You must still credit the source, however.
2. If your Web site is for your economic benefit, then you would be in violation of copyright laws because no credit was given for the recipes, and you are presenting them as your own.
3. You are guilty of plagiarism because you copied from another source and implied it was your own work.
4. Again, because it is for a school project, you are not in violation because of the academic fair use provision. However, it's always important to document your sources.

searches the indexed data, pulling out relevant information according to your search. The resulting list appears in your Web browser as a list of **hits**, or sites that match your search.

Why don't I get the same results from all search engines? Each search engine uses a unique formula, or algorithm, to formulate the search and create the resulting index of related sites. In addition, search engines differ in how they rank the search results. Most search engines rank their results based on the frequency of the appearance of your queried keywords in Web sites as well as the location of those words in the sites. Thus, sites that include the keywords in their URL or site name most likely appear at the top of the **hit list**. After that, results vary because of differences in each engine's proprietary formula.

In addition, search engines differ as to which sites they search. For instance, Google and Ask.com search nearly the entire Web, whereas specialty search engines search only sites that are specifically relevant to the particular specialty subject. Specialty search engines exist for almost every industry or interest. For example, **www.dailystocks.com** is a search engine used primarily by investors that searches for corporate information to help them make educated decisions. Search Engine Watch (**www.searchenginedirectory.com**) has a list of many specialty search engines organized by industry.

Can I use a search engine to search for images and videos? With the increasing popularity of multimedia, search engines such as Google, Ask.com, and Yahoo! have capabilities to search the Web for digital images and audio and video files. YouTube (**www.youtube.com**) is one of many sites that has gained recent popularity because of its wealth of video content. In addition to the amusing videos that are captured in popular news, YouTube contains instructional and informational videos.

SUBJECT DIRECTORIES

How can I use a subject directory to find information on the Web? As mentioned earlier, a subject directory is a guide to the Internet organized by topics and subtopics. Yahoo! was one of the original subject directories, and although it still has a subject directory, it now acts more as a

search engine. Google, which started as a search engine, also has a subject directory feature.

So when is it good to use a subject directory? With a subject directory, you do not use keywords to search the Web. Instead, after selecting the main subject from the directory, you narrow your search by successively clicking on subfolders that match your search until you have reached the appropriate information. For example, to find previews on newly released movies in Google's subject directory, you would click on the main category of Arts, select the subcategory Movies, select the further subcategory Previews, and then open one of the listed Web sites.

Can I find the same information with a subject directory as I can with a search engine? Most subject directories organize commercial and consumer information rather than academic or research information. Some of the main categories in Yahoo's subject directory, for example, are Education, Computers & Internet, Recreation & Sports, and Society & Culture. Even within categories such as Reference, you can find consumer-oriented subcategories such as Phone Numbers and Quotations. Many Web sites that began strictly as subject directories such as Yahoo! and MSN are now part of a larger Web site that focuses on offering its visitors a variety of information such as the weather, news, sports, and shopping guides. This type of Web site is referred to as a portal.

When should I use a subject directory instead of a traditional search engine? Directory searches are great for finding information on general topics (such as sports and hobbies) rather than narrowing in on a specific or unusual piece of information. For example, conducting a search on the keyword *hobbies* with a search engine does not provide a convenient list of hobbies like a subject directory does. Although most subject directories tend to be commercially oriented, there are academic and professional directories that use subject experts to select and annotate sites. These directories are created specifically to facilitate the research process. The Librarians' Internet Index (**www.lii.org**), in Figure 3.26, for example, is an academic directory whose index lists librarian-selected Web sites that have little if any commercially sponsored content.

SOUND BYTE

Finding Information on the Web

In this Sound Byte, you'll learn how and when to use search engines and subject directories. Through guided tours, you'll learn effective search techniques, including how to use Boolean operators and meta search engines.

ACTIVE HELPDESK

Using Subject Directories and Search Engines

In this Active Helpdesk call, you'll play the role of a helpdesk staffer, fielding calls about how to search the Internet using search engines and subject directories, as well as about how to use Boolean operators to search the Web more effectively.

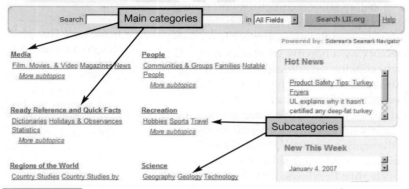

FIGURE 3.26

Subject directories are best for searches that are more general, or just for browsing within a topic. Some academic subject directories, such as **www.lii.org**, are annotated by experts.

BITS AND BYTES

Citing Web Site Sources

After you've evaluated a Web site and determined it to be a credible source of information that you will use in your paper, you will need to list the source in the Works Cited section of your paper. There are formal guidelines as to how to cite Web content; unlike books and periodicals, however, the standards are still being developed. At a minimum, the following components should be included in the citation: author, title of document or publication, date of publication or last revision, complete URL, and date accessed. The following are examples of Web citations in both Modern Language Association (MLA) and American Psychological Association (APA) style forms for an article found in *BusinessWeek* online:

Example of MLA style
MacMillian, Douglas. "Hybrids Cost-Efficient Over Long Haul." *BusinessWeek*. 09 January 2007. 12 February 2007. **http://www.businessweek.com/autos/content/jan2007/ bw20070108_774581.htm**

Example of APA Style
MacMillian, D. (January 9, 2007). Hybrids Cost-Efficient Over Long Haul. *BusinessWeek*. Retrieved February 12, 2007, from **http://www.businessweek.com/autos/content/jan2007/ bw20070108_774581.htm**.

For further assistance, go to **www.citationmachine.net**, which is an interactive tool designed to output the proper MLA or APA citation format with information you provide in an online form. Word 2007 also includes citation and bibliography formatting for most of the standard formats.

EVALUATING WEB SITES

How can I make sure the Web site is appropriate to use for research?

When you're using the Internet for research, you shouldn't assume that everything you find is accurate and appropriate to use. Before you use an Internet resource, consider the following.

1. **Authority:** Who is the author of the article or the sponsor of the site? If the author is well known or the site is published by a reputable news source (such as the *New York Times*), then you can feel more confident using it as a source than if you are unable to locate such information. *Note:* Some sites include a page with information about the author or the site's sponsor.

2. **Bias:** Is the site biased? The purpose of many Web sites is to sell products or services or to persuade rather than inform. These sites, though useful in some situations, present a biased point of view. Look for sites that offer several sets of facts or consider opinions from several sources.

3. **Relevancy:** Is the information in the site current? Material can last a long time on the Web. Some research projects (such as historical accounts) depend on older records. However, if you're writing about cutting-edge technologies, you need to look for the most recent sources. Therefore, look for a date on information to make sure it is current.

4. **Audience:** For what audience is the site intended? Ensure that the content, tone, and style of the site match your needs. You probably wouldn't want to use information from a site geared toward teens if you're writing for adults or use a site that has a casual style and tone for serious research.

5. **Links:** Are the links available and appropriate? Check out the links provided on the site to determine whether they are still working and appropriate for your needs. Don't assume that the links provided are the only additional sources of information. Investigate other sites on your topic as well.

The answers to these questions will help you decide whether you should consider a Web site to be a good source of information.

The Internet and How it Works

The Internet is such an integral part of our lives that it's hard to imagine life without it. Looking forward, our ability to use and interact with the Internet and the World Wide Web will converge even more with our daily lives. Therefore, it's important to understand how the Internet works and the choices available for connecting to it.

THE INTERNET'S CLIENTS AND SERVERS

How does the Internet work?
Computers connected to the Internet communicate (or "talk") to each other in turns, just as we do when we ask a question and get an answer. Thus, a computer connected to the Internet acts in one of two ways: it is a **client**, a computer that asks for data, or it is a **server**, a computer that receives the request and returns the data to the client. Because the Internet uses clients and servers, it is referred to as a **client/server network**. (We'll discuss such networks in more detail in Chapter 7.)

How do computers talk to each other? Suppose you want to access the Web to check out snow conditions at your favorite ski area. As Figure 3.27 illustrates, when you type the Web site address of the ski area in your Web browser, your computer acts as a client computer because you are asking for data from the ski area's Web site. Your browser's request for this data travels along several pathways that can be likened to interstate highways. The largest and fastest pathway is the main artery of the Internet called the **Internet backbone**; all intermediary pathways connect to this backbone. All data traffic flows along the

FIGURE 3.27

How the Internet's client/server network works.

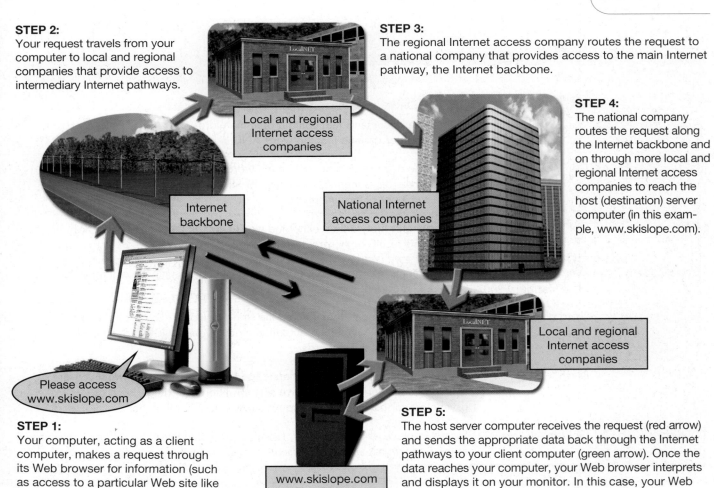

STEP 2:
Your request travels from your computer to local and regional companies that provide access to intermediary Internet pathways.

Local and regional Internet access companies

STEP 3:
The regional Internet access company routes the request to a national company that provides access to the main Internet pathway, the Internet backbone.

STEP 4:
The national company routes the request along the Internet backbone and on through more local and regional Internet access companies to reach the host (destination) server computer (in this example, www.skislope.com).

Internet backbone

National Internet access companies

Please access www.skislope.com

STEP 1:
Your computer, acting as a client computer, makes a request through its Web browser for information (such as access to a particular Web site like www.skislope.com).

Local and regional Internet access companies

www.skislope.com server

STEP 5:
The host server computer receives the request (red arrow) and sends the appropriate data back through the Internet pathways to your client computer (green arrow). Once the data reaches your computer, your Web browser interprets and displays it on your monitor. In this case, your Web browser displays the Web site www.skislope.com.

Refining Your Web Searches: Boolean Operators

When you conduct Web searches, you often receive a list of hits that includes thousands—even millions—of Web pages that have no relevance to the topic you're trying to search. **Boolean operators** are words you can use to refine your searches, making them more effective. These words—AND, NOT, and OR—describe the relationships between keywords in a search. Figure 3.28 shows examples of these operators being used and the results the searches would produce.

Narrowing and Expanding Searches

Using the Boolean operators AND, NOT, and OR alone or in combinations in your keyword searches can help to expand or limit your search results. The Boolean AND operator helps you narrow (or limit) the results of your search. When you use the AND operator to join two keywords, the search engine returns only those documents that include both keywords (not just one).

You can also narrow your search by using the NOT operator. When you use the NOT operator to join two keywords, the search engine doesn't show the results of any pages containing the word following NOT. Be aware, however, that when you use the NOT operator, you may eliminate documents that contain the unwanted keyword but that also contain important information that may have been useful to you. Note that some search engines also let you use the plus sign (+) and minus sign (–) instead of the words AND and NOT, respectively.

The OR operator expands a keyword search so that the search results include either or both keywords. Boolean OR searches are particularly helpful if there are a variety of synonymous keywords you could use in your search.

FIGURE 3.28 Using Boolean Operators

Operator	Example	Results
AND	Car AND Ford	Only those documents that contain both the words **Car** AND **Ford**. Most search engines assume that the word AND is used as a default.
NOT	Car NOT Ford	Only those documents that contain the word **Car** but do NOT also contain the word **Ford**. This is the most restrictive of all searches and will return the smallest number of documents.
OR	Car OR Ford	All documents that contain either the word **Car** OR the word **Ford** OR both words. This results in the greatest number of documents.
Combinations	(Car AND Ford) NOT Gerald	All documents referring to **Car** and **Ford**, but no documents relating to the 38th U.S. president, Gerald Ford.
Quotation Marks	"Lord of the Rings"	Only those documents that contain the string of words "Lord of the Rings" in that exact order. Without the quotation marks, you would get documents containing any of those words.
Wildcard*	Psych*	Stands in place of a series of letters. Good for those searches when you are searching for a term that can have several different endings, such as psychology or psychiatry, and you want to research all of them.
Wildcard%	Goldsm%th	Stands in place of a single letter. Good to use when there are different spellings of the same word, such as *Goldsmith* and *Goldsmyth*.

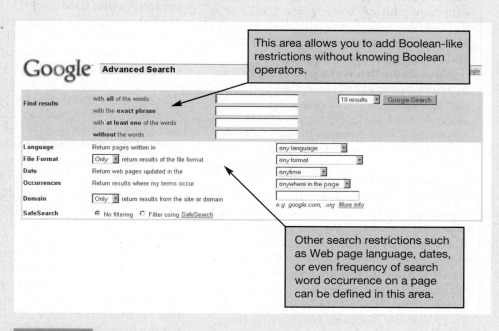

This area allows you to add Boolean-like restrictions without knowing Boolean operators.

Other search restrictions such as Web page language, dates, or even frequency of search word occurrence on a page can be defined in this area.

FIGURE 3.29

Most search engines have an advanced search form that you can fill out. The form uses the Boolean operators but in a more user-friendly format.

Other Helpful Search Strategies

Combining search terms produces more specific results. To do so, however, you must use parentheses to add order to your search. For example, if you are looking for tutorials or lessons to better use the Microsoft Excel program, you can search for (*Tutorials OR Lessons) AND Excel.* Similarly, if you want to know how to better use the entire Microsoft Office suite with the exception of Access, you can search for (*Tutorials OR Lessons) AND (Office NOT Access).*

To search for an exact phrase, place quotation marks around your keywords. The search engine will look for only those Web sites that contain the words in that exact order. For example, if you want information on the movie *Lord of the Rings* and you type these words without quotation marks, your search results will contain pages that include any of the words *Lord, of, the,* and *Rings* although not necessarily in that order. Typing "*Lord of the Rings*" in quotes guarantees that search results will include this exact phrase.

Some search engines let you use an asterisk (*) to replace a series of letters and a percent sign (%) to replace a single letter in a word. These symbols, called **wildcards**, are helpful when you're searching for a keyword but are unsure of its spelling, or if a word can be spelled in different ways or may contain different endings. For example, if you're doing a genealogy project and are searching for the name *Goldsmith*, you might want to use *Goldsm%th* to take into consideration alternative spellings of the name (such as Goldsmyth). Similarly, if you're searching for sites related to psychiatry and psychology and you type *psych**, the search results will include all pages containing the words *psychology, psychiatry, psychedelic,* and so on.

Using Boolean search techniques can make your Internet research a lot more efficient. With the simple addition of a few words, you can narrow your search results to a more manageable and more meaningful list. Meanwhile, most search engines offer an advanced search page that provides the same type of strategies in a well-organized form (see Figure 3.29).

backbone and then on to smaller pathways until it reaches its destination, which is the server computer for the ski area's Web site. The server computer returns the requested data to your computer by using the most expedient pathway system (which may be different from the pathway the request took). Your Web browser then interprets the data and displays it on your monitor.

How does the data get sent to the correct computer? Each time you connect to the Internet, your computer is assigned a unique identification number. This number, called an **Internet Protocol address** (or **IP address**), is a set of four numbers separated by periods and commonly referred to as a *dotted quad*, such as 123.45.245.91. IP addresses are the means by which all computers connected to the Internet identify each other. Similarly, each Web site is assigned an IP address that uniquely identifies it. However, because the long strings of numbers that make up IP addresses are difficult for humans to remember, Web sites are given text versions of their IP addresses. So the ski area's Web site mentioned earlier may have an IP address of 66.117.154.119 and a text name of **www.skislope.com**. When you type "www.skislope.com" into your browser window, your computer (with its own unique IP address) looks for the ski area's IP address (66.117.154.119). Data is exchanged between the ski area's server computer and your computer using these unique IP addresses.

Connecting to the Internet

To take advantage of the resources the Internet offers, you need a means to connect your computer to it. Home users nowadays have several connection options available. Originally, the only means to connect to the Internet was with a **dial-up connection**. With dial-up connections, you connect to the Internet using a standard telephone line. However, other connection options, collectively called **broadband connections**, offer faster means to connect to the Internet. Broadband connections include cable, satellite, and DSL. In many parts of the world, broadband connections are quickly becoming the preferred method of connecting to the Internet. By the end of 2007, nearly 305 million people worldwide connected to the Internet via broadband.

SOUND BYTE

Connecting to the Internet

In this Sound Byte, you'll learn the basics of connecting to the Internet from home, including useful information on the various types of Internet connections and selecting the right ISP.

BROADBAND CONNECTIONS

What broadband options do I have?
The three leading broadband home Internet connection technologies are (1) **digital subscriber line (DSL)**, which uses a standard phone line to connect your computer to the Internet; (2) cable, which uses your television's cable service provider to connect to the Internet; and (3) fiber-optic, which uses plastic or glass cables to transfer the data at the speed of light. Some users, especially those located in rural areas, connect to the Internet by satellite.

Why would I choose a broadband connection? A cable Internet connection promises better speed than a DSL connection, DSL is faster than satellite, and fiber-optic is the fastest of all. No matter which type of broadband technology you use, any broadband connection is much faster than dial-up, and the quality of your Web experience will be greatly enhanced with a broadband connection because the capabilities of the Web are designed with the assumption that the majority of Internet users are accessing the Internet via some form of broadband connection.

Depending on the area in which you live, you might not have a choice as to the type of broadband connection that is available. Check with your local cable TV provider, phone company, and satellite TV providers to determine what broadband options are available where you live and what the transfer rates are in your area. It might also be good to check with your neighbors to see what kind of broadband connections they are using. Speeds vary by neighborhood, sometimes exceeding advertised rates, so it's always good to check actual experiences.

Cable

If I have cable TV, do I have access to cable Internet? Although both cable TV and a **cable Internet connection** use coaxial cable, they are separate services. In fact, even though you may have cable TV in your home, cable Internet service may not be available in your area. Coaxial cable is a one-way service in which the cable company feeds your television programming signals. To bring two-way Internet connections to homes, cable companies must upgrade their networks for two-way data transmission capabilities and with fiber-optic lines. Because data sent through fiber-optic lines is transmitted at the speed of light, transmission speeds are much faster than are those along conventional copper wire technologies.

What do I need to hook up to cable Internet? A cable Internet connection requires a **cable modem**, as shown in Figure 3.30. Generally, the modem is located somewhere near your computer. The cable modem is then connected to an expansion (or adapter) card called a **network interface card (NIC)**, which is located inside your system unit. The cable modem works to translate the cable signal into digital data and back again. Because the cable TV signal and Internet data can share the same line, you can watch cable TV and be on the Internet at the same time. If you want to share your Internet connection with more than one computer, then you will also need a router.

Are there any disadvantages to cable Internet? Because you share your cable Internet connection with your neighbors, you may experience periodic decreases in connection speeds during peak usage times. Although cable Internet connection speeds are still faster than the dial-up alternative, your ultimate speed depends on how many other users are trying to transmit data at the same time as you are.

DSL

How does DSL work? Similar to a dial-up connection, DSL uses telephone lines to connect to the Internet. However, unlike dial-up, DSL allows phone and data transmission to share the same line, thus eliminating the need for an additional phone line. Phone lines are made of twisted copper wires known as *twisted pair wiring*. Think of this twisted copper wiring as a three-lane highway with only one lane being used to carry voice data. DSL uses the remaining two lanes to send and receive data separately at much higher frequencies. Thus, although it uses a standard phone line, a DSL connection is much faster than a dial-up connection.

Can anyone with a phone line have DSL? Just because you have a traditional phone line in your house doesn't mean that you have access to DSL service. Your local phone company must have special DSL technology to offer you the service. Although more phone companies are acquiring DSL technology, many areas in the United States, especially rural ones, still do not have DSL service available.

What special equipment do I need for DSL service? You need a special DSL modem like the one shown in Figure 3.31. A **DSL modem** is a device that connects the computer data to the DSL line and then separates the types of signals into voice and data signals so that they can travel in the right "lane" on the twisted pair wiring. Voice data is sent at the lower speed, while digital data is sent at data transfer rates ranging from 500 Kbps to 6 megabits per second (Mbps), which is 6,000 Kbps. Sometimes a DSL filter is required in DSL installations. Filters are necessary to reduce interference caused when the DSL equipment shares the same lines as the standard phone line. If a filter is required, the phone line is fit into the filter, and the filter plugs into the phone wall jack. As with cable, your computer will need a network interface card.

Are there different types of DSL service? The more typical DSL transmissions download (or receive) data from the Internet faster than they upload (or send) data. Such transmissions are referred to as *asymmetric digital subscriber line* (ADSL). Other DSL transmissions called *symmetric digital subscriber line* (SDSL) upload and download data at the same speed. If you upload data to the Internet often (if you design and update your own Web site, for example), then you may want to investigate the range of your DSL connection's sending-speed capabilities or check to see if your DSL provider offers SDSL service.

What are the advantages of DSL? With data transfer rates that reach 1.5 Mbps, DSL beats the slow speeds of dial-up by a great deal, and DSL service allows you to connect to the Internet without tying up your phone line. In addition, unlike cable and satellite, DSL service does not share the

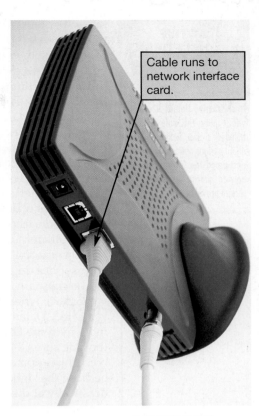

Cable runs to network interface card.

FIGURE 3.30

A cable Internet connection. To gain cable Internet access, you need a cable modem. This modem connects to a network interface card located inside your computer's system unit.

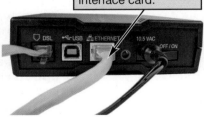

Cable runs to network interface card.

FIGURE 3.31

You need a special DSL modem to connect to the Internet using DSL.

ACTIVE HELPDESK

Connecting to the Internet

In this Active Helpdesk call, you'll play the role of a helpdesk staffer, fielding calls about various options for connecting to the Internet and how to choose an Internet service provider.

line with other network users in your area. In times of peak Internet usage, DSL speed is not affected, whereas cable and satellite hookups often experience reduced speeds during busy times. Because you are not sharing a line with DSL as you are with cable, some people maintain that DSL is less subject to denial of service attacks, service theft, and the like. In addition, bad weather does not affect DSL service as it can with satellite, and DSL service is less susceptible to the radio frequency interference that hinders cable.

Are there drawbacks to DSL? As mentioned earlier, DSL service is not available in all areas. If you do have access to DSL service, the quality and effectiveness of your service depend on your proximity to a phone company's central office (CO). A CO is the place where a receiving DSL modem is located. Data is sent through your DSL modem to the DSL modem at the CO. For the DSL service to work correctly, you must be within approximately three miles of a CO because the signal quality and speed weaken drastically at distances beyond 18,000 feet. A simple call to your local phone company can determine your proximity to a CO and whether DSL service is available. You can also find out whether DSL is available in your area by checking **www.dsl.com** or **www. getconnected.com**.

Fiber-Optic Service

What is fiber-optic service? Fiber-optic service (FiOS) uses fiber-optic lines, which are strands of optically pure glass that are as thin as a human hair. They are arranged in bundles called *optical cables* and transmit data via light signals over long distances. Because light travels so quickly, this technology can bring an enormous amount of data to your home at superfast speeds. When the data reaches your house, it's converted to electrical pulses that transmit digital signals your computer can "read."

What are the advantages of fiber-optic service? One of the main benefits of FiOS is its speed. Verizon claims that speeds delivered over FiOS lines can reach 30 Mbps. This is a huge improvement over traditional cable and DSL service. The higher speeds achieved with FiOS lines can enable users to download full-length movies in just a few minutes. Most providers offer several packages of varying speed and costs, and they can be bundled with TV and phone services.

Are there disadvantages to fiber-optic service? Right now, for the fastest transmission speeds, cost might be the main disadvantage. For data transmission speeds of 30 Mbps, the cost can be expensive. Also, because fiber-optic lines must be laid in place before service is available, the service is available only in select areas. The first town to go with fiber-optic was Keller, Texas, in 2004. Since then, fiber-optic has become available to parts of many East and West Coast areas.

Satellite

What is satellite all about? Satellite Internet is another way to connect to the Internet. Most people choose satellite Internet when other high-speed options are unavailable. To take advantage of satellite Internet, you need a satellite dish, which is placed outside your home and connected to your computer with coaxial cable, the same type of cable used for cable TV. Data from your computer is transmitted between your personal satellite dish and the satellite company's receiving satellite dish by a satellite that sits in a geosynchronous orbit thousands of miles above the Earth.

What are the advantages of satellite Internet connections? Because several major telecommunications companies maintain satellites in orbit above the equator, almost anyone in the United States can receive satellite service. This makes it a particularly popular choice for those who live in rural areas where neither cable nor DSL service is available.

Are there any drawbacks to satellite? Unfortunately, limitations to this service do apply. Because it takes longer for data to be transferred with satellite broadband than with cable or DSL, this type of connection is not best for such Internet uses as online gaming and online securities trading. In addition, because download transmissions are not "wired," but rather are sent as radio waves, the strength and reliability of the signal are more vulnerable to interference. Last, if you live in North America, your satellite dish must face south for the best line of sight to the satellites circling the Earth's equator. If high buildings, mountains, or other tall objects obstruct your southern exposure, then your signal may be blocked. Unfavorable weather conditions also can block or interfere with the satellite transmission signal.

Wireless

Why is wireless Internet access necessary? In our ever mobile lifestyles, accessing the Internet wirelessly can make our lives more productive, and perhaps a bit more fun, while away from our desk. Students can send instant messages to each other across campus, and business travelers can quickly grab their e-mail between flights while eating a hamburger or sipping a mocha frappuccino. At home, wireless networks allow us to share an Internet connection and print from our notebooks from any room without having to attach and detach wires.

How does one access the Internet wirelessly? To access the Internet wirelessly, you need to be in a wireless fidelity (WiFi) hot spot and have the right equipment on your mobile device. Most notebooks, PDAs, game systems, and MP3 players sold in the past several years come equipped with a network interface card, but if your notebook does not have wireless capability built in, several wireless adapters are available that can fit into the PC card slot or a USB port.

It's simple to set up a wireless network at home (see Chapter 7 for details), and most businesses and schools and many public places such as airports, libraries, bookstores, and restaurants offer WiFi. WiFi411 (**www.wifi411.com**) will help you locate a hot spot wherever you are planning to go. Some public places offer free access to WiFi, but many others require you buy wireless access through a wireless access service plan. For example, McDonald's provides WiFi access through AT&T, and Starbucks provides WiFi through T-Mobile. To access these WiFi services you can pay for a single session or a monthly membership, or you can sign up for a longer-term subscription in which you are billed monthly.

If you need to access the Internet wirelessly but will not be in a location with a convenient WiFi hot spot, then you can also purchase an **aircard** such as the one shown in Figure 3.32. Aircards are devices that enable users to have wireless Internet access with mobile devices such as PDAs and notebooks. They require a service plan like your cell phone plan. When considering purchasing an aircard and service plan, be sure to check the coverage and costs before deciding because they can vary among the different providers.

What are concerns with wireless? Most public hot spots are unsecured, so caution should be used when accessing the Internet from public locations. Although casually surfing the Internet is fine, it's best not to use your credit card, for example, to purchase items online from a pubic hot spot as the credit card information can be captured by a lurking identity thief. See additional information on wireless security in Chapter 7.

DIAL-UP CONNECTIONS

How does a dial-up connection work? A dial-up connection is the least costly method of connecting to the Internet, needing only a standard phone line and a modem. A **dial-up modem** is a device that converts (*mod*ulates) the digital signals the computer understands to the analog signals that can travel over phone lines. In turn, the computer on the other end also must have a modem to translate (*dem*odulate) the received analog signal back to a digital signal that the receiving computer can understand.

Modern desktop computers generally come with internal modems built into the system unit. Notebooks today usually have internal modems; if not, then small credit card–sized devices called **PC cards** (sometimes called **PCMCIA cards**) can be inserted into a special slot on the notebook.

What are the advantages of a dial-up Internet connection? A dial-up connection is the least costly way to connect to the Internet. Although slower than broadband connections, dial-up connections are often fine for casual Internet users who do not need a fast connection.

What are the disadvantages of dial-up? In a word: speed. Dial-up modems have a maximum data transfer rate that is at least five times slower than a basic broadband connection. Web pages can take a long time to load, especially if they contain multimedia, which is the norm for most Web pages today. Similarly, if you visit many Web sites at the same time or receive or send large files through e-mail, then you'll find that a dial-up connection is especially slow. Another disadvantage of dial-up

FIGURE 3.32

Aircards like the one pictured here fit into the PC card slot on your notebook to allow you to access the Internet wirelessly, even without having access to a WiFi hot spot.

FIGURE 3.33 Comparing Cable, DSL, and Fiber-Optic Internet Connection Options

	DSL	Cable	Fiber-Optic
Maximum upload speeds	Average speeds of 1.5 Mbps, with a maximum of 6+ Mbps	Average speeds of 3 Mbps, with a maximum of 12+ Mbps	Average speeds of 20 Mbps, with a maximum speed of 30 Mbps
Pros	Lets you surf the Net and talk on the same phone line simultaneously.	Speeds are not dependent on distance from central office.	Increased speeds. Service is not shared or dependent on distance from central office.
Cons	Speed drops as you get farther from phone company's central office.	Line shared with others in neighborhood; speeds may vary.	Cost, although this is a diminishing concern as the technology continues to be deployed and accepted.
	Not every phone line will work; no easy way to find out if yours will.	May require professional installation if cable not already present.	Not available in all areas.

Note: The data transfer rates listed in this table are approximations. As technologies improve, so do data transfer rates.

is that when you're on the Internet, you tie up your phone line if you don't have a separate line.

CHOOSING THE RIGHT INTERNET CONNECTION OPTION

How do I choose which Internet connection option is best for me? In 2007 approximately half of all U.S. households connected to the Internet used some form of broadband connection. If you are thinking about making the switch to broadband, then you might not have the luxury of a choice between services. Many areas will have access to only one type of service.

One factor to consider in choosing the right Internet connection is speed. **Data transfer rate** is the measurement of how fast data travels between computers. It is also informally referred to as *connection speed.* For example, dial-up modems have a maximum data transfer rate of 56 kilobits per second (Kbps, usually referred to as 56K). A kilobit is 1,000 bits and is normally used to represent the amount of data that is transferred in 1 second between two telecommunication points. Satellite Internet is about 10 times faster than dial-up but is still significantly slower than DSL and cable. Although DSL is catching up, cable wins out over DSL for speed. However,

the availability of fiber-optic service through DSL providers increases download rates to as high as 30 Mbps.

Finally, you may also need to consider which other services you want bundled into your payment, such as phone or TV. The table in Figure 3.33 compares several features of cable, DSL, and fiber-optic to help you with your decision.

Finding an Internet Service Provider

After you have chosen the method by which you'll connect to the Internet, you need a way to access the Internet. **Internet service providers (ISPs)** are national, regional, or local companies that connect individuals, groups, and other companies to the Internet. EarthLink, for example, is a well-known national ISP.

As mentioned earlier, the Internet is a network of networks, and the central component of the Internet network is the Internet backbone, or the main pathway of high-speed communications lines through which all Internet traffic flows. Large communications companies such as AT&T, Qwest, and Sprint are backbone providers that control access to the main lines of the Internet backbone. These backbone providers supply Internet access to ISPs, which, in turn, supply access to other users.

Where do I find an ISP? If you have a broadband connection, then your broadband provider *is* your ISP. If you're accessing the Internet from a dial-up connection, you need to determine which ISPs are available in your area. Look in the phone book, check ads in the newspaper, or ask friends which ISP they use. In addition, you can go to sites such as **www.thelist.com** or **www.all-free-isp.com** for listings of national and regional dial-up ISPs.

The Future of the Internet

Certainly, the Internet of the future will have more bandwidth and offer increased services. One thing is certain: Because of the prevalence of wireless technologies, the Internet will be more accessible, and we will become more dependent on it. With the increase of commerce and communication activities dominating the Internet, the concern is that there will be no bandwidth left for one of the Internet's original purposes: exchange of scientific and academic research. Two major projects currently under way in the United States to develop advanced technologies for the Internet are the large scale networking (LSN) program and Internet2.

What are the large scale networking and Internet2 programs? Out of a project titled the Next Generation Internet (which ended in 2002), the U.S. government created the **large scale networking (LSN)** program. LSN's aim is to fund the research and development of cutting-edge networking and wireless technologies and to increase the speed of networks.

The **Internet2** is an ongoing project sponsored by more than 200 universities (supported by government and industry partners) to develop new Internet technologies and disseminate them as rapidly as possible to the rest of the Internet community. The Internet2 backbone supports extremely high-speed communications (up to 9.6 gigabits per second, or Gbps) and provides an excellent testing area for new data transmission technologies. It is hoped that the Internet2 will solve the major problem plaguing the current Internet: lack of bandwidth. Once the Internet2 is fully integrated with the current Internet, greater volumes of information should flow more smoothly.

How else will the Internet become a more integral part of our lives? As this chapter explained, the Internet is already an integral part of our lives. It is the way we communicate, shop, research, entertain, and express ourselves. Many of the tools on the Web that have been described in this chapter—social networking sites, wikis, podcasts, and user content databases such as YouTube (for videos) and Flikr (for photos)—are part of a new wave of Web-based services that emphasize online collaboration and sharing among users. These and more services have been collectively referred to as **Web 2.0**. The future Internet will continue to evolve with more Web-based applications driven by user input, interaction, and content.

In the future, you can expect to use the Internet to assist you with many day-to-day tasks that you now do manually. No longer will PCs and mobile devices be our primary access to the Internet. We can already see the convergence of the Internet with the telephone, television, and gaming devices.

As other less obvious Internet-enabled devices become popular and more accessible to the common consumer, our lives will become more Internet dependent. For example, Internet-enabled appliances and household systems are now available that allow your home virtually to run itself. Today, there are refrigerators that can monitor their contents and go online to order more diet soda when they detect that the supply is getting low. Meanwhile, Internet heating and cooling systems can monitor weather forecasts and order fuel deliveries when supplies run low or bad weather is expected. These appliances will become more widespread as the price of equipment drops.

The uses for the Internet are limited only by our imaginations and the current constraints of technology. At some point, the Internet will no longer be a place we "go" to, but truly an integral part of our lives.

1. What is the origin of the Internet?

The Internet is the largest computer network in the world, connecting millions of computers. Government and military officials developed the Internet as a reliable means of communications in the event of war. Eventually, scientists and educators used the Internet to exchange research. Today, we use the Internet and the Web (which is a part of the Internet) to shop, research, communicate, and entertain ourselves.

2. How can I communicate through the Internet?

Communication was one of the reasons the Internet was developed and is one of the primary uses of the Internet today. E-mail allows users to communicate electronically without the parties involved being available at the same time, whereas chat rooms are public areas on the Web in which different people communicate. Blogs are journal entries posted to the Web that are generally organized by a topic or area of interest and are publicly available. Instant messaging enables you to communicate in real time with friends who are also online. Listservs are electronic mailings to groups of people, and newsgroups are online discussion forums in which people post messages and read and reply to messages from other newsgroup members. Both listservs and newsgroups are organized by topic or areas of interest. Listservs are private, whereas newsgroups are public.

3. What are the various kinds of multimedia files found on the Web, and what software do I need to use them?

The Web is appealing because of its enriched multimedia content. Multimedia is anything that involves one or more forms of media in addition to text, including graphics, audio, and video clips. Sometimes you need a special software program called a *plug-in* (or *player*) to view and hear multimedia files. Plug-ins are often installed in new computers or are offered free of charge at manufacturers' Web sites.

4. What is e-commerce, and what e-commerce safeguards protect me when I'm online?

E-commerce is the business of conducting business online. E-commerce includes transactions between businesses (B2B), between consumers (C2C), and between businesses and consumers (B2C). Because more business than ever before is conducted online, numerous safeguards have been put in place to ensure that transactions are protected.

5. How do I manage online annoyances, such as spam?

The Web is filled with annoyances such as spam, pop-ups, cookies, spyware, and scams such as phishing that make surfing the Web frustrating and sometimes dangerous. Software tools help to prevent or reduce spam, adware, and spyware, while exercising caution can prevent serious harm being done because of phishing and other Internet scams and hoaxes.

6. What is a Web browser?

Once you're connected to the Internet, in order to locate, navigate to, and view Web pages, you need special software called a *Web browser* installed on your system. The most common Web browsers are Microsoft Internet Explorer, Mozilla Firefox, and Safari.

7. What is a URL, and what are its parts?

You gain access to a Web site by typing in its address or Uniform Resource Locator (URL). A URL is composed of several parts, including the protocol, the domain, the top-level domain, and, occasionally, paths (or subdirectories).

8. How can I use hyperlinks and other tools to get around the Web?

One unique aspect of the Web is that you can jump from place to place by clicking on specially formatted pieces of text or images called *hyperlinks*. You can also use tools such as Back and Forward buttons, History

lists, breadcrumb lists, and Favorites or Bookmarks to navigate the Web.

9. How do I search the Internet using search engines and subject directories?

A search engine is a set of programs that searches the Web using specific keywords you wish to query and then returns a list of the Web sites on which those keywords are found. Search engines can be used to search for images, podcasts, and videos in addition to traditional text-based Web content. A subject directory is a structured outline of Web sites organized by topic and subtopic. Metasearch engines search other search engines.

10. How do I evaluate a Web site?

Not all Web sites are equal, and some are better sources for research than others. To evaluate whether it is appropriate to use a Web site as a resource, determine whether the author of the site is reputable and whether the site is intended for your particular needs. In addition, make sure that the site content is not biased, the information in the site is current, and all the links on the site are available and appropriate.

11. How does data travel on the Internet?

A computer connected to the Internet acts as either a client (a computer that asks for information) or a server (a computer that receives the request and returns the information to the client). Data travels between clients and servers along a system of communication lines or pathways. The largest and fastest of these pathways is the Internet backbone. To ensure that data is sent to the correct computer along the pathways, IP addresses (unique ID numbers) are assigned to all computers connected to the Internet.

12. What are my options for connecting to the Internet?

Home users have many options for connecting to the Internet. A dial-up connection, in which you connect to the Internet using a standard phone line, was at one time the standard way to connect to the Internet. Now other connection options called *broadband connections* are faster and will soon make dial-up a legacy connection technology. Broadband connections include cable, DSL, and satellite. Fiber-optic service is being deployed in select areas around the country and will become a standard of Internet delivery in the near future. WiFi allows users to connect to the Internet wirelessly.

13. How do I choose an Internet service provider?

Internet service providers (ISPs) are national, regional, or local companies that connect individuals, groups, and other companies to the Internet. Factors to consider in choosing an ISP include cost, quality of service, and availability.

14. What will the Internet of the future look like?

The Internet of the future will have higher bandwidth and will be able to provide additional services as a result of projects such as the large scale networking program and Internet2. The Internet will become more ingrained into our daily lives as Internet-enabled appliances and household systems will provide more remote-control features for our homes.

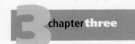

Key Terms

Buzzwords

Word Bank

- AOL
- Bookmark
- breadcrumb list
- browser
- buddy list
- cable modem

- cookies
- dial-up
- DSL
- hyperlink
- instant messaging
- keyword

- Internet service provider
- satellite
- search engine
- spam
- subject directory
- URLs

Instructions: Fill in the blanks using the words from the Word Bank above.

The day finally arrived when Juan no longer was a victim of slow Internet access through a traditional (1) _____ connection. He could finally hook up to the Internet through his new high-speed (2) _____. He had been investigating broadband access for awhile and thought that connecting through his existing phone lines with (3) _____ would be convenient. Unfortunately, it was not available in his area. Where Juan lives, a clear southern exposure does not exist, so he did not even entertain the idea of a (4) _____ connection.

Juan was looking forward to the speedy access provided by the cable company, his new (5) _____, but he was faced with the need to change his e-mail from (6) _____, his old ISP, because he didn't want to pay for duplicate services. Although he needed to change his e-mail address, he was glad he didn't have to give up instant messaging because his (7) _____ of online contacts had grown to be quite extensive. With the new speed of his broadband connection, Juan especially liked being able to quickly scan the Internet with Firefox, his preferred (8) _____.

Juan clicked on his list of favorite Web sites and found the movie review site he had saved as a (9) _____ the day before. He prefers to use this browser feature rather than entering in the (10) _____ of the sites he visits often. Juan navigated through the site, clicking on the (11) _____ that took him immediately to the page he was most interested in. Finding the movie he wanted to see, Juan ordered tickets online. The account information he input during an earlier visit to the site automatically appeared. In this case, Juan is glad that Web sites use (12) _____ to capture such information.

Then, using the (13) _____ at the top of the Web site, he traced his steps back to his starting point. Juan next typed in the address for Google, his preferred (14) _____, and typed the (15) _____ to begin his search for a good restaurant in the area.

Becoming Computer Literate

Using keywords from the chapter, write a letter to your local cable company imploring it to bring cable modem service to your neighborhood. In the letter, include your dissatisfaction with dial-up as well as your opinion on why cable is better than satellite and DSL, which are currently being offered in your neighborhood. Also include the activities on the Internet you think people in the community could benefit from by using high-speed cable access.

Instructions: Answer the multiple-choice and true–false questions below for more practice with key terms and concepts from this chapter.

MULTIPLE CHOICE

1. Which one of the following statements is NOT true about instant messaging?
   a. It is a popular form of communication.
   b. You communicate in real time.
   c. More than two people can IM at the same time.
   d. Unlike e-mail, IM is good for private conversations.

2. When you are shopping online, which of the following does NOT indicate that you have a secure connection?
   a. A closed padlock icon in the status bar.
   b. The URL begins with *https*.
   c. The word "secure" in the title bar.
   d. The VeriSign seal on the Web page.

3. With a podcast, you can
   a. subscribe to video and audio content.
   b. have the most recent content "delivered" automatically.
   c. play the video and audio content on an MP3 player.
   d. All of the above.

4. A Web page that enables online collaboration is
   a. a podcast.   b. a wiki.
   c. a blog.   d. an IM chat.

5. Which of the following is annoying, but really doesn't render any harm to your computer?
   a. Viruses   b. Spyware
   c. Sneakware   d. Malware

6. One scam that lures Internet users into revealing personal information is
   a. malware.   b. phishing.
   c. spam.   d. Internet hoax.

7. When searching the Internet, which of the following is true?
   a. It doesn't matter which search engine you use; they all provide the same results.
   b. A subject directory is best to use when you can provide keywords.
   c. Boolean operators and advanced search pages will help to narrow your results.
   d. Search engines are best to use when you need to narrow the search by specific topics.

8. In the Web address **http://www.irs.gov**, which part is considered the top-level domain?
   a. www   b. .gov
   c. http   d. www.irs.gov

9. Which of the following provides the fastest broadband Internet connection by transmitting data at the speed of light?
   a. Cable   b. DSL
   c. Fiber-optics   d. Satellite

10. The primary disadvantage to cable Internet access is that the quality and effectiveness of the service
   a. are affected by the number of users on the same cable line at any time.
   b. depend on your proximity to a phone company central office.
   c. can be affected by adverse weather conditions.
   d. depend on the Internet service provider you select.

TRUE–FALSE

_____ 1. The Web and the Internet are interchangeable terms.

_____ 2. DSL service is not affected by the number of users on the line at the same time.

_____ 3. Because Google generates the most search results of any of the search engines, it is called a metasearch engine.

_____ 4. Cookies store personal information to help customize Web pages for users.

_____ 5. You cannot connect to the Internet wirelessly unless you're in a WiFi hot spot.

Making the Transition to... Next Semester

1. Online Support Facilities

Your school most likely has many online support facilities. Do you know what they are? Go to your school's Web site and search for online support.

a. Is online tutoring available?
b. Can you reserve a book from the library online?
c. Can you register for classes online?
d. Can you take classes online?
e. Can you buy books online?

2. Plagiarism Policies

Does your school have a plagiarism policy?

a. Search your school's Web site to find the school's plagiarism policy. What does it say?
b. How well do you paraphrase? Find some Web sites that help test or evaluate your paraphrasing skills.

3. Advanced Web Searches

Using search engines effectively is an important tool. Some search engines help you with Boolean-type searches using advanced search forms. Choose your favorite search engine and select the advanced search option. (If your favorite search engine does not have an advanced search feature, then try Yahoo! or Google.)

a. Conduct a search for inexpensive vacation spots for spring break using Boolean search terms. Record your results along with your search queries.
b. Conduct the same search but this time use the advanced search form with your favorite search engine. Were the results the same? If there were any differences, what were they? Which was the best search method to use in this case, and why?

4. Free Speech Online

Jeanne was suspended from school for several days because her posts on MySpace about her teacher and a few of her classmates were "vulgar" and "derogatory." Tom was expelled from his school because the picture he posted of himself was in violation of his school's code of conduct. Similarly, Bill, a local employer, changed his mind about a job offer to a recent graduate after seeing questionable content on the candidate's Facebook.com page.

a. Should a person be penalized for his or her content on any Web site?
b. Is the issue denial of free speech or prudent reactions to improper behavior?

5. Using Web 2.0 in Education

Social networking sites, blogs, wikis, and file sharing sites are commonly referred to as "Web 2.0," the "second generation" of the Internet. These sites offer opportunities for collaboration, creativity, and enterprise. Describe how Web 2.0 sites such as Wikipedia, YouTube, and Digg might change how you learn and manage information.

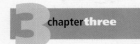

Making the Transition to... the Workplace

1. **Online Résumé Resources**

   Using a search engine, locate several Web resources that offer assistance in writing a résumé. For example, the University of Minnesota (**http://www1.umn.edu/ohr/careerdev/ resources/resume**) has a résumé tutor that guides you as you write your résumé.

   a. What other Web sites can you find that help you write a résumé?
   b. Do these sites all offer the same services and have the same features?

2. **Online Cover Letter Resources**

   Your résumé will need to be accompanied by a cover letter. Research Web sites that offer advice for and samples of cover letters.

   a. Which Web sites do you feel offer the best advice on how to write a cover letter? Which style cover letter works best for you?
   b. What do the Web sites say you should include in your cover letter, and why?

3. **Evaluating Web Content**

   You have noticed that your co-workers are using the Internet to conduct research. However, they are not careful about checking the validity of the Web sites they find before using the information.

   a. Research the Internet for Web site evaluation guidelines. Print out your sources and findings.
   b. Using the material from step a, create a scorecard or set of guidelines that will help others determine whether a Web site is reliable.

4. **Internet Connection Option**

   Now that you've graduated, you are planning to move into your first apartment and leave behind the comforts of broadband access at the residence halls. Evaluate the Internet options available in your area.

   a. Create a table that includes information on cable Internet, DSL, and satellite broadband service providers, as well as dial-up ISPs. The table should include the name of the provider, the cost of the service, the upload and download transfer rates, and the installation costs (service and parts). Also include whether a Web-based e-mail account will be available. Include the URL of each ISP or broadband service provider's Web site.
   b. Based on the table you create, write a brief paragraph describing which service you would choose and why.

5. **Internet Connection Speed**

   You would like to know how fast your Internet connection speed is. Your co-worker in the information technology (IT) department recommended that you check out **www. bandwidthplace.com** and **www.pcpitstop.com**.

   a. Choose one of the recommended sites and test your connection speed. How is the test conducted? What is used to measure the connection speed?
   b. List reasons why you would be interested in measuring your Internet connection speed.

6. **E-Mail Privacy**

   Take a moment to think about this statement: An e-mail is no more private than a postcard.

   a. Search the Web for resources that can help you support and oppose the preceding statement. Print out sources for both sides of the argument.
   b. Write a paragraph that summarizes your position.

Critical Thinking Questions

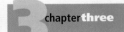

Instructions: Albert Einstein used *Gedanken experiments*, or critical thinking questions, to develop his theory of relativity. Some ideas are best understood by experimenting with them in our own minds. The following critical thinking questions are designed to demand your full attention but require only a comfortable chair—no technology.

1. Internet and Society

The Internet was initially created in part to enable scientists and educators to share information quickly and efficiently. The advantages the Internet brings to our lives are evident, but does Internet access also cause problems?

a. What advantages and disadvantages does the Internet bring to your life?
b. What positive and negative effects has the Internet had on our society as a whole?
c. Some people argue that conducting searches on the Internet provides answers but does not inspire thoughtful research. What do you think?
d. Should use of the Internet be banned, or at least limited, for research projects in schools? Why or why not?

2. File-Swapping Ethics

Downloading free music, movies, and other electronic media from the Internet, although illegal, still occurs by using sites such as Limewire and Bit Torrents.

a. What's your opinion on having the ability to download free music files of your choice? Do you think the musicians who oppose online music sharing have made valid points?
b. Discuss the differences you see between sharing music files online and sharing CDs with your friends.
c. The current price to buy a song online is about $1. Is this a fair price? If not, what price would you consider to be fair?

3. The Power of Google

Google is the largest and most popular search engine on the Internet today. Because of its size and popularity, some people claim that Google has enormous power to influence a Web user's search experience solely by its Web site ranking processes. What do you think about this potential power? How could it be used in negative or harmful ways?

a. Some Web sites pay search engines to list them near the top of the results pages. These sponsors therefore get priority placement. What do you think of this policy?
b. What effect (if any) do you think that Google has on Web site development? For example, do you think Web site developers intentionally include frequently searched words in their pages so that they will appear in more hits lists?
c. When you "google" someone, you type their name in the Google search box to see what comes up. What privacy concerns do you think such "googling" could present? Have you ever "googled" yourself or your friends?

4. Charging for E-Mail?

Should there be a charge placed on sending e-mail or on having IM conversations? What would be an appropriate charge? If a charge was placed on e-mail and IM conversations, what would happen to their use?

5. Internet and Politics

What role has and will the Internet play in political campaigns? Do you see the day when voting will happen through the Internet? Why or why not?

Team Time Comparing Internet Search Methods

Problem:

With millions of sites on the Internet, finding useful information can be a daunting—and at times, impossible—task. However, there are methods to make searching easier, some of which have been discussed in this chapter. In this Team Time, each team will search for specific items or pieces of information on the Internet and compare search methodologies.

Process:

Split your group into three or more teams, depending on class size. Each group will search for the same items.

Search Items:

1. What was America's first penny candy to be individually wrapped?

2. At which fraternity and which college was the movie *Animal House* based?

3. What were the previous names for the American League baseball team the Los Angeles Angels of Anaheim?

4. What is the cheapest price to purchase a copy of the latest version of Microsoft Office Professional?

5. What are Kingda Ka and Son of Beast, and what do they have in common?

Process:

1. Teams are positioned at computers connected to the Internet.

2. Each team is given the list of search items. Each team should use a different search strategy from the following list: (1) use only a subject directory, (2) use only a search engine, or (3) use only the advanced search feature of a search engine. If more teams are allowed, you could also add a team that only uses a metasearch engine. Other than these restrictions, teams can use whichever search strategies they feel will best reach the desired goal with the most accuracy in the least amount of time.

3. Print the results from each search page. Teams compare printouts and notes to determine which search methods worked best for each item.

Conclusion:

Were subject directories better than search engines for certain searches? Which methods were used to narrow down choices? How were final answers determined?

Multimedia

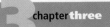

In addition to the review materials presented here, you'll find more materials featured with the book's multimedia, including the *Technology in Action* Student Resource CD and the Companion Website (**www.prenhall.com/techinaction**), which will help reinforce your understanding of the chapter content. These materials include the following:

ACTIVE HELPDESK

In Active Helpdesk calls, you'll assume the role of helpdesk operator, taking calls about the concepts you've learned in this chapter. You'll apply what you've learned and receive feedback from a supervisor to review and reinforce those concepts. The Active Helpdesk calls for this chapter are as follows and can be found on your Student Resource CD:

- Staying Secure on the Internet
- Getting Around the Web
- Using Subject Directories and Search Engines
- Connecting to the Internet

SOUND BYTES

Sound Bytes are dynamic multimedia tutorials that help demystify even the most complex topics. You'll view video clips and animations that illustrate computer concepts and then apply what you've learned by reviewing with the Sound Byte Labs, which include quizzes and activities specifically tailored to each Sound Byte. The Sound Bytes for this chapter are as follows and can be found on your Student Resource CD:

- Blogging
- Creating a Web-Based E-mail Account
- The Best Utilities for Your Computer
- Welcome to the Web
- Finding Information on the Web
- Connecting to the Internet

COMPANION WEBSITE

The *Technology in Action* Companion Website includes a variety of additional materials to help you review and learn more about the topics in this chapter. The resources available at **www.prenhall.com/techinaction** include:

- **Online Study Guide.** Each chapter features an online true–false and multiple-choice quiz. You can take these quizzes, automatically check the results, and e-mail the results to your instructor.
- **Web Research Projects.** Each chapter features several Web research projects that ask you to search the Web for information on computer-related careers, milestones in computer history, important people and companies, emerging technologies, and the applications and implications of different technologies.

TECHNOLOGY IN FOCUS

Computer Abuse

Security

Information Technology

ethics

In this Technology in Focus, we explore what ethics are, how your personal ethics develop, and how your personal ethics fit into the world around you. We'll also examine how technology and ethics affect each other and how technology can be used to support ethical conduct. Finally, we'll examine several key issues in technology ethics today, including the areas of social justice, intellectual property rights, privacy, Internet commerce, free speech, and computer abuse.

Gambling

Censorship

People speak of ethics—and the lack of ethics—casually all the time, but the ethical choices that individuals make is an extremely serious matter and can have a far-reaching impact. It is important to have a clear idea of what ethics are, what your personal ethics are, and how personal ethics fit into the world at large.

ETHICS IN COMPUTING

You just bought a new notebook computer. You know you can go to BitTorrent or Limewire to download the latest summer blockbuster movie and its soundtrack. You also probably know this is unethical. Although pirating music and videos is a valid example of unethical behavior, it has been overused as an illustration of the ethical challenges of technology. There is a vast range of ethical issues surrounding technology (as shown in Figure 1), several of which we will discuss in this section.

WHAT IS ETHICS?

Ethics is the study of the general nature of morals and of the specific moral choices made by individuals. Morals involve conforming to established or accepted ideas of right and wrong (as generally dictated by society) and are usually viewed as black and white. Ethics usually involves subtle distinctions such as fairness and equity; ethical values are the guidelines you use to make decisions each day. For example, the person in front of you at Starbucks drops a dollar on the floor and doesn't notice it. Do you tell him about it, or do you pick up the dollar and use it to pay for your coffee?

Doesn't everyone have the same basic ethics? There are many systems of ethical conduct. On one extreme is moral relativism, a theory that holds that there is no universal moral truth and that instead there are only beliefs, perspectives, and values. Everyone has his or her own ideas of right and wrong, and so who are we to judge anyone else? Another ethical philosophy is situational ethics, which states that decision making should be based on the circumstances of a particular situation and not on fixed laws.

Many other ethical systems have been proposed over time, some of which are defined by religious traditions. For example, the expression "Judeo-Christian ethics" refers to the common set of basic values shared across both Jewish and Christian religious traditions. These include behaviors such as respecting property and relationships, honoring one's parents, and being kind to others.

Don't some people behave with no ethics at all? Although many valid systems of ethical conduct exist, it is still true that sometimes people act in a manner that violates the beliefs they hold or the beliefs of the ethical system they say they follow. Unethical behavior can be defined as not conforming to a set of approved standards of social or professional behavior. For instance, using your phone to text message your friend during an exam is prohibited by most college rules of student conduct. This behavior is different from amoral behavior, when a person has no sense of right and wrong and no interest in the moral consequences of their actions.

PERSONAL ETHICS

What are personal ethics? Every day you say certain things and take specific actions, and at each point you are making decisions based on some criteria. It may be that you are trying to care for the people around you, or you are trying to eliminate a source of pain or anger in your life. Or your words and actions may be driven by a combination of criteria. As you choose your words and actions, you are following a set of personal ethics, a checklist of personal decisions you have compiled to organize your life. Some people have a clear, well-defined set of principles they follow. Others' ethics are inconsistent or are applied differently in similar situations.

It can be challenging to adhere to your own ethical system if the consequences of your decisions today might lead to an unhappy result for you in the short term.

FIGURE 1

Ethics in computing covers a wide range of areas, not just privacy and security.

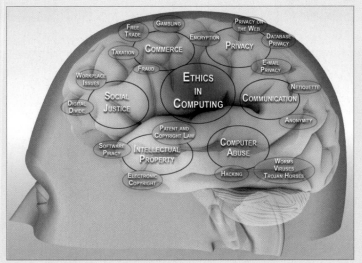

For instance, to get the job of your dreams, should you exaggerate a bit on your résumé and say you've already finished your college degree, even though you are still one credit short? Is this lying? Is such behavior justified in this setting? After all, you do intend to finish that last credit, and you would work really hard for this company if you were hired. If you tell the truth and state that you haven't finished college yet, then you might be passed over for the position. Making this choice is an ethical decision (see Figure 2).

How do a person's ethics develop?
Many elements contribute to your ethical development (see Figure 3). Naturally, your family has a major impact in establishing the values you cherish in your own life, and these might include a cultural bias toward certain moral positions. Your religious affiliation is another major influence in your ethical life because most religions have established specific codes of ethical conduct. How these sets of ethics interact with the values of the larger culture is often challenging. Issues such as abortion, the death penalty, or war all force confrontations between personal ethical systems and the larger society's established legal ethical system.

As you mature, your life experiences also affect your personal ethics. Does the behavior you see around you make sense within the ethical principles that your family, your church, or your first-grade teacher taught you? Has your experience led you to abandon some ethical rules while adopting others? Have you modified how and when you apply these laws of conduct, depending on what is at stake?

FIGURE 2
It would be nice if there were signposts to ethical conduct, but the issues are complex.

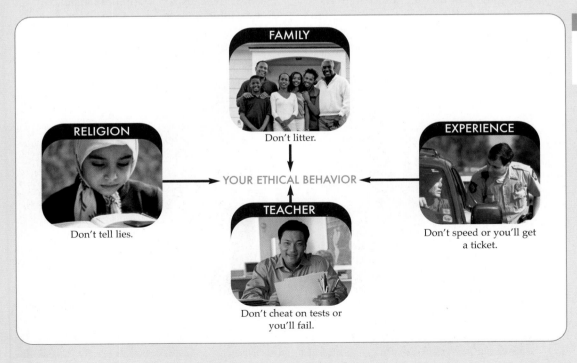

FIGURE 3
Many different forces shape your ethical worldview.

FAMILY
Don't litter.

RELIGION
Don't tell lies.

YOUR ETHICAL BEHAVIOR

EXPERIENCE
Don't speed or you'll get a ticket.

TEACHER
Don't cheat on tests or you'll fail.

What if I'm not sure what my personal ethics are? When you have a clear and firm idea of what values are most important to you, it may be easier to handle situations in your professional and your personal life that demand ethical action. Follow these steps to help define your personal ethics:

1. **Describe yourself.** Write down a description of who you are based on how others view you. Would a friend describe you as honest or helpful or kind?

2. **List your beliefs.** Make a list of all the beliefs that influence your decision making. For example, would you be okay with working as a research assistant in a lab that infected dogs with diseases to use them for medical research? How important is it to you that you never speak a lie? Consider whether your answers to each of these questions are "flexible." Are there situations where your answers might change (say, if a friend was ill or in danger)?

3. **Identify external influences.** Consider the places you work and live and how you relate to the people you see during the day. Are there things that you would like to change about these relationships that would involve listing them in a code of ethics?

4. **Consider "why."** After writing down your beliefs, think about why you believe them. Have you accepted them without investigation, or do they stand up to the test of real-world experiences in your life? Which of these values are worthy of short-term sacrifice in order to uphold your beliefs?

5. **Prepare a statement of values.** It can be useful to distill what you have written into a short list. By having a well-defined statement of the values you hold most important in your own life that you can refer to in times of challenge, it will be easier for you to make ethical decisions.

Are there tangible benefits to ethical living? Society has established its own set of rules of conduct as laws. Ignoring or being inconsistent in following these principles can surely have an immediate impact. Whether it is complying with a law that affects the way your business is run or with a law that impacts your personal life (don't exceed the speed limit or you'll receive a fine), decision-making principles that work with society's legal boundaries can make your life much simpler.

More and more research is showing the health benefits of ethical living. When your day-to-day decisions are in conflict with the values you consider most important as a human being, you often develop stress and anger. Constant conflict between what you value and what actions you are forced to take can lead to a variety of mental and physical damages.

Perhaps even happiness itself is a result of living ethically (see Figure 4). "Positive psychology" is a new focus in the field of psychology. Pioneered by Dr. Martin Seligman of the University of Pennsylvania, this field works to discover the causes of happiness instead of addressing the treatment of mental dysfunctions. Dr. Seligman's research has shown that, by identifying your personal strengths and values and by aligning your life so that you

FIGURE 4

The field of positive psychology shows that living and working ethically affects your happiness.

Cheating
Stealing
Selfish
Lying

Generosity
Honesty
Trust

can apply them every day, you can experience an increase in happiness (and a decrease in depression) equivalent to the effects of antidepressant medication and therapy. So, finding a way to identify and then apply your ethics and values to your daily life has an impact on your health and happiness.

PERSONAL ETHICS IN THE WORLDVIEW

How do my personal ethics fit into the world at large? All of your actions, words, and even thoughts are controlled by your personal ideas of right and wrong. But do your ethics shift when you go to work? Your responsibility at work is to follow the ethics that the owner has established for the business. Although each person at your workplace may be trying to follow the corporate ethical guidelines, each person will follow them differently based on his or her personal ethics. Person A may feel it is acceptable to tell white lies to get his project more funding, whereas Person B might believe that telling the truth at all times is the only and best way that she can foster teamwork and cooperation to get a project completed. But overall, when dealing in a business environment, your ethics are guided by the ethical principles that are defined by the business owner or management.

How do employers affect personal ethics? Should your boss have control (or even input) about your conduct outside of the office? Do behavior, integrity, and honesty off the job relate to job performance? They might. But even if they don't, your actions could reflect poorly on your employer from your employer's perspective. Consider Ellen Simonetti, who was fired by Delta Airlines for blogging. Even though Ms. Simonetti never mentioned Delta Airlines by name on her blog (Queen of the Sky: Diary of a Dysfunctional Flight Attendant), Delta Airlines objected to photos that she posted of herself and fellow flight attendants in their Delta uniforms. Delta Airlines felt that the photos were inappropriate and portrayed negative images of Delta Airlines employees. Another example is Jillian Tomlinson, the Australian surgeon who was suspended by her employer for discussing medical procedures, the work environment, and fellow employees and for posting CAT scans of patients on her blog (although patient names were not revealed). So although your ethics might dictate one mode of behavior, you need to consider how your actions might be viewed by your employer (see Figure 5).

FIGURE 5

Is your boss watching you? Does that make you more or less inclined to behave ethically?

TECHNOLOGY AND ETHICS: HOW ONE AFFECTS THE OTHER

Technology is all around us and affects almost every aspect of our daily lives. Because technology moves faster than rules can be formulated to govern it, how technology is used is left up to the individual with the guidance of his personal ethics. In both good and bad ways, technology affects our community life, family life, work environment, education, and medical research, to name only a few areas of our lives.

Technology constantly challenges our ethics as individuals and as a society. In the rest of this Technology in Focus feature, we will explore the different relationships between technology and ethics. Specifically, we present different viewpoints of situations with regard to social justice, intellectual property (fair use), privacy, e-commerce (online gambling), electronic communication issues (free speech), and computer abuse (protection versus access) in which ethics and technology impact each other.

Ethical considerations are never black and white. They are complex, and reasonable people can have different valid views. We present alternative viewpoints of situations in which ethics and technology impact each other for you to consider and discuss. The table shown in Figure 6 summarizes these issues.

USING COMPUTERS TO SUPPORT ETHICAL CONDUCT

Although there are many opportunities to use computers and the Internet unethically, many more ways are available to use technology to support ethical conduct.

Many charitable organizations use the Internet for fund raising. When Hurricane Katrina struck the Gulf Coast in 2005, the American Red Cross (see Figure 7) and other charities supporting relief efforts used their Web pages to enable donors to quickly, easily, and securely make contributions to aid hurricane victims. Using technology to garner contributions enabled these charities to quickly raise more than $2.6 billion for relief efforts.

When you spot unethical behavior at your company, you need a fast, secure way to report it to the appropriate members of management. The Sarbanes-Oxley Act of 2002 requires companies to provide mechanisms for employees and third parties to report

FIGURE 6		
Ethics in Computing		
Topic	**Ethical Discussion**	**Debate Issue**
Social justice	Can technology be used to benefit everyone?	Does technology provide economic opportunity for all?
Intellectual property	What is fair about fair use?	What kind of fair use standards are beneficial?
Privacy	Is personal privacy a casualty of the modern age?	Should personal privacy be protected?
E-commerce	Is online gambling a problem?	Should online gambling be banned or regulated?
Electronic communication	When does big business limit free speech?	Did Google make the right choice in China?
Computer abuse	Does restricting online information protect children?	Is filtering or monitoring software helpful?

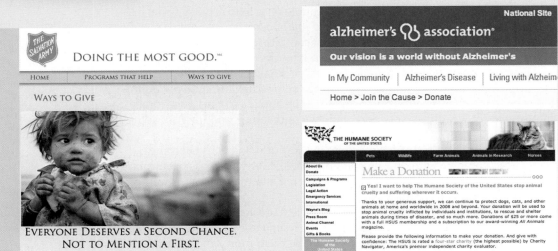

FIGURE 7

Most major charities facilitate donations through the Internet.

complaints, including ethics violations. And these mechanisms are required to provide the employees with anonymity. Many businesses are using their Web sites to allow whistleblowers to report wrongdoing anonymously, replacing their previous e-mail and telephone hotline systems that did not shield employees from being identified. With an electronic system, it is easier for a company to sort and classify complaints and designate them for appropriate action.

Electronic systems such as intranets and e-mail are also excellent mechanisms for informing employees about ethics policies. Storing ethics guidelines electronically on a company intranet ensures that employees have access to information whenever they need it. And by using e-mail, new policies or changes to existing policies can be quickly and efficiently communicated to employees.

Throughout your life, you will encounter many ethical challenges relating to information technology. Your personal ethics—combined with the ethical guidelines your company provides and the general ethical environment of society—will guide your decisions.

For further information on ethics, check out the following Web sites:

- **http://ethics.csc.ncsu.edu**
- **www.ethicscenter.net**
- **www.business-ethics.com**
- **www.business-ethics.org**

Can Technology Be Used to Benefit Everyone?

SUMMARY OF THE ISSUE

Does our society have a responsibility to use technology to help achieve social justice? Freeman Dyson, an American physicist and mathematician, has sparked discussion about this issue by saying that science is concentrating too much on "making toys for the rich" instead of addressing the necessities of the poor. One has the promise of great financial reward in creating an even smaller cellular phone, but one has little incentive to find solar energy solutions to help struggling rural communities. Dyson proposes that three technologies could be applied to turn poor rural areas into sources of wealth: solar energy, genetic engineering, and Internet access (see Figure 8).

Solar energy is available virtually anywhere in the world and could become cheap enough to compete with oil. The spiraling price of oil, which has been caused primarily by increased worldwide demand, has created a barrier against elevating poor rural communities above the poverty level.

Through genetic engineering, it might be possible to design new plants (or modify existing plants) to achieve novel biological processes such as converting sunlight into fuel efficiently. If plants could be engineered to make them more efficient sources of energy or provide other qualities in demand (such as being better sources of protein and fiber when consumed), rural residents would be able to produce items with high market demand and would have greater opportunities to increase their standard of living.

The Internet can help businesses and farms in remote areas become part of the modern economy. Currently, it is difficult for rural farmers in Third World countries to determine the best place to take their crops to market. By consulting the Internet, however, they could obtain price quotes for markets within their reach and determine which ones would provide the best prices for their crops.

QUESTIONS TO THINK ABOUT AND RESEARCH

1. Are the types of technology suggested by Dyson plausible or out of the reach of current scientific methods?

2. Would Dyson's suggested use of technology help people or spark social revolution?

3. What impact would a widespread distribution of solar-powered cell phones have on a country that lacks the infrastructure for telephone and electrical wires? Has any country ever experienced such a leap in technology in a short period of time?

4. Dyson was a winner of the Templeton Prize in 2000. What kind of award is the Templeton, and what was the basis for Dyson's selection?

POINT

Technology Provides Economic Opportunity for All

The advocates of Dyson's position maintain that a lack of technology or resources is not what keeps the majority of the world's population in poverty. Instead, they would argue that it is a lack of commitment and focus on the problem of social justice that allows poverty to continue.

1. If people all agree that poverty is unacceptable, the world possesses the technology and resources to eliminate it.

2. Technology can improve the quality of life of poor countries (and poor people in rich countries) if scientists and business leaders join together.

3. Technology can be an ethical force to humanize us, giving us the ability to deeply affect the lives of all. Francis Bacon, the 16th- and 17th-century English philosopher, once wrote that science can "endow the human family with new mercies."

COUNTERPOINT

Technology Doesn't Provide Economic Opportunity for All

Dyson's critics maintain that his suggestions on using technology for social change are impractical and cannot be achieved with the current resources. They even feel his plan might be dangerous inasmuch as it may have unforeseen scientific and political results.

1. No one can solve the problems of poverty. The proof is that it has never been done.

2. The problem of poverty is not an issue for technologists. It should be addressed by religious leaders, education experts, and politicians.

3. Genetic engineering may hold the promise of great benefits, but it should not be explored because of its potential risks.

4. Any move away from an oil-centered energy plan threatens the stability of the world economies.

 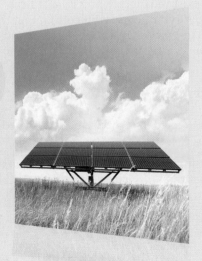 

FIGURE 8

Should technology focus on "toys for the rich" or the needs of the poor?

Intellectual Property

What Is Fair about Fair Use?

SUMMARY OF THE ISSUE

Intellectual property (such as music, writing, and art) is protected through copyright law. This means that creative works such as songs, video productions, television programs, and written manuscripts cannot be reproduced without the permission of the creator and usually not without payment to the copyright owner (see Figure 9).

Historically, the policy of fair use has allowed a range of exceptions to this copyright provision. Fair use is based on the belief that the public is entitled to freely use portions of copyrighted materials for certain purposes. If you wish to criticize a novelist, for example, under fair use, you have the freedom to quote a portion of the novelist's work without asking permission. Without this provision, copyright owners could prevent any negative comments about their work. Fair use decisions are guided by four criteria:

- What is the purpose of the fair use of the work (for example, is it a for-profit use or an educational use)?
- What is the nature of the proposed work (for example, will it be a published document or an unpublished product)?
- How much of the copyrighted material is being used?
- What is the effect of the fair use of the material (for example, would it decrease the number of copies of the original that would be sold)?

In this age of easy digital media creation and distribution, however, the interpretation of fair use is being questioned. For example, Kevin Ryan found himself at odds with Dr. Seuss Enterprises. He created a set of songs that imitated the style of Bob Dylan singing such Seuss classics as *Green Eggs and Ham* and *The Cat in the Hat.* He posted the MP3 files to a Web site, and soon bloggers found the songs and publicized them widely. A cease-and-desist letter from Dr. Seuss Enterprises for alleged copyright violations was issued quickly, and Ryan quickly removed the material from his Web site (**http://dylanhearsawho.com**) rather than enter into a potentially lengthy legal battle. So in today's fast-paced digital world, the question of the proper role of the fair use exclusion in copyright law may have to be reconsidered.

QUESTIONS TO THINK ABOUT AND RESEARCH

1. How should the four factors of fair use be interpreted in the age of electronic media distribution?

2. Can an online music reviewer post a song's audio to illustrate his criticism of the artist's album? Does that infringe on the artist's right to earn income from her work?

3. Should a documentary film maker be allowed to pull pieces of television interviews and organize them in a way that criticizes the person featured?

4. Should a parody of the original be allowed to quote or play sections of the original work? By its nature, a parody can be negative or mocking in tone. Does this invite too much criticism when made publicly available on the Internet?

POINT

Liberal Fair Use Standards Are Beneficial

Artists and critics will be silenced if they are forced to fear legal action every time they use a portion of copyrighted material. The aggressive—and expensive—style of enforcement that copyright holders now use limits the free expression of ideas that is a cornerstone of most democratic societies.

1. Allowing an open interpretation of fair use encourages a wide dissemination of information.

2. Creative work and open criticism together allow the flourishing of the most democratic, free society. If copyright owners can shut down the use of any part of their works, then they have too much control of the creative process of others.

3. Although the existing laws on fair use worked well in the past, they cannot cope with the widespread dissemination of information that is possible with the modern Internet.

COUNTERPOINT

Strict Fair Use Standards Are Beneficial

Guidelines for what defines fair use already exist. Because these guidelines have worked well to protect the interests of both the creators and users/critics, there is no need to modify them.

1. The existing laws on fair use have worked well for print media and do not need to be modified because of modern electronic distribution techniques.

2. The copyright holders are within their rights to be as aggressive as they wish in enforcing control of their own work. They should be allowed to set whatever licensing fee they wish. The artists or critics can still use the material but must be able to pay the licensing fee set.

FIGURE 9

The issues of intellectual property have become critical because all the media we produce has become digital.

Is Personal Privacy a Casualty of the Modern Age?

SUMMARY OF THE ISSUE

Like respect for others and being treated with dignity, privacy is a basic human right. But what exactly is privacy? Simply stated, privacy is the right to be left alone to do as one pleases. The idea of privacy is often associated with hiding something (a behavior, a relationship, or a secret). But privacy really means not being required to explain your behavior to others. With the advent of the digital society, however, is there any such thing as personal privacy (see Figure 10)? Like Hansel and Gretel, we leave a veritable trail of electronic breadcrumbs almost everywhere we go.

Debit and credit cards are fast replacing cash, and they leave records of our purchases at merchants and transactions at the bank. E-mail is fast replacing snail mail, so now your correspondence (and your secrets) may live on indefinitely in Web servers around the world. Have you visited a Web site lately? Chances are that the owner of that site kept track of what you looked at while you were visiting the site.

Can't we just modify our behavior to protect our privacy? We could, but a recent survey by the Ponemon Institute revealed that only about 7 percent of Americans are willing to change their behavior to protect privacy. Many people freely give up personal information (such as their name, address, and phone number) to obtain buyer loyalty cards that qualify them for discounts at supermarkets and pharmacies. And to obtain a discount on tolls and speed up their trips, many people sign up for electronic toll passes (which are actually RFID devices) that can be used to track where they have been at a specific point in time. Information gathered by these programs could then be used against you in a divorce case to prove you were a bad parent because you were routinely out in your car at 2 A.M. on school nights or because you bought mostly junk food at the supermarket. Although many Americans say they are concerned about a loss of privacy, few moves have been made in the United States to preserve privacy rights.

QUESTIONS TO THINK ABOUT AND RESEARCH

1. Is privacy protected by the U.S. Constitution? If it isn't currently protected, would you be willing to join a group that was working toward a constitutional amendment on privacy?

2. Which is more important to you: protecting the United States from potential terrorists by surrendering some personal privacy or keeping all of your personal privacy rights?

3. Should U.S. citizens have the right to access personal information collected about them by companies and make corrections if the information is erroneous? How would you manage such a process if you ran a company that collected this information?

POINT

Protect Personal Privacy

The advocates for protecting privacy in the United States argue that the right to privacy is a basic human right that should be afforded to everyone. As long as individuals aren't hurting anyone or breaking any laws, people should be entitled to do what they want without fear of being monitored.

1. If I'm not doing anything wrong, then you have no reason to watch me.

2. If the government is collecting information by watching citizens, it might misuse or lose control of the data.

3. By allowing the government to determine what behaviors are right and wrong, we open ourselves to uncertainty because the government may arbitrarily change the definition of which behaviors are unacceptable.

4. Requiring national ID cards is reminiscent of the former Nazi and Soviet regimes.

5. Implementing privacy controls (such as national ID cards) is extremely expensive and a waste of taxpayer funds.

COUNTERPOINT

Reduced Privacy Is a Fact of Modern Life

Advocates for stronger monitoring of private citizens usually cite national security concerns and the prevention of terrorist activities. Inconveniencing ordinary people who are doing nothing wrong is just a price that must be paid to ensure that society is free from malicious acts by a few malcontents.

1. If you aren't doing anything wrong, then you don't have anything to hide.

2. Electronic enhancements to identification documents are essential in the digital world we live in so that government agencies can more efficiently exchange information to enhance their detection and apprehension of suspected terrorists.

3. Laws protect citizens from being abused or taken advantage of by overzealous government officials who are involved in monitoring activities.

4. It is not possible to put a price on freedom or security; therefore, projects such as a national ID system are worth the cost of implementation.

FIGURE 10

Is personal privacy possible any longer?

Should Online Gambling Be Banned or Regulated?

SUMMARY OF THE ISSUE

Internet gambling is currently a multibillion-dollar industry. With wireless Internet connectivity increasingly available, online gambling via cell phones will make online gambling even more accessible. The basic online gambling activities are predominantly sports betting, casino games, the lottery, bingo, and poker (see Figure 11).

Internet gambling is already illegal in the United States. Legislation was passed in October 2006 to reinforce the prohibition of online gambling, yet it remains a viable and growing industry worldwide. Because there are no boundaries to the Internet and Internet activity, restrictive legislation cannot ban a user (the gambler) or a provider (the online casino, which is based outside the boundaries of the United States) but rather seeks punitive damages against those who promote the activity— namely, the financial intermediaries (banks and credit card companies)—thereby making it more difficult for an online Internet casino to operate. The debate remains whether such activity should continue to be banned altogether or whether it should be allowed to operate legally but under the regulated environment of the U.S. government.

Internet gambling's characteristics are unique, and advocates of both sides of this issue acknowledge the obvious concerns of online gambling. Online gambling, unlike gambling done in brick-and-mortar facilities, encourages gamblers to play 24 hours a day from home and facilitates addictive gambling. Betting with a credit card can undercut a player's perception of the value of cash, further leading to gambling addiction, bankruptcy, and crime. In addition, children may play without sufficient age verification.

QUESTIONS TO THINK ABOUT AND RESEARCH

1. What are the important differences between online and traditional gambling?

2. In what ways can Internet gambling businesses be used to facilitate other illegal activities?

3. How might the prohibition of online gambling be compared to the prohibition of alcohol in the United States in the 1920s?

4. Why is online gambling legalized in other countries, and how do those countries handle concerns voiced by opponents to legalized online gambling in the United States?

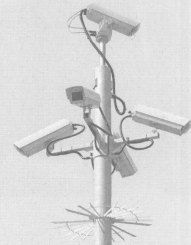

POINT

Ban Online Gambling

The advocates for continuing the ban on online gambling in the United States argue that thorough and extensive enforcement of the current prohibition would stop online gambling and hence eliminate the source of the problems.

1. Internet gambling is too easily accessible to minors and compulsive gamblers (brick-and-mortar casinos provide restrictions that help control access to minors and compulsive or addictive gamblers).

2. Offshore Internet gambling facilities could be used to support criminal activities such as illegal money laundering and identity theft.

3. Unlike physical gambling facilities, it is difficult to put controls in place to ensure that the operations are "honest"—for example, odds being unfairly tweaked in the favor of the "house" or money being collected from players but winnings never paid out.

4. Online gambling facilitates the hiding of gambling addiction from family members, thereby adding to the potential financial burden on families and society (through loss of jobs, homes, and marriages).

COUNTERPOINT

Legalize Online Gambling

Advocates for legalizing online gambling in the United States argue that legalizing it will bring it out of the underworld and place stricter controls on the industry. Enforced governmental regulations placed on current onsite gambling facilities could be applied to online sites and eliminate the source of the problems.

1. Current multibillion-dollar public online gambling companies exist outside the United States. Increased regulatory action would bring to light the legitimate organizations that can and do protect consumers, restrict access by minors, and protect those lured into gambling addiction. Enhanced regulation would make the illegitimate operations more difficult to operate.

2. Online gambling is "transparent"—every transaction is logged and available for scrutiny.

3. Regulation would standardize the industry and bring in tax revenues to the U.S. government.

4. Online gambling is regulated in 64 countries, including the United Kingdom.

5. Prohibiting online gambling would send it underground and leave the vulnerable unprotected.

6. It's much easier to regulate online activity than prohibit it.

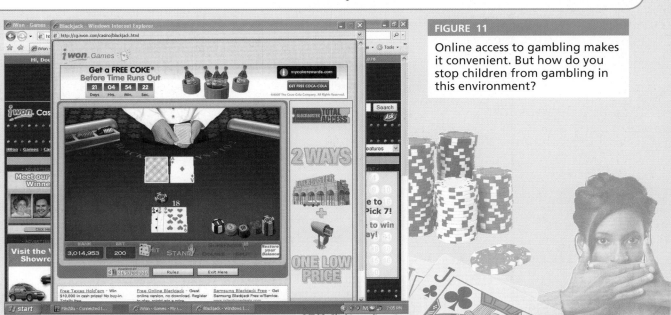

FIGURE 11

Online access to gambling makes it convenient. But how do you stop children from gambling in this environment?

Electronic Communication

When Does Big Business Limit Free Speech?

SUMMARY OF THE ISSUE

In early 2006, Google conceded to Beijing's demands that it self-censor its search engine. Google was following in the footsteps of other large U.S. high-tech companies that had previously collaborated with the Chinese government in suppressing dissent in return for access to the booming Chinese Internet market. Corporate America's definition of the price it is willing to pay to obtain Chinese business has stirred up a vigorous controversy. Google justified its decision by stating that when a company decides to do business, it must operate within the rules of that market.

Chinese policies include

- filters that block objectionable foreign Web sites,

- regulations that ban what the Chinese government considers subversive and pornographic content, and

- a requirement that the Internet service providers enforce government censorship.

How big is the Chinese Internet market? More than 172 million people in China are online, representing approximately 13 percent of the Chinese population. In comparison, 215 million people in the United States—90 percent of the U.S. population—are online. Thus, there is much room for expansion of Chinese access to the Internet. In fact, near the end of this decade, Chinese e-commerce is expected to have more Internet users than the United States. Google and others decided to give in to the government demands because otherwise they would lose out on a huge market. History has shown that many businesses will put monetary gain (for shareholders) over protecting basic human rights such as free speech (see Figure 12).

QUESTIONS TO THINK ABOUT AND RESEARCH

1. Does the presence of U.S. tech companies in China contribute to the overall expansion of access to information in China?

2. What kind of parallels can be drawn to the U.S. corporate response to apartheid in South Africa in the 1970s?

3. Can U.S. government action help by pressing U.S. concerns on censorship during talks with foreign governments?

POINT

Google Acted Unethically

Those who have protested Google's actions are those who fight for human rights at any level. They feel that Google's compliant behavior only condones China's censorship policies and continues to thwart the effort to promote human rights initiatives in China.

1. Google sacrificed free speech for business. This action violates human rights, international law, and corporate ethics.

2. Cooperating with China violates human rights.

3. If international businesses can't stand up to China, then how will China ever have the incentive to change?

4. Most other rights hang on the community's ability to have open discussions. Preventing that from happening is a serious assault on human rights.

5. If the policy were to make children work or to kill women, would the companies choose not to comply? Are human rights and the freedom of speech any different?

COUNTERPOINT

Google's Actions Were Justified

The advocates of Google's actions tend to be other businesses and those with large economic interests that can relate to Google's business predicament. They feel that Google acted in accordance with "doing business" and should abide by the laws of the local governments.

1. Companies are free to pursue profits as long as they follow a country's laws.

2. Withdrawing from China would further restrict speech.

3. Google's presence, as muted as it is, continues to advance the slow progress the Chinese government is making toward democracy. U.S. companies can ethically stay in China if they make an effort to improve human rights there. U.S. companies operating in China should agree on guidelines that respect human rights.

GOT FREE SPEECH?

FIGURE 12

As globalization brings us all in closer contact, how will our ethics and values come into conflict with others?

Computer Abuse

Does Restricting Online Information Protect Children?

SUMMARY OF THE ISSUE

Computer abuse is loosely defined as using a computer or the Internet to harm another individual. By providing anonymity, the Internet facilitates such unsavory activities as

- the ability of sexual predators to contact potential victims;
- the distribution of pornography;
- cyberbullying (harassing individuals through electronic means);
- phishing, or tricking individuals out of sensitive information; and
- the dissemination of hate speech.

Although computer abuse is a threat to everyone, children are especially vulnerable because they tend to use technology more than adults, are more trusting than many adults, and may lack the real-life experience to identify malicious intent or behavior. No one argues that protecting children from harm is not a laudable goal, but the question is how best to accomplish it. Laws restricting the Internet's content have largely failed when they are overturned by courts on the grounds that they violate free speech. Therefore, controlling access to objectionable material has been the avenue pursued.

Content-filtering software is designed to block objectionable content from view and is usually designed for shielding children (see Figure 13). To receive discounts for affordable Internet access, the government requires schools and libraries to have filtering software on their computers. But problems have arisen as these types of public institutions have installed such software to protect children. When objectionable material is blocked, the free speech rights of the individual are affected—not by preventing them from exercising their right of free speech but rather by infringing on their rights of free access to information. The courts have usually viewed access to information as a First Amendment (free speech) issue.

Filtering software presents a problem when it is unable to discriminate between information that should be blocked and information that is not objectionable but rather informational. Blocking software has blocked informational sites such as the Safer Sex Page, groups supporting gay rights, sites with information about breast cancer, and even the home pages of politicians such as former Representative Richard (Dick) Armey (R–Texas). Furthermore, designers of objectionable Web sites (such as pornography sites) are often clever enough to disguise their objectionable content so that it fools the filters. The public has raised a huge outcry, demanding that publicly funded institutions must protect children from objectionable content. So what is the best way to satisfy this demand if filtering isn't the answer?

QUESTIONS TO THINK ABOUT AND RESEARCH

1. Does your school use filtering software in computer labs on campus? Do you think your school should restrict objectionable content if it receives public funds?
2. Who should decide what types of sites should be blocked by filtering software? Educators? Librarians? Software programmers? The government?
3. If you have children (or if you have children in the future), will you install filtering software on computers in your home?
4. What alternatives to filtering software would be effective in protecting children from objectionable content?

POINT

Monitoring Software Protects Children

Most advocates of filtering software in publicly funded institutions cite the need to protect minors from material deemed objectionable by accepted public standards.

1. Because laws have proven ineffective, filtering software is the only way to protect children from objectionable material, such as pornography or violence.

2. Parents need to be assured that publicly funded institutions such as schools and libraries are "safe havens" where their children will not be allowed to access or be exposed to objectionable material.

3. Publicly funded institutions have a right to uphold the moral standards of the public.

4. Filtering Internet content is a logical extension of the existing library screening process, whereby librarians decide what books to put on the shelves.

COUNTERPOINT

Monitoring Software Restricts Access to Information

Opponents of filtering software cite the First Amendment, which guarantees free speech and hence free access to information.

1. Filtering software routinely blocks Web sites with informational content as opposed to objectionable material.

2. Filtering software is akin to censorship, which violates the First Amendment.

3. Filtering software is not 100 percent reliable and fails to screen out a lot of objectionable material.

4. Filtering widens the "digital divide" by adversely affecting the poor. Wealthier individuals tend to have Internet access in their homes and are less affected by filters in public institutions.

5. Educating children about using the Internet carefully and responsibly will be more effective in the long run than filtering software.

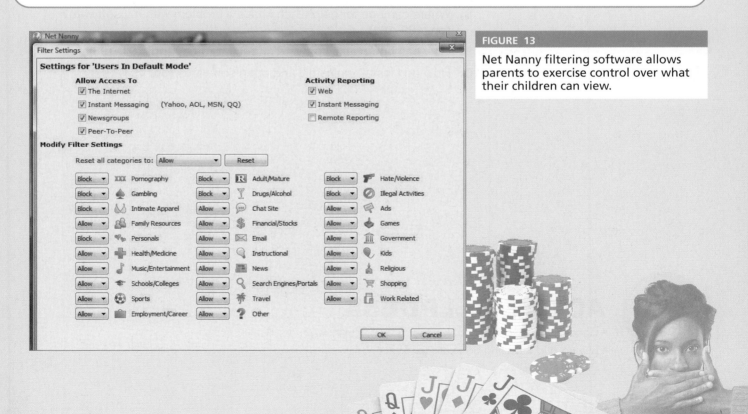

FIGURE 13

Net Nanny filtering software allows parents to exercise control over what their children can view.

chapter four

Application Software:

Programs That Let You Work and Play

Objectives

After reading this chapter, you should be able to answer the following questions:

1. What's the difference between application software and system software? **(p. 166)**

2. What kinds of applications are included in productivity software I might use at home? **(pp. 166–178)**

3. What are the different types of multimedia software? **(pp. 178–183)**

4. What are the different types of entertainment software? **(pp. 183–185)**

5. What are the different types of drawing software? **(pp. 185–186)**

6. What kinds of software do small and large businesses use? **(pp. 186–189)**

7. What kind of software is available online? **(pp. 192–193)**

8. Where can I go for help when I have a problem with my software? **(pp. 189–191)**

9. How can I purchase software or get it for free? **(pp. 191–196)**

10. How do I install, uninstall, and open software? **(pp. 196–199)**

ACTIVE HELPDESK

- Choosing Software **(p. 185)**
- Buying and Installing Software **(p. 197)**

Using Application Software

Finals are this week. Jenna sits down to tackle the last project for her computer literacy class, a research assignment on "simulation" software. She's a fan of *The Sims* software games and is researching how different professions are using simulation software to train workers. Her instructor said students could use any format for the project, so Jenna decides to do a PowerPoint presentation. With the Insert Slides from the Outline feature, she transfers the outline she has already prepared in Word to PowerPoint slides. Using that as the basis for her presentation, she adds visual interest to the slides with photographs and other illustrations, being careful to include references to her sources.

With the presentation complete, she saves it to a flash drive and then checks off the project as "complete" in the tasks list in Outlook. While in Outlook, Jenna turns to her calendar to check out tomorrow's activities and answers a few e-mail messages that have accumulated in her Inbox. Last, she checks her debit card balance online and reviews her spending habits in the Web-based financial planning application **wesabe.com** that she has just begun to use to monitor her budget. Later, she will use TurboTax, a tax preparation software program, to do her taxes herself. She has saved a lot of money by doing her own taxes, and the program was simple to learn.

Before going to dinner, Jenna quickly checks into Blackboard, the management software program her online class uses to manage assignments, homework, and discussions. Not seeing anything new to do, Jenna relaxes by playing a bit of *The Sims.*

How often do you use software, and what kinds of software are you familiar with? Do you know what software programs are on the market and what their most important features are? In this chapter, you'll learn about the kinds of software you can use to perform a variety of tasks, from simple word processing to digital image editing—at home, school, and work. We'll then discuss how you can buy software, what the different versions of software mean, and how you can legally get software for free off the Web. Finally, we'll look at how you can install and uninstall software safely on your system.

SOUND BYTES

- Creating Web Queries in Excel 2007 **(p. 168)**
- Using Speech-Recognition Software in Windows Vista **(p. 178)**
- Enhancing Photos with Image Editing Software **(p. 182)**

The Nuts and Bolts of Software

A computer without software is like a sandwich without filling. Although the computer hardware is obviously critical, a computer system does nothing without software. What is software? Technically speaking, the term **software** refers to a set of instructions that tells the computer what to do. These instruction sets, also called **programs**, provide a means for us to interact with and use the computer, all without specialized computer-programming skills. Your computer has two basic types of software: system software and application software.

- **System software** includes software such as Windows Vista and Mac OS X, which help run the computer and coordinate instructions between application software and the computer's hardware devices. System software includes the operating system and utility programs (programs in the operating system that help manage system resources). We discuss system software in detail in Chapter 5.

- **Application software** is the software you use to do tasks at home, school, and work. You can do a multitude of things with application software such as writing letters, sending e-mail, paying taxes, creating presentations, editing photos, and taking an online course, to name a few.

Figure 4.1 shows the various types of application software available. In this chapter, we look at all of these types in detail, starting with productivity software.

More Productivity at Home

One reason to have a computer is to make it easier to tackle the tasks you have in your day-to-day life. Productivity software is all about helping you do that, making it easier to keep your budget, send letters, or keep track of the kids' school events. It's safe to say you regularly use some form of productivity software already. **Productivity software** includes programs that enable you to perform various tasks generally required in home, school, and business. This category includes word-processing, spreadsheet, presentation, database, and personal information manager (PIM) programs.

WORD-PROCESSING SOFTWARE

What is the best software to use to create general documents? Most students use **word-processing software** to create and edit documents such as research papers, letters, and résumés. *Microsoft Word* and *Corel WordPerfect* are popular word-processing programs. *Writer*, a word-processing program from the OpenOffice

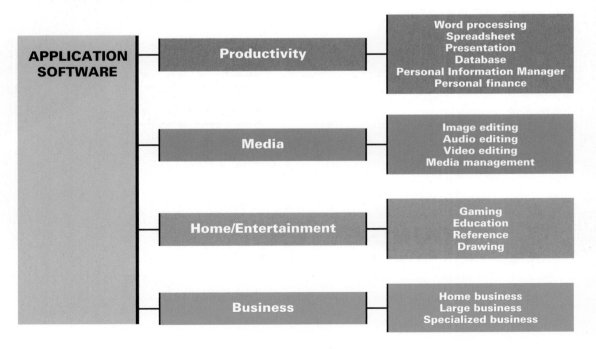

FIGURE 4.1

Organization of Application Software

suite (**www.openoffice.org**), and *AbiWord* (**www.abisource.com**) are gaining in popularity because they are available as free downloads from the Internet. Both AbiWord and Writer have many of the same features as their higher-priced Word and WordPerfect competitors, making either a great choice for cost-conscious consumers.

Because of its general usefulness, word-processing software is the most widely used software application. Word-processing software has a key advantage over its ancestral counterpart, the typewriter: You can make revisions and corrections without having to retype an entire document. You can quickly and easily insert, delete, and move pieces of text. Similarly, you can remove and insert text from one document into another seamlessly.

How do I control the way my documents look? Another advantage of word-processing software is that you can easily format, or change the appearance of, your document. As a result, you can produce professional-looking documents without having to send them to a professional. With formatting options, you can change fonts, font styles, and sizes; add colors to text; adjust margins; add borders to portions of text or entire pages; insert bulleted and

numbered lists; and organize your text into columns. You also can insert pictures from your own files or from a gallery of images—clip art—that is included with the software. You also can enhance the look of your document by creating an interesting background or by adding a "theme" of coordinated colors and styles throughout your document. Figure 4.2 shows an example of some of the formatting options.

What special tools do word-processing programs have? You're probably familiar with the basic tools of word-processing software. Most applications come with some form of spelling and grammar checker and a thesaurus, for example. Another popular tool is the search-and-replace tool that allows you to search for text in your document and automatically replace it with other text.

The average user is unaware of many interesting word-processing software tools. For example, did you know that you could translate words or phrases to another language or automatically correct your spelling as you type? You also can automatically summarize key points in a text document. Writer, the word-processing program in the OpenOffice suite, has many of the same tools you're used to seeing in Microsoft

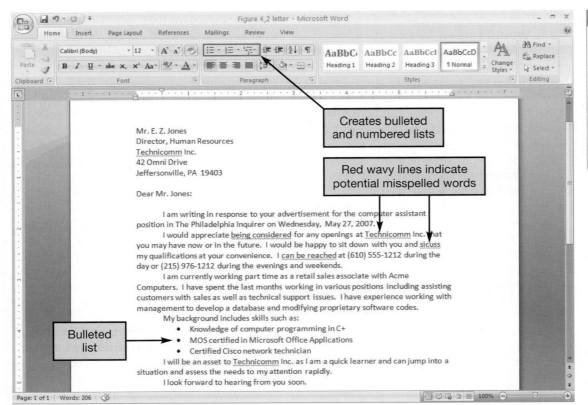

FIGURE 4.2

Nearly every word-processing software application has basic features to help you make your document look professionally formatted and to ensure that words are spelled correctly and used grammatically.

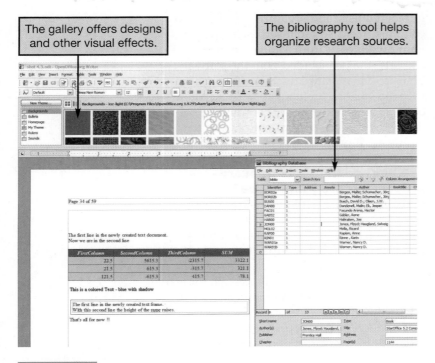

The gallery offers designs and other visual effects.

The bibliography tool helps organize research sources.

FIGURE 4.3

Writer, the word-processing program in the OpenOffice suite, has many of the same features as Word and WordPerfect as well as some unique ones.

row 1, is referred to as "cell A1." You can enter several types of data into a cell:

- **Labels:** Descriptive text that identifies the components of the worksheet.

- **Values:** Numerical data either typed in directly or entered by the program as a result of a calculation.

- **Formulas:** Equations that you build yourself using addition, subtraction, multiplication, and division, as well as values and cell references. For example, in Figure 4.4, you would type the formula "=B8-B22" to calculate net income for September.

- **Functions:** Formulas that are pre-programmed into the spreadsheet software. Functions help you with calculations ranging from the simple (such as adding groups of numbers) to the complex (such as determining monthly loan payments), without you needing to know the exact formula. So, in Figure 4.4, to calculate your average earned income in September, you could use the built-in AVERAGE function, which would look like this: =AVERAGE(B4:B7).

The primary benefit of spreadsheet software is its ability to recalculate all functions and formulas in the spreadsheet automatically when values for some of the inputs are changed. For example, in Figure 4.4, you can insert an additional row (Memberships) and change a value (September clothing expense), and then recalculate the results for Total Expenses and Net Income without having to redo the worksheet from scratch.

Because automatic recalculation enables you to see immediately the effects that different options have on your spreadsheet, you can quickly test different assumptions in the same analysis. This is called a *what-if analysis.* Look again at Figure 4.4 and ask, "What if I add $50 to my clothing budget? What impact will such an increase have on my budget?" By adding another $100 to tuition, as shown in the budget in Figure 4.4, you will automatically know the impact a tuition increase will have on your expenses and net income.

What kinds of graphs and charts can I create with spreadsheet software? Sometimes it's easier to see the meaning of numbers when they are shown in a graphical format such as in a chart. As

Word and Corel WordPerfect, as well as some unique ones (see Figure 4.3).

SPREADSHEET SOFTWARE

Why would I need to use spreadsheet software? Spreadsheet software—for example, *Microsoft Excel* and *Lotus 1-2-3*—enables you to do calculations and numerical analyses easily. You can use spreadsheet software to track your expenses and create a simple budget. You also can use spreadsheet software to determine how much you should be paying on your student loans, car loan, or credit card bills each month. You know you should pay more than the minimum payment to spend less on interest, but how much more should you pay and for which loan? Spreadsheet software can help you evaluate different scenarios such as planning the best payment strategy.

How do I use spreadsheet software? The basic element in a spreadsheet program is the worksheet, which is a grid consisting of columns and rows. As shown in Figure 4.4, the columns and rows form individual boxes called *cells.* Each cell can be identified according to its column and row position. For example, a cell in column A,

SOUND BYTE

Creating Web Queries in Excel 2007

In this Sound Byte, you'll learn what Excel Web queries are, as well as how to use them effectively.

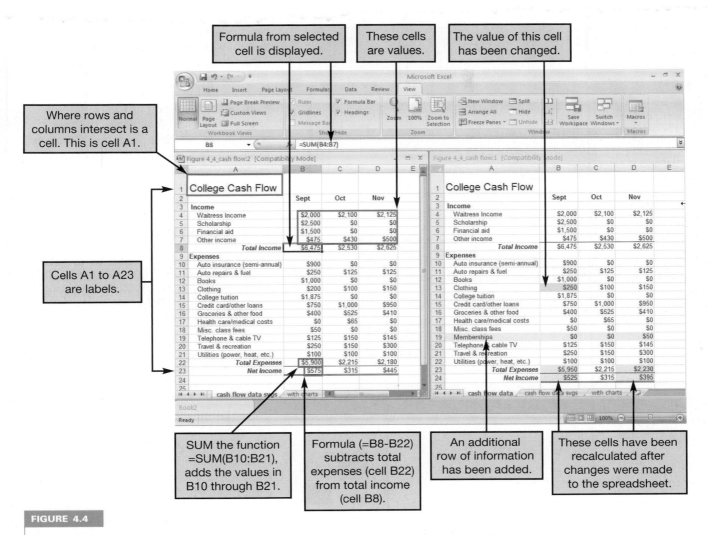

Where rows and columns intersect is a cell. This is cell A1.

Cells A1 to A23 are labels.

Formula from selected cell is displayed.

These cells are values.

The value of this cell has been changed.

SUM the function =SUM(B10:B21), adds the values in B10 through B21.

Formula (=B8-B22) subtracts total expenses (cell B22) from total income (cell B8).

An additional row of information has been added.

These cells have been recalculated after changes were made to the spreadsheet.

FIGURE 4.4

Spreadsheet software enables you to calculate and manipulate numerical data easily with the use of built-in formulas.

shown in Figure 4.5, most spreadsheet applications allow you to create a variety of charts, including basic column charts, pie charts, and line charts—with or without three-dimensional (3D) effects. In addition to these basic charts, you can use stock charts (for investment analysis) and scatter charts (for statistical analysis), as well as create custom charts.

Are spreadsheets used for anything besides financial analysis?

There are so many powerful mathematical

FIGURE 4.5

(a) Column charts show comparisons. (b) Pie charts show how parts contribute to the whole. (c) Line charts show trends over time.

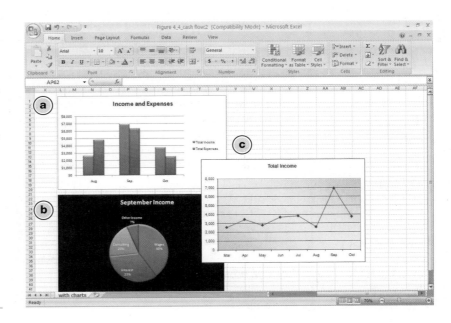

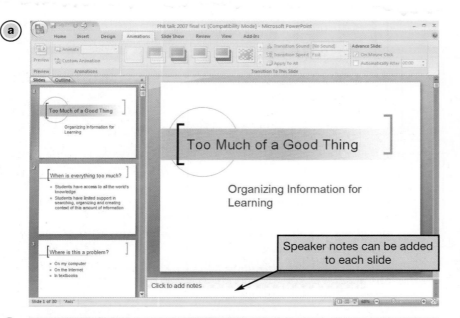

Speaker notes can be added to each slide

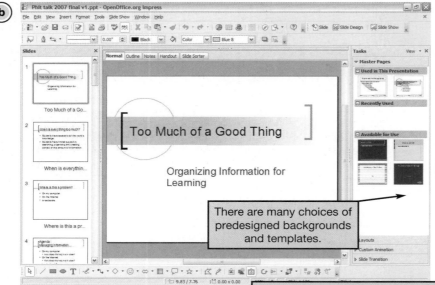

There are many choices of predesigned backgrounds and templates.

Simpler feature set but still very useful are online web-based presentation products.

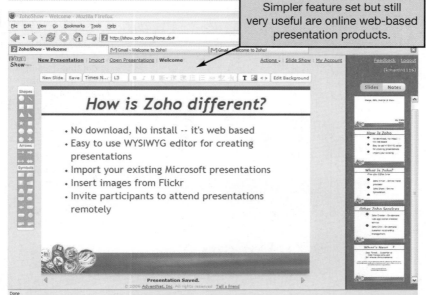

functions built into spreadsheet programs that they can be used for serious numerical analyses or simulation. For example, an Excel spreadsheet could be designed to compute the output voltage at a point in an electrical circuit or to simulate customer arrival and wait times. In these settings, spreadsheet programs can often solve problems that formerly required custom programming. Many spreadsheet applications have database capabilities to sort, filter, and group data.

PRESENTATION SOFTWARE

What software do I use to create presentations? You've probably sat through presentations during which the speaker's dialogue is displayed in slides projected on a screen. These presentations can be the most basic of outlines, containing only a few words and simple graphics, or elaborate multimedia presentations with animated text, graphic objects, and colorful backgrounds. You use **presentation software** such as *Microsoft PowerPoint*, *OpenOffice Impress*, or *Zoho Show* (shown in Figure 4.6) to create these types of dynamic slide shows. Because these applications are simple to use, you can produce high-quality presentations without a lot of training.

How do I create a presentation? Using the basic features included in presentation software, creating a slide show is simple. To arrange text and graphics on your slides, you can choose from a variety of slide layouts. These layouts give you the option of using a single or double column of bulleted text, various combinations of bulleted text, and other content such as clip art, graphs, photos, and even video clips.

You also can lend a theme to your presentation by choosing from different design templates. You can use animation effects to control how and when text and other objects enter and exit each slide. Similarly, slide transitions add different effects as you move from one slide to the next during the presentation.

FIGURE 4.6

Several programs allow you to create presentation materials: (a) Microsoft Office PowerPoint 2007, (b) OpenOffice Impress, and (c) Zoho.com's Show.

DATABASE SOFTWARE

How can I use database software?

Database software such as *Oracle*, *Corel Paradox*, and *Microsoft Access* is basically a complex electronic filing system. As mentioned earlier, spreadsheet applications include many database features and are easy to use for simple database tasks such as sorting, filtering, and organizing data. However, you need to use a more robust, fully featured database application to manage larger and more complicated groups of data that contain more than one table or to group, sort, and retrieve data and to generate reports.

Traditional databases are organized into fields, records, and tables, as shown in Figure 4.7. A field is a data category such as "First Name," "Last Name," or "Street Address." A record is a collection of related fields such as "Douglas Seaver, Printing Solutions, 7700 First Avenue, Topeka, KS, (888) 968-2678." A table groups related records such as "Sales Contacts."

How do you benefit when businesses use database software?

FedEx, UPS, and other shipping companies let customers search their online databases for tracking numbers, allowing customers to get instant information on the status of their packages. Other businesses use databases to keep track of clients, invoices, and personnel information. Often that information is available to a home computer user. For example, at Amazon.com you can use the company's Web site to access the entire history of all the purchases you have ever made.

BITS AND BYTES

Looking for a Free or More Affordable Productivity Suite?

If you're looking for a more affordable software alternative to the big three (Microsoft Office, Corel WordPerfect Office, and Lotus SmartSuite), you may want to consider downloading a free open source productivity suite. **Open source software** is program code made publicly available with few restrictions. The code can be copied, distributed, or changed without the stringent copyright protections of software products you purchase. OpenOffice is a popular open source software suite. In addition, there are Web-based products that are available free of charge. These Web-based applications, such as Google Docs and the Zoho suite, are accessible from wherever you are and are easily shared, so they are perfect for virtual workgroups.

Compared to Microsoft Office, you won't find all the features you're used to seeing, but OpenOffice offers most of the features required by the average user. And if you use OpenOffice, you can easily read, write, and edit files created in other applications, although you may lose some formatting when migrating or transferring files to OpenOffice. Similarly, users of other productivity suites can open files created in OpenOffice.

Keep one thing in mind when you choose a free or Web-based software product: support. Unlike Microsoft Office and other proprietary software applications, there is no formal support. Instead, open source and Web-based applications are supported from their community of users across Web sites and newsgroups. For more information on alternative software, see the Technology in Focus feature "Computing Alternatives" on page 258.

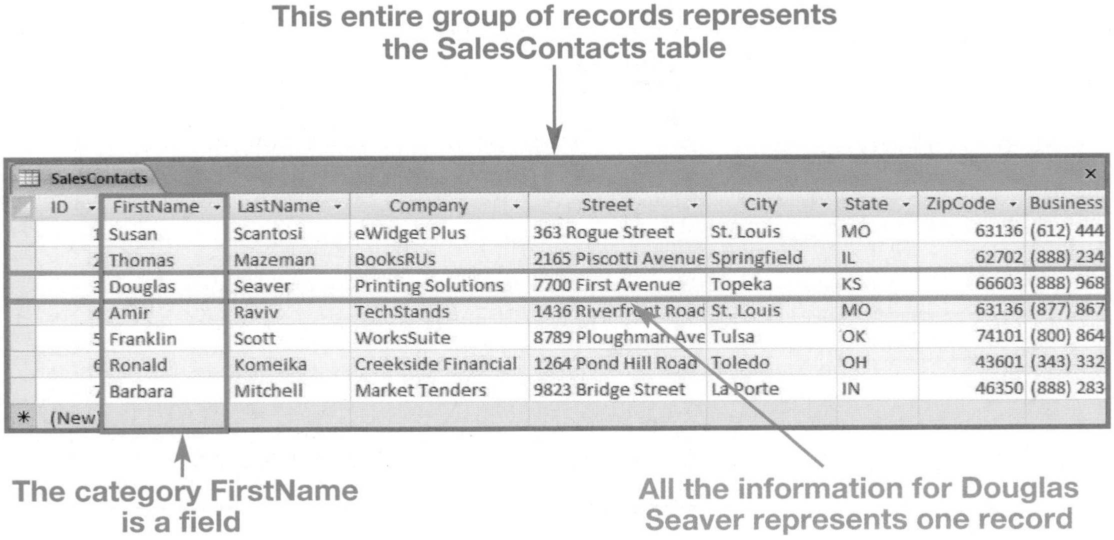

This entire group of records represents the SalesContacts table

ID	FirstName	LastName	Company	Street	City	State	ZipCode	Business
1	Susan	Scantosi	eWidget Plus	363 Rogue Street	St. Louis	MO	63136	(612) 444
2	Thomas	Mazeman	BooksRUs	2165 Piscotti Avenue	Springfield	IL	62702	(888) 234
3	Douglas	Seaver	Printing Solutions	7700 First Avenue	Topeka	KS	66603	(888) 968
4	Amir	Raviv	TechStands	1436 Riverfront Road	St. Louis	MO	63136	(877) 867
5	Franklin	Scott	WorkSuite	8789 Ploughman Ave	Tulsa	OK	74101	(800) 864
6	Ronald	Komeika	Creekside Financial	1264 Pond Hill Road	Toledo	OH	43601	(343) 332
7	Barbara	Mitchell	Market Tenders	9823 Bridge Street	La Porte	IN	46350	(888) 283
*	(New)							

The category FirstName is a field

All the information for Douglas Seaver represents one record

FIGURE 4.7

In databases, similar information is organized by main topic into tables and grouped into categories called *fields*. Each individual row of data is called a *record*. Some databases have multiple tables that "relate" to each other through common fields.

PERSONAL INFORMATION MANAGER (PIM) SOFTWARE

Which applications should I use to manage my time, contact lists, and tasks? Most productivity software suites contain some form of **personal information manager (PIM) software** such as *Microsoft Outlook* or *Lotus Organizer*. These programs strive to replace the management tools found on a traditional desk—a calendar, address book, notepad, and to-do list, for example. Some PIMs contain e-mail management features so that you not only can receive and send e-mail messages but also organize them into various folders, prioritize them, and coordinate them with other activities in your calendar (see Figure 4.8).

If you share a common network at home or at work and are using the same PIM software as others on the network, then you can use a PIM program to check people's availability before scheduling meeting times. Whether coordinating a team project or a family event, you can create and electronically assign tasks to group members by using a PIM. You can even track each person's progress to ensure that the tasks are finished on time.

Are there Web-based PIM programs? Many Web-based e-mail clients such as Yahoo!, Google, and AOL have developed coordinating calendar and contacts programs similar to Microsoft Outlook. Yahoo! also includes Notepad for jotting down notes and tasks, Google's calendar and contacts sync with Outlook so that you can access your Outlook calendar information simply by logging into Google, and AOL's Instant Messenger, AIM, has coordinating e-mail, calendar, and contact functions.

PRODUCTIVITY SOFTWARE FEATURES

What tools can help me work more efficiently with productivity software? Whether you are working on a word-processing document, spreadsheet, database, or slide presentation, you can make use of several tools to increase your efficiency:

- **Wizards** are step-by-step guides that walk you through the necessary steps to complete a complicated task. At each step, the wizard asks you questions. Based on your responses, the wizard helps you complete that portion of the task. Many productivity software applications include wizards. For example, you can easily create charts in Excel using the Excel Chart Wizard.

- **Templates** are forms that are included in many productivity applications that provide the basic structure for a particular kind of document, spreadsheet, or presentation. Templates can include specific page layout designs, special formatting and styles relevant to that particular document, and automated tasks (macros). Typical templates allow you to lay out a professional-looking résumé, structure a home budget, or communicate the results of a project in a presentation.

- **Macros** are small programs that group a series of commands to run as a single command. Macros are best used to automate a routine task or a complex series of commands that must be run frequently. For example, a teacher may write a macro to sort the grades in her grade book automatically in descending

---

FIGURE 4.8

The Outlook Today feature in Microsoft Outlook includes common PIM features such as a summary of your appointments, a list of your tasks, and the number of new e-mail messages you have.

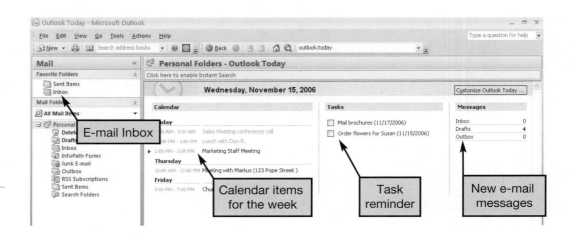

order and to highlight those grades that are below a C average. Every time she adds the results of an assignment or test, she can set up the macro to run through that series of steps automatically.

INTEGRATED SOFTWARE APPLICATIONS

What's an integrated software application? An **integrated software application** is a single software program that incorporates the most commonly used tools of many productivity software programs into one integrated stand-alone program. Note that integrated software applications are not substitutes for the full suite of applications they replace. Generally, because they don't include many of the more complex features of the individual productivity software applications, they can be thought of as "software lite." To have access to the full functionality of word-processing and spreadsheet software, for example, you should get the individual applications or a suite that includes each of these applications.

Microsoft Works 9 is an example of an integrated software application. This integrated

BITS AND BYTES

Productivity Software Tips and Tricks

Looking for tips on how to make better use of your productivity software? Many Web sites send subscribers daily e-mails full of tips, tricks, and shortcuts to their favorite software programs. Nerdy Books (**www.nerdybooks.com**), for example, sends a free tip each day to the e-mail accounts of its subscribers. Nerdy Books also has Bob's Blog of software tips and podcasts for those tips that can't be written in just a few sentences. Dummies eTips (**http://etips.dummies.com**), based on the *For Dummies* series of help books, offers subscribers tips on a variety of topics, including productivity software applications. Most of these services are free, although some require that you subscribe to an ancillary product.

software application includes word-processing, spreadsheet, and database functionality as well as templates, a calendar, a dictionary, and map features. *iWork '08* is an integrated software application from Apple that includes word-processing (Pages), presentation (Keynote), and spreadsheet (Numbers) functionality. Figure 4.9 shows the multifunctionality of Apple iWork. The

FIGURE 4.9

Although an integrated software application such as Apple iWork is one program, it contains the most commonly used features of several individual productivity software applications.

FIGURE 4.10

Software suites provide users with a cheaper method of obtaining all of the software they want to buy in one bundle.

Task Launcher is the first window that opens when you launch Microsoft Works.

Why would I use an integrated software application instead of individual, stand-alone programs? Integrated software applications are perfect if you don't need the more advanced features found in the individual productivity software applications. Like stand-alone applications, integrated software programs provide templates for frequently developed documents such as résumés and invoices. Integrated software programs also are less expensive than their individual fully featured counterparts. If you find your needs go beyond the limited capabilities of an integrated program, you might want to consider buying the individual programs that meet your particular requirements, or you may want to consider buying a software suite.

SOFTWARE SUITES

What's a software suite? A **software suite** is a group of software programs that have been bundled as a package. You can buy software suites for many different categories of applications, including productivity, graphics, and virus protection (see Figure 4.10). There are three primary developers of productivity software suites: Microsoft, Corel, and Lotus. Microsoft and Corel offer different packages with different combinations of software applications, whereas Lotus offers only SmartSuite.

Which software applications do productivity software suites contain? Most productivity software suites contain the same basic software programs such as word-processing, spreadsheet, presentation, and PIM software. However, depending on the version and manufacturer, some suites also include other programs such as database programs and desktop publishing software. When you are shopping for software, it can be difficult to figure out which bundle is the right one for your needs. For example, *Microsoft Office 2007* is bundled in eight different ways; four of these are described in the table in Figure 4.11. Be sure to research carefully the bundling options for software you are buying.

Why would I buy a software suite instead of individual programs? Most people buy software suites because suites are cheaper than buying each program

FIGURE 4.11 A Sampling of Microsoft Office Suites

	Word Processing, Spreadsheet, Presentation	Database	PIM	Desktop Publishing	Note Taking	Other (Info Path, Groove)
Microsoft Office 2007	**Word, Excel, PowerPoint**	**Access**	**Outlook**	**Publisher**	**One Note**	
Ultimate 2007	X	X	X	X	X	X
Professional 2007	X	X	X	X		
Standard 2007	X		X			
Home and Student 2007	X				X	

individually. In addition, because the programs bundled in a software suite come from the same developer, they work well together (that is, they provide for better integration) and share common features, toolbars, and menus. For example, when using applications in the Microsoft Office suite, you can seamlessly create a spreadsheet in Excel, import it into Access, and then link a query created in Access to a Word document. It would be much harder to do the same thing using different applications from a variety of software developers.

PERSONAL FINANCIAL SOFTWARE

What software can I use to prepare my taxes? Everyone has to face doing their taxes, and having the right computer software can make this burden much simpler and keep it completely under your control. **Tax preparation software** such as *Intuit TurboTax* and *H&R Block TaxCut* enable you to prepare your state and federal taxes on your own rather than having to hire a professional. Both programs offer a complete set of tax forms and instructions, as well as videos that contain expert advice on how to complete each form. In addition, error-checking features are built into the programs to catch mistakes. TurboTax also can run a check for audit alerts, file your return electronically, and offer guidance on financial planning to help effectively plan and manage your financial resources

FIGURE 4.12

Tax preparation software, such as Intuit TurboTax, enables you to prepare and file your taxes by using a guided, step-by-step process.

for the following year (see Figure 4.12). Remember, however, that the tax code changes annually so you must purchase the current tax year's version of the software each year.

Speech-Recognition Software

Dragon Naturally Speaking is a leading **speech-recognition software** (or **voice-recognition software**) that translates your spoken words into typed text. With this software, you can dictate documents and e-mail messages, use voice commands to start and switch between applications and control the operating system, and even surf or fill out forms on the Web. Speech-recognition software is available in different languages, so Chinese, Japanese, and Spanish commands work just as well as English. Accuracy levels of 95 percent to 99 percent can be achieved in quiet environments with a quality microphone.

Microsoft has incorporated a powerful speech-recognition system into Windows Vista. After starting speech recognition (from the Start menu, type "speech" in the search box and click on "Windows Speech Recognition"), the speech-recognition toolbar appears and indicates whether or not the computer is "listening" for voice input. Just click the microphone icon to make the computer listen to or ignore voice input.

Figure 4.13 shows how you can use Vista's speech-recognition to instruct the software to run commands within an application. If you aren't sure what speech commands are available, just say "What can I say?" to display the speech reference card.

Speech-recognition software is complicated. As you speak, the software divides each second of your speech into 100 individual samples, or sounds. It then compares these individual sounds with a database (called a *codebook*) that contains samples of every sound a human being can make. When a match is made, your voice sound is given a number that corresponds to the number of the similar sound in the database.

After your voice sounds are assigned values, these values are matched with another database containing phonemes for the language being spoken. A phoneme is the smallest phonetic unit that distinguishes one word from another. For example, "b" and "m" are both phonemes that distinguish the words *bad* and *mad* from

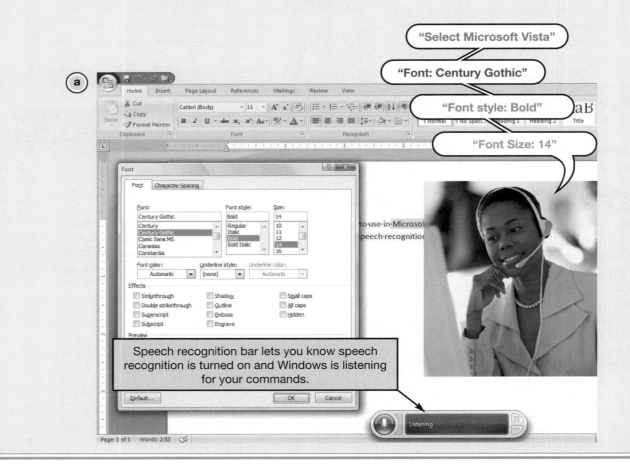

"Select Microsoft Vista"

"Font: Century Gothic"

"Font style: Bold"

"Font Size: 14"

Speech recognition bar lets you know speech recognition is turned on and Windows is listening for your commands.

each other in the English language. A typical language such as English is made up of thousands of different phonemes. And because of differences in pronunciation, some phonemes may actually have several different corresponding matching sounds.

Once all the sounds are assigned to phonemes, word and phrase construction can begin. The phonemes are matched against a word list that contains transcriptions of all known words in a particular language. Because pronunciation can vary (for example, the word *the* can be pronounced so that it rhymes with *duh* or *see*), the word list must contain alternative pronunciations for many words. Each phoneme is worked on separately; the phonemes are then chained together to form words that are contained in the word list. Because a variety of sounds can be put together to form many different words, the software analyzes all the possible values and picks the one value that it determines has the best probability of correctly matching your spoken word. The word is then displayed on the screen or is acted upon by the computer as a command.

But there are problems with speech-recognition software. We don't always speak every word the same way,

and accents and regional dialects result in great variations in pronunciations. Therefore, speech recognition is not perfect and requires training. Training entails getting the computer to recognize your particular way of speaking, a process that involves reading prepared text into the computer so the phoneme database can be adjusted to your specific speech patterns.

Another approach to improve speech inconsistencies is to restrict the word list to a few keywords or phrases and then have the computer guess the probability that a certain phrase is being said. This is how cell phones that respond to voice commands work. The phone doesn't really figure out that you said "call home" by breaking down the phonemes. It just determines how likely it is that you said "call home" as opposed to "call office." This cuts down on the processing power needed and reduces the chance of mistakes. However, it also restricts the words you can use to achieve the desired results.

Though not perfect, speech-recognition software programs can be of invaluable service for individuals who don't type well or who have physical limitations that prevent them from using a keyboard or mouse. For those whose careers depend on a lot of typing, using speech-recognition software reduces the chances of their incurring debilitating repetitive strain injuries. In addition, because most people can speak faster than they can write or type, speech-recognition software can help individuals work more efficiently. It also can help you to be productive during generally non-productive times. For example, you can dictate into a digital recording device while doing other things such as driving and then later download the digital file to your computer and let the program type up your words for you.

Speech recognition should continue to be a hot topic for research over the next decade. Aside from the obvious benefits to persons with disabilities, many people are enamored with the idea of talking to their computers!

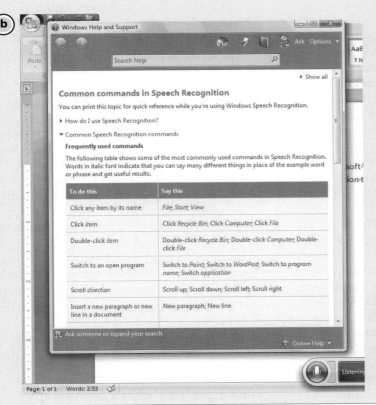

FIGURE 4.13

(a) Speech-recognition software allows you to create documents using simple voice commands. (b) Forget what speech command to use? Just say "What can I say?" to display the speech reference card.

FIGURE 4.14

Wesabe.com is an online financial management tool that provides useful data about spending habits from your uploaded bank and credit card statements. An extensive online community provides helpful tips and discussions with other people in similar situations.

SOUND BYTE

Using Speech-Recognition Software in Windows Vista

In this Sound Byte, you'll see a demonstration of the speech-recognition software included with Windows Vista. You'll also learn how to access and train speech-recognition software so that you can create and edit documents without typing.

What software can I use to help keep track of my personal finances?

Financial planning software helps you manage your daily finances. *Intuit Quicken* and *Microsoft Money* are popular examples. Financial planning programs include electronic checkbook registers and automatic bill payment tools, as shown in Figure 4.14. With these features, you can print checks from your computer or pay recurring monthly payments, such as rent or student loans, with automatically scheduled online payments. The software automatically records all transactions, including online payments, in your checkbook register. In addition, you can assign categories to each transaction and then use these categories to analyze your spending patterns. You even can set up a budget and review your spending habits.

Web-based programs such as **mint.com** and **wesabe.com** are rapidly gaining in popularity. Although they do not offer bill-paying services or help track your investment portfolio like Quicken and Money do, they are great at analyzing your spending habits and offering advice on how to manage your spending better. Because they are Web-based, you can monitor and update your finances from any computer in a private and secure setting. Users also have access to a network of other users with whom to exchange tips and advice.

Financial planning software applications also coordinate with tax preparation software. Quicken, for example, integrates seamlessly with TurboTax, so you never have to go through your checkbook and bills to find tax deductions, tax-related income, or expenses. Many banks and creditcard companies also offer online services that download a detailed monthly statement into Quicken or Money. Quicken even offers a credit card. All of your purchases are organized into categories and are downloaded automatically to your Quicken file to further streamline your financial planning and recordkeeping. You can also purchase Pocket Quicken to install on your PDA/smartphone so that your financial records are always at your fingertips.

More Media at Home

From movies and television to music and photography, the entertainment world is becoming all digital. Your computer can help you create, organize, and modify digital images, songs, and movies, if you have the right software. **Multimedia software** includes image, video, and audio editing software; animation software; and other specialty software required to produce computer games, animations, and movies. In this section, we look at several popular types of multimedia software as shown in Figure 4.15.

DIGITAL IMAGE EDITING SOFTWARE

What can I do with a digital image that I can't do with a photograph?

Once the image information is in a digital format (the image is taken with a digital camera or scanned), you can use it easily with all your other software. With the digital file, it is simple to store a picture of each person in your Outlook contacts list or add an image you captured into a newsletter you are writing.

Products such as *Microsoft Photo Story* and *Google's Picasa*, which are both free downloads, make it easy for you to use your collection of digital images in new ways. In Photo Story, you can add text, music, and camera movement to create a full-featured slide show that will let you use your images. Using Picasa, you can create a poster from an image or several different styles of collages.

What software do I use to edit my photos? As its name implies, **image editing software** (sometimes called **photo editing software**) enables you to edit photographs and other images. Image editing software includes tools for basic modifications to digital images such as removing red-eye; modifying contrast, sharpness, and color casts; or removing scratches or rips from scanned images of old photos. Many of these software packages now also include an extensive set of painting tools such as brushes, pens, and artistic media (e.g., paints, pastels, oils) that allow you to create realistic-looking images as well. Often graphic designers use digital photos and

images as a basis for their design and then modify these images within image editing software to create their final products.

Adobe Photoshop CS3 and *Corel Paint Shop Pro* are fully featured image editing software applications. They each offer sophisticated tools such as those for layering images (placing pictures on top of each other) and masking images (hiding parts of layers to create effects such as collages). See Figure 4.16. Designers use these more sophisticated tools

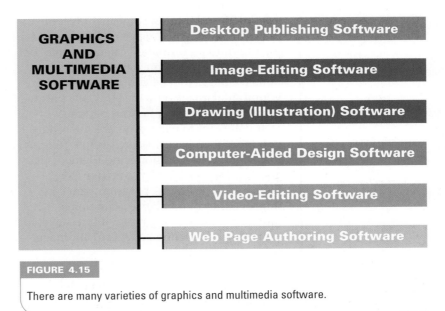

GRAPHICS AND MULTIMEDIA SOFTWARE

- Desktop Publishing Software
- Image-Editing Software
- Drawing (Illustration) Software
- Computer-Aided Design Software
- Video-Editing Software
- Web Page Authoring Software

FIGURE 4.15

There are many varieties of graphics and multimedia software.

Background layer

Clipping layer

Both layers combined

FIGURE 4.16

With some image editing software, you can take two individual pictures and combine them into one picture.

to create the enhanced digital images used commercially in logos, advertisements, and on book and CD covers.

Can a nonprofessional use image editing software? Image editing programs such as *Adobe Photoshop Elements* and *Roxio PhotoSuite* are programs geared toward the casual home user. With these applications, you can perform the most common image editing tasks such as taking out red-eye and cropping and resizing pictures. These programs enable you to add creative effects such as borders and frames. Some include templates in which you can insert your favorite pictures into preformatted calendar pages or greeting cards. They may also have photo fantasy images that let you paste a face from your digital image onto the body of a professional athlete or other famous person.

If you want to use a program that offers you more than basic features but is still easy to use, then Adobe Photoshop Elements is a good starting point for the novice (see Figure 4.17). With this program, you can improve the color balance of an image, touch up an image (by removing red-eye, for example), add creative effects to an image,

or group images together to create montages. If you later decide to upgrade to the professional Adobe Photoshop CS3, you will already be familiar with the user interface.

DIGITAL AUDIO SOFTWARE

Why would I have digital audio files on my computer? Best-selling novels, newspapers, and radio shows all can be purchased as audio files from sellers such as Audible, Inc. (**www.audible.com**). Huge numbers of free sources of audio files are also available through the phenomenon of *podcasting*, which is the distribution of audio files such as radio shows and music videos over the Internet. By subscription, these audio files are delivered to your machine free with the release of each edition. You may also choose to digitize (or *rip*) your CD collection to store on your computer. In addition, with programs such as *Magix Music Maker* or *Apple's GarageBand*, you can compose your own songs or soundtracks with virtual instruments, voice recorders, synthesizers, and special audio effects. So you may quickly have several gigabytes of audio files on your hard drive before you even know it!

Why are MP3 files so popular? MP3 is a type of audio compression format that reduces the file size of traditional digital audio files so that more files will take up less storage capacity. For example, a typical CD stores between 10 and 15 songs in uncompressed format, but with files in MP3 format, the same CD can store between 100 and 180. The smaller file size not only lets you store and play music in less space, but also distributes it quickly and easily over the Internet. You can find hundreds of digital audio software applications that allow you to copy (also called *ripping*), play, edit, and organize MP3 files, as well as record and distribute your own music online. Most digital audio software programs support one of the following functions, whereas others, such as iTunes, incorporate many of these capabilities into one multifunctional program:

- **MP3 recording** allows you to record directly from streaming audio and other software or microphone sources to MP3 format.

- **CD ripping** allows you to encode CDs to the MP3 format.

- **CD burning** allows you to create your own CDs from your MP3 collection.

FIGURE 4.17

Image editing software such as Adobe Photoshop Elements enables you to easily create (a) calendars, (b) greeting cards and postcards, (c) slide shows, and (d) more from your digital photos.

- **Encoding and decoding** is done by encoders, or programs that convert files to MP3 format at varying levels of quality. Most ripping software has encoders built in to convert the files directly into MP3 format.

- **Format conversion** programs allow you to convert MP3 files to other digital audio formats such as WAV (short for WAVE form audio format), WMA (Windows Media Audio), and AIFF (Audio Interchange File Format).

Can I edit audio files? Audio editing software includes tools that make editing your audio files as easy as editing your text files. Software such as the open source *Audacity* (**http://audacity.sourceforge.net**) and *Sony Sound Forge Audio Studio* (**www.sonycreativesoftware.com**) enables you to perform such basic editing tasks as cutting dead-air space from the beginning or end of the song or cutting a portion from the middle. You also can add special sound effects, such as echo or bass boost, and remove static or hiss from your MP3 files. Both of these applications support recording sound files from a microphone or any source you can connect through the input line of the sound card.

DIGITAL VIDEO EDITING SOFTWARE

What kind of software do I need to edit my digital videos? With the boom of digital camcorders and the improved graphics capabilities on home computers, many people are experimenting with **digital video editing software**. Several video editing software applications are available and at a wide range of prices and capabilities. Although the most expensive products (such as *Adobe Premiere Pro CS3*) offer the widest range of special effects and tools, some moderately priced video editing programs have enough features to keep the casual user happy. *Microsoft Movie Maker* and *Apple iMovie HD* have intuitive drag-and-drop features that make it simple to create professional-quality movies with little or no training (see Figure 4.18). Microsoft Movie Maker is included with Windows XP and Vista. Other software developers offer free trial versions so that you can decide whether the product meets your needs before purchasing it.

Does video editing software support all kinds of video files? Video files come in a number of formats. Many of the affordable video editing software packages support only a few types of video files. For example, one application may support Windows Media Player video files, whereas another may support Apple QuickTime or RealPlayer video files instead. Fortunately,

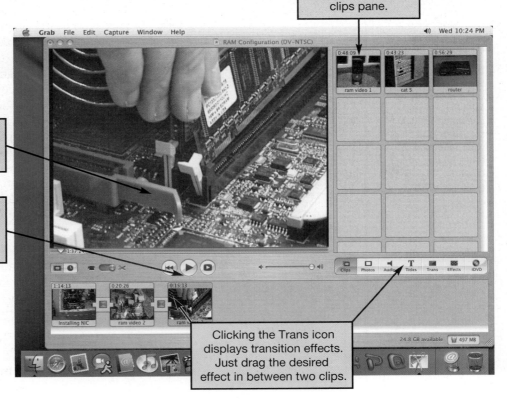

Available video clips are shown in the clips pane.

The iMovie monitor displays the current clip for viewing or editing.

Clips added to the movie being made are shown in the clip viewer. Just drag and drop!

Clicking the Trans icon displays transition effects. Just drag the desired effect in between two clips.

FIGURE 4.18

Video editing programs such as Apple iMovie make it easy even for novice users to create and edit movies.

SOUND BYTE

Enhancing Photos with Image Editing Software

In this Sound Byte, you'll learn tips and tricks on how to best use image editing software. You'll learn how to remove the red-eye from photos and incorporate borders, frames, and other enhancements to produce professional effects.

software boxes list which types of video files are supported by the software. You should buy the least expensive application with the greatest number of supported file formats.

For more information on video editing software, see the Technology in Focus feature "Digital Entertainment" on page 420.

MEDIA MANAGEMENT SOFTWARE

How do I manage the audio, video, and image files on my system?
Many people add hundreds or even thousands of files to their systems by purchasing music and downloading images and video. Your hard disk drive is a convenient place to store all your music and images, but only if you can find what you're looking for!

Software such as *Windows Media Player*, *Nullsoft Winamp*, and *Apple iTunes* allows you to organize audio and video files so that you can sort, filter, and search your music collection by artist, album, or category (see Figure 4.19). Using these programs, you can manage individual tracks, generate playlists, and even export the files to a database or spreadsheet application for further manipulation. Then you can burn the songs to a CD, and the program will print

liner notes that you can place inside the CD case.

Are there Web-based programs available to edit, share, and store my photos?
One great advantage of taking digital images is the ability to easily share the images via the Internet. Initially, we had to send images as attachments—and our exuberance in sending several images at the same time often clogged someone's inbox. Several online photo sharing and photo storing sites such as **Snapfish.com**, **Kodak.com**, and **Shutterfly.com** enable you to upload your digital images from your computer, create photo albums, and share them with friends and family. These sites offer printing services as well.

Flickr.com is probably one of the best online photo management and photo sharing applications that lets you organize your images and then share them with millions of users, or just with your closest of friends and family. Discussion boards are available so that groups can exchange comments about the images, just as you would if you were passing them around the dinner table. Finally, taking advantage of online mapping technologies, Flickr enables you to link your images to a map so that you can show exactly where you took the images or see where others have taken theirs.

FIGURE 4.19

Software programs such as iTunes help you manage all the MP3 files on your computer. You can sort, filter, and search your collection by artist, album, or category, as well as create playlists.

Album covers flow by in a smooth display

Smart playlists can select a list of songs from library on specific criteria

Google Picasa (**http://picasa.google.com**) is another popular player in the online photo editing, storing, and sharing field. Picasa helps you send the image to your friends, your mobile devices, or your blog! Picasa automatically resizes a huge 5-megapixel image to a more manageable size for e-mail, attaches it to your outgoing message, and sends it. Also, Picasa allows you to transfer images directly to your blog or to mobile devices such as an iPod or PDA.

More Fun at Home

As the term implies, **entertainment software** is designed to provide users with thrills, chills, and all-out fun! Computer games make up the vast majority of entertainment software. These digital games began with Pong, Pac-Man, and Donkey Kong and have evolved to include many different categories, including action, driving, puzzles, role-playing, card-playing, sports, strategy, and simulation games. Entertainment software also includes other types of computer applications such as **virtual reality programs** that turn artificial environments into a realistic experience.

GAMING SOFTWARE

Do I need special equipment to run entertainment software? As with any computer software, you need to make sure your system has enough processing power, memory (RAM), and hard drive capacity to run the program. Because games often push the limit of sound and video quality, be sure your system has the appropriate sound cards, video cards, speakers, monitor, and CD or DVD drives.

Some software may require a special controller to play the game. In the gaming console world, games such as *Steel Battalion* and *Rock Band* actually are sold with their own specialized controllers (see Figure 4.20). These controllers also can be adapted to your PC. Complex simulation programs can benefit from configurable, wireless controllers such as the Cyborg Evo.

How do I tell what computer games are appropriate for a certain user? The Entertainment Software Rating Board (ESRB) is a self-regulatory body established in 1994 by the Entertainment Software Association (**www.esrb.org**). The ESRB's rating system helps consumers choose the computer and video games that are right for their families by providing information about game content so that they can make informed purchasing decisions. ESRB ratings have two parts: rating symbols suggest age appropriateness, and content descriptors indicate elements in a game that may have triggered a particular rating or may be of interest or concern. It's important to check both the rating symbol (on the front of the game box) and the content descriptors (on the back of the game box). The rating symbols currently in use by the ESRB include ratings for Everyone (E), Teens (T), Mature (M), and Adult Only (AO).

Can I make video games? Now that video games represent an industry with revenue of more than $10 billion each year, designing and creating video games is emerging as a desirable career opportunity. Professionally created video games involve artistic storytelling and design, as well as sophisticated programming. Major production houses such as Electronic Arts use software applications that are not easily available to the casual home enthusiast. However, you can use the editors and game engines available for games such as *EverQuest*, *Oblivion*, and *Unreal Tournament* to create custom levels and characters, as well as extend the game.

If you want to try your hand at creating your own video games, multimedia software applications such as *Adobe Flash CS3* and *RPG Maker VX* provide the tools you

FIGURE 4.20

Computer joysticks can be specialized. Rock Band controllers include a guitar, a drum set, and a microphone.

need to explore game design and creation. The program *GameMaker* (**www.yoyogames.com**) is a free product that allows you to build a game with no programming at all; key elements of the new game creation are dragged and dropped into place. *Alice* (**www.alice.org**) is another free environment to check out. It lets you easily create 3D animations and simple games and will soon have the actual Sims characters included!

EDUCATIONAL SOFTWARE

What kinds of educational software applications are there? Although a multitude of educational software products are geared toward the younger set, software developers have by no means ignored adult markets. In addition to all the products relating to the younger audience, there are software products that teach users new skills such as typing, languages, cooking, and playing the guitar. Preparation software is also popular for students who will be taking the SAT, GMAT, LSAT, and MCAT exams.

Popular programs are also available to help students during lectures, organizing and maintaining their notes and the recordings they create from lectures. For example, *Microsoft OneNote* allows students with Tablet PCs to write their notes directly onto the tablet, using it as an electronic notebook. Pieces of text can be easily moved around the page, Web links can be quickly integrated, and audio or video recordings of lectures can be added with one click. Students can search for a term across the full set of notebooks they have created during this term, helping to find connecting ideas from course to course.

What types of programs are available to train you to use software or special machines? Many programs provide tutorial-like training for popular computer software applications. These programs use illustrated step-by-step instructions to guide users through unfamiliar skills. Some training programs known as **simulation programs** allow users to experience or control the software as if it were the actual software or an actual event. Such simulation programs include commercial and military flight training, surgical instrument training, and machine operation training. Often these simulators can be delivered locally on CD or DVD or over the Internet.

One benefit of these simulated training programs is that they safely allow users to experience potentially dangerous situations such as flying a helicopter during high winds. Consequently, users of these training programs are more likely to take risks and learn from their mistakes—something they could not afford to do in real-life situations. Simulated training programs also help prevent costly errors. Should something go awry, the only cost of the error is restarting the simulation program.

Do I need special software to take courses online? As long as you have a compatible Web browser, online classes will be accessible to you. Depending on the content and course materials, however, you may need a password or special plug-ins to view certain videos or demos.

Taking classes over the Internet is rapidly becoming a popular method of learning because it offers greater schedule flexibility for busy students. Although some courses are run from an individually developed Web

BITS AND BYTES

How to Open the Unknown

Normally, when you double-click a file icon on your desktop, the program that knows how to read the selected file is automatically run. For example, when you double-click a *.doc or *.docx file, Microsoft Word starts and displays the file. Sometimes, however, a pop-up appears with the message "Unknown File Type." Or a document may open with a program other than the one you wanted to open it with. To assign a program to a file type or to change the program opening that type of file, follow these instructions.

1. Click the Start button, and then click Search.
2. Use the search and navigation tools in this folder to locate the file you want to change (you can search for all Word files by searching for *.doc or *.docx). Right-click on a file of the correct type, and then, depending on the type of file, either click Open With or point to Open With, and then click Choose Default Program.
3. Click the program that you want to use to open this type of file. A list of programs installed on your computer will be provided.
4. Although you can choose to open individual files with a certain program, normally you would select the "Always use the selected program to open this kind of file" check box, and then click OK.
5. When you double-click that type of file in the future, the file will open in the program you selected.

site, many online courses are run through **course management software** programs such as *Blackboard*, *Moodle*, and *Angel*. These programs provide traditional classroom tools such as calendars and grade books over the Internet (see Figure 4.21). Special areas are available for students and professors to exchange ideas and information, including the use of chat rooms and discussion forums, and sending e-mail messages. Other areas are available for posting assignments, lectures, and other pertinent class information.

REFERENCE SOFTWARE

How can I use software to research information? Encyclopedias are no longer those massive sets of books in the library. Now you can find full sets of encyclopedias on CDs and DVDs. In addition to containing all the information found in traditional paper encyclopedias, electronic encyclopedia reference software includes multimedia content such as interactive maps, and video and audio clips. When researching famous sports figures, for example, not only can you read about Jackie Robinson but also you can view a video of him in action. World Book, Britannica, and Grolier all offer their encyclopedias on CD or DVD.

Is reference software available online? In addition to the traditional atlases, dictionaries, and thesauri available on CD and DVD, many other types of reference software are available online. Many traditional encyclopedias have online components. Encarta, for example, can be found on the Web at **encarta.msn.com**, and most of us are familiar with wiki-based online encyclopedic information found on **Wikipedia.org** and **Citizendium.org.** Other types of reference information are also available online. The American Sign Language dictionary, for example, is available online and includes video clips that show finger spelling and the modeling of

FIGURE 4.21

Management software such as Blackboard provides a method of accessing traditional classroom features, including participating in discussions and taking tests in an online environment.

each gesture. **WebMD.com** offers medical information, and **FindLaw.com** has basic legal information, and forms that you previously would have had to pay a professional to obtain are available online.

DRAWING SOFTWARE

What kind of software should I use for simple illustrations? Drawing **software** (or **illustration software**) programs let you create or edit two-dimensional, line-based drawings. You use drawing software to create technical diagrams or original nonphotographic drawings, animations, and illustrations using standard drawing and painting tools such as pens, pencils,

ACTIVE HELPDESK

Choosing Software

In this Active Helpdesk call, you'll play the role of a helpdesk staffer, fielding calls about the different kinds of multimedia software, educational and reference software, and entertainment software.

and paintbrushes. You also can drag geometric objects from a toolbar onto the canvas area to create images and use paint bucket, eyedropper, and spray can tools to add color and special effects to the drawings.

Are there different types of drawing software? Drawing software is used in both creative and technical drawings. Software applications such as *Adobe Illustrator CS3* include tools that let you create professional-quality creative and technical illustrations. The Illustrator tools help you create complex designs, such as muscle structures in the human body, and use special effects, such as charcoal sketches. Its warping tool allows you to bend, stretch, and twist portions of your image or text. Because of its many tools and features, Illustrator is one of the preferred drawing software programs of most graphic artists.

There are many software packages to help plan the layout of rooms, homes, and landscapes such as those offered by Broderbund. *Microsoft Visio* is a program used to create technical drawings, maps, basic block diagrams, networking and engineering flowcharts, and project schedules, but it can also be used by the more casual designer. Visio uses project-related templates with special objects that you drag onto a canvas. For example, by using the Visio floor template and dragging furniture and other interior objects onto it, you can create an interior design like the one shown in Figure 4.22. Visio also provides mind-mapping templates that help you organize your thoughts and ideas.

FIGURE 4.22

The drawing program Visio lets you create different types of diagrams easily with drag-and-drop options.

Business Software

With the amount of power available in a typical home computer, you have more opportunities than ever to run a business from your home. No matter what service or product you provide, there are common types of software you'll want to consider. Accounting software will help manage the flow of money, and desktop publishing and Web page creation tools will help you market and grow your new enterprise. A number of software packages are designed to organize and help with the day-to-day operations of a typical business. If you ever plan to run a business from your own home, or even if you are just a user of large business products and services, it is helpful to know what functions business software can perform.

HOME BUSINESS SOFTWARE

What programs are good for people with small businesses? If you have a small business or a hobby that produces income, then you know the importance of keeping good records and tracking your expenses and income. **Accounting software** helps small-business owners manage their finances more efficiently by providing tools for tracking accounts receivable and accounts payable. In addition, these applications also offer inventory management plus payroll and billing tools. Examples of accounting software applications include *Intuit QuickBooks* and *Peachtree by Sage*. Both programs include templates for invoices, statements, and financial reports so that small-business owners can create common forms and reports.

What software can I use to lay out and design newsletters and other publications? Desktop publishing (DTP) software allows you to incorporate and arrange graphics and text in your documents in creative ways. Although many word-processing applications allow you to use some of the features that are hallmarks of desktop publishing, specialized desktop publishing software such as *QuarkXPress* and *Adobe InDesign* allows professionals to design books and other publications with complex layouts (see Figure 4.23).

What tools do desktop publishing programs include? Desktop publishing programs offer a variety of tools

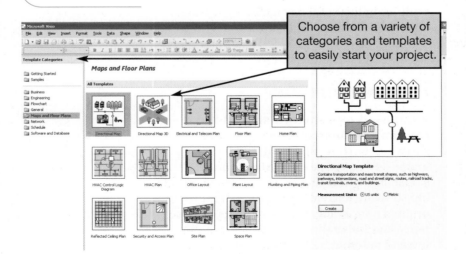

Choose from a variety of categories and templates to easily start your project.

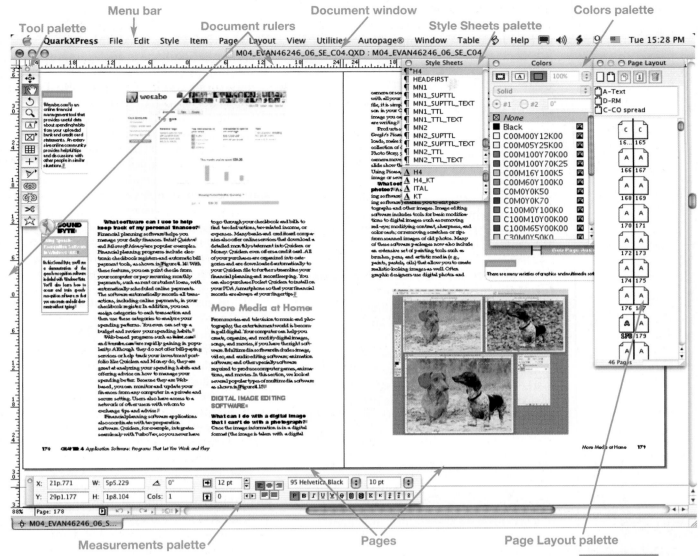

Tool palette

Menu bar

Document rulers

Document window

Style Sheets palette

Colors palette

Measurements palette

Pages

Page Layout palette

FIGURE 4.23

Major publishing houses use professional publishing programs such as QuarkXPress to lay out the pages of textbooks.

with which you can format text and graphics. With text formatting tools, you easily can change the font, size, and style of your text as well as arrange text on the page in different columns, shapes, and patterns. You also can import files into your documents from other sources, including elements from other software programs (such as a chart from Excel or text from Word) and image files. You can readily manipulate graphics with tools that can crop, flip, or rotate images or modify the image's color, shape, and size. Desktop publishing programs also include features that allow you to publish to the Web.

What software do I use to create a Web page? Web page authoring software allows even the novice to design interesting and interactive Web pages, without knowing any HyperText Markup Language (HTML) code. Web page authoring applications often include wizards, templates, and reference materials to help you easily complete most Web page authoring tasks. More experienced users can take advantage of the advanced features in this software, including features that enable you to add headlines and weather information, stock tickers, and maps to make your Web content current, interactive, and interesting. *Microsoft Expression Web* and *Adobe Dreamweaver* are two of the leading programs to which both professionals and casual page designers turn.

Are there other ways to create Web pages? If you need to produce only the occasional Web page and do not need a separate page authoring program, you'll find that many software applications include features that enable you to convert your document easily into a Web page. For example, in some Microsoft Office applications, you can choose to save the file as a Web page, and the application will automatically convert the file to a Web-compatible format.

Large Business Software

There is a software application for almost every aspect of business. There are specialized programs for marketing and sales, finance, point of sale, general productivity, project management, security, networking, data management, e-commerce, and human resources to name just a few. In the following sections, we discuss this seemingly endless list.

What software do businesses use for planning and management? Planning is a big part of running a successful business. Software programs such as *Palo Alto Software's Business Plan Pro* and *Marketing Plan Pro* help businesses write strategic and development business and marketing plans. Another good example of business planning software is **project management software** such as *Microsoft Project*. This type of software helps project managers easily create and modify scheduling charts like the one shown in Figure 4.24, which help managers plan and track specific tasks and coordinate personnel resources.

Customer relationship management (CRM) software stores sales and client-contact information in one central database. Sales professionals use CRM programs to get in touch with and follow up with their clients. These programs also include tools that enable businesses to assign quotas and create reports and charts to document and analyze actual and projected sales data.

CRM programs coordinate well with PIM software such as Outlook and can be set up to work with PDAs. GoldMine from FrontRange Solutions is one example of a CRM program.

Enterprise resource planning (ERP) systems are important to businesses as they consolidate multiple systems into one and improve coordination of these business areas across multiple departments. ERP systems are used to control many "back-office" operations and processing functions such as billing, production, inventory management, and human resources management. ERP systems are implemented by third-party vendors and matched directly to the specific needs of a company. Oracle and SAP are well-known companies that sell ERP software.

What software helps business travelers? Mapping programs such as *DeLorme Street Atlas USA* and *Microsoft Streets & Trips* are perfect for businesses that require employees to travel frequently. These programs provide street maps and written directions to locations nationwide, and you can customize maps to include landmarks and other handy traveling sites such as airports, hotels, and restaurants. **Online mapping services** such as MapQuest, Yahoo! Maps, and Google Maps and Google Earth are now more popular than the more traditional mapping software programs because they are easily accessible with any Internet connection and are updated more frequently. Mapping programs are available in versions for PDAs and for cars and work in conjunction with a global positioning system (GPS) device to help you navigate your way around unfamiliar territory. Mapping programs are essential for sales representatives or delivery-intensive businesses but also are useful for nonprofessionals traveling to unfamiliar locations.

What software is used with e-commerce? Seemingly every business has an online presence to display company information or products, handle online sales, or offer customer service and support. Depending on the size of the company and its specific needs, there are products such as *IBM's WebSphere*, *goEmerchant* from EVS Holding Company, and *ProStores Business* from Kurant Corporation that offer Web site creation and hosting services, shopping cart setup, and credit card processing services in

FIGURE 4.24

A Gantt chart in Microsoft Project provides project managers with a visual tool for assigning personnel and scheduling and managing tasks.

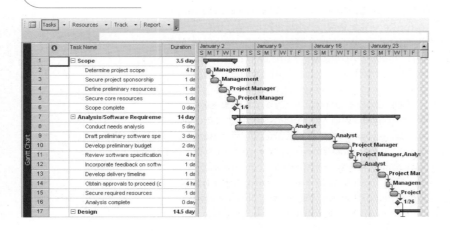

one complete bundle. For larger businesses, specialized software to handle each aspect of e-commerce is available, or they might develop their own software tailored to their specific needs.

SPECIALIZED BUSINESS SOFTWARE

What kinds of specialized business software are there? Some software applications are tailored to the needs of a particular company or industry. Such software designed for a specific industry is called **vertical market software**. For example, the construction industry uses software such as *Sage Master Builder*, which features estimating tools to help construction companies bid on jobs. It also integrates project management functions and accounting systems that are unique to the construction industry.

Other examples of vertical market software include property management software for real estate professionals; ambulance scheduling and dispatching software for emergency assistance organizations; and library automation software for cataloging, circulation, inventory, online catalog searching, and custom report printing at libraries.

In addition to these specific business software applications that companies can buy off the shelf, programs often are custom developed to address a particular company's specific needs. These custom applications are referred to as **proprietary software** because they are owned and controlled by the company that uses them.

What software is used to make 3D models? Computer-aided design (CAD) programs are a form of 3D modeling that engineers use to create automated designs, technical drawings, and model visualizations. Specialized CAD software such as *Autodesk's AutoCAD* is used in areas such as architecture, automotive, aerospace, and medical engineering.

With CAD software, architects can build virtual models of their plans and readily visualize all aspects of design before actual construction. Engineers use CAD software to design everything from factory components to bridges. The 3D nature of these programs allows engineers to rotate their models and make adjustments to their designs where necessary, thus eliminating costly building errors.

BITS AND BYTES

Need a Way to Share Files? Try PDF

Say you've created a file in Microsoft Excel, but the person to whom you want to send it doesn't have Excel, or any spreadsheet software, installed on his computer. Or say your sister owns a Mac and you own a PC. You constantly are running into file-sharing problems. What do you do in these situations? One solution is to create a PDF file. Portable Document Format (PDF) is a file format you can create with Adobe Acrobat or Cutepdf Writer, a freeware program available from **www.cutepdf.com**. These programs transform any file, regardless of its application or platform, into a document that can be shared, viewed, and printed by anyone who has Adobe Reader. If you are using Microsoft Word 2007, OpenOffice Writer, or Corel WordPerfect, then you can create PDF files easily with the built-in feature. Adobe Reader, the program you need to read all PDF files, is a free download available at **www.adobe.com**.

CAD software also is being used in conjunction with GPS devices for accurate placement of fiber-optic networks around the country. The medical engineering community uses CAD to create anatomically accurate solid models of the human anatomy to develop medical implants quickly and accurately. The list of CAD applications keeps growing as more and more industries realize the benefits CAD can bring to their product development and manufacturing processes.

Many graphics, animation, video, and gaming systems use an application from AutoDesk called *3D Studio Max* to create 3D models with complex textures and lighting models. A 30-day free trial version of the software is available at **www.autodesk.com**. 3D Studio Max is a complex and rich program. A slightly simpler package is the open source program *Blender*, which is available free of charge at **www.blender.org**.

Getting Help with Software

If you need help while you work with software, you can access several different resources to find answers to your questions. For general help or information about the product, many Web sites offer **frequently asked questions (FAQs)** for answers to the most common questions.

Emerging Technologies: Is It Real or Is It Virtual?

Software can take us beyond what is familiar to us and into alternate realities. Virtual reality uses software to allow people to interact in a simulated three-dimensional environment that users can manipulate and explore as if they were in that world. Beyond video games, the applications of virtual reality are almost endless. Three-dimensional environments created by computers are getting better and better at helping people experience new things or experience familiar things in new ways.

Virtual environments are used in military training programs, the space program and, as discussed in Chapter 1, in the medical field. Studies show that soldiers who have gone through virtual reality (VR) training are just as effective as those who have trained in traditional combat situations. Flight simulators are used by airlines to prepare commercial pilots to fly in a wide range of flight conditions, as well as by the military and NASA. The obvious benefit of simulators and VR is that there is little machine and human expense when a mistake is made in virtual conditions as there would be in "live" conditions.

Engineers and designers are also using virtual reality technologies. Car manufacturers build virtual prototypes of new vehicles, test them, and make alterations in design before producing a single physical part. Architects create virtual models of building plans so that clients or potential buyers can "walk through" and get a more realistic idea of how moving through the building will be.

Second Life, a virtual world launched in 2003 by Linden Research, Inc., has gained worldwide popularity. Users create avatars, or virtual representations of themselves, with which they interact in the

virtual world. Second Life has its own economy, where users have created "in-world" businesses and residents can legally trade in the world's own currency, called Linden dollars.

Second Life has also begun to permeate into the "outside world." "Outside world" businesses now assist and advise "in-world" businesses. For example, real-world programmers build complex in-world projects for clients such as Dartmouth College, Major League Baseball, and Lego. Real-world accountants offer services to advise "in-world" businesses on finance, strategic planning, or budget forecasting. It is "fertile ground" for innovative and entrepreneurial thinkers both inside and outside Second Life.

Finally, businesses and educational institutions also recognize the marketing potential in Second Life, and they use the virtual world to test new ideas. Educational institutions such as Harvard, Princeton, and Ohio University have built virtual campuses with the intention of holding "virtual tours" for prospective students or for current students to take courses (see Figure 4.25), participate in student organizations, or meet and collaborate online just as they would if they met in the real-world student center.

Virtual worlds such as Second Life are innovative ways to hold distance-learning classes. Online classes held in a virtual world environment can provide the same online convenience of not having to travel to class while providing a more enjoyable and perhaps even more effective experience. In a virtual world, students

---

Where can I find help while working in an application? Some programs also offer online help and support. Sometimes online help is comparable to a user's manual. However, many times online help allows you to chat over the Internet with an online support team member. Some applications are context-sensitive and offer task-specific help or screen tips to explain where your cursor is resting.

In Microsoft Office applications, a question mark icon is found on the far top right of the program screen. This icon takes you to the main Help interface. **Integrated help** means that the documentation for the product is built directly into the software so

that you won't need to keep track of bulky manuals. You can type your question, search for a term, or browse the Help topics (see Figure 4.26). Like many software packages, Microsoft Office offers help documentation, which is installed locally on your machine, and online help resources, which are updated continually.

Finally, the Help menu on the menu bar of most applications enables you to choose to search an index or content outline to find out the nature of almost any Microsoft application feature.

Where do I go for tutorials and training on an application? If you need help learning how to use a product,

are able to convene in traditional classrooms, on sandy Malibu beaches or in fresh air venues—environments limited only by the imagination of the instructor and the students. With more enjoyable instructional venues, students might actually make the time to attend virtual classrooms, thus increasing their productivity and the interactivity of an online classroom.

Additionally, virtual classroom environments add an additional technological experience that students may be able to bring with them into their profession. Seton Hall University, for example, uses Second Life in an emergency-preparedness course that allows the students to experience working in simulated catastrophic situations, which would otherwise be difficult to experience in the real-world.

FIGURE 4.25

Virtual worlds are innovative ways to hold distance learning classes.

Just as in the real world, the virtual world has its problems. However, it is likely that virtual reality and virtual environments will continue to find uses in entertainment, education, distance learning, design, and manufacturing.

sometimes the product's developer offers online tutorials or program tours that show you how to use the software features. Often you can find good tutorials simply by searching the Internet. **MalekTips.com**, for example, includes a vast array of multimedia help files, you can find podcasts for applications such as Excel and Photoshop in iTunes, and even YouTube has some helpful videos.

Buying Software

These days, you no longer need to go to a computer supply store to buy software. You can find software in almost any retail environment. In addition, you can purchase software online, through catalogs, and at auctions.

SOFTWARE LICENSES

Don't I own the software I buy? Most people don't understand that, unlike other items they purchase, the software applications they buy don't belong to them. The only thing they're actually purchasing is a license that gives them the right to use the software for their own purposes as the *only* user of that copy. The application is not

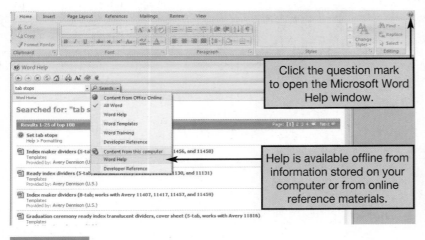

Click the question mark to open the Microsoft Word Help window.

Help is available offline from information stored on your computer or from online reference materials.

FIGURE 4.26

Microsoft Office gives you tips on tasks you're working on and answers specific questions you have using online and offline resources.

theirs to lend or copy for installation on other computers, even if it's another one of their own.

What are software licenses? Software licenses are agreements between you, the user, and the software developer. You accept this agreement before installing the software on your machine. It is a legal contract that outlines the acceptable uses of the program and any actions that violate the agreement. Generally, the agreement will state who the ultimate owner of the software is, under what circumstances copies of the software can be made, and whether the software can be installed on any other machine. Finally, the license agreements will state what, if any, warranty comes with the software.

Do you always buy just one license? Most individuals will buy single licenses to cover their specific use. These licenses cannot be shared and you cannot "extend" the license to install the software on more than one of your computers. However, Apple also offers a "family license" to legally install some of its software on as many as five computers, and some versions of Microsoft Office come with three licenses. Businesses and educational institutions often buy multiuser licenses that allow more than one person to use the software. Some multiuser licenses are per-seat and limit the number of users to a specific amount, while concurrent licenses limit the number of users accessing the software at any given time.

PREINSTALLED SOFTWARE

What application software comes with my computer? Virtually every new computer comes with some form of application software, although the applications depend on the hardware manufacturer and computer model. You usually can count on your computer having some form of productivity software preinstalled, such as Microsoft Works or Corel WordPerfect Office.

Multimedia-enriched computers also may offer graphics software or a productivity suite that includes page authoring software. Many new computers also include some form of software that is useful to the home user such as image editing software or financial planning software.

Can I get the manufacturer to install software before shipping? If you know you'll need a particular type of software not offered as standard on your new computer, then you may want to see if the computer manufacturer has a special offer that will allow you to add that particular software at a reduced price. Sometimes, initially buying software through the hardware manufacturer is less expensive than buying software on the retail market, but this is not always the case, so do some comparative pricing before you buy.

WEB-BASED APPLICATION SOFTWARE

Does all application software require installation on my computer? Most application software you acquire, whether by purchasing a CD or DVD at a retail store or by downloading the software from a Web site, requires the software to be installed on your computer before use. However, Web-based application software is growing in popularity. **Web-based application software** is a program hosted on a Web site that does not require a large installation on your computer. In some cases, a Web application will add nothing at all to your system; sometimes a small plug-in or control software module will be quickly downloaded.

Is all Web-based software free? Some Web sites charge a fee to use their application software. *TurboTax Online* (**www.turbotax.com**) is a version of the popular tax preparation software that you can access online to prepare your tax returns. Aside from saving the hassle of software installation on your computer, TurboTax Online also stores your information in a secure location so that you can retrieve it anytime.

More and more of your software needs might be met by some of the emerging Web-based providers. Many Web sites offer no-charge Web-based applications, such as the mapping software *Mapquest* (**www.mapquest.com**) and *Yahoo! Maps* (**www.maps.yahoo.com**), that allow you to generate driving directions from point to point. Sites such as **zoho.com** (see Figure 4.27), **ThinkFree.com**, and **docs.google.com** offer Web-based applications that cover a range of word-processing, presentation, project management, and spreadsheet needs.

These products are run from software stored completely on the Web server instead of your hard drive. They are typically free of charge. They are a reflection of a movement toward a new software distribution model. Perhaps we will see the day that software is available online and rented for the period of time you need access to it.

The features of these programs are generally a subset of what the installed versions offer, but they do offer other advantages. Google Docs, for example, is a free application with word-processing, spreadsheet, and presentation capabilities. You can invite people to share your files and work together in real time, watching as others make changes to the document. As long as you have a Web browser, you can access your files, which are stored securely online. Although these free applications are not as full featured as the products from Microsoft, they can read and export to many different file formats and be used with other packages. The trend toward Web-based applications is interesting to watch.

DISCOUNTED SOFTWARE

Is it possible to buy software at a discount?
Software manufacturers understand that students and educators often need to use software for short periods of time because of specific classes or projects. In addition, software developers want to encourage you to learn with their

FIGURE 4.27

Zoho.com is one of the many emerging Web sites that offers free Web-based productivity software.

product, hoping you'll become a long-term user of their software. Therefore, if you're a student or an educator, you can purchase software that is no different from regularly priced software at prices that are sometimes substantially less than general consumer prices.

Sometimes, campus computer stores or college bookstores also offer discounted prices to students and faculty who possess a valid ID. Online software suppliers such as Journey Education Marketing (**www.journeyed.com**), CampusTech, Inc. (**www.campustech.com**), and Academic Superstore (**www. academicsuperstore.com**) also offer the same software applications available in the store to students at reduced prices. You also can find software through mail-order companies. Check out Google Catalogs (**http://catalogs.google.com**) for an extensive listing of companies that offer software by mail order.

Can I buy used software? Often you can buy software through online auction sites such as eBay. If you do so, be sure that you are buying licensed (legal) copies. Computer shows that display state-of-the-art computer equipment are generally good sources for software. However, here, too, you must exert a bit of caution to make sure you are buying licensed copies and not pirated versions.

BITS AND BYTES

Software 911

If your software problem is more technical, such as an error message, lots of resources are available on the Web. Most software manufacturers have support on their Web sites that include FAQs, discussion boards monitored by employees of the company, and collections of tutorials and troubleshooting advice. For example, to resolve problems with Microsoft products, check the Microsoft Help and Support located at **support.microsoft.com** to find a collection of more than 250,000 articles written by Microsoft support professionals reflecting their resolution of customer issues and problems. To search Microsoft's Help and Support most effectively, use a search engine such as Google. To do so, go to Google (**www.google.com**) and select the Advanced Search option. Specify **support.microsoft.com** as the domain to be searched and then type your search terms. Technical communities in the form of blogs, newsgroups, webcasts, and forums are also available on the Web to provide opportunities for you to interact with employees, experts, and peers. Access Microsoft's technical communities at **www.microsoft.com/communities**.

Can I buy software directly from the Internet? As with many other retail products, you can buy and download software applications directly from many developers and retail store Web sites. You also can use the Internet to buy software that is custom developed to your specific needs. Companies such as Ascentix Corporation (**www.ascentix.com**) act as intermediaries between you (the software user) and a software developer. With custom-developed software, the developer tweaks open source software code to meet your particular needs.

The *Microsoft .NET* program (**www. microsoft.com/net**) offers software over the Internet for all devices—not just computers—that have a connection to the Internet. Therefore, you can download software specifically for your PDA or wireless phone by using .NET. In addition, if you have a Microsoft .NET account (available free of charge at the Microsoft Web site), you can connect to any other .NET-connected device.

FREEWARE AND SHAREWARE

Can I get software for free legally?
Freeware is any copyrighted software that you can use for free. Plenty of freeware exists on the Web, ranging from games and screen savers to business, educational, graphics, home and hobby, and system utility software programs. To find free software, type "freeware" in your search engine. One good source of freeware offering a large variety of programs is Freeware Home (**www. freewarehome.com**).

Although they do not charge a fee, some developers release free software and request that you mail them a postcard or send them an e-mail message to thank them for their time in developing the software and to give them your opinion of it. Such programs are called *postcardware* and *e-mailware*, respectively.

Another option is to search for an open source program to fit your needs. Open source programs are free to use on the condition that any changes you make to improve the source code also must be distributed for free. SourceForge.net (**http://sourceforge.net**) is an excellent site to begin your hunt for a group that may already have built a solution that will work for you!

Can I try new software before it is really released? Some software developers offer **beta versions** of their software free of charge. Beta versions are software applications that are still under development. By distributing free beta versions, developers hope users will report errors or bugs they find in their programs, helping the developers correct any errors before they launch the software on the market at retail prices.

Is it still freeware if I'm asked to pay for the program after using it for awhile? One model for distributing software is to allow users to test software first (run it for a limited time, free of charge). Large corporations do this by offering free trial software products. These are fully functional packages, but they expire if not purchased within a certain timeframe. Small software developers also use this kind of distribution. This is referred to as **shareware**. Shareware software is distributed freely but with certain conditions. Sometimes the software is released on a trial basis only and must be registered after a certain period of time; in other cases, no support is available unless the software is registered. In some cases, direct payment to the author is required. Shareware is not freeware. If you use the software after the initial trial period is over, then you are breaking the software license agreement.

Software developers put out shareware programs to get their products into users' hands without the added expense and hassle of marketing and advertising. Therefore, quite a few great programs are available as shareware, and they can compete handily with programs on retail shelves. For example, TechSmith Corporation (**www.techsmith.com**) offers screen capture and desktop recording software applications as shareware such as *SnagIt Screen Capture* and *Camtasia Studio* screen recording and presentation. You can try these products for free for a 30-day period, after which time you must purchase the software to continue using it. For a listing of other shareware programs, visit the CNET Tucows.com (**www.Tucows.com**), as shown in Figure 4.28, or the CNET Shareware.com (**www.shareware.com**) Web sites.

Can shareware programmers make me pay for the shareware once I have it? The whole concept of shareware assumes that users will behave ethically and abide by the license agreement. However, to protect themselves, many developers have incorporated code into the program to stop it from working completely or to alter the output slightly after the trial period expires.

Are there risks associated with installing or downloading from the Internet beta versions, freeware, and shareware? Not all files available as shareware and freeware will work on your computer. You easily can crash your system and may even need to reinstall your operating system as a result of loading a freeware or shareware program that was not written for your computer's operating system.

Of course, by their very nature, beta products are most likely not bug-free, so you always run the risk of something going awry with your system. Unless you're willing to deal with potential problems, it may be best to wait until the last beta version is released. By that time, most of the serious bugs have been worked out.

As a matter of precaution, you should be comfortable with the reliability of the software developer before downloading a freeware, shareware, or beta version of software. If it's a reliable developer whose software you are already familiar with, then you can be more certain that a serious bug or virus is not hiding in the software. However, downloading software from an unknown source could potentially put your system at risk for contracting a virus. (We discuss viruses in detail in Chapter 7.)

A good practice to establish before installing any software on your system is to use the Windows Vista operating system's Restore feature and create a *restore point*. That way, if anything goes wrong during installation, you can restore your system back to how it was before you started. (We discuss the System Restore utility in Chapter 5.) Also, make sure that your virus protection software is up-to-date.

SOFTWARE VERSIONS AND SYSTEMS REQUIREMENTS

What do the numbers after software names indicate? Software developers change their software programs to repair

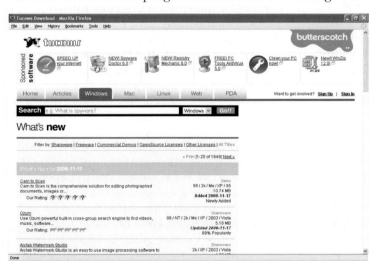

FIGURE 4.28

Tucows.com is a useful site for finding freeware applications. The site provides product reviews, hardware requirements, and details about the limitations of the free version of the software.

BITS AND BYTES

Keeping Your Software Up-to-Date

Bugs in software occur all the time. Software developers are constantly testing their product, even after releasing the software to the retail market, and users report errors they find. In today's environment in which security is a large concern, companies test their products for vulnerabilities against hackers and other malicious users. Once a fix or patch to a bug or vulnerability is created, most software developers will put the repair in downloadable form on the Internet, available at no charge. You should check periodically for any software updates or service packs to ensure your software is up-to-date. For your convenience, many products have an automatic update feature that downloads and installs updates automatically.

problems (or bugs) or add new or upgraded features. Generally, they keep the software program's name but add a number to it to indicate that it is a different version. Originally, developers used numbers only to indicate different software versions (major upgrades) and releases (minor upgrades). Today, however, software developers also use years (such as Microsoft Office 2007) and letters (such as WordPerfect Office X3) to represent version upgrades.

When is it worth buying a newer version? Although software developers suggest otherwise, there is no need to rush out and buy the latest version of a software program every time one is released. Depending on the software, some upgrades are not significantly different from the previous version to make it cost-effective for you to buy the newest version. Unless the upgrade adds features that are important to you, you may be better off waiting to upgrade every other release. You also should consider how frequently you use the software to justify an upgrade and whether your current system can handle the new system requirements of the upgraded version.

If I have an older version of software and someone sends me files from a newer version, can I still open them? Software vendors recognize that people work on different versions of the same software. Vendors therefore make the

newest version backward-compatible, meaning the newest software can recognize (open) files created with older versions. However, many software programs are not forward-compatible, meaning that older versions cannot recognize files created on newer versions.

How do I know whether the software I buy will work on my computer? Every software program has a set of **system requirements** that specify the minimum recommended standards for the operating system, processor, primary memory (RAM), and hard drive capacity. Sometimes there are other specifications for the video card, monitor, CD drive, and other peripherals. These requirements generally are printed on the software packaging or are available at the publisher's Web site. Before installing software on your computer, ensure that your system setup meets the minimum requirements by having sufficient storage, memory capacity, and processing capabilities.

Installing, Uninstalling, and Opening Software

Before you use your software, you must permanently place it, or install it, on your system. The installation process is slightly different, depending on whether you've purchased the software from a retail outlet and have an installation CD or whether you are downloading it from the Internet. Deleting or uninstalling software from your system requires certain precautions to ensure you remove all associated programs from your system.

How do I install software? When you purchase software, the program files may come on a CD or a DVD. For most programs being installed on a PC, an installation wizard automatically opens when you insert the CD, as shown in Figure 4.29. By following the steps indicated by the wizard, you can install the software application on your system. If the wizard doesn't open automatically for some reason, then the best way to install the software is to go to the Programs and Features icon located in the Control Panel on the Start menu. This

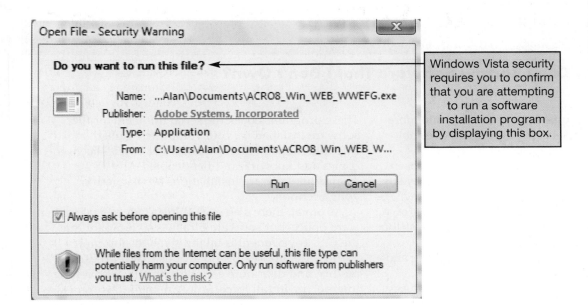

FIGURE 4.29

Installation wizards guide you through the installation process and generally appear automatically when you install new software.

Windows Vista security requires you to confirm that you are attempting to run a software installation program by displaying this box.

feature locates and launches the installation wizard.

How is the installation process different for software I download from the Web? When you download software from the Web, you typically do not get an installation disc. Instead, everything you need to install and run the downloaded program is contained in one file that has been compressed (or zipped) to make the downloading process quicker. For the most part, these downloaded files unzip or decompress themselves and automatically start or launch the setup program. During the installation and setup process, these programs select or create the folder on your computer's hard drive in which most of the program files will be saved. Usually, you can select a different location if you desire. Either way, note the name and location of the files, because you may need to access them later.

What do I do if the downloaded program doesn't install by itself? Some programs you download do not automatically install and run on your computer. Although the compressed files may unzip automatically as part of the download process, the setup program may not run without some help from you. In this case, you need to locate the files on the hard drive (this is why you must remember the location of the files) and find the program that is

controlling the installation (sometimes named *setup.exe* or *install.exe*). Files ending with the .exe extension are executable files or applications. All other files in the folder are support, help, and data files. Once the setup program begins, you will be prompted with the necessary actions to complete the installation.

What's the difference between a custom installation and a full installation? One of the first steps in the installation wizard is deciding between a full installation and a custom installation. A **full installation** will copy all the files and programs from the distribution disc to the computer's hard drive. By selecting **custom installation**, you can decide which features you want installed on the hard drive. Installing only the features you know you want allows you to save space on your hard drive.

ACTIVE HELPDESK

Buying and Installing Software

In this Active Helpdesk call, you'll play the role of a helpdesk staffer, fielding calls about how to best purchase software or get it for free, how to install and uninstall software, and where you can go for help when you have a problem with your software.

Ethics: Can I Borrow Software That I Don't Own?

A computer user who copies an application onto more than one computer, if the license agreement does not permit this, is participating in **software piracy**. Historically, the most common way software has been pirated among computer users has been when they supplement each other's software library by borrowing CDs and installing the borrowed software on their own computers. Larger-scale illegal duplication and distribution by counterfeiters also is quite common. The Internet also provides a means of illegally copying and distributing pirated software.

Is it really a big deal to copy a program or two? As reported by the Business Software Alliance, 40 percent of all software is pirated. Not only is pirating software unethical and illegal, but also the practice has financial impacts on all software application consumers. The reduced dollars from pirated software lessen the amount of money available for further software research and development while increasing the up-front costs to legitimate consumers.

To determine whether you have a pirated copy of software installed on your computer at work or at home, you can download a free copy of GASP (a suite of programs designed to help identify and track licensed and unlicensed software and other files) from the Business Software Alliance Web site (**www.bsa.org/usa**). A similar program is available at the Microsoft Web site (**www.microsoft.com/piracy**).

These programs check the serial numbers for the software installed on your computer against software manufacturer databases of official licensed copies and known fraudulent copies. Any suspicious software installations are flagged for your attention.

As of yet, there's no such thing as an official software police, but software piracy is so rampant that the U.S. government is taking steps to stop piracy worldwide. Efforts to stop groups that reproduce, modify, and distribute counterfeit software over the Internet are in full force. Software manufacturers also are becoming more aggressive in programming mechanisms into software to prevent repeated installations. For instance, with many Microsoft products, installation requires the activation of the serial number of your software with a database maintained at Microsoft. This is different from the traditional "registration" that enrolled you voluntarily and allowed you to be notified of product updates, for example. Activation is required, and failure to activate your serial number or attempting to activate a serial number that has been used previously results in the software going into a "reduced functionality mode" after the 50th time you use it. So without activation, you would not be able to save documents in Office—a strong motivator to let Microsoft watch how many times you install the software you purchased!

Can I just delete a program to uninstall it? A software application contains many different files—library files, help files, and other text files—in addition to the main file you use to run the program. By deleting only the main file, or simply deleting the icon on your desktop, you are not ridding your system of all the pieces of the program. In addition, some applications make changes to a variety of settings, and none of these are restored if you just delete the desktop icon or remove the main file.

Sometimes, programs have an Uninstall Program icon in the main program folder on the Start menu. Using this icon will run the proper cleanup to clear out all of the files associated with the application as well as

restore any settings that have been changed. If you can't locate the uninstall program for your particular software application, click the Start menu, click Control Panel, and then click Programs and Features. This will give you a list of software applications installed on your system; from this list you can choose which software application you would like to uninstall.

Is there a best way to open an application? The simplest way to open an application is by clicking its icon in the All Programs list found on the Start menu. Every program that you install on your system is listed on the Start menu. However, if you find you use only a few programs the most often, you can place a shortcut to that program either on the Quick Launch toolbar on the taskbar or on your desktop. To place a program in the Quick Launch toolbar on the taskbar, right-click the program icon on your desktop or right-click the program name on the Start menu. From the shortcut menu that is displayed, select Add to Quick Launch to place an icon for this program on the Quick Launch toolbar (see Figure 4.30a).

To create a shortcut on the desktop, right-click the icon of the desired program and click Send To, and then select Desktop (see Figure 4.30b). This places the shortcut icon directly on the Desktop. You can identify a shortcut icon by the little black arrow in the lower-left corner of the icon, as shown in Figure 4.30a.

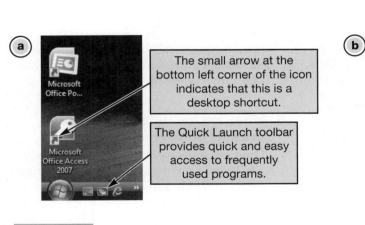

The small arrow at the bottom left corner of the icon indicates that this is a desktop shortcut.

The Quick Launch toolbar provides quick and easy access to frequently used programs.

To create a shortcut to the program on your desktop, right-click the program icon from the Start menu and select Send To then Desktop.

FIGURE 4.30

To quickly access an application you use often, you can place a shortcut in (a) the Quick Launch toolbar or (b) on your desktop.

Summary

1. What's the difference between application software and system software?

System software is the software that helps run the computer and coordinates instructions between application software and the computer's hardware devices. System software includes the operating system and utility programs. Application software is the software you use to do everyday tasks at home, school, and work. Application software is productivity software, such as word-processing and finance programs; media software, such as those used for image editing; home and entertainment software, such as games or educational programs; and business software.

2. What kinds of applications are included in productivity software I might use at home?

Productivity software programs include word-processing, spreadsheet, presentation, personal information manager (PIM), and database programs. You use word-processing software to create and edit written documents. Spreadsheet software enables you to do calculations and numerical and what-if analyses easily. Presentation software enables you to create slide presentations. Personal information manager (PIM) software helps keep you organized by putting a calendar, address book, notepad, and to-do lists within your computer. Database programs are electronic filing systems that allow you to filter, sort, and retrieve data easily. Individuals can also use software to help with business-like tasks such as preparing taxes and managing personal finances.

3. What are the different types of multimedia software?

Multimedia software includes digital image, video, and audio editing software; animation software; and other specialty software required to produce computer games. A wide variety of software programs is used to play, copy, record, edit, and organize MP3 files. Modern users have so many audio, video, and image files that many software solutions are available for organizing and distributing these types of files.

4. What are the different types of entertainment software?

Beyond the games that most of us are familiar with, entertainment software includes virtual reality programs that use special equipment to make users feel as though they are actually experiencing the program in a realistic 3D environment.

5. What are the different types of drawing software?

Drawing software lets you create and edit line-based drawings to produce both imaginative and technical illustrations. Floor plans, animations, and mind maps are some of the types of images that can be created.

6. What kinds of software do small and large businesses use?

Many businesses, including home businesses, use software to help them with finance, accounting, strategic planning, marketing, and Web-based tasks common to most businesses. In addition, businesses may use specialized business software (or vertical market software) that is designed for their specific industry.

7. What kind of software is available online?

Web-based software is a program that is hosted on a Web site and does not require installation on your computer. Many software applications are available as Web-based software such as productivity software, tax preparation, and financial planning. Digital photos and videos can be manipulated, saved, and stored online. The features of many Web-based applications are not as robust as their traditionally offered counterparts, but this is likely to change.

8. Where can I go for help when I have a problem with my software?

Most software programs have a Help menu built into the program with which you can search through an index or subject directory to find answers. Some programs group the most commonly asked questions into a single frequently asked questions (FAQ) document. In addition, vast resources of free or fee-based help and training are available on the Internet or at booksellers.

9. How can I purchase software or get it for free?

Almost every new computer system comes with some form of software to help you accomplish basic tasks. You must purchase all other software unless it is freeware or open source code, which you can download from the Web for free. You can also find special software called *shareware* that lets you run it free of charge for a test period. Although you can find software in almost any store, as a student you can purchase the same software at a reduced price with an academic discount.

10. How do I install, uninstall, and open software?

When installing and uninstalling software, it's best to use the specific Add or Remove Program feature that comes with the operating system. Most programs are installed using an installation wizard that steps you through the installation. Other software programs may require you to activate the setup program, which will begin the installation wizard. Using the Add or Remove Programs feature when uninstalling a program will help you ensure that all ancillary program files are removed from your computer.

Buzzwords

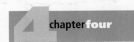

Word Bank

- application software
- beta version
- freeware
- illustration software
- image editing software
- integrated help

- integrated software
- productivity software
- shareware
- software piracy
- software suite
- speech-recognition software

- spreadsheet
- system requirements
- system software
- templates
- wizards
- word processing

Instructions: Fill in the blanks using the words from the Word Bank above.

Roxanne is so pumped! Her aunt is upgrading to a newer computer and is giving Roxanne her old one. Roxanne has just enrolled in college and knows she's going to need at least (1) a(n) _____ program to help her write papers and (2) a(n) _____ program to help her keep track of expenses while at school. Because both of these software applications are part of a larger group of applications called (3) _____, she knows she can buy them as a group. She's been told that it's cheaper to buy them as (4) a(n) _____ than to buy them individually. Because she knows she'll need the stable, tested versions of the software, she cannot get by using (5) a(n) _____ of the program.

Because she's not a great typist, Roxanne is interested in (6) _____ that will convert her dictated words into typed text. As a graduation present, Roxanne received a new digital camera. She needs to install the (7) _____ that came with her camera to edit and manage her digital pictures. Although she's used the software a couple of times on her parents' computer, she is still glad for the (8) _____ feature to assist her with specific feature questions and the (9) _____ that provide step-by-step guides to help her do things.

Roxanne especially likes the decorative preformatted (10) _____ she can use to insert pictures and make them seem professional. She also knows of some (11) _____ games she can download without cost from the Internet and other (12) _____ programs that she could try but eventually pay for. There are some really useful utility programs she found under the category of (13) _____ programs that she can download for no charge and would like to install and try out. It's tempting for her to borrow software from her friends, but she knows that it's considered (14) _____. She also knows that before installing any of the programs she must check the (15) _____ to determine if the software is compatible with her system as well as whether the system has enough resources to support the software.

Becoming Computer Literate

Using key terms from this chapter, write a letter to one of your friends or relatives about which software applications he or she may need to be able to work more productively. Also include which software application(s) that individual may need to modify, review, and store the pictures taken with a digital camera he or she just purchased.

Instructions: Answer the multiple-choice and true–false questions below for more practice with key terms and concepts from this chapter.

MULTIPLE CHOICE

1. Application software
   a. is another name for system software.
   b. helps maintain the resources of the computer.
   c. includes products such as Microsoft Office, tax software, and editing packages.
   d. Both A and C.

2. Which of the following is an example of a software suite?
   a. Microsoft SharePoint
   b. Google Docs
   c. WordPerfect Office X3
   d. None of the above

3. A Web-based software program is
   a. a stand-alone program developed to work exclusively for one company.
   b. an application designed specifically for a Web-based business or industry.
   c. a program that helps you design Web pages.
   d. an application that does not need to be installed but is run directly from the Web.

4. An integrated software application such as Microsoft Works is
   a. an individual program.
   b. meant only for business purposes.
   c. sold in specific collections, which reduces the price.
   d. only available in open source format.

5. The type of software you would use to help you coordinate many people on a single project is
   a. project management.
   b. spreadsheet.
   c. database.
   d. system.

6. What software is the best for creating a newsletter?
   a. Word-processing software
   b. Desktop publishing software
   c. Computer-aided design software
   d. Media management software

7. The ESRB is responsible for providing
   a. licensing of entertainment software.
   b. educational software standards.
   c. ratings for game software.
   d. resolution of complaints about software products.

8. Which of the following is true?
   a. MP3 files contain audio data.
   b. MP3 files are the only recognized format for digital audio.
   c. Windows Media player is able to organize large collections of audio files.
   d. Only A and C are true.

9. Where can you find help on how to use the software and solve specific software problems?
   a. An index or subject directory found in the Help menu.
   b. Documents of frequently asked questions.
   c. Resources on the Web
   d. All of the above

10. Once you install a shareware software program, you
   a. have to pay an introductory fee.
   b. can install it on all computers in your home.
   c. can lend it to your friends as long as they are using it for academic purposes only.
   d. can use the software legally until the trial period expires.

TRUE–FALSE

_____ 1. Microsoft SharePoint is a bundled package of word-processing, spreadsheet, database, and presentation software applications.

_____ 2. Open source software such as Audacity is used to organize video files.

_____ 3. The best way to delete a program from your system is to delete the shortcut on the desktop.

_____ 4. When you buy software, it's yours to do whatever you'd like, including making a copy for a friend to have.

_____ 5. Web application software runs from any computer without any installation from CD.

Making the Transition to... Next Semester

1. Installing Software

You have just spent $285 on a software package. You have a desktop computer that you use at home and a notebook that you use only at work.

a. Are you allowed to install the software on both computers? Should you be allowed to do that?

b. What if you wanted to install the software on two computers that you own and use exclusively at home?

c. Can you install the software on two computers if you use only one computer at a time?

d. Are you allowed to install the software package on your computer and also on a friend's computer if she is interested in buying her own copy but wanted to test it first?

2. Software Training

You are most likely familiar with many software applications. Undoubtedly, you will use many more applications before your coursework is done. Make two lists. In one list, itemize by category the software applications you are already familiar with. In the other list, identify at least three other software applications you think you may need or would want to try in the future. Research the types of on-campus or online training or help features that may be offered for those programs you have on your second list.

3. Upgrading Software

You are trying to decide whether you want to upgrade some software that you used this past semester. How do the following items weigh into your decision to upgrade the software or not?

a. The cost of the upgrade

b. The length of time the upgrade has been available

c. Hardware requirements

d. Features of the upgrade versus the stability of your current system

4. Choices, Choices

You have many options of software available for doing word processing. Describe the decision process you would use to select between a free Web-based word-processing application, an open source word-processing application, and a standard packaged software application if you are:

a. traveling abroad for a semester, visiting 15 different cities, and not carrying a notebook with you.

b. staying at home for the term and compiling a capstone report using several hundred researched sources of information.

c. working with three people from other colleges on a joint paper that will be presented at a conference at the end of the term.

5. Choosing the Best Software

This past semester you spent a lot of time doodling and created a comic strip character that all your friends love. You've decided to start releasing a small newsletter, including some articles and a few comics each week. Which software applications would be the best fit for the following tasks:

a. Designing and laying out the newsletter

b. Creating the text articles

c. Creating the comic strip

After the first five issues, the newsletter is clearly a smash. You decide to expand it into a *zine*, an Internet-delivered magazine. Now which software applications are important to you for the same tasks?

Making the Transition to... the Workplace

1. Surveying the Competition

You are asked to develop a departmental report that analyzes the key competitors in your market. You will need to:

a. identify the major competitors in your market;
b. gather information on their companies, their sales, and the features of their products;
c. organize your data so it can be easily sorted and filtered;
d. analyze the trends in the marketplace and predict future direction of growth; and
e. create a final report and presentation to deliver to the department heads.

Identify what software products you would use to complete each of these tasks. How would you use them, and how would they work together to support your efforts?

2. Integrating Applications

Some software applications work well together and some do not. Certainly, all of the applications within a given suite such as Microsoft Office are well integrated. Give an example of a business office need that would benefit from the following:

a. Integrating Excel with Word
b. Integrating Access with Excel
c. Integrating Access with Word

3. Choosing the Best Software for the Job

For each of the following positions, describe the set of software applications you would expect to encounter if you were:

a. a photographer opening a new business to sell your own photography.
b. an administrative assistant to a college president.
c. a graphic designer at a large publishing house.
d. a director in charge of publicity for a new summer camp for children.
e. a presenter discussing your year living abroad to elementary students.
f. a Web page designer for a small not-for-profit organization.
g. a construction site manager.
h. a person in the career you are pursuing.

4. The Right Productivity Suite

You are asked to research the cost and use of productivity software for your small company. Right now, the company has been using Microsoft Works, but the need to expand to a full-fledged productivity suite is evident. Research the major productivity suites on the market. Look at cost, the ability to exchange files between customers and other employees easily (for example, does file type make a difference?), and the various features within each version of software. Explore the major developers' products as well as the open source option OpenOffice and a set of Web-based packages. Which productivity suite would you recommend? Be specific in your recommendation.

Critical Thinking Questions

Instructions: Albert Einstein used *Gedanken experiments* or critical thinking questions, to develop his theory of relativity. Some ideas are best understood by experimenting with them in our own minds. The following critical thinking questions are designed to demand your full attention but require only a comfortable chair—no technology.

1. Software Ethics 1

The cost of new software applications can be prohibitively high. You need to do a project for school that requires the use of a software application you don't own, but your roommate has a copy that her dad gave her from his work. She is letting you install it on your machine.

a. Is it okay for you to borrow this software?
b. Would it be okay if you uninstalled the application after you were finished using it?
c. Would it be okay if the software was on the school's network and you could copy it from there?

2. Software Ethics 2

Currently, there is no true system to check for illegal installations of software programs. What kind of program or system do you think could be developed to do this type of checking? Who would pay to develop, run, and maintain the program: the developers or the software users?

3. Media Management

Less than a decade ago, home users had no media files on their computer systems. Today, many users have a library of music, a collection of digitized movies, personal photo collections, and even a large set of recorded television shows. Examine three different software packages on the market today for managing these materials. What features do they need to make the PC the primary entertainment device for a home? What would make users move their PC from the office into the living room?

4. Software and Microcredit

The 2006 Nobel Peace Prize was awarded to Muhammad Yunus, who created the Grameen Bank. This bank makes quite small loans to the poor of Bangladesh, without requiring collateral. Often these loans are less than $200 but allow women to begin small businesses and climb out of poverty. How has software made the Grameen Bank productive and able to serve almost 7 million borrowers? What other ways could software make a difference to the struggling peoples of the world?

5. Software for the Hearing and Visually Impaired

The World Wide Web Consortium (W3C) currently has an initiative to ensure that all Web pages are accessible to everyone, including those with visual and hearing impairments. The W3C site has a list of currently available commercial and free Web accessibility evaluation tools (**www.w3.org/WAI/ER/tools**) that Web site developers can use to ensure their Web sites conform to the disability standards.

a. Pick a favorite Web site and see how it checks out using one of the freeware programs on the W3C list. What changes would be necessary for that Web site to conform to W3C standards?
b. Can you think of other unique uses of software that might make the world a better place for those with visual and hearing impairments?
c. How might recommendations made by the W3C also benefit people without physical limitations?

Problem:

Gizmos, Inc. is a start-up company in the business of designing, building, and selling the latest gizmos. You have been hired as director of information systems. As such, one of your responsibilities is to ensure that all necessary software applications are purchased and installed on the company's server.

Task:

Split your class into as many groups of four or five as possible. Each group is to perform the same activity and present and compare results with each other at the end of the project.

Process:

1. Identify a team leader who will coordinate the project and record and present results.

2. Each team is to identify the various kinds of software that Gizmos, Inc. needs. Ensure that all activities and departments of the company have software to meet their needs. Consider software that employees will need for several tasks: software they can use to design the gizmos, productivity software they may need, and software the sales reps will need to help keep track of their clients. Also consider software that human resources personnel can use to keep track of employee data and that software product managers can use to track projects. In addition, think of other software that might be useful to Gizmos, Inc.

3. Create a detailed and organized list of required software applications. If possible, include licensing fees, assuming the company has 50 users.

Conclusion:

Software applications help us do the simplest and most complex tasks every day. It's important to understand how dependent we are becoming on computers and technology. Compare your results with those of other team members. Were there software applications that you didn't think about that other members did? How expensive is it to ensure that even the smallest company has all the software required to carry out daily activities?

Multimedia

In addition to the review materials presented here, you'll find additional materials featured with the book's multimedia, including the *Technology in Action* Student Resource CD and the Companion Website (**www.prenhall.com/techinaction**), which will help reinforce your understanding of the chapter content. These materials include the following:

ACTIVE HELPDESK

In Active Helpdesk calls, you'll assume the role of helpdesk operator, taking calls about the concepts you've learned in this chapter. You'll apply what you've learned and receive feedback from a supervisor to review and reinforce those concepts. The Active Helpdesk calls for this chapter are listed below and can be found on your Student Resource CD:

- Choosing Software
- Buying and Installing Software

SOUND BYTES

Sound Bytes are dynamic multimedia tutorials that help demystify even the most complex topics. You'll view video clips and animations that illustrate computer concepts, and then apply what you've learned by reviewing with the Sound Byte Labs, which include quizzes and activities specifically tailored to each Sound Byte. The Sound Bytes for this chapter are listed below and can be found on your Student Resource CD:

- Creating Web Queries in Excel 2007
- Using Speech-Recognition Software in Windows Vista
- Enhancing Photos with Image Editing Software

COMPANION WEBSITE

The *Technology in Action* Companion Website includes a variety of additional materials to help you review and learn more about the topics in this chapter. The resources available at **www.prenhall.com/techinaction** include:

- **Online Study Guide.** Each chapter features an online true–false and multiple-choice quiz. You can take these quizzes, automatically check the results, and e-mail the results to your instructor.

- **Web Research Projects.** Each chapter features several Web research projects that ask you to search the Web for information on computer-related careers, milestones in computer history, important people and companies, emerging technologies, and the applications and implications of different technologies.

Using System Software:

The Operating System, Utility Programs, and File Management

ACTIVE HELPDESK

Working with System Software

Franklin begins his workday as he does every morning, powering on his computer and watching it boot up. Once he sees the welcoming image of his desktop, he opens Microsoft Outlook to check his e-mail, Internet Explorer to access his company's Web site, and Microsoft Word to bring up the proposal he needs to finish. As he reads his e-mail, a warning pops up alerting him that one message may contain a file with a virus. He deletes the file without opening it, glad that his antivirus software had been automatically updated yesterday.

Using Windows Explorer, Franklin easily finds a proposal he worked on because he has been creating folders for his projects and diligently saving his files in their proper folder. Last year, his desktop was a complete mess. He was constantly losing time trying to find files because he couldn't remember where he saved them, and he gave them names he easily forgot. His organized folders now make finding his files a snap.

Later, at the end of the workday, Franklin has one more thing to do. Recently, his computer has been running sluggishly, so he is hoping to improve its performance. Last night, he ran Disk Cleanup, a utility program that removes unneeded files from the hard drive, as well as Error-checking, a utility program that checks for disk errors. Although he had seen an improvement in his computer's performance, he decides to use Disk Defragmenter to defrag his hard drive, hoping it will give him more space and allow his system to work more efficiently.

Yesterday, Franklin heard that a new version of Windows was about to be released. He wonders if he should consider upgrading to the new version to take advantage of its new features. But he remembers his friend Tanya had several challenges when she upgraded to Windows Vista, like when her DVD drive stopped working. Franklin can't decide if he should take the time and trouble to upgrade or just wait until the next time he buys a new machine to get a new operating system.

Can you take advantage of the features in your operating system as much as Franklin has? In this chapter, you'll learn all about system software and how vital it is to your computer. We'll start by examining the operating system (OS), looking at the different operating systems on the market as well as the tasks the OS manages. We'll then look at how you can use the OS to keep your files and folders organized so that you can use your computer more efficiently. Finally, we'll look at the many utility programs included as system software on your computer. Using these utility programs, you'll be better able to take care of your system and extend its life.

SOUND BYTES

- Customizing Windows Vista **(p. 215)**
- File Management **(p. 235)**
- File Compression **(p. 240)**
- Hard Disk Anatomy Interactive **(p. 243)**
- Letting Your Computer Clean Up After Itself **(p. 245)**

System Software Basics

As you learned in the last chapter, there are two basic types of software on your computer: application software and system software. **Application software** is the software you use to do everyday tasks at home and at work. **System software** is the set of software programs that helps run the computer and coordinates instructions between application software and the computer's hardware devices. From the moment you turn on your computer to the time you shut it down, you are interacting with system software, which consists of two primary types of programs: the operating system and utility programs.

What does an operating system do? The **operating system (OS)** is a group of programs that controls how your computer system functions. The OS manages the computer's hardware, including the processor (also called the central processing unit, or CPU), memory, and storage devices, as well as peripheral devices such as the monitor and printer. The OS also provides a consistent means for software applications to work with the CPU, and it is responsible for the management, scheduling, and interaction of tasks as well as system maintenance. Your first interaction with the OS is the user interface—that is, the features of the program that allow the user to communicate with the computer system.

System software also includes **utility programs**. These are small programs that perform many of the general housekeeping tasks for the computer, such as system maintenance and file compression.

Do all computers have operating systems? Every computer, from the smallest notebook to the largest supercomputer, has an operating system. Even tiny personal digital assistants (PDAs) and some appliances have operating systems. The role of the OS is critical; the computer cannot operate without it. As explained more fully in the later section "What the Operating System Does," the operating system coordinates the flow of data and information through the computer system by coordinating the hardware, software, user interface, processor, and the system's memory. But first, let's look at the types of operating systems and what kinds of computers they are used with.

Operating System Categories

Although most computer users can name only a few operating systems, many types exist. As Figure 5.1 illustrates, these operating systems can be classified into four categories, depending on the number of users they service and the tasks they perform. Some operating systems coordinate resources for many users on a network (a multiuser operating system); other operating systems, such as those found in some household appliances and car engines, don't require the intervention of any users at all (a real-time operating system). Some operating systems are available commercially for personal and business use (single-user, multitask operating systems), whereas others are proprietary systems developed specifically for the devices they manage (single-user, single-task operating systems).

REAL-TIME OPERATING SYSTEMS

Do machines with built-in computers need an operating system? Machinery that is required to perform a repetitive series of specific tasks in an exact amount of time requires a **real-time operating system (RTOS)**. This type of operating system is a program with a specific purpose and must guarantee certain response times for particular computing tasks; otherwise the machine's application is useless. Devices that must perform regimented tasks or record precise results—such as measurement instruments found in the scientific, defense, and aerospace industries—require real-time operating systems. Examples include digital storage oscilloscopes and the Mars Reconnaissance Orbiter.

Do robots have operating systems? Real-time operating systems are also found in many types of robotic equipment. Television stations use robotic cameras with real-time operating systems that glide within a suspended cable system to record sports events from many angles. You also encounter real-time operating systems in your everyday life in devices such as fuel-injection systems in car engines, video game consoles, and home appliances (see Figure 5.2).

Real-time operating systems require minimal user interaction. The programs are

FIGURE 5.1 **Operating System Categories**

Category of Operating System	Examples of Operating System Software	Examples of Devices Using the Operating System
Real-time operating system (RTOS)	Nucleus RTOS is one of the few commercially available programs. Noncommercially available programs include QNX Neutrino and Lynx.	Scientific instruments Automation and control machinery, robotic devices Video games
Single-user, single-task operating system	Palm OS Pocket PC (Windows CE) Windows Mobile MS-DOS Symbian OS Linux	PDAs Embedded computers in cell phones, cameras, appliances, and toys
Single-user, multitask operating system	Windows Vista, XP, and 2000 Mac OS X Linux	Personal desktop computers Notebooks
Multiuser operating system	SUSE Linux Enterprise Windows Server 2008 i5/OS z/OS Linux/UNIX Unicos (offshoot of Unix)	Networks (both home and business) Mainframes Supercomputers

written specifically to the needs of the devices and their functions. Therefore, there are no commercially available standard RTOS software programs.

SINGLE-USER OPERATING SYSTEMS

What type of operating system controls my personal computer? Because your computer—whether it's a desktop, notebook, or even a Tablet PC—can handle only one person working on it at a time but performs a variety of tasks simultaneously, it uses a **single-user, multitask operating system**. The Microsoft Windows and Macintosh operating systems are most commonly used as single-user multitask operating systems. (Note, however, that the newer versions such as Windows XP and Windows Vista have networking capabilities, so technically they also could be considered multiuser operating systems.) We will discuss the features of single-user, multitask operating systems in more detail in the next section of this chapter.

Usually, when you buy a desktop or notebook computer, its operating system software

FIGURE 5.2

Devices such as the space shuttle, cars, and robots use real-time operating systems.

FIGURE 5.3

Although PDAs use a single-user, single-task operating system in which only one user can perform one task at a time, the operating system has a similar look to that of a traditional desktop operating system.

is already installed on the computer's hard drive so that you can just turn on the computer and start using it. Sometimes you may need to install the OS yourself if you change or upgrade to a different version, or you might reinstall it in the case of a system problem.

Does the same kind of operating system also control my PDA? All computers on which one user is performing just one task at a time require a **single-user, single-task operating system**. PDAs currently can perform only one task at a time by a single user, so they require single-user, single-task operating system software such as Palm OS or BlackBerry Desktop Software (see Figure 5.3).

Microsoft's Windows Mobile is an application that includes both operating system software and application components bundled specifically for PDAs. Besides the address book, date book, memo pad, and to-do list that are standard with Windows Mobile, the bundled application software also includes versions of Word, Excel, PowerPoint, Outlook, Internet Explorer, and Windows Media Player (so you can take your tunes along with you) that are designed specifically for PDAs.

Palm OS is another operating system found in many PDAs. Palm OS includes an address book, clock, notepad, sync capability, memo viewer, and security software. Palm OS, unlike Windows Mobile, does not include any other applications, such as productivity software. However, their Documents To Go feature does allow importing and limited editing of Microsoft Office documents. The BlackBerry PDAs, which are manufactured by Research In Motion (RIM), feature their own proprietary OS. The unique feature of this OS is its always-on wireless capability.

Cell phones also use a single-user, single-task operating system that not only manages the functions of the phone but also provides other functionality such as built-in phone directories, games, and calculators. Symbian OS is the leading OS software for mobile phones or smartphones, although the BlackBerry OS and Windows Mobile are found on smartphones.

Are there any other single-user, single-task operating systems? Another example of a single-user, single-task operating system is **Microsoft Disk Operating System (MS-DOS)**. MS-DOS (or DOS) was the first widely installed operating system in personal computers. Compared to the operating systems we are familiar with today, DOS was a highly user-"unfriendly" OS. To use it, you needed to type specific commands. For example, to copy a file named "letter" from the hard drive to a flash drive, you would type the following command after the C prompt:

```
C:\>copy letter.txt F:
```

Although DOS is used infrequently today as a primary operating system, information technology (IT) professionals still use it to edit and repair system files and programs.

MULTIUSER OPERATING SYSTEMS

What kind of operating system do networks use? A **multiuser operating system** (also known as a **network operating system**) enables more than one user to access the computer system at one time by efficiently handling and prioritizing all the requests from multiple users. Networks (groups of computers connected to each other for the purposes of communicating and sharing resources) require a multiuser operating system because many users access the server computer at the same time and share resources such as printers. A network operating system is installed on the server and manages all user requests, ensuring they do not interfere with each other. For example, on a network on which users share a printer, the printer can produce only one document at a time. The OS is therefore responsible for managing all the printer requests and making sure they are processed one at a time.

Examples of network operating systems include Linux, UNIX, and Windows Server. Windows Vista and Mac OS X also can be considered network operating systems because they enable users to create a home network without needing to install a different OS.

What other kinds of computers require a multiuser operating system? Large corporations with hundreds or thousands of employees often use powerful computers known as *mainframes*. These computers are responsible for storing, managing, and simultaneously processing data from all users. Mainframe operating systems fall into the multiuser category. Examples include UNIX and IBM's i5/OS and z/OS.

Supercomputers also use multiuser operating systems. Scientists and engineers use supercomputers to solve complex problems or to perform massive computations. Some supercomputers are single computers with multiple processors, whereas others consist of multiple computers that work together.

Desktop and Notebook Operating Systems

As mentioned earlier, desktop computers (and notebooks) use multitask operating systems, of which several are available, including Windows, Linux, and Mac OS. The type of processor in the computer determines which operating system a particular desktop computer uses. The combination of operating system and processor is referred to as a computer's **platform**.

For example, Microsoft Windows operating systems are designed to coordinate with a series of processors from Intel Corporation and Advanced Micro Devices (AMD) that share the same or similar sets of instructions. However, up until a few years ago, Apple Macintosh operating systems worked primarily with processors from the Motorola Corporation and IBM that were designed specifically for Apple computers. Now Apple is making Intel-based Macs. Still, the two operating systems (Windows and Mac OS) are not interchangeable. If you attempt to load a Windows OS on a Mac, for example, the Mac processor would not understand the operating system and would not function properly. Most application software is also platform dependent. However, the use of the Intel chip in Apple computers may change this proprietary relationship. In addition, Mac OS X Leopard provides a variety of features and technologies that enable Macs and PCs running Windows to work seamlessly together. A utility called Boot Camp is available with OS X Leopard and allows you to run Windows on a Mac while also being able to run OS X. In addition, Macs and PCs can easily share files, the same network, and even the same peripherals such as printers, scanners, and cameras.

MICROSOFT WINDOWS

What is the difference between the various Windows operating systems?
With each new version of its operating system, Microsoft continues to make improvements. Figure 5.4 outlines the features and

SOUND BYTE

Customizing Windows Vista

In this Sound Byte, you'll find out how to customize your desktop. You'll learn how to configure the desktop, set up a screen saver, change pointer options, customize the Start menu, and manage user accounts.

FIGURE 5.4 **Windows Vista**		
Versions	**Description**	**Windows XP Comparable Version**
Windows Vista Home Basic	This version is for low-level budget home users who do not require advanced media support.	Windows XP Home Edition
Windows Vista Home Premium	This version combines the media features of Windows XP Media Center Edition with the Windows XP Home Edition to support advanced home media uses such as HDTV and DVD authoring.	Windows XP Home Edition with features from Windows XP Media Center Edition
Windows Vista Business	As its name implies, this version is aimed at the business market. Similar to Windows XP Professional, this version has added support for networking capabilities.	Windows XP Professional
Windows Vista Enterprise	This edition is aimed at the enterprise segment of the business market and is not available through retail stores or original equipment manufacturers (OEMs). It comes with Microsoft Virtual PC, which enables it to run on any platform.	
Windows Vista Ultimate	This is the "ultimate" operating system for high-end PC users, gamers, multimedia professionals, and PC enthusiasts. Vista Ultimate comes with RSS (Really Simple Syndication) support for easy access to podcasts and weblogs, and a game-performance tweaker.	

Icons

Files

Windows

Click icons on the "Dock"
to launch programs

FIGURE 5.5

The most recent version of the Mac operating system, Leopard, is based on the UNIX operating system. Although not compatible with each other, Windows OS and the Mac OS have many similar features.

benefits of each version of Windows Vista, its newest operating system. What was once only a single-user, single-task operating system is now a powerful multiuser operating system. Over time, Windows improvements have concentrated on increasing user functionality and friendliness, improving Internet capabilities, and enhancing file privacy and security. Unlike the versions of Windows XP that were built around features (such as Windows XP Tablet PC Edition, Windows XP Media Center Edition, Windows XP Home Edition, and Windows XP Professional), Windows Vista comes in a number of versions to accommodate the user: the home user (Home Basic, Home Premium), the business user (Business and Enterprise), or the combination user (Ultimate).

MAC OS

How is Mac OS different from Windows? Although the Apple **Mac OS** and the Windows operating systems are not compatible, they are extremely similar in terms of functionality. In 1984, Mac OS became the first commercially available operating system to incorporate a graphical user interface (GUI) with its user-friendly point-and-click technology in an affordable

computer. Both operating systems now have similar window work areas on the desktop that house individual applications and support users working in more than one application at a time (see Figure 5.5).

Despite their similarities, there are many subtle and not-so-subtle differences that have created loyal fans of each product. Macs have long been recognized for their superior graphics display and processing capabilities. Users also attest to Mac's greater system reliability, superior file-backup utilities, and better document recovery. Despite these advantages, fewer software applications are available for the Mac platform, and Mac systems tend to be more expensive than Windows-based PCs.

Mac OS X Leopard, the most recent version of the OS, is based on the UNIX operating system. Mac OS X includes a streamlined user interface with a Dock for the most commonly used programs and a Dashboard with widgets, or mini-applications, for quick access to up-to-the-minute information such as stock prices or flight tracking. For more information on Mac OS X, see the Technology in Focus feature "Computing Alternatives" on page 258.

LINUX

What is Linux? **Linux** is an open source operating system. The Linux operating system uses a Linux kernel (the central programming code of an operating system), and the rest of the code is from the GNU (pronounced "gunoo") Project and other sources. Linux is designed for use on personal computers and as a network operating system. **Open source software** is freely available for developers to use or modify as they wish. Linux began in 1991 as a part-time project by Finnish university student Linus Torvalds, who wanted to create a free OS to run on his home computer. He posted his OS code to the Web for others to use and modify. It has since been tweaked by scores of programmers as part of the Free Software Foundation GNU Project.

Today, Linux is gaining a reputation as a stable OS that is not subject to crashes and failures. Because the code is open and available to anyone, Linux is quickly tweaked to meet virtually any new operating system need. For example, when Palm PDAs emerged, the Linux OS was promptly modified to run on this new device.

TRENDS IN IT

Emerging Technologies: Open Source Software— Why Isn't Everyone Using Linux?

Proprietary software such as Microsoft Windows and Mac OS is developed by corporations and sold for profit. This means that the **source code**, the actual lines of instructional code that make the program work, is not accessible to the general public. Without being able to access the source code, it's difficult to modify the software or see exactly how the program author constructed various parts of the system.

Restricting access to the source code protects companies from having their programming ideas stolen and prevents customers from using modified versions of the software. This benefits the companies that create the software because their software code can be pirated (or stolen). However, in the late 1980s, computer specialists became concerned over the fact that large software companies (such as Microsoft) were controlling a large portion of market share and driving out competitors. They also felt that proprietary software was too expensive and contained too many bugs (errors).

These people felt that software should be developed without a profit motive and distributed with its source code free for all to see. The theory was that if many computer specialists examined, improved, and changed the source code, a more full-featured, bug-free product would result. Hence, the open source movement was born.

Open source software is freely distributed (no royalties accrue to the creators), contains the source code, and can in turn be redistributed freely to others. Most open source products are created by teams of programmers and are modified (updated) by hundreds of other programmers around the world. You can download open source products for free off the Internet. Linux is probably the most widely recognized name in open-source software, but other products such as MySQL (a database program) and OpenOffice.org (a suite of productivity applications) are also gaining in popularity.

So, if an operating system such as Linux is free, then why does Windows (which you must pay for) have such a huge market share (more than 91 percent) and Linux have less than 1 percent of the desktop market? Corporations and individuals have grown accustomed to one thing that proprietary software makers can provide: technical support. It is almost impossible to provide technical support for open source software because it can be freely modified, and there is no one specific developer to take responsibility for technical support (see Figure 5.6). Therefore, corporations have been reluctant to install open source software extensively

because of the cost of the internal staff of programmers that must support it.

Companies such as Red Hat have been combating this problem. The company provides a warranty and technical support for its version of Linux (which Red Hat programmers modified from the original source code). Packaging open source software in this manner has made its use much more attractive to businesses. Today, many Web servers are hosted on computers running Linux.

So when will free versions of Linux (or another open-source operating system) be the dominant OS on home computers? The answer is maybe never. Most casual computer users won't feel comfortable without technical support; therefore, any open source products for home use would need to be marketed the way Red Hat markets Linux. Also, many open source products are not easy to maintain.

However, companies such as Linspire (**www.linspire. com**) are making easy-to-use visual interfaces that work with the Linux operating system. If one of these companies can develop an easy-to-use product and has the marketing clout to challenge Microsoft, then you may see more open source OSs deployed in the home computer market in the future.

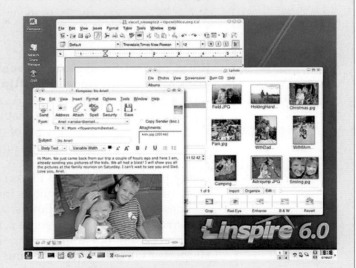

FIGURE 5.6

Companies like Ubuntu and Linspire provide free (or low-cost) Linux software, but a lack of name-brand technical support scares many companies away from wide-scale adoption.

Similarly, only a few weeks were necessary to get the Linux OS ready for the new Intel Xeon processor, a feat unheard of in proprietary OS development. Some Linux-based operating systems have been modified to run iPods and gaming systems. Linux is also gaining popularity among computer manufacturers, which have begun to ship it with some of their latest PCs.

Where can I buy Linux? You can download the open source versions of Linux for free off the Internet. However, several versions of Linux are more proprietary in nature. These versions come with support and other products that are not generally associated with the open source Linux. Red Hat has been packaging and selling versions of Linux since 1994 and is probably the most well-known Linux distributor. Red Hat Enterprise Linux 5 is the current version on the market. Other Linux distributors include Mandriva, Suse, Debian GNU/Linux, and Gentoo Linux. For a full listing and explanation of all Linux distributors, visit **www.distrowatch.com**. For more information on Linux, see the Technology in Focus feature "Computing Alternatives" on page 258.

Operating Systems for Servers and Mainframes

What operating system is best for computers that handle multiple users and multiple tasks? As mentioned in the beginning of the chapter, there are several different types of operating systems. So far, we've described operating systems for single-user, single-task computers (cell phones and PDAs) and single-user, multitask computers (notebooks and desktops). Larger computers, which are known as mainframes and servers, need a different type of operating system that supports multiple users requesting multiple tasks simultaneously. **Servers** are computers on a network that manage network resources, and **mainframes** are extremely large computers that handle the requests of hundreds or thousands of users simultaneously. Mainframe computers run operating systems developed by IBM and Unisys. The most common operating systems that

run large servers and networks are Windows Server and UNIX (or Linux, which was developed from UNIX). Since the release of Windows 2000, home users have had access to operating systems that could support a small network—multiple users, multiple tasks—allowing home and small-business users to create small networks.

What is UNIX? UNIX is a multiuser, multitask operating system used primarily with mainframes as a network operating system, although it is also often found on PCs. Developed in 1969 by Ken Thompson and Dennis Ritchie of AT&T's Bell Labs, the UNIX code was initially not proprietary—in other words, no company owned it. Rather, any programmer was allowed to use the code and modify it to meet his or her needs. Later, AT&T licensed the UNIX source code to the Santa Cruz Operation Group. UNIX is a brand that belongs to the company The Open Group, but any vendor that meets testing requirements and pays a fee can use the UNIX name. Individual vendors then modify the UNIX code to run specifically on their hardware. HP/UX from Hewlett-Packard, Solaris from Sun, and AIX from IBM are some of the UNIX systems currently available in the marketplace. Linux and UNIX are often used as operating systems on supercomputers, as well as on mainframes and servers.

What the Operating System Does

As shown in Figure 5.7, the operating system is like a traffic cop coordinating the flow of data and information through the computer system. In doing so, the OS performs several specific functions:

- It provides a way for the user to interact with the computer.
- It manages the processor, or CPU.
- It manages the memory and storage.
- It manages the computer system's hardware and peripheral devices.
- It provides a consistent means for software applications to work with the CPU.

In this section, we look at each of these functions in detail.

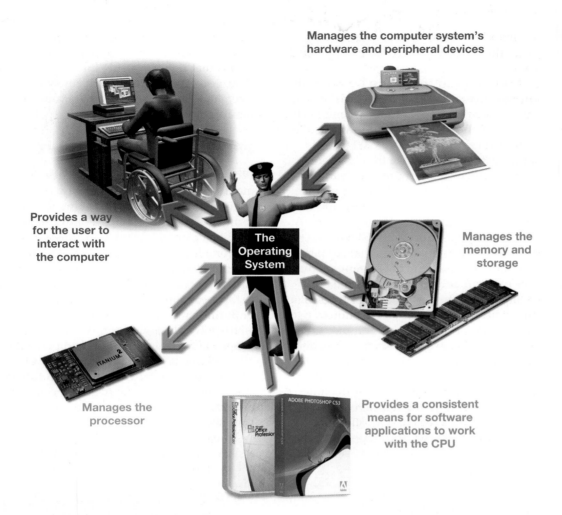

Manages the computer system's hardware and peripheral devices

Provides a way for the user to interact with the computer

The Operating System

Manages the memory and storage

Manages the processor

Provides a consistent means for software applications to work with the CPU

FIGURE 5.7

The operating system is the traffic cop of your computer, coordinating its many activities and devices.

THE USER INTERFACE

How does the operating system control how I interact with my computer?

The operating system provides a **user interface** that enables you to interact with the computer. As noted earlier, the first personal computers had a DOS operating system with a command-driven interface, as shown in Figure 5.8a. A **command-driven interface** is one in which you enter commands to communicate with the computer system. The commands were not always easy to understand; as a result, the interface proved to be too complicated for the average user. Therefore, PCs were used primarily in business and by professional computer operators.

The command-driven interface was later improved by incorporating a menu-driven interface, as shown in Figure 5.8b. A **menu-driven interface** is one in which you choose a command from menus displayed on the screen. Menu-driven interfaces eliminated the need to know every command because you could select most of the commonly used

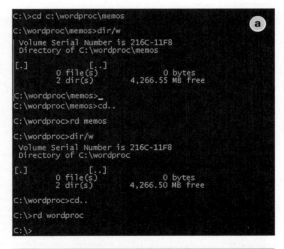

FIGURE 5.8

(a) Example of a command-driven interface. Such interfaces were not user-friendly. (b) Menu-driven interfaces were a step toward today's user-friendly interfaces.

commands from a menu. However, they were still not easy enough for most people to use.

What kind of interface do operating systems use today? Most current personal computer operating systems such as Mac OS and Microsoft Windows use a **graphical user interface**, or **GUI** (pronounced "gooey"). Unlike the command- and menu-driven interfaces used earlier, GUIs display graphics and use the point-and-click technology of the mouse and cursor, making them much more user-friendly. As illustrated in Figure 5.9, a GUI uses **windows** (rectangular boxes that contain programs displayed on the screen), **menus** (lists of commands that appear on the screen), and **icons** (pictures that represent an object such as a software application or a file or folder).

Unlike Windows or Mac OS, Linux does not have a single default GUI interface. Instead, users are free to choose among many commercially available or free interfaces, such as GNOME and KDE, each of which provides a different look and feel. For example, GNOME (pronounced "gah-NOHM") actually allows you to select

which desktop appearance (Windows or Mac) you'd like your system to display. This means that if you're using Linux for the first time, you don't have to learn a new interface; you just use the one you're most comfortable with already.

PROCESSOR MANAGEMENT

Why does the operating system need to manage the processor? When you use your computer, you are usually asking it to perform several tasks at once. For example, you might be printing a Word document, waiting for a file to download from the Internet, listening to a CD from your CD drive, and working on a PowerPoint presentation—all at the same time, or at least what appears to be at the same time. Although the processor is the powerful brains of the computer, processing all of its instructions and performing all of its calculations, it needs the OS to arrange for the execution of all these activities in a systematic way to give the appearance that everything is happening simultaneously.

To do so, the operating system assigns a slice of its time to each activity requiring

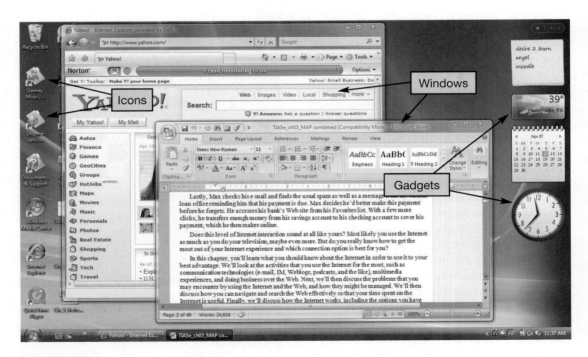

FIGURE 5.9

Today's operating systems coordinate a user's experience through a graphical user interface. GUIs are more user-friendly than command- and menu-driven interfaces because they include features such as icons, windows, and other helpful graphical programs known as *gadgets*.

the processor's attention. The OS must then switch between different processes thousands of times a second to make it appear that everything is happening seamlessly. Otherwise, you wouldn't be able to listen to a CD and print at the same time without experiencing delays in the process. When the OS allows you to perform more than one task at a time, it is said to be **multitasking**.

How exactly does the operating system coordinate all the activities? When you type and print a document in Word while also listening to a CD, for example, many different devices in the computer system are involved, including your keyboard, mouse, CD drive, and printer. Every keystroke, every mouse click, and each signal to the printer and from the CD drive creates an action, or **event**, in the respective device (keyboard, mouse, CD drive, or printer) to which the operating system responds.

Sometimes these events occur sequentially (such as when you type characters one at a time), but other events require two or more devices working simultaneously (such as the printer printing while you continue to type and listen to a CD). Although it looks as though the keyboard, CD drive, and printer are working at the same time, in effect, the OS switches back and forth between processes, controlling the timing of events the processor works on.

For example, assume you are typing and want to print another document. When you tell your computer to print your document, the printer generates a unique signal called an **interrupt** that tells the operating system that it is in need of immediate attention. Every device has its own type of interrupt, which is associated with an interrupt handler, a special numerical code that prioritizes the requests. These requests are placed in the interrupt table in the computer's primary memory (or random access memory, RAM). The operating system processes the task assigned a higher priority before processing a task that has been assigned a lower priority. This is called **preemptive multitasking**.

In our example, the operating system pauses the CPU from its typing activity and from the CD activity when it receives the interrupt from the printer and puts a "memo" in a special location in RAM called a *stack*. The memo is a reminder of where

the CPU was before it left off so that it can work on the printer request. The CPU then retrieves the printer request from the interrupt table and begins to process it. On completion of the printer request, the CPU goes back to the stack, retrieves the memo it placed about the keystroke or CD activity, and returns to that task until it is interrupted again.

What happens if there is more than one document waiting to be printed? The operating system also coordinates multiple activities for peripheral devices such as printers. When the processor receives a request to send information to the printer, it first checks with the operating system to ensure that the printer is not already in use. If it is, the OS puts the request in another temporary storage area in RAM called the *buffer*. It will wait in the buffer until the **spooler**, a program that helps coordinate all print jobs currently being sent to the printer, indicates the printer is available. If more than one print job is waiting, a line (or *queue*) is formed so that the printer can process the requests in order.

MEMORY AND STORAGE MANAGEMENT

Why does the operating system have to manage the computer's memory? As the operating system coordinates the activities of the processor, it uses RAM as a temporary storage area for instructions and data the processor needs. The processor then accesses these instructions and data from RAM when it is ready to process them. The OS is therefore responsible for coordinating the space allocations in RAM to ensure that there is enough space for all of the waiting instructions and data. It then clears the items from RAM when the processor no longer needs them.

Can my system ever run out of RAM space? RAM has limited capacity. As you add and upgrade your software applications and usage of the computer system, you will likely find that the amount of RAM you once found to be quite sufficient is no longer enough. Most computers sold for home use have between 1 and 4 gigabytes (GB) of RAM. A system with 1 or 2 GB of RAM is usually sufficient if you're running several applications at the same time.

Ethics: Sugar—The Sweet OS for Every Child

The Internet is a fantastic tool, but only if you can access it. In an effort to give children in developing countries a better opportunity to "learn, share, and create," the One Laptop Per Child (OLPC) initiative was founded by Nicholas Negroponte and other faculty from MIT Media Lab, in conjunction with partners such as Google, AMD, and News Corporation. The mission of OLPC (**www. laptop.org**) is to ensure that all school-age children in lesser-developed communities receive their own personal computers so that they are no longer excluded from the educational, economic, and entertainment benefits that computers can provide.

This ambitious project to develop and distribute a low-cost notebook computer (currently, the cost is $200) would provide access to electronic textbooks and other learning aids—and eventually the Internet. The project has expanded to include a wide variety of professionals from academia, business, the arts, and technology. The main thrust of the project is to overcome the so-called digital divide (the gap between people who have access to computers and those who don't) and provide computing resources to everyone regardless of their financial means.

The notebook itself is revolutionary in design (see Figure 5.10). Called the XO, the notebook is small and has a comfortable, child-sized, built-in handle. It also has a tablet-like monitor that can twist to turn the notebook into an electronic book (e-book), which is critical in areas where books are hard to come by. The outside of the notebook is rugged and child-friendly. In addition, it is power efficient, running on less than one-tenth the power a standard notebook requires. Because access to electricity is minimal in many of the project's target areas, the notebook is also self-powered by a pull-string, which is easy for the children to use.

At the core of the project is the operating system—Sugar—which completely rethinks the computer-user interface. Credit goes to the developers, who really thought about how the users of the notebook would interact with the device. The operating system is based on open source code components from Red Hat's Fedora Core 6 version of the Linux operating system. The OLPC notebooks will most likely be the first computer that many of these children have used. Because children have no idea of what to do with the machine and may not have anyone to tell them, the user interface was designed to be as intuitive as possible.

The operating system focuses on activities rather than applications. When the machine powers up, the first image is that of the XO man (an O on top of an X) in the middle of a circle surrounded by icons that represent

FIGURE 5.10

The revolutionary design of the XO notebook is rugged yet child-friendly. The XO can be easily converted from a traditional notebook to an e-book. It is extremely power-efficient but can also be self-powered.

If you're running Windows Vista, however, the minimum requirement just to run the minimum capabilities of the operating system alone is 1 GB, and if you want to incorporate the Aero capabilities of Windows Vista, it's recommended that your system have at least 2 GB of RAM. Systems with 1 GB that run Windows Vista may be challenged by limited RAM resources, especially with graphic-intensive programs such as Adobe Photoshop, many gaming applications, and even the latest version of

home, friends, and neighborhood. The computer includes a built-in microphone and webcam for children to create their own multimedia. For example, the multimedia tool allows children to add music to their drawings. Other activities include browsing the Internet, chatting, text editing, and playing games. At the core of each activity is the ability to collaborate, which facilitates the community learning experience. To further enhance collaboration, the notebooks are all interconnected in a wireless mesh network, providing the potential for every activity to be a networked activity. Browsing, for example, would no longer be an isolated, individual activity; it could also be a collaborative group experience (see Figure 5.11a). Wireless capabilities also help extend the community beyond the physical borders. These computers make it possible for a child in Africa, for example, to connect with another child in Europe.

In addition, the operating system uses a journaling technique for file management (see Figure 5.11b). The file system records what the child has done (rather than just what the student has saved), reading more as a scrapbook of the student's interactions with the computer as well as with peers. The journal can be tagged, searched, and sorted in a variety of ways.

Another general concept behind the operating system is that children learn through doing, so the software puts an emphasis on tools for exploring and expressing, as well as learning by helping each other. Because Sugar is built on an open source platform, it also encourages students to explore how it works and to modify the code to meet their individual preferences.

The OLPC is not the only organization interested in increasing the reach of technology to those in less-developed nations. Intel has gone forward with its own program and produced the Classmate PC. Although the Classmate PC is more closely aligned with a traditional Windows-based PC—running on either Windows or the open source OS Mandravia Discovery 2007 (a version of Linux)—it offers some of the same user-friendly hardware features of the XO machine. Some reviewers and followers of both projects have offered the opinion that the Classmate PC is better-

FIGURE 5.11

(a) The user is sharing a browsing experience with several others. (b) The journaling file management system chronicles what the student saves as well as the student's interaction with the machine and with others.

suited for the older student user, whereas the XO laptop is geared toward a younger, less sophisticated user. With so many children waiting to be exposed to technology and to a more fun and intuitive learning process, there is most likely room in the market for both machines.

Microsoft Office. Like most users, over time, you will expand how you use your computer by adding new software and new peripherals, so it's best to consider adding as much RAM as you can afford to your system.

What happens if my computer runs out of RAM? When there isn't enough RAM for the operating system to store the required data and instructions, the operating system borrows room from the more spacious hard drive. This process of optimizing

FIGURE 5.12

Virtual memory borrows excess storage capacity from the hard drive when there is not enough capacity in RAM.

RAM

Data and instructions not recently used

OS

Data and instructions needed now

Hard drive's swap file

RAM storage by borrowing hard drive space is called **virtual memory**. As shown in Figure 5.12, when more RAM is needed, the operating system swaps out from RAM the data or instructions that have not been recently used and moves them to a temporary storage area on the hard drive called the **swap file** (or **page file**). If the data or instructions in the swap file are needed later, the operating system swaps them back into active RAM and replaces them in the hard drive's swap file with less active data or instructions. This process of swapping is known as **paging**.

Can I ever run out of virtual memory? Only a portion of the hard drive is allocated to virtual memory. You can manually change this setting to increase the amount of hard drive space allocated, but eventually your computer system will become sluggish as it is forced to page more and more often. This condition of excessive paging is called **thrashing**. The solution to this problem is to increase the amount of RAM in your system so that it will not be necessary for it to send data and instructions to virtual memory. You'll learn how to monitor your RAM and virtual memory requirements in Chapter 6.

How does the operating system manage storage? If it weren't for the operating system, the files and applications you save to the hard drive and other storage locations would be an unorganized mess. Fortunately, the OS has a file management system that keeps track of the name and location of each file you save and the programs you install. We will talk more about file management later in the chapter.

HARDWARE AND PERIPHERAL-DEVICE MANAGEMENT

How does the operating system manage the hardware and peripheral devices? Each device attached to your computer comes with a special program called a **device driver** that facilitates the communication between the hardware device and the operating system. Because the OS must be able to communicate with every device in the computer system, the device driver translates the device's specialized commands to commands that the operating system can understand, and vice versa. Thus, devices will not function without the proper device driver because the OS would not know how to communicate with them.

Do I always need a driver? Today, most devices such as flash drives, mice, keyboards, and many digital cameras come with the driver already installed in Windows. The devices whose drivers are included in Windows are called **Plug and Play (PnP)**. Plug and Play is a software and hardware standard that Microsoft created with the Windows 95 OS. PnP is designed to facilitate the installation of new hardware in PCs by including the driver the device needs to run into the OS. Because the OS includes this software, incorporating a new device into your computer system seems automatic. Plug and Play enables users to plug in their new device to a port on the system unit, turn on the computer, and immediately play, or use, the device. The OS automatically recognizes the device and its driver without any further user manipulations to the system.

What happens if the device is not Plug and Play? Some current devices, such as many types of printers, and many older devices are not Plug and Play. When you install a non–Plug and Play device, you will be prompted to insert the driver that was provided with the device. If you obtain a non–Plug and Play device secondhand and did not receive the device driver, or if you are required to update the device driver, you can often download the necessary driver from the manufacturer's Web site. You can also check out Web sites such as **www.driverzone.com** or **www.driverguide.com** to locate drivers.

Can I damage my system by installing a device driver? Occasionally, when you install a driver, your system may become unstable (that is, programs may stop responding, certain actions may cause a crash, or the device or the entire system may stop working). Although this is uncommon, it can happen. Fortunately, Windows Vista has a Roll Back Driver feature that reinstalls the old driver and remedies the problem (see Figure 5.13).

SOFTWARE APPLICATION COORDINATION

How does the operating system help software applications run on the computer? Software applications feed the CPU the instructions it needs to process data. These instructions take the form of computer code. Every software application, no matter what its type or manufacturer, needs to interact with the CPU. For programs to work with the CPU, they must contain code that the CPU recognizes. Rather than having the same blocks of code for similar procedures in each software application, the operating system includes the blocks of code—called **application programming interfaces** (APIs)—that software applications need to interact with it. Microsoft DirectX, for example, is a group of multimedia APIs built into the Windows operating system that improves graphics and sounds when you're playing games or watching video on your PC.

What are the advantages of using APIs? To create programs that can communicate with the operating system, software

programmers need only refer to the API code blocks in their individual application programs rather than including the entire code in the application itself. APIs not only avoid redundancies in software code but also make it easier for software developers to respond to changes in the operating system.

Large software developers such as Microsoft have many software applications under their corporate umbrella and use the same APIs in all or most of their software applications. Because APIs coordinate with the operating system, all applications that have incorporated these APIs have common interfaces such as similar toolbars and menus. Therefore, many features of the software applications have the same look. An added benefit to this system is that applications sharing these same formats also can easily exchange data between different programs. As such, it's easy to create a chart in Microsoft Excel from data in Microsoft Access and incorporate the finished chart into a Microsoft Word document.

ACTIVE HELPDESK

Managing Hardware and Peripheral Devices: The OS

In this Active Helpdesk call, you'll play the role of a helpdesk staffer, fielding calls about how the operating system manages memory, storage, hardware, and peripheral devices.

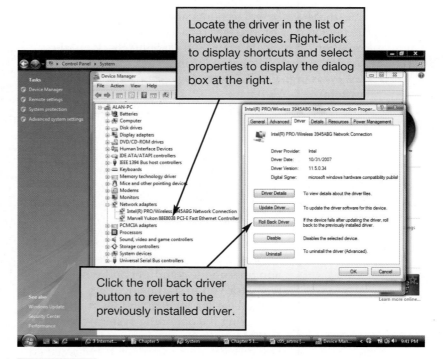

Locate the driver in the list of hardware devices. Right-click to display shortcuts and select properties to display the dialog box at the right.

Click the roll back driver button to revert to the previously installed driver.

FIGURE 5.13

If you think a recent driver update may be making your computer unstable, you can use the Roll Back Driver feature (accessible through the System icon in the Control Panel) to get rid of the new driver and replace it with the last one that worked. However, Roll Back Driver permits only one level of rollback and does not work for printer drivers.

BITS AND BYTES

A Web-Based Operating System

Now that broadband Internet access is becoming commonplace, the concept of a more universal operating system, called a *Web-based OS*, is being discussed and some prototype sites are in their infancy. So what is a Web-based operating system? Actually, the terms *Web-based operating environment* or *portable desktop* might be more accurate. Nonetheless, the concept behind this movement is to make the Web the primary application interface through which users can view content, manage data, and use various services (calendars, e-mail, and picture sharing and storage) on their local machine and on the Web without noticing any difference.

Currently, we can use applications that have been installed on a specific computer only. A Web-based operating environment would allow users access to applications and content via the Web, regardless of the machines they are using. This means business travelers would not need to lug their notebooks everywhere they went. Instead, they would need only to find a computer that had Internet access to be able to work on documents, see their calendar, read their e-mail, and so on. All of their settings and preferences (even a customized desktop image), as well as working documents, could be stored in an individual Web-based account for them to access anywhere and on any machine at any time. Because security measures have not been completely worked out, it's advisable that Web-based accounts not be used to store or manipulate personal or proprietary data and information. For more information, or to begin your own account, check out the Web sites of the current Web-based OS innovators, including eyeOS (**www.eyeos.org**), GoGUI (**www.gogui.com**), and YouOS (**www.youos.com**).

The Boot Process: Starting Your Computer

Although it only takes a minute or two, a lot of things happen quickly between the time you turn on the computer and when it is ready for you to start using it. As you learned earlier, all data and instructions (including the operating system) are stored in RAM while your computer is on. When you turn off your computer, RAM is wiped clean of all its data (including the OS). So, how does the computer know what to do when you turn it on if there is nothing in RAM? It runs through a special **boot process** (or start-up process) to load the operating system into RAM. The term *boot*, from *bootstrap loader* (a small program used to start a larger program), alludes to the straps of leather, called *bootstraps*, that men used in former times to help them pull on their boots. The use of bootstraps in this way created the expression to "pull oneself up by the bootstraps."

What are the steps involved in the boot process? As illustrated in Figure 5.14, the boot process consists of four basic steps:

1. The basic input/output system (BIOS) is activated by powering on the CPU.
2. The BIOS checks that all attached devices are in place (called a *power-on self-test,* or POST).
3. The operating system is loaded into RAM.
4. Configuration and customization settings are checked.

How can I tell my computer is entering the boot process? As the computer goes through the boot process in Windows operating systems, indicator lights on the keyboard and disk drives will illuminate and the system will emit various beeps. If you have a version of Windows earlier than XP, text will scroll down the screen as well. When you boot up on a PC with Windows Vista or on a Mac, you won't hear any beeps or see any keyboard lights illuminate. Instead, a welcome screen will appear, indicating the progress of the start-up process. Once the boot process has completed these steps, it is ready to accept commands and data. Let's look at each of these steps in more detail.

STEP 1: ACTIVATING BIOS

What's the first thing that happens after I turn on my computer? In the first step of the boot process, the CPU activates the **basic input/output system** (BIOS). BIOS (pronounced "bye-OSE") is a program that manages the data between the operating system and all the input and output devices attached to the system, hence its name. BIOS is also responsible for loading the OS from its permanent location on the hard drive into RAM.

BIOS itself is stored on a special read-only memory (ROM) chip on the motherboard. Unlike data stored in RAM, data stored in ROM is permanent and does not get erased when the power is turned off.

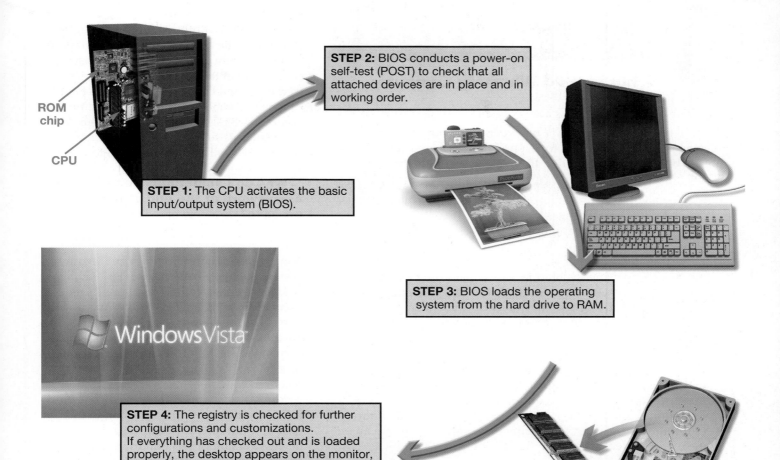

ROM chip

CPU

STEP 1: The CPU activates the basic input/output system (BIOS).

STEP 2: BIOS conducts a power-on self-test (POST) to check that all attached devices are in place and in working order.

STEP 3: BIOS loads the operating system from the hard drive to RAM.

Windows Vista

STEP 4: The registry is checked for further configurations and customizations. If everything has checked out and is loaded properly, the desktop appears on the monitor, and the system is ready to accept your first command.

FIGURE 5.14

The Boot Process

STEP 2: PERFORMING THE POWER-ON SELF-TEST

How does the computer determine whether the hardware is working properly? The first job BIOS performs is to ensure that essential peripheral devices are attached and operational. This process is called the **power-on self-test**, or POST. The POST consists of a test on the video card and video memory, a BIOS identification process, and a memory test to ensure that memory chips are working properly.

The BIOS compares the results of the POST with the various hardware configurations that are permanently stored in CMOS (pronounced "see-moss"). CMOS, which stands for *complementary metal-oxide semiconductor*, is a special kind of memory that uses almost no power. A little battery provides enough power so that its contents will not be lost after the computer is turned off. CMOS contains information about the system's memory, types of disk drives, and other essential input and output hardware components. If the results of the POST compare favorably to the hardware configurations stored in CMOS, the boot process continues. If new hardware has been installed, this will cause the POST to disagree with the hardware configurations in CMOS, and you will be alerted that new hardware has been detected.

STEP 3: LOADING THE OPERATING SYSTEM

How does the operating system get loaded into RAM? When the previous steps are successfully completed, BIOS goes through a preconfigured list of devices in its search for the drive that contains the **system files**, the main files of the operating system. When it is located, the operating system loads from its permanent storage location on the hard drive to RAM.

BITS AND BYTES

What Do I Do When My Computer Freezes?

At some point in time, we have all experienced our computers freezing up—nothing seems to respond to a mouse click or tap on any keyboard key. What to do? Try following these steps:

1. Press the Ctrl+Alt+Del keys at the same time to access the Task Manager. On the Applications tab, close the application that is listed as Not Responding.
2. If the non-responding application will not close from the Task Manager, press Ctrl+Alt+Del again to restart the computer. Restarting the computer is called a "soft" or "warm" boot. You might also try using the Start menu and choosing Restart.
3. If the computer will not restart from the Task Manager or from the Start menu, then press the power button one time to try to reset the computer (older computers may have a separate Restart button).
4. If the computer still won't restart, press and hold down the Power button until the power is completely turned off. You may have to hold down the power button for several seconds.
5. Leave the computer turned off for a minute or so to allow all the internal components to shut down completely. Then turn the computer on again. (Powering the computer on from an off position is called a "cold" or "hard" boot.)

Once the system files are loaded into RAM, the **kernel** (or **supervisor program**) is loaded. The kernel is the essential component of the operating system. It is responsible for managing the processor and all other components of the computer system. Because it stays in RAM the entire time your computer is powered on, the kernel is said to be *memory resident*. Other parts of the OS that are less critical stay on the hard drive and are copied over to RAM on an as-needed basis so that RAM is not entirely filled. These programs are called *nonresident*. Once the kernel is loaded, the operating system takes over control of the computer's functions.

STEP 4: CHECKING FURTHER CONFIGURATIONS AND CUSTOMIZATIONS

When are the other components and configurations of the system checked? CMOS checks the configuration of memory and essential peripherals in the beginning of the boot process. In this last phase of the boot process, the operating system checks the registry for the configuration of other system components. The **registry** contains all of the different configurations (settings) used by the OS and by other applications. It contains the customized settings you put into place such as mouse speed and the display settings for your monitor and desktop, as well as instructions as to which programs should be loaded first.

Why do I sometimes need to enter a password at the end of the boot process? In a networked environment, such as that found at most colleges, the operating system services many users. To determine whether a user is authorized to use the system (that is, whether a user is a paying student or college employee), authorized users are given a login name and password. The verification of your login name and password at the end of the boot process is called **authentication**. The authentication process blocks unauthorized users from entering the system.

You also may need to insert a password following the boot process to log in to your user account on your computer. The newest version of the Windows operating system, Windows Vista, is a multiuser system. Even in a home environment, all users with access to a Windows Vista computer (such as family members or roommates) can have their own user accounts. Users can set up a password to protect their account from being accessed by another user without permission. For more information on selecting a good password, see the Technology in Focus feature "Protecting Your Computer and Backing up Your Data" on page 364.

How do I know if the boot process is successful? The entire boot process takes only a minute or two to complete. If the entire system is checked out and loaded properly, the process completes by displaying the desktop. The computer system is now ready to accept your first command.

HANDLING ERRORS IN THE BOOT PROCESS

What should I do if my computer doesn't boot properly? Sometimes problems occur during the boot process. Fortunately, you have several options for correcting the situation. If you have recently installed new software or hardware, try uninstalling it. (Make sure you use the Add or Remove Programs feature in the Control Panel to remove the software.) If the problem no longer occurs when rebooting, then you have determined the cause of the problem and can reinstall the device or software. If the problem does not go away, then the first option is to restart your computer in Safe mode.

What is Safe mode? Sometimes Windows does not boot properly, and you end up with a screen with "Safe Mode" appearing in the corners as shown in Figure 5.15. (Alternatively, you can boot directly into Safe mode by pressing the F8 key during the boot process.) **Safe mode** is a special diagnostic mode designed for troubleshooting errors. When it is in Safe mode, only the system's essential devices—such as the mouse, keyboard, and monitor—function. Even the regular graphics device driver will not be activated in Safe mode. Instead, the system runs in the most basic graphics mode, resulting in a neutral screen, eliminating any desktop images and nonessential icons. While in Safe mode, you can use the **Device Manager**, a feature in the operating system that lets you view and change the properties of all devices attached to your computer. Safe mode boots Microsoft Windows with only the necessary original Microsoft Windows drivers to boot.

If Windows detects a problem in the boot process, it will add Last Known Good Configuration to the Windows Advanced Options Menu (found also by pressing the F8 key during the boot process). **Last Known Good Configuration** is a feature in Windows XP and Vista. Every time your computer boots successfully, a configuration of the boot process is saved. When you choose to boot with the Last Known Good Configuration, the operating system starts your computer by using the registry information that was saved during the last shutdown. Using Safe mode and Last Known Good Configuration are the two most widely used methods of booting into Windows when you're unable to do so with your current configuration.

Finally, if all other attempts to reboot fail, try a System Restore. **System Restore** can be used to roll back to a past configuration. Because it doesn't restore any personal data files, you can be assured that your personal

BITS AND BYTES

Upgrading Your Operating System

At some point, a new version of the operating system you are using will be released. You are then faced with the decision of whether to upgrade to the new version (such as going from Windows XP to Windows Vista). Here are a few key things to consider before taking the plunge:

- **Are there significant features in the new version that will make your life easier?** If the only features the new version offers are ones you don't need, why bother upgrading?
- **Will your hardware work with the new OS?** Check the minimum operating requirements (required RAM, processor speed, hard drive space, etc.) of the new version to ensure that your computer can handle the workload of the new software. You will also need to make sure drivers for the new OS are available for all your hardware devices and peripherals to ensure they will work properly with the new OS.
- **Is your application software compatible with the new version of the OS?** Sometimes software works fine with a new version of an OS; as many Vista users found out, however, sometimes it does not. Check with the software vendors regarding compatibility.

Before starting the upgrade, you should back up all your data files. Upgrades are usually designed to not disturb data files, but upgrades do not always go smoothly. Make sure you have current backups of all your data files so you won't lose anything accidentally during the upgrading process.

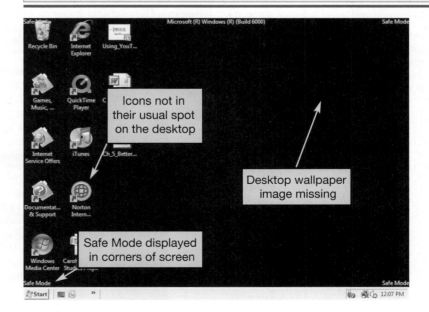

FIGURE 5.15

If there is an error in the boot process, your system might boot into Safe mode. Safe mode offers limited functionality but enough to allow you to perform diagnostic testing.

ACTIVE HELPDESK

Starting the Computer: The Boot Process

In this active helpdesk call, you'll play the role of a helpdesk staffer, fielding calls about how the operating system helps the computer start up.

data will stay intact, meaning the files will match the files the last time you changed them, regardless of System Restore. A System Restore point is made every day you use your computer. You also can create a custom restore point if needed.

What should I do if my keyboard or other device doesn't work after I boot my computer? Sometimes during the boot process, BIOS skips a device (such as a keyboard) or improperly identifies it. Your only indication that this sort of problem has occurred is that the device won't respond after the system has been booted. When that happens, you can generally resolve the problem by rebooting. If the problem persists, you may want to check the operating system's Web site for any patches (or software fixes) that may resolve the issue. If there are no patches or the problem persists, then you may want to get technical assistance.

The Desktop and Windows Features

The **desktop** is the first interaction you have with the operating system and the first image you see on your monitor. As its name implies, your computer's desktop puts at your fingertips all of the elements necessary for a productive work session that are typically found on or near the top of a traditional desk such as files and folders.

What are the main features of the desktop? The very nature of a desktop is that it enables you to customize it to meet your individual needs. As such, the desktop on your computer may be different from the desktop on your friend's computer. However, most desktops share common features, some of which are illustrated in Figure 5.16.

Windows Vista includes new features called the Sidebar and Gadgets. The **Sidebar** is a pane on the right side of the desktop that organizes gadgets for easy access. **Gadgets** can be any items you refer to frequently, including weather information, calendar items, calculators, games, photo albums, and more.

What are common features of a window? As noted earlier, one feature introduced by the graphical user interface is windows (with a lowercase w), the rectangular panes on your computer screen that display applications running on your system. Windows provide for a flexible, user-friendly, multitasking environment.

FIGURE 5.16

The Windows desktop puts the most commonly used features of the operating system at your fingertips.

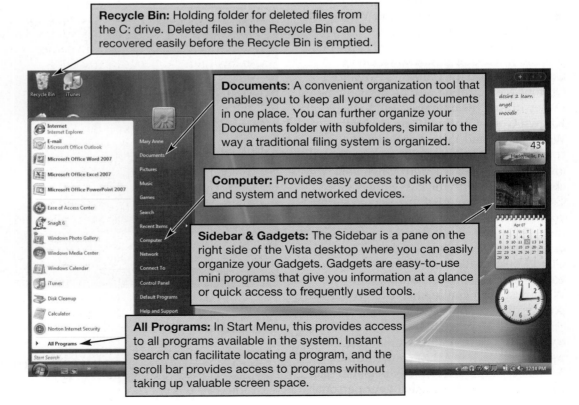

Recycle Bin: Holding folder for deleted files from the C: drive. Deleted files in the Recycle Bin can be recovered easily before the Recycle Bin is emptied.

Documents: A convenient organization tool that enables you to keep all your created documents in one place. You can further organize your Documents folder with subfolders, similar to the way a traditional filing system is organized.

Computer: Provides easy access to disk drives and system and networked devices.

Sidebar & Gadgets: The Sidebar is a pane on the right side of the Vista desktop where you can easily organize your Gadgets. Gadgets are easy-to-use mini programs that give you information at a glance or quick access to frequently used tools.

All Programs: In Start Menu, this provides access to all programs available in the system. Instant search can facilitate locating a program, and the scroll bar provides access to programs without taking up valuable screen space.

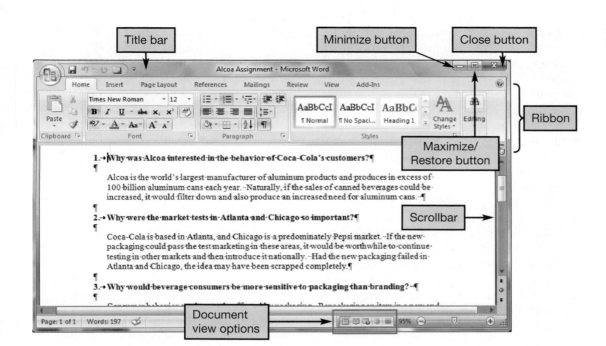

FIGURE 5.17

Most windows in a graphical user interface share the same common elements.

Figure 5.17 illustrates some of the features of windows, including **toolbars** or **ribbons** (groups of icons collected for easy access) and **scrollbars** (bars that appear at the side or bottom of the screen that control which part of the information is displayed on the screen). Using the Minimize, Maximize and Restore, and Close buttons, you can open, close, and resize windows.

How can I see more than one window on my desktop at a time? You can easily arrange the windows on a desktop by tiling them, which means arranging separate windows so that they sit next to each other either horizontally or vertically. You also can arrange windows by cascading them so that they overlap one another, or you can simply resize two open windows so that they appear on the screen at the same time.

Tiling windows makes accessing two or more active windows more convenient. To untile the windows, or to bring a window back to its full size, click the Restore button in the top right corner of the window.

Windows Vista offers two more ways to navigate through open windows. Windows Flip allows you to scroll through open windows by using Alt+Tab. Although the Alt+Tab feature was available in Windows XP, Vista's improvements include live thumbnail images of the open windows instead of an icon and file name, which appeared in Windows XP. Windows Vista Flip 3D lets you "flip" through open windows in a stack by using the scroll wheel

on your mouse. The open windows appear in a three-dimensional configuration as shown in Figure 5.18.

Can I move or resize the windows once they are tiled? Regardless of whether the windows are tiled, you can resize and move them around the desktop. You can reposition windows on the desktop by pointing to the title bar at the top of the window with your cursor and, when holding down the left mouse button, drag them to a different location. To resize a window, place your cursor over any side or corner of a window until it changes to a double-headed arrow [↕]. You can then left-click and drag the window to the new desired size.

ORGANIZING YOUR COMPUTER: FILE MANAGEMENT

So far you have learned that the operating system is responsible for managing the processor, memory, storage, and devices, and that it provides a mechanism for applications and users to interact with the computer system. An additional function of an operating system is to enable **file management**, which entails providing organizational structure to the computer's contents. The OS allows you to organize the contents of your computer in a hierarchical structure of **directories** that includes files, folders, and drives. In this section, we discuss how you can use this hierarchical structure to create a more organized and efficient computer.

FIGURE 5.18

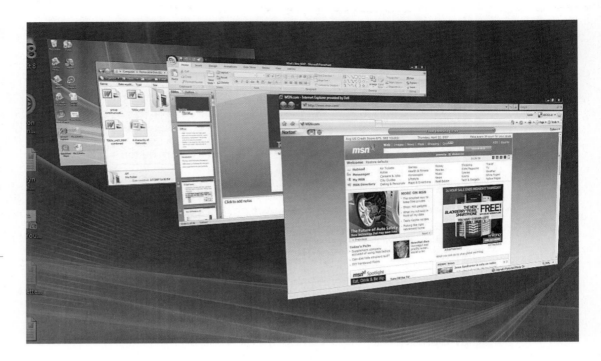

ORGANIZING YOUR FILES

What exactly is a file? Technically, a **file** is a collection of related pieces of information stored together for easy reference. A file in an operating system is a collection of program instructions or data stored and treated as a single unit. Files can be generated from an application such as a Word document or Excel workbook. In addition, files can represent an entire application, a Web page, a set of sounds, or an image. Files are stored on the hard drive, a flash drive, or another storage medium for permanent storage. As the number of files you save increases, it is important to keep them organized in **folders**, or collections of files.

How does the operating system organize files? Windows organizes the contents of the computer in a hierarchical structure with drives, folders, subfolders, and files. The hard drive, represented as the C drive, is where you permanently store most of your files. Other storage devices on your computer are also represented by letters. The A drive has traditionally been reserved for the floppy drive. Any additional drives (flash, CD, or DVD drives) installed on your computer are represented by other letters (D, E, F, and so on).

How is the hard drive organized? The C drive, or hard drive, is like a large filing cabinet in which all files are stored. As such, the C drive is the top of the filing

structure of the computer system and is referred to as the **root directory**. All other folders and files are organized within the root directory. There are areas in the root directory that the operating system has filled with folders holding special OS files. The programs within these files help run the computer and generally shouldn't be touched. The Windows Vista operating system also creates other folders such as Documents, Pictures, and Music (My Documents, My Pictures, and My Music in Windows XP). These are available for you to begin to store and organize your text, image, and audio files, respectively.

How can I easily locate and see the contents of my computer? If you use a Windows PC, **Windows Explorer** is the main tool for finding, viewing, and managing the contents of your computer by showing the location and contents of every drive, folder, and file. As illustrated in Figure 5.19, Windows Explorer is divided into two panes, or sections.

The navigation pane on the left shows the contents of your computer in a traditional hierarchical tree structure and also the new Searches Folders. It displays all the drives of the system, as well as other commonly accessed areas such as the Desktop and the Documents folder. There are shortcut folders that take you to Documents, Pictures, or Music folders. The Searches link lets you see all the Search Folders on your PC. A Search

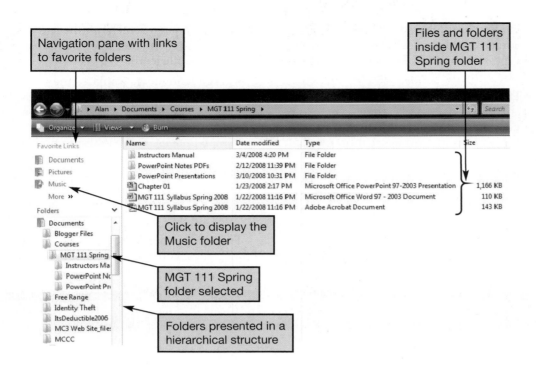

Navigation pane with links to favorite folders

Files and folders inside MGT 111 Spring folder

Click to display the Music folder

MGT 111 Spring folder selected

Folders presented in a hierarchical structure

FIGURE 5.19

Windows Explorer lets you see the contents of your computer.

>Right-click the **Start** button and choose **Explore**.

Folder organizes your files logically and without physically rearranging the files to expedite searches of a particular file type. For example, if you have picture files stored not only in the Pictures folder but also in other folders, then it might take you awhile to find a particular picture file you need. By clicking on the Picture Search folder, all of the picture files, no matter where they are stored on your computer, will appear in the Picture Search folder.

How should I organize my files?
Creating folders is the key to organizing your files because they keep related documents together. Again, think of your computer as a big filing cabinet to which you can add many separate filing drawers, or subfolders. Those drawers, or subfolders, have the capacity to hold even more folders, which can hold other folders or individual files. For example, you might create one folder called Classes to hold all of your class work. Inside the Classes folder, you could create folders for each of your classes (such as Intro to Computers, MGT 111, and British Literature). Inside each of those folders, you could create subfolders for each class's assignments, completed homework, research, notes, and so on.

Grouping related files into folders makes it easier for you to identify and find files. Which would be easier—going to the MGT 111 folder to find a file or searching through

the 143 individual files in Documents hoping to find the right one? Grouping files in a folder also allows you to move them more efficiently, so you can quickly transfer critical files needing frequent backup to a CD, for instance.

VIEWING AND SORTING FILES AND FOLDERS

Are there different ways I can view and sort my files and folders? A new feature in Windows Vista is Live Icons. Live Icons allows you to preview the actual contents of a specific file or folder without actually opening the file. Live Icons can be displayed in a variety of views, which are discussed in more detail below.

• **Tiles view:** Displays files and folders as icons in list form. Each icon includes the file name, the application associated with the file, and the file size. The display information is customizable. The Tiles view also displays picture dimensions, a handy feature for Web page developers.

• **Details view:** The most interactive view. Files and folders are displayed in list form, and the additional file information is displayed in columns alongside the file name. You can sort and display the contents of the folder by any of the column headings, so you may sort the contents alphabetically by file name or type, or hierarchically by date last modified or by file size (see Figure 5.20).

- **List view:** Another display of even smaller icons and file names. This is a good view if you have a lot of content in the folder and need to see most or all of it at once.

- **Small and Medium Icon views:** Also display files and folders as icons in list form, but the icons are either a small or medium size and include no other file information than the file name. However, additional file information is displayed in a ScreenTip (the text that appears when you place your cursor over the file icon).

- **Large Icon view:** Replaces the Thumbnails view in Windows XP as illustrated in Figure 5.21. Large Icon view shows the contents of folders as small images. There is also Extra Large Icon view, which shows folder contents and other icons as even larger images. Large and Extra Large icon views are the best to use if your folder contains picture files.

For those folders that contain collections of MP3 files, you can download the cover of

FIGURE 5.20

Details view enables you to sort and list your files in a variety of ways to enable quick access to the correct file.

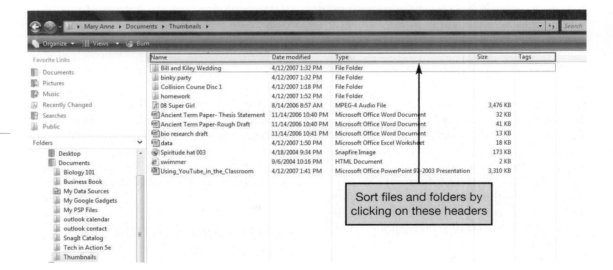

Sort files and folders by clicking on these headers

FIGURE 5.21

In Windows Vista, Large Icons is an especially good way to display folders containing different files. Live Icons display a thumbnail image of actual contents, making it easier to find a given item. The preview pane on the right enables you to see the first page of your document without first opening it.

>To access Large Icon view, from the command bar in any folder dialog box, click **View**, and then select **Large Icon** view. You may also use the scalable feature to adjust the size of the icons.

Folders with live preview of contents

Preview pane shows first page of selected document without opening it

Folders with live preview of contents (Excel spreadsheet, image, and PowerPoint presentation)

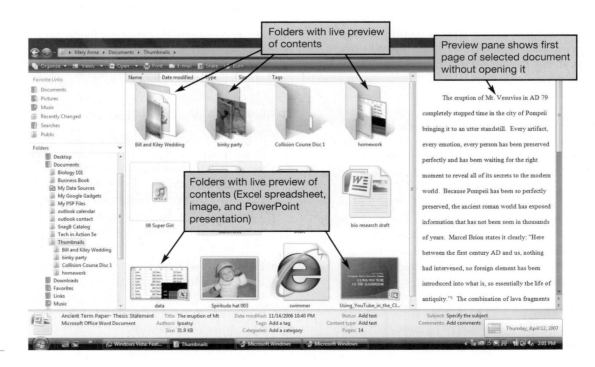

the CD or an image of the artist to display on any folder to further identify that collection.

What's the best way to search for a file? You've no doubt saved a file and forgotten where you saved it, or you have downloaded a file from the Internet and are not sure where it was saved. What's the quickest way to find a file? Looking through every file stored on your computer could take hours, even with a well-organized file management system. Fortunately, Windows Vista includes Instant Search, found on the Start menu, that searches through your hard drive or other storage device (CD or flash drive) to locate files that match criteria you provide. Your search can be based on a part of the file name or just a word or phrase in the file. You can also narrow your search by providing information about the type of file, which application was used to create the file, or even how long ago the file was saved. (Mac OS Leopard has a similar feature called Spotlight, known as Sherlock in earlier versions.) Instant Search can also find e-mails based on your criteria. Instant Search is also found in Windows Explorer and is used to search the contents of current folders.

NAMING FILES

Are there special rules I have to follow when I name files? Files have names just like people. The first part of a file, or the **file name**, is similar to our first names and is generally the name you assign to the file when you save it. For example, "bioreport" may be the name you assign a report you have completed for a biology class.

In a Windows application, an **extension**, or **file type**, follows the file name and a period or dot (.). Like our last name, this extension identifies what kind of family of files the file belongs to or which application should be used to read the file. For example, if "bioreport" is a document created in Works, then it has a .wks extension and is named "bioreport.wks." If the bioreport file is a Word 2007 document, then it has a .docx extension and is named "bioreport.docx." Figure 5.22 lists some common file extensions and the types of documents they indicate.

SOUND BYTE

File Management

In this Sound Byte, you'll examine the features of file management and maintenance. You'll learn the various methods of creating folders, how to turn a group of unorganized files into an organized system of folders, and how to maintain your file system.

FIGURE 5.22 Common File Name Extensions

Extension	Type of Document	Application that Uses the Extension
.doc	Word-processing document	Microsoft Word 2003
.docx	Word-processing document	Microsoft Word 2007 document
.wpd	Word-processing document	Corel WordPerfect
.xlsx	Spreadsheet	Microsoft Excel 2007 workbook
.accdb	Database	Microsoft Access 2007
.pptx	PowerPoint presentation	Microsoft PowerPoint 2007 presentation
.pdf	Portable Document Format	Adobe Acrobat or Adobe Reader
.rtf	Text	Any program that can read text documents
.txt	Text	Any program that can read text documents
.htm or .html	Web page	Any program that can read HTML
.jpg	Joint Photographic Experts Group (JPEG) image	Most programs capable of displaying images
.gif	Graphic Interchange Format (GIF) image	Most programs capable of displaying images
.bmp	Bitmap image	Windows
.zip	Compressed file	WinZip

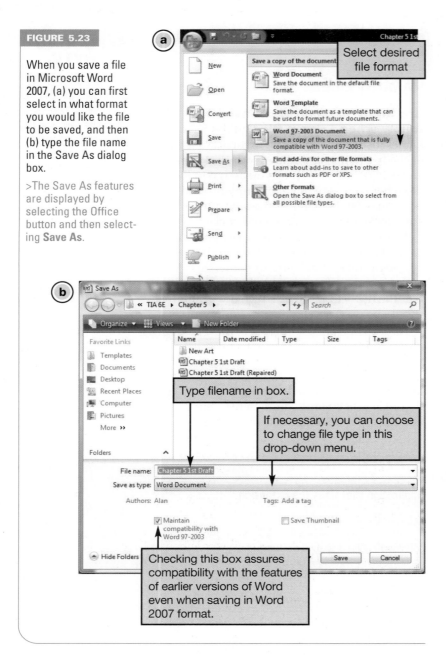

FIGURE 5.23

When you save a file in Microsoft Word 2007, (a) you can first select in what format you would like the file to be saved, and then (b) type the file name in the Save As dialog box.

>The Save As features are displayed by selecting the Office button and then selecting **Save As**.

Select desired file format

Type filename in box.

If necessary, you can choose to change file type in this drop-down menu.

Checking this box assures compatibility with the features of earlier versions of Word even when saving in Word 2007 format.

Do I need to know the extensions of all files to save them? As shown in Figure 5.23, when you save a file created in most applications running under the Windows operating system, you do not need to add the extension to the file name; it is added automatically for you. Mac and Linux operating systems do not require file extensions. This is because the information as to the type of application the computer should use to open the file is stored inside the file itself. However, if you're using these operating systems and will be sending files to Windows users, you should add an extension to your file name so that Windows can more easily open your files. To ease the frustration of users of previous versions of Office, when using any Office 2007 application, you can choose to save the file in either a 2007 format or a 2003 or earlier format.

Are there things I shouldn't do when naming my file? Each operating system has its own naming conventions, or rules, which are listed in Figure 5.24. Beyond those conventions, it's important that you name your files so that you can easily identify them. A file name such as "research.docx" may be descriptive to you if you're only working on one research paper. However, if you create other research reports later and need to identify the contents of these files quickly, you'll soon wish you had been more descriptive. Giving your files more descriptive names, such as bioresearch.docx or, better yet, bio101research.docx, is a good idea.

Keep in mind, however, that every file in the same folder or storage device (hard drive, CD, and so on) must be uniquely identified. Therefore, files may share the

FIGURE 5.24 File-Naming Conventions

	Mac OS	Windows
File and folder name length	As many as 255 characters*	As many as 255 characters
Case sensitive?	Yes	No
Forbidden characters	Colon (:)	" / \ * ? < > | :
File extensions needed?	No	Yes
Path separator	Colon (:)	\

*Note: Although Mac OS X supports file names with as many as 255 characters, many applications running on OS X still support only a maximum of 31-character file names.

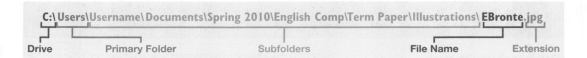

FIGURE 5.25

Understanding File Paths

C:\Users\Username\Documents\Spring 2010\English Comp\Term Paper\Illustrations\ EBronte.jpg

| Drive | Primary Folder | Subfolders | File Name | Extension |

same file name (such as "bioreport.docx" or "bioreport.xlsx") or share the same extension ("bioreport.xlsx" or "budget.xlsx"); however, no two files stored on the same device and folder can share both the same file name and the same extension.

How can I tell where my files are saved? When you save a file for the first time, you give the file a name and designate where you want to save it. For easy reference, the operating system includes default folders where files are saved unless you specify otherwise. In Windows Vista, the default folders are "Documents" for files, "Downloads" for files downloaded from the Internet, "Music" for audio files, "Pictures" for graphic files, and "Videos" for video files. Although you can create your own folders, these default folders are the beginning of a well-organized system.

You can determine the location of a file by its **file path**. The file path starts with the drive in which the file is located and includes all folders, subfolders (if any), the file name, and extension. For example, if you were saving a picture of Emily Brontë for a term paper for an English composition course, the file path might be C:\Users\ Username\Documents\Spring 2010\ English Comp\Term Paper\Illustrations\ EBronte.jpg.

As shown in Figure 5.25, the C indicates the drive on which the file is stored (in this case, the hard drive), and Documents is the file's primary folder. Spring 2010, English Comp, Term Paper, and Illustrations are successive subfolders within the Documents main folder. Last is the file name, EBronte, separated from the file extension (in this case, .jpg) by a period. Notice that

in between the drive, primary folder, subfolders, and file name are backslash characters (\). These backslash characters, used by Windows and DOS, are referred to as **path separators**. Mac files use a colon (:), whereas UNIX and Linux files use the forward slash (/) as the path separator.

WORKING WITH FILES

How can I move and copy files? Once you've located your file with Windows Explorer, you can perform many other file-management actions such as opening, copying, moving, renaming, and deleting files. You open a file by double-clicking the file from its storage location. Based on the file extension, the operating system then determines which application needs to be loaded to open the requested file and opens the file within the correct application automatically. You can copy a file to another location using the Copy command. When you copy a file, a duplicate file is created and the original file remains in its original location. To move a file from one location to another, you use the Move command. When you move a file, the original file is deleted from its original location.

Where do deleted files go? The **Recycle Bin** is a folder on the desktop where files deleted from the hard drive reside until you permanently purge them from your system. Unfortunately, files deleted from other drives (such as the CD, flash drive, external hard drive, and network drive) do not go to the Recycle Bin but are deleted from the system immediately. (Mac systems have something similar to the Recycle Bin, called Trash, which is represented by a wastebasket icon. To delete files on a Mac, drag the files to Trash on the Dock.)

How do I permanently delete files from my system? Files in the Recycle Bin or Trash are being held only until they are permanently deleted. To delete your files from the Recycle Bin permanently, select Empty the Recycle Bin after right-clicking the desktop icon. On Macs, select Empty Trash from the Finder menu in OS X.

ACTIVE HELPDESK

Organizing Your Computer: File Management

In this Active Helpdesk call, you'll play the role of a helpdesk staffer, fielding calls about the desktop, windows features (such as scrollbars and the Minimize and Maximize buttons), and how the operating system helps keep the computer organized.

BITS AND BYTES

A File Type for Everyone

Imagine you are sending an e-mail to a diverse group of individuals. You are not sure what word-processing software each of them uses, but you assume that there will be a mix of people who use Word, WordPerfect, and even Writer. How can you be sure that everyone will be able to open the attachment regardless of the program installed on his or her computer? Save the file in Rich Text Format (.rtf), Portable Document Format (.pdf), or Text (.txt) format. Rich Text and Text files can be read by any modern word-processing program, although some formatting may be lost when saving as a Text (.txt) format. And anyone can read a PDF file by downloading the Acrobat Reader from the Adobe Web site (**www.adobe.com**). To save files as RTF, PDF, or TXT files, simply change the file type when saving your file. In Microsoft Word, for example, you can change the file type in the Save As dialog box shown in Figure 5.26.

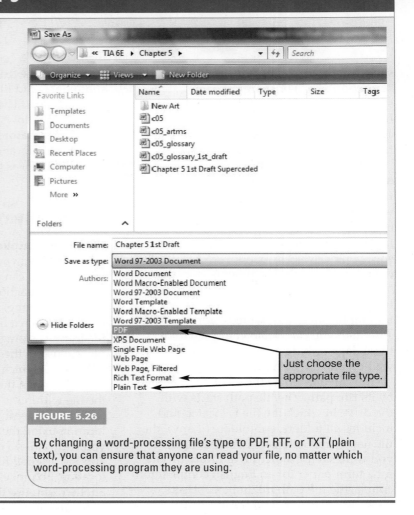

FIGURE 5.26

By changing a word-processing file's type to PDF, RTF, or TXT (plain text), you can ensure that anyone can read your file, no matter which word-processing program they are using.

Is it possible to retrieve a file that I've accidentally deleted? The benefit of the Recycle Bin is that you can restore the files you place there—as long as you've not emptied the Recycle Bin. To restore a file, open the Recycle Bin, locate and select the file, and select Restore. Take note that once the Recycle Bin has been emptied, deleted files are not easily retrievable, although it's not impossible to get them back with the right software.

Utility Programs

You have learned that the operating system is the single most essential piece of software in your computer system because it coordinates all the system's activities and provides a means by which other software applications

and users can interact with the system. However, there is another set of programs included in system software. Utility programs are small applications that perform special functions. Some utility programs help manage system resources (such as disk defragmenter utilities, or *defrag* utilities), others help make your time and work on the computer more pleasant (such as screen savers), and still others improve efficiency (such as file compression utilities).

Some of these utility programs are incorporated into the operating system. For example, Windows Vista has its own firewall and file-compression utility. Other utility programs, such as antivirus and security programs, have become so large and require such frequent updating that they are sold as stand-alone off-the-shelf programs in stores or as Web-based services available for an annual fee.

FIGURE 5.27 Utility Programs Available within Windows and as Stand-Alone Programs

Windows Utility Program	Off-the-Shelf (Stand-Alone) Windows Utility Program	Function
File Management		
Add or Remove Programs		Properly installs and uninstalls software
Windows Explorer File Compression	WinZip	Reduces file size
Windows System Maintenance and Diagnostics		
Automatic Backup	Norton Ghost	Backs up important information
Disk Cleanup	CCleaner, McAfee Quick Clean	Removes unnecessary files from hard drive
Disk Defragmenter	Norton SystemWorks	Arranges files on hard drive in sequential order
Error-checking (previously ScanDisk)		Checks hard drive for unnecessary or damaged files
System Restore	FarStone RestoreIT!	Restores system to a previously stable state
Task Manager		Displays performance measures for processes; provides information on programs and processes running on computer
Task Scheduler		Schedules programs to run automatically at prescribed times

Sometimes utility programs, such as Norton SystemWorks, are offered as software suites, bundled with other useful maintenance and performance-boosting utilities. Still other utilities, like Lavasoft's Ad-Aware, are offered as freeware or shareware programs and are available as downloads from the Web.

Figure 5.27 illustrates some of the various types of utility programs available within the Windows operating system as well as those available as off-the-shelf programs in stores. In general, the basic utilities designed to manage and tune the computer hardware are incorporated in the operating system. The off-the-shelf utility programs typically offer more features, or an easier user interface, for backup, security, diagnostic, or recovery functions.

In this section, we explore many of the utility programs you'll find installed on a Windows operating system. Unless otherwise noted, you can find these utilities in the Control Panel or on the Start menu by selecting Programs, Accessories, and then System Tools. (We also take a brief look at some Mac utilities.) We will discuss antivirus and personal firewall utility programs in Chapter 7.

DISPLAY UTILITIES

How can I change the appearance of my desktop? The Display icon, found in Appearance and Themes in the Control Panel, has all the features required to change the appearance of your desktop, providing different options for the desktop background, screen savers, windows colors, font sizes, and screen resolution. Although Windows comes with many different background themes and screen saver options preinstalled, hundreds of downloadable options are available on the Web. Just search for "backgrounds" or "screen savers" on your favorite search engine to customize your desktop. Another way to access the background and screen saver options and all display utilities is to right-click an empty space on your desktop and choose Properties from the shortcut menu.

BITS AND BYTES

Need to Recover a Deleted Recycle Bin File?

Once you empty the Recycle Bin, because you don't see the file name anymore, it looks as if the file has been erased from the hard drive. However, only the reference to the deleted file is deleted permanently, so the operating system has no easy way to find the file. The file data actually remains on the hard drive until otherwise written over. Should you delete a file from the Recycle Bin in error, you can immediately restore the deleted file by clicking Restore all Items from the Task pane. For those files that have been deleted for awhile and are not recoverable with Restore all Items, programs such as FarStone's RestoreIT! or Norton's GoBack can be used; however, the longer you wait to recover a deleted file, the chances of a full recovery decrease. That's because the probability that your file has been overwritten by other data increases.

Do I really need to use a screen saver? Screen savers are animated images that appear on a computer monitor when no user activity has been sensed for a certain time. Originally, screen savers were used to prevent burn-in, the result of an image being burned into the phosphor inside the monitor's cathode ray tube when the same image was left on the monitor for long periods of time. Screen savers are now used almost exclusively for decoration.

You can control how long your computer sits idle before the screen saver starts. For example, if you don't want people looking at what's on your screen when you leave your computer unexpectedly for a time, you may want to program your screen saver to run after only a minute or two of inactivity. (Right-click on the Windows desktop to access Display Properties and click the Screen Saver tab.) However, if you find that you let your computer sit inactive for awhile but need to look at the screen image (while you study or read a document or spreadsheet, for example), you may want to extend the period of inactivity.

Can I make the display on my LCD monitor clearer? If you use a notebook computer or have a flat-panel liquid crystal display (LCD) monitor, you may be interested in the Clear Type feature in Windows Vista. Clear Type is a default setting that smoothes the edges of screen fonts to make text easier to read.

SOUND BYTE

File Compression

In this Sound Byte, you'll learn about the advantages of file compression and how to use Windows Vista to compress and decompress files. If you own an earlier operating system, this Sound Byte will teach you how to find and install file compression shareware software programs.

THE ADD OR REMOVE PROGRAMS UTILITY

What is the correct way to add new programs to the system? These days, when you install a new program, the program automatically runs a wizard (a step-by-step guide) that walks you through the installation process. If a wizard does not start automatically, however, you should go to the Add or Remove Programs folder in the Control Panel. This prompts the operating system to look for the setup program of the new software and starts the installation wizard.

What is the correct way to remove unwanted programs from my system? Some people think that deleting a program from the Program Files folder on the C drive is the best way to remove a program from the system. However, most programs include support files such as a help file, dictionaries, and graphics files that are not located in the main program folder found in Program Files. Depending on the supporting file's function, support files can be scattered throughout various folders within the system. You would normally miss these files by just deleting the main program file from the system. By selecting the Windows uninstaller utility, Add or Remove Programs (found in the Control Panel), you delete not only the main program file but also all supporting files.

FILE COMPRESSION UTILITIES

What is file compression? A file compression utility is a program that takes out redundancies in a file to reduce the file size. File compression is helpful because it makes a large file more compact, making it easier and faster to send over the Internet, upload to a Web page, or save onto a disk. As shown in Figure 5.28, Windows Vista has built-in compression (or zip) file support. There are also several stand-alone freeware and shareware programs, such as WinZip (for Windows) and StuffIt (for Windows or Mac), that you can obtain to compress your files.

How does file compression work? Most compression programs look for repeated patterns of letters and replace these patterns with a shorter placeholder. The repeated patterns and the associated placeholder are cataloged and stored temporarily

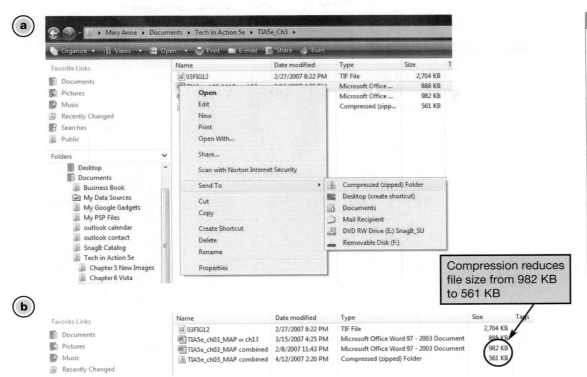

FIGURE 5.28

(a) File compression is a built-in utility of the Windows operating system. (b) Compressing the Word document reduced the file size from 982 KB to 561 KB.

>To access the Windows file compression utility, right-click the file or folder that is to be compressed, select **Send to** from the short-cut menu, and then select **Compressed (zipped) Folder**.

Compression reduces file size from 982 KB to 561 KB

in a separate file called the *dictionary*. For example, in the following sentence, you can easily see the repeated patterns of letters:

The rain in Spain falls mainly on the plain.

Although this example contains obvious repeated patterns (**ain** and **the**), in a large document, the repeated patterns may be more complex. The compression program's algorithm (a set of instructions designed to complete a solution in a step-by-step manner) therefore runs through the file several times to determine the optimal repeated patterns to obtain the greatest compression.

How effective are file compression programs? The effectiveness of file compression—that is, how much a file's size is reduced—depends on several factors, including the type and size of the individual file and the compression method used. Current compression programs can reduce text files by as much as 50 percent. However, some files such as PDF files already contain a form of compression, so they do not need to be compressed further. Other file types, especially some graphics and audio formats, have gone through a compression process that reduces file size by permanently discarding data. For example, image files such as Joint Photographic Experts Group (JPEG), Graphics Interchange Format (GIF), and

Portable Network Graphics (PNG) files discard small variations in colors that the human eye may not pick up. Likewise, MP3 files permanently discard sounds that the human ear cannot hear. These graphic and audio files do not need further compression.

How do I decompress a file I've compressed? When you want to restore the file to its original state, you need to decompress the file so that the pieces of file that the compression process temporarily removed are restored to the document. Generally, the same program you used to compress the file has the capability to decompress the file as well (see Figure 5.29).

SYSTEM MAINTENANCE UTILITIES

Are there any utilities that make my system work faster? Disk Cleanup is a Windows utility that cleans, or removes, unnecessary files from your hard drive. These include files that have accumulated in the Recycle Bin as well as temporary files, which are files created by Windows to store data temporarily when a program is running. Windows usually deletes these temporary files when you exit the program, but sometimes it forgets or doesn't have time if

FIGURE 5.29

The Extraction Wizard in Windows Vista makes unzipping compressed folders and files easy.

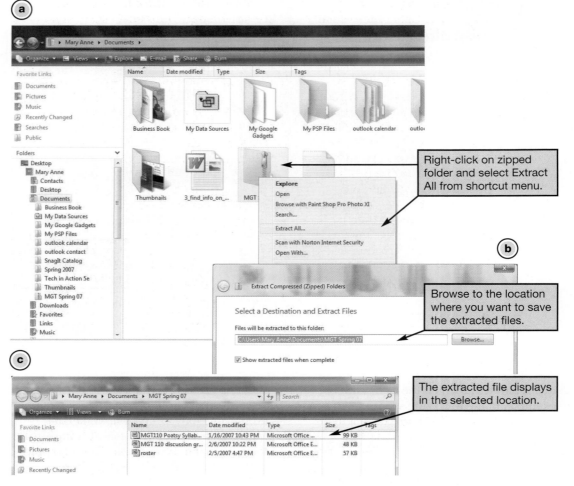

Right-click on zipped folder and select Extract All from shortcut menu.

Browse to the location where you want to save the extracted files.

The extracted file displays in the selected location.

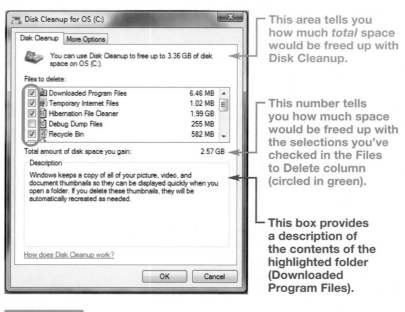

This area tells you how much *total* space would be freed up with Disk Cleanup.

This number tells you how much space would be freed up with the selections you've checked in the Files to Delete column (circled in green).

This box provides a description of the contents of the highlighted folder (Downloaded Program Files).

FIGURE 5.30

Using Disk Cleanup will help free space on your hard drive.

>Disk Cleanup is accessed by clicking **Start**, **All Programs**, **Accessories**, and then **System Tools**.

your system freezes up or incurs a problem preventing you from properly exiting a program. Disk Cleanup, found in System Tools in the Accessories folder in the Start Menu, also removes temporary Internet files (Web pages stored on your hard drive for quick viewing) as well as offline Web pages (pages stored on your computer so you can view them without being connected to the Internet). If not deleted periodically, these unnecessary files can deter efficient operating performance.

How can I control which files Disk Cleanup deletes? When you run Disk Cleanup, the program scans your hard drive to determine which folders have files that can be deleted and calculates the amount of hard drive space that would be freed by doing so. You check off which type of files you would like to delete as shown in Figure 5.30.

What else can I do if my system runs slowly? Over time, as you add and delete information in a file, the file pieces are saved in scattered locations on the hard drive. Locating all the pieces of the file takes extra time, making the operating system less efficient. **Disk defragmenter** regroups related pieces of files on the hard disk, allowing the OS to work more efficiently. You can find the Windows Disk Defragmenter utility under System Tools in the Accessories folder of the Start menu. Using the Windows Disk Defragmenter Analyzer feature, you should check several times a year to determine whether your drive needs to be defragmented. Unfortunately, Macs do not have a defrag utility built into the system because the thought is that the file system used by Mac OS X is so efficient that defragging the hard drive is unnecessary. Still, for those users who feel the need to defrag their Mac, iDefrag is an external program that can be purchased from Coriolis Systems.

How do I diagnose potential errors or damage on my storage devices? **Error-checking**, once known as ScanDisk, is a Windows utility that checks for lost files and fragments as well as physical errors on your hard drive. Lost files and fragments of files occur as you save, resave, move, delete, and copy files on your hard drive. Sometimes the system becomes confused, leaving references on the **file allocation table** or **FAT** (an index of all sector numbers in a table) to files that no longer exist or have been moved. Physical errors on the hard drive occur when the mechanism that reads the hard drive's data (which is stored as 1s or 0s) can no longer determine whether the area holds a 1 or a 0. These areas are called *bad sectors*. Sometimes Error-checking can recover the lost data, but more often it deletes the files that are taking up space unnecessarily. Error-checking also makes a note of any bad sectors so that the system will not use them again to store data.

Where can I find Error-checking? In Windows XP and Vista, the Error-checking utility can be found in Disk Properties. In earlier versions of a Windows operating system, Error-checking can be found in System Tools. To locate Error-checking in Windows Vista or XP, after clicking Computer from the Start menu, right-click the disk you want to diagnose, select Properties, select Tools, and select Check Now. On Macs, you can use the Disk Utility to test and repair disks. You will find Disk Utility in the Utilities folder in the Applications folder on your hard drive.

How can I check on a program that has stopped running? If a program has stopped working, you can use the Windows **Task Manager utility** to check on the program or to exit the nonresponsive program. Although you can access Task Manager from the Control Panel, it is more easily accessible by pressing the Ctrl+Alt+Del keys on your keyboard at the same time, or by right-clicking an empty space on the taskbar at the bottom of your screen. The Applications tab of Task Manager lists all programs that you are using and indicates whether they are working properly (running) or have stopped improperly (not responding). You can terminate programs that are not responding by clicking the End Task button in the dialog box.

If you need outside assistance because of a program error, Dr. Watson for Windows, a tool that is included in Microsoft Windows XP, and Problem Reports and Solutions, a tool in Windows Vista, gather information about the computer when there is a program error. When an error occurs, these tools automatically create and save a text log. The log can then be viewed, printed, or delivered electronically to any technical support professional who can then use this information to help diagnose the problem.

SYSTEM RESTORE AND BACKUP UTILITIES

Is there an undo command for the system? Say you have just installed a new software program and your computer freezes. After rebooting the computer, when you try to start the application, the system freezes once again. You uninstall the new program, but your computer continues to freeze after rebooting. What can you do now?

Windows Vista and XP have a utility called System Restore that lets you restore your system settings back to a specific date when everything was working properly. You can find System Restore under System Tools on the Accessories menu. If the computer was running just fine before you installed software or a new hardware device, you would restore your computer back to the settings before the software or hardware installation. System Restore does not affect your personal data files (such as Microsoft Word documents, browsing history, or e-mail), so you won't lose changes made to these files when you use System Restore.

SOUND BYTE

Hard Disk Anatomy Interactive

In this Sound Byte, you'll watch a series of animations that show various aspects of a hard drive, including the anatomy of a hard drive, how to read and write data to a hard drive, and the fragmenting and defragmenting of a hard drive.

ACTIVE HELPDESK

Using Utility Programs

In this Active Helpdesk call, you'll play the role of a helpdesk staffer, fielding calls about the utility programs included in system software and what they do.

DIG DEEPER

How Disk Defragmenter Utilities Work

To understand how disk defragmenter utilities work, you must first understand the basics of how a hard disk drive stores files. A hard disk drive is composed of several *platters*, or round thin plates of metal, that are covered with a special magnetic coating that records the data. The platters are about 3.5 inches in diameter and are stacked onto a spindle. There are usually two or three platters in any hard disk drive, with data being stored on one or both sides. Data is recorded on hard disks in concentric circles called **tracks**, which are further broken down into pie-shaped wedges called **sectors** (see Figure 5.31). The data is further identified by *clusters*, which are the smallest segments within the sectors.

When you want to save (or write) a file, the bits that make up your file are recorded onto one or more clusters of the drive. To keep track of which clusters hold which files, the drive also stores an index of all sector numbers in a table. To save a file, the computer will look in the table for clusters that are not already being used and will then record the file information on those clusters. When you open (or read) a file, the computer searches through the table for the clusters that hold the desired file and reads that file. Similarly, when you delete a file, you are actually not deleting the file itself, but rather the reference in the table to the file.

So, how does a disk become fragmented? When only part of an older file is deleted, the deleted section of the file creates a gap in the sector of the disk where the data was originally stored. In the same way, when new information is added to an older file, there may not be space to save the new information sequentially near

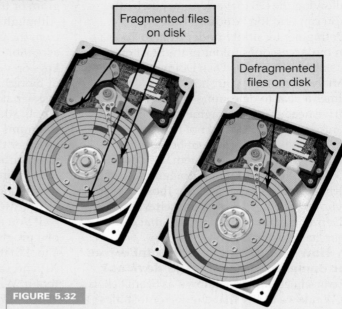

FIGURE 5.32

Over time, as files are saved, deleted, and modified, the fragments of information for various files fall out of sequential order on the hard disk and the disk becomes fragmented. Defragmenting the hard drive arranges file fragments so that they are located next to each other. This makes the hard drive run more efficiently.

where the file was originally saved. In that case, the system writes the added part of the file to the next available location on the disk, and a reference is made in the table as to the location of this file fragment. Over time, as files are saved, deleted, and modified, the bits of information for various files fall out of sequential order and the disk becomes fragmented.

Disk fragmentation is a problem because the operating system is not as efficient when a disk is fragmented. It takes longer to locate a whole file because more of the disk must be searched for the various pieces, greatly slowing down the performance of your computer.

How can you make the files line up more efficiently on the disk? At this stage, the disk defragmenter utility enters the picture. The defragmenter tool takes the hard drive through a defragmentation process in which pieces of files that are scattered over the disk are placed together and arranged sequentially on the hard disk. Also, any unused portions of clusters that were too small in which to save data before are grouped, increasing the available storage space on the disk. Figure 5.32 shows before and after shots of a fragmented disk having gone through the defragmentation process.

For more about hard disks and defragmenting, be sure to check out the Sound Byte "Hard Disk Anatomy Interactive."

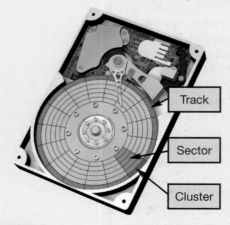

FIGURE 5.31

On a hard disk platter, data is recorded onto tracks, which are further broken down into sectors and clusters.

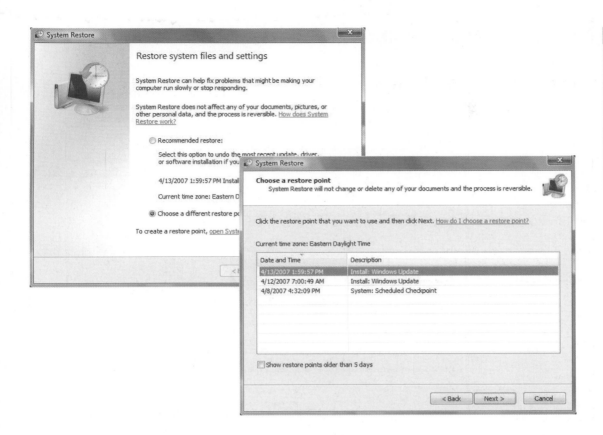

FIGURE 5.33

Setting a restore point is good practice before installing any hardware or software.

>The Restore Point Wizard is found by clicking **Start**, **All Programs**, **Accessories**, **System Tools**. In the System Tools folder, click **System Restore**. The System Restore wizard displays, with Restore Point shown on the first page of the Wizard.

How does the computer remember its previous settings? Every time you start your computer or when a new application or driver is installed, Windows Vista (or XP) automatically creates a snapshot of your entire system's settings. This snapshot is called a **restore point**. You also can create and name your own restore points at any time. Creating a restore point is a good idea before making changes to your computer such as installing hardware or software. If something goes wrong with the installation process, Windows can reset your system to the restore point. As shown in Figure 5.33, Windows includes a Restore Point Wizard that walks you through the process of setting restore points.

How can I protect my data in the event something malfunctions with my system? When you use the Windows Vista **Automatic Backup utility**, you create a duplicate copy of all the data on your hard disk and copy it to another storage device, such as a DVD or external hard drive. A backup copy protects your data in the event your hard disk fails or files are accidentally erased. Although you may not need to back up every file on your computer, you should back up the files that are most important to

you and keep the backup copy in a safe location. Mac OS X Leopard includes a backup utility called Time Machine that will automatically back up your files to a specified location. Apple also offers backup hardware called Time Capsules, which are wireless devices designed to work with Time Machine and record your backup data. (For more information on backing up your files, see the Technology in Focus "Protecting Your Computer and Backing Up Your Data," on page 364.)

THE TASK SCHEDULER UTILITY

How can I remember to perform all these maintenance procedures? To keep your computer system in top shape, it is important to routinely run some of the utilities described previously. Depending on your usage, you may want to defrag your hard drive or clean out temporary Internet files periodically. However, many computer users forget to initiate these tasks. Luckily, the Windows **Task Scheduler utility**, shown in Figure 5.34, allows you to schedule tasks to run automatically at predetermined times, with no interaction necessary on your part.

SOUND BYTE

Letting Your Computer Clean Up After Itself

In this Sound Byte, you'll learn how to use the various maintenance utilities within the operating system. In addition, you'll learn how to use Task Scheduler to clean up your hard disk automatically. You'll also learn the best times of the day to schedule these maintenance tasks and why they should be done on a routine basis to make your system more efficient.

FIGURE 5.34

To keep your machine running in top shape, use Task Scheduler to schedule maintenance programs to run automatically at selected times and days.

>Task Scheduler is found by clicking **Start**, **All Programs**, **Accessories**, and then **System Tools**.

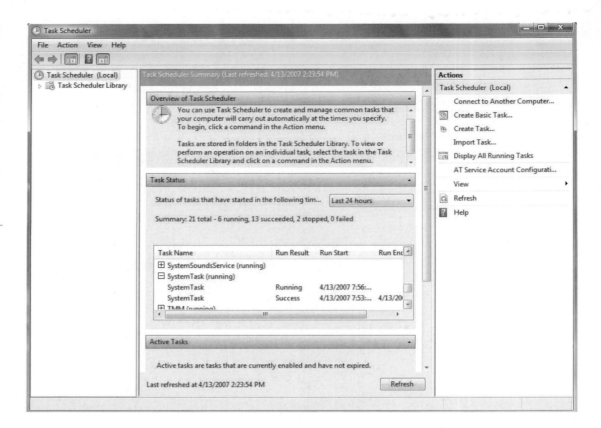

BITS AND BYTES

Need a System Software Update?

Bugs, or problems, in software occur all the time. Software developers are constantly testing their products, even after releasing the software to the retail market, and as users report errors they find. Windows Update is Microsoft's service (utility) for updating operating system software. For Windows Vista users, Windows Update automatically notifies you when updates are available for download. Mac users can update their system with Software Update found under System Preferences.

ACCESSIBILITY UTILITIES

Are there utilities designed for users with special needs? Windows Vista has created an Ease of Access Center, which is a centralized location for assistive technology and tools to adjust accessibility settings. In the Ease of Access Center, you can find tools to help you adjust the screen contrast, magnify the screen image, have screen contents read to you, and display an on-screen keyboard as more fully explained in the

following list. If you're not sure where to start or what settings might help, a questionnaire asks you about routine tasks and provides a personalized recommendation for settings that will help you use your computer (see Figure 5.35). Some of these features are described below:

- **High Contrast:** Allows you to select a color scheme setting in which you can control the contrast between text and background. Because some visually impaired individuals find it easier to see white text on a dark background, there are color schemes that invert screen colors.

- **Magnifier:** A display utility that creates a separate window that displays a magnified portion of your screen. This feature makes the screen more readable for users who have impaired vision. The Narrator utility is a very basic speech program that reads what is on-screen, whether it's the contents of a window, menu options, or text you have typed. The Narrator coordinates with text utilities such as Notepad and WordPad as well as with Internet Explorer, but it may not work correctly with other programs. For this reason, Narrator is

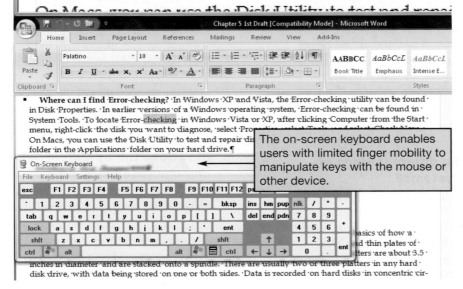

The magnifier window enlarges the text of the document.

The on-screen keyboard enables users with limited finger mobility to manipulate keys with the mouse or other device.

FIGURE 5.35

Microsoft Windows includes such handy accessibility features as a magnifier and an on-screen keyboard to help those with disabilities. These features are not meant to be sufficient for users with severe disabilities. Full-blown software applications are available to fill those needs.

not meant for individuals who must rely solely on a text-to-speech utility to operate the computer.

- **On-Screen Keyboard:** Displays a keyboard on the screen. You type by clicking on or hovering over the keys with a pointing device (mouse or trackball) or joystick. This utility, which is similar to the Narrator, is not meant for everyday use for individuals with severe disabilities. A separate program with more functionality is better in those circumstances.

- **Windows Speech Recognition:** An effective tool that allows you to

dictate text and control your computer by voice. The speech recognition utility is in the Ease of Access folder, which can be found in the Control Panel.

Whether you use Windows, OS X, Linux, or another operating system, a fully featured operating system is available to meet your needs. As long as you keep the operating system updated and regularly use the available utilities to fine-tune your system, you should experience little trouble from your OS.

1. What software is included in system software?

System software is the set of software programs that helps run the computer and coordinates instructions between application software and hardware devices. It consists of the operating system (OS) and utility programs. The OS controls how your computer system functions. Utility programs are programs that perform general housekeeping tasks for the computer such as system maintenance and file compression.

2. What are the different kinds of operating systems?

Operating systems can be classified into four categories. Real-time operating systems (RTOSs) require no user intervention and are designed for systems with a specific purpose and response time (such as robotic machinery). Single-user, single-task OSs are designed for computers on which one user is performing one task at a time (such as PDAs). Single-user, multi-task OSs are designed for computers on which one user is performing more than one task at a time (such as desktop computers). Multiuser OSs are designed for systems in which multiple users are working on more than one task at a time (such as networks).

3. What are the most common desktop operating systems?

Microsoft Windows is the most popular OS. It has evolved from being a single-user, single-task OS into a powerful multi-user operating system. The most recent release is Windows Vista. Another popular OS is the Mac OS, which is designed to work on Apple computers. Apple's most recent release, Mac OS X Leopard, is based on the UNIX operating system. You'll find various versions of UNIX on the market, although it is most often used on networks. Linux is an open source OS based on UNIX and designed primarily for use on personal computers, although it is often found as the operating system on servers.

4. How does the operating system provide a means for users to interact with the computer?

The operating system provides a user interface that enables you to interact with the computer. Most OSs today use a graphical user interface (GUI). Unlike the command- and menu-driven interfaces used earlier, GUIs display graphics and use the point-and-click technology of the mouse and cursor, making the OS more user-friendly. Common features of GUIs include windows, menus, and icons.

5. How does the operating system help manage resources such as the processor, memory, storage, hardware, and peripheral devices?

When you use your computer, you are usually asking it to perform several tasks at the same time. When the OS allows you to perform more than one task at a time, it is multitasking. To provide for seamless multitasking, the OS controls the timing of events the processor works on.

As the OS coordinates the activities of the processor, it uses RAM as a temporary storage area for instructions and data the processor needs. The OS is therefore responsible for coordinating the space allocations in RAM to ensure that there is enough space for the waiting instructions and data. If there isn't sufficient space in RAM for all the data and instructions, then the OS allocates the least necessary files to temporary storage on the hard drive, called virtual memory.

The OS manages storage by providing a file management system that keeps track of the names and locations of files and programs. Programs called *device drivers* facilitate the communication between devices attached to the computer and the OS. Device drivers translate the specialized commands of devices to commands that the OS can understand and vice versa, enabling the OS to communicate with every device in the computer system. Device drivers for common devices are included in the OS software, whereas other devices come with a device driver that you must install or download off the Web.

6. How does the operating system interact with application software?

All software applications need to interact with the CPU. For programs to work with the CPU, they must contain code the CPU recognizes. Rather than having the same blocks of code appear in each software application, the OS includes the blocks of code to which software applications refer. These blocks of code are called *application programming interfaces (APIs)*.

7. How does the operating system help the computer start up?

When you start your computer, it runs through a special process called the *boot process*. The boot process consists of four basic steps: (1) the basic input/output system (BIOS) is activated by powering on the CPU; (2) in the POST test, the BIOS checks that all attached devices are in place; (3) the operating system is loaded into RAM; and (4) configuration and customization settings are checked.

8. What are the main desktop and windows features?

The desktop is the first interaction you have with the OS and the first image you see on your monitor once the system has booted up. It provides you with access to your computer's files, folders, and commonly used tools and applications. Windows are the rectangular panes on your screen that display applications running on your system. Common features of windows include toolbars (or ribbons) and scrollbars, and minimize, maximize, and restore buttons.

9. How does the operating system help me keep my computer organized?

The OS allows you to organize the contents of your computer in a hierarchical structure of directories that includes files, folders, and drives. Windows Explorer helps you manage your files and folders by showing the location and contents of every drive, folder, and file on your computer. Creating folders is the key to organizing files because folders keep related documents together. Following naming conventions and using proper file extensions are also important aspects of file management.

10. What utility programs are included in system software, and what do they do?

Some utility programs are incorporated into the OS; others are sold as stand-alone off-the-shelf programs. Common Windows utilities include those that enable you to adjust your display, add or remove programs, compress files, defrag your hard drive, clean unnecessary files off your system, check for lost files and errors, restore your system to an earlier setting, back up your files, schedule automatic tasks, and check on programs that have quit running.

Buzzwords

Word Bank

- defrag
- Error-checking
- file compression
- file management
- files
- folders
- Linux
- Mac OS
- platform
- sectors
- system software
- Task Manager
- Task Scheduler
- tracks
- utility programs
- Windows
- Windows Explorer
- Vista

Instructions: Fill in the blanks using the words from the Word Bank above.

Veena was looking into buying a new computer and was trying to decide what
(1) _____ to buy—a PC or a Mac. She had used PCs all her life, so she was more familiar with the (2) _____ operating system. Still, she liked the way the (3) _____
looked and was considering switching. Her brother didn't like either operating system, so
he used (4) _____, a free operating system, instead.

After a little research, Veena decided to buy a PC. With it, she got the most recent version
of Windows, (5) _____. She vowed that with this computer, she'd practice better
(6) _____ because she often had a hard time finding files on her old computer. To view
all of the folders on her computer, she opened (7) _____. She made sure that she gave
descriptive names to her (8) _____ and placed them in organized (9) _____.

Veena also decided that with her new computer, she'd pay more attention to the (10)
_____, those little special-function programs that help with maintenance and repairs.
These special-function programs, in addition to the OS, make up the (11) _____.
Veena looked into some of the more frequently used utilities. She thought it would be a
good idea to (12) _____ her hard drive regularly so that all the files lined up in sequentially ordered (13) _____ and so that it was more efficient. She also looked into
(14) _____ utilities, which would help her reduce the size of her files when she sent
them to others over the Internet. Finally, she decided to use the Windows (15) _____
utility to schedule tasks automatically so that she wouldn't forget.

Becoming Computer Literate

Using key terms from the chapter, write a letter to your computer-illiterate aunt explaining
the benefits of simple computer maintenance. First, explain any symptoms her computer
may be experiencing (such as a sluggish Internet connection); then include a set of steps she
can follow in setting up a regimen to remedy the problems. Make sure you explain some of
the system utilities described in this chapter, including, but not limited to, defrag, Disk
Cleanup, and Task Scheduler. Include any other utilities she might need and explain why
she should have them.

Self-Test

Instructions: Answer the multiple-choice and true–false questions below for more practice with key terms and concepts from this chapter.

MULTIPLE CHOICE

1. PDAs use which category of operating system?
   a. Single-user, single task
   b. Multiuser, multitask
   c. Single-user, multitask
   d. Real-time

2. Which of the following would be found in a GUI operating system?
   a. Icons
   b. Windows
   c. Scrollbars
   d. All of the above

3. Virtual memory is
   a. unlimited in capacity.
   b. created by sectioning off an area of the hard drive.
   c. another name for RAM.
   d. synonymous with cache memory.

4. Plug and Play devices
   a. don't require drivers.
   b. have drivers included in the Windows OS.
   c. must be installed using Add or Remove Programs.
   d. None of the above

5. Which of the following is NOT done during the boot process?
   a. Checks that all attached devices are in place and working
   b. Verifies the user's login name and password

   c. Loads the OS from the hard drive
   d. Checks for customized settings put in place for the monitor and desktop

6. Swapping files from virtual memory back to RAM is known as
   a. thrashing.   b. multitasking.
   c. caching.   d. paging.

7. Which view option would be best to sort files by date modified and type of application?
   a. Details   b. Tiles
   c. Large Icons   d. All of the above

8. Which of the following file extensions indicates a file created by a program in the Office 2007 suite?
   a. bioreport.xlsx
   b. bioreport.docx
   c. bioreport.pptx
   d. All of the above

9. To return to a state when your OS was previously stable, which utility would you use?
   a. System Restore
   b. Disk Defragmenter
   c. Windows Explorer
   d. Disk Cleanup

10. Which utility is NOT an accessibility utility?
   a. Magnifier
   b. Narrator
   c. Windows Speech Recognition
   d. File Compression

TRUE–FALSE

_____ 1. Restore points can be set manually.

_____ 2. Linux is a multiuser, multitasking operating system.

_____ 3. Open source operating systems are expensive.

_____ 4. It is possible for a computer to run out of space in RAM.

_____ 5. All files deleted from any device end up in the Recycle Bin.

Making the Transition to... Next Semester

1. Organizing Files and Folders

It's the beginning of a new semester and you promise yourself that you are going to keep all files related to your schoolwork more organized this semester. Develop a plan that outlines how you'll set up folders and subfolders for each subject. Identify at least three different folders for each class. If time and schedule permit, discuss your organization scheme with your instructor.

2. OS Compatibility Issues

Your school requires that you purchase a notebook to run on the school's system. The required machine runs on the Windows operating system. At home you have an Apple computer with OS X Leopard.

a. Research the compatibility issues between the two computers.
b. How does a PDA running with Palm OS fit into the equation?
c. Can you synch the PDA with either or both machines?
d. Explore the application Boot Camp. What does it do? Would it be helpful in this situation?

3. Understanding Safe Mode

It is the night before the major term paper for your philosophy class is due. Your best friend comes screaming down the hall, begging for help. His only copy of his draft paper is on his desktop computer, and it is suddenly booting up with the words Safe Mode in the corners of the screen. What would be the most useful questions to ask him? What steps would you take to debug the problem? If you cannot get the computer to come out of Safe mode, is there a way to retrieve the draft? How many times will you say "Make backups!" that evening?

4. Software Requirements

This semester you have added six new applications to your notebook. You know which courses you'll be taking next semester, and you realize they will require an additional eight major software applications. A friend who is in a similar position tells you she's not worried about putting that much software on her computer because she has a really big hard drive.

a. Is hard disk storage your only concern? Should it be your main concern, or should you worry more about having sufficient RAM? How does your use of the programs impact your answer?
b. Does virtual memory management by your operating system allow you to ignore RAM requirements?

5. Connecting Peripherals

You are considering upgrading to the latest version of Windows. Your current notebook computer is approximately three years old.

a. What concerns would you have about upgrading?
b. How would you determine if your peripheral devices would work with the new OS?
c. Would you consider switching to Linux instead? What are the pros and cons of this decision?

1. Organizing Files and Folders

You started a new job and are given a new computer. You never kept your files and folders organized on the computer you used when in college, but now you are determined to do a better job at keeping your files organized. You know you need folders for the several clients with whom you will be working. For each client, you'll need to have folders for billing information, client documents, and account information. In addition, you need folders for the MP3 files you will listen to when you're not working, as well as a folder for the digital pictures you'll take for personal and company reasons. Finally, you're working toward an advanced degree and will be taking business finance and introduction to marketing courses at night, so you'll need folders for all the homework assignments for both courses. Determine the file structure you would need to create to accommodate your needs. Start with the C drive and assume that Documents, Pictures, and Music are the default folders for documents, pictures, and music files, respectively.

2. Using Mac Utility Programs

Your company has been having trouble with some of its Mac computers running inefficiently. Your boss asks you to research the utility programs your company could use on its Macs to make them run better. In particular, your boss would like you to determine what utilities are available in the Mac OS and then determine what utilities the company may need to purchase. Also, your boss wants to ensure the availability of a disk defrag utility, a file compression utility, and a diagnostic utility you could run to check the hard drive for errors. Using the Internet for your research, what utilities are already in the Mac OS, and what stand-alone utilities can you find? Will they run on all versions of the Mac OS?

3. Monitoring Activities with the OS

The company that you work for has just announced a new internal accounting structure. From now on, each department will be charged individually for the costs associated with computer usage such as backup storage space, Internet usage, and so on.

a. Research how the operating system may be set up to monitor such activity by department.
b. What other activities do you think the operating system can be set up to monitor?

4. Choosing the Best OS

Your new boss is considering moving some of the department operations to Linux-based computer systems. He asks you to research the advantages and disadvantages of moving to Linux or Mac OS X. How would these choices impact his department in the following areas?

a. Budget for technical support for the systems
b. Choice and budget for hardware for the systems
c. Costs of implementation
d. Possibility for future upgrades

Critical Thinking Questions

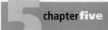

Instructions: Albert Einstein used *Gedanken experiments* or critical thinking questions, to develop his theory of relativity. Some ideas are best understood by experimenting with them in our own minds. The following critical thinking questions are designed to demand your full attention but require only a comfortable chair—no technology.

1. Open Source Pros and Cons

Open source programming embraces a philosophy that states programmers should make their code available to everyone rather than keeping it proprietary. The Linux operating system has had much success as an open source code. The chapter mentions some of the advantages of open source code such as quicker code updates in response to technological advances and changes.

a. What are other advantages of open source code?
b. Can you think of disadvantages to open source code?
c. Why do you think that companies such as Microsoft maintain proprietary restrictions on their code?
d. Are there disadvantages to maintaining proprietary code?

2. The OS of the Future

Operating system interfaces have evolved from a text-based console format to the current graphical user interface. What direction do you think they will move toward next? How could operating systems be organized and used in a manner that is more responsive to humans and better suited to how we think? Are there alternatives to hierarchical file structures for storage? Can you think of ways in which operating systems could adapt and customize themselves based on your usage?

3. Which OS Would You Choose?

Suppose you are building a computer system from scratch and have complete discretion as to your choice of operating system. Which one would you install and why?

4. The OS: With or Without Utilities?

Which environment do you think is better for consumers: to have companies develop smaller, more inexpensive operating systems and then allow competing companies to develop and market utility programs, or to have extremely large full-featured operating systems that include most utilities as part of the operating system itself? Do you think that including utility programs with the operating system makes the cost of the operating system higher?

Team Time   Choosing the Best OS

Problem:

You have been hired to help set up the technology requirements for a small advertising company. The company is holding off buying anything until the decision has been made as to the platform on which the computers should run. Obviously, one of the critical decisions is the operating system.

Task:

Recommend the appropriate operating system for the company.

Process:

1. Break up into three teams. Each team will represent one of the three primary operating systems today: Windows, Mac, and Linux.

2. As a team, research the pros and cons of your operating system. What features does it have that would benefit your company? What features does it not have that your company would need? Why (or why not) would your operating system be the appropriate choice? Why is your OS better (or worse) than either of the other two options?

3. Develop a presentation that states your position with regard to your operating system. Your presentation should have a recommendation and include facts to back it up.

4. As a class, decide which operating system would be the best choice for the company.

Conclusion:

Because the operating system is the critical piece of software in the computer system, the selection should not be taken lightly. The OS that is best for an advertising agency may not be best for an accounting firm. It is important to make sure you consider all aspects of the work environment and the type of work that is being done to ensure a good fit.

Multimedia

In addition to the review materials presented here, you'll find more materials featured with the book's multimedia, including the *Technology in Action* Student Resource CD and the Companion Website (**www.prenhall.com/techinaction**), which will help reinforce your understanding of the chapter content. These materials include the following:

ACTIVE HELPDESK

In Active Helpdesk calls, you'll assume the role of helpdesk operator, taking calls about the concepts you've learned in this chapter. You'll apply what you've learned and receive feedback from a supervisor to review and reinforce those concepts. The Active Helpdesk calls for this chapter are as follows and can be found on your Student Resource CD:

- Managing Hardware and Peripheral Devices: The OS
- Starting the Computer: The Boot Process
- Organizing Your Computer: File Management
- Using Utility Programs

SOUND BYTES

Sound Bytes are dynamic multimedia tutorials that help demystify even the most complex topics. You'll view video clips and animations that illustrate computer concepts and then apply what you've learned by reviewing with the Sound Byte Labs, which include quizzes and activities specifically tailored to each Sound Byte. The Sound Bytes for this chapter are as follows and can be found on your Student Resource CD:

- Customizing Windows Vista
- File Management
- File Compression
- Hard Disk Anatomy Interactive
- Letting Your Computer Clean Up After Itself

COMPANION WEBSITE

The *Technology in Action* Companion Website includes a variety of additional materials to help you review and learn more about the topics in this chapter. The resources available at **www.prenhall.com/techinaction** include:

- **Online Study Guide.** Each chapter features an online true–false and multiple-choice quiz. You can take these quizzes, automatically check the results, and e-mail the results to your instructor.
- **Web Research Projects.** Each chapter features a number of Web research projects that ask you to search the Web for information on computer-related careers, milestones in computer history, important people and companies, emerging technologies, and the applications and implications of different technologies.

Computing | Alternatives

You may think that there are no viable alternatives to buying computers running Microsoft Windows and using Microsoft Office applications such as Word and Excel. However, in this Technology in Focus feature, we explore software and hardware alternatives to Microsoft products that may provide you with cheaper and more flexible options. Let's get started by looking at alternatives to Microsoft Office products.

Application Software Alternatives

Commercial (or proprietary) software is developed by corporations such as Microsoft and Apple to be sold for a profit. Opponents of proprietary software contend that software should be developed without profit motive and that the source code (the actual lines of instructional code that make the program work) should be made available so that others may modify or improve the software. **Open source software** is freely distributed (no royalties accrue to the creators), contains the source code, and can in turn be distributed to others. Therefore, you can download open source software for free from various Web sites, install it on as many computers as you wish, make changes to the source code if you know how, and redistribute it to anyone you wish (as long as you don't charge for distributing it). In this section, we look at some open source software that you can download and use on your computer. For a list of open source resources available on the Web, visit **www.sourceforge.net**.

PRODUCTIVITY SOFTWARE ALTERNATIVES: OPENOFFICE

As mentioned in Chapter 4, the OpenOffice.org suite (OpenOffice) is a free suite of productivity software programs that provide similar functionality to Microsoft Office. Versions of OpenOffice are available for a variety of operating systems, including Windows, Linux, and Mac. It currently offers support in more than 90 languages besides English, with more being added all the time by the development community. You can download the installation file you'll need to run OpenOffice at **www.openoffice. org**. The minimum system requirements for installing OpenOffice 3 in a Windows environment are less than those required for Microsoft Office Professional Edition 2007.

The main components of OpenOffice are word-processing (Writer), spreadsheet (Calc), and presentation (Impress) programs that provide similar functionality to the Word, Excel, and PowerPoint applications you're familiar with in Microsoft Office. The OpenOffice 3 suite now also includes three additional programs. Draw provides the typical tools to communicate with graphics and diagrams, Math creates equations and formulas for your documents, and Base allows you to create and manipulate database tables.

The great advantage of OpenOffice is its compatibility with most programs. This means that if your friend uses Microsoft Office 2007 and you send her an OpenOffice file, she can still read it, and you can read all of her Microsoft Office files, too. Unlike previous versions, OpenOffice 3 is now able to open Microsoft Office 2007 files without the need for a conversion program. Although the individual applications in OpenOffice are not as full-featured as those in Microsoft Office, and although they do not have the new ribbon interface found in Office 2007 applications, it is still a powerful productivity software suite, and the price is right.

When you launch OpenOffice via the Quickstarter icon (see Figure 1), you are presented with a list of document types from which to choose. Once you select the appropriate document type (such as spreadsheet, presentation, or text) and click Open, the appropriate application and a new, blank document will open so that you can begin working.

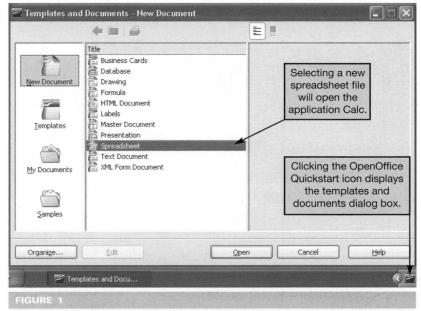

FIGURE 1

The Templates and Documents dialog box in OpenOffice 3 allows you to select the type of document you wish to start. The appropriate application will then open.

Writer

Writer, the OpenOffice word-processing application, is extremely similar in look and feel to Microsoft Word 2003. As is the case in Word, you can easily change text appearance in Writer by altering font type, style, alignment, and color. You can also easily insert graphics (pictures or clip art), tables, and hyperlinks into documents. Writer's wizards provide you with several templates you can use to create standard documents such as faxes, agendas, and letters. Special tools in

Writer also allow you to create bibliographic references, indexes, and tables of contents.

When saving a document in Writer, the default file format has an .odt extension. By using the Save As command, you can save files in other formats, such as various versions of Word (.doc), Pocket Word (.psw) for mobile devices, Rich Text Format (.rtf), Text (.txt), and HTML Document (.htm). The handy Export Directly as PDF icon in Writer allows you to save documents as PDF files (see Figure 2).

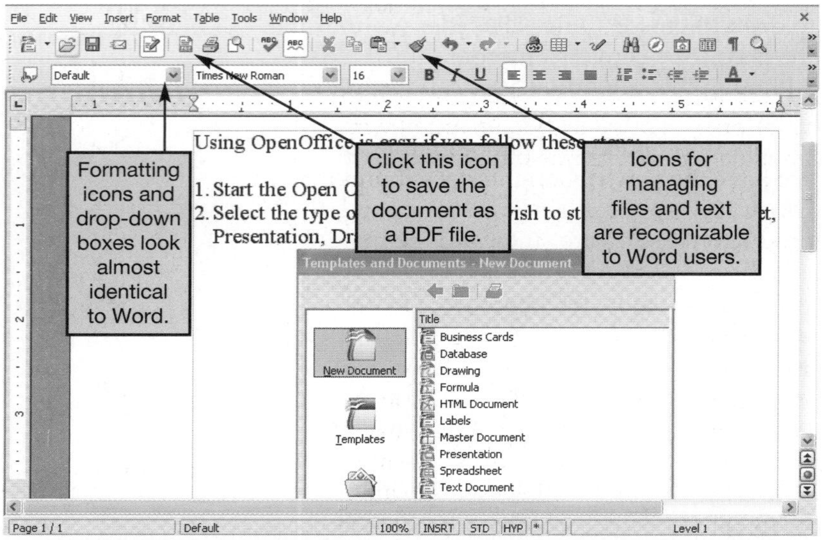

Calc

Opening a blank spreadsheet with Calc is just like starting one in Microsoft Excel. Once you open a spreadsheet, you enter text, numbers, and formulas into the appropriate cells. You also can apply a full range of formatting options (font size, color, style, and so on) to the cells, making it easy to create files such as the monthly budget spreadsheet shown in Figure 3. Built-in formulas and functions simplify the job of creating spreadsheets, and Calc's Function Wizard guides you through the wide range of available functions, providing suggestions as to which function to use.

When saving a document in Calc, the default file format has an .ods extension. By using the Save As command, you can save files in other formats, such as various versions of Excel (.xls), including Pocket Excel (.pxl) for use on mobile devices. The handy Export Directly as PDF icon is also available in Calc.

Impress

To start Impress, select Presentation from the OpenOffice start-up interface, and you'll be presented with a wizard that offers you the option of creating a blank presentation or building one from supplied templates. When compared to the vast array of stunning templates in Microsoft PowerPoint, the templates supplied with Impress are less than impressive. Still, it is easy to construct attractive slides and save them as templates yourself. Or just Google the words "OpenOffice Impress Templates" and you'll find a wide variety of templates for Impress that others have created and that you can download free of charge. To help you in the search, OpenOffice installation includes the option of installing Google search (Web or Desktop), which will appear in the taskbar, making it easily accessible while working in any of the OpenOffice applications. It is also easy to construct attractive slides and save them as templates yourself.

FIGURE 2

Writer provides similar functionality and icons to Microsoft Word 2003 and allows users to create versatile documents that can be saved in a variety of formats.

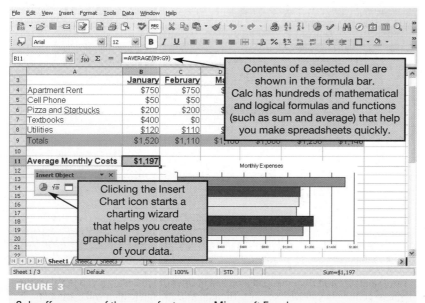

FIGURE 3

Calc offers many of the same features as Microsoft Excel.

Web-Based Alternatives

Although open source alternatives to Microsoft Office applications are cost-effective options—that is, free—they are also convenient because of their accessibility and transferability. Open source alternatives like Open Office are cost-effective—that is, free. There are also Web-based Office software alternatives. All you need is a computer and an Internet connection, and you can be productive almost anywhere. Moreover, with Web-based applications you can invite others to access and edit the same documents online, thus avoiding the coordination mess when collaborating on a project with others. As mentioned in Chapter 4, Google Docs includes a Web-based word processor and spreadsheet and presentation applications. Zoho (**www.zoho.com**) is another great Web-based productivity suite that features project management software, customer relationship management solutions, Web conferencing, online database, group chat, and wikis in addition to the traditional word processing, spreadsheet, and presentations applications. My Office and Workspace from ThinkFree (**www.thinkfree.com**) are a unique combination of online, offline, and mobile productivity. ThinkFree is fully compatible with Microsoft Office—including 2007 formats—and runs on Mac, Windows, and Linux platforms. The sync tool, included with ThinkFree, automatically uploads any changes you make to your offline documents to your online documents. Going mobile? ThinkFree has a mobile Office application that can run on your iPhone or other PDA/smartphone device.

DATABASE SOFTWARE ALTERNATIVES: BASE AND MYSQL

OpenOffice 3 contains Base, a database product similar to Microsoft Access or SQL Server. Like the other OpenOffice programs, Base works seamlessly with database files created in other applications except Access 2007, which needs a separate converter. Alternatively, if you're interested in getting your hands on a free high-end SQL database application, the most popular open source option is MySQL (**www.mysql.com**). Sporting many of the features contained in SQL Server and Oracle Database 11g, MySQL is a powerful database program you can use to develop serious database applications (see Figure 4). Although it is more difficult to learn and use than Microsoft Access, many books and online tutorials are available to help you get MySQL up and running.

E-MAIL CLIENT ALTERNATIVES: EUDORA AND THUNDERBIRD

If you are exploring other choices for Microsoft Office productivity applications, don't overlook other e-mail clients as alternatives to Microsoft Outlook. Mozilla Thunderbird 2 is an open source e-mail client that has many enhancements to organize e-mail with tagging, folders, search, and saved search features. In addition, Mozilla Thunderbird 2 has upped its security and privacy measures so that messages received and sent remain safe. Available from the Mozilla Web site are plenty of add-ons, including a blog editor, calendar, calculator, and multimedia tools.

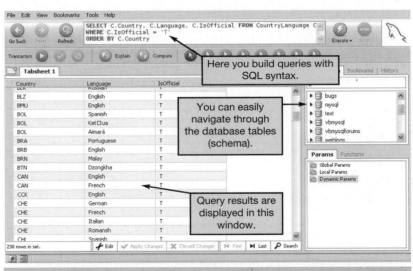

FIGURE 4

The two main components that you should download and install with MySQL are the Database Server and the Query Browser, which is shown here. You use the Database Server to create tables for your database and enter your data. The Query Browser provides a visual interface with the database to display the results of queries you create.

Thunderbird can run on Windows, Mac, and Linux platforms. Eudora, another popular e-mail client, is currently being retrofitted by Qualcomm and other contributors into an open source application. Future versions of

Eudora will be based on the same technology that Mozilla Thunderbird is based on.

DRAWING SOFTWARE ALTERNATIVES: DRAW AND DIA

Microsoft Visio is a popular program for creating flowcharts and diagrams. However, Visio is not cheap. OpenOffice includes a program called Draw that allows you to create simple graphs, charts, and diagrams. Another option is Dia, a free program that allows you to create Visio-like diagrams and charts (see Figure 5). You can download a Windows-compatible version of Dia from **http://live.gnome.org/Dia**. The Web site also offers a tutorial to get you up and running.

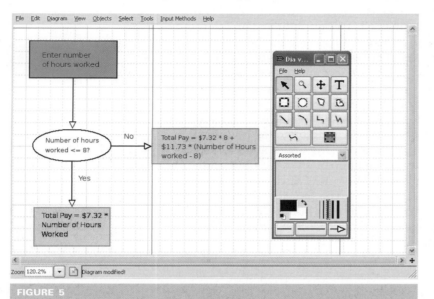

FIGURE 5

With Dia, you can create simple flowcharts, which a computer programmer might use in developing algorithms. Although not as powerful as Visio, Dia is available at no charge.

WEB PAGE AUTHORING SOFTWARE ALTERNATIVES: NVU

Although Microsoft Word and OpenOffice Writer can save documents as HTML files, sometimes you need a more versatile tool for creating Web pages, especially for larger sites with many linked pages. Adobe Dreamweaver is a popular commercial package for building Web sites, and Expression Web is a Web authoring application that is complementary to the Microsoft Office 2007 suite. But SeaMonkey Composer is a free, open source WYSIWYG ("what you see is what you get") Web authoring application that is compatible with the Windows, Mac, and Linux platforms. SeaMonkey Computer (see Figure 6) supports cascading style sheets, positioned layers, and dynamic image and table resizing. SeaMonkey Composer is part of the SeaMonkey Internet application suite (**www.seamonkey-project.org**).

IMAGE EDITING SOFTWARE ALTERNATIVES: GIMP

Need to create or edit some digital art but can't afford a high-end package such as Adobe Photoshop or even a consumer package such as Adobe Photoshop Elements? Download a free copy of GIMP (short for GNU Image Manipulation Program) at **www.gimp.org** and you'll find a set of tools almost as powerful as Photoshop. In addition, GIMP is available for systems running Windows, Mac, Linux, or UNIX. Many good tutorials are deployed

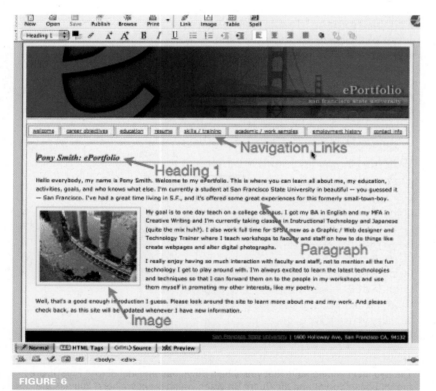

FIGURE 6

SeaMonkey Composer is an open source Web page authoring program that contains many features similar to those of leading commercial packages and is available at no cost.

at **www.gimp.org/tutorials** to get you up to speed in no time.

Here are some handy things you can do with GIMP in five minutes or less:

- Crop or change the size of an image (see Figure 7).

- Reduce the file size of an image by decreasing its quality.

- Flip an image or rotate an image 90 degrees.

GIMP also enables you to use more advanced skills such as applying image filters, creating textures and gradients, drawing digital art, creating animated images through layer manipulation, and changing photos into a painting or sketch.

Operating System Alternatives

Installing open source application software such as OpenOffice on a Windows machine is simple. A bit more complex is changing your OS from Windows to an open source OS such as Linux. Why would you want to switch to Linux if you already own Windows?

Before Windows XP, many people felt Windows was not stable. Citing lockups and forced reboots, many users searched for an

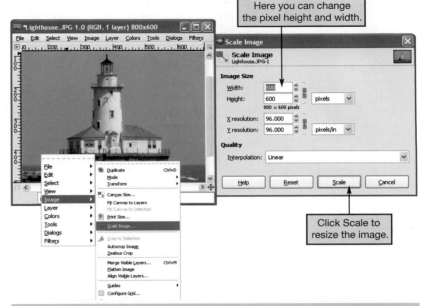

FIGURE 7

Using the Scale Image feature of GIMP, you can easily change an image (such as this image of a lighthouse) to the exact pixel size you need in order to fit the image on a Web site, for example.

OS that would not crash as often. With Windows XP (especially with Service Pack 2 installed), Microsoft has done a great deal to address stability issues. Now, with Windows Vista, the instability that comes with a new OS is back, although Service Pack 1 should help remedy some of the initial release issues.

Photo Management Software Alternatives: JAlbum

If you're like many people, you have gigabytes of digital photos on your hard drive. But how can you easily organize photos for display on a Web site so that you can share them with friends and family? An open source option is JAlbum (available at **http://jalbum.net**), a program that allows you to create Web albums of your digital images easily using simple drag-and-drop tools. JAlbum is available for the Windows, Mac, Linux, UNIX, and Solaris operating systems and supports 30 languages.

JAlbum provides significant advantages over some commercial photo management systems because it provides a high degree of control over the look and feel of the album you create. It also offers many templates if you don't have the time, energy, or artistic flair to create your own. You also can use JAlbum to create index and slideshow pages, and the software uploads your album to the Internet. Best of all, your friends and family don't need any software other than a current Web browser to view your album. You can also choose to burn your albums onto a CD for sharing.

Stability issues aside, Windows is still plagued by security issues. A lot of spyware, computer viruses, and other hacker nuisances are designed to take advantage of security flaws in Windows. Although Windows Vista has reportedly addressed many of the security issues in Windows XP, because Windows (Vista or XP) is the most widely used OS, it's still a prime target for viruses and other annoyances. From a virus creator's or hacker's perspective, nuisances that spread through Windows have the greatest chance of causing the most aggravation. An open source OS alternative such as Linux that is not as widely used as Windows might be less of a target for these annoyances.

Another reason to install an open source OS is portability. Depending on which version of Linux you use, you may be able to take it with you on a CD or flash drive and use it on almost any computer. This portability feature appeals to people who use a lot of different computers (such as lab computers at school). Instead of getting used to a new configuration every time you're away from your home computer, wouldn't it be nice to have the same environment you're used to everywhere you go? In the next section, we explore the different varieties of Linux and how to install them.

WHICH LINUX TO USE

Linux is available for download in various packages known as distributions, or distros. Think of distros as different makes and models of cars. Distros include the underlying Linux kernel (the code that provides Linux's basic functionality) and related programs. Distros also often contain special modifications or additional open source software (such as OpenOffice). So which distro is right for you?

A good place to start researching distros is **http://distrowatch.com**. This site tracks Linux distros and provides helpful tips for beginners in choosing one. Figure 8 lists some popular Linux distros and their home pages.

Before you can decide which distro is right for you, there are a few things to consider. The general overall requirements to run Linux are relatively modest:

- a 1.2-GHz processor,
- 384 MB of RAM (text mode) and 192 MB RAM (graphical mode),
- 8 GB of hard drive space, and
- VGA graphics card capable of 640×480 resolution.

Just like any other software program, however, Linux performs better with a faster processor and more memory. Also, depending on how much additional software is deployed in the distro you choose to use, your system requirements may be higher and you may need more hard drive space. Check the specific recommendations for the distro you're considering on the distro's Web site.

EXPERIMENTING WITH LINUX

Some Linux distros (such as Ubuntu and PCLinuxOS) are designed to be run from a CD or DVD. This alleviates having to install files on the computer's hard drive. Therefore, you can boot up from a DVD on an existing Windows PC and run Linux without disturbing the existing Windows installation. However, depending on the distro you use,

FIGURE 8

Distro	Home Page
Mandriva Linux, (formerly Mandrake Linux)	**www.mandrivalinux.com**
Fedora Core (Red Hat)	**http://fedoraproject.org**
Debian GNU/Linux	**www.debian.org**
Ubuntu	**www.ubuntu.com**
Gentoo Linux	**www.gentoo.org**
Slackware Linux	**www.slackware.com**
KNOPPIX	**www.knoppix.com**
PCLinuxOS	**www.pclinuxonline.com**

you may not have full access to the files on your Windows hard drive.

Booting your existing computer from a CD- or DVD-based version of Linux is a low-risk way to experiment with Linux and see how well you like it. Ubuntu, which you can download and burn onto a DVD from **www.ubuntu.com**, uses an extremely familiar-looking Windows-like desktop. When you download Ubuntu, you get the Firefox browser as well as GIMP, OpenOffice, and many other software packages, including utilities and games. The minimum system requirements to run Ubuntu are:

- an Intel-compatible CPU;
- at least 4 GB of disk space (if you are installing Ubuntu and not just running it off of a CD or DVD);
- 256 MB of RAM for the alternate install CD or 384 MB to use the live, CD-based installer;
- a bootable CD/DVD-ROM drive; and
- a standard graphics card.

Figure 9 shows Ubuntu in action. This computer is connected to the Internet via a high-speed connection as part of a home network. The computer booted from the Ubuntu CD when it detected the CD in the drive. As part of the installation sequence, Ubuntu automatically detects components of the computer (such as the network card) and configures Linux to recognize them. You'll have no trouble connecting to the Internet, and any files you create with OpenOffice can be saved to a flash drive.

3D LINUX

Mandriva Linux (**www.mandriva.com**) offers several versions of its OS. Mandriva Linux One 2008 is the company's most basic product and is free and remains true to the original open source principles. (Other versions are available.) PowerPack 2008 for individual users offers a more complete package that includes added multimedia and gaming software. Mandriva Flash is Mandriva's portable OS option, which is installed on a convenient 4 GB flash drive. This portable version does not make changes on the host computer, so you can bring your computer environment anywhere you go. Mandriva Flash takes

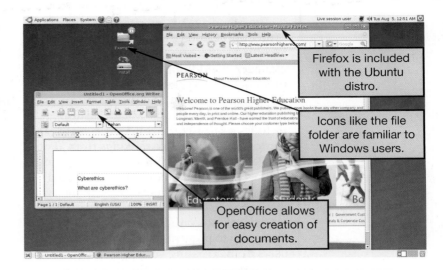

Firefox is included with the Ubuntu distro.

Icons like the file folder are familiar to Windows users.

OpenOffice allows for easy creation of documents.

FIGURE 9

Notice how the Ubuntu user interface resembles the Windows desktop.

FIGURE 10

The Mandriva operating system has an innovative 3D desktop environment.

up one-quarter of the flash drive, allowing the remaining 3 GB for you to conveniently store and take with you all your office work and Internet and multimedia files. All Mandriva versions run simultaneously with Windows, so you don't need to worry about partitioning your hard drive, as was the case with earlier versions. The 2007 versions of Mandriva introduced Metisse, an innovative 3D desktop environment (see Figure 10).

The Mandriva OS also includes other open source applications, such as OpenOffice, Mozilla Firefox browser, and KMail e-mail manager. In addition, there are several multimedia programs including those used to create photo albums and digital music.

In addition to all this, Mandriva also includes security features. The OS divides security levels into five rankings from "Poor" to "Paranoid." Your choice depends on how you're using the system (select "Paranoid" if you're running business transactions through your computer). You also can set up a simple-to-configure firewall called Shorewall to prevent unauthorized Internet users from accessing your personal network.

If you don't like Mandriva Linux or Ubuntu, head out to **www.distrowatch.com** and find another free Linux distro to install. With the hundreds of distros available, you're sure to find one that fits your needs.

Hardware Alternatives

Tired of your Windows-based PC? Old computer too slow for your current needs and not worth upgrading? If so, you may be in the market for some new hardware. Before you head off to the store to buy another Windows-based computer, why not consider two alternatives: (1) moving to an Apple platform or (2) building your own computer.

APPLE COMPUTERS

The best way to decide whether a Mac is right for you is to actually get your hands on one and take it for a test drive. Chances are that someone you know has a Mac. If not, then Apple has retail stores chock full of employees who are only too happy to let you test out the equipment. Be sure to check out the entry-level Macs, as shown in Figure 11.

Some people are switching to Macs because they love their iPods so much. Apple is leveraging the popularity of these digital devices by designing software for its computers to work seamlessly with the iPods. In addition, many Apple fans think Macs are more user-friendly and stylish than their PC competitors. Others change to Macs because many applications (especially for digital artists and graphic designers) deliver superior features on the Apple platform.

Mac OS X Leopard

Most Mac users, however, have switched from Windows because of the OS, Mac OS X. It's latest version, Leopard, has many slick and innovative features that are tempting to even the most loyal Windows users. If you've been using Windows for awhile, you shouldn't have any problem making the transition to Leopard. You'll notice immediately that the Mac OS uses the same desktop

FIGURE 11

(a) Apple's newest notebook—MacBook Air—is the thinnest notebook on the market but still has a 13-inch screen and a full-sized keyboard. (b) The MacBook weighs slightly more than 5 pounds and features the Intel Core 2 Duo processor and a 13-inch screen. (c) The iMac line features sleek, space-saving desktop units sporting fast Intel Core 2 Duo processors.

metaphors as Windows, including icons for folders and a Trash can (instead of a Recycle Bin) to delete documents. Screen real estate is managed using familiar-looking windows you're already accustomed to using on Windows.

Like earlier versions of Mac OS, Leopard is based on the UNIX OS, which is exceptionally stable and reliable. Aside from being stable, security and safety are great reasons to switch to the Mac OS because it does not seem to suffer from the exploitation of security flaws as much as Windows does. This doesn't necessarily mean that the Mac OS is better constructed than Windows; it could just be that because Windows has a lead-in market share, it is a more attractive target for hackers. Regardless of the reason, you're probably somewhat less likely to be inconvenienced by viruses, hacking, and spyware if you're running Mac OS. Of course, you won't have any better protection from spam, phishing, or other Internet scams, so you still need to stay alert. Leopard offers a 3D desktop environment as well as a new automated backup utility called Time Machine (see Figure 12).

When you start a Mac, a program called the Finder automatically starts. This program is like Windows Explorer and controls the desktop and the Finder windows with which you interact. It's always running when the Mac is on. Using the new Quick Look feature, it's now possible to view the contents of a file without ever opening it. This allows you to flip through multipage documents, watch videos, and view an entire presentation with just a single click of the mouse. Spaces is another new feature that helps to keep order when projects pile up. With Spaces you can group your application windows.

Leopard has kept other features from previous versions such as Spotlight, a desktop search feature that allows you to find anything on your computer from one spot. The Dashboard and widgets enable you to have easy access to many mini-applications that allow you to perform common tasks and get quick access to real-time information such as the weather, stock prices, or sports updates.

At the top of the desktop is the menu bar. The options on the menu bar change according to which program is "active" at the moment (that is, foremost on your screen). When you click the Apple icon in the upper left corner, a drop-down menu is displayed,

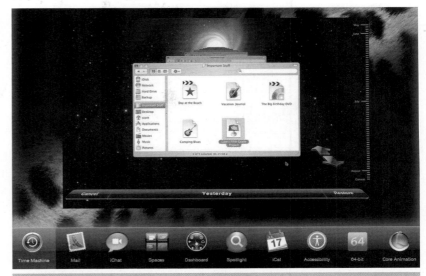

FIGURE 12

Time Machine, an automated backup and restore utility, is one of the new features in Mac OS X Leopard.

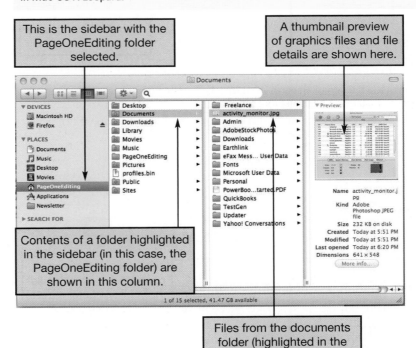

This is the sidebar with the PageOneEditing folder selected.

A thumbnail preview of graphics files and file details are shown here.

Contents of a folder highlighted in the sidebar (in this case, the PageOneEditing folder) are shown in this column.

Files from the documents folder (highlighted in the column to left) appear here.

FIGURE 13

The Sidebar holds any folders you specify (such as the PageOneEditing folder shown here). You can choose to view the contents of files and folders in three different views: icon view, list view, and column view.

>To access the Sidebar, double-click the hard drive icon on the desktop.

from which you can select several options. The Dock is similar to the Taskbar in Windows and includes a strip of icons that displays across the bottom of the desktop.

Each Finder window has an area on the left known as the Sidebar (see Figure 13).

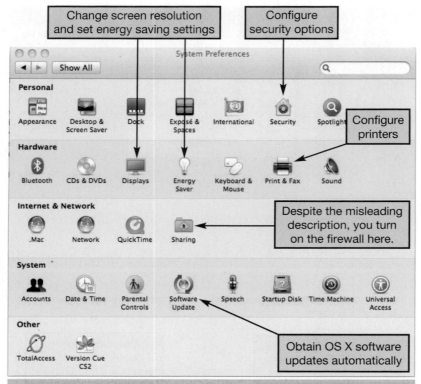

Change screen resolution and set energy saving settings

Configure security options

Configure printers

Despite the misleading description, you turn on the firewall here.

Obtain OS X software updates automatically

FIGURE 14

Much like the Control Panel in Windows, the System Preferences window allows you to customize and configure Leopard.

>To get to System Preferences, click the **Apple** menu icon in the top left corner of the screen and choose **System Preferences**.

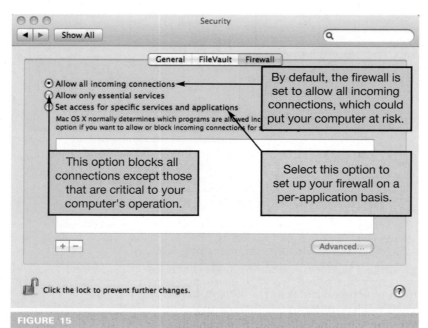

By default, the firewall is set to allow all incoming connections, which could put your computer at risk.

This option blocks all connections except those that are critical to your computer's operation.

Select this option to set up your firewall on a per-application basis.

FIGURE 15

Macs have a firewall, but be sure to configure the firewall before going out onto the Internet.

The Sidebar holds any folders you specify (even though the icons don't look like folders) to make navigation easier and faster. Navigating around a Finder window and copying or moving files work almost exactly the same way as in Windows.

Configuring a Mac

In Windows, you make changes to settings and preferences through the Control Panel. In Mac OS X Leopard, you use System Preferences, which is an option on the Apple menu. Selecting System Preferences from the Apple menu displays the window shown in Figure 14.

Protecting Your Mac

Although Macs tend to be attacked less frequently by viruses and other hacker nuisances, you can still be vulnerable if you don't take precautions. Leopard comes with a firewall. To configure it, click on the Security icon under the Personal section of the System Preferences window. When the Security window opens, click on the Firewall button to display the Firewall configuration screen shown in Figure 15. Be sure to set up the firewall before going out onto the Internet for the first time, because the firewall is set up by default to allow all incoming connections.

In addition, hackers may be creating viruses and other nuisances to exploit security holes in the Mac OS. Mac users should therefore keep their software up to date with the latest fixes and software patches by setting their system to check automatically for software updates on a periodic basis. On Macs, this feature is available through the System Preferences window by clicking the Software Update icon, which is under the System section. Figure 16 shows the options you choose to make sure the Mac OS is kept up to date.

Utility Programs

Just like Windows Vista, Leopard contains a wide variety of utility programs to help users maintain and evaluate their Macs. In Macs, utility programs are located in a folder named Utilities within the Applications folder on the hard drive.

If you're a Windows user, you know that the Windows Task Manager utility can help

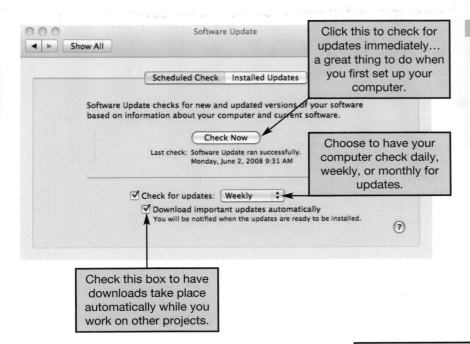

Click this to check for updates immediately... a great thing to do when you first set up your computer.

Choose to have your computer check daily, weekly, or monthly for updates.

Check this box to have downloads take place automatically while you work on other projects.

FIGURE 16

Keeping the Mac OS up to date with the latest software fixes and patches greatly decreases your chances of being the target of hackers.

>From the **Apple** menu, choose **System Preferences** and then click **Software Update**. In addition to these precautions, antivirus software such as Norton is available for Leopard.

you determine how your system is performing. In Macs, this utility is called the Activity Monitor, shown in Figure 17. It shows what programs (processes) are currently running and how much memory they're using. The CPU, System Memory, Disk Activity, Disk Usage, and Network buttons indicate the activity in each of these crucial areas.

Like the Systems Properties box in Windows, the Mac OS System Profiler shown in Figure 18 displays all the hardware (and software) installed in a Mac, including the type of processor, the amount of RAM installed, and the amount of VRAM on the video card.

As you can see, operating a Mac is fairly simple and is similar to the Windows environment. There are many books that will help you make a smooth transition to an Apple computer.

DO IT YOURSELF!

The do-it-yourself craze has swept across America, so why not stop repainting the house and apply those do-it-yourself skills to building a computer? Of course, building a computer isn't for everyone, but for those who enjoy working with their hands and don't mind doing some up-front research, it can be a rewarding experience.

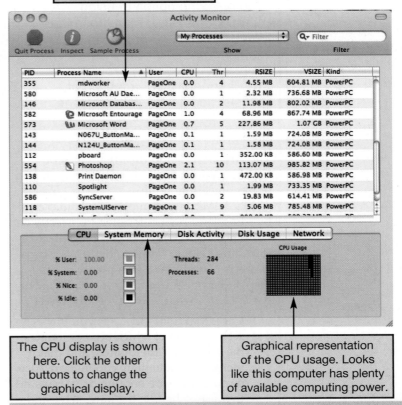

All running processes are shown here as well as the memory they are using.

The CPU display is shown here. Click the other buttons to change the graphical display.

Graphical representation of the CPU usage. Looks like this computer has plenty of available computing power.

FIGURE 17

Similar to the Task Manager in Windows, the Activity Monitor analyzes the performance of a Mac.

>Go to the **Utilities** folder found in the **Applications** folder on your hard drive and double-click **Activity Monitor** to open the utility.

FIGURE 18

The System Profiler is similar to the Systems Properties dialog box in Windows and reveals a wealth of information about the hardware and software in your computer.

>To launch System Profiler, from the **Apple** menu, click **About this Mac**, and then click the **More Info** button.

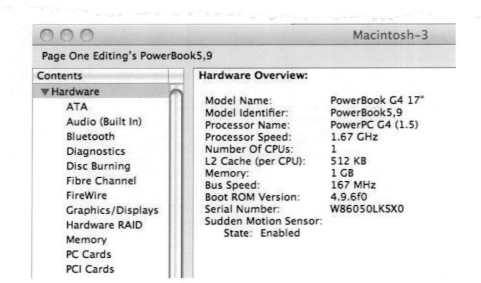

Advantages	Disadvantages
You get exactly the configuration and features you want.	There is no technical support when things go wrong.
You have the option of using components other than those that are used in mass-produced computers.	You'll need to examine technical higher-quality specifications (such as which CPU works with the motherboard you want), which may overwhelm the average computer user.
You'll hopefully get a feeling of satisfaction from a job well done.	You won't necessarily save money.

The advantages and disadvantages of building your own computer are as shown in the preceding table.

Many Web sites can provide guidance for building your own computer. PC Mechanic (**www.pcmech.com/byopc**) is a good place to start. Just Google "How to build your own computer" and you'll find plenty of online help and advice. To start, you need a list of parts. Here's what you'll typically need:

1. **Case:** Make sure the case you buy is an ATX-style case, which accommodates the newest motherboards, and that it includes an adequate cooling fan. Also be sure there are enough drive bays in the case to handle the hard drive and any other peripheral drives (CD, DVD, and so on) you'll be installing.

2. **Power Supply:** A power supply provides power to the computer. Many cases come with a power supply installed. Make sure to get a power supply with adequate wattage to handle the load generated by all the of computer's components.

3. **Processor (CPU):** Get the fastest one you can afford, because it will help to greatly extend the life of your computer. To cool the processor, many come with a fan installed; if not, you'll need to purchase a processor cooling fan.

4. **Motherboard:** Many motherboards come with sound, video, and network cards. These work fine for basic computing, but if you're building a PC for gaming, opt for a motherboard into which you can plug higher-end graphics and sound cards. Also make sure the motherboard you buy can accommodate the CPU you have chosen. And make sure the motherboard has expansion slots (PCI slots and a separate AGP) for a high-end graphics card.

5. **USB Ports:** Make sure that your motherboard has at least two to four USB ports and install a separate bay with USB and FireWire ports for flash drives and other devices. Other devices, such as your monitor and keyboard, may also have USB ports incorporated for additional flexibility.

6. **RAM:** Check your motherboard specifications before buying RAM to ensure you buy the correct type and an amount that will fit into the available slots.

7. **Video Card:** Low-end cards with 128 or 256 MB of video memory are fine for normal computer use, but for gaming or displaying high-end graphics or videos, get a card with 512 MB or more, depending on your budget. If you will be using a digital LCD monitor or hooking your gaming system to your computer, then you should make sure that the video card has a DVI connection or an HDMI port.

8. **Sound Card:** Make sure to get a PCI card that is compatible with Sound Blaster (the standard for sound cards).

9. **Optical Drives (CD, DVD, and Blu-ray):** A CD or DVD drive is a must for software installation. You can install individual drives or a combination drive that has CD and DVD capabilities. For portable storage, make sure the CD/DVD drive has the capability to write CDs and DVDs. You may want to install a Blu-ray drive to view your favorite movies using high-definition technology. Blu-ray discs offer five times the storage capacity of a DVD, holding as much as 50 GB of data. Currently, Blu-ray burners are expensive, but they are available if you have the need.

10. **Hard Drive:** The price per gigabyte has been rapidly coming down in recent years, so get a large-volume drive. For optimal performance, choose a hard drive with the fastest RPM you can afford.

11. **Modem:** You need a modem only if you're connecting to the Internet via a dial-up connection or if you want to use your computer to fax documents.

12. **Network Interface Card:** Network cards are sometimes integrated in the motherboard, so check before you buy one.

In addition to these components, you'll need a keyboard, mouse or other pointing device, monitor, and OS software.

You can buy these components at national stores such as Best Buy or Circuit City or at reputable Web sites such as **www.tigerdirect.com or www.newegg.com**. Once you have the components, it is almost as simple as bolting them into the case and connecting them properly. Make sure you read all the installation instructions that come with your components before beginning installation. Don't forget to check YouTube or the Web sites of component manufacturers for handy how-to videos and step-by-step installation guides. Then read through a complete installation tutorial such as the one found at The Tech Report Web site (**http://techreport.com/articles.x/13671**), which provides an excellent visual guide to assembling a computer. Then grab your screwdriver and get started—you'll be up and running in no time.

So, as you can see, there are many options beyond a Windows-based computer running commercial software applications. We hope you spread your wings and try a few of them.

Understanding and Assessing Hardware:

Evaluating Your System

ACTIVE HELPDESK

Does Your Computer Fit You?

After saving up for a computer, Natalie took the leap a few years ago and bought a new desktop PC. Now she is wondering what to do. Her friends with newer computers are burning CDs and Blu-ray discs, and they're able to hook up their digital cameras directly to their computers and create multimedia. They seem to be able to do a hundred things at once without their computers slowing down at all.

Natalie's computer can't do any of these things—or at least she doesn't think it can. And lately it seems to take longer to open files and scroll through Web pages. Making matters worse, her computer freezes often and takes a long time to reboot. Now she's wondering whether she should buy a new computer, but the thought of spending all that money again makes her think twice. As she looks at ads for new computers, she realizes she doesn't know what such things as "CPU" and "RAM" really are, or how they affect her system. Meanwhile, she's heard it's possible to upgrade her computer, but the task seems daunting. How will she know what she needs to do to upgrade, or whether it's even worth it?

How well is your computer meeting your needs? Are you unsure whether it's best to buy a new computer or upgrade your existing system? If you don't have a computer, do you fear purchasing one because computers are changing all the time? Do you know what all the terms in computer ads mean and how the different parts affect your computer's performance?

In this chapter, you'll learn how to evaluate your computer system to determine whether it is meeting your needs. You'll start by figuring out what you want your ideal computer to be able to do. You'll then learn about important components of your computer system—its CPU, memory, storage devices, audio and video devices, and ports—and how these components affect your system. Along the way, worksheets will help you conduct a system evaluation, and multimedia Sound Bytes will show you how to install various components in your system and how to increase its reliability. You'll also learn about the various utilities available to help speed up and clean up your system. If you don't have a computer, this chapter will provide you with important information you need about computer hardware to make an informed purchasing decision.

SOUND BYTES

- Using Windows Vista to Evaluate CPU Performance **(p. 281)**
- Memory Hierarchy Interactive **(p. 282)**
- Installing RAM **(p. 285)**
- CD and DVD Reading and Writing Interactive **(p. 291)**
- Installing a DVD-RW Drive **(p. 292)**

Is It the Computer or Me?

Do you ever wonder whether your computer is fine and you just need more knowledge to get it to work smoothly? Is that true, or do you really need a more sophisticated computer system? And is now a good time to buy a new one? There never seems to be a good time to buy a new computer. It seems that if you can just wait a year, computers will inevitably be faster and cost less. But is this actually true?

As it turns out, it is true. In fact, a rule of thumb often cited in the computer industry, called **Moore's Law**, describes the pace at which CPUs (the central processing units)—the small chips that can be thought of as the "brains" of the computer—improve. Named for Gordon Moore, the cofounder of the CPU chip manufacturer Intel, this rule predicts that the number of transistors inside a CPU will increase so fast that CPU capacity will double every 18 months. (The number of transistors on a CPU chip helps determine how fast it can process data.)

As you can see in Figure 6.1, this rule of thumb has held true since 1965, when Moore first published his theory. Imagine, what if you could find a bank that would agree to treat your money this way? If you put 10 cents in that kind of savings account in 1965, you would have a balance of more than $3.3 million today! Moore, himself, however, has predicted that around the year 2020 CPU chips will be manufactured in a different way, thus changing or eliminating the effects of Moore's Law altogether.

In addition to the CPU becoming faster, other system components also continue to improve dramatically. For example, the capacity of memory chips such as dynamic random access memory (DRAM)—the most common form of memory found on personal computers—increases about 60 percent every year. Meanwhile, hard drives have been growing in storage capacity by some 50 percent each year.

So, with technology advancing so quickly, how do I make sure I have a computer that matches my needs? No one wants to buy a new computer every year just to keep up

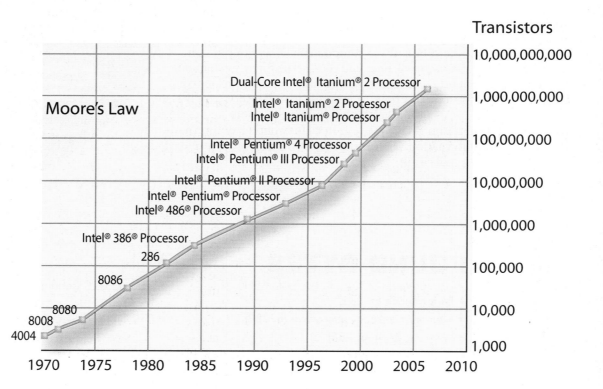

FIGURE 6.1

Moore's Law predicts that CPUs will continue to get faster. The number of transistors on a CPU chip helps determine how fast it can process data. With the Intel Dual-Core Itanium 2 chip, more than a billion transistors can be fabricated into one chip. *Source:* Adapted from the Moore's Law animated demo at **www.intel.com**.

with technology. Even if money weren't a consideration, the time it would take to transfer all of your files and reinstall and reconfigure your software would make buying a new computer every year terribly inefficient. Extending the life of a computer also reduces or postpones the environmental and security concerns involved in the disposal of computers.

Of course, no one wants to keep doing costly upgrades that won't significantly extend the life of a system either. So how can you determine if your system is suitable or needs upgrading? And how can you know which is the better option: upgrading or buying a new computer? In this chapter, you'll determine how to answer these questions by learning useful information about computer systems. The first step is figuring out what you want your computer to do for you.

What Is Your Ideal Computer?

As you decide whether your computer suits you, it's important to know exactly what you want your ideal computer system to be able to do. Later, as you perform a system evaluation, you can compare your existing system to your ideal system. This will help you determine whether you should purchase hardware components to add to your system or buy a new system.

But what if I don't have a computer? Even if you're a new computer user and are looking to buy your first system, you will still need to evaluate what you want your system to do for you before you purchase a computer. Being able to understand and evaluate computer systems will make you a more informed buyer. You should be comfortable answering questions such as: What is a CPU, and how does it affect your system? How much RAM do you need, and what role does it play in your system? It's important for you to be able to answer such questions before you buy a computer.

How do I know what my ideal system is? To determine your ideal system, consider what you want to be able to do with your computer. For example, do you need to bring your computer with you? Do you want to be able to edit digital photos? Do you want to watch and record Blu-ray discs? Or are you just using your computer for word processing? The worksheet in Figure 6.2 lists a number of ways in which you may want to use your computer. In the second column, place a check next to those computer uses that apply to you. Also, set a priority of high, medium, or low in the rightmost column so that you can determine which features are most important to you.

Next, look at the list of desired uses for your computer and determine whether your current system can perform these activities. If there are things you can't do, then you may need to purchase additional hardware or a better computer. For example, if you want to play CDs and DVDs, all you need is a DVD-R drive. However, you need a CD-RW or DVD-RW drive if you want to burn (record) CDs or DVDs. Likewise, if you plan to edit digital video files or play games that include a lot of sounds and graphics with large files, you may want to add more memory, buy a better set of speakers, get a DVD or Blu-ray burner, add a high-speed hard drive, and possibly invest in a new monitor. Depending on the costs of the individual upgrade components, you may be better off buying a new system.

Note that you also may need new software and training to use new system components. Many computer users forget to consider the training they'll need when they upgrade their computer. Missing any one of these pieces might be the difference between your computer enriching your life or becoming another source of stress.

How do I know if I need training? Although computers are becoming increasingly user-friendly, you still need to learn how to use them to your best advantage. Say you want to edit digital photos. You know image editing software exists, but how do you know if your computer's hardware can support the software? What will happen if you can't get it installed or don't know how to use it? If you have questions like these, you know you need training. Training shouldn't be an afterthought. Consider the time and effort involved in learning about what you want your computer to do before you buy hardware or software. If you don't, you may have a wonderful computer system but lack the skills necessary to take full advantage of it.

FIGURE 6.2 What Should Your Ideal Computer System Be Able to Do?

Computer Uses	Do You Want Your System to Do This?	Can Your System Do This Now?	Priority (High, Medium, Low)
Portability Uses			
Take your computer with you			
Access the Internet wirelessly			
Entertainment Uses			
Access the Internet, send e-mail			
Play and record CDs and DVDs			
Play and record Blu-ray discs			
Produce digital videos			
Record and edit digital music			
Edit digital photos			
Play graphics-intensive games			
Transfer digital photos (or other files) to your computer using flash memory cards			
Connect all your peripheral devices to your computer at the same time			
Purchase music or videos from the Internet			
Other			
Educational Uses			
Perform word-processing tasks			
Use other educational software			
Create backups of all your files			
Access library and newspaper archives			
Create multimedia presentations			
Other			
Business Uses			
Create spreadsheets or databases			
Work on multiple software applications quickly and simultaneously			
Conduct online banking, pay bills online, or self-prepare taxes			
Conduct online job searches or post résumés			
"Synchronize" your mobile device (PDA, PSP, or iPod) with your computer			
Other			

Evaluating a Desktop or Notebook System

The first decision in evaluating your system is whether you want a desktop or a notebook. To make the best decision, it's important to evaluate how and where you will use the computer. The main distinction between desktops and notebooks is portability. If you indicated in the chart in Figure 6.2 that you need to take your computer with you to work or school, or even want the flexibility to move from room to room in your house, then a notebook is the best choice. If portability is not an absolute factor, then you should consider a desktop. Review Figure 6.3 to better understand the advantages and disadvantages of desktops and notebooks to help you determine which type of system may best suit your needs. More discussion of notebooks can be found in Chapter 8.

Assessing Your Hardware: Evaluating Your System

With a better picture of your ideal computer system in mind, you can make a more informed assessment of your current computer. To determine whether your computer system has the right hardware components to do what you ultimately want it to do, you need to conduct a **system evaluation**. To do so, you look at your computer's subsystems, what they do, and how they perform. These subsystems include the following:

- CPU subsystem,
- memory subsystem (the computer's random access memory, or RAM),
- storage subsystem (hard drive and other drives),
- video subsystem (video card and monitor),
- audio subsystem (sound card and speakers), and
- computer ports.

In the rest of this chapter, we examine each subsystem. At the end of each section, you'll find a small worksheet you can use to evaluate each subsystem on your computer. *Note:* This chapter discusses tools you can use to assess a Windows-based PC. For information on how to assess a Mac, refer to the Technology in Focus feature "Computing Alternatives" on page 258.

Evaluating the CPU Subsystem

As you begin to determine whether your computer system adequately meets your needs, you'll want to consider early on the type of processor in your system. As mentioned earlier, your computer's **central processing unit** (**CPU** or **processor**) is critically important because it processes instructions, performs calculations, manages the flow of information through a computer system, and is responsible for processing the data you input into information. As shown in Figure 6.4, the CPU is located on the **motherboard**, the primary circuit board of the computer system. There are several types of processors on the market: Intel processors (such as the Pentium family, the Core Duo family, the Centrino line, and the Itanium family) and AMD processors (such as the Athlon and Phenom, both of which are used on PCs).

FIGURE 6.3 Considerations When Purchasing Desktop and Notebook Computers

Notebooks	Desktops
Portable	Best value: more speed, memory, and storage capacity for lower price
Take up less physical space	More difficult to steal, less susceptible to damage from dropping or mishandling
Easier to ship or transport if the system needs repair	Easier to expand and upgrade

How does the CPU work? The CPU is composed of two units: the **control unit** and the **arithmetic logic unit (ALU)**. The control unit coordinates the activities of all the other computer components. The ALU is responsible for performing all the arithmetic calculations (addition, subtraction, multiplication, and division). The ALU also makes logic and comparison decisions such as comparing items to determine if one is greater than, less than, equal to, or not equal to another.

Every time the CPU performs a program instruction, it goes through the same series of steps. First, it fetches the required piece of data or instruction from RAM, the temporary storage location for all the data and instructions the computer needs while it is running. Next, it decodes the instruction into something the computer can understand. Once the CPU has decoded the instruction, it executes the instruction and stores the result to RAM before fetching the next instruction. This process is called a **machine cycle**. (We will discuss the machine cycle in more detail in Chapter 9.)

How is CPU speed measured? The computer goes through these machine cycles at a steady and constant pace. Known as **clock speed**, this pace is controlled by the system clock, which works like a metronome in music. The system clock keeps a steady beat, regulating the speed at which the processor goes through machine cycles. Processors work incredibly fast, going through millions or billions of machine cycles each second. Processor speed is measured in units of hertz (Hz). Hertz means "machine cycles per second." Older machines ran at speeds measured in **megahertz (MHz)**, or 1 million hertz, whereas current systems run at speeds measured in **gigahertz (GHz)**, or 1 billion hertz. So a 3.8 GHz processor performs work at a rate of 3.8 billion machine cycles per second. It's important to realize, however, that CPU clock speed alone doesn't determine the performance of the CPU.

What else affects CPU performance? In addition to pure processing speed, CPU performance also is affected by the speed of the **front side bus (FSB)** and the amount of **cache memory**. The FSB connects the processor (CPU) in your computer to the system memory. Think of the front

side bus as the highway on which data travels between the CPU and RAM. With a wider highway, traffic can move faster because more cars can travel at the same time. Consequently, the faster the FSB is, the faster you can get data to your processor. The faster you get data to the processor, the faster your processor can work on it. FSB speed is measured in megahertz (MHz).

Cache memory is another important consideration that determines CPU performance. Cache memory is a form of random access memory but is more accessible to the CPU than regular RAM. Because of its ready access to the CPU, cache memory is even faster than RAM to get data to the CPU for processing. There are several levels of cache memory; these levels are defined by a chip's proximity to the CPU. Level 1 cache is a block of memory that is built onto the CPU chip for the storage of data or commands that have just been used. Level 2 cache is located on the CPU chip but is slightly farther away from the CPU, or it's on a separate chip next to the CPU and therefore takes somewhat longer to access. Level 2 cache contains more storage area than does level 1 cache. Today's processors are defined by the combination of processor speed, front side bus speed, and the amount of cache memory. For example, Intel's Core 2 Duo processors come in a range of speeds, cache memory, and front side bus. The E8500 Core 2 Duo processor has 3.16 GHz processor speed, 6 MB L2 cache, and 1333 MHz front side bus, whereas the E6700 Core 2 Duo processor has 2.66 GHz processor speed, 4 MB L2 cache, and 1066 MHz front side bus. We will discuss more of these factors that contribute to CPU performance in Chapter 9.

What else might affect processor performance? In addition to the front side bus and cache memory that play a part in CPU performance, CPU designers make many other choices that impact how the CPU will fit into the bigger picture of overall system performance. For example, some CPUs are optimized to process multimedia instructions and can handle audio and video processing commands much more quickly than other processors. Another design approach is to try to build a processor that can work on two separate sets of instructions at the same time, in parallel.

Both Intel and AMD have a variety of CPUs with two cores that use less power than having two CPUs running at once, and

FIGURE 6.4

The CPU is a small chip that sits on the motherboard inside your system unit.

they deliver a substantial increase in performance. Figure 6.5 shows how commands coming from two different applications are processed at the same time with a Core Duo processor. Now applications such as virus protection software and your operating system, which are always running behind the scenes, can have their own processor, freeing up the other processor to run other applications such as a Web browser, Word, or iTunes more efficiently. Some higher-end processors such as the Intel Core 2 Quad and Core 2 Extreme processors have four cores for even more efficient processing power.

How fast should my CPU be? First, you need to know how fast your computer is. You can easily identify the speed of your current system's CPU by accessing the system properties. As shown in Figure 6.6, you can view basic information about your computer, including which CPU is installed in your system as well as its speed.

At a minimum, your CPU should meet the requirements of your system's software and hardware. If your system is older and you are buying new software and peripheral devices, then your CPU may not be able to handle the load.

For example, say your computer is three years old. For the past three years, you've been using it primarily for word processing and to surf the Internet. You recently purchased a digital camera. Now you want to edit your digital photos, but your system doesn't seem to be able to handle this. You check the system requirements on the photo editing software you just installed

Single path vs. the dual path processors for data

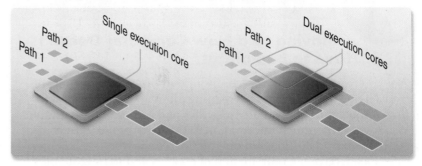

Single core processor   Dual core processor

and realize that the software runs best with a more powerful processor. In this case, if everything else in your system is running properly, a faster CPU would help improve the software's performance. Pentium D processors or Pentium Core 2 Duo processors running at 2 GHz or higher are good for the average user, and Pentium Extreme Edition or Core 2 Quad processors running at any speed are good processors for the higher-end user.

How can I tell whether my CPU is meeting my needs? Several factors determine whether your CPU is meeting your needs, as shown in Figure 6.7. Although speed determines how fast your CPU is capable of performing operations, you need to determine whether that speed is capable of handling the tasks you need to perform. Even though your CPU meets the minimum requirements specified for a particular software application, if you're

FIGURE 6.5

Two is faster than one! With the dual-core processors, Intel CPUs can work in parallel, processing two separate programs at the same time instead of switching back and forth between them.

FIGURE 6.6

The System Properties window identifies which CPU you have, as well as its speed. The computer in this example contains an Intel Core 2 running at 2.0 GHz.

>Click the **Start** button and then click **Computer** from the right panel of the **Start** menu. On the top toolbar, click **System Properties**.

BITS AND BYTES

Moving to a New Computer Doesn't Have to Be Painful

Are you ready to buy a new computer but dread the prospect of transferring all your files and redoing all of your Windows settings? You could transfer all those files and settings manually, but Windows stores much information in the registry files, which can be tricky to update. So what do you do? Windows Vista incorporates Easy Transfer Companion that enables you to migrate files and settings from a Windows XP system to a Windows Vista system via a network connection by using a flash drive or external hard drive or using optical media such as a CD or DVD.

Alternatively, other PC migration software is also available such as Acronis Migrate Easy 7.0 and Easy PC Transfer, both of which are designed to make transitioning to a new computer easier. For the latest information on such utilities, search on migration software at **www.pcmag.com**. You'll be ready to upgrade painlessly in no time. Or, if you prefer to avoid the do-it-yourself option, support technicians at retail stores such as Best Buy's Geek Squad will often perform the migration for a nominal charge.

A utility that can provide this kind of information is incredibly useful when considering whether you should upgrade and if your performance suddenly seems to drop off for no apparent reason. In Windows (XP or Vista), a program called Task Manager gives you easy access to all this data. Mac OS X has a utility similar to Task Manager called Activity Monitor, which is located in the Utilities folder in your Applications folder.

To view information on your CPU usage, right-click an empty area of the taskbar, select Task Manager, and click the Performance tab as shown in Figure 6.8. The CPU Usage graph records your CPU usage for the past several seconds. Of course, there will be periodic peaks of high CPU usage, but if you see that your CPU usage levels are greater than 90 percent during most of your work session, a faster CPU will contribute a great deal to your system performance. To see exactly how to use the Task Manager step by step, watch the Sound Byte "Using Windows Vista to Evaluate CPU Performance."

ANALYZING YOUR CPU

Is it expensive or difficult to upgrade a CPU? Replacement CPUs are expensive. In addition, although it is reasonably easy to install a CPU, it can be difficult to determine which one to install. Not all CPUs are interchangeable, and the replacement CPU must be compatible with the motherboard. Some people opt to upgrade the entire motherboard, but motherboards are a lot more difficult to install. As we discuss at the end of this chapter, if you plan to upgrade your computer in other ways in addition to upgrading the CPU, then you may want to consider buying a new computer.

Are the fastest CPUs the best to use? If you decide to upgrade your CPU, then consider buying one that is not the most recently released with the fastest speed but a slightly slower one of the same type. For example, if the Intel Pentium Core 2 dual-core family has just released a 3.16 GHz CPU, then you would pay a premium to buy this newest processor. The release of this newest CPU, however, will drive down the prices on earlier Pentium Core 2 dual-core chips running at speeds of 3 GHz and 2.66 GHz. Buying a slightly slower CPU and investing the savings in other system components (such as additional RAM) will often

FIGURE 6.7 Do You Need to Upgrade Your CPU?

	Current System	Upgrade Required?
CPU speed (in MHz or GHz)		
Cache memory (in MB)		
FSB speed (in MHz)		
CPU processing style: Quad core? dual core? hyperthreaded?		
CPU Usage at appropriate level?		

running other software (in addition to the operating system, which is always running), you'll need to check to see how well the CPU is handling the entire load. You can tell whether your CPU speed is limiting your system performance if you periodically watch how busy it is as you work on your computer. Keep in mind that the workload your CPU experiences will vary considerably depending on what you're doing. So, even though it might run Word just fine, it may not be able to handle running Word, a Web browser, iTunes, and IM at the same time. The percentage of time that your CPU is working is referred to as **CPU usage**.

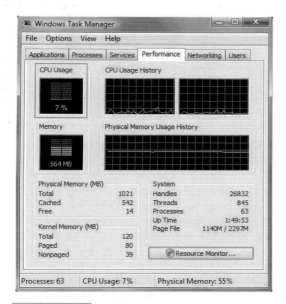

FIGURE 6.8

The Performance tab of the Windows Task Manager utility shows you how busy your CPU actually is when you're using your computer. In this case, current CPU usage level is at 7 percent. If CPU usage levels are above 90 percent for long periods of time, you may want to consider getting a faster, more powerful processor.

>In an empty area of the taskbar, right-click, select **Task Manager**, and click the **Performance** tab.

result in a better-performing system. The same is true if you're buying a new computer: Often you can save money without losing a great deal of performance by buying a computer with a CPU slightly slower than the fastest one on the market.

Will improving the speed of the CPU be enough to improve my computer's performance? You may think that if you have the fastest processor, you will have a system with the best performance. However, upgrading your CPU will affect only the processing portion of the system performance, not how quickly data can

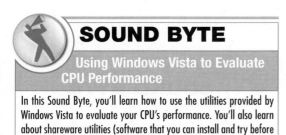

SOUND BYTE

Using Windows Vista to Evaluate CPU Performance

In this Sound Byte, you'll learn how to use the utilities provided by Windows Vista to evaluate your CPU's performance. You'll also learn about shareware utilities (software that you can install and try before you purchase it) that expand on the capabilities the Task Manager utility provides.

move to or from the CPU. Your system's overall performance depends on many other factors, including the amount of RAM installed as well as hard drive speed. Therefore, your selection of a CPU may not offer significant improvements to your system's performance if there is a bottleneck in processing because of insufficient RAM or hard drive capacity.

Are there different choices of CPUs for a notebook and desktop? Both Intel and AMD make processors that are specific to a notebook computer. Notebook processors not only need to perform quickly and efficiently, like their desktop counterparts, but also need better power savings to improve battery life. Intel's Pentium M, Celeron, or Core mobile processors and AMD's Turion 64 Mobile, Mobile AMD Sempron, and AMD Athelon 64 processors are used in notebooks. Desktop processors include Intel's Core 2 Extreme, Quad, and Duo processors; some Pentium D, Celeron D, and dual-core processors; and AMD's Athlon, Phenom, Sempron, and ATI Radeon processors.

Evaluating RAM: The Memory Subsystem

Random access memory (RAM) is your computer's temporary storage space. Although we refer to RAM as a form of storage, it really is the computer's short-term memory. As such, it remembers everything that the computer needs to process the data into information, such as data that has been entered and software instructions, but only when the computer is on. This means that RAM is an example of **volatile storage**. When the power is off, the data stored in RAM is cleared out. This is why, in addition to RAM, systems always include **nonvolatile storage** devices for permanent storage of instructions and data when the computer is powered off. Hard drives provide the greatest nonvolatile storage capacity in the computer system.

Why not use a hard drive to store the data and instructions? It's about one million times faster for the CPU to retrieve a piece of data from RAM than from a hard drive. The time it takes the CPU to retrieve data from RAM is measured in nanoseconds (billionths of seconds), whereas retrieving data from a fast hard

ACTIVE HELPDESK

Evaluating Your CPU and RAM

In this Active Helpdesk call, you'll play the role of a helpdesk staffer, fielding calls about what the CPU does and how to evaluate its performance. You'll also field calls about how memory works and how to evaluate how much memory a computer needs.

drive takes an average of 10 milliseconds (ms), or thousandths of seconds. This difference is influential in designing a balanced computer system and can have a tremendous impact on system performance. Therefore, it's critical that your computer has more than enough RAM.

Where is RAM located? You can find RAM inside the system unit of your computer on the motherboard. **Memory modules** (or **memory cards**), the small circuit boards that hold a series of RAM chips, fit into special slots on the motherboard (see Figure 6.9). Most memory modules in today's systems are called *dual inline memory modules (DIMMs)*.

FIGURE 6.9

Memory modules hold a series of RAM chips and fit into special slots on the motherboard.

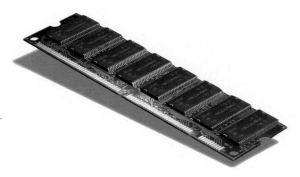

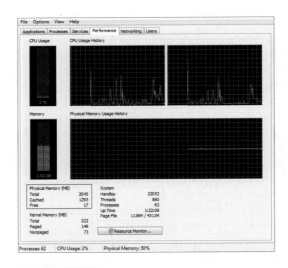

FIGURE 6.10

The Performance tab of the Windows Task Manager shows you how much physical memory is installed in your system, as well as how much is currently being used and how much is available. Windows Vista uses memory much more efficiently than previous versions, which is why only 17 MB of physical memory is shown as free.

>In the **Taskbar** area, right-click. Select **Task Manager**. Click the **Performance** tab.

Are there different types of RAM?

Like most computer components, RAM has gone through a series of transitions. In current systems, the RAM memory used most often comes in the form of double data rate (DDR) or DDR2 memory modules. In older systems, other types of RAM may have been used including DRAM, static RAM (SRAM), and synchronous DRAM (SDRAM).

All types of RAM are slightly different in how they function and in the speed at which memory can be accessed. Although you don't have a choice as to the type of RAM you get when buying a new system, if you're adding RAM to any system, you must determine what type your system needs. Consult your user's manual or the manufacturer's Web site. In addition, many online RAM resellers (such as **www.crucial. com**) can help you determine the type of RAM your system needs based on the model number and brand of your computer. We will discuss the different kinds of RAM in more detail in Chapter 9.

How can I tell how much RAM I have installed in my computer?

The amount of RAM that is actually sitting on memory modules in your computer is your computer's **physical memory**. The easiest way to see how much RAM you have is to look in the System Properties window. (On the Mac, choose About This Mac from the Apple menu.) This is the same tab you looked in to determine your system's CPU type and speed and is shown in Figure 6.6. RAM capacity is measured in megabytes (MB), or gigabytes (GB), though most machines today, especially those running Windows Vista, are sold with at least 1 GB of RAM. The computer in Figure 6.6 has 2045 MB (or 2 GB) of RAM installed.

More detailed information on physical memory is displayed in the Physical Memory table in the Performance tab of Windows Task Manager, shown in Figure 6.10. The Physical Memory table shows

SOUND BYTE

Memory Hierarchy Interactive

In this Sound Byte, you'll learn about the different types of memory used in a computer system.

both the total amount of physical memory you have installed as well as the available physical memory you have. If you are used to using Windows XP and have only a couple of applications running, then you expect to see lots of available memory. But with even just one application running under Windows Vista, it appears you have little available memory because Windows Vista manages memory differently from previous versions of Windows by using a memory-management technique known as Superfetch.

Because RAM is the fastest memory that you have in your computer, it would be helpful to have as much information as possible about the programs you are currently using in RAM so your computer will respond faster. Windows Vista now manages memory this way by anticipating what information you will need next and storing it in RAM instead of in cache memory or on your hard drive. So if you have MS Word running, Windows stores as much of the information related to Word in RAM as it can, thereby almost filling up your RAM. But don't worry, as other needs arise (you start Excel, for instance), Windows Vista reallocates the contents of RAM to account for you using multiple programs.

How much memory does the operating system need to run? The memory that your operating system uses is referred to as **kernel memory**. This memory is listed in a separate Kernel Memory table in the Performance tab. In Figure 6.10, the Kernel Memory table tells you that approximately 222 MB (total kernel memory) of the total 2 GB of RAM is being used to run Windows Vista.

As you know from Chapter 5, the operating system is the main software application that runs the computer. Without it, the computer would not work. At a minimum, the system needs enough RAM to run the operating system. Therefore, the amount of kernel memory that the system is using is the absolute minimum amount of RAM that your computer can run on. However, because you run additional applications, you need to have more RAM than the minimum.

How much RAM do I need? Because RAM is the temporary holding space for all the data and instructions that the computer uses while it's on, most computer users need quite a bit of RAM. In fact,

FIGURE 6.11 Sample RAM Requirements

Application	Minimum RAM Required
Windows Vista Home Basic	512 MB
Microsoft Office Professional 2007	256 MB
Internet Explorer 7	128 MB
iTunes	256 MB
Microsoft Picture It!	128 MB
Total RAM required to run all programs simultaneously	1,280 MB or 1.28 GB

systems running all the new features of Windows Vista should have a minimum of 1 GB of RAM, but for peak performance, systems are recommended to have at least 2 GB of RAM. Ultimately, the amount of RAM your system needs depends on how you use it. At a minimum, you need enough RAM to run the operating system (as explained earlier), plus whatever other software applications you're using, and then a bit of additional RAM to hold the data you're inputting.

To determine how much RAM you need, list all the software applications you might be running at one time. Figure 6.11 shows an example of RAM requirements. In this example, if you are running your operating system, word-processing and spreadsheet programs, a Web browser, a music player, and photo editing software simultaneously, then you will need a minimum of 1.28 GB RAM. It's always best to check the system requirements of any software program before you buy it to make sure your system can handle it. System requirements can be found on the software package or on the manufacturer's Web site.

However, it's a good idea to have more than the minimum amount of RAM so you can use more programs in the future. When upgrading RAM, the rule of thumb is to buy as much as you can afford but no more than your system will handle.

VIRTUAL MEMORY

Would adding more RAM improve my system performance? As shown in Figure 6.12, several factors should be considered when determining if your system needs more RAM.

FIGURE 6.12 Do You Need to Upgrade Your RAM?

Application	Current System
Type of RAM your system is using	
Maximum amount of RAM you need	
Amount of RAM in your system now	
Amount of RAM you want to add	
Number of currently empty memory module slots	
Memory module size	
Page file usage amount	
Total amount of RAM you can add	

When there's not enough RAM installed in your system, it will become sluggish, freeze more often, or just shut down as you perform certain tasks. When this happens, the system becomes **memory bound**—that is, limited in how fast it can send data to the CPU because there is not enough memory. If this is the case, then adding more RAM to your system will immediately affect performance.

How do I know whether my system is memory bound? As you recall from Chapter 5, if you don't have enough RAM to hold all of the programs you're currently trying to run, then the operating system will begin to store the data that doesn't fit in RAM into a space on the hard drive called **virtual memory**. When it is using virtual memory, your operating system builds a file called the **page file** on the hard drive to allow processing to continue. This enables the system to run more applications than can actually fit in your computer's RAM.

So far, this system of memory management sounds like a good idea, especially because hard drives are much cheaper than RAM per megabyte of storage. The drawback is speed. Remember that accessing data from the hard drive to send it to the CPU is more than one million times slower than accessing data from RAM. Another drawback is that some applications do not run well on virtual memory. So, using virtual memory is a method of last resort. If your system is running with a large page file (that is, if it is using a lot of virtual memory), then adding more RAM will dramatically increase performance.

ADDING RAM

Is there a limit to how much RAM I can add to my computer? Every computer is designed with a maximum limit on the amount of RAM it can support. Each computer is designed with a specific number of slots on the motherboard in which the memory cards fit, and each slot may have a limit on the amount of RAM it can support. In addition, the operating system running on that machine may impose its own limit. (For example, the maximum amount of RAM for Windows Vista ranges from 4 GB to 128 GB, depending on the particular version.) To determine these limits, check your owner's manual or the manufacturer's Web site.

Once you know how much RAM your computer can support, you can determine the

FIGURE 6.13

Adding RAM to a desktop computer (a) or a laptop (b) is quite simple and relatively inexpensive. You simply line up the notches and push in the memory module. Just be sure that you're adding a compatible memory module to your computer.

best configuration of memory cards to achieve the greatest amount of RAM. For example, say you have a total of four memory card slots: Two are already filled with 512 MB RAM cards and the other two are empty. Maximum RAM allowed for your system is 2 GB. This means you can buy two more 512 MB RAM modules for the two empty slots, for a total of 2 GB (4 × 512 MB) of RAM. If all of the memory card slots are already filled, you may be able to replace the old modules with greater-capacity RAM modules, depending on your maximum allowed RAM.

Is it hard to add RAM? Adding RAM to a computer is fairly easy (see Figure 6.13). RAM comes with installation instructions, which you should follow carefully. RAM is also relatively inexpensive compared with other system upgrade options. Still, the cost of RAM fluctuates in the marketplace as much as 400 percent over time, so if you're considering adding RAM, you should watch the prices of memory in online or print advertisements. For a demonstration on how easy it is to add RAM to your system, watch the Sound Byte "Installing RAM."

Adding RAM to a personal computer is quite simple and relatively inexpensive. You simply line up the notches and push in the memory module. Just be sure that you're adding a compatible memory module to your computer.

Evaluating the Storage Subsystem

As you've learned, there are two ways data is saved on your computer: temporary storage and permanent storage. RAM is a form of temporary (or volatile) storage—thus, anything residing in RAM is not permanently saved. Therefore, it's critical to have the means to store data and software applications *permanently.*

Fortunately, several storage options exist within every computer system. Storage devices for a typical personal computer include the hard drive, USB flash drives, optical drives, and external hard drives. When you turn off your computer, the data stored to these devices is saved. These devices are therefore referred to as *nonvolatile* storage devices. Of all the nonvolatile storage devices, the hard drive is used the most.

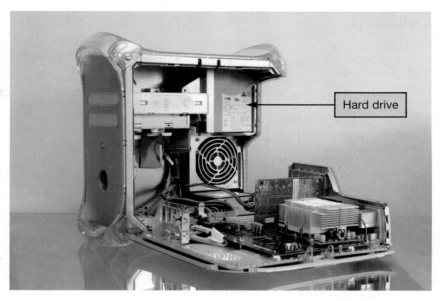

Hard drive

FIGURE 6.14

Hard drives are the most popular storage device for personal computers. The hard drive is installed permanently inside the system unit.

SOUND BYTE
Installing RAM

In this Sound Byte, you'll learn how to select the appropriate type of memory to purchase, how to order memory online, and how to install it yourself. As you'll discover, the procedure is a simple one and can add great performance benefits to your system.

THE HARD DRIVE

What makes the hard drive the most popular storage device? With storage capacities of up to 1.5 terabytes (TB), **hard drives**, shown in Figure 6.14, have the largest storage capacity of any storage device. The hard drive is also a much more economical device than other storage drives because it offers the most gigabytes of storage per dollar.

Second, the hard drive's **access time**, or the time it takes a storage device to locate its stored data and make it available for processing, is also the fastest of all permanent storage devices. Hard drive access times are measured in milliseconds, or thousandths of seconds. For large-capacity drives, access times of approximately 9.5 milliseconds—that's less than one-hundredth of a second—are not unusual. This is much faster than the access times of other popular storage devices such as flash drives.

FIGURE 6.15

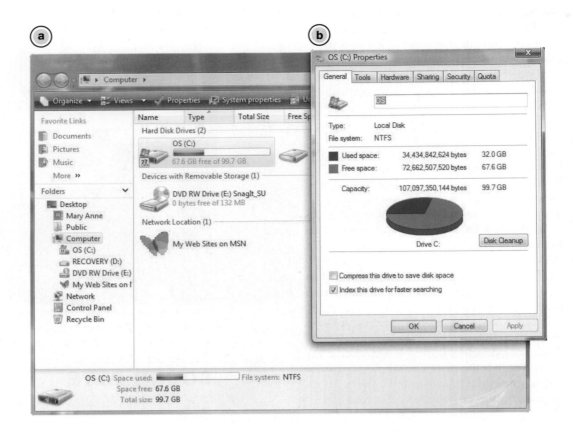

(a) In Vista, the free and used capacity of each device in the computer system is shown in the Computer window. (b) Alternatively, you can determine the capacity of your hard drive using the pie chart in the General tab of the Properties dialog box. The hard drive shown has 99.7 GB of space, with 67.6 GB of free space.

>To view the Computer window, click **Start**, and click **Computer**. To view the pie chart from the **Start Menu**, right-click the **C** drive, and select **Properties**.

Another reason hard drives are popular is that they transfer data to other computer components (such as RAM) much faster than the other storage devices do. This speed of transfer is referred to as **data transfer rate**; depending on the manufacturer, the rate is expressed in either megabits or megabytes per second.

How is data stored on hard drives? As you learned in Chapter 5, a hard drive is composed of several coated **platters** (round, thin plates of metal) stacked onto a spindle. When data is saved to a hard drive platter, a pattern of magnetized spots is created on the iron oxide coating of each platter. Each of these spots represents a 1, whereas the spaces not "spotted" represent a 0. These 0s and 1s are bits (or binary digits) and are the smallest pieces of data that computers can understand. When data stored on the hard drive platter is retrieved (or read), your computer translates these patterns of magnetized spots into the data you have saved.

How do I know how much storage capacity I need? Typically, hard drive capacity is measured in gigabytes (GB),

with some high-end systems having a hard drive with capacity in the terabytes (TB). To check how much total capacity your hard drive has, as well as how much is being used, click the Start button and select Computer from the right side of the Start menu. The hard drives, their capacity, and usage are shown, similar to those shown in Figure 6.15.

To determine the storage capacity your system needs, calculate the amount of storage capacity that basic computer programs will need to reside on your computer. Because the operating system is the most critical piece of software, your hard drive needs enough space to store that program. The demands on system requirements have grown with new versions of operating systems. Windows Vista, the latest Microsoft operating system, requires a 40 GB hard drive with a whopping 15 GB of available hard drive capacity. Five years ago, such software wouldn't have fit on most hard drives.

In addition to having space for the operating system, you need enough space to store the software applications you use such

DIG DEEPER

How a Hard Drive Works

The thin metal platters that make up a hard drive are covered with a special magnetic coating that enables the data to be recorded onto one or both sides of the platter. Hard drive manufacturers prepare the disks to hold data through a process called *low-level formatting*. In this process, **tracks** (concentric circles) and **sectors** (pie-shaped wedges) are created in the magnetized surface of each platter, setting up a gridlike pattern used to identify file locations on the hard drive. A separate process called *high-level formatting* establishes the catalog that the computer uses to keep track of where each file is located on the hard drive. More detail on this is presented in the Dig Deeper feature "How Disk Defragmenter Utilities Work" on page 244.

Hard drive platters spin at a high rate of speed, some as fast as 15,000 revolutions per minute (rpm). Sitting between each platter are special "arms" that contain **read/write heads** (see Figure 6.16). The read/write heads move from the outer edge of the spinning platters to the center, as many as 50 times per second, to retrieve (read) and record (write) the magnetic data to and from the hard drive platter. As noted earlier, the average total time it takes for the read/write head to locate the data on the platter and return it to the CPU for processing is the access time. A new hard drive should have an average access time of approximately 10 ms.

Access time is mostly the sum of two factors: seek time and latency. The time it takes for the read/write heads to move over the surface of the disk, between tracks, to the correct track is called the **seek time** (sometimes people incorrectly refer to this as access time). Once the read/write head locates the correct track, it may need to wait for the correct sector to spin to the read/write head. This waiting time is called **latency** (or *rotational delay*). The faster the platters spin (or the faster the rpm), the less time you'll have to wait for your data to be accessed. Currently, most hard drives for home systems spin at 7,200 rpm. Some people include an even faster hard drive that spins as fast as 10,000 rpm as a system drive and then add a slower drive with greater capacity for storage.

The read/write heads do not touch the platters of the hard drive; rather, they float above them on a thin cushion of air at a height of 0.5 microinches. As a matter of comparison, a human hair is 2,000 microinches thick and a particle of dust is larger than a human hair. Therefore, it's critical to keep your hard drive free from all dust and dirt, as even the smallest particle could find its way between the read/write head and the disk platter, causing a **head crash**—a stoppage of the hard drive that often results in data loss.

Capacities for hard drives in personal computers exceed 500 GB. Increasing the amount of data stored in a hard drive is achieved either by adding more platters or by increasing the amount of data stored on each platter. How tightly the tracks are placed next to each other, how tightly spaced the sectors are, and how closely the bits of data are placed affect the measurement of the amount of data that can be stored in a specific area of a hard drive platter. Modern technology continues to increase the standards on all three levels, enabling massive quantities of data to be stored in small places.

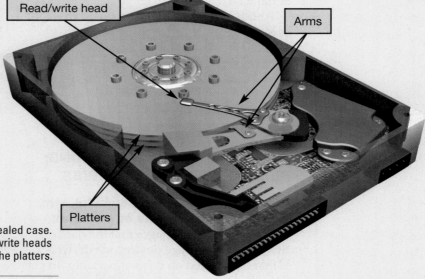

Read/write head

Arms

Platters

FIGURE 6.16

The hard drive is a stack of platters enclosed in a sealed case. Special arms fit in between each platter. The read/write heads at the end of each arm read from and save data to the platters.

FIGURE 6.17 **Sample Hard Drive Requirements**

Application	Hard Drive Space Required
Windows Vista	15 GB
MS Office 2007 Professional	2 GB
Adobe Photoshop Elements	2 GB
Roxio Easy Media Creator 9	1 GB installation and as much as 9 GB to copy CDs or DVDs
Total required	20–28 GB

as Microsoft Office, a Web browser, music, and games. Figure 6.17 shows an example of hard drive requirements for someone storing a few programs on a hard drive.

Are some hard drives faster than others? There are several types of hard drives. Integrated Drive Electronics (IDE), which is also called *parallel advanced technology attachment (PATA)*, is an older style that used wide cables to connect the hard drive to the motherboard. *Serial Advanced Technology Attachment (Serial ATA)* hard drives use much thinner cables and can transfer data more quickly than IDE drives. A slower drive is fine if you use your computer primarily for word processing, spreadsheets, e-mail, and the Internet. However, "power users" such as graphic designers and software developers will benefit from the faster Serial ATA hard drive.

Another factor that affects a hard drive's speed is access time (or the speed with which it locates data for processing). As noted earlier, access time is measured in milliseconds. The faster the access time the better, although often hard drives have similar access times.

PORTABLE STORAGE OPTIONS: FLASH AND OPTICAL DRIVES

If my hard drive is so powerful, why do I need other forms of storage? Despite all the advantages that the hard drive has as a storage device, one drawback is that data stored on it is not portable. To get data from one computer to another (assuming the computers aren't networked), you'll need a portable storage device such as a

flash drive. Equally important, you need alternative storage options for backing up data on your hard drive in case it experiences a head crash or other system problems. Finally, despite the massive storage capacity of hard drives, you should remove infrequently used files from your hard drive to maintain optimal storage capacity.

What forms of portable storage are best? Several portable storage formats (or media) are popular, with varying ranges of storage capacity (see Figure 6.18).

CD-R, CD-RW, DVD-R, and DVD-RW discs are optical media storage devices with storage capacities ranging from 700 MB to 17.08 GB. These are popular for storing large files, especially audio and video files.

Flash memory cards are another form of portable storage. Flash memory is non-volatile memory that can be electrically erased and reprogrammed. These tiny removable memory cards are often used in digital cameras, portable media players, and PDAs. Some flash cards can hold 8 GB or more of data. As the technology becomes more popular, capacities will continue to increase.

FIGURE 6.18 **Portable Storage Capacities**

Storage Media	Capacity
CD	700 MB
DVD single-sided:	
Single layer	4.7 GB
Double layer	8.54 GB
DVD double-sided:	
Single layer	9.4 GB
Double layer	17.08 GB
Blu-ray disc	
Single layer	25 GB
Dual layer	50 GB
Flash memory	512 MB–16 GB (and more)
Portable hard drive	20 GB and more

Note: Capacities are accurate as of publication date but are expected to continue to increase.

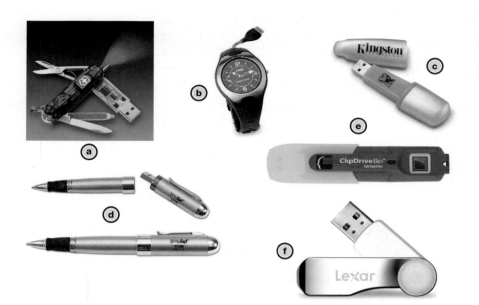

FIGURE 6.19

Flash drives, also known as *thumb drives* or *jump drives,* allow you to carry 16 GB or more of data in a variety of convenient packaging options. (a) Swiss Army knife with integrated flash drive, (b) watch with integrated flash drive, (c) conventional flash drive, (d) pen containing flash drive, (e) flash drive with fingerprint recognition reader, (f) folding flash drive.

This same technology is also packaged as **flash drives** (sometimes called *thumb drives* or *jump drives*). Small enough to fit on a key chain, a flash drive can hold 16 GB or more of data (and the capacities are increasing all the time) and can be plugged into any USB port (see Figure 6.19). Windows Vista instantly recognizes flash drives when they are plugged into a USB port and treats them as another hard drive on the system. For a modest cost, you can easily carry 8 GB with you and have enough room to store a huge PowerPoint presentation, some pictures and videos, and even a bunch of MP3 songs. For these reasons, flash drives are fast becoming the most preferred means of portable storage.

What if you need more portable capacity than a flash drive? For large amounts of portable storage, external hard drive devices sometimes are the best solution. Hard drives are now available in tiny and light packages and can connect quickly to a USB 2.0 or FireWire port. Light devices such as the Apple iPod, which fits in your pocket, are another option for portable storage, especially audio and video files, and can hold 160 GB of data. Larger external hard drives that are small enough to carry in a purse or backpack still can hold 1 TB or more of data. Connect them to a free USB port and they are recognized by the operating system as just another hard drive. Other larger external

BITS AND BYTES

Taking Care of Flash Drives

The following guidelines will help you keep your flash drives safe:

- A flash drive fits into a USB port only one way—do not force it if you feel resistance.
- When removing the drive, be sure any activity LED that may be on the drive is no longer lit. Then click the Safely Remove Hardware icon on the taskbar (see Figure 6.20). Only remove the drive itself once the Safely Remove Drive message appears. Pulling the drive out of the port earlier could corrupt your data.
- When not using the drive, keep the cap in place. Moisture and dust can damage the data stored on the drive.

FIGURE 6.20

Before taking out your flash drive, click the Safely Remove Hardware icon on your system tray.

hard drives are perfect to use as devices to which you can back up all your important files.

So many choices are available to you for portable data storage. Consider the amount

BITS AND BYTES

Store It Online

Another trend in storage is letting someone else provide the space for you! With online storage, a company provides you with space on its servers, which you use to store your backup data, your photos and movies, large files—whatever you need. Companies such as Xdrive (**www.xdrive.com**) offer 5 GB free online space, or you can rent 50 GB of secure storage for less than $10 a month. Because your data is accessible from any Web browser, online storage is a mobile solution as well.

Web-based e-mail providers are moving in this direction also. Yahoo Mail (**www.mail.yahoo.com**)

provides users with a free account and free unlimited online space for storing messages.

Photo storage sites such as Shutterfly (**www.shutterfly. com**) provide online storage for your digital photos, and All You Can Upload (**www.webshots.com**) is a popular site for storing pictures that will be hosted on blogs, eBay, MySpace, etc. You can specify who is allowed to view your images, and family and friends can order copies and merchandise with your photos directly from the site.

To read information stored on a disk, a laser inside the disk drive sends a beam of light through the spinning disk.

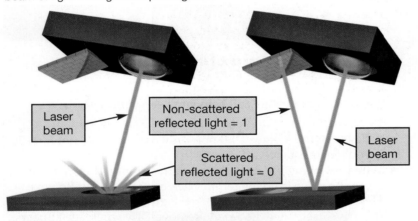

If the light reflected back is scattered in all directions (which happens when the laser hits a pit), the laser translates this into the binary digit 0.

If non-scattered light is reflected back to the laser (which happens when the laser hits an area in which there is no pit), the laser translates this into the binary digit 1.

In this way, the laser reads the pits and non-pits as a series of bits (0s and1s), which the computer can then process.

FIGURE 6.21

Data is read from a CD using focused laser light.

of data you want to routinely transport and then select the device that meets your needs at the lowest cost.

Optical Storage

How is data saved onto an optical disc? Like the hard drive, data is saved to **compact discs (CDs)**, **digital video discs (DVDs)**, and **Blu-ray discs (BDs)**, which are the newest means to store digital data, within established tracks and sectors. However, unlike hard drives, which store their data on magnetized platters, optical discs store data as tiny pits that are burned into the disc by a high-speed laser. These pits are extremely small. For CDs and DVDs, they are less than 1 micron in diameter, so nearly 1,500 pits fit across the top of a pinhead. The pits on a Blu-ray disc are only 0.15 microns, more than twice as small as the pits on a DVD. As you can see in Figure 6.21, data is read from a disc by a laser beam, with the pits and nonpits translating into the 1s and 0s of the binary code computers understand. CDs and DVDs use a red laser to read and write data. Blu-ray discs get their name because they are read with a blue laser light. All of them collectively are referred to as **optical media**.

What's the difference among all the optical discs? The biggest differences among all the optical discs are storage capacity and media quality. A DVD's storage capacity is much greater than a CD's, and Blu-ray discs have the greatest capacity of all. DVDs can have data on just one side or both sides of the disc, with one or two layers on each side for a maximum capacity of 17 GB per disc. Blu-ray discs were created to store high-definition video. An average two-hour standard definition movie can fit on a standard DVD, but the newer high-definition movies require a disc with about five times more storage space. A single-layer Blu-ray disc can hold 25 GB of data, while a double-layer disc can hold 50 GB, enough for four hours of high-definition video. In addition, Blu-ray audio and video quality is superior to that of a DVD or CD. Currently taking place are experiments using fluorescent optical discs that can store data in as many as 100 different layers, for a final capacity of 450 GB!

Why can I store data on some discs but not others? All forms of optical media come in pre-recorded, recordable, and rewritable formats. The pre-recorded discs—known as **CD-ROM, DVD-ROM,** and **BD-ROM discs**—are read-only optical discs, meaning you can't save any data onto them. Pre-recorded CDs usually contain audio content, software programs, or games, whereas DVD-ROMs and BD-ROMs typically contain movies or pre-recorded TV shows in regular or high definition, respectively. Recordable formats such as CD-R, DVD-R, and BD-R allow data to be written (saved or burned) to them. If you want to be able to use a form of optical media repetitively, writing and rewriting data to many times, then there is the read/writeable format such as CD-RW, DVD-RW, and BD-RE.

Do I need separate players and burners for CD/DVD and now BD formats? Although CDs and DVDs are based on the same optical technology, CD drives cannot read DVDs. If your system has only a CD drive, then you need to add a DVD drive to view DVDs. However, if your system has a DVD drive, then that is all you need, even just to listen to CDs, because DVD drives can read them. Although Blu-ray discs are read with a different type of laser than CDs and DVDs, most Blu-ray players are backward-compatible and can play DVDs and CDs. There are different types of optical drives for playing or recording to discs. If you want to record to CDs, DVDs, or Blu-ray discs, then you need to make sure your drive is capable of recording (or burning) and not just playing. Because recording drives are also

SOUND BYTE
CD and DVD Reading and Writing Interactive

In this Sound Byte, you'll learn about the process of storing and retrieving data from CD-R, CD-RW, and DVD discs. You'll be amazed to see how much precision engineering is required to burn MP3 files onto a disc.

backward-compatible, you do not need separate burners for each form of media. A DVD burner will also record CDs, and a Blu-ray burner will most likely record both CDs and DVDs (although there may be some compatibility issues).

Are there different standards of optical media? Unfortunately, technology experts have not agreed on a standard DVD format. Currently, there are two recognized formats, **DVD-R/RW** (pronounced "DVD dash") and **DVD+R/RW** (pronounced "DVD plus"). **DVD-RAM** is a third format. You can record, erase, and rewrite on DVD-RAM, similar to the plus and minus formats, but DVD-RAM discs are generally encased in a plastic cartridge. Web sites such as **www.videohelp. com** list the compatibility of various DVD players and the various DVD formats. However, you must make sure you purchase blank DVD discs that match the type of drive you own.

BITS AND BYTES
Taking Care of Optical Discs

The following guidelines will help you keep your optical discs safe:

- Exercise care in handling your optical discs. Dirt or oil on CDs, DVDs, and BDs can keep data from being read properly, and large scratches can interrupt data completely. Hold the disc by the edge or the center ring only.
- To keep CDs, DVDs, and BDs from warping, avoid placing them near heat sources and store them at room temperature.
- Clean CDs, DVDs, and BDs by taking a bit of rubbing alcohol on a cotton ball and wiping them from the center to the edge of the disc in long swipes. Don't rub the optical disc in a circular motion, because you may cause more scratches.
- Use a felt-tip marker to label optical discs and write on the area provided for the label. Don't put stickers or labels on optical discs unless they're specifically designed for that purpose.

SOUND BYTE

Installing a DVD-RW Drive

In this Sound Byte, you'll learn how to install a DVD-RW drive in your computer.

Are some CD and DVD drives faster than others? When you buy an optical drive, knowing the drive speed is important. Speeds are listed on the device's packaging. Record (write) speed is always listed first, rewrite speed is listed second (except for CD-R drives and DVD-R, which cannot rewrite data), and playback speed is listed last. For example, a CD-RW drive may have speeds of 52X32X52X, meaning that the device can record data at 52X speed, rewrite data at 32X speed, and play back data at 52X speed. For CDs, the X after each number represents the transfer of 150 kB of data per second. So, for example, a CD-RW drive with a 52X32X52X rating records data at 52 X 150 KB per second, or 7,800 KB per second.

DVD drives are much faster than CD drives. For example, a 1X DVD-ROM drive provides a data transfer rate of approximately 1.3 MB of data per second, which is roughly equivalent to a CD-ROM speed of 9X. CD and DVD drives are constantly getting faster. If you're in the market for a new CD or DVD burner, then you'll want to investigate the drive speeds on the market and make sure you get the fastest one you can afford.

Blu-ray drives are the fastest. Blu-ray technology defines 1X speed as 36 MB per second. Because BD movies will require data transfer rates of at least 54 MB per second, most Blu-ray disc players will have a minimum of 2X speeds (72 MB per second).

UPGRADING YOUR STORAGE SUBSYSTEM

How can I upgrade my storage devices? The table in Figure 6.22 will help you determine if your computer's storage subsystem needs upgrading.

If you need to upgrade, there are several ways in which you can increase your storage capacity or add extra drives to your computer.

If you find your hard drive is running out of space, or you want a place to back up or move files to create more room on your hard drive, then you have several options. You can replace the hard drive installed in your system unit with a bigger one. However, replacing your internal hard drive requires backing up your entire hard drive and reloading all the data onto your new hard drive. Instead, you may want to install an additional hard drive in your current system, if you have an extra drive bay (the space reserved on the inside of your system unit for hard drives). Instead of installing a bigger hard drive, you might just choose to add an external hard drive you can plug directly into a free USB 2.0 or FireWire port. Figure 6.23 shows an example of such an external hard drive.

You can also upgrade your storage subsystem by adding a DVD burner or other drive to your system. If your computer did not come with an internal optical disc drive, and if you have an open (unused) drive bay in your system, then you can easily install an additional drive there. Many people upgrade to a DVD-RW or BD-RE not for more storage but because they want additional multimedia capabilities (such as the ability to burn CDs, DVDs, or BDs). If you don't have open bays in your system, then you can still add CD, DVD, and Blu-ray drives. As with hard

FIGURE 6.22 **Do You Need to Upgrade Your Storage Subsystem?**	Current System	Upgrade Required?
Hard drive capacity		
CD-R/CD-RW drive		
DVD-ROM drive		
DVD-/+RW Drive		
Blu-ray R/RW drive		
Other storage devices needed?		

FIGURE 6.23

This external hard drive offers you up to 1TB extra storage and includes a system to back up your files simply with the push of one button.

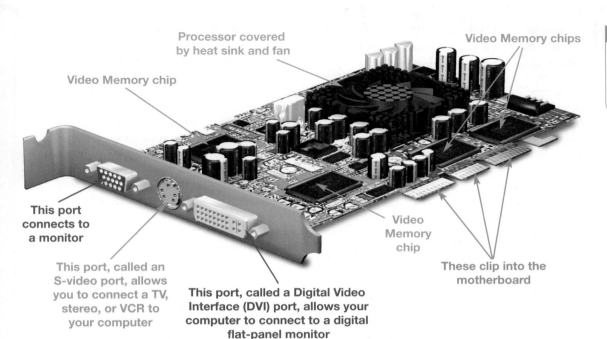

Video Memory chip

Processor covered
by heat sink and fan

Video Memory chips

FIGURE 6.24

Video cards have
grown to be highly
specialized subsys-
tems.

This port
connects to
a monitor

This port, called an
S-video port, allows
you to connect a TV,
stereo, or VCR to
your computer

This port, called a Digital Video
Interface (DVI) port, allows your
computer to connect to a digital
flat-panel monitor

Video
Memory
chip

These clip into the
motherboard

drives, these drives are available as
external units you attach to your computer
through an open USB port.

**What if I want to use flash
memory?** As flash memory becomes
more popular, you may want your
computer to be able to read flash memory
cards. Many desktop computers include
internal memory card readers, but if yours
does not, then you can purchase external
memory card readers that connect to your
system through an open USB port. As
discussed earlier, some flash memory
comes as mini portable hard drives that just
plug directly into a USB port.

Evaluating the Video
Subsystem

How video is displayed depends on two
components: your video card and your
monitor. It's important that your system
have the correct monitor and video card to
meet your needs. If you are considering
loading Windows Vista to your system, or
use your computer system to display files
that have complex graphics, such as videos
on DVD or from your camcorder, or even
play graphics-rich games with a lot of fast
action, then you may want to consider
upgrading your video subsystem.

FIGURE 6.25

Because of the large
amount of graphics
memory and the fast
graphics processing
units on modern video
cards, they have their
own fan to remove
heat.

VIDEO CARDS

What is a video card? A **video card** (or
video adapter) is an expansion card that is
installed inside your system unit to translate
binary data into the images you view on your
monitor. Today, almost all computers ship
with an installed video card. Modern video
cards like the ones shown in Figure 6.24 and
Figure 6.25 are extremely sophisticated. They
include ports that allow you to connect to different video equipment such as the DVI ports
for digital LCDs, S-video ports for connecting
your computer to the TV, and Super VGA
ports for CRT and analog LCD monitors. In
addition, video cards include their own
RAM, called **video memory**. Several standards of video memory are available, including graphics double data rate 3 (GDDR3)

FIGURE 6.26 Bit Depth and Color Quality

Bit Depth	Color Quality Description	Number of Colors Displayed
4-bit	Standard VGA	16
8-bit	256-color mode	256
16-bit	High color	65,536
24-bit	True color	16,777,216
32-bit	True color	16,777,216 plus 8 bits to help with transparency

and DDR2 memory. Because displaying graphics demands a lot of the CPU, video cards also come with their own graphics processing units (GPUs). Calls to the CPU for graphics processing are redirected to the GPU, significantly speeding up graphics processing. GPUs are covered in more detail in Chapter 9.

How can I tell how much memory my video card has? Information about your system's video card can be found in the Advanced Settings of the Display Settings dialog box. To get to the Display Settings dialog box, right-click on your desktop and select Personalize. Under Personalize appearance and sounds, click Display Settings, and then click the Advanced Settings button. A window will display, showing you the type of graphics card installed in your system, as well as memory information including the Total Available Graphics Memory, Dedicated Video Memory, and Shared System Memory. The documentation that came with your computer should also contain specifications for the video card, including the amount of video memory it has installed.

How much memory does my video card need? The amount of memory your video card needs depends on what you want to display on your monitor. If you work primarily in Microsoft Word and conduct general Web searches, 64 MB is a realistic minimum. For the serious gamer, no less than a 512 MB video card is essential, although cards with as much as 1 GB are available in the market and are preferred. These high-end video cards with greater amounts of memory allow games to generate smoother animations and more sophisticated shading and texture. Before purchasing new software, check the specifications to ensure your

video card has enough video memory to handle the load.

What else does the video card do? The video card also controls the number of colors your monitor can display. The number of bits the video card uses to represent each pixel (or dot) on the monitor, referred to as **bit depth**, the color quality of the image displayed. The more bits, the better an image's color detail. A 4-bit video card displays 16 colors, the minimum number of colors your system works with (referred to as Standard VGA). Most video cards today are 24-bit cards, displaying more than 16 million colors. This mode is called *true color mode* (see Figure 6.26).

The most recent generation of video cards can add some great features to your computer if you are a TV fan. Multimedia cards such as the ATI All-In-Wonder X1900 can open a live TV window on your screen, including features such as picture-in-picture. Using this video card, you can record programs to your hard drive or pause live TV. The card even comes with a wireless remote control.

So how do I know if I need a new video card? If your monitor takes awhile to refresh when editing photos, surfing the Web, or playing a graphics-rich game, then the video card could be short on memory. You also may want to upgrade if added features such as television viewing or importing analog video are important to you. If you want to use two monitors at the same time, then you also may need to upgrade your video card. On a desktop computer, replacing a video card is fairly simple: You simply insert the new video card in the correct expansion slot on the motherboard.

MONITORS

How do I evaluate my monitor?
You've evaluated your video card to ensure the best display. However, if the monitor is no good, you're still out of luck. As you learned in Chapter 2, there are two types of monitors: liquid crystal display (LCD) and cathode ray tube (CRT). If you currently have a CRT monitor but would rather have an LCD, you may want to upgrade.

When evaluating your monitor, you need to consider its size. The most common monitor sizes are 17, 19, and 21 inches, although there are 30-inch monitors in use. If your

ETHICS IN IT

Ethics: Optical Technology: A Free Lunch—Or at Least a Free Copy

Decades ago, when the electronic photocopier made its debut, book publishers and others who distributed the printed word feared they would be put out of business. They were worried that people would no longer buy books and other printed matter if they could simply copy someone else's original. Years later, when audiocassette and VCR players and recorders arrived on the market, those who felt they would be negatively affected by these new technologies expressed similar concerns. Now, with the arrival of CD-RW, DVD-RW, and BD-RE technology, the music and entertainment industries are worried because users can copy CDs, DVDs, and Blu-ray discs in a matter of minutes.

Although photocopiers and VCRs certainly didn't put an end to the industries they affected, some people still say the music and entertainment industries will take a significant hit with CD-RW, DVD-RW, and BD-RE technology. Industry insiders are claiming that these technologies are unethical, and they're pressing for increased federal legislation against such copying. And it's not just the CD-RW, DVD-RW, BD-RE technology that's causing problems—"copies" are not necessarily of the physical sort. Thanks to the Internet, file transferring copyrighted works— particularly music and films—is now commonplace. According to Music United (**www.musicunited.org**), more than 243 million

files are downloaded illegally every month, and about one-quarter of all Internet users worldwide have downloaded a movie from the Internet.

In a separate survey, the Recording Industry Association of America (RIAA), a trade organization that represents the interests of recording giants such as Sony, Capitol Records, and other major producers of musical entertainment, reported that 23 percent of music fans revealed they were buying less music because they could download it or copy a CD-ROM from a friend.

As you would expect, the music and entertainment industries want to be fairly compensated for their creative output. They blame the technology industry for the creation of means by which artists, studios, and the entertainment industry in general are being "robbed." Although the technology exists that readily allows consumers to transfer and copy music and videos, the artists who produce these works do not want to be taken advantage of. However, others claim that the technology industry should not bear the complete burden of protecting entertainment copyrights. The RIAA sums up the future of this debate nicely: "Goals for the new millennium are to work with [the recording] industry and others to enable technologies that open up new opportunities but at the same time to protect the rights of artists and copyright owners."

---

monitor is 15 inches or smaller, you may want to upgrade to a larger size if you find that you need to scroll horizontally and vertically to see an entire Web page, for example. LCD monitors are measured diagonally; unlike a CRT, the measurement is equal to the viewing size. Because the price of LCD monitors has dropped considerably and Windows Vista makes it simple to set up, if you have the desk space, you might want to consider using two monitors, especially if you like to have two separate windows open at full size at the same time. If you can't afford to buy a larger screen but want to see more on the screen itself, then you can try adjusting the resolution of your monitor. There are other factors, outlined in Figure 6.27 and discussed in the following sections, that will also affect your decision to upgrade your video subsystem.

FIGURE 6.27 **Do You Need to Upgrade Your Video Subsystem?**		
	Current System	**Upgrade Required?**
Monitor type (CRT or LCD)		
Monitor size (viewable area)		
LCD monitor pixel response rate		
LCD monitor brightness		
LCD monitor contrast ratio		
DVI or VGA hookup		
Video card memory		
TV tuner		

How would changing my screen resolution help me see more on my screen? Most monitors can display different resolutions (the number of pixels displayed on the screen). Changing the screen resolution can make a difference in how much is displayed. If you notice that you are scrolling more often to see all of a Web page, for example, then increasing the screen resolution will enable you to see more of the Web page without scrolling. In Figure 6.28, you can see the same Web page shown at different screen resolutions. Although increasing the screen resolution allows more to be displayed on the monitor, it also makes the images and text on the screen smaller and perhaps more difficult to read. One other consideration when changing screen resolutions is that video cards have maximum resolutions. Just

FIGURE 6.28

Adjusting screen resolution will allow you to see more on your screen. In these images, the same Web page is shown at (a) 1,024 × 768 pixels and (b) 1,600 × 1,200 pixels.

because you have a monitor that can display 1600 × 1200, it doesn't mean that your video card can.

Are there different features to consider when choosing an LCD monitor? When choosing an LCD monitor, in addition to resolution (discussed above and in Chapter 2), the main specifications and features to watch out for include aspect ratio (the standard proportion in width to height for a computer monitor) and contrast ratio. The standard aspect ratio is 4:3, but some monitors can display a wider format of 16:9 or 16:10. Contrast ratio should be between 400:1 and 600:1. Another feature to consider when buying an LCD monitor is brightness. If you want to watch movies on your LCD monitor, choose one with a brightness measure of at least 250 for basic computing needs and 500 for movies and TV. Pixel response rates are improving all the time, but the serious gamer should have a max of 12 ms to 15 ms. Keeping these specifications in mind, you also might want to ensure that your new monitor has a *digital* (DVI) as well as *analog* (VGA) hookup. If viewing from the side of the monitor is critical for you, then make sure the monitor has a good viewing angle.

Evaluating the Audio Subsystem

Computers output sound by means of speakers (or headphones) and a sound card. For many users, the preinstalled speakers and sound card are adequate for the sounds produced by the computer itself—the beeps and so on that the computer makes. However, if you're listening to music, viewing DVDs, hooking into a household stereo system, or playing games with sophisticated sound tracks, you may want to upgrade your speakers or your sound card.

SPEAKERS

What kinds of computer speakers are available? Two types of speakers ship with most personal computers: amplified speakers (which use external power) or unamplified speakers (which use internal power). Amplified speakers are easy to identify because they come with a separate power transformer and must be plugged into an electrical outlet before they'll function. Unamplified speakers merely plug into the speaker jack on your sound card and require no extra outside power.

Which type of speaker is better? Amplified speakers generally produce better quality sound. However, they usually do not adequately reproduce the low-frequency bass sounds that make gaming and musical scores sound richer and fuller. For better bass sounds, consider purchasing a speaker system that includes a **subwoofer**, a special type of speaker designed to more faithfully reproduce low-frequency sounds.

SOUND CARDS

What does the sound card do? Like video cards, **sound cards** are expansion cards that attach to the motherboard inside your system unit. Just as the video card enables your computer to produce images on the monitor, a sound card enables the computer to produce sounds.

Can I hook up a surround-sound system to my computer? Most computers ship with a basic sound card, most of which are **3D sound cards**. The 3D sound technology advances sound reproduction beyond traditional stereo sound (where the human ear perceives sounds as coming from the left or the right of the performance area) and is better at convincing the human ear that sound is omnidirectional, meaning that you can't tell from which direction the sound is coming. This tends to produce a fuller, richer sound than stereo sound. However, 3D sound is not surround sound.

What is surround sound then? The current surround-sound standard is from Dolby. There are many formats available, including Dolby Digital EX and Dolby Digital Plus for high-definition audio. Dolby TrueHD is the newest standard and features high-definition and lossless technology, in which no data is lost in the compression process. To create surround sound, Dolby takes digital sound from a medium (such as a DVD-ROM) and reproduces it in eight channels. Seven channels cover the listening field with placement to the left front, right front, and center of the audio stage, as well as the left rear and right rear, and then two extra side speakers are added, as shown in

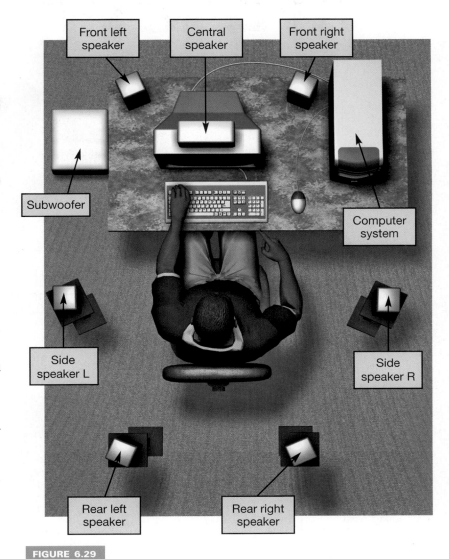

FIGURE 6.29

Dolby Digital surround sound gives you better quality audio output.

Figure 6.29. The eighth channel holds extremely low-frequency sound data and is sent to a subwoofer, which can be placed anywhere in the room. To set up surround sound on your computer, you need two things: a set of surround-sound speakers and, for the greatest surround sound experience, a sound card that is Dolby digital–compatible.

I don't need surround sound on my computer. Why else might I need to buy an upgraded sound card? Most basic sound cards contain the following input and output jacks (or ports): microphone in, speaker out, and line in. This allows you to hook up a set of stereo

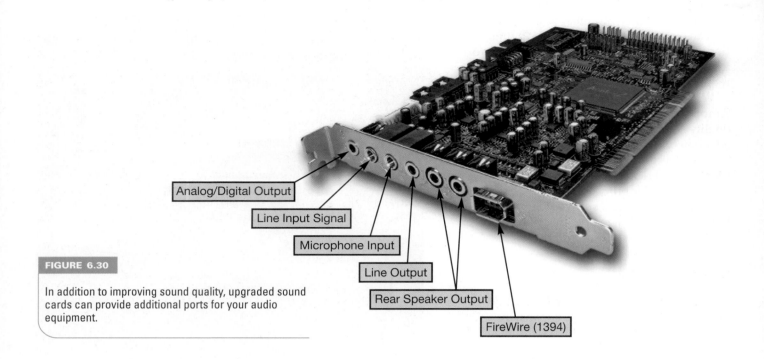

Analog/Digital Output

Line Input Signal

Microphone Input

Line Output

Rear Speaker Output

FireWire (1394)

FIGURE 6.30

In addition to improving sound quality, upgraded sound cards can provide additional ports for your audio equipment.

FIGURE 6.31 Do You Need to Upgrade Your Audio Subsystem?

	Current System	Upgrade Required?
Speakers (amplified or unamplified)		
3D sound card		
Dolby Digital		
Sufficient ports?		

speakers and a microphone. However, what if you want to hook up a right and left speaker individually or attach other audio devices to your computer? To do so, you need more ports, which are provided on upgraded sound cards like the one shown in Figure 6.30.

With an upgraded sound card, you can connect portable minidisc players, portable media players, portable jukeboxes, headphones, and CD players to your computer. Musicians also create music on their computers by connecting special devices (such as keyboards) directly to sound card ports. To determine whether your audio subsystem is meeting your needs, review the table in Figure 6.31.

Evaluating Port Connectivity

New computer devices are being introduced all the time, and the system you purchased last year may not support the hardware you're interested in today. A **port** is an interface through which external devices are connected to your computer. To evaluate your system's port connectivity, check the camera, camcorder, printer, scanner, and other devices you'd like to be able to connect to your computer and look for the type of port connection they require. Does your system have the ports necessary to connect to all of these devices?

What types of ports are there? Although the most common types of ports on new computer systems include universal serial bus, FireWire, and Ethernet, some older systems still have parallel ports. Each type of port operates at a certain speed, which is measured in either kilobits per second (Kbps) or megabits per second (Mbps). Figure 6.32 lists the basic characteristics of these ports.

The **universal serial bus (USB) port** is fast becoming the most common port on computers today. The original USB (version 1.1) port could transfer data at only 12 Mbps and was quickly replaced with USB version 2 (USB 2.0), which increased throughput to

FIGURE 6.32 **Ports and Their Uses**

Port Name	Port Shape	Connector Shape	Data Transfer Speed	Typical Devices Attached to Port
Current Technologies				
USB 2.0 Maintains backward compatibility with USB 1			480 Mbps	Mice Keyboards Printers Scanners Game controllers Digital video camcorders Digital cameras
FireWire			400 Mbps or 800 Mbps	Digital video camcorders Digital cameras
Ethernet or Gigabit Ethernet			As much as 1,000 Mbps	Network connections Cable modems
DVI			As much as 4.95 GB	Digital LCD monitor
Super VGA			NA	Analog LCD monitor or CRT monitor
S-video			NA	Connects PC to TV
Legacy Technologies				
Parallel			12 Mbps (12,000 Kbps)	Printers

FIGURE 6.33

Bluetooth-equipped devices communicate wirelessly with one another using radio waves.

newer FireWire 800, which transfers data at 800 Mbps, is faster but struggles to compete against the more universal USB 2.0 ports. FireWire is most commonly used to connect digital video devices (such as digital cameras) or hard drives to the computer.

The **Ethernet port** (technically called an RJ-45 jack) is used to connect your computer to a local network or cable modem. Because one of the most common uses of RJ-45 jacks is for connecting Ethernet networks, it is often referred to simply as an *Ethernet jack*. Ethernet originally offered a transfer rate of 10 Mbps. Fast Ethernet (called 100Base-T), with a transfer rate of 100 Mbps, is the standard used in most personal computers today.

If you have a network that needs to transfer lots of large files such as video files, then Gigabit Ethernet networking would be useful. Gigabit Ethernet can transfer at a rate as high as 1,000 Mbps.

Bluetooth technology uses radio waves to send data over short distances (see Figure 6.33). The maximum transfer rate of the original Bluetooth 1.0 is 1 Mbps. The newer standard Bluetooth 2.0 is three times faster, with a maximum transfer rate of 3 Mbps. Many notebooks and PDAs include a small Bluetooth chip that allows them to transfer data wirelessly to any other device with a Bluetooth chip, such as a cell phone, PDA, or Bluetooth-enabled keyboard or mouse. The advantage of Bluetooth devices is that a clear line of sight isn't needed between the two devices, although the distance between the devices is limited to about 30 feet.

WiFi (Wireless Fidelity), another wireless transmission standard, differs slightly from Bluetooth. WiFi is designed to cover much longer distances and to allow much faster data transfer: as high as 200 Mbps. Although WiFi is a great way to connect your notebook from the back porch to the PC in the upstairs bedroom, Bluetooth is a better solution for a short-distance connection such as from a wireless keyboard to the system unit.

480 Mbps. A newer USB 3.0 standard that takes advantage of fiber-optic technology, with anticipated throughput of as much as 5 Gbps, is currently being tested. Printers, scanners, digital cameras, keyboards, mice, and hard drives can all be connected to the computer using USB ports. Parallel ports were traditionally used to connect printers and scanners to computers. Most parallel ports achieved data transfer rates of 12 Mbps, much faster than obsolete serial ports, which moved data at speeds only as high as 56 kbps. Parallel ports have been phased out in favor of higher-speed USB ports.

FireWire (previously called **IEEE 1394**) is based on a standard developed by the Institute of Electrical and Electronics Engineers (IEEE). Until the introduction of USB 2.0, FireWire was the fastest port available, with a transfer rate of 400 Mbps. The

ADDING PORTS: EXPANSION CARDS AND HUBS

What if I don't have all the ports I need? New port standards are developed every few years, and special expansion cards

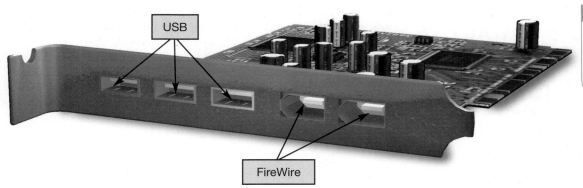

USB

FireWire

are usually the only way to add the newest ports to an older computer or to expand the number of ports on your computer. For example, your computer may have only USB 1.0 ports, but you may have several devices that would run better with USB 2.0 ports. Just as sound cards and video cards provide ports for sound and video equipment to connect to the computer, you also can install expansion cards in your system unit to provide additional ports (such as USB 2.0 and FireWire). Like the other expansion cards, these cards clip into an open expansion slot on the motherboard. Figure 6.34 shows an example of such an expansion card.

What if there are no open slots on the motherboard for me to insert an expansion card? If there are no open slots on the motherboard and you still need extra ports, then you can add an expansion hub (shown in Figure 6.35). An **expansion hub** is a device that connects to one port, such as a USB port, to provide four or eight new ports, similar to a multiplug extension cord used with electrical appliances. Because almost everything connects to your computer using USB ports, you should have at least six USB ports and have an expansion hub handy to cover any additional needs.

You also can connect multiple USB devices through a single USB port by connecting the devices in a daisy chain. In a daisy chain, you attach one device to another through its USB port, with the last device connecting to a USB port on the computer.

Is there a limit to the number of ports I can add? Using expansion hubs, you can expand your computer so that it can handle more USB and FireWire devices. Note, however, that even if your USB hub device is USB 2.0–compliant, if you are plug-

FIGURE 6.35

If you don't have enough USB ports to support your USB devices, then consider getting an expansion hub, which can add four or eight USB ports to your system.

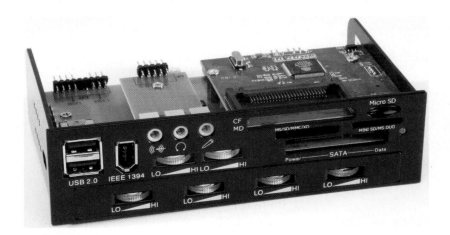

FIGURE 6.36

You also can use an empty drive bay to add additional ports and even a flash card reader to the front panel of the system unit.

ging the hub into a USB 1.1 port on your computer, the transfer rate will be that of the USB 1.1 port. For installation of other ports, you're limited by the number of open expansion slots in your computer.

You also can add ports to an empty drive bay, giving you easy-to-reach new ports. The Koutech 10-in-1, shown in Figure 6.36,

ACTIVE HELPDESK

Evaluating Your Storage Subsystem and Ports

In this Active Helpdesk call, you'll play the role of a helpdesk staffer, fielding calls about the computer's storage devices and ports.

fits into a regular drive bay and adds front-panel access to two USB 2.0 ports, two FireWire ports, three audio jacks, and a 6-in-1 digital media card reader.

Which devices benefit most from high-speed ports? Any device that requires the transfer of large amounts of data will significantly benefit from using a high-speed port such as a FireWire or USB 2.0 port. For example, digital video cameras produce large files that need to be transferred to a computer. If your video camera has a FireWire port, but your computer doesn't, then investing in a FireWire expansion port would definitely be worth the cost based on the time you'll save during downloads.

Evaluating System Reliability

Many computer users decide to buy a new system not necessarily because they need a faster CPU, more RAM, or a bigger hard drive, but because they are experiencing problems such as slow performance, freezes, and crashes. Over time, your computer builds up excess files and becomes internally disorganized just from normal everyday use. This excess clutter and disorganization can lead to deteriorating performance or, far worse, system failure. Therefore, before you buy a new system because you think yours may be unreliable, make sure the problem is not one you can fix. Proper upkeep and maintenance also may postpone an expensive system upgrade or replacement.

What can I do to ensure my system performs reliably? There are several procedures you can follow to ensure your system performs reliably:

1. **Clean out your Startup folder.** Some programs install themselves into your Startup folder and are automatically run each time the computer reboots, whether you are using them or not. This unnecessary load causes extra stress on RAM. Check your Startup folder by clicking on Start, All Programs, and then click on the Startup folder and make sure all the programs listed are important to you. Right-click on any unnecessary program and select Delete to remove it from the Startup folder. Make sure you delete *only* programs you know without a doubt are unnecessary.

2. **Clear out unnecessary files.** Temporary Internet files can accumulate quickly on your hard drive, taking up unnecessary space. Running the Disk Cleanup utility is a quick and easy way to ensure your temporary Internet files don't take up precious hard drive space. Likewise, you should delete any unnecessary files from your hard drive regularly, because they can make your hard drive run slower.

3. **Run spyware and adware programs.** These often detect and remove different pests and should be used in addition to your regular antivirus package.

4. **Run the Disk Defragmenter utility on your hard drive.** When your hard drive becomes fragmented, its storage capacity is negatively impacted. When you defrag your hard drive, files are reorganized, making the hard drive work more efficiently. For more complete coverage of the Disk Defragmenter, refer to Chapter 5.

My system crashes often during the day. What can I do? Computer systems are complex. It's not unusual to have your system stop responding occasionally. If rebooting the computer doesn't help, you'll need to begin troubleshooting:

1. Check that you have enough RAM, which you learned how to do in the section "Evaluating RAM: The Memory Subsystem" earlier in this chapter. Systems with insufficient amounts of RAM often crash.

2. Make sure you have properly installed any new software or hardware. If you're using a PC system, use the System Restore utility in Windows

Vista to "roll back" to a time when the system worked more reliably. Mac OS X Time Machine, as shown in Figure 6.37, provides automatic backup and enables you to look through and restore (if necessary) files, folders, libraries, or the entire system.

3. If you see an error code in Windows, visit the Microsoft Knowledge Base (**http://support.microsoft.com**), an online resource for resolving problems with Microsoft products. This may help you determine what the error code indicates and how you may be able to solve the problem. If you don't find a satisfactory answer in the Knowledge Base, try copying the entire error message into Google and searching the larger community for solutions.

Can my software affect my system reliability? Having the latest version of software products makes your system much more reliable. You should upgrade or update your operating system, browser software, and application software as often as new patches (or fixes) are reported for resolving errors. Sometimes these errors are performance-related; sometimes they're tied to maintaining better security for your system.

How do I know whether updates are available for my software? You can configure Windows Vista so that it automatically checks for, downloads, and installs any available updates for itself, Internet Explorer, and other Microsoft applications such as Microsoft Office. Many other applications now also include the ability to check for updates. Check under the Help menu of the product, and often you will find a Check for Updates command.

What if none of this helps? Is buying a new system my only option? If your system is still unreliable after these changes, then you have two options:

1. **Upgrade your operating system to the latest version.** There are substantial increases in reliability with each major release of a new operating system. However, upgrading the operating system may require hardware upgrades such as additional RAM, an updated graphics processor, and an even larger hard drive. The Microsoft Windows Vista Upgrade Advisor will perform a

FIGURE 6.37

Mac's Time Machine restores files, folders, libraries and, if necessary, the entire system.

scan of your system to determine what upgrades might be required before converting to Windows Vista. Be sure to examine the *recommended* (not required) specifications of the new operating system.

2. **Reinstall the operating system. As a last resort, you might need to reinstall the operating system.** To do so, you'll want to back up all of your data files before the installation and be prepared to reinstall your software after the installation. Make sure you have all of the original discs for the software installed on your system, along with the product keys, serial numbers, and any other activation codes so that you can reinstall them.

Making the Final Decision

Now that you have evaluated your computer system, you need to shift to questions of *value.* How closely does your system come to meeting your needs? How much would it cost to upgrade the system you have to match what you'd ideally like your computer to do not only today but also several years from now? How much would it

Computers in Society: How to Donate Your Old Computer Safely

What happened to your last computer? If you threw it away hoping it would be safely recycled with your empty water bottles, think again. Mercury in screens, cadmium in batteries and circuit boards, and flame retardant in plastic housing are all toxic, as are the four to eight pounds of lead in the cathode ray tube of nearly every monitor. An alarming trend emerging is that discarded machines are beginning to create an "e-waste" crisis.

Instead of throwing your computer away, you may be able to donate it to a nonprofit organization. Some manufacturers, such as Dell, offer recycling programs and have formed alliances with nonprofit organizations to help distribute your old technology to those who need it. You can also take your computer to an authorized computer recycling center in your area (find a local one at **www.usedcomputer.com**).

However, before donating or recycling a computer, make sure you carefully remove all data from your hard drive, or you may end up having your good deed turn bad, making you the victim of identity theft. Credit card numbers, bank information, Social Security numbers, tax records, passwords, and personal identification numbers (PINs) are just a few of the pieces of sensitive information that we casually record to our computer's hard drive. Just deleting files that contain proprietary personal information is not protection enough. Even reformatting or erasing your hard drive does not totally remove data as was proved by two MIT graduate students. In 2003, they bought more than 150 used hard drives from various sources. Although some of the hard drives were reformatted or damaged so the data was supposedly irrecoverable, the two students were able to retrieve medical records, financial information, pornography, personal e-mails, and more than 5,000 credit card numbers!

The U.S. Department of Defense suggests a seven-layer overwrite for a "secure erase." In other words, they suggest that you fill your hard drive *seven times over* with a random series of 1s and 0s. Fortunately, several software programs exist for PCs running Windows such as Active @ KillDisk, Eraser, and CyberScrub. Wipe is available for Linux, and Shredit X can be used for OS X. These programs provide secure hard drive erasures, either of specific files on your hard drive or of the entire hard drive.

Keep in mind that even these data erasure software programs can't provide the ultimate level in security. Computer forensic specialists or supercybercriminals can still manage to retrieve some data from your hard drive with the right tools. The ultimate level of protection is to destroy the hard drive altogether. Suggested methods include drilling holes in the hard drive, burning or melting the hard drive, or just taking an old-fashioned sledgehammer to it! For large companies that need to upgrade large quantities of computers and are faced with destroying or recycling their old computers, the problem becomes much worse. In these cases, recycling isn't a good option, and throwing them away can become an environmental hazard. Companies such as GigaBiter (**www.gigabiter.com**) eliminate security and environmental risks associated with electronic destruction by first delaminating the hard drive and then breaking down the computer e-waste into recyclable products. The result of the final step is a sandlike substance that is 100-percent recyclable.

cost to purchase a new system that meets these specifications?

To decide which option (upgrading or buying a new system) has better value for you, you need to price both scenarios. Figure 6.38 provides an upgrade worksheet you can use to evaluate both the upgrade path and the new purchase path. Be sure to consider what benefit you might obtain by having two systems if you were to buy a new computer. Would you have a use for the older system? Would you donate it to a charitable organization? Would you be able to give it to a family member? Purchasing a new system is an important investment of your resources, and you want to make a well-reasoned, well-supported decision.

Needs	Hardware Upgrade Cost	Included on a New System?	Additional Expense for Item If Not Included on a New System
FIGURE 6.38 Upgrade Versus New Purchase Comparison Worksheet			
Portability			
Notebook			
Wireless connectivity			
CPU and Memory Subsystems			
CPU upgrade			
RAM upgrade			
Storage Subsystem			
Hard drive upgrade			
CD-R or CD-RW drive			
DVD-ROM drive			
DVD-RW drive			
Blu-ray drive			
Flash card reader			
Other storage device			
Video and Audio Subsystems			
New monitor			
Video card upgrade			
Speaker upgrade			
Sound card upgrade			
Port Connectivity			
USB 2.0			
FireWire			
Ethernet			
Bluetooth			

1. How can I determine whether I should upgrade my existing computer or buy a new one?

To determine whether you need to upgrade or purchase a new system, you need to define your ideal system and what it can do. Then you need to perform a system evaluation to assess the subsystems in your computer, including the CPU, memory, storage, video, audio, and ports. Last, you need to determine if it's economically practical to upgrade or whether buying a new computer would be best.

2. What does the CPU do, and how can I evaluate its performance?

Your computer's CPU processes instructions, performs calculations, manages the flow of information through a computer system, and is responsible for processing the data you input into information. It is composed of two units: the arithmetic logic unit and the control unit. CPU speed is measured in megahertz or gigahertz, or millions or billions of machine cycles a second. A machine cycle is the process the CPU goes through to fetch, decode, execute, and store data. You can tell whether your CPU is limiting your system performance by watching how busy it is as you work on your computer. The percentage of time that your CPU is working is referred to as CPU usage, which you can determine by checking the Task Manager.

3. How does memory work in my computer, and how can I evaluate how much memory I need?

RAM is your computer's short-term memory. It remembers everything that the computer needs to process data into information. However, it is an example of volatile storage. When the power is off, the data stored in RAM is cleared out. The amount of RAM sitting on memory modules in your computer is your computer's physical memory. The memory your OS uses is kernel memory. At a minimum, you need enough RAM to run the OS plus the software applications you're using, plus a bit more to hold the data you will input.

4. What are the computer's main storage devices, and how can I evaluate whether they match my needs?

Storage devices for a typical computer system include a hard drive, flash drives, and CD and DVD drives. Blu-ray drives are gaining in popularity for viewing and burning high-density media. When you turn off your computer, the data stored in these devices is saved. These devices are referred to as *nonvolatile* storage devices. Hard drives have the largest storage capacity of any storage device and the fastest access time and data transfer rate of all nonvolatile storage options. CDs and DVDs have capacities from 700 MB to 17 GB. Portable flash drives allow easy transfer of as much as 16 GB or more of data from machine to machine. To determine the storage capacity your system needs, calculate the amount of storage your software needs to reside on your computer. To add more storage or to provide more functionality for your system, you can install additional drives, either internally or externally.

5. What components affect the output of video on my computer, and how can I evaluate whether they match my needs?

How video is displayed depends on two components: your video card and monitor. A video card translates binary data into the images you see. These cards include their own RAM (video memory) as well as ports that allow you to connect to video equipment. The amount of video memory you need depends on what you want to display on the monitor. More powerful cards allow you to play graphics-intense games and multimedia. Your monitor's size, resolution, and refresh rate all affect how well the monitor performs. For a clearer, brighter image, buy a monitor with a high refresh rate.

6. **What components affect the quality of sound on my computer, and how can I evaluate whether they match my needs?**

Your computer's sound depends on your speakers and sound card. Two types of speakers ship with most computers: amplified speakers and unamplified speakers. If you're listening to music, viewing DVDs, or playing games, you may want to have speakers with a subwoofer. Sound cards enable the computer to produce sounds. Users upgrade their sound cards to provide for 3D sound, surround sound, and additional ports for audio equipment.

7. **What are the ports available on desktop computers and notebook computers, and how can I determine what ports I need?**

A port is an interface through which external devices connect to the computer. Common ports include universal serial bus (USB), FireWire, Bluetooth, and Ethernet. Parallel ports, used mostly with printers, have been phased out in favor of the faster USB 2.0 port. To evaluate your port connectivity, check the devices you'd like to connect to your computer and look for the type of port they require. If your system doesn't have enough ports, then you can add ports through expansion cards (which you install in your system unit) and expansion hubs (which connect to your system through a port).

8. **How can I improve the reliability of my system?**

Many computer users decide to buy a new system because they are experiencing problems with their computer. However, before you buy a new system because you think yours may be unreliable, make sure the problem is not one you can fix. Make sure you have installed any new software or hardware properly, check that you have enough RAM, run system utilities such as Disk Defragmenter and Disk Cleanup, clean out your Startup folder, remove unnecessary files from your system, and keep your software updated with patches. If you continue to have troubles with your system, reinstall or upgrade your OS, and, of course, seek technical assistance.

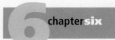

Key Terms

Buzzwords

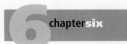

Word Bank

- access time
- Bluetooth
- CD-RW drive
- CPU
- expansion card
- expansion hub

- FireWire
- flash drive
- hard drive
- LCD
- monitor
- motherboard

- RAM
- sound card
- subwoofer
- system evaluation
- upgrading
- USB

Instructions: Fill in the blanks using the words from the Word Bank above.

Joe already has a PC but just heard about a great deal on a new one. He decides to perform a(n) (1) _____ on his computer to see whether he should keep it or buy the new one. First, he right-clicks Computer in the Start menu to check his System Properties. By doing so, he can check what (2) _____ is in his computer. He sees he has a Core Duo processor running at 2.0 GHz. Next he checks his internal memory, or (3) _____. He then turns to the Task Manager to evaluate his CPU and RAM usage to see if he needs to add more RAM should he keep his PC.

He continues to evaluate his system by checking out what components he has and what he'll need. He notes the storage capacity of the (4) _____. Recently, he has been using a(n) (5) _____ to store files because his hard drive is nearing capacity. But the (6) _____, or the amount of time it takes for the disk to find the right data, is so slow that the larger hard drive of a new computer is appealing. Joe also notes that he is unable to download large files from the Internet and save them onto a CD like his friends do. His current system does not have a(n) (7) _____ with which to burn CDs, but the new system would. The new system would also include speakers with a(n) (8) _____ to improve the sound. He also sees that it would include a(n) (9) _____ that would allow him to connect more of his audio equipment to his PC.

Joe's 19-inch (10) CRT _____ doesn't fit well on his desktop, and having a(n) (11) _____ monitor would conserve space. He also knows that if he wants to attach more devices to his PC in the future, he'll need more (12) _____ ports, because his current system has only a few of these faster ports. He notes, however, that it may be just as cost-effective to install a(n) (13) _____ in his system to give it more ports or to buy a(n) (14) _____ he could attach to his system unit to add more ports. Finally, Joe considers the cost of buying the new computer versus (15) _____ his current system. He realizes it's more economical right now to keep his current system.

Becoming Computer Literate

Jen lives across the hall from you. She heard you worried last semester that your PC wasn't fast enough. Between the simulation program for math, the reports you did for English, and your programming class, your computer was running slowly and you were out of storage space. She's offered to help you upgrade your system, but she needs you to tell her what you want upgraded and why.

Instructions: Using the preceding scenario, write a letter to Jen using key terms from the chapter. Be sure your sentences are grammatically correct and technically meaningful.

Instructions: Answer the multiple-choice and true–false questions below for more practice with key terms and concepts from this chapter.

MULTIPLE CHOICE

1. The amount of RAM recommended for most systems today is measured in
   a. gigabytes.
   b. gigahertz.
   c. megahertz.
   d. kilobytes.

2. When evaluating CPU performance, which is NOT a feature you need to consider?
   a. Amount of cache memory
   b. Speed of the processor
   c. Speed of the front side bus
   d. Size of the processor

3. RAM is classified as what kind of storage in a computer system?
   a. Volatile
   b. Nonvolatile
   c. Permanent
   d. Flash

4. Physical memory is:
   a. the amount of RAM that is actually sitting on memory modules in your computer.
   b. the memory needed to run the key components of the operating system.
   c. the amount of space on the hard drive to temporarily store data when there isn't enough RAM.
   d. the memory stored on the hard drive.

5. From which location is it slowest to get data to the CPU for processing?
   a. RAM
   b. Cache memory
   c. Hard drive
   d. Virtual memory

6. Which of the following would you want to purchase if you're looking for more than 100 GB of portable storage?
   a. External hard drive
   b. Apple iPod
   c. Flash drive
   d. Online storage account

7. Flash memory cards are NOT a form of storage for what kind of devices?
   a. Portable media players
   b. Notebook computers
   c. Digital cameras
   d. Personal digital assistants

8. Blu-ray technology is required to store what kind of media?
   a. Standard definition video
   b. High-definition video
   c. Analog audio
   d. Digital audio

9. Which of the following is becoming the most common port on a computer system because most peripheral devices connect to it?
   a. Parallel port
   b. Ethernet port
   c. USB 2.0 port
   d. FireWire port

10. Which of the following should you do to ensure the reliability of your system?
    a. Run Disk Defragmenter
    b. Run Disk Cleanup
    c. Install software upgrades and patches
    d. All of the above

TRUE–FALSE

_____ 1. The Task Manager provides information for the Windows Vista operating system about programs and processes running on your computer.

_____ 2. Installing a second hard drive in your system will have an immediate impact on system performance if your system is memory bound.

_____ 3. Data is stored in the same manner on hard drives, CDs, and flash memory cards.

_____ 4. Video cards have their own separate memory and processor.

_____ 5. FireWire ports are used for Internet connectivity.

Making the Transition to... Next Semester

1. Evaluating Your System

A small worksheet follows the end of each section in this chapter to guide you as you evaluate your own system. These smaller worksheets have been combined into one complete worksheet that is on the book's Companion Website (**www.prenhall.com/ techinaction**). Download the worksheet and fill it in based on the computer you are currently using when taking this class.

a. Research the costs of replacement parts for those components you feel should be upgraded.
b. Research the cost of a new system that would be roughly equivalent to your current computer after upgrades.
c. Determine whether it would be more cost-effective to upgrade your computer or buy a new one.

2. Your Software Needs

What software do you need for the courses you're taking this semester? Will you need any different software for next semester? How many of these software applications do you run at one time? Examine the requirements for those software packages. Prepare a table that lists the software applications you are currently using as well as any you may need to use in the future. For each, list the minimum RAM and hard drive space requirements. How does your system measure up against those requirements?

3. Campus Computer Use

What kinds of computers do students use in college, and how do different people budget for their computer needs? To find an answer to these questions, interview several college students in different years of school. Ask them the following questions:

a. Did you need your own computing equipment, or did you use your college's equipment when you first started school? Would you recommend I do the same?
b. Did you need to upgrade your computer before you came to college? How did you do this?
c. Was the computer you used in your first year of college able to handle your workload in later years?
d. If you used one computer, what upgrades did you need to perform?
e. If you had to buy a new computer, how much money did you budget and how much did you spend? What did you do with your old computer?

4. Buying Computers Online

Visit an online seller of computer systems and components (such as **www. coolcomputing.com**, **www.pricewatch.com**, **www.newegg.com**, and **www.tigerdirect.com**) and answer the following questions:

a. What is the current cost of RAM?
b. How much additional RAM could you add to your system?
c. What are the prices of the most popular CPU upgrades?
d. How much would you need to spend to upgrade to a new operating system?
e. How would each of these help you in your work?

5. Comparing Monitor Specs

You want to add a second monitor to your system. Using the Web, research several different LCD monitors. Compare specifications for the monitors, including screen size, contrast ratio, brightness, and cost. From your list, identify the one monitor you would choose to add to your system and explain why. Check to see if your graphics card could support a second monitor. If not, what kind of replacement graphics card would you need?

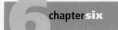

Making the Transition to... the Workplace

1. Using Your Computer for Education and Business

As you move from an educational environment to a business environment, how you use your computer will inevitably change. Write one or two paragraphs that describe what your computer system is like now. Then write one or two paragraphs that describe what your ideal computer system would be like after you've graduated and entered the workforce. What different components, if any, would your system need? Could you upgrade your current system to incorporate these new components, or would you need to buy a new system? Make sure you defend either position you take with information covered in this chapter. To help you in your decision, fill out the worksheet similar to Figure 6.2 that is available on the book's companion Website (**www.prenhall.com/techinaction**).

2. Assessing Memory Use

Your home office computer is running a bit sluggish, and you want to determine which application is the memory hog so you can either avoid using it or use it without any other programs running to preserve RAM. You've been told you can do this in the Processes tab in the Task Manager utility. On your computer, open the Task Manager utility and determine which application currently running is using the most memory. Can you tell how much it is using? Note that because the names of the programs have been shortened (for example, Microsoft Word is referred to as *winword.exe*), you may not immediately recognize the program names.

3. IT Support at Work

When you are evaluating potential employers, one consideration will be how well they support you as an employee and provide the environment you need to do productive work. What questions would you ask in an interview to determine what kind of IT support you can expect in your new position?

4. Web Programming Software at Home

You are a Web programmer and you often work from home. You need to investigate whether your home computer would be able to run three programs you use most frequently at work: Adobe Photoshop, Microsoft Visual Basic .NET, and Microsoft Word. Use the Web to research RAM and hard drive requirements for these programs. Will your computer be able to handle the load?

5. Build an Ideal System

Imagine that a client tells you she wants a system that has at least 2 GB of RAM, the fastest processor on the market, and enough storage space to edit hours of video and music files. In table format, compare the components and pricing of three systems that would meet the client's needs by visiting manufacturer Web sites such as **www.dell.com**, **www.gateway.com**, and **www.alienware.com**. Make a final selection and justify why this is the best solution.

Critical Thinking Questions

Instructions: Albert Einstein used *Gedanken experiments*, or critical thinking questions, to develop his theory of relativity. Some ideas are best understood by experimenting with them in our own minds. The following critical thinking questions are designed to demand your full attention but require only a comfortable chair—no technology.

1. **Your Ideal System**

   If you could buy any new system on the market, not worrying about the price, what would you buy? What kind of monitor would you have? How much RAM and CPU? What kind of ports would you require? Which sound system would fit your needs? Would you know how to use your ideal system?

2. **Future Systems**

   Given current trends in technology, what kind of system can you imagine upgrading to or buying new in 10 years? Which components would change the most? Which components would need to stay the same, if any? What do you imagine the entire system would look like?

3. **Impacts of New Technology**

   We are constantly being bombarded with new technology. We hear of new tools and system improvements from our friends, relatives, and advertisements almost daily. This chapter talks about upgrading current systems so that we can take advantage of some of the newer technology. Some improvements we absolutely need (more RAM, perhaps), whereas others we may just really want (such as a Blu-ray burner). What do you think are the societal, economic, and environmental impacts of our wanting to have the latest and greatest computers? Do you think the push toward faster and more powerful machines is a good thing?

4. **New Technologies: Putting Industries at Risk?**

   The Trends in IT feature in this chapter discusses the impact that CD, DVD, and the new Blu-ray technologies have had on the music and entertainment industries. Can you think of other industries that might be at risk because of these new technologies?

5. **Recycling Computers**

   Mercury in screens and switches, cadmium in batteries and circuit boards, and four to eight pounds of lead in CRT monitors are all metals that are environmentally toxic. Discarded machines are beginning to create an e-waste crisis. Who do you think should assume the cost of recycling computers? Should it be the consumer, the government, or the industry? What other options are there besides just throwing older computers away?

6. **System Longevity**

   If you purchase a computer system for business purposes, the Internal Revenue Service (IRS) allows you to depreciate its cost over five years. The IRS considers this a reasonable estimate of the useful lifetime of a computer system. What do you think most home users expect in terms of how long their computer systems should last? How does the purchase of a computer system compare with other major household appliances in terms of cost, value, benefit, life span, and upgrade potential?

Problem:

In a large organization, whether it is a company or a college, the IT department often has to install several different types of computing systems. There certainly would be advantages to having every computer be identical, but because different departments have different needs and items are purchased at different times, it is typical for there to be significant differences between two computers in the same corporation.

Process:

Split your class into teams.

1. Select a department or computer lab on campus (or within your company, at the public library, and so on). *Note:* If you are physically unable to go to the various labs, describe the type of components that would be needed by that particular department. (For example, if you choose the computer art department, you know you will need good graphics software. You also know you will need certain levels of RAM and so forth to accommodate that graphics software.)

2. Following the worksheet in Figure 6.2, analyze the computing needs of that particular computer lab.

3. Using the System Evaluation worksheet (found on the book's Companion Website at **www.prenhall.com/techinaction**), develop a complete systems evaluation of the computers at the lab.

4. Consider possible upgrades in hardware, software, and peripherals that would make this lab better able to meet the needs of its users.

5. Write a report that summarizes your findings. If purchasing a new system is more economical, then recommend which system the lab should buy.

Conclusion:

The pace of technological change can make computer science an uncomfortable field for some. For others, it is precisely the pace of change that is exciting. Being able to evaluate a computer system and match it to the current needs of its users is an important skill.

Multimedia

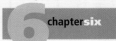

In addition to the review materials presented here, you'll find other materials featured with the book's multimedia, including the Technology in Action Student Resource CD and the Companion Website (**www.prenhall.com/techinaction**), which will help reinforce your understanding of the chapter content. These materials include the following:

ACTIVE HELPDESK

In Active Helpdesk calls, you'll assume the role of helpdesk operator, taking calls about the concepts you've learned in this chapter. You'll apply what you've learned and receive feedback from a supervisor to review and reinforce those concepts. The Active Helpdesk calls for this chapter are as follows and can be found on your Student Resource CD:

- Evaluating Your CPU and RAM
- Evaluating Your Storage Subsystem and Ports

SOUND BYTES

Sound Bytes are dynamic multimedia tutorials that help demystify even the most complex topics. You'll view video clips and animations that illustrate computer concepts and then apply what you've learned by reviewing with the Sound Byte Labs, which include quizzes and activities specifically tailored to each Sound Byte. The Sound Bytes for this chapter are listed here and can be found on your Student Resource CD:

- Using Windows Vista to Evaluate CPU Performance
- Memory Hierarchy Interactive
- Installing RAM
- CD and DVD Reading and Writing Interactive
- Installing a DVD-RW Drive

COMPANION WEBSITE

The *Technology in Action* Companion Website includes a variety of additional materials to help you review and learn more about the topics in this chapter. The resources available at **www.prenhall.com/techinaction** include:

- **Online Study Guide.** Each chapter features an online true–false and multiple-choice quiz. You can take these quizzes, automatically check the results, and e-mail the results to your instructor.
- **Web Research Projects.** Each chapter features a number of Web research projects that ask you to search the Web for information on computer-related careers, milestones in computer history, important people and companies, emerging technologies, and the applications and implications of different technologies.

7

chapter *seven*

Networking and Security:

Connecting Computers and Keeping Them Safe
from Hackers and Viruses

Objectives

After reading this chapter,
you should be able to
answer the following
questions:

1. What is a network, and what are the advantages of setting up one? **(p. 318)**

2. What is the difference between a client/server network and a peer-to-peer network? **(pp. 319–320)**

3. What are the main hardware components of every network? **(pp. 320–322)**

4. What are the most common home networks? **(p. 322)**

5. What are wired Ethernet networks, and how are they created? **(pp. 322–326)**

6. What are wireless Ethernet networks, and how are they created? **(pp. 326–329)**

7. How are power-line networks created, and are they a viable alternative to Ethernet networks? **(p. 330)**

8. How do I configure my computer's software to set up a network? **(pp. 331–335)**

9. How can hackers attack a network, and what harm can they cause? **(pp. 336–340)**

10. What is a firewall, and how does it keep my computer safe from hackers? **(pp. 340–345)**

11. Why are wireless networks more vulnerable than wired networks, and what special precautions are required to ensure my wireless network is secure? **(pp. 345–346)**

12. From which types of viruses do I need to protect my computer? **(pp. 347–350)**

13. What can I do to protect my computer from viruses? **(pp. 350–352)**

ACTIVE HELPDESK

- Understanding Networking **(p. 327)**
- Understanding Firewalls **(p. 344)**
- Avoiding Computer Viruses **(p. 349)**

The Problems of Sharing

The Kato family is facing computer-sharing problems. Koji and Yukari realized that they both needed computers, and they bought their children, Mari and Toshio, their own computers, too. Still, there is trouble in this "paradise."

Scarce Resources: Toshio was using his computer to scan photos for a school Web site project. Just then, his sister Mari burst into his room and demanded to use his scanner because she didn't have one and needed to scan images for an art project. Toshio wouldn't budge. The ensuing shouting match brought their mother, Yukari, to the room. Because both projects were due the next day, Yukari told Toshio he would have to let Mari use the scanner at some point. In exchange, Mari would have to let Toshio use her computer so he could print from the color printer attached to it. Neither teen was happy, but it was the best Yukari could do.

Mobility Issues: Koji and Yukari stared at their network's router. They had it installed in the den where both of their desktop computers were located, and they spent a considerable amount of money having a computer technician run wires from it to Mari and Toshio's rooms so they could be connected, too. But since the teens now both had new notebook computers that they received as back-to-school gifts, they both now disliked being tied down to their rooms for Internet access. Koji had wanted to buy a new wireless router, but Yukari was concerned about the report they just saw on the news about the security issues surrounding wireless networks. How would they know if they were safe from hackers with their network signals floating around the neighborhood?

Virus Attack: Later that night, Koji booted up his computer to make some changes to a marketing plan that he brought home from work. Right away, he noticed that many of his icons had disappeared from his desktop. As he launched Microsoft Word, a message flashed on the screen that read, "The Hacker of Death Was Here!" Suddenly, his screen went black. When he rebooted his computer, it was unable to recognize the hard drive. The next day, Koji called the computer support technician at work and learned he had caught the "Death Squad" virus, which had erased the contents of his hard drive. Koji mused that he should have bought an antivirus program instead of the latest version of World of Warcraft.

If this scenario doesn't exactly reflect the situation in your home now, it may in the future. As the price of computers continues to drop, more families will have multiple home computers. To avoid inconvenience and the expense of redundant equipment, computers need to be able to communicate with each other and share peripherals (such as scanners and printers) and resources (such as Internet connections). Thus, this chapter explores how you can network computers. In addition, you'll learn strategies for keeping unauthorized outsiders from prying into your computer when you're sharing resources with the outside world, as well as how to keep your computer safe from viruses.

SOUND BYTES

- Installing a Computer Network **(p. 322)**
- Installing a Personal Firewall **(p. 340)**
- Securing Wireless Networks **(p. 345)**
- Protecting Your Computer **(p. 351)**

Networking Fundamentals

Although you may not yet have a home network, you use and interact with networks all the time. In fact, every time you use the Internet you're interacting with the world's largest network. But what exactly *is* a network? A computer **network** is simply two or more computers that are connected via software and hardware so that they can communicate with each other. Devices connected to a network are referred to as **nodes**. A node can be a computer, a peripheral (such as a printer), a game console (such as an Xbox 360), a digital video recorder (such as a TiVo), or a communications device (such as a modem). The main function for most networks is to facilitate information sharing, but networks provide other benefits.

What are the benefits of networks? Networks allow users to share peripherals. For example, in Figure 7.1a, the computers are not networked. Computer 1 is connected to the printer, but Computer 2 is not. To print files from Computer 2, users have to transfer them using a flash drive or another storage medium to Computer 1, or they have to disconnect the printer from Computer 1 and connect it to Computer 2. By networking Computer 1 and Computer 2, as shown in Figure 7.1b, both computers can print from the printer attached to Computer 1 without transferring files or moving the printer (although Computer 1 must be powered on).

By networking computers, you can transfer files from one computer to another without using external storage media such as flash drives. And you can set up shared folders in Windows that allow the user of each computer on the network to store files that other computers on the network may need to access, as shown in Figure 7.2.

Can I use a network to share an Internet connection? If you install a device called a *router* on your network, you

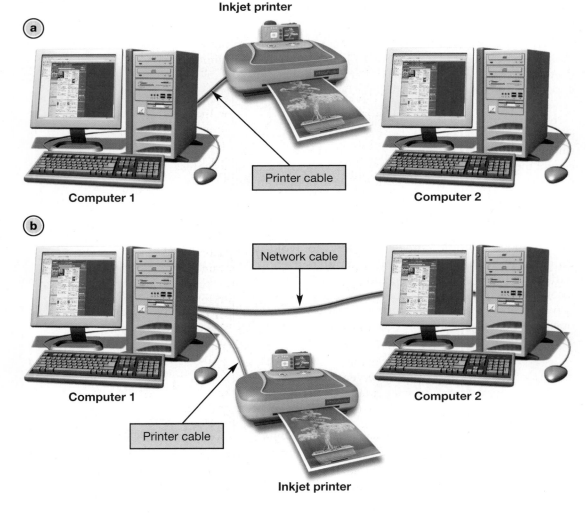

FIGURE 7.1

(a) Computer 1 and Computer 2 are not networked. Only Computer 1 can use the printer unless the printer is disconnected from Computer 1 and reconnected to Computer 2. (b) Computer 1 and Computer 2 are networked. Both computers can use the printer without having to move it.

Inkjet printer

a

Printer cable

Computer 1

Computer 2

b

Network cable

Computer 1

Computer 2

Printer cable

Inkjet printer

can share broadband Internet connections. Unfortunately, dial-up connections don't have sufficient bandwidth to support sharing an Internet connection. We'll discuss routers in detail later in the chapter.

Network Architectures

The term **network architecture** refers to the design of a network. Network architectures are classified according to the way in which they are controlled and the distance between their nodes.

DESCRIBING NETWORKS BASED ON NETWORK ADMINISTRATION

What do we mean by networks being "administered"? A network can be administered (or run) in either of two main ways: locally or centrally. A peer-to-peer network is the most common example of a locally administered network. The most common type of centrally administered network is a client/server network.

What are peer-to-peer networks? In **peer-to-peer (P2P) networks**, each node connected to the network can communicate directly with every other node on the network instead of having a separate device exercise central control over the entire network. Thus, all nodes on this type of network are in a sense peers. When printing, for example, a computer on a P2P network doesn't have to go through the computer that's connected to the printer. Instead, it can communicate directly with the printer. Figure 7.1b shows a very small peer-to-peer network.

Because they are simple to set up, P2P networks are the most common type of home network. We discuss different types of peer-to-peer networks that are popular in homes later in this chapter.

What are client/server networks? Very small schools and offices may have P2P networks. However, most networks that have 10 or more nodes are client/server networks. A **client/server network** contains two different types of computers: clients and servers. The **client** is the computer on which users accomplish specific tasks (such as construct spreadsheets) and make specific requests (such as printing a file). The **server** is the computer that provides information or

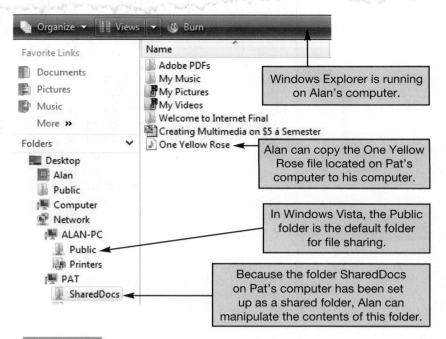

Windows Explorer is running on Alan's computer.

Alan can copy the One Yellow Rose file located on Pat's computer to his computer.

In Windows Vista, the Public folder is the default folder for file sharing.

Because the folder SharedDocs on Pat's computer has been set up as a shared folder, Alan can manipulate the contents of this folder.

FIGURE 7.2

This Windows network has two computers attached to it: ALAN-PC, which is running Windows Vista, and PAT, which is running Windows XP. The Public and the SharedDocs folders have been enabled for file sharing. When Alan is working on his computer, he can easily access the files located in the shared directory on Pat's computer such as the file called One Yellow Rose.

resources to the client computers on the network. The server on a client/server network also provides central administration for functions on the network (such as printing). Figure 7.3 illustrates a client/server network in action.

As you learned in Chapter 3, the Internet is an example of a client/server network. When your computer is connected to the Internet, it is functioning as a client computer. When connecting to the Internet through an Internet service provider (ISP), your computer connects to a server computer maintained by the ISP. The server "serves up" resources to your computer so that you can interact with the Internet.

Are client/server networks ever used as home networks? Although client/server networks can be configured for home use, P2P networks are more often used in the home because they cost less than client/server networks and are easier to configure and maintain. To set up a client/server network in your home, you have to buy an extra computer to act as the server. Although a computer could function both as a server and a client, its performance would be significantly degraded because of the

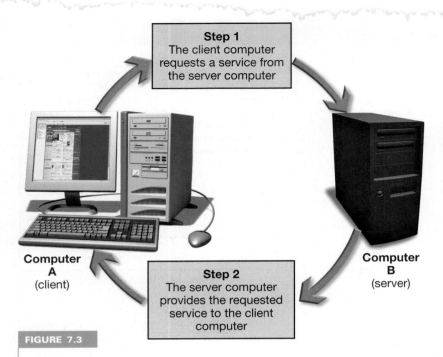

Step 1
The client computer requests a service from the server computer

Computer A (client)

Step 2
The server computer provides the requested service to the client computer

Computer B (server)

FIGURE 7.3

In a client/server network, a computer acts as either a client making requests for resources or as a server providing resources.

complexity of the server-related functions it would have to perform. Therefore, it is impractical to use a single computer as both a client and a server. In addition, you need training to install and maintain the special software required by client/server networks.

The major benefits a client/server network provides (such as centralized security and administration) are not necessary in most home networks. However, because of the expansion of media files on home computers (from digital cameras, camcorders, music downloads, etc.), home server options are now being marketed. Windows Home Server and Sony's media servers, although not as fully featured as servers used in business networks, are becoming more popular choices for managing an entire family's personal media.

DESCRIBING NETWORKS BASED ON DISTANCE

How does the distance between nodes define a network? The distance between nodes on a network is another way to describe a network. **Local area networks (LANs)** are networks in which the nodes are located within a small geographic area. Examples include a network in your home or a computer lab at school.

Is it possible to connect LANs together? Wide area networks (WANs) are made up of LANs connected over long distances. Say a school has two campuses

(east and west) located in different towns. Connecting the LAN at the east campus to the LAN at the west campus (by telecommunications lines) would allow the users on the two LANs to communicate. The two LANs would be described as a single WAN.

Are wireless networks that cover large portions of cities considered WANs? Technically, wireless networks like the one deployed in Philadelphia, which is designed to provide access to city residents and visitors, are WANs. However, when a network is sponsored by a government entity to provide access to a specific geographic area, these networks are usually called *metropolitan area networks (MANs)*. Many cities in the United States are now deploying MANs to provide access to residents and provide convenience for tourists.

Network Components

To function, all networks include (1) a means of connecting the nodes on the network (by cables or wireless technology), (2) special devices that allow the nodes to communicate with each other and to send data, and (3) software that allows the network to run. We discuss each of these components next (see Figure 7.4).

TRANSMISSION MEDIA

How are nodes on a network connected? All network nodes (computers and peripherals) are connected to each other and to the network by **transmission media**. A transmission medium establishes a communications channel between the nodes on a network and can take several forms:

1. Networks can use existing wiring, such as power lines, to connect nodes.
2. Networks can use additional cable to connect nodes, such as twisted pair cable, coaxial cable, or fiber-optic cable. You have probably seen twisted pair and coaxial cable. Normal telephone wire is **twisted pair cable** and is made up of copper wires that are twisted around each other and surrounded by a plastic jacket. If you have cable TV, the cable running into your TV or cable box is **coaxial cable**. Coaxial cable consists of a single copper wire surrounded by layers of plastic. **Fiber-optic cable** is made up of plastic

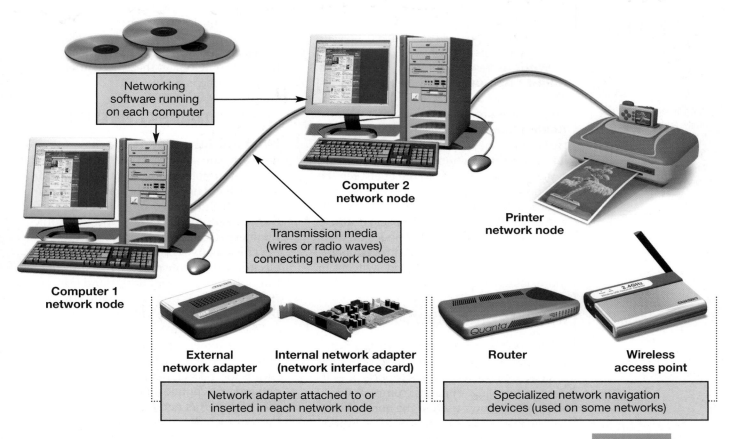

Networking software running on each computer

Computer 2 network node

Printer network node

Transmission media (wires or radio waves) connecting network nodes

Computer 1 network node

| External network adapter | Internal network adapter (network interface card) | Router | Wireless access point |

Network adapter attached to or inserted in each network node

Specialized network navigation devices (used on some networks)

FIGURE 7.4

Network Components

or glass fibers that transmit data at extremely fast speeds.

3. Wireless networks use radio waves instead of wires or cable to connect nodes.

Do all modern networks transfer data quickly? Different types of transmission media transmit data at different speeds. **Data transfer rate** (also called **bandwidth**) is the maximum speed at which data can be transmitted between two nodes on a network. **Throughput** is the actual speed of data transfer that is achieved and is usually less than the data transfer rate. Data transfer rate and throughput are usually measured in megabits per second (Mbps). A megabit, when applied to data transfer rates, represents 1 million bits. Twisted pair cable, coaxial cable, and wireless media provide enough bandwidth for most home networks, whereas fiber-optic cable is sometimes used in client/server networks.

NETWORK ADAPTERS

How do the different nodes on the network communicate? Network **adapters** are devices connected to or installed in network nodes that enable the nodes to communicate with each other and to access the network. Most desktop and notebook computers (and many peripherals) sold today contain network adapters installed *inside* as expansion cards. These adapters are referred to as **network interface cards (NICs)**.

What if I don't have a network adapter installed inside my computer? Network adapters are also available as external devices that plug into an available USB port. These are often used to provide older computing devices with wireless connectivity. We discuss network adapters in more detail throughout the chapter.

NETWORK NAVIGATION DEVICES

How is data sent through a network? Data is sent over transmission media in bundles called **packets**. For computers to communicate, these packets of data must be able to flow between computers. **Network navigation devices** help make this data flow possible. These devices, which are attached to the network, enable the transmission of data. Some simple peer-to-peer networks do not require network navigation devices because

SOUND BYTE

Installing a Computer Network

Installing a network is relatively easy if you've seen someone else do it. In this Sound Byte, you'll learn how to install the hardware and configure Windows for a wired or wireless home network.

the network adapters serve that purpose. More sophisticated networks need specialized navigation devices.

What network navigation devices might I use on my home network? The two most common specialized navigation devices are routers and switches. **Routers** transfer packets of data between two or more networks. For example, if a home network is connected to the Internet, a router is required to send data between the two networks (the home network and the Internet). **Switches** are the "traffic cops" of networks. They receive data packets and send them to their intended nodes on the same network (not between different networks). We discuss routers and switches in more detail later in the chapter.

NETWORKING SOFTWARE

What software do home networks require? Home networks need operating system (OS) software that supports peer-to-peer networking. The most common versions of Windows used in the home (Vista Home Basic or Premium, XP Home Edition, and 2000) support P2P networking. You can connect computers running any of these OSs to the same network. Mac OS X and the various versions of Linux also support P2P networking.

Is the same software used in client/server networks? Client/server networks, on the other hand, are controlled by a central server that has specialized **network operating system (NOS)** software installed on it. This software handles requests for information, Internet access, and the use of peripherals for the rest of the network nodes. Examples of NOS software include Windows Server 2008 and SUSE Linux Enterprise.

Types of Peer-to-Peer Networks

The most common type of network you will probably encounter is a peer-to-peer network, because this is the network you would set up in your home. Therefore, we'll focus on P2P networks in this chapter. There are three main types of P2P networks:

1. wired Ethernet networks,
2. wireless Ethernet networks, and
3. power-line networks.

The major differences in these networks are the transmission media by which the nodes are connected. In the following sections, we will look at these networks and how each one is set up.

WIRED ETHERNET NETWORKS

What are Ethernet networks? **Ethernet networks** are so named because they use the Ethernet protocol as the means (or standard) by which the nodes on the network communicate. The Ethernet protocol was developed by the Institute of Electrical and Electronics Engineers (IEEE). This nonprofit group develops many standard specifications for electronic data transmission that are adopted throughout the world. Each standard the IEEE develops is numbered, with 802.3 being the standard for wired Ethernet networks.

The Ethernet protocol makes Ethernet networks extremely efficient at moving data. However, to achieve this efficiency, the algorithms for moving data through an Ethernet network are complex. Because of this complexity, Ethernet networks require additional devices such as switches and routers.

Ethernet networks are slightly more complicated to set up than other home network options, but they're faster, more reliable, and less expensive, making them the most popular choice for home networks. Although 100 Mbps Ethernet networks are most commonly installed in homes, prices are falling quickly on 1-gigabit-per-second (1 Gbps, or 1,000 Mbps) Ethernet components. In fact, home computers now routinely ship with 1 Gb Ethernet equipment preinstalled. The potential high throughput of Gigabit Ethernet is useful if you're moving around large files such as downloaded movies on your home network.

How do I create an Ethernet network? An Ethernet network requires that you install or attach network adapters to each computer or peripheral you want to connect to the network. Because Ethernet networks are so common, most computers sold today come with Ethernet adapters preinstalled. As noted earlier, such internal network adapters are referred to as *network interface cards (NICs)*. Modern Ethernet NICs are usually 10/100/1000 Mbps cards (see Figure 7.5a). This means they can handle the old 10 Mbps and 100 Mbps data transfer rates as well as the newer 1 Gbps data transfer rate.

If your computer doesn't have a NIC (or the NIC installed in your motherboard fails), you can buy one and install it or you can use a USB adapter, which you plug into any open USB port on the system unit (see Figure 7.5b). Although you can use USB versions in notebooks, PC Card versions of Ethernet NICs are made especially for notebooks (see Figure 7.5c). PC Cards are about the size of a credit card and fit into specially designed slots on a notebook. However, most new notebooks include built-in Ethernet adapters.

How are nodes connected on wired Ethernet networks? The most popular transmission media option for wired Ethernet networks is **unshielded twisted pair (UTP) cable**. UTP cable is composed of four pairs of wires that are twisted around each other to reduce electrical interference. You can buy UTP cable in varying lengths with RJ-45 connectors (Ethernet connectors) already attached. RJ-45 connectors resemble standard phone connectors (called *RJ-11 connectors*) but are slightly larger, as shown in Figure 7.6.

Do all wired Ethernet networks use the same kind of UTP cable? Figure 7.7 lists the three main types of UTP cable used in home-wired Ethernet networks—Cat 5, Cat 5E, and Cat 6—and their data transfer rates. In general, it's better to install Cat 5E cable than Cat 5 because they're about the same price, and installing Cat 5E cable enables you to take advantage of higher-bandwidth Ethernet systems when upgrading equipment. However, if you're planning on using a Gigabit Ethernet network, use Cat 6 cable, which supports higher throughput. Cat 7 cable is designed for Ultra-Fast Ethernet (10 Gigabit Ethernet) networks that run at speeds as fast as 10 Gbps. Installing a 10 Gigabit Ethernet network in the home is probably unnecessary because home applications don't require this level of data transfer rate.

Is UTP cable difficult to install? UTP cable is no more difficult to install than normal phone cable. You just need to take a few precautions. Avoid putting sharp bends into the cable when running it around corners because this can damage the copper wires inside and lead to breakage. Also, run the cable around the perimeter of the room

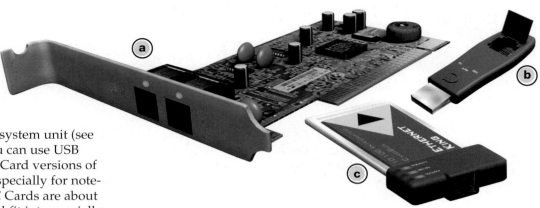

FIGURE 7.5

Ethernet network adapters come in a variety of versions, including (a) a 100/1000 NIC, which is installed in an expansion slot inside the system unit; (b) a USB adapter, which you plug into an open USB port; and (c) a PC Card, which you slide into a specially designed slot on a notebook.

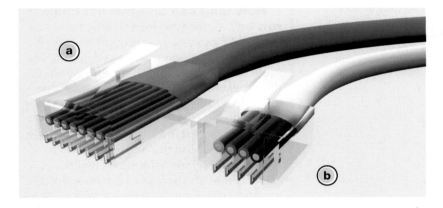

FIGURE 7.6

(a) An RJ-45 (Ethernet) connector, which is used on UTP cable; and (b) a typical RJ-11 connector, which is used on standard phone cord. Note that the RJ-45 is larger and has contacts for eight wires (four pairs) instead of four wires. You must use UTP cable with RJ-45 connectors on an Ethernet network because a phone cable will not work.

FIGURE 7.7 Data Transfer Rates for Popular Network Cable Types

UTP Cable Category	Data Transfer Rate
Category 5 (Cat 5)	As fast as 100 Mbps
Category 5E (Cat 5E)	100 to 1,000 Mbps
Category 6 (Cat 6)	1,000 Mbps (1 Gbps) and higher
Category 7 (Cat 7)	10 Gbps and higher

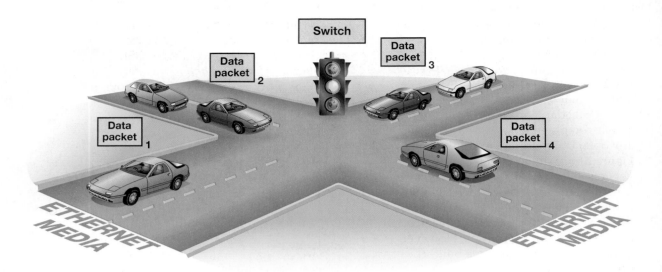

Switch

Data packet 2

Data packet 1

Data packet 3

Data packet 4

ETHERNET MEDIA

ETHERNET MEDIA

FIGURE 7.8

Switches (working in conjunction with NICs) act like traffic signals. They enforce the rules of the data road on an Ethernet network and help prevent data packets from crashing into each other.

(instead of under a rug, for example) to avoid damaging the wires from foot traffic.

How long can an Ethernet cable run be? Cable runs for Ethernet networks using UTP cable can't exceed 100 meters (328 feet) or the signal starts to degrade. For cable runs of more than 100 meters, you can use **repeaters**, devices that are installed on long cable runs to amplify the signal. In effect, repeaters act as signal boosters. Repeaters can extend run lengths to 600 feet, but they do add to the cost of a network. When possible, use continuous lengths of cable. Although two cables can be spliced together with a connecting jack, this presents a source of failure for the cable, because connectors can loosen in the connecting jack and moisture or dust can accumulate on the contacts. Usually, extending your wired network using wireless technology is a better option than using repeaters or splicing cable.

ETHERNET SWITCHES

How do Ethernet networks use switches? Data is transmitted through the wires of an Ethernet network in packets. Imagine the data packets on an Ethernet network as cars on a road. If there were no traffic signals or rules of the road (such as driving on the right-hand side), we'd see a lot more collisions between vehicles, and people wouldn't get where they were going as readily (or at all). Data packets can also suffer collisions. If data packets collide, the data in them is damaged or lost. In either case, the network doesn't function efficiently.

As shown in Figure 7.8, a switch in an Ethernet network acts like a traffic signal by enforcing the rules of the data road on the transmission media. The switch keeps track of the data packets and, in conjunction with network interface cards, helps the data packets find their destination without running into each other. This keeps the network running efficiently.

Switches are often mistakenly referred to as *hubs*. A hub, though, is a network navigation device that merely retransmits a signal to all other nodes attached to it. Switches, on the other hand, are essentially "smart hubs" because they transmit data only to the node to which it should be sent. When Ethernet networks first came out, switches were much more expensive than hubs, so many home networks used hubs, but today there is virtually no cost differential. Therefore, most navigation devices sold for home networks are switches (even if they are mistakenly referred to as hubs).

How many computers and peripherals can be connected to a switch? Switches are differentiated by the number of ports they have for connecting network devices. Four- and eight-port switches are often used in home networks. A four-port switch can connect a maximum of four devices to the network, whereas an eight-port switch can handle eight devices. You should buy a switch that has enough ports for all the devices you want to connect to the network. Many people buy switches with more ports than they currently need so that they can expand their network in the future.

A wonderful feature of switches is that you can chain them together. Usually, one port on a switch is designated for plugging into a second switch. You can chain two four-port switches together to provide connections for a total of six devices. Most switches can be chained to provide hundreds of ports, which would far exceed the needs of most home networks, but may provide you with needed expandability in a small business network.

ETHERNET ROUTERS

How does data from an Ethernet network get shared with the Internet or another network? As mentioned earlier, routers are devices that transfer packets of data between two or more networks. If a home network is connected to the Internet, then you need a router to send data between the home network and the Internet.

Because so many people are sharing Internet access in home networks, manufacturers are making devices that combine switches and routers and that are specifically designed to connect to DSL or cable modems. These are often referred to as **DSL/cable routers**. If you want your Ethernet network to connect to the Internet through a DSL or cable modem, then obtaining a DSL/cable router is a good idea. Because you already need a switch to connect multiple devices on an Ethernet network, these routers (which include switching capabilities) fulfill a dual role by controlling your network traffic and allowing your Internet connection to be shared. Figure 7.9 shows an example of an Ethernet network configured using a DSL/cable router.

Besides computers, what other devices can I attach to a router? Because sharing peripherals is a major benefit of installing a network, many peripheral devices, such as scanners and printers, now come with Ethernet capability installed. Such devices are usually described as network-ready devices. A **network-ready device** can

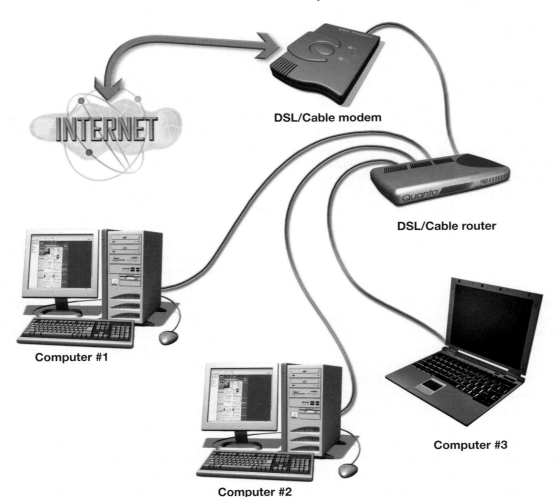

DSL/Cable modem

INTERNET

DSL/Cable router

Computer #1

Computer #2

Computer #3

FIGURE 7.9

This configuration shows two desktop computers and a notebook connected to a DSL/cable router. This configuration allows all three computers to share a broadband Internet connection easily.

BITS AND BYTES

Surfing in Public? Beware of Social Engineering Tactics

You're at the coffee shop working on a project on your notebook, and you notice that the person sitting next to you is staring at your screen. It is just idle curiosity on their part, or do they have a more nefarious motive? As more and more users go wireless, the potential for cyber-crimes increases. Social engineering refers to a group of activities that essentially trick users into divulging sensitive information through ordinary communication means such as conversations and e-mail.

Shoulder surfing, which involves looking over someone's shoulder while they type in access codes on notebooks—or enter calling card numbers at pay phones—can be a problem in any public place. Sometimes, less-than-honest people are more overt in obtaining your personal information. Pretexting is the act of creating an invented scenario (the pretext) to convince someone to divulge information. Although usually done over the telephone, this can easily be done in

person. Travelers at airports and people at coffee shops all around the country are often trying to connect computers to public wireless networks; when they do connect, other people may be around to take advantage of them. A friendly person pretending to be an airport employee, for example, may ask you to divulge password or other sensitive information on the pretext of helping you make a wireless connection.

And now that USB drives are so inexpensive, many would-be thieves leave them around in public places loaded with software designed to capture sensitive information when a curious person picks it up and inserts it into their USB port.

So be wary of your surroundings when using electronic devices in public so you don't fall victim to these scams. Don't accept advice from strangers and never divulge any passwords or access codes to anyone even if they appear to be helpful.

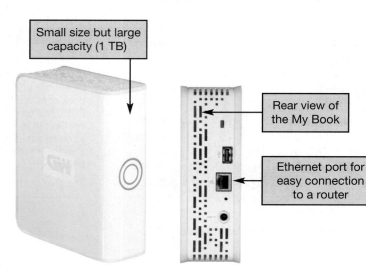

Small size but large capacity (1 TB)

Rear view of the My Book

Ethernet port for easy connection to a router

FIGURE 7.10

The My Book World Edition is an NAS device from Western Digital that can store 1 TB of data in a device the size of a small book.

be connected directly to a router instead of connecting it to a computer on the network. These devices can then be accessed by any computer on the network.

Network attached storage (NAS) devices are also becoming popular in home networks. People are generating tremendous quantities of digital data today with digital cameras and camcorders, and these digital files need to be stored. Although they could be stored on individual hard drives in computers on a network, NAS devices provide for centralized data storage and access.

Popular for years on business networks, NAS devices are specialized computing devices designed to store and manage data. You can think of them as specialized external hard drives. NAS devices, like the My Book series from Western Digital, connect directly to the network through a router or switch. Specialized software can then be installed on computers attached to the network to ensure that all data saved to an individual computer is also stored on the NAS as a backup. Aside from creating backups, NAS devices facilitate the sharing of files such as movies, music, and digital photos. Some NAS devices, such as the one from Western Digital shown in Figure 7.10, are accessible over the Internet, making it possible to retrieve your data wherever you have an Internet connection.

WIRELESS ETHERNET NETWORKS

What is a wireless network? A **wireless network** uses radio waves instead of wires or cables as its transmission media. Just as it established the 802.3 standard for wired Ethernet networks, the IEEE has established standards for wireless Ethernet networks. Current wireless networks in the

United States are based on the **802.11 standard**, which was established in 1997. The 802.11 standard is also known as **WiFi** (short for *wireless fidelity*).

Four standards are currently defined under 802.11: 802.11a, 802.11b, 802.11g, and 802.11n (in use but not yet ratified by IEEE members as of the publication of this text). The main differences between these standards are the maximum data transfer rates and the types of security that they support. For home networking, 802.11g and 802.11n are the standards most commonly used.

The 802.11g standard, which supports a data transfer rate of 54 Mbps, is a well established standard for home use because it is much faster than the original 802.11b standard. Before 802.11n was developed, many manufacturers also introduced products in the Super G (also called Extreme G or Enhanced G) category, which can be confusing to buyers. These devices were still based on the 802.11g standard but used proprietary hardware and software tweaks to increase the maximum data transfer rate to 108 Mbps. However, because Super G is not standards-based (that is, it is not based on its own IEEE standard), Super G devices from one manufacturer might not work with those of another manufacturer.

Despite 802.11n not being ratified by the IEEE, devices have been released in advance of the 802.11n standard ratification. Such devices are labeled as *pre-n* or *draft-n.* Proprietary versions of 802.11n routers are also on the market called Extreme N (or Xtreme N). These devices may not necessarily work with devices based on the final approved 802.11n standard. However, as 802.11n devices usually achieve much higher throughput (in excess of 100 Mbps) than 802.11g devices with signal coverage over a much wider area, a pre-n device might be just what you need to get good wireless coverage throughout your home. With all devices that adhere to an unapproved standard (such as pre-n devices), it is critical to buy all the components from one manufacturer to ensure they work correctly together. To check the status of standard approvals, go to **www.ieee.org**.

What do I need to set up a wireless network? Just like other networks, each node on a wireless network requires a **wireless network adapter**. If not built into the motherboard of the computer, these adapters are available as NICs that are inserted into expansion slots on the computer (see Figure 7.11a) or as USB devices that plug into an open USB port (see Figure 7.11b). Most notebooks today come with a built-in 802.11g or 802.11 draft-n network adapter.

Wireless network adapters differ from other network adapters in that they contain transceivers. A **transceiver** is a device that translates the electronic data that needs to be sent along the network into radio waves and then broadcasts these radio waves to other network nodes. Transceivers serve a dual function because they also receive the signals from other network nodes. As shown in Figure 7.11, many add-on wireless network adapters have antennae poking out of them, which are necessary for the transmission and reception of these radio waves.

Do all nodes on the wireless network have to be computers? A node on a wireless network can also be a peripheral device such as a printer, storage device, or scanner. The peripheral will need to be connected to a wireless network adapter so that other nodes on the network can communicate with it.

How do I share an Internet connection on a wireless network? Just as with wired Ethernet networks, wireless Ethernet networks require the installation of

FIGURE 7.11

Wireless network adapters added to desktop computers have antennae. If your computer came with an internal wireless network card, it will not have an antenna sticking out of it. Wireless network adapters are available as (a) NICs, which are inserted into an open expansion slot on the computer, or as (b) USB devices, which plug into an open USB port.

ACTIVE HELPDESK

Understanding Networking

In this Active Helpdesk call, you'll play the role of a helpdesk staffer, fielding calls about home networks—their advantages, the main components, and the most common types of home networks—as well as about wireless networks and how they are created.

a router to share an Internet connection. A **wireless router** (sometimes called a **gateway**) is a device that combines the capabilities of a wired router with the ability to receive wireless signals. Note that it is important that you do not mistakenly buy a wireless access point (which we discuss later) instead of a wireless router because a wireless access point does not perform the same function.

What types of problems can I run into when installing wireless networks? The maximum range of wireless devices under the 802.11g standard is about 250 feet. However, as the distance between nodes increases, throughput decreases markedly. Draft-n equipment provides greater bandwidth over longer distances.

Also, 802.11g devices work on a bandwidth of 2.4 GHz. This is the same bandwidth that many cordless phones use, so your phone and wireless network may interfere with each other. The best solution is to buy a cordless phone that uses a bandwidth of 5 GHz, or you can purchase 802.11n equipment, which uses the 5 GHz band.

Obstacles between wireless nodes also decrease throughput. Walls and large metal objects are the most common sources of interference with wireless signals. For example, placing a computer with a wireless network adapter next to a refrigerator may prevent the signals from reaching the rest of the network. And a node that has four walls between it and the Internet connection will most likely have lower than the maximum throughput. The 802.11n devices have much better range than 802.11g devices and are less susceptible (but not immune) to interference.

What if a node on the network can't communicate with other nodes or with the router? Repositioning the node or the wireless network adapter within the same room (sometimes even just a few inches from the original position) can often affect communication between the nodes. If this doesn't work, try moving the computers closer together or to other rooms in your house. Many newer routers support the addition of external antennae, which are either directional (focus signal in a certain direction) or omnidirectional (spread the signal out over a wide area). If you have a single problem area, plugging a directional antenna into your router and placing the antenna as close to the problem area as possible and facing directly toward it may solve the reception problem.

If these solutions don't work, then you may need to add a wireless access point. A **wireless access point (WAP)** is a device that attaches to a network and provides wireless nodes (such as a notebook with a wireless NIC installed) with a means of wirelessly connecting to the network. When you have connection problems (say the notebook on your porch can't connect to the wireless router), adding a WAP to the network will often solve the problem. Essentially, you're extending the range of the wireless network by providing a second point to which nodes can connect to the network. The WAP must be connected to the network either directly to the switch on the router or to another node that is within range of the router.

For example, as you can see in Figure 7.12, Notebook C on the back porch and

FIGURE 7.12

With a wireless access point installed on Computer B, data can travel from Notebook C (on the back porch) to the wireless router (in the bedroom).

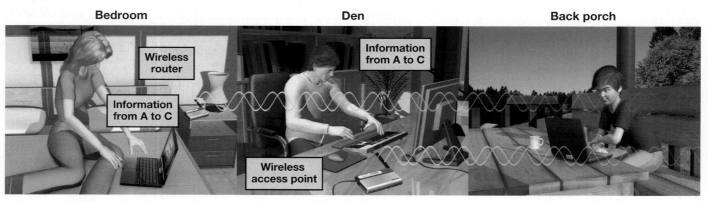

Bedroom · Den · Back porch

Wireless router

Information from A to C

Information from A to C

Wireless access point

Computer A with wireless network adapter — Computer B with wireless access point — Notebook C with wireless network adapter

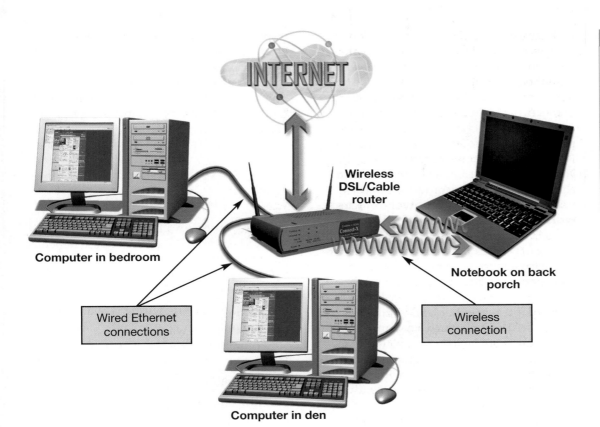

INTERNET

Wireless DSL/Cable router

Computer in bedroom

Wired Ethernet connections

Computer in den

Notebook on back porch

Wireless connection

FIGURE 7.13

Using a wireless DSL/cable router, the computers in the den and bedroom still maintain a high-speed wired Ethernet connection. However, the notebook can connect to the network wirelessly and be used in many areas of the home.

the wireless router (connected to Computer A in the bedroom) can't make contact. However, Notebook C can connect to Computer B in the den. By connecting a WAP to Computer B, all traffic from Notebook C is relayed to the wireless router through the WAP connected to Computer B.

Can I have wired and wireless nodes on one network? Many users want to create a network in which some computers (such as desktops) connect to the network with wires, whereas other computers (such as notebooks) connect to the network wirelessly. Most wireless DSL/cable routers allow you to connect wireless and wired nodes to the same network. This type of router contains both a WAP and ports that allow you to connect wired nodes to the router. Figure 7.13 shows an example of a network with a wireless DSL/cable router attached. As you can see, the notebook maintains a wireless connection to the router, whereas the other two computers are connected by wires. Using this type of router is a cost-effective way to have some wireless connections while preserving the high-speed attributes of wired Ethernet where needed.

BITS AND BYTES

One Brand Equals Fewer Headaches

Networking standards set by organizations such as the IEEE make it easier for manufacturers to produce devices that work with a variety of computers and peripherals. In theory, such standards should benefit consumers as well because equipment from different manufacturers should work together when placed on the same network. The reality, however, is that devices from different manufacturers—even if they follow the same standards—don't always work together perfectly because manufacturers sometimes introduce proprietary hardware and software that deviate from the standards (such as in the case of Super G or Extreme N wireless). This means that a wireless NIC from manufacturer A might not work with a DSL/cable router from manufacturer B. The safe course of action is to use equipment manufactured by the same company or at least save your packaging and receipt in case you need to return a component that doesn't work with the rest of your network.

POWER-LINE NETWORKS

What are power-line networks? Power-line networks use the existing electrical wiring in your home to connect the nodes in the network. Thus, in a power-line network, any electrical outlet provides a network connection. The HomePlug Power Line Alliance (**www.homeplug.org**) sets standards for home power-line networking. The original power-line networks had a maximum data transfer rate of 14 Mbps. However, recently adopted new standards provide for power-line networks with data transfer rates approaching 200 Mbps, which can make them a viable alternative to wireless or wired Ethernet.

How do I create a power-line network? To create a power-line network, you connect a power-line network adapter (similar to a network adapter in an Ethernet network) to each computer or peripheral that you're going to attach to the network (see Figure 7.14). You can buy power-line network adapters in either USB or Ethernet versions. After you attach a network adapter to each node on the network, you plug the adapters into an electrical outlet. Most power-line network adapters will be recognized automatically by the Windows operating system.

Why would I use a power-line network instead of an Ethernet network? Because of the low bandwidth of the original power-line networks and the lower costs of Ethernet networks, power-line networks declined in popularity. However, with the introduction of power-line equipment that supports much higher data throughput, power-line networks are becoming popular again. So if you're in a situation in which running new wires is impractical and you're experiencing too much interference to run a wireless network, you may want to consider installing a power-line network.

Choosing a Peer-to-Peer Network

If you're setting up a home network, the type of network you should choose depends on your particular needs. In general, consider the following factors in determining your network type:

- whether existing wiring is available,
- whether you want wireless communications,
- how fast you want your network connection to be, and
- how much money you can spend on your network.

What if I want to use existing wiring for my home network? As noted earlier, you can use power lines (electrical wiring) as media for a home network. Obviously, you need an electrical outlet available in each room where you want to connect a node to the network. Because you have to plug most nodes (computers, printers, and so on) into an electrical outlet to operate them anyway, connecting a power-line network is usually convenient. However, these networks might be more expensive than wired or wireless Ethernet networks.

What are the pros and cons of wireless networks? Wireless networks free you from having to run wires in your home. In addition, you can use any flat surface as a workstation. However, wireless networks may not work effectively in every home, so you need to install and test the wireless network to figure out whether it will work. To avoid unnecessary expenses, make sure you can return equipment for a refund if it doesn't work properly in your home.

Which network provides the highest data transfer rate? Most routine home computing tasks such as Web browsing and e-mailing require minimal throughput (less than 10 Mbps is sufficient). However, if

Plug the adapter into any power outlet to create a network of up to 16 nodes.

Connection to computers or peripherals is easily achieved by plugging in a standard Ethernet cable.

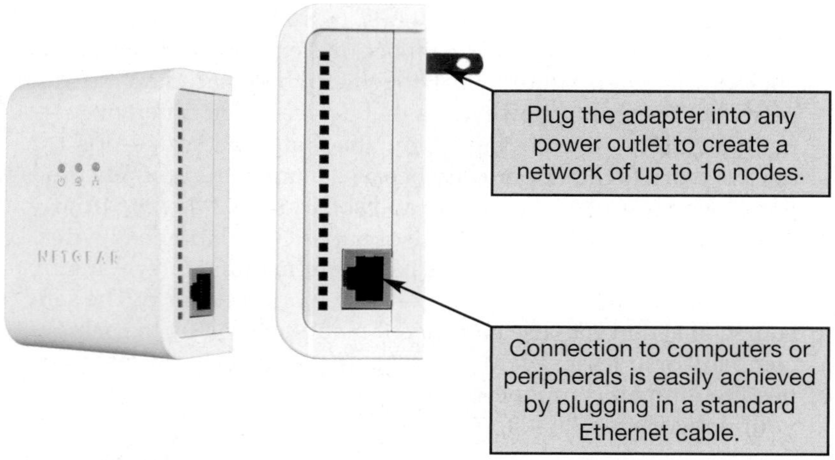

FIGURE 7.14

Power-line adapters such as the Netgear HDX101 plug into any electrical outlet and are then connected to your computer (or peripheral) via an Ethernet cable. Although maximum throughput of 200 Mbps is usually unattainable, the throughput is often superior to 802.11g wireless networks.

high-speed data transmission is important (for example, if you play computer games or exchange large files), then you may want a network with high throughput. With data transfer rates as high as 1,000 Mbps, wired Ethernet networks are the fastest home networks. You may want to consider a Gigabit network if you engage in a lot of multiplayer gaming or transfer of video. Without high throughput, streaming video can appear choppy, games can respond slowly, and files can take a long time to transfer.

What cost factors do I need to consider in choosing a network? You may need to consider your budget when deciding what type of network to install. Figure 7.15 lists the approximate costs of installing the various types of peer-to-peer networks and their various advantages and disadvantages.

Do I need to consider the type of broadband connection I have? Whether you connect to the Internet by DSL, cable, or satellite makes no difference in terms of the type of network you select. The differences occur with your particular network's hardware and software requirements.

Configuring Software for Your Home Network

Once you install the hardware for your network, you need to configure your operating system software for networking on your computers. In this section, you'll learn how to do just that using special Windows tools. Although configuration is different with Mac OS X, the setup is quick and easy. Linux, though not insurmountable, is the most complex operating system to configure for a home network.

Is configuring software difficult? Windows Vista makes configuring software relatively simple by almost automating the

FIGURE 7.15 Comparing the Major Types of Home Networks

	Wired			Wireless	
	100 Mbps Ethernet	**Gigabit Ethernet**	**Power-Line**	**802.11g**	**802.11n**
Maximum data transfer rate (bandwidth)	100 Mbps	1,000 Mbps or 1 Gbps	200 Mbps	54 Mbps	540 Mbps
Actual expected throughput	50 to 60 Mbps	500 to 600 Mbps	100 Mbps	15 to 25 Mbps	150 to 200 Mbps
Operational frequency	N/A	N/A	N/A	2.4 GHz	5 GHz
Cost of basic access point, router or switch	$40 to $60 (switch)	$100 to $200 (switch)	$100 to $200 (adapter or router)	$30 to $60	$80 to $150
Pros	Mature, proven technology; low cost	Fastest practical home technology available	No additional wiring required	Backward-compatible with 802.11b devices and significantly faster	Significantly faster than 802.11g
Cons	Cat 5E wiring required. Can be expensive to install hidden wiring.	Cat 5E or 6 wiring required. Can be expensive to install hidden wiring.	May not have outlets in the correct locations.	Interference from walls and other structures can cause signal to degrade (especially over greater distances).	Products based on final standard may not be backward-compatible.

Source: Table adapted from "Pump Up Your Home Network" by Erik Rhey, *PC Magazine*, October 3, 2006.

entire process of setting up a network using various wizards. As you learned in Chapter 4, a wizard is a utility program included with Microsoft software that you can use to help you accomplish a specific task. You can launch the Vista wizards from the Network and Sharing Center, which can be accessed via the Control Panel. Before running any wizards, you should do the following:

1. Install network adapters on each node.
2. For a wired network, plug all the cables into the router, network adapters, and so on.
3. Make sure your cable/DSL modem is connected to your router and that it is connected to the Internet.

4. Turn on your equipment in the following order (allowing the modem and the router each about one minute to power up and configure):

   a. your cable/DSL modem,

   b. your router, and

   c. all computers and peripherals (printers, scanners, and so on).

Completing these steps enables the wizards to make decisions about how best to configure your network. After you have completed these steps, open the Network and Sharing Center from the Control Panel (see Figure 7.16a). From there, select *Set up a connection or network* (see Figure 7.16b) to access the Vista networking wizards. *Note:* If you already have a wired network set up and are connected to the Internet, plugging your Vista computer into the router is all you need to do. Vista will automatically detect an existing wired network.

What if I don't have Windows Vista on all my computers? Windows XP and Windows Vista are the most common OSs found in the home that support P2P networking. Therefore, you can network these computers with other computers using Windows Vista. If you have one computer with Windows Vista but your other computers run on other versions of Windows, then you should set up your Windows Vista computer first. Windows Vista can automatically detect computers running other versions of Windows on your network; however, you may have to make adjustments to the non-Vista computers on your network to enable them to see the Windows Vista computers on your network (such as installing Windows XP Service Pack 2 or 3). Check the Microsoft Web site for instructions.

What if I don't have Windows Vista on any of my computers? Windows XP features wizards for setting up wired and wireless networks just like Windows Vista does. If you're networking all Windows 2000 machines, however, there is no wizard, so you have to set up your computers manually. Various resources on the Internet can assist you in setting up Windows 2000 networks. Not surprisingly, one of the best resources is the Microsoft Web site (**www.microsoft.com**).

How do I differentiate my computers on my network? When you set up your Windows Vista computer, you gave it a

BITS AND BYTES

Wireless Hot Spots—Convenient but Exercise Caution

Public places such as Starbucks where you can wirelessly connect to the Internet are known as *hot spots*. Sometimes the service is free; other times there is a small charge. How can you tell? Just fire up your wireless-equipped notebook or PDA, start your browser, and try to access a Web site. If the service is not free, the store's "wireless gateway sentinel" software provides you with rates and an opportunity to pay for access. Either way, you are surfing in minutes while enjoying your latte.

Some cities are installing WiFi equipment to turn large areas—sometimes entire cities—into hot spots. One of the largest hot spots in the United States covers 700 square miles surrounding the rural town of Hermiston, Oregon. Philadelphia and San Francisco are among the major cities that have undertaken citywide WiFi initiatives.

Because most hot spots are designed to be easily found and recognized by computers, however, they often offer little or no security. User data can be visible to anyone using the networks and is often transmitted as clear text. Hackers will often use packet sniffers (software designed to intercept and read the contents of data packets) on unsecured wireless networks in an attempt to gather sensitive data such as access codes and credit card numbers. Therefore, when you are surfing on a public hot spot, never engage in sensitive transactions that involve revealing credit card numbers or other personal information. Also, hackers sometimes set up their own hot spots to look like they are provided by retail establishments. Check with employees to verify the name of the legitimate network to which you should be connecting.

Going out of town and need to know where you can find a hot spot? Visit a site that offers hot spot directories such as **www.wifinder.com**, **www.wififreespot.com**, or **www.jiwire.com**. But make sure to use common sense and surf carefully!

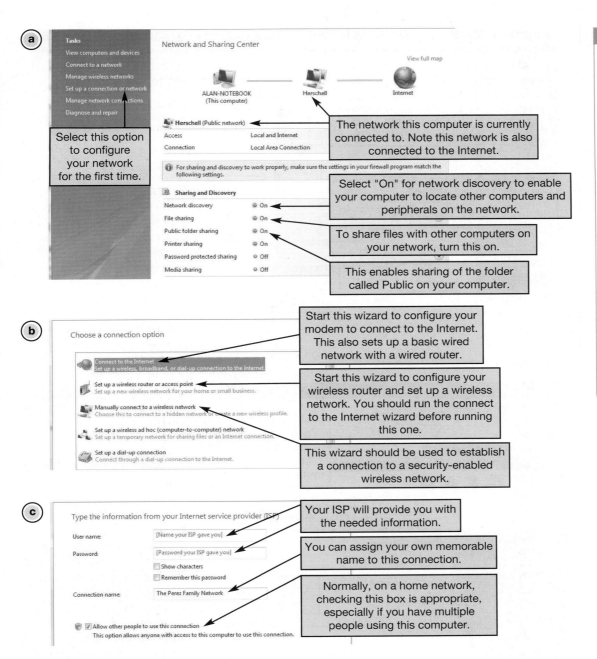

(a) Network and Sharing Center

Tasks
View computers and devices
Connect to a network
Manage wireless networks
Set up a connection or network
Manage network connections
Diagnose and repair

ALAN-NOTEBOOK (This computer) — Herschell — Internet

View full map

Herschell (Public network)
Access   Local and Internet
Connection   Local Area Connection

For sharing and discovery to work properly, make sure the settings in your firewall program match the following settings.

Sharing and Discovery
Network discovery   On
File sharing   On
Public folder sharing   On
Printer sharing   On
Password protected sharing Off
Media sharing   Off

Select this option to configure your network for the first time.

The network this computer is currently connected to. Note this network is also connected to the Internet.

Select "On" for network discovery to enable your computer to locate other computers and peripherals on the network.

To share files with other computers on your network, turn this on.

This enables sharing of the folder called Public on your computer.

(b) Choose a connection option

Connect to the Internet
Set up a wireless, broadband, or dial-up connection to the Internet.

Set up a wireless router or access point
Set up a new wireless network for your home or small business.

Manually connect to a wireless network
Choose this to connect to a hidden network or create a new wireless profile.

Set up a wireless ad hoc (computer-to-computer) network
Set up a temporary network for sharing files or an Internet connection.

Set up a dial-up connection
Connect through a dial-up connection to the Internet.

Start this wizard to configure your modem to connect to the Internet. This also sets up a basic wired network with a wired router.

Start this wizard to configure your wireless router and set up a wireless network. You should run the connect to the Internet wizard before running this one.

This wizard should be used to establish a connection to a security-enabled wireless network.

(c) Type the information from your Internet service provider (ISP)

User name: [Name your ISP gave you]
Password: [Password your ISP gave you]
                  Show characters
                  Remember this password
Connection name: The Perez Family Network

Allow other people to use this connection
This option allows anyone with access to this computer to use this connection.

Your ISP will provide you with the needed information.

You can assign your own memorable name to this connection.

Normally, on a home network, checking this box is appropriate, especially if you have multiple people using this computer.

FIGURE 7.16

(a) The **Network and Sharing Center** in Windows Vista helps you configure your home network. (b) Selecting **Set up a connection or network** provides you access to wizards that will assist you. (c) Fill in the information provided by your ISP, give the connection a name, and check the box to allow all users of the computer to access the connection. The wizard will then set up your connection and connect your computer to the Internet.

>The Windows **Network and Sharing Center** is found in the **Control Panel**.

name. Each computer on a network needs a unique name (different from the names of all other computers on the network) so that the network can identify it. This unique name ensures that the network knows which computer is requesting services and data so that the data can be delivered to the correct computer. Also, computers on a network can be located in various workgroups. For simplicity on a home network, you should assign all your computers to the same workgroup. If you don't recall your computer's name or the workgroup to which it is assigned, open the Control Panel and click the System icon (see Figure 7.17). You will be able to change the name of the computer or the workgroup from here.

Is that it? Assuming you installed and configured everything properly, your home network should be up and running, allowing you to share files, Internet connections, and peripherals. Most routers will work fine right out of the box. However, with some routers you may have to alter the configuration to connect to the Internet.

How do I set up my router so that I can use it to connect to the Internet? First, contact your ISP to help you with any special settings that may be needed to configure your router to work

FIGURE 7.17

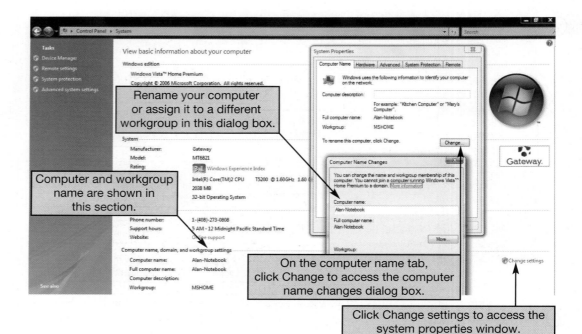

Accessing the System screen from the Control Panel allows you to check your computer and workgroup name and change it if necessary.

>The **Windows System** screen can be accessed by clicking the **System** icon in the **Control Panel**.

Rename your computer or assign it to a different workgroup in this dialog box.

Computer and workgroup name are shown in this section.

On the computer name tab, click Change to access the computer name changes dialog box.

Click Change settings to access the system properties window.

FIGURE 7.18

Although setups differ from router to router, basic information such as the logon information and the type of IP addressing is required to configure the router to work with your network and your ISP.

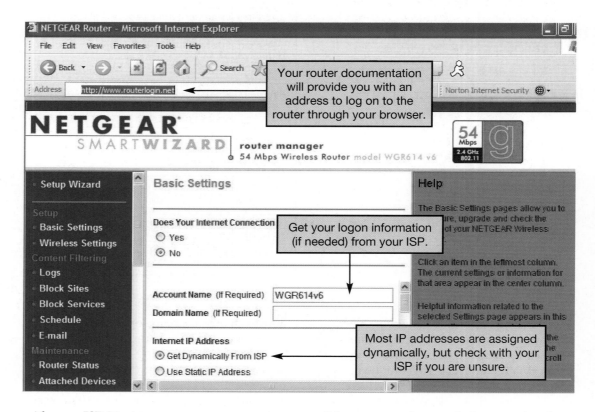

Your router documentation will provide you with an address to log on to the router through your browser.

Get your logon information (if needed) from your ISP.

Most IP addresses are assigned dynamically, but check with your ISP if you are unsure.

with your ISP. Next, you can access your router from Internet Explorer (or another Web browser) by entering the router's IP address or default URL. You can usually find this information in the documentation that came with the router. You'll also need a username and password to log on to the router, both of which you'll also find in the documentation that came with the router.

Many routers feature their own wizard (which is different from the Windows Networking wizards) that takes you through unique configuration screens. A sample screen from a Netgear router is shown in Figure 7.18. If you're unsure of any information that needs to be entered to configure the router, call your ISP and ask for guidance.

Ethics: Don't Let Data Walk Out the Front Door

The weakest link in any computer security system is the user. Whether using your home network or the computer system at your workplace, you have the potential to do the most damage through unsafe computing practices such as surfing questionable sites, downloading infected files from unscrupulous file sharing sites, or accepting CD-ROMs (maybe with free music or games) from strangers and then running them on the company network, thereby causing infection. Flash drives are another threat. Because these devices are everywhere and are so inexpensive, they are often used (either intentionally or unintentionally) to infect computer networks. Think you won't fall victim to this security threat? Think again!

Secure Network Technologies, a security consulting firm, decided to test a client's security procedures by leaving 20 flash drives at random locations around the client's office. By the end of the day, employees had picked up 15 of the flash drives and plugged them into computers on the company network. The flash drives contained a simple program to display images as well as a Trojan horse program. While employees were viewing the images, the consultants were able to access the company network (if they wanted to do so) and steal or compromise data. It isn't hard to imagine hackers leaving flash drives around your company to act as their way into your company's network.

Another problem that flash drives pose is theft of data or intellectual property. With the devices being so portable and now coming in such large capacities, it is easy for a disgruntled employee to literally walk out the front door with stacks of valuable documents tucked right in his or her pants pocket. Industrial espionage has never been easier . . . no spy cameras are needed!

So what should companies do to prevent their data from being compromised or stolen via flash drives? First, educate employees to the dangers posed by portable media devices, and other untrusted media, and create policies regulating the use of media in the workplace. Second, all computers in the company need to have security measures installed such as personal firewalls or antivirus software. The firewalls should be able to prevent malicious programs from running, should they be introduced to the computer. Last, administrators should lock down and monitor the use of USB devices. Although Microsoft networking software allows network administrators to shut off access on computers to their USB ports, this prevents employees from using flash drives and other USB devices for legitimate purposes.

Other software products, such as DeviceLock and Safend, can be deployed on a network to provide options such as:

- detailed security policies,
- monitoring USB device connections, and
- tracking users who connected devices to the network (including devices other than flash drives).

And don't forget to inform the employees that the use of these devices is being monitored. That alone is enough to scare many employees from connecting untrusted devices to the network.

In the next section, we explore how you can protect your computers and your network from intruders and hackers.

Keeping Your Home Computer Safe

The media is full of stories about computer viruses damaging computers, criminals stealing people's identities online, and attacks on corporate Web sites that have brought major corporations to a standstill. These are examples of **cybercrime**, which is formally defined as any criminal action perpetrated primarily through the use of a computer. The existence of cybercrime means that computer users must take precautions to protect themselves.

Who perpetrates computer crimes? **Cybercriminals** are individuals who use computers, networks, and the Internet to perpetrate crime. Anyone with a computer and the wherewithal to arm themselves with the appropriate knowledge can be a cybercriminal.

How serious a problem is cybercrime in the United States? The Internet Crime Complaint Center (IC3) is a partnership between the Federal Bureau of Investigation (FBI) and the National White Collar Crime Center (NW3C). In 2006 (the latest year for which data is available), IC3 processed more than 200,400 complaints related to Internet crime. Many complaints were fraud-related, such as auction fraud, nondelivery of ordered items, and credit and debit card fraud. Nonfraud-related complaints pertained to issues such as computer intrusions, unsolicited email, and child pornography. The majority of complaints (more than 44 percent) were related to Internet auction fraud, which is a growing problem. In the next sections, we discuss cybercriminals and the damage they can wreak on your computer. We also discuss methods for protecting your computer from attacks.

Computer Threats: Hackers

Although there is a great deal of disagreement as to what a hacker actually is (especially among hackers themselves), a **hacker** is most commonly defined as anyone who unlawfully breaks into a computer system, whether an individual computer or a network (see Figure 7.19).

Are there different kinds of hackers? Some hackers are offended by being labeled as criminals and therefore attempt to divide hackers into classes. Many

hackers who break into systems just for the challenge of it (and who don't wish to steal or wreak havoc on the systems) refer to themselves as **white-hat hackers**. They tout themselves as experts who are performing a needed service for society by helping companies uncover the vulnerabilities in their systems.

These white-hat hackers look down on those hackers who use their knowledge to destroy information or for illegal gain. These hackers are known as **black-hat hackers**. (The terms *white hat* and *black hat* are references to old Western movies in which the heroes wore white hats and the outlaws wore black hats.) Regardless of the hackers' opinions, the laws in the United States and in many other countries consider any unauthorized access to computer systems a crime.

What about the teenage hackers who get caught every so often? These amateur hackers are often referred to as **script kiddies**. Script kiddies don't create programs used to hack into computer systems; instead, they use tools created by skilled hackers that enable unskilled novices to wreak the same havoc as professional hackers. Unfortunately, it is easy to find these tools on the Web.

Fortunately, because the users of these programs are amateurs, they're usually not

FIGURE 7.19

Although not necessarily destroying civilization, hackers can cause problems for corporations and individuals alike.

BRINGING CIVILIZATION TO ITS KNEES...

BITS AND BYTES

Be Careful When Joining Social Networking and Video Sites

Making contacts and meeting friends online has never been easier. Social networking services such as MySpace (**www.myspace.com**) and Facebook (**www.facebook.com**) are signing up users at a rapid pace. And YouTube (**www.youtube.com**) allows you to post videos of yourself and your friends. These services have you list personal information about yourself (interests, hobbies, photos, what school you attend, and so on) and encourage you to list connections to your friends. When your friends log on and view your profile, they can see themselves and long chains of other acquaintances. The idea is that your friends can see who else you know and get you to make appropriate introductions (or do it themselves).

Although the sites offer fairly tight protection of personal information (such as not revealing last names), think carefully about making your personal information visible on the site and be wary of disclosing additional information to people you meet online. Often children and young adults, who account for a large percentage of the users on these sites, are too trusting about revealing personal information. Cybercriminals are combing these sites with the sole purpose of using the information to perpetrate identity theft. Therefore, always avoid giving out personal information such as your full name, address, Social Security number, and financial information to people you have never met. Also, be careful when uploading videos of you and your friends. Identity thieves often like to steal younger people's identities because it often takes longer for the theft to be detected.

Finally, be wary of accepting computer files from people you've met online because these files could contain viruses or other malware. Just because you meet someone who is a friend of a friend of your second cousin doesn't mean that person isn't a hacker or a scam artist. So, enjoy meeting new people, but exercise the appropriate amount of caution.

---

proficient at covering their electronic tracks. Therefore, it's relatively easy for law enforcement officials to track them down and prosecute them. Still, script kiddies can cause a lot of disruption and damage to computers, networks, and Web sites before they're caught.

Why would a hacker be interested in breaking into my home computer? Some hackers just like to snoop. They enjoy the challenge of breaking into systems and seeing what information they can find. Other hackers are hobbyists seeking information about a particular topic wherever they can find it. Because many people keep proprietary business information on their home computers, hackers bent on industrial espionage may break into home computers. For other hackers, hacking is a way to pass time.

WHAT HACKERS STEAL

Could a hacker steal my credit card number? If you perform financial transactions online such as banking or buying goods and services, then you probably do so using a credit card. Credit card and bank account information can thus reside on your hard drive and may be detectable by a hacker. Also, many sites that you access require you to provide a logon ID and password to gain access. Even if this data is not stored on your computer, a hacker may be able to capture it when you're online by using a packet sniffer.

What's a packet sniffer? As you learned earlier, data travels through the Internet in small pieces called *packets*. The packets are identified with a string of numbers, in part to help identify the computer to which they are being sent. Once the packets reach their destination, they are reassembled into cohesive messages. A **packet sniffer** is a program that looks at (or sniffs) each packet as it travels on the Internet—not just those that are addressed to a particular computer, but all packets. Some packet sniffers are configured to capture all the packets into memory, whereas others capture only certain packets that contain specific content (such as credit card numbers). Wireless networks can be particularly vulnerable to this type of exploitation.

What do hackers do with the information they "sniff"? Once a hacker has your credit card information, he or she can either use it to purchase items illegally or sell the number to someone who will. Also, if a hacker steals the logon ID and password to an account where you have your credit card

BITS AND BYTES

Prevention of Identity Theft . . . Don't Overlook Photocopiers!

We are constantly bombarded with identity theft warnings regarding suspicious e-mail, phishing sites, and telephone scams. But many people are unaware that photocopiers present potential danger for identity theft. This is because most photocopiers manufactured today contain hard drives just like your computer. Documents are scanned, stored on the hard drive, and then printed by the copier. So, unless the copier has been specially configured to have the hard drive overwritten to destroy data or to use encryption, copies of your tax return may be lurking on the public copier at your local library or copy shop that you used before mailing your returns to the IRS. A clever hacker could retrieve a wealth of potential information off of just one public copy machine.

So what should you do to protect yourself? Ask the local copy shop or the IT department at your office about the security measures they have set up on their copiers before you use them to copy sensitive documents. If you are buying a copier for your business, investigate security options that are available to protect your employees. And for small copying jobs (like your tax return), consider buying an all-in-one device (printer, copier, scanner, fax machine) for your home office because you can more easily keep that machine protected from wily hackers.

hackers need to control many computers at the same time. To this end, hackers often use Trojan horses to install other programs on computers. A **Trojan horse** is a program that appears to be something useful or desirable (like a game or a screen saver), but at the same time does something malicious in the background without your knowledge. The term *Trojan horse* derives from Greek mythology and refers to the wooden horse that the Greeks used to sneak into the city of Troy and conquer it. Therefore, computer programs that contain a hidden (and usually dreadful) "surprise" are referred to as Trojan horses.

What damage can Trojan horses do? Often, the malicious activity perpetrated by a Trojan horse program is the installation of **backdoor programs** that allow hackers to take almost complete control of your computer without your knowledge. Using a backdoor program, hackers can access and delete all files on your computer, send e-mail, run programs, and do just about anything else you can do with your computer. Computers that hackers control in this manner are referred to as **zombies**.

DENIAL OF SERVICE ATTACKS

What else can hackers do? Hackers can also launch an attack from your computer called a **denial-of-service (DoS) attack**. In a denial-of-service attack, legitimate users are denied access to a computer system because a hacker is repeatedly making requests of that computer system through a computer he or she has taken over as a zombie. Computers can handle only a certain number of requests for information at one time. When they are flooded with requests in a denial-of-service attack, they shut down and refuse to answer any requests for information, even if the requests are from legitimate users. Thus, the computer is so tied up responding to the bogus requests for information that authorized users can't gain access.

Couldn't a DoS attack be traced back to the computer that launched it? Launching a DoS attack on a computer system from one computer is easy to trace. Therefore, most savvy hackers use a **distributed denial-of-service (DDoS) attack**. DDoS attacks are automated attacks that are launched from more than one zombie at the same time. Figure 7.20 illustrates how a

information stored (such as eBay or Amazon), then he or she can use your accounts to purchase items and have them shipped to him or herself instead of you. If hackers can gather enough information in conjunction with your credit card information, then they may be able to commit **identity theft**. Identity theft is characterized by someone using personal information about you (such as your name, address, and social security number) to assume your identity for the purpose of defrauding others.

Although this sounds scary, you can protect yourself from packet sniffing by simply installing a firewall and using data encryption (converting data into a form that is difficult for unauthorized persons to decode), which we discuss later in this chapter.

TROJAN HORSES

Is there anything else hackers can do if they break into my computer? Hackers often use individuals' computers as a staging area for mischief. To perpetrate widespread computer attacks, for example,

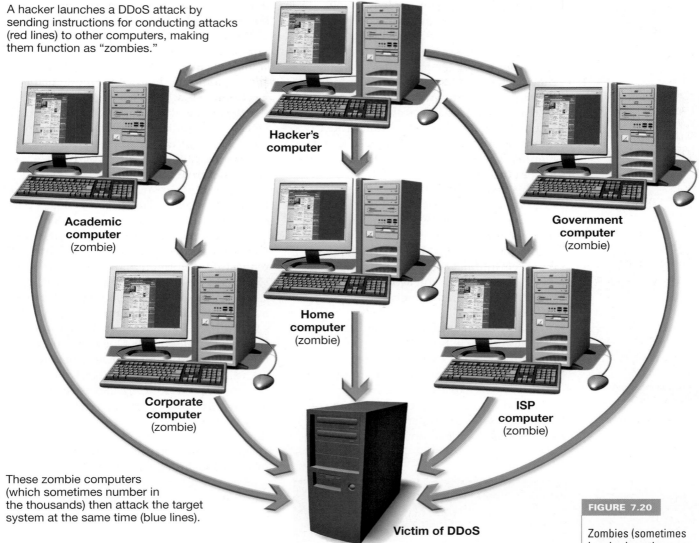

A hacker launches a DDoS attack by sending instructions for conducting attacks (red lines) to other computers, making them function as "zombies."

Hacker's computer

Academic computer (zombie)

Government computer (zombie)

Home computer (zombie)

Corporate computer (zombie)

ISP computer (zombie)

These zombie computers (which sometimes number in the thousands) then attack the target system at the same time (blue lines).

Victim of DDoS

FIGURE 7.20

Zombies (sometimes hundreds or thousands of them) can be used to facilitate a distributed denial of service (DDoS) attack.

DDoS attack works. A hacker creates many zombies (sometimes hundreds or thousands) and coordinates them so that they begin sending bogus requests to the same computer at the same time. Administrators of the victim computer often have a great deal of difficulty stopping the attack because it comes from so many computers. Often the attacks are coordinated automatically by botnets, which direct software programs (called *robots* or *bots*) that run autonomously on zombie computers. Some botnets have been known to span 1.5 million computers.

DDoS attacks are a serious problem. In January 2008, Scientology Web sites found themselves the victims of DDoS attacks by a group that called itself "Anonymous" and whose members are linked to an anti-Scientology campaign called Project Chanology. In February 2007, users of online games such Return to Castle Wolfenstein, Halo, Counter-Strike, and many others found they could not access the games because of a DDoS attack by the "RUS" hacker group. This DDoS attack was launched from more than one thousand different computers mostly located in former Soviet Union countries such as Russia, Uzbekistan, and Belarus. Because many Web sites receive revenue directly from users (such as subscriptions to online games) or indirectly (such as Web surfers clicking on advertisements), DDoS attacks can be financially distressing for the owners of the affected Web sites.

HOW HACKERS GAIN ACCESS

How exactly does a hacker gain access to a computer? Hackers
can gain access to computers directly or

SOUND BYTE

Installing a Personal Firewall

Firewalls provide excellent protection against hackers on a home network. In this Sound Byte, you'll learn how to install and configure software firewalls to protect your computer.

FIGURE 7.21

Open logical ports are an invitation to hackers.

indirectly. Direct access involves sitting down at a computer and installing hacking software. This rarely occurs in your home. However, to deter unauthorized use, you may want to lock the room that your computer is in or remove key components (such as the power cord) when strangers (repairmen and so on) are in your house and may be unobserved for periods of time. You might also set up your computer so that it requires a password for a user to gain access to your desktop.

The most likely method a hacker will take to access a computer is indirectly through its Internet connection. When connected to the Internet, your computer is potentially open to attack by hackers. Many people forget that their Internet connection is a two-way street. Not only can you access the Internet, but also people on the Internet can access your computer.

Think of the computer as a house. Common sense tells you to lock your doors and windows when you aren't home to deter theft. Hooking your computer up to the Internet is like leaving the front door to your house wide open. Anyone passing by can access your computer and poke around for valuables. Your computer obviously

doesn't have doors and windows like a house, but it does have logical ports.

What are logical ports? Logical **ports** are virtual—that is, not physical—communications gateways or paths that allow a computer to organize requests for information (such as Web page downloads, e-mail routing, and so on) from other networks or computers. Unlike physical ports (USB, FireWire, and so on), you can't see or touch a logical port; it is part of a computer's internal organization.

Logical ports are numbered and assigned to specific services. For instance, logical port 80 is designated for hypertext transfer protocol (HTTP), the main communications protocol (or standard) for the Internet. Thus, all requests for information from your browser to the Web flow through logical port 80. E-mail messages sent by simple mail transfer protocol (SMTP), the protocol used for sending e-mail on the Internet, are routed through logical port 25. Open logical ports, like open windows in a home, invite intruders, as illustrated in Figure 7.21. Unless you take precautions to restrict access to your logical ports, other people on the Internet may be able to access your computer through them.

Fortunately, you can thwart most hacking problems by installing a firewall.

Computer Safeguards: Firewalls

Firewalls are software programs or hardware devices designed to keep computers safe from hackers. Firewalls specifically designed for home networks are called **personal firewalls** and are made to be easy to install. By using a personal firewall, you can close open logical ports to invaders and potentially make your computer invisible to other computers on the Internet.

Firewalls are named after a housing construction feature. When houses were first being packed densely into cities (attached to each other with common walls), fire was a huge hazard because wood (the major construction component for houses) burns readily. An entire neighborhood could be lost in a single fire. Thus, builders started building common walls of nonflammable or slow-burning material to stop, or at least slow, the spread of fire. These came to be known as firewalls.

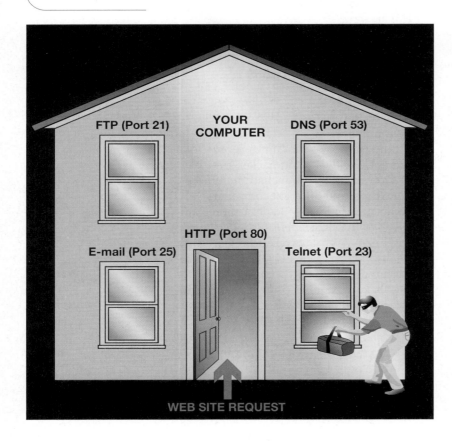

FTP (Port 21)   YOUR COMPUTER   DNS (Port 53)

HTTP (Port 80)

E-mail (Port 25)   Telnet (Port 23)

WEB SITE REQUEST

Computers in Society: Identity Theft—Is There More Than One You Out There?

You've no doubt heard of identity theft. A thief steals your name, address, Social Security number, and bank account and credit card information and runs up debts in your name. This leaves you holding the bag as you're hounded by creditors collecting on the fraudulent debts. It sounds horrible—and it is. In fact, one of the authors of this textbook had his identity stolen and spent about 50 hours filing police reports, talking to credit agencies, closing bogus accounts, and convincing companies that the $25,000 of debt run up on six bogus credit card accounts was done by an identity thief. Many victims of identity theft spend months (or even years) trying to repair their credit and eliminate fraudulent debts. And if an identity thief uses your identity to obtain medical services at a hospital, you may find yourself denied coverage later on because the thief's treatment has exceeded the limit of covered services on your policy.

Stories of identity theft abound in the media—such as the Long Island, New York, man accused of stealing more than 30,000 identities—and should serve to make the public wary. However, many media pundits would have you believe that the only way your identity can be stolen is by a computer. This is simply not true. The U.S. Federal Trade Commission (**www.ftc.gov**) has identified the following as methods thieves use to obtain others' personal information. Identity thieves may:

1. steal purses and wallets in which people often keep unnecessary valuable personal information such as their ATM PIN codes;
2. steal mail or look through trash for bank statements and credit card bills, which provide valuable personal information; and
3. pose as bank or credit card company representatives and trick people into revealing sensitive information over the phone.

Although none of these methods involve using a computer, you're at risk from online attacks, too. For example, you can give personal information to crooks by responding to bogus e-mails purportedly from your bank, credit card company, or ISP in a practice known as *phishing*. Once identity thieves obtain your personal information, they can use it in many different ways.

- Identity thieves can request a change of address for your credit card bill or bank statement. By the time you realize that you aren't receiving your statements, the thieves have rung up bogus charges on your account or emptied your bank account.

- They can open new credit card accounts in your name.
- They can open bank accounts in your name and write bad checks, ruining your credit rating.
- They can take out mortgages in your name and then disappear with the proceeds, leaving you with the debt.
- They can counterfeit bank cards or checks for your legitimate accounts.

Although foolproof protection methods don't exist, the following precautions will help you minimize your risk:

1. Never reveal your password or PIN code to anyone or place it in an easy-to-find location.
2. Never reveal personal information unless you're sure that a legitimate reason exists for a business to know the information and you can confirm you're actually dealing with a legitimate representative. Banks and credit card companies usually request information by standard mail, not over the phone or online. If someone calls or e-mails asking you for personal information, decline and call the company where you opened your account.
3. Create hard-to-guess passwords for your accounts. Use a combination of letters and numbers and avoid using obvious passwords such as first or last names, birth dates, and so on.
4. When shopping online, be wary of unfamiliar merchants whom you can't contact through a mailing address or phone number or businesses whose prices are too good to be true. These can be attempts to collect your personal information for use in fraudulent schemes.

If you have been the victim of identity theft, most states now allow you to freeze your credit history so that no new accounts can be opened until you lift the credit freeze. Even if you live in a state where you can't freeze your account, you can still place an extended fraud alert on your credit history for seven years, which also warns merchants that they should check with you (at your home address or phone number) before opening an account in your name.

Using common sense and keeping personal information in the hands of as few people as possible are the best defenses against identity theft. For additional tips on preventing identity theft or for procedures to follow if you are a victim, check out the U.S. federal government site on identity theft at **www.consumer.gov/idtheft**.

DIG DEEPER

How Firewalls Work

Firewalls are designed to restrict access to a network and its computers. Firewalls protect you in two major ways: by blocking access to logical ports and by keeping your computer's network address secure.

To block access to logical ports, firewalls examine data packets that your computer sends and receives. Data packets contain information such as the address of the sending and receiving computers and the logical port that the packet will use. Firewalls can be configured so that they filter out packets sent to specific logical ports in a process referred to as **packet filtering**.

For example, file transfer protocol (FTP) programs are a typical way in which hackers access a computer. If a firewall is configured to ignore *all* incoming packets that request access to port 21 (the port designated for FTP traffic), no FTP requests will get through to your computer. This process is referred to as **logical port blocking**. If port 21 were a window on your home, you would have effectively locked it so that a burglar couldn't get in. If you need port 21 for a legitimate purpose, you could instruct the firewall to allow access to that port for a specified period of time or by a certain user.

For the Internet to share information seamlessly, data packets must have a way of getting to their correct location. Therefore, all computers connected to the Internet have a unique address. These addresses are called **Internet Protocol addresses** (or **IP addresses**). As noted earlier, data packets contain the IP address of the computer to which they are being sent. Routing servers on the Internet make sure the packets get to the correct address. This is similar to the way addresses work on a conventional letter. A unique street address (such as 123 Main St., Anywhere, CA 99999) is placed on the envelope and the postal service routes it to its correct destination. Without such addressing, data packets, like letters, would not reach the intended recipients.

IP addresses are assigned when users log on to their Internet service provider (ISP) in a procedure known as **dynamic addressing**, which is illustrated in Figure 7.22. IP addresses are assigned out of a pool of available IP addresses licensed to the ISP. Because hackers use IP addresses to find victims and come back to their computers for more mischief, frequently switching IP addresses helps make users less vulnerable to attacks.

However, because many broadband (cable and DSL) users leave their modems on for long periods of time (consecutive days or weeks), their IP addresses tend to

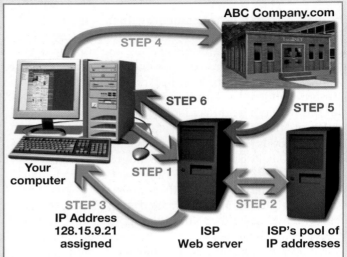

STEP 1: When you connect to your ISP, your computer requests an IP address.

STEP 2: The ISP's Web server consults its list of available IP addresses and selects one.

STEP 3: The selected IP address is communicated to your computer. The address remains in force for as long as you are connected to the ISP.

STEP 4: Once on the Internet, your Web browser requests access to ABC Company's Web site.

STEP 5: The ABC Company server consults an IP address listing and determines that the IP address of your computer is assigned to your ISP. It then forwards the requested information to the ISP's Web server.

STEP 6: The ISP's Web server knows to whom it assigned the IP address and therefore forwards the requested information on to your computer.

FIGURE 7.22

How Dynamic Addressing Works

change less frequently than those of dial-up users. This is similar to having an IP address assigned by **static addressing** (your IP address is always the same and is assigned by your ISP) which is often used by businesses who are hosting a Web site. When broadband users have a static address (one that changes less frequently than a true dynamic address, which changes every time), they are more vulnerable to hackers because the hackers have a more permanent IP address with which

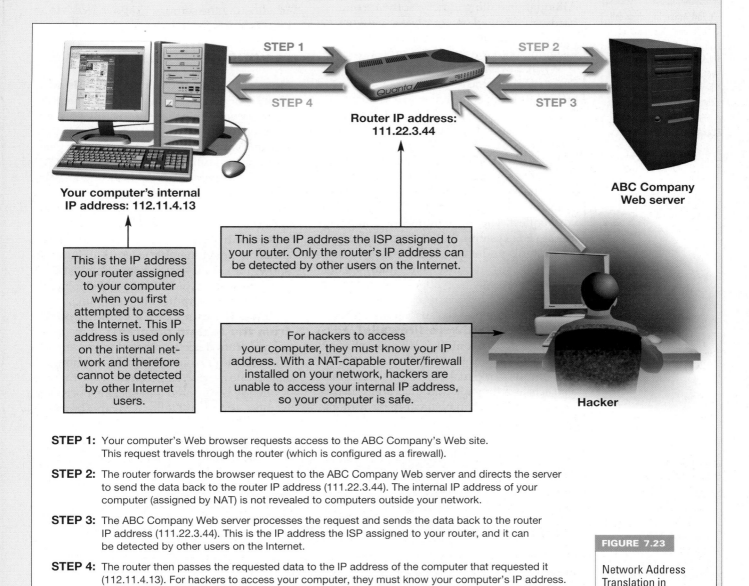

Your computer's internal IP address: 112.11.4.13

This is the IP address your router assigned to your computer when you first attempted to access the Internet. This IP address is used only on the internal network and therefore cannot be detected by other Internet users.

Router IP address: 111.22.3.44

This is the IP address the ISP assigned to your router. Only the router's IP address can be detected by other users on the Internet.

ABC Company Web server

For hackers to access your computer, they must know your IP address. With a NAT-capable router/firewall installed on your network, hackers are unable to access your internal IP address, so your computer is safe.

Hacker

STEP 1: Your computer's Web browser requests access to the ABC Company's Web site. This request travels through the router (which is configured as a firewall).

STEP 2: The router forwards the browser request to the ABC Company Web server and directs the server to send the data back to the router IP address (111.22.3.44). The internal IP address of your computer (assigned by NAT) is not revealed to computers outside your network.

STEP 3: The ABC Company Web server processes the request and sends the data back to the router IP address (111.22.3.44). This is the IP address the ISP assigned to your router, and it can be detected by other users on the Internet.

STEP 4: The router then passes the requested data to the IP address of the computer that requested it (112.11.4.13). For hackers to access your computer, they must know your computer's IP address. With a NAT-capable router/firewall installed on your network, hackers are unable to access your internal IP address, so your computer is safe.

FIGURE 7.23

Network Address Translation in Action

to locate the computer. It also makes it easier for hackers to make repeated visits to a computer.

To combat the problems associated with static addressing, firewalls use a process called **network address translation (NAT)** to assign internal IP addresses on a network. These internal IP addresses are not shared with other devices that aren't part of the network, so the addresses are safe from hackers. Figure 7.23 shows how NAT works. You can use NAT in your home by purchasing a firewall with NAT capabilities. As noted earlier, many routers sold for home use are also configured as firewalls, and many feature NAT as well.

ACTIVE HELPDESK

Understanding Firewalls

In this Active Helpdesk call, you'll play the role of a helpdesk staffer, fielding calls about how hackers can attack networks and what harm they can cause, as well as what a firewall does to keep a computer safe from hackers.

TYPES OF FIREWALLS

What kinds of firewalls are there?

As noted earlier, firewalls can be configured using software or hardware devices. Although installing either a software or a hardware firewall on your home network is probably sufficient, you should consider installing both for maximum protection.

What software firewalls are there?

Firewalls for home networks are mostly offered through comprehensive security packages such as Norton Internet Security, McAfee Internet Security, and ZoneAlarm Internet Security Suite. Windows Vista also includes a reliable firewall. These products are easy to set up and include options that allow the software to make security decisions for you based on the level of security you request. These programs also come with monitoring systems that alert you if your computer is under attack. The newest versions of these programs have "smart agents" that automatically stop attacks as they are detected by closing the appropriate logical ports or disallowing the suspicious activity.

What are hardware firewalls?

You can also buy and configure hardware firewall devices. For example, when buying a router for your network, make sure to buy one that also acts as a firewall. Manufacturers such as Linksys, D-Link, and Netgear make routers that double as firewalls. Just like software

firewalls, the setup in hardware firewalls is designed for novices, and the default configuration is to keep unnecessary logical ports closed. Documentation accompanying the firewalls can assist more experienced users in adjusting the settings to allow access to specific ports if needed. .

IS YOUR COMPUTER SECURE?

How can I tell if my computer is at risk?

For peace of mind (and to ensure that your firewall setup was successful), you can visit several Web sites that offer free services that test your computer's vulnerability. One popular site is Gibson Research (**www.grc. com**). The company's ShieldsUP and LeakTest programs are free and easy to run and can pinpoint security vulnerabilities in a system connected to the Internet. If you get a clean report from these programs, your system is probably not vulnerable to attack. Figure 7.24 shows the results screen from a ShieldsUP port probe test, which checks which logical ports in your computer are vulnerable.

What if I don't get a clean report from the testing program?

If the testing program detects potential vulnerabilities and you don't have a firewall, you should install one as soon as possible. If the firewall is already configured and specific ports (such as those shown in Figure 7.25) are shown as being vulnerable, consult your firewall

FIGURE 7.24

This screen shows results from a ShieldsUP common ports test. This test was run on a computer connected to the Internet with no firewall installed. Any ports that are reported as open (such as port 1025) by this test represent vulnerabilities that could be exploited by hackers.
Installation of a hardware or software firewall should close any open ports.

Port	Service	Status	Description
143	IMAP	Closed	Your computer has responded that this port exists but is currently closed to connections.
389	LDAP	Closed	Your computer has responded that this port exists but is currently closed to connections.
443	HTTPS	Closed	Your computer has responded that this port exists but is currently closed to connections.
445	MSFT DS	Stealth	There is NO EVIDENCE WHATSOEVER that a port (or even any computer) exists at this IP address!
1002	ms-ils	Closed	Your computer has responded that this port exists but is currently closed to connections.
1024	DCOM	Closed	Your computer has responded that this port exists but is currently closed to connections.
1025	Host	OPEN!	One or more unspecified Distributed COM (DCOM) services are opened by Windows. The exact port(s) opened can change, since queries to port 135 are used to determine which services are operating where. As is the rule for all exposed Internet services, you should arrange to close this port to external access so that potential current and future security or privacy exploits can not succeed against your system.
1026	Host	Closed	Your computer has responded that this port exists but is currently closed to connections.
1027	Host	Closed	Your computer has responded that this port exists but is currently closed to connections.

Ports reported as closed or in stealth mode are safe from attack

Ports reported as open are subject to exploitation by hackers

documentation for instructions on how to close or restrict access to those ports.

Securing Wireless Networks

When running a wireless network, installing a firewall is a key precaution. But wireless networks present special vulnerabilities that wired networks do not. Therefore, you should take additional specific steps to keep your wireless network safe.

Why is a wireless network more vulnerable than a wired network? If you're keeping a wired network secure with a firewall, you're fairly safe from most hacker attacks. However, wireless networks, especially with 802.11n equipment, have wide ranges, including areas outside of your house. This makes it possible for a hacker to access your network without you even knowing it.

Why should I be worried about strangers using my wireless network? Some use of other people's wireless networks is unintentional. Houses are built close together. Apartments are clustered even closer together. Wireless signals can easily reach a neighbor's residence. Most wireless network adapters are set up to access the strongest wireless network signal detected. If your router is on the east side of your house and you and your notebook are on the west side, then you may be end up getting a stronger signal from your neighbor's wireless network than from your own. **Piggybacking** is connecting to a wireless network (that is not your own) without the permission of the owner. This practice is illegal in many jurisdictions but often happens inadvertently between neighbors.

So why should you care if your neighbor is logged onto your network instead of his? Your neighbor probably isn't a hacker, but he might be using a lot of bandwidth—your bandwidth! If he's downloading a massive movie file while you're trying to do research for a term paper, he's probably slowing you down. Also, when some less than honest neighbors discover they can log onto your wireless network, they may cancel their own Internet service to save money by using yours.

In addition, because cyberattacks are traceable, criminals love to launch attacks

FIGURE 7.25 Common Logical Ports

Port Number	Protocol Using the Port
21	FTP (file transfer protocol) control
23	Telnet (unencrypted text communications)
25	SMTP (simple mail transfer protocol)
53	DNS (domain name system)
80	HTTP (hypertext transfer protocol)
443	HTTPS (HTTP protocol with transport layer security, or TLS, encryption)

(such as DDoS attacks) from public computers (such as in a library) so they can't be identified. If a criminal is sitting in his car outside your house and logging on to your wireless network, any cyberattacks he launches might be traced back to your IP address and you may find law enforcement officials knocking on your door.

Won't a firewall protect me? Firewalls will protect you from a lot of cyberattacks. However, on a wireless network, because your packets of information are being broadcast through the airwaves, savvy hackers can intercept and decode information from your transmissions that may allow them to bypass your firewall. Therefore, to secure a wireless network, you should take the following additional precautions:

1. **Change your network name (SSID).** Each wireless network has its own name to identify it. Unless you change this name when you set up your router, the router uses a default network name (also known as the *service set identifier* or SSID) that all routers from that manufacturer use (such as "Wireless"). Hackers know the default names and access codes for routers. If you haven't changed the SSID, it's advertising the fact that you probably haven't changed any of the other default settings for your router either.

2. **Disable SSID broadcast.** Most routers are set up to broadcast their SSID so that other wireless devices can find them. If your router supports disabling SSID broadcasting, turn it off. This makes it more difficult for a hacker to detect your network.

SOUND BYTE

Securing Wireless Networks

In this Sound Byte, you'll learn what "war drivers" are and why they could potentially be a threat to your wireless network. You'll also learn the simple steps to secure your wireless network against intruders.

3. **Change the default password on your router.** Hackers know the default passwords of most routers, and if they can access your router, they can probably break into your network. Change the password on your router to something hard to guess (use at least 8 characters with a combination of letters and numbers).

4. **Turn on security protocols.** Most routers ship with security protocols such as Wired Equivalent Privacy (WEP) or Wi-Fi Protected Access (WPA). Both use encryption (a method of translating your data into code) to protect data in your wireless transmissions. WPA is a much stronger protocol than WEP, so enable WPA if you have it; enable WEP if you don't. When you attempt to connect a node to a WEP- or WPA-enabled network for the first time, you're required to enter the encryption key. The encryption key (see Figure 7.26) is the code that computers on your network need to decrypt (decode) data transmissions. Without this key, it is extremely difficult, if not impossible, to decrypt the data transmissions from your network (see Figure 7.27). This prevents unauthorized access to your network because hackers won't know the correct key to use.

5. **Implement media access control.** Each network adapter on your network has a unique number (like a serial number) assigned to it by the manufacturer. This is called a *media access control address* (or MAC address), and it is a number printed right on the network adapter. Many routers allow you to restrict access to the network to only certain MAC addresses. This helps ensure that only authorized devices can connect to your network.

6. **Limit your signal range.** Most newer routers allow you to adjust the transmitting power to low, medium, or high. Cutting down the power to low or medium could prevent your signal from reaching too far away from your home, making it tougher for interlopers to poach your signal.

7. **Apply firmware upgrades.** Your router has read-only memory that has software written to it. This software is known as *firmware*. As bugs are found in the firmware (which hackers might exploit), manufacturers issue patches, just as the makers of operating system software do. Periodically check the manufacturer's Web site and apply any necessary upgrades to your firmware.

If you follow these steps, you will greatly improve the security of your wireless network. In the next section, we'll explore another major threat to your network: computer viruses.

FIGURE 7.26

By running your router configuration wizard, you can configure the security protocols available on your router and change the SSID, which helps protect your wireless network.

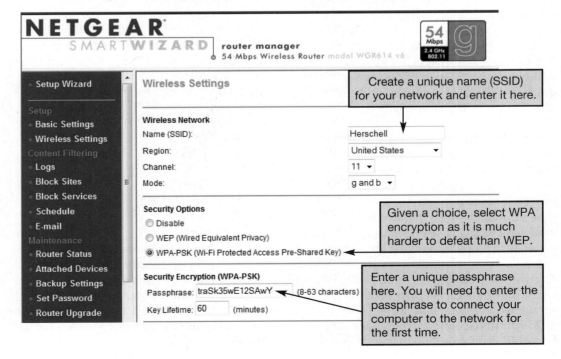

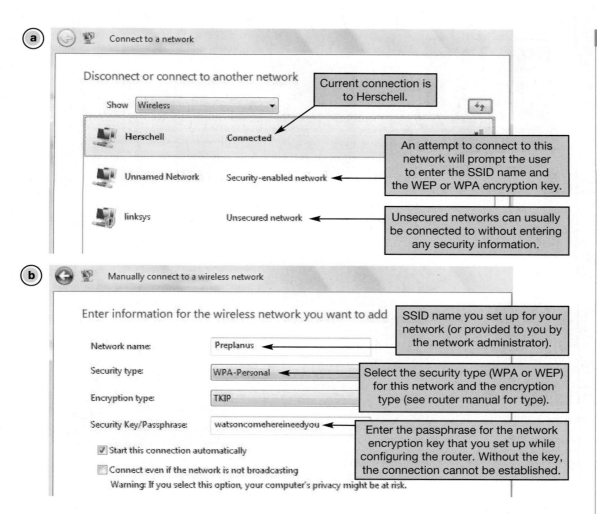

(a) Connect to a network

Disconnect or connect to another network

Current connection is to Herschell.

Show | Wireless

	Herschell	Connected
	Unnamed Network	Security-enabled network
	linksys	Unsecured network

An attempt to connect to this network will prompt the user to enter the SSID name and the WEP or WPA encryption key.

Unsecured networks can usually be connected to without entering any security information.

(b) Manually connect to a wireless network

Enter information for the wireless network you want to add

Network name:	Preplanus
Security type:	WPA-Personal
Encryption type:	TKIP
Security Key/Passphrase:	watsoncomehereineedyou

☑ Start this connection automatically

☐ Connect even if the network is not broadcasting

Warning: If you select this option, your computer's privacy might be at risk.

SSID name you set up for your network (or provided to you by the network administrator).

Select the security type (WPA or WEP) for this network and the encryption type (see router manual for type).

Enter the passphrase for the network encryption key that you set up while configuring the router. Without the key, the connection cannot be established.

FIGURE 7.27

(a) The Windows Vista Connect to a network dialog box shows all wireless networks within range. Clicking on one allows you to connect to it or prompts you for more information such as the SSID name and security key.
(b) Manually connecting to a wireless network allows you to establish a connection if you know the network encryption key and the SSID name.

>You can access the **Connect to a network** dialog box by right-clicking the **Network Connection** icon on the taskbar and selecting **Connect to a network** from the shortcut menu. You can access the **Manually connect to a wireless network** dialog box by accessing the **Control Panel**, selecting **Network and Sharing Center**, choosing **Set up a connection or network option**, and then clicking on **Manually connect to a wireless network**.

Computer Threats: Computer Viruses

Keeping your computer safe entails keeping it safe from more than just hackers. You must also guard against computer viruses. A computer **virus** is a computer program that attaches itself to another computer program (known as the *host program*) and attempts to spread itself to other computers when files are exchanged. Viruses normally attempt to hide within the code of a host program to avoid detection.

What do computer viruses do? A computer virus's main purpose is to replicate itself and copy its code into as many other files as possible. Although virus replication can slow down networks, it is not usually the main threat. The majority of viruses have secondary objectives or side effects, ranging from displaying annoying messages on the computer screen to the destruction of files or the contents of entire hard drives. Because computer viruses do cause disruption to computer systems, including data destruction and information theft, virus creation and deployment is a form of cybercrime.

How does my computer catch a virus? If your computer is exposed to a file infected with a virus, the virus will try to copy itself and infect a file on your computer. If you never expose your computer to new files, then it will not become infected. However, this would be the equivalent of a human being living in a bubble to avoid catching viruses from other people—quite impractical.

Shared disks or flash drives are a common source of virus infection, as is e-mail, although many people have misconceptions about how e-mail infection occurs. Just opening an e-mail message will not infect your computer with a virus. Downloading or running a file that is attached to the e-mail is how your computer becomes infected. Thus, be extremely wary of e-mail attachments, especially if you don't know the sender. Figure 7.28 shows how computer viruses are often passed from one computer to the next.

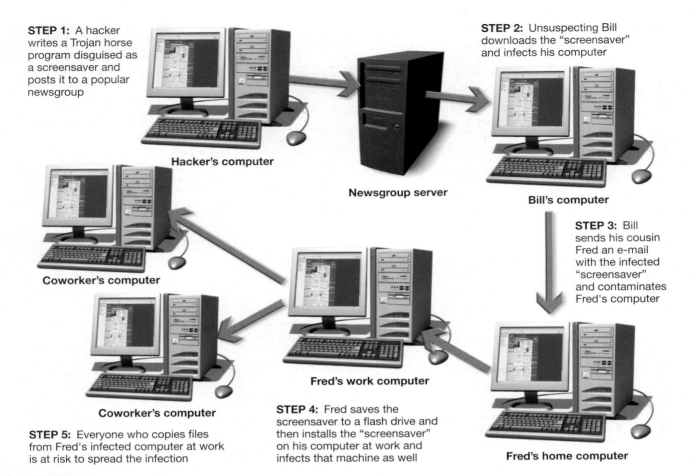

STEP 1: A hacker writes a Trojan horse program disguised as a screensaver and posts it to a popular newsgroup

Hacker's computer

Newsgroup server

STEP 2: Unsuspecting Bill downloads the "screensaver" and infects his computer

Bill's computer

STEP 3: Bill sends his cousin Fred an e-mail with the infected "screensaver" and contaminates Fred's computer

Coworker's computer

Coworker's computer

Fred's work computer

Fred's home computer

STEP 5: Everyone who copies files from Fred's infected computer at work is at risk to spread the infection

STEP 4: Fred saves the screensaver to a flash drive and then installs the "screensaver" on his computer at work and infects that machine as well

FIGURE 7.28

Computer viruses and other dangerous programs, such as Trojan horses, are passed from one unsuspecting user to the next.

TYPES OF VIRUSES

Although thousands of computer viruses and variants exist, they can be grouped into six broad categories based on their behavior and method of transmission.

Boot-Sector Viruses

What are boot-sector viruses? Boot-**sector viruses** replicate themselves into a hard drive's master boot record. The **master boot record** is a program that executes whenever a computer boots up, ensuring that the virus will be loaded into memory immediately, even before some virus protection programs. Boot-sector viruses are often transmitted by a floppy disk left in a floppy drive or by a flash drive left in a USB port. When the computer boots up with the disk in the drive, it tries to launch a master boot record from the floppy, which is usually the trigger for the virus to infect the hard drive. Boot-sector viruses can be extremely destructive: They can erase your entire hard drive.

Logic Bombs and Time Bombs

What are logic bombs? Logic bombs are viruses that are triggered when certain logical conditions are met—such as opening a file, booting your computer, or accessing certain programs. **Time bombs** are viruses that are triggered by the passage of time or on a certain date. For example, the Michelangelo virus, first launched in 1992, was a famous time bomb that was set to trigger every year on March 6, Michelangelo's birthday. In 2006, the BlackWorm virus (otherwise known as Kama Sutra, Mywife, or CME-24) started spreading through e-mail attachments. Opening the attachment infects the computer, and on the third day of every month, the virus seeks out and deletes certain file types on Windows computers. The effects of logic bombs and time bombs range from annoying messages being displayed on the screen to reformatting of the hard drive, causing complete data loss.

Worms

What are worms? Worms are slightly different from viruses in that they attempt to travel between systems through network connections to spread their infections. Viruses infect a host file and wait for that file to be executed on another computer to replicate. Worms can run independently of host file execution and are much more active in spreading themselves. The Storm worm broke out in January 2007 and eventually infected as many as 10 million individual computers. This worm spread by e-mail attachment, and compromised computers were included in a network of zombie computers. Fortunately, having antivirus software and a firewall installed and also applying software patches (code issued by the manufacturers of software programs, such as Windows, that repairs known security problems) as they are issued can protect you from most worms.

Script and Macro Viruses

What are script and macro viruses?
Some viruses are hidden on Web sites in the form of scripts. **Scripts** are a series of commands—actually, miniprograms—that are executed without your knowledge. Scripts are often used to perform useful, legitimate functions on Web sites such as collecting name and address information from customers. However, some scripts are malicious. For example, say you receive an e-mail encouraging you to visit a Web site full of useful programs and information. Unknown to you, clicking a link to display a video runs a script that infects your computer with a virus.

Macro viruses are attached to documents (such as Word and Excel documents) that use macros. A macro is a short series of commands that usually automates repetitive tasks. However, macro languages are now so sophisticated that viruses can be written with them. In March 1999, the Melissa virus became the first major macro virus to cause problems worldwide. It attached itself to a Word document. Anyone opening an infected document triggered the virus, which infected other Word documents on the victim's computer.

The Melissa virus was also the first practical example of an **e-mail virus**. E-mail viruses use the address book in the victim's e-mail system to distribute the virus. When executed, the Melissa virus sent itself to the first 50 people in the address book on the infected computer. This helped ensure that

BITS AND BYTES

Virus Symptoms

If your computer displays any of the following symptoms, it may be infected with a virus:

1. Existing program icons or files suddenly disappear. Viruses often delete specific file types or programs.
2. Changes appear in your browser. If you fire up your browser and it takes you to an unusual home page (one you didn't set) or it has new toolbars, then you may have a virus.
3. Odd messages or images are displayed on the screen or strange music or sounds play.
4. Data files become corrupted. Although files become corrupt for many reasons, a virus is one cause.
5. Programs don't work properly. This could be caused by either a corrupted file or a virus.

If you think you have a virus, boot up your computer with an antivirus software CD in your CD-ROM drive. This allows you to run the antivirus software before potential viruses load on the computer. Looking for free antivirus software? Check out avast! 4 Home Edition, available for download at **www.avast.com**.

Melissa became one of the most widely distributed viruses ever released.

Encryption Viruses

What are encryption viruses?
Encryption viruses are the newest form of virus. When these viruses infect your computer, they run a program that searches for common data files (such as Microsoft Word and Excel documents) and compresses them into a file using a complex encryption key. This renders your files unusable. You then receive a message asking you to send money to an account to receive the program to decrypt your files. The flaw with this type of virus, which keeps it from being widespread, is that law-enforcement officials can trace the payments to an account and potentially catch the perpetrators. Still, these types of viruses are seen from time to time.

Virus Classifications

How else are viruses classified?
Viruses can also be classified by the methods they take to avoid detection by antivirus software:

- **Polymorphic viruses** change their own code (or periodically rewrite themselves) to avoid detection. Most

ACTIVE HELPDESK

Avoiding Computer Viruses

In this Active Helpdesk call, you'll play the role of a helpdesk staffer, fielding calls about different types of viruses and what users should do to protect their computer from them.

polymorphic viruses infect one certain type of file (.exe files, for example).

- **Multipartite viruses** are designed to infect multiple file types in an effort to fool the antivirus software that is looking for them.

- **Stealth viruses** temporarily erase their code from the files where they reside and hide in the active memory of the computer. This helps them avoid detection if only the hard drive is being searched for viruses. Fortunately, antivirus software developers are aware of these tricks and have designed software to watch for them.

Given the creativity of virus programmers, you can be sure we'll see other types of viruses emerging in the future. In the next section, we'll discuss preventing virus infections.

FIGURE 7.29

By setting up a schedule in the antivirus module of Norton Internet Security, complete virus scans can be set up to run automatically. This computer will be scanned every Tuesday at 8 P.M.

Computer Safeguards: Antivirus Software and Other Security Measures

Certain viruses merely present minor annoyances, such as randomly sending an ambulance graphic across the bottom of the screen, as is the case with the Red Cross virus. Other viruses can significantly slow down a computer or network or destroy key files or the contents of entire hard drives. The best defense against viruses is to install **antivirus software**, which is specifically designed to detect viruses and protect your computer and files from harm. Antivirus software is usually included in most comprehensive computer security packages such as Norton Internet Security.

ANTIVIRUS SOFTWARE

How often do I need to run antivirus software? You should run a virus check on your entire system at least once a week. By doing so, all files on your computer are checked for undetected viruses. Because these checks take time, you can configure the software to run these checks automatically when you aren't using your system—for example, late at night (see Figure 7.29).

How does antivirus software work? Most antivirus software looks for **virus signatures** in files. Signatures are portions of the virus code that are unique to a particular computer virus. Antivirus software scans files for these signatures and thereby identifies infected files and the type of virus that is infecting them.

The antivirus software scans files when they're opened or executed. If it detects a virus signature or suspicious activity (such as launching an unknown macro), it stops the execution of the file and virus and notifies you that it has detected a virus. It also places the virus in a secure area on your hard drive so that it won't spread infection to other files. This procedure is known as **quarantining**. Usually the antivirus software then gives you the choice of deleting or repairing the infected file. Unfortunately, antivirus programs can't always fix infected files so that the files are usable again. You should keep backup copies of critical files so that you can restore them in case a virus damages them irreparably.

Some antivirus software will also attempt to prevent infection by inoculating key files on your computer. In **inoculation**, the antivirus software records key attributes about files on your computer (such as file size and date created) and keeps these statistics in a safe place on your hard drive. When scanning for viruses, the antivirus software compares the files to the attributes it

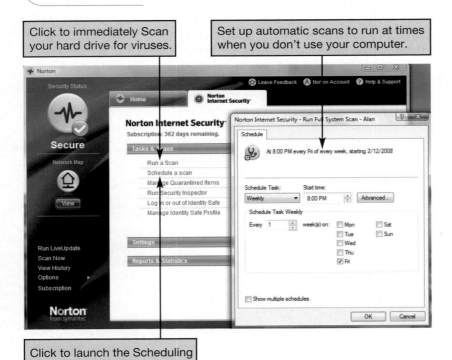

Click to immediately Scan your hard drive for viruses.

Set up automatic scans to run at times when you don't use your computer.

Click to launch the Scheduling dialog box (shown at right).

previously recorded to help detect attempts by virus programs to modify your files.

Does antivirus software always stop viruses? Antivirus software catches known viruses effectively. Unfortunately, new viruses are written all the time. To combat unknown viruses, modern antivirus programs search for suspicious virus-like activities as well as virus signatures. However, virus authors know how antivirus software works. They take special measures to disguise their virus code and hide the effects of a virus until just the right moment. This helps ensure that the virus spreads faster and farther. Thus, your computer can still be attacked by a virus that your antivirus software doesn't recognize. To minimize this risk, you should keep your antivirus software up-to-date.

How do I make sure my antivirus software is up-to-date? Most antivirus programs have an automatic updates feature that downloads a list of upgrades you can install on your computer while you're online (see Figure 7.30). Automatic updates ensure that your programs are up-to-date.

What should I do if I think my computer is infected with a virus? Boot up your computer with the antivirus CD that came with your antivirus software in your CD drive. This should prevent most virus programs from loading and will allow you to run the antivirus software directly from the CD drive. If viruses are detected, you may want to research them further to determine whether your antivirus software will eradicate them completely or if you need to take additional manual steps to eliminate the virus. Most antivirus company Web sites (such as **www.symantec.com**) contain archives of information on viruses and provide step-by-step solutions for removing viruses.

OTHER SECURITY MEASURES

Is there anything else I should do to protect my system? Many viruses exploit weaknesses in operating systems. And malicious Web sites can be set up to attack your computer by downloading harmful software onto your computer. These attacks, known as *drive-by downloads*, are common and affect almost one in a thousand Web pages (per Google's research in early 2008). To combat these threats, make sure your operating system is up-to-date and contains the latest security patches (or fixes). Windows

Click to Run LiveUpdate immediately.

FIGURE 7.30

Norton's LiveUpdate provides automatic updates on all virus and security products installed on the computer. It can be set to automatically update every time you connect to the Internet.

Vista makes this easy by providing a utility called Windows Update. When you enable automatic updates, your computer searches for Windows updates on the Microsoft Web site every time it connects to the Internet.

How do I enable automatic updates? To enable automatic updates, click the Start button, select Control Panel, and double-click the Windows Update icon. Then click the Change Settings option to display the dialog box shown in Figure 7.31. It is strongly recommended that you select the Install updates automatically option.

How can I ensure I've covered all aspects of my computer protection? The checklist in Figure 7.32 should provide you with a guide to ensure you didn't miss any critical aspects of security. Additional information on protecting your computer and its data can be found in the Technology in Focus feature "Protecting Your Computer and Backing Up Your Data" beginning on page 364.

Taking a few precautions regarding your network and online security can provide huge benefits such as peace of mind and the avoidance of time spent correcting problems. So enjoy your network and your online experiences, but do it safely.

SOUND BYTE

Protecting Your Computer

In this Sound Byte, you'll learn how to use a variety of tools to protect your computer, including antivirus software and Windows utilities.

FIGURE 7.31

The Windows Vista Automatic Updating screen makes it easy for users to configure Windows to update itself.

>To enable automatic updates, click the **Start** button, select **Control Panel**, double-click the **Windows Update** icon, and click the **Change Settings** link.

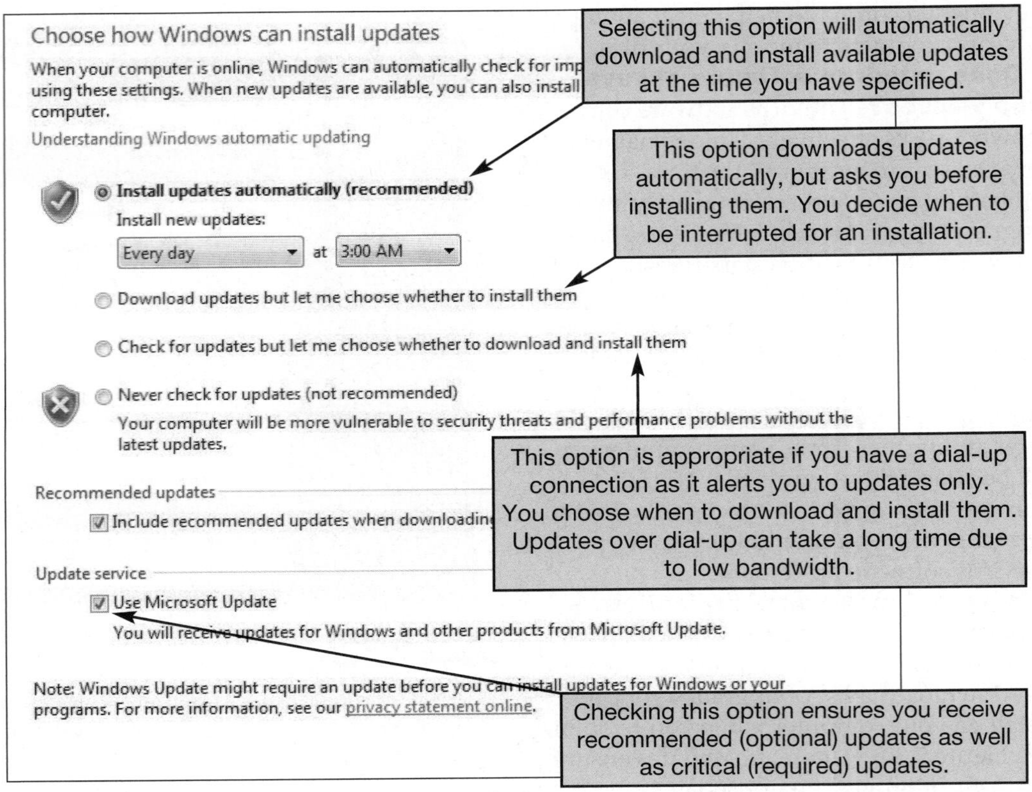

Choose how Windows can install updates

When your computer is online, Windows can automatically check for imp using these settings. When new updates are available, you can also install computer.

Understanding Windows automatic updating

◉ **Install updates automatically (recommended)**
Install new updates:
[Every day ▾] at [3:00 AM ▾]

○ Download updates but let me choose whether to install them

○ Check for updates but let me choose whether to download and install them

○ Never check for updates (not recommended)
Your computer will be more vulnerable to security threats and performance problems without the latest updates.

Recommended updates
☑ Include recommended updates when downloading

Update service
☑ Use Microsoft Update
You will receive updates for Windows and other products from Microsoft Update.

Note: Windows Update might require an update before you can install updates for Windows or your programs. For more information, see our privacy statement online.

Selecting this option will automatically download and install available updates at the time you have specified.

This option downloads updates automatically, but asks you before installing them. You decide when to be interrupted for an installation.

This option is appropriate if you have a dial-up connection as it alerts you to updates only. You choose when to download and install them. Updates over dial-up can take a long time due to low bandwidth.

Checking this option ensures you receive recommended (optional) updates as well as critical (required) updates.

FIGURE 7.32 Computer Security Checklist

	Yes	No
Virus and Spyware Protection		
Is antivirus and antispyware software installed on all your computers?	☐	☐
Is the antivirus and antispyware software configured to automatically and regularly update itself?	☐	☐
Is the software set to scan your computer on a regular basis (at least weekly) for viruses and spyware?	☐	☐
Firewall		
Do all your computers have firewall software installed and turned on before going on the Internet for the first time?	☐	☐
Is your router also able to function as a hardware firewall?	☐	☐
Have you tested your firewall security by using the free software available at **www.grc.com**?	☐	☐
Wireless Security		
Have you changed the default password to access your router?	☐	☐
Have you changed the name (SSID) of your network and turned off SSID broadcasting?	☐	☐
Have you enabled WPA or WEP encryption for your network?	☐	☐
Software Updates		
Have your configured your operating systems (Windows, OS X) to automatically install new software patches and updates?	☐	☐
Is other software installed on your computer (such as Microsoft Office) configured for automatic updates?	☐	☐
Is the Web browser you are using the latest version?	☐	☐

TRENDS IN IT

Careers: Cybercops on the Beat—Computer Security Careers

With billions of dollars being spent on e-commerce initiatives every year, companies have a vested interest in keeping their information technology (IT) infrastructures humming along. The rise in terrorism has shifted the focus slightly from protecting just virtual assets and access to protecting physical assets and access points as well. The increased need for virtual and physical security measures means there should be a robust job market ahead for computer security experts.

The National Security Agency and the Office of Homeland Security are both encouraging information security professionals to be proficient in information assurance. As defined by the NSA, **information assurance** is "the set of measures intended to protect and defend information and information systems by ensuring their availability, integrity, authentication, confidentiality, and non-repudiation. This includes providing for restoration of information systems by incorporating protection, detection, and reaction capabilities." The five key attributes of secure information systems are as follows:

1. **Availability:** The extent to which a data-processing system is able to receive and process data. A high degree of availability is usually desirable.
2. **Integrity:** A quality that an information system has if the processing of information is logical and accurate and the data is protected against unauthorized modifications or destruction.
3. **Authentication:** Security measures designed to protect an information system against acceptance of a fraudulent transmission of data by establishing the validity of a data transmission, message, or the identity of the sender.
4. **Confidentiality:** The assurance that information is not disclosed to unauthorized persons, processes, or devices.
5. **Nonrepudiation:** A capability of security systems to guarantee that a message or data can be proven to have originated from a specific person and was processed by the recipient. The sender of the data receives a receipt for the data, and the receiver of the data gets proof of the sender's identity. The objective of nonrepudiation is to prevent either party from later denying having handled the data.

The Global Information Assurance Certification, or GIAC (**www.giac.org**), is an industry-recognized certification that provides objective evidence (through examinations) that security professionals have mastered key skills in various aspects of information assurance.

What skill sets will be most in demand for security professionals? Aside from information assurance technical skills (with an emphasis on network engineering and data communications), broad-based business experience is also extremely desirable. IT security professionals need to understand the key issues of e-commerce and the core areas of their company's business (such as marketing, sales, and finance). Understanding how a business works is essential to pinpointing and correcting the security risks that could be detrimental to a company's bottom line. And because of the large number of attacks by hackers, security forensic skills and related certifications are in high demand. Working closely with law enforcement officials is essential to rapidly solving and stopping cybercrime.

Another important attribute of security professionals is the ability to lead and motivate teams. Security experts need to work with diverse members of the business community, including customers, to forge relationships and understanding among diverse groups. Security professionals must conduct skillful negotiations to ensure that large project implementations are not unduly delayed by security initiatives or pushed through with inadequate security precautions. Diplomacy is therefore a sought-after skill.

Look for more colleges and universities to roll out security-based degrees and certificate programs as the demand for security professionals increases. These programs will most likely be appropriate for experienced networking professionals who are ready to make the move into the IT security field. If you're just starting to prepare for a career, consider a degree in network engineering, followed by network security training while you're working at your first job. A degree program that is also designed to prepare you for security certification exams is particularly desirable. Networking and security degrees, combined with passing grades on certification exams, should help you ensure a smooth transition into the exciting world of cybersecurity.

1. What is a network, and what are the advantages of setting up one?

A computer network is simply two or more computers that are connected using software and hardware so that they can communicate. Networks allow users to (1) share peripherals, (2) transfer files easily, and (3) share an Internet connection.

2. What is the difference between a client/server network and a peer-to-peer network?

In peer-to-peer networks, each node connected to the network can communicate directly with every other node instead of having a separate device exercise central control over the network. P2P networks are the most common type of network installed in homes. Most networks that have 10 or more nodes are client/server networks. A client/server network contains two types of computers: a client computer on which users accomplish specific tasks, and a server computer that provides resources to the clients and central control for the network.

3. What are the main hardware components of every network?

To function, any network contains four components: (1) transmission media (cables or radio waves) to connect and establish communication between nodes; (2) network adapters that allow the nodes on the network to communicate; (3) network navigation devices (such as routers and hubs) that move data around the network; and (4) software that allows the network to run.

4. What are the most common home networks?

The two most common home networks are wired Ethernet and wireless Ethernet. Modern power-line networks, boasting faster data throughput, are now a viable option in certain situations. The major difference in these networks is the transmission media by which the nodes are connected.

5. What are wired Ethernet networks, and how are they created?

Ethernet networks use the Ethernet protocol as the means by which the nodes on the network communicate. This protocol makes Ethernet networks efficient but also slightly complex. Because of this complexity, additional devices (switches or routers) are required in Ethernet networks. To create a wired Ethernet network, you connect or install network adapters or NICs to each network node. Network adapters connect via cables to a central network navigation device such as a switch or a router. Data flows through the navigation device to the nodes on the network.

6. What are wireless Ethernet networks, and how are they created?

A wireless network uses radio waves instead of wires or cable as its transmission media. Current wireless protocols provide for networks with a maximum of 108 Mbps. To create a wireless network, you install or attach wireless network adapters to the nodes that will make up the network. If the nodes are unable to communicate because of distance, then you can add a wireless access point to the network to help relay data between nodes. Wireless networks are susceptible to interference from other wireless devices such as phones.

7. How are power-line networks created, and are they a viable alternative to Ethernet networks?

Power-line networks use the electrical wiring in your home to connect the nodes in the network. To create a power-line network, you connect special network adapters to each node on the network. These adapters are then plugged into an electrical outlet, and data is transmitted through the electrical wires. Modern power-line networks can often exceed the throughput achieved in wireless Ethernet networks, making them a viable option when interference with wireless signals is present.

8. **How do I configure my computer's software to set up a network?**

Windows Vista and XP both feature software wizards that facilitate the setup of both wired and wireless networks. Plug in the modem, routers, and all cables and then switch on the modem, router, and computers (in that order). Run the wizards, which should guide you through the process. Make sure each computer has a distinct name and ensure that all computers are in the same workgroup.

9. **How can hackers attack a network, and what harm can they cause?**

A hacker is defined as anyone who breaks into a computer system unlawfully. Hackers can use software to break into almost any computer connected to the Internet (unless proper precautions are taken). Once hackers gain access to a computer, they can potentially (1) steal personal or other important information; (2) damage and destroy data; or (3) use the computer to attack other computers.

10. **What is a firewall, and how does it keep my computer safe from hackers?**

Firewalls are software programs or hardware devices designed to keep computers safe from hackers. By using a personal firewall, you can close open logical ports to invaders and potentially make your computer invisible to other computers on the Internet.

11. **Why are wireless networks more vulnerable than wired networks, and what special precautions are required to ensure my wireless network is secure?**

Wireless networks are even more susceptible to hacking than wired networks because the signals of most wireless networks extend beyond the walls of your home. Neighbors may unintentionally (or intentionally) connect to the Internet through your wireless connection, and hackers may try to access it. To prevent unwanted intrusions into your network, you should change the default password on your router (to make it tougher for hackers to gain access), use a hard-to-guess SSID (network name), turn off SSID broadcasting (to make it harder for outsiders to detect your network), and enable security protocols such as WPA or WEP.

12. **From which types of viruses do I need to protect my computer?**

A computer virus is a program that attaches itself to another program and attempts to spread itself to other computers when files are exchanged. Computer viruses can be grouped into six categories: (1) boot-sector viruses, (2) logic bombs and time bombs, (3) worms, (4) scripts and macros, (5) encryption viruses, and (6) Trojan horses. Once run, they perform their malicious duties in the background, often invisible to the user.

13. **What can I do to protect my computer from viruses?**

The best defense against viruses is to install antivirus software. You should update the software on a regular basis and configure it to examine all e-mail attachments for viruses. You should periodically run a complete virus scan on your computer to ensure that no viruses have made it onto your hard drive.

Buzzwords

Word Bank

- antivirus software
- distributed denial of service (DDoS)
- firewall
- hacker(s)
- identity theft
- information assurance
- logical port(s)
- network adapter(s)
- peer-to-peer (P2P)
- phone cable
- repeater
- router
- switch
- throughput
- virus
- wired Ethernet
- wireless Ethernet
- zombies

Instructions: Fill in the blanks using the words from the Word Bank above.

Cathi needed to network three computers for herself and her roommates, Sharon and Emily. She decided that a(n) (1) _____ network was the right type to install in their apartment because a client/server network was too complex. Because none of them were gamers or transferred large files, they didn't need high (2) _____. Still, they decided to use the fastest type of home network, a(n) (3) _____ network, because it is reliable and easy to install. Because Sharon already had high-speed Internet access through the cable TV company, she needed to buy a(n) (4) _____ for the network to ensure all users could share the connection. The router also doubled as a(n) (5) _____, preventing the need to purchase a separate device. Fortunately, all their computers already had (6) _____ installed, making it easy to connect the computers to the network.

Cathi's roommate Emily was skeptical of being hooked up to the Internet because she had been the victim of (7) _____, which destroyed her credit rating. A(n) (8) _____ had obtained her credit card information by posing as an employee of her bank. Cathi assured Emily that the router could be configured as a(n) (9) _____ to repel malicious hacking mischief and assist in providing (10) _____ for the data on her computer. Turning off the unused (11) _____ would repel most attacks on their home network. With this protection, it was unlikely that a hacker would turn their PCs into (12) _____ to launch (13) _____ attacks. But after the scare with the Melissa (14) _____, Cathi was careful to warn the others not to open files from untrusted sources. She also made sure they all installed (15) _____ on their PCs to protect them from viruses.

Becoming Computer Literate

While attending college, you are working at the Snap-Tite company, a small manufacturer of specialty fasteners. Currently, the employees must copy files to flash drives to transfer them among the four PCs the company owns. Only the company president has access to the Internet. The accounts payable clerk is the only one who has a printer and is constantly being interrupted by other employees when they want to print their files. Your boss heard that you were taking a computer course and asked you to create a solution.

Instructions: Using the preceding scenario, draft a networking plan for Snap-Tite using as many of the keywords from the chapter as you can. Be sure that the company president, who is unfamiliar with many networking terms, can understand the report.

Instructions: Answer the multiple-choice and true–false questions below for more practice with key terms and concepts from this chapter.

MULTIPLE CHOICE

1. Which type of sharing is NOT a benefit of installing a home network?
   a. Peripheral   b. Internet connection
   c. CPU   d. File

2. Which of the following is NOT a reason peer-to-peer networks are generally installed in homes?
   a. Client/server networks are less expandable than peer-to-peer networks.
   b. Client/server networks are designed for larger numbers of users.
   c. Client/server networks provide more security than is needed in a home network.
   d. Servers are too difficult for most home users to set up.

3. All networks contain the following elements EXCEPT
   a. network adapters.
   b. transmission media.
   c. networking software.
   d. wireless connectivity.

4. Which is an example of a network navigation device required to move data between two networks?
   a. Wireless signal sender   b. Switch
   c. Router   d. 5E cable

5. Wireless Ethernet networks are more challenging to set up than wired networks because
   a. the navigation devices they use are more complicated to set up.
   b. they have more security vulnerabilities.
   c. there are many sources of signal interference in most houses.
   d. None of the above.

6. Power-line networks are viable alternatives to Ethernet networks because they
   a. are less expensive than Ethernet networks.
   b. don't require running any new wires to install.
   c. provide six times the throughput of wired Ethernet networks.
   d. All of the above.

7. When hackers use a program that controls many other computers and uses them to launch an attack on another computer, this is called a
   a. zero-day attack.
   b. Trojan horse attack.
   c. distributed denial-of-service attack.
   d. boot-sector virus attack.

8. Which is NOT a benefit of firewalls?
   a. They make it harder for a hacker to locate specific computers on a network.
   b. They repeatedly change the IP address of the router.
   c. They close unused logical ports to decrease network vulnerability.
   d. They filter out unauthorized requests for data.

9. Wireless Ethernet networks are attractive to hackers because
   a. the 802.11 protocol has weak security rules.
   b. you can't install a firewall on a wireless Ethernet network.
   c. wireless Ethernet networks have much greater bandwidth than wired.
   d. it is much easier for a hacker to establish a connection with a wireless network.

10. Viruses that are triggered by a certain event (such as a date) or condition being achieved are called
    a. worms.
    b. stealth viruses.
    c. logic bombs.
    d. macro viruses.

TRUE–FALSE

_____ 1. Actual data throughput is usually higher on wireless networks.

_____ 2. All home networks require each computer on the network to be equipped with its own network adapter.

_____ 3. Installing a firewall on your network will stop most viruses from being planted on your network.

_____ 4. Never opening e-mail attachments will ensure a computer never catches a virus.

_____ 5. Some wireless Ethernet networks are subject to interference from cordless phones.

Making the Transition to...
Next Semester

1. Dormitory Networking

Dave, Jerome, and Thomas were sitting in the common room of their campus suite staring at $100 piled up on the coffee table. Selling last semester's books back to the bookstore had been a good idea. As they waited for their other roommate Phil to come home, Dave said, "Wouldn't it be cool if we could network our notebooks? Then we could play Ultra Super Robot Kill-Fest in team mode!" Jerome pointed out it would be even more useful if they could all have access to Dave's laser printer because he owned the only one. "And Jerome's always bugging me to use my scanner when I'm trying to sleep," remarked Thomas. "And I can't believe the only high-speed Internet connection is out here in the lounge!" The three roommates ran down the hall and rapped on your door looking for some guidance. Consider how you would answer their questions:

a. Is $100 enough to set up a wireless network for four notebooks in four separate rooms? (Assume each computer contains a wireless network adapter already.)
b. Can the roommates share a printer and a scanner if they set up a wireless network? Will they need any additional equipment for the printer and the scanner to share them across the network if they are already connected to one of the notebook computers?
c. How would they share the one high-speed Internet connection wirelessly?
d. Phil just returned from the campus post office with a check from his aunt for $75. Do the roommates now have enough money to set up a network attached storage (NAS) device that would allow them to have their files automatically backed up?

To answer these questions, use the chapter text and the following resources: **www.coolcomputing.com**, **www.pricewatch.com**, **www.westerndigital.com**, **www.netgear.com**, **www.bestbuy.com**, **www.tigerdirect.com**.

2. Connecting Your Computer to Public Networks

In the course of your education, you are constantly connecting your notebook to various wireless public networks such as those in the school library and neighborhood coffee shop. As you know from reading this chapter, you are more vulnerable to hackers when connected to a wireless network. Conduct research on the Internet about surfing at public hot spots and prepare a list of sensible precautions for you and your classmates to take when surfing on an open network.

3. Identity Theft Awareness

Two students in your residence hall have recently been the victims of identity theft. You have been assigned to create a flyer telling students how they can protect themselves from identity theft in the residence hall. Using the information found in this chapter, materials you find on the U.S. federal government Web site on identity theft (**www.consumer.gov/idtheft**), as well as other Web resources, create a flyer that lists five to 10 ways in which students can avoid having their identities stolen.

Making the Transition to...
the Workplace

1. Antivirus Protection

Your employer recently installed high-speed Internet access at the office where you work. There are 50 workstations connected to the network and the Internet. Within a week, half the computers in the office were down because of a virus that was contracted by a screen saver. In addition, network personnel from a university in England contacted the company, claiming that your employer's computer systems were being used as part of a denial of service (DDoS) attack on their Web site.

a. Price out security suite software on the Internet and determine the most cost-effective package for the company to implement protection on 50 workstations.

b. Write a "virus prevention" memo to all employees that suggests strategies for avoiding virus infections.

c. Draft a note to the CEO to explain how a firewall could prevent DDoS attacks from being launched on the company network.

2. Public Wireless Access

Many corporations are using wireless technology to enhance or drive their businesses. Assume you are opening a local coffee shop in your town. Investigate the following:

a. Starbucks (**www.starbucks.com**) currently provides wireless access (for a fee) in many of its locations. Using **www.wifinder.com** or **www.wi-fihotspotlist.com**, find the closest Starbucks to your home that features wireless access. Will this store compete with your proposed store, or is it too far away?

b. Visit your local Starbucks (or check the Starbucks Web site at **www.starbucks.com**) and find out the cost of its wireless access. Use the Internet to research whether wireless access is profitable for Starbucks and whether it drives customers to their stores (many articles have been written about this). Compare this with Panera Bread, which offers free wireless access to its customers. Why does one company charge for Internet access while another does not?

c. As part of your business plan, write one or two paragraphs explaining why you will (or will not) offer wireless connectivity at your coffee shop and whether it will be a pay service or a free service.

d. Can you find any free alternatives for wireless access within a 10-mile radius of your proposed store location? How will this affect your decision to offer wireless connectivity at your business?

3. Testing Your Computer

Visit Gibson Research at **www.grc.com** and run the company's ShieldsUP and LeakTest programs on your computer.

a. Did your computer get a clean report? If not, what potential vulnerabilities did the testing programs detect?

b. How could you protect yourself from the vulnerabilities these programs can detect?

Critical Thinking Questions

Instructions: Albert Einstein used *Gedanken experiments,* or critical thinking questions, to develop his theory of relativity. Some ideas are best understood by experimenting with them in our own minds. The following critical thinking questions are designed to demand your full attention but only require a comfortable chair—no technology.

1. Protecting Your Wireless Home Network

Many people have installed wireless networks in their homes. Consider the wireless network installed in your home (or in a friend's home if you don't have wireless).

a. Is your network set up to provide adequate protection against hackers? If not, what would you need to do to make it secure?

b. Are there other wireless networks within range of your home? If so, are they set up with an adequate level of security, or can you connect to them easily? How would you go about informing your neighbors that their networks are vulnerable?

2. Upgrading Your Wireless

You have just finished purchasing and installing a new wireless network in your home. A new wireless standard of networking will be launched next month that is 10 times as fast as the wireless network you installed.

a. What types of applications would you need to be using heavily to make it worth upgrading to the new standard?

b. Suppose your neighbor upgraded to the new standard but does not have his network secured. Is tapping into your neighbor's wireless connection ethical? Is it illegal where you live?

3. Ethical Hacking?

Hackers and virus authors cause millions of dollars worth of damage to PCs and networks annually. But hacking is a highly controversial subject. Many hackers believe they are actually working for the "good of the people" or "exercising their freedom" when they engage in hacking activities. However, in most jurisdictions in the United States, hacking is punishable by stiff fines and jail terms.

a. Hackers often argue that hacking is for the good of all people because it points out flaws in computer systems. Do you agree with this? Why or why not?

b. What should the punishment be for convicted hackers and why?

c. Who should be held accountable at a corporation whose network security is breached by a hacker?

4. Keeping Networks Safe from Cyberterrorists

Many of us rely on networks every day, often without realizing it. Whether researching a term paper on the Internet, ordering a book from Amazon.com, or accessing your college e-mail from home, you are relying on networks to relay information. But what if terrorists destroyed key components of the Internet or other networks on which we depend?

a. What economic problems would result from DDoS attacks launched by terrorists on major e-commerce sites?

b. Research the precautions that the U.S. military and intelligence agencies (FBI and CIA) are taking to ensure that networks involving national defense remain secure from terrorist attacks. What else should they do?

5. Protection for Your Computer?

Do you have a firewall, antispyware, and antivirus software installed on the computer you use most often? If not, why not? What types of problems can you experience from not having this software installed? Have you ever been a victim of a hacker or a virus?

Team Time

Problem:

Wireless technology is being adopted by leaps and bounds both in the home and in the workplace. Offering easy access free of physical tethers to networks seems to be a solution to many problems. However, wireless computing also has problems, ranging from poor reception to hijackers stealing your bandwidth.

Task:

Your campus has recently undertaken a wireless computing initiative. As part of the plan, your dorm has just been outfitted with wireless access points (base stations) to provide students with connectivity to the Internet and the college network. However, since the installation, students have reported poor connectivity in certain areas and extremely low bandwidth at other times. Your group has volunteered to research the potential problems and to suggest solutions to the college IT department.

Process:

Break the class into three teams. Each team will be responsible for investigating one of the following issues:

1. **Detecting poor connectivity:** Research methods that can be used to find areas of poor signal strength such as signal sniffing software (**www.netstumbler.com**) and handheld scanning devices such as WiFi Finder (**http://us.kensington.com**). Investigate maximum distances between access points and network nodes (equipment manufacturers such as **www.netgear.com** and **www.linksys.com** provide guidelines) and make appropriate recommendations.

2. **Signal boosters:** Research alternatives that can be used to increase signal strength in access points, antennae, and wireless cards. Signal boosters are available for access points. You can purchase or construct replacement antennae or antenna enhancements. WiFi cards that offer higher power than conventional cards are now available.

3. **Security:** "War drivers" (people who cruise neighborhoods looking for open wireless networks from which to steal bandwidth) may be the cause of the bandwidth issues. Research appropriate measures to keep wireless network traffic secure from eavesdropping by hackers. In your investigation, look into the new Wi-Fi Protected Access (WPA) standard developed by the Wi-Fi Alliance. Check out the security section on the Wi-Fi Alliance Web site to start (**www.weca.net**).

Present your findings to your class and discuss possible causes and preventive measures for the problems encountered at your dorm. Provide your instructor with a report suitable for eventual presentation to the college IT department.

Conclusion:

As technology improves, wireless connectivity should eventually become the standard method of communication between networks and network devices. As with any other technology, security risks exist. Understanding those risks and how to mitigate them will allow you to participate in the design and deployment of network technology and provide peace of mind for your network users.

Multimedia

In addition to the review materials presented here, you'll find additional materials featured with the book's multimedia, including the *Technology in Action* Student Resource CD and the Companion Website (**www.prenhall.com/techinaction**), which will help reinforce your understanding of the chapter content. These materials include the following:

ACTIVE HELPDESK

In Active Helpdesk calls, you'll assume the role of helpdesk operator taking calls about the concepts you've learned in this chapter. You'll apply what you've learned and receive feedback from a supervisor to review and reinforce those concepts. The Active Helpdesk calls for this chapter are listed below and can be found on your Student Resource CD:

- Understanding Networking
- Understanding Firewalls
- Avoiding Computer Viruses

SOUND BYTES

Sound Bytes are dynamic multimedia tutorials that help demystify even the most complex topics. You'll view video clips and animations that illustrate computer concepts, and then apply what you've learned by reviewing with the Sound Byte Labs, which include quizzes and activities specifically tailored to each Sound Byte. The Sound Bytes for this chapter are listed here and can be found on your Student Resource CD:

- Installing a Computer Network
- Installing a Personal Firewall
- Securing Wireless Networks
- Protecting Your Computer

COMPANION WEBSITE

The *Technology in Action* Companion Website includes a variety of additional materials to help you review and learn more about the topics in this chapter. The resources available at **www.prenhall.com/techinaction** include:

- **Online Study Guide.** Each chapter features an online true–false and multiple-choice quiz. You can take these quizzes, automatically check the results, and e-mail the results to your instructor.

- **Web Research Projects.** Each chapter features a number of Web research projects that ask you to search the Web for information on computer-related careers, milestones in computer history, important people and companies, emerging technologies, and the applications and implications of different technologies.

PROTECTING YOUR COMPUTER AND BACKING UP YOUR DATA

Just like any other valuable asset, computers and the data they contain require protection from damage, thieves, and unauthorized users. Although it's impossible to protect your computer and data completely, following the suggestions outlined in this Technology in Focus will provide you with peace of mind that you have done all you can to protect your computer from theft and keep it in working order.

PHYSICALLY PROTECTING YOUR COMPUTER

Your computer isn't useful to you if it is damaged. Therefore, it's essential to select and ensure a safe environment for it. This includes protecting it from environmental factors, power surges, and power outages.

Environmental Factors

You need to consider a number of environmental factors when protecting your computer.

1 Sudden movements (such as a fall) can damage your notebook computer or mobile device's internal components. Certain computers, such as those in the Panasonic Toughbook line, are designed for rugged conditions and to resist damage from falls. But to avoid problems, make sure that the computer sits on a flat, level surface, and carry your notebook in a padded case to protect it should you drop it. If you do drop your computer or notebook, have it professionally tested by a computer repair facility to uncover any hidden damage.

2 Electronic components do not like excessive heat or excessive cold. Unfortunately, computers generate a lot of heat, which is why they have fans to cool their internal components. Make sure that you place your computer so that the fan's input vents (usually found on the rear of the system unit) are unblocked so that air can flow inside. And don't leave computing devices in a car during especially hot or cold weather because components can be damaged by extreme temperatures.

3 Naturally, a fan drawing air into a computer also draws in dust and other particles, which can wreak havoc on your system. Therefore, keep the room in which your computer is located as clean as possible. Even in a clean room, the fan ducts can become packed with dust, so vacuum it periodically to keep a clear airflow into your computer.

4 Because food crumbs and liquid can damage keyboards and other computer components, consume food and beverages away from your computer.

Power Surges

Power surges occur when electrical current is supplied in excess of normal voltage (120 volts in the United States). Old or faulty wiring, downed power lines, malfunctions at electric company substations, and lightning strikes can all cause power surges. **Surge protectors** are devices that protect your computer against power surges (see Figure 1). To use a surge protector, you simply plug your electrical devices into the outlets of the surge protector, which in turn plugs into the wall.

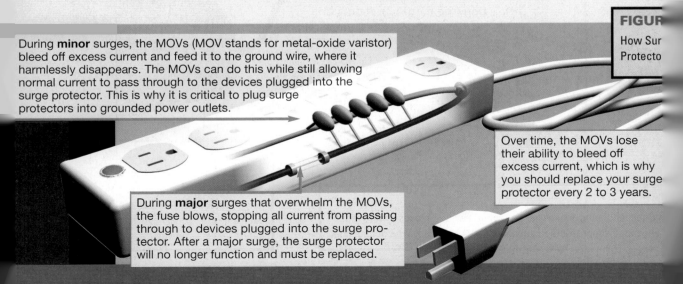

FIGUR

How Sur
Protecto

During **minor** surges, the MOVs (MOV stands for metal-oxide varistor) bleed off excess current and feed it to the ground wire, where it harmlessly disappears. The MOVs can do this while still allowing normal current to pass through to the devices plugged into the surge protector. This is why it is critical to plug surge protectors into grounded power outlets.

During **major** surges that overwhelm the MOVs, the fuse blows, stopping all current from passing through to devices plugged into the surge protector. After a major surge, the surge protector will no longer function and must be replaced.

Over time, the MOVs lose their ability to bleed off excess current, which is why you should replace your surge protector every 2 to 3 years.

Surge protectors wear out over time (usually in fewer than five years), so buy a surge protector that includes indicator lights. Indicator lights illuminate when the surge protector is no longer functioning properly. (Note that old surge protectors can still function as multiple-outlet power strips, delivering power to your equipment without protecting it.) A power surge could ruin your computer and other devices if you don't protect them. At $20 to $40, a quality surge protector is an excellent investment.

It's important to protect *all* your electronic devices, not just computers, from surges. Printers and other computer peripherals all require protection. However, it can be inconvenient to use individual surge protectors on everything. A more practical method is to install a **whole-house surge protector** (see Figure 2). Whole-house surge protectors function like other surge protectors, but they protect *all* electrical devices in the house. Typically, you need an electrician to install a whole-house surge protector, which will cost $200 to $300 (installed).

Data lines (transmission media), such as the coaxial cable that attaches to your modem, also can carry surges. Installing a **data line surge suppressor** for each data line connected to your computer through another device (such as a modem) will provide additional protection (see Figure 3). A data line surge suppressor is connected to the data line at a point before it reaches the modem or other device. In this way, it intercepts surges on the data line before they reach sensitive equipment.

Surge protectors won't necessarily guard against all surges. Lightning strikes can generate such high amounts of voltage that they can overwhelm a surge protector. As tedious as it sounds, unplugging computers and peripherals during an electrical storm is the only way to achieve absolute protection.

Power Outages

Like power surges, power outages can wreak havoc on a system. Mission-critical computers such as Web servers often are protected by **uninterruptible power supplies (UPSs)**, as shown in Figure 4. A UPS is a device that contains surge protection equipment and a large battery. When power is interrupted (such as during a blackout), the UPS continues to send power to the attached computer from its battery. Depending on the battery capacity, you have between about 20 minutes and 3 hours to save your work and shut down your computer properly.

Surge protector

FIGURE 2
A whole-house surge protector usually is installed at the breaker panel or near the electric meter. It protects all appliances in the home from electrical surges.

SOUND BYTE
Surge Protectors

In this Sound Byte, you'll learn about the major features of surge protectors and how they work. You'll also learn about the key factors you need to consider before buying a surge protector, and you'll see how easy it is to install one.

FIGURE 3
APC, a large manufacturer of surge protection devices, makes a wide range of data line surge suppressors to accommodate almost any type of data line.

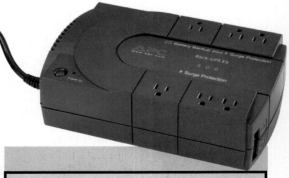

FIGURE 4
Although it looks like a fat surge protector, a UPS device contains a large battery that kicks in during power outages. If your computer is plugged into such a device, you'll have time to save your work before you lose power.

DETERRING THEFT

Because they are portable, notebooks are easy targets for thieves. Common sense dictates that you don't leave your notebook unattended or in places where it can be stolen easily (such as in hotel rooms or coffee shops). Three additional approaches to deterring computer theft include alarming them, locking them down, or installing devices that alert you when they are stolen.

Alarms

To prevent your notebook from being stolen, you can attach a motion alarm to it (see Figure 5). When you leave your notebook, you use a small device called a *key fob activator* to activate the alarm. If your notebook is moved while the alarm is activated, it emits a wailing 85-decibel sound. The fact that the alarm is visible acts as an additional theft deterrent, just like a "Beware of Dog" sign in a front yard.

Locks and Surrounds

Chaining a notebook to your work surface can be another effective way to prevent theft. As shown in Figure 6, a special locking mechanism is attached to the notebook (some notebooks are even manufactured with locking ports), and a hardened steel cable is connected to the locking mechanism. The other end of the cable is looped around something large and heavy, such as a desk. The cable lock requires the use of a key or knowing the combination to free the notebook. You should consider taking a cable lock with you when traveling to help deter theft in hotel rooms.

Many people associate computer theft only with notebooks or mobile devices. But desktop computers are vulnerable to theft also, especially theft of internal components such as RAM. Cable locks connect through special fasteners on the back of desktop computers, but components can still be stolen because these cables often don't prevent the system unit case from being opened. A more effective theft deterrent for desktops is a **surround** (or **cage**) such as that shown in Figure 7. A surround is a metal box that encloses the system unit, making it impossible to remove the case while still allowing access to ports and devices such as CD players.

Alarm

FIGURE 5
A notebook alarm sends out an ear-piercing sound if your notebook is moved before you deactivate the alarm.

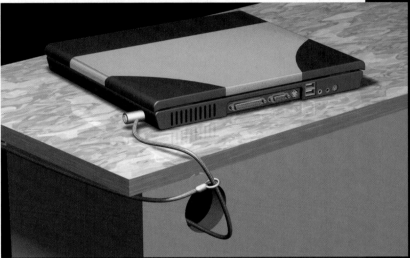

FIGURE 6
Cable locks are an effective deterrent to theft. New models have combination locks that alleviate keeping track of your keys.

FIGURE 7
Computer surrounds deter theft by making access to the internal components of the computer difficult while still allowing access to ports and drives.

Computers That "Phone Home"

You've probably heard of LoJack, the theft-tracking device used in cars. Car owners install a LoJack transmitter somewhere in their vehicle. If the vehicle is stolen, police activate the transmitter and use its signal to locate the car. Similar systems now exist for computers. Tracking software such as Computrace Complete or Computrace LoJack for Laptops (**www.absolute.com**) and PC or Mac PhoneHome (**www.pcphonehome.com**) enables the computer it is installed on to alert authorities as to its location if it is stolen.

To have your computer help with its own recovery, you install the tracking software on your computer's hard drive. After you install the software, it contacts a server at the software manufacturer's Web site each time you connect to the Internet. If your computer is stolen, you notify the software manufacturer. The software manufacturer instructs your computer to transmit tracking information (such as an IP address) that will assist authorities in locating and retrieving the stolen computer.

The files and directories holding the software are not visible to thieves looking for such software. What if the thieves reformat the hard drive in an attempt to destroy all files on the computer? The tracking software is written in such a way that it detects a reformat and hides the software code in a safe place in memory or on the hard drive (some sectors of a hard drive are not rewritten during most formats). That way, it can reinstall itself after the reformatting is completed.

KEEPING MOBILE DEVICES SAFE

PDAs and smartphones present their own unique hazards. Here are a few tips for keeping them secure.

Foiling Data Theft of Mobile Devices

PDA/smartphones can be vulnerable to unauthorized access if they are left unattended or are stolen. Although some devices offer basic protection features (such as password protection), sensitive business information often requires an additional level of protection. Security software such as TealLock from TealPoint Software (**www.tealpoint.com**) offers additional protection features such as data encryption and protection against attempts to break into a device through "brute force" attacks (running a program to guess all possible passwords). Most programs feature optional data self-destruct modes (sometimes known as **bomb software**) that destroy data on both internal memory and external data cards if repeated attempts are made to crack passwords.

Preventing Bluetooth Attacks

Bluetooth is a transmission medium for exchanging data wirelessly over short distances. Most PDA/smartphones are Bluetooth-enabled. Although progress is being made, Bluetooth hardware and software still are riddled with security holes, especially on smartphones. If you have a Bluetooth-enabled device, you are susceptible to two severe types of mischief:

1 **Bluesnarfing:** Bluesnarfing involves exploiting a flaw in the Bluetooth access software for the purpose of accessing a Bluetooth device and stealing the information contained on it. Think how much valuable information is contained on your smartphone (names, contact information, and meeting notes) that might be valuable to a business competitor. Unfortunately, Bluesnarfing is relatively easy (and cheap) because a lot of Bluesnarfing software is available on the Internet.

2 **Bluebugging:** Although much more difficult and expensive to execute, Bluebugging presents much more serious dangers. The process involves a hacker actually taking over control of a Bluetooth-enabled device so that he or she can do some or all of the following:

- make phone calls;
- send, receive, or read short message service (SMS) messages;
- establish Internet connections;
- write phonebook entries; or
- set call forwarding.

This is a real risk in Europe because Bluetooth and SMS are wildly popular there, but the rise of Bluetooth usage in the United States is making this a risk here as well. Many Europeans use their phones to make micropayments (small purchases from merchants that eventually appear on their cell phone bill) by a process known as *reverse SMS*. If a hacker Bluebugs your phone, he could potentially send payments to fake accounts he controls using reverse SMS.

So how can you protect yourself from Bluetooth attacks? Most devices with Bluetooth capability give you the option of making your device invisible to other Bluetooth devices. This does not affect your ability to use your devices paired to your Bluetooth device (such as a wireless headset for a phone). As vulnerabilities are discovered, PDA/smartphone manufacturers issue software patches. You must ensure that you update the software in your mobile devices just as you do for your computer's OS. Antivirus software also is also available for mobile devices, so you may wish to purchase this for your PDA/smartphone. For more information on securing your Bluetooth devices, go to **www.bluetomorrow.com**.

PROTECTING YOUR COMPUTER FROM UNAUTHORIZED ACCESS

To protect yourself even further, you may want to restrict access to the sensitive data on your computer. Both software and hardware solutions exist to restrict others from accessing your computer, helping you keep its contents safe.

Password Protection and Access Privileges

Windows Vista has built-in password protection of files as well as the entire desktop. If your computer is set up for multiple users with password protection, the Windows logon screen requires users to enter a password to gain access to the desktop. The computer can be set to default back to the Welcome screen after it is idle for a set period of time. This forces users to reenter a password to regain access to the computer. If someone attempts to log on to your computer without your password, that person won't be able to gain access. It is an especially good idea to use passwords on notebook computers or any computer that may be unattended for periods of time. Figure 8 shows the Control Panel screen used to set up a password on your user account.

There are two types of users in Windows Vista: administrators and standard users. Setting up a password on a user account prevents other standard users from being able to access that user's files. However, users with administrator privileges (perhaps your parents) could still see your files if you are a standard user. So be aware that your files may not be safe from all prying eyes!

Of course, password protection works only as well as your password does. Password cracking programs have become more sophisticated lately. In fact, some commonly available programs, such as John the Ripper, can test more than 1 million password combinations per second! Creating a secure password

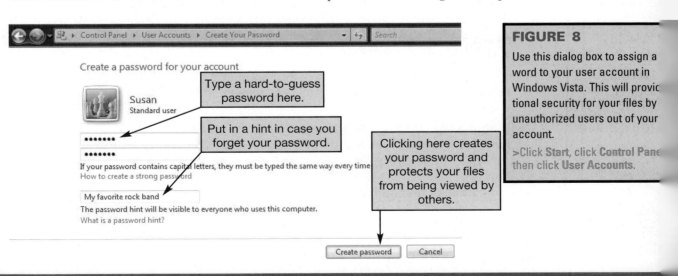

Create a password for your account

Susan
Standard user

Type a hard-to-guess password here.

Put in a hint in case you forget your password.

If your password contains capital letters, they must be typed the same way every time
How to create a strong password

My favorite rock band

The password hint will be visible to everyone who uses this computer.
What is a password hint?

Clicking here creates your password and protects your files from being viewed by others.

Create password   Cancel

FIGURE 8

Use this dialog box to assign a word to your user account in Windows Vista. This will provic tional security for your files by unauthorized users out of your account.

>Click **Start**, click **Control Pane** then click **User Accounts**.

ARE KLINGONESE PASSWORDS SAFE?

Many computer users are diehard science fiction fans. *Star Trek*, *Babylon 5*, and *Battlestar Galactica* have provided computer users with loads of planet names, alien races, alien vocabulary (Klingon words from the *Star Trek* series are especially popular), and starship names to use as passwords. Unfortunately, hackers are onto this ploy. Recently developed hacking programs use dictionaries of "geek-speak" to attempt to break passwords. Although "Qapla" (Klingonese for "success" and also used as "good-bye") might seem like an unbreakable password, don't bet your data on it! You can still use these words if you incorporate multiple words into a password that also contains symbols and numbers.

Use a different password for each system or Web site you need to access. This prevents access to every account you maintain if one of your passwords is discovered. (If you can't remember them all, use the password management feature of Windows Vista or the Firefox browser.)

Never tell anyone your password or write it down in a place where others might see it.

Change your password if you think someone may know it.

Check the strength of your password by using the free password checker found on the Security at Home section of the Microsoft Web site (**www.microsoft.com**).

Figure 9 shows some possible passwords and explains why they make good or bad candidates.

is therefore more important than ever. To do so, follow the basic guidelines shown here:

Your password should contain at least 14 characters and include numbers, symbols, and upper- and lowercase letters.

Your password should not be a single word or any word found in the dictionary.

Ideally, use a combination of several words with strategically placed uppercase characters.

Your password should not be easily associated with you (such as your birth date, the name of your pet, or your nickname).

Managing Your Passwords

Good security practices suggest that you have different passwords for different Web sites that you access and that you change your passwords frequently. The problem with well-constructed passwords is that they can be hard to remember. Fortunately, password management is now built into most browsers (or soon will be available). This takes the worry out of forgetting passwords because your browser does the remembering for you.

FIGURE 9
GOOD AND BAD PASSWORD CANDIDATES

GOOD PASSWORD	REASON
L8t2meGaNDalf351	Uses letters and numbers to come up with memorable phrase "Late to me" and adds it to a character name from *Lord of the Rings* plus a random number.
IwaLR8384GdY	First initials of first line of Green Day song *I Walk a Lonely Road* plus a random number and an abbreviation for Green Day
P1zzA244Water ShiPDowN	Easily remembered word with mix of alphanumeric characters and upper- and lowercase letters, your locker number at your gym, plus the title of a book that you like (with upper- and lowercase letters)
S0da&ICB3N&J3RRY	Mix of numbers, symbols, and letters. Stands for soda and ice cream and the names of famous ice cream makers with the number 3 instead of the letter E

BAD PASSWORD	REASON
Jsmith	Combination of first initial and last name
4smithkids	Even though this has alphanumeric combination, it is too descriptive of a family.
Brown5512	Last name and last four digits of phone number is easily decoded.
123MainSt	Your street address is an easily decoded password.

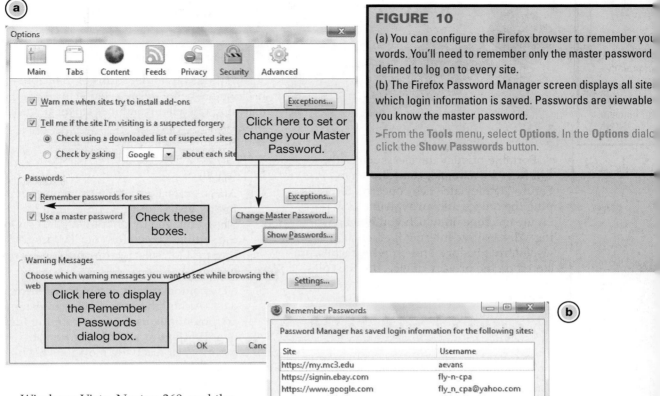

FIGURE 10
(a) You can configure the Firefox browser to remember you[r] words. You'll need to remember only the master password defined to log on to every site.
(b) The Firefox Password Manager screen displays all site[s] which login information is saved. Passwords are viewable [if] you know the master password.

>From the **Tools** menu, select **Options**. In the **Options** dial[og] click the **Show Passwords** button.

Windows Vista, Norton 360, and the Firefox browser make it easy to keep track of passwords by providing password management tools. From the Tools menu in Firefox, select Options, and then click the Security icon (the closed padlock) shown in Figure 10a. In the Passwords section, check **Remember passwords for sites** to have Firefox remember passwords when you log onto Web sites. Check **Use a master password**, which causes a dialog box to display, and enter a well-designed, secure password. The next time you go to a Web site that requires a login, Firefox displays a dialog box prompting you to have Firefox remember the login name and password for this site. The next time you return to the site and select a login option, just enter the master password and the Firefox Password Manager fills in the login and password information for you.

You also can see a list of sites maintained by the Firefox Password Manager by clicking the Show Passwords button, which displays the Remember Passwords dialog box (Figure 10b). Passwords for each site are displayed after you click the Show Passwords button and enter the master password.

So start using secure passwords and let your browser relieve you of the problem of trying to remember them all.

Keep Prying Eyes from Your Web Surfing Habits

If you use shared computers in such public places as libraries, coffee shops, and college student unions, you should be concerned about a subsequent user of the computer spying on your surfing habits. You never know what nefarious tools have been installed by hackers on a public computer. And when you are surfing wirelessly with your notebook at a public hot spot, shouldn't you protect yourself from hackers trying to intercept or spy on your data? Wouldn't it be nice if protection tools for Web surfing could be carried in your pocket?

FIGURE 11

Products such as the IronKey help to protect your privacy when working on computers away from your home or office.

Portable privacy devices, such as the IronKey (**www.ironkey.com**) shown in Figure 11, alleviate such concerns. Simply plug the device into an available USB port on the machine on which you will be working. All sensitive Internet files, such as cookies, Internet history, and browser caches, are stored on the privacy device, not the computer you are using. Privacy devices such as these often come preloaded with software such as Anonymizer Safe Surfing Suite (**www.anonymizer.com**), which shields your IP address from prying eyes, making it difficult (if not impossible) for hackers to tell where you are surfing on the Internet. These privacy devices also have password management tools that store all of your logon information and encrypt it in the event your privacy device falls into someone else's hands.

Keeping Instant Messenger Sessions Safe

Virus attacks and other forms of malicious hacking are being perpetrated at an alarming rate via instant messenger (IM) programs such as AOL Instant Messenger and Windows Live Messenger. To keep your IM sessions safe, follow these precautions:

1 **Allow contact only from users on your Buddy List.** This prevents you from being annoyed by unknown parties. On the settings screen for your IM program (Figure 12a), select **Allow only users on my Buddy List**.

2 **Never automatically accept transfers of data.** Although file and video transfers are potentially useful for swapping files over IM (Figure 12b), they are a common way of receiving malicious files, which can then infect your computer with viruses.

FIGURE 12

When you use AOL IM, check all of the preference screens for appropriate settings to ensure that your computer stays secure.

Settings - Privacy

🔍

General IM
Enhanced IM
Buddy List
Address Book
Expressions
Sounds
Sign In / Sign Out
Notifications
Privacy

Privacy:

Who can contact me
○ Allow all users to contact me
◉ Allow only users on my Buddy List ◀
○ Allow only the users below

Allow List:

[Add]

> Whenever you have a choice, restrict your contacts to people on your Buddy List. This makes it much tougher for scam artists and hackers to trick you.

Settings - Enhanced IM   – □ ✕

> Setting auto-acceptance options is never a good idea. You want to control exactly what is coming to your computer.

General IM
Enhanced IM
Offline IM
Mobile

Enhanced IM: ◀
☐ Auto-accept all Video invitations from Buddies on my Buddy List®
☐ Auto-accept all Talk invitations from Buddies on my Buddy List®
☐ Auto-accept all Instant Images and Direct IM invitations from Buddies on my Buddy List®
☐ Auto-accept all File Transfer invitations from Buddies on my Buddy List®

Keeping Windows Up to Date

Software patches to close security holes in Windows (or other operating systems) are issued periodically. To be sure you are protected from spreading threats, make sure these patches are installed on your computer. With Windows Vista (see Figure 13), this can be an automatic process. From the **Start** menu, select **Control Panel**, and then click the **Windows Update** icon to display the **Windows Update** window. Click the **Change settings** option to display the **Choose how Windows can install updates** dialog box (see Figure 13). Pick the best option for your situation (the first two options are good for broadband connections; the third option is better for dial-up).

Biometric Authentication Devices

Biometric authentication devices are devices you can attach to your computer or portable computing device that read a unique personal characteristic such as a fingerprint or the iris pattern in your eye and convert its pattern to a digital code. When you use the device, your pattern is read and compared to the one stored on the computer. Only users having an exact fingerprint or iris pattern match are allowed to access the computer.

Because no two people have the same biometric characteristics (fingerprints and iris patterns are unique), these devices provide a high level of security. They also eliminate the human error that can occur in password protection. (You might forget your password, but you won't forget to bring your fingerprint to the computer!) Some notebooks feature built-in fingerprint readers, and Figure 14a shows a mouse that includes a fingerprint reader. Another useful device is the APC Touch Biometric Pod Password Manager (see Figure 14b); after it identifies you by your fingerprint, the device provides logon information to password-protected Web sites you need to access.

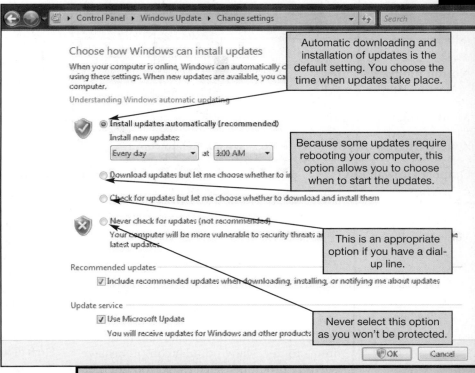

Control Panel ▶ Windows Update ▶ Change settings

Choose how Windows can install updates

When your computer is online, Windows can automatically c using these settings. When new updates are available, you ca computer.

Understanding Windows automatic updating

○ Install updates automatically (recommended)

Install new updates:

Every day ▼ at 3:00 AM ▼

○ Download updates but let me choose whether to i

○ Check for updates but let me choose whether to download and install them

○ Never check for updates (not recommended)

Your computer will be more vulnerable to security threats a latest updates

Recommended updates

☑ Include recommended updates when downloading, installing, or notifying me about updates

Update service

☑ Use Microsoft Update

You will receive updates for Windows and other products

OK   Cancel

Automatic downloading and installation of updates is the default setting. You choose the time when updates take place.

Because some updates require rebooting your computer, this option allows you to choose when to start the updates.

This is an appropriate option if you have a dial-up line.

Never select this option as you won't be protected.

FIGURE 13

Turning on the Automatic Updates feature of Windows Vista is an essential part of protecting your computer.

>From the Windows Vista **Control Panel**, click the **Windows Update** icon, and then select **Change settings**.

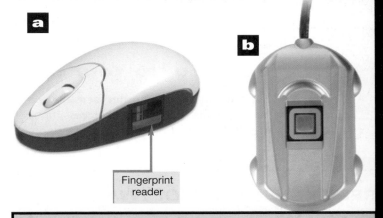

Fingerprint reader

FIGURE 14

(a) The SecuGen OptiMouse III is a two-button mouse with a scroll wheel that includes a digital fingerprint reader. (b) The APC Touch Biometric Pod Password Manager uses a fingerprint reader to recognize authorized users. The device stores all your logon names and passwords so that you don't have to keep track of them. As many as 20 users can use the same device, making it perfect for shared computers.

Other biometric devices include voice authentication and face pattern recognition systems, which are now starting to appear as installations in notebook computers.

FIGURE 15
POPULAR PERSONAL PROTECTION SOFTWARE

FIREWALL	URL
Norton Internet Security, Norton 360	www.symantec.com
McAfee Internet Security Suite	www.mcafee.com
ZoneAlarm Internet Security Suite	www.zonelabs.com
Outpost Firewall PRO	www.agnitum.com/products/outpost

Firewalls

As noted in Chapter 7, unauthorized access often occurs when your computer is connected to the Internet. You can best prevent such cases of unauthorized access by using either hardware or software personal firewalls. Hardware firewalls are often built into a router. Many popular comprehensive security programs, such as Norton Internet Security and McAfee Internet Security Suite, include firewalls as part of their protection packages. Figure 15 lists popular security software suites and stand-alone firewall programs. Setting up either a hardware or software firewall should be an integral part of your security arsenal when you are connected to the Internet.

Backing Up Your Data

The data on your computer faces three major threats: unauthorized access, tampering, and destruction. As noted in Chapter 7, a hacker can gain access to your computer and steal or alter your data. However, a more likely scenario is that you will lose your data unintentionally. You may accidentally delete files; your hard drive may break down, resulting in complete data loss; a virus may destroy your original file; or a fire may destroy the room that houses your computer. Because many of these factors are beyond your control, you should have a strategy for backing up your files. Backups are especially important if you are running a small business; the backup strategy for small businesses is quite similar to the procedures recommended for individuals.

Making file **backups**—copies of files that you can use to replace the originals, if they are lost or damaged—is important. To be truly secure, backups must be stored away from your home or office. You wouldn't want a fire or a flood destroying the backups along with the original data. Removable storage media, such as external hard drives, DVDs, CDs, and flash drives, are popular choices for backing up files because they hold a lot of data and can be transported easily.

Two types of files need backups—program files and data files.

- **Program files** are used to install software and usually come on CDs or DVDs or download from the Web. If any programs came preinstalled in your computer, then you may have received a CD or DVD that contains the original program. As long as you have the original media in a safe place, you shouldn't need to back up these files. If you have downloaded a program file from the Internet, however, you should make a copy of the program installation files on a removable storage device as a backup. If you didn't receive discs for installed programs with your computer, then see the next section for suggested strategies for backing up your entire computer.

- **Data files** are files created by you and include such files as spreadsheets, music files, contact lists, address books, e-mail archives, and your Favorites list from your browser.

You should back up your data files frequently, depending on how much work you can afford to lose. You should always back up data files when you make changes to them, especially if those changes involve

FREE PROTECTION SOFTWARE

If you want to protect your computer but don't want to buy software, you're not out of luck. You can download plenty of programs for free off the Web. Many companies offer free versions of their software that either expire after a certain time or offer fewer features than commercial versions. In many cases, these free versions are sufficient for home use. One site for downloading free software is **www.download.com**. This should be your first stop when looking for free software you can use to protect your computer. But be aware that some free software can contain malware, so make sure to use anti-malware software to keep yourself protected.

PROTECTION FROM PHISHING SITES

As you learned in Chapter 3, phishing attacks are attempts to lure you to Web sites that look legitimate (such as banking sites) and then trick you into revealing information that can be used in identity thefts. Because phishing has become such a problem, most Internet browsers have a built-in phishing filter that examines Web sites to see if they are known or suspected fraudulent sites. The major Internet security packages—for example, McAfee and Norton (see Figure 16)—also offer phishing protection tools. When you have the Norton Toolbar displayed in your browser, you are constantly informed about the legitimacy of the site. In fact, if you have an Internet security package installed, you can turn off the phishing filter in your browser to speed up the loading of Web pages.

Another way to protect yourself is to never use your credit card number when you shop online. Although it sounds impossible, credit card providers such as Citibank are offering services such as "Virtual Account Numbers" for their customers. Before purchasing a product online, you visit an online site, where you are assigned a new virtual account number each time you visit. This number is tied to your real credit card account but can be used only once. That means that if the number is stolen, it's no good to thieves because they can't use the virtual account number because you've already used it.

The Norton Internet Security Suite provides protection against phishing sites by preventing suspected fraudulent sites from loading in your browser.

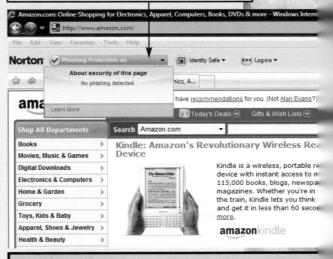

FIGURE 16

Not sure if you are on the Amazon Web site or a cleverly disgui[sed] phishing site? The Norton fraud toolbar reassures you that all is

hours of work. It may not seem important to back up your history term paper file when you finish it, but do you really want to do all that work again if your computer crashes before you have a chance to turn in your paper?

To make backups easier, store all your data files in one folder on your hard drive. For example, on your hard drive you can create a folder called Documents. You can then create subfolders (such as History Homework, Music Files, and so on) within the Documents folder. If you store all your data files in one place, to back up your files, you simply copy the Documents folder and all of its subfolders onto an alternative storage medium.

Remembering to schedule backups is often the toughest part of file-safety procedures. Windows Vista includes a backup utility that provides a quick and easy way to schedule backups of files on a regular basis. Unfortunately, this utility lacks features that allow you to select only certain folders or directories for backup. A better choice is a free product called Cobian Backup (**www.educ.umu.se/~cobian/ index.htm**), shown in Figure 17. Cobian allows you to easily configure backup tasks and select directories or individual files to back up on a regular basis.

Backup Software— Not Just for Data Files

Your OS and software applications also need to be protected by backups. Although you can create restore points in Windows Vista to take your system back to the time before it had a problem, this doesn't help in the case of a hard drive failure. If you

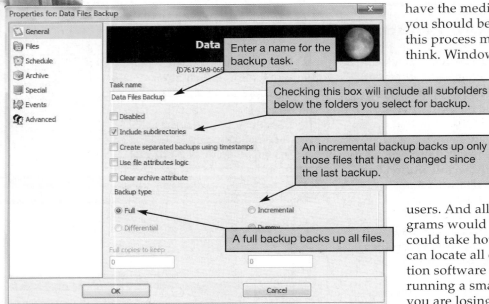

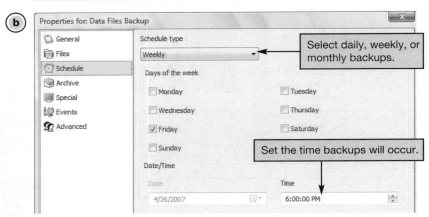

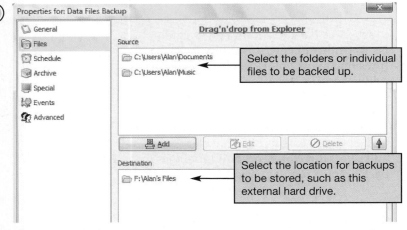

FIGURE 17

(a) The General tab in Cobian Backup lets you choose the type of backup and name it. (b) The Schedule window makes it easy to schedule backups on a regular basis. (c) Dragging and dropping files from Windows Explorer makes it easy to define folders and files that should be backed up, as well as the destination for the backup files.

have the media to reinstall Windows, then you should be in good shape—although this process may take more time than you think. Windows has many settings that need to be reinstated to get your machine functioning the way you had it set up. Working with these settings can be intimidating for the average user and just plain time consuming for experienced users. And all of your application programs would need to be reinstalled, which could take hours (or days), assuming you can locate all of the discs for your application software CDs and DVDs. If you are running a small business, then the time you are losing reconfiguring the computers probably means lost revenue. For complete protection, you should use backup software such as Genie Backup Manager (**www.genie-soft.com**) or Safety Drill, which comes with Maxtor external hard drives. These products create an image of your entire system. Taking an image of your entire system and storing it on another hard drive provides you with the ultimate protection. With a backup of your entire hard drive, including your system image, you won't need to reinstall all of the program software from the original media. Instead, you just replace the broken hard drive with the backup hard drive (or copy the contents of the backup drive to a new drive).

Online Backups

A final backup solution is to store backups of your files online, which is often the most convenient solution for small businesses. For a fee, companies such as Iron Mountain (**http://backup.ironmountain.com**) or IBackup (**www.ibackup.com**) can provide you with such online storage. If you store a backup of your entire system on the Internet, then you won't need to buy an additional hard drive for backups. This method also takes the worry out of keeping your backups in a safe place because they're always stored in an area far away from your computer (such as on the backup company's server). However, if you'd like to store your backups online, make sure you have high-speed Internet access.

ADDITIONAL RESOURCES

Hackers, spammers, and advertisers constantly develop new methods for circumventing the protection that security software provides. Although the manufacturers of such software constantly update and improve security, you should keep abreast of new techniques being employed that could threaten your privacy and security. *SC Magazine* is a security magazine available in a free online version at **www.scmagazine.com**. Take a few minutes each month and scan the articles to make sure you have taken the appropriate protective measures on your computer to keep it safe and secure.

SHOULD YOU BACK UP YOUR FILES STORED ON THE SCHOOL NETWORK?

Most likely, if you're allowed to store files on your school's network, these files are backed up on a regular basis. However, you should check with your school's network administrators to determine how often they're backed up and how you would go about requesting files be restored from the backup media if they're damaged or deleted. But don't rely on these network backups to bail you out if your data files are lost or damaged. It may take days for the network administrators to get around to restoring your files. It is better to keep backups of your data files yourself (especially for homework and project files) so that you can immediately restore them. Buy a large-capacity flash drive and carry it with you!

8

Mobile Computing:

Keeping Your Data on Hand

Objectives

After reading this chapter, you should be able to answer the following questions:

1. What are the advantages and limitations of mobile computing? **(pp. 380–382)**

2. What are the various mobile computing devices? **(p. 382)**

3. How do cell phone components resemble a traditional computer, and how do they work? **(pp. 382–388)**

4. What can I carry in a portable media player, and how does it store data? **(pp. 388–393)**

5. Why would I use a PDA/smartphone, and what internal components and features do they have? **(pp. 393–402)**

6. How can I synchronize my PDA/smartphone with my computer? **(pp. 396–397)**

7. What is a Tablet PC, and why would I want to use one? **(pp. 402–403)**

8. How powerful are notebooks, and how do they compare to desktop computers? **(pp. 402–408)**

ACTIVE HELPDESK

- Using Portable Media Players **(p. 391)**
- Using PDA/Smartphones **(p. 393)**

Using Mobile Computing Devices

Kendra wakes up at 5 A.M. to get an early start on what will be a long day. She's taking a business trip for her new job, and it's a long flight from Boston to Los Angeles. She's packed her smartphone and her notebook (laptop), and she has updated the information for all her L.A. contacts. Despite her preparation, when she arrives at the airport, she finds her flight has been canceled. Trying not to get upset, she pulls out her smartphone, accesses the Internet via a wireless Internet service provider, and rebooks a ticket on a competing airline while fellow passengers are racing off to the ticket counter. The airline ticket site was recently enhanced, so her booking information was automatically downloaded to her Microsoft Outlook files. With an e-mail to her business contacts in L.A. letting them know she'll be late, she smoothes the first wrinkle in her trip.

As Kendra waits for her new flight, she checks her work schedule on her smartphone and e-mails a few clients. Because she'll be driving from the airport to the hotel on unfamiliar streets, she uses the map software in her smartphone that shows her the best route. She calls the rental car agency and tells them she'll be picking up the car later than planned, then checks out some L.A. restaurant reviews on the Internet. With an hour left before her plane takes off, she does some work on her notebook. She updates her expense report file, including the new flight information. Although canceled flights are never convenient, at least she's had a few hours to take care of some work before arriving in L.A.

As this scenario indicates, mobile devices can offer you a great deal of convenience and can increase your productivity when you're away from the office. And going mobile is increasingly becoming the norm because more people are buying cell phones and other mobile devices. In fact, the current number of subscribers to cell phone services in the United States exceeds the number of those who use wired telephone service lines. With more than 250 million Americans currently owning cell phones, mobility is here to stay!

In this chapter, we discuss the advantages and disadvantages of going mobile. We also look at the range of mobile computing devices you can choose from and discuss their components, features, and capabilities. Along the way, you'll learn how you can synchronize your mobile devices to make even better use of them. Whether you have already gone mobile or are still considering your options, this chapter will help you become a savvy consumer, taking full advantage of the world of mobile computing.

SOUND BYTES

- PDA/Smartphones on the Road and at Home **(p. 394)**
- Connecting with Bluetooth **(p. 397)**
- Tablet and Notebook Tour **(p. 407)**

Mobile Computing: Is It Right for You?

Just 30 years ago, the idea of a powerful personal computer that could fit on a desktop was a dream. Today, you can carry computers around in your backpack, fit them in your pocket, and even incorporate them into your clothes. **Mobile computing devices**—portable electronic tools such as cell phones, PDA/smartphones, portable media players, and notebooks—are dramatically changing our day-to-day lives, allowing us to communicate with others, remain productive, and access a wide array of information no matter where we are.

Still, going mobile isn't for everyone. Although having instant access to your e-mail, schedule, and the Internet wherever you are during the day can be convenient and boost your productivity, there is a downside associated with mobile computing. Because mobile devices have been miniaturized, they're more expensive and less rugged than stationary desktop equipment, so it's important that you assess the advantages of how going mobile fits with your lifestyle.

How do I know whether mobile devices are right for me? Before you buy any mobile device, consider whether your needs match what mobile devices can offer. To do so, ask yourself these questions:

- **Do I need to communicate with others when I'm away from my home or office?** Whether it means talking on the phone or checking your e-mail, if you need to communicate no matter where you are, mobile devices may be right for you.

- **Do I need to access my electronic information when I'm away from my desk?** If you need to access and make changes to electronic information (such as an Outlook schedule or Excel report) when you're out and about, then a more powerful mobile device such as a PDA/smartphone or notebook would be a valuable tool. However, if it's as efficient for you to keep paper records when you're away from your computer and later enter that data into your computer, you may not need mobile devices.

- **Do I need to access the Internet when I'm away from my desk?** Mobile devices that are **Web-enabled** allow you to have constant access to the Internet wherever you are. Of course, you'll access the Internet at greater speeds and for less cost when you're at home or in the office. However, if you need quickly changing information when you're away from your desk, Web-enabled mobile devices may be right for you.

- **Are the convenience and productivity offered by mobile devices important to me?** Mobile devices can provide you with a great deal of convenience and help you to be more productive. For example, a nursing student would have an easier time performing a diagnostic interview with a patient if the reference codes she needed were available in her PDA rather than in a huge stack of books. Likewise, students who take online classes with course management products such as Blackboard can download their courses and carry them on an ultramobile 2-pound computer such as the Asus Eee PC so that they can work on their assignments anywhere, with or without Internet access.

- **Is the information I need to carry already in an electronic format?** Do you currently use personal information management (PIM) software such as Microsoft Outlook to store your daily schedule and contact list? Or are your schedule and contact list currently in paper form? Converting information to an electronic format and learning how to use mobile devices are hidden costs of going mobile.

You also need to consider your needs when determining the type of device to select. If you are a salesperson who constantly demonstrates multimedia products to clients, then perhaps you need a high-powered multimedia notebook such as the Dell XPS M2010 (see Figure 8.1a)—despite its hefty price tag and weight. Or maybe you just need to keep in touch with your friends while listening to music and watching videos, so the Motorola MotoRazr V3 might suffice (see Figure 8.1b). Perhaps you don't need a phone but want a larger screen for video watching, in which case the Apple iPod Touch is best (see Figure 8.1c). Consider the activities you'll be pursuing while mobile before selecting a device.

FIGURE 8.1

The portable device that is right for you depends on your needs. (a) With a 20.1-inch monitor, eight speakers, and a detachable wireless keyboard, the Dell XPS M2010 is a portable computer that easily has the power of a multimedia desktop system. It also weighs 18 lbs. (b) The Motorola MotoRazr V3 features picture caller ID, Bluetooth connectivity, and a 3D graphics engine to display photos and video. (c) The iPod Touch is a personal media player that delivers music, video, games, and Internet connectivity.

MOBILE DEVICE LIMITATIONS

What are the limitations of mobile devices? It's important that you consider the following when figuring out whether your needs match the limitations of mobile devices:

- Battery life limits the usefulness of some mobile devices.
- The screen is small on most devices.
- The speed of Internet connection available to mobile devices, although increasing, is still low compared to wired high-speed Internet access available in your home or office.

The benefits of Internet connectivity also are dependent on the wireless Internet coverage in your area. For example, if you travel in rural areas, it may be difficult to take advantage of wireless Internet connectivity. So if you are considering wireless Internet access, make sure you check the areas of coverage for the providers you are considering.

As a student, you should consider how much of your campus is covered by wireless connectivity. Is your residence hall covered? your classrooms? the library? Some schools create "wireless clouds" that enable you to be covered no matter where you are on campus. Other schools offer little coverage, making wireless connectivity to the Internet more difficult.

You must decide whether the extra cost of going mobile is worth the value and convenience. Mobile computing devices are more expensive and less rugged than

FIGURE 8.2 Are Mobile Devices Right for You?

Consideration	Yes	No
When I'm away from my desk, I need to communicate with others both with voice and e-mail.		
I need to access my electronic information wherever I am.		
I need to access the Internet when I'm away from my desk.		
The added convenience and productivity of mobile devices are important to me.		
My needs match the limitations of devices (such as short battery life, small display screen, and slower Internet connection speeds).		
Most of my living and travel locations are covered by wireless Internet access.		
It is worth the added expense for me to go mobile.		

desktop systems. Vibration, falls, dust, and liquids can all destroy your notebook, iPod, or smartphone. If the environment you live in or travel through is dusty or bumpy, for example, then you should be prepared to spend money on equipment designed for rugged conditions, on additional warranty coverage, or on repair and replacement costs. Finally, desktop systems always boast more expandability and better performance for the same cost when compared with mobile computers.

So, is mobile computing right for me? Figure 8.2 presents a checklist of the factors you need to consider when deciding whether to go mobile. Do your needs to communicate and access electronic information and the Internet when you're away from your desk make mobile devices a good investment?

Mobile Computing Devices

When you do decide to go mobile, you'll find a wide range of mobile computing devices on the market today:

- **Cellular phones** feature traditional phone services such as call waiting and voice mail. Many now come with calendars, contact databases, text messaging, e-mail, GPS, and Internet browsing capabilities.
- **Portable media players (PMPs)** allow you to carry music, video, and other digital files.

- **PDA/smartphones** are a result of the **convergence** (or combination of features) of various portable devices such as PMPs and cellular phones. These handheld devices provide solutions when running software such as Excel or Word is important as well as Web browsing, e-mail, and multimedia viewing.
- **Subnotebooks** run fully featured operating systems but weigh in at 2 pounds or less.
- **Notebooks and Tablet PCs** are more powerful and have larger screens than PDA/smartphones and subnotebooks.

Figure 8.3 lists the main features of these mobile devices. In the next sections, we look at each device in detail.

Cellular Phones

Cellular phones (or **cell phones**) have evolved from clunky, boxlike devices to compact, fully featured communication and information storage devices. Cell phones offer all of the features available on a traditional telephone system, including auto-redial, call timers, and voice-mail capabilities. Some cell phones also feature voice-activated dialing, which is important for hands-free operation. In addition, cell phones can offer Internet access, text messaging, PIM features, voice recording, GPS services, and digital image and video capture.

FIGURE 8.3 Mobile Devices: Price, Size, Weight, and Capabilities

Device	Relative Price	Approximate Size	Approximate Weight	Standard Capabilities
Cell phone	$$ (Includes cost for the phone, a monthly plan, and Internet access)	5" × 2" × 0.5"	0.25 lb.	Provides voice, e-mail, limited access to application software, and Internet connectivity
PMP	$$–$$$	3" × 2" × 0.5"	0.25 lb. or more	Provides storage of digital music, video, and other digital files
PDA/smartphone	$$–$$$	4.5" × 2" × .75"	0.25 lb.	Provides PIM capabilities, access to application software, and access to the Internet
Subnotebook	$$$$	7" × 5"	1–2 lbs.	Have 7" or smaller screens and run fully functioning operating system and applications
Tablet PC	$$$$$	10" × 8" × 1"	3 lbs.	Provides PIM capabilities, access to application software, access to the Internet, and special handwriting- and speech-recognition capabilities
Notebook	$$$$–$$$$$	10" × 13" × 2"	5 to 8 lbs.	Provides all the capabilities of a desktop computer while also being portable

CELL PHONE HARDWARE

Is a cell phone considered a computer? Cell phones are so advanced that they have many of the same components as a computer: a processor (central processing unit, or CPU), memory, and input and output devices, as shown in Figure 8.4. A cell phone also requires software and has its own operating system (OS).

What does the processor inside a cell phone do? Although the processor inside a cell phone is obviously not as fast or as high-powered as a processor in a desktop computer, it is still responsible for a great number of tasks. The processor coordinates sending all of the data between the other electronic components inside the phone. It also runs the cell phone's operating system, which provides a user interface so that you can change phone settings, store information, play games, and so on.

Is there a standard operating system for phones? No, each cell phone manufacturer makes its own tweaks to an operating system and designs its own user interface. This can make switching phones daunting because you have to learn how to use a different set of commands and icons.

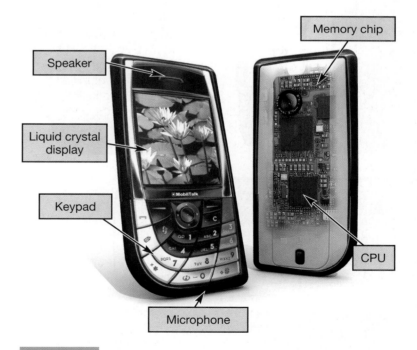

FIGURE 8.4

Inside your cell phone, you'll find some familiar components, including a CPU, a memory chip, input devices such as a microphone and a keypad, and output devices such as a display screen and a speaker.

FIGURE 8.5

A phone with the OpenMoko operating system installed. Why learn a new system each time you buy a phone ... and why pay for it?

One popular operating system for PDA/smartphones is the **Symbian OS**. PDA/smartphones often use the Windows Mobile operating system. Apple's iPhone uses a version of the OS X operating system. These operating systems are required to translate the user's commands into instructions for the processor.

One open source group of coders has formed an open source project to develop the first free phone operating system. The goal for the OpenMoko operating system (see Figure 8.5) is to provide a consistent operating system and interface that users can install on compatible phones when they upgrade to avoid relearning tasks.

What does the memory chip inside a cell phone do? The operating system and the information you save into your phone (such as phone numbers and addresses) need to be stored in memory. The operating system is stored in read-only memory (ROM) because the phone would be useless without that key piece of software. As you learned earlier in this text, there are two kinds of memory used in computers: volatile memory, which requires power to save data, and nonvolatile memory, which can store data even when the power is turned off. ROM is nonvolatile, or permanent, memory. This means that when you turn off your cell phone, the data that is stored in ROM (including the operating system) does not get lost.

Other phone data, such as ring tones, are stored in separate internal memory chips. Full-featured phones have as much as 20 megabytes (MB) of memory (smartphones generally have more) that you can use to store contact data, ring tones, images, songs, video, and even small software applications such as currency converters or a world clock.

What input and output devices do cell phones use? The input devices for a cell phone are primarily the microphone and a keypad. Some phones such as the Pantech Duo (see Figure 8.6a) feature a hidden

FIGURE 8.6

(a) The Pantech Duo includes a built-in QWERTY keyboard. (b) The Nokia N73 can input both still photographs and video to your phone. With an added memory card, you can even watch movies. (c) Apple iPhone 3G provides fast connections to the Internet for a full-featured browsing experience. Why wait to get to a computer when you can update your Facebook page on the go?

keyboard to make sending e-mail or text messages more efficient. Other phones feature touch-sensitive screens that allow you to input data. Cell phones often include a digital camera. The Nokia N73 (see Figure 8.6b) offers a high-quality 3.2 megapixel camera that can input photographs or capture live video to your phone. Picture or video messaging is popular with cell phone users. Phone users can transmit photos and video files via e-mail, post the files to Web sites (such as **www.myspace.com**), or send them directly to other phones. The Apple iPhone 3G (see Figure 8.6c) is much more than a phone; it provides the ability to surf the Web, check e-mail, play music, and watch video.

Cell phone output devices include a speaker and a liquid crystal display (LCD). Higher-end models include full-color, high-resolution plasma displays. Such displays are becoming increasingly popular as more people are using their cell phones to send and receive the digital images included in multimedia text messages and e-mail, and even watch TV. Cell phone and cable providers are teaming up to deliver broadcast TV programs directly to cell phones through services such as Verizon V Cast and Sprint TV Live. Cell phones such as the LG VX9400 (see Figure 8.7) are optimized for TV reception and viewing.

HOW CELL PHONES WORK

How do cell phones work? When you speak into a cell phone, the sound enters the microphone as a sound wave. Because analog sound waves need to be digitized (that is, converted into a sequence of 1s and 0s that the cell phone's processor can understand), an **analog-to-digital converter chip** converts your voice's sound waves into digital signals. Next, the digital data must be compressed, or squeezed, into the smallest possible space so that it will transmit more quickly to another phone. The processor cannot perform the mathematical operations required at this stage quickly enough, so a specialized chip called the **digital signal processor** is included in a cell phone to handle the compression work. Finally, the digital data is transmitted as a radio wave through the cellular network to the destination phone.

When you receive an incoming call, the digital signal processor decompresses the incoming message. An amplifier boosts the signal to make it loud enough, and it is then passed on to the speaker.

What's "cellular" about a cell phone? A set of connected "cells" makes up a cellular network. Each cell is a geographic area centered on a **base transceiver station**, which is a large communications tower with antennas, amplifiers, and receivers and transmitters. When you place a call on a cell phone, a base station picks up the request for service. The station then passes the request to a central location called a **mobile switching center**. (The reverse process occurs when you receive an incoming call on a cell phone.) A telecommunications company builds its network by constructing a series of cells that overlap in an attempt to guarantee that its cell phone customers have coverage no matter where they are.

As you move during your phone call, the mobile switching center monitors the strength of the signal between your cell phone and the closest base station. When the signal is no longer strong enough between your cell phone and the base station, the mobile switching center orders the next base station to take charge of your call. When your cell phone "drops out," it sometimes does so because the distance between base stations was too great to provide an adequate signal.

CELL PHONE TEXT MESSAGING

What is text messaging? Short message service (SMS)—often just called *text messaging*—is a technology that allows you to send short text messages (as many as 160 characters) over mobile networks. To send SMS messages from your cell phone, you use the numeric keypad or a presaved template and type your message. You can send SMS messages to other mobile devices (such as cell phones or pagers) or to any e-mail address. You also can use SMS to send short text messages from your home computer to mobile devices such as your friend's cell phone.

FIGURE 8.7

With a swiveling screen and extendable antenna, the LG VX9400 is a phone first but a TV second!

How does SMS work? SMS uses the cell phone network to transmit messages. When you send an SMS message, an SMS calling center receives the message and delivers it to the appropriate mobile device using something called store-and-forward technology. This technology allows users to send SMS messages to any other SMS device in the world.

Many SMS fans like text messaging because it can be cheaper than a phone call (see Figure 8.8), and it allows the receivers to read messages when it is convenient for them. In fact, in some countries such as Japan, text messaging is more popular than voice messaging. If you plan to do a lot of texting, look for a phone with a good text prediction algorithm. Typing a single letter pulls up a list of popular words beginning with that letter, saving you typing time. For example, the T9 algorithm also "learns" from your usage patterns and displays the most used word first.

Can I send and receive multimedia files over a cell phone? SMS technology allows you to send only text messages. However, an extension of SMS called **multimedia message service (MMS)** allows you to send messages that include text, sound, images, and video clips to other phones or e-mail addresses. MMS messages actually arrive as a series of messages; you view the text, then the image, and then the sound, and so on. You can then choose to save just one part of the message (such as the image), all of it, or none of it. MMS users can subscribe to financial, sports, and weather

BITS AND BYTES

Make Your Phone Deliver

Carriers offer many additional services for your cell phone. Music ID, for example, allows you to identify a song easily. Just hold your phone close to the speaker for 15 seconds. You will then receive a text message with the name of the artist and the song. Music ID has a database of more than 3 million songs, so you can be the first to grab those new titles.

Other services can be added to your phone plan. For example, you can subscribe to high-definition radio stations over your cell phone. The extra fee allows you to stream more than 50 channels of commercial free digital radio through your phone. Many phones are equipped for navigation services such as Telenav Navigator. Telenav delivers turn-by-turn instructions to you over your phone and displays real-time traffic information.

The Apple iPhone offers a few unique services. Movies can be rented from the iTunes store and delivered directly to your phone. A new program being tested with Apple and Starbucks is the Now Playing service. With Now Playing, iPhone users can click on a special application that will identify, purchase, and download the song they are currently listening to at their Starbucks location. Phones are not just for texting!

FIGURE 8.8 Free Text Messaging Services

SMS Code	Service Name	Web Site	Description
46645 (googl)	Google SMS	www.google.com/sms	Obtain information such as addresses, phone numbers, driving directions, sports scores, and movie listings from the Google search engine.
6107267837 (610 Smarter)	Smarter SMS	www.smarter.com/sms	Send product part number to find out which companies offer the product for the lowest price.
44636 (4Info)	4INFO	www.4info.net	Similar to Google SMS but also handles flight information and horoscopes.
242 242 (cha cha)	Cha cha	www.chacha.com	Human "guides" provide answers to any question in conversational English.
3109043113	411sms	www.411sms.com	Offers many services, including address and phone listings, turn-by-turn directions, movie show times, stock quotes, hotspot locations, dictionary definitions, horoscopes, and foreign language translations.

---

services that will "push" information to them, sending it automatically to their phones in MMS format.

CELL PHONE INTERNET CONNECTIVITY

How do I get Internet service for my phone? Just as you pay an Internet service provider (ISP) for Internet access for your desktop or notebook computer, connecting your cell phone to the Internet requires that you have a **wireless Internet service provider** (or **wireless ISP**). Phone companies that provide cell phone calling plans (such as T-Mobile, Verizon, and AT&T) usually double as wireless ISPs. Internet connectivity plans, and often text messaging plans, are usually known as **data plans**. Data charges are separate from cell phone calling charges and are provided at rates different from voice calls. You should assess your data needs and select a plan that provides an adequate amount of data usage.

At what speed can my phone connect to the Internet? As noted earlier, accessing the Internet on a mobile device comes with limitations. First, the connection often is slower than what you experience at your home. Although broadband speeds of 15 megabits per second (Mbps) are achievable at home, your cell phone probably will connect at a much lower speed, which usually won't exceed 200 to 300 Kbps.

Providers have introduced many new phones that support faster data transfer technologies based on two standards: EDGE (short for enhanced data rate for global evolution) and EVDO (evolution data optimized). EDGE and EVDO have brought mobile devices much faster data transfer: as high as 700 Kbps (or more) under ideal conditions. Using phones that support EDGE or EVDO and a phone plan that allows data transfer, both uploading information (such as e-mail messages that include photos) and downloading information (such as from a company intranet or the Internet) can take place much more quickly. These technologies could replace WiFi for Internet connectivity on mobile devices because they are more reliable and less susceptible to interference. And you won't have to hunt for a WiFi hotspot because these technologies are used to blanket major urban areas with connectivity.

What is the Internet like on a phone? On phones that have a limited amount of screen space, it is difficult to view Web pages without a great deal of horizontal scrolling. This is because most Web sites are designed for viewing on desktop monitors, which have much wider pixel widths than mobile screens. To enhance your Internet browsing experience on mobile devices, special **microbrowser** software runs on your cell phone. Microbrowser software provides a Web browser, which is optimized to display Web content effectively on the smaller screen (see Figure 8.9). Popular versions of microbrowser software include Internet Explorer Mobile (included with the Windows Mobile OS) and Opera Mobile. Opera Mobile uses special small screen rendering technology to reformat the Web images to fit on your cell phone screen, eliminating the need for horizontal scrolling. For the best Web experience, consider a PDA/smartphone that has a larger screen such as an iPhone, which boasts a 3.5-inch diagonal measure screen.

FIGURE 8.9

Microbrowser software helps you access the Internet from your cell phone or PDA/smartphone.

More commonly, Web sites are being created with content specifically designed for wireless devices. This specially designed content, which is text-based and contains no graphics, is written in a format called **Wireless Markup Language (WML)**. Content is designed so that it fits the smaller display screens of handheld mobile devices.

Can I keep my e-mail up to date using my cell phone? A popular feature of cell phones with Internet access is checking e-mail. BlackBerry handhelds were the original devices that were optimized to check e-mail, and they used to be the e-mail devices of choice. However, Windows Mobile now delivers a solid e-mail experience on a cell phone (and it syncs with your Outlook e-mail on your computer), so even though BlackBerrys are still an excellent option, they aren't the only option. If checking and sending e-mail while on the go is mission critical for you, then check out PDA/smartphones with larger displays and integrated keyboards that make it easier to manage your e-mail. Most portable e-mail

BITS AND BYTES

Phoning Home—Accessing Your Home Computer from Your Cell Phone

An estimated 1 billion cellular phones currently are deployed that aren't considered smartphones. But don't count your cheap phone out of the running if it doesn't have advanced software capabilities. You can still use it to access your home computer remotely and retrieve that big presentation you need for this afternoon. Remote access services such as GoToMyPC (**www.gotomypc.com**) and LogMeIn (**www.logmein.com**) can help and are free of charge. As long as you have a browser on your phone and a data plan with your provider, you can access the files on your computer from your phone without installing any software on the phone. So, you may not have to trade in that low-end phone yet. Just try getting it to work a little harder!

devices now feature special "push" technology (pioneered by BlackBerry) to automatically deliver your e-mail to your phone so that your e-mail finds you whether or not you're thinking about it.

Can I get a virus on my cell phone? Although viruses can already target cell phones, manufacturers and software engineers are bracing themselves for a tidal wave of viruses targeted to cell phones. With half of users reporting they send confidential e-mails by using their cell phones and one-third of users indicating they access bank account or credit card information, cell phones are the next most likely realm of attack by cybercriminals. The potential of cell phone viruses ranges from the mildly annoying (certain features of your phone stop working) to the expensive (your phone is used without your knowledge to make expensive calls).

How can you prevent cell phone viruses? Symantec, McAfee, and F-Secure are the leading companies currently providing antivirus software for mobile devices. Products are designed for specific phone operating systems such as Symantec Mobile Security for Symbian, which is designed for phones running the Symbian OS. Although viruses plaguing cell phones have not yet reached the volume of viruses attacking PC operating systems, with the proliferation of mobile devices it is expected that cell phone virus attacks will increase. If no antivirus program is available for your

phone's operating system, then the best precautions are common sense ones. Don't download ring tones, games, or other software from unfamiliar Web sites, and check the phone manufacturer's Web site frequently to see whether your phone needs any software upgrades that could patch security holes.

Portable Media Players

Portable media players have taken the electronics market by storm! Originally, these devices were known as MP3 players and were named after the MP3 format used for efficiently storing music as digital files (or a series of bits). **Portable media players (PMPs)** are small portable devices (such as an iPod) that enable you to carry your MP3 files around with you. But digital media isn't limited to music. Digital files (using special data formats such as AVI or MPEG-4) can hold video, audio, and images. Therefore, many companies now manufacture PMPs that handle video and still images, as well as music files. Many smartphones are capable of storing and playing media files, but for the best experience, a dedicated media player is often the optimal choice because PMPs tend to offer more features and storage.

Depending on the player, you can carry several hours of music or video—or possibly your entire CD collection—in an incredibly small device. For example, the Apple iPod (with a 160 GB hard drive) is 4.1 inches by 2.4 inches (and only 0.53 inch thick), yet it can hold as many as 40,000 songs, 50,000 images, or 200 hours of video. The most compact players are slightly larger than a flash drive (although they hold far less music than the iPod). Figure 8.10 shows several models of PMPs, all of which connect to computers via USB 2.0 ports.

Are all music files MP3 files? The letters at the end of a filename (the file extension) indicate how the data in the file is organized. MP3 is the name of just one type of file format used to store digital music, but many others exist, such as AAC and WMA. There are also many video formats such as DivX, MPEG-4 (which usually has an .mp4 extension), WMV, and XviD.

FIGURE 8.10 Some Portable Media Players and Their Characteristics

	Media Capacity	Built-In Flash Memory	Hard Drive Capacity	Connection to Computer	Other Features
Creative Labs Digital MP3 Zen Nano Plus 	As many as 500 songs	512 MB to 1 GB	None	USB 2.0 port	Built-in FM radio, voice recorder, and four-band equalizer.
Oregon Scientific MP121 	Up to 32 hours of music	1 GB	None	USB 2.0 port	Waterproof to 3 feet deep, built-in pedometer, built-in FM radio, and equalizer.
Apple iPod Nano 	As many as 2,000 songs or 8 hours of video	4 GB to 8 GB	None	USB 2.0 port	Weighs only 1.5 ounces; flash memory provides for skip-free playback.
Apple iPod 	As many as 40,000 songs, 50,000 images, or 200 hours of video	None	80 GB to 160 GB	USB 2.0 port	Has calendar feature that syncs with Outlook; can serve as a small, portable hard drive.
Zen Vision W 	As many as 15,000 songs or 240 hours of movies	None	30 GB to 60 GB	USB 2.0 port	Includes 4.3"-wide screen display, integrated FM radio and a voice recorder; syncs with Outlook.

All file formats compete on sound and video quality and compression, which relates to how small the file can be and still provide high-quality playback. If you buy a song from the iTunes Music Store, for example, you receive an .aac format file. AAC files can be played only on iPods but can be converted to the more widely seen MP3 or Windows Media Audio (WMA) formats. WMA files can be played on a wide variety of MP3 players. Most PMPs that support video playback can play a wide range of video formats.

Are all PMP devices music players? No, there are a number of electronic devices with other capabilities that now incorporate the capability to carry electronic files and play music and video files. Some models of digital cameras, such as the Samsung NV3, have support for playing both music and videos. Gaming devices such as the Sony PlayStation Portable (PSP) allow you to play video games, play music and video files, and browse the Internet.

In the last few years, standalone GPS devices have dropped dramatically in price and size. Now these small, handheld units organize music and photos as well as deliver turn-by-turn instructions and real-time traffic information. Full-featured GPS models such as the Bushnell Onix 400 include

MP3 players, audio book players, and the capability to display photos and connect to the Internet (see Figure 8.11). Using Internet services such as MSN Direct, your GPS can keep you informed about the weather, traffic backups, local movie times, and even local gas prices.

PMP HARDWARE

How do I know how much digital media a PMP can hold? The number of songs or hours of video a portable media player can hold obviously depends on how much storage space it has. Most MP3 players use built-in **flash memory**, a type of nonvolatile memory, to store files. Most PMPs that support video use a hard drive and can store a much larger amount of music and video. Less expensive PMPs use flash memory (ranging from 1 GB to 16 GB), whereas more expensive models use a built-in hard drive, which provides as much as 160 GB of storage. Some of the PMPs that use flash memory allow you to add storage capacity by purchasing removable flash memory cards.

Another factor that determines how much music a player can hold is the quality of the MP3 music files. The size of an MP3 file depends on the digital sampling of the song. The **sampling rate** is the number of times per second the music is measured and converted to a digital value. Sampling rates are measured in kilobits per second (Kbps). The same song could be sampled at 256 Kbps or 64 Kbps. The size of the song file will be four times larger if it is sampled at 256 Kbps than the lower sampling rate of 64 Kbps. The higher the sampling rate, the better quality the sound—but the larger the file size.

How do you control the size of an MP3 file? If you are ripping, or converting, a song from a CD into a digital MP3 file,

you can select the sampling rate yourself. You decide by considering what quality sound you want as well as how many songs you want to fit onto your MP3 player. For example, if your player has 1 GB of storage and you have ripped songs at 192 Kbps, then you can fit about 694 minutes of music onto the player. The same 1 GB could store 2,083 minutes of music if it were sampled at 64 Kbps. Whenever you are near your computer, you can connect your player and download a different set of songs, but you always are limited by the amount of storage your player has.

PMP FLASH MEMORY AND FILE TRANSFER

What if I want to store more music or video than what the memory on my PMP allows? Some PMPs allow you to add memory by inserting removable flash memory cards. Flash memory cards are noiseless and featherlight, use tiny amounts of power, and slide into a special slot in the player. If you've ever played a video game on PlayStation or Xbox and saved your progress to a memory card, then you have used flash memory. Because flash memory is nonvolatile, when you store data on a flash memory card, you won't lose it when you turn off the player. In addition, flash memory can be erased and rewritten with new data.

What types of flash memory cards do PMPs use? Several different types of flash cards are used with different PMP models, as shown in Figure 8.12. One popular type is CompactFlash cards. These are about the size of a matchbook and can hold between 4 GB and 64 GB of data. They are highly durable, so the data you store on them is safe. Multimedia cards and SmartMedia cards are about the same size as CompactFlash cards but are thinner and less rugged. A newer type of memory card called Secure Digital is faster and offers encryption capabilities so that your data is secure even if you lose the card.

PMP devices by Sony use a special format of flash memory called the *Memory Stick.* These tiny rectangular "sticks" are currently used only in Sony devices. Particular models of PMPs can support only certain types of flash cards, so check your manual to be sure you buy compatible memory cards.

FIGURE 8.11

The Bushnell Onix 400 GPS keeps you up to date on weather and other information via an Internet connection.

How do I transfer media files to my portable media player? All portable media players come with software that enables you to transfer your audio and video files from your computer onto the player. As noted earlier, players that hold thousands of songs and hours of video use internal hard drives to store music. For example, devices such as Apple iPods can hold gigabytes of data. To move large volumes of data between your computer and your PMP, you want a high-speed port. Most PMPs use a USB 2.0 port, but some players may use FireWire ports, which provide comparable throughput. Using a USB 2.0 port, you can transfer two dozen MP3 files to the iPod in fewer than 10 seconds.

PMP ETHICAL ISSUES: NAPSTER AND BEYOND

What was Napster all about? The initial MP3 craze was fueled by sites such as MP3.com, which originally stored its song files on a public server with the permission of the original artist or recording company. Therefore, you were not infringing on a copyright by downloading songs from sites such as MP3.com (which still exists and now provides free music in streaming format).

When originally introduced, Napster was a file exchange site created to correct some of the annoyances found by users of MP3.com and similar sites. One such annoyance was the limited availability of popular music in MP3 format. With the MP3 sites, if you found a song you wanted to download, the links to the sites on which the file was found often no longer worked. Napster differed from MP3.com because songs or locations of songs were not stored in a central public server but instead were "borrowed" directly from other users' computers. This process of users transferring files between computers is referred to as **peer-to-peer (P2P) sharing**. Napster also provided a search engine dedicated to finding specific MP3 files. This direct search and sharing eliminated the inconvenience of searching links only to find them unavailable.

The problem with Napster was that it was so good at what it did. Napster's convenient and reliable mechanism to find and download popular songs in MP3

FIGURE 8.12

(a) CompactFlash memory cards offer rugged, portable storage. They can be dropped and exposed to hot and cold weather and still protect your data. (b) Secure Digital cards are faster and offer security protection for your data. (c) Memory Sticks are currently used only in Sony devices.

format became a huge success. The rapid acceptance and use of Napster—at one point, it had nearly 60 million users—led the music industry to sue the site for copyright infringement, and Napster was closed in June 2002. Napster has since reopened as a music site that sells music downloads and is sanctioned by the recording industry.

So now all downloaded music and video must be purchased? Although you need to pay for most music you download, some artists post songs for free. Business models are still evolving as artists and recording companies try to meet audience needs while also protecting their own intellectual property rights. Several different approaches exist. One is to deliver something called *tethered downloads* in which you pay for the music and own it but are subject to restrictions on its use.

Another approach is to purchase DRM-free music, which is music without any digital rights management. These song files can be moved freely from system to system. For example, Apple's iTunes store currently sells both types of music, but at different prices. The cheaper $0.99 song purchase allows you to give songs to anyone on audio CD but

ACTIVE HELPDESK

Using Portable Media Players

In this Active Helpdesk call, you'll play the role of a helpdesk staffer, fielding calls about portable media players, what they can carry, and how they store data.

BITS AND BYTES

Trick Out Your iPod

Portable media players are no longer just for playing music and videos. Add-on products such as iPodSync (**www.ipod-sync.com**) are constantly being developed to provide your iPod with new features. Although this product is used mainly for synchronizing your iPod with Outlook and transferring weather forecasts, Web feeds, and pictures to your iPod, it has an additional useful feature called *PowerPoint Exporter*, which is available as a free download, that enables you to export PowerPoint presentations as images to your iPod. You can then use your iPod as a mobile presentation tool. So pass your iPod over to your customer while sipping coffee at Starbucks and close that big deal with a slick presentation!

Since Linux became popular, enthusiasts want to install it on everything—including iPods. The iPod Linux Project (**www.ipodlinux.org**) is an open source project dedicated to developing versions of Linux to install on iPods. The current version of the OS includes a user interface called Podzilla, and many applications and modules have been written to provide functionality that the creators at Apple never dreamed of for the iPod. So if you're feeling adventurous, install it and see what else you can do with your iPod.

sharing environment in which computers connect directly to other computers.

The argument these P2P networks make to defend their legality is that they do not run a central server like the original Napster but only facilitate connections between users. Therefore, they have no control over what the users choose to trade, and not all P2P file sharing is illegal. For example, it is perfectly legal to trade photos or movies you have created with other folks over a P2P site. People who oppose such file-sharing sites contend that the sites know their users are distributing files illegally and breaking copyright laws. Be aware that having illegal content on your computer, deliberately or by accident, is a criminal offense in many jurisdictions.

Will PMPs eliminate radio stations? Radio stations have always had the advantages of early access to new music and the personalities and conversations they add to the listening experience. However, the Internet allows artists to release new songs to their fans immediately (on sites such as **www.mp3.com**) and without relying on radio airtime. This opens up new channels for artists to reach an audience and changes the amount of power radio stations have in the promotion of music. And many radio stations have gained increased listenership by making their stations available through Internet sites and by broadcasting in high-definition quality.

Another development that competes with radio (and television) is podcasting, which allows users to download audio and video content and then to listen to those broadcasts on their PMPs whenever they want. Podcasting is paving the way for anyone to create a radio or television show at home and to distribute it easily to an audience. Using free software such as Audacity (**http://audacity.sourceforge.net**) and a microphone, you can record voice-overs, sequence songs, and "publish" your show to the Internet. Loyal fans can use podcasting software—Juice (**http://juicereceiver.sourceforge.net**) or iTunes (for Windows or Mac), for example—to find their latest episode and automatically transfer it to their portable media players. Plugging your iPod into a data port on your computer causes the iPod to search iTunes for new content and automatically transfers the new files to your iPod. This process is known as *synchronization*.

only to share the media electronically with five other computers. The $1.29 DRM-free song can be placed on as many computers or players as you wish. Other sites offer subscription services. For a monthly fee, Napster to Go allows you to download as many songs as you like to your MP3 player. These songs will be usable, however, only as long as you are paying the monthly subscription fee.

If the original Napster site was illegal, then why are peer-to-peer (P2P) sharing sites still operating? When Napster was going through its legal turmoil, other P2P Web sites were quick to take advantage of a huge opportunity. Napster was "easy" to shut down because it used a central index server that queried other Napster computers for requested songs. Current P2P protocols (such as LimeWire and BearShare) differ from Napster in that they do not limit themselves to sharing only MP3 files. Video files are obtainable easily on P2P sites. More important, these sites don't have a central index server. Instead, they operate in a true P2P

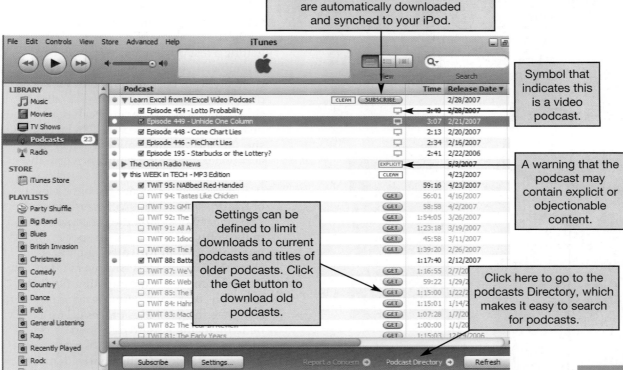

After you've added a podcast to the list, click here to subscribe. Episodes are automatically downloaded and synched to your iPod.

Symbol that indicates this is a video podcast.

A warning that the podcast may contain explicit or objectionable content.

Settings can be defined to limit downloads to current podcasts and titles of older podcasts. Click the Get button to download old podcasts.

Click here to go to the podcasts Directory, which makes it easy to search for podcasts.

FIGURE 8.13

iTunes makes it easy to subscribe to and manage podcasts. Podcasts can be played through iTunes (on your computer), or because they are transferred automatically to your iPod when you synchronize it to your computer, podcasts can be played on your iPod.

Podcasts are easy to subscribe to and download using iTunes (see Figure 8.13). And iTunes is free of charge!

PDA/Smartphones

A **personal digital assistant (PDA)** is a small device that allows you to carry and process digital information. **Smartphones** are cell phones that have advanced memory and processing power. PDA/smartphones are about the size of your hand and usually weigh fewer than 5 ounces. Although small, they are powerful and can carry all sorts of information—from calendars to contact lists to specially designed personal productivity software programs (such as Excel and Word), songs, photos, videos, and games. And you can easily synchronize (the process of making sure the data on two devices is exactly the same) your PDA/smartphone and your home computer so that the changes you make to your schedules and files on your mobile device are made on your home or office computer files as well. Over the past several years, PDAs and smartphones have grown to overlap greatly in their capabilities.

Now one term—**PDA/smartphone**—covers both categories of devices.

HARDWARE

What hardware is inside a PDA/smartphone?
Like any computing device, a PDA/smartphone includes a processor (CPU), operating system software, storage capabilities, input and output devices, and ports. Because of their small size, PDA/smartphones must use specially designed processors and operating system software. They store their operating system software in ROM and their data and application programs in random access memory (RAM).

What kinds of input devices do PDA/smartphones use?
PDA/smartphones feature touch-sensitive screens that allow you to enter data directly with a penlike device called a **stylus**. To make selections, you simply tap or write on the screen with the stylus. Other models include integrated keyboards or support small, portable, folding keyboards. Figure 8.14 shows various input options.

ACTIVE HELPDESK

Using PDA/Smartphones

In this Active Helpdesk call, you'll play the role of a helpdesk staffer, fielding calls about PDA/smartphones— what you can use them for, what internal components and features they have, and how you can synchronize mobile devices with a desktop computer.

FIGURE 8.14

For entering text, PDA/smartphones offer different options: (a) a stylus and text entry window, (b) an integrated keyboard (shown here on a Sharp Zaurus SL-5500), and (c) a virtual keyboard accessory.

What kinds of displays do PDA/smartphones have?

PDA/smartphones come with LCD screens in a variety of resolutions. High-end color displays are the norm today and can measure almost 4 inches and have resolutions as high as 640×480 pixels.

How do I compare processors for PDA/smartphones?

Popular processors (CPUs) include the Samsung SC, the Texas Instruments OMP, and the Intel XScale processor. When comparing processors, keep processor speed in mind. **Processor speed**, which is measured in hertz (Hz), is the number of operations (or cycles) the processor completes each second. Just as with computers, you should get the fastest processor your budget allows.

If you're interested in running demanding software such as games, Microsoft Office applications, or image editing applications, getting a fast processor is essential. For -example, if you will be doing large sets of calculations in Excel workbooks, the speed difference between a fast processor and a slower one is especially noticeable. The type of application software you plan on running should help you determine whether the additional processing power is worth the cost.

Processor speed is not the only aspect of the processor that affects performance. The internal design of the processor, both in the software commands it speaks and its internal hardware, are other factors. To measure performance, reviewers often run the same task on competing devices and then compare the time it takes to complete the task. This process is called **benchmarking** and gives a good indication of the unit's overall system performance. Look for benchmarks in magazines (such as *PC Magazine*) in addition to online reviews (such as those found at **www.wired.com**).

As well as having different speeds, each processor uses different amounts of power, which affects how long the device can run on a single battery. Compare the expected operating time on one battery charge with your typical travel day to determine whether a particular device will work for you.

OPERATING SYSTEMS

How do I compare PDA/smartphone operating systems?

The two main operating system competitors on the PDA/smartphone market have traditionally been

SOUND BYTE

PDA/Smartphones on the Road and at Home

In this Sound Byte, you'll learn how to use your PDA/smartphone as a powerful tool, how to use flash memory, and how to synchronize your PDA/smartphone with your home computer.

the **Palm OS** from Palm and the **Windows Mobile** (formerly known as Pocket PC) system from Microsoft. Palm OS is now found only on PDAs made by Palm. Windows Mobile is a popular operating system and is used by Compaq, HP, Dell, and Toshiba—and now even by Palm—on their PDA/smartphones. As you can see in Figure 8.15, Windows Mobile sports a typical graphical user interface.

So which operating system is better? The Palm OS clearly ruled a few years ago primarily because of the Palm OS's ability to work more efficiently on slower processors and PDAs with less memory. However, now several operating systems such as the BlackBerry OS, the OS X variation on the iPhone, Windows Mobile, and the Symbian OS are popular. Today's PDA/smartphones sport fast processors with 128 MB of RAM or more, which allows larger, more complex operating systems to deliver speedy performance. In addition, many operating systems are embracing support for new technologies such as hardware graphics acceleration and EVDO high-speed networking. Many operating systems can now handle Word, Excel, and PowerPoint files.

FIGURE 8.15

Windows Mobile is a popular operating system on PDA/smartphones.

BITS AND BYTES

How Do You Find Your WiFi?

Detecting a nearby WiFi signal is important if you are looking for Internet connectivity while you are on the move. Some notebooks have a built-in WiFi scanner that displays a row of lights on the case whenever a WiFi signal is available. Also available are keychain fobs that light up when they detect WiFi signals in the vicinity.

If you are running Windows Vista, the Connect to a Network dialog box (accessible from the Network and Sharing Center) shows the strength of all wireless networks within range of your computer.

At **www.thinkgeek.com** you may find the most easy-to-use WiFi detector ever. The WiFi Detector t-shirt has a logo that lights up to indicate the signal strength of a nearby WiFi network (see Figure 8.16). Find your WiFi and look … well, look geeky while doing so!

FIGURE 8.16

The WiFi Detector T-shirt makes a statement—a geeky statement.

MEMORY AND STORAGE

What kinds of memory do PDA/smartphones use?

ROM is used to hold the operating system as well as the most basic programs the PDA/smartphone runs such as the calendar, to-do list, and contact list. These devices do not contain internal hard drives. Therefore, RAM holds additional applications and any data you load. However, because RAM is volatile storage and you do not want your data to disappear when you shut the device off, a small amount of power is taken from the battery to keep the data "alive."

The main advantage of using RAM in this way is speed. RAM is incredibly fast compared with hard drives, so programs load and run quickly. Because the price of RAM has decreased over the last few years, most top-of-the-line PDA/smartphones contain at least 128 MB of RAM. Still, applications for mobile devices (such as Excel) do not have all the functions that desktop versions include precisely because of their limited amount of RAM.

What if I need more memory?

PDA/smartphones cannot expand the amount of internal memory they contain. For memory needs beyond built-in RAM and ROM, PDA/smartphones use removable flash memory. For example, if you want your smartphone to hold a large MP3 collection and some videos, then you might not have enough built-in RAM. But you could add the storage space you need by inserting a 4 GB micro SDHC memory card, as shown in Figure 8.17. Before buying a flash card,

consult your user manual or the manufacturer's Web site to make sure you select the style of memory that is supported. Not all devices allow you to add memory. The Apple iPhone, for example, is limited to the amount of memory installed when you purchase it.

FILE TRANSFER AND SYNCHRONIZATION

How do I transfer data from my PDA/smartphone to my computer?

If the computer accepts the type of flash card you're using, you can simply pull the flash card out of your mobile device and slip it into the flash card reader on your computer. If your desktop does not include a built-in card reader, then you might want to purchase an external memory card reader that connects to your computer using a USB port.

You also can transfer your data from your PDA/smartphone to a desktop computer by using a special device called a **cradle**. Most PDAs/smartphones come with a cradle or sync cable that connects the device to the desktop using a USB port as shown in Figure 8.18.

FIGURE 8.17

Different PDA/smartphones use different types of flash memory. Here a 4 GB micro SDHC card is being inserted into a smartphone.

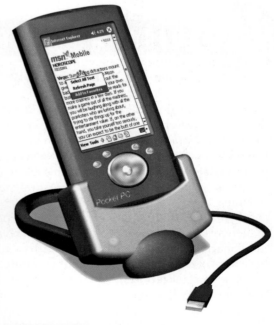

FIGURE 8.18

A cradle connects your PDA/smartphone to your computer for easy synchronization and transfer of files.

How do I synchronize a PDA/smartphone with a computer?

PDA/smartphones let you coordinate the changes you make to your to-do lists, schedules, and other files with the files on your home or office computer. This process of updating your data so that the files on your PDA/smartphone and computer are the same is called **synchronizing**. To synchronize your desktop and the device, you simply place the PDA/smartphone in its cradle (or attach it to the computer via a USB cable) and touch a "sync" button. This begins the process of data transfer that updates both sets of files to the most current version.

Microsoft has recognized the vast increase in portable computing devices by integrating synchronization into Windows Vista. The Sync Center (see Figure 8.19), which is accessed from the Control Panel, allows you to set up automatic or manual synchronization. Ensure that the device for which you are trying to set up synchronization parameters is connected to your computer and then launch the Sync Center. Select the *Set up new sync partnerships* option to view available devices and configure their synchronization options.

Can I transfer files wirelessly?

Some PDA/smartphones include an infrared (IrDA) port that transmits data signals using infrared light waves. To transfer data between two devices, you can use the infrared port and "beam" data directly across. For example, if you missed a class, a fellow student could send you the assignment file by simply pointing her PDA/smartphone at yours.

Another type of wireless connection is **Bluetooth**. This technology uses radio waves to transmit data signals over short

SOUND BYTE

Connecting with Bluetooth

In this Sound Byte, you'll learn what freedoms Bluetooth affords you, how to decide whether you want Bluetooth on equipment you purchase, and how to use Bluetooth devices.

distances (as far as 30 feet or so). Most PDA/smartphones on the market today are Bluetooth-enabled, meaning they include a small Bluetooth chip that allows them to transfer data wirelessly to any other Bluetooth-enabled device. One benefit Bluetooth has over infrared is that direct line of sight does not have to be present between the two devices for them to communicate. You also can use Bluetooth to synchronize your device with your computer. Bluetooth accessories such as ear pieces and even stereo headsets are also available.

SOFTWARE AND ACCESSORIES

What PDA/smartphone software is available?

Most devices come with a standard collection of software such as a to-do list, contacts manager, and calendar. Modified versions of application software such as Word, Excel, Outlook, and PowerPoint also are available. Although these programs are not as fully featured as their desktop counterparts, they can read and edit files that can be transmitted to full-version applications on your computer. In addition, a variety of games, tools, and reference applications are available from numerous software companies. A good source to locate software applications for your

FIGURE 8.19

The Windows Vista Sync Center makes it easy to arrange for synchronization of all your mobile devices.

>To launch Sync Center, click the **Start** button, select **Control Panel**, and double-click the **Sync Center** icon.

BITS AND BYTES

411 for Answers

Most phone services charge as much as $2.00 for a 411 call for information on a phone listing or address. But now there is competition. The Google 411 service is a free way to find out the address, directions, or phone number of a business or person. A call to GOOG-411 gets you the same information at no charge. If you say "text" into the phone, it kicks back a text message with the address and a map.

If you are looking for a different kind of information, try the service Cha Cha. You can either call (1.800. cha cha) or text (242 242) any kind of question, and real human "guides" will find the answer and send it back to you. So, answers to questions like

- How many calories are there in a slice of pizza?
- When is *American Idol* on tonight?
- Is there a way to get acrylic paint out of jeans?

are just a free call or text away!

PDA/smartphone is **www.pdastreet.com**. In addition, Web sites such as **www.download. com** and **www.tucows.com** feature plenty of shareware and freeware applications for mobile platforms.

USES OF CONVERGENT DEVICES

Where do people use PDAs? PDAs have caught on in a variety of professions over the last few years, often in situations that involve time-sensitive data collection. Medical professionals use PDAs loaded with patient management software. These

programs provide quick access to patient records when visiting patient rooms or supervising tests (such as MRIs and CAT scans) and allow for fast updating of patient records. Package delivery companies such as Federal Express and United Parcel Service provide employees with specialized versions of PDAs that can record information about packages being picked up or delivered, which enhances package tracking capabilities and stream-lines billing information. Scientists use PDAs to collect and summarize data observed during experiments either in the lab or in the field, which provides for much more accurate data recording than relying on notes that must be input at a later time at a desktop computer. Also, anyone who needs reference material probably would find it easier to carry an electronic version of a paper reference source that also would be instantly searchable.

For the 2010 census, the U.S. Bureau of the Census will outfit 500,000 census takers with specially designed PDA/smartphones made by High Tech Computer Corporation (a Taiwan-based company). The devices will run on Windows Mobile software and will transmit data wirelessly via a cellular net-work. It is hoped that allowing census takers to record information electronically as it is collected will reduce the number of people missed in the count (estimated to be several million in the 2000 census).

Does a regular person need a smartphone? Smartphones are expensive solutions. Because they cost more to pur-chase than a basic cell phone and then require a high-volume monthly data plan to

FIGURE 8.20

The Apple iPhone (a) and the AT&T Tilt (b) are part of the new generation of smart-phone devices. These devices combine the features of a cell phone, PMP, and PDA into a single handheld unit.

get full use out of them, unless you need the added features a typical cell phone is a better choice. But if you need to read e-mail and e-mail attachments on the go, a smartphone such as the Apple iPhone or the AT&T Tilt (see Figure 8.20) is a great option. These smartphones offer full keyboards and sport high-speed EVDO Internet access capabilities, a camera, and Bluetooth capabilities to free you from wires. You can add on navigation services, reach the Internet almost any time, and play your music and videos—all with just one device to carry.

Are there other devices besides PDA/smartphones that I could consider before purchasing a notebook computer? Specialized computing devices designed for mobility are hitting the market more regularly. There are tiny Internet enabled devices appearing that don't bother to include cell phone features at all. The Nokia n800 Internet tablet series (see Figure 8.21), for example, uses Skype for voice communications instead of a cell phone service. It has a high-resolution screen and WiFi connectivity so you can stream audio and video, use Web e-mail clients, and access Web sites. Memory expands with SD expansion cards.

If you require a larger screen and more processing power, then look at a category of emerging computer systems known as ultra mobile or subnotebooks. The **ultramobile** and **subnotebook** categories consist of notebooks that weigh 2 pounds or less. Examples include the Asus Eee PC and the OQO model 02 (see Figure 8.22). Ultramobiles pack major computing power into a tiny package and try to extend battery life as long as possible. Although some models can be expensive, they may be just what you need if size is your biggest consideration. But be prepared to put up with a cramped keyboard and relatively small screen.

For avid readers of e-books (books stored in electronic files), the Sony Portable Reader System (see Figure 8.23) could be just what you are looking for. Featuring 128 MB of internal memory, it can hold 160 e-books. And if that isn't enough, it accepts flash memory cards for even more storage. Its 9-ounce weight certainly qualifies it as portable. And through clever technology, keeping a page displayed requires no energy, so you can get approximately 7,500 turned pages on one charge.

FIGURE 8.21

The Nokia n800 series Internet tablet features a touch screen and keypad and is designed primarily for Web surfing and sending e-mail.

FIGURE 8.22

Subnotebooks like the (a) Asus Eee PC and the (b) OQO model 02 weigh in at less than 2 pounds but run fully featured operating systems.

FIGURE 8.23

The Sony Portable Reader is designed to store as many as 160 e-books; it weighs approximately 9 ounces (without the cover).

Ethics: The Power of GPS ... and the Threats

Most people know where the closest supermarket is in relation to their home. But if you are out of town, how can you find a local supermarket when you get a craving for potato chips? Many people aren't whizzes at geography, but knowing your current location and the location of your destination can often come in handy. Luckily for those who are "directionally impaired," **Global positioning system (GPS)** technology enables you to carry a powerful navigational aid in your pocket.

You've probably heard of GPS, but what is it exactly and how does it work? The global positioning system is a system of 21 satellites (plus three working spares) built and operated by the U.S. Department of Defense that constantly orbits the Earth. GPS devices use an antenna to pick up the signals from these satellites and special software to transform those signals into latitude and longitude. Using the information obtained from the satellites, GPS devices can tell you what your geographical location is anywhere on the planet to within 10 feet (see Figure 8.24). Because they provide such detailed positioning information, GPS devices are now used as navigational aids for aircraft, recreational boats, and automobiles, and they even come in handheld models for hikers.

Although this precise positioning information clearly redefines the fields of surveying and search-and-rescue operations, it also has changed other fields. Wildlife researchers now tag select animals and watch their migration patterns and how populations are distributed. Meanwhile, GPS was important to the two teams that created the Chunnel, the tunnel under the English Channel that connects England to France. One team worked from France toward England and the other from England toward France. They used GPS information along the way to make sure they were on target; in 1990, the two sections joined to become the first physical link between England and the continent of Europe since the ice age.

GPS has made its way into several commercial products as well. Hertz rental cars offer in-car GPS assistance with the NeverLost system. The unit is mounted on the front dashboard and displays your location on a map that is updated in real time as you drive. Enter your

destination, and a voice warns you of lane changes and approaching turns. If you miss a turn, it automatically recalculates the required route and gives you directions to get back on course. Flip to another screen, and it shows you how far you have to drive to the next gas station, restaurant, or amusement park. Most automotive companies now offer GPS systems as installed options in their vehicles. And GPS navigation can be added to any vehicle using a portable GPS device, a

FIGURE 8.24

GPS computes your location anywhere on Earth from a system of orbiting satellites.

PDA/smartphone equipped with GPS (see Figure 8.25), or by adding GPS software and accessories to your notebook.

But Who Is Watching?

Having the ability to locate and track an object anywhere on Earth does bring with it societal implications, however. The Federal Communications Commission (FCC) mandated that every cell phone had to include a GPS chip by the end of 2005. This enabled the complete rollout of the Enhanced 911 (E911) program. E911 automatically gives dispatchers precision location information for any 911 call. It also means your cell phone records may include precise tracking information that indicates where you are when you make a call. But is that information that you would want the government or other people to know? Consider if you were at a park playing baseball with your friends and you made a phone call. At the same time, in another part of the park, an organization with suspected terrorist ties was holding a rally. Would you want the government to assume because you made a phone call from the park that you are a member of that organization?

Because phones now have GPS chips, cellular phone providers offer plans (for a monthly fee) that allow you to track where a cell phone is at any given time via a Web site. This could be a real boon for tracking a lost child who wandered off into the woods during a group hike. But are other uses of the technology ethical? Did your daughter really go to the library, or is she actually at the local skate park hanging with her friends? Is your spouse really working late at the office or watching the baseball game with friends at the ballpark? Now, with a few clicks of the mouse, you can tell where a family member's phone is located. But is this an invasion of privacy? Is it ethical to track the whereabouts of your family members? This is something that you need to decide.

GPS technology begs several questions: What limits and supervision of the government need to be in place to ensure the ethical use of GPS technologies? In what ways could the tracking information provided by GPS devices be used unethically? If GPS tracking information is recorded in your phone data, then should the criteria for allowing government agencies to subpoena phone records be changed? Should users be allowed to turn off location information from their phones? Already, location records such as these were used in determining that the *New York Times* reporter Jayson Blair had been fabricating stories, resulting in his resignation. Car rental companies such as Acme Car Rental of New Haven, Connecticut, are using GPS records to fine customers for speeding violations. As a nation, we now need to decide how we should balance the benefits and costs (to our privacy) of using this new level of tracking information.

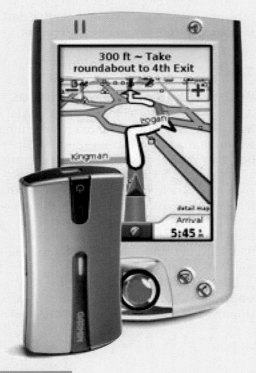

FIGURE 8.25

The Garmin Mobile 10 software allows you to turn your Bluetooth-enabled PDA into a fully functional GPS.

You can expect to see more of these types of specialty portable computing devices in the near future. Although not right for every situation, they may be a good fit for your needs. Web sites such as Gizmodo, the Gadget Guide (**www.gizmodo.com**), are a great resource for keeping abreast of new developments.

Notebooks

The most powerful mobile computing solution is a **notebook computer**, sometimes called a **laptop computer**. Notebooks offer large displays and all of the computing power of a full desktop system (see Figure 8.26).

NOTEBOOK HARDWARE

What hardware comes in a notebook? Notebooks can be equipped with Blu-ray and DVD/CD-RW drives; large hard drives (many as large as 160 GB); more than 2 GHz processor speed featuring dual core CPUs; and 4 GB or more of RAM. Input devices on notebooks include keyboards with built-in mouse functionality. In terms of output devices, many notebooks include large display screens measuring as large as a whopping 20.1 inches diagonally.

What are common CPUs for notebooks? CPUs available for notebooks are usually a bit slower than the latest available CPU offered for desktop units. Whereas existing desktops can currently run a 3.4 GHz processor, most notebook CPUs run at speeds less than 2.8 GHz. You won't notice the difference if you're using

word-processing programs, but if you run many applications at the same time or use programs that make heavy demands on the CPU (such as video editing software), the notebook's performance will be slower than a desktop computer. However, many notebooks now use dual-core CPUs, which makes the difference in processing speed less noticeable. In addition, the new memory management schemes of Windows Vista allow the computer to use RAM more efficiently, which has also helped reduce the performance differences between notebooks and desktops.

Many notebook systems use low-power processors designed to consume less power than other CPUs. Often CPUs in mobile computers feature integrated wireless capability as well. When combined with specially designed video chipsets, the total package consumes less power than comparable desktop units, thereby extending battery life.

TABLET PCS

What is different about a Tablet PC? A **Tablet PC** is a portable computer that is lightweight, features advanced handwriting recognition, and can be rotated into a clipboard style (see Figure 8.27). Tablet PCs are available from a variety of manufacturers, come in a variety of designs, and are about the same size as a clipboard. Newer models weigh slightly more than three pounds, including the integrated keyboard, making them ultrathin and lightweight computing solutions.

When would a Tablet PC be the best mobile solution? Manufacturing employees, medical employees, educators

FIGURE 8.26

Notebook computers offer larger displays and more powerful processors than desktops could offer just a few years ago. Here you see
(a) a PC notebook and
(b) a MacBook Air notebook.

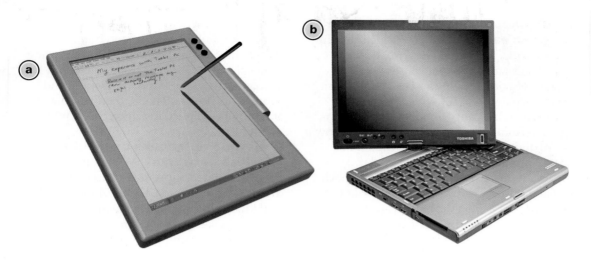

FIGURE 8.27

A Tablet PC can be held like a (a) tablet or rotated into traditional (b) notebook mode.

and students, sales representatives who call on clients (and take notes during the calls), and employees who fill out electronic forms are the major purchasers of Tablet PCs (see Figure 8.28). They are exceptionally light and, with their handwriting-recognition capabilities, allow you to take notes silently without distracting keystrokes. **Digital ink**, the text-entry system that allows you to easily draw images and enter text by "writing" on the surface of the tablet, is a great match for these settings.

How do software products support digital ink? Windows Vista has support for digital ink built in. When using Office 2007 products such as Word or OneNote, you can annotate (mark up) existing documents with digital ink. The original document can remain unchanged, but your digital ink annotations on the document are still saved. Using this feature, you can mark up an article and send it to a co-worker, add notes to a meeting agenda, or draw a route on a map.

FIGURE 8.28

You input data into a Tablet PC by writing on the touch-sensitive screen with a digital pen. The tablet then uses handwriting recognition to convert your writing to typewritten text.

NOTEBOOK OPERATING SYSTEMS AND PORTS

Are there special operating systems for notebooks? Notebooks use the same operating systems that run on desktop systems. However, notebook operating systems do have some special settings, such as power management profiles. A power management profile contains recommended power-saving settings, such as turning off your hard drive after 15 minutes of no use, shutting down the display after 20 minutes of no movement, and switching the machine to sleep or hibernation mode after a certain length of time.

Can the operating system help me keep track of how much battery time I have left? Windows Vista has a feature called the Windows Mobility Center that is designed to help keep track of system functions that are particularly important when you are on the go with your system (see Figure 8.29). When the Windows Mobility Center is open, you can see at a glance details on battery status, display brightness (which affects battery life), power management settings, wireless network connections, external displays, and connected presentation systems (projectors).

Can notebooks connect to other devices easily? Notebooks include a full set of ports, including FireWire, USB 2.0, RJ-11 jacks for a modem connection, and Ethernet ports for wired networking connections (see Figure 8.30). Video ports often include high-quality S-video connectors as well as digital DVI connectors, which allow a pure digital signal to run to a digital flat-panel monitor.

Often, the size limitations of notebooks mean that they don't offer as many of each type of port as in a desktop system. Therefore, if you buy a notebook, you should consider how you will use your machine and whether you will need an expansion hub. An expansion hub is a device that connects to a USB port, creating three or four USB ports from one. If you will be connecting a USB mouse, printer, and scanner to your notebook, then you may be short one USB port, in which case a hub would come in handy.

How do notebooks connect to wireless networks? Most notebooks have integrated support for wireless connectivity. As you saw in Chapter 7, the 802.11g WiFi wireless standard is the most common standard used in wireless networks today, but 802.11n is gaining in popularity. The 802.11g standard allows wireless connections to operate as high as 54 Mbps, and 802.11n provides even faster transfer rates and an extended range. Many notebooks also offer built-in Bluetooth, which allows you to wirelessly connect to other Bluetooth-enabled devices like printers.

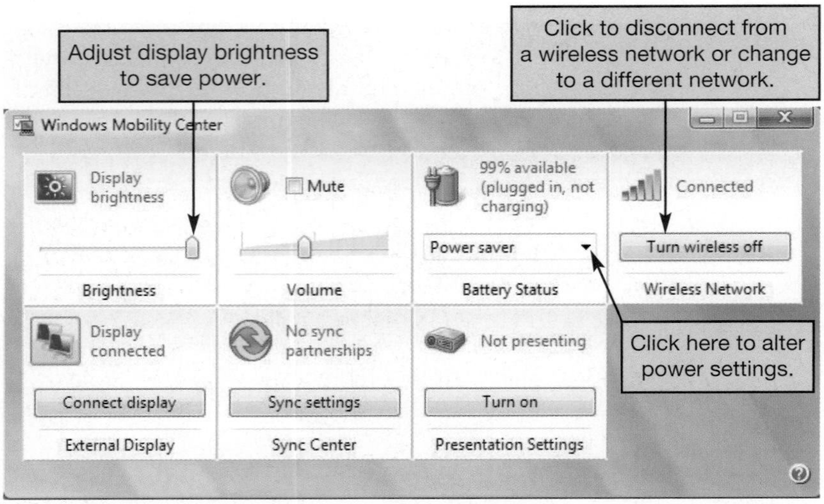

NOTEBOOK BATTERIES AND ACCESSORIES

What types of batteries are there for notebooks? Rechargeable batteries today come in two main types: lithium ion (Li-ion) and nickel metal hydride (NiMH). The new lithium and nickel-based batteries are lighter than previous generation batteries and do not show the "memory effect" that old batteries did. **Memory effect** means that the battery must be completely used up before it is recharged. If not, the battery won't hold as much charge as it originally did.

Adjust display brightness to save power.

Click to disconnect from a wireless network or change to a different network.

Click here to alter power settings.

FIGURE 8.29

The Windows Mobility Center makes it easy to manage various operations of your notebook OS.

>Click the **Start** button and select **All Programs.** Click the **Accessories** folder and select **Windows Mobility Center.**

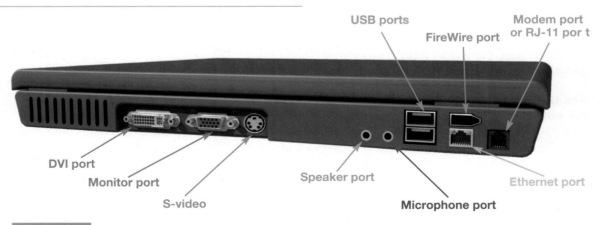

USB ports
FireWire port
Modem port or RJ-11 por t
DVI port
Monitor port
S-video
Speaker port
Microphone port
Ethernet port

FIGURE 8.30

Notebooks include many of the ports you're used to seeing on desktop computers.

TRENDS IN IT

Ubiquitous Networking: Wherever You Go, There You Are

With the rise of portable computing devices, the idea of ubiquitous networking has been generating a lot of interest. Ubiquity in computing essentially means being able to access and exchange information wherever you happen to be and having the key information that you need accessible when you need it. But how do we achieve this ultimate goal? There are two popular approaches.

The Network Is Watching You (How Orwellian)

Instead of having to move the files and programs you need onto mobile devices, how about having a network that "watches" your movements and moves the data so that it follows you? Researchers at telecommunications companies such as the AT&T Laboratories at Cambridge University are attempting to make this possible by creating a detection system that can track your location within a building, moving your files wherever you go. To take advantage of the network, users will carry a small device called a "bat," shown in Figure 8.31. This device will have a unique ID number and contain a radio transceiver and transmitter. A detection system (or central controller) installed in the building will keep track of the physical location of the bats and hence the people who carry them.

Bats are about the size of a pager device and therefore small enough to be carried comfortably. They allow the detection system to locate the bat owners wherever they roam in the facility.

How does this system work? Suppose you go into a conference room that contains a computer and a phone. The controller is tracking the bat you have in your pocket, so it knows you entered the conference room and therefore routes all your phone calls to the phone in the conference room. It also sends your files and desktop settings to the computer in the conference room.

What if two people are in the conference room at the same time? The controller assigns available devices to the first person who enters the room. However, using interactive buttons on your bat, you can indicate to the controller that you wish to take temporary possession of a device assigned to another person.

Take Your Computer's Soul with You

The other option for ubiquity nirvana would be to take not just your data files with you (say, on a flash drive), but instead take your entire computer with you (virtually, of course). IBM is conducting a research project called SoulPad that attempts to achieve this miracle of portability. Using a portable storage device (IBM has used iPods in its testing), you save a suspended image of your computer, including all desktop settings and data files (essentially the "soul" of your computer), before leaving your home computer. When you arrive at another computer, you attach the portable storage device, and then your computer data and settings are loaded onto the remote computer so that you can pick up exactly where you left off. In testing, this has been piloted on computers running Windows and Linux. What is making this technology possible is the availability of tiny, high-capacity storage devices, high-speed data transfer (via FireWire or USB 2.0), and virtualization software. Eventually, it will probably be possible to deploy the SoulPad on a smartphone. This is convergence at the next level!

As we achieve ubiquity in computing, we will have to rethink our territorial approach to work and living spaces, as well as some of our ideas about privacy. In the future, because our data might follow us around (or we'll take it all with us), access to our personal information may always be right where we are.

FIGURE 8.31

Bats are about the size of a pager device and therefore small enough to be carried comfortably. They allow the detection system to locate the bat owners wherever they roam in the facility.

01223 343222

BITS AND BYTES

Tips to Stretch Your Notebook's Battery Life

Your notebook stores data both in RAM and on the hard drive. Increasing your RAM capacity makes your notebook perform more quickly because data can be read from RAM much faster than from a hard drive. Adding more RAM to your notebook also will make your battery last longer. This is because if the data needed is not in RAM, the hard drive must be powered up, requiring some 30 times as much battery power as simply reading directly from RAM.

Also, do not expose your notebook batteries to extreme heat and cold (such as leaving them in a parked car) because this tends to shorten battery life. Turn off all programs that are automatically loaded (check the taskbar) that you don't currently need to lessen the chances the hard drive will be accessed and waste precious power. For instance, on flights you can't connect to the Internet so you probably don't need your antivirus or antispyware programs. Finally, turn off your wireless capabilities if you won't be connecting to the Internet. The wireless unit in your computer will constantly search for wireless connections and drain power in the process.

FIGURE 8.32

(a) The Monster To Go power strip lets you create more outlets at a crowded airport.
(b) The three-port USB car adapter lets you charge multiple devices as you drive.

How long does a notebook battery last? The capacity of a battery is measured in ampere-hours (A-hrs). Ampere is a measure of current flow, so a battery rated at 5 A-hrs can provide 5 amps of current for an hour. Battery power depends on the device you're using and the work you're doing. A high-performance battery can operate a notebook for as long as five hours if fully charged. However, using the notebook's DVD drive can consume a high-performance battery in as few as 90 minutes. Manufacturers also describe batteries as

having cells (for example, 6-cell versus 9-cell). The more cells, the more capacity the battery has but also the more it weighs. Some notebook systems allow you to install two batteries at the same time, doubling the battery life but forcing you to purchase a second battery and have both fully charged.

Do I need to use my battery everywhere I go? Some environments support easy access to power for notebooks. For example, you can use an AC/DC or DC/DC converter to enable a notebook to run in a car without using battery power. Many airplanes provide DC power connections at each seat, although you have to buy a special adapter to use these connections with your devices.

Of course, power outlets are always at a premium in places such as airports and coffee shops, so you may want to consider a portable outlet strip such as the Monster To Go (see Figure 8.32a). For those occasions where you spend a lot of time in a car, consider using a three-port car outlet charger that includes a USB connector so that you can charge several devices as you drive (see Figure 8.32b)

What special purchases might a notebook require? Because a notebook is so easily stolen, purchasing a security lock is a wise investment. And as is the case with regular desktops, power surges can adversely affect notebooks, so investing in a portable surge protector is also a good idea. (Be sure to read the Technology in Focus feature "Protecting Your Computer and Backing Up Your Data," page 364, for more information about protecting your notebook.)

Docking stations are available for most notebooks. This piece of hardware allows you to connect printers, scanners, full-size monitors, mice, and other peripherals directly to the docking station. As shown in Figure 8.33, you then simply slide your notebook into the docking station to connect it to all the peripheral devices, rather than connecting all of their cables individually.

If you frequently make presentations to large groups, adding a lightweight projector to your notebook will prove useful. Printers have also become travel-sized. Figure 8.34 shows some of these special notebook accessories.

What if I need to collaborate with colleagues while I'm on the road? At the office, collaborating with your co-workers is easier because most likely

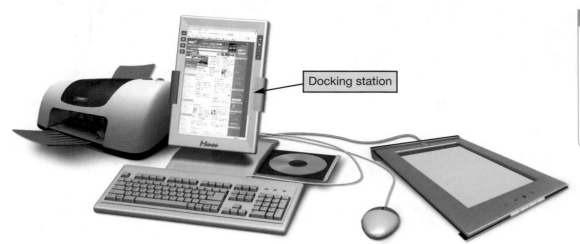

FIGURE 8.33

A docking station makes it easy to connect your notebook to your desktop monitor and any other peripherals. Just slide the notebook in place, and you're ready to go.

Docking station

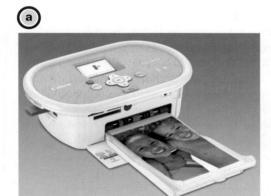

FIGURE 8.34

(a) The Canon Selphy CP770 printer features Bluetooth, memory card slots, and USB interfaces to make transfering images to the printer easy and without requiring a computer. At only 3.2 lbs., it is easy to transport to wherever a printer is needed. (b) Projectors can now weigh one pound and be as small as 4.8 × 3.9 inches, and yet they are powerful enough to project to a conference room or small auditorium.

everyone is connected to your office network. But there are software **collaboration tools** available to allow you to set up ad hoc networks almost anywhere. Products such as Colligo Workgroup Edition (**www.colligo.com**), shown in Figure 8.35, and Microsoft Groove (included in some versions of Microsoft Office) make it easy to configure secure networks of notebooks or tablets in the field (airports, client sites, and classrooms). Once the network is established, you can share files and printers, update Outlook calendars, and chat with other members of

the network. You even have a simple whiteboard tool for sketching your ideas. Working together was never easier!

NOTEBOOK OR DESKTOP?

How does a notebook compare to a desktop? Desktop systems are invariably a better value than notebooks in terms of computing power gained for your dollar. Because of the notebook's small **footprint** (the amount of space on the desk it takes up),

SOUND BYTE

Tablet and Notebook Tour

In this Sound Byte, you'll take a tour of a Tablet PC and a notebook computer, learning about the unique features and ports available on each.

FIGURE 8.35

The Colligo Workgroup Edition software allows you to set up a secure wireless network wherever you are so that you can work together with your peers.

FIGURE 8.36

ExpressCards add functionality to your notebook.

you pay more for each component. Each piece has had extra engineering time invested to make sure it fits in the smallest space. In addition, a desktop system offers more expandability options. It's easier to add new ports and devices because of the amount of room available in the desktop computer's design.

Desktop systems also are more reliable. Because of the amount of vibration that a notebook experiences, as well as the added exposure to dust, water, and temperature fluctuations, notebooks do not last as long as desktop computers. Manufacturers offer extended warranty plans that cover accidental damage and unexpected drops, although at a price.

How long will I be able to keep my notebook? The answer to that question depends on how easy it is to upgrade your system. Take note of the maximum amount of memory you can install in your notebook and generally install as much as you can afford. This will help extend the useful life of your notebook. Internal hard drives are not easy for novices to install in a notebook, but if you have a FireWire or USB 2.0 port, you can add an external hard drive for more storage space. Historically, notebooks have been equipped with PC Card slots, which are slots on the side of the notebook that accept special credit card–sized devices called PC Cards.

A new standard has emerged called ExpressCard. **ExpressCards** (shown in Figure 8.36) are smaller and transfer data faster than the PC Cards they are replacing. ExpressCards can add fax modems, network connections, wireless adapters, USB 2.0 and FireWire ports, and other capabilities to your notebook. You can add an ExpressCard that allows you to read flash memory cards such as CompactFlash, Memory Sticks, and Secure Digital cards. As new types of ports and devices are introduced, many will be manufactured in ExpressCard formats so that you can make sure your notebook does not become obsolete before its time.

In a world that's becoming ever more mobile, notebooks and other mobile devices will play an increasing role. So be sure to stay on top of mobile technology.

Emerging Technologies: Nanotubes—The Next Big Thing Is Pretty Darn Small!

In the classic 1967 film *The Graduate*, Dustin Hoffman is a young man uncertain about which career he should embark on. At a cocktail party, an older gentleman provides him with some career advice, telling him, "I've got just one word for you ... plastics!" This made sense at the time because plastics were coming on strong as a replacement for metal. If *The Graduate* were remade today, the advice would be, "I've got just one word for you ... nanotubes!"

As you learned in Chapter 1, nanoscience involves the study of molecules and structures (called *nanostructures*), whose size ranges from 1 nanometer to 100 nanometers (or one-billionth of a meter). Using nanotechnology, scientists are hoping to one day build resources from the molecular level by manipulating individual atoms instead of using raw materials already found in nature (such as wood or iron ore). This would allow us to create microscopic computers, the ultimate in portable devices. Imagine nano-sized robotic computers swimming through your arteries, clearing them of plaque. Consider carrying with you a supercomputer the size of a pencil eraser—or, even better, having the power of your desktop computer implanted in your body as a nano-sized chip.

The possibilities of miniaturization are endless, but what materials would be used to construct the computer circuits for these devices? Carbon nanotubes are poised to be the building blocks of the future. You're familiar with carbon from pencils. The graphite core in a pencil is composed of sheets of carbon atoms laid out in a honeycomb pattern. Individual sheets of graphite are extremely strong but don't bond well to other sheets. This makes them ideal for use in a pencil because, as you write, the graphite flakes off and leaves marks on the paper. Unfortunately, graphite doesn't conduct electricity well. This inability, coupled with the lack of strong bonding principles, makes graphite unsuitable as a material to manufacture circuits.

Carbon nanotubes were discovered in the 1950s. Nanotubes are essentially a sheet of carbon atoms (much like graphite) laid out in a honeycomb pattern but rolled into a spherical tube, as shown in Figure 8.37. Arranging the carbon in a tube increases its strength astronomically. It is estimated that carbon nanotubes are as much as 10 to 100 times stronger per unit of weight than steel. This should make them ideal for constructing many types of devices and building materials. Some day we may have earthquake-proof buildings constructed from nanotubes or virtually indestructible clothing woven from nanotube fibers.

But how does this help us build a computer? Aside from strength, the most interesting property of nanotubes is that they are good conductors of electricity. Nanotubes are actually classified as semimetal, meaning they can have properties that are a cross between semiconductors (such as silicon, which is used to create computer chips) and metals. In fact, depending on how a nanotube is constructed, it can change from a semiconductor to a metal along the length of the tube. These properties make it vastly superior to silicon for the construction of transistor pathways in computer chips because they provide engineers with more versatility.

In addition, although the smallest silicon transistors that are likely to be produced in the future will be millions of atoms wide, scientists believe that transistors constructed of nanotubes would be only 100 to 1,000 atoms wide. This represents a quantum leap in miniaturization that even surpasses the original invention of the transistor. Just imagine what can be done when nanotube transistors replace silicon transistors!

So, when can you buy that pencil eraser-sized computer? Not for quite a while. At this point, researchers can manufacture nanotubes only in extremely small quantities at a large cost. But the U.S. government and many multinational corporations are expected to pour billions of dollars into nanoscience research over the next decade. The ongoing research will hopefully lead to breakthroughs in manufacturing technology that will result in nano-scale computers within your lifetime.

FIGURE 8.37

Here is a highly magnified close-up of a carbon nanotube. Rolling the sheets of carbon atoms into a tube shape gives them incredible strength.

1. What are the advantages and limitations of mobile computing?

Mobile computing allows you to communicate with others, remain productive, and have access to your personal information and schedules, Internet-based information, and important software no matter where you are. However, because mobile devices have been miniaturized, they are more expensive and less rugged than desktop equipment. In addition, battery life limits the usefulness of mobile devices, the screen area is small on most devices, the speed of Internet connection is currently lower than is available in the home, and wireless Internet coverage can be limited in some areas.

2. What are the various mobile computing devices?

A range of mobile computing devices are on the market today, including cell phones, portable media players (PMPs), personal digital assistants (PDAs) and smartphones, subnotebooks, notebooks, and Tablet PCs.

3. How do cell phone components resemble a traditional computer, and how do they work?

Just like a computer system, cell phones include a processor (CPU), memory, input and output devices, software, and an operating system. When you speak into a cell phone, the sound enters as a sound wave. Analog sound waves need to be digitized, so an analog-to-digital converter chip converts these sound waves into digital signals. The digital information is then compressed (by a digital signal processor) so that it transmits more quickly to another phone. Finally, the digital information is transmitted as a radio wave through the cellular network to the destination phone.

4. What can I carry in a portable media player, and how does it store data?

A portable media player (PMP) is a device that enables you to carry digital music, image, and video files around with you. Some PMPs also allow you to carry contact databases and calendars as well. The most inexpensive players use only flash memory to store data, whereas more expensive models use a built-in hard drive, which provides more storage.

5. Why would I use a PDA/smartphone, and what internal components and features do they have?

PDA/smartphones are powerful devices that can carry calendars, contact lists, personal productivity software programs, songs, photos, games, and more. Like any computer, they includes a processor, operating system software, input and output devices, and ports. Most PDA/smartphones feature touch-sensitive screens that allow you to enter data with a stylus. You can use either handwritten text or special notation systems to enter data. In terms of output devices, they come with LCD screens in a variety of resolutions and sizes. The two main PDA/smartphone operating systems are the Symbian OS and Windows Mobile. PDA/smartphones do not come with built-in hard drives; for memory needs beyond their built-in RAM and ROM, many use removable flash memory.

6. How can I synchronize my PDA/smartphone with my computer?

The process of updating your data so that the files on your mobile device and desktop computer are the same is called *synchronizing*. To synchronize your desktop and your mobile device, you place the device in a cradle and touch a "sync"

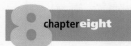

button. This begins the process of information transfer that updates both sets of files to the most current version. Other options for synchronizing or transferring files include using a USB cable, an IrDA port, and the Bluetooth wireless connectivity option.

7. What is a Tablet PC, and why would I want to use one?

A Tablet PC is a portable computer that includes advanced handwriting recognition and incorporates the use of digital ink. Tablets are so named because the display monitor can be used in either a traditional notebook mode or tablet mode. The most innovative input technology on the Tablet PC is digital ink. Supporting digital ink, the tablet's screen is pressure-sensitive and reacts to a digital pen. A Tablet PC can be the ideal solution when you require a lightweight, portable computer with full desktop processing power.

8. How powerful are notebooks, and how do they compare to desktop computers?

The most powerful mobile computing solution is a notebook computer. Notebooks offer large displays and can be equipped with Blu-ray or DVD/CD-RW drives, hard drives, and 4 GB or even more of RAM. Many models feature a full set of ports for easy connectivity. Still, desktop systems are more reliable and cost-effective than notebooks. In addition, it is easier to upgrade and add new ports and devices to a desktop than to a notebook. And though powerful, CPUs for notebooks are usually a bit slower than the latest CPU offered for desktop units. Still, many users feel that the mobility notebooks offer is worth the added expense.

Buzzwords

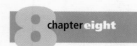

Word Bank

- Bluetooth
- cell phone
- cradle
- flash memory card
- GPS
- microbrowser

- MMS
- mobile computing devices
- notebook
- PDA/smartphone
- PMP
- processor speed

- SMS
- stylus
- subnotebook
- synchronize
- Tablet PC

Instructions: Fill in the blanks using the words from the Word Bank above.

Kathleen's new job as a sales rep is going to mean a lot of travel. She knows she'll need to buy one or more of the (1) _____ available today to stay productive when she's out of the office. Because she needs voice communication, e-mail, and Office to review documents on the road, she'll be selecting a(n) (2) _____ rather than a(n) (3) _____. With her smartphone, she'll be able to exchange text messages with her co-workers using (4) _____. When she accesses the Internet from her phone, she'll use (5) _____ software to check the latest stock prices.

Because Kathleen travels a lot and loves music, she has been considering buying a digital (6) _____. However, she has instead decided to purchase a more expensive (7) _____ that includes a full version of Vista and weighs only 1 pound. That way, she can use the device as more than just an MP3 player. She also invests in a removable (8) _____ on which she'll store her MP3 files. Because she's a hiker, she wants to use a separate mobile device for navigation information, so she may buy a(n) (9) _____ as well.

To make sure she is getting the best device with the most powerful processor, Kathleen has been comparing benchmarks that measure (10) _____. In addition, she wants to make sure she can (11) _____ her PDA/smartphone with her desktop computer so that the files on both match. Thus, she bought a device that includes the wireless (12) _____ technology as well as an external (13) _____ that connects her PDA/smartphone to her PC through a USB port. Because she needs to use digital ink to take notes on the production floor at work, she bought a(n) (14) _____ as well. It was a better choice than a full-sized (15) _____ because she carries it with her all day, taking notes while standing on the production floor.

Becoming Computer Literate

You have a job as a sales rep at a large publishing company and are on the road constantly calling on customers. Your boss is considering investing in some kind of mobile device with Internet access to help you perform your duties. However, first she requires a justification. What mobile device(s) would be best suited for your position? Would you need Internet access for it? Does it depend on which type of device you're using or your job responsibilities? What advantages would there be for the company? What hardware would be required?

Instructions: Using the preceding scenario, write a report using as many of the key terms from the chapter as you can. Be sure the sentences are grammatically and technically correct.

Self-Test

Instructions: Answer the multiple-choice and true–false questions below for more practice with key terms and concepts from this chapter.

MULTIPLE CHOICE

1. Mobile computing is useful only in professions
   a. that don't rely on Internet access.
   b. where work requires intensive graphics and large display screens.
   c. where work requires intensive computer processing power.
   d. None of the above.

2. Currently, cell phones contain ALL of the following except
   a. a CPU.
   b. output devices.
   c. hard drives.
   d. input devices.

3. Cell phones store data
   a. on memory cards.
   b. in RAM.
   c. in ROM.
   d. All of the above.

4. To fit more songs on a personal media player, you can
   a. decrease the sampling rate of digitized music files.
   b. install additional RAM in the PMP.
   c. increase the sampling rate of digitized music files.
   d. install a larger hard drive in the PMP.

5. Flash memory is
   a. nonvolatile and is not erased when power is disconnected.
   b. volatile and is erased when power is disconnected.
   c. used only in PDA/smartphones and Tablet PCs.
   d. the main storage medium in notebook computers.

6. The device best suited for a salesperson who has to demonstrate processor-intensive multimedia to clients is a
   a. smartphone with Internet capabilities.
   b. PDA/smartphone with an external monitor.
   c. Tablet PC.
   d. notebook computer.

7. GPS chips are
   a. installed in all newly manufactured automobiles.
   b. installed in all newly manufactured cell phones.
   c. reliable only when installed in Tablet PCs.
   d. available only for PDA/smartphones.

8. For Internet access, you should obtain
   a. a Tablet PC.
   b. a PDA/smartphone.
   c. an Internet tablet.
   d. All of the above can have Internet capability.

9. When a notebook does not have enough USB ports, you can
   a. have two devices share one USB port.
   b. add ports only if the notebook is configured with flash memory.
   c. NOT add ports unless your computer uses Windows Vista.
   d. add ports using a PC card or external hub.

10. Portable devices that can be synchronized with your home computer are
    a. PDAs and GPS units.
    b. iPods and PDA/smartphones.
    c. ultramobiles and GPS units.
    d. any device with Bluetooth.

TRUE–FALSE

____ 1. Hard drives are found only in desktops, notebooks, and Tablet PCs.

____ 2. PMPs with a hard drive are able to carry fewer songs than those with flash memory.

____ 3. A PDA/smartphone and a notebook can exchange data wirelessly if they both have Bluetooth.

____ 4. Tablet PCs are commonly used for text messaging.

____ 5. Smartphones run Windows Vista as an operating system.

Making the Transition to... Next Semester

1. Choosing Devices to Fit Your Needs

As a student, which devices discussed in this chapter would have the most immediate impact on the work you do each day? Which would provide the best value (that is, the greatest increase in productivity and organization per dollar spent)? Consider two other mobile devices as well: the Nintendo DS and the Sony PlayStation Portable (PSP). How do these mobile gaming consoles rate as devices to help you carry, store, and display electronic information?

2. Choosing the Best Notebook

Compare the Apple MacBook series of notebook computers with the Dell Inspiron series. Consider price, performance, expandability, and portability. Explain which would be the better investment for your needs next semester.

3. Choosing the Best Cell Phone Plan

Major national cellular providers include AT&T, Verizon, T-Mobile, and Sprint. Visit their Web sites and compare the prices and features of their popular cellular plans for both minimal users and power users. Based on your research, which cell phone plan would be best for your needs? Which company has the most cost-effective data plan? Would an "unlocked" phone (one not tied to a specific vendor) work best for you?

4. Choosing the Best PDA/Smartphone

Your friend wants to trim down the number of different devices she keeps carrying around. Visit the cellular providers' Web sites that you found for the preceding question and research options. Which PDA/smartphone would you recommend to your friend and why? Compare at least three different models of phones and list their price, music storage capacity, built-in memory, and expandability options.

a. Which of the three models you compared is the best value for your friend?
b. What special features does the phone you chose have? What accessories would you recommend your friend buy to make the phone more useful?
c. Would you consider buying a refurbished PDA/smartphone? Why or why not?

5. iTunes U

Download a free copy of iTunes software. In the iTunes Store, explore the iTunes U podcast directory, which contains audio and video lectures freely published from major universities.

a. Look for the MIT Open Courseware video podcasts. How many lectures are available from MIT (Massachusetts Institute of Technology)?
b. If each lecture is 90 minutes on average and approximately 200 MB in size, how much storage would it take to save all of the video lectures in every course published from MIT?
c. Is there a mobile device that can store and play that much content? What devices could store the lectures from all of the courses in mathematics offered by MIT Open Courseware?

Making the Transition to... the Workplace

1. Corporate Mobile Computing Needs

Imagine your company is boosting its sales force and looking to the future of mobile technology. Your boss has asked you to research the following issues surrounding mobile computing for the company:

a. Do mobile computing devices present increased security risks? What would happen if you left a flash memory card at a meeting and a competitor picked it up? Are there ways to protect your data on mobile devices?

b. Can viruses attack mobile devices? Is there any special software on the market to protect mobile devices from viruses? How much would it cost to equip 20 devices with protection?

c. Is there a role for mobile computing devices even if employees don't leave the building? Which devices would be important for a company to consider for use within corporate offices?

d. Should employees be allowed to use mobile devices provided by the company for personal use even though these files related to personal use might eat up potentially valuable memory and space? What restrictions should be put on personal use to protect the privacy of proprietary company information contained on the devices?

2. 3G Communications

The current generation of telecommunications (nicknamed "3G" for third generation) allows the speed of cellular network transmissions to hit 3 Mbps. How does that compare to dial-up and cable modem access for wired networks? What implications does it have for information access and e-commerce?

3. Mobile Speed Limits

Using the Internet, research what speed limitations are expected to exist in the future with regard to mobile devices. Also, report on the average speeds obtained during testing on two popular mobile devices. (Good sources of testing information include **www.pcmag.com** and **www.consumerreports.org**.)

4. Too Much Mobile?

Imagine you are a manager of 18 employees, all of whom work in open-air cubicles (that is, there are no fixed walls or separate offices). As a manager, what concerns might you have about their personal cell phone usage? Do you think your employees would respond well to a "Quiet Zone," an area in which no personal cell phone usage is allowed? What about conduct during important meetings? Should employees be allowed to text message each other during the meeting? As a manager, are there concerns you might have if employees have digital cameras on their cell phones?

5. Mobile Devices on the Highway

Mobile devices used in vehicles are becoming the norm in today's society. Consider the following:

a. Several car manufacturers provide Bluetooth option packages for their vehicles. What advantages are there to having Bluetooth connectivity in your car? Are there any disadvantages?

b. Examine the Microsoft Sync software package. List the features and services it provides. If you were a salesperson with a territory you covered by car, how would Sync help you?

Critical Thinking Questions

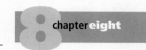

Instructions: Albert Einstein used *Gedanken experiments,* or critical thinking questions, to develop his theory of relativity. Some ideas are best understood by experimenting with them in our own minds. The following critical thinking questions are designed to demand your full attention but require only a comfortable chair—no technology.

1. **Mobile Devices and Society**

   Do you think we will ever become a completely wireless society? Will there always be a need for some land lines (physical wired connections)? How will broadband wireless communication infrastructure impact a city's social and economic development? Will there be more or less social interaction? Will mobile computing promote increased understanding between people or create more isolation?

2. **The Ultimate Mobile Devices**

   As devices become lighter and smaller, we are seeing a convergence of multiple functions into one device.

   a. What would the ultimate convergent mobile device be for you? Is there a limit in weight, size, or complexity?

   b. America Online Instant Messenger (AIM) service is now available on many cellular phone systems. Would the ability to be alerted to IM buddies on your cell phone be useful to you? What would you be willing to pay for this feature? What other alerts might be useful to you (eBay auctions, for instance)? Does your college offer a texting service to alert students to important events or safety alerts?

3. **Protecting Intellectual Property**

   The recording industry, recording artists, the motion picture industry, and consumers find themselves in a complex discussion when the topic of peer-to-peer sharing systems is brought up.

   a. What solution would you propose to safeguard the business interests of industry, the intellectual property rights of artists, and the freedoms of consumers?

   b. Have you ever downloaded music or video off the Web? If so, did you download from a legal site? Do you think illegal download sites should be allowed to exist?

4. **Privacy Concerns: GPS Tracking at Work**

   You drive a delivery vehicle for your employer. How would you feel if your employer installed a GPS device in all of its delivery vehicles to monitor employee work habits? How would you feel if your employer disciplined you for speeding based on data obtained from the GPS device installed in your delivery vehicle? Should employers have the right to monitor their employees in this way? Why or why not?

5. **Privacy Concerns: GPS Tracking at Home**

   Consider the following questions related to GPS security risks:

   a. Your spouse carries a GPS-enabled cell phone. The GPS chip inside allows a private service (**www.ulocate.com**) to gather information on your spouse's last location, the path he or she took to get there, and their average speed from point to point. Would you use the service to check on your spouse's activities? What if it was your spouse monitoring you?

   b. Would you agree to insert a GPS-enabled tracking device into your pet? your child? What legislation do you think should be required if tracking data were available on you? Would you be willing to sell that information to marketing agencies? Should that data be available to the government if you were suspected of a crime?

6. **Electronic Publishing**

   Explore the specifications of the Sony Portable Reader and the Amazon Kindle. How would your study habits change if your textbooks were delivered to you in electronic format only on one of these eReader machines? What unique advantages would there be? What disadvantages would there be? How would using an eReader compare with just receiving the book as an electronic file such as a PDF document?

Problem:

You have formed a consulting group that advises clients on how to move their businesses into the new mobile computing age.

Task:

Each team will be defined as an expert resource in one of the mobile devices presented in this chapter: cell phones (including smartphones), PMPs, PDA/smartphones, subnotebooks, or notebooks. For each scenario described by a client, the group should assess how strong a fit its device is to that client's needs.

Process:

Divide the class into three or four teams and assign each group a different mobile device (PMP, PDA/smartphone, subnotebook, or notebook).

1. Research the current features and prices for the mobile device your team has been assigned.

2. Consider the following three clients:
   - An elementary classroom that wants to have students carry mobile devices to the nearby creek to do a science project on water quality.
   - A manufacturing plant that wants managers using a mobile device to be able to report back hourly on the production line's performance and problems.
   - A pharmaceutical company that wants to outfit its sales reps with the devices they need to be prepared to promote their products when they visit physicians.

3. Discuss the advantages and disadvantages of your device for each client. Consider value, reliability, computing needs, and communication needs as well as expandability for the future.

4. As a group, prepare a final report that considers the costs, availability, and unique features of the device that led you to recommend or not recommend it for each client.

5. Bring the research materials from the individual team meetings to class. Looking at the clients' needs, make final decisions as to which mobile device is best suited for each client.

Conclusion:

Many mobile computing devices are on the market today. Finding the best mobile device to use in any given situation depends on factors such as value, reliability, expandability, and the computing and communication needs of the client.

Multimedia

In addition to the review materials presented here, you'll find additional materials featured with the book's multimedia, including the *Technology in Action* Student Resource CD and the Companion Website (**www.prenhall.com/techinaction**), which will help reinforce your understanding of the chapter content. These materials include the following:

ACTIVE HELPDESK

In Active Helpdesk calls, you'll assume the role of helpdesk operator taking calls about the concepts you've learned in this chapter. You'll apply what you've learned and receive feedback from a supervisor to review and reinforce those concepts. The Active Helpdesk calls for this chapter are listed below and can be found on your Student Resource CD:

* Using Portable Media Players
* Using PDA/Smartphones

SOUND BYTES

Sound Bytes are dynamic multimedia tutorials that help demystify even the most complex topics. You'll view video clips and animations that illustrate computer concepts, and then apply what you've learned by reviewing with the Sound Byte Labs, which include quizzes and activities specifically tailored to each Sound Byte. The Sound Bytes for this chapter are listed here and can be found on your Student Resource CD:

* PDAs/Smartphones on the Road and at Home
* Connecting with Bluetooth
* Tablet and Notebook Tour

COMPANION WEBSITE

The *Technology in Action* Companion Website includes a variety of additional materials to help you review and learn more about the topics in this chapter. The resources available at **www.prenhall.com/techinaction** include:

* **Online Study Guide.** Each chapter features an online true–false and multiple-choice quiz. You can take these quizzes, automatically check the results, and e-mail the results to your instructor.

* **Web Research Projects.** Each chapter features a number of Web research projects that ask you to search the Web for information on computer-related careers, milestones in computer history, important people and companies, emerging technologies, and the applications and implications of different technologies.

Digital
Entertainment

When did everything go "digital"? It used to be that you'd only find analog forms of entertainment. Today, no matter what you're interested in—music, movies, television, radio—a digital version is popular (see Figure 1). MP3 files encode digital forms of music, and digital cameras and video camcorders are now commonplace. In Hollywood, some feature films are now being shot entirely with digital equipment, and many movie theaters use digital projection equipment.

George Lucas, a great proponent of digital technology, filmed *Star Wars Episode II: Attack of the Clones* all the way back in 2002 completely in digital format. It played in special digital release at digital-ready theaters. And in January 2005, the digital film *Rize*, by David LaChapelle, premiered at the Sundance Film Festival. It was streamed from computers in Oregon to a full-size cinema screen in Park City, Utah, beginning a new age of movie distribution. Also gaining in popularity is the MOD Films site (**www.modfilms.com**), a gathering place for people who see "remixable" films in our future. The components of these feature films—from production footage to soundtrack, dialogue, and sound effects—will be available to the audience online, and each person will be able to interact with and modify the film, creating a new plotline or a different ending. Digital entertainment is here to stay.

Meanwhile, satellite radio systems such as XM Satellite Radio and HD Radio are digital formats. And at the time of publication, digital television (DTV), a digital encoding of television signals, is expected to become the standard in February 2009. In this Technology in Focus, we look at two popular forms of digital entertainment: digital photography and digital video. But first, let's consider what makes digital so unique.

What's So Special About Digital?

So what *is* so special about digital? Think about the information captured in music and film: sounds and images. Sound is carried to

FIGURE 1
Analog Versus Digital Entertainment

	ANALOG	DIGITAL
MUSIC	Vinyl record albums Cassette tapes	CDs MP3 files
PHOTOGRAPHY	35-mm single lens reflex (SLR) cameras Photos stored on film	Digital cameras, including digital SLRs Photos stored as digital files
VIDEO	8-mm, Hi8, or VHS camcorders Film stored on VHS tapes	Digital video (DV) camcorders Film stored as digital files; often distributed on DVD and Blu-ray discs
RADIO	AM/FM radio	HD Radio XM Radio
TELEVISION	Conventional broadcast analog TV	Digital television (DTV)

your ears by sound waves, which are actually patterns of pressure changes in the air. Images are our interpretation of the changing intensity of light waves around us. These sound and light waves are called *analog* or *continuous* waves. They illustrate the loudness of the sound or the brightness of the colors in the image at a given moment in time. They are continuous signals because you would never have to lift your pencil off the page to draw them—they are just long continuous lines.

First-generation recording devices such as vinyl records and analog television broadcasts were designed to reproduce these sound and light waves. The needle in a groove of a vinyl record vibrates in the same pattern as the original sound wave. Television signals are actually waves that tell your TV how to display the same color and brightness as seen in the original studio. But it's difficult to describe a wave, even mathematically. The simplest sounds, such as the C note of a piano, have the simplest shapes, like that shown in Figure 2a. However, something like the word *hello* generates a highly complex pattern, like that shown in Figure 2b.

Digital formats are descriptions of these signals as a long string of numbers. This is the main reason why digital recording has such an advantage over analog. Digital gives us a simple way to describe sound and light waves *exactly* so that sounds and images can be reproduced perfectly each time. We already have easy ways to distribute digital information (on CDs and DVDs and using e-mail, for example). But how could a digital format, a sequence of numbers, act as a convenient way to express these complicated wave shapes?

The answer is provided by something called **analog-to-digital conversion**. In analog-to-digital conversion, the incoming analog signal is measured many times each second. The strength of the signal at each measurement is recorded as a simple number. The series of numbers produced by the analog-to-digital conversion process gives us the digital form of the wave. Figure 3 shows an analog and digital version of the same wave. In Figure 3a, you see the original continuous analog wave. You could draw the wave in Figure 3a without lifting your pencil from the page. In Figure 3b, the wave has been digitized and now is not a single line but is represented instead as a series of points or numbers.

So, how does this all work? Let's take music as an example. Figure 4 shows how

FIGURE 2

(a) This is an analog wave showing the simple, pure sound of a piano playing middle C. (b) This is the complex wave produced when a person says "Hello."

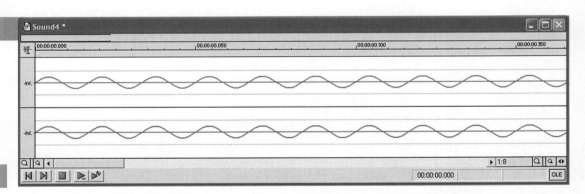

a

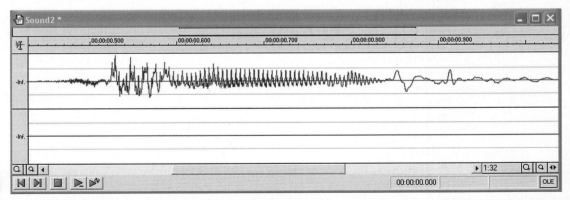

b

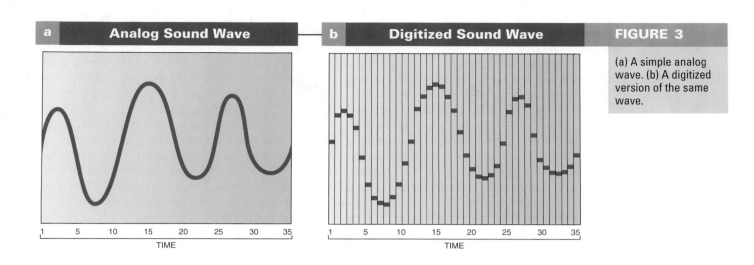

a Analog Sound Wave   **b** Digitized Sound Wave   **FIGURE 3**

(a) A simple analog wave. (b) A digitized version of the same wave.

TIME   TIME

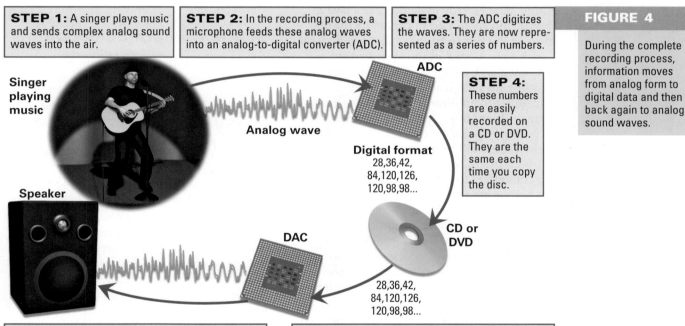

STEP 1: A singer plays music and sends complex analog sound waves into the air.

STEP 2: In the recording process, a microphone feeds these analog waves into an analog-to-digital converter (ADC).

STEP 3: The ADC digitizes the waves. They are now represented as a series of numbers.

FIGURE 4

During the complete recording process, information moves from analog form to digital data and then back again to analog sound waves.

STEP 4: These numbers are easily recorded on a CD or DVD. They are the same each time you copy the disc.

Singer playing music

ADC

Analog wave

Digital format
28,36,42,
84,120,126,
120,98,98...

CD or DVD

Speaker

DAC

28,36,42,
84,120,126,
120,98,98...

STEP 6: These analog waves tell your receiver how to move the speaker cones to duplicate the same sound waves as in the original music.

STEP 5: To play the CD, your CD player must have a digital-to-analog converter (DAC) to convert the numbers back to the analog wave.

the process of creating digital entertainment begins with the physical act of playing music, which creates analog waves. Next, a chip inside the recording device called an *analog-to-digital converter (ADC)* digitizes these waves into a series of numbers. This series of numbers can be recorded onto CDs and DVDs or sent electronically. On the receiving end, a playback device such as a CD player or DVD player is fed that same series of numbers. Inside the playback device, a *digital-to-analog converter (DAC)*, a chip that converts the digital numbers to a continuous wave, reproduces the original wave exactly.

More precisely, the digital wave will be *close* to exact. How accurate it is, or how close the digitized wave is in shape to the original analog wave, depends on the **sampling rate** of the ADC. The sampling rate specifies the number of times the analog wave is measured each second. The higher the sampling rate, the more accurately the original wave can be re-created. However, higher sampling rates also produce much more data and therefore result in bigger files. For example, sound waves on CDs are sampled at a rate of 44,000 times a second. This produces a huge list of numbers—44,000 of them each second!

When sounds or image waves are digitized, it means that analog data is changed into digital data—from a wave into a series of numbers. The digital data is perfectly reproducible and can be distributed easily on CDs and DVDs or through the airwaves. The data also can be easily processed by a computer.

These digital advantages have revolutionized photography, music, movies, television, and radio. For example, digital television has a sharper picture and superior sound quality. However, there is a cost in the shift from analog to digital technologies. At the time of publication, the Federal Communications Commission had set February 2009 as the target date when all over-the-air broadcasters were to end analog transmission and transmit solely in digital format. When this happens, consumers receiving broadcast signals (i.e., not cable subscribers) will be forced to choose between upgrading to DTV sets or purchasing converters for older televisions. The digital revolution in television will bring better quality and additional conveniences, but at a cost, as the older analog equipment is phased out. (Visit **www.fcc.gov/dtv** and **www.dtv.gov** for more information.)

The same tension exists in the migration from analog to digital technology in photography. Let's take a look at this form of entertainment and explore the advantages and investment required in migrating to a digital format.

Digital Photography

Before digital cameras hit the market, most people used some form of 35-mm single-lens reflex (SLR) camera. When you take a picture using a traditional SLR camera, a shutter opens, creating an aperture (a small window in the camera), which allows light to hit the 35-mm film inside. Chemicals coating the film react when exposed to light. Later, additional chemicals develop the image on the film, and it is printed on special light-sensitive paper. A variety of lenses and processing techniques, special equipment, and filters are needed to create printed photos from traditional SLR cameras.

Digital cameras, on the other hand, do not use film. Instead, they capture images on electronic sensors called *charge-coupled device (CCD) arrays* and then convert those images to digital data, a long series of numbers that represent the color and brightness of millions of points in the image. Unlike traditional cameras, digital cameras allow you to see your images the instant you shoot them. Most camera models can now record digital video as well as digital photos.

Digital Camera Selection

With hundreds of models to choose from, where do you begin? The first question to answer is whether you want a compact "point-and-click" model camera or a more serious digital SLR. The larger digital SLR cameras allow you to switch between different lenses and offer features important to serious amateur and professional photographers (such as depth of field previewing). Although having such flexibility in moving up to a larger zoom lens is a great advantage, these cameras are also larger, heavier, and use more battery power than the tiny point-and-click models. Think about how you will be using your camera and decide which will serve you best in the long run.

Next, you'll want to evaluate the quality of the camera on a number of levels. One great resource to use is Digital Photography Review (**www.dpreview.com**). The site's camera reviews evaluate a camera's construction, its features, image quality, ease of use, and value for the cost.

In addition, you will find comparisons to similar camera models by other manufacturers and feedback from owners of those models. Links are provided to several resellers, making it easy to compare prices as well.

Digital Camera Resolutions

Part of what determines the image quality of a digital camera is its **resolution**, or the

FIGURE 5

Digital Camera
Resolutions

Nikon Coolpix S4 (6.1 MP)

Kodak V1273 (12 MP)

Canon EOS-1Ds (21.9 MP)

Sony Cyber-shot
DSC-T100 (8.1 MP)

number of data points it records for each image captured. A digital camera's resolution is measured in megapixels (MP). The prefix *mega* is short for millions. The word *pixel* is short for picture element, which is a single dot in a digital image. Point-and-click models typically offer resolutions from 6 MP to 12 MP. Professional digital SLR cameras, such as the Canon EOS-1Ds Mark III, can take photos at resolutions as high as 21.1 MP, but they sell for thousands of dollars. Figure 5 shows some popular digital camera models and the number of pixels they record at their maximum resolution.

If you're interested in making only 5 × 7" or 8 × 10" prints, a lower resolution camera is fine. However, low-resolution images become grainy and pixelated when pushed to make larger size prints. For example, if you tried to print an 11 × 14" enlargement from a 2 MP shot taken using your cell phone's camera, the image would look grainy—you would see individual dots of color instead of a clear, sharp image. The 6 MP to 12 MP cameras on the market now have plenty of resolution to guarantee sharp, detailed images even with enlargements as big as 11 × 14".

Storage of Digital Images

When a digital camera takes a photo, it stores the images on a flash memory card inside the camera, as shown in Figure 6.

FIGURE 6

Flash memory slides into a digital camera and is used to store images.

Flash memory cards are tiny and convenient, allowing you to easily transfer digital information between your camera and your computer or printer. Flash memory therefore takes the place of film used in traditional cameras.

To fit more photos on the same size of flash memory card, digital cameras allow you to choose from several different file types in order to compress, or squeeze, the image data into less memory space. When you choose to compress your images, you will lose some of the detail, but in return you'll be able to fit more images on your flash card. The most common file types supported by digital cameras are the RAW uncompressed data and the Joint Photographic Experts Group (JPEG). RAW files record all of the original image information, so they are larger than compressed JPEG files. JPEG files can be compressed just a bit, keeping most of the details, or compressed a great deal, losing some detail. Most cameras allow you to select from a few different JPEG compression levels.

Often cameras also support a very low-resolution storage option, creating files that you can easily attach to e-mail messages. This low-resolution setting typically provides images that are not useful for printing but are so much smaller in size that they are easily e-mailed. Even people who have slow Internet connections are able to quickly download and view such images on-screen.

Preparing Your Camera and Taking Your Photos

Preparing your camera includes ensuring that your camera's batteries are charged and the settings are correct. Digital cameras consume a great deal of power, so you might want to carry a spare, charged battery pack. Also make sure that the flash card is installed and has enough space for the number of photos you plan to take.

Next, set the resolution on your camera. Most cameras offer two or three different resolution settings. For example, a 10 MP camera might be able to shoot images at six different resolutions varying from 10 MP down to 1.5 MP. If you're taking a photo that will be enlarged and that needs to be of an extremely high quality, use the full power of your camera. Shoot the image at 10 MP and save it as uncompressed data at the highest resolution. If you're planning to use the image for a Web page, where having a smaller file would be helpful, use a lower resolution and the space-saving compressed JPEG format. If you're unsure how you're going to use your images, then record them with the maximum resolution your camera allows.

Most cameras include an autofocus feature and automatically set the aperture and correct shutter speed. Several cameras now also incorporate image stabilization

algorithms to reduce the amount of vibration seen in the image if your hands are a bit shaky. Newer models have face-recognition software that recognizes a face is in the image and uses that to adjust focus. Some models have a feature called *smile shutter*, which takes a shot only once your subject is smiling. This makes taking a digital photo as simple as pressing a button. The great thing about digital cameras, of course, is that they let you instantly examine your photos in a display window on the camera. If you don't like a certain photo, you can delete it immediately, freeing space on your flash card.

Transferring Your Photos to Your Computer

If you just want to print your photos, you may not need to transfer them to your computer. Many photo printers can make prints directly from your camera or from the flash memory card. However, transferring the photos to your computer allows you to store them and frees your flash card for reuse.

Transferring your photos to your computer is simple. All current model digital cameras have a built-in universal serial bus (USB) 2.0 port (some high-end models may also include a FireWire port). Using a USB 2.0 cable, you can connect the camera to your computer and copy the converted images as uncompressed files or in a compressed format as JPEG files. Another option is to transfer the flash card from your camera to the computer. Some desktops have flash card slots on the front of the system unit. However, if yours does not, you can buy an external memory card reader like the one shown in Figure 7 and attach it to your computer using an available USB port. Many newer model cameras also support wireless network connections to your computer so that you can transfer the images without the fuss of putting a cable in place. The Panasonic Lumix TZ50 goes one step further. It uses its integrated WiFi to connect to Google's online photo service, Picasa, and upload your images up to a Picasa Web photo album automatically.

When you connect your camera to your computer, with the Microsoft Windows Vista operating system, the rest of the transfer is automatic (see Figure 8). Assuming your sound is turned on, you'll hear an attention sound telling you the computer

FIGURE 7

If your computer does not have a built-in flash card reader, you can buy an external reader that attaches to your computer using a USB cable and port.

a

b

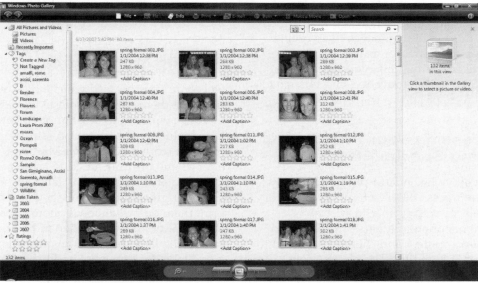

FIGURE 8

The Windows Vista OS makes it simple to import digital images to a file on your hard drive. (a) Vista enables you to import or view images. (b) Images are imported directly to Windows Photo Gallery in which you can rate and add captions to your images.

How Do My Old Photos Become Digital?

Obviously, not every document or image you have is in an electronic form. What about all the photographs you have already taken? Or an article from a magazine or a hand-drawn sketch? How can these be converted into digital format?

Digital scanners such as the one shown in Figure 9 convert paper text and images into digital formats. You can place any flat material on the glass surface of the scanner and convert it into a digital file. Most scanner software allows you to store the converted images as RAW files or in compressed form as JPEG files. And some scanners include hardware that allows you to scan film negatives or slides as well or even insert a stack of photos to be scanned in sequence.

Scanner quality is measured by its resolution, which is given in dots per inch (dpi). Most modern scanners can digitize a document at resolutions as high as 4,800 × 9,600 dpi, in either color or grayscale modes. You can easily connect a scanner to your computer using USB 2.0 or FireWire ports. Scanners also typically come with software supporting optical character recognition (OCR). OCR software converts pages of handwritten or typed text into electronic files. You can then open and edit these converted documents with traditional word-processing programs such as Microsoft Word. In addition, many scanners have a Copy button that allows you to scan and sometimes print documents, taking the place of a copy machine.

FIGURE 9

Scanners can convert paper documents, photo prints, or strips of film negatives into digital data.

and camera are connected and can communicate. Next, a dialog box appears, asking you whether you want to view the images or import them to your computer. If you choose to import, you have the ability to tag the group of images. Once they've been downloaded into Windows Photo Gallery, you can add details to each image with captions and ratings. If you're satisfied with the photos and want to share them, you can send them to your friends as e-mail attachments or upload the images to an online Web photo album, for example. If you're not satisfied with them, you can process them further to remove red-eye, change to sepia tones, or add special effects.

Processing Your Photos and Adding Special Effects

Once you've taken your photos, you may want to process them—cropping them, for example, or adding special effects. Traditional photographers often invest in special equipment and chemicals needed to develop 35-mm film. The photographer can then resize or crop the photo, add different filtering effects, or combine photos. With digital photography, you can do all of this using inexpensive image editing software.

Hundreds of image editing programs are available, from freeware to highly sophisticated software suites. Many times the manufacturer of your camera will include an image editing program on a CD that comes with your camera. If you want to purchase a more powerful program, Adobe Photoshop Elements and Corel Paint Shop Pro Photo X2

are two well-reviewed packages suitable for home use. They allow you to remove flaws such as red-eye; crop images; correct poor color balance; apply filtering effects such as mosaics, charcoal, and an impressionistic style; and merge components from multiple images to create collages. Figure 10 shows just a few examples of the filtering effects you can apply to an image. The exact set of filtering effects you will have depends on the software you're using.

Printing Your Photos

Once you've processed your photos, you can print them using a professional service or your own printer. Most photo printing labs, including the film-processing departments at stores such as Wal-Mart and Target, offer digital printing services, as do many high-end online processing labs. These sites accept original or edited image files and print them on professional photo paper with high-quality inks. The paper and ink used at processing labs are higher quality than what is available for home use and produce heavier, glossier prints that won't fade. In addition, Kodak and Sony have kiosks in department stores and photography stores that you can use yourself. These kiosks accept image files directly from your flash cards, allow you to do a small amount of editing such as cropping the image or correcting red-eye, and then print the finished photos on the spot. From the Windows Vista Photo Gallery, you can send your digital photo directly to local merchants such as CVS and Walgreens for printing.

FIGURE 10

Using image editing software, you can add filtering effects such as color pencil, collage, and oil painting.

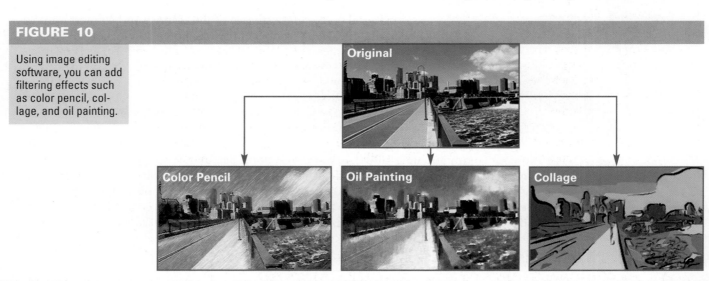

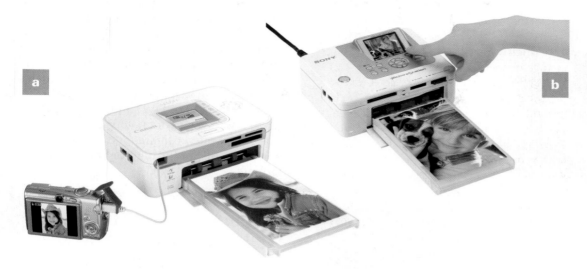

FIGURE 11

Many photo printers incorporate displays to let you see the images before you print. (a) The Kodak EasyShare system allows you to transfer and print pictures quickly and easily. (b) The Sony DPP-FP90 dye-sublimation printer produces professional-quality images that resist fading, water stains, and fingerprints.

In addition, you can find online services, such as **Flickr.com** and **Shutterfly.com**, which let you upload your images to their Web site. On the site, you then can organize your images as an online photo album for others to view for free; if you want hard-copy prints, mugs, T-shirts, or calendars sporting your shot, you can order them directly from the site.

Photo printers for home use are available in two technologies: inkjet and dye sublimation (see Figure 11). Most popular and inexpensive are inkjet printers. As noted in Chapter 2, some inkjet printers are capable of printing high-quality color photos, although they vary in speed and quality. Some include a display window so that you can review the image as you stand at the printer, whereas others are portable, allowing you to print your photos wherever you are. Some printers even allow you to crop the image right at the printer without having to use special image editing software.

Unlike inkjet printers, dye-sublimation printers produce images using a heating element instead of an inkjet nozzle. The heating element passes over a ribbon of translucent film that has been dyed with bands of colors. By controlling the temperature of the element, dyes are vaporized from a solid into a gas. The gas vapors penetrate the photo paper before they cool and return to solid form, producing glossy, high-quality images. If you're interested in a printer to use for printing only photographs, a dye-sublimation printer is a good choice. However, some models print only specific photo sizes, such as 4 × 6" prints, so be sure

the printer you buy will fit your long-term needs.

Transferring images to a printer is similar to transferring them to your computer. If you have a direct-connection camera, you can plug the camera directly into the printer with a cable. Some printers have slots that accept different types of flash memory cards. Of course, you also can transfer your images to the printer from your computer if you have stored them there.

You may decide not to print your photos at all. As noted earlier, online albums let you share your photos without having to print them. And portable devices such Apple's iPod and many cell phones enable you to carry and display your photos. The iPod, for example, can be connected to a TV and deliver slide shows of your photographs complete with musical soundtracks you have selected.

Digital Video

Digital video comes from several sources, not just digital camcorders. Most cell phones can record video, and most digital cameras take video as well as digital still shots. Webcams are inexpensive devices for creating digital video as well. With all of these possibilities, it is useful to know what to do with digital video files once you have recorded them—how to transfer them, process them, and distribute them to an audience. We'll start by looking at video camcorders.

Digital video camcorders deliver the highest quality video. The first camcorders

FIGURE 12

(a) First-generation home video camcorders recorded on full-size VHS cassettes.
(b) Modern digital video camcorders can record in high definition and still be small and light.

were analog video cameras such as the one shown in Figure 12a. These were large, heavy units that held a full-size VHS tape. The push to produce smaller, lighter models led to the introduction of compact VHS tapes and then to 8-mm and Hi8 formats. Still, all of these are analog formats, and each records to its own specific type of tape.

The newest generation of video equipment for home use is the digital video (DV) format. Introduced in 1995, the digital video standard led to a new generation of recording equipment. Today, digital video cameras offer many advantages over their VHS counterparts. They are incredibly small and light, and most don't require any tapes at all. They store hours of video onto built-in hard drives. Some models even record directly to DVD discs.

Using digital video, you can easily transfer video files to your computer. Then, using video editing software, you can edit the video at home, cutting out sections, resequencing segments, and adding titles. To do the same with analog videotape would require expensive and complex audio/video equipment usually seen only in video production studios. And with digital video, you can save (or *write*) your final product on a CD or DVD and play it in your home DVD system or on your computer. For true videophiles, cameras and burners are now available for the high-definition video formats.

Preparing to Shoot Video Footage

Preparing your digital video camera involves making sure you have enough battery power and storage capacity. Batteries for digital video cameras are rechargeable and can provide between one and nine hours of shooting time. Longer-lasting batteries cost and weigh more, so you'll want to think about how you use your camera before deciding which batteries to purchase. Most videographers recommend carrying two spare batteries, though having one spare is fine if you can recharge it while you're using the second.

Digital video cameras most often record onto built-in hard drives, although some models use tape, memory cards, or write directly to DVDs. Make sure you have enough storage capacity to cover the event you're shooting. Check the user guide for your particular camera to see how much memory you need to store video. For example, on the Sony DCR-SR45 Handycam, the 30 GB hard drive can store 20 hours of video in its lowest resolution mode, 10 hours in standard mode, and 7 hours of highest-quality video.

Shooting video with a digital video camera is similar to shooting video with an analog camera. Automated programs control the exposure settings for different environments (nighttime shots, action events, and so on), while automatic focusing and telephoto zoom lens features are common as well. Many cameras include an antishake feature that stabilizes the image when you're using the camera without a tripod. Using these features, you can capture great footage by just pointing and pressing Record.

Transferring Your Video to Your Computer

Digital video cameras already hold your video as digital data, so transferring the data to your computer is simple (see Figure 13). Most cameras use a USB 2.0 port to connect the camera to your computer. Some models offer the convenience of one-button DVD transfer. With the push of just one button on the camcorder, all of the recorded video is automatically sent through your computer and written to a DVD. Data can also be transferred to your computer using a flash memory card if your camcorder supports it.

Once you connect your camera to your computer, Microsoft Vista automatically identifies it, recognizing its manufacturer and model. The OS then scans the software on your system and presents a list of all the programs you can use to import your video. You may have received a video editing program when you purchased your digital video camera. If you installed the program,

it will appear on this list (see Figure 13a). Windows Import Video is the default program for importing if you have no other software installed. Windows Movie Maker is another video editing program and is included as part of Windows Vista. Other digital video editing programs such as Adobe Premiere Elements and Pinnacle Studio can import video as well. These are more powerful, full-featured programs that you purchase separately.

Windows Video Import (or other software programs) allows you to fast-forward, pause, and rewind, moving to the segment you wish to transfer (or record) to your hard drive (Figure 13b). You can use the digital video camera control arrows at the top to locate the exact piece of footage you want to transfer. Click the Start Video Import button and the video file transfers to the hard drive.

Some camcorders on the market today make it even easier to get data to a DVD directly. Made by Sony, the DVD Handycam Camcorder DCR-DVD 910 writes its digital

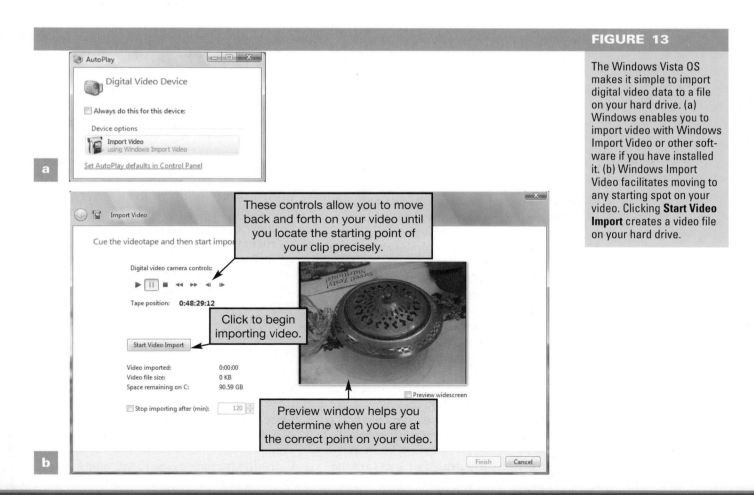

FIGURE 13

The Windows Vista OS makes it simple to import digital video data to a file on your hard drive. (a) Windows enables you to import video with Windows Import Video or other software if you have installed it. (b) Windows Import Video facilitates moving to any starting spot on your video. Clicking **Start Video Import** creates a video file on your hard drive.

These controls allow you to move back and forth on your video until you locate the starting point of your clip precisely.

Click to begin importing video.

Preview window helps you determine when you are at the correct point on your video.

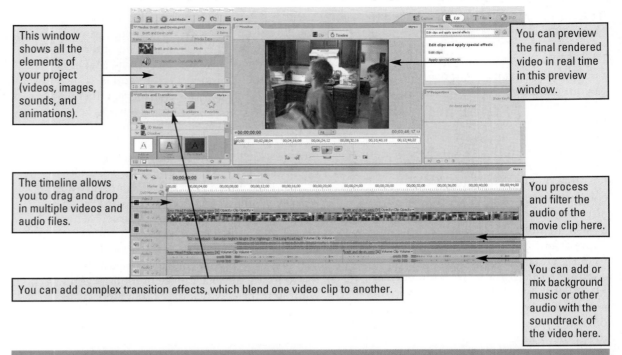

This window shows all the elements of your project (videos, images, sounds, and animations).

You can preview the final rendered video in real time in this preview window.

The timeline allows you to drag and drop in multiple videos and audio files.

You process and filter the audio of the movie clip here.

You can add or mix background music or other audio with the soundtrack of the video here.

You can add complex transition effects, which blend one video clip to another.

FIGURE 14

Adobe Premiere allows you to build a movie from video clips and add sound tracks and special effects such as three-dimensional transitions between scenes.

data directly onto 3-inch DVDs. It can record as much as 60 minutes of video per disc when using the standard quality setting. You can then drop the DVD into most DVD players and view it immediately.

Editing Your Video and Adding Special Effects

Once the digital video data is in a file on your computer's hard drive, the fun really begins. Video editing software presents a storyboard, or *timeline*, with which you can manipulate your video file, as shown in Figure 14. Using this software, you can review your clips frame by frame or trim them at any point. You can order each segment on the timeline in whichever sequence you like and correct segments for color balance, brightness, or contrast.

In addition, you can add transitions to your video such as those you're used to seeing on TV—fades to black, dissolves, and so on. Figure 14 shows how easy it is to add transitions in Adobe Premiere. Just select the type of transition you want from the drop-down list and drag that icon into the

timeline where you want the transition to occur.

Video editing software also lets you add titles, animations, and audio tracks to your video, including background music, sound effects, and additional narration. Figure 14 shows two audio tracks: the original voices on the video and an additional audio clip. You can adjust the volume of each audio track to switch from one to the other or have both playing together. Finally, you can preview all of these effects in real time.

There is a lot to learn about digital video editing, and it is easy to be overwhelmed with the number of choices available. Examine online tutorial resources such as Izzy's Video podcasts (**www.izzyvideo.com**) to learn how to make the most impact with the editing and effects you apply to your raw video footage.

Distributing Your Video

Once you're done editing your video file, you can save (or export) it in a variety of formats. Figure 15 shows some of the popular video file formats in use today, along with

FIGURE 15
Typical File Formats for Digital Video

FORMAT	FILE EXTENSION	NOTES
QuickTime	.mov .qt	You can download QuickTime player without charge from **www.apple.com/quicktime**. The pro version allows you to build your own QuickTime files.
Moving Picture Experts Group (MPEG)	.mpg .mpeg	MPEG-4 video standard adopted internationally in 2000; recognized by most video player software.
Windows Media Video	.wmv	Microsoft file format recognized by Windows Media Player (included with the Windows OS).
Microsoft Video for Windows	.avi	Microsoft file format recognized by Windows Media Player (included with the Windows OS).
RealMedia	.rm	Format from RealNetworks is popular for streaming video. You can download the player for free at **www.real.com**.
Adobe Flash Video	.flv	Adobe Flash video format, sometimes embedded in Shockwave files (*.swf).

the file extensions they use. (File extensions are the letters that follow the period in a file name, such as in Movie1.*mpg*. These extensions indicate the type of data inside the file.)

Your choice of file format for your finished video will depend on what you want to do with your video. For example, the RealMedia RM streaming file format is a great choice if your file is really large and you plan to post it on the Web. The Microsoft AVI format is a good choice if you're sending your file to a wide range of users because it's extremely popular and commonly accepted as the standard video format for the Windows Media Player.

When you export your video, you have control over every aspect of the file you create, including its format, window size, frame rate, audio quality, and compression level. You can customize any of these if you have specific production goals, but most often just using the default values works well.

When would you want to customize some of the audio and video settings?

If you're trying to make the file as small as possible so that it will download quickly or so that it can fit on a single CD, then you would select values that trade off audio and video quality for file size. For example, you could drop the frame rate to 15 fps, shrink the window size to 320 × 240 pixels, and switch to mono audio instead of stereo.

You also can try different compression choices to see which one does a better job of compressing your particular file. **Codecs** (**co**mpression/**dec**ompression) are rules, implemented in either software or hardware, that squeeze the same audio and video information into less space. Some information will be lost using compression, and there is a variety of different codecs to choose from, each claiming better performance than its competitors. Commonly used codecs include MPEG, Indeo, DivX, and Cinepak. There is no one codec that is always superior—a codec that works well for a simple interview may not do a good job compressing a live-action scene.

If you'd like to save your video onto a DVD, you can use special DVD authoring software such as Ulead DVD Workshop or Adobe Encore DVD. These DVD software packages often include preset selections for producing video for mobile devices (like the Apple iPod or the Sony PSP). These programs can also create final DVDs that have animated menu systems and easy navigation controls, allowing the viewer to move quickly from one movie or scene to another. Home DVD players as well as gaming systems such as PlayStation and Xbox can read these DVDs, so your potential audience is even greater!

New Options for Quick Video Delivery

Because of the popularity of videos on the Web, products and services are now available that let you quickly upload your videos. One such product is the Flip video camcorder from Pure Digital Technologies, shown in Figure 16.

The Flip camcorder, which retails at about $100, can record 60 minutes of video. After recording, the USB connector is flipped out and connected to your computer. Flip has built-in software that lets you transfer the video file directly to YouTube (**www.youtube.com**) or e-mail the file. It's a simple solution that takes advantage of the easy Web-based distribution of video.

Even if you don't have a camcorder, you may already have a device that records digital video and not realize it—your cell phone. Many cell phone models record low-resolution video. YouTube has a special Mobile Upload Profile that you can set up for your account. Once your unique e-mail address has been assigned, any video you have on your phone can be submitted to YouTube by merely e-mailing the file to the account address. If you have captured a breaking news story, this is the fastest way to get the word out!

Webcasting, or broadcasting your video live to an audience, is another option that has become simpler. Sites like Justin.tv let

FIGURE 16

The Flip video camera is an inexpensive way to capture 60 minutes of video and easily post it on the YouTube service.

you quickly set up to webcast your video as it is captured to an Internet audience. You can also display an interactive chat next to the video feed. Both the chat and the video are captured and archived for viewers who couldn't see the live broadcast.

Web cameras are another option for quickly pushing video up to the Web. Inexpensive webcams (from $25 to $100) can be easily attached to your desktop or notebook computer. Many models of monitors have built-in webcams. More expensive webcam models have motors that allow you to automatically rotate to track the sound, so you are always in the frame even if you are moving around the room. Services such as YouTube offer Quick Capture buttons, so with one click, your video is shot and delivered to the Internet.

Digital imaging and video allow us fantastic control over the way we use information. In addition they offer new and exciting means of entertainment. So whether you're working or just having fun, be sure to take advantage of all that digital technology has to offer.

Behind the Scenes:

A Closer Look at System Hardware

Objectives

After reading this chapter, you should be able to answer the following questions:

1. What is a switch, and how does it work in a computer? **(pp. 438–439)**

2. What is the binary number system, and what role does it play in a computer system? **(pp. 439–444)**

3. What is inside the CPU, and how do these components operate? **(pp. 444–446)**

4. How does a CPU process data and instructions? **(pp. 446–449)**

5. What is a GPU, and how does it boost performance? **(pp. 445–446)**

6. What is cache memory? **(pp. 449–450)**

7. What types of RAM are there? **(pp. 451–455)**

8. What is a bus, and how does it function in a computer system? **(pp. 455–457)**

9. How do manufacturers make CPUs so that they run faster? **(pp. 457–459)**

ACTIVE HELPDESK

- Understanding the CPU **(p. 451)**
- Understanding Types of RAM **(p. 454)**

Technology in Action: Taking a Closer Look

Although Jim and Joe are twins, they are completely different in certain ways. Joe checks the oil in his car regularly, knows the air pressure in his tires, and can tell when the fan belt should be replaced. Jim, on the other hand, asks, "Oil level? What oil?" and drives from place to place relying on service departments to keep his car running. Although Jim's lack of maintenance hasn't resulted in any catastrophic problems, Joe warns his brother that by not learning a few things about cars, he'll end up paying more to keep up his car, if it even lasts that long.

Similarly, after taking a class in college, Joe has a strong but basic understanding of his computer and keeps his PC running well through periodic maintenance and upgrades. Not surprisingly, Jim is hands-off when it comes to his computer. He's happy to just turn it on and open the files he needs. He can't be bothered with all the acronyms: CPU, RAM, and all the rest. When there's a problem, Jim just calls his brother. He hates waiting and paying for technical service and is afraid he'll mess up his system if he tries to fix things himself. But after making another 2 A.M. call to Joe after his computer crashed, Joe told him, "Take a class or pay a technician!"

When it comes to your computer, are you most like Jim or Joe? Joe found out how easy it is to understand his computer and isn't dependent on anyone else to keep it running. But if you use a computer without understanding the hardware inside, you'll have to pay a technician to fix or upgrade it. Meanwhile, it won't be as efficient as if you were fine-tuning it yourself, and you may find yourself buying a new computer sooner than necessary.

There are other advantages to having a deeper understanding of computer hardware. If you're preparing for a career in programming, for example, understanding computer hardware will affect the speed and efficiency of the programs you design. In addition, if you're interested in computers, you're no doubt excited by advances you hear about. How do you evaluate the impact of a new type of memory or a new processor? A basic appreciation of how a computer system is built and designed is a good start.

In this chapter, we'll build on what you've learned about computer hardware in other chapters and go behind the scenes, looking at the components of your system unit in more detail. First, we examine how computers translate the commands you input into the digits they can understand: 1s and 0s. Next, we analyze the internal workings of the central processing unit (CPU) and memory. We then look at buses—the highways that transport data between the CPU, memory, and other devices connected to the computer. But first, let's look at the building blocks of computers: switches.

SOUND BYTES

- Binary Numbers Interactive **(p. 440)**
- Where Does Binary Show Up? **(p. 439)**
- Computer Architecture Interactive **(p. 457)**

Digital Data: Switches and Bits

In earlier chapters, you learned that the **system unit** is the box that contains the central electronic components of the computer. But how exactly does the computer perform all of its tasks? How does it process the data you input? In this section, we discuss how the CPU performs its functions—adding, subtracting, moving data around the system, and so on—using nothing but a large number of on/off switches. In fact, as you'll learn, a computer system can be viewed as just an enormous collection of on/off switches.

ELECTRICAL SWITCHES

What are switches, and what do they do? You learned earlier that, unlike humans, computers work exclusively with numbers (not words). To process data into information, computers need to work in a language they understand. This language, called **binary language**, consists of just two numbers: 0 and 1. Everything a computer does, such as process data or print a report, is broken down into a series of 0s and 1s. **Electrical switches** are devices inside the computer that can be flipped between these two states: 1 or 0, on or off.

Why do computers use 0s and 1s to process data? Because modern computers are electronic, digital machines, they understand only two states of existence: on and off. Computers represent these two possibilities, or states, using the binary switches (or digits) 1 and 0.

Although the notion of switches may seem complex, you use various forms of switches every day. For example, the on/off button on your DVD player is a mechanical switch: pushed in, it could represent the value 1 (on), whereas popped out, it could represent the value 0 (off). Another switch you use each day is a water faucet. As shown in Figure 9.1, shutting off the faucet so that no water flows could represent the value 0, whereas turning it on could represent the value 1.

Because computers are built from a huge collection of switches, using buttons or water faucets obviously would limit the amount of data computers could store. It would also make computers huge and cause them to run at extremely slow speeds. Thus,

FIGURE 9.1

Water faucets can be used to represent binary switches. Turning on the faucet could represent the value 1, whereas shutting off the faucet so that no water flows could represent the value 0.

the history of computers is really a story about creating smaller and faster sets of electrical switches so that more data can be stored and manipulated quickly.

What were the first switches used in computers? The earliest generation of electronic computers used devices called **vacuum tubes** as switches. Vacuum tubes act as computer switches by allowing or blocking the flow of electrical current. The problem with vacuum tubes is that they take up a lot of space. The first high-speed digital computer, the Electronic Numerical Integrator and Computer (ENIAC), was deployed in 1945 and used nearly 18,000 vacuum tubes as switches, which filled approximately 1,800 square feet of floor space. That's about one-half of a standard high school basketball court! In addition to being large, the vacuum tubes produced a lot of heat and burned out frequently. So vacuum tubes are impractical switching devices in personal computers because of their size and reliability.

What do personal computers use as switching devices? Since the introduction of ENIAC's vacuum tubes, two major revolutions have occurred in the design of switches and consequently computers to make them smaller and faster: the invention of the transistor and the fabrication of integrated circuits.

What are transistors? Transistors are electrical switches that are built out of layers of a special type of material called a **semiconductor**, which is any material that can be controlled to either conduct electricity or act as an insulator (to prohibit electricity from passing through). Silicon, which is found in common sand, is the semiconductor material used to make transistors.

By itself, silicon does not conduct electricity particularly well, but if specific chemicals are added in a controlled way to the silicon, it begins to behave like a switch. The silicon allows electrical current to flow easily when a certain voltage is applied, and it prevents electrical current from flowing otherwise, thus behaving as an on/off switch. This kind of behavior is exactly what is needed to store digital information, the 0s (off) and 1s (on) in binary language.

Early transistors were built in separate units as small metal rods, with each rod acting as a single on/off switch. These first transistors were much smaller than vacuum tubes, produced little heat, and could be switched from on to off (allowing or blocking electrical current) quickly. They also were less expensive than vacuum tubes.

It wasn't long, however, before transistors reached their limits. Continuing advances in technology began to require more transistors than circuit boards could reasonably handle at the time. Something was needed to pack more transistor capacity into a smaller space. Thus, integrated circuits, the next technical revolution in switches, were developed.

What are integrated circuits? **Integrated circuits** (or **chips**) are tiny regions of semiconductor material such as silicon that support a huge number of transistors. Along with all the many transistors, other components critical to a circuit board (such as resistors, capacitors, and diodes) are also located on the integrated circuit. Most integrated circuits are no more than one-quarter inch in size.

Why are integrated circuits important? Because so many transistors can fit into such a small area, integrated circuits have enabled computer designers to create small yet powerful **microprocessors**, which are chips that contain a CPU. In 1971, the Intel 4004 was the first complete microprocessor to be located on a single integrated circuit, marking the beginning of the true miniaturization of computers. The Intel 4004 contained slightly more than 2,300 transistors. Today, more than 500 million transistors can be manufactured in a space as tiny as the nail of your smallest finger!

This incredible feat has fueled an industry like none other. In 1951, the Univac I computer was the size of a large room—the processor memory unit itself was 14 feet long by 8 feet wide by 8.5 feet high and could perform about 1,905 operations per second. Thanks to advances in integrated circuits, the IBM PC released 30 years later took up just 1 cubic foot of space, cost $3,000, and performed 155,000 times more quickly. (For more information about computer history, see the Technology in Focus feature "The History of the PC" on page 36.)

But how can computers store information in a set of on/off switches? So computers use on/off switches to perform their functions. But how can these simple switches be organized so that they enable you to use a computer to pay your bills online or write an essay? How

BITS AND BYTES

Does Your Computer Need More Power? Team It Up!

If one computer is powerful, then two are twice as powerful—but only if you can get them to work together. A computing cluster is a group of computers, connected by specialized clustering software, that work together to solve complex equations. Most clusters work on something called the balancing principle, which means that computational work is transferred from overloaded (busy) computers in the cluster to computers with more available computing resources. Computing clusters, although not as fast as supercomputers (single computers with extremely high processing capabilities), can perform computations faster than one computer working alone and are used for complex calculations such as weather forecasting and graphics rendering. You can even set up a computing cluster at home, as long as you have at least two computers. Using the Linux operating system and clustering software based on openMosix (**http://openmosix.sourceforge.net**), you can build your own computing cluster for free.

could a set of switches describe a number or a word or give a computer the command to perform addition? Recall that to manipulate the on/off switches, the computer works in binary language, which uses only two digits, 0 and 1. Therefore, to understand how a computer works, it's necessary to first look at how the computer uses a special numbering system called the *binary number system* to represent all of its programs and data.

THE BINARY NUMBER SYSTEM

What is a number system? A number **system** is an organized plan for representing a number. Although you may not realize it, you are already familiar with one number system. The **base 10 number system**, also known as **decimal notation**, is the system you use to represent all of the numeric values you use each day. It's called base 10 because it uses 10 digits, 0 through 9, to represent any value.

To represent a number in base 10, you break the number down into groups of ones, tens, hundreds, thousands, and so on. Each digit has a place value depending on where it shows up in the number. For example, using base 10, in the whole number 6,954, there are 6 sets of thousands, 9 sets of hundreds, 5 sets of tens, and 4 sets of ones.

SOUND BYTE

Where Does Binary Show Up?

In this Sound Byte, you'll learn how to use tools to work with binary, decimal, and hexadecimal numbers. (These tools come with the Windows operating system.) You'll also learn where you might see binary and hexadecimal values showing up as you use a computer.

Working from right to left, each place in a number represents an increasing power of 10, as shown here:

$$6{,}954 = 6 * (1{,}000) + 9 * (100) + 5 * (10) + 4 * (1)$$
$$= 6 * 10^3 + 9 * 10^2 + 5 * 10^1 + 4 * 10^0$$

Note that in this equation, the final number 1 is represented as 10^0 because any number raised to the zero power is equal to 1.

Anthropologists theorize that humans developed a base 10 number system because we have 10 fingers. But computer systems, with their huge collections of on/off switches, are not well suited to thinking about numbers in groups of 10. Instead, computers describe a number as powers of 2 because each switch can be in one of two positions: on or off. This numbering system is referred to as the **binary number system**. It is the number system used by computers to represent all data.

How does the binary number system work? Because it only includes two digits (0 and 1), the binary number system is also referred to as the **base 2 number system**. However, even with just two digits, the binary number system can still represent all the same values that a base 10 number system can (see Figure 9.2). Instead of breaking the number down into sets of ones, tens, hundreds, and thousands, as is done in base 10 notation, the binary number system describes a number as the sum of

SOUND BYTE

Binary Numbers Interactive

This Sound Byte helps remove the mystery surrounding binary numbers. You'll learn about base conversion between decimal, binary, and hexadecimal interactively using colors, sounds, and images.

powers of 2. Binary numbers are used to represent every piece of data stored in a computer: all of the numbers, all of the letters, and all of the instructions that the computer uses to execute work.

Representing Numbers in the Binary Number System

How does the binary number system represent a whole number? As noted earlier, in the base 10 number system, a whole number is represented as the sum of ones, tens, hundreds, and thousands—sums of powers of 10. The binary system works in the same way but describes a value as the sum of groups of 64s, 32s, 16s, 8s, 4s, 2s, and 1s—that is, powers of 2: 1, 2, 4, 8, 16, 32, 64, and so on.

Let's look at the number 67. In base 10, the number 67 would be 6 sets of 10s and 7 sets of 1s, as follows:

$$\text{Base 10: } 67 = 6 * 10^1 + 7 * 10^0$$

One way to figure out how 67 is represented in base 2 is to find the largest possible power of 2 that could be in the number 67. Two to the eighth power is 256, and there are no groups of 256 in the number 67. Two to the seventh power is 128, but that is bigger than 67. Two to the sixth power is 64, and there is a group of 64 inside a group of 67. So,

67 has	1 group of	64	That leaves 3 and
3 has	0 groups of	32	
	0 groups of	16	
	0 groups of	8	
	0 groups of	4	
	1 group of	2	That leaves 1 and
1 has	1 group of	1	And now nothing is left

Therefore, the binary number for 67 is written as 1000011 in base 2:

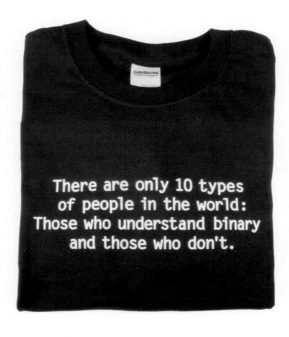

FIGURE 9.2

Only two digits are available in binary: 1 and 0. Together they can be used to represent any number. The joke here is that the decimal value 2 is written as 10 in binary.

There are only 10 types of people in the world: Those who understand binary and those who don't.

$$\text{Base 2: } 67 = 64 + 0 + 0 + 0 + 0 + 2 + 1$$
$$= (1 * 2^6) + (0 * 2^5) + (0 * 2^4) + (0 * 2^3) + (0 * 2^2) + (1 * 2^1) + (1 * 2^0)$$
$$= (1000011) \text{ base 2}$$

You can also convert base 10 numbers to binary manually by repeatedly dividing the number by 2 and examining the remainder at each stage. An example will make this clearer. Let's convert the base 10 number 67 into binary:

$$67 \div 2 = 33 \text{ remainder } 1$$
$$33 \div 2 = 16 \text{ remainder } 1$$
$$16 \div 2 = 8 \text{ remainder } 0$$
$$8 \div 2 = 4 \text{ remainder } 0$$
$$4 \div 2 = 2 \text{ remainder } 0$$
$$2 \div 2 = 1 \text{ remainder } 0$$
$$1 \div 2 = 0 \text{ remainder } 1$$
$$1\ 0\ 0\ 0\ 0\ 1\ 1$$

The binary number is then read from the bottom up. Therefore, 1000011 is the binary (base 2) equivalent of the base 10 number 67. In computer memory, bytes store data as a set of eight bits, so the same value would be stored inside a byte of RAM with a leading 0 as 01000011.

Is there a faster way to convert between base 10 (decimal) and binary? Programmers and engineers who work with binary codes daily learn to convert between decimal and binary mentally. However, if you use binary notation less often, it is easier to use a calculator. Some calculators identify this operation with a button labeled DEC (for decimal) and one labeled BIN (for binary). You can access the Scientific Calculator that supports conversion between decimal (base 10) and binary (base 2) by choosing Start, All Programs, Accessories, then clicking Calculator, and then clicking the View menu to select Scientific.

Representing Letters and Symbols: ASCII and Unicode

How can the binary number system represent letters and punctuation symbols? We have just been converting numbers from base 10, which we understand, to base 2 (binary state), which the computer understands. Similarly, we need a system that converts letters and other symbols that we understand to a binary state that

the computer understands. To provide a consistent means for representing letters and other characters, certain codes dictate how to represent characters in binary format. Older mainframe computers use Extended Binary-Coded Decimal Interchange Code (EBCDIC, pronounced "Eb-sih-dik"). However, most of today's personal computers use the American National Standards Institute (ANSI, pronounced "An-see") standard code, called the **American Standard Code for Information Interchange** (ASCII, pronounced "As-key"), to represent each letter or character as an 8-bit (or 1-byte) binary code.

As you know by now, binary digits correspond to the on and off states of your computer's switches. Each of these digits is called a **binary digit**, or **bit** for short. Eight binary digits (or bits) combine to create one **byte**. In the previous discussions, we have

BITS AND BYTES

Why Doesn't My 200 GB Drive Have 200 GB?

If you look at the properties of your hard drive (right-click Computer and then click Properties), you'll see one number reporting the size of the hard drive in bytes—say, 203,871,289,344—and a different value listed in gigabytes—say, 189 GB. But isn't 200 billion bytes equal to 200 GB?

Well, not exactly. Historically, the sizes of computer storage devices were measured in bytes using the standard international (SI) prefixes: *kilo* for one thousand, *mega* for one million, and *giga* for one billion. Notice that the numbers 1,000, 1,000,000, and 1,000,000,000 are all powers of ten. In computer memory devices, though, the capacity is most often a power of 2. A gigabyte has been used to mean the power of 2 that is nearest to a billion. That number is 2^{30}, or 1,073,741,824 bytes, which is a difference of 7 percent.

So 203 billion bytes and 189 GB are the same, but the situation is confusing. That is why a special set of binary prefixes has been introduced. The new prefixes are *kibi*, *mebi*, and *gibi*. One kibibyte is exactly $1,024 = 2^{10}$ bytes, one mebibyte is exactly 2^{20} bytes, and one gibibyte is exactly 2^{30} bytes. This notation has been adopted by governing bodies (like the IEEE), but most manufacturers still use the traditional SI prefixes.

DIG DEEPER

Advanced Binary and Hexadecimal Notations

You understand how the binary number system represents a positive number, but how can it represent a negative number? In the decimal (base 10) system, a negative value is represented by a special symbol, the minus sign (−). In the binary (base 2) system, a negative number is represented using a **sign bit**. The sign bit is usually the left-most bit. Several methods can determine the sign bit. In each method, when the sign bit is 1, the binary number has a negative (or nonpositive) value; when the sign bit is 0, the binary number has a positive value.

The binary pattern 11101 can represent both a positive number and a negative number. So how does the computer know that what it is looking at is a negative number and not a positive binary number? If we know the number is a binary number using a sign bit, then we read the first bit (the sign bit) as 1 and therefore know that the number is a negative number. Following the sign bit are the digits that represent the value of the number itself. Because 1101 in binary (base 2) has the value 13 in the decimal (base 10) system, the final interpretation of the bits 11101 would be −13.

But what if we were told in advance that 11101 is definitely a positive number? We would then read this number differently and compute 1 * 16 + 1 * 8 + 1 * 4 + 0 * 2 + 1 * 1 and get the base 10 value of 29. The bits themselves are exactly the same. The only thing that has changed is our agreement on what the same five digits mean: The first time they represented a negative number, and the second time they represented a positive number. In a program's code, the computer is told ahead of time whether to expect a sign bit.

The binary number system also can represent a decimal number. How can a string of 1s and 0s capture the information in a value such as 99.368? Because every computer must store such numbers in the same way, the Institute of Electrical and Electronics Engineers (IEEE) has established a standard called the *floating-point standard* that describes how numbers with fractional parts should be represented in the binary number system. Using a 32-bit system, we can represent an incredibly wide range of numbers. The method dictated by the IEEE standard works the same for any number with a decimal point, such as the number −0.75. The first digit, or bit (the sign bit), is used to indicate whether the number is positive or negative. The next eight bits store the magnitude of the number, indicating whether the number is in the hundreds or millions, for example. The standard says to use the next 23 bits to store the value of the number.

been converting base 10 numbers to a binary format. In such cases, the binary format has no standard length. For example, the binary format for the number 2 is two digits (10), whereas the binary format for the number 10 is four digits (1010). Although binary numbers can have more or less than 8 bits, each single alphabetic or special character is 1 byte (or 8 bits) of data and consists of a unique combination of a total of eight 0s and 1s.

The ASCII code represents the 26 uppercase letters and 26 lowercase letters used in the English language, along with many punctuation symbols and other special characters, using 8 bits. Figure 9.4 shows several examples of ASCII code representation of printable letters and characters.

Can ASCII represent the alphabets of different languages? Because it represents letters and characters using only 8 bits, the ASCII code can assign only 256 (or 2^8) different codes for unique characters and letters. Although this is enough to represent English and many other characters found in the world's languages, ASCII code cannot represent all languages and symbols because some languages require more than 256 characters and letters. Thus, a new encoding scheme, called **Unicode**, was created. By using 16 bits instead of the 8 bits used in ASCII, Unicode can represent nearly 1,115,000 code points and currently assigns more than 96,000 unique character symbols. The first 128 characters of Unicode are identical to ASCII, but because of its depth, Unicode is also able to represent the alphabets of all modern and historic languages and notational systems, including such languages as Tibetan, Tagalog, Japanese, and Canadian-Aboriginal syllabics. As we continue to become a more global society, it is anticipated that Unicode will replace

As you can imagine, some numbers in binary result in quite a long string of 0s and 1s. For example, the number 123,456 is a 17-digit sequence of 1s and 0s in binary code: 11110001001000000. When working with these long strings of 0s and 1s, it is easy for a human to make a mistake. Thus, many computer scientists use hexadecimal notation, another commonly used number system, as a form of shorthand.

Hexadecimal notation is a base 16 number system, meaning it uses 16 digits to represent numbers instead of the 10 digits used in base 10 or the 2 digits used in base 2. The 16 digits it uses are the 10 numeric digits, 0 to 9, plus six extra symbols: A, B, C, D, E, and F. Each of the letters A through F corresponds to a numeric value, so that A equals 10, B equals 11, and so on (see Figure 9.3). Looking back at the number we started with, 123,456 is represented as 1E240 in hexadecimal notation. This is much easier for computer scientists to use than the long string of binary code. The Scientific Calculator in Windows also can perform conversions to hexadecimal notation. (You can watch a video showing you how to perform conversions between bases using the Windows Calculator in the Sound Byte "Where Does Binary Show Up?")

When will you ever use hexadecimal notation? Unless you become a professional programmer, com-

FIGURE 9.3 Sample Hexadecimal Values

Decimal Number	Hexadecimal Value	Decimal Number	Hexadecimal Value
00	00	08	08
01	01	09	09
02	02	10	0A
03	03	11	0B
04	04	12	0C
05	05	13	0D
06	06	14	0E
07	07	15	0F

puter hardware designer, or you write your own Web pages (where hexadecimal notation is used to represent colors), you will likely encounter hexadecimal notation only when you see an error code on your computer. Generally, the location of the error will be represented in hexadecimal notation.

ASCII as the standard character formatting code.

So *all* data inside the computer is stored as bits? Yes! As noted in the Dig Deeper feature, both positive and negative numbers can be stored using signed integer notation, with the first bit (the sign bit) indicating the sign and the rest of the bits indicating the value of the number. Decimal numbers are stored according to the IEEE floating-point standard, whereas letters and symbols are stored according to the ASCII code or Unicode. All of these different number systems and codes exist so that computers can store different types of information in their on/off switches. No matter what kind of data you input in a computer—a color, a musical note, or a street address—that data will be stored as a string of 1s and 0s. The important lesson is that the interpretation of 0s and 1s is what matters. The same binary

FIGURE 9.4 ASCII Standard Code for a Sample of Letters and Characters

ASCII Code	Represents This Symbol	ASCII Code	Represents This Symbol
01000001	A	01100001	a
01000010	B	01100010	b
01000011	C	01100011	c
01011010	Z	00100011	#
00100001	!	00100100	$
00100010	"	00100101	%

Note: For the full ASCII table, see **www.asciitable.com**.

pattern could represent a positive number, a negative number, a fraction, or a letter.

How does the computer know which interpretation to use for the 1s and 0s? When your brain processes language, it takes sounds you hear and uses the rules of English along with other clues to build an interpretation of the sound as a word. If you are in New York City and hear someone shout, "Hey, Lori!" you expect someone is saying hello to a friend. If you are in London and hear the same sound—"Hey! Lorry!"—you jump out of the way because a truck is coming at you! You knew which interpretation to apply to the same sound because you had some other information—that you were in England.

Likewise, the CPU is designed to understand a specific language, a set of instructions. But certain instructions tell the CPU to expect a negative number next or to interpret the following bit pattern as a character. Because of this extra information, the CPU always knows which interpretation to use for a series of bits.

The CPU: Processing Digital Information

The **central processing unit** (**CPU**, or **processor**), the "brains" of the computer, executes every instruction given to your computer. As you learned earlier, the entire CPU fits on a tiny chip called the *microprocessor*. The microprocessor contains all of the hardware (including millions of transistors—the switches we discussed earlier) that is responsible for processing information.

The CPU is located in the system unit on the computer's **motherboard**, the main circuit board that connects all of the electronic components of the system: the CPU, memory, the expansion slots where you can insert expansion (or adapter) cards, and all of the electrical paths that connect these components. Figure 9.5 shows a typical motherboard and the location of each of these components.

Looking at a CPU chip gives you little information about how exactly it accomplishes its work. However, understanding more about how the CPU is designed and how it operates will give you greater insight into how computers work, what their limitations are, and what technological advances may be possible in the future.

What CPUs are used in desktop and notebook computers? Only a few major companies manufacture CPUs for desktop computers. Intel manufactures the Xeon, Core 2 Extreme (shown in Figure 9.6a), Celeron, Itanium, and Pentium processors. Advanced Micro Devices (AMD) produces the AMD-Penom, Athlon, Sempron, and Turion processors. Intel and AMD chips are used in the majority of Windows-based PCs.

Apple computers used a different CPU design in the past. The G4 and PowerPC G5 chips were used by Apple machines for more than 10 years. But in 2005, Apple shook up the CPU playing field when it announced that all of its systems would be redesigned to use Intel CPUs. Versions of the PowerPC chip (shown in Figure 9.6b) still live on in some version in video gaming system consoles such as the Nintendo Wii and the Xbox 360.

As you learned in earlier chapters, the processor used on a computer also determines what operating system is used. The combination of operating system and processor is referred to as a computer's *platform*.

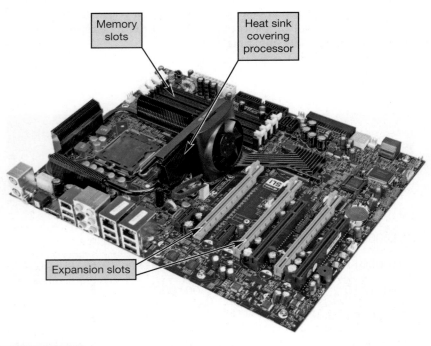

FIGURE 9.5

The motherboard is the home of all the most essential computer hardware, including the CPU socket, memory card slots, and expansion slots where you can insert expansion (or adapter) cards.

Labels: Memory slots; Heat sink covering processor; Expansion slots

FIGURE 9.6

(a) The Core 2 Extreme chip is used in many Windows-based PCs. (b) The Microsoft Xbox 360 gaming console uses a custom PowerPC—based CPU to perform 1,000 billion calculations per second.

BITS AND BYTES

Work with Several Languages?

Windows supports multinational environments in several different ways. If you want to change the language used by Windows to a language other than English, you can change the display language. The display language is the language used for dialog boxes, wizards, and so on and can be selected from 33 choices. You can also change the keyboard input language, the language used to enter text, and switch between different keyboard layouts with just a click of the taskbar. What does all this mean? You can read and type in your native language and work in multilanguage documents—whether it's Tibetan stacked symbols, Chinese characters, or standard English—with just a few simple clicks! For more information, visit **http://windowshelp.microsoft.com**.

What makes one CPU different from another? The primary distinction between CPUs is processing power, which is determined by the number of cores on each CPU. A core is a complete processing section from a CPU embedded into the same physical chip. In addition to core design, as you'll learn in the next section, other factors differentiate CPUs, but the greatest differentiators are how quickly the processor can work (called its clock speed) and the amount of immediate access memory the CPU has (called its cache memory).

Until recently, the latest advancement in processors was *hyperthreading,* which provides quicker processing of information by enabling a new set of instructions to start before the previous set has finished. The most recent design innovation for PC processors, an improvement upon hyperthreading, is known as **core technology**. With core technology, there are two or more processors on the same chip, enabling the execution of two sets of instructions at the exact same time. Figure 9.7 shows these different approaches.

In Figure 9.7c, hyperthreading allows two different programs to be processed at one time, but they are sharing the computing resources of the chip. With multi-cores each program has the full attention of its own processing core (see Figure 9.7a and Figure 9.7b) . This results in faster processing and smoother multitasking.

Is a GPU different from a CPU? A **graphics processing unit (GPU)** performs the same kind of computational work that a CPU performs. However, a GPU is specialized to speedily handle 3 D graphics and image and video processing. Figure 9.8

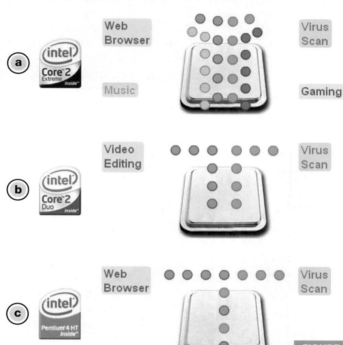

shows that the CPU can run much more efficiently with a GPU doing all of the graphics computation.

Special lighting effects can be achieved with a modern GPU. Designers can now change the type of light and the texture and color of objects based on complex interactions, as shown in Figure 9.8. Some GPU designs incorporate dedicated hardware to allow high-definition movies to be decoded.

Does the GPU live on the motherboard with the CPU? Basic video processing is sometimes integrated into the motherboard. However, high-end video

FIGURE 9.7

(a) The Intel Core 2 Extreme is a four-core processor, running four programs simultaneously. (b) The Intel Core 2 Duo is a two-core processor. (c) The Intel Pentium 4 Hyperthreading operates with only one core but hyperthreads, trying to simulate working on two processes at once.

FIGURE 9.8

The GPU is specialized to handle processing of photos, videos, and video game images. It frees the CPU to work on other system demands.

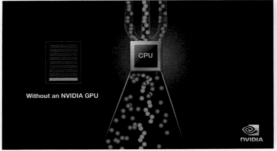

Without a GPU

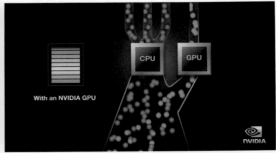

With a GPU

FIGURE 9.9

These two images show the difference in displayed gaming environments with a basic video card and one with an advanced GPU. The NVIDIA GeForce GPUs allow the more detailed water ripples, shadowing effects and the more realistic terrain texture.

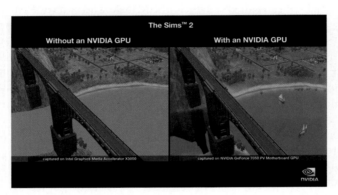

The Sims™ 2

Without an NVIDIA GPU | With an NVIDIA GPU

captured on Intel Graphics Media Accelerator X3000 | captured on NVIDIA GeForce 7050 PV Motherboard GPU

cards that have their own GPUs are separate from the motherboard. These sophisticated video cards connect through the ultrafast PCI Express bus. Top-end cards such as the NVIDIA GeForce 8800 series use two separate GPUs to add even more processing punch. These cards carry their own processing RAM space: between 512 MB and 1 GB, depending on the model. Together they provide an unprecedented level of realism and detail in gaming environments (see Figure 9.9).

THE CPU MACHINE CYCLE

What exactly does the CPU do? Any program you run on your computer is actually a long series of binary code, 1s and 0s, describing a specific set of commands the CPU must perform. Each CPU is somewhat different in the exact steps it follows to perform its tasks, but all CPUs must perform a series of similar general steps. These steps, referred to as a CPU **machine cycle** (or **processing cycle**), are shown in Figure 9.10 and are described here:

1. When any program begins to run, the 1s and 0s that make up the program's binary code must be "fetched" from their temporary storage location in random access memory (RAM) and moved to the CPU before they can be executed.

RAM

1002
1003
1004
1005
1006
1007
1008
1009
1010

CPU

Registers
R1
R2
R3
R4
R5
R6
R7
R8
R9
R10

Arithmetic Logic Unit (ALU)

+ −
* /

Control Unit

① ② ③ ④

Step 1: FETCH: When a program begins to run, the program's binary code must be "fetched" from RAM and moved to the CPU's control unit before it can be executed.

Step 2: DECODE: Once the program's binary code is in the CPU, it is "decoded" into the commands the CPU understands. The control unit then tells the registers which data to feed to the arithmetic logic unit (ALU), the part of the CPU designed to perform mathematical operations.

Step 3: EXECUTE: The ALU performs the work described in the command.

Step 4: STORE: The result is stored in the registers. The CPU is then ready to fetch the next set of bits encoding the next instruction.

FIGURE 9.10

The CPU Machine Cycle

Ethics: Which Strategy Makes More Money—Sharing or Hiding?

In system design, both in hardware and software, corporations need to make a decision about how they will work with the world: Will they provide an open system or be "closed"? It speaks to an ethical view of the world and how it operates by the company leadership. Is it better for businesses to be open about their design specifications, even though others may copy their system? Or will it lead to more profit if they hide the details of what has been done and protect their investments?

Different companies have taken widely different approaches to this question. One example in hardware is the system design of the original IBM PC. It was not a closed system, and the specifications on how to build a system and how to interface were available to other companies. This led to a huge number of similar "clone" systems that were manufactured by competitors but were able to run the same software and operating system, and basically do the same work. The availability of cheap clones fueled the market for home PCs tremendously. Although IBM did not profit from clone systems directly, it benefited from the larger market. Many users found the lack of quality in knockoff systems a problem and eventually bought IBM hardware. IBM was able to push ahead with its deep R&D pockets and produce new systems with more advanced features, keeping a continual performance edge over clone systems. Third-party companies popped up like crazy, creating a huge number of peripheral devices, boards, and add-ons because they knew the hardware details for the system and could design their own products to match them.

The main competitor, Apple Computers, took the opposite approach. The Apple Macintosh was a "closed" design, and no other company was able to manufacture a similar system. This meant every person who wanted a Macintosh had to purchase it from Apple, at the company's selling price, with no competition. It kept the price higher than the plunging PC costs, which were driven down by the proliferation of clone manufacturers. Apple systems won some niche markets in graphics design and education, but today the market is about 95 percent Windows-based PCs.

Neither strategy is without advantages. The Apple iPhone was released as a closed system. "You don't want your phone to be an open platform," says Apple CEO Steve Jobs, meaning that anyone can write applications for it and potentially gum up the provider's network. "You need it to work when you need it to work. AT&T doesn't want to see its West Coast network go down because some application messed up." But within a month of its release, there were hundreds of available hacked software modules for the iPhone. On his blog site Rough Type, Nick Carr says, "In Jobs's world, users are users, creators are creators, and never the twain shall meet." But will that view continue to be viable over the next several years?

The advantage of product stability can be more easily guaranteed with a closed system. Others argue that the collective synergy of allowing any company to design for your system results in better choices, lower prices to consumers, and widespread market penetration of products. External developers and content providers have already worked with AT&T and its network to provide applications for devices such as Windows Mobile and Palm OS smartphones.

The Web 2.0 ideology—in which every user is a creator and user-generated content is an essential component of products—provides challenges for hardware and software system designers. Consider the following:

- How much do you as a consumer value product stability versus the ability to have choices from many third-party vendors?
- Do you think more innovative product design comes from a closed-system approach or an open system?
- Do you think one system would always lead to more profit for a company?
- How will the push toward more user-generated content impact the design of computer systems and mobile devices?

2. Once the program's binary code is in the CPU, it is decoded into the commands the CPU understands.

3. Next, the CPU actually performs the work described in the commands. Specialized hardware on the CPU performs addition, subtraction, multiplication, division, and other mathematical and logical operations at incredible speeds.

4. The result is stored in **registers**, special memory storage areas built into the CPU, which are the most expensive, fastest memory in your computer. The CPU is then ready to fetch the next set of bits encoding the next instruction.

BITS AND BYTES

The Future of RAM

As the demand for portable computing devices accelerates, researchers are constantly looking for ways to save space and power consumption (to increase battery life). Magnetoresistive Random Access Memory (MRAM) or Nano Random Access Memory (NRAM) may soon provide solutions to these common challenges.

Most RAM used today is DRAM (dynamic RAM). DRAM uses electrical charges to store data, whereas MRAM uses magnetic plates to store data. NRAM uses carbon nanotubes, which are only one carbon atom thick, to store data (see more on nanotubes in Chapter 1. A significant advantage of both MRAM and NRAM technologies is that they use almost 99 percent less power, making them ideal for portable computing devices. Imagine a camera with 2 TB of storage—unimaginable today but perhaps part of the near future.

Does the CPU always perform these steps? No matter what program you are running, be it a Web browser or a word-processing program, and no matter how many programs you are using at one time, the CPU performs these four steps over and over at incredibly high speeds. Shortly, we'll look at each stage in more detail so that you can understand the complexity of the CPU's design, how to compare different CPUs on the market, and what enhancements to expect in CPU designs of the future. But first, let's examine a few of the CPU's other components that help it perform its tasks.

The System Clock

How does the CPU know when to begin the next stage in the machine cycle? To move from one stage of the machine cycle to the next, the motherboard contains a built-in **system clock**. This internal clock is actually a special crystal that acts like a metronome, keeping a steady beat and thereby controlling when the CPU moves to the next stage of processing.

These steady beats or "ticks" of the system clock, known as the **clock cycle**, set the pace by which the computer moves from process to process. The pace, known as **clock speed**, is measured in hertz (Hz), a unit of measure that describes how many times something happens per second. Today's system clocks are measured in gigahertz (GHz), or one billion clock ticks per second. Therefore, in a 3 GHz system, there are three billion clock ticks each second. Computers with older processors would sometimes need one or more cycles to process one instruction. Today, however, CPUs are designed to handle more instructions more efficiently, therefore executing more than one instruction per cycle.

The Control Unit

How does the CPU know which stage in the machine cycle is next? The CPU, like any part of the computer system, is designed from a collection of switches. How can simple on/off switches "remember" the fetch-decode-execute-store sequence of the CPU machine cycle? How can they perform the work required in each of these stages?

The **control unit** of the CPU manages the switches inside the CPU. It is programmed by CPU designers to remember the sequence of processing stages for that CPU and how each switch in the CPU should be set, on or off, for each stage. With each beat of the system clock, the control unit moves each switch to the correct on or off setting and then performs the work of that stage.

Let's now look at each of the stages in the machine cycle in a bit more depth.

STAGE 1: THE FETCH STAGE

Where does the CPU find the necessary information? The data and program instructions the CPU needs are stored in different areas in the computer system. Data and program instructions move between these areas as needed or not needed by the CPU for processing. Programs (such as Microsoft Word) are permanently stored on the hard drive because it offers nonvolatile storage, meaning the programs remain stored there even when you turn the power off. However, when you launch a program (that is, when you double-click an icon to execute the program), the program, or sometimes only the essential parts of a program, is transferred from the hard drive into RAM.

The program moves to RAM because the CPU can access the data and program instructions stored in RAM more than one million times faster than if they are left on the hard drive. This is because RAM is much closer to the CPU than is the hard drive. Another reason for the delay in access of data and program instructions from the hard drive to the CPU has to do with the fact that the hard drive is a physical device. The hard drive has read/write heads that have to sweep over the platters, which takes longer. RAM is faster because it's electrical, not physical.

As specific instructions from the program are needed, they are moved from RAM into registers (the special storage areas located on the CPU itself), where they wait to be executed.

Why doesn't the CPU chip just contain enough memory to store an entire program? The CPU's storage area is not big enough to hold everything it needs to process at the same time. If enough memory were located on the CPU chip itself, an entire program could be copied to the CPU from RAM before it was executed. This certainly would add to the computer's speed and efficiency because there would not be any delay to stop and fetch instructions from RAM to the CPU. However, including so much memory on a CPU chip would make these chips extremely expensive. Also, CPU design is so complex that only a limited amount of storage space is available on the CPU itself.

Cache Memory

So the CPU needs to fetch every instruction from RAM each time it goes through a cycle? Actually, there is another layer of storage that has even faster access than RAM called **cache memory**. The word *cache* is derived from the French word *cacher*, meaning "to hide." Cache memory consists of small blocks of memory located directly on and next to the CPU chip. These memory blocks are holding places for recently or frequently used instructions or data that the CPU needs the most. When these instructions or data are stored in cache memory, the CPU can retrieve them more quickly than would be the case if it had to access the instructions or data in RAM.

Taking data you think you'll be using soon and storing it nearby is a simple idea but a powerful one. This is a strategy that shows up in other places in your computer

BITS AND BYTES

Why Does Caching Work?

Did you know that 80 percent of the time your CPU spends processing it is working on the same 20 percent of code? Software monitoring programs have been built to test this conjecture for specific systems, and it generally holds up well. This is the concept that cache memory exploits. It would be much too expensive to design a system with enough memory on the CPU to store an entire program. But if careful management of a cache of fast memory can make sure that the majority of the 20 percent of the program used the most often is already sitting in the cache (and is therefore closer to the CPU), the improvement in overall performance is great.

system. For example, when you are browsing Web pages, it takes longer to download images than text. Your browser software automatically stores images on your hard drive so that you don't have to wait to download them again if you want to go back and view a page you've already visited. Although this cache of files is not related to the cache storage space designed into the CPU chip, the idea is the same.

How does cache memory work? Modern CPU designs include several types of cache memory. If the next instruction to be fetched is not already located in a CPU register, instead of looking directly to RAM to find it, the CPU first searches Level 1 cache. **Level 1 cache** is a block of memory that is built onto the CPU chip for the storage of data or commands that have just been used.

If the command is not located in Level 1 cache, the CPU searches **Level 2 cache**. Depending on the design of the CPU, Level 2 cache is located on the CPU chip but is slightly farther away from the CPU, or it's on a separate chip next to the CPU and therefore takes somewhat longer to access. Level 2 cache contains more storage area than does Level 1 cache. For the Intel Core 2 Duo, for example, the Level 1 cache is 32 kilobytes (KB), and the Level 2 cache is 2 megabytes (MB).

Only if the CPU doesn't find the next instruction to be fetched in either Level 1 or

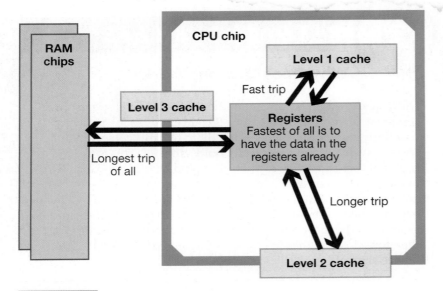

RAM chips

CPU chip

Level 1 cache

Fast trip

Level 3 cache

Registers
Fastest of all is to have the data in the registers already

Longest trip of all

Longer trip

Level 2 cache

FIGURE 9.11

Modern CPUs have two or more levels of cache memory, which leads to faster CPU processing.

Level 2 cache will it make the long journey to RAM to access it.

Are there any other types of cache memory? The current direction of processor design is toward larger and larger multilevel CPU cache structures. Therefore, some newer CPUs, such as Intel's Xeon processor for workstations and servers, have an additional third level of cache memory storage called **Level 3 cache**. On computers with Level 3 cache, the CPU checks this area for instructions and data after it looks in Level 1 and Level 2 cache, but before it makes the longer trip to RAM (see Figure 9.11). The Level 3 cache holds between 2 and 8 megabytes (MB) of data. With 8 MB of Level 3 cache, there is virtually enough storage for an entire program to be transferred to the CPU for its execution.

How do I use cache memory? As an end user of computer programs, you do nothing special to use cache memory. In fact, you will not even be able to notice that caching is being used—nothing special lights up on your system unit or keyboard. However, the advantage of having more cache memory is that you'll experience better performance because the CPU won't have to make the longer trip to RAM to get data and instructions as often. Unfortunately, because it is built into the CPU chip or motherboard,

you can't upgrade cache: It is part of the original design of the computer system. Therefore, like RAM, it's important when buying a computer to consider buying the one, everything else being equal, with the most cache memory.

STAGE 2: THE DECODE STAGE

What happens during the decode stage? The main goal of the decode stage is for the CPU's control unit to translate (or **decode**) the program's instructions into commands the CPU can understand. A CPU can understand only a tiny set of commands. The collection of commands a specific CPU can execute is called the **instruction set** for that system. Each CPU has its own unique instruction set. For example, the AMD Athlon 64 X2 Dual-Core processor used in an Alienware Aurora gaming computer has a different instruction set than does the Intel Core 2 Duo used in a Dell Inspiron notebook. The control unit interprets the code's bits according to the instruction set the CPU designers laid out for that particular CPU. Based on this process of translation, the control unit then knows how to set up all the switches on the CPU so that the proper operation will occur.

What does the instruction set look like? Because humans are the ones to write the instructions initially, all of the commands in an instruction set are written in a language that is easier for humans to work with called **assembly language**. However, because the CPU knows and recognizes only patterns of 0s and 1s, it cannot understand assembly language, so these human-readable instructions are translated into long strings of binary code. The control unit uses these long strings of binary code called **machine language** to set up the hardware in the CPU for the rest of the operations it needs to perform. Machine language is a binary code for computer instructions, much like the ASCII code is a binary code for letters and characters. Similar to each letter or character having its own unique combination of 0s and 1s assigned to it, a CPU has a table of codes consisting of combinations of 0s and 1s for each of its commands. If the CPU sees that pattern of bits arrive, then it knows the work it must do. Figure 9.12 shows a few commands in both assembly language and machine language.

Many CPUs have similar commands in their instruction sets, including the commands listed here:

ADD	Add
SUB	Subtract
MUL	Multiply
DIV	Divide
MOVE	Move data to RAM
STORE	Move data to a CPU register
EQU	Check if equal

CPUs differ in the choice of additional assembly language commands selected for the instruction set. Each CPU design team works to develop an instruction set that is both powerful and speedy.

STAGE 3: THE EXECUTE STAGE

Where are the calculations performed in the CPU? The **arithmetic logic unit (ALU)** is the part of the CPU designed to perform mathematical operations such as addition, subtraction, multiplication, and division and to test the comparison of values such as greater than, less than, or equal to. For example, in performing calculations on grade point averages, the ALU would decide whether a grade point average of 3.9 was greater than, less than, or equal to the grade point average of 3.5. The ALU also performs logical OR, AND, and NOT operations. For example, in determining whether a student can graduate, the ALU would need to ascertain whether the student had taken all required courses AND obtained a passing grade in each of them. The ALU is specially designed to execute such calculations flawlessly and with incredible speed.

Where does the data come from that feeds the ALU? The ALU is fed data from the CPU's registers. The amount of data a CPU can process at a time is based in part on the amount of data each register can hold. The number of bits a computer can work with at a time is referred to as its **word size**. Therefore, a 64-bit processor can process more information faster than a 32-bit processor.

STAGE 4: THE STORE STAGE

What happens in the last stage of CPU processing? In the final stage, the result produced by the ALU is stored back

FIGURE 9.12 Representations of Sample CPU Commands

Human Language for Command	CPU Command in Assembly Language (Language Used by Programmers)	CPU Command in Machine Language (Language Used in the CPU's Instruction Set)
Add	ADD	1110 1010
Subtract	SUB	0001 0101
Multiply	MUL	1111 0000
Divide	DIV	0000 1111

ACTIVE HELPDESK
Understanding the CPU

In this Active Helpdesk call, you'll play the role of a helpdesk staffer, fielding calls about what is inside the CPU and how these components operate, as well as how a CPU processes data and instructions and how cache memory works.

in the registers. The instruction itself will explain which register should be used to store the answer. Now the entire instruction has been completed. The next instruction will be fetched, and the fetch-decode-execute-store sequence will begin again.

RAM: The Next Level of Temporary Storage

By now you are aware of **random access memory (RAM)** and the role it plays in your computer system. As you'll recall, RAM is volatile, meaning that when you turn off your computer, the data stored in RAM is erased. RAM is located as a set of chips on the system unit's motherboard, and its capacity is measured in megabytes and gigabytes, with most modern systems containing 1 GB to 8 GB of RAM. The type of memory chips your computer uses is tied to the type and speed of your CPU.

Figure 9.13 shows a hierarchy of the different types of memory found in your computer system in addition to the more permanent storage devices. You've already read about the top two tiers: CPU registers

TRENDS IN IT

Emerging Technologies: Printable Processors—The Ultimate in Flexibility

You know that the CPU is the "brains" of the computer. Without this important little chip, the computer couldn't process information. The innovations of the transistor and the integrated circuit have shrunk the processor so much that even a pen-sized instrument can house processing capabilities. Miniaturization has made technology very much a part of our lives.

Manufacturing tiny bits of electronic circuitry on silicon is a time-consuming and costly process. But imagine if making microprocessors were as easy as printing them out on your inkjet printer. Or for larger projects, imagine printing out computer components on rolls similar to those that are fed through newspaper presses. Sound crazy? Such a technology is under development. What will one day be possible with printable computer technology makes even the Jetsons seem old-fashioned.

If computer processors could be printed on such common materials as flexible plastic or even paper rather than manufactured on silicon, then computers could be cheaper, smaller, and more completely incorporated into objects we use every day. In fact, the computer would be nearly invisible. You might, for example, download a processor from the Internet and print this processor directly onto a plastic-type substance using your desktop printer. You could then incorporate these plastic-based processors into everything—even wallpaper that could change images or provide lighting for a room.

Printable processors might even have uses you would expect to see in a James Bond movie, such as wearable computers. Your jacket might have a processor with a built-in thermostat that "reads" your body temperature, and your sunglasses could include processors in the lenses that display visual information.

The printable processor technology is anticipated to lead to other innovations, including lightweight medical devices such as programmable heart and

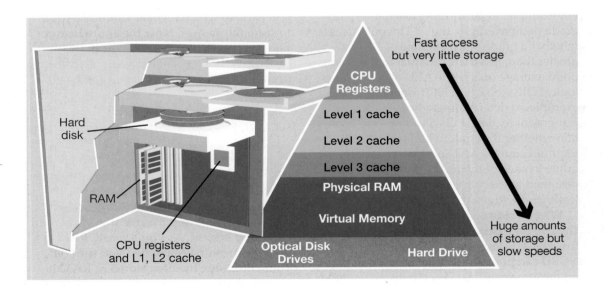

FIGURE 9.13

A computer system's memory has many different levels, ranging from the minute amounts in the CPU to the much slower but more plentiful storage of a hard drive.

and cache memory. The following section describes the various types of physical RAM in your system.

The CPU accesses RAM extremely rapidly, which is why your computer uses RAM as a temporary storage location for data and instructions. The time it takes a device to locate data and instructions and make those data and instructions available to the CPU for processing is known as its **access time**. Recall that getting data and instructions from the hard drive to the CPU takes about 10 milliseconds (ms), or ten-thousandths of a second. The time it takes to get instructions from RAM to the CPU is expressed in nanoseconds (ns), or billionths of seconds. RAM is fast! Remember, however, that

Optimized fin design to maximize air flow

Aluminum heat sink to dissipate heat

Dedicated heat sink

FIGURE 9.15

Corsair DDR2 memory modules have special heat exchangers to keep the memory chips cool. This lets them run at higher speeds, resulting in a performance boost.

Most RAM chips reside on small circuit boards called *memory modules.* Newer computers generally use DIMMs (dual inline memory modules). DIMMs replaced SIMMs (single inline memory modules) when Pentium processors became so prevalent. Pentium processors have a 64-bit bus width, which matches the 64-bit data path of the DIMMs. SIMMs with a 32-bit data path could be used but would need to be installed in matched pairs.

On high-end systems, manufacturers offer an option to purchase Corsair Dominator DDR2. These modules, shown in Figure 9.15, are screened and tested to high levels to guarantee optimum performance. A special heat exchanger is designed into the RAM module to help it operate at a lower temperature, making it more stable and more reliable. The extra heat management lets the RAM be overclocked, meaning it can operate at the faster speed of 1066 MHz instead of 800 MHz. All of these pieces boost the performance of the system and are popular with demanding video gamers.

Does ROM help the CPU work? As you've learned, read-only memory (ROM) is a set of memory chips located on the motherboard that stores data and instructions that cannot be changed or erased. ROM chips can be found on most digital devices and usually contain the start-up instructions the computer needs. ROM chips do not provide any other form of data storage.

Buses: The CPU's Data Highway

A **bus** is an electrical wire in the computer's circuitry—the highway that data (or bits) travels on between the computer's various components. Computers have two different kinds of buses. **Local buses** (or **front side buses** or **FSB**) are on the motherboard and run between the CPU and the main system memory. Most systems also have another type of bus called an **expansion bus** that expands the capabilities of your computer by allowing a range of different expansion cards (such as video cards and sound cards) to communicate with the motherboard.

Do buses affect a computer's performance? Some buses can move data along more quickly than others, whereas others can move more data at one time. The rate of speed that data moves from one location to another, known as *bus clock speed*, affects the overall performance of the computer. Bus clock speed is measured in units of megahertz (MHz), or millions of clock cycles per second. Systems on the market now have FSB speeds ranging from 667 MHz to 1066 MHz. The width of the bus (or the **bus width**) determines how many bits of data can be sent along a given bus at any one time. The wider the bus, the more data that can be sent at one time.

FIGURE 9.16

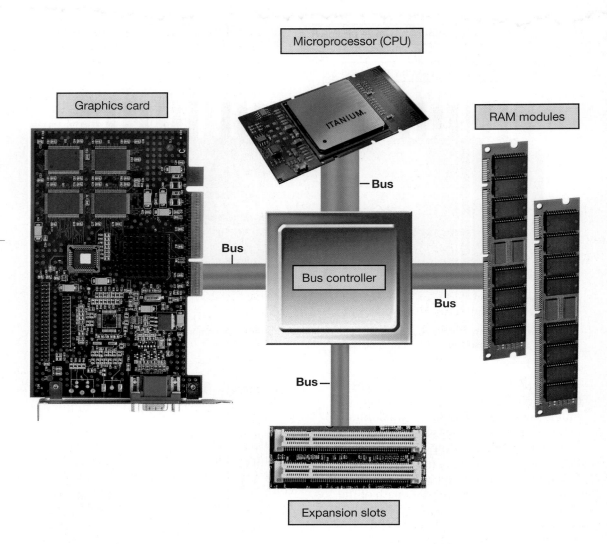

Bus width is measured in terms of bits, so a 32-bit bus can carry more data at one time than a 16-bit bus. Together, bus clock speed and bus width determine how quickly any given amount of data can be transferred on a bus (see Figure 9.16). This data transfer rate (measured in units of megabytes per second) is calculated by multiplying the speed of the bus by the bus width.

The bus width also affects the processor's word size, or the number of bits a processor can manipulate at one time. Even if a processor can manipulate 64 bits at a time, if the bus width allows only 32 bits of data to be sent at one time, the processor's performance will be affected.

What kinds of expansion buses do I need to know about? As noted earlier, the motherboard contains expansion slots in which you insert expansion cards. These expansion cards (such as a graphics card) enable you to connect peripheral devices

(such as a monitor) by providing pathways to the CPU in your computer. For the peripherals to be able to communicate (send and receive data) with your CPU, the motherboard includes expansion buses.

Expansion buses have evolved to provide faster transfer speeds and wider bit widths to deliver higher data transfer rates to the many peripheral devices you may connect to your computer. There are several types of expansion buses. Older computers include buses such as the **Industry Standard Architecture (ISA)** bus and the **Extended Industry Standard Architecture (EISA)** bus to connect devices such as the mouse, modem, and sound cards. These are being replaced by faster, more efficient connections.

The **Accelerated Graphics Port (AGP)** bus design was specialized to help move three-dimensional graphics data quickly. In a modern computer system, you'll find **Peripheral Component Interconnect**

Express (PCIe) buses. PCIe expansion buses connect directly to the CPU and support such devices as network cards, and sound and video cards. They extend the speeds of the original PCI bus design, which has been used for much of the past decade. There are PCIe x8 and PCIe x16 buses, which are 8 times and 16 times faster than the original PCIe specification.

Making Computers Even Faster: Advanced CPU Designs

Knowing how to build a CPU that can run faster than the competition can make a company rich. However, building a faster CPU is not easy. When a company decides to design a faster processor, it must take into consideration the time it will take to design, manufacture, and test that processor. When the processor finally hits the market, it must be faster than the competition to even hope to make a profit. To create a CPU that will be released 36 months from now, it must be built to perform at least twice as fast as anything currently available.

In fact, as you learned in Chapter 6, Gordon Moore, the cofounder of processor manufacturer Intel, predicted more than 40 years ago that the number of transistors on a processor would double every 18 months. Known as Moore's Law, this prediction has been remarkably accurate—but only with tremendous engineering ingenuity. The first 8086 chip had only 29,000 transistors and ran at 5 MHz. Advances in the number of transistors on processors through the 1970s, 1980s, and 1990s continued to align with Moore's prediction.

However, there was a time near the turn of the 21st century when skeptics questioned how much longer Moore's Law would hold true. These skeptics were proved wrong with the microprocessor's continued growth in power. Today's Penryn chip (for notebook computers) has 820 million transistors and runs at 2.6 GHz—more than 200 times faster than its original counterpart. And Intel's Tukwila flaunts a whopping 2 billion transistors! How much longer can Moore's prediction hold true? Only time will tell.

Processor manufacturers can increase CPU performance in many different ways.

One approach is to use a technique called **pipelining** to boost performance. Another approach is to design the CPU's instruction set so that it contains specialized, faster instructions for handling multimedia and graphics. In addition, some CPUs, such as Intel's Core 2 Extreme processors, now have four independent processing paths inside, with one CPU chip doing the work of four separate CPU units. Some heavy computational problems are attacked by actually clustering together large numbers of computers working at the same time.

PIPELINING

What is pipelining? Earlier in the chapter you learned that as an instruction is processed, the CPU runs sequentially through the four stages of processing: fetch, decode, execute, store. Pipelining is a technique that allows the CPU to work on more than one instruction (or stage of processing) at a time, thereby boosting CPU performance.

For example, without pipelining, it may take four clock cycles to complete one instruction (one clock cycle for each of the four processing stages). However, with a four-stage pipeline, the computer can process four instructions at the same time. Like an automobile assembly line, instead of waiting for one car to go completely through each process of assembly, painting, and so on, you can have four cars going through the assembly line at the same time. When every component of the assembly line is done with its process, the cars all move on to the next stage.

How does pipelining speed up computer operations? Pipelined architectures allow several instructions to be processed at the same time. The ticks of the system clock (the clock cycle) indicate when all instructions move to the next process. The secret of pipelining is that the CPU is allowed to be fetching one instruction while it is simultaneously decoding another, executing a third, storing a fourth, and so on. Using pipelining, a four-stage processor can potentially run up to four times faster because some instruction is finishing every clock cycle rather than waiting four cycles for each instruction to finish (see Figure 9.17).

How many stages can a pipeline have? This depends entirely on design decisions. In this chapter we discussed a

SOUND BYTE

Computer Architecture Interactive

In this Sound Byte, you'll take animated tours that illustrate many of the hardware concepts introduced in this chapter. Along the way you'll learn about the machine cycle of the CPU, the movement of data between RAM and the CPU, and the hierarchy of the different types of memory in computer systems.

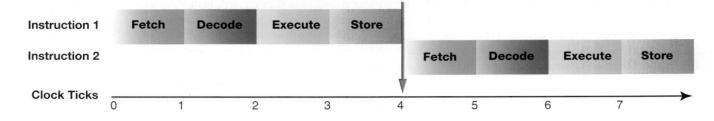

(a) Instruction Cycle, Non-Pipelined: At the end of four clock cycles, Instruction 1 has completed a cycle and Instruction 2 is about to be fetched from RAM.

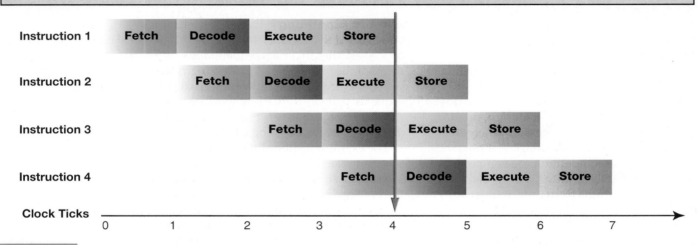

(b) Instruction Cycle, Pipelined: At the end of four clock cycles, Instruction 1 has completed a cycle, Instruction 2 has just finished executing, Instruction 3 has finished decoding, and Instruction 4 has been fetched from RAM.

FIGURE 9.17

The Effects of Pipelining

CPU that went through four stages in the execution of an instruction. The Intel Pentium 4 with hyperthreading features a 31-stage pipeline, and the PowerPC G5 processor uses a 10-stage pipeline. Thus, similar to an assembly line, in a 31-stage pipeline, as many as 31 different instructions can be processed at any given time, making the processing of information much faster. However, because so many aspects of the CPU design interact, you cannot predict performance based solely on the number of stages in a pipeline.

How does pipelining impact the design of the CPU chip? There is a cost to pipelining a CPU. The CPU must be designed so that each stage (fetch, decode, execute, store) is independent. This means that each stage must be able to run at the same time that the other three stages are running. This requires more transistors and a more complicated hardware design.

SPECIALIZED MULTIMEDIA INSTRUCTIONS

How are some processors designed to process multimedia more quickly than others? Each design team developing a new CPU tries to imagine what users' greatest needs will be in four or five years. Currently, several processors on the market reflect this consideration in the incorporation of specialized multimedia instructions into the basic instruction set.

What kinds of changes would help the processor? Hardware engineers have redesigned the chip so that the instruction set contains new commands that are specially designed to speed up the work needed for video and audio processing. For example, Intel has integrated the Streaming Single Instruction Multiple Data (SIMD) Extensions 3 set of commands into the newer Pentium 4 processor design, adding a special group of

157 commands to the base instruction set. These multimedia-specific instructions work to accelerate video, speech, and image processing in the CPU.

MULTIPLE PROCESSING EFFORTS

Can I have more than one CPU in my desktop computer? Many high-end server systems employ a **dual-processor design** that has two completely separate CPU chips on one motherboard. Often, these server systems can later be scaled so that they can accommodate four, six, or even eight processors. Some of the most powerful mainframes support as many as 32 processors!

Meanwhile, Intel is promoting a technology called *multi-core processing* in its Core 2 Duo line of chips. Chips with dual-core processing capabilities have two separate parallel processing paths inside them, so they are almost as fast as two separate CPUs. Combining this with another Intel approach called *hyperthreading* (or HT), these chips can run as many as four tasks (fetch, decode, execute, store) at one time. Dual-core processing is especially helpful because antivirus software and other security programs are often running in the background as you use your system. A dual-core processor enables these multiple applications to execute much more quickly than with traditional CPUs. Quad-core processors are appearing in high-performance home-based systems now as well.

When do I need all that processing power? Dual or core processor systems are often used when intensive computational problems need to be solved in such areas as computer simulations, video production, and graphics processing. Having two processors allows the work to be done almost twice as quickly, but not quite. It is not quite twice as fast because the system must do some extra work to decide which processor will work on which part of the problem and to recombine the results each CPU produces.

Could I have more than one machine working on a single task? Certain types of problems are well suited to a parallel-processing environment. In **parallel processing**, there is a large network of computers, with each computer working

BITS AND BYTES

Today's Supercomputers: The Fastest of the Fast

Supercomputers are the biggest and most powerful type of computer. Scientists and engineers use these computers to solve complex problems or to perform massive computations. Some supercomputers are single computers with multiple processors, whereas others consist of multiple computers that work together.

The fastest supercomputer today is the IBM-developed Blue Gene/L, which is used for computing the safety of the nation's nuclear-weapons stockpile. It operates at more than 596 teraflops (or 596 trillion operations per second). That's almost 280,000 times faster than the average personal computer! Of course, the Blue Gene/L does use more than 131,000 separate processors at the same time. The supercomputer Columbia uses its 10,000 processors to compute the impact of space shuttle damage on the craft's orbit in 24 hours, instead of the three months required by older systems. Check out the world's fastest supercomputers at **www.top500.org**.

on a portion of the same problem simultaneously. To be a good candidate for parallel processing, a problem must be one that can be divided into a set of tasks that can be run simultaneously. If the next step of an algorithm can be started only after the results of the previous step have been computed, parallel processing will present no advantages.

A simple analogy of parallel processing is a laundromat. Instead of taking all day to do five loads of laundry with one machine, you can bring all your laundry to a laundromat, load it in five separate machines, and finish it all in approximately the same time it would have taken you to do just one load on a single machine. In real life, parallel processing is used for complex weather forecasting to run calculations over many different regions around the globe, in the airline industry to analyze customer information in an effort to forecast demand, and by the government in census data compilation.

So what you can continue to expect from CPUs in the future is that they will continue to get smaller and faster and consume less power. This fits with the current demands of consumers for more powerful portable computing devices. By understanding these and other hardware components that make up your computer system, you can use your system more effectively and make better buying decisions.

Emerging Technologies: Computer Technology—Changing the Face of Medicine

As you know by now, computers are no longer just for gaming and spreadsheets. Microprocessors, nanotechnology, and other technologies developed during the personal computing explosion of the last two decades are rapidly being adapted to the medical field. Aside from the surgical robotic techniques and patient simulators discussed in Chapter 1, you can look forward to the appearance of the following medical advancements within the next decade:

1. **Mechanisms that deliver drugs:** Although drugs such as insulin are self-administered by patients, the current injection delivery method can be uncomfortable or difficult to handle, especially for young and elderly patients. Many physicians view inhalation of insulin as the answer (because most people do not find this unpleasant), but the difficulty is in developing an efficient aerosol delivery method. Aradigm, a California manufacturer, is developing an inhaler called AerX that uses the same technology as inkjet printer nozzles to process liquid medication into an aerosol (required for appropriate absorption of the medication through the membranes in the lungs). For many diabetics, this may mean saying good-bye to syringes.

2. **Chips that let you forget to take your pills:** Many drugs must be delivered in precise doses on a regular basis to be effective in treating disease. Although you may be able to remember to take a pill three times a day, not everyone is capable of adhering to this schedule, especially the elderly, young children, and individuals with mental challenges. Therefore, researchers are developing new technologies to deliver medication automatically without any patient intervention. One such promising technology is a dime-sized silicon wafer implant being developed by MicroCHIPS, a Massachusetts-based company. The implants, which are produced using the same methods used to produce silicon microchips for CPUs, contain hundreds of storage areas (called *reservoir arrays*) that store individual doses of medication. The chips are implanted beneath the skin in your abdominal area. Preprogrammed microprocessors on the chip tell the wafer when to administer the doses of medication. No human interaction needed!

3. **Invasive medical procedures:** If you need to have an endoscopy (an examination of your gastrointestinal tract), doctors today normally insert a rather large hose that holds a camera into your body. The Food and Drug Administration has approved a camera that uses small-scale (not yet nano scale) computer technologies to shrink the camera to the size of a small pill. A patient swallows the camera, which then beams images of the small intestine to a recording device worn on a belt. Now that's an easier pill to swallow.

4. **Computers monitoring your body functions:** Israeli scientists have devised a computer that runs on DNA molecules and enzymes instead of silicon chips. Although it has no practical applications just yet, the computer is extremely fast—in fact, it can perform 330 trillion operations per second, approximately 100,000 times as fast as any personal computer on the market today. Also, where silicon chips are reaching their limit of miniaturization, DNA computers can be constructed using only a few molecules—you don't get much smaller than that! As shown in Figure 9.18, DNA computers are combinations of DNA and specially constructed enzymes. Within a single drop of this special fluid, chemical reactions are taking place in billions of DNA computers that generate data and perform rudimentary calculations.

DNA computers use chemical reactions caused by mixing enzymes and DNA molecules. The reactions are designed to provide data and the needed energy for any calculations. Because chemical reactions can be measured precisely and their outcomes predicted reliably,

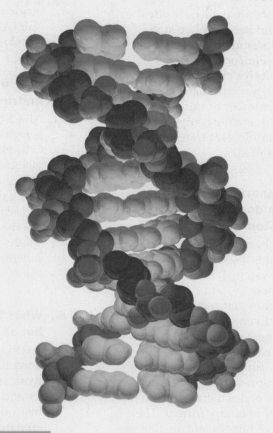

FIGURE 9.18

Here you see a representation of the inside of a DNA-based computer. The double-stranded DNA is combined with enzymes, and together they become the CPU for this biological computing device.

there is no need for conventional hardware and software. All information can be passed at the molecular level. Although DNA computing is today in its infancy, doctors envision devices constructed from DNA computers that will patrol our bodies and make repairs (such as clearing plaque from arteries) as soon as a problem is detected.

So, as you can see, computing technology can be used not only to improve the quality of your life, but also to improve the quality of your health.

1. What is a switch, and how does it work in a computer?

Electrical switches are devices inside the computer that flip between two states: 1 or 0, on or off. Transistors are switches built out of layers of semiconductor material. Integrated circuits (or chips) are tiny regions of semiconductor material that support a huge number of transistors. Integrated circuits enable computer designers to fit millions of transistors into an extremely small area.

2. What is the binary number system, and what role does it play in a computer system?

The binary number system uses only two digits, 0 and 1. It is also referred to as the base 2 number system. It is used instead of the base 10 number system to manipulate the on–off switches that control the computer's actions. Even with just two digits, the binary number system can still represent all the same values that a base 10 number system can. To provide a consistent means for representing letters and other characters, codes dictate how to represent characters in binary format. The ASCII code uses 8 bits (0s and 1s) to represent 255 characters. Unicode uses 16 bits of data for each character and can represent more than 65,000 character symbols.

3. What is inside the CPU, and how do these components operate?

The CPU executes every instruction given to your computer. CPUs are differentiated by their processing power (how many transistors are on the microprocessor chip), how quickly the processor can work (called *clock speed*), and the amount of immediate access memory the CPU has (called *cache*

memory). The CPU consists of two primary units: the control unit controls the switches inside the CPU, and the arithmetic logic unit (ALU) performs logical and arithmetic calculations.

4. How does a CPU process data and instructions?

All CPUs must perform a series of similar general steps. These steps, referred to as a *CPU machine cycle* (or *processing cycle*), include: fetch (loading program and data binary code into the CPU), decode (translating the binary code into commands the CPU can understand), execute (carrying out the commands), and store (placing the results in special memory storage areas, called *registers*, before the process starts again).

5. What is a GPU, and how does it boost performance?

A GPU, or graphics processing unit, functions similarly to a CPU but is created to work specifically with complex 3D graphics and image and video processing. Instead of being integrated into the motherboard, GPUs are part of high-end video cards. This level of video processing power brings an unprecedented level of detail and realism to video gaming and other graphics-intensive environments.

6. What is cache memory?

Cache memory consists of small blocks of memory that are located directly on and next to the CPU chip and hold recently or frequently used instructions or data that the CPU needs the most. The CPU can more quickly retrieve data and instructions from cache memory than from RAM.

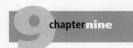

7. What types of RAM are there?

RAM is volatile storage, meaning that when you turn off your computer, the data stored there is erased. The cheapest and most basic type of RAM is DRAM (dynamic RAM). There are many types of RAM, including SDRAM, DDR SRAM, and DDR2 SDRAM. All of these forms of RAM store data that the CPU can access quickly.

8. What is a bus, and how does it function in a computer system?

A bus is an electrical wire in the computer's circuitry through which data (or bits) travels between the computer's various components. Local buses are on the motherboard and run between the CPU and the main system memory. Expansion buses expand the capabilities of your computer by allowing a range of different expansion cards to connect to the motherboard. The width of the bus (or the bus width) determines how many bits of data can be sent along a given bus at any one time.

9. How do manufacturers make CPUs so that they run faster?

Pipelining is a technique that allows the CPU to work on more than one instruction (or stage of processing) at a time, thereby boosting CPU performance. A dual-processor design has two separate CPU chips installed on the same system. Core systems are often used when intensive computational problems need to be solved. In parallel processing, computers in a large network each work on a portion of the same problem at the same time.

Buzzwords

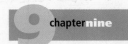

Word Bank

- AGP
- ALU
- ASCII
- binary
- buses
- byte

- cache
- control unit
- decoded
- DRAM
- fetch
- instruction set

- Level 1 cache
- Level 2 cache
- Level 3 cache
- number system
- registers

Instructions: Fill in the blanks using the words from the Word Bank above.

Computers are based on a system of switches, which can be either on or off. The
(1) _____ number system, which has only two digits, models this well. A(n)
(2) _____ is a set of rules for the representation of numbers. Eight binary digits are
combined to create one (3) _____, so they are easier to work with. The (4) _____
code organizes bytes in unique combinations of 0s and 1s to represent characters, letters,
and numerals.

The CPU organizes switches to execute the basic commands of the system. No matter what
command is being executed, the CPU steps through the same four processing stages. First it
needs to (5)_____ the instruction from RAM. Next the instruction is (6) _____, and
the (7) _____ sets up all of the CPU hardware to perform that particular command.
The actual execution takes place in the (8) _____. The result is then saved by storing it
in the (9) _____ on the CPU. Another form of memory the CPU uses is (10) _____
memory. (11) _____ is the form of this type of memory located closest to the CPU.
(12) _____ is located a bit farther from the CPU.

RAM comes in several different types. (13) _____ must be refreshed each cycle to keep
the data it stores valid. The pathways connecting the CPU to memory are known as
(14) _____. The speeds at which they can move data, or the data transfer rates, vary.
(15) _____ is a bus designed primarily to move three-dimensional graphics data
quickly.

Becoming Computer Literate

Your new boss is unsure what the differences between high-end systems are and would like
you to compile a report on two high-end systems, a Macintosh desktop and a Windows-
based PC. She has asked you to compare the price-to-performance ratio, the hardware
features including CPU design, and memory capacities.

Instructions: Using the preceding scenario, write a report using as many of the key
words from the chapter as you can. Be sure the sentences are grammatically correct and
technically meaningful.

Self-Test

Instructions: Answer the multiple-choice and true–false questions below for more practice with key terms and concepts from this chapter.

MULTIPLE CHOICE

1. Switching can be done by
   a. using transistors built of semiconductors.
   b. turning on and off the flow of water.
   c. using vacuum tubes to allow electricity to flow or not flow.
   d. All of the above

2. Hexadecimal notation is based on
   a. powers of 16.   b. powers of 10.
   c. powers of 8.   d. powers of 2.

3. Bits can be encoded in different ways to represent
   a. numeric values.
   b. the letters and symbols of the ASCII table.
   c. the alphabets of all modern languages.
   d. All of the above

4. A video card
   a. has its own memory section.
   b. has its own processor called the GPU.
   c. might have multiple GPUs.
   d. All of the above

5. The decode stage of the CPU cycle is used to
   a. gather data from the registers.
   b. execute an instruction in the ALU.
   c. pull data from the Level 1 cache.
   d. translate the program's binary code into instructions the CPU understands.

6. Dynamic RAM is called "dynamic" because
   a. it is faster than static RAM (SRAM).
   b. it must be refreshed to keep the data valid.

   c. it has a great personality.
   d. it changes its value every clock cycle.

7. Which of the following is a computer bus standard?
   a. PCIe
   b. FIS
   c. HTT
   d. All of the above

8. Corsair Dominator RAM is
   a. DDR2 that is overclocked and designed with its own exchange system.
   b. a brand of ROM.
   c. found on some video cards.
   d. an SDRAM module that is inexpensive but a bit slower than most RAM.

9. Multi-core CPU design means
   a. more than one processing path can run at the same time in the CPU.
   b. only one CPU is used in the system but there are several different types of RAM.
   c. there are multiple, separate CPU chips on the motherboard.
   d. there are multiple CPUs, but only if each has its own OS.

10. There are different types of memory in a computer system because
   a. RAM is more economical and better for larger temporary storage needs.
   b. cache memory is used only for most needed instructions.
   c. there is a need for both volatile and nonvolatile storage.
   d. All of the above

TRUE–FALSE

____ 1. A binary number can be only two digits long.

____ 2. SDRAM is the fastest memory available for a home system.

____ 3. The system clock runs at different speeds depending on the workload.

____ 4. The GPU does memory management to help lighten the load of the CPU.

____ 5. All of the different types of buses inside a computer system run at the same speed.

Making the Transition to... Next Semester

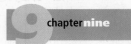

1. Upgrading RAM

As your college career continues, are you finding your computer needs increasing? Upgrading the RAM in your machine can greatly improve performance. What kind of RAM is installed in the computer you use for schoolwork (your own or the lab system you use)? How much would an upgrade to 2 GB of RAM cost for that type of RAM? An upgrade to 4 GB of RAM? Use the supplier Crucial Technology (**www.crucial.com**) to get information about the type of RAM in your system.

2. Lab Processors

It is always challenging for administrators to keep computer laboratories up-to-date. Investigate the type of processor installed in the computer systems you use in your lab. Visit the manufacturer's Web site to get detailed specifications about the design of that processor—the number of cores in its design, how many levels of cache it has, how much total cache memory it has, its speed, and the number of pipeline stages in the CPU. How does that processor compare with the latest model available from the manufacturer?

3. Comparison Shopping for Systems

Do some comparison shopping. Pick three relatively comparable, moderately priced computer systems—one a Macintosh desktop computer, one a Windows-based desktop computer, and the other a notebook that uses either the Windows or Macintosh OS. Create a spreadsheet that outlines all the specific features of each machine. What kind of processor does each machine include? How fast is it? How many levels of cache and how much storage capacity does each cache level have? Look at the RAM: What kind and how much RAM does each machine have? What is the bus architecture of each machine?

4. Game Time

The next generation of video gaming consoles is on the market, and you want to reward yourself for having worked hard all semester. Consider the three main entries in the market: Microsoft Xbox 360, Sony PlayStation 3, and Nintendo Wii. For each gaming console, find out what CPU is being used and what features it has that support high-end gaming. What overall processing power can the system achieve (measured in units of FLOPS, or floating-point operations per second)? What kind of graphics card is used? What kind of ports are included? How does the system handle Internet connectivity? Consider research sources such as **www.extremetech.com**, **www.gameinformer.com**, and the Sony, Microsoft, and Nintendo Web sites.

5. Which Video Card?

Word gets out that you know a lot about computer hardware, and you are suddenly the one everyone is coming to with questions. One of your friends wants to buy a high-end gaming system, and another friend needs an inexpensive desktop solution. To prepare yourself to be the "computer guru," find out which video card would be the best recommendation for each friend. Use manufacturer Web sites as well as **www.pcmag.com** and **www.tomshardware.com** for information.

Making the Transition to... the Workplace

1. Finding Your Network Adapter Address

Almost every business today uses networks to connect the computer systems they own. Each machine is assigned its own identifying number called a *network adapter address*. This value is a long binary number that uniquely labels each adapter card in the business. On the networked machine, click Start, click Run, and then type "command" in the Open text box of the Run dialog box. Then type "ipconfig" in the console window to find your own network adapter address. Is it presented in binary? hexadecimal? decimal? Why?

2. CPUs: The Next Generation

In an effort to stay technologically current, you have been asked to research the most recently released CPUs to determine whether it's worth buying new machines with the new CPUs or waiting for perhaps the next generation. Investigate the newest CPUs released by Intel and AMD. Compare these new CPUs with the current "best" CPUs. What technological advancements are present in the latest CPUs? From a cost perspective, does it make sense to replace the old systems with these new CPUs? What is the buzz on the next-generation CPUs? Would it be better to wait for these future CPUs to come out?

3. Using Pipelining

You work in a assembly plant, so production lines are a familiar concept to your boss. However, he still doesn't understand the concept of pipelining and how it expedites a computer's processing cycle. Create a presentation for your boss that describes pipelining in enough detail so that your boss will understand it. In doing so, compare it with the automobile assembly process.

4. Super Power

Your team at work is exploring a sophisticated price prediction model. But the algorithm requires a supercomputer or a computing cluster (multiple computers joined by software working together) to achieve maximum efficiency. Your boss is not interested in spending department funds on this, but if you can find a way to explore this cheaply by using open source software that runs on Linux, then he'll support it. Research low-cost cluster computing solutions (like Beowulf clusters) at sites such as **www.beowulf.org**, **http://openmosix.sourceforge.net**, and **http://bofh.be/clusterknoppix**. Would it be feasible to use existing Windows computers to run the cluster? Describe how to set up a small cluster and the benefits of doing so, including cost estimates for a 16-node cluster (using cheap PCs that can run Linux).

5. Error Handling Using Binary Numbers

At work you have been bothered by an error message that occasionally pops up from one of your programs. It displays the following message:

```
Error code Number 0011 1010 1111 0011 Please call tech support
help line.
```

Before you call in, take each group of four binary digits and write down the equivalent hexadecimal digit. You can do this by computing the base 10 equivalent of the four binary digits first and then figuring out the base 16 representation of that number.

Critical Thinking Questions

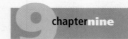

Instructions: Albert Einstein used *Gedanken experiments*, or critical thinking questions, to develop his theory of relativity. Some ideas are best understood by experimenting with them in our own minds. The following critical thinking questions are designed to demand your full attention but require only a comfortable chair—no technology.

1. **Processors of the Future**

   Consider the current limitations of the design of memory, how it is organized, and how a CPU operates. Think radically—what extreme ideas can you propose for the future of processor design? What do you think the limit of clock speed for a processor will be? How could a CPU communicate more quickly with memory? What could future cache designs look like?

2. **Increasing Processor Speed**

   SIMD and 3DNow! (used by AMD in its processors) are two approaches to modifying the instruction set to speed up graphics operations. What do you think will be the next important type of processing users will expect from computers? How could you customize the commands the CPU understands so that processing occurs faster on the CPU you are designing?

3. **The Impact of Registers**

   How would computer systems be different if we could place 4 GB of registers on a single CPU? How would that impact the design of video cards? Would it change the way RAM is used in the system?

4. **The CPU Processing Cycle**

   The four stages of the CPU processing cycle are fetch, decode, execute, and store. Think of some real-world tasks you perform that could be described the same way. For each example, describe how it would be changed if it were pipelined. What additional resources would the pipelined task require?

5. **Binary Events**

   Binary events, things that can be in one of only two positions, happen around you all the time. A common example is a light switch that is toggled on or off. How about a coin? It must always be either heads up or heads down. What other events or objects behave in a binary style?

6. **Lots of Ways to Remember**

   Why does there need to be a memory hierarchy within a computer system, such as the one drawn in Figure 9.13? How would you design a system if it were very inexpensive to produce lots of CPU registers and very expensive to build hard drives? What if someone discovered a way to make hard drives a million times faster than they are today? How would you design a system then?

Team Time Balancing Systems

Problem:

For a system to be effective, it must be balanced—that is, the performance of each subsystem must be well matched so that there are no bottlenecks in the overall performance. In this exercise, teams will develop balanced hardware designs for specific systems within several different price ranges.

Task:

Each group will select one part of a computer: the CPU, the memory, or the bus architecture. The group will be responsible for researching the available options and collecting information on both price and performance specifications. The group will write a report that recommends a specific product for each of three price ranges—entry level, midrange, and high performance. Finally, the three groups will combine their reports so that the team has developed a specification for the entire system.

Process:

1. Divide into three groups: processor, memory, and bus design.

2. Consider the following three price ranges:
   - $500 to $1,000
   - $1,001 to $2,500
   - Unlimited

   For each price range, try to specify at least two components that would keep the system cost in range and would provide the best performance. Keep track of all performance information so that you can later meet with the other groups and make sure each subsystem is well matched.

3. Bring the research materials from the group meetings to one final team meeting. Looking at the system level, make final decisions on the system design for each of the three price ranges. Each range is the sum of total cost that can be expended for hardware for the system unit (monitor and other peripherals not included). The system case, power supply, motherboard, RAM, video card, and storage must be included. Research vendors that supply parts to home developers such as TigerDirect.com (**www.tigerdirect.com**) or NewEgg (**www.newegg.com**).

4. Produce a report that documents the decisions and trade-offs evaluated en route to your final selections.

Conclusion:

A performance increase in one subsystem contributes to the overall performance, but only in proportion to how often it is used. This affects system design and how limited financial resources can be spent to provide the most balanced, best-performing system.

Multimedia

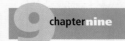

In addition to the review materials presented here, you'll find additional materials featured with the book's multimedia, including the *Technology in Action* Student Resource CD and the Companion Website (**www.prenhall.com/techinaction**), which will help reinforce your understanding of the chapter content. These materials include the following:

ACTIVE HELPDESK

In Active Helpdesk calls, you'll assume the role of helpdesk operator taking calls about the concepts you've learned in this chapter. You'll apply what you've learned and receive feedback from a supervisor to review and reinforce those concepts. The Active Helpdesk calls for this chapter are listed below and can be found on your Student Resource CD:

* Understanding the CPU
* Understanding Types of RAM

SOUND BYTES

Sound Bytes are dynamic multimedia tutorials that help demystify even the most complex topics. You'll view video clips and animations that illustrate computer concepts, and then apply what you've learned by reviewing with the Sound Byte Labs, which include quizzes and activities specifically tailored to each Sound Byte. The Sound Bytes for this chapter are listed here and can be found on your Student Resource CD:

* Binary Numbers Interactive
* Where Does Binary Show Up?
* Computer Architecture Interactive

COMPANION WEBSITE

The *Technology in Action* Companion Website includes a variety of additional materials to help you review and learn more about the topics in this chapter. The resources available at **www.prenhall.com/techinaction** include:

* **Online Study Guide.** Each chapter features an online true–false and multiple-choice quiz. You can take these quizzes, automatically check the results, and e-mail the results to your instructor.

* **Web Research Projects.** Each chapter features a number of Web research projects that ask you to search the Web for information on computer-related careers, milestones in computer history, important people and companies, emerging technologies, and the applications and implications of different technologies.

TECHNOLOGY IN FOCUS
Careers in IT

It's hard to imagine an occupation in which computers are not used in some fashion. Even such previously low-tech industries as junkyards and fast food use computers to manage inventories and order commodities. In this Technology in Focus feature, we explore various information technology (IT) career paths open to you.

What to Consider First: Job Outlook

If you want to investigate a career with computers, the first question you probably have is "Will I be able to get a job?" With all the media hoopla surrounding the loss of IT jobs, many people think the boom in computer-related jobs is over. However, current projections of the U.S. Department of Labor's Bureau of Labor Statistics show that three out of the top 17 fastest-growing occupations through 2016 are still in a computer field (Figure 1). Recently, *Money* magazine rated the top 10 best jobs in the United States; computer IT analysts came in at number 7, and software engineers were number 1! *Money* projects growth rates for these jobs over the next 10 years at 36.1 percent and 46.07 percent, respectively. And an annual survey of college recruiters recently revealed that employers were looking to hire more graduates with computer-related degrees.

Despite these forecasts, recent surveys by the Higher Education Research Institute at the University of California at Los Angeles of incoming college freshmen who declared they would major in computer science has fallen 60 percent since the fall of 2000. This trend developed mainly because of the intense media discussion about the demise of Internet start-up companies in the early 2000s. Because of declining enrollment, critical shortages of computing professionals in the United States are projected over the next 5 to 10 years. In terms of job outlook, this is a perfect time to consider an IT career.

Regardless of whether you choose to pursue a career in IT, you should visit the Bureau of Labor Statistics site at **www.bls.gov**. One of the site's most useful features is the *Occupational Outlook Handbook*. Aside from projecting job growth in a career field, it describes typical tasks that workers perform, the amount of training and education needed, and salary estimates.

In the global economy in which we now operate, job outlook also includes the risk of jobs being outsourced, possibly to other countries (known as *offshoring*). **Outsourcing** is a process whereby a business hires a third-party firm to provide business services (such as customer support call

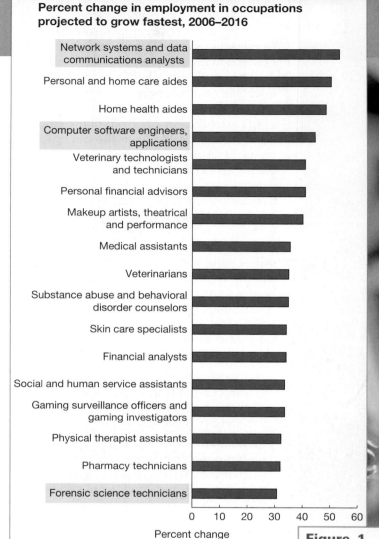

Percent change in employment in occupations projected to grow fastest, 2006–2016

(Bar chart, "Percent change" on x-axis from 0 to 60, occupations listed top to bottom)

- Network systems and data communications analysts
- Personal and home care aides
- Home health aides
- Computer software engineers, applications
- Veterinary technologists and technicians
- Personal financial advisors
- Makeup artists, theatrical and performance
- Medical assistants
- Veterinarians
- Substance abuse and behavioral disorder counselors
- Skin care specialists
- Financial analysts
- Social and human service assistants
- Gaming surveillance officers and gaming investigators
- Physical therapist assistants
- Pharmacy technicians
- Forensic science technicians

Percent change

Figure 1

As this chart shows, huge growth is expected in three different computer-related occupations, according to the Bureau of Labor Statistics.

centers) that were previously handled by in-house employees. **Offshoring** occurs when the outsourcing firm is located (or uses employees) outside the United States. India was the first country to offer its workforce and infrastructure for offshoring, and countries such as China, Romania, and other former Eastern Bloc countries now vie for a piece of the action. The big lure of outsourcing and offshoring is cost savings: The outsourcing firm can do the work more cheaply than in-house employees can. Considering that the standard of living and salaries are much lower in many countries than in the United States, offshoring is an attractive option for many U.S. employers.

But outsourcing and offshoring do not always deliver the vast cost savings that chief executive officers (CEOs) envision. TPI, a global sourcing advisory firm, conducted a survey that showed the average cost savings

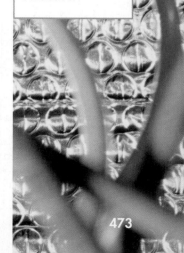

from outsourcing was only 15 percent. Often, however, other less-tangible factors can out-weigh the cost savings from outsourcing. Communications problems can arise between internal and external employees, for example, and cultural differences between the home country and the country doing the offshoring can result in software code that needs extensive rework by in-house employees to make it usable. Data also can be less secure in an external environment or during the transfer between the company and an external vendor. A study by Deloitte Consulting found that 70 percent of survey participants had "negative experiences" with overseas outsourcing, and 44 percent of participants saw no cost savings as a result of outsourcing. Although outsourcing and off-shoring won't be going away, companies are approaching it with more caution.

So, what IT jobs will be staying in the United States? According to *InformationWeek* magazine, most of the jobs in these three categories (Figure 2) will stay put:

1. **Customer facing:** Jobs that require direct input from customers or that involve systems with which customers interface daily.

2. **Enablers:** Jobs that involve getting key business projects accomplished, often requiring technical skills beyond the realm of IT and good people skills.

3. **Infrastructure jobs:** Jobs that are the nuts and bolts of moving and storing information that U.S.-based employees need to do their jobs.

Common Myths about IT Careers

Many people have misconceptions about pursuing a career in IT that scare them away from considering a career in computing or convince them to pursue a computing career for the wrong reasons. Do you share any of these misconceptions?

Is an IT Career Right for You?

A career in IT can be a difficult path. Before preparing yourself for such a career, consider the following.

1. **Salary range:** What affects your salary in an IT position? Your skill set and experience level are the obvious answers, but the size of your employer and geographic location also are factors. Large companies tend to pay more, so if you're pursuing a high salary, set your sights on

FIGURE 2

Jobs That Should Remain Onshore

Customer Interaction	Software and Systems	Hardware/Networking Jobs
Web application developers	Business process analysts	Network security
Web interface designers	Application developers (when customer interaction is critical)	Network installation technicians
Database and data warehouse designers/developers	Project managers (for systems with customers and business users who are located predominately in the U.S.)	Network administrators (engineers)
Customer Relationship Management (CRM) analysts		Wireless infrastructure managers and technicians
Enterprise Resource Planning (ERP) implementation specialists		Disaster recovery planners/responders

COMMON MYTHS ABOUT IT CAREERS

Myth 1: Getting a computer science degree means you're going to be rich. Computer-related careers often offer high salaries, but choosing a computer career isn't a guarantee you'll get a high-paying job. Just as in other professions, you probably will need years of training and on-the-job experience to earn a high salary. However, starting salaries in certain IT professions are robust.

Myth 2: All of the jobs are going offshore. Although many IT jobs have been lost to international competition over the past few years, most networking, analyst (business, systems, and database), and creative jobs (digital media creation and game development) have stayed in the United States. As demand for IT professionals has increased overseas, this has driven up foreign wages, making "offshoring" jobs less attractive. The bottom line is that plenty of IT jobs remain in the United States.

Myth 3: You have three professional certifications . . . you're ready to work. Many freshly minted technical school graduates sporting IT certifications feel ready to jump into a job. But employers routinely cite experience as being more desirable than certification. Experience earned through an internship or a part-time job will make you much more marketable when your certification program is complete.

Myth 4: Women are at a disadvantage in an IT career. Currently, women make up less than 20 percent of the IT workforce, and the percentage is not showing signs of increasing. This presents a huge opportunity for women who have IT skills because many IT departments are actively seeking to diversify their workforces. Also, although a salary gender gap (that is, the difference between what men and women earn for performing the same job) exists in IT careers, it's smaller than in many other professions.

Myth 5: People skills don't matter in IT jobs. Despite what many people think, IT professionals are not locked in lightless cubicles, basking in the glow of their monitors. Most IT jobs require constant interaction with other workers, often in team settings. People skills are important, even when you work with computers.

Myth 6: Mathematically impaired people need not apply. It is true that a career in programming involves a fair bit of math, but even if you're not mathematically inclined, you can explore other IT careers. IT positions also value such attributes as teamwork, creativity, leadership ability, and artistic style.

Myth 7: Working in IT means working for a computer company or in an IT department. Computers and information systems are used across all industries and in most job functions. For example, as an accounting major, if you minor in IT, employers may be more willing to consider hiring you because working in accounting today means constantly interfacing with management information systems and manipulating data.

Resolving myths is an important step toward considering a job in IT. But you need to consider other issues related to IT careers before you decide to pursue a particular path.

a large corporation. But remember that making a lot of money isn't everything—be sure to consider other quality-of-life issues such as job satisfaction.

2. **Gender bias:** Many women view IT departments as Dilbert-like microcosms of antisocial geeks and don't feel they would fit in. Unfortunately, some mostly male IT departments do suffer from varying degrees of gender bias. Although some women may thrive on the challenge of enlightening these "male enclaves" and bringing them forward to the 21st century, others find such environments difficult to work in.

3. **Location:** In this case, *location* refers to the setting in which you work. IT jobs can be office-based, field-based, project-based, or home-based. Not every situation is perfect for every individual. Figure 4 summarizes the major job types and their locations.

4. **Changing workplace:** In IT, the playing field is always changing. New software and hardware are constantly being developed. It's almost a full-time job to keep your skills up-to-date. You can expect to spend a lot of time in training and self-study trying to learn new systems and techniques.

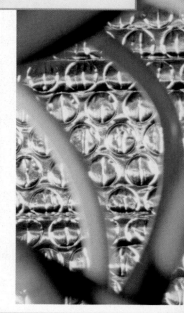

HOW MUCH WILL I EARN?

Like many other professional jobs, IT employees can earn a very good living. Although starting salaries for some IT positions (computer desktop support and helpdesk analysts) are in the modest $34,000 to $38,000 range, starting salaries for students with bachelor's degrees in computer science are fairly robust. A recent article in *Money* magazine showed that the highest annual starting salaries belong to engineers (chemical, electrical, and mechanical). But coming in at a respectable fourth place is computer science, at slightly more than $50,000. And the recent *Money* magazine survey of the best jobs in the United States ranked several IT positions as highly desirable for young employees.

IT salaries vary widely, depending on experience level and the geographic location of the job. To obtain the most accurate information, research salaries yourself. Job posting sites such as **Monster.com** can provide guidance, but a better site is **Salary.com**. As shown in Figure 3, you can use the salary wizard on this site to determine what IT professionals in your area are making compared with national averages. Hundreds of IT job titles are listed so that you can fine-tune your search to the specific job in which you're interested.

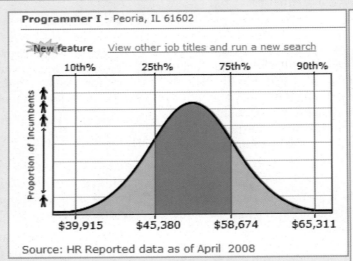

Programmer I - Peoria, IL 61602

New feature   View other job titles and run a new search

10th%   25th%   75th%   90th%

Proportion of Incumbents

$39,915 $45,380 $58,674 $65,311

Source: HR Reported data as of April 2008

Figure 3

The salary wizard at **Salary.com** shows that for an entry-level programming position (programmer I) in Peoria, Illinois, you could expect to earn a median salary of approximately $52,027 (midway between the 25th and 75th percentiles). The wizard is easy to tailor to your location and job preferences.

FIGURE 4

Where Do You Want to Work?

Type of Job	Location and Hours	Special Considerations
Office-based	Report for work to the same location each day and interact with the same people on a regular basis Requires regular core hours of attendance (such as 9 A.M. to 5 P.M.)	May require working beyond "normal" working hours Some positions require workers to be on call 24/7
Field-based	Travel from place to place as needed, and perform short-term jobs at each location	Involves a great deal of travel and working independently
Project-based	Work at client sites on specific projects for extended periods of time (weeks or months) Contractors and consultants fall into this area.	Can be especially attractive to individuals who like workplace situations that vary on a regular basis
Home-based (Telecommuting)	Work from home	Involves very little day-to-day supervision and requires an individual who is self-disciplined

5. **Stress:** Whereas the average American works 42 hours a week, a survey by *InformationWeek* shows that the average IT staff person works 45 hours a week and is on call for another 24 hours. On-call time (hours an employee must be available to work in the event of a problem) has been increasing in recent years because more IT systems (such as e-commerce systems) require 24/7 availability. See Figure 5.

The good news is that despite the stress and changing nature of the IT environment, most computing skills are portable from industry to industry. A networking job in the clothing manufacturing industry uses the same primary skill set as a networking job for a supermarket chain. So, if something disastrous happens to the industry you're in, you should be able to transition to another industry with little trouble.

What Realm of IT Should You Work In?

Figure 7 provides an organizational chart for a modern IT department that should help you understand the careers currently available.

Figure 5

Stress comes from multiple directions in IT jobs.

The chief information officer (CIO) has overall responsibility for the development, implementation, and maintenance of information systems and infrastructure. Usually the CIO reports to the chief operating officer (COO).

The responsibilities below the CIO are generally grouped into two units: development and integration (responsible for the development of systems and Web sites) and technical services (responsible for the day-to-day operations of the company's information infrastructure and network, including all hardware and software deployed).

MATCHING A CAREER TO YOUR SKILLS

Totally unsure about what career you would like to pursue? Online tools such as the ISEEK Skills Assessment (**www.iseek.org**) can help you identify careers based on your skills. This tool has you fill out a skills matrix (see Figure 6), rating your skills in various categories. The program then evaluates the skills matrix and suggests job titles for you to explore.

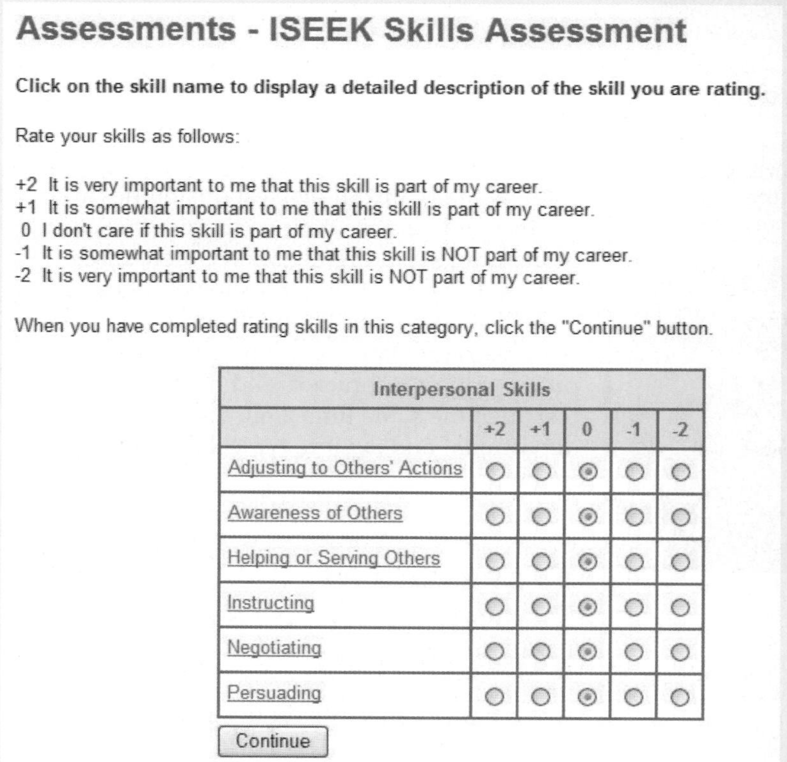

Figure 6

This is one of 10 categories on the ISEEK skills matrix that you can complete to help you assess which career paths match your talents.

Assessments - ISEEK Skills Assessment

Click on the skill name to display a detailed description of the skill you are rating.

Rate your skills as follows:

+2 It is very important to me that this skill is part of my career.
+1 It is somewhat important to me that this skill is part of my career.
 0 I don't care if this skill is part of my career.
-1 It is somewhat important to me that this skill is NOT part of my career.
-2 It is very important to me that this skill is NOT part of my career.

When you have completed rating skills in this category, click the "Continue" button.

Interpersonal Skills	+2	+1	0	-1	-2
Adjusting to Others' Actions	○	○	◉	○	○
Awareness of Others	○	○	◉	○	○
Helping or Serving Others	○	○	◉	○	○
Instructing	○	○	◉	○	○
Negotiating	○	○	◉	○	○
Persuading	○	○	◉	○	○

Continue

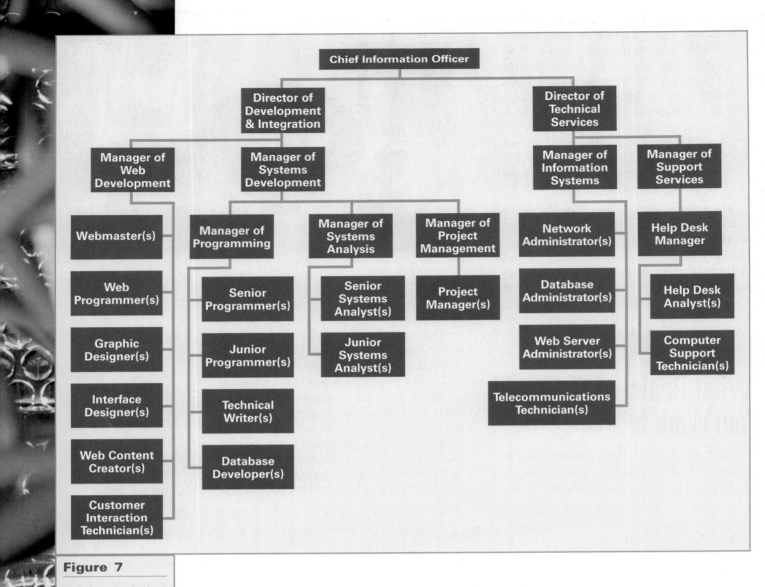

Chief Information Officer

Director of Development & Integration

Director of Technical Services

Manager of Web Development

Manager of Systems Development

Manager of Information Systems

Manager of Support Services

Webmaster(s)

Manager of Programming

Manager of Systems Analysis

Manager of Project Management

Network Administrator(s)

Help Desk Manager

Web Programmer(s)

Senior Programmer(s)

Senior Systems Analyst(s)

Project Manager(s)

Database Administrator(s)

Help Desk Analyst(s)

Graphic Designer(s)

Junior Programmer(s)

Junior Systems Analyst(s)

Web Server Administrator(s)

Computer Support Technician(s)

Interface Designer(s)

Technical Writer(s)

Telecommunications Technician(s)

Web Content Creator(s)

Database Developer(s)

Customer Interaction Technician(s)

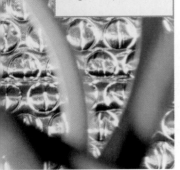

Figure 7

This is a typical structure for an IT department at a large corporation.

In large organizations, responsibilities are distinct and jobs are defined more narrowly. In medium-sized organizations, there can be overlap between position responsibilities. At a small shop, you might be the network administrator, database administrator, computer support technician, and helpdesk analyst all at the same time. Let's look at each department and explore typical jobs found in them.

Working in Development and Integration

Two distinct paths exist in this division: Web development and systems development. Because everything involves the Web today,

there is often a great deal of overlap between these departments.

Web Development

When most people think of Web development careers, they usually equate them to being a *webmaster*. However, today's webmasters usually are supervisors with responsibility for certain aspects of Web development. At smaller companies, they may be responsible for tasks that the other folks in a Web development group usually do:

- **Web content creators** generate the words and images on the Web. Journalists, other writers, editors, and marketing personnel prepare an enormous amount of Web content, whereas **video producers**, **graphic designers**, and **animators** create Web-based multimedia. **Interface designers** work with graphic designers and animators to create a look and feel for the site and make it easy to navigate. Content creators have a thorough understanding of their own fields as well as HTML/XHTML and JavaScript. They also need to be familiar with the capabilities and limitations of modern Web development tools so that they know what the Web publishers can accomplish.

- **Web publishers** build Web pages to deploy the materials that the content creators develop. They wield the Web tools (such as Adobe Dreamweaver and Microsoft Expression) that develop the Web pages and create links to databases (using products such as Oracle and SQL Server) to keep information flowing between users and the Web page. They must possess a solid understanding of client- and server-side Web languages (HTML/XHTML, XML, Java, JavaScript, ASP, and PERL) and development environments such as the Microsoft .NET Framework.
- **Customer interaction technicians** provide feedback to a Web site's customers. Major job responsibilities include answering e-mail, sending requested information, funneling questions to appropriate personnel (technical support, sales, and so on), and providing suggestions to Web publishers for site improvements. Extensive customer service training is essential to work effectively in this area.

As you can see in Figure 8, many different people can work on the same Web site. The education required varies widely for these jobs. Web programming jobs often require a four-year college degree in computer science, whereas graphic designers with two-year art degrees often are hired.

Systems Development

Ask most people what systems developers do and they will say "programming," but this is only one aspect of systems development. Because large projects involve many people, there are many job opportunities in systems development. An explanation of each key area follows.

- **Systems analysts** spend most of their time in the beginning stages of the

Interface designers create navigation schemes.

Graphic designers create art as needed.

Content creators generate text for the site.

Figure 8

As you can see, it takes a team to create and maintain a Web site.

systems development life cycle (SDLC). They talk with end users to gather information about problems and existing information systems. They document systems and propose solutions to problems. Having good people skills is essential to success as a systems analyst. In addition, analysts work with programmers during the development phase to design appropriate programs to solve the problem at hand. Therefore, many organizations insist on hiring systems analysts who have both solid business backgrounds and previous programming experience (at least at a basic level). For entry-level jobs, a four-year degree is usually required. Many colleges and universities offer degrees in management information systems (MIS) that include a mixture of systems development, programming, and business courses.

- **Programmers** participate in the SDLC, attending meetings to document user needs and working closely with systems analysts during the design phase. Programmers need excellent written communication skills because they often generate detailed systems documentation for end-user training purposes. Because programming languages are mathematically based, it is essential for programmers to have strong math skills and an ability to think logically.

Programmers should also be proficient at more than one programming language. A four-year degree is usually required for entry-level programming positions.

- **Project managers** usually have years of experience as programmers or systems analysts. This job is part of a career path upward from entry-level programming and systems analyst jobs. Project managers manage the overall systems development process: assigning staff, budgeting, reporting to management, coaching team members, and ensuring deadlines are met. Project managers need excellent time-management skills because they are pulled in several directions at once. Many project managers obtain master's degrees to supplement their undergraduate degrees in computer science or MIS.

In addition to these key players, the following people are also involved in the systems development process:

- **Technical writers** generate systems documentation for end users and for programmers who may make modifications to the system in the future.
- **Network engineers** help the programmers and analysts design compatible systems, because many systems are required to run in certain environments (UNIX or Windows, for instance) and

must work well in conjunction with other programs.

- **Database developers** design and build databases to support the software systems being developed.

Large development projects may have all of these team members on the project. Smaller projects may require an overlap of positions (such as a programmer also acting as a systems analyst). The majority of these jobs require four-year college degrees in computer science or management information systems. As shown in Figure 9, team members work together to build a system.

It is important to emphasize that all systems development careers are stressful. Deadlines are tight for development projects, especially if they involve getting a new product to market ahead of the competition. But if you enjoy challenges and can endure a fast-paced, dynamic environment, there should be plenty of opportunities for good systems developers in the decade ahead.

Working in Technical Services

Technical services jobs are vital to keeping IT systems running. The people in these jobs install and maintain the infrastructure behind the IT systems and work with end

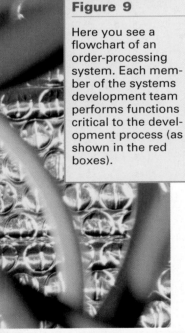

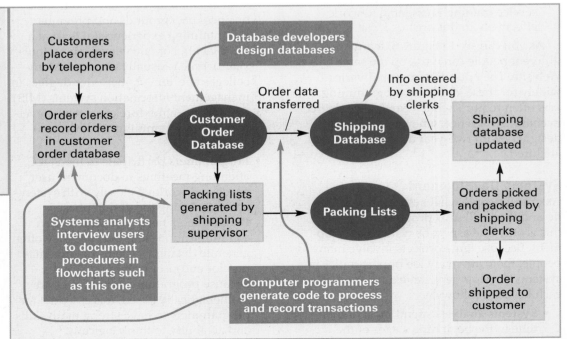

Figure 9

Here you see a flowchart of an order-processing system. Each member of the systems development team performs functions critical to the development process (as shown in the red boxes).

Customers place orders by telephone

Order clerks record orders in customer order database

Database developers design databases

Systems analysts interview users to document procedures in flowcharts such as this one

Customer Order Database

Order data transferred

Packing lists generated by shipping supervisor

Packing Lists

Computer programmers generate code to process and record transactions

Shipping Database

Info entered by shipping clerks

Shipping database updated

Orders picked and packed by shipping clerks

Order shipped to customer

users to make sure they can effectively interact with the systems. These also are the least likely IT jobs to be outsourced because hands-on work with equipment and users is required on a regular basis. The two major categories of technical services careers are information systems and support services.

GET IN THE GAME: CAREERS IN GAME DEVELOPMENT

The video gaming industry in the United States is gaining rapidly on the earning power of the Hollywood movie industry; both achieved slightly more than $9 billion in sales for 2007. Although some aspects of game development such as scenery design and certain aspects of programming are being sent offshore, the majority of game development requires a creative team that needs to work in close proximity to each other. Therefore, it is anticipated that most game development jobs will stay in the United States. The release of the Xbox 360 and PlayStation 3 consoles have doubled development budgets for games because the new consoles support more sophisticated games. As the majority of development costs are personnel-related, this translates into more job opportunities.

Game development jobs usually are split along two paths: designers and programmers. Game designers tend to be artistic and are responsible for creating 2D and 3D art, game interfaces, video sequences, special effects, game levels, and scenarios. Game designers must master software packages such as Autodesk 3ds Max, Autodesk Maya, NewTek LightWave 3D, Adobe Photoshop, and Adobe Flash (see Figure 10). Programmers are then responsible for coding the scenarios developed by these designers. Using languages such as C, C++, Assembly, and Java, programmers build the game and ensure that it plays accurately.

Aside from programmers and designers, play testers and quality assurance professionals play the games with the intent of breaking them or discovering bugs within the game interfaces or worlds. *Play testing* is an essential part of the game development process because it assists designers in determining which aspects of the game are most intriguing to players and which parts of the game need to be repaired or enhanced.

No matter what job you may pursue in the realm of gaming, you will need to have a two- or four-year college degree. If you're interested in gaming, then look for a school with a solid animation or 3D art program or computer game programming curriculum.

So how can you get started on a game development career? One key task that is often performed by high school and college students is beta testing. Just before a game is ready to go to market, the beta version (the last version tested before release) is distributed to volunteers for testing. The objective is to play the game and report any problems in game play or design. Although beta testing is an unpaid job, play testers (who are compensated) often are recruited from the beta testers who provide good feedback. For more information on gaming careers, check out **www.igda.org** and **www.gamecareerguide.com**.

Figure 10

LightWave is a popular package that is used to create realistic graphics for games such as the one shown here.

Information Systems

The information systems department keeps the networks and telecommunications up and running at all times. Within the department, you'll find a variety of positions:

- **Network administrators** (sometimes called *network engineers*) install and configure servers, design and plan networks, and test new networking equipment (see Figure 11).
- **Database administrators (DBAs)** install and configure database servers and ensure that the servers provide an adequate level of access to all users.
- **Web server administrators** install, configure, and maintain Web servers and ensure that the company maintains Internet connectivity at all times.
- **Telecommunications technicians** oversee the communications infrastructure, including training employees to use telecommunications equipment. They are often on call 24 hours a day.

Support Services

As a member of the support services team, you interface with users (external customers or employees) and troubleshoot their computer problems. These positions include the following:

- **Helpdesk analysts** staff the phone (or e-mail) and solve problems for customers or employees, either remotely or in person. Often helpdesk personnel are called on to train users on the latest software and hardware.
- **Computer support technicians** go to a user's physical location and fix software and hardware problems. They also often

have to chase down and repair faults in the network infrastructure.

As important as these people are, they often receive a great deal of abuse by angry users whose computers are not working. When working in support services, you need to be patient and have a "thick skin."

Technical services jobs often require two-year college degrees or training at trade schools or technical institutes. At smaller companies, job duties tend to overlap between the helpdesk and technician jobs. And these jobs are in demand. A survey of 1,400 chief information officers sponsored by Robert Half Technology identified Windows administration, wireless network management, and database management (SQL) as the top skills needed by U.S. IT departments.

How Should You Prepare for a Job in IT?

A job in IT requires a robust skill set and formal training and preparation. Most employers today have an entry-level requirement of a college degree, a technical institute diploma, appropriate professional certifications, experience in the field, or a combination of these. How can you prepare for a job in IT?

1. **Get educated.** Two- and four-year colleges and universities normally offer three degrees to prepare students for IT careers: computer science, MIS, and computer engineering (although titles vary). Alternatives to colleges and universities are privately licensed technical (or trade) schools. Generally, these programs focus on building skill sets rapidly and obtaining a job in a specific field. The main advantage of technical schools is that their programs usually take less time to complete than college degrees. However, to have a realistic chance of employment in IT fields other than networking or Web development, you should attend a degree-granting college or university.

2. **Investigate professional certifications.** Certifications attempt to provide a consistent method of measuring skill levels in specific areas of IT. Hundreds of IT certifications are available, most of which you get by passing a written exam. Software and hardware vendors (such as Microsoft and Cisco) and

Figure 11

At smaller companies, you may be fixing a user's computer in the morning, installing and configuring a new network operating system in the afternoon, and troubleshooting a router problem (shown here) in the evening.

SO YOU WANT TO BE A NETWORK ADMINISTRATOR?

You know that network administrators are the people who design, install, and maintain the network equipment and infrastructure. But what *exactly* do they do?

Network administrators are involved in every stage of network planning and deployment. They decide what equipment to buy and what type of media to use, and they determine the correct topology for the network. They also often develop policies regarding network usage, security measures, and hardware and software standards.

After the planning is complete, network administrators help install the network (either by supervising third-party contractors or by doing the work themselves). Typical installation tasks include configuring and installing client computers and peripherals, running cable, and installing wireless media devices.

Installing and configuring security devices and software are also critical jobs.

When equipment and cables break, network administrators must locate the source of the trouble and fix the problem. They also obtain and install updates to network software, and they evaluate new equipment to determine whether the network should be upgraded. In addition, they monitor the network performance to ensure that users' needs are met.

Given the importance of the Internet to most organizations, network administrators also ensure that the Internet connection is maintained at all times, which usually is a high priority on their to-do list. Finally, network administrators plan disaster recovery strategies (such as what to do if a fire destroys the server room).

professional organizations (such as the Computing Technology Industry Association) often establish certification standards. (Visit **www.microsoft.com**, **www.cisco.com**, **www.comptia.org**, and **www.sun.com** for more information on certifications.)

Employees with certifications generally earn more than employees who aren't certified. However, most employers don't view a certification as a substitute for a college degree or a trade school program. You should think of certifications as an extra edge beyond your formal education that will make you more attractive to employers. To ensure you're pursuing the right certifications, ask employers which certifications they respect or explore online job sites to see which certifications are listed as desirable or required.

3. **Get experience.** Aside from education, employers want you to have experience, even for entry-level jobs. As you're completing your education, consider getting an internship or part-time job in your field of study. Many colleges will help you find internships and allow you to earn credit toward your degree through internship programs.

4. **Do research.** Find out as much about the company and the industry it is in before going on an interview. Start with the company's Web site and then expand your search to business and trade publications (such as *Business Week* and *CIO* magazines).

How Do You Find a Job in IT?

Training for a career is not useful unless you can find a job at the end of your training. Here are some tips on getting a job.

1. **Visit your school's placement office.** Many employers recruit at schools, and most schools maintain a placement office to help students find jobs. Employees in the placement office can help you with résumé preparation and interviewing skills as well as provide you with leads for internships and jobs.

2. **Visit online employment sites.** Most IT jobs are advertised online at sites such as **Monster.com** and **CareerBuilder.com** (see Figures 12 and 13). Begin searching

FIGURE 12

Online IT Career Resources

www.computerjobs.com

www.jobcircle.com

www.techcareers.com

www.justtechjobs.com

www.linkedin.com

www.tech-engine.com

www.dice.com

www.gamasutra.com

Figure 13

Employment sites such as **CareerBuilder.com** enable you to search for specific jobs within a defined geographic area. These sites also allow you to store your résumé at the site and apply for positions with one click.

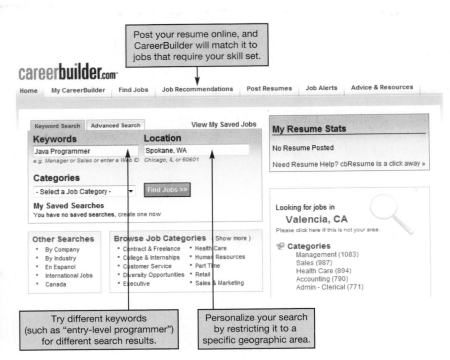

for jobs on these sites early in your education because the job listings detail the skill sets employers require. Focusing on coursework that will provide you with desirable skill sets will make you more marketable.

3. **Start networking.** Many jobs are never advertised but instead are filled by word of mouth. Seek out contacts in your field and discuss job prospects with them. Find out what skills are needed and ask them to recommend others in the industry with whom you can speak. Professional organizations such as the Association for Computing Machinery (ACM) are one way to network. These organizations often have chapters on college campuses and offer reduced membership rates for students. The contacts you make there could lead to your next job. Local user groups that are made up of working professionals with similar interests (such as Microsoft programmers or Linux administrators) also are good sources of contacts. Figure 14 lists major professional

FIGURE 14

Professional Organizations

Organization Name	Purpose	Web Site
Association for Computing Machinery (ACM)	Oldest scientific computing society. Maintains a strong focus on programming and systems development.	www.acm.org
Association for Information Systems (AIS)	Organization of professionals who work in academia and specialize in information systems.	www.aisnet.org
Association of Information Technology Professionals (AITP)	Heavy focus on IT education and development of seminars and learning materials.	www.aitp.org
Institute of Electrical and Electronics Engineers (IEEE)	Provides leadership and sets engineering standards for all types of network computing devices and protocols.	www.ieee.org
Information Systems Security Association (ISSA)	Not-for-profit, international organization of information security professionals and practitioners.	www.issa.org

FIGURE 15

Resources for Women in IT

Organization Name	Purpose	Web Site
Anita Borg Institute for Women and Technology	Organization whose aim is to "increase the impact of women on all aspects of technology."	www.anitaborg.org
Association for Women in Computing (AWC)	A not-for-profit organization dedicated to promoting the advancement of women in computing professions.	www.awc-hq.org
Center for Women and Information Technology (CWIT)	Established at the University of Maryland, Baltimore County (UMBC), the organization is dedicated to providing global leadership in achieving women's full participation in all aspects of IT.	www.umbc.edu/cwit
Diversity/Careers in Engineering & Information Technology	An online magazine whose articles cover career issues focused on technical professionals who are members of minority groups, women, or people with disabilities.	www.diversitycareers.com
Women in Technology International (WITI)	A global trade association for tech-savvy, professional women.	www.witi.com

organizations you should consider investigating.

If you are a woman considering pursuing an IT career, there are many resources and groups that cater to female IT professionals and students. The oldest and best known organization is the Association for Women in Computing, founded in 1978. Figure 15 provides a list of resources to investigate.

4. **Check corporate Web sites for jobs.** Many corporate Web sites list current job opportunities. For example, Apple features a searchable site (see Figure 16) that you can tailor to a specific job type. Check the sites of companies in which you are interested and then do a search on the site for job openings or, if provided, click the Employment link.

The outlook for IT jobs should continue to be positive in the future. We wish you luck with your education and job search.

Figure 16

Corporate Web sites often list available jobs. The Apple site arranges jobs into broad categories and then provides easy search tools to zero in on the right job for you.

10

chapter ten

Behind the Scenes:

Building Applications

Objectives

After reading this chapter, you should be able to answer the following questions:

1. What is a system development life cycle, and what are the phases in the cycle? **(pp. 488–491)**

2. What is the life cycle of a program? **(p. 492)**

3. What role does a problem statement play in programming? **(pp. 493–494)**

4. How do programmers create algorithms? **(pp. 494–500)**

5. How do programmers move from algorithm to code, and what categories of language might they code in? **(pp. 500–504)**

6. How does a programmer move from code in a programming language to the 1s and 0s the CPU can understand? **(pp. 506–509)**

7. How is a program tested? **(pp. 509–510)**

8. What steps are involved in completing the program? **(p. 510)**

9. How do programmers select the right programming language for a specific task? **(pp. 510–512)**

10. What are the most popular programming languages for Windows and Web applications? **(pp. 512–517)**

ACTIVE HELPDESK

- Understanding Software Programming **(p. 509)**
- Selecting the Right Programming Language **(p. 512)**

Understanding Software Programming

Every day we face a wide array of tasks. Some tasks are complex and need a human touch; others require creative thought and higher-level organization. However, some tasks are routine, such as alphabetizing a huge collection of invoices. Tasks that are repetitive, work with electronic information, and follow a series of clear steps are candidates for automation with computers.

Well-designed computer programs already exist for many tasks. For example, if you want to write a research paper, Microsoft Word allows you to do just that. The program has already been designed to translate the tasks you want to accomplish into computer instructions. To do your work, you need only be familiar with the interface of Word; you do not have to create a program yourself.

However, for users who cannot find an existing software product to accomplish a task, programming is mandatory. For example, imagine that a medical company comes up with a new smart bandage that is designed to transmit medical information about a wound directly to a diagnostic computer (these are under development). No software product on the market is designed to accumulate and relay information in this manner. Therefore, the company will need to deploy a team of software developers to generate the appropriate software for this bandage to function as designed.

Even if you'll never create a program of your own, knowing the basics of computer programming is still helpful. For example, most modern software applications enable you to customize and automate various features by using small custom-built mini-programs called *macros*. By creating macros, you can ask the computer to execute a complicated sequence of steps with a single command. Understanding how to program macros enables you to add custom commands to Word or Excel, for example, and to automate frequently performed tasks, providing a huge boost to your productivity.

Understanding programming is therefore an important piece of getting the most out of your computer system. If you plan to use only off-the-shelf software (existing software), having a basic knowledge of programming enables you to understand how application software is constructed and to add features that support your personal needs. If you plan to create custom applications from scratch, then a detailed knowledge of programming is key to the successful completion of any project. Thus, in this behind-the-scenes chapter, we explore the stages of program development and survey the most popular programming languages.

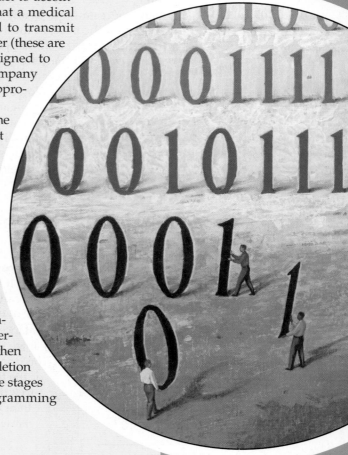

SOUND BYTES

- Programming for End Users **(p. 493)**
- Looping Around the IDE **(p. 507)**

The Life Cycle of an Information System

Generally speaking, a system is a collection of pieces working together to achieve a common goal. Your body, for example, is a system of muscles, organs, and other organized groups of cells working together. Or the college you attend is a system with administrators, faculty, students, and maintenance personnel working together. An **information system** includes data, people, procedures, hardware, and software. You interact with information systems all the time, whether you are at a grocery store, bank, or restaurant. In any of these instances, the parts of the system work together toward a similar goal. Because teams of individuals are required to develop such systems, an organized process (or set of steps) needs to be followed to ensure that development proceeds in an orderly fashion.

This set of steps is usually referred to as the **system development life cycle (SDLC)**. In this section, we provide you with an overview of systems development and show you how programming fits into the cycle.

SYSTEM DEVELOPMENT LIFE CYCLE

Why do you need a process to develop a system? If you have programming skills, you can sit down in a day, perhaps, to write a little program to balance your checkbook or to organize your CD collection. If you don't have such skills or the time or inclination to write a program, then you can buy one. However, one person

does not develop in a day the programs you buy in a store. Those programs are generally far more complex than you would write yourself, and they require many phases to make the product complete and saleable. Therefore, an entire team of people and a systematic approach are necessary. As noted earlier, this set of steps is often referred to as the *system development life cycle (SDLC)*.

What steps constitute the SDLC? All six steps of the SDLC are shown in Figure 10.1. As the figure shows, this system is sometimes referred to as a "waterfall" system because each step is dependent on the previous step being completed first. A brief synopsis of each step follows.

1. **Problem and Opportunity Identification:** Corporations are always attempting to break into new markets, develop new sources of customers, or launch new products. For example, when the founders of eBay developed the idea of an online auction community, they needed a system that could serve customers and allow them to interact with each other. At other times, systems development is driven by a company's desire to serve its existing customers more efficiently or to respond to problems with a current system. For example, when traditional brick-and-mortar businesses want to launch e-commerce sites, they need to develop systems for customers to purchase products.

    Whether solving an existing problem or exploiting an opportunity, corporations usually generate more ideas for systems than they have the time and money to implement. Large corporations typically form a development steering committee to evaluate systems development proposals. The committee reviews ideas and decides which projects to take forward based on available resources such as personnel and funding.

2. **Analysis:** In this phase, analysts explore in depth the problem to be solved and develop a program specification. The program specification is a clear statement of the goals and objectives of the project. It is also at this stage that the first feasibility assessment is performed. The feasibility assessment determines whether the project should go forward. You might have a great idea, but that doesn't mean that the company has the

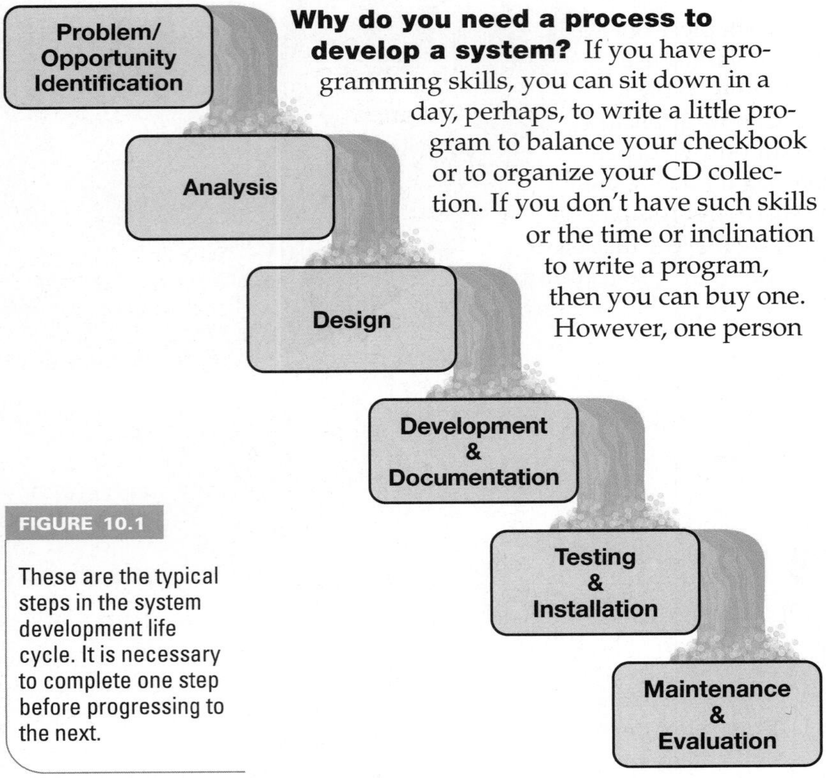

FIGURE 10.1

These are the typical steps in the system development life cycle. It is necessary to complete one step before progressing to the next.

Problem/
Opportunity
Identification

Analysis

Design

Development
&
Documentation

Testing
&
Installation

Maintenance
&
Evaluation

technical expertise or the financial or operational resources to develop it. Similarly, there may not be enough time to develop the product fully.

Assuming the project is feasible, the analysis team studies the current system (if there is one) and defines the user requirements of the proposed system. Finally, the analysts recommend a solution or plan of action, and the process moves to the design phase.

3. **Design:** Before a house is built, blueprints are developed so that the workers have a plan to follow. The design phase of the SDLC has the same objective: generating a detailed plan for programmers to follow. The current and proposed systems are documented using flowcharts and data-flow diagrams. Flowcharts are visual diagrams of a process, including the decisions that need to be made along the way. Data-flow diagrams trace all data in an information system from the point at which data enters the system to its final resting place (storage or output). The data-flow diagram in Figure 10.2 shows the flow of concert ticket information.

The ultimate goal of the design phase with respect to software development is to design documents that programmers can follow in developing the actual system. It is also in this phase that the "make or buy" decision is made. Once the system plan is designed, a company evaluates existing

BITS AND BYTES

The More Minds the Better

In each phase of the software development life cycle, a style of interaction named *joint application development (JAD)* is useful in creating successful, flexible results. JAD is popular because it helps designers adapt to changes in program specifications quickly. In JAD the customer is intimately involved in the project right from the beginning. Slow communication and lengthy feedback time is one reason the traditional development process is so time-consuming. In JAD "workshops," there are no communication delays. Such workshops usually include end users, developers, subject experts, observers (such as senior managers), and a facilitator. The facilitator enforces the rules of the meeting to make sure all voices are heard and agreement is reached as quickly as possible. Also called *accelerated design* or *facilitated team techniques*, the goal of JAD is to improve design quality by fostering clear communication. For more details, refer to **http://www.credata.com/research/jad.html**.

software packages (off-the-shelf software) to determine whether it needs to develop a new piece of software or buy something already on the market and adapt it to fit its own needs.

For instance, if you want to start an online auction site to compete with eBay, you might not have to build your own system. Numerous online auction software packages that are for sale now might meet your needs. If you cannot find an existing package that meets

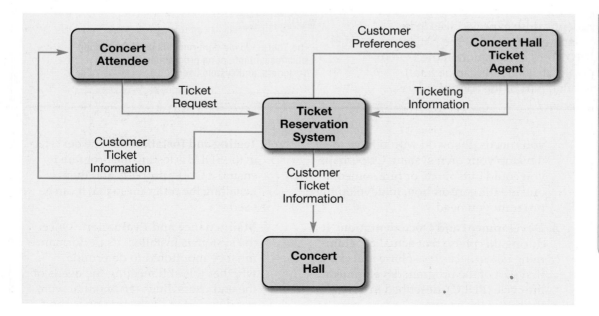

FIGURE 10.2

Data-flow diagrams trace the flow of data, such as ticketing information. This is a top-level overview diagram. More detailed diagrams would be prepared later for each piece of the system, showing specific pieces of information being tracked (such as customer name, payment information, and so on).

ETHICS IN IT

Ethics: When Software Kills

Earlier we discussed the SDLC and the range of careers in software development. Building a software application is a process that involves many people and requires many decisions. But what happens when the released product is defective—tragically defective?

The most infamous example of this is the computerized radiation therapy machine, the Therac-25 (see Figure 10.3). Between June 1985 and January 1987, six known accidents in the United States and Canada led to massive radiation overdoses by the Therac-25, resulting in the death of three patients and serious injuries to the others. This error has been described as the worst series of radiation accidents in the history of medical accelerators.

The software was responsible for monitoring the machine status, accepting input about the treatment desired, and setting the machine up for treatment. It turned on the beam in response to an operator command and also turned off the beam when treatment was completed, when an operator commanded it, or when a malfunction was detected.

In the first accident, a 61-year-old woman was receiving follow-up radiation after surgery for breast cancer. When the machine turned on, she said that she felt a "tremendous force of heat . . . this red-hot sensation." When the technician came in, and the patient said that she had been burned, the technician replied that that was not possible. The patient went home but was soon in so much pain she went to the local hospital. Hospital staff determined that the patient was experiencing a normal reaction to the radiation therapy and advised her to continue treatments.

Although the therapeutic dose expected was to be about 200 rads, it was later estimated that the patient had received one or two doses of radiation in the 15,000 to 20,000 rad range (doses of 1,000 rads can be fatal). The hospital explained that part of the confusion was because staff members had never seen a radiation overdose of that magnitude before. Eventually the patient lost her breast, lost the use of her shoulder and arm, and was in constant pain. Other patients had similar incidents, some dying as a result of complications from the error in the dosage.

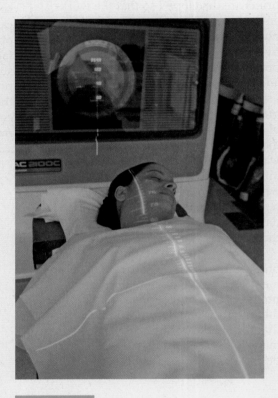

FIGURE 10.3

The Therac-25 incident reminds us of the responsibilities incumbent on programmers, system designers, and system users.

---

your needs, then you would have to develop your own system. Or perhaps you could outsource, or hire someone outside the corporation, to develop the program you need.

4. **Development and Documentation:** It is during this phase that actual programming takes place. This phase is also the first part of the program development life cycle (PDLC), described in detail in the rest of the chapter.

5. **Testing and Installation:** The next step in the SDLC is testing the program to ensure it works properly and then installing the program so that it can be used.

6. **Maintenance and Evaluation:** Once the system is installed, its performance must be monitored to determine whether it is still meeting the needs of the end users. Bugs (errors) that were not detected in the testing phase and

In the years since these accidents, much analysis has been done to see how the tragedy could have been avoided. One notable item is that remarkably little software documentation was produced by the two manufacturing companies during development. A memo by the Food and Drug Administration reviewing the incident said, "Unfortunately, the company response also seems to point out an apparent lack of documentation on software specifications and a software test plan."

In addition, testing was not done in a rigorous manner. A "small amount" of software testing was done on a simulator, but most testing was done as a system rather than examining software and hardware separately. It appears that the machine and software testing was minimal, with most effort directed at the integrated system test.

Although the basic mistakes involved poor software engineering practices, many different factors explained the full set of accidents including:

- simple programming errors,
- inadequate safety engineering,
- poor human–computer interaction design,
- too little focus on safety by the manufacturing organization, and
- inadequate reporting structure at the company level and as required by the U.S. government.

In events such as this one, who should be held responsible for producing defective software? Is it the corporate management that does not institute a defined software process? Is it the production managers who forced tight schedules that demanded risky software engineering practices? What about the software engineers who wrote the defective code? The very first article of the code of ethics of the Institute of Electrical and Electronic Engineers (IEEE) states, "[We] accept responsibility in making engineering decisions consistent with the safety, health, and welfare of the public, and to disclose promptly factors that might endanger the public or the environment." Or what about users of the software? Can they be held responsible for accidents? What if they made changes to the system?

The Association of Computing Machinery (ACM) and the IEEE have established eight principles for ethical software engineering practices:

1. **Public:** Software engineers shall act consistently with the public interest.
2. **Client and Employer:** Software engineers shall act in a manner that is in the best interests of their client and employer consistent with the public interest.
3. **Product:** Software engineers shall ensure that their products and related modifications meet the highest professional standards possible.
4. **Judgment:** Software engineers shall maintain integrity and independence in their professional judgment.
5. **Management:** Software engineering managers and leaders shall subscribe to and promote an ethical approach to the management of software development and maintenance.
6. **Profession:** Software engineers shall advance the integrity and reputation of the profession consistent with the public interest.
7. **Colleagues:** Software engineers shall be fair to and supportive of their colleagues.
8. **Self:** Software engineers shall participate in lifelong learning regarding the practice of their profession and shall promote an ethical approach to the practice of the profession.

Only through constant vigilance on the part of each software programmer, manager, and testing professional will situations such as the Therac-25 be prevented.

---

that the users discover subsequently must be corrected. Additional enhancements that users request are evaluated so that appropriate program modifications can be made.

The waterfall model is an idealized view of software development. Most developers follow some variation of it, however. For example, a design team may "spiral," so a group that is supporting the work of a different group will develop software together rather than working independently, one after the other. Often there is a "backflow" up the waterfall because even well-designed projects can require redesign and specification changes midstream.

Some people criticize the waterfall model for taking too long to feed actual running code back to the client. This may contribute to an ever-changing set of features and requests from the clients as they wait longer and longer to see a working prototype.

Other developmental models, such as rapid application or RAD, are being used in the industry to address these issues.

The Life Cycle of a Program

Programming often begins with nothing more than a problem or a request: "We can't get our budget reports out on time," or "Can you tell me how many transfer students have applied to our college?" When problems or requests such as these arise, someone realizes that computer programs could solve these problems more efficiently and reliably than the procedures currently in place.

What is programming? As you have just read, once the project has been deemed to be feasible and a plan is in place, the work of programming begins. **Programming** is the process of translating a task into a series of commands a computer will use to perform that task. It involves identifying which parts of a task a computer can perform, describing those tasks in a highly specific and complete manner, and, finally, translating this description into the language spoken by the computer's central processing unit (CPU).

How do programmers tackle a programming project? Just as an information system has a development life cycle, each programming project follows several stages from conception to final deployment. This process is sometimes referred to as the **program development life cycle (PDLC)**:

1. **The Problem:** First, programmers must develop a complete description of the problem. The problem statement identifies the task to be automated and describes how the software program will behave.

2. **A Plan:** The problem statement is next translated into a set of specific, sequential steps that describe exactly what the computer program must do to complete the work. This is known as an *algorithm*. At this stage, the algorithm is written in natural language (that is, whatever language the programmer speaks, such as English).

3. **The Coding:** The algorithm is then translated into programming code, a language that is friendlier to humans than the 1s and 0s that the CPU speaks but that is still highly structured. By coding the algorithm, programmers must think in terms of the operations that a CPU can perform.

4. **The Debugging:** The code then goes through a process of debugging in which the programmers find and repair any known errors in the code.

5. **The Project:** The software is then tested, both by the programming team and by the people who will use the program. The results of the entire project are documented for the users and the development team. Finally, users are trained so that they can use the program efficiently.

Figure 10.4 illustrates the steps of a program's life cycle. Now that you have an overview of the process involved in developing a program, let's look at each step in more detail.

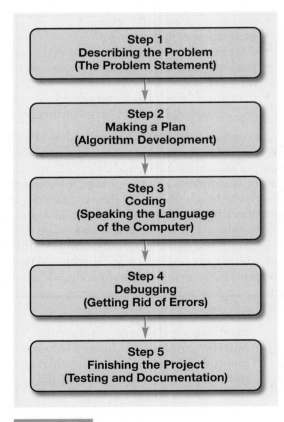

Step 1
Describing the Problem
(The Problem Statement)

Step 2
Making a Plan
(Algorithm Development)

Step 3
Coding
(Speaking the Language of the Computer)

Step 4
Debugging
(Getting Rid of Errors)

Step 5
Finishing the Project
(Testing and Documentation)

FIGURE 10.4

The stages followed by each programming project from conception to final deployment are collectively referred to as the program development life cycle.

Describing the Problem: The Problem Statement

The **problem statement** is the starting point of programming work. It is a clear description of what tasks the computer program must accomplish and how the program will execute these tasks and respond to unusual situations. Programmers develop problem statements so that they can better understand the goals of their programming efforts.

What kind of problems can computer programs solve? Not every problem is well suited to a computerized solution. The strengths of computing machines are that they are fast and work without error—unlike humans, computers don't introduce mistakes because they're tired or stressed. As mentioned earlier, tasks that are repetitive, work with electronic information, and follow a series of clear steps are candidates for computerization.

This might sound as if computers only help us with the dullest and most simplistic tasks. However, computer programs also can help solve sophisticated problems. For example, pharmaceutical companies design drugs using complex computer programs that model molecules. Using program simulations, chemists can "create" new drugs in the computer and quickly determine whether they will have the desired pharmacological effects. Based on the program's data, chemists select the most promising choices and begin to test those compounds in the real laboratory. This is not exactly simple stuff.

Still, computers cannot yet act with intuition or be spontaneously creative. They can attack highly challenging problems such as making weather predictions or playing chess, but only in a manner that takes advantage of what computers do best— making fast, reliable computations.

How do programmers create problem statements? Most computer users understand what jobs (or problems) they want to computerize but not the details of the programming process. Therefore, the goal in creating a useful problem statement is to have programmers interact with users to describe three things relevant to creating a useful program: data, information, and method.

1. **Data** is the information that users have at the start of the job. It will be fed into the program.

2. **Information** is the result that the users require at the end of the job. The program produces this information from data.

3. **Method**, described precisely, is how the program converts the inputs into the correct outputs.

For example, say you want to compute how much money you'll earn working at a parking garage. Your salary is $7.32 per hour for an eight-hour shift, but if you work more than eight hours a day, you will earn $11.73 per hour for the overtime work. To determine how much money you make in any given day, you could multiply this in your mind, write it on a piece of paper, or use a calculator; or you could create a simple computer program to do the work for you. In this example, what are the three elements of the problem statement?

1. **Input:** The data that you know at the beginning of the problem, which is the number of hours you worked.

2. **Output:** The information you need to have at the end of the problem, which is your total pay for the day.

3. **Processing:** The set of steps that will take you from your input to an output. In this case, the computer program would check if you worked more than eight hours (that is, it would determine whether you worked any overtime). If you did not work overtime, then the output would be $7.32 multiplied by the total number of hours you worked ($58.56). If you did work overtime, then the program would calculate your pay at $58.56 (8 hours at $7.32 per hour) for the regular part of your shift plus an additional $11.73 multiplied by the number of overtime hours you worked. This processing thereby transforms your input into your desired output.

How do programmers handle bad inputs? In the problem statement, programmers also must describe what the program should do if the input data is invalid or just gibberish (users do make mistakes). This part of the problem statement is referred to as **error handling**. The problem statement also includes a **testing plan** that lists specific input numbers the program would typically expect the user to enter. It then lists the precise output values that a perfect program will return for those input

SOUND BYTE

Programming for End Users

In this Sound Byte, you'll be guided through the creation of a macro in the Microsoft Office 2007 suite. You'll learn how Office enables you to program with macros to customize and extend the capabilities it offers.

Program Goal:	To compute the total pay for a fixed number of hours worked at a parking garage.		
Inputs:	Number of Hours Worked.................... a positive number		
Outputs:	Total Pay Earned................................ a positive number		
Process:	The Total Pay Earned is computed as $7.32 per hour for the first eight hours worked each day. Any hours worked beyond the first eight are calculated at $11.73 per hour.		
Error Handling:	The input Number of Hours Worked must be a positive real number. If it is a negative number or other unacceptable character, the program will force the user to re-enter the information.		
Testing Plan:	**Input**	**Output**	**Notes**
	8	8*7.32	Testing positive input
	3	3*7.32	Testing positive input
	12	8*7.32 + 4*11.73	Testing an overtime input
	-6	Error message/ask user to re-enter value	Handling error

values. Later, in a testing process, programmers use the input and output data values from the testing plan to determine whether the program they created works in the way it should. (We discuss the testing process later in the chapter.)

Does the testing plan cover every possible use of the program? The testing plan cannot list every input that the program could ever encounter. Instead, programmers work with users to identify the categories of inputs that will be encountered, find a typical example of each input category, and specify what kind of output must be generated. In the preceding parking garage example, the error-handling process would describe what the program would do if the user happened to enter "-8" (or any other nonsense character) for the number of hours you worked. The error handling would specify whether the program would return a negative value, prompt you to reenter the input, or yell at you and shut down (well, maybe not exactly that last option). We could expect three categories of inputs in the parking garage example. The user might enter:

1. a negative number for hours worked that day,

2. a positive number equal to or less than eight, or

3. a positive number greater than eight.

The testing plan would describe how the error would be managed or how the output would be generated for each input category.

Is there a standard format for a problem statement? Most companies (and instructors) have their own format for documenting a problem statement. However, all problem statements include the same basic components: the data that is expected to be provided (inputs), the information that is expected to be produced (outputs), the rules for transforming the input into output (processing), an explanation of how the program will respond if users enter data that doesn't make sense (error handling), and a testing plan. Figure 10.5 shows a sample problem statement for our parking garage example.

Making a Plan: Algorithm Development

Once programmers understand exactly what the program must do and have finalized the problem statement, they can begin developing a detailed **algorithm**, a set of specific, sequential steps that describe in natural language exactly what the computer program must do to complete its task. Let's look at some ways in which programmers design and test algorithms.

Do algorithms appear only in programming? Although the term *algorithm* may sound like it would fall only under the domain of computing, you design and execute algorithms (or problem-solving procedures) in your daily life. For example, say you are planning your morning. You know you need to (1) get gas for your car, (2) swing past the café and pick up a mocha latté, and (3) stop by the bookstore and buy the textbook before your 9 A.M. accounting lecture. In what order will you accomplish all these tasks? How do you decide? Should you try to minimize the distance you'll travel or the time you'll spend driving? What happens if you forget your credit card?

Figure 10.6 presents an algorithm you could develop to make decisions about how to accomplish these tasks. This algorithm lays out a specific plan that encapsulates all of the choices you need to make in the course of completing a particular task and shows the specific sequence in which these tasks will occur. At any point in the morning, you could gather your current information (your inputs)—"I have $20 and my Visa card, but the ATM machine is down"—and the algorithm would tell you unambiguously what your next step should be.

What are the limitations of algorithms? The deterministic nature of an algorithm enables us to describe it completely on a simple piece of paper. An algorithm is a series of steps that is completely known—at each point we know *exactly* what step to take next. However, not all problems can be described as a fixed sequence of predetermined steps; some involve random and unpredictable events. For example, although the program that computes your parking garage take-home pay each day works flawlessly, programs that predict the stock prices are often wrong because many random events (inputs), such as a flood in Costa Rica or a shipping delay in California, change the outcomes (outputs).

DEVELOPING AN ALGORITHM: DECISION MAKING AND DESIGN

How do programmers develop an algorithm? By now you understand that when programmers develop an algorithm, they convert the problem statement into a

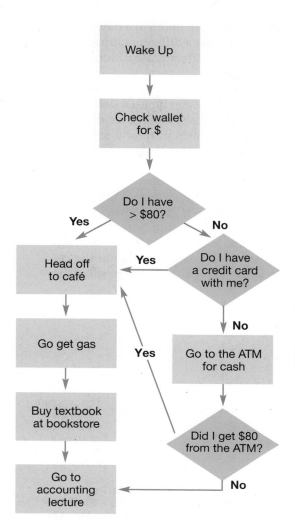

FIGURE 10.6

An algorithm you might use to plan your morning would include several steps that encapsulate all of the decisions you might need to make and show the specific sequence in which these steps would occur.

list of steps (or actions) the program will take. For simple problems, this list is straightforward—the program completes this action first, this action second, this action third, and so on. However, only the simplest of algorithms execute the same series of actions every time they run.

More complex problems involve choices and therefore cannot follow a sequential list of steps to generate the correct output. Instead, the list of steps created for complex problems includes **decision points**, or points at which the program must choose from an array of different actions based on the value of its current inputs. Programmers convert a problem into an algorithm by listing the sequence of actions that must be taken and recognizing the places where decisions must be made.

So, in our parking garage example, if the number of hours you worked in a given day is eight or less, the program performs one simple calculation: It multiplies the number of hours worked by $7.32. If you worked more than eight hours in a day, then the program takes a different path and performs a different calculation as shown in Figure 10.7.

What kinds of decision points are there? Two main types of decisions change the flow of an algorithm. One decision point that appears often in algorithms is a "fork in the road," or a branch. Such decision points are called **binary decisions** because they can be answered in one of only two ways: yes (true) or no (false). For example, the answer to the question, "Did you work at most eight hours today?" (Is number of hours worked <= 8 hours?), shown in Figure 10.7, is a binary decision because the answer can be only "yes" or "no." The result of the decision determines which of the branch paths the algorithm follows. If the answer is yes, the program follows one sequence of steps; if the answer is no, it follows a different path.

A second decision point that often appears in algorithms is a repeating loop. In a **loop**, a question is asked and if the answer is yes, a set of actions is performed. Once the set of actions has been performed, the question is asked again (creating a loop). As long as the answer to the question is yes, the algorithm continues to loop around and repeat the same set of actions. When the answer to the question is no, the algorithm breaks free of the looping and moves on to the first step that follows the loop.

In our parking garage example, the algorithm would require a loop if you wanted to compute the total pay you earned in a full week of work rather than just in a single day. This is because for each day of the week, you would want to perform the same set of steps. Figure 10.8 shows how the idea of looping would be useful in this part of our parking garage program. On Monday, the program would set the Total Pay to $0.00. It would then perform the following set of steps:

1. Read the number of hours worked that day.
2. Determine whether you qualified for overtime pay.
3. Compute the pay earned that day.
4. Add that day's pay to the Total Pay for the week.

FIGURE 10.7

Decision points force the program to travel down one branch of the algorithm or another.

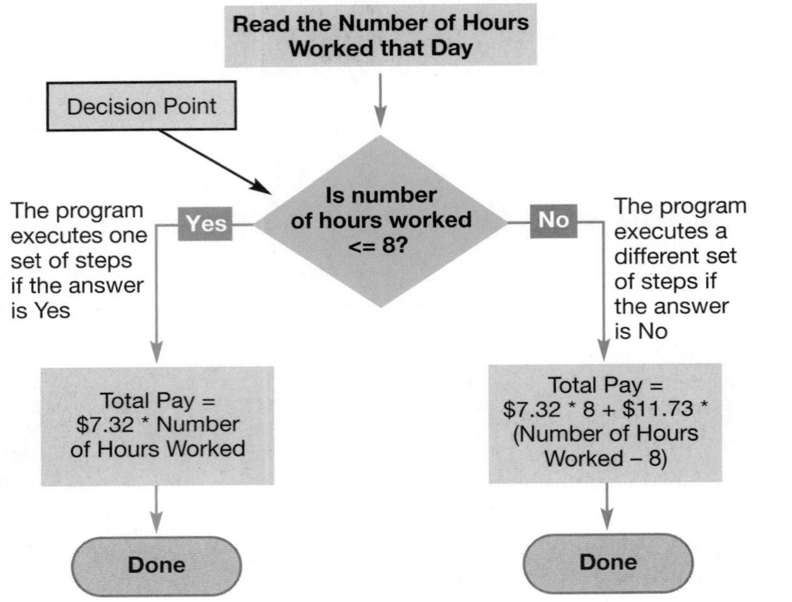

Read the Number of Hours Worked that Day

Decision Point

The program executes one set of steps if the answer is Yes

Yes

Is number of hours worked <= 8?

No

The program executes a different set of steps if the answer is No

Total Pay = $7.32 * Number of Hours Worked

Total Pay = $7.32 * 8 + $11.73 * (Number of Hours Worked − 8)

Done

Done

FIGURE 10.8

In this example of a loop, we stay in the loop until the test condition is no longer true. We then break free from the loop and move on to the next step in the algorithm outside of the loop.

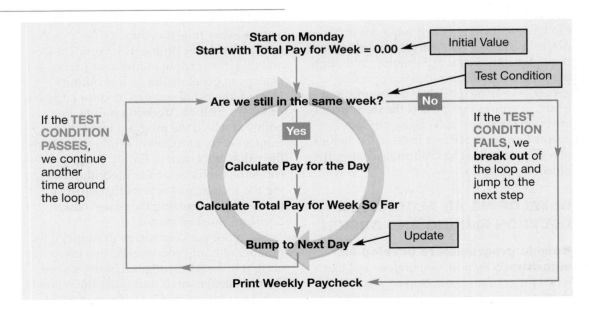

Start on Monday
Start with Total Pay for Week = 0.00   Initial Value

Test Condition

Are we still in the same week?   No

If the **TEST CONDITION PASSES**, we continue another time around the loop

Yes

Calculate Pay for the Day

Calculate Total Pay for Week So Far

Bump to Next Day   Update

If the **TEST CONDITION FAILS**, we **break out** of the loop and jump to the next step

Print Weekly Paycheck

On Tuesday, the algorithm would loop back, repeating the same sequence of steps it performed on Monday, adding the amount you earned on Tuesday to the Total Pay amount. The algorithm would continue to perform this loop for each day (seven times) until it hits Monday again. At that point the decision "Are we still in the same week?" becomes false. The program would stop and calculate the Total Pay for the entire week of work and print the weekly paycheck. As you can see, there are three important features to look for in a loop:

1. A beginning point, or **initial value**. In our example, the Total Pay for the week starts at an initial value of $0.00.

2. A set of actions that will be performed. In our example, the algorithm computes the daily pay each time it passes through the loop.

3. A check to see whether the loop is completed, or a **test condition**. In our example, the algorithm should run the loop seven times, no more and no less.

Note that almost every higher-level programming language supports both making binary yes/no decisions and handling repeating loops. **Control structures** is the general term used for keywords in a programming language that allow the programmer to control, or redirect, the flow of the program based on a decision.

How do programmers keep track of all these decision points and changes in flow in an algorithm? Programmers have several visual tools at their disposal to help them document the decision points and flow of their algorithm.

Flowcharts provide a visual representation of the patterns the algorithm comprises. Figure 10.9 presents an example of a flowchart used to depict the flow of an algorithm. As you can see, specific shape symbols indicate program behaviors and decision types. Diamonds indicate that a binary decision and branching action will be performed, and rectangles indicate a program instruction. Figure 10.10 lists additional flowcharting symbols and what they indicate.

Many software packages make it easy for programmers to create and modify flowcharts. Microsoft Visio is one popular flowcharting program.

Pseudocode is a text-based approach to documenting an algorithm. In pseudocode,

words describe the actions that the algorithm will take. Pseudocode is organized like an outline, with differing levels of indentation to indicate the flow of actions within the program. There is no standard set of vocabulary for pseudocode. Programmers use a combination of common words in their natural language, and the special words that are commands in the programming language they are using.

How do programmers create algorithms for specific tasks? As we've discussed, it's difficult for human beings to force their problem-solving skills into the highly structured, detailed algorithms that computing machines require. Therefore, several different methodologies have been developed to support programmers, including top-down design and object-oriented analysis.

TOP-DOWN DESIGN

What is top-down design? Top-down design is a systematic approach in which a problem is broken down into a series of high-level tasks. In top-down design,

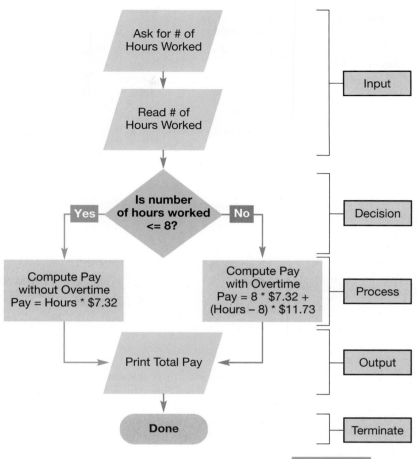

FIGURE 10.9

Programmers use flowcharts like this one to depict visually the flow of actions and decision points in their algorithms.

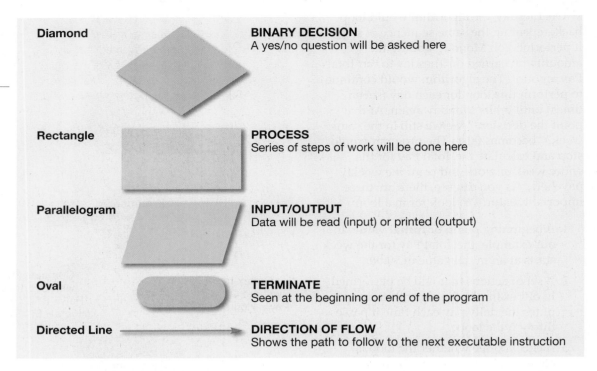

FIGURE 10.10

Standard Symbols Used in Flowcharts

Diamond

BINARY DECISION
A yes/no question will be asked here

Rectangle

PROCESS
Series of steps of work will be done here

Parallelogram

INPUT/OUTPUT
Data will be read (input) or printed (output)

Oval

TERMINATE
Seen at the beginning or end of the program

Directed Line

DIRECTION OF FLOW
Shows the path to follow to the next executable instruction

programmers apply the same strategy repeatedly, breaking down each task into successively more detailed subtasks. They continue until they have a sequence of steps that are close to the types of commands allowed by the programming language they will use for coding. (Previous coding experience helps programmers know the appropriate level of detail to specify in the algorithm generated by top-down design.)

How is top-down design used in programming? Let's consider our parking garage example again. Initially, top-down design would identify three high-level tasks: Get Input, Process Data, and Output Results (see Figure 10.11a).

Applying top-down design to the first operation, Get Input, we'd produce the more detailed sequence of steps shown in Figure 10.11b: Announce Program, Give Users Instructions, Read the Input NumberHoursWorkedToday. When we try to refine each of these steps, we find that they are at the level of commands that most programming languages support (that is, they tell the computer to print and read statements). So the operation Get Input has been converted to an algorithm.

Next we move to the second high-level task, Process Data, and break it into subtasks. In this case, we need to determine whether overtime hours were worked and compute the pay accordingly. We continue to apply top-down design on all tasks until we can no longer break tasks into subtasks as shown in Figure 10.11c.

FIGURE 10.11

(a) In this figure, top-down design is applied to the highest level of task in our parking garage example. (b) Here the tasks are further refined into subtasks. (c) Finally, the subtasks are refined into a sequence of instructions, or an algorithm.

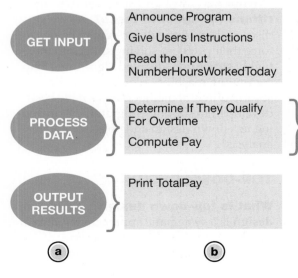

GET INPUT
Announce Program
Give Users Instructions
Read the Input NumberHoursWorkedToday

PROCESS DATA
Determine If They Qualify For Overtime
Compute Pay

```
if (NumberHoursWorkedToday <= 8)
   Pay = $7.32 * NumberHoursWorkedToday

else
   Pay = 7.32 * 8 +
         $11.73 * (NumberHoursWorkedToday – 8)
```

OUTPUT RESULTS
Print TotalPay

(a)   (b)   (c)

OBJECT-ORIENTED ANALYSIS

What is object-oriented analysis? A very different approach to generating an algorithm is object-oriented analysis. With **object-oriented analysis**, programmers first identify all of the categories of inputs that are part of the problem the program is trying to solve. These categories are called **classes**. For example, the classes in our parking garage example might include a TimeCard and an Employee.

Classes are further defined by information (**data**) and actions (**methods** or **behaviors**) associated with the class. For example, data for an Employee would include a Name, Address, and Social Security Number, whereas the methods for the Employee would be GoToWork(), LeaveWork(), or CollectPay(). Think of classes as nouns: persons, places, or things. Data describes classes, so it is characterized as an adjective, whereas methods are often characterized as verbs—the ways that the class acts and communicates with other classes. Figure 10.12 shows the data and methods the Employee class would contain.

In the object-oriented approach, programmers identify and define each class, as well as their data and methods. Programmers then determine how classes interact with each other. For example, when an Employee does GoToWork(), the Employee class must "talk" to the TimeCard class and punch in for the day, setting the StartTime on the TimeCard.

Programmers may need to create several different examples of a class. Each of these examples is an **object**. In Figure 10.12, John Doe, Jane Doe, and Bill McGillicutty are each Employee objects (specific examples of the Employee class). Each object from a given class is described by the same pieces of data and has the same methods; for example, John, Jane, and

Bill are all Employees and can use the GoToWork, LeaveWork, and CollectPay methods. However, because John and Jane have different pay grades (PayGrade 5 and 10, respectively), and because they all have different Social Security numbers, they are all unique objects.

Why would a developer select the object-oriented approach over top-down design? Object-oriented analysis forces programmers to think in general terms about their problem, which tends to lead to more general and reusable solutions. An important aspect of object-oriented design is that it leads to **reusability**. Because object-oriented design generates a family of classes for each project, programmers can easily reuse existing classes from other projects, enabling them to produce new code quickly.

To take advantage of reuse, programmers must study the relationships between objects. Hierarchies of objects can be built quickly in object-oriented languages using the mechanism of inheritance. **Inheritance** means that a new class can automatically pick up all of the data and methods of an existing class, and then extend and customize those to fit its own specific needs.

The original class is called the **base class**, and the new, modified class is called the **derived class**. You can compare this with

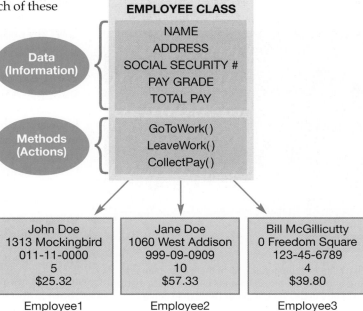

EMPLOYEE CLASS

Data (Information):
NAME
ADDRESS
SOCIAL SECURITY #
PAY GRADE
TOTAL PAY

Methods (Actions):
GoToWork( )
LeaveWork( )
CollectPay( )

Objects (Specific Employees):

John Doe 1313 Mockingbird 011-11-0000 5 $25.32	Jane Doe 1060 West Addison 999-09-0909 10 $57.33	Bill McGillicutty 0 Freedom Square 123-45-6789 4 $39.80
Employee1	Employee2	Employee3

FIGURE 10.12

The Employee class includes the information (data) and actions (methods or behaviors) that completely describe an Employee. It provides a blueprint for a programmer to build an Employee object. The objects are the actual employees, with real data.

making cookies. For example, you have a basic recipe for sugar cookies (base class: sugar cookies). However, in your family, some people like chocolate-flavored sugar cookies (derived class: chocolate cookies), and others like almond-flavored sugar cookies (derived class: almond cookies). All the cookies share the same attributes with the basic sugar cookie. But instead of creating two entirely new recipes—one for chocolate cookies and one for almond cookies—the two varieties inherit the basic sugar cookie (base class) recipe, and then the recipe is customized to make the chocolate- and almond-flavored sugar cookies (derived classes).

With the object-oriented approach, the majority of design time is spent in identifying the classes required to solve the problem, modeling them as data and methods, and thinking about what relationships they need to be able to have with each other. Constructing the algorithm becomes a process of enabling the objects to interact.

Coding: Speaking the Language of the Computer

Once programmers create an algorithm, they select the best programming language for the problem and then translate the algorithm into that language.

FIGURE 10.13

What's the best language? All of them offer humans more understandable commands and translate them into binary codes for computer CPUs to execute.

How is a person's idea translated into CPU instructions? Translating an algorithm into a **programming language** is the act of **coding**. As Figure 10.13 indicates, programming languages are (somewhat!) readable to humans but then are translated into patterns of 1s and 0s to be understood by the CPU. Figure 10.13 shows the pattern of bits in base 16, or hexadecimal.

Although programming languages free programmers from having to think in binary language (the 1s and 0s that computers understand), they force programmers to translate the ideas of the algorithm into a highly precise format. Programming languages are quite limited, allowing programmers to use only a few specific words while still demanding a consistent structure.

How exactly do programmers move from algorithm to code? Once programmers have an algorithm, either in the form of a flowchart or as a series of pseudocode statements, they scan the algorithm and identify the key pieces of information it uses to make decisions. What steps are required in the calculation of new information? What is the exact sequence of the steps? Are there points where decisions have to be made? What kinds of decisions are made? Are there places where the same steps are repeated several times? Identifying the required information and the flow of how it will be changed by each step of the algorithm leads the programmer to begin converting the algorithm into computer code in a specific programming language.

CATEGORIES OF PROGRAMMING LANGUAGES

What exactly is a programming language? A programming language is a kind of "code" for the set of instructions the CPU knows how to perform. Computer programming languages use special words and strict rules to enable programmers to control the CPU without having to know all of its hardware details.

What kinds of programming languages are there? Programming languages are classified in several major groupings, sometimes referred to as *generations*. With each generation in language development, programmers have been relieved of more of the burden of keeping track of what the hardware requires. The earliest

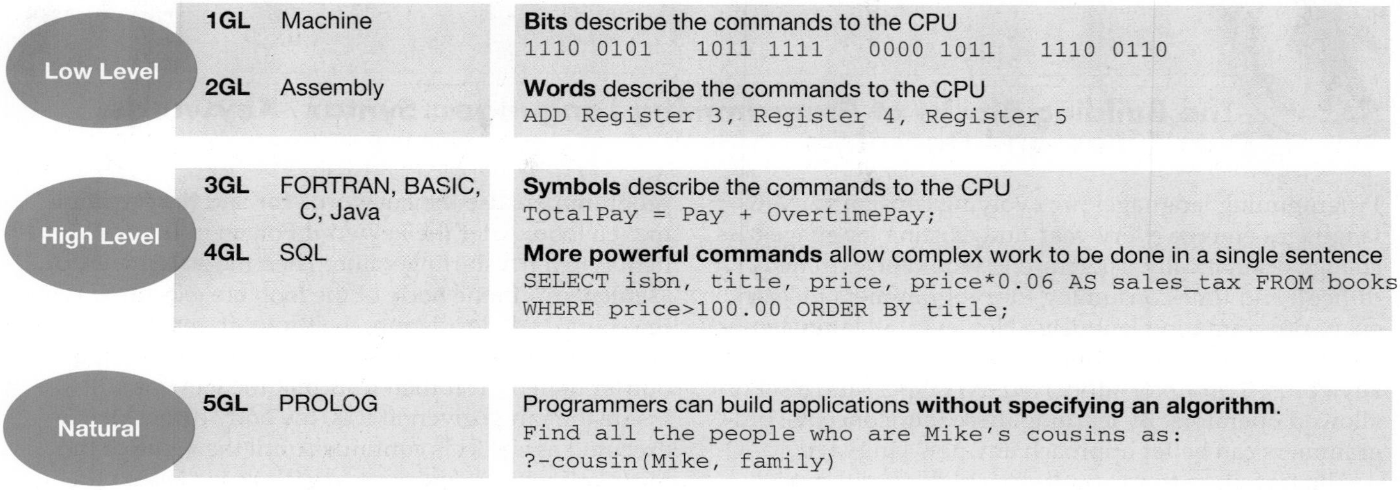

Low Level	**1GL** Machine	**Bits** describe the commands to the CPU `1110 0101    1011 1111    0000 1011    1110 0110`	
	2GL Assembly	**Words** describe the commands to the CPU `ADD Register 3, Register 4, Register 5`	
High Level	**3GL** FORTRAN, BASIC, C, Java	**Symbols** describe the commands to the CPU `TotalPay = Pay + OvertimePay;`	

	4GL SQL	**More powerful commands** allow complex work to be done in a single sentence
		`SELECT isbn, title, price, price*0.06 AS sales_tax FROM books`
		`WHERE price>100.00 ORDER BY title;`	

Natural	**5GL** PROLOG	Programmers can build applications **without specifying an algorithm.**
		`Find all the people who are Mike's cousins as:`
		`?-cousin(Mike, family)`	

languages, assembly language and machine languages, required the programmer to know a great deal about how the computer was constructed internally and how it stored data. Programming is becoming "easier" as languages continue to become more closely matched to how humans think about problems. Figure 10.14 shows small code samples of each generation of language.

How have modern programming languages evolved? First-generation languages (1GLs) are the actual **machine languages** of a CPU, the sequence of bits—1s and 0s—that the CPU understands. **Second-generation languages (2GLs)** are also known as **assembly languages**. Assembly languages allow programmers to write their programs using a set of short, English-like commands that speak directly to the CPU and give the programmer direct control of hardware resources. **Third-generation languages (3GLs)** use symbols and commands to help programmers tell the computer what to do, making 3GL languages easier to read and remember. Most programming languages today are considered third generation—BASIC, FORTRAN, COBOL, C/C++, and Java.

Many database query languages and report generators are **4GLs**, or **fourth-generation languages**. **Structured Query Language (SQL)** is a database programming language that is an example of a 4GL. The following single SQL command would check a huge table of data on the employees and build a new table showing all those employees who worked overtime:

```
SELECT * EMPLOYEES WHERE
"TotalHours" TOTAL MORE THAN 8
```

But programmers must always work from algorithms, correct? **Fifth-generation languages (5GLs)** are considered the most "natural" of languages. With 5GLs, problems are presented as a series of facts or constraints instead of as a specific algorithm. The system of facts can then be queried, or asked questions. PROLOG (PROgramming LOGic) is an example of a 5GL. A PROLOG program could be a list of family relationships and rules such as "Mike is Sally's brother. A brother and a sister have the same mother and father." After a huge collection of facts and rules has been collected, a user could ask for a list of all Mike's cousins, for example. PROLOG would find the answers by repeatedly applying the principles of logic instead of following a step-by-step algorithm that the programmer provided.

Do programmers have to use a higher-level programming language to solve a problem with a computer? No, experienced programmers sometimes write a program directly in the CPU's assembly language. However, the main advantage of higher-level programming languages—C or Java, for example—is that they allow programmers to think in terms of the problem they are solving rather than worrying about the internal design and specific instructions available for a given CPU. In addition, higher-level programming languages have the capability to produce a program easily that will run on both an Intel Pentium CPU and a Sun UltraSPARC T1 CPU. If programmers wrote directly in the assembly language for an Intel Pentium CPU, then they would have to rewrite the program completely if they wanted it to run on a Sun workstation with the UltraSPARC CPU. Thus, higher-level

FIGURE 10.14

Programming languages continually evolve toward more efficient and easier-to-use solutions.

The Building Blocks of Programming Languages: Syntax, Keywords, Data Types, and Operators

Programming languages are evolving constantly. New languages emerge every year, and existing languages change dramatically. Therefore, it would be extremely difficult and time consuming for programmers to learn every programming language. However, all languages have several common elements: rules of syntax, a set of keywords, a group of supported data types, and a set of allowed operators. By learning these four concepts, programmers can better approach any new language.

The transition from a well-designed algorithm to working code requires a clear understanding of the rules (syntax) of the programming language being used. **Syntax** is an agreed-upon set of rules defining how a language must be structured. The English language has a syntax; it defines which symbols are words (for example, "poodle" is a word but "oodlep" is not) and in what order words and symbols (such as ; and ,) are allowed.

Likewise, all programming languages have a formal syntax that programmers must follow when creating code **statements**, or sentences in a code. Syntax errors are violations of the strict, precise set of rules that define the language. Even misplacing a single comma or using a lowercase letter where a capital letter is required will generate a syntax error and make the program unusable.

Keywords are the set of specific words that have predefined meanings for a particular language. Keywords translate the flow of the algorithm into the structured code of the programming language. For example, when the algorithm indicates that a binary decision (decision point) must be made, the programmer translates that binary decision into the appropriate keyword or keywords from the language.

For example, in the programming language C++, the binary decision asking whether you worked enough hours to qualify for overtime pay would use the keywords **if else**. At this point in the code, the program can follow one of two paths: *if* you indicated through your input that you worked fewer than or equal to eight hours, it takes one path; if not (*else*), it follows another. Figure 10.15 shows the binary decision in the algorithm and the lines of C++ code for this decision using the *if else* keywords.

Loops are translated from algorithm to code by using the appropriate keyword from the language as well. For example, in the programming language Visual Basic,

programmers use the keywords **For** and **Next** to implement a loop. After the keyword For, an input or output item is given a starting value. Then the statements, or "sentences," in the body of the loop are executed. When the command Next is run, the program returns to the For statement and increments the value of the input or output item by 1. It then tests that the value is still inside the range given. If it is, the body of the loop is executed again. This continues until the value of the input or output item is outside the range listed. The loop is then ended, and the statement that follows the loop is run. If we think back to the parking garage example, the following lines of Visual Basic code loop to sum the total pay for the entire week. In this statement the starting value of the input item Day is 1, and the program loops until Day equals 7:

```
For Day = 1 to 7
  TotalPay = TotalPay + Pay;
Next Day
```

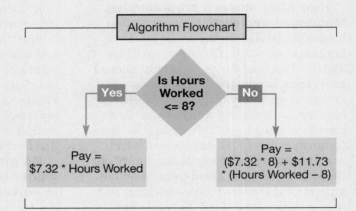

Algorithm Flowchart

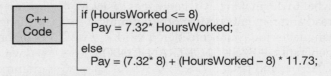

FIGURE 10.15

The binary decision in the algorithm has been converted into C++ code.

Often, a quick overview of a language's keywords can reveal the unique focus of that language. For example, the language C++ includes the keywords "public," "private," and "protected," which indicate that the language includes a mechanism for controlling security. Although people who are new to a language might not immediately understand how these keywords are used, examining the keywords of a language you are learning will often tell you what special features the language has and will help you ask important questions about it.

Each time programmers want to store data in their program, they must ask the operating system for storage space at a random access memory (RAM) location. **Data types** describe the *kind* of data that is being stored at the memory location. Each programming language has its own unique data types (although there is some degree of overlap among languages). For example, C++ includes data types that represent integers, real numbers, characters, and Boolean (true–false) values. These C++ data types show up in code statements as *int* for integer, *float* for real numbers, *char* for characters, and *bool* for Boolean values.

Because it takes more room to store a real number such as 18,743.23 than it does to store the integer 1, programmers use data types in their code to indicate to the operating system how much memory it needs to allocate. Programmers must be familiar with all of the data types available in the language so that they can assign the most appropriate data type for each input and output value so as not to waste memory space.

Operators are the coding symbols that represent the fundamental actions of the language. Each programming language has its own set of operators. Many languages include common algebraic operators such as +, −, *, / to represent the mathematical operations of addition, subtraction, multiplication, and division, respectively. Some languages, however, introduce new symbols as operators. The language A Programmer's Language (APL) was designed to solve multidimensional mathematical problems. APL includes unfamiliar operators such as rho, sigma, and iota, each representing a complex mathematical operation. Because it contains many unique operators, APL requires programmers to use a special keyboard (see Figure 10.16).

Programming languages sometimes include other unique operators. For example, the C++ operator && is used to tell the computer to read data from the keyboard or from a file. The C++ operator && is used to tell the computer to check whether two statements are both true. "Is your age greater than 20 AND less than 30?" is a question that requires the use of the && operator.

In the following C++ code, several operators are being used. The > operator checks whether the number of hours worked is greater than 0. The && operator checks that the number of hours worked is both positive AND less than or equal to 8 at the same time. If that happens, then the = operator sets the output Pay equal to the number of hours paid at $7.32 per hour:

```
if (Hours > 0 && Hours <= 8)
  Pay = Hours * 7.32;
```

Knowing operators such as these, as well as the other common elements described earlier, helps programmers learn new programming languages.

APL Keyboard

FIGURE 10.16

APL requires programmers to use a unique APL keyboard that includes the many specialized operators in the language.

programming languages offer **portability**—the capability to move a completed solution easily from one type of computer to another.

CREATING CODE: WRITING THE PROGRAM

What happens first when writing a program? All of the inputs a program receives and all of the outputs the program produces need to be stored in the computer's RAM while the program is running. Each input and each output item that the program manipulates, also known as **variables**, needs to be announced early in the program so that memory space can be set aside. A **variable declaration** tells the operating system that the program needs to allocate storage space in RAM. The following line of code is a variable declaration:

```
int Day;
```

This variable's name is Day. The "int" that precedes the Day variable indicates that this variable will always be an integer, a whole number such as 15 or –4. This statement asks for enough RAM storage space to hold an integer. After the RAM space is found, it is reserved. As long as the program is running, these RAM cells will be saved for the Day variable; no other program can use that memory until the program ends. From that point on, when the program encounters the symbol Day, it will access the memory it reserved as Day and find the integer stored there.

The following line of C++ code asks that a real number (represented by the keyword "float") be stored in RAM:

```
float TotalPay;
```

This line asks the operating system to find enough storage space for one real number.

Can programmers leave notes to themselves inside a program? Programmers often insert **comments** (or **remarks**) into program code to explain the purpose of sections of code, to indicate the date they wrote the program, and to include other important information about the code so that fellow programmers can more easily understand and update it should the original programmer no longer be available. Comments are written into the code in plain English. The *compiler*, a program that translates codes into binary 1s and 0s, just ignores comments. Comments are intended to be read only by human programmers. Languages provide a special symbol or keyword to indicate the beginning of a comment. In C++, the symbol // at the beginning of a line indicates that the rest of the line is a comment. In Visual Basic, a single apostrophe or the keyword "REM," short for "REMark," does the same thing.

What would completed code for a program look like? Figure 10.17 presents a completed C++ program for our example parking garage problem. Each statement in a program is executed sequentially (that is, in order from the first statement to the last) unless the program encounters a keyword that changes the flow. In the figure, the program begins (step 1) by declaring the variables needed to store the program's inputs and outputs in RAM. Next, the "for" keyword begins a looping pattern (step 2). All of the steps between the very first bracket { and the last bracket } (indicated by a blue bracket for better identification) will be repeated seven times to gather the total pay for each day of the week.

The next section (step 3) collects the input data from the user. The program then (step 4) checks that the user entered a reasonable value (in this case, a positive

BITS AND BYTES

Some Software with That Lego?

Programming lessons can begin at an early age. The LEGO Group conducts a programming competition each year using its MindStorms series of LEGO kits. These kits include gears, wheels, several motors, and a motorized programmable LEGO "brick" that contains a microprocessor. Sensors feed the robots; you build the sounds and visual stimuli around them. Teams then use ROBOLAB software to develop programs and send them to the brick's microprocessor. You can try out this software in a small demo housed at **www.robolabonline.com**. The unit can be told to turn the motor on or off, switch the direction of a wheel's rotation, or turn on sensors to measure temperature or light levels. The ROBOLAB software even allows beginning programmers to drag and drop elements such as "if" statements and loops. Together with an understanding of motors and a talent for logical thinking, teams design robots that can travel through mazes, cross bridges, and deliver packages—whatever tasks the LEGO Group has come up with for that year's tournament! For more information, see **www.firstlegoleague.org**.

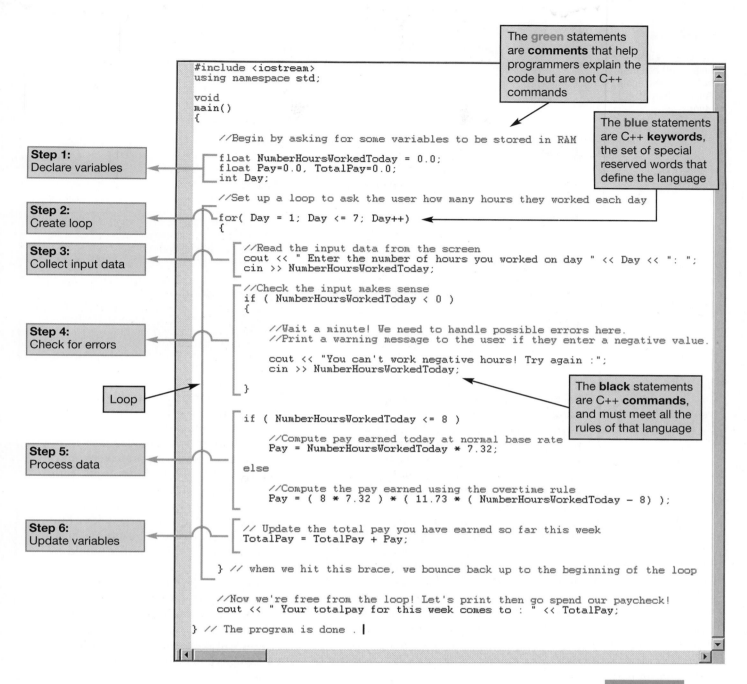

The **green** statements are **comments** that help programmers explain the code but are not C++ commands

The **blue** statements are C++ **keywords**, the set of special reserved words that define the language

The **black** statements are C++ **commands**, and must meet all the rules of that language

Step 1:
Declare variables

Step 2:
Create loop

Step 3:
Collect input data

Step 4:
Check for errors

Loop

Step 5:
Process data

Step 6:
Update variables

```cpp
#include <iostream>
using namespace std;

void
main()
{

    //Begin by asking for some variables to be stored in RAM

    float NumberHoursWorkedToday = 0.0;
    float Pay=0.0, TotalPay=0.0;
    int Day;

    //Set up a loop to ask the user how many hours they worked each day

    for( Day = 1; Day <= 7; Day++)
    {

        //Read the input data from the screen
        cout << " Enter the number of hours you worked on day " << Day << ": ";
        cin >> NumberHoursWorkedToday;

        //Check the input makes sense
        if ( NumberHoursWorkedToday < 0 )
        {

            //Wait a minute! We need to handle possible errors here.
            //Print a warning message to the user if they enter a negative value.

            cout << "You can't work negative hours! Try again :";
            cin >> NumberHoursWorkedToday;

        }

        if ( NumberHoursWorkedToday <= 8 )

            //Compute pay earned today at normal base rate
            Pay = NumberHoursWorkedToday * 7.32;

        else

            //Compute the pay earned using the overtime rule
            Pay = ( 8 * 7.32 ) * ( 11.73 * ( NumberHoursWorkedToday - 8) );

        // Update the total pay you have earned so far this week
        TotalPay = TotalPay + Pay;

    } // when we hit this brace, we bounce back up to the beginning of the loop

    //Now we're free from the loop! Let's print then go spend our paycheck!
    cout << " Your totalpay for this week comes to : " << TotalPay;

} // The program is done . |
```

number for hours worked) and, if needed, reads another input value. Now (step 5) the program processes the data. If the user worked eight hours or less, he or she is paid at the rate of $7.32, whereas hours exceeding eight are paid at $11.73.

The final statement (step 6) updates the value of the TotalPay variable. The last bracket } indicates that the program has reached the end of a loop. The program will repeat the loop to collect and process the information for the next day. When the seventh day of data has been processed, the Day variable will be bumped up to the next

value, 8. The program then fails the test (Day <= 7?). At that point, the program exits the loop, prints the results, and quits.

Are there ways in which programmers can make their code more useful for the future? One aspect of converting an algorithm into good code is the programmer's ability to design general code that can adapt easily to new settings. Sections of code that will be used repeatedly, with only slight modification, can be packaged into reusable "containers" or components. These reusable components, depending on the language, are referred to as

FIGURE 10.17

A complete C++ program that solves the parking garage pay problem.

FIGURE 10.18

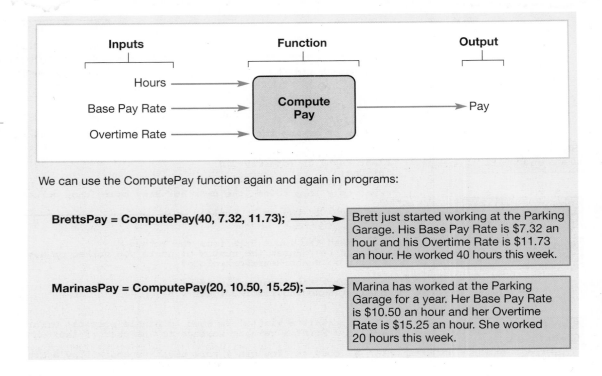

We can use the ComputePay function again and again in programs:

BrettsPay = ComputePay(40, 7.32, 11.73); ⟶ Brett just started working at the Parking Garage. His Base Pay Rate is $7.32 an hour and his Overtime Rate is $11.73 an hour. He worked 40 hours this week.

MarinasPay = ComputePay(20, 10.50, 15.25); ⟶ Marina has worked at the Parking Garage for a year. Her Base Pay Rate is $10.50 an hour and her Overtime Rate is $15.25 an hour. She worked 20 hours this week.

functions, procedures, subroutines, modules, or *packages.*

In our program, we could create a function that implements the overtime pay rule. As it stands in Figure 10.17, the code works only in situations where the hourly pay is exactly $7.32 and the bonus pay is exactly $11.73. However, if we rewrote this part of the processing rules as a function, we could have code that would work for any base pay rate and any overtime rate. If the base pay rate or overtime rate changed, the function would use whichever values it was given as input to compute the output pay variable. Such a function, as shown in Figure 10.18, could be reused in many settings without changing any of the code.

COMPILATION

How does a programmer move from code in a programming language to the 1s and 0s the CPU can understand? Compilation is the process by which code is converted into machine language—the language the CPU can understand. The **compiler** is the program that understands both the syntax of the programming language and the exact structure of the CPU and its machine language. It can "read" the **source code**—the instructions programmers have written in the higher-level language—and

translate the source code directly into machine language—the binary patterns that will execute commands on the CPU.

Each programming language has its own compiler. In addition, separate versions of the compiler are required to compile code that will run on each different type of processor. One version of the compiler would create finished programs for a Sun UltraSPARC processor, for example, and another version of the compiler would create programs for an Intel Pentium CPU.

At this stage, programmers finally have produced an **executable program**, the binary sequence that instructs the CPU to run their code. Executable programs cannot be read by human eyes because they are pure binary codes. They are stored as *.exe or *.com files on Windows systems.

Does every programming language have a compiler? Some programming languages do not have a compiler but use an interpreter instead. An **interpreter** translates the source code into an intermediate form, line by line. Each line is then executed as it is translated. The compilation process takes longer than the interpretation process because, in compilation, all of the lines of source code are translated into machine language before any lines are executed. However, the finished compiled program runs faster than an interpreted program because the interpreter is constantly translating and executing as it goes.

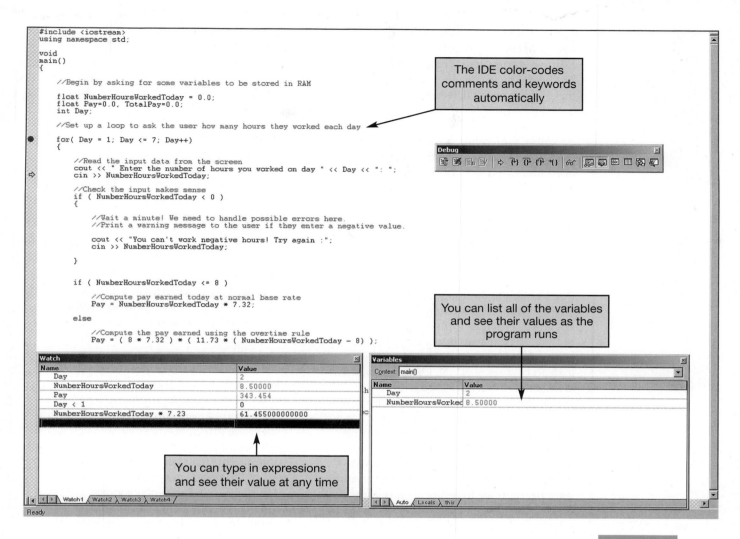

```
#include <iostream>
using namespace std;

void
main()
{

    //Begin by asking for some variables to be stored in RAM

    float NumberHoursWorkedToday = 0.0;
    float Pay=0.0, TotalPay=0.0;
    int Day;

    //Set up a loop to ask the user how many hours they worked each day

    for( Day = 1; Day <= 7; Day++)
    {

        //Read the input data from the screen
        cout << " Enter the number of hours you worked on day " << Day << ": ";
        cin >> NumberHoursWorkedToday;

        //Check the input makes sense
        if ( NumberHoursWorkedToday < 0 )
        {

            //Wait a minute! We need to handle possible errors here.
            //Print a warning message to the user if they enter a negative value.

            cout << "You can't work negative hours! Try again :";
            cin >> NumberHoursWorkedToday;

        }


        if ( NumberHoursWorkedToday <= 8 )

            //Compute pay earned today at normal base rate
            Pay = NumberHoursWorkedToday * 7.32;

        else

            //Compute the pay earned using the overtime rule
            Pay = ( 8 * 7.32 ) * ( 11.73 * ( NumberHoursWorkedToday - 8) );
```

The IDE color-codes comments and keywords automatically

Debug

You can list all of the variables and see their values as the program runs

Watch

Name	Value
Day	2
NumberHoursWorkedToday	8.50000
Pay	343.454
Day < 1	0
NumberHoursWorkedToday * 7.23	61.455000000000

Watch1 / Watch2 / Watch3 / Watch4 /
Ready

You can type in expressions and see their value at any time

Variables

Context: main()

Name	Value
Day	2
NumberHoursWorked	8.50000

Auto / Locals / this /

FIGURE 10.19

The IDE for Microsoft Visual C++ helps when the programmer is entering the code and when logical errors are found.

If producing the fastest executable program is important, then programmers will choose a language that uses a compiler instead of an interpreter. For developmental environments in which a lot of changes are still being made to the code, interpreters have an advantage: Programmers do not have to wait for the entire program to be recompiled each time they make a change. With interpreters, programmers can immediately see the results of their program changes as they are making them.

CODING TOOLS: INTEGRATED DEVELOPMENT ENVIRONMENTS

Are there any tools that make the coding process easier? Modern programming is supported by a collection of tools that make the writing and testing of software easier. Compiler products feature an **integrated development environment (IDE)**, a developmental tool that helps

programmers write, compile, and test their programs. As is the case with compilers, every language has its own specific IDE. Figure 10.19 shows the IDE for Microsoft Visual Studio using C++.

How does an IDE help programmers when they are typing the code? The IDE includes tools that support programmers at every step of the coding process. **Code editing** is the step in which programmers actually type the code into the computer. IDEs include an **editor**, a special tool that helps programmers as they enter the code, highlighting keywords and alerting them to typos. Modern IDE editors also automatically indent the code correctly, aligning sections of code appropriately, and color code comments to remind programmers that these lines will not be executed as code. In addition, IDEs provide help files that document and provide examples of the proper use of keywords and operators.

SOUND BYTE

Looping Around the IDE

In this Sound Byte, you'll work in the Microsoft Visual Studio integrated development environment (IDE) with the C++ programming language and examine how the basic control structures of programming languages do their work.

How does the IDE help programmers after code editing is finished?
Editing is complete when the entire program has been keyed into the editor. At that time, the programmer clicks a button in the IDE, and the compilation process begins. A pop-up window shows the compilation progress, which line is currently being compiled, how many syntax errors have been identified, and how many warnings have been generated. A warning is a suggestion from the compiler that the code might not work in the way the programmer intended, although there is no formal syntax error on the line.

As mentioned earlier, **syntax errors** are violations of the strict, precise set of rules that define the language. Programmers create syntax errors when they misspell keywords (such as typing BEEGIN instead of BEGIN) or use an operator (such as +) incorrectly (such as typing x = y ++ 2 instead of x = y + 2). Once compilation is finished, the IDE presents all of the syntax errors in one list. The programmer can then click any item in the list to see a detailed explanation of the type of error. When the programmer double-clicks an item in the list, the editor jumps to the line of code that contains the error, enabling the programmer to repair syntax errors quickly.

Debugging: Getting Rid of Errors

Once the program compiles without syntax errors, it has met all of the syntax rules of the language. However, this doesn't mean that the program behaves in a logical way or that it appropriately addresses the task the algorithm described. If programmers made errors in the strategy used in the algorithm or in how they translated the algorithm to code, then problems will occur. The process of running the program over and over to find errors and to make sure the program behaves in the way it should is termed **debugging** (see Figure 10.20).

How do programmers know whether there is anything wrong with their program? At this point in the process, the testing plan that was documented as part of the problem statement becomes critically important to programmers. As you'll recall from earlier in the chapter, the testing plan clearly lists input and output values, showing how the users expect the program to behave in each input situation. It is important that the testing plan contains enough specific examples that every part of the program is tested.

In the parking garage problem, we want to make sure the program calculates the correct pay for a day when you worked fewer than or equal to eight hours and a day when you worked more than eight hours. Each of these input values forces the program to make different decisions in its

FIGURE 10.20

Debugging is the process of using logic combined with an understanding of the problem to be solved to correct errors in a program.

processing path, the sequence of steps that turns inputs into outputs. To be certain the program works as intended, programmers try every possible path.

For example, once we can successfully compile the example code for the parking garage problem, we can begin to use our testing plan. The testing plan indicates that an input of 3 for NumberHours WorkedToday must produce an output of Pay = 3 * $7.32 = $21.96. In testing, we run the program and make sure that an input value of 3 yields an output value of $21.96. To check that the processing path involving overtime is correct, we input a value of 12 hours. That input must produce Pay = 8 * $7.32 + (12 − 8) * $11.73 = $105.48.

A complete testing plan includes sample inputs that exercise all of the error handling required as well as all of the processing paths. Therefore, we would also want to check how the program behaves when NumberHoursWorkedToday is entered as -2.

If the testing plan reveals errors, then why does the program compile? The compiler is itself a program. It cannot think through code or decide whether what the programmer wrote is logical. The compiler only can make sure that the specific rules of the language are followed, that all of the keywords are spelled correctly, and that the operators being used are meaningful to that language.

For example, if in the parking garage problem we happened to type the if statement as:

```
if (NumberHoursWorkedToday > 88)
   //Use the Overtime Pay rule
```

instead of

```
if (NumberHoursWorkedToday > 8)
   //Use the Overtime Pay rule
```

the compiler would not see a problem. It doesn't seem strange to the compiler that you only get overtime after working 88 hours a day. These **logical errors** in the problem are caught only when the program executes. Another kind of error caught when the program executes is a **runtime error**. For example, it is easy for programmers to accidentally write code for a loop that loops one time too many or one time too few. This can lead to a problem such as dividing a number by zero, a big "no-no" mathematically! That kind of forbidden operation leads to a runtime error message.

Are there tools that help programmers find logic errors? Most IDEs include a tool called a **debugger** that helps programmers dissect a program as it runs. The debugger pauses the program as it is running and allows programmers to examine the values of all the variables. The programmers can then run the program in slow motion, moving it forward just one line at a time. Stepping through the program enables programmers to see exactly the sequence of steps being executed and the outcome of each calculation. They can then isolate the exact place in which a logical error occurs, correct the error, and recompile the program.

Finishing the Project: Testing and Documentation

Once debugging has detected all of the runtime errors in the code, it is time for users to test the program. This process is called *internal testing*. In internal testing, a group within the software company uses the program in every way it can imagine—both as it was intended to be used and in ways only new users may think up. The internal testing group makes sure the program behaves as described in the original testing plan. Any differences in how the program responds are reported back to the programming team, which makes the final revisions and updates to the code.

The next round of testing is external testing. In this testing round, the people who eventually will purchase and use the software must work with it to determine whether it matches their original vision.

ACTIVE HELPDESK

Understanding Software Programming

In this Active Helpdesk call, you'll play the role of a helpdesk staffer, fielding calls about the life cycle of a program, the role a problem statement plays in programming, how programmers create algorithms and move from algorithm to code to the 1s and 0s the CPU can understand, and the steps involved in completing the program.

BITS AND BYTES

Many Languages on Display

At the site **www.99-bottles-of-beer.net**, you can find a simple program that displays the lyrics to the song *99 Bottles of Beer on the Wall*. If you have ever sat through round after round of this song on a long school bus trip, you know how repetitive it is. That means the code to write this song can take advantage of looping statements. This site presents the program in more than 1,000 different languages. Take a tour and see how much variety there is in programming!

What other testing does the code undergo? Before its final commercial release, software is often provided at a reduced cost or no cost in a **beta version** to certain test sites or to interested users. By providing users with a beta version of software, programmers can collect information about the remaining errors in the code and make a final round of revisions before officially releasing the program.

What happens if problems are found after beta testing? Users often discover problems in a program after its commercial release. These problems are addressed with the publication of **software updates** or **service packs**. Users can download these software modules to repair errors identified in the program code. For example, the Windows XP operating system had a major revision released as Service Pack 2 that added many new security features and updates.

After testing, is the project finished? Once testing is completed but before the product is officially released, the work of **documentation** still exists. At this point, technical writers are responsible for creating internal documentation for the program, including describing the development and technical details, how the code works, and how the user interacts with the program. In addition, the technical publishing department produces all of the necessary user manuals that will be distributed to the program users. User training begins once the software is distributed. Software trainers work as instructors who take the software to the user community and teach others how to use it efficiently.

Programming Languages: Many Languages for Many Projects

In any programming endeavor, programmers want to create a solution that meets several competing objectives. They want the software to run quickly and reliably and to be simple to expand later when the demands on the system change. They also want it to be completed on time, for minimal cost, and to use the smallest amount of system resources possible.

Because it will always be difficult to balance these conflicting goals, a wide variety of programming languages has been developed. Earlier in the chapter, you learned about the five main categories (generations) of programming languages. In this section, we discuss the specific programming languages that are members of these different generations. Although programming languages often share many common characteristics, each language has specific traits that allow it to be the best fit for certain types of projects. Figure 10.21 hints at the fact that sometimes a language builds a loyal following, and that pushes a programmer to apply the same language to every situation.

The ability to understand enough about each language to match it to the appropriate style of problem is an exceptionally powerful skill for programmers.

What languages are popular today? There are far too many languages for one person to become expert at them all, but understanding the range of languages and how they relate to one another is especially useful. One quick way to determine which languages are popular is to examine job postings for programmers. At the moment, languages most in demand include C/C++, Java, and knowledge of Active Server Pages (ASP). In specific industries, certain languages tend to dominate the work. In the banking and insurance industries,

FIGURE 10.21

When attacking a problem, you can choose from many different programming languages. Sometimes, though, people become attached to one language in an almost "religious" way!

for example, the programming language COBOL is still common, although most other industries typically no longer use it.

How do I know which language to study first? A good introductory programming course will emphasize many skills and techniques that will carry over from one language to another. You should find a course that includes an emphasis on design, algorithm development, debugging techniques, and project management. All of these aspects of programming will help you in any language environment. **Pascal** is the only modern language that was specifically designed as a teaching language, but it is no longer often taught at the college level. Many colleges and universities have opted to have students begin with Java or C++.

How does anyone learn so many languages? Professional programmers can work in a great number of different languages. They become proficient at learning new languages because they have become familiar with the basic components, discussed in this chapter's Dig Deeper, that are common to all languages: syntax, keywords, operators, and data types. The Bits and Bytes piece "Many Languages on Display" on page 509 directs you to a site that displays an old song in more than 1,000 different languages.

SELECTING THE RIGHT LANGUAGE

How do programmers know which language to select for a specific project? A programming team considers several factors before selecting the language it will use for a specific project:

- **Space available:** Not all languages take up the same amount of space. Therefore, the target language should be well matched to the amount of space available for the final program. For example, if the program will be embedded in a chip for use in a toaster, then it is important for the language to be space efficient.
- **Speed required:** Similarly, some projects require a focus on speed rather than size. Some languages can execute faster than others. Therefore, some projects require the selection of a language that can produce code that executes in the fastest possible time. Although poorly written code executes inefficiently in any

language, it is still true that some languages produce faster code than others.

- **Organizational resources available:** Other considerations for managers are the resources available in their group. Selecting a language that is easy to use and easy to maintain if there is a turnover in programmers is an important consideration. Managers also may factor in the existing pool of talent available for the project. Having to train five programmers in a new language to tackle a project would have significant disadvantages over allowing them to work in a familiar language.
- **Type of target application:** Certain languages are customized to support a specific environment (UNIX or Windows, for instance). Knowing which languages are most commonly used for which environments can be a helpful guide.

WINDOWS APPLICATIONS

What languages do programmers use if they want to build a Windows application? Software programs that run under the Windows OS are extremely popular. These programs often have a number of common features—scroll bars, title bars, text boxes, buttons, and expanding or collapsing menus, to name a few. Several languages include customized controls that enable programmers to easily include these features in their programs. Although Figure 10.22 pokes

FIGURE 10.22

This poster mocks the image of a harsh, difficult road to learning programming. Modern tools allow it to be much more fun and simple.

PROGRAMMING
YOU'RE DOING IT COMPLETELY WRONG

fun at some stereotypic ideas of learning programming, the experience has become much more manageable in recent years.

Can I just point and click to create a Windows application? In languages that support Windows programming, programmers can simply use the mouse to lay out on the screen where the scroll bars and buttons will be in the application. The code needed to explain this to the computer is then written automatically when the programmer says the layout is complete. This is referred to as **visual programming**, and it helps programmers produce a final application much more quickly. In this section we'll discuss a few languages that are used to develop Windows applications and that take advantage of visual programming.

Visual Basic

What if programmers want to have a model of their program before it's fully developed? Earlier in the chapter, you read about how information systems are developed through the SDLC. Although the SDLC has been around for quite some time, it doesn't necessarily work for all environments and instances. Programmers often like to build a **prototype**, or small model, of their program at the beginning of a large project.

Although the entire project won't be finished for several months, it can be useful to have a simple shell or skeleton of what the final program will look like to help with design. Prototyping is a form of **rapid application development (RAD)**, which is an alternative to the waterfall approach of systems development described at the beginning of the chapter. Instead of developing detailed system documents before the production of the system, developers create a prototype first, and they generate system documents as they use and remodel the product.

Prototypes for Windows applications are often coded in **Microsoft Visual Basic (VB)**, which is a powerful programming language used to build a wide range of Windows applications. The strengths of VB include a simple, quick interface that is easy for a programmer to learn and use. It has grown from its roots in the language BASIC (short for Beginner's All-purpose Symbolic Instruction Code) to become a sophisticated and full-featured object-oriented language. It is often used in the creation of graphical user interfaces for Windows.

Visual Basic 2008 is the current version of Visual Basic and is designed for building object-oriented applications for Windows, the Web, and mobile devices. Visual Basic 2008 provides a multitude of new or improved features over the previous version. These changes make development with Visual Basic easier and more powerful than any earlier version. Visual Basic 2008 and the .NET Framework are both part of Visual Studio 2008, which provides a complete set of developer tools.

How does the Microsoft .NET Framework help programmers? The .NET Framework is a software development environment designed to enable Web sites to talk to each other easily. Too often, computer systems cannot exchange information. It might be because they have different operating systems or because they use different rules for packaging data. The .NET Framework introduces a standard way for software to interact through Web services. **Web services** are programs that a Web site uses to make information available to other Web sites. For example, your Web site could use the Google Web service to search for information or to check the spelling of a word. The Google Web service returns the requested information to your program in a standard package that you then decode. Instead of a human being submitting a search to Google and reading over the results, programs can now do that themselves.

The power of .NET and Web services will continue to grow as more companies make some or all of their data available this way. The VB.NET programming tool has many supports for the programmer who is interested in using Web services.

C and C++

What languages do programmers use if the problem requires a lot of "number crunching"? A Windows application that demands raw processing power because there are difficult repetitive numerical calculations is most often a candidate for C/C++. For example, applications that simulate human cells and drug interactions have to solve elaborate mathematical equations many thousands of times each second. All of that mathematical work makes the program a good candidate for C/C++. Several companies sell C/C++ compilers equipped with a design environment that makes Windows programming as visual as with VB.

ACTIVE HELPDESK

Selecting the Right Programming Language

In this Active Helpdesk call, you'll play the role of a helpdesk staffer, fielding calls about how programmers select the right programming language for a specific task and what the most popular Windows and Web applications are.

Why was the C language developed? As the predecessor of C++, C was originally developed for system programmers. It was defined by Brian Kernighan and Dennis Ritchie of AT&T Bell Laboratories in 1978 as a language that would make accessing the operating system easier. It provides higher-level programming language features (such as *if* statements and *for* loops) but still allows programmers to manipulate the system memory and CPU registers directly. This mix of high- and low-level access makes C highly attractive to "power" programmers. Most modern operating systems (Windows Vista, Mac OS X, and Linux) have been written in C.

C++ (pronounced "sea plus plus") takes C to the next level. Bjarne Stroustrup, the developer of C++, used all of the same symbols and keywords as C, but he extended the language with additional keywords, better security, and more support for the reuse of existing code through object-oriented design.

Are C and C++ natural choices when I'm looking to learn my first language? Neither C nor C++ was intended as a teaching language. The notation and compactness of the languages make them relatively difficult to master. They are in demand in industry, however, because C/C++ can produce fast-running code that uses a small amount of memory. Programmers often choose to learn C/C++ because their basic components (operators, data types, and keywords) are common to many other languages.

Java

What language do programmers use for applications that need to collect information from networked computers? Say a program that an insurance company runs each night needs to communicate with networked computers in many offices around the country, collect the policy changes and updates from that day's business, and update the company's main records. The programming team writing this program would want to use a language that already provides support for network communications.

Java would be a good choice. James Gosling of Sun Microsystems introduced Java in the early 1990s. It quickly became popular because its object-oriented model enables Java programmers to benefit from its large set of existing classes. For example, a Java programmer could begin to use the existing

BITS AND BYTES

Really Want to Learn? Work for Free!

The open source software movement is a grassroots collection of developers who believe that software projects can be managed start to finish by groups of individuals instead of companies. Open source software is developed and maintained at no charge by groups of people who are brought together by common interests such as editing photographs. When completed, the software product and its source code are distributed free of charge.

The development, testing, and maintenance of the open source code are managed through resources such as SourceForge (**http://sourceforge.net**), a development Web site that hosts more than 100,000 programs. To support development of open source projects, SourceForge provides services to its more than 1 million users in support of their development of projects. For example, version control tools allow specific versions of a project to be checked in or out, as in a library, allowing many people to work on the project at the same time. Also provided are communication tools and publicity tools to help the project succeed in reaching its audience.

Most types of software in the marketplace have an open source equivalent. (See the Technology in Focus section called "Computing Alternatives" on page 258 for more information.) So if you are looking to learn about developing software by doing it, investigate SourceForge and volunteer for a project!

"network connection" class with little attention to the details of how that code itself was implemented. Classes exist for many graphical objects, such as windows and scroll bars, and network objects, such as a connection to a remote machine. Microsoft has since released a language named C# (pronounced "sea sharp") that competes with Java.

Can a Java application work on any type of computer? An attractive feature of Java is that it is architecture neutral. This means that Java code needs to be compiled only once, and it can run on many CPUs (see Figure 10.23). The Java program does not care which CPU, operating system, or user interface is running on the machine where it lands. This is possible because the target computer runs a Java Virtual Machine (VM), software that can explain to the Java program how to function on any specific system. A Java VM installed with Microsoft Internet Explorer, for example, allows Internet Explorer to execute any **Java applet** (a small Java-based program) it encounters on the Internet. Although Java code does not perform as fast as C++, the advantage of needing to compile only once before it can

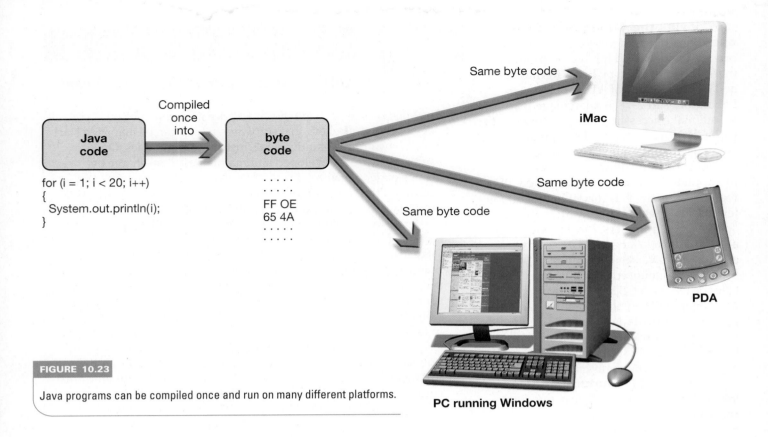

FIGURE 10.23

Java programs can be compiled once and run on many different platforms.

be distributed to any system is extremely important.

WEB APPLICATIONS: HTML/XHTML AND BEYOND

What is the most basic language for developing Web applications? A document that will be presented on the Web must be written using special symbols called *tags* that control how a Web browser will display the text, images, and other content tagged in the **HyperText Markup Language (HTML)** or **eXtensible HyperText Markup Language (XHTML)**. Although knowledge of HTML/XHTML is required to program for the Web, they are not in themselves programming languages. HTML/XHTML is just a series of tags that modify the display of text. HTML was the original standard defining these tags. XHTML is a newer standard that corrects some of the problems of inconsistency found in HTML. To see more detail of XHTML tags, flip to page 637 of Chapter 13.

Many good HTML/XHTML tutorials are available on the Web at sites such as **www.learnthenet.com**, **www.webmonkey.com**, and **www.w3c.org**. These sites include lists of the major HTML/XHTML tags that can be used to create HTML/XHTML documents.

Are there tools that help programmers write in HTML/XHTML? Several different programs are available to assist in the generation of HTML/XHTML. Adobe Dreamweaver CS3 and Microsoft Expression Web present Web page designers with an interface that is similar to a word-processing program. Web designers can place text, images, and hyperlinks freely, and the corresponding HTML/XHTML tags are inserted automatically, as shown in Figure 10.24. For simple, static (nonchanging) Web pages, no programming is required.

Scripting Languages for the Web

Which programming languages do programmers use to make complex Web pages? To make their Web pages more visually appealing and interactive, programmers use scripting languages to add more power and flexibility to their HTML code. **Scripting languages** are simple programming languages that are limited to performing a specific set of specialized tasks. Scripts allow decisions to be made and calculations to be performed. Several popular scripting languages work well with

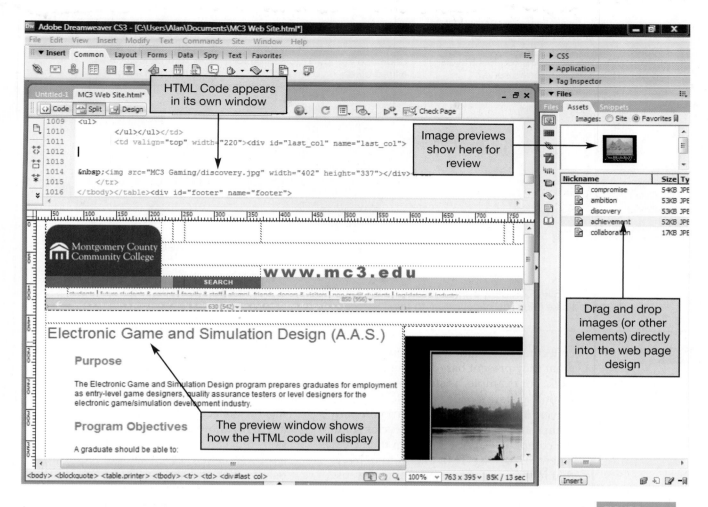

HTML Code appears in its own window

Image previews show here for review

Drag and drop images (or other elements) directly into the web page design

The preview window shows how the HTML code will display

HTML, including JavaScript, VBScript, and PHP (Hypertext Preprocessor).

JavaScript is a scripting language that is often used to add interactivity to Web pages. JavaScript is not as fully featured as Java, but its syntax, keywords, data types, and operators are a subset of Java's. In addition, JavaScript has a set of classes that represent the objects often used on Web pages: buttons, check boxes, and drop-down lists.

The JavaScript button class, for example, describes a button with a name and a type (whether it is a regular button or a Submit or Reset button). The language includes behaviors—such as click ()—and can respond to user actions. For example, when a user moves his or her mouse over a button and clicks to select it, the button "knows" the user is there and jumps in and performs a special action (such as playing a sound).

Are there other scripting languages besides JavaScript? Programmers who are more familiar with Visual Basic than Java or C++ often use **VBScript**, a subset of Visual Basic, to introduce dynamic decision making into Web pages. **Dynamic decision making** means that the page can decide how to display itself based on the choices the reader makes. PHP is another scripting language that has become extremely popular.

ASP, JSP, and PHP

How are interactive Web pages built? To build Web sites with interactive capabilities, programmers use **Active Server Pages (ASP)**, **Java Server Pages (JSP)**, or the scripting language PHP (Hypertext Preprocessor) to adapt the HTML/XHTML page to the user's selections. The user's supplied information is translated into a request from the company's main computer, often using a database query language such as SQL. Scripting code in ASP, JSP, or PHP controls the automatic writing of the custom HTML/XHTML page that is returned to the user's computer.

What does additional programming bring to my Web page? The most advanced Web pages interact with the user,

FIGURE 10.24

Adobe Dreamweaver CS3 is a popular tool for creating Web pages.

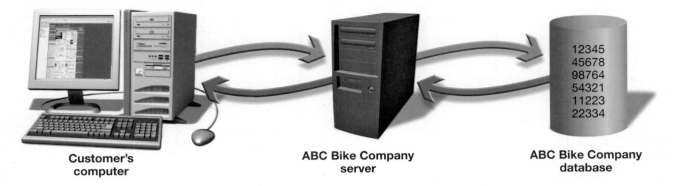

STEP 1: A customer clicks on an option to see all the red bikes on ABC Bike Company's Web page. The request travels to the ABC Bike Company's server.

STEP 2: The ABC Bike Company's server sends a request to its database computer to search for all red bikes.

STEP 3: The database computer returns a list of all red bikes.

Customer's computer

ABC Bike Company server

ABC Bike Company database

12345
45678
98764
54321
11223
22334

The ABC Bike Company's server uses an ASP program to write the HTML page displaying the red bike info. The page is sent to the customer, where it appears on his or her screen.

FIGURE 10.25

An online store is an example of the three-tier client/server type of Internet application.

collecting information and then customizing what they present based on the user's feedback. For example, as shown in Figure 10.25, an online store's page will collect a customer bicycle inquiry and then ask the company's main server for a list of red bicycles sold by the company. An ASP program then creates a new HTML/XHTML page and delivers that to the user's browser, telling the customer what red bicycles (including details such as model and size) are currently sold by ABC.

Thus, ASP programs can have HTML/XHTML code as their output. They use what the user has told them from the list boxes, check boxes, and buttons on the page to make decisions. Based on those results, the ASP program decides what HTML/XHTML to write. A small example of ASP writing its own HTML/XHTML code is shown in Figure 10.26.

Flash and XML

What if a programmer wants to create a Web page that includes sophisticated animation? Many Web sites feature elaborate animations that interact with visitors. These sites include buttons and hyperlinks, along with animation effects. These components can be designed with **Adobe Flash**, a software product for developing Web-based multimedia. Flash includes its own programming language named ActionScript, which is similar to JavaScript in its selection of keywords, operators, and classes.

Microsoft has unveiled a competing product named SilverLight that supports the development of rich multimedia and interactive Web applications..Other advances, like the collection of technologies referred to as AJAX, allow the creation of Web applications that can create an interaction between a browser and a server without requiring a user to click on a link, giving users a much more responsive experience.

Is HTML/XHTML the only markup language for the Web? When Web sites communicate with humans, HTML/XHTML work well because the formatting they control is important. People respond immediately to the visual styling of textual information; its layout, color, size, and font design all help to transfer the message off the page to the reader. When computers want to communicate with each other, however, all of these qualities just interfere. **Extensible Markup Language** (**XML**) enables designers to define their own data-based tags, making it much easier for a Web site to transfer the key information on its page to another site.

Without XML, a Web site that wanted to look up current stock pricing information at another site would have to retrieve the HTML/XHTML page, sort through the formatting information, and try to recognize which text on the page identified the data needed. With XML, groups can agree on standard systems of tags that represent important data elements. For example, the XML tags <stock> and </stock> might

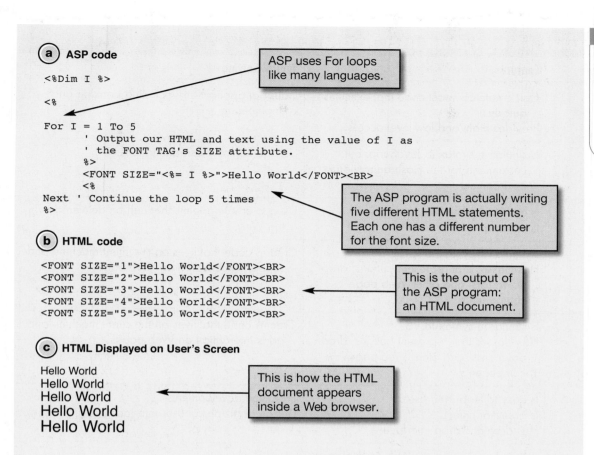

FIGURE 10.26

(a) ASP code

ASP uses For loops like many languages.

```
<%Dim I %>

<%

For I = 1 To 5
        ' Output our HTML and text using the value of I as
        ' the FONT TAG's SIZE attribute.
        %>
        <FONT SIZE="<%= I %>">Hello World</FONT><BR>
        <%
Next ' Continue the loop 5 times
%>
```

The ASP program is actually writing five different HTML statements. Each one has a different number for the font size.

(b) HTML code

```
<FONT SIZE="1">Hello World</FONT><BR>
<FONT SIZE="2">Hello World</FONT><BR>
<FONT SIZE="3">Hello World</FONT><BR>
<FONT SIZE="4">Hello World</FONT><BR>
<FONT SIZE="5">Hello World</FONT><BR>
```

This is the output of the ASP program: an HTML document.

(c) HTML Displayed on User's Screen

Hello World
Hello World
Hello World
Hello World
Hello World

This is how the HTML document appears inside a Web browser.

(a) An ASP program can write (b) HTML/XHTML code as its output. (c) The HTML/XHTML page it writes would show up in a browser.

delimit key stock quote information. Mathematicians have created a standardized set of XML tags for their work named MathML, whereas biometrics groups are developing an XML standard to describe and exchange biometric data such as DNA and face scans. We discuss HTML/ XHTML and XML in more detail in Chapter 13.

Figure 10.27 shows a table of popular programming tools as well as their features and the typical settings in which they are used.

THE NEXT GREAT LANGUAGE

What will be the next great language? It is never easy to predict which language will become the next "great" language, but software experts predict that as software projects continue to grow in size, the amount of time needed to compile a completed project will also grow. It is not uncommon for a large project to require 30 minutes or more to recompile. Interpreted languages, however, have virtually no compile time because compilation occurs while the code is being edited. As

projects get larger, this capability to be compiled instantaneously will become even more important. Thus, interpreted languages such as Python, Ruby, and Smalltalk could become more important in the coming years.

Will all languages someday converge to one? Certain characteristics of modern programming languages correspond well with how programmers actually think. These traits support good programming practices and are emerging as common features of most modern programming languages. The object-oriented paradigm is one example. Both Visual Basic and COBOL have moved toward a support of objects.

There will always be a variety of programming languages, however. Figure 10.28 illustrates that idea in lighthearted fashion, trying to give each language a "personality."

Forcing a language to be so general that it can work for any task also forces it to include components that make it slower to compile, produce larger final executables, and require more memory to run. Having a variety of languages and mapping a

FIGURE 10.27 Popular Programming Tools

Programming Language	Features	Typical Setting
C/C and C#	Can create compact code that executes quickly. Provides high- and low-level access.	Industrial applications including banking and engineering.
Flash ActionScript Microsoft SilverLight	Is similar in syntax to JavaScript but customized for the Flash animation environment.	Used to control Flash animations.
Java	Is architecture neutral. Is object-oriented.	Used to create applets that can be delivered over the Web.
JavaScript	Is similar in syntax to Java. Has classes that represent buttons, drop-down lists, and other Web page components.	Creates code that lives on the client machine and supports interaction on Web pages.
VBScript	Is similar in syntax to VB. Has classes that represent buttons, drop-down lists, and other Web page components.	Creates code that lives on the client machine and adds interaction on Web pages.
Visual Basic .NET	Is easy to learn and use. Is object-oriented. Has drag-and-drop interface.	Prototype development. Design of graphical user interfaces.
Web Technologies		
ASP, JSP, PHP	Set of rules and standards that allow Web sites to create their own HTML code based on user actions.	Controls the automated writing of HTML pages.
HTML/XHTML	Set of tags that control the display of text on a Web page.	Controls layout and style of information presented on a Web page.
XML	Enables users to define their own tags. Facilitates exchange of information between Web sites.	Used in the construction of Web services.

FIGURE 10.28

There will always be a variety of languages, each with its own "personality."

problem to the best language create the most efficient software solutions.

So what do I do if I want to learn languages that will be relevant in the future? No absolute set of languages is best to learn, and there is no one best sequence in which to learn them. The Association for Computing Machinery (ACM), which can be found at **www.acm.org**, encourages educators to teach a core set of mathematical and programming skills and concepts, but departments are free to offer a variety of languages.

Some geographical and industry-related considerations come into play when selecting which programming language courses you

TRENDS IN IT

Will It Blend? Writing Your First Video Game in Blender

Blender is a free open source application that supports home video game production by combining many tools into one package. By working just in Blender, you have what you need for each of the various stages of beginning 3D video game development: creating three-dimensional objects with textures and then moving them around a 3D world with realistic physics.

First, Blender allows you to easily construct three-dimensional models (see Figure 10.29). Meshes are used to begin any model and can be customized to represent any 3D shape or object. You can add specific textures and shading to make the model more realistic. Blender then allows you to animate the object. That animation can be saved as a movie or connected to specific control keys or movements. You can also play a complete video game within Blender by using the built-in game engine. Finally, Blender incorporates a physics engine that understands basic concepts such as particle collisions and gravity modeling. This is useful, for example, when a game character tosses a plasma grenade toward a target!

The programming rules used to describe object behavior in the game are made simpler by Blender's Logic Bricks. For example, using Logic Bricks you can, in just a few clicks, create a rule that makes one object disappear when it collides with another. You can also use Logic Bricks to map key movements to control objects or cameras in the environment.

Blender is available for download from **www.blender.org**, where you will find an active community to support you as you learn. The Blender Foundation is involved in releasing to the public games that were developed for free using Blender. These open source games include titles such as Orange, Peach, and Apricot. These are available for anyone to reuse and learn from. For example, the **apricot.blender.org** blog provides more information about the Apricot game project.

Many resources are available for Blender, including free books such as *Blender 3D: Noob to Pro*, available on Wiki Books (**http://en.wikibooks.org/wiki/Main_Page**).

In addition, YouTube has posts for a huge number of video tutorials on working with Blender, and libraries of Blender routines and objects are freely distributed on the Internet.

So if you are interested in video game development, three-dimensional art, or just creating animations, download Blender and realize the power of the open source software movement.

FIGURE 10.29

Blender allows you to create 3D models, animate them, and apply real physics to create playable video games.

---

should study. For example, in an area in which a large number of pharmaceutical companies exist, there may be a demand for Massachusetts General Hospital Utility Multi-Programming System, or MUMPS. This language is often used to build clinical databases, an important preoccupation of the pharmaceutical industry. Review the advertisements for programmers in area newspapers and investigate resources such as ComputerJobs (**www.computerjobs.com**) to identify languages in demand in your area. Also stay current on the direction of software engineering in general.

Whether or not you'll pursue a career in programming, having an understanding of software engineering is important in many IT careers. Software is the set of instructions that allow us to make use of our hardware. Programming skills give you the power to understand, create, and customize a computer system.

Summary

1. What is a system development life cycle, and what are the phases in the cycle?

An information system includes data, people, procedures, hardware, and software. Teams of individuals are required to develop systems, and an organized process (or set of steps) needs to be followed to ensure that development proceeds in an orderly fashion. This set of steps is usually referred to as the system development life cycle (SDLC). There are six steps in the SDLC: (1) A problem or opportunity is identified; (2) the problem is analyzed, and a program specification document is created to outline the project objectives; (3) a detailed plan for programmers to follow is designed using flowcharts and data-flow diagrams; (4) using this plan, the program is developed and documented; (5) the program is then tested to ensure that it works properly, and the program is installed so that it can be used; (6) maintenance and evaluation continue to ensure a working product.

2. What is the life cycle of a program?

Each programming project follows several stages from conception to final deployment. The problem statement identifies the task to be computerized and describes how the software program will behave. An algorithm specifies the sequential steps that describe what the program must do to complete the work and then is translated into highly structured programming code. The code then goes through a process of debugging, in which the programmers find and repair any errors in the code, and further testing, both by the programming team and by the people who will use the program. The results of the entire project are documented for the users and the development team. Finally, users are trained so that they can use the program efficiently.

3. What role does a problem statement play in programming?

The problem statement is an explicit description of what tasks the computer program must accomplish and how the program will execute these tasks and respond to unusual situations. It describes the input data that users will have at the start of the job, the output that the program will produce, and the exact processing that converts these inputs to outputs. In addition, potential errors and plans to address these errors are identified.

4. How do programmers create algorithms?

For simple problems, programmers create an algorithm by converting the problem statement into a list of steps (or actions) the program will take. For more complex problems, the programmer must identify where decision points occur in the list of steps. Some decisions are yes/no (binary), whereas others create a repeating action (loop). Algorithms are documented in the form of a flowchart or in pseudocode. Programmers either use a top-down or object-oriented analysis to produce the algorithm.

5. How do programmers move from algorithm to code, and what categories of language might they code in?

Computer code uses special words and strict rules to enable programmers to control the CPU without having to know all of its hardware details. Programming languages are classified in several major groupings, sometimes referred to as *generations*, with the first generation being machine language, the binary code of 1s and 0s that the computer understands. Assembly language is the next generation; it uses short, English-like commands that speak directly to the CPU and give the programmer direct control of hardware resources. Each successive generation in language development relieves programmers of the burden of keeping track of what the hardware requires and becomes more closely matched to how humans think about problems.

6. How does a programmer move from code in a programming language to the 1s and 0s the CPU can understand?

Compilation is the process by which code is converted into machine language, the language the CPU can understand. The compiler is the program that understands both the syntax of the programming language and the exact structure of the CPU and its machine language. It can translate the instructions written by programmers in the higher-level language into machine language, the binary patterns that will execute commands on the CPU. Each programming language has its own compiler with separate versions that are required to compile code that will run on each different type of processor.

7. How is a program tested?

If programmers make errors in the algorithm or in translating the algorithm to code, problems will occur. Programmers debug the program by running it constantly to find errors and to make sure the program behaves in the way it should. Once debugging has detected all the code errors, users, both within the company and outside the company, test the program in every way they can imagine—both as it was intended to be used and in ways only new users may think up. Before its commercial release, software is often provided at a reduced cost or no cost in a beta version to certain test sites or to interested users for a last round of testing.

8. What steps are involved in completing the program?

Once testing has been completed, technical writers create internal documentation for the program and the user manuals that will be distributed to users of the program. User training begins once the software is distributed to teach the user community how to use the software efficiently.

9. How do programmers select the right programming language for a specific task?

A programming team reviews several considerations before selecting the language. Certain languages are best used with certain problems. The target language should be well matched to the amount of space available for the final program. Some projects require the selection of a language that can produce code that executes in the fastest possible time. Selecting a language with which the programmers are familiar is also helpful.

10. What are the most popular programming applications for Windows and Web applications?

Visual Basic, C/C++, and Java are among those languages that enable programmers to easily include Windows control features such as scroll bars, title bars, text boxes, buttons, and expanding and collapsing menus. To develop Web applications, programmers use HTML/XHTML for basic Web design. For more complex Web designs, scripting programs such as JavaScript and VBScript are popular programs. Web page animations are done with ASP, JSP, PHP, Flash, and XML.

Key Terms

Buzzwords

Word Bank

- algorithm
- beta version
- C/C++
- classes
- compiler
- debugger

- documentation
- HTML/XHTML
- inheritance
- interpreter
- JavaScript
- machine language

- object-oriented
- problem statement
- testing plan
- top-down design
- Visual Basic

Instructions: Fill in the blanks using the words from the Word Bank above.

Things are not running smoothly at the Whizgig factory. We need to keep track of how many Whizgigs are made every hour and how many are defective. We begin by calling in the programming team to work with users. Together they begin to build a software solution by creating a(n) (1) _____. All of the input and output information required is identified as well as the (2) _____, which lists specific examples of what outputs the program will produce for certain inputs. The team then begins to design the (3) _____ by listing all the tasks and subtasks required to complete the job. This approach is called (4) _____.

An alternative to this design method is the (5) _____ design, which develops the program based on objects. Objects that have similar attributes and behaviors can be grouped into (6) _____. The benefit of using this type of design approach is that objects and classes can be reused in other programs. If necessary, new classes can be made by first "borrowing" the attributes of an existing class and then adding differentiating attributes. This concept is known as (7) _____.

To select the best language for this problem, the team considers the resources at Whizgig. Although a lot of the programmers know the visual programming language of (8) _____, the most important factors for this application will be how fast it runs, so the language (9) _____ is selected. Because Whizgig has no Web presence, the programmers will not be using (10) _____. Once the program has been written in programming language, the (11) _____ translates it to (12) _____, or the binary code that the CPU understands. Now the program is ready to be tested.

The (13) _____ looks for errors in the program code. Then the programmers put together the necessary (14) _____ that explains the program and how to use it. However, because this is a program that is to be used internally, the program does not need to go through a test of the (15) _____ by a group of potential outside users.

Becoming Computer Literate

Your new manager wants to design and deploy an Internet application to collect marketing information about potential customers. She wants to gather data and analyze it in one report, which can be shipped to the marketing department.

Instructions: Write a memo to the manager describing what will have to be considered in the creation of this project. Write the memo using as many of the key terms from the chapter as you can.

Instructions: Answer the multiple-choice and true–false questions below for more practice with key terms and concepts from this chapter.

MULTIPLE CHOICE

1. In the SDLC, translating from an algorithm to a programing language is considered:
   a. coding.
   b. debugging.
   c. building a testing plan.
   d. All of the above

2. Algorithms document
   a. the programming languages to be used in the program.
   b. testing operations to be conducted by the program.
   c. the sequence of decisions and actions the program will take.
   d. the documentation to be included in the program.
   e. All of the above

3. Programmers can easily debug program code using
   a. flowcharts.
   b. pseudocode.
   c. IDE.
   d. None of the above

4. A compiler for a programming language
   a. is the same no matter which CPU the program is running on.
   b. is the actual machine language of the CPU.
   c. translates from a human-friendly pro-gramming language to binary 1s and 0s.
   d. None of the above

5. An object, defined by a specific class, is a collection of
   a. data and methods.
   b. ideas and a testing plan.
   c. programming languages.
   d. class variables.

6. To make code more reusable, programmers use modules called
   a. functions.
   b. subroutines.
   c. procedures.
   d. Any of the above, depending on the specific language.

7. HTML/XHTML has no compiler because
   a. HTML/XHTML is written using English words.
   b. most programming languages do not use compilers.
   c. it is a series of tags that can be understood directly by a browser.
   d. Wait! HTML/XHTML does have to be compiled!

8. Debugging a program is not necessary if
   a. there is a testing plan.
   b. it is a beta version of software.
   c. the program compiles.
   d. Debugging is always needed.

9. Which of the following is used in the design of Web applications?
   a. HTML/XHTML
   b. JavaScript
   c. PHP
   d. All of the above
   e. None of the above

10. Which of the following languages is used if a problem requires a lot of number crunch-ing?
   a. Cobol
   b. C/C++
   c. HTML/XHTML
   d. Windows Vista

TRUE–FALSE

____ 1. Algorithms are represented visually by using flowcharts.

____ 2. Programmers debug a program by delivering it to users to find errors and to make sure the program behaves in the way it should.

____ 3. Object-oriented programming produces more reusable code than that generated by top-down design.

____ 4. Python is the ideal development language, which is why other programming languages are beginning to lose their importance.

____ 5. Visual Basic is only useful for rapid application development (RAD), which enables program-mers to build software that executes incredibly quickly.

Making the Transition to... Next Semester

1. Pipeline of Programming Courses

Research the core programming sequence at the college you are attending.

a. How many courses are in the core sequence?
b. How many languages does the sequence cover?
c. How many sections of each of the classes are offered?
d. What can you infer about the percentage of students that stay in the programming tract over time?
e. What does that result mean to the future of your community and country?

2. ACM Recommendations

How will you follow up an introductory programming class at your current school? Examine the recommendations from the Association for Computing Machinery (**www.acm.org/education/curric_vols/CC2005-March06Final.pdf**) and compare them with the course content at your school.

3. A Ruby and a Perl

Perl is an especially useful and convenient language to use for specific types of programming problems. Ruby is another new programming language that has specific advantages for some settings. On the Web, research Ruby and Perl and determine what the key features are of these languages. Determine also which programming situations would demand Ruby and which would be best suited for Perl.

4. Beta Testing

Companies use beta testing to detect remaining problems in their programs before releasing the final version to the retail market. Go to **www.betanews.com** or to any other site that offers beta versions of your favorite software title. What programs would you be interested to beta test? Why do you think it would make sense to beta test a software program? What, if any, are the risks involved in beta testing a software program?

5. Creating a Problem Statement

Create a problem statement for the process of registering for courses next semester. It should describe the inputs, outputs, and decision rules that need to be followed to register successfully for the correct courses.

6. Code Reusability

This semester you will write a program that plays a game of blackjack with the user. Next semester's course has an instructor who always assigns a more sophisticated version of this problem, for which you will need to develop much more complex logic in the blackjack strategy engine of your game. How could you design your code this semester so that it would be the most reusable and helpful to you next term? Discuss how the importance of reusability would impact your choice of language. How would the object-oriented design model be beneficial here?

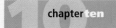

Making the Transition to... the Workplace

1. Programming Is Not Just for Programmers

Think about the range of jobs in the place where you currently work.

a. How many of the employees use computers?
b. How many individuals create macros, scripts, or shortcuts for doing their work in a faster, more automated fashion?
c. How many people actually program in a modern programming language?

2. Algorithm Design

Identify the most commonly performed task at your place of business. Think of a way to document it as an algorithm. Then study it to see if you can find a way to make it even slightly more efficient. A small improvement to the most often performed task means big productivity gains.

3. Choosing the Best Language

Using resources from the Web, determine which programming languages would be best to learn if you were going to program for the following industries:

a. Animated movies
b. Computer games
c. Database management
d. Robotics

4. Testing Software

Your company has a division that designs software to control the automatic transmission in a line of automobiles. How would you develop a testing plan for this software? What conditions would you need to examine to be sure you were minimizing the probability of software failure in the field?

5. Software Development

This chapter presents the traditional software development life cycle (SDLC) in six stages. Review the areas you would examine in the company to see if they are better suited to the traditional SDLC or the model of joint application development (JAD). What qualities in the corporate culture would you look for to see if they are "agile," in the sense of being able to adapt to changes quickly? What kind of employee qualities and experience would be important for a team that is taking the JAD approach to a project?

6. Accessibility

Web designers and developers can take specific steps to allow visually impaired users to access Web sites more easily. Examine the information on accessibility at Adobe's Web site (**www.adobe.com**). What is accessibility? Explore the details of existing assistive technologies, such as screen readers. What are the legal requirements to which Web sites must comply in order to meet the needs of the disabled? Why is maximizing accessibility important?

Critical Thinking Questions

Instructions: Albert Einstein used *Gedanken experiments*, or critical thinking questions, to develop his theory of relativity. Some ideas are best understood by experimenting with them in our own minds. The following critical thinking questions are designed to demand your full attention but require only a comfortable chair—no technology.

1. Using Data and Methods

Think about what classes would be important in modeling a band that is about to go on a national concert tour. What data and methods would each class need? How are the classes related to each other?

2. Class Hierarchy

A common test for deciding the structure of a class hierarchy is the "is a" versus "has a" test. For example, a motorcycle "has a" sidecar, so Sidecar would be a data field of a Motorcycle object. However, a motorcycle "is a" kind of vehicle, so Motorcycle would be a subclass of the base class Vehicle. Use the "is a" versus "has a" test to decide how a class structure could be created for computer peripherals. Work to separate the unique features into objects and to extract the most common features into higher-level classes.

3. Future Programming Languages

What do you think the computer programming language of the future should be able to do? How simple would it be? Would it use a graphical interface? Would it combine voice-recognition software with the coding process? Do you think computers will ever be able to create their own programs, or will humans always have to play a role in computer programming?

4. Programming Ethics

Some companies make their programmers sign agreements to prevent them from competing with the company later by working for a competitor. Is this ethical conduct on the part of the company? What if the company fires the programmer and she then has trouble finding work? How would this kind of agreement change the employee's work habits and professional development decisions?

5. Debugging

You learned how programs go through a testing process to rid the program of errors. Which parts of the SDLC waterfall model presented on page 488 incorporate debugging? How do the results of these stages of debugging change the flow of the SDLC? How would that be changed with the joint application development programming model?

6. Understanding Algorithms

Are there some problems whose solutions cannot be expressed as algorithms? Are there problems that cannot be solved with a fixed algorithm but could be described with an algorithm that incorporates probability and chance?

Problem:

You and your team have just been selected to write a software program that tells a vending machine how to make proper change from the bills or coins the customer inserts. The program needs to deliver the smallest possible amount of coins for each transaction.

Task:

Divide the class into three teams: Algorithm Design, Coding, and Testing. The responsibilities of each team are outlined as follows.

Process:

1. The Algorithm Design team is required to develop two documents. The first document should present the problem as a top-down design sequence of steps. The second document should use object-oriented analysis to identify the key objects in the problem. Each object needs to be represented as data and behaviors. Inheritance relationships between objects should be noted as well. You can use flowcharts to document your results.

   Also, consider using a product such as Alice (**www.alice.org**) to try to develop the code for a prototype of the system.

2. The Coding team needs to decide which programming language would be the most appropriate for the project. This program needs to be fast and take up only a small amount of memory. Make sure your team defends its position by finding information about the language you select on the Web.

   If the Algorithm Design team created prototype code with Alice, be sure to study the choices team members made and how their code would match the language you recommend.

3. The Testing team must create a testing plan for the program. What set of inputs would you test with to be sure the program is completely accurate? Develop a table listing combinations of inputs and correct outputs.

4. As a group, discuss how each team would communicate its results to the other teams. Once one team has completed its work, are the team members finished or do they need to interact with the other teams? How would the tools of a site such as SourceForge (**www.sourceforge.net**) help your development team across the life of the project?

Conclusion:

Any modern programming project requires programming teams to produce an accurate and efficient solution to the problem. The interaction of the team members within the team as well as with the other teams is vital to successful programming.

Multimedia

In addition to the review materials presented here, you'll find additional materials featured with the book's multimedia, including the *Technology in Action* Student Resource CD and the Companion Website (**www.prenhall.com/techinaction**), which will help reinforce your understanding of the chapter content. These materials include the following:

ACTIVE HELPDESK

In Active Helpdesk calls, you'll assume the role of helpdesk operator taking calls about the concepts you've learned in this chapter. You'll apply what you've learned and receive feedback from a supervisor to review and reinforce those concepts. The Active Helpdesk calls for this chapter are listed below and can be found on your Student Resource CD:

- Understanding Software Programming
- Selecting the Right Programming Language

SOUND BYTES

Sound Bytes are dynamic multimedia tutorials that help demystify even the most complex topics. You'll view video clips and animations that illustrate computer concepts, and then apply what you've learned by reviewing with the Sound Byte Labs, which include quizzes and activities specifically tailored to each Sound Byte. The Sound Bytes for this chapter are listed here and can be found on your Student Resource CD:

- Programming for End Users
- Looping Around the IDE

COMPANION WEBSITE

The *Technology in Action* Companion Website includes a variety of additional materials to help you review and learn more about the topics in this chapter. The resources available at **www.prenhall.com/techinaction** include:

- **Online Study Guide.** Each chapter features an online true–false and multiple-choice quiz. You can take these quizzes, automatically check the results, and e-mail the results to your instructor.
- **Web Research Projects.** Each chapter features a number of Web research projects that ask you to search the Web for information on computer-related careers, milestones in computer history, important people and companies, emerging technologies, and the applications and implications of different technologies.

Behind the Scenes:

Databases and Information Systems

Objectives

After reading this chapter, you should be able to answer the following questions:

1. What is a database, and why is it beneficial to use databases? **(pp. 532–533)**

2. What components make up a database? **(pp. 533–537)**

3. What types of databases are there? **(pp. 537–539)**

4. What do database management systems do? **(pp. 539–547)**

5. How do relational databases organize and manipulate data? **(pp. 547–553)**

6. What are data warehouses and data marts, and how are they used? **(pp. 553–557)**

7. What is an information system, and what types of information systems are used in business? **(pp. 557–562)**

8. What is data mining, and how does it work? **(pp. 562–563)**

ACTIVE HELPDESK

- Understanding Database Management Systems **(p. 539)**
- Using Databases **(p. 540)**
- Data Warehouses, Data Marts, and Information Systems **(p. 562)**

Using Databases

We're constantly inundated with information. The rapid rise of the Internet and the widespread use of computers have only accelerated the flow of information into our lives.

In a typical week, you constantly come into contact with databases. On Monday, when you purchased a book from **Amazon.com**, you accessed a database to find the book you wished to buy. When calling the phone company on Wednesday to check on your phone bill, you accessed a database using the phone company's voice menu system, which looked up your billing information based on your account number. On Friday, when you signed up for season tickets at your community theater, information about your subscription was recorded in a database so that the theater could mail out your tickets when they were printed. Even something as simple as the burger you bought at a fast-food restaurant on Saturday involved interaction with a database. The cashier recorded the items in your order in a sales database just by keying them into the point-of-sale terminal.

In fact, the ability of modern businesses to thrive and grow depends on the quality and efficiency of their databases. Gaining an understanding of how databases work and the information systems that they support will assist you in understanding how any business captures and manages data. In addition, you will gain an appreciation for the design issues surrounding the construction and deployment of databases, which may help you determine whether pursuing a career in database administration is right for you.

In this chapter we explore the basic building blocks from which databases are created. You'll see how a database is designed and walk through the process of creating a simple database. Along the way, we discuss important features of databases and the types of database programs used by organizations. We also discuss the various types of information systems that use databases and explore modern data storage designs such as data warehouses. Then we'll examine how data can be further analyzed (or "mined") to yield information beyond the original scope of the database design. Finally, we'll show you how you can protect your privacy against the proliferation of databases.

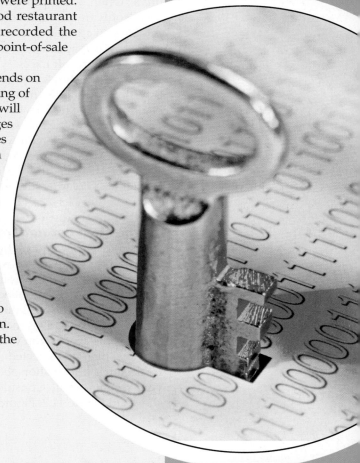

SOUND BYTES

• Creating an Access 2007 Database **(p. 546)**
• Improving an Access 2007 Database **(p. 550)**

Life Without Databases

Databases are collections of related data that can be easily stored, sorted, organized, and queried. By creating an organized structure for data, we hope to make data more meaningful and therefore more useful. In other words, we are attempting to turn data into information.

However, not every instance in which related data needs to be turned into organized information demands the complexity of a database. For simple tasks, lists are adequate. Often, word-processing or spreadsheet software is used to create simple lists. A table you create in Microsoft Word can serve as a list, as can a spreadsheet you create in Microsoft Excel.

Figure 11.1 shows a simple "Books to Buy" list you might create in Excel before beginning college. This list works well because it is simple and suited for just one purpose: to provide you with a list of the books you need to buy for a particular semester. If all the information that needed to be tracked was as simple as the information in Figure 11.1, then there would be no need for databases.

When is a list not appropriate? Any time *complex* information needs to be organized or more than one person needs to access it, a list no longer is efficient. For example, when you enrolled in college, you provided information about yourself to a number of people. This included your name, address, the classes you wished to take, and the meal plan you selected. Your school also tracks other information about you, such as your residence hall. Consider the two lists shown in Figure 11.2. Figure 11.2a is a list the registrar's office uses to keep track of students, the classes they are taking, and the meal plan they selected. Figure 11.2b is a list the residence hall manager uses to track where students are housed.

What's the problem with having two lists? First, there is a great deal of duplicated data between the two lists in Figure 11.2. For example, each time William Wallace registers for a class, his name and address are entered. He needs to provide the same data to the residence hall manager when he receives his residence hall assignment. This **data redundancy**, though not a problem in the small lists in Figure 11.2, can be problematic when a college has 10,000 students. Imagine the wasted time in entering data multiple times, semester after semester, not to mention the increased likelihood of making a mistake.

Second, each time information in the list changes, multiple lists must be updated. If Li Chan moves, his data will need to be updated in *all* the lists that contain his address. It would be easy to overlook one or more lists or even one or more rows in the same list. This would lead to a state of **data inconsistency**. It would not be possible to easily tell which data was correct. Also notice that Jennifer Evans's last record in Figure 11.2a contains a different street address from her other records. It's impossible to tell which address is correct, again resulting in data inconsistency.

In addition, correct data can be entered into a list but in an inconsistent format. Look at students Jennifer Evans and Donald Lopez in Figure 11.2a. Both are registered for PSY 110, but two different course names have been entered (Intro to Psychology and Intro to Psych). Is this the same course? Which one is the correct name? Confusion arises when data is inconsistently entered. Establishing data consistency is therefore difficult to do with a list.

Aside from data redundancy and inconsistency, are there any other problems with using lists instead of databases? What if someone accidentally entered Jennifer Evans's enrollment data twice in the list in Figure 11.2a? Any reports (such as student bills) that are generated based on this list will be inaccurate because of the duplicate data. For example, Jennifer would be sent two separate bills for her

	A	B	C	D
1	Books To Buy			
2				
3	Class	Title	Author	Bought
4	English Comp 1	The Prose Reader: Essays for Thinking, Reading, and Writing	Flachmann	Yes
5	Computer Programming 1	Java: How to Program	Deitel	Yes
6	Western Civilizations 1	The Western Heritage	Kagan, Ozment, Turner	
7	Intro to Psychology	Psychology	Wade	Yes
8	Inorganic Chemistry	Chemistry	McMurry, Fay	
9				

FIGURE 11.1

A simple list created in Microsoft Excel (as a spreadsheet) or a table created in Microsoft Word is often sufficient to organize simple tasks.

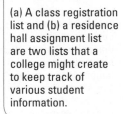

FIGURE 11.2

Class Registration List - Fall

SID #	Last Name	First Name	Home Address	City	State	Zip Code	Class Code	Class Name	# Of Credits	Meal Plan #
234567891	Chan	Li	123 Main Street	Tuba City	NV	49874-7643	LAN 330	Japanese 1	3	2
234567891	Chan	Li	123 Main Street	Tuba City	NV	49874-7643	REL 216	Early Buddhism	3	2
234567891	Chan	Li	123 Main Street	Tuba City	NV	49874-7643	ENG 102	English Comp 2	3	2
456789123	Coyle	Diane	745 Station Drive	Springfield	MA	18755-5555				
123456789	Evans	Jennifer	123 Oak Street	Gotham City	PA	19999-8888	CIS 111	Programming	3	1
123456789	Evans	Jennifer	123 Oak Street	Gotham City	PA	19999-8888	ENG 101	English Comp 1	3	1
123456789	Evans	Jennifer	123 Oak Street	Gotham City	PA	19999-8888	HIS 103	Western Civ	3	1
123456789	Evans	Jennifer	123 Oak Street	Gotham City	PA	19999-8888	CHE 140	Chemistry	4	1
123456789	Evans	Jennifer	124 Oak Street	Gotham City	PA	19999-8888	PSY 110	Intro to Psychology	3	1
567891234	Lopez	Donald	3421 Lincoln Court	Spalding	ND	87564-2546	HIS 401	16th Century Europe	3	1
567891234	Lopez	Donald	3421 Lincoln Court	Spalding	ND	87564-2546	SOC 310	Interpersonal Relationships	3	1
567891234	Lopez	Donald	3421 Lincoln Court	Spalding	ND	87564-2546	PSY 110	Intro to Psych	3	1

Residence Hall Assignment List - Fall

SID #	Last Name	First Name	Home Address	City	State	Zip Code	Residence Hall Name	Room Number
234567891	Chan	Li	123 Main Street	Tuba City	NV	49874-7643	Wilson Hall	218
456789123	Coyle	Diane	745 Station Drive	Springfield	MA	18755-5555	Montgomery Hall	231
123456789	Evans	Jennifer	123 Oak Street	Gotham City	PA	19999-8888	Montgomery Hall	312
567891234	Lopez	Donald	3421 Lincoln Court	Spalding	ND	87564-2546	Stone House	102
345678912	Wallace	William	654 Front Street	Locust Glen	MI	67744-3584	Forsman Quad	124

(a) A class registration list and (b) a residence hall assignment list are two lists that a college might create to keep track of various student information.

classes, resulting in confusion and potential headaches.

In Figure 11.2a, each student has selected one of the college's meal plans, and this data must be entered into each row. What if someone enters a meal plan that doesn't exist on one of the rows pertaining to Donald Lopez? This is not only wrong, but also can be confusing to anyone viewing the list. With a list, anything can be entered in a row or column, even if that information is incorrect.

In addition, information can be organized in many ways. Consider the residence hall assignment list in Figure 11.2b, which is organized alphabetically by last name. This works well for the accounting clerk who needs to generate bills for student housing. But for the residence manager who wants to see which residence hall rooms are still vacant, it would be more useful to have the data organized by residence hall and room number. Reorganizing multiple lists in this way can be labor intensive.

A final problem with lists is how to handle incomplete data. In Figure 11.2a, Diane Coyle has enrolled in the college but has not yet selected a meal plan or registered for courses. Her known information has been entered, but it's impossible to tell by looking at her record whether data relating to her course registrations and meal plans was available and just not entered or is truly missing.

Can't I just exercise caution and set rules for updating lists? Carefully following the rules when you update a list like the ones shown in Figure 11.2 can address many of the problems mentioned, but there is still room for error. And it would not avoid the most pressing problems of lists: (1) the inability of the data to be shared and (2) data redundancy. Even if you could surmount all of these problems, you cannot easily change lists to accommodate the disparate needs of many users.

How can I solve the problems associated with lists? For single topics, a list is sufficient. But for any complex data that needs to be organized or shared, using a database is the most practical and efficient way to avoid the pitfalls associated with using lists.

Database Building Blocks

Almost any kind of data that needs organization and analysis can be put into a database. For example, Yahoo! maintains an online database (called Yahoo! People Search) that

FIGURE 11.3

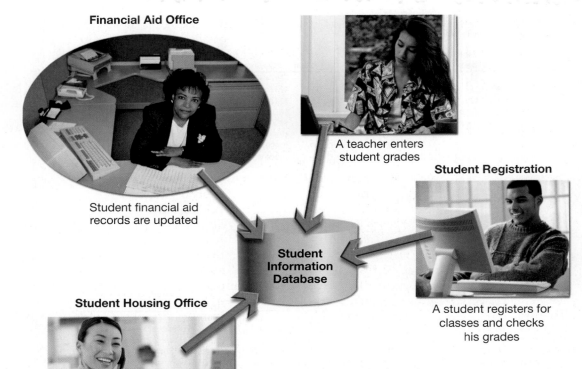

Financial Aid Office

Student financial aid records are updated

A teacher enters student grades

Student Registration

Student Information Database

A student registers for classes and checks his grades

Student Housing Office

A student is assigned to a residence hall

assists you in finding a person's street address or e-mail address. Publishers such as Ziff Davis Media, Inc., which publishes *PC Magazine,* store subscribers' mailing addresses and payment information in a database. In this section, we explore the advantages of using databases as well as the terminology databases use to categorize data.

ADVANTAGES OF USING DATABASES

How do databases make our lives easier? Without databases, you could not store and retrieve large quantities of information easily. Consider airline reservation systems. Thousands of people fly across the United States on any given day. Without a database, it would be extremely difficult to keep track of such a large number of airline reservations. In addition, although you can look up information fairly quickly in a list, even extremely large electronic databases

can provide the information you request in seconds. Databases provide three main advantages: They enable information sharing, they promote data integrity, and they allow the flexible use of data.

How do databases make information sharing possible? Consider student records at a college. As noted earlier, without databases, financial aid, admissions, and student housing would all need their own student files. The information in these files might not match because each department would maintain its own records. If a change had to be made in a student's address, all three files (the financial aid file, the admissions file, and the student housing file) would have to be changed.

As shown in Figure 11.3, with a database, only one file is maintained, which reduces the possibility of errors when data is entered or updated. It also increases efficiency, because there are no files to reconcile with each other. A database therefore provides for data centralization. There is no need for multiple lists. Each department that needs to use the student information accesses the same set of data.

How do databases promote data integrity? **Data integrity** means that the data contained in the database is accurate and reliable. **Data centralization** goes a long way toward ensuring data integrity. Instead of having to update multiple lists, your name and address information is maintained in only one place. If you move, your address must be changed only once.

How do databases provide flexibility? Another significant advantage of databases is that they are flexibly organized, enabling you to reorganize the information they contain in a variety of ways to suit the needs of the moment. Think back to the earlier example regarding lists. The registrar and housing manager need to see different information. With a list, you can organize information in only one way. If information is in a database, the registrar can easily view just the information she needs (such as the courses the student is taking), whereas the housing manager can easily view just the information he needs (such as the residence hall to which the student is assigned).

Data flexibility also makes information dissemination tasks easier. Suppose your school wants to send out a mailing about a new course to all business majors. Having the contact information of students available in a database makes it easy to merge the data with Microsoft Word and create personalized letters and address labels. Obviously, this would be much faster than generating these items manually, and the results should contain fewer errors. Thus, databases can manage larger amounts of data and process that data more efficiently.

Are there any disadvantages associated with databases? Databases are more complex to construct and administer than lists. They also can be time-consuming and expensive to set up. Great care must be

exercised in the design of databases to ensure they will function as intended. Although average individuals can design small databases, it is helpful to have an experienced **database administrator** (or **database designer**), an individual trained in the design and building of databases, to assist with the construction of large databases.

Data privacy concerns also arise when using databases. Think about how much information you've provided to your school. The school probably has records of your Social Security number, birth date, address, and credit card information. These are all the things an identify thief would love to have to steal your identity. For this reason, many colleges and universities no longer use Social Security numbers as a student identification (ID) number. Instead, they create a unique student ID number when you register, which helps protect your Social Security number from falling into the wrong hands. Despite the increased complexity of databases and the issues surrounding privacy, however, the advantages of databases far outweigh the administrative disadvantages.

DATABASE TERMINOLOGY

How is data stored in a database?
Understanding how databases store information requires knowing the unique terminology developed to describe databases. As shown in Figure 11.4, databases have three main components: fields, records, and tables (or files).

FIGURE 11.4

In a database, a category of information is stored in a *field*. A group of related fields is called a *record*, and a group of related records is called a *table* (or *file*).

Li Chan's contact information and class registration information constitute one record

The column City represents one field in this database

Class Code is a field name

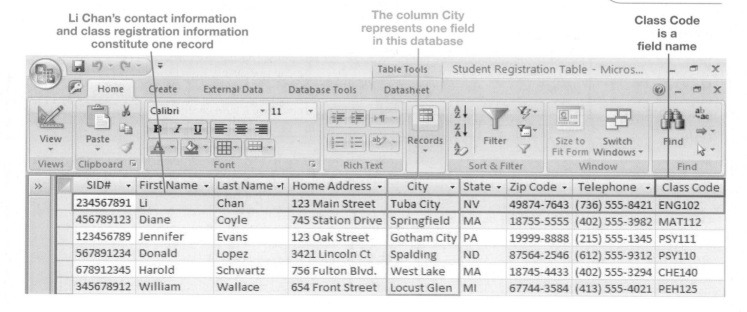

SID#	First Name	Last Name	Home Address	City	State	Zip Code	Telephone	Class Code
234567891	Li	Chan	123 Main Street	Tuba City	NV	49874-7643	(736) 555-8421	ENG102
456789123	Diane	Coyle	745 Station Drive	Springfield	MA	18755-5555	(402) 555-3982	MAT112
123456789	Jennifer	Evans	123 Oak Street	Gotham City	PA	19999-8888	(215) 555-1345	PSY111
567891234	Donald	Lopez	3421 Lincoln Ct	Spalding	ND	87564-2546	(612) 555-9312	PSY110
678912345	Harold	Schwartz	756 Fulton Blvd.	West Lake	MA	18745-4433	(402) 555-3294	CHE140
345678912	William	Wallace	654 Front Street	Locust Glen	MI	67744-3584	(413) 555-4021	PEH125

Fields

What is a field? A category of information in a database is stored in a **field**. Fields are displayed in columns. The city where a student lives can be found in the City field in the class registration list shown in Figure 11.4. Each field is identified by a **field name**, which is a way of describing the field. Class Code is a field name in the class registration list database in Figure 11.4. In a database, fields have other characteristics to describe them, including field data types and field size.

What are data types? When fields are created in the database, the user assigns those fields a **data type** (or **field type**). The data type indicates what type of data can be stored in the field.

Common data types are as follows and are listed in Figure 11.5:

- **Text fields** can hold any combination of alphanumeric data (letters or numbers) and are most often used to hold text. Although text fields can contain numbers (such as telephone numbers), they are stored as text and therefore cannot be used to store numbers that will be used in calculations.

- **Numeric fields** store numbers. Unlike in text fields, values in numeric fields can be used to perform calculations. For instance, the numbers stored in numeric fields can be used to calculate tuition owed.

- **Computational fields** (or **computed fields**) are numeric fields that store the contents of a calculation, which is generated with a formula in the numeric field. This is similar to a formula computation in a spreadsheet cell.

- **Date fields** hold date data such as birthdays, due dates, and so on.

- **Memo fields** are text fields that are used to hold long pieces of text. For example, a paragraph describing your high school achievements would be stored in a memo field.

- **Object fields** hold items such as pictures, video clips, or entire documents.

- **Hyperlink fields** store hyperlinks to Web pages.

What is meant by field size? Field size defines the maximum number of characters or numbers that a field can hold. If a numeric field has a size of 5, it can hold a number as high as 99999. As a rule, you should tailor the field size to the length of the data it will contain. If you define a field size of 50, space is reserved for 50 characters in that field, whether or not all 50 characters are used. Therefore, if you know that a character field will have a maximum of two characters, defining the field size as 50 wastes space and makes the files unnecessarily larger. The larger files can cause decreased database performance, especially in large databases.

FIGURE 11.5 Common Data Types and Examples of the Types of Information They Can Contain

Data Type	Used to Store	Example of Data Stored in the Field
Text	Alphabetic or alphanumeric data	Mary, CIS110
Numeric	Numbers	256, 1.347, $5600
Computational	Computational formulas	Credit hours x per-credit tuition charges
Date	Dates in standard date notation	4/15/2012
Memo	Long blocks of text	Four score and seven years ago our fathers brought forth on this continent a new nation, conceived in liberty, and dedicated to the proposition that all men are created equal.
Object	Multimedia files or entire documents	MP3 file, AVI file
Hyperlink	A hyperlink to a Web page on the Internet	**www.prenhall.com/techinaction**

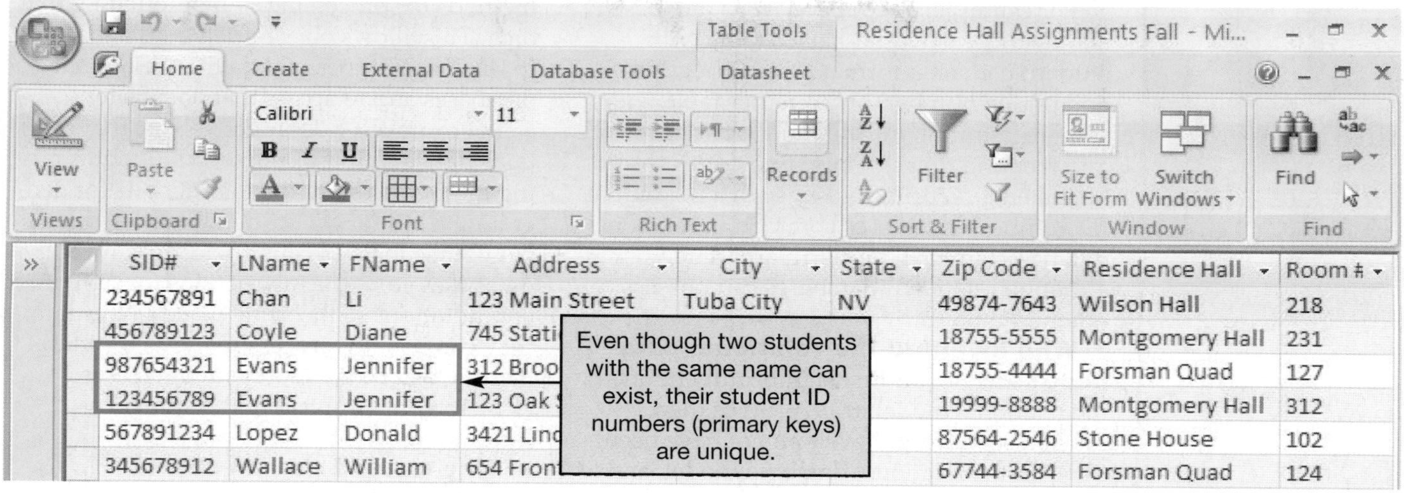

SID#	LName	FName	Address	City	State	Zip Code	Residence Hall	Room #
234567891	Chan	Li	123 Main Street	Tuba City	NV	49874-7643	Wilson Hall	218
456789123	Coyle	Diane	745 Stati			18755-5555	Montgomery Hall	231
987654321	Evans	Jennifer	312 Broo			18755-4444	Forsman Quad	127
123456789	Evans	Jennifer	123 Oak			19999-8888	Montgomery Hall	312
567891234	Lopez	Donald	3421 Lind			87564-2546	Stone House	102
345678912	Wallace	William	654 Fron			67744-3584	Forsman Quad	124

Even though two students with the same name can exist, their student ID numbers (primary keys) are unique.

FIGURE 11.6

This table of residence hall assignments uses SID# as the primary key. Unique student ID numbers make ideal primary keys because even students with the same name won't have the same ID number.

Records and Tables

What are records and tables in databases? A group of related fields is called a **record**. A student's name, address, and class registration information is a record. A group of related records is called a **table** (or **file**). Tables usually are organized by a common subject. Figure 11.4 shows a table that contains records for all students registered for classes in the current semester.

PRIMARY KEYS

Can fields have the same values in the same table? Yes, they can. It is possible that two students will live in the same town or have the same last name. However, to keep records distinct, each record must have one field that has a value unique to that record. This unique field is called a **primary key** (or a **key field**). For example, as shown in Figure 11.6, in student records, the primary key is the student ID number (field name SID#). Establishing a primary key and ensuring that it is unique make it impossible to duplicate records.

What makes a good primary key? We already have many numbers that follow us through our lives that make excellent primary keys. Social security numbers were often selected as primary keys when data was captured about individuals. Concerns about identity theft, however, led many businesses to abandon social security numbers as the primary means of identifying individuals. Driver license numbers are unique (within a particular state), as are the license plate numbers on our cars. State government agencies often use these numbers to track individuals and their transactions.

Primary keys don't have to be numbers that already represent something. For example, when you place an order with **Amazon.com**, your transaction gets a unique order number. This number is the Amazon database's primary key. You refer to this number when checking your order status, returning merchandise, and so on. It is essential to have a unique number for each order because it would be difficult to keep track of it without one.

Database Types

Many different types of electronic databases have been used since the invention of the computer. The three major types of databases currently in use are relational, object-oriented, and multidimensional databases. Of these three, relational databases still have the largest market share, but the market share of multidimensional databases is growing at a fast pace.

RELATIONAL DATABASES

What is a relational database? A **relational database** organizes data in table format by logically grouping similar data into **relations** (or tables that contain related data). As discussed earlier, each record in a database table is assigned a primary key to ensure that the record is unique. In relational databases, tables are logically linked to each other by including their primary keys in other tables with related information.

For example, at your college, a database about students would have a table with student contact information (name, address, and phone number) and another table with class registration information (class number and meeting times). These two tables would be linked by a primary key such as a student ID number. Data types common in relational databases are text, numeric, and date, although relational databases can possess other data types.

Who invented the relational database? E. F. Codd first significantly defined the relational model in 1970. Since then, much research and development have been done on the relational database model, and the theories surrounding the model have proven to be extremely reliable for storing and manipulating data.

OBJECT-ORIENTED DATABASES

What is an object-oriented database? An **object-oriented database** stores data in objects, not in tables. The models on which these databases are formed derive from the object-oriented programming paradigm, discussed in Chapter 10, which was catching on in the programming community in the late 1980s. Objects contain not only data but also methods for processing or manipulating that data. This allows object-oriented databases to store more types of data than relational databases and to access that data faster.

For example, a "student" object that contains data about the courses a student is taking might also store the instructions for generating a bill for the student based on his or her course load. Because object-oriented databases store the instructions for doing computations in the same place as the data, they can usually process requests for information faster than relational databases (which would only store the student information).

Why would I use an object-oriented database? Also, whereas relational databases excel in the storage of **structured (analytical) data** (such as "Bill" or "345"), object-oriented databases are more adept at handling unstructured data. **Unstructured data** includes nontraditional data such as audio clips (including MP3 files), video clips, pictures, and extremely large documents. Data of this type is known as a **binary large object (BLOB)** because it is actually encoded in binary form.

Object-oriented databases are based on complex models for manipulating data—much more complex than relational database models. As businesses need to store a greater variety of data, object-oriented databases are becoming more popular. Many relational database systems have been expanded to include object-oriented components. For a business to use its data in an object-oriented database, it needs to undergo a costly conversion process. But once this initial cost is overcome, the faster access and reusability of the database objects can provide advantages for large businesses.

Object-oriented databases also need to use a query language to access and manage data. Many object-oriented databases use **object query language (OQL)**, which is similar in many respects to SQL (structured query language, a standard language used to construct queries to extract data from databases).

MULTIDIMENSIONAL DATABASES

What is a multidimensional database? A **multidimensional database** stores data in multiple dimensions as opposed to relational databases, which store data in two-dimensional tables. Multidimensional

BITS AND BYTES

When a Number Isn't Really a Number

You might think that phone numbers should be defined as numeric data types. However, the data type you assign a phone number depends on what data needs to be stored *with* the phone number. If the phone number will be stored as a 10-digit number with no formatting (such as 3175553456), then a numeric field is appropriate. However, if you want to store the phone number so that it contains formatting to separate the area code, such as (317) 555-3456, then the data type should be a text field because the parentheses and dash are text characters that can't be stored in a numeric field.

Numbers that will be used in a calculation must *always* be defined as numeric data types. For instance, the number of credits for a course is often used to compute a student's bill. If you stored this value as text, you couldn't multiply it by the cost per credit hour to generate a bill. However, text fields store data more efficiently than numeric fields; therefore, if size is a consideration, a text field might be more appropriate to store data. So think carefully about how the data in fields will be used before assigning a data type.

databases organize data in a cube format. Each data cube has a *measure attribute,* which is the main type of data that the cube is tracking. Other elements of the cube are known as *feature attributes,* which all describe the measure attribute in some meaningful way. For example, sales of automobiles (measure attribute) could be categorized by various dimensions such as region, automobile color, automobile model, time period (such as current month), or salesperson (all feature attributes). In addition, the database could be constructed to define different levels within a particular feature attribute (such as state and town within a region).

What are the advantages of multidimensional databases? The two main advantages of multidimensional databases are that they can easily be customized to provide information to a variety of users (based on their need), and they can process data much faster than pure relational databases. The need for processing speed is especially critical when deploying a large database that will be accessed via the Internet. Therefore, large databases such as eBay that are accessed by many users needing to view data in different ways are usually designed as multidimensional databases. Oracle Corporation has slowly morphed its tried and true relational database into a multidimensional database in response to customer demand. This was primarily in response to customers who were using an Oracle database for applications deployed on the Web and needed better ways of storing and accessing image, audio, and video files. With multidimensional databases such as the current Oracle Database 11g, businesses do not have to abandon the proven relational database model because multidimensional databases are based on proven relational database theory.

Database Management Systems: Basic Operations

Databases are created and managed using a **database management system (DBMS)**. A DBMS is specially designed application software (such as Oracle Database or Microsoft Access) that interacts with the user, other applications, and the database to capture

and analyze data. The four main operations of a DBMS are:

1. creating databases and entering data,
2. viewing (or browsing) and sorting (or indexing) data,
3. extracting (or querying) data, and
4. outputting data.

In the next section, we look at each of these operations in detail.

CREATING DATABASES AND ENTERING DATA

How do I create a database with a DBMS? To create a database with a DBMS, you must first define the data to be captured. Therefore, you must create a description of the data. This description is contained in the database's files and is referred to as the **data dictionary** (or the **database schema**). The data dictionary defines the name, data type, and length of each field in the database. Describing the data helps to categorize and analyze it and set parameters for entering valid data into the database (such as a 10-digit number in a phone number field).

How do I know what fields are needed in my database? Careful planning is required to identify each distinct piece of data you need to capture. Each field should describe a unique piece of data and should never combine two separate pieces of data.

For example, for student registration at a college, capturing the student's name, street address, city, state, and zip code is important. But should a student's name be placed in one field or two? Because first and last names are separate pieces of data, you would want to create a separate field for each. For instance, suppose you wish to send a form letter to students addressing them by their first name (such as "Dear Susan"). If Susan's first and last name are in the same field in the database, it will be difficult to extract just her first name for the salutation.

What does a data dictionary look like, and how do I create one? In Microsoft Access, the data dictionary is called the Field Properties box. Figure 11.7a shows the Field Properties box for a database table in Access. The first step in creating an entry in the data dictionary is to create a field name. Field names should be unique within a table. In the table in Figure 11.7a, the field

ACTIVE HELPDESK

Understanding Database Management Systems

In this Active Helpdesk call, you'll play the role of a helpdesk staffer, fielding calls about database management systems, what they do, and how people can use them.

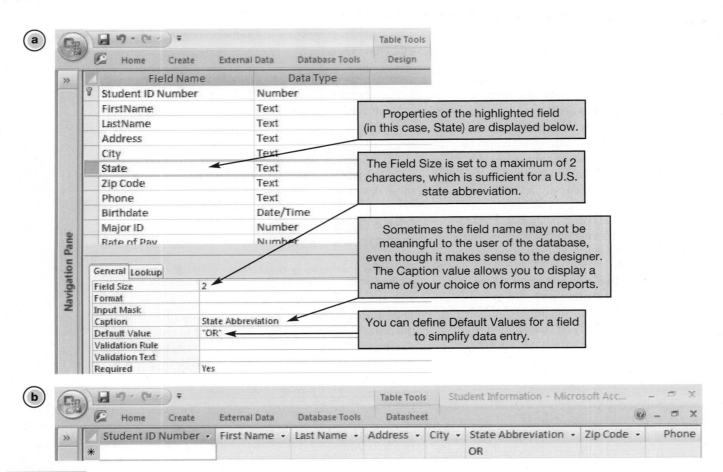

Properties of the highlighted field (in this case, State) are displayed below.

The Field Size is set to a maximum of 2 characters, which is sufficient for a U.S. state abbreviation.

Sometimes the field name may not be meaningful to the user of the database, even though it makes sense to the designer. The Caption value allows you to display a name of your choice on forms and reports.

You can define Default Values for a field to simplify data entry.

FIGURE 11.7

(a) The Field Properties box is shown for the Student Information table in an Access database. The Field Properties box represents the database's data dictionary. (b) The Student Information table, ready for data input, results from setting up the data dictionary in Figure 11.7a. Notice that the default value for the State field is already filled in.

name State is used to store the abbreviation for the state where the student lives.

Next, you must define a data type for each field. For the State field, you use a text data type because names are expressed using characters. Third, you should set a maximum field size (in this case, two characters) for the field. Data in the field can be shorter than the maximum but can never exceed it.

Finally, you can set **default values** for a field. These are the values the database will use for the field unless the user enters another value. Though not appropriate for first names, because they vary widely, default values are useful for numbers that are frequently the same. For example, setting a default value for a State field saves users from having to enter it for each student if most students live in one state (common at community colleges).

You need to repeat these steps for each field in the table. When completed, the resulting Student Information table, shown in Figure 11.7b, is ready for data entry.

The attributes (such as data type and field size) shown in Figure 11.7a and 11.7b, which are actually data describing other data, are

called **metadata**. Metadata is an integral part of the data dictionary. You need to build the data dictionary for each table you will use in a database before you enter data into the database. However, this also has the benefit of forcing you to consider up front the data you need to capture and the metadata that describes it.

What happens if I forget to define a field in the data dictionary or if I want to add another one later? Databases are extremely flexible. You can add additional fields (or ones you forgot) as needed. However, don't forget that you will need to populate (enter data into) these new fields with the appropriate data. This could be difficult if you suddenly need to add a

ACTIVE HELPDESK

Using Databases

In this Active Helpdesk call, you'll play the role of a helpdesk staffer, fielding calls about databases, their benefits, and components, and how relational databases organize and manipulate data.

Birth Date field to a database that already contains records for 10,000 individuals. If you plan to use the Birth Date field to analyze the data, then you need to have a plan for accumulating birth dates to ensure the completeness of the data.

INPUT FORMS

How do I get data into the database?
After you create a data dictionary for each table (or file) in the database and establish the fields you want the database to contain, you can begin creating individual records in the database. There's an old-fashioned way to get data into these records: You can key it directly into the database. However, today, a great deal of data already exists in some type of electronic format (such as a word-processing document, spreadsheet, and so on). Fortunately, most databases can import data electronically from other application files, which can save an enormous amount of keying.

When importing data, most databases usually apply filters to the data to determine that it is in the correct format as defined by the data dictionary. Nonconforming data is flagged (either on-screen or in a report) so that you can modify the data to fit the database's format.

How can I make manual entry into a database more convenient?
For small databases, or databases in which no electronic information is to be imported, you can create an input form to speed data entry. An **input form** provides a view of the data fields to be filled, with appropriate labels to assist database users in populating the database. Figure 11.8 shows an example of an input form for the Student Information table shown in Figure 11.7.

DATA VALIDATION

How can I ensure that only valid data is entered into the database?
One feature of most DBMSs is the capability to perform data validation. **Validation** is the process of ensuring that data entered into the database is correct (or at least reasonable) and complete. When you registered for college, for example, the admissions clerk most likely asked you for your phone number. A phone number in the United States usually comprises 10 digits formatted in the following fashion: (610) 555-1234. **Validation rules** are set up in the student database to alert the user if clearly wrong entries, such as "Joh- nS-mith" or "2345," are entered in the phone number field.

Validation rules are generally defined as part of the data dictionary. Violations of validation rules usually result in an error message being displayed on the screen so that the error can be addressed. Common types of validation checks include range,

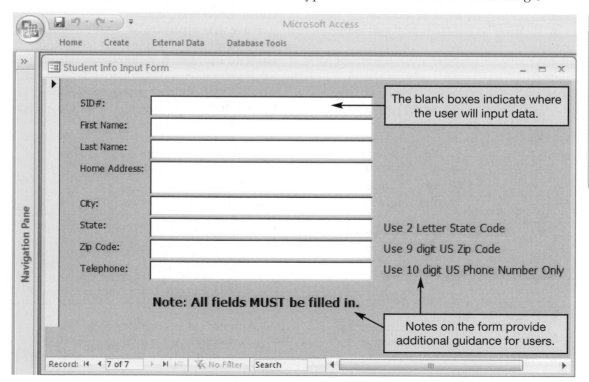

FIGURE 11.8

This input form is for entering data into the Student Information table. Each field has a label that indicates the data to be placed in the field (represented by the blank boxes). Notes can be added to the form as needed to guide the users.

completeness, consistency, and alphabetic and numeric checks.

How does a range check work?

Range checks ensure that the data entered into the database falls within a certain range of numbers. For instance, rates of pay for student jobs usually fall within a certain range. Therefore, in a student pay database,

you could set the **field constraints** (properties that must be satisfied for an entry to be accepted into the field) to restrict pay rates to a range you define.

Figure 11.9 shows how you set up a range check in a data dictionary (in the field properties box) for an Access database. If users tried to enter a rate of pay less than $7.25 or greater than $20, they would be notified of an invalid range error and the input would not be accepted.

What does a completeness check accomplish?

If you have ever bought anything online, you have probably encountered error messages generated by completeness checks. In database systems, fields can be defined as "required," meaning data must be entered into them. A **completeness check**, such as the one shown in Figure 11.10, ensures that all fields defined as "required" have data entered into them.

What is the function of a consistency check?

A **consistency check** compares the values of data in two or more fields to see if these values are reasonable. For example, your birth date and the date you enrolled in school are often in a college's database. It is not possible for you to have enrolled in college before you were born. Also, most college students are at least 16 years old. Therefore, a consistency check on these fields might ensure that your birth date is at least 16 or more years before the date you enrolled in college.

How are alphabetic and numeric checks used?

You may want to restrict fields to only alphabetic or numerical data (such as for names and student ID numbers). An **alphabetic check** confirms that only textual characters are entered in a field

FIGURE 11.9

Here a validation rule is set to restrict rates of pay to a certain range.

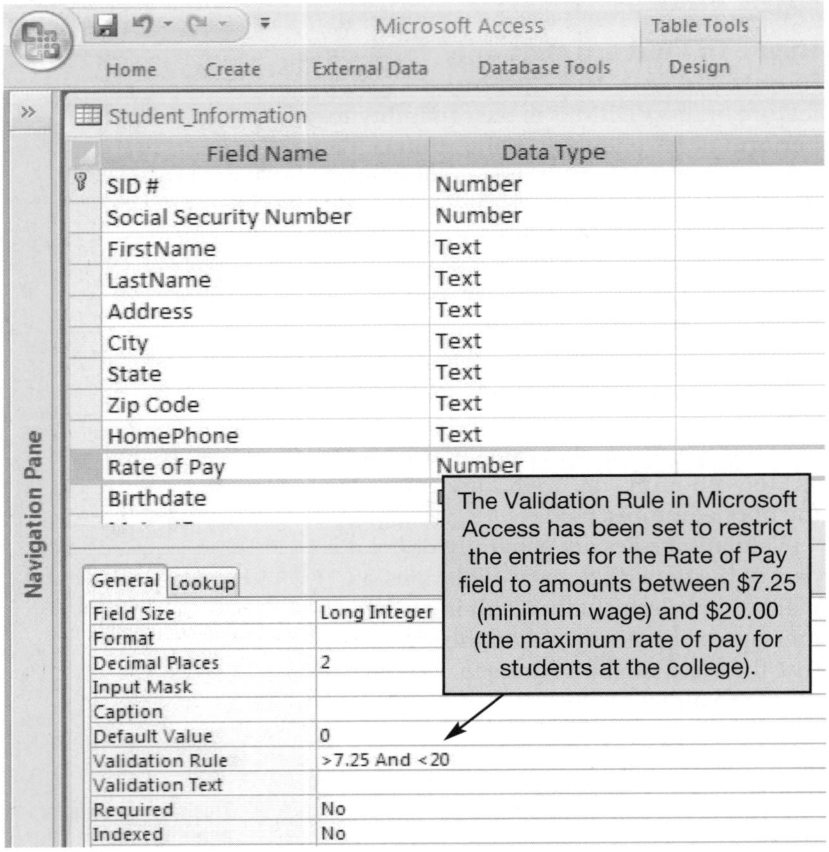

FIGURE 11.10

A database completeness check, like this one shown for Yahoo! Mail, ensures that all fields defined as "required" have data entered into them.

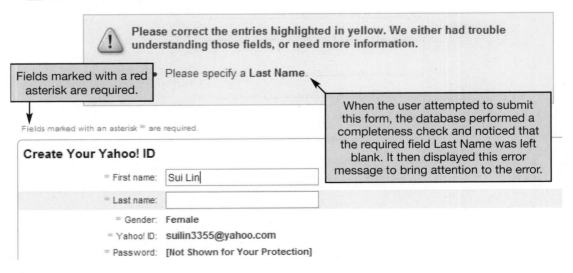

(such as "Gwen"). A **numeric check** confirms that only numbers are entered in the field. With these checks in place, "St3v3" would not be accepted as a first name or a zip code. Figure 11.11 shows how you can set such checks and customize error messages in Access.

VIEWING AND SORTING DATA

How can I view the data in a database? Displaying the tables on-screen and **browsing** through the data (viewing records) is an option with most databases. In many instances you'll only want to view the data. For example, if you want to register for an additional course for the current semester, the admissions clerk would browse the roster database to determine which courses you are already taking. But browsing through a large database is time consuming unless the records are in an order that makes your task easy.

How can I reorder records in a database? You can easily **sort** (or **index**) a database into the order that you need. Sorting a database involves organizing it in a new fashion. Figure 11.12a shows an Access data table in which the records were input in no particular order. By clicking the drop-down arrow next to the field name (in this case, Last Name) and selecting Sort Ascending (the first option on the menu), the database displays the records in alphabetical order by last name, as shown in Figure 11.12b.

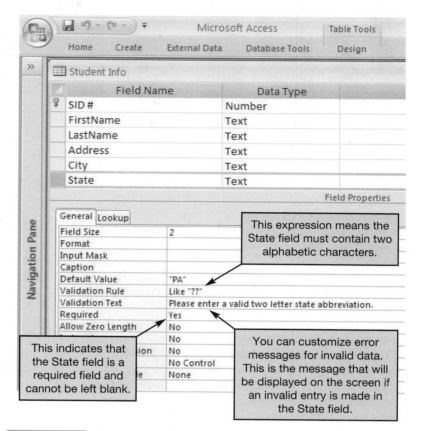

FIGURE 11.11

The field properties table in Access is shown for the State field. Although several types of validation rules have been activated here, you probably wouldn't find it necessary to use all of them at once.

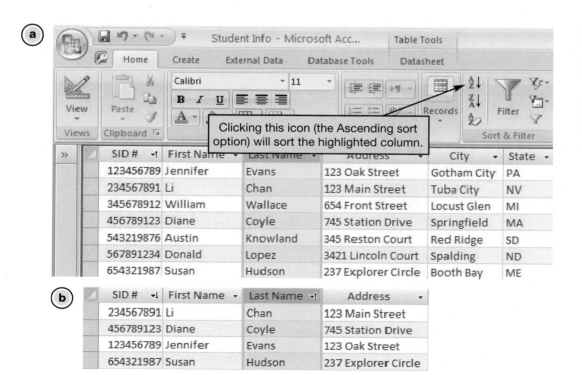

FIGURE 11.12

(a) Shown is an unsorted table. Notice that the Last Name column (which we want to sort on) is selected (shaded). Selecting the highlighted sorting option (Ascending) produces the sorted output (b) with the records sorted in ascending alphabetical order by last name.

Structured Query Language (SQL)

To extract records from a database, you use a query language. Almost all relational and object relational databases today use **structured query language**, or **SQL**. For example, Oracle, Microsoft SQL Server, Microsoft Access, IBM DB2, and Sybase are all popular databases that use SQL.

When relational databases were first developed in the early 1970s, each DBMS software product contained its own query language. This meant that database administrators had to learn a new language whenever they worked with a different DBMS. Also, the early query languages were mathematically based and often difficult to master. E. F. Codd, who has been called the father of relational databases, proposed a standardized query language when working at IBM in the mid-1970s.

The original language was called SEQUEL, short for structured English query language. The idea was to make queries easy by using English language–like sentence structure. Database software designers enthusiastically accepted the concept, and a modified version of the original SEQUEL language, named SQL, was developed. Oracle first introduced SQL in a commercial database product in 1979. It has been the de facto standard language for relational databases since then.

SQL uses relational algebra to extract data from databases. **Relational algebra** is the use of English-like expressions that have variables and operations, much like algebraic equations. Variables include table names, field names, or selection criteria for the data you wish to display. Operations include directions such as *select* (which enables you to pick variable names), *from* (which tells the database which table to use), and *where* (which enables you to specify selection criteria). The two most common queries used to extract data using relational algebra are select queries and join queries.

A **select query** displays a subset of data from a table (or tables) based on the criteria you specify. A typical select query has the following format:

SELECT (Field Name 1, Field Name 2, …)
FROM (Table Name)
WHERE (Selection Criteria)

The first line of the query contains variables for the field names you want to display. The FROM statement enables you to specify the table name from which the data will be retrieved. The last line (the WHERE statement) is used only when you wish to specify which records need to be displayed (such as all students with GPAs greater than 3.2). If you wish to display all the

FIGURE 11.13

When the query on the left is applied to the Student Information table (a), it restricts the output to only a phone list (b). The query on the right, which uses a WHERE statement, further restricts the phone list to only students from Massachusetts (c).

rows (records) in the table, then you do not use the WHERE statement.

Suppose you want to create a telephone list from the Student Information table in Figure 11.13a that includes all students. The SQL query you would send to the database would look like this:

SELECT (First Name, Last Name, Telephone)
FROM (Student Information Table)

Figure 11.13b shows the output from this query.

But what if you want a phone list only of students from Massachusetts? In that case, you would add a WHERE statement to the query as follows:

SELECT (First Name, Last Name, Telephone)
FROM (Student Information Table)
WHERE (State = MA)

This query restricts the output to students who live in Massachusetts, as shown in Figure 11.13c. Notice that the State field in the Student Information table can be used by the query (in this case, as a limiting criterion), but the contents of the State field are not required to be displayed in the query results. This explains why the output shown in Figure 11.13c doesn't show the State field.

When you want to extract data that is in two or more tables, you use a **join query**. The query actually links (or joins) the two tables using the common field in both tables and extracts the relevant data from each. The format for a simple join query for two tables is as follows:

SELECT (Field Name 1, Field Name 2)
FROM (Table 1 Name, Table 2 Name)
WHERE (Table 1 Name.Common Field Name = Table 2 Name.Common Field Name)
AND (Selection Criteria)

Notice how similar this is to a select query, although the FROM statement must now contain two table names. Also, in a join query, the WHERE statement is split into two parts. In the first part (right after WHERE), the relation between the two tables is defined by identifying the common fields between the tables. The second part of the statement (after AND) is where the selection criteria are defined.

The AND means that both parts of the statement must be true for the query to produce results (i.e., the two related fields must exist and the selection criteria must be valid). Figure 11.14 illustrates a join query for the Student Information and Roster Master tables to produce a class roster for students.

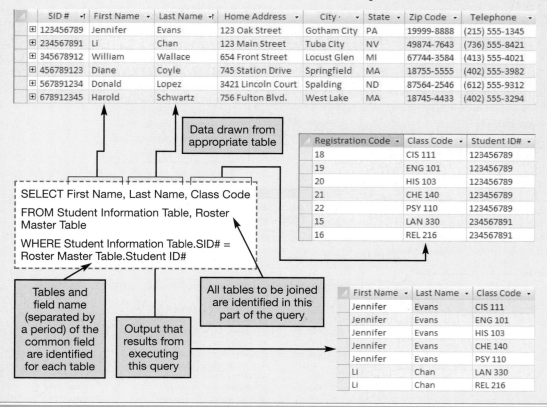

FIGURE 11.14

This join query will display a student roster for each student in the Student Information table. Notice that the WHERE statement creates the join by defining the common fields (in this case SID # and Student ID#) in each table.

SOUND BYTE

Creating an Access 2007 Database

In this Sound Byte, you'll learn how to create an Access database to catalog a collection of CDs and DVDs. The Sound Byte will take you through a step-by-step process that will result in a fully functional small database.

What if I want to find a particular piece of data in a database? Browsing records works for small databases, but if the amount of data you are managing is small, then you probably would just maintain it in a list anyway. To find data in a large database quickly and efficiently, however, you need to be able to request only the data you are seeking. Therefore, database management systems let you query the data to enable you to find what you're looking for.

EXTRACTING OR QUERYING DATA

What is a query? A **query** is simply a question or inquiry. A **database query** is a question or inquiry you ask the database so that it provides you with the records you wish to view. When you query a database, you instruct it to search for a particular piece of data such as a student's grade point average (GPA). Queries also enable you to have the database select and display records that match certain criteria such as all of the students whose GPAs are 3.2 or higher.

Is querying a database as simple as just asking the proper question? All modern DBMSs contain a **query**

language that the software uses to retrieve and display records. A query language consists of its own vocabulary and sentence structure, which you use to frame the requests. Query languages are similar to full-blown programming languages but are usually much easier to learn. The most popular query language today is structured query language, or **SQL** (pronounced "sequel").

Do I have to learn a query language to develop queries for my database? Fortunately, modern database systems provide wizards to guide you through the process of creating queries. Figure 11.15 shows an example of an Access wizard being used to create a query. Not only does the wizard speed up the process of creating queries, but also you don't have to learn a query language.

Did the Simple Query Wizard use SQL to create the query? When you use Access, you're actually using SQL commands without realizing it. The Simple Query Wizard takes the criteria you specify and creates the appropriate SQL commands behind the scenes.

However, you may want to create your own SQL queries in Access, modify existing

FIGURE 11.15

(a) The Simple Query Wizard in Microsoft Access makes creating queries easy. The wizard displays all fields available in your table so that you can select the ones you need to see. (b) In this example, name and address information are selected.

>The Simple Query Wizard can be found on the **Create** tab, in the **Other** group. Click **Query Wizard** and select **Simple Query Wizard**.

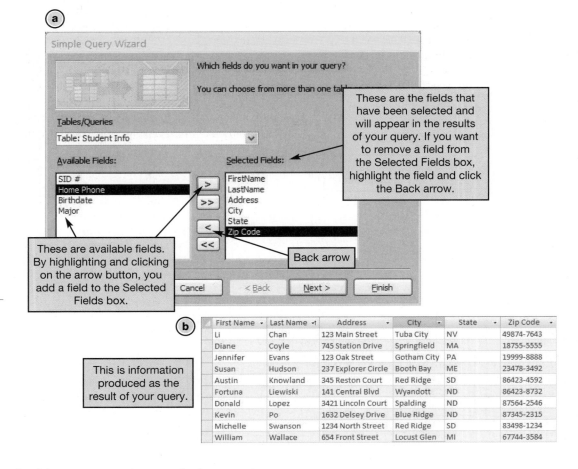

queries at the SQL language level, or view the SQL code that the wizard created. To do so, with a query open, select SQL View from the View drop-down box on the ribbon. This displays the SQL code that makes up the query. Figure 11.16 shows the SQL code that the query in Figure 11.15 created.

OUTPUTTING DATA

How do I get data out of a database?
The most common form of output for any database is a printed (or electronic) report. Businesses routinely summarize the data within their databases and compile **summary data reports**. For instance, at the end of each semester your school prints a grade report for you that shows the classes you took and the grades you received.

Can I transfer data to another software application? Database systems also can be used to **export** data to other applications. Exporting data involves putting it into an electronic file in a format that another application can understand. For example, the query shown in the wizard in Figure 11.15 may be used to generate a list of recipients for a form letter. In that case, the query output would be directed to a file that could be easily **imported** into Microsoft Word so that the data could be used in a mail merge process to generate letters.

In the next section, we look at the operation of relational databases and explore how relationships are established among tables in these databases.

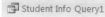

SELECT [Student Info].FirstName, [Student Info].LastName, [Student Info].Address, [Student Info].City, [Student Info].State, [Student Info].[Zip Code]
FROM [Student Info];

Relational Database Operations

As explained earlier, relational databases operate by organizing data into various tables based on logical groupings. For example, all student address and contact information (phone numbers, e-mail addresses, and so on) would be grouped into one table. Because not all of the data in a relational database is stored in the same table, a methodology must be implemented to link data between tables.

In relational databases, the links between tables that define how the data is related are referred to as **relationships**. To establish a relationship between two tables, both tables must have a common field (or column). Common fields contain the same data (such as student ID numbers), as shown in Figure 11.17.

Relationships in databases can take three forms: one-to-one, one-to-many, or many-to-many. A **one-to-one relationship** indicates that for each record in a table there is only one corresponding record in a related table. For example, a parking space can be occupied by only one car at a time, so a table that links assigned parking spaces to a table of faculty members would have a one-to-one relationship. One-to-many relationships occur most frequently in relational databases.

FIGURE 11.16

The SQL View window shows the SQL code that the wizard created for the query in Figure 11.15. Although it is a relatively simple SELECT statement, it is much easier to create with the wizard.

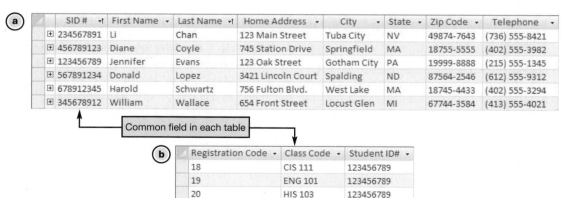

FIGURE 11.17

(a) The Student Information table and the (b) Roster Master table share the common field of student ID number. This allows a relationship to be established between the two tables.

TRENDS IN IT

Computers in Society: Can a Database Catch a Criminal?

When you watch police dramas on TV, detectives often use fingerprints to catch criminals. But until recently, the process of identifying suspects by their fingerprints was time consuming and ineffective in catching criminals who moved from state to state.

The use of fingerprints as a method of identification dates back to the beginning of the 20th century when the "Henry" method of fingerprint classification (still in use today) was developed in England. Fingerprints are unique to each individual and do not change during the course of a lifetime. Therefore, they are ideally suited for identification purposes in criminal investigations.

Originally, investigators collected fingerprints by placing ink on a person's fingertips and rolling his or her fingers on a piece of card stock. Fingerprint identification experts then manually compared new suspects' fingerprints with existing paper files of fingerprints. This was a time-consuming process, and the pool of potential suspects was limited to the fingerprints that the particular law enforcement agency had collected.

Lack of a large pool of fingerprints was less of a problem in the United States during the early 1900s because the population was not particularly mobile. However, in the 1930s, criminals became more mobile. The Federal Bureau of Investigation (FBI) thus undertook the maintenance of a large centralized manual database of fingerprint cards and photos of these cards and provided fingerprint identification services to local law enforcement agencies. However, identification was still performed manually, and many local law enforcement agencies had

neither the manpower nor the money to submit their fingerprint records to the FBI. Although it still identified many criminals, the system was inefficient.

During the 1960s and 1970s, the FBI began researching methods for using computers to perform fingerprint identification. These early efforts led to the Integrated Automated Fingerprint Identification System (IAFIS). Thanks to the IAFIS, instead of using ink and card stock, new fingerprints are now digitally scanned directly into a computer. In addition, existing fingerprint cards can be scanned and captured in the database. The IAFIS made fingerprint searching and identification much quicker through the use of its computer-searching algorithms.

In the late 1990s, the FBI released a software package called Remote Fingerprint Editing Software (RFES). The RFES package (shown in Figure 11.18) enables local law enforcement agencies to capture fingerprints electronically and perform searches in the IAFIS database. Law enforcement agencies use electronic readers to scan fingerprints lifted from crime scenes into the computer. The software then searches the IAFIS database for prints that match.

As more law enforcement agencies scan old fingerprint cards and post them to the IAFIS, the odds of finding a fingerprint match increases. In fact, criminal investigators are submitting fingerprints from old, unsolved cases to the IAFIS database in attempts to find a match to fingerprints collected in cases where no suspects were found by conventional methods. In Pennsylvania, this approach resulted in the arrest and conviction of a

A **one-to-many relationship** is characterized by a record in one table (such as the student information table in Figure 11.17). There is only one instance of a student ID in the Student Information table, but there can be many instances of the same student ID in the Master Roster table. Students can register for many classes, but each registration record can be related to only one student.

Many-to-many relationships are characterized by records in one table being related to multiple records in a second table and vice versa. For instance, a table of students could be related to a table of student employers. The employers could employ many students, and students could work for more than one employer.

NORMALIZATION OF DATA

How do I decide which tables I need and what data to put in them? You create database tables (or files) for two reasons: to hold unique data about a person or thing and to describe unique events or transactions. In databases, the goal is to reduce data redundancy by recording data only once. This process is called **normalization** of the data. Yet the tables must still work well enough together to enable you to retrieve the data when you need it. Tables should be grouped using logical data that can be identified uniquely.

Let's look at an example. In Figure 11.19, the Class Registration - Fall table contains a

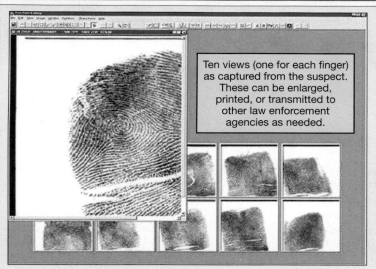

FIGURE 11.18

Law enforcement agencies can use the FBI's Remote Fingerprint Editing Software to search the IAFIS database, capture fingerprints from new suspects, and scan in information from existing fingerprint cards.

suspect for a murder that had been unsolved for 14 years!

Even more cutting edge on the technology front is the identification of suspects purely by the DNA evidence (such as hair or skin cells—from people or their pets!) left behind at a crime scene. Put simply, DNA is essentially an instruction manual and blueprint for how everything in your body is assembled and works.

Although much of human DNA does not vary from person to person, 3 million base pairs of DNA (or about 0.10 percent of your entire DNA structure) does vary from person to person, which is enough to allow identification of a specific individual from a DNA sample.

The FBI maintains a database called the Combined DNA Index System (CODIS) that accumulates DNA profiles based on DNA samples collected from felons by federal, state, and local law enforcement agencies. CODIS enables federal, state, and local crime labs to exchange and compare DNA profiles electronically, which assists in the identification of suspects when no other leads are available. Aside from convicting offenders, DNA evidence has also been used to prove the innocence of people who have been wrongly convicted, usually resulting in their release from prison. A prime example is William Gregory, a Kentucky resident, who was convicted of rape in 1993. He was subsequently released from prison after DNA tests showed that hairs found at the rape scene were not his. Had DNA evidence been available at the time of his arrest, he might never have been incarcerated.

Developing an efficient, nationwide system of fingerprint and DNA identification would not be possible without the use of computerized databases. Databases enable the information to be stored, sorted, and retrieved quickly. Next time you're watching a police drama on television, don't forget that databases are working behind the scenes to identify the criminals. For more information on DNA identification, see **http://science.howstuffworks.com/dna-evidence.htm**.

	A	B	C	D	E	F	G	H	I	J
1	Class Registration - Fall									
2										
3	SID #	Last Name	First Name	Home Address	City	State	Zip Code	Class Code	Class Name	# of Credits
4	234567891	Chan	Li	123 Main Street	Tuba City	NV	49874-7643	LAN 330	Japanese 1	3
5	234567891	Chan	Li	123 Main Street	Tuba City	NV	49874-7643	REL 216	Early Buddhism	3
6	234567891	Chan	Li	123 Main Street	Tuba City	NV	49874-7643	ENG 102	English Comp 2	3
7	456789123	Coyle	Diane	745 Station Drive	Springfield	MA	18755-5555			
8	123456789	Evans	Jennifer	123 Oak Street	Gotham City	PA	19999-8888	CIS 111	Programming	3
9	123456789	Evans	Jennifer	123 Oak Street	Gotham City	PA	19999-8888	ENG 101	English Comp 1	3
10	123456789	Evans	Jennifer	123 Oak Street	Gotham City	PA	19999-8888	HIS 103	Western Civ	3
11	123456789	Evans	Jennifer	123 Oak Street	Gotham City	PA	19999-8888	CHE 140	Chemistry	4
12	123456789	Evans	Jennifer	124 Oak Street	Gotham City	PA	19999-8888	PSY 110	Intro to Psychology	3
13	567891234	Lopez	Donald	3421 Lincoln Court	Spalding	ND	87564-2546	HIS 401	16th Century Europe	3
14	567891234	Lopez	Donald	3421 Lincoln Court	Spalding	ND	87564-2546	SOC 310	Interpersonal Relationships	3
15	567891234	Lopez	Donald	3421 Lincoln Court	Spalding	ND	87564-2546	PSY 110	Intro to Psych	3

FIGURE 11.19

Data from unrelated topics is located in the Class Registration - Fall list. The column headings in blue are related to student contact data, whereas the column headings in red relate to enrollment information. To construct a database, these topics should be contained in separate tables.

FIGURE 11.20

Student contact data is grouped in the Student Information table and needs to be entered only once for each student. The primary key for each record is a unique student ID number.

SID#	First Name	Last Name	Home Address	City	State	Zip Code	Telephone
⊞ 234567891	Li	Chan	123 Main Street	Tuba City	NV	49874-7643	(736) 555-8421
⊞ 456789123	Diane	Coyle	745 Station Drive	Springfield	MA	18755-5555	(402) 555-3982
⊞ 123456789	Jennifer	Evans	123 Oak Street	Gotham City	PA	19999-8888	(215) 555-1345
⊞ 567891234	Donald	Lopez	3421 Lincoln Court	Spalding	ND	87564-2546	(612) 555-9312
⊞ 678912345	Harold	Schwartz	756 Fulton Blvd.	West Lake	MA	18745-4433	(402) 555-3294
⊞ 345678912	William	Wallace	654 Front Street	Locust Glen	MI	67744-3584	(413) 555-4021

FIGURE 11.21

Although it contains related data (registration information), this table still contains a great deal of duplicate data and no usable primary key.

Student ID #	Class Code	Class Name	# Of Credits
123456789	PSY 110	Intro to Psychology	
123456789	CIS 111	Programming	
123456789	ENG 101	English Comp 1	
123456789	HIS 103	Western Civ	
123456789	CHE 140	Chemistry	
234567891	LAN 330	Japanese 1	3
234567891	ENG 102	English Comp 2	
234567891	REL 216	Early Buddhism	
345678912	SOC 220	The Art of Negotiation	
345678912	HIS 204	Scottish History	
345678912	PEH 125	Fencing 1	
567891234	PSY 110	Intro to Psychology	

Names and course numbers must be duplicated for each student taking the course.

Also, there is no unique field that can be used as a primary key. Student ID# cannot be used as the primary key because the same ID# will be entered on multiple records when a student enrolls in more than one course.

great deal of data related to individual students and their course registration. However, each table in a relational database should contain a related group of data on a single topic. There are two distinct topics in this list: student contact information and student registration information. Therefore, this list needs to be divided into two tables so that the distinct data (contact data and registration data) can be categorized appropriately. Also, data about each student is duplicated in this table, and normalizing the data eliminates this duplication.

The Student Information table in Figure 11.20 organizes all of the student contact information found in Figure 11.19 into a separate table. Notice that the information for each student needs to be shown only once instead of multiple times as in the list in the figure. The unique primary key for this table is the student's ID number. Student information might be needed in a variety of instances and by a variety of departments, but it needs to reside only in this one database table, which many departments of the school can share.

Next, we could put the registration data found in Figure 11.19 for each student in a separate table, as shown in Figure 11.21. There is no need to repeat student name and address data in this table. Instead, each student can be identified by his or her student ID number. However, there are problems with this table. Each class name and class code has to be repeated for every student taking the course, and there is no unique field that can be used as a primary key for this table. This presents another opportunity to further normalize the data.

What can be done to fix the table in Figure 11.21? In Figure 11.21, we have identified more data that should be grouped

SOUND BYTE

Improving an Access 2007 Database

In this Sound Byte, you'll learn how to create input forms, queries, and reports to simplify maintenance of your CD and DVD database. You'll follow along step by step using Microsoft Access wizards to create and modify queries to suit your needs.

Computers in Society: Need Cash? Use Databases to Find Your Property

Did you ever lose a check before cashing it and forget to get it replaced (or figure you couldn't)? Did you ever relocate quickly and forget to get your security deposit back on your apartment? Did your grandmother open a bank account in your name and forget to tell you about it? These are all examples of unclaimed property. And thanks to the Internet and databases, it has never been easier to look for this "found money."

In most states, unclaimed property (bank accounts, security deposits on apartments, uncashed checks, and so on) is required by law to be turned over to the state treasury for safekeeping after a certain period of time. The state treasury is required to hold the property for a period of time (sometimes forever) so that the rightful owner can make a claim. Until a few years ago, searching for your unclaimed property meant sifting through mountains of paper records at the state capitol.

But today, many states have unclaimed property databases deployed on the Web. Go to the official state Web site for the state where you think you may have unclaimed property and search on the terms "unclaimed property" or "abandoned property." Pennsylvania's site, located at **www.patreasury.org/unclaimed/search.html**, features a simple search box where you can enter your name to search for your pot of gold (see Figure 11.22a). Scan the resulting search list (see Figure 11.22b), and if you find an item that might be yours, follow the procedures set down by that state to make a claim and prove ownership.

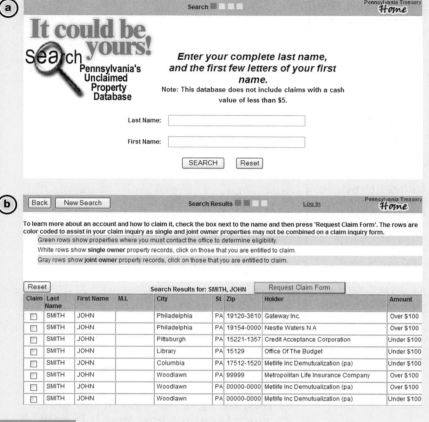

FIGURE 11.22

The state of Pennsylvania's unclaimed property Web site starts with a simple search form (a). The search results (b) might be just the place to find your missing funds.

If you are unsure which state your property is located in, then try the National Association of Unclaimed Property Administrators (**www.unclaimed. org**). This site provides the capability to search for money in all 50 states.

logically into another separate table: class code and class name. Therefore, we should create another table for just this information. This enables us to avoid repeating class names and codes. Figure 11.23 shows the Course master table. Note that the class code is unique for every course and acts as a primary key in this table.

To solve the other problems with the table in Figure 11.21, we need a way to uniquely identify each student registration for a specific course. This can be solved by creating a course registration number that will be unique and assigned by the database as records are entered. Figure 11.24 shows the resulting Roster master table.

FIGURE 11.23

Related information about courses (class code, class name, and the credits for the class) is grouped logically in one table. The unique class code is the primary key.

Class Code	Class Name	Credits
CHE 140	Chemistry	4
CIS 111	Programming	3
ENG 101	English Comp 1	3
ENG 102	English Comp 2	3
HIS 103	Western Civ	3
HIS 204	Scottish History	3
HIS 401	16th Century Europe	3
LAN 330	Japanese 1	3
PEH 125	Fencing 1	3
PSY 110	Intro to Psychology	3
REL 216	Early Buddhism	3
SOC 220	The Art of Negotiation	2
SOC 310	Interpersonal Relationships	3

FIGURE 11.24

The Roster master table shows only pertinent data related to a student's registration. Only three fields are needed: the registration code number (which is the unique primary key), the class code, and the student's ID number. This approach greatly minimizes duplicate data.

Registration Code	Class Code	Student ID#
18	CIS 111	123456789
19	ENG 101	123456789
20	HIS 103	123456789
21	CHE 140	123456789
22	PSY 110	123456789
15	LAN 330	234567891
16	REL 216	234567891
17	ENG 102	234567891
28	HIS 204	345678912
29	PEH 125	345678912
30	SOC 220	345678912

How do I get the data in the tables to work together now that it is split up? The entire premise behind relational databases is that relationships are established among the tables to allow the data to be shared. As noted earlier, to establish a relationship between two tables, the tables must have a common field (column). This usually involves the primary keys of a table.

For instance, to track registrations by student in the Roster master table in Figure 11.24, the student ID number is the logical piece of data to use. The student ID number is the primary key in the Student Information table in Figure 11.20; however, in the Roster master table, the student ID number is called a **foreign key**—the primary key of another table that is included for purposes of establishing relationships with that other table. Figure 11.25 shows the relationships that exist among the Course master, Roster master, and Student Information tables. Relationships among tables can be established whenever you need them.

Because relationships are vital to the operation of the database, it is important to ensure that there are no inconsistencies in the data entered in the common fields of two tables. Each foreign key (Student ID# in the Roster master table in Figure 11.24) entered into a table must be a valid primary key from the related table (SID# from the Student Information table in Figure 11.20).

For instance, if 392135684 is not a valid student ID number for any student listed in the Student Information table, then it should not be entered into the Roster master table. Each entry in the Roster master table must correspond to a student (linked by his or her SID#) in the Student Information table. If this requirement is not applied to foreign keys, then a relationship cannot be established between tables.

How do I ensure that a foreign key field contains a valid primary key from the related table? To apply this restraint, when defining a relationship in a database, you have the option of enforcing referential integrity for that relationship. **Referential integrity** means that for each value in the foreign key of one table, there is a corresponding value in the primary key of the related table.

For instance, if you attempt to enter a record in the Roster master table with an SID# of 156784522 and referential integrity is being enforced, the database checks to ensure that a record with SID# 156784522 exists in the Student Information table. If the corresponding record does not exist, then an error message displays. Establishing referential integrity between two tables helps prevent inconsistent data from being entered.

All of the data that is collected in databases needs to be stored and managed. Database administrators (DBAs) are the IT professionals responsible for designing, constructing, and maintaining databases. They review and manage data on an ongoing basis to ensure data is flowing smoothly in and out of the database. Figure 11.26 shows a view of an Oracle 11g database that is used primarily by DBAs when reviewing the performance of a database. In the next section, we explore the types of systems where databases are typically used today.

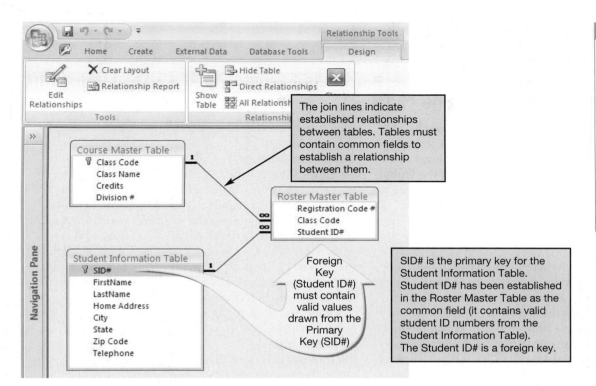

FIGURE 11.25

The join lines indicate established relationships between tables. Tables must contain common fields to establish a relationship between them.

SID# is the primary key for the Student Information Table. Student ID# has been established in the Roster Master Table as the common field (it contains valid student ID numbers from the Student Information Table). The Student ID# is a foreign key.

Foreign Key (Student ID#) must contain valid values drawn from the Primary Key (SID#)

FIGURE 11.25

The Relationships screen in Microsoft Access visually represents the relationships established between tables. Notice that foreign keys in related tables do not have to have the same field names as the primary keys in the other table. They merely have to contain the same type of data.

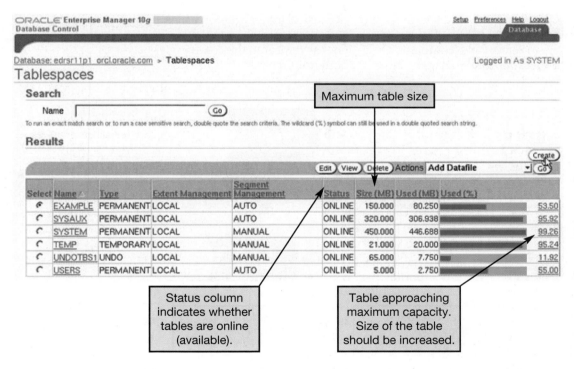

Maximum table size

Status column indicates whether tables are online (available).

Table approaching maximum capacity. Size of the table should be increased.

FIGURE 11.26

The Tablespaces section of Enterprise Manager (in Oracle 11g) makes it easy for DBAs to review data about tables in a glance and make adjustments where appropriate.

Data Storage

At the simplest level, data is stored in a single database on a database server, and you retrieve the data as needed. This works fine for small databases and when all of the data you are interested in is in a single database. But problems arise when all the data you need is not in one convenient spot. Large storage repositories called *data warehouses* and *data marts* help solve this problem.

DATA WAREHOUSES

What is a data warehouse? A **data warehouse** is a large-scale electronic repository of data that contains and organizes all

Emerging Technologies: Web Portal Enables Krispy Kreme to Manage Its Dough ... Without Going Nuts!

Krispy Kreme didn't build its doughnut empire by managing information poorly. Now that the company operates more than 470 stores in the United States, Australia, South Korea, Canada, Mexico, and the United Kingdom, effectively managing information is even more critical to making "dough." To combine all its information systems and make them accessible, Krispy Kreme created its own enterprise portal (see Figure 11.27).

A portal is a Web site where many types of data services or applications can be accessed at one time. One of the best-known consumer portals is Yahoo!, which provides visitors with everything from telephone directory listings to games in a one-stop shop. But portal technology is not just for the consumer market. Enterprise portals integrate traditional back-office operations (such as supply ordering and deliveries) with services such as e-mail and employee training, which front-line employees need to function.

Krispy Kreme's enterprise portal is called **myKrispy Kreme.com**. One of the main reasons the company created the portal was to provide store managers and

franchise owners with an easy way to place orders. The company also hoped the portal would increase the speed of its order processing by transmitting all data electronically over the Internet. After deploying the portal, ordering errors decreased by almost 90 percent, and distribution representatives (who are responsible for filling orders and having the materials distributed to the stores) were able to handle at least 10 additional stores each. Meanwhile, an inventory management system that is part of the portal provides store managers and corporate management with real-time views of inventory levels down to the specific doughnut type.

Other functions of the Krispy Kreme portal provide e-mail services, news updates, contest information, and employee training. Training videos are streamed over the Internet to ensure that employees are trained consistently from outlet to outlet. And multilingual portions of the portal are deployed to support the overseas expansion into markets such as Mexico and South Korea. The portal and information management are now as critical to the company's success as its secret doughnut recipe!

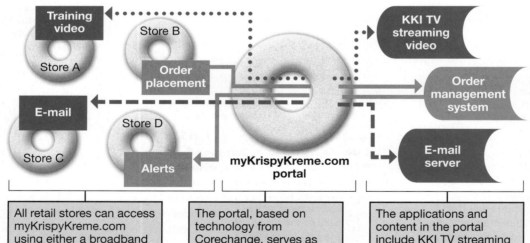

FIGURE 11.27

Doughnuts aren't the only thing hot at Krispy Kreme. The company's portal keeps information flowing among stores, corporate offices, and vendors.

All retail stores can access myKrispyKreme.com using either a broadband or dial-up connection to the Internet. Employees can watch training videos, place orders, check existing orders, assess inventory levels, and receive alerts.

The portal, based on technology from Corechange, serves as the conduit to multiple applications and data sources as well as the Web.

The applications and content in the portal include KKI TV streaming training videos, an order management system based on software from Integrated Visual Systems, e-mail, weather, and news.

the data related to an organization in one place. Individual databases contain a wealth of information, but each database's information usually pertains to one topic.

For instance, the order database at **Amazon.com** contains such information about book orders as your name, address, and payment information, and the book name. However, the order database does not contain information on inventory levels of books, nor does it list suppliers from which out-of-stock books can be obtained. Data warehouses, therefore, consolidate information from disparate sources to present an enterprise-wide view of business operations.

Is data in a data warehouse organized the same way as in a normal database? Data in the data warehouse is organized by subject. Most databases focus on one specific operational aspect of business operations. For example, insurance companies sell many types of insurance, such as life, automobile, and homeowners' insurance. Different divisions of the insurance company are responsible for each type of insurance and track the policies they sell in different databases (one for automobile insurance policy sales and one for life insurance policy sales, for example), as shown in Figure 11.28.

These databases capture specific information about each type of policy. The Automobile Policy Sales database captures information about driving accident history, car model, and the age and gender of the drivers because this information is pertinent to the pricing of car insurance policies. The Life Insurance Policy Sales database captures information about the age and gender of the policyholder and whether the insured smokes, but it does not include details about cars or driving records.

However, total policies sold (and the resulting revenue generated) is critical to the management of the insurance company no matter what type of policy is involved. Therefore, an insurance company's data warehouse would have a subject called Policy Sales Subject (see Figure 11.28) that would contain information about *all* policies sold throughout the company. The Policy Sales Subject is a database that contains information from the other databases the company maintains. However, all data in the Policy Sales Subject database is specifically related to policy sales.

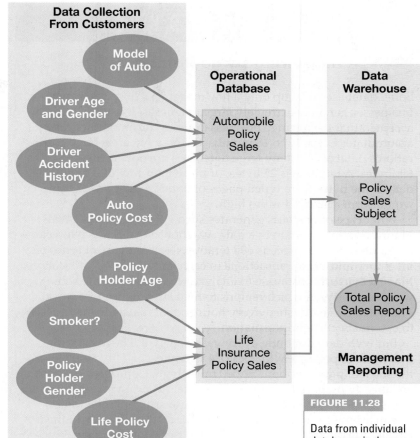

FIGURE 11.28

Data from individual databases is drawn together under appropriate subject headings in a data warehouse. Managers can then produce comprehensive reports that would be impossible to create from the individual databases.

From the Policy Sales Subject database, it is easy for managers to produce comprehensive reports such as the Total Policy Sales Report, as shown in Figure 11.28, that can contain information pertaining to all policy sales.

Are data warehouses much larger than conventional databases? Data warehouses, like conventional warehouses, are vast repositories of information. The data contained within them is not operational in nature, but rather archival. Data warehouse data is **time-variant data**, meaning it doesn't all pertain to one period in time.

The warehouse contains current values, such as amounts due from customers, as well as **historical data**. If you want to examine the buying habits of a certain type of customer, then you need data about both current and prior purchases. Having time-variant data in the warehouse enables you to analyze the past, examine the present in light of historical data, and make projections about the future.

BITS AND BYTES

Measuring Large Databases

Some databases take up only a few megabytes of space. However, businesses generate extremely large databases. It is widely accepted that the average business doubles the amount of data it accumulates every 12 to 18 months. So, how big are a large corporation's databases? Many large databases are now measured in terabytes. A terabyte is 2^{40} bytes, or more than 1 trillion bytes of data. If the bytes were typed pages of paper, a terabyte of pages would form a stack 51 miles high!

What type of business generates such volumes of data? Wal-Mart tracks information in a data warehouse that holds two years of records—which exceeds 600 terabytes—relating to all types of inventory and sales transactions in each and every Wal-Mart store. Managers use the database to analyze what products are selling well (or poorly) in which regions to help streamline store stock. The database is refreshed every hour so that managers have access to extremely current information.

But with data doubling every year, soon we'll be measuring databases in petabytes (that's 1,024 terabytes, or 2^{50} bytes). Now the stack of paper is about 52,000 miles high. Computer scientists are already prepared for even more data: An exabyte is a staggering 1,024 petabytes, or 2^{60} bytes. Large government scientific research projects, such as those conducted at the Stanford Linear Accelerator Center, already have databases containing petabytes of information. If databases double in size every year, then it won't be long before there is an exabyte of data stored somewhere near you.

POPULATING DATA WAREHOUSES

How are data warehouses populated with data? Source data for data warehouses can come from three places:

1. internal sources (such as company databases),

2. external sources (suppliers, vendors, and so on), and

3. customers or visitors to a company's Web site.

Internal data sources are obvious. Sales, billing, inventory, and customer databases all provide a wealth of information. However, internal information is not contained exclusively in databases. Spreadsheets and other ad hoc analysis tools may contain data that needs to be loaded into the warehouse.

External data sources include vendors and suppliers that often provide data regarding product specifications, shipment methods and dates, electronic billing information, and so on. In addition, a virtual wealth of customer (or potential customer) information is available by monitoring the clickstream of the company Web site.

What is a clickstream, and why is it important? Companies can use software on their Web sites to capture information about each click that users make as they navigate through the site. This information is referred to as **clickstream data**. Monitoring the clickstream helps managers assess the effectiveness of a Web site. Using clickstream data-capture tools, a company can determine which pages users visit most often, how long users stay on each page, which sites directed users to the company site, and the user demographics. Such data can provide valuable clues to what a company needs to improve on its site to stimulate sales.

DATA STAGING

Does all source data fit into the warehouse? No two source databases are the same. Although two databases might contain similar information (such as customer names and addresses), the format of the data is most likely different in each database. Therefore, source data must be "staged" before entering the data warehouse. **Data staging** consists of three steps:

1. extraction of the data from source databases,

2. transformation (reformatting) of the data, and

3. storage of the data in the warehouse.

Many different software programs and procedures may have to be created to extract the data from varied sources and to reformat it for storage in the data warehouse. The nature and complexity of the source data determine the complexity of the data staging process.

Once the data is stored in the data warehouse, how can it be extracted and used? Managers can query the data warehouse in much the same way you query an Access database. However, because there is more data in the warehouse, significantly more flexible tools are needed to perform such queries. Online analytical processing

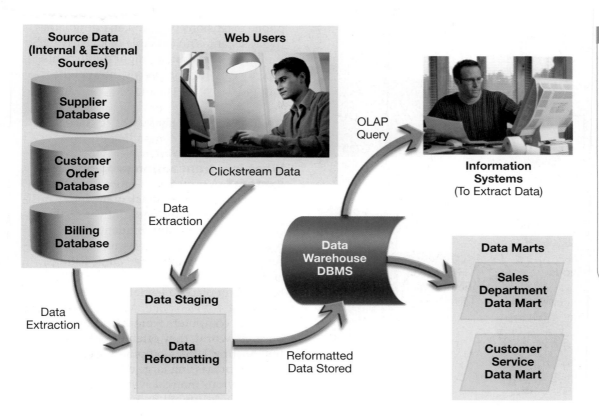

FIGURE 11.29

Source Data (Internal & External Sources)

Supplier Database

Customer Order Database

Billing Database

Web Users

Clickstream Data

Data Extraction

Data Extraction

Data Staging

Data Reformatting

Reformatted Data Stored

Data Warehouse DBMS

OLAP Query

Information Systems (To Extract Data)

Data Marts

Sales Department Data Mart

Customer Service Data Mart

Shown here is an overview of the data warehouse process. Data staging is vital because different data must be extracted and then reformatted to fit the data structure defined in the data warehouse DBMS. Data can be extracted using powerful OLAP query tools, or it can be stored in special-ized data marts for use by specific employee groups.

(OLAP) software provides standardized tools for viewing and manipulating data in a data warehouse. The key feature of OLAP tools is that they enable flexible views of the data, which the software user can easily change.

DATA MARTS

Is finding the right data in a huge data warehouse difficult? Looking for the data you need in a data warehouse can be daunting when there are terabytes of data. Therefore, small slices of the data warehouse called **data marts** are often created. Whereas data warehouses have an enterprise-wide depth, the information in data marts pertains to a single department.

For instance, if you work in the sales department, you need accurate sales-related information at your fingertips—and you would not want to wade through customer service data, accounts payable data, and product shipping data to get it. Therefore, a data mart that contains infor-mation relevant only to the sales depart-ment can be created to make the task of finding this data easier. An overview of the data-warehousing process is illustrated in Figure 11.29.

Managing Data: Information Systems

Making intelligent decisions about develop-ing new products, creating marketing strate-gies, and buying raw materials requires timely, accurate information. **Information systems** are software-based solutions used to gather and analyze information. A system that delivers up-to-the-minute sales data on books to the computer of **Amazon.com**'s pres-ident is one example of an information sys-tem. Databases, data warehouses, and data marts are integral parts of information sys-tems because they store the information that makes information systems functional.

All information systems perform similar functions, including acquiring data, process-ing that data into information, storing the data, and providing the user with a number of output options with which to make the information meaningful and useful (see Figure 11.30). Most information systems fall into one of five categories: (1) office support systems, (2) transaction processing systems, (3) management information systems, (4) decision support systems, and (5) enterprise resource planning (ERP) systems. Each type of system almost always involves the use of one or more databases.

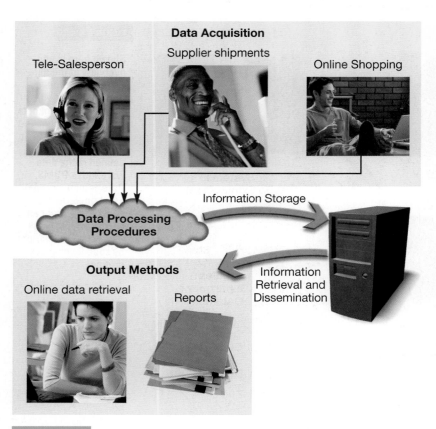

Data Acquisition

Tele-Salesperson   Supplier shipments   Online Shopping

Data Processing Procedures

Information Storage

Output Methods

Online data retrieval

Reports

Information Retrieval and Dissemination

FIGURE 11.30

All information systems perform similar functions, including acquiring data, processing that data into information, storing the data, and providing the user with a number of output options with which to make the information meaningful and useful.

OFFICE SUPPORT SYSTEMS

What does an office support system accomplish? An **office support system (OSS)** is designed to assist employees in accomplishing their day-to-day tasks and improve communications. Microsoft Office is an example of an OSS because it assists employees with routine tasks such as maintaining an employee phone list in Excel, designing a sales presentation in PowerPoint, and writing customer letters using Word.

Modern OSSs include software tools with which you are probably familiar, including e-mail, word-processing, spreadsheet, database, and presentation programs. OSSs had their roots in manual, paper-based systems that were developed before computers. After all, maintaining a company phone listing was necessary long before computers were invented. A paper listing of employee

phone extensions typed by an administrative assistant is an example of an early OSS. A modern OSS system might publish this directory on the company's intranet (its internal network).

TRANSACTION PROCESSING SYSTEMS

What is a transaction processing system? A **transaction processing system (TPS)** is used to keep track of everyday business activities. For example, at your college, transactions that occur frequently include registering students for classes, accepting tuition payments, mailing course listings, and printing course catalogs. Your college has TPSs in place to track these types of activities.

When computers were introduced to the business world, they often were put to work first hosting TPSs. Computers were much faster at processing large chunks of data than previous manual systems. Imagine having clerks typing up tuition invoices for each student at a 10,000-student university. Obviously, a computer can print invoices much quicker from a database.

How do transactions enter a TPS? Transactions can be entered manually or electronically. When you call a company and order a sweater, for example, the call taker enters your data into a TPS. When you purchase gasoline at a pay-at-the-pump terminal, the pump captures your credit card data and transmits it to a TPS, which automatically records a sale (gallons of gasoline and dollar value). Transactions are processed either in batches or in real time. Various departments in an organization then access the TPSs to extract the information they need to process additional transactions, as shown in Figure 11.31.

What is batch processing? **Batch processing** means that transaction data is accumulated until a certain point is reached, and then several transactions are processed all at once. Batch processing is appropriate for activities that are not time sensitive, such as developing a mailing list to mail out the new course catalogs that students have requested. A mailing label could be printed for each person as he or she requests a catalog, but it is more efficient to batch the requests and process them all at once when the catalogs are ready to be addressed.

How does real-time processing work? For most activities, processing and recording transactions in a TPS occur in real time. **Real-time processing** means that the database is queried and updated while the transaction is taking place. For instance, when you register for classes, the registration clerk checks to make sure seats are still available for the classes you want and records your registration in the class immediately. This **online transaction processing (OLTP)** ensures that the data in the TPS is as up-to-date as possible.

MANAGEMENT INFORMATION SYSTEMS

What is a management information system? A **management information system (MIS)** provides timely and accurate information that enables managers to make critical business decisions. MISs were a direct outgrowth of TPSs. Managers quickly realized that the data contained in TPSs was an extremely powerful tool only if the information could be organized and output in a useful form. Today's MISs are often built in as a feature of TPSs.

What does an MIS provide that a TPS does not? The original TPSs were usually designed to output detail reports. A **detail report** provides a list of the transactions that occurred during a certain time period. For example, during registration periods at your school, the registrar might receive a detail report that lists the students who registered for classes each day. Figure 11.32a shows an example of a detail report on daily enrollment.

Going beyond the detail reports provided by TPSs, MISs provide summary reports and exception reports. **Summary reports** provide a consolidated picture of detailed data. These reports usually include some calculation (totals) or visual displays of information (such as charts and graphs). Figure 11.32b shows an example of a summary report displaying total daily enrollment.

Exception reports show conditions that are unusual or that need attention by users of the system. The registrar at your college may get an exception report when all sections of a course are full, indicating that it may be time to schedule additional sections. Figure 11.32c shows an example of such an exception report.

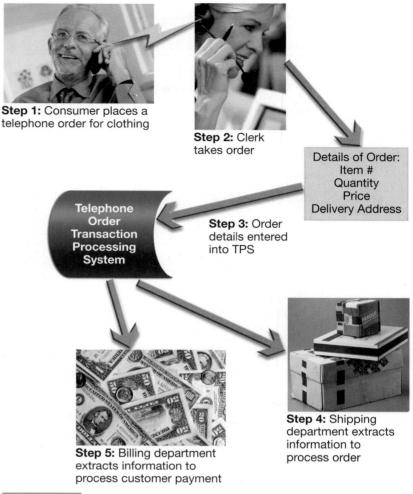

Step 1: Consumer places a telephone order for clothing

Step 2: Clerk takes order

Details of Order:
Item #
Quantity
Price
Delivery Address

Step 3: Order details entered into TPS

Telephone Order Transaction Processing System

Step 4: Shipping department extracts information to process order

Step 5: Billing department extracts information to process customer payment

FIGURE 11.31

TPSs help capture and track critical business information needed to complete business transactions successfully, such as the selling of merchandise over the telephone.

DECISION SUPPORT SYSTEMS

What is a decision support system? A **decision support system (DSS)** is designed to help managers develop solutions for specific problems. A DSS for a marketing department might provide statistical information on customer attributes (such as income levels, buying patterns, and so on) that would assist managers in making decisions regarding advertising strategy. A DSS not only uses data from databases and data warehouses but also enables users to add their own insights and experiences and apply them to the solution.

What does a decision support system look like? Database management systems, while playing an integral part of a

Daily Enrollment Report

Class Code	Class Name	Student ID#
CHE 140	Chemistry	123456789
CIS 111	Programming	123456789
ENG 101	English Comp 1	123456789
ENG 102	English Comp 2	234567891
ENG 102	English Comp 2	678912345
HIS 103	Western Civ	123456789
HIS 204	Scottish History	345678912
HIS 401	16th Century Europe	567891234

(b)

Enrollment Summary Report

Division Name	Total Credits
Chemistry	4
Computer Information Systems	5
English	9
History	9
Languages	3
Physical Education	3
Psychology	9
Religion	3
Sociology	3
Grand Total Credits	48

(c)

Class Sections Fully Enrolled Fall Semester

Class Code	Class Name
CHE 140	Inorganic Chemistry
ENG 101	English Comp 1
SOC 310	Interpersonal Relationships

FIGURE 11.32

The three types of management information system reports are (a) detail report, (b) summary report, and (c) exception report.

DSS, are supplemented by additional software systems in a DSS. In a DSS, the user interface provides the means of interaction between the user and the system. An effective user interface must be easy to learn. The other major components of a DSS are internal and external data sources, model management systems, and knowledge-based

systems. As shown in Figure 11.33, all of these systems work together to provide the user of the DSS with a broad base of information on which to base decisions.

INTERNAL AND EXTERNAL DATA SOURCES

What are internal and external data sources for DSSs? Data can be fed into the DSS from a variety of sources. Internal data sources are maintained by the same company that operates the DSS. For example, internal TPSs can provide a wealth of statistical data about customers, ordering patterns, inventory levels, and so on. **External data sources** include any source not owned by the company that owns the DSS, such as customer demographic data purchased from third parties, mailing lists, or statistics compiled by the federal government. Internal and external data sources provide a stream of data that is integrated into the DSS for analysis.

MODEL MANAGEMENT SYSTEMS

What function does a model management system perform? A model management system is software that assists in building management models in DSSs. A management model is an analysis tool that provides a view of a particular business situation (through the use of internal and external data) for the purposes of decision making. Models can be built to describe any business situation, such as the classroom space requirements for next semester or a listing of alternative satellite campus locations.

Internal models are developed inside the organization (such as a spreadsheet that shows current classroom use on a college campus). External models are purchased from third parties (such as statistics about student populations for two-year college students in the United States). Model management systems typically contain financial and statistical analysis tools used to analyze the data provided by models or to create additional models.

KNOWLEDGE-BASED SYSTEMS

What is a knowledge-based system, and how is it used in DSSs? A knowledge-based system provides

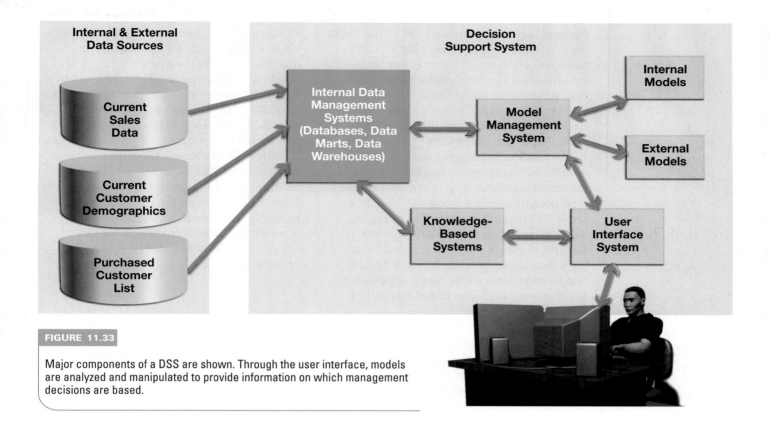

Internal & External Data Sources

Current Sales Data

Current Customer Demographics

Purchased Customer List

Decision Support System

Internal Data Management Systems (Databases, Data Marts, Data Warehouses)

Model Management System

Internal Models

External Models

Knowledge-Based Systems

User Interface System

FIGURE 11.33

Major components of a DSS are shown. Through the user interface, models are analyzed and manipulated to provide information on which management decisions are based.

additional intelligence that supplements the user's own intellect and makes the DSS more effective. It can be an **expert system** that tries to replicate the decision-making processes of human experts to solve specific problems. For example, an expert system might be designed to take the place of a physician in remote locations such as a scientific base on Antarctica. A physician expert system would ask the patient about symptoms just as a live physician would, and the system would make a diagnosis based on the algorithms programmed into it.

Another type of knowledge-based system is a **natural language processing (NLP) system**. NLP systems enable users to communicate with computer systems using a natural spoken or written language as opposed to using computer programming languages. Individuals with disabilities who cannot use a keyboard benefit greatly from NLP systems because they can just speak to the computer and have it understand what they are saying without using specific computer commands. Using an NLP system can simplify the user interface, making it much more efficient and user-friendly. The speech-recognition feature of Microsoft Office is a type of NLP system.

All knowledge-based systems fall under the science of artificial intelligence. **Artificial intelligence (AI)** is the branch of computer science that deals with the attempt to create computers that think like humans. To date, no computers have been constructed that can replicate the thinking patterns of a human brain because scientists still do not fully understand how humans store and integrate knowledge and experiences to form human intelligence.

How does a knowledge-based system help in the decision-making process? Databases and the models provided by model management systems tend to be extremely analytical and mathematical in nature. If we relied solely on databases and models to make decisions, then the answers would be derived with a "yes or no" mentality, allowing no room for human thought. Fortunately, human users are involved in these types of systems, providing an opportunity to inject human judgment and experience into the decision-making process.

The knowledge-based system also provides an opportunity to introduce experience into the mix. Knowledge-based systems support the concept of fuzzy logic.

Normal logic is highly rigid: If "x" happens, then "y" will happen. **Fuzzy logic** enables the interjection of experiential learning into the equation by considering probabilities. Whereas an algorithm in a database has to be specific, an algorithm in a knowledge-based system could state that if "x" happens, 70 percent of the time "y" will happen.

For instance, managers at Amazon.com would find it extremely helpful if their DSSs informed them that 40 percent of customers who bought a certain book also bought the sequel. This could suggest that designing a discount program for sequels bought with the original book might spur sales. Fuzzy logic enables a system to be more flexible and to consider a wider range of possibilities than would conventional algorithmic thinking.

ENTERPRISE RESOURCE PLANNING SYSTEMS

What is an enterprise? An enterprise is any business entity large or small. It could be the pizza shop on the corner or a Fortune 500 manufacturer of sports apparel. All businesses have data and information to manage, and large and complex organizations can benefit from managing that information with a central piece of software.

What does an enterprise resource planning system do? Enterprise resource planning (ERP) systems are broad-based software systems that integrate multiple data sources and tie together the various processes of an enterprise to enable information to flow more smoothly. ERP systems use a common database to store and integrate information to enable the information to be used across multiple areas of an enterprise.

For instance, human resource functions (such as the management of hiring, firing, promotions, and fringe-benefits) and accounting functions (such as payroll) are often the first processes integrated into an ERP system. Historically, human resource records and accounting records were kept in separate databases, but having the information reside in one database makes the management and paying of employees more streamlined. If manufacturing operations were then integrated into the ERP system, the data that is already in place regarding the employees and payroll could be easily used for accumulating the costs of running

an assembly line (the workers on the assembly line get paid) or for scheduling the manpower to run the assembly line. The objective of ERP systems is to accumulate all information relevant to running a business in a central location and make it readily available to whomever needs that information to make decisions.

Almost all Fortune 500 companies have implemented ERP systems, and many medium-sized companies are implementing them also. Although the corner pizza shop probably does not need an ERP system, it would be difficult to coordinate the activities of a multinational corporation without one.

Data Mining

Just because you captured data in an organized fashion and stored it in a certain format that seems to make sense doesn't mean that an analysis of the data will automatically reveal everything you need to know. Trends can sometimes be hard to spot if the data is not organized or analyzed in a unique way. To make data work harder, companies employ data-mining techniques.

Data mining is the process by which great amounts of data are analyzed and investigated. The objective is to spot significant patterns or trends within the data that would otherwise not be obvious. For instance, through mining student enrollment data, a school may discover that 40 percent of new nursing degree students are Latino.

Why do businesses mine their data? The main reason businesses mine data is to understand their customers better. If a company can better understand the types of customers who buy its products and what motivates them to do so, it can market effectively by concentrating its efforts on the populations that are most likely to buy.

ACTIVE HELPDESK

Data Warehouses, Data Marts, and Information Systems

In this Active Helpdesk call, you'll play the role of a helpdesk staffer, fielding calls about data warehouses, data marts, and information systems.

How do businesses mine their data? Data mining enables managers to sift through data in several ways. Each method produces different information that managers can then base their decisions on. Managers make their data meaningful through the following activities:

1. **Classification:** To analyze data, managers need to classify it. Therefore, before mining, managers define data classes that they think will be helpful in spotting trends. They then apply these class definitions to all unclassified data to prepare it for analysis. For example, "good credit risk" and "bad credit risk" are two data classes that managers could establish to determine whether to grant mortgages to applicants. Managers would then identify factors (such as credit history and yearly income) that they could use to classify applicants as good or bad risks.

2. **Estimation:** When managers classify data, the record either fits the classification criteria or it doesn't. Estimation enables managers to assign a value, based on some criterion, to data. For example, assume a bank wants to send out credit card offers to people who are likely to be granted a credit card. The bank may run the customers' data through a program that assigns them a score based on where they live, their household income, and their average bank balance. This provides managers with an estimate of the most likely credit card prospects so that they can include them in the mailing.

3. **Affinity grouping (or association rules):** When mining data, managers also can determine which data goes together. In other words, they can apply affinity grouping or association rules to the data. For example, suppose analysis of a sales database indicates that two items are bought together 70 percent of the time. Based on this data, managers might decide that these items should be pictured on the same page in their next mail-order catalog.

4. **Clustering:** Clustering involves organizing data into similar subgroups, or clusters. It is different from classification in that there are no predefined classes. The data-mining software makes the decision about what to group, and it is up to managers to determine whether the clusters are meaningful. For example, the data-mining software may identify clusters of customers with similar buying patterns. Further analysis of the clusters may reveal that certain socioeconomic groups have similar buying patterns.

5. **Description and visualization:** Often, the purpose of data mining is merely to describe data so that managers can visualize it. Sometimes having a clear picture of what is going on with the data helps people to interpret it in new and different ways. For example, if large amounts of data revealed that left-handed males who live in suburban environments never take automotive technology courses, then it would most likely spark a heated discussion about the reasons why. It would certainly provide plenty of opportunities for additional study on the part of psychologists, sociologists, and college administrators!

You may have noticed that products are frequently moved around in supermarkets. This is usually the result of data mining. With electronic scanning of bar codes, each customer's purchase is recorded in a database. By classifying the data and using cluster analysis, supermarket managers can determine which products people usually purchase with other products. The store then places these products close to each other so that shoppers can find them easily. For instance, if analysis shows that people often buy coffee with breakfast cereal, it makes sense to place these items in the same aisle.

As the human race continues to accumulate data, the development of faster and bigger databases will be a necessity. You can expect to interact with more and more databases every year even if you don't realize you are doing so.

Ethics: Data, Data Everywhere—But Who Is Viewing It and Why?

As databases have become commonplace, there is an ever-increasing amount of information about you and your habits located in various databases. Every time you purchase something with a credit card, there is a record of that transaction, and both the merchant from whom you purchased the item and the credit card company have information about your buying habits (see Figure 11.34). Have you used a toll service that allows you to pay your tolls electronically by just driving through a lane without stopping? Toll records are routinely subpoenaed in court cases. Toll records were used in an Illinois court by a husband in a divorce case to prove his wife was rarely home and therefore unfit for custody of their son. All banking transactions are handled by computers (and hence databases) in the United States, and there is a high probability that your employer is electronically transferring your pay to your bank by direct deposit. And if you engage in online banking and bill paying, then there is another electronic trail of your financial life being generated in databases.

Think you can avoid scrutiny by paying cash? Not if you are a member of a frequent buyer club (popular with supermarkets and drug stores for granting discounts) and are providing the checkout clerk with your personal information in exchange for coupons or a few dollars off your purchases. And you never can be sure what this data may be used for. In October 2004, a firefighter was arrested after his supermarket purchase records revealed he purchased the same type of fire starters used in an arson case. After three months, the charges were dropped when another person pleaded guilty to committing the arson.

And if financial information isn't sensitive enough, the majority of physicians and hospitals in the United States are tracking medical records in electronic databases. Your entire prescription history (and hence hints to your medical history) is in a database at the local pharmacy. Applied for insurance lately? Your doctor was probably able to provide (with your permission, of course) your entire medical history to the insurance company with a few clicks of a mouse. All of the data that exists in the world around us should give us pause, and we need to stop and consider the ethical implications of the electronic society we live in.

Data Convergence—The Perfect Storm of Privacy Invasion?

Discrete pieces of data such as filling your gas tank last Thursday or buying a copy of *War and Peace* last month don't mean much in and of themselves. But with so much data in electronic form, it is getting much easier to combine data from various data sources and build powerful profiles of an individual to which data-mining techniques can be applied. For instance, suppose a marketing company purchased data about your buying habits from the supermarket, pharmacy, and bookstore where you shop and your credit card company. In addition, the marketing company also purchased information about you from the company where you bought your lawn mower (it got that from your credit card information). What information did the lawn mower

FIGURE 11.34

Workman disassembling a house reveal the contents hidden inside, which is similar to the eroding of our privacy rights. If our personal information is in multiple databases and viewable by many people, is the information still private?

company have about you? The personal information you gave when you filled out your warranty card online (household income, age, rent or own a home, etc.)! By combining all of this information into one database, the marketing company is able to build an extremely detailed picture of who you are.

For example, based on your purchases at the pharmacy, a marketing company might determine there are both males (shaving gel) and females (cosmetics) living in your home. It also might notice that you have been buying pregnancy test kits once a month for 18 months and conclude you are trying to have a baby (and not having much luck, by the way). By your address and the car you drive (you had charges on your credit card at a Lexus dealer), the company has estimated that you have a household income of more than $100,000 per year, making you affluent. It also noticed you shop at a lot of stores that feature outdoor and sports equipment and have recently bought a mountain bike, and the company has concluded that you have an active lifestyle. Based on this analysis, you start receiving mail and phone solicitations for canoes, baby clothing, fertility treatments, and plasma TVs. But just because this type of analysis can be done, should we be doing it? Do you want people marketing to you based on fairly sensitive personal information (such as trying to become pregnant)? Where does marketing stop and an invasion of privacy begin?

What Can You Do?

Providing information and having it recorded in databases are part of our way of life now. Because refusing to give information out at all is bound to be impractical, you should ask the following questions related to data you are providing:

1. **For what purpose is the data being gathered?** When the clerk at the electronics superstore asks for your zip code, ask why she wants it (it is probably for some marketing purpose).

2. **Are the reasons for gathering the data legitimate or important to you?** For warranty purposes on a large-screen TV, you may need to give a clerk your address and zip code. For purchasing a CD, is asking for your zip code really a legitimate request? However, disclosing medical information to key people (such as your pharmacist) may be important to receiving good care and therefore is extremely important to you. If you don't see the advantage,

then ask more questions or don't reveal the information.

3. **How will the information gathered be protected once it has been obtained?** Ask about data protection policies before you give information. Most Web sites provide access to their data protection policies—readily available through clickable links or pop-up boxes—when they ask for information. If an organization doesn't have a data protection policy, then be wary of providing them sensitive information unless there is a compelling advantage to doing so (such as receiving good medical care). And data protection doesn't just refer to keeping data secure. It also means restricting access to the data to employees of the organization that need to use that data. A shipping clerk might need to see your address, for example, but doesn't need to see your credit card information.

4. **Will the information collected be used for purposes other than the purpose for which it was originally collected?** This might be covered in a data protection policy. If it isn't, then ask about it. Will your information be sold to other companies? Will it be used for marketing other products to you?

5. **Could the information asked for be used for identity theft?** Identity thieves usually need Social Security numbers and your birth date to open credit card accounts in your name. Be especially wary when asked for this information and make sure there is a legitimate need for this information. Most organizations and businesses are shying away from using Social Security numbers to track customers because of the risk of identity theft.

6. **Are organizations that already have your data safeguarding it?** Don't just consider new requests for information. Think about organizations that already have your information and monitor their performance. Have they been in the news lately because of a major data breach (inadvertently exposing information to inappropriate or unauthorized individuals)? You might want to consider switching institutions (such as a bank) if they have poor track records of data security.

So think carefully before providing information and be vigilant about monitoring your data when you can. It may mean the difference between invasion of privacy and peace of mind.

1. What is a database, and why is it beneficial to use databases?

Databases are electronic collections of related data that can be organized so that it is more easily accessed and manipulated. Properly designed databases cut down on data redundancy and duplicate data by ensuring relevant data is recorded in only one place. This also helps eliminate data inconsistency, which comes from having different data about the same transaction recorded in two different places. And when databases are used, multiple users can share and access information at the same time. Databases are used any time complex information needs to be organized or more than one person needs to access it. In these cases, lists (which are used to keep track of simple information) are no longer efficient.

2. What components make up a database?

The three main components of a database are fields, records, and tables. A category of information in a database is stored in a field. Each field is identified by a field name, which is a way of describing the field. Fields are assigned a data type that indicates what type of data can be stored in the field. Common data types include text, numeric, computational, date, memo, object, and hyperlink. A group of related fields is a record. A group of related records is a table or file. To keep records distinct, each record must have one field that has a value unique to that record. This unique field is a primary key (or a key field).

3. What types of databases are there?

The three major types of databases currently in use are relational, object-oriented, and multidimensional databases. Relational databases are characterized by two-dimensional tables of data in which a common field is maintained in each of two tables and the information in the tables is linked by this field. Object-oriented databases store data in objects, not in tables. The objects also contain instructions about how the data is to be manipulated or processed. Multidimensional databases represent data in three-dimensional cubes to enable faster retrieval of information from the database.

4. What do database management systems do?

Database management systems (DBMSs) are specially designed applications (such as Oracle or Microsoft Access) that interact with the user, other applications, and the database itself to capture and analyze data. The main operations of a DBMS are creating databases, entering data, viewing (or browsing) data, sorting (or indexing) data, extracting (or querying) data, and outputting data. A query language is used to extract records from a database. Almost all relational databases today use structured query language, or SQL. However, most DBMSs include wizards that enable you to query the database without learning a query language. The most common form of output for any database is a printed report.

5. How do relational databases organize and manipulate data?

Relational databases operate by organizing data into various tables based on logical groupings. Because not all of the data in a relational database is stored in the same table, a methodology must be implemented to link data between tables. In relational databases, the links between tables that define how the data is related are referred to as *relationships*. To establish a relationship between two tables, both tables must have a common field (or column). Once linked, information can be drawn from multiple tables through the use of queries (for on-screen viewing of data) or report generators (used to produce printed reports).

6. What are data warehouses and data marts, and how are they used?

A data warehouse is a large-scale electronic repository of data that contains and organizes in one place all the relevant data related to an organization. Data warehouses often contain information from multiple databases. Because it can be difficult to find information in a large data warehouse, small slices of the data warehouse called *data marts* are often created. The information in data marts pertains to a single department within the organization, for example. Data warehouses and data marts consolidate information from a wide variety of sources to provide comprehensive pictures of operations or transactions within a business.

7. What is an information system, and what types of information systems are used in business?

Information systems are software-based solutions that are used to gather and analyze information. Information systems fall into one of five categories. An office support system is designed to assist employees in accomplishing their day-to-day tasks and improve communications. A transaction processing system (TPS) is a system that is used to keep track of everyday business activities. A management information system (MIS) provides timely and accurate information that enables managers to make critical business decisions. A decision support system (DSS) is a system designed to help managers develop solutions for specific problems. An enterprise resource planning (ERP) system is a large software system that gathers information from all parts of a business and integrates it to make it readily available for decision making.

8. What is data mining, and how does it work?

Data mining is the process by which large amounts of data are analyzed to spot otherwise hidden trends. Through processes such as classification, estimation, affinity grouping, clustering, and description (visualization), data is organized so that it provides meaningful information that can be used by managers to identify business trends.

Buzzwords

Word Bank

- data dictionary
- data inconsistency
- data mining
- data warehouse
- decision support
- field

- join query
- memo field
- metadata
- numeric field
- object field
- primary key

- relational algebra
- select query
- SQL
- table
- text field
- transaction processing

Instructions: Fill in the blanks using the words from the Word Bank above.

When constructing a database (1) _____ it is important to ensure each record is identified uniquely. A(n) (2) _____ should be established as a unique field to be included with each record. In a database, digits such as 1234 are normally stored in a(n) (3) _____, but they also could be stored in a(n) (4) _____ if calculations do not need to be performed on the number. Extremely lengthy textual data is stored in a(n) (5) _____ whereas video files are appropriately stored in a(n) (6) _____. The (7) _____ fully describes each field in the database and its attributes. Data used to describe other data in this manner is referred to as (8) _____.

Queries are used to prepare data for viewing or printing. A(n) (9) _____ usually displays requested information from only one table. For displaying related information that is stored in multiple tables, a(n) (10) _____ must be used. The most popular query language in use today is (11) _____. Queries generated by this language make use of English-language statements driven by the mathematical principles of (12) _____.

When individual databases are not sufficient to maintain all the data that needs to be tracked, a(n) (13) _____ should be created. Databases are often key components of (14) _____ systems, which record routine business activities. A(n) (15) _____ system utilizes databases and other related systems to assist management with building business models and making critical decisions.

Becoming Computer Literate

Everyone loves the pottery that your best friend, Kimdra, makes, and she has decided to start selling it to the general public. Kimdra has a few existing customers already (mostly family and friends), but she plans to put her work in a few art shows and make some deals with area stores to feature it. Keeping track of all this information is going to be important, but she is not computer literate. Kimdra has approached you to be her database consultant and to design a database for her new business. Write a proposal that outlines what you intend to do for your friend. What kind of database will you create? What kind of information will your friend need in the database to run her business? How should that information be organized? As her business grows, how do you imagine the database will grow with the business?

Instructions: Answer the multiple-choice and true–false questions below for more practice with key terms and concepts from this chapter.

MULTIPLE CHOICE

1. Two lists reflecting different data about the same person is an example of
   a. data redundancy.
   b. data inconsistency.
   c. data disparity.
   d. data duplication errors.

2. Which of the following is NOT an advantage of using a database versus lists?
   a. Information can be easily shared among users.
   b. Data entry errors can be minimized with databases.
   c. Data integrity can be ensured with a database.
   d. Databases are easier to build and maintain than lists.

3. A group of related fields in a relational database is called a
   a. primary key.
   b. record.
   c. master key.
   d. table.

4. In databases, tables are related using
   a. primary keys and foreign keys.
   b. Boolean logic.
   c. data marts.
   d. database logic.

5. A field that has a unique value for each record in a database is called the
   a. logical key.
   b. master field.
   c. key field.
   d. primary key.

6. A primary key of one table that is also found in a related table is a
   a. linked key.
   b. foreign key.
   c. secondary key.
   d. subordinate key.

7. Which of the following is one of the four main operations of a database management system?
   a. Querying data
   b. Dissecting data
   c. Structuring data
   d. Consolidating data

8. Ensuring that a field must contain a number that is between two values is an example of a(n)
   a. existence check.
   b. completeness check.
   c. range check.
   d. consistency check.

9. A system that is designed to help perform routine daily tasks is known as
   a. a decision support system.
   b. an office support system.
   c. a data warehouse.
   d. a management information system.

10. An electronic system used to record sales of products through a Web site is an example of a
    a. transaction processing system.
    b. decision support system.
    c. management information system.
    d. knowledge-based system.

TRUE–FALSE

____ 1. A query is designed to make data entry into a database easier.

____ 2. Consistency checks ensure that only reasonable data values are entered into a database.

____ 3. Reducing data redundancy by recording data only once is called *data normalization*.

____ 4. A data warehouse is a smaller slice of a data mart.

____ 5. The main reason businesses use data mining is to simplify transaction processing systems.

Making the Transition to...
Next Semester

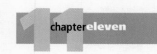

1. Researching the Alumni Database

Many schools try to maintain contact with former students to keep them informed of new programs and courses being offered at the institution. Visit your school's alumni office and determine the following:

a. Is a separate database maintained for the purposes of communicating with alumni?
b. What type of database software is used?
c. What data is captured in this database?
d. How often is the data contained in the database verified with the alumni?

2. Developing an Alumni Database

If the alumni office doesn't maintain a separate database for the purposes of communicating with graduates, use the previous questions as a guideline for developing an alumni database design for your school.

3. Creating a Database

Imagine that you own 400 DVDs and want to track them in a database. Determine the following:

a. What fields do you need in your database for categorizing and tracking your DVDs? What would be a good primary key to use for this "DVD" table?
b. What fields do you need for capturing information about your friends to whom you have loaned DVDs? What would be the primary key of this "borrower" table?
c. What common field would you include in both tables to relate the "DVD" table to the "borrower" table? Justify your answer.

4. Database Conversion

You've just volunteered to assist the director of a club at your school with a membership drive. The first order of business is to convert the existing paper membership records into an Access database. Consider the following issues:

a. What fields do you need in your "membership" table for tracking valid members?
b. How would you distinguish active members in the "membership" table from members who have not attended meetings in more than a year? Would it be more efficient to put the inactive members into a separate table? Justify your answer.
c. After the Access database is constructed, what software would you suggest be used to generate appeal letters for the club's fund-raising campaign to benefit a homeless shelter? How would you suggest the results of the fund-raising campaign be stored in the member database? Explain your answer sufficiently to convince the director of your decision.

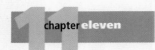

Making the Transition to... the Workplace

1. Data Warehousing

You are a summer intern in the information technology group of an athletic apparel manufacturer. At the weekly staff meeting, the chief information officer (CIO) indicates that the president is requesting information about sales of all lines of goods for the past 10 years. Unfortunately, data more than three years old is not maintained in the current sales database and has been archived to tape. A volunteer is needed (and everyone looks to you) to extract the data from the backup tapes and prepare the needed reports.

As you are spending your 16th evening extracting the data, the CIO mentions that manufacturing, shipping, and accounts receivable may need their own reports that include different data but span the same time period as your current assignment. The CIO assures you that most of the information is available on tape; if it isn't, then it can be located in the mountains of paper stored in the old warehouse. You know that this tedious work could be avoided by the introduction of a data warehousing system!

a. Prepare a data warehousing plan for the CIO. Describe briefly the benefits of data warehousing and provide an overview of the process.
b. For sales, manufacturing, shipping, and accounts receivable data, suggest the types of information that should be captured in the data warehouse.
c. What types of data marts would you suggest setting up for this company?

2. Creating a Data Access Policy

You have an internship in the information technology department at the regional office of Mammoth Insurance Company, which sells automobile, life, and medical insurance. Colossal Insurance Company, one of your firm's competitors, was recently raked over the coals in the news media because a few employees were looking up medical records of insurance customers for the purpose of developing a mailing list for people with certain illnesses. The employees were then using the list to market a new online mail-order prescription drug Web site (owned by the employees, not Colossal) directly to Colossal's customers. Many customers were upset by the solicitations, which they viewed as an invasion of their privacy. The Colossal employees contended that no one ever told them they couldn't use the company records for this purpose.

The CIO of Mammoth wants to ensure that such a controversy doesn't happen to her company. She has asked your supervisor (who in turn drafted you to help) to prepare a data access policy for Mammoth. Prepare a draft of the policy and consider the following:

a. Who should have access to the medical information of insurance company customers? The insurance underwriters (the people who approve or disapprove policies) need the information. Does anyone else?
b. Should marketing personnel be granted access to medical and driving records for the purposes of marketing Mammoth's products? If so, who should approve the access? Should customers be informed before conducting marketing campaigns using their "sensitive" information? Who should be responsible for notifying customers?
c. Describe the types of uses of customer information that would be deemed inappropriate by the company. What should the penalties be for violating the policy?

Critical Thinking Questions

Instructions: Albert Einstein used *Gedanken experiments*, or critical thinking questions, to develop his theory of relativity. Some ideas are best understood by experimenting with them in our own minds. The following critical thinking questions are designed to demand your full attention but require only a comfortable chair—no technology.

1. Database Ethics

Internet databases abound with personal information about you. You probably provided some of this information, but it may have been sold to other companies. Other information about you may have been obtained without your knowledge while you surfed Web sites. Consider the following:

a. Is it ethical for a company to sell personal information (such as household income) that you voluntarily provide?

b. Is gathering information about people's surfing and buying habits by tracking their clicks through a Web site an invasion of privacy?

c. Should Web sites be legally required to inform users that they are tracking surfing habits? Why or why not?

2. IRS Database

The Internal Revenue Service (IRS) maintains large databases about taxpayers that include a wealth of information on personal income that can be easily sorted by geographic location. This information would be of great value to marketing professionals for targeting marketing programs to consumers. Currently, the IRS is prohibited from selling this information to third parties. However, the IRS (and other government agencies) are under increasing pressure to find ways to increase revenue or decrease expenses.

a. Do you favor a change in the laws that would permit the IRS to sell names and addresses with household income information to third parties? Why or why not?

b. Would it be acceptable for the IRS to sell income information to marketing firms if it did not include personal information (such as names and addresses) but only included income statistics for certain geographic areas? How is this better (or worse) than selling personal information?

c. How would you feel about the IRS marketing financial products (such as tax software) directly to consumers? Would this be a conflict of interest with the IRS's main mission (the collection of tax revenue and enforcement of tax compliance)?

3. The Total Information Awareness Program

After the terrorist attacks on September 11, 2001, some U.S. citizens began demanding more scrutiny of foreign nationals and people wishing to emigrate to the United States. In response to these concerns, the Department of Defense launched the Total Information Awareness (TIA) program through the Defense Advanced Research Projects Agency (DARPA). The program was created to develop data-mining techniques to probe massive federal databases as well as commercial and private employment, medical, and financial databases. The objective was to spot trends that would identify people who were threats to national security. TIA gave rise to many protests from the American public and privacy advocates about the potential invasion of privacy that such programs could engender. Although TIA's funding was terminated by Congress in 2004, various other programs live on as the government uses other databases to monitor activity. For instance, in May 2006 it was revealed that millions of Americans' phone calls were being monitored, causing further public outcry about invasion of privacy.

a. Research government monitoring programs that are currently in place. What data-mining efforts is the U.S. government currently using to monitor data?

b. Do you think the government should institute programs like the TIA program? Why or why not?

c. Which is more important to you: safeguarding your privacy or protecting the United States from terrorists? Why?

Team Time Student Data Tracking

Problem:

Many schools use student data information systems that were installed more than 10 years ago. When preparing to transition to a newer system, additional information is often identified that needs to be captured in the new system that was not recorded in the old system (such as e-mail addresses). Also, in preparing to transfer legacy data to a new system, the data often needs to be "groomed." Grooming data means verifying the data accuracy, ensuring data consistency, and correcting problems.

Task:

Your class has volunteered to assist the IT department with the transition to a new student information system. Customers (students) often provide unique perspectives and should always be consulted (when possible) during the design and implementation of new systems. The school administration feels your input into the design process will enhance the usability of the new system.

Process:

Divide the class into small groups.

1. Your group should examine your school's current student information system (from a user perspective). Identify the data that is being captured from students (when enrolling or registering for courses). Compile a list of suggestions for data that does not need to be captured (but currently is being captured) and for additional data that should be gathered (but is not currently). Determine the extent to which student services can be accessed over the Internet and suggest services that require Internet accessibility but are not currently offered.

2. Investigate whether your school has a written data access policy and obtain a copy if possible. If your school does not have an access policy, have members of your group draft a policy that addresses the types of data that various groups of employees (faculty, administrators, business office workers, etc.) should be able to access.

3. Present your group's findings to the class. Compare your suggestions to those of other groups. Be sure to address the needs of all groups of students (residents, commuters, and online students).

4. Prepare a list of recommendations for improvements to the current student information system for the director of student affairs. Clearly indicate how the proposed changes will benefit both students and the school employees who are interacting with the system.

Conclusion:

Colleges and universities are competing for students more fiercely than ever before. Those institutions that listen to their students and find innovative ways to serve their needs will have a distinct advantage in attracting and retaining students. Listening to customers is a basic principle of business that educational institutions should not overlook.

Multimedia

In addition to the review materials presented here, you'll find additional materials featured with the book's multimedia, including the *Technology in Action* Student Resource CD and the Companion Website (**www.prenhall.com/techinaction**), which will help reinforce your understanding of the chapter content. These materials include the following:

ACTIVE HELPDESK

In Active Helpdesk calls, you'll assume the role of a helpdesk operator taking calls about the concepts you've learned in this chapter. You'll apply what you've learned and receive feedback from a supervisor to review and reinforce those concepts. The Active Helpdesk calls for this chapter are listed below and can be found on your Student Resource CD:

- Understanding Database Management Systems
- Using Databases
- Data Warehouses, Data Marts, and Information Systems

SOUND BYTES

Sound Bytes are dynamic multimedia tutorials that help demystify even the most complex topics. You'll view video clips and animations that illustrate computer concepts, and then apply what you've learned by reviewing with the Sound Byte Labs, which include quizzes and activities specifically tailored to each Sound Byte. The Sound Bytes for this chapter are listed here and can be found on your Student Resource CD:

- Creating an Access 2007 Database
- Improving an Access 2007 Database

COMPANION WEBSITE

The *Technology in Action* Companion Website includes a variety of additional materials to help you review and learn more about the topics in this chapter. The resources available at **www.prenhall.com/techinaction** include:

- **Online Study Guide.** Each chapter features an online true–false and multiple-choice quiz. You can take these quizzes, automatically check the results, and e-mail the results to your instructor.

- **Web Research Projects.** Each chapter features a number of Web research projects that ask you to search the Web for information on computer-related careers, milestones in computer history, important people and companies, emerging technologies, and the applications and implications of different technologies.

chapter *twelve*

Behind the Scenes:

Networking and Security

Objectives

After reading this chapter, you should be able to answer the following questions:

1. What are the advantages of a business network? **(p. 578)**

2. How does a client/server network differ from a peer-to-peer network? **(pp. 579–580)**

3. What are the different classifications of client/server networks? **(pp. 581–583)**

4. What components are needed to construct a client/server network? **(pp. 583–584)**

5. What do the various types of servers do? **(pp. 584–586)**

6. What are the various network topologies (layouts), and why is network topology important in planning a network? **(pp. 586–592)**

7. What types of transmission media are used in client/server networks? **(pp. 592–597)**

8. What software needs to be running on computers attached to a client/server network, and how does this software control network communications? **(pp. 597–599)**

9. How do network adapters enable computers to participate in a client/server network? **(pp. 599–600)**

10. What devices assist in moving data around a client/server network? **(pp. 600–603)**

11. What measures are employed to keep large networks secure? **(pp. 603–611)**

ACTIVE HELPDESK

- Using Servers **(p. 586)**
- Selecting a Network Topology and Cable **(p. 592)**
- Selecting Network Navigation Devices **(p. 604)**

Understanding How Networks Work

Computer networks are everywhere. Actually, the Internet is a large network of networks—in fact, it's the largest. Most people interact with other, smaller computer networks on a daily basis, whether or not they are aware of it. Even something as simple as buying gas involves interacting with a network. The pay-at-the-pump convenience of purchasing gas with a debit card is made possible because the gas pump can connect to a network. When you swipe your card at the pump, the network interface in the pump connects to the network at the oil company that owns the gas station. That network connects with the network at your bank and checks to ensure that you have sufficient funds in your bank account to cover a gasoline purchase. Assuming you have a sufficient account balance, the oil company network sends an authorization back to the pump to enable you to buy gas.

When your transaction is complete, the pump sends the purchase information to the corporate network. The amount of gas you purchased is then recorded in an inventory control database and is used to help determine when a gas delivery needs to be made to the gas station. Without networks, you couldn't use your debit card to buy gas conveniently at the pump because there would be no fast way to check your bank balance. Also, without the corporate network tracking gas purchases, your neighborhood station might run out of gas more frequently. As you can see, networks assist in making your life easier.

Why is it important to understand networks and their capabilities? For one, it will help you interact with the information technology professionals who are responsible for configuring and maintaining the networks where you work or go to school. In the business world, understanding the capabilities and limitations of networks will assist you when working with IT professionals, who will assist you in deploying or gathering information to accomplish your job objectives (say, gathering and analyzing market research for a new marketing campaign). In addition, a fundamental grasp of network principles can help you decide whether you want to pursue additional coursework or even a career in networking. Finally, it can enhance your productivity by keeping you connected with today's fast-moving world.

This chapter builds on the information you learned about networks in Chapter 7 and takes you behind the scenes of networking principles. We look at how client/server networks work and examine exactly how these networks are designed and built. Along the way, we discuss the various kinds of servers used in such networks as well as the layout and equipment used to create them. Finally, we discuss how large networks are kept secure.

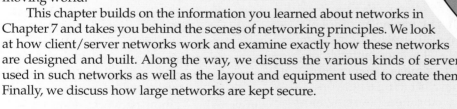

SOUND BYTES

- Network Topology and Navigation Devices **(p. 588)**
- What's My IP Address? (and Other Interesting Facts about Networks) **(p. 601)**
- A Day in the Life of a Network Technician **(p. 605)**

Networking Advantages

As you learned in Chapter 7, a **network** is a group of two or more computers (or nodes) that are configured to share information and resources such as printers, files, and databases. Essentially, a network enables computers and other devices to communicate with each other. But why do we network computers? As discussed in Chapter 7, home networks enable users to share peripherals (such as printers), transfer files simply, and share Internet connections.

What advantages do businesses gain from networks? Large business networks provide similar and additional advantages over individual stand-alone computers:

- **Networks increase productivity.** Computers are powerful stand-alone resources. However, to increase productivity, people need to be able to share data and peripherals with co-workers and communicate with them efficiently. Without a network, only one person at a time can access information because it would reside on a single computer. Information sharing is therefore the largest benefit a company gains by installing a network.

- **Networks enable expensive resources to be shared.** Networks enable people to share peripherals such as printers, eliminating the need for duplicate devices. You probably have a printer hooked up to your home computer. Think about how often it sits idle. Compound that by having an office of 20 employees, each with his or her own printer. Having 20 printers sitting idle 90 percent of the time is a tremendous waste of money. Installing a network that enables two printers (working most of the time) to serve all 20 employees saves money.

- **Networks facilitate knowledge sharing.** The databases you learned about in Chapter 11 become especially powerful when deployed on a network. Networked databases can serve the needs of many people at one time and increase the availability of data. Your company's databases are much more useful when you and your co-workers can look up customer records at the same time.

- **Networks enable software sharing.** Installing a new version of software on everyone's desktop in a company with 1,000 employees can be time consuming. However, if the computers are networked, all employees can access the same copy of a program from the server. Although companies must still purchase a software license for each employee, with a network they avoid having to install the program on every desktop. This also saves space on individual desktops, because the software doesn't reside on every computer.

- **Networks facilitate Internet connectivity.** Most employees need to connect to the Internet to perform their jobs. Providing each employee's computer with its own dedicated connection to the Internet (using a modem) is costly. Through a network, large groups of employees can share one Internet connection, reducing Internet connectivity expenses.

- **Networks enable enhanced communication.** E-mail and text messaging are extremely powerful applications when deployed on a network (especially one that is connected to the Internet). You can easily exchange information with your co-workers, and valuable data can be easily shared by transferring files between users.

Are there disadvantages to businesses using networks? Because business networks are often complex, additional personnel are usually required to maintain them. These people, called **network administrators**, have training in computer and peripheral maintenance and repair, networking design, and the installation of networking software. In addition, networks require additional equipment and software to operate. However, most companies feel that the cost savings of peripheral sharing and the ability to have employees access information simultaneously outweigh the costs associated with network administrators and equipment.

Aside from the smallest networks such as peer-to-peer networks, which are typically used in homes and small businesses, the majority of computer networks are based on the client/server model of computing.

Client/Server Networks

As you've learned, a server is a computer that both stores and shares resources on a network, whereas a **client** is a computer that requests those resources. A **client/server network** (also called a **server-based network**) contains servers as well as client computers. The inclusion of servers is what differentiates a client/server network from a typical peer-to-peer (P2P) network. (As you'll recall, each node connected to the P2P network can communicate directly with every other node on the network, instead of having a separate device exercise control over the network.) Figure 12.1 illustrates the client/server relationship.

The main advantage of a client/server relationship is that it makes data flow more efficiently than in peer-to-peer networks. Servers can respond to requests from a large number of clients at the same time. Also, servers are configured to perform specific tasks (such as handling e-mail or database requests) efficiently.

For instance, say you are hungry and go to a fast-food restaurant. As the customer ordering food, you are the client making a request. The cook, in the role of the server, responds to the request and prepares the meal. Certainly, you could go to the restaurant and cook your own meal, but this would hardly be efficient. You would be floundering around in the kitchen with other customers trying to cook their meals. By assigning specialized tasks to a fast-food cook (the server), many customers (clients) can be served efficiently at the same time. This is how servers work. One server can provide services efficiently to a large number of clients at one time.

Does my home network have a server? As you'll recall from Chapter 7, peer-to-peer networks, which are typically set up in homes or very small businesses, do not require servers. In these networks, computers act as both clients and servers when appropriate.

Why don't businesses use peer-to-peer networks? P2P networks become difficult to administer when they are expanded beyond 10 users. Each individual computer may require updating for changes to the network, which is not efficient. Also, security can't be implemented centrally on a P2P network but instead must be handled by

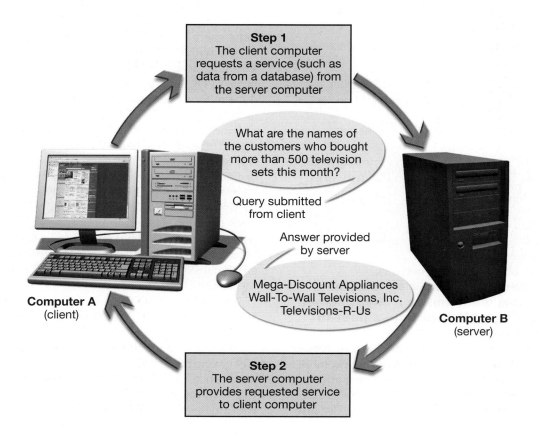

Step 1
The client computer requests a service (such as data from a database) from the server computer

What are the names of the customers who bought more than 500 television sets this month?

Query submitted from client

Answer provided by server

Mega-Discount Appliances
Wall-To-Wall Televisions, Inc.
Televisions-R-Us

Computer A
(client)

Computer B
(server)

Step 2
The server computer provides requested service to client computer

FIGURE 12.1

Basic Client/Server Interaction

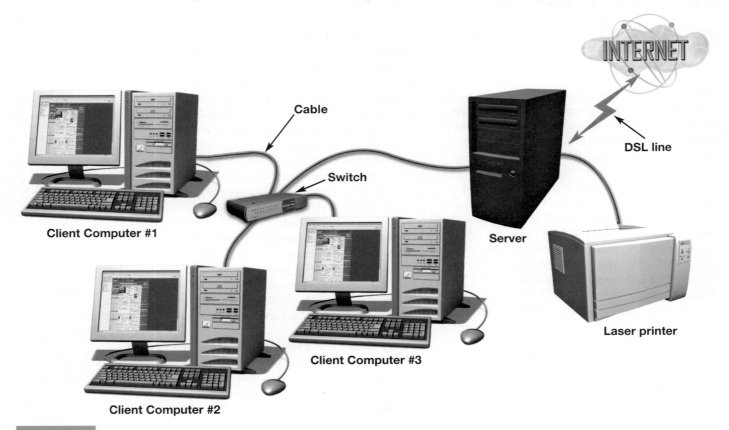

Cable

Switch

Client Computer #1

Client Computer #2

Client Computer #3

Server

DSL line

INTERNET

Laser printer

FIGURE 12.2

This small client/server network enables users to share a printer and an Internet connection.

each individual user. As noted earlier, client/server networks contain at least one server that provides shared resources and services (including security) to the client computers that request them.

In addition, client/server networks move data more efficiently than P2P networks, making them appropriate for large numbers of users. For example, Figure 12.2 shows a small client/server arrangement. The server in this figure provides printing and Internet connection services for all the client computers connected to the network.

Besides having a centralized server, what makes a client/server network different from a peer-to-peer network? The main difference is that client/server networks have increased scalability. With a **scalable network**, more users can be added easily without affecting the performance of the other network nodes (computers or peripherals). Because

servers handle the bulk of tasks performed on the network (printing, Internet access, and so on), it is easy to accommodate more users by installing additional servers to help with the increased workload. Installing additional servers on a network is relatively simple and can usually be done without disrupting services for existing users.

In addition, peer-to-peer networks are **decentralized**. This means that users are responsible for creating their own data backups and for providing security for their computers. In client/server networks, all clients connect to a server that performs tasks for them. Therefore, client/server networks are said to be **centralized**. Many tasks that individual users must handle on a P2P network can be handled centrally at the server.

For instance, data files are normally stored on the server. Therefore, backups for all users on a network can be performed by merely backing up all the files on the server. Also, security can be exercised over the server instead of on each user's computer; this way, the server, not the individual user, coordinates file security.

Classifications of Client/Server Networks: LANs, WANs, and MANs

Networks are generally classified according to their size and the distance between the physical parts of the network. The three main classifications are local area networks, wide area networks, and metropolitan area networks.

Local area networks (LANs) are generally small groups of computers and peripherals linked together over a relatively small geographic area. The computer lab at your school or the network on the floor of the office where you work is probably a LAN.

For large companies that operate at diverse geographic locations, a LAN is not sufficient for meeting their computing needs. **Wide area networks (WANs)** comprise large numbers of users or separate LANs that are miles apart and linked together. A large college campus would have a WAN that spans all of its lecture halls, residence halls, and administrative offices.

Similarly, corporations often use WANs to connect two or more geographically diverse branches. For example, ABC Shoe Company has manufacturing plants and administrative offices all over the globe. The LAN at each ABC Shoe Company office is connected to other ABC Shoe Company LANs, forming a global ABC Shoe Company WAN. Figure 12.3 shows an example of what part of the ABC Shoe Company WAN might look like.

FIGURE 12.3

WANs are several LANs in different geographic locations connected by telecommunications media. Satellite communication is often used to transmit data over long distances.

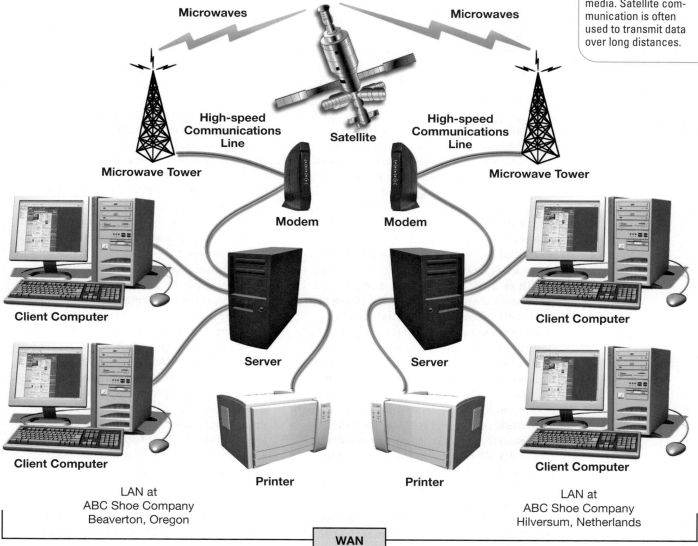

Microwaves · Microwaves · Satellite · High-speed Communications Line · High-speed Communications Line · Microwave Tower · Microwave Tower · Modem · Modem · Client Computer · Client Computer · Server · Server · Client Computer · Client Computer · Printer · Printer

LAN at ABC Shoe Company Beaverton, Oregon

LAN at ABC Shoe Company Hilversum, Netherlands

WAN

BITS AND BYTES

Too Much Data? Here Comes the SAN

Databases can become so large that conventional database servers can't handle the information flowing in and out of them. A **storage area network** (**SAN**) is specifically designed to store and distribute large amounts of data to client computers or servers. SANs are made up of several **network attached storage (NAS) devices**, which are specialized devices attached to a network whose sole function is to store and disseminate data. Picture a computer that contains nothing but hard drives and you have a pretty good idea of what a NAS device looks like. NAS devices are the filing cabinets of the new millennium and exist merely to store the huge amounts of data network users generate.

NAS devices are now available for use in the home. The Western Digital My Book external hard drives come in versions that act as an NAS for home networks, allowing all users on the network to store files on a single drive. And the Time Machine feature of OS X Leopard allows your computers to make any hard drive (attached to your network) function as an NAS device by storing backups of everything you do on your Mac.

Sometimes government organizations or civic groups establish WANs to link users in a specific geographic area (such as within a city or county). These special types of WANs are known as **metropolitan area networks (MANs)**. Many MANs are implemented as wireless networks that provide Internet access to large portions of cities. San Diego's Traffic Management Center (TMC) uses a MAN to analyze traffic patterns. You can check out the traffic maps they generate at **www.dot.ca.gov/sdtraffic**.

What sort of network connects personal digital assistants (PDAs) and cell phones? Personal area networks (PANs) are used to connect wireless devices (such as Bluetooth-enabled devices) in close proximity to each other. (Bluetooth technology uses radio waves to transmit data over short distances.) PANs are wireless and operate in the personal operating space of an individual, which is generally defined to be within 30 feet (or 10 meters) of your body. Today, PANs free you from having wires running to and from the devices you're using. One day, PANs may use the human body to transmit and receive signals.

What other sort of networks do businesses use? An **intranet** is a private corporate network that is used exclusively by company employees to facilitate information sharing, database access, group scheduling, videoconferencing, or other employee collaborations. Intranets are deployed using Transmission Control Protocol/Internet Protocol (TCP/IP) networks (which we discuss in Chapter 13) and generally include links to the Internet. The intranet is not accessible to nonemployees; a firewall (software or hardware used to prevent unauthorized entry) protects it from unauthorized access through the Internet.

One of the main uses of intranets is groupware (software that enables users to share and collaborate on documents). Software such as Lotus Notes, a type of groupware, facilitates sharing of employee information and brainstorming to solve problems. Most groupware programs also support messaging and group calendaring.

Extranets are pieces of intranets that only certain corporations or individuals can access. The owner of the extranet decides who will be permitted to access it. Customers and suppliers are typical entities that would benefit from accessing information on an extranet. Extranets are useful for enabling electronic data interchange (EDI). EDI provides for the exchanging of large amounts of business data (such as orders for merchandise) in a standardized electronic format. Other uses of extranets include providing access to catalogs and inventory databases and sharing information among partners or industry trade groups.

How are intranets and extranets kept secure? Because of security concerns, intranets and extranets often use virtual private networks to keep information secure. A **virtual private network (VPN)** uses the public Internet communications infrastructure to build a secure, private network between various locations. Although wide area networks (WANs) can be set up using private leased communications lines, these lines are expensive and tend to increase in price as the distance between points increases. VPNs use special security technologies and protocols that enhance security, enabling data to traverse the Internet as securely as if it were on a private leased line. Installing and configuring a VPN requires special hardware such as VPN-optimized routers and firewalls. In addition, VPN software must be installed on users' PCs.

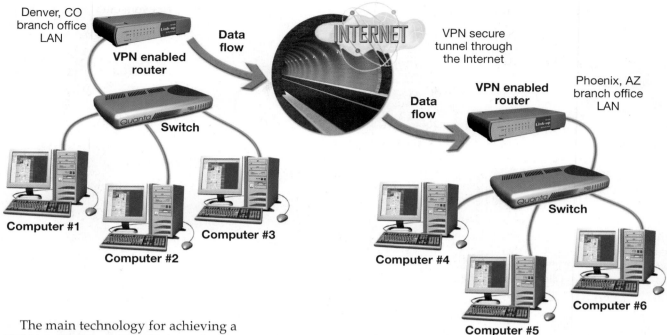

Denver, CO branch office LAN

VPN enabled router

Data flow

INTERNET

VPN secure tunnel through the Internet

Data flow

VPN enabled router

Phoenix, AZ branch office LAN

Switch

Switch

Computer #1

Computer #2

Computer #3

Computer #4

Computer #5

Computer #6

FIGURE 12.4

Local area networks (LANs) in different cities can communicate securely over the Internet using VPN technology.

The main technology for achieving a VPN is called *tunneling*. Data packets are placed inside new data packets. The format of the new data packets is encrypted and is only understood by the sending and receiving hardware, known as *tunnel interfaces*. The hardware is optimized to seek efficient routes of transmission through the Internet. This provides a high level of security and makes information much more difficult to intercept and decrypt.

Imagine you have to deliver a message to a branch office. You could have one of your employees drive to the other office and deliver the message. But suppose he has to go through a bad neighborhood or has never been to the office before? The messenger could be waylaid by a carjacker or could become hopelessly lost. Using a VPN (as shown in Figure 12.4) is the equivalent of hiring a limousine and an armed guard to drive your employee through a private tunnel directly to the destination. Of course, a VPN avoids the enormous cost associated with this method!

Constructing Client/Server Networks

In Chapter 7, we discussed the main components of peer-to-peer networks. Client/server networks share many of the same components of P2P networks as well as some components specific to client/server networks:

- **Server:** Unlike peer-to-peer networks, client/server networks contain at least one computer that functions solely as a server.

- **Network topology:** Because client/server networks are more complex than peer-to-peer networks, the layout and structure of the network, which is called the **network topology**, must be carefully planned.

- **Transmission media:** Data needs a way to flow between clients and servers on networks. Therefore, an appropriate type of transmission media (cable or wireless communications technology) based on the network topology is needed. Client/server networks use a wider variety of cable types than do simpler P2P networks.

- **Network operating system (NOS) software:** All client/server networks require network operating system (NOS) software, which is specialized software that is installed on servers and client computers that enables the network to function. Most modern

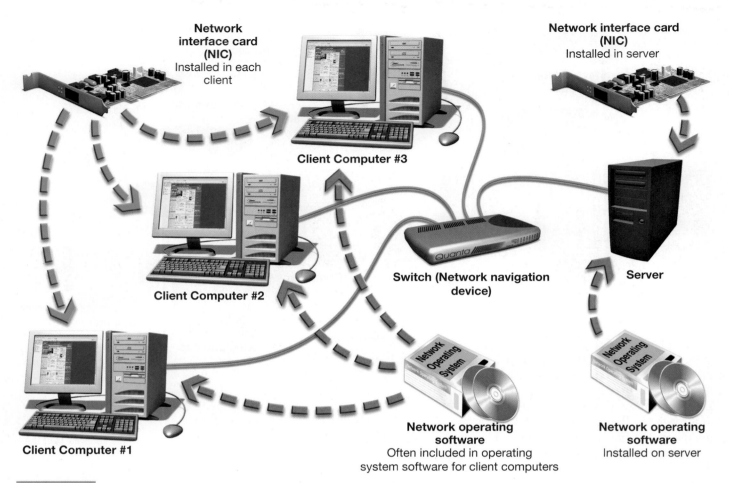

Network interface card (NIC)
Installed in each client

Client Computer #3

Network interface card (NIC)
Installed in server

Client Computer #2

Switch (Network navigation device)

Server

Client Computer #1

Network operating software
Often included in operating system software for client computers

Network operating software
Installed on server

FIGURE 12.5

The basic components of a typical client/server network are shown in this small network. The method of connecting the computers to the server defines a network's topology.

operating systems (such as Windows Vista and OS X) include the software needed for computers to function as clients on a network.

- **Network adapters:** As is the case with peer-to-peer networks, network adapters (or network interface cards) must be attached or installed to each device on the network. These adapters enable the computer (or peripheral) to communicate with the network using a common data communication language, or protocol.

- **Network navigation devices:** Because of the complexity of a client/server network, specialized network navigation devices (such as routers, switches, and bridges) are needed to move data signals around the network.

Figure 12.5 shows the components of a simple client/server network. In the following sections, we explore each component in more detail.

Servers

Servers are the workhorses of the client/server network. They serve many different network users and assist them with accomplishing a variety of tasks. The number and types of servers on a client/server network depend on the network's size and workload. Small networks (such as the one pictured in Figure 12.2) would have just one server to handle all server functions such as file storage, delivery of applications to the clients, printing, and so on.

As more users are added to a network, dedicated servers are also added to take the load off of the main server. **Dedicated servers** are used to fulfill one specific function (such as handling e-mail). When dedicated servers are deployed, the main server then becomes merely an authentication server or a file server.

What are authentication and file servers? **Authentication servers** keep track of who is logging on to the network

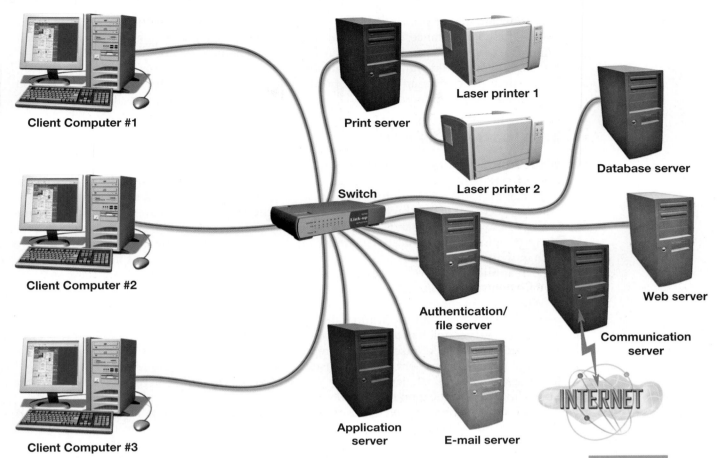

Client Computer #1

Client Computer #2

Client Computer #3

Print server

Laser printer 1

Laser printer 2

Switch

Database server

Authentication/ file server

Web server

Communication server

Application server

E-mail server

INTERNET

FIGURE 12.6

This is a typical large-scale client/server network with several dedicated servers installed.

and which services on the network are available to each user. Authentication servers also act as overseers for the network. They manage and coordinate the services provided by any other dedicated servers located on the network. **File servers** store and manage files for network users. On the network at your workplace or school, you may be provided with space on a file server to store files you create.

What functions do dedicated servers handle? Any task that is repetitive or demands a lot of time from the server's processor (CPU) is a good candidate to relegate to a dedicated server. Common types of dedicated servers are print servers, application servers, database servers, e-mail servers, communications servers, and Web servers. Servers are connected to a client/server network so that all client computers that need to use their services can access them, as shown in Figure 12.6.

PRINT SERVERS

How does a print server function?
Printing is a function that takes a large

quantity of central processing unit (CPU) time and that most people do quite often. Setting up a **print server** to manage all client-requested printing jobs for all printers on the network helps enable client computers to complete more productive work than printing. When you tell your computer to print a document, it passes off the task to the print server. This frees the CPU on your computer to do other jobs.

When the print server receives a printing request (or job) from a client computer, it puts the job into a print queue on the print server. A print queue is a software holding area for printing jobs. Normally, each printer on a network has its own uniquely named print queue. Jobs receive a number when entering the queue and are sent to the printer in the order in which they are received. Print queues thus function like the "take a number" machines at a supermarket deli. Thus, print servers organize print jobs into an orderly sequence to make printing more efficient on a shared printer. Another useful aspect of print servers is that they can prioritize print jobs. Different users and types of print jobs can be assigned different priorities, and higher-priority jobs are printed first. For instance, in a company in which documents are printed on demand for clients, you would want these print jobs to take precedence over an employee printing routine correspondence.

APPLICATION SERVERS

What function does an application server perform? In many networks, all users run the same application software (such as Microsoft Office) on their computers. In a network of thousands of personal computers, installing application software on each individual computer is time consuming. An **application server** acts as a repository for application software.

When a client computer connects to the network and requests an application, the application server delivers the software to the client computer. Because the software does not reside on the client computer itself, this eases the task of installation and upgrading. The application needs to be installed or upgraded only on the application server, not on each network client.

DATABASE SERVERS

What does a database server do? As its name implies, a **database server** provides client computers with access to information stored in a database. Often, many people need to access databases at the same time. For example, airline ticketing clerks can serve multiple people at the same time because they all have access to the ticket reservation database. This is achieved by storing the database on a database server, which each clerk's computer can access through the network. If the database were on a stand-alone computer instead of a network, only one clerk could use it at a time, making the ticketing system terribly inefficient.

E-MAIL SERVERS

When is an e-mail server necessary? The volume of e-mail on a large corporate network could quickly overwhelm a server that was attempting to handle other functions as well. Therefore, the sole function of an **e-mail server** attached to the network is to process and deliver incoming and outgoing e-mail. On a network with an e-mail server, when you send an e-mail from your computer, it goes to the e-mail server, which then handles the routing and delivery of your message. The e-mail server functions much like a postal carrier, who picks up your mail and sees that it finds its way to the correct destination.

COMMUNICATIONS SERVERS

What types of communications does a communications server handle? A **communications server** handles all communications between the network and other networks, including managing Internet connectivity. All requests for information from the Internet and all messages being sent through the Internet pass through the communications server. Because Internet traffic is substantial at most organizations, the communications server has a heavy workload.

The communications server often is the only device on the network connected to the Internet. E-mail servers, Web servers, and other devices needing to communicate with the Internet usually route all their traffic through the communications server. Providing a single point of contact with the outside world makes it easier to secure the network from hackers.

WEB SERVERS

What function does a Web server perform? A **Web server** is used to host a Web site available through the Internet. Web servers run specialized software such as Apache (open source server software) and Microsoft Internet Information Services (IIS) that enable them to host Web pages. Not every large network has a Web server. Many companies use an Internet service provider (ISP) to host their corporate Web sites instead.

Network Topologies

Just as buildings have different floor plans depending on their uses, networks have different blueprints denoting their layout. *Network topology* refers to the physical or logical arrangement of computers, transmission media (cable), and other network components. *Physical topology* refers to the layout of the "real" components of the network,

---

ACTIVE HELPDESK

Using Servers

In this Active Helpdesk call, you'll play the role of a helpdesk staffer, fielding calls about various types of servers and client/server software.

---

whereas *logical topology* pertains to virtual connections between network nodes. Logical topologies usually are determined by network protocols instead of the physical layout of the network or the paths electrical signals follow on the network. Because networks have different uses, not all networks have the same topology.

For example, assume that your class has to send a message to the class next door. You decide to arrange your class in a straight line from your classroom to the other classroom. Each student will whisper the message to the next student in the line until the message is eventually passed to a student in the other classroom. The arrangement of the students in a straight line is the topology. The passing of the message from student to student using the English language is the protocol.

In this section, we explore the most common network topologies (bus, ring, and star) and discuss when each topology is used. As you'll see, the type of network topology used is important because it can affect the network's performance and scalability. Knowing how the basic topologies work and the strengths and weaknesses of each will help you understand why particular network topologies were chosen on the networks you use.

BUS TOPOLOGY

What does a bus topology look like?

In a **bus** (or **linear bus**) **topology**, all computers are connected in sequence on a single cable, as shown in Figure 12.7. This topology is deployed most often in peer-to-peer networks (not client/server networks). Each computer on the bus network can communicate with every other computer on the network directly. A limitation of bus networks is that data collisions can occur easily if two computers transmit data at the same time because a bus network is essentially composed of one main communication medium (single cable).

Think of a data collision as having a group of three people (e.g., Emily, Reesa, and Luis) sitting in a room having a conversation. For the conversation to be effective, only one person can speak at a time; otherwise, they would not be able to hear and understand each other. Therefore, if Emily is speaking, Reesa and Luis must wait until she finishes before presenting their ideas, and so on.

Because two signals transmitted at the same time on a bus network may cause a data collision, an **access method** has to be established to control which computer is

FIGURE 12.7

A Linear Bus Topology

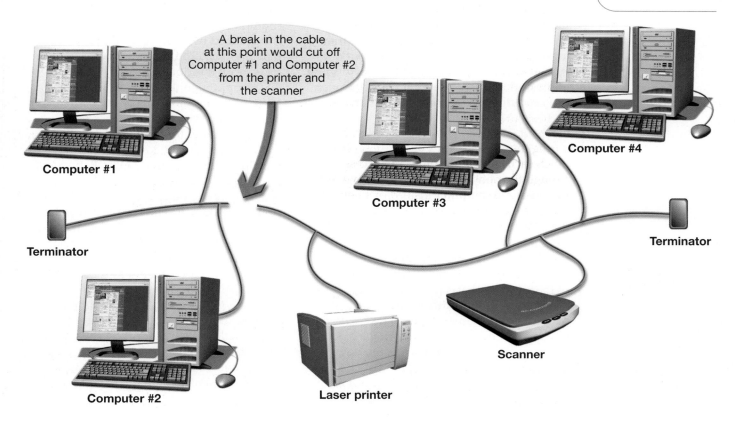

A break in the cable at this point would cut off Computer #1 and Computer #2 from the printer and the scanner

Computer #1

Terminator

Computer #2

Laser printer

Computer #3

Scanner

Computer #4

Terminator

SOUND BYTE

Network Topology and Navigation Devices

In this Sound Byte, you'll learn about common network topologies, the types of networks they are used with, and various network navigation devices.

allowed to use the transmission media at a certain time. Computers on a bus network behave the same way as a group of people having a conversation. The computers "listen" to the network data traffic on the media. When no other computer is transmitting data (that is, when "conversation" stops), the computer knows it is allowed to transmit data on the media. This means of taking turns "talking" avoids **data collisions**, which happen when two computers send data at the same time and the sets of data collide somewhere in the media. When data collides, it is often lost or irreparably damaged.

How does data get from point to point on a bus network? When it is safe to send data (that is, when no other computers are transmitting data), the sending computer broadcasts the data onto the media. The data is broadcast throughout the network to all devices connected to the network. The data is broken into small segments called **packets**. Each packet contains the address of the computer or peripheral device to which it is being sent. Each computer or device connected to the network listens for data that contains its address. When it "hears" data addressed to it, it takes the data off the media and processes it.

For example, say your computer needs to print something on the printer attached to the network. Your computer "listens" to the network to ensure no other nodes are transmitting. It then sends the print job out onto the network. When the printer "hears" a job addressed to it (the print job your computer just sent), it pulls the data off the network and executes the job.

The devices (nodes) attached to a bus network do nothing to move data along the network. This makes a bus network a **passive topology**. The data merely travels the entire length of the medium and is received by all network devices. The ends of the cable in a bus network are capped off by terminators (as shown in Figure 12.7). A **terminator** is a device that absorbs the signal so that it is not reflected back onto parts of the network that have already received it.

What are the advantages and disadvantages of bus networks? The simplicity and low cost of configuring a bus network are the major reasons this topology is deployed most often in P2P networks. The major disadvantage is that if there is a break in the cable, the bus network is effectively

disrupted, because some computers are cut off from others on the network.

Also, because transmission signals degrade as the distance of the cable increases, a bus network is difficult to expand to a large number of users. And because only one computer can communicate at a time, adding a large number of nodes to a bus network limits performance and causes delays in sending data. Therefore, you rarely see a bus network deployed except in small networks that are not expected to grow.

RING TOPOLOGY

What does a ring topology look like? Not surprisingly, given its name, the computers and peripherals in a **ring** (or **loop**) **topology** are laid out in a configuration resembling a circle, as shown in Figure 12.8. Data flows around the circle from device to device in one direction only. Because data is passed using a special data packet called a **token**, this type of topology is commonly referred to as a **token-ring topology**. The original token-ring networks achieved **data transfer rates** (bandwidth) of either 4 Mbps or 16 Mbps, but more recent token technologies can deliver speeds as high as 100 Mbps.

How is a token used to move data around a ring? A token is passed from computer to computer around the ring until it is grabbed by a computer that needs to transmit data. The computer holds onto the token until it is done transmitting data. Only one computer on the ring can "hold" the token at a time, and usually only one token exists on each ring.

If a computer (or node) has data to send, it waits for the token to be passed to it. It then takes the token out of circulation and sends data to its destination. When the receiving node receives a complete transmission of the data, it sends an acknowledgment to the sending node. The sending node then generates a new token and starts it going around the ring again. This **token method** is the access method that ring networks use to avoid data collisions.

A ring topology is an **active topology** because each node on the network is responsible for retransmitting the token or the data to the next node on the ring. Large ring networks have the capability to use multiple tokens to help move more data faster.

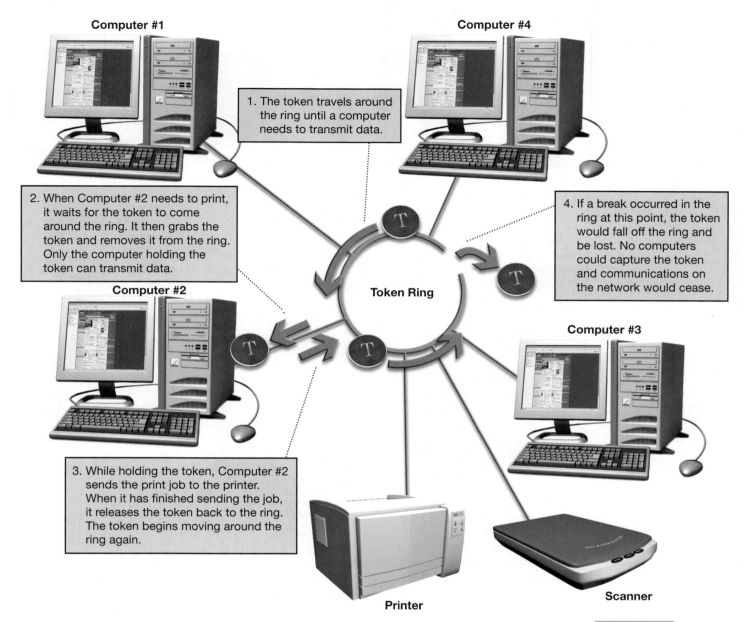

Computer #1

Computer #4

1. The token travels around the ring until a computer needs to transmit data.

2. When Computer #2 needs to print, it waits for the token to come around the ring. It then grabs the token and removes it from the ring. Only the computer holding the token can transmit data.

4. If a break occurred in the ring at this point, the token would fall off the ring and be lost. No computers could capture the token and communications on the network would cease.

Computer #2

Token Ring

Computer #3

3. While holding the token, Computer #2 sends the print job to the printer. When it has finished sending the job, it releases the token back to the ring. The token begins moving around the ring again.

Printer

Scanner

FIGURE 12.8

A Token-Ring Topology

Is a ring topology better than a bus topology? A ring topology provides a fairer allocation of network resources than does a bus topology. By using a token, a ring network enables all nodes on the network to have an equal chance to send data. One "chatty" node cannot as easily monopolize the network bandwidth because it must pass the token on after sending a batch of data.

In addition, the ring topology's performance remains acceptable even with large numbers of users. However, if one computer fails on a ring network, it can bring the entire network to a halt because that computer is unavailable to retransmit tokens and data. Problems in the ring can also be hard for network administrators to find. It's easier to expand a ring topology than a bus topology, but adding a node to a ring does cause the ring to cease to function while the node is installed.

STAR TOPOLOGY

What is the layout for a star topology? A **star topology** is the most widely deployed client/server network layout in businesses today because it offers the most flexibility. In a star topology, the nodes connect to a central communications device called a switch, thus resembling a star, as shown in Figure 12.9. The switch receives a signal from the sending node and retransmits it to all other nodes on the network. The

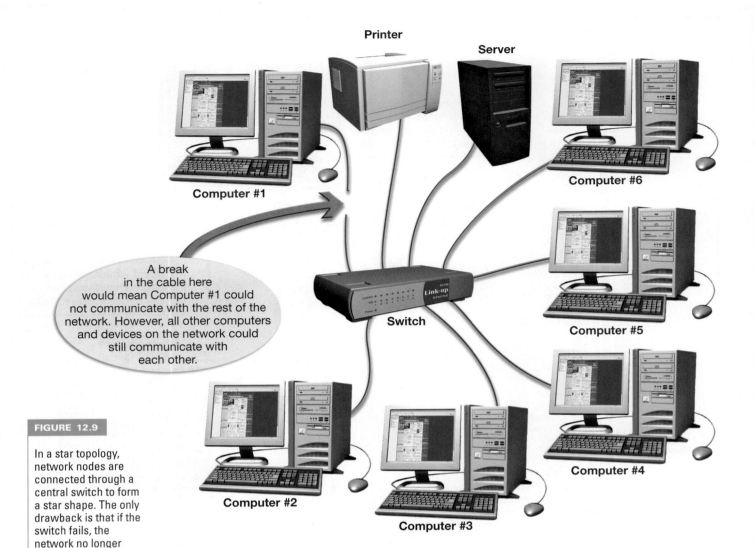

Printer

Server

Computer #1

Computer #6

A break in the cable here would mean Computer #1 could not communicate with the rest of the network. However, all other computers and devices on the network could still communicate with each other.

Switch

Computer #5

Computer #4

Computer #2

Computer #3

FIGURE 12.9

In a star topology, network nodes are connected through a central switch to form a star shape. The only drawback is that if the switch fails, the network no longer functions. However, it is relatively easy to replace a switch.

network nodes examine data and only pick up the transmissions addressed to them. Because the switch retransmits data signals, a star topology is an active topology. (We discuss switches in more detail later in this chapter.)

Many star networks use the Ethernet protocol. Networks using the Ethernet protocol are by far the most common type of network in use today. Although many students think that Ethernet is a type of network topology, it is actually a communications protocol. A topology is a physical design of a network, whereas a **protocol** is a set of rules for exchanging communication. Therefore, an Ethernet network can be set up using a bus, a ring, or a star topology. The original Ethernet networks achieved maximum data transfer rates of 10 Mbps. However, newer equipment delivers 100 Mbps and even 1 Gigabit transfer rates at especially affordable prices. For businesses that need even

more speed, the new 10 Gigabit standard supports a transfer rate of up to 10 Gbps, but the equipment supporting this standard is still relatively expensive and therefore is not seen in small businesses unless very high bandwidth is required.

How do computers on a star network avoid data collisions? Because most star networks are Ethernet networks, they use the method used on all Ethernet networks to avoid data collisions: **CSMA/ CD** (short for *carrier sense multiple access with collision detection*). With CSMA/CD, a node connected to the network listens (that is, has carrier sense) to determine that no other nodes are currently transmitting data signals. If the node doesn't hear any other signals, then it assumes it is safe to transmit data. All devices on the network have the same right (that is, they have multiple access) to transmit data when they deem it safe. It is therefore possible for two devices to begin

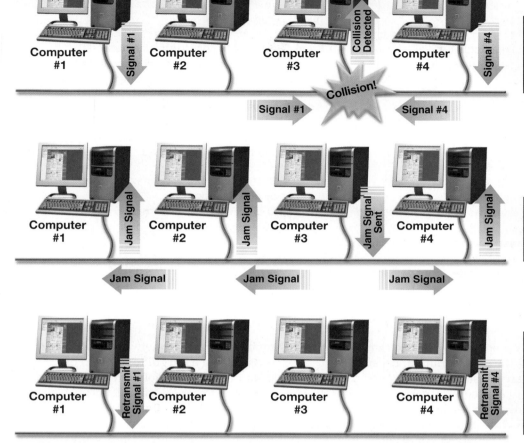

Step 1: Computer #1 and Computer #4 begin transmitting data signals at the same time. A data collision occurs, which is detected by Computer #3.

Step 2: Computer #3 sends a jam signal to all nodes on the network, informing them that a collision has occurred.

Step 3: Computer #1 and Computer #4 wait random amounts of time, then send their signals again. Since the signals are resent at different times, a second collision should not occur.

14 nanoseconds later   18 nanoseconds later

FIGURE 12.10

Avoiding Data Collisions on an Ethernet Network

transmitting data signals at the same time. If this happens, the two signals collide.

What happens when the signals collide? As shown in Figure 12.10, when signals collide, a node on the network detects the collision. It then sends a special signal called a **jam signal** to all network nodes, alerting them that a collision has occurred. The nodes then stop transmitting and wait a random amount of time before retransmitting their data signals. The wait time needs to be random; otherwise, both nodes would start transmitting at the same time and another collision would occur.

What are the advantages and disadvantages of a star topology? Because of the complexity of the layout of star networks, they require more cable and are often more expensive than bus or ring networks. However, a star topology generally is considered to be superior to a ring topology because if one computer fails it

doesn't affect the rest of the network. This is extremely important in a large network, in which one disabled computer affecting the operations of several hundred other computers would be totally unacceptable.

It is also easy to add nodes to star networks, and performance remains acceptable even with large numbers of users. In addition, the centralization of communications (through a switch) makes troubleshooting and repairs on star networks easier for network technicians. Technicians can usually pinpoint a communications problem just by examining the switch, as opposed to searching for a particular length of cable that broke in a ring network.

COMPARING TOPOLOGIES

So which topology is the best one?
Figure 12.11 lists the advantages and disadvantages of bus, ring, and star topologies. In

FIGURE 12.11 **Advantages and Disadvantages of Bus, Ring, and Star Topologies**

Topology	Advantages	Disadvantages
Bus	Uses a minimal amount of cabling. Easy, reliable, and inexpensive to install.	Breaks in the cable can disable the network. Large numbers of users will greatly decrease performance because of high volumes of data traffic.
Ring	Allocates access to the network fairly. Performance remains acceptable even with large numbers of users.	Adding or removing nodes disables the network. Failure of one computer can bring down the entire network. Problems in data transmission can sometimes be difficult to find.
Star	Failure of one computer does not affect other computers on the network. Centralized design simplifies troubleshooting and repairs. Easy to add more computers or groups of computers as needed (high scalability). Performance remains acceptable even with large numbers of users.	Requires more cable and is often more expensive than a bus or ring topology. The switch is a central point of failure. If it fails, all computers connected to that switch are affected.

all but the smallest networks, star topologies are the most common. Because networks are constantly adding new users, the ability to add new users simply (that is, by installing a new switch) without affecting users already on the network is the deciding factor. The networks you'll encounter at school and in the workplace will almost certainly be laid out in a star topology. However, bus topologies are becoming obsolete as even most simple home networks have moved to a star topology. Ring topologies are popular when fair allocation of network access is a major requirement of the network.

Can topologies be combined within a single network? Because each topology has its own unique advantages, topologies are often combined to construct business networks. Combining multiple topologies into one network is known as constructing a **hybrid topology**. For instance, fair allocation of resources may be critical for reservation clerks at an airline (requiring a token-ring network), whereas a purchasing department's network may require a star topology. One disadvantage of hybrid topologies is that hardware changes must usually be made to switch a node from one topology to another.

Transmission Media

When constructing a house, a variety of building material is available, depending on the needs of the builder. Similarly, when building a network, network engineers can use different types of media. **Transmission media**, whether it is cable or wireless communications technology, comprise the routes data takes to flow between devices on the network. Without transmission media, network devices would be unable to communicate.

WIRED TRANSMISSION MEDIA

What types of cable are commonly used for networks? In Chapter 7, you learned that most home networks use either twisted pair cable (phone wire or Ethernet)

ACTIVE HELPDESK

Selecting a Network Topology and Cable

In this Active Helpdesk call, you'll play the role of a Helpdesk staffer, fielding calls about how a client/server network differs from a peer-to-peer network, the different classifications of client/server networks, various network topologies, and the types of transmission media used in client/server networks.

or electrical wires as transmission media. For business networks, the three main cable types that are used today are twisted pair, coaxial, and fiber optic.

What are the important factors in choosing a cable? Although each type is different, they share many common factors that need to be considered when choosing a cable type:

- **Maximum run length:** Each type of cable has a maximum run length over which signals sent across it can be "heard" by devices connected to it. Therefore, when designing a network, network engineers must accurately measure the distances between devices to ensure that appropriate cable is selected.

- **Bandwidth:** As you learned in earlier chapters, **bandwidth** is the amount of data that can be transmitted across a transmission medium in a certain amount of time. Each cable is different and is rated by the maximum bandwidth it can support. Bandwidth is measured in bits per second, which represents how many bits of data can be transmitted along the cable each second.

- **Bend radius (flexibility):** When installing cable, it is often necessary to bend the cable around corners, surfaces, and so on. The bend radius of the cable defines how many degrees a cable can be bent in a one-foot segment before it is damaged. If many corners need to be navigated when installing a network, network engineers use cabling with a high bend radius.

- **Cable cost:** The cost per foot of different types and grades of cable varies widely. Cable selection may have to be made on the basis of cost if adequate funds are not available for the optimal type of cabling.

- **Installation costs:** Certain cable (such as twisted pair) is easy and inexpensive to install. Fiber-optic cable requires special training and equipment to install, which increases the installation costs.

- **Susceptibility to interference:** Signals traveling down a cable are subject to two types of interference. Electromagnetic interference (EMI), caused by the cable

BITS AND BYTES

A Network on the Move!

When you think of cutting-edge technology, do you think of city buses? If you visited Portsmouth, England, you would. Portsmouth is a small city visited by more than 6.5 million tourists each year. Because the city is always full of people, 320 buses are deployed in it, each one equipped with a highly sophisticated wireless network, including an onboard computer and wireless network card. And each bus stop is equipped with an Internet terminal that enables patrons to check e-mail, buy bus tickets, and find out exactly where the bus they are waiting for is located and when it will arrive.

The network keeps track of the exact location of all the network nodes (the computers on the buses) by sending test signals (pings) to them and measuring the time communications take to travel back and forth. The network doesn't use 802.11 technology; instead, it uses a competing standard developed for the military called QDMA (quad-division multiple access). The main advantage of QDMA is that it can network devices moving as fast at 250 miles an hour without losing the link. However, there are plans to add 802.11-compatible wireless access points at bus kiosks and on the buses to allow riders to use their own computers, PDAs, and cell phones to surf the Net.

being exposed to strong electromagnetic fields, can distort or degrade signals on the cable. Fluorescent lights and machinery with motors or transformers are the most common sources of EMI emissions. Cable signals also can be disrupted by radio frequency interference (RFI), which is usually caused by broadcast sources (television and radio signals) being located near the network. Cable types are rated as to how well they resist interference.

- **Signal transmission methods:** Both coaxial cable and twisted pair cable send electrical impulses down conductive material to transmit data signals. Fiber-optic cable transmits data signals as pulses of light.

In the sections that follow, we discuss the characteristics of each of the three major types of cable. We also discuss the use of wireless media as an alternative to cable.

Twisted Pair Cable

What does twisted pair cable look like? Twisted pair cable should be familiar to you because the telephone cable (or wire)

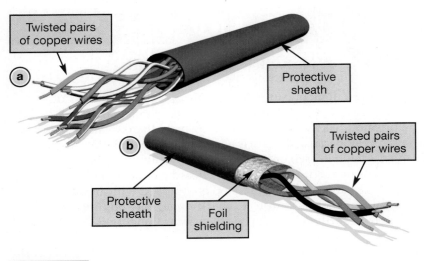

Twisted pairs
of copper wires

(a)

Protective
sheath

Protective
sheath

(b)

Foil
shielding

Twisted pairs
of copper wires

FIGURE 12.12

Anatomy of (a) unshielded twisted pair (UTP) cable and (b) shielded twisted pair (STP) cable.

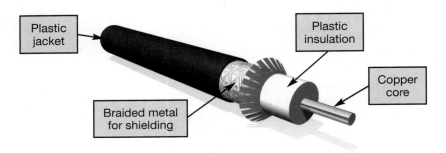

Plastic
jacket

Plastic
insulation

Copper
core

Braided metal
for shielding

FIGURE 12.13

Coaxial cable consists of four main components: the core, an insulated covering, a braided metal shielding, and a plastic jacket.

in your home is one type of twisted pair cable. **Twisted pair cable** consists of pairs of copper wires twisted around each other and covered by a protective jacket (or sheath). The twists are important because they cause the magnetic fields that form around the copper wires to intermingle, which makes them less susceptible to outside interference. It also reduces the amount of crosstalk interference, or the tendency of signals on one wire to interfere with signals on a wire next to it.

If the twisted pair cable contains a layer of foil shielding to reduce interference, it is known as **shielded twisted pair (STP)**

cable. If it does not contain a layer of foil shielding, it is known as **unshielded twisted pair (UTP) cable**, which is more susceptible to interference. Figure 12.12 shows illustrations of both types of twisted pair cable. Because of its lower price, UTP is more widely used, unless significant sources of interference must be overcome (such as in a production environment where machines create magnetic fields). However, there are different standard categories of UTP cable from which to choose.

What types of UTP cable are available? The two most common types of UTP cable in use today are Category 5E (Cat 5E) and Category 6 (Cat 6). Cat 6 cable can handle a bandwidth of 1 gigabit per second (Gbps), whereas Cat 5E can handle a bandwidth of just 200 megabits per second (Mbps).

Unless severe budget constraints are in place, network engineers usually install the highest-bandwidth cable possible because reinstalling cable later (and the subsequent tearing up of walls and ceilings) can be very expensive. Therefore, since the fall of 2002, when the standard for Cat 6 cable was approved, new cable runs in businesses have been made with Cat 6 cable. Home networks that use twisted pair cable generally use Cat 5E cable because it's less expensive and most home networks don't need gigabit networks.

Coaxial Cable

What does coaxial cable look like? **Coaxial cable** should be familiar to you if you have cable television, because most cable television installers use coaxial cable. Coaxial cable (as shown in Figure 12.13) consists of four main components:

1. The core (usually copper) is in the very center and is used for transmitting the signal.

2. A solid layer of nonconductive insulating material (usually a hard, thick plastic) surrounds the core.

3. A layer of braided metal comes next to reduce interference with signals traveling in the core.

4. Finally, an external jacket of lightweight plastic covers the internal cable components to protect them from damage.

Although coaxial cable used to be the most widely used cable in business networks, advances in twisted pair cable shielding and transmission speeds, as well as twisted pair's lower cost, have reduced the popularity of coaxial cable.

Are there different types of coaxial cable? The two main coaxial cable types are ThinNet and ThickNet. ThinNet is a category of cable that covers several cable types, such as RG58 10Base2 or RG-6. If you have cable television or cable Internet service in your home, you have some type of ThinNet cable. It is usually covered by a black or white plastic jacket. ThickNet, usually distinguished by a yellow jacket, is similar to ThinNet but is more rigid and better shielded to protect against interference. ThickNet, because it is better shielded, is used in industrial settings where there is a lot of electrical interference. ThinNet cables are used in homes because they are cheaper and because most houses do not have significant sources of interference (such as industrial machinery).

Fiber-Optic Cable

What does fiber-optic cable look like? As shown in Figure 12.14, **fiber-optic cable** is composed of a glass (or plastic) fiber (or a bundle of fibers) that comprises the core of the cable (where the data is transmitted). Cladding, a protective layer made of glass or plastic, is wrapped around the core to protect it. Finally, for additional protection, an outer jacket (sheath) is added, often made of durable materials such as Kevlar (the substance used to make bulletproof vests). Data transmissions can pass through fiber-optic cable in only one direction. Therefore, usually at least two cores are located in each fiber-optic cable to enable transmission of data in both directions.

How does fiber-optic cable differ from twisted pair and coaxial cable? As noted earlier, the main difference between fiber-optic cable and other types of cable is the method of signal transmission. Twisted pair and coaxial cable use copper wire to conduct electrical impulses. In a fiber-optic cable, electrical data signals from network devices (client computers, peripherals, and so on) are converted to light pulses before they are transmitted. Because EMI and RFI do not affect light waves, fiber-optic cable is virtually immune to interference.

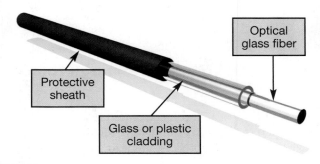

FIGURE 12.14

Fiber-optic cable is made up of a glass or plastic fiber (or a bundle of fibers), a glass or plastic cladding, and a protective sheath.

WIRELESS MEDIA OPTIONS

What wireless media options are there? Although the word *wireless* implies no wires, in businesses, **wireless media** are usually add-ons to extend or improve access to a wired network. In the corporate environment, wireless access is often provided to give employees a wider range to their working area. For instance, if conference rooms offer wireless access, employees can bring their notebooks (laptops) to meetings and gain access to the network during the meeting. However, when they go back to their offices, they may connect to the regular wired network through a wired connection. So, today's corporate networks are often a combination of wired and wireless media.

Are there standards defined for wireless communication? As you learned in earlier chapters, wireless devices must use the same communications standard to communicate with each other. Wireless networks in the United States are currently based on the **802.11 standard**, also known as **WiFi** (short for Wireless Fidelity), established by the Institute of Electrical and Electronics Engineers (IEEE). Wireless devices attached to networks using the 802.11 standard communicate with each other using radio waves.

The 802.11 standard is actually divided into a number of separate standards. The 802.11g standard is the most common standard in use now. With a maximum **throughput** (bandwidth) of 54 Mbps, 802.11g standard is widely deployed in corporate and personal networks. 802.11g

DIG DEEPER

The OSI Model: Defining Protocol Standards

The Institute of Electrical and Electronics Engineers (IEEE) has taken the lead in establishing recognized worldwide networking protocols, including a standard of communications called the Open Systems Interconnection (OSI) reference model. The OSI model, which was quickly adopted as a standard throughout the computing world, provides the protocol guidelines for all modern networks. All modern network operating system (NOS) protocols are designed to interact in accordance with the standards set out by the OSI model.

The OSI model divides communications tasks into seven distinct processes called layers. Each layer of an OSI network has a specific function. Figure 12.15 shows the layers of the OSI model and their functions. Each layer knows how to communicate with the layer above and below it.

This layering approach makes communications more efficient because specialized pieces of the NOS perform specific tasks. The layering approach is akin to assembly-line manufacturing. For example, producing thousands of cars per day would be difficult if one person had to build a car on his or her own. However, by splitting up the work of assembling a car into specialized tasks (such as installing the engine, bolting on the bumpers, and so on) and assigning them to people who perform exceptionally well at certain tasks, greater efficiency is achieved. This is how the OSI layers work. By handling specialized tasks and communicating only with the layers above and below them, the layering approach makes communications more efficient.

FIGURE 12.15 The Layers of the OSI Model and Their Functions

Application layer	Handles all interfaces between the application software and the network Translates user information into a format the presentation layer can understand
Presentation layer	Reformats data so that the session layer can understand it Compresses and encrypts data
Session layer	Sets up a virtual (not physical) connection between the sending and receiving devices Manages communications sessions
Transport layer	Creates packets Handles packet acknowledgment
Network layer	Determines where to send the packets on the network
Data link layer	Assembles the data into frames, addresses them, and sends them to the physical layer for delivery
Physical layer	Transmits (delivers) data on the network so it can reach its intended address

devices include Super G (also called Extreme G or Enhanced G) devices, which use proprietary algorithms and hardware to increase maximum throughput to 108 Mbps. However, 802.11g devices are being replaced by 802.11n devices. The 802.11n standard supports much higher throughput and greatly increased range (often by using multiple antennas to send and receive signals), which makes it an ideal choice for providing wireless coverage over an entire office, or in environments where large data files (such as video) are being transmitted.

COMPARING TRANSMISSION MEDIA

So which medium is best for client/server networks? Network engineers specialize in the design and deployment of networks and are responsible for selecting network topology and media types. Their decision as to which transmission medium the network will use is based on the topology selected, the length of the cable runs needed, the amount of interference present, and the need for wireless connectivity.

Let's look at how each OSI layer functions by following an e-mail you create and send to your friend:

- **Application layer:** Handles all interaction between the application software and the network. It translates the data from the application into a format that the presentation layer can understand. For example, when you send an e-mail, the application layer takes the e-mail message you created in Microsoft Outlook, translates it into a format your network can understand, and passes it to the presentation layer.
- **Presentation layer:** Reformats the data so that the session layer can understand it. It also handles data encryption (changing the data into a format that makes it harder to intercept and read the message) and compression, if required. In our e-mail example, the presentation layer notices that you selected an encryption option for the e-mail message and encrypts the data before sending it to the session layer.
- **Session layer:** Sets up a virtual (not physical) connection between the sending and receiving devices. It then manages the communication between the two. In our e-mail example, the session layer would set up the parameters for the communications session between your computer and the Internet service provider (ISP) where your friend has her e-mail account. The session layer then tracks the transmission of the e-mail until it is satisfied that all the data in the e-mail was received at your friend's ISP.
- **Transport layer:** Breaks up the data into packets and sequences them appropriately. It also handles acknowledgment of packets (that is, it determines whether the packets were received at their destination) and decides whether packets need to be sent again. In our e-mail example, the transport layer breaks up your e-mail message into packets and sends them to the network layer, making sure that all the packets reach their destination.
- **Network layer:** Determines where to send the packets on the network and the best way to route them there. In our e-mail example, the network layer examines the address on the packets (the address of your friend's ISP) and determines how to route the packets so they get to your ISP and can ultimately get to the receiving computer.
- **Data link layer:** Responsible for assembling the data packets into frames (a type of data packet that holds more data), addressing the frames, and delivering them to the physical layer so they can be sent on their way. It is the equivalent of a postal worker who reads the address on a piece of mail and makes sure it gets sent to the proper recipient. In our e-mail example, the data link layer assembles the e-mail data packets into frames, which are addressed with appropriate routing information received from the network layer.
- **Physical layer:** Takes care of delivering the data. It converts the data into a signal and transmits it onto the network so that it can reach its intended address. In our e-mail example, the physical layer sends out the data over the Internet to its ultimate destination (your friend's ISP).

By following standardized protocols set forth by the OSI model, NOS software can communicate happily with the computers and peripherals attached to the network as well as with other networks.

Figure 12.16 compares the attributes of the major cable types. Most large networks have a mix of media. For example, coaxial cable may be appropriate for the portion of the network that traverses the factory floor where interference from magnetic fields is significant. However, unshielded twisted pair cable may work fine in the general office area. And wireless media may be required in conference rooms and other areas where employees are likely to connect their notebooks or where it is impractical or expensive to run cable.

Network Operating Systems

Merely connecting computers and peripherals with media does not create a client/server network. Special software known as a **network operating system (NOS)** needs to be installed on each client computer and server connected to the network to provide the services necessary for them to communicate. Many modern operating systems (such as Windows Vista and Mac OS X) include

FIGURE 12.16 Characteristics of Major Cable Types

Cable Characteristics	Twisted Pair (Cat 6)	Coaxial (ThinNet)	Coaxial (ThickNet)	Fiber Optic
Maximum run length	328 feet (100 m)	607 feet (185 m)	1,640 feet (500 m)	Up to 62 miles (100 km)
Bandwidth	1,000 Mbps	10 Mbps	10 Mbps	100 Mbps to 2 Gbps
Bend radius (flexibility)	No limit	360 degrees/foot	30 degrees/foot	30 degrees/foot
Cable cost	Extremely low	Low	Moderate	High
Installation cost	Extremely low	Low	Slightly higher than ThinNet	Most expensive because of installation training required
Susceptibility to interference	High	Low	Extremely low	None (not susceptible to EMI and RFI)

NOS client software as part of the basic installation. However, if your operating system does not include NOS client software, it must be installed on each client. The NOS provides a set of common rules (a protocol) that controls communication between devices on the network. The major NOSs on the market today include Windows Server 2008, UNIX, and Novell Open Enterprise Server.

Do peer-to-peer networks need special NOS software? The software that P2P networks require is built into the Windows and Macintosh operating systems. Therefore, there is no need to purchase specialized NOS software.

How does NOS software differ from operating system software? Operating system (OS) software is designed to facilitate communication between the software and hardware components of your computer. NOS software is specifically designed to provide server services, network communications, management of network peripherals, and storage. To provide network communications, the client computer must run a small part of the NOS in addition to the OS. Windows Vista is an OS and is installed on home computers. As noted above, because it also has some NOS functionality, client computers (in a client/server network) that have Windows Vista installed as the OS do not need an additional NOS. Windows Server 2008 is an NOS that is deployed on servers in a client/server network.

How does the NOS control network communications? Each NOS has its own proprietary communications language, file management structure, and device management structure. The NOS also sets and controls the protocols (rules) for all devices wishing to communicate on the network. Many different proprietary networking protocols exist, such as Novell Internetwork Packet Exchange (IPX), Microsoft NetBIOS Extended User Interface (NetBEUI), and the Apple File Protocol (AFP). These protocols were developed for a specific vendor's operating system. For example, IPX was developed for networks running the Novell NOS. Proprietary protocols such as these do not work with another vendor's NOS.

However, because the Internet uses an open protocol (called TCP/IP) for communications, many corporate networks use TCP/IP as their standard networking protocol regardless of the manufacturer of their NOS. All modern NOSs support TCP/IP. (We discuss TCP/IP in more detail in Chapter 13.)

Can a network use two different NOSs? Many large corporate networks use several different NOSs at the same time. This is because different NOSs provide different features, some of which are more useful in certain situations than others. For instance, although the employees of a corporation may be using a Microsoft Windows environment for their desktops and e-mail, the file servers and print servers may be running a Novell NOS.

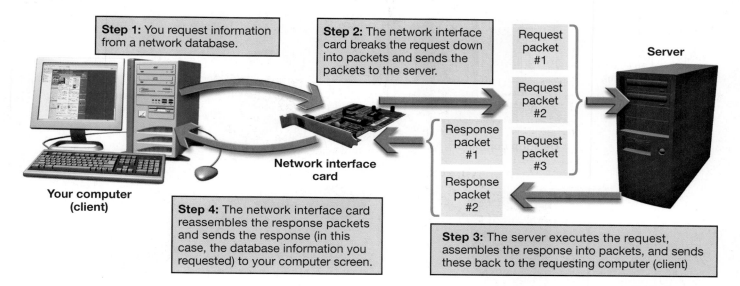

Step 1: You request information from a network database.

Step 2: The network interface card breaks the request down into packets and sends the packets to the server.

Request packet #1

Request packet #2

Request packet #3

Response packet #1

Response packet #2

Server

Your computer (client)

Network interface card

Step 4: The network interface card reassembles the response packets and sends the response (in this case, the database information you requested) to your computer screen.

Step 3: The server executes the request, assembles the response into packets, and sends these back to the requesting computer (client)

FIGURE 12.17

A NIC is responsible for breaking down data into packets and preparing the packets for transmission across the network. It also is responsible for receiving incoming data packets and reconstructing them.

Because NOSs use different internal software languages to communicate, they can't communicate directly with each other. However, if both NOSs are using the same protocol (such as TCP/IP), they can pass information between the networks and it can be interpreted by the other network.

Network Adapters

As we noted in Chapter 7, client computers and peripherals need an interface to connect with and communicate on the network. **Network adapters** are devices that perform specific tasks to enable computers to communicate on a network. Most network adapters are installed *inside* computers and peripherals as expansion cards. These adapters are referred to as network interface cards (NICs).

Although you could use network adapters that plug into universal serial bus (USB) ports on a client/server network, most network adapters are NICs. That's because external devices are more susceptible to damage.

What do network adapters do? Network adapters perform three critical functions:

1. **They generate high-powered signals to enable network transmissions.** Digital signals generated inside the computer are fairly low-powered and would not travel well on network media (cable or wireless technology) without network adapters. Network adapters convert the signals from inside the computer to higher-powered signals that have no trouble traversing the network media.

2. **They are responsible for breaking the data into packets and preparing them for transmission across the network.** They also are responsible for receiving incoming data packets and, in accordance with networking protocols (rules), reconstructing them, as shown in Figure 12.17.

3. **They act as gatekeepers for information flowing to and from the client computer.** Much like a security guard in a gated community, network adapters are responsible for permitting or denying access to the client computer (the community) and controlling the flow of data (visitors).

Are there different types of network adapters? Although there are different types of network adapters, almost without exception, Ethernet (either wired or wireless) is the standard communications protocol used on most current networks. Therefore, the adapter cards shipping with computers today are always Ethernet compliant. The majority of Ethernet adapters provide connection ports that accept RJ-45 (Ethernet) connector plugs for connection to twisted pair cable. However, adapters that provide other types of connectors for direct connections to other types of network media (such as fiber-optic cables) are available.

Do wireless networks require network adapters? Most corporate networks are not entirely wireless, but they do provide

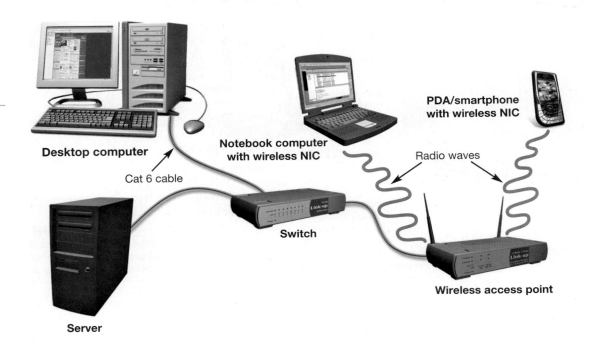

FIGURE 12.18

This small corporate network has an added wireless access point.

Desktop computer

Cat 6 cable

Notebook computer with wireless NIC

PDA/smartphone with wireless NIC

Radio waves

Switch

Wireless access point

Server

wireless connectivity to some computers and portable devices (such as smartphones). Computers that connect to the network using wireless access need special network adapter cards, called **wireless network interface cards (wireless NICs)**, installed in the system unit. Unlike wired NICs, wireless NICs don't connect to the network with cables. Instead, the network must be fitted with devices called **wireless access points (WAPs)** that give wireless devices a sending and receiving connection point to the network.

Figure 12.18 shows an example of a typical corporate network with a wireless access point. The access point is connected to the wired network through a conventional cable. As we discussed in Chapter 7, when a notebook (or other device with a wireless NIC) is powered on near a wireless access point, it establishes a connection with the access point using radio waves. Many devices can communicate with the network through a single wireless access point.

Do network adapters require software? Because the network adapter is responsible for communications between the client computer and the network, it needs to speak the same language as the network's special operating system software. Therefore, special communications software called a **device driver** is installed on all client computers in the client/server net-

work. Device drivers enable the network adapter to communicate with the server's operating system and with the operating system of the computer in which the adapter is installed.

What are my options if I'm not located in range of a wireless network? You can bring your own wireless network with you! Most cellular telephone companies, such as AT&T and Sprint, offer broadband PC cards for your notebook that will keep you connected (for a fee, of course). PC cards fit into expansion slots on your notebook and enable it to send and receive data using your cellular provider's wireless network. Broadband download speeds now can reach a respectable 1.4 Mbps, making this a truly viable option if you need to ensure you have connectivity wherever you go—or virtually everywhere. Check with the cellular provider to ensure they have coverage most places you will travel.

Network Navigation Devices

Earlier in this chapter, you learned that to flow through the network, data is broken into small segments called packets. Data packets are like postal letters. They don't get to their destinations without some help.

SOUND BYTE

What's My IP Address? (and Other Interesting Facts about Networks)

In this Sound Byte, you'll learn how to determine your IP address, which is commonly requested when setting up online gaming. You'll also explore several Web sites that can reveal interesting information about your connection to the Internet.

In this section, we explore the various conventions and devices that help speed data packets on their way through the network.

MAC ADDRESSES

How do data packets know where to go on the network? Each network adapter has a physical address similar to a serial number on an appliance. This is called a **media access control (MAC) address**, and it is made up of six two-position characters such as 01:40:87:44:79:A5. The first three numbers (in this case, 01:40:87) specify the manufacturer of the network adapter, whereas the second set of numbers (in this case, 44:79:A5) makes up a unique address. Because all MAC addresses must be unique, the IEEE runs a committee that is responsible for allocating blocks of numbers to network adapter manufacturers. MAC should not be confused with Apple computers of the same name.

Are MAC addresses the same as IP addresses? MAC addresses and Internet Protocol (IP) addresses are not the same thing. A MAC address is used for identification purposes *internally* on a network, which is similar to giving people different names to differentiate them. An IP address is the address *external* entities use to communicate with your network and is similar to your home street address. Think of it this way: The postal carrier delivers a package (data packet) to your dorm building based on its street address (IP address). The dorm's mail clerk delivers the package to your room because it has your name on it (MAC address) and not that of your neighbor. Both pieces of information are necessary to ensure that the package (or data) reaches its destination.

How does a data packet get a MAC address? Data packets are not necessarily sent alone. Sometimes groups of data packets are sent together in a group called a frame.

Frames are containers that can hold multiple data packets. This is similar to placing several letters going to the same postal address in a big envelope. When the data packets are being assembled into frames, the NOS software assigns the appropriate MAC address to the frame. The NOS keeps track of all devices and their addresses on the network. Much like a letter placed into the postal service, the frame is delivered to the MAC address that the NOS assigned to the frame.

What delivers the frames to the correct device on the network? In a small bus network, frames just bounce along the wire until the correct client computer notices the frame is addressed to it and pulls the signal off the wire. This is inefficient in a larger network. Therefore, many types of devices have been developed to deliver data to its destination efficiently. These devices are designed to amplify signals, route signals, and exchange data with other networks.

Are MAC addresses useful for anything besides identifying a particular network device? On networks with wireless capabilities, MAC addresses can be used to enhance network security. Most wireless routers and access points can be used to filter MAC addresses to eliminate ones from unauthorized devices. Because each MAC address is unique, you can input a list of authorized MAC addresses into the router. If someone who is using an unauthorized network adapter (i.e., one with an unauthorized MAC address) attempts to connect to the network, they will be unable to make a connection. Although impractical for a large organization with many employees being hired and leaving constantly, MAC address filtering is a useful security tool on home networks and small business networks.

REPEATERS AND HUBS

What types of devices amplify signals on a single network? Repeaters are relatively simple devices whose sole function is to amplify a signal and retransmit it. Repeaters are used to extend cable runs beyond the maximum run length (over which a signal would degrade and be unreadable). Repeaters do not transmit signals to specific devices; they just forward the signals along the media.

Which devices transmit signals to specific nodes on networks? As you learned in Chapter 7, **hubs** are devices that

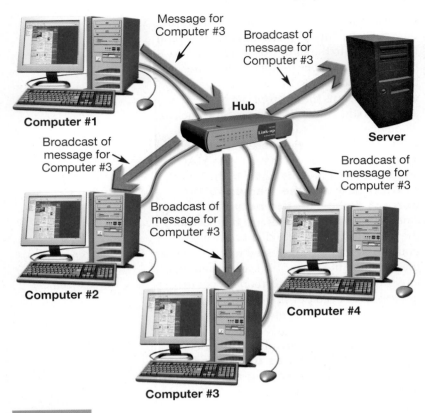

also transmit signals. In addition, they have multiple ports to which devices are connected. As shown in Figure 12.19, the hub receives the signal from a device, reconstructs it, and transmits it to all other ports on the hub.

SWITCHES AND BRIDGES

Which devices are used to route signals through a single network?
Switches and bridges are used to send data on a specific route through the network. A **switch** can be viewed as a "smart" hub. It makes decisions, based on the MAC address of the data, as to where the data is to be sent. Therefore, only the intended recipient of the data receives the signal as opposed to a hub, which sends out data to all devices connected to it. This improves network efficiency by helping ensure that devices receive data intended only for them.

Do I need a switch on my home network? Switches are technically unnecessary on small networks (such as home networks) because there is not a large amount of data traffic, making increasing efficiency unnecessary. However, as switches are so inexpensive today, most home networks have switches built into their routers. Figure 12.20 shows a switch being used to rebroadcast a message.

FIGURE 12.19

A hub broadcasts messages to all devices attached to it regardless of the intended recipient.

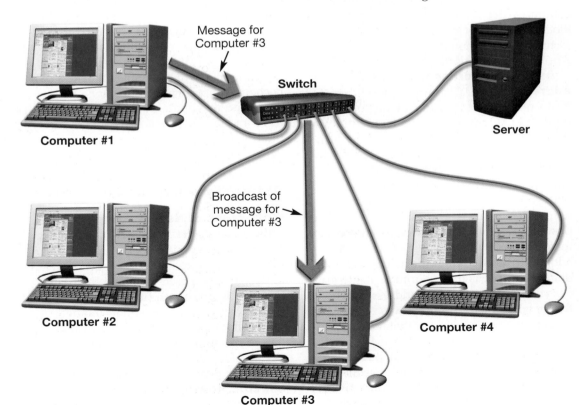

FIGURE 12.20

Like hubs, switches rebroadcast messages—but only to the device for which the message is addressed. Because the cost of switches has fallen significantly, you are most likely to encounter switches rather than hubs on networks today.

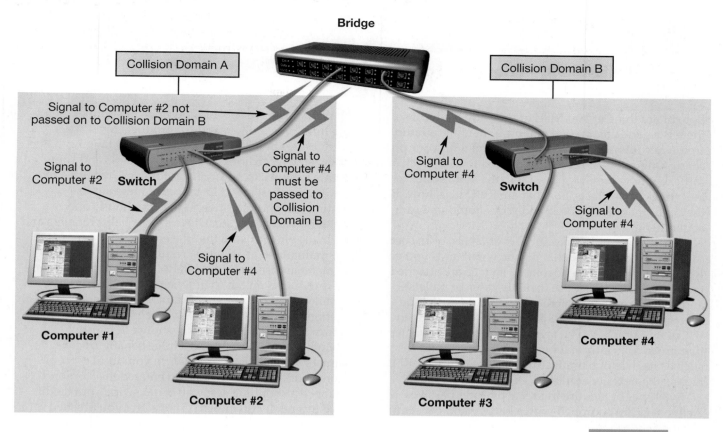

Bridge

Collision Domain A

Collision Domain B

Signal to Computer #2 not passed on to Collision Domain B

Signal to Computer #2

Switch

Signal to Computer #4 must be passed to Collision Domain B

Signal to Computer #4

Signal to Computer #4

Switch

Signal to Computer #4

Computer #1

Computer #2

Computer #3

Computer #4

FIGURE 12.21

Bridges are devices that are used to send data between different network collision domains. Here signals received by the bridge from collision domain A are forwarded only to collision domain B if the destination computer is located in that domain.

As a corporate network grows in size, performance can decline as many devices compete for transmission time on the network media. To solve this problem, a network can be broken into multiple segments known as collision domains. **Bridges** are devices that are used to send data between these different collision domains. A bridge sends data between collision domains depending on where the recipient device is located, as indicated in Figure 12.21. Most home networks contain only one segment and therefore do not require bridges.

ROUTERS

What device is designed to move data to another network? Whereas repeaters, hubs, switches, and bridges perform their functions within a single network, **routers** are designed to send information between two networks. To accomplish this, routers must look at higher-level network addresses (such as IP addresses), not MAC addresses. When the router notices data with an address that does not belong to a device on the network from which it originated, it sends the data

to another network to which it is attached (or out onto the Internet).

Network Security

A major advantage that client/server networks have over peer-to-peer networks is that they contain a higher level of security. With client/server networks, users can be required to use a user ID and a password to gain access to the network. Also, the security can be centrally administered by network administrators, freeing individual users of the responsibility of maintaining their own data security (as they must do on a peer-to-peer network).

In the next section, we explore the challenges network administrators face to keep a client/server network secure. We use a college network as our example, but note that the same principles apply to all client/server networks.

What sources of security threats do all network administrators need to watch for? Threats can be classified into three main groups as shown here:

• **Human errors and mistakes:** Everyone makes mistakes. For example, the clerk

Ethics: RFID—Friend or Foe?

Bought anything at Wal-Mart or Best Buy lately? If so, there is a good chance that you brought home a **radio frequency identification tag (RFID tag)** with your purchase. Originally, RFID tags were used to keep track of cattle, but now they've moved into the retail sector to keep track of products. So what are RFID tags, how did they end up in retail stores, and why should you care about them?

RFID tags can look like stickers or labels, or in some cases they look like the thin plastic wristbands you get when you check into a hospital. The tags are attached to batches of merchandise (usually cases or pallets), and all tags contain a microchip that holds a unique sequence of numbers used to identify the product to which it is attached. The tags also contain a tiny antenna that broadcasts information about the merchandise, such as its date of manufacture or price. Think of RFID tags as the next generation of UPC codes.

Two types of tags are in use: active and passive. Active tags are equipped with a battery and constantly transmit information. Passive tags don't have their own power source but instead get their energy from tag readers. Passive tags are more common because they are cheaper. Tag readers are devices that scan the information on the tags as the tags are passed by the reader. They do this through antennas that generate magnetic fields, which the passive tags sense. In response, the passive tags transmit their product code to the tag reader. The reader then sends the digital information to a computer system, most likely a database.

So how do RFID tags help retailers? Inventory for large retailers can be daunting to manage. Retailers such as Wal-Mart have tens of thousands of suppliers sending hundreds of thousands of products to its warehouses and stores. The use of RFID tagging allows the recording of inventory receipts and shipments to stores to be largely automated, resulting in fewer mistakes, fewer instances of merchandise getting lost and forgotten in the warehouse, and tighter control over stock levels. This helps retailers and their suppliers ensure that the correct inventory levels are maintained at all times, resulting in fewer shortages of merchandise and, ultimately, increased sales because the product is on the shelf when you go to buy it. Retailers also can use the product serial number information that can be embedded in tags to speed repair or return service. This process is shown in Figure 12.22.

Someday, RFID could be a huge benefit for consumers. Imagine if all products in your local grocery store had RFID tags. When you entered the store and grabbed a shopping cart, you could swipe your credit card in a reader on the cart. Then, after you finished shopping, you could walk out the door, at which time an RFID reader would take an inventory of the contents of your cart and charge your credit card for what you purchased. No more waiting in checkout lines! And the streamlining of payment could result in lower costs for consumers. After you got home, if your refrigerator was equipped with RFID equipment, it could scan your purchases and keep track of your groceries, including expiration dates. Your refrigerator might contact your PDA (via the Internet) and let you know that your milk was out of date so you could buy more on the way home. Now that's a smart fridge!

In this Active Helpdesk call, you'll play the role of a Helpdesk staffer, fielding calls about how network adapters enable computers to participate in a client/server network and what devices assist in moving data around a client/server network.

processing your tuition payment could accidentally delete your records. A member of the computer support staff could mistakenly install an old database on top of the current one. Even physical accidents fall into this category, such as losing control of a car and driving it through the wall of the main server room.

- **Malicious human activity:** Malicious actions can be perpetrated by current employees, former employees, or third parties. For example, a disgruntled employee could introduce a virus to the network. A hacker could break into the student database server to steal credit card records. A former employee who feels he or she was unjustly fired could deliberately destroy data.

- **Natural events and disasters:** Some events—such as broken water pipes or fire, or disasters such as hurricanes, floods, earthquakes, and other acts of nature—are beyond human control. All can lead to the inadvertent destruction of data.

Who does a college network need to be secure from? A college network, like any network, is vulnerable to unauthorized users and manipulation or misuse of the data contained on it. The person who sat next to you last semester in

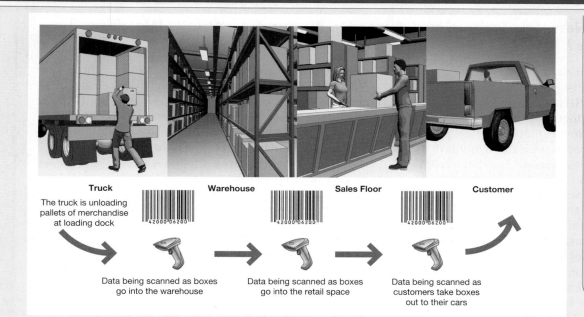

FIGURE 12.22

As merchandise equipped with RFID tags enters the warehouse, the tags are scanned, and the inventory database is updated. When merchandise is moved to the sales floor, scanning updates the inventory database again for the new stock location. One last scan occurs when customers purchase items which triggers the stock ordering system to place another order with a supplier if inventory is too low.

Truck
The truck is unloading pallets of merchandise at loading dock

Data being scanned as boxes go into the warehouse

Warehouse

Data being scanned as boxes go into the retail space

Sales Floor

Data being scanned as customers take boxes out to their cars

Customer

But convenience could come with a price. There is concern that people might gather information about consumers' buying habits without their knowledge, similar to the concerns people have about spyware on computers today, because the RFID tags would be operational outside of the retail store. For example, someone could sit in the parking lot with a tag reader and detect exactly what you purchased as you unknowingly pushed your shopping cart by the car. If this person were from a competing retailer, this competitive information could be especially valuable. Or this person could be from a government enforcement agency that was trying to determine whether underage consumers were purchasing alcoholic beverages. And depending on the range of the tags, some pundits have speculated that thieves could drive by houses and scan for desirable items to steal, such as large-screen TVs. However, this is unlikely with the state of the current RFID technology.

Many consumers resent any potential invasion of their privacy. Therefore, retailers will need to educate consumers about RFID tags and their benefits. Retailers also will need to ensure that consumers have the option to deactivate or remove tags to protect their privacy if so desired.

English class who failed may be interested in changing his grade to an A. Hackers may be interested in the financial and personal information (such as social security numbers and credit card numbers) stored in college financial office databases on the network. Thus, one of the network administrator's key functions is to keep network data secure.

AUTHENTICATION

How does a college ensure that only authorized users access its network? Authentication is the process whereby users prove they have authorization to use a computer network. The type of authentication most people are familiar with is providing a password. However, authentication can also be achieved through the use of biometric devices (discussed later in this chapter) and through **possessed objects**. A possessed object is any object that a user carries to identify himself and that grants him access to a computer system or computer facility. Examples include identification badges, magnetic key cards, and smart keys (similar to flash drives).

How do most colleges handle authentication on their networks? As mentioned earlier, to gain access to a typical college client/server network, you have to enter a user ID and a password. This is a

SOUND BYTE

A Day in the Life of a Network Technician

In this Sound Byte, you'll learn firsthand about the exciting, fast-paced job of a computer technician. Interviews with actual network technicians and tours of networking facilities will provide you with a deeper appreciation for the complexities of the job.

ETHICS IN IT

Ethics: Network Technicians' Access to Networks—Who Is Watching the Watchers?

According to **Salary.com**, the majority of employers report monitoring their employees in some fashion. The monitoring of phone calls, e-mail, and Web usage by employers is legal in almost all jurisdictions in the United States. Employers that suspect employees are "goofing off" can install spyware to monitor employee computer keystrokes and keep track of Web sites visited down to the individual computer level. Naturally, network administrators are often involved in employee monitoring. Consider the case of Vernon Blake, the network administrator at the Alabama Department of Transportation. His boss was constantly playing computer games at work. This was common knowledge, yet no action was taken. Vernon installed software on his boss's computer and captured screen images that verified the boss was playing solitaire about 70 percent of the time. When Blake reported the results to management, the boss was reprimanded and Blake was fired! The company cited Blake's lack of authority or permission to install the monitoring software.

In addition, businesses are constantly receiving from their customers sensitive information such as social security numbers, birth dates, and credit card numbers—all valuable information for identify thieves. The job of protecting this data ultimately falls on the network administrators who are in charge of network and data security. Another example involves the American Institute of Certified Public Accountants (AICPA), a professional organization of CPAs. The AICPA maintains membership lists that include names, addresses, birth dates, and social security numbers. The AICPA has clearly defined written policies that

forbid equipment containing member information (such as a hard drive on a computer) from being sent out to external vendors for repair. Yet, an IT staff member violated this policy and sent a hard drive containing membership information on 330,000 members to an external vendor. The hard drive was lost in transit when being returned to the AICPA. The AICPA quickly notified members of the security breach and offered them a free year of credit monitoring service to head off any problems—most likely at considerable expense to the AICPA. Although the AICPA has not indicated the disciplinary action taken against staff involved, it would seem likely that the penalties were severe.

So who is in charge of monitoring the network administrators so that they don't abuse their access to sensitive information or fail to exercise proper safeguards over sensitive data? Savvy companies put written policies in place for employees regarding computer usage. These policies need to include guidelines for network administrators who have higher levels of access than normal employees. Procedures for safeguarding data and guidelines for investigating employee misuse of computers must be clearly explained, and management needs to periodically review the activities of the network administrators to ensure compliance with polices. Although all employees need to follow approved company procedures regarding computer usage, it is especially important to ensure employees with high levels of access and high-level security responsibilities are adhering to company guidelines.

---

process known as authentication. By correctly inputting your ID and password, you prove to the network who you are and show that you have authorized access (because the ID was generated by the network administrator when you became a student).

Can hackers use my account to log on to the network? If a hacker knows your user ID and password, he or she can log on and impersonate you. Sometimes network user IDs are easy to figure out because they have a certain pattern (such as your last name and first initial of your first name). Because of this potential vulnerability, network administrators often configure accounts to disable themselves after several logon attempts with invalid passwords have

been tried. This prevents hackers from using **brute force attacks** to attempt to crack passwords. Brute force attacks are delivered by specialized hacking software that attempts to try many combinations of letters, numbers, words, or pieces of your user ID in an attempt to discover your password. If network accounts aren't set to disable themselves after a small number of incorrect passwords is tried, these attacks may eventually succeed.

ACCESS PRIVILEGES

How can I gain access to everything on the college network? The simple answer is, you can't! When your account was set up, certain access privileges were granted to indicate which systems you are allowed to use. For example, your access privileges probably include the ability to access the Internet. You also might have access privileges to view your transcript and grades online, depending on the sophistication of your college network. However, you definitely were not granted access to the grade reporting system, which would enable you to change your grades. Likewise, you do not have access to the financial systems; otherwise, you might be able to change your account, indicating that your bill was paid when it had not been.

How does restricting access privileges protect a network? Because network access accounts are centrally administered on the authentication server, it is easy for the network administrator to set up accounts for new students and grant them access only to the systems and software they need. The centralized nature of the creation of access accounts and the ability to restrict access to certain areas of the client/server network make it more secure than a peer-to-peer network. If you shouldn't go somewhere (such as into the files that record student grades), you can't get there on your school network!

PHYSICAL PROTECTION MEASURES

Are any physical measures taken to protect the network? Restricting physical access to servers and other sensitive equipment is critical to protecting the network. Where are the servers that power your college network? They are most likely behind locked doors to which only authorized personnel have access. Do you see any routers or hubs lying about in computer labs? Of course you don't. These devices are securely tucked away in ceilings, walls, or closets, safe from anyone who might tamper with them in an attempt to sabotage the network or breach its security.

As shown in Figure 12.23, access to sensitive areas must be controlled. Many different devices can be used to control access. **Access card readers** are relatively cheap devices that read information from a magnetic strip on the back of a credit card–like access card (such as your student ID card). The card reader, which can control the lock on a door, is programmed to admit only authorized personnel to the area. Card readers are easily

BITS AND BYTES

Connecting to Wireless Networks on the Road? Beware of "Evil Twins"!

When you are at the airport or Starbucks, you may need to connect to a wireless network and check your e-mail. So you switch on your notebook, and the wireless network adapter finds a network called "star bucks" or "airport wireless." You connect, enter your credit card information, and start merrily surfing away. Three days later your credit card company calls asking about the $4,800 big screen TV you just bought at Sam's Club and the $6,300 of power tools charged at Home Depot. You didn't make either of these purchases, but you probably fell prey to an "evil twin" wireless hotspot.

Hackers know the areas where people are likely to seek access to wireless networks. They will often set up their own wireless networks in these areas with sound-alike names to lure unsuspecting Web surfers and get them to enter credit card information to gain access. Other times these "evil twins" offer free Internet access and the hackers just monitor traffic looking for sensitive information they can use.

So how can you protect yourself? Check with authorized personnel at places where you will be connecting to hotspots to determine the names of the legitimate hotspots. And if you run across "free" access to a hotspot that isn't provided by a legitimate merchant, you are better off not connecting at all because you can't be sure your information won't be used against you.

programmed by adding authorized ID card numbers, social security numbers, and so on.

Biometric access devices are becoming more popular, although they are still cost prohibitive to many organizations, especially colleges. Biometric devices use some unique characteristic of human biology to identify authorized users. Some devices read fingerprints or palm prints when you place your hand on a scanning pad. Other devices shine a beam of laser light into your eye and read the unique patterns of your retina to identify you. Facial recognition systems store unique characteristics of an individual's face for later comparison and identification. All of these devices are preprogrammed when authorized individuals use them for the first time and then their fingerprints, face patterns, or retinal patterns are scanned and stored in a database.

Financial institutions and retail stores are considering using such devices to attempt to eliminate the growing fraud problem from theft and counterfeiting of credit and debit cards. If fingerprint authorization were required at Wal-Mart to make a purchase, a

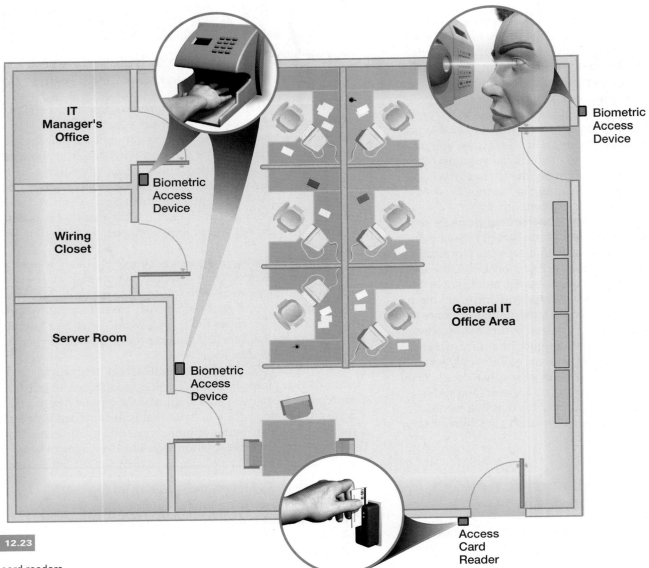

IT Manager's Office

Wiring Closet

Server Room

Biometric Access Device

Biometric Access Device

Biometric Access Device

General IT Office Area

Biometric Access Device

Access Card Reader

FIGURE 12.23

Access card readers can be used to limit access to semisensitive areas such as the IT office. Higher-security areas, such as the server room, may deserve the additional protection that biometric access devices offer.

thief who stole your wallet and attempted to use your credit card would be unsuccessful.

Biometric devices currently on the market, however, don't always function as intended. Facial recognition and retinal systems can sometimes be fooled using pictures or videos of an authorized user. Fingerprint readers have been fooled by researchers using fingers made out of Play-Doh, using the fingers of cadavers, or by having unauthorized persons breathing on the sensor, which makes the previous user's fingerprint visible (fingers leave an oily residue behind when they touch a surface). Research institutions, such as Clarkson University, are designing next-generation fingerprint readers that are much more difficult to fool. These will use specially designed algorithms that will detect moisture patterns on a person's fingers.

Another approach may involve readers that will detect an electrical current when a finger touches the reader, which is possible because the human body conducts electrical current. Future retinal readers will check to see whether the person blinks or if a person's eyes contract when a bright light is shone on them. Suffice it to say, these devices have a ways to go before they are foolproof.

FIREWALLS

Is the college Internet connection vulnerable to hackers? Just like a home network, when a college network is connected to the Internet, this creates an attractive nuisance. A college network will most likely have a high-bandwidth connection to the Internet that will attract hackers. A

Emerging Technologies: WiFi Phones Keep Doctors and Nurses Connected

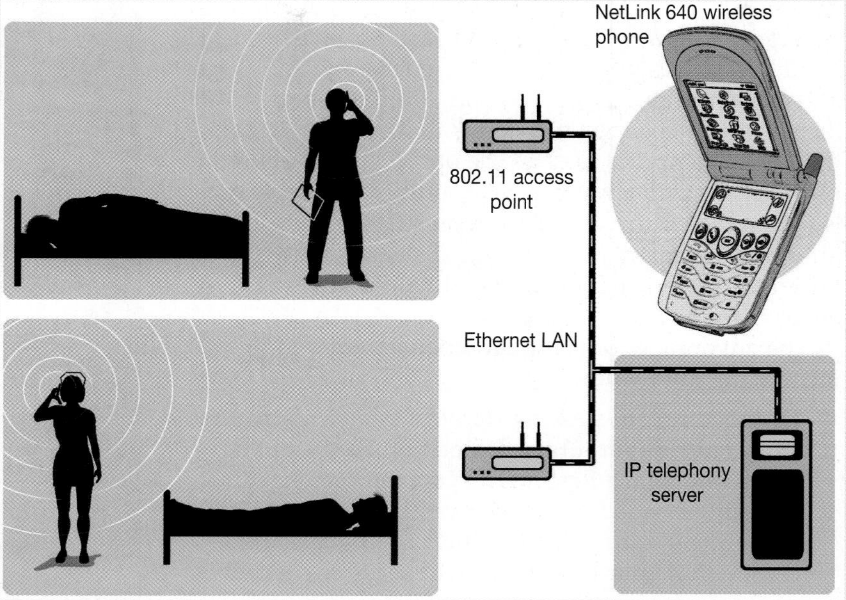

Have you ever noticed that you can't make cell phone calls when you're in a hospital? Cell phone signals can interfere with sensitive electronic equipment such as heart monitors and IV monitors, rendering them ineffective. Unfortunately, this means doctors and nurses can't communicate quickly with cell phones in the hospital either. However, using a WiFi network, they can.

A number of U.S. hospitals, such as Mission Community Hospital in Panorama City, California, are providing their nurses and doctors with SpectralLink's NetLink WiFi-enabled cell phones that enable communications over the hospital's wireless network (instead of by conventional cell phone signals). These phones cause no interference with medical equipment, and, unlike conventional cell phones, the phones offer a special feature that allows users to broadcast a message to multiple phones throughout the hospital. This is especially useful for emergency situations (such as a "code blue" cardiac arrest alert) when various personnel must be gathered quickly to deal with a crisis.

How does this all work? Unlike traditional cell phone calls that flow through a telephone company's switching or microwave system, WiFi-enabled cell phones route calls through the Internet either to landlines or out to other cell phones (see Figure 12.24), avoiding the interference associated with traditional cell phone calls. In addition, the NetLink system can be integrated with conventional phone systems.

Any business or college with a physical campus could potentially benefit from the connectivity achieved by such a network. And with concerns about responding to emergencies growing since 9/11, being able to

FIGURE 12.24

Keeping connected, especially in emergencies, is safe and easy when doctors and nurses can use special WiFi-enabled cell phones to communicate.

alert an entire organization at once by pushing a button and talking makes this type of network communications highly attractive. And especially with sensitive medical data, appropriate security measures need to be implemented on the wireless network. There is a need to prevent hackers from cruising around the hospital, connecting to wireless networks, and then scanning them for medical and billing information. And in addition to the expense of beefing up wireless security, this does require all participants in the network to have a WiFi-enabled phone. Time will tell whether more organizations decide that it is worth the cost of equipping key personnel (such as security guards) when the time comes to replace their existing phones.

---

welldefended college network, just like a home network, includes a firewall. Firewalls can be composed of software or hardware, and many sophisticated firewalls include both. Routers are often equipped to act as hardware firewalls.

Does the firewall on my college network work the same way as a personal firewall installed on a home network? Although the firewall at your

school may contain a few extra security options, making it even harder to breach than a personal firewall, the school's firewall works on the same basic principles as a home network. At a minimum, most firewalls work as packet screeners. **Packet screening** involves examining incoming data packets to ensure they originated from or are authorized by valid users on the internal network. The router is the device that performs

BITS AND BYTES

Enhanced Security—Carry an Operating System in Your Pocket

Surfing the Web or running applications (to generate documents) on public computers is somewhat risky. You can't be sure what security measures have been instituted on the public computer (such as antivirus and anti-spyware protection) and, therefore, you increase your chances of creating an infected file. Also, the public computer may not be optimally configured to protect your privacy. A practical solution available now is taking the Linux OS with you on a flash drive. The interfaces for many Linux builds such as Ubuntu (see Figure 12.25) look almost exactly like Windows and are easy to use.

The advantages of using Linux on a public computer include the following:

- **Reduced risk of picking up viruses and malware from public computers.** When you boot a public computer from a flash drive, you completely eliminate any interaction with the public computer's operating system. This significantly reduces the chance that your flash drive will become infected by any malware running on the public computer.
- **Attacks to Linux are far less likely.** Because Windows has a 91 percent market share, people who write malware tend to target Windows systems.
- **Enhanced privacy.** When you run off your own storage medium (flash drive), you avoid reading and writing to the hard disk of the public computer. Therefore, you don't leave traces of your activity behind.

An excellent resource is **www.pendrivelinux.com**, which has many different versions of Linux available

FIGURE 12.25

Ubuntu is a version of Linux that has a Windows-like interface and familiar browser tools like Firefox.

for download and includes step-by-step instructions on how to install them to your flash drive. If you are a Mac user, there is an option for you, too! gOS is a version of Linux that provides a close approximation of OS X so you can feel right at home.

---

the packet screening. Unauthorized or suspect packets are discarded by the firewall before reaching the network.

Packet screening also can be configured for outgoing data to ensure that requests for information to the Internet are from legitimate users. This helps detect Trojan horse programs that may have been installed by hackers. As you learned in Chapter 7, Trojan horses masquerade as harmless programs but have a more sinister purpose. They often try to disguise where they are sending data from by using bogus IP addresses on the packets the programs send instead of an authorized IP address belonging to the network.

If packet screening is working, packets going in and out of the network are checked to ensure they are either from or addressed

to a legitimate IP address on the network. If the addresses are not valid addresses for the network, the firewall discards them.

What other security measures does the firewall on a client/server network use? To increase security even further, most large networks add a **bastion host**—a heavily secured server located on a special perimeter network between the company's secure internal network and the firewall. A bastion host gets its name from the fortified towers (called bastions), located along the outer walls of medieval castles, which were specifically designed to defend the castles against attackers.

To external computers, the bastion host gives the appearance of being the internal network server. Hackers can waste a lot of

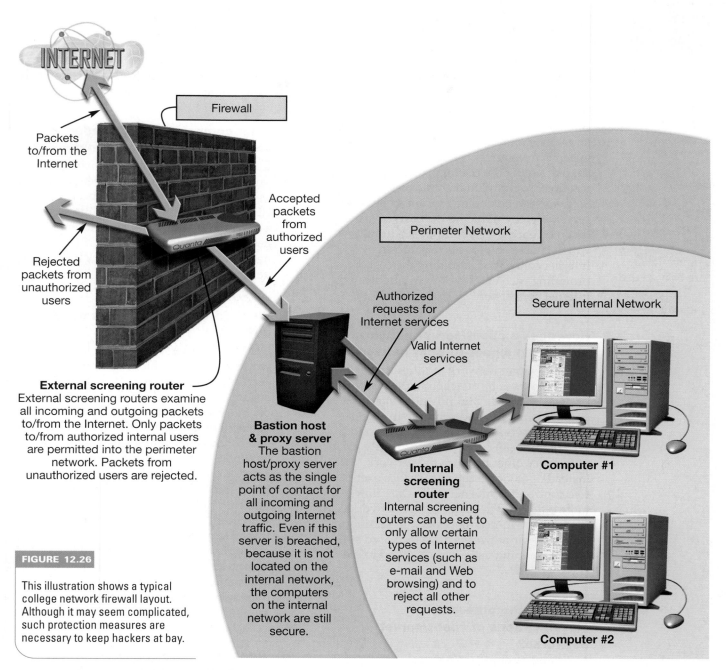

Firewall

Packets to/from the Internet

Rejected packets from unauthorized users

External screening router
External screening routers examine all incoming and outgoing packets to/from the Internet. Only packets to/from authorized internal users are permitted into the perimeter network. Packets from unauthorized users are rejected.

Accepted packets from authorized users

Perimeter Network

Authorized requests for Internet services

Valid Internet services

Secure Internal Network

Bastion host & proxy server
The bastion host/proxy server acts as the single point of contact for all incoming and outgoing Internet traffic. Even if this server is breached, because it is not located on the internal network, the computers on the internal network are still secure.

Internal screening router
Internal screening routers can be set to only allow certain types of Internet services (such as e-mail and Web browsing) and to reject all other requests.

Computer #1

Computer #2

FIGURE 12.26

This illustration shows a typical college network firewall layout. Although it may seem complicated, such protection measures are necessary to keep hackers at bay.

time and energy attacking the bastion host. However, even if a hacker breaches the bastion host server, the internal network is not vulnerable because the bastion host is not on the internal network. And during the time the hackers spend trying to penetrate the bastion host, network administrators can detect and thwart their attacks.

Bastion hosts are often configured as proxy servers. A **proxy server** acts as a go-between for computers on the internal network and the external network (the Internet). All requests from the internal network for Internet services are directed through the proxy server. Similarly, all

incoming requests from the Internet must pass through the proxy server. It is much easier for network administrators to maintain adequate security on one server than it is to ensure that security is maintained on hundreds or thousands of computers in a college network. Figure 12.26 shows a network secured by a firewall, a bastion host, and a screening router.

Now that you know a bit more about business network computing, you should be able to comfortably navigate the network at your college or your place of employment and understand why certain security measures have been taken to protect the network data.

Summary

1. What are the advantages of a business network?

A network enables employees to communicate with each other more easily even over large distances. Networks also enable expensive resources, such as printers, to be shared, saving the cost of providing these resources to individual employees. Software can be deployed from a network server, thereby reducing the costs of installation on each user's computer. And networks enable employees to share an Internet connection, avoiding the cost of providing each employee with a dedicated Internet connection.

2. How does a client/server network differ from a peer-to-peer network?

A client/server network requires that at least one server be attached to the network. The server coordinates functions such as data transmission and printing. In a peer-to-peer network, each node connected to the network can communicate directly with every other node on the network, instead of having a separate device exercise control over the network. Data flows more efficiently in client/server networks than in peer-to-peer networks. In addition, client/server networks have increased scalability, meaning users can be added to the network easily.

3. What are the different classifications of client/server networks?

Local area networks (LANs) are small groups of computers (as few as two) and peripherals linked together over a small geographic area. A group of computers on the floor of the office where you work is most likely a LAN. Wide area networks (WANs) comprise large numbers of users or of separate LANs that are miles apart and linked together. Corporations often use WANs to connect two or more branches (such as an office in California and one in Ohio). Sometimes government organizations or civic groups establish WANs to link users in a specific geographic area (such as within a city or county). These special WANs are known as metropolitan area networks (MANs).

4. What components are needed to construct a client/server network?

Client/server networks have many of the same components of peer-to-peer networks as well as some components specific to client/server networks, including servers, a network topology, transmission media, network operating system (NOS) software, network adapters, and network navigation devices.

5. What do the various types of servers do?

Dedicated servers are used on large networks to increase efficiency. Authentication servers control access to the network and ensure that only authorized users can log on. File servers provide storage and management of user files. Print servers manage and control all printing jobs initiated on a network. Application servers provide access to application software (such as Microsoft Office). Database servers store database files and provide access to users who need the information in the databases. E-mail servers control all incoming and outgoing e-mail traffic. Communications servers are used to control the flow of information from the internal network to outside networks (such as the Internet). Web servers are used to host a Web site.

6. What are the various network topologies (layouts), and why is network topology important in planning a network?

In a bus topology, all nodes are connected to a single linear cable. Ring topologies are comprised of nodes arranged roughly in a circle in which the data flows from node to node in a specific order. In a star topology, nodes are connected to a central communication device (a switch) and branch out like points of a star. A hybrid topology is a blending of two or more types of topologies in one network. Each topology has its own advantages and disadvantages.

Topology selection depends mainly on two factors: (1) the network budget and (2) the specific needs of network users (speed, fair allocation of resources, and so on).

7. What types of transmission media are used in client/server networks?

In addition to wireless media, three main cable types are used: twisted pair cable, coaxial cable, and fiber-optic cable. Twisted pair cable consists of four pairs of wires twisted around each other to reduce interference. Coaxial cable is the same type of cable used by your cable TV company to run a signal into your house. It provides better shielding from interference than twisted pair cable but is more expensive. Fiber-optic cable uses glass or plastic bundles of fiber to send signals using light waves. It provides the largest bandwidth but is expensive and difficult to install. Wireless media utilizes radio waves to send data between nodes on a network.

8. What software needs to be running on computers attached to a client/server network, and how does this software control network communications?

Network operating system (NOS) software needs to be installed on each computer and server connected to a client/server network to provide the services necessary for the devices to communicate. The NOS provides a set of common rules (called a *protocol*) that controls communication between devices on the network.

9. How do network adapters enable computers to participate in a client/server network?

Network adapters provide three critical functions: (1) They take low-power data signals generated by the computer and convert them into higher-powered signals that can traverse network media easily. (2) They break the data generated by the computer into packets and package them for transmission across the network media. (3) They act as gatekeepers to control the flow of data to and from the computer. Without a network adapter, a computer could not communicate on a network.

10. What devices assist in moving data around a client/server network?

Repeaters are used to amplify signals on a network ensuring that signals are received even at the end of a long cable run. Hubs receive and retransmit signals to all devices attached to them. Switches are "smart" hubs in that they can read the address of data packets and retransmit a signal to its destination instead of to every device connected to the switch. Routers are used to route data between two different networks such as between a corporate network and the Internet.

11. What measures are employed to keep large networks secure?

Access to most networks requires authentication procedures (such as entering a user ID and password) to ensure that only authorized users access the network. The system administrator defines access privileges for users so that they can access only specific files. Network equipment is physically secured behind locked doors, which are often protected by biometric access devices. Biometric devices, such as fingerprint and palm readers, use unique physical characteristics of individuals for identification purposes. Firewalls are also employed to keep hackers from attacking networks through Internet connections. Packet screeners review traffic going to and from the network to ascertain whether it was generated by a legitimate user.

Buzzwords

Word Bank

- application server
- bastion host
- bridges
- bus
- database server
- fiber-optic

- LAN
- network administrator
- packet screener
- packets
- repeaters
- routers

- scalable
- star
- switches
- twisted pair
- WAN
- wireless access points

Instructions: Fill in the blanks using the words from the Word Bank above.

As a(n) (1) _____, Susan's first task was to configure her company's new network. Because the company had branch offices in three different states, she knew it would be necessary to configure the network as a(n) (2) _____. However, to handle all of the wireless devices the sales representatives carried, (3) _____ would need to be installed throughout the building. Software would need to be shared among 50 employees, so a robust (4) _____ would be a necessity. And because the company was experiencing rapid growth, the network would have to be highly (5) _____, which would require the selection of a(n) (6) _____ topology as opposed to a(n) (7) _____ topology, which would only work for a small network.

Powerful electrical fields on the factory floor would mean that using (8) _____ cabling would be an absolutely necessity in the manufacturing plant, whereas (9) _____ cabling would be sufficient for the office areas. Because the company had experienced hacking on its old network, Susan insisted that a(n) (10) _____ be installed to further bolster the network defenses by filtering unauthorized transmissions of data. Combined with a(n) (11) _____ installed as part of the perimeter network, she felt they would be adequately protected from wily hackers.

(12) _____ would be necessary to shift data (13) _____ between collision domains on the network. For the farthest reaches of the building, (14) _____ would need to be installed to amplify the network data signals. If a star topology was to be used, several (15) _____ would need to be deployed to handle all 50 network users.

Becoming Computer Literate

Chemco Brothers, Inc., a manufacturer of specialty chemicals, has decided that to increase the accuracy of its production records, the network used for management and clerical workers should extend onto the manufacturing floor. Although most employees do not travel more than a few feet from their main work areas during their shift, the three supervisors roam the entire plant and need access to computers wherever they go.

Instructions: Draft a memo (with supporting diagrams, if necessary) that details how to deploy 15 computers (12 for workers, 3 for supervisors) in the factory areas. Justify the network topology you select, explain your choice of transmission media, and indicate the device(s) needed to connect the computers to the existing network.

Instructions: Answer the multiple-choice and true–false questions below for more practice with key terms and concepts from this chapter.

MULTIPLE CHOICE

1. Which of the following is an advantage of installing a network in a business?
   a. Decreased productivity
   b. Decreased network security protection
   c. Sharing of peripherals
   d. Increased cost to buy peripherals

2. Why are client/server networks often installed in businesses instead of peer-to-peer networks?
   a. Security is stronger on client/server networks.
   b. They eliminate the need for dedicated servers.
   c. They are less scalable than peer-to-peer networks.
   d. Less cabling is needed on client/server networks.

3. When the networks on two campuses of a college are connected to form one large network, this network would be classified as a
   a. WAN.   b. MAN.
   c. PAN.   d. LAN.

4. Which of the following is NOT necessary in every client/server network?
   a. Network operating software
   b. Network adapters
   c. Transmission media
   d. E-mail server

5. To ensure only authorized users can access a network, a corporate network would include which server?
   a. Database
   b. Authentication
   c. Communications
   d. Application

6. Which type of network topology is most scalable?
   a. Star   b. Ethernet
   c. Token-ring d. Bus

7. Fiber-optic cable most likely would be used in a corporate network when
   a. cost is more important than speed.
   b. electrical or magnetic interference is not present.
   c. especially short cable runs are required.
   d. speed is more important than cost.

8. NOS software is
   a. not absolutely essential for running a client/server network.
   b. needed only on the servers in a client/server network.
   c. needed on all computers in a client/server network.
   d. needed only when configuring a network in a bus topology.

9. Network adapters are NOT
   a. necessary to connect computers to all types of networks.
   b. needed for connecting computers wirelessly to networks.
   c. used only in client/server networks.
   d. necessary in networks using the star topology.

10. Providing adequate security on a corporate network involves all of these issues except
    a. limiting network access by requiring passwords.
    b. authentication.
    c. proprietary software lockout.
    d. restricting access to servers.

TRUE–FALSE

_____ 1. Hubs are used to route data between two or more network collision domains.

_____ 2. Two different types of network operating software can be deployed on the same network.

_____ 3. Fiber-optic cable is less susceptible to interference than twisted pair cable.

_____ 4. Client/server networks are harder to administer than peer-to-peer networks.

_____ 5. A communications server is used to host Web sites on a client/server network.

Making the Transition to... Next Semester

1. Internet Usage Policy

Schools face many potential liability issues when they connect students to the Internet. Your school most likely has a written policy (perhaps posted on the school's Web site) on appropriate usage of the network and the Internet by students. Other issues that network usage policies typically address include guidelines on student file storage, antivirus protection, and backups. Obtain a copy of your school's policy (or speak with the appropriate IT personnel) and answer the following questions:

a. What types of sites are students not permitted to access?

b. Are restrictions in effect for using peer-to-peer file-sharing sites? What are those restrictions?

c. How much storage space is provided for student files (if any)?

d. How often are student files backed up (if ever)? Are these incremental backups (only new files or files that have changed are backed up) or full backups (all files are backed up)?

e. Are files deleted after each semester?

f. Are students prohibited from commenting about the school and professors on blogs, wikis, or other Web sites? If so, how do you feel about that?

2. Wireless Connections at School

Wireless networks are growing in popularity as more and more students are bringing notebooks and other portable devices onto campus. Investigate the following:

a. Does your school offer wireless connectivity to students? If so, what areas of the campus are currently covered by wireless access?

b. What technologies are being deployed for connectivity (802.11b, 802.11g, or 802.11n)? If 802.11b/g is currently deployed, is there a plan to upgrade to a faster standard in the future?

c. Is access to the wireless network restricted (i.e., is authentication required to log on)? If not, is this under consideration to prevent poaching of bandwidth by neighbors and unauthorized visitors?

3. Internet Security Measures at School

Visit your IT services department and investigate the current security measures in place for the following:

a. **Firewall protection of the Internet connection.** What hardware and software are installed? Have there been any recent hacking attempts? If so, were they successful?

b. **Antivirus protection.** Is antivirus software installed on all computers deployed on campus? If so, what package is being used, and how often is it updated? What measures (if any) are in place to prevent users who bring their own computers onto campus (such as notebooks connected wirelessly) and connect to the network from infecting the network with a virus? Are products (other than antivirus software) installed to detect and prevent the installation of other malware products such as adware and spyware?

Making the Transition to... the Workplace

1. Security Issues at Work

You have been interning in the IT department of an insurance company, and you have applied for a full-time job at the company. One morning, you come to work and are told to clean out your desk and that your internship is ended effective immediately and that you will not be considered for a full-time position. Your boss explains that the human resources director was checking your references when she located your profile on **Facebook.com**. She noted that you had made derogatory comments about certain company personnel and that you described your current work assignments as boring. Although this is not covered by the computer usage policy at your workplace, company management feels you are disgruntled.

a. Using the Internet, research employment laws in your state. Can you be fired for what you wrote on your Facebook page? Do you have any legal recourse against the company?

b. Would the company be more justified in firing you if you had been warned (in the company's computer usage policy) that the types of activities for which you were fired were not permitted? Would the company be in a better legal position had it included these infractions in its written policies?

2. Client/Server Networks

The owner of the company for which you work announces that the company will be hiring another 25 workers over the next six months. Currently, your peer-to-peer network is adequately handling the needs of the 10 employees who now work at the company. However, you know that adding 25 more employees to the network would overload it.

a. Write a memo explaining why a switch to a client/server network would be appropriate. Be sure to explain which topology you think would be best to install.

b. In the memo, estimate the costs of constructing a 35-person client/server network, including the costs of one server, cabling, workstations for the 25 new employees, and switches. Use resources such as **www.dell.com** and **www.compaq.com** for designing and pricing network components.

3. Antivirus Solutions at Work

Recently, the company you work for had its network brought to a halt by an employee who inadvertently infected the server after opening an e-mail attachment containing a worm. Your boss has charged you with the task of locating a cost-effective antivirus solution to protect the corporate network. Complete the following tasks:

a. Compare the costs of installing antivirus products from the two industry leaders, McAfee (**www.mcafee.com**) and Norton (**www.symantec.com**), on each of the 20 computers and the one server in your corporate network.

b. Would your company consider using a free antivirus program such as avast! or AVG? What are the risks associated with relying on a free product?

c. Write a draft memo to employees explaining the types of e-mail messages and attachments they should avoid opening and passing on to others. Make sure to include warnings about phishing, attachments containing viruses, and hoaxes.

Critical Thinking Questions

Instructions: Albert Einstein used *Gedanken experiments*, or critical thinking questions, to develop his theory of relativity. Some ideas are best understood by experimenting with them in our own minds. The following critical thinking questions are designed to demand your full attention but require only a comfortable chair—no technology.

1. Internet Risks at School

Internet access is deemed essential to enable students to research projects and papers adequately. But granting that access potentially invites people to engage in dangerous or unacceptable behaviors.

a. Do you think your school should restrict access to certain Internet sites (such as peer-to-peer file-sharing services) to prevent students from violating laws by illegally sharing copyrighted material?

b. Plagiarism is thought to be spreading because of the easy exchange of information on the Internet. What should the penalty be for a student who plagiarizes material from a Web site and why? Should a student who plagiarizes have his or her Internet access privileges revoked? Why or why not?

c. Should schools prohibit students from writing negative comments about faculty and administrators on their blogs and Facebook pages? Why or why not?

2. Ethical Hackers?

Some hackers argue that hacking should not be a crime because they are performing a service to the companies that they are hacking by pointing out weaknesses in network security.

a. Should hackers be punished for gaining unapproved access to computer systems?

b. Are there any instances in which hacking is a "necessary evil" and the law enforcement officials should just look the other way?

c. Is it unethical for software companies not to share with users known security risks in their software?

3. Acceptable Use Internet Policies

Many companies are drafting acceptable use policies for computers and Internet access to inform employees of the approved uses for corporate computing assets. Consider these areas of a potential company policy:

a. Should employees be allowed to use their computers and Internet access for personal use (such as checking noncompany e-mail, shopping online, or playing games)? If so, how much time per day is reasonable for employees to spend on personal tasks? Should employees be permitted to use their computers for personal tasks only during personal time (such as breaks and lunch hours)?

b. Should employee computer and Internet usage be monitored to ensure compliance with the personal use policies? Should employers inform employees that they are being monitored? What should the penalties be for violating these policies? Should your productivity (and pay raises) be determined based on what activities you perform during the day as monitored by the company (via computers, cameras, tracking devices, etc.)?

c. Many corporations block access to Internet Web sites that would enable employees to participate in potentially illegal activities (such as downloading music, gambling, or viewing pornography). Should corporations have the right to block users from Web sites when they are at work? Why or why not?

4. Network Layout Designs

Assume you are designing the network layout for a local coffee shop. In which areas of the store would you provide wireless network access? Would you charge customers for access or provide it free of charge? Should customers and employees access the same network, or should a separate one be established for business activities? Would you provide all employees with Internet access? If not, whom would you exclude?

Problem:

As wireless devices become more prevalent, increased demands for wireless access will be placed on networks. Although many schools already deploy adequate wireless access, there is room for improvement of coverage in numerous areas.

Task:

The network manager at your school has requested that you assist in developing a plan for deploying or expanding wireless coverage for the campus. Your group has been selected to assist with the research. Before presenting your findings to the network manager, your group needs to fine-tune its recommendations.

Process:

Divide the class into small teams.

1. Explore the areas of your campus where students congregate to socialize or engage in research. Determine if these areas are covered by wireless Internet access and the speed (802.11b/g/n) at which connections are offered (this may require interviewing your school's network manager or just testing for connectivity with a notebook). For areas of the school that are covered by wireless technology (such as the library), test the signal strength of the connection by attempting to connect to the Internet in various locations.

2. Present your findings to your class. Lead a discussion with the other students and solicit feedback as to their experiences with wireless connectivity on the campus. In which other areas of the campus do you feel wireless technology should be deployed?

3. Prepare a report for the network manager that includes your suggestions for improvements and upgrades to the wireless network on your campus. If possible, address options for wireless connectivity when students are off campus for field trips, seminars, and so on.

Conclusion:

Being tied down to a wired computer terminal just doesn't cut it in the 21st century. Although wireless technology can be difficult and expensive to deploy in some instances (such as in old campus buildings), today's students will continue to demand the portable connections that they need to function effectively. Someday we'll probably wonder why we even bothered with wired connections at all!

Multimedia

In addition to the review materials presented here, you'll find additional materials featured with the book's multimedia, including the *Technology in Action* Student Resource CD and the Companion Website (**www.prenhall.com/techinaction**), which will help reinforce your understanding of the chapter content. These materials include the following:

ACTIVE HELPDESK

In Active Helpdesk calls, you'll assume the role of helpdesk operator taking calls about the concepts you've learned in this chapter. You'll apply what you've learned and receive feedback from a supervisor to review and reinforce those concepts. The Active Helpdesk calls for this chapter are listed below and can be found on your Student Resource CD:

- Using Servers
- Selecting a Network Topology and Cable
- Selecting Network Navigation Devices

SOUND BYTES

Sound Bytes are dynamic multimedia tutorials that help demystify even the most complex topics. You'll view video clips and animations that illustrate computer concepts, and then apply what you've learned by reviewing with the Sound Byte Labs, which include quizzes and activities specifically tailored to each Sound Byte. The Sound Bytes for this chapter are listed here and can be found on your Student Resource CD:

- Network Topology and Navigation Devices
- What's My IP Address? (and Other Interesting Facts about Networks)
- A Day in the Life of a Network Technician

COMPANION WEBSITE

The *Technology in Action* Companion Website includes a variety of additional materials to help you review and learn more about the topics in this chapter. The resources available at **www.prenhall.com/techinaction** include:

- **Online Study Guide.** Each chapter features an online true–false and multiple-choice quiz. You can take these quizzes, automatically check the results, and e-mail the results to your instructor.
- **Web Research Projects.** Each chapter features a number of Web research projects that ask you to search the Web for information on computer-related careers, milestones in computer history, important people and companies, emerging technologies, and the applications and implications of different technologies.

Behind the Scenes:

The Internet: How It Works

Objectives

After reading this chapter, you should be able to answer the following questions:

1. Who owns, manages, and pays for the Internet? **(p. 624)**
2. How do the Internet's networking components interact? **(pp. 624–627)**
3. What data transmissions and protocols does the Internet use? **(pp. 627–630)**
4. Why are IP addresses and domain names important for Internet communications? **(pp. 630–635)**
5. What are FTP and Telnet, and how do I use them? **(p. 635)**
6. What are HTML/XHTML and XML used for? **(pp. 636–641)**
7. How do e-mail, instant messaging, and Voice over Internet Protocol work, and how is information using these technologies kept secure? **(pp. 641–649)**

ACTIVE HELPDESK

- Understanding IP Addresses, Domain Names, and Protocols **(p. 634)**
- Keeping E-Mail Secure **(p. 645)**

Sheryl has decided not to pursue a career in IT. Although she found the information she learned in her Introduction to Computers course fascinating, she did not want to pursue additional coursework in such classes as Web development and networking. She would leave those jobs to other people.

Regardless, in her new position in marketing management, Sheryl realizes she will be continually interacting with IT employees, and she is thankful she has some understanding about the topic. The other day, for example, Sheryl and her boss were talking with the IT manager about a newly proposed sales system. Unfortunately, the IT manager explained to them that the proposed system wouldn't be feasible because the router could not handle the expected volume of outgoing requests. Sheryl was glad she had some understanding and was familiar with what a router is and what it does. That understanding put her at a greater advantage because it was clear her boss wasn't following what the IT manager was saying. Because Sheryl did, she was able to ask pertinent questions and later revise the proposal to satisfy her requirements and still work within the restrictions of the IT department.

Sheryl was also able to help the IT department explain some basic information about Web page design to the other business managers as the company began to redesign its Web site. She was glad she could discuss the various ways to make their Web site more interactive by using the more robust markup languages HTML/XHTML, CGI scripts, and applets. Moreover, she was able to conclusively explain why the company needed to add a virtual private network so that the employees could exchange company information among themselves in a secure and private manner.

At this point, you know what the Internet is, and you've certainly used some of its features such as the Web and e-mail. So why do you need to know how the Internet works? Most people can drive a car without knowing how an internal combustion engine is designed and built. However, a more thorough understanding of auto mechanics is useful when you're making decisions about buying a car or when you need to fix it when it breaks down. Similarly, understanding the mechanics behind the Internet can assist you in whatever job you hold, as it did for Sheryl.

This chapter builds on what you learned in Chapter 3 and takes you behind the scenes of the Internet. We look at who manages the Internet and discuss in detail how the Internet works and the various standards it follows. Along the way, we go behind the scenes of some Internet communication features such as e-mail, instant messaging services, and Voice over Internet Protocol. We also discuss just how safe these features are and what you can do to make your communications even more secure. Finally, we'll look at how the Internet will be changing in the future so that you'll be poised to take advantage of new technologies as they emerge.

SOUND BYTES

• Creating Web Pages with HTML **(p. 637)**

The Management of the Internet

To keep the Internet functioning at peak efficiency, it must be governed and regulated. However, there is no one single entity that is in charge of the Internet. In addition, new uses are created every day by a variety of individuals and companies.

Who owns the Internet? Even though the U.S. government funded the development of the technologies that spawned the Internet, no one really owns it. The particular local networks that constitute the Internet are all owned by different individuals, universities, government agencies, and private companies. Government entities such as the National Science Foundation (NSF) and the National Aeronautics and Space Administration (NASA), as well as many large, privately held companies, own pieces of the communications infrastructure (the high-speed data lines that transport data between networks) that makes the Internet work.

Does anyone manage the Internet? Because all of the individual networks that participate in the Internet are owned by several different entities, the Internet would cease to function without some sort of organization. Therefore, several nonprofit organizations and user groups, each with a specialized purpose, are responsible for its management. Figure 13.1 shows the major organizations that play a role in the governance and development of the Internet.

Many of the functions handled by these nonprofit groups were previously handled by U.S. government contractors because the Internet developed out of a U.S. government military project. However, because the Internet now serves the global community, not just the United States, assigning responsibilities to organizations with global memberships is helping to speed along the Internet's internationalization. Through close collaboration of the organizations listed in Figure 13.1 (and a few others), the Internet's vast collection of users and networks is managed.

Who pays for the Internet? You do! The U.S. government pays for a large portion of the Internet infrastructure, as well as funds research and development for new technologies. The primary source of these funds is your tax dollars. Originally, U.S. taxpayers footed the entire bill for the Internet, but as the Internet grew and organizations were formed to manage it, businesses, universities, and other countries began paying for Internet infrastructure and development.

FIGURE 13.1 Major Organizations That Play a Role in Internet Governance and Development

Organization's Name	Organization's Purpose	Web Address
Internet Society (ISOC)	Professional membership society comprising more than 100 organizations and more than 20,000 individual members in more than 180 countries. Provides leadership for the orderly growth and development of the Internet.	**www.isoc.org**
Internet Engineering Task Force (IETF)	A subgroup of ISOC made up of individuals and organizations that research new technologies for the Internet to improve capabilities or to keep the infrastructure functioning smoothly.	**www.ietf.org**
Internet Architecture Board (IAB)	Technical advisory group to the ISOC and a committee of the IETF. Provides direction for the maintenance and development of the protocols that are used on the Internet.	**www.iab.org**
Internet Corporation for Assigned Names and Numbers (ICANN)	Organization responsible for management of the Internet's domain name system (DNS) and the allocation of IP addresses.	**www.icann.org**
World Wide Web Consortium (W3C)	Consortium whose more than 400 member organizations set standards and develop protocols for the Web.	**www.w3.org**

Internet Networking

The Internet's response to our requests for information seems almost magical at times. By simply entering a URL in your browser or going to Yahoo! or Google and entering a search topic, you can summon up information that is stored on servers anywhere around the world. But there is no magic involved, just a series of communication transactions that enable the Internet to function as a global network. In this section, we explore the various networks that make up the Internet and how to connect to them, and we examine the workings of Internet data communications.

CONNECTING TO THE INTERNET

How are computers connected to the Internet? As a network of networks, the Internet is similar to the highway system in the United States. The highway system consists of interstate highways, which are the fastest and largest roadways—such as I-95, which runs up and down the East Coast; I-80, which runs from the Northeast to the West Coast; and I-5, which runs north and south along the West Coast. Regional highways connect to the Interstate highways, and local roads connect to the regional highways. As shown in Figure 13.2, the main paths of the Internet along which data travels the fastest, analogous to the Interstate highways, are known collectively as the **Internet backbone**. The backbone is a collection of large national and international networks, which are usually owned by commercial, educational, or government (such as NASA) organizations. These backbone providers are required to be connected with other backbone providers and have the fastest high-speed connections. Among the large companies that provide backbone connectivity are UUnet (a division of Verizon), AT&T, Sprint Nextel, and Qwest.

How do the ISPs that form the Internet backbone communicate? Backbone ISPs initially connected with T lines. **T lines** carried digital data over twisted pair wires. T-1 lines were the first to be used and transmitted data at a throughput rate of 1.544 Mbps. T-3 lines were later developed to transmit data at 45 Mbps. Today, backbones are typically high-speed fiber-optic lines, designated as **OC (optical carrier) lines**. OC lines come in a variety of speeds, as shown in Figure 13.3. Although most large ISPs connect to the Internet with

FIGURE 13.2

When you connect to the Internet in your home or at work or school, you most likely are connecting through intermediate or local Internet service providers. Just as there are regional and local highways connecting to the interstate highways, there are local and regional Internet service providers that connect to the backbone.

OC-192 lines, AT&T has begun to use OC-768 connections in its Internet backbone network.

The bandwidth of the connections between ISPs and end users depends on the amount of data traffic required. Whereas your home might connect with DSL, cable, or even fiber-optic lines, the volume of Internet traffic at your college probably requires that it use at least T-3 lines or even an OC line to move data to the school's ISP. Large companies usually need high-throughput OC lines running to their ISPs.

How are the ISPs connected to each other? The points of connection between ISPs were once known as *network access points (NAPs)*. Network access points were designed to move large amounts of data quickly between networks and bridged the Internet's beginnings as a government-funded academic experiment to the modern Internet of many commercial companies working together to form the Internet that we all know and use today. Now, private sector companies make up the Internet system and exchange data via **Internet exchange points (IXPs)**. A typical IXP is made up of one or more network switches to which ISPs connect. As you'll recall from Chapter 12, **switches** are devices that send data on a specific route through the network. By interconnecting directly to each other through IXPs, networks can reduce their costs and improve the speed and efficiency with which data is exchanged.

How do individuals connect to an ISP? Whether they dial up through a conventional modem or connect through high-speed access (such as cable or DSL), individual Internet users enter an ISP through a **point of presence (POP)**, which is a bank of modems (shown in Figure 13.4) through which many users can connect to an ISP simultaneously. ISPs maintain multiple POPs throughout the geographic area they serve.

THE NETWORK MODEL OF THE INTERNET

What type of network model does the Internet use? The majority of Internet communications follows the **client/server model** of network communications, which we defined in earlier chapters as client computers requesting services and servers providing those services to the clients. In the case of the Internet, the clients are devices such as computers, cell phones, and PDAs using browsers (or other interfaces) that request services (Web pages and so on). Various types of servers are

FIGURE 13.3 Speed and Configuration of OC Lines	
OC-1	51.85 Mbps
OC-3	155.52 Mbps
OC-12	622.08 Mbps
OC-24	1.244 Gbps
OC-48	2.488 Gbps
OC-96	4.976 Gbps
OC-192	9.953 Gbps
OC-768	39.813 Gbps

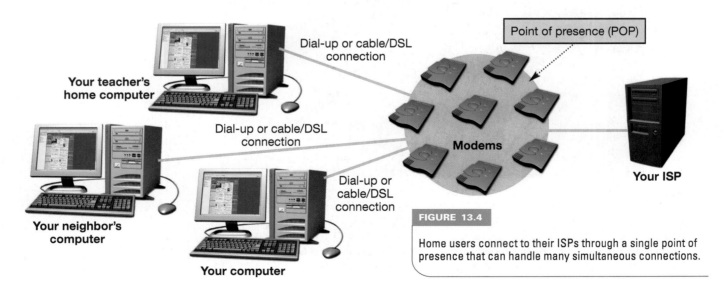

FIGURE 13.4

Home users connect to their ISPs through a single point of presence that can handle many simultaneous connections.

STEP 1: Your computer, acting as a client, runs the BitTorrent software (which you downloaded from BitTorrent's Web site). Using this software, you request access to a particular music file. Your computer transmits this request to BitTorrent's server.

STEP 2: The BitTorrent server makes your computer aware of other users (Users A and B) running BitTorrent software.

BitTorrent server

Your computer

STEP 3: Your computer determines that User A has the music file you wish to access. Acting as a client, your computer requests the file from User A.

STEP 4: User A's computer, acting as a server, sends the requested file to your computer.

User A

STEP 5: User B's computer (having been alerted to your presence by the BitTorrent server) determines you have a file it wants. Acting as a client, it requests the file from your computer.

STEP 6: Your computer receives the request from User B. It then switches roles from client to server and serves the requested file up to User B.

User B

FIGURE 13.5

File Sharing Services in Action

deployed (installed) on the networks that make up the Internet from which clients can request services:

- **Web servers:** Computers that run specialized operating systems that enable them to host (provide Web space for) Web pages (and other information) and provide requested Web pages to clients.

- **Commerce servers:** Computers that host software that enables users to purchase goods and services over the Web. These servers generally use special security protocols to protect sensitive information (such as credit card numbers) from being intercepted.

- **File servers:** Computers that are deployed to provide remote storage space or to act as a storehouse for files that users can download. For example, Yahoo! provides its users with a file storage option called Yahoo! Briefcase. Storing files in your personal "briefcase" (file folder) enables you to access these files from anywhere you can access the Web with a browser. When you use the Yahoo! Briefcase, you're storing files remotely on a file server. Google, Snapfish, and Delicious also offer online storage services for productivity documents, pictures, and Web pages, respectively.

Do all Internet connections take place in a client/server mode? Certain services on the Internet operate in a peer-to-peer mode, as depicted in Figure 13.5. For example, BitTorrent (**www.bittorrent.com**) is a popular file-sharing service through which Internet users can exchange files. BitTorrent and other file-sharing services require the user's computer to act as both a client and a server. When requesting files from another user, the computer behaves like a client. It switches to server mode when it provides a file stored on its hard drive to another computer.

Data Transmission and Protocols

Just like any other network, the Internet follows standard protocols to send information between computers. A **computer protocol** is a set of rules for exchanging electronic information. If the Internet is the information superhighway, then protocols are the rules of the road.

Why were Internet protocols developed? To accomplish the early goals of the Internet, protocols needed to be written and agreed upon by users. The protocols had to be **open systems**, meaning their designs would be made public for access by any interested party. This was in direct opposition to the **proprietary systems**, or private systems, that were the norm at the time.

As we mentioned in earlier chapters, when common communication protocols (rules) are followed, networks can communicate even if they have different topologies, transmission media, or operating systems. The idea of an open-system protocol is that everyone can use it on their computer systems and be able to communicate with any other computer using the same protocol. The three biggest Internet tasks—communicating, seeking information, and shopping—are all being done the same way on any system that is following accepted Internet protocols.

Were there problems developing an open-system Internet protocol?

Agreeing on common standards was relatively easy. The tough part was developing a new method of communication because the current technology—circuit switching—was not efficient for computer communication. Circuit switching has been used since the early days of the telephone for establishing communication. In **circuit switching**, a dedicated connection is formed between two points (two people on telephones), and the connection remains active for the duration of the transmission. This method of communication is extremely important when communications must be received in the order in which they are sent (such as in telephone conversations).

When applied to computers, however, circuit switching is inefficient. Computer processing and communication take place in bursts. As a computer processor performs the operations necessary to complete a task, it transmits data in a group (or burst). The processor then begins working on its next task and ceases to communicate with output devices or other networks until it is ready to transmit data in the next burst. Circuit

FIGURE 13.6

Packets can each follow their own route to their final destination. Sequential numbering of packets ensures they are reassembled in the correct order at their destination.

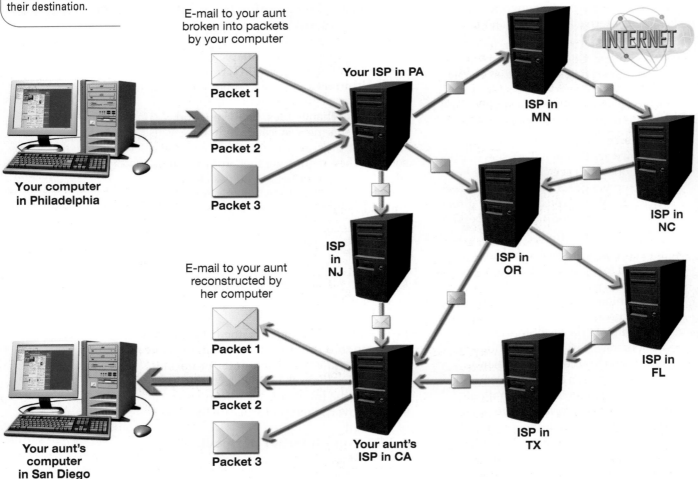

E-mail to your aunt broken into packets by your computer

Packet 1
Packet 2
Packet 3

Your computer in Philadelphia

Your ISP in PA

INTERNET

ISP in MN

ISP in NC

ISP in NJ

ISP in OR

ISP in FL

E-mail to your aunt reconstructed by her computer

Packet 1
Packet 2
Packet 3

Your aunt's computer in San Diego

Your aunt's ISP in CA

ISP in TX

switching is inefficient for computers because the circuit either would have to remain open (and therefore be unavailable to any other system) with long periods of inactivity, or it would have to be reestablished for each burst.

PACKET SWITCHING

If they can't use circuit switching, what do computers use to communicate? Packet switching is the communications methodology that makes computer communication efficient. Packet switching doesn't require a dedicated communications circuit to be maintained. With packet switching, data is broken into smaller chunks (called **packets** or **data packets**) that are sent over various routes at the same time. When the packets reach their destination, they are reassembled by the receiving computer. This technology resulted from one of the original goals of creating the Internet: If Internet nodes are disabled or destroyed (such as through an act of warfare or terrorism), the data can travel an alternate route to reach its destination.

What information does a packet contain? Packet contents vary depending on the protocol being followed. At a minimum, all packets must contain (1) an address to which the packet is being sent, (2) reassembling instructions if the original data was split between packets, and (3) the data that is being transmitted.

Sending a packet is sort of like sending a letter. Assume you are sending a large amount of information in written format from your home in Philadelphia to your aunt in San Diego. The information is too large to fit in one small envelope, so you mail three different envelopes to your aunt. Each envelope includes your aunt's address, a return address (your address), and the information being sent inside it. The pages of the letters sent in each envelope are numbered so that your aunt will know in which order to read them.

Each envelope may not find its way to San Diego by the same route (the letters may be routed through different post offices), but they will all eventually arrive in your aunt's mailbox. Your aunt will then reassemble the message (put the pages of the letters in order) and read it. The process of sending a message through the Internet works in much the same way. This is illustrated in

Figure 13.6, which traces an e-mail message sent from a computer in Philadelphia to a computer in San Diego.

Why do packets take different routes, and how do they decide which route to use? The routers that connect ISPs with each other monitor traffic and decide on the most efficient route for packets to take to their destination. The router works in the same way as a police officer during a traffic jam. When routes are clogged with traffic, police officers are deployed in areas of congestion to direct you to an alternate route to get to your destination.

TCP/IP

What protocol does the Internet use for transmitting data? Although many protocols are available on the Internet, the main suite of protocols used is **TCP/IP**. The suite is named after the original two protocols that were developed for the Internet: the **Transmission Control Protocol (TCP)** and the **Internet Protocol (IP)**. Although most people think that the TCP/IP suite consists of only two protocols, it actually comprises many interrelated protocols, the most important of which are listed in Figure 13.7.

FIGURE 13.7 The Main Protocols Contained in the TCP/IP Protocol Suite	
Internet Protocol (IP)	Sends data between computers on the Internet.
Transmission Control Protocol (TCP)	Prepares data for transmission and provides for error checking and resending lost data.
User Datagram Protocol (UDP)	Prepares data for transmission—no resending capabilities.
File Transfer Protocol (FTP)	Enables files to be downloaded to a computer or uploaded to other computers.
Telnet	Enables logging in to a remote computer and working on it as if sitting in front of it.
HyperText Transfer Protocol (HTTP) and Secure HTTP (S-HTTP)	Transfers HyperText Markup Language (HTML) data from servers to browsers. S-HTTP is an encrypted protocol for secure transmissions.
Simple Mail Transfer Protocol (SMTP)	Used for transmission of e-mail messages across the Internet.

Which particular protocol actually sends the information? The Internet Protocol (IP) is responsible for sending the information from one computer to another. The IP is like a postal worker who takes a letter (a packet of information) that was mailed (created by the sending computer) and sends it on to another post office, which in turn routes it to the addressee (receiving computer). The postal worker never knows whether the recipient actually receives the letter. The only thing the postal worker knows is that the letter was handed off to an appropriate post office that will assist in completing the delivery of the letter.

IP Addresses and Domain Names

Each computer, server, or device (router, etc.) connected to the Internet is required to have a unique identification number. But since humans are better at remembering and working with words, not numbers, the numeric IP addresses were given more human-friendly, word-based addresses.

IP ADDRESSES

What is an IP address? You will recall from Chapter 3 that an **IP address** is a unique identification number that defines each computer, service, or other device that connects to the Internet. IP addresses fulfill the same function as street addresses. For example, to send a letter to John Doe's house in Walla Walla, Washington, you have to know his address. John might live at 123 Main Street, which is not a unique address (many towns have a Main Street); but 123 Main Street, Walla Walla, WA 99362 *is* unique.

The numeric zip code is the unique postal identification for a specific geographic area and is governed by the U.S. Postal Service. Similarly, IP addresses must be registered with the **Internet Corporation for Assigned Names and Numbers (ICANN)** to ensure they are unique and have not been assigned to other users. The ICANN is responsible for allocating IP addresses to network administrators, just as the U.S. Postal Service is responsible for assigning zip codes to geographic areas.

What does an IP address look like? A typical IP address is expressed as follows:

$$197.24.72.157$$

An IP address expressed like this is called a **dotted decimal number** (also known as a **dotted quad**). However, recall that computers work with binary numbers. The same IP address in binary form is as follows:

$$11000101.00011000.01001000.10011101$$

The four numbers in the dotted decimal notation are each referred to as an **octet**. This name derives from the fact that each number would have eight positions when shown in binary form. Because 32 positions are available for IP address values (four octets with eight positions each), IP addresses are considered 32-bit numbers. A position is filled either by a 1 or a 0, resulting in 256 (2^8) possible values for each octet. Values start at 0 (not 1); therefore, each octet can have a value from 0 to 255. The entire 32-bit address can represent 4,294,967,296 values (or 2^{32}), which is quite a few Internet addresses!

BITS AND BYTES

What's Your IP Address?

Curious as to what your IP address is? You could go through the operating system to find out, or more simply, go to one of many Web sites such as **www.whatismyip.com** or **www.ipchicken.com** that provide this information. Figure 13.8 displays the output from WhatIsMyIP.com, which shows the IP address your PC is currently using.

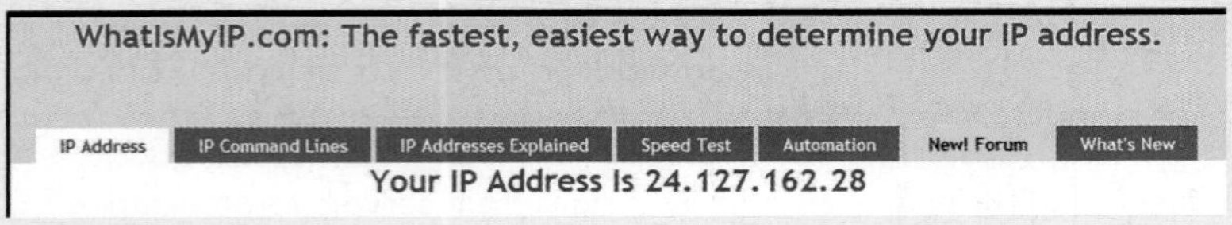

WhatIsMyIP.com: The fastest, easiest way to determine your IP address.

| IP Address | IP Command Lines | IP Addresses Explained | Speed Test | Automation | New! Forum | What's New |

Your IP Address Is 24.127.162.28

FIGURE 13.8

Some Web sites, such as WhatIsMyIP.com, determine your IP address for you.

Will we ever run out of IP addresses? When the original IP addressing scheme, **Internet Protocol version 4 (IPv4)**, was created in the early 1980s, no one foresaw the explosive growth of the Internet in the 1990s. (Of course, the Internet wasn't yet the exciting visual medium that it is today.) Therefore, 4 billion values for an address field seemed like enough to last forever. However, as the Internet grew rapidly, it quickly became apparent that we were going to run out of IP addresses.

Because the unique IP addressing system described earlier offers only a fixed number of IP addresses, a different addressing scheme known as **classless interdomain routing (CIDR,** pronounced "cider") was developed. CIDR, or supernetting, allows a single IP address to represent several unique IP addresses by adding a **network prefix** (a slash and a number) to the end of the last octet. The network prefix identifies how many of the possible 32 bits in a traditional IP address are to be used as the unique identifier, leaving the remaining bits to identify the specific host. For example, in the IP address 206.13.01.48/25, "/25" is the network prefix and indicates that the first 25 bits are used as the unique network identifier; the remaining 7 bits identify the specific host site.

Are there other Internet addressing systems? Internet Protocol version 6 **(IPv6)** is an IP addressing scheme (developed by the Internet Engineering Task Force, or IETF) that makes IP addresses longer, thereby providing more available IP addresses. IPv6 uses eight groups of 16-bit numbers, referred to as **hexadecimal notation** (or *hex* for short), which you learned about in Chapter 9. An IPv6 address would have the following format:

0000:0000:0000:0000:0000:0000:0000:0000

Hex addressing provides a much larger field size, which will enable a much larger number of IP addresses (approximately 340 followed by 36 zeros). This should provide a virtually unlimited supply of IP addresses and will allow many different kinds of non-PC devices such as cell phones and home appliances to more easily join the Internet in the future.

How does my computer get an IP address? You learned in Chapter 7 that IP addresses are either assigned statically or dynamically. **Static addressing** means that the IP address for a computer never changes and is most likely assigned manually by a network administrator. **Dynamic addressing**, in which your computer is assigned an address from an available pool of IP addresses, is more common. A connection to an ISP could use either method. If your ISP uses static addressing, then you were assigned an IP address when you applied for your service and had to configure your computer manually to use that address. More often, though, your ISP assigns your computer a temporary (dynamic) IP address, as shown in Figure 13.9.

How exactly are dynamic addresses assigned? Dynamic addressing is normally handled by the **dynamic host configuration protocol (DHCP)**, which belongs to the TCP/IP protocol suite. DHCP takes a pool of IP addresses and shares them with hosts on the network on an as-needed basis. ISPs don't need to maintain a pool of

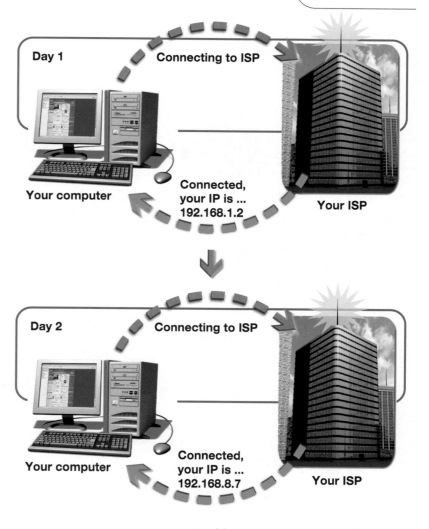

FIGURE 13.9

Dynamic IP addressing changes your IP address every time you connect to the Internet.

Day 1   Connecting to ISP
Your computer
Connected, your IP is ... 192.168.1.2
Your ISP

Day 2   Connecting to ISP
Your computer
Connected, your IP is ... 192.168.8.7
Your ISP

Making the Connection: Connection-Oriented Versus Connectionless Protocols

The Internet Protocol is responsible only for *sending* packets on their way. The packets are created by either the TCP or the **User Datagram Protocol (UDP)**. You don't decide whether to use TCP or UDP. The choice of protocol was made for you by the developers of the computer programs you are using or by the other protocols (such as those listed in Figure 13.7) that interact with your data packet.

As explained earlier, data transmission between computers is highly efficient, if connections do not need to be established (as in circuit switching). However, there are benefits to maintaining a connection, such as less data loss. The difference between TCP and UDP is that TCP is a connection-oriented protocol, whereas UDP is a connectionless protocol.

A **connection-oriented protocol** requires two computers to exchange control packets, which set up the para-

meters of the data exchange session, before sending packets that contain data. This process is referred to as **handshaking**. TCP uses a process called a **three-way handshake** to establish a connection, as shown in Figure 13.10a. Perhaps you need to report sales figures to your home office. You phone the sales manager and tell him or her that you are ready to report your figures. The sales manager then prepares to receive the information by getting a pencil and a piece of paper. By confirming that he or she is ready and by your beginning to report the figures, a three-way (three-step) handshaking process is completed.

Your computer does the same thing when it sends an e-mail through your ISP, as shown in Figure 13.10b. It establishes a connection to the ISP and announces it has e-mail to send. The ISP server responds that it is ready to receive the e-mail. Your computer then acknowledges

FIGURE 13.10

(a) Colleagues in Hamburg and Tokyo are establishing communication using a three-way handshake. (b) Here two computers are establishing communication the same way.

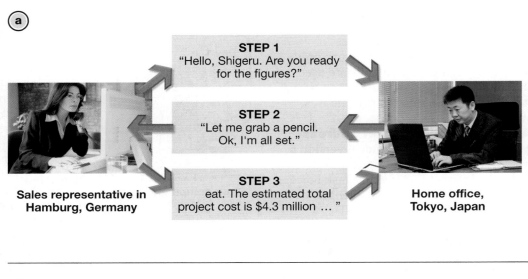

a

STEP 1
"Hello, Shigeru. Are you ready for the figures?"

STEP 2
"Let me grab a pencil. Ok, I'm all set."

STEP 3
eat. The estimated total project cost is $4.3 million … "

Sales representative in Hamburg, Germany

Home office, Tokyo, Japan

b

STEP 1
I want to send e-mail.

STEP 2
Ok, I'm ready to receive.

STEP 3
Here's the e-mail message for Aunt Sally.

Your computer

Your ISP's server

the ready state of the server and begins to transmit the e-mail.

A **connectionless protocol** does not require any type of connection to be established or maintained between two computers that are exchanging information. Just like mailing a letter, the data packets are sent without notifying the receiving computer or receiving any acknowledgment that the data was received. UDP is the Internet's connectionless protocol.

Besides establishing a connection, TCP provides for reliable data transfer. Reliable data transfer means that the application that uses TCP can rely on this protocol to deliver all the data packets to the receiver free from errors and in the correct order. TCP achieves reliable data transfer by using acknowledgments and providing for the retransmission of data, as shown in Figure 13.11.

Assuming that two systems, X and Y, have established a connection, when Y receives a data packet that it can read from X, it sends back a **positive acknowledgment (ACK)**. If X does not receive an ACK in an appropriate period of time, it resends the packet. If the packet is unreadable (damaged in transit), then Y sends a **negative acknowledgment (NAK)** to X, indicating the packet was not received in understandable form. X then retransmits that packet. Acknowledgments assure that the receiver has received a complete set of data packets. If a packet is unable to get through after being resent several times, the user is generally presented with an error message indicating the communications were unsuccessful.

You may wonder why you wouldn't always want to use a protocol that provides for reliable data transfer. On the Internet, speed is often more important than accuracy. For certain applications (such as e-mail), it's critically important that your message be delivered completely and accurately. For streaming multimedia, it's not always important to have every frame delivered accurately because most streaming media formats provide for error correcting caused by data loss. It is, however, extremely important for streaming media to be delivered at a high rate of speed; otherwise, playback quality can be affected. Therefore, a protocol such as TCP, which uses handshakes and acknowledgments, would probably not be appropriate when viewing a movie trailer over the Internet.

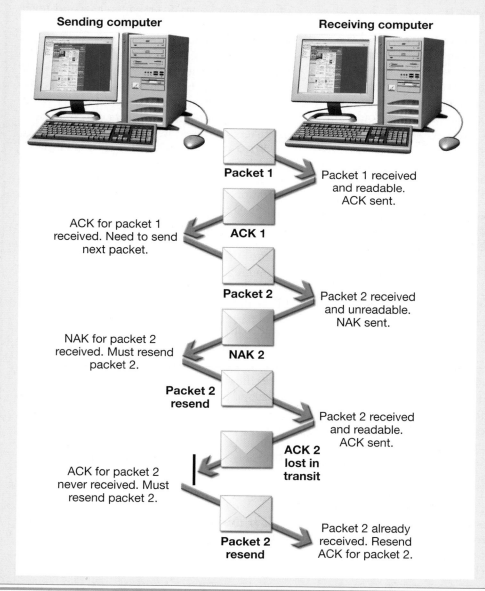

Sending computer **Receiving computer**

Packet 1 → Packet 1 received and readable. ACK sent.

ACK for packet 1 received. Need to send next packet. ← ACK 1

Packet 2 → Packet 2 received and unreadable. NAK sent.

NAK for packet 2 received. Must resend packet 2. ← NAK 2

Packet 2 resend → Packet 2 received and readable. ACK sent.

ACK for packet 2 never received. Must resend packet 2. ← ACK 2 lost in transit

Packet 2 resend → Packet 2 already received. Resend ACK for packet 2.

FIGURE 13.11

Packet Acknowledgment in Action

ACTIVE HELPDESK

Understanding IP Addresses, Domain Names, and Protocols

In this Active Helpdesk call, you'll play the role of a helpdesk staffer, fielding calls about which data transmissions and protocols the Internet uses, and why IP addresses and domain names are important for Internet communications.

IP addresses for all of their subscribers because not everyone is logged on to the Internet at one time. Thus, when a user logs on to an ISP's server, the DHCP server assigns that user an IP address for the duration of the session. Similarly, when you log on to your computer at work in the morning, DHCP assigns your computer an IP address. These temporary IP addresses may or may not be the same from session to session.

What are the benefits of dynamic addressing? Although having a static address would seem to be convenient, dynamic addressing provides for better security measures to keep hackers out of computer systems. Imagine how hard it would be for burglars to find your home if you changed your address every day!

DOMAIN NAMES

I've been on the Internet, so why have I never seen IP addresses? Computers are fantastic at relating to IP addresses and other numbers. However, humans remember names better than they remember strings of numbers. (Would you rather call your friend 1236231 or Maria?) As the Web was being formed, a naming system needed to be developed to enable people to work with names instead of numbers. Hence, domain names were born.

BITS AND BYTES

How to Register a Domain Name

Have you wanted to create a Web site with your own domain name (**www.me.com**)? The process of creating your own Web site is straightforward, but finding a name that you like and that is available may prove to be difficult.

The first thing you need to do is to create a list of domain names that are acceptable to you. If you are creating the Web site for business purposes, then you might want to keep search strategies in mind. With your list of acceptable domain names in hand, go to **www.whois.org** to determine if your preferred name has already been taken. If the search results indicate that there is no match, then the name is available. If the name is already taken, then try making small variations to the name.

After you find a name you like that's available, find an official Internet registrar (InterNIC has a link to the Accredited Registrar Directory). Registrars offer a variety of services for a range of prices, so compare prices among the registrars that offer the services you want. Once you provide the registrar with their required information, you've got yourself a Web site.

As you learned in Chapter 3, a **domain name** is simply a name that takes the place of an IP address, making it easier for people to remember. You've most likely visited **www.yahoo.com**. Yahoo.com is a domain name. The server where Yahoo!'s main Web site is deployed has an IP address (such as 123.45.67.89), but it's much easier for you to remember to tell your browser to go to Yahoo.com than it is the nine-digit IP address.

How are domains organized? Domains are organized by level. As you'll recall from Chapter 3, the portion of the domain name after the dot is the top-level domain (TLD). The TLDs are standardized pools (such as .com and .org) that have been established by ICANN. (Refer back to Figure 3.21 in Chapter 3 for a list of the TLDs that are currently approved and in use.) Within the top-level domains are many **second-level domains**. In the .com domain are popular sites such as **Amazon.com**, **Google.com**, and **Microsoft.com**. Each of the second-level domains needs to be unique within that particular domain but not necessarily unique to all top-level domains. For example, **Mycoolsite.com** and **Mycoolsite.org** could be registered as separate domain names.

Who controls domain name registration? ICANN assigns companies or organizations to manage domain name registration. Because names can't be duplicated within a top-level domain, one company is assigned to oversee each TLD and maintain a listing of all registered domains. VeriSign is the current ICANN-accredited domain name registrar for the .com and .net domains. VeriSign provides a database that lists all the registered .net and .com domains and their contact information. However, for simplicity you can look up any .com or .net domain at **www.networksolutions.com** to see if it is registered and who owns it. Country-specific domains such as .nz for New Zealand and .sg for Singapore are controlled by groups in those countries. You can find a complete list of country-code top-level domains on the Internet Assigned Numbers Authority Web site at **www.iana.org**.

DNS SERVERS

How does my computer know the IP address of another computer? Say you want to get to Yahoo.com. To do so, you type the company URL—www.yahoo.com—into your browser's address box. However,

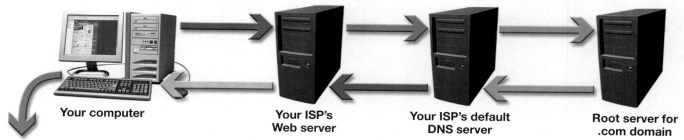

STEP 1: Your browser requests information from ABC.com.

STEP 2: Your ISP doesn't know the IP address of ABC.com, so it requests the address from its default DNS server.

STEP 3: The default DNS server doesn't know the IP address of ABC.com either, so it queries the root server of the .com domain.

Your computer

Your ISP's Web server

Your ISP's default DNS server

Root server for .com domain

STEP 7: Your computer then routes its request to ABC.com and stores the IP address in cache for later use.

STEP 6: Your ISP's Web server also stores the correct IP address for ABC.com for future reference and returns it to your computer.

STEP 5: The default DNS server stores the correct IP address for ABC.com for future reference and returns it to your ISP's Web server.

STEP 4: The root server provides the default DNS server with the appropriate IP address of ABC.com.

FIGURE 13.12

DNS Servers in Action

the URL is not important to your computer; only the IP address of the computer hosting the Yahoo! site is. When you enter the URL in your browser, your computer must convert the URL to an IP address. To do this, your computer consults a database that is maintained on a **DNS server** that functions like a phone book for the Internet.

Your ISP's Web server has a default DNS server (one that is convenient to contact) that it goes to when it needs to translate a URL to an IP address (illustrated in Figure 13.12). Your ISP or network administrator defines the default DNS server. If the default DNS server does not have an entry for the domain name you requested, then it queries another DNS server.

If all else fails, your ISP's Web server contacts one of the many root DNS servers maintained throughout the Internet. The **root DNS servers** know the location of all the DNS servers that contain the master listings for an entire top-level domain. Your default DNS receives the information from the master DNS (say, for the .com domain) and then stores that information in its cache for future use and communicates the appropriate IP address to your computer.

Other Protocols: FTP and Telnet

The TCP/IP protocol suite contains numerous protocols, although some of them are used infrequently. Two of the more

commonly used protocols on the Internet are the File Transfer Protocol and Telnet.

FILE TRANSFER PROTOCOL

How does FTP work? The **File Transfer Protocol (FTP)** enables users to share files that reside on local computers with remote computers. If you're attempting to download files using FTP to your local computer, the FTP client application (most likely a Web browser) first establishes a TCP session with the remote computer. FTP provides for authentication and password protection, so you may be required to log in to an FTP site with a username and password.

Can I upload files with FTP? Most FTP sites allow you to upload files. To do so, you either need a browser that handles FTP transfer (current versions of Internet Explorer and Firefox do), or you need to obtain an FTP client application. Many FTP client programs are available as freeware or shareware. Searching on the term "FTP" on **www.download.com** will produce a list of programs to choose from. Smart FTP Client (**www.smartftp.com**) is an FTP shareware program that is free for personal, educational, and nonprofit use.

TELNET

What is Telnet? Telnet is both a protocol for connecting to a remote computer and a TCP/IP service that runs on a remote computer to make it accessible to other computers. At colleges, students sometimes use Telnet to connect to mainframe

```
C:\Windows\system32\telnet.exe
Welcome to Microsoft Telnet Client

Escape Character is 'CTRL+]'

Microsoft Telnet> ?/

Commands may be abbreviated. Supported commands are:

c    - close              close current connection
d    - display            display operating parameters
o    - open hostname [port] connect to hostname (default port 23).
q    - quit               exit telnet
set  - set                set options (type 'set ?' for a list)
sen  - send               send strings to server
st   - status             print status information
u    - unset              unset options (type 'unset ?' for a list)
?/h  - help               print help information
Microsoft Telnet> _
```

FIGURE 13.13

This Telnet command window shows available commands.

computers or servers from their personal computers. The Telnet client application (which runs on your personal computer) connects to the Telnet server application (running on a remote computer). Telnet enables you to take control of a remote computer (the server) with your computer (the client) and manipulate files and data on the server as if the server were your own computer.

How do I use Telnet? To establish a Telnet session, you need to know the domain name or IP address of the computer to be connected to using Telnet. In addition, logon information (ID and password) is generally required. With Windows Vista, you also need to turn on the Telnet feature. To do so, click the Start button in the taskbar, select Control Panel, and then select Programs. In the Programs and Features group, select the option to turn windows features on or off. In the list of features, click Telnet Client and then click OK. After Telnet has been configured in Vista, click the Start button and enter "telnet" in the quick search box. This will then display the window shown in Figure 13.13. Typing ?/ at the command prompt displays the

BITS AND BYTES

What Is an Internet Cache?

Your **Internet cache** is a section of your hard drive that stores information that you may need again for surfing (such as IP addresses, frequently accessed Web pages, and so on). However, caching of domain name addresses also takes place in DNS servers. This helps speed up Internet access time because the DNS server doesn't have to constantly query master DNS servers for TLDs. However, caches do have limited storage space, so entries are held in the cache only for a fixed period of time and then are deleted. The time component associated with cache retention is known as the time to live (TTL). Without caches, surfing the Internet would take a lot longer.

available Telnet commands. To connect to a remote computer, type "open" and the host name (or IP address) of the remote computer and follow the logon instructions (which vary from system to system).

HTTP, HTML, and Other Web Jargon

Although most people think that the Internet and the Web are the same thing, the World Wide Web (WWW or the Web) is a grouping of protocols and software that resides on the Internet. The Web provides an engaging interface for exchanging graphics, video, animations, and other multimedia on the Internet. One aspect that distinguishes the Web from the Internet is the use of special languages such as HTML (HyperText Markup Language) and protocols such as HTTP (HyperText Transfer Protocol) that allow different computers to talk to each other.

HTTP AND SSL

Which Internet protocol does a browser use to send requests? The **HyperText Transfer Protocol (HTTP)** was created especially for the transfer of hypertext documents across the Internet. **Hypertext** documents are documents in which text is linked to other documents or media (such as video clips, pictures, and so on). Clicking a specific piece of text (called a *hyperlink*) that has been linked elsewhere takes you to the linked file.

When the browser sends a request, does it do anything to make the information secure? As you read in Chapter 3, some Web sites require extra layers of security to ensure that banking or purchasing transactions can be done safely and without personal and financial information being mishandled. Commerce servers use security protocols to protect sensitive information from being intercepted by hackers.

Secure HyperText Transfer Protocol (S-HTTP) is an extension to the HTTP protocol and supports sending data securely over the Web. A similar protocol with wider usage is the **secure sockets layer (SSL)**. SSL creates a secure connection between a client and a server, and any amount of data can be sent securely over that connection. S-HTTP is designed to transmit individual messages securely. SSL and S-HTTP, therefore, can be seen as complementary rather than as competing technologies. Both protocols have been approved by the IETF as a standard. Online shopping sites frequently use SSL technology to safeguard credit card information, whereas S-HTTP is more likely to be used in situations where the server represents a bank and requires authentication from the user that is more secure than a user ID and password.

HTML/XHTML

How are Web pages formatted? A Web page is merely a text document that is formatted using the **HyperText Markup Language (HTML)**. HTML describes the content of a Web page (mainly text and graphic images) in terms of how it is to be marked up—or displayed and interacted with. Another markup language that extends HTML is called the **eXtensible HyperText Markup Language (XHTML)**. XHTML has much more stringent rules than HTML regarding markup tags. Style sheets (described in more detail later on) provide developers an easier way to update and revise Web pages. Although XHTML is the development environment of choice for Web developers today, many people still refer to Web site formatting as "HTML tagging."

HTML and XHTML are not programming languages; rather, they are sets of rules for marking up blocks of text so that a browser knows how to display them. Blocks of text in HTML/XHTML documents are surrounded by pairs of **HTML tags** (such as <b> and </b> to indicate bolding). HTML tags surround and define HTML content. These tags and the text between them are referred to as **elements**. The elements are interpreted by the browser, and appropriate effects are applied to the text. The following is an element from an HTML/XHTML document:

```
<i>This should be italicized.</i>
```

The browser would display this element as:

This should be italicized.

The first tag, <i>, tells the browser that the text following it should be italicized. The ending </i> tag indicates that the browser should cease applying italics to the text. Note that multiple tags can be combined in a single element such as the following:

```
<b><i>This should be bolded and
italicized.</i></b>
```

The browser would display this element as

This should be bolded and italicized.

Obviously, the <b> tag indicates bolding. Tags for creating hyperlinks appear as follows:

```
<a href="http://www.
prenhall.com">Prentice Hall
Publishing</a>
```

The code <a href = "http://www.prenhall.com"> defines the link's destination. The <a> tag is the anchor tag and creates a link to another resource on the Web (denoted by the "href" attribute), such as an HTML page, an image, or a sound. In this case, the link is to the **prenhall.com** Web page. The text between the open and close of the anchor tag (Prentice Hall Publishing) is the link label. The link label is the text (or image) that is displayed on the Web page as clickable text for the hyperlink.

Can I see the HTML/XHTML coding of a Web page? HTML/XHTML documents are merely text documents with tags applied to them. If you want to look at the HTML/XHTML coding behind your favorite Web page, just right-click anywhere on the page, select View Source from the shortcut menu, and the HTML/XHTML code for that page will be displayed, as shown in Figure 13.14. Alternatively, you can select View Source from your browser menu. For more information on how to build Web pages, see the Sound Byte "Creating Web Pages with HTML."

SOUND BYTE

Creating Web Pages with HTML

Creating simple Web pages using Microsoft Word is relatively easy. In this Sound Byte, you'll learn the basics of Web page creation by setting up a Web site featuring a student résumé.

FIGURE 13.14

From the **View** menu in your browser, click **Source** to display the source code in a browser. A Notepad window that contains the HTML document opens.

XML

Can I create my own HTML/XHTML tags to fit my special needs? For HTML/XHTML, you're required to use the predefined tags that constitute the HTML/XHTML standard. This works fairly well for displaying information on Web pages but is less optimal if two Web pages need to exchange information. Information exchange has become much more common with the rise of business-to-business (B2B) electronic commerce. B2B transactions involve two businesses selling products and services to each other without a retail customer involved. Because HTML/XHTML was not designed for information exchange, **eXtensible Markup Language** (**XML**) was created.

How is XML different from HTML/XHTML? Extensible markup language (XML) is another markup language, but it describes the content in terms of what data is being described rather than how it is to be displayed. Instead of being locked into standard tags and formats for data, users can build their own markup languages to accommodate particular data formats and needs.

For example, three pieces of typical information that need to be captured for an e-commerce transaction are a credit card number, price, and zip code. In HTML/XHTML, the paragraph tags (<p> and </p>) are used to define text and numeric elements. Almost any text or graphic can fall between these tags and be treated as a paragraph. So, in our example, the HTML/XHTML code would appear as follows:

```
<p>1234567890123456</p>
(credit card number)
<p>12.95</p> (price)
<p>19422</p> (zip code)
```

The browser will interpret the data contained within the <p> and </p> tags as separate paragraphs. But the paragraph tags tell us nothing about the data contained within them. Without the labels added (not part of the HTML/XHTML code), we may not realize what data was contained within. Also, tags don't provide any methodology for data validation. Credit card numbers are usually 16 numbers long. But any length of data could be inserted between <p> and </p> tags. How would we know if the credit card number was a valid length? The answer lies in creating tags that are specific to the task at hand and that actually describe

the data contained within them. Here's how our data might look in XML:

```
<credit_card_number>
1234567890123456
</credit_card_number>
<price>12.95</price>
<zip_code>19422</zip_code>
```

We have created the tags we need for data capture. Our XML specification provides a tag called "credit card number" that is used exclusively for credit card data.

How has XML impacted other Web page developments? XML has spawned quite a few custom packages for specific communities. For example, Mathematical Markup Language (MathML) is an XML-based markup language that is used to describe mathematical symbols and formulas so that they can be presented in a familiar way in Web documents. Wireless Markup Language (WML) uses XML to output Web resources on mobile devices; MusicXML is used to create and publish musical scores online; and GraphML is an XML-based format for creating graphs. These are just a few of the many examples that illustrate the very nature of XML—that information exchange standards can be easily constructed and customized to meet a variety of growing online applications.

THE COMMON GATEWAY INTERFACE

Can you use HTML/XHTML to make a Web page interactive? Because HTML/XHTML was originally designed to link text documents, HTML/XHTML by itself can't do all the amazing things we expect modern Web pages to do. As we mentioned earlier, HTML and XHTML are not programming languages; rather, they are sets of tags for determining how text is displayed and where elements are placed. Fortunately, the limitations of HTML/XHTML were recognized early, and the common gateway interface (CGI) was developed.

Most browser requests merely result in a file being displayed in your browser (such as the **eBay.com** main Web page). Displaying a file is fine if you're just going to be reading text. However, to make a Web site interactive, you may need to run a software program to perform a certain action (such as gathering a name and address and adding it to a database). The **common gateway interface (CGI)**

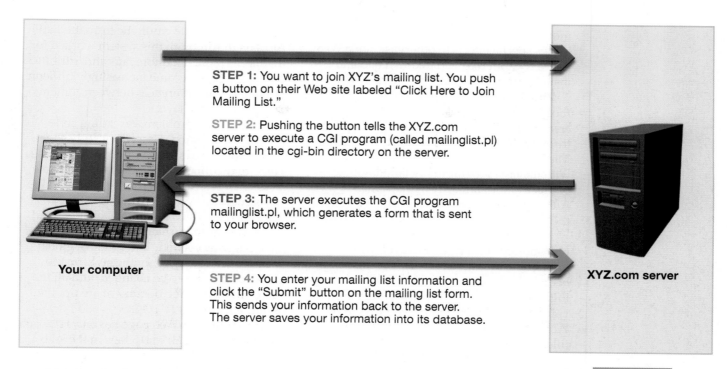

STEP 1: You want to join XYZ's mailing list. You push a button on their Web site labeled "Click Here to Join Mailing List."

STEP 2: Pushing the button tells the XYZ.com server to execute a CGI program (called mailinglist.pl) located in the cgi-bin directory on the server.

STEP 3: The server executes the CGI program mailinglist.pl, which generates a form that is sent to your browser.

STEP 4: You enter your mailing list information and click the "Submit" button on the mailing list form. This sends your information back to the server. The server saves your information into its database.

Your computer

XYZ.com server

FIGURE 13.15

Information Flow When a CGI Program Is Run

provides a methodology by which your browser can request that a program file be executed (or run) instead of just being delivered to the browser. This enables functionality beyond simply displaying information.

CGI files can be created in almost any programming language, and the programs created are often referred to as **CGI scripts**. Common languages that are used to create CGI scripts are PERL, C, and C++. Because programming languages are extremely powerful, almost any task can be accomplished by writing a CGI script. You have probably encountered CGI scripts on Web pages without realizing it. Have you ever left an entry in a guest book on a Web page? Have you used a search engine to create a customized results page based on keywords you entered? Have you filled out a form to be added to a mailing list? All of these tasks are commonly done using CGI scripts.

How do CGI programs get executed? On most Web servers, a directory called **cgi-bin** is created by the network administrator who configures the Web server. All CGI scripts are placed into this directory. The Web server knows that all files in this directory are not to be merely read and sent, but also need to be run. Because these programs are run on the Web server as opposed to running inside your browser, they are referred to as **server-side programs**.

For instance, a button on a Web site may say "Click Here to Join Mailing List" (see step 1 in Figure 13.15). Clicking the button may call a script file (perhaps called "mailinglist.pl") from the cgi-bin directory on the Web server hosting the site (step 2). This file generates a form that is sent to your browser, which includes fields for a name and e-mail address and a button that says "Submit" (step 3). After filling in the fields and clicking the Submit button, the mailinglist.pl program sends the information back to the server. The server then records the information in a database (step 4).

DYNAMIC HTML

Can Web pages be made more interactive without accessing Web servers? Dynamic HTML (DHTML) is a combination of technologies—HTML/XHTML, cascading style sheets, and JavaScript—that is used to create lively and interactive Web sites. Recall that the Web is based on a client/server network. Once a Web server processes a Web page and sends the page to the computer requesting it (the client), the receiving computer cannot get any new data from the server unless a new request is made. When interactivity is required on a Web page, this exchange of data between the client and server can make the interactivity inefficient and slow. DHTML technologies allow the Web page to change after it's been loaded, generally in response to such user actions as clicking a mouse or mousing over objects on a page. DHTML brings special effects to otherwise static Web pages without the need to download and install plug-ins or other special software.

What is JavaScript? JavaScript is the most commonly used scripting language for creating DHTML effects. It was developed through the joint efforts of Netscape and Sun Microsystems. JavaScript is often confused with the Java programming language because of the similarity in the name. Although they share some common elements, the two languages function quite differently.

Pure HTML/XHTML documents don't respond to user input. However, with JavaScript, HTML/XHTML documents can be made responsive to mouse clicks and typing. For example, JavaScript is often used to validate when information you fill out on a Web form is validated (say to make sure you filled in all required fields).

When JavaScript code is embedded in an HTML/XHMTL document, it is downloaded with the HTML/XHTML page to the browser. All actions dictated by the embedded JavaScript commands are executed on the client computer (the one with the browser). Without JavaScript and other scripting languages, Web pages would be pretty lifeless.

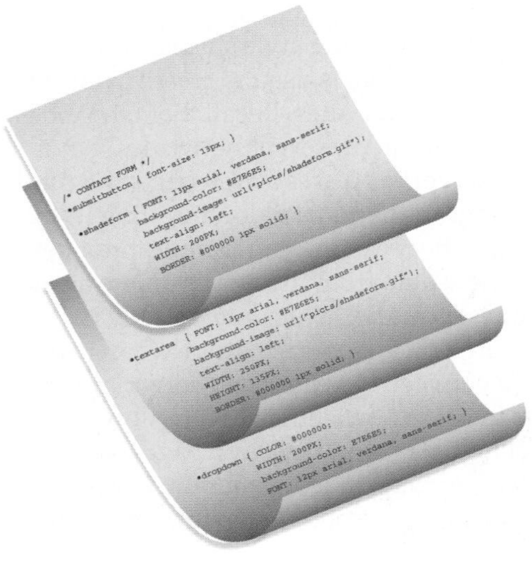

How can I easily change the formatting of HTML/XHTML elements? In addition to the HTML/XHTML formatting tags described earlier, some tags describe areas of a Web page to help with layout. For example, the tag <h1> declares an area as a header. Similarly, <p> says, "This is a paragraph," and <table> says, "This is a table." In addition to defining certain areas as a header, paragraph, or table, additional tags were needed to indicate how the header,

paragraph, or table would be formatted and displayed. Although this system worked for awhile, as more and more tags and attributes were created, it became increasingly difficult to manage the differences between content and presentation layout.

To solve this problem, cascading style sheets were created. **Cascading style sheets (CSS)** are lists of statements (also known as *rules*) that define in one single location how to display HTML/XHTML elements. Style rules enable a Web developer to define a style for each HTML/XHTML element and apply it to as many elements on as many Web pages as needed. Then when a global change is necessary, only the style on the style sheet needs to be changed, and all the elements in the Web document are updated automatically.

For example, a Web page has an <H1> heading tag, and all <H1> tags in the Web page are formatted with a white background and an orange border (see Figure 13.16). Before CSS, if you wanted to change the border color from orange to yellow, you would have to change the background color of every <H1> tag. Instead, the change from orange to yellow only needs to happen once on the style sheets, and all the <H1> tags update to yellow without individual changes.

Where does the cascading come in? In Web documents, there are different layers of styles (external, embedded, and inline), so it's possible that different rules can be created for the same type of element. In other words, in an external style sheet, there might be a rule that defines the background color for all paragraphs as blue. But somewhere else in an embedded style sheet, the rule for background color for paragraphs might be defined as white; in an inline style sheet, the background color might be light pink. Eventually, all these style sheets must be merged to form one style sheet for the document, creating conflicts between rules. Therefore, rules are assigned weights so that when the rules are collected and merged, the rule or style with a higher weight overrides the rule or style that carries a lower weight. This hierarchy of competing styles is formed, creating a "cascade" of styles according to their assigned weights.

How are the individual components of a Web page organized? Just as cascading style sheets organizes and combines the attributes of objects of a Web page,

FIGURE 13.16

Cascading style sheets place formatting for specific document elements together in one place to simplify Web page development and revisions.

DHTML uses the **document object model (DOM)** to organize the objects and page elements. The document object model defines every item on a Web page—including graphics, tables, and headers—as an object. Then with DOM, similar to CSS, Web developers can easily change the properties of these objects.

CLIENT-SIDE APPLICATIONS

Aside from CGI scripts, are there other ways to make a Web site interactive? Sometimes running programs on the server is not optimal. Server-side program execution can require many communication sessions between the client and the server to achieve the goal. Often it is more efficient to run programs on your computer (the client). Therefore, client-side programs were created. A **client-side program** is a computer program that runs on the client computer and requires no interaction with a Web server. Client-side programs are fast and efficient because they run on your desktop and don't depend on sending signals back and forth to the Web server. Two main types of client-side methods exist. The first involves embedding programming language code directly within the HTML or XHTML code of a Web page using an **HTML/XHTML embedded scripting language**. The most popular embedded language is JavaScript, which is used extensively in dynamic HTML files.

The second type of client-side program is an **applet**, a small application that resides on a server. When requested, a compiled version of the program is downloaded to the client computer and run there. The Java language is the most common language used to create applets for use in browsers. The applets can be requested from the server when a Web page is loaded, and they will be run once they're downloaded to the client computer.

Although there can be some delay in functionality while waiting for the Java applet to download to the client, once the applet arrives, it can execute all its functions without further communication with the server. Games are often sent to your browser as applets. As an example, in Figure 13.17 your browser makes contact with a game on the game site ArcadePod.com (**www.arcadepod.com**) and makes your request to play a game (step 1). The Web server returns the Java applet (step 2) that contains all the code to run the game on your computer. Your computer executes the applet code, and the game runs on your computer.

Communications over the Internet

A new communications revolution was started when Internet use began to explode in the mid-1990s. The volume of Internet e-mail is growing exponentially every month (unfortunately, over 80 percent of it is spam),

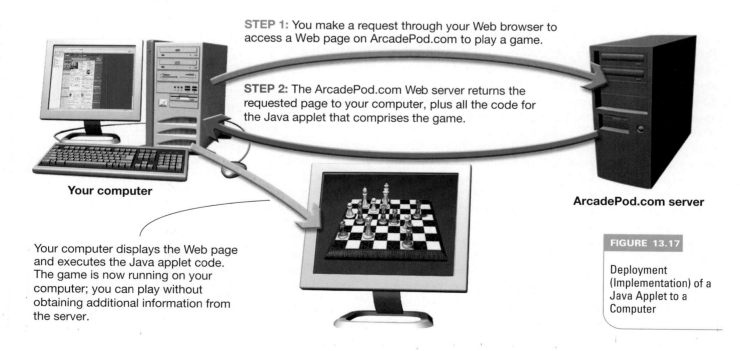

STEP 1: You make a request through your Web browser to access a Web page on ArcadePod.com to play a game.

STEP 2: The ArcadePod.com Web server returns the requested page to your computer, plus all the code for the Java applet that comprises the game.

Your computer

Your computer displays the Web page and executes the Java applet code. The game is now running on your computer; you can play without obtaining additional information from the server.

ArcadePod.com server

FIGURE 13.17

Deployment (Implementation) of a Java Applet to a Computer

instant messaging is a major method of communication, and the popularity of Voice over Internet Protocol is also on the rise. In the following sections, we explore all of these communications media in more detail and show you how to keep your information exchanges efficient and secure.

E-MAIL

Who invented e-mail? In 1971, Ray Tomlinson, a computer engineer who worked on the development of the ARPANET (the precursor to the Internet) for the U.S. government, created e-mail. E-mail grew from a simple program that Tomlinson wrote to enable computer users to leave text messages for each other on a single machine. The logical extension of this was sending text messages between machines on the Internet. Tomlinson created the convention of using the @ sign to distinguish between the mailbox name and the destination computer. E-mail became the most popular application on ARPANET; by 1973, it accounted for 75 percent of all data traffic.

How does e-mail travel the Internet? Just like other kinds of data that flow along the Internet, e-mail has its own protocol. The **Simple Mail Transfer Protocol (SMTP)** is responsible for sending e-mail along the Internet to its destination. As in most other Internet applications, e-mail is a client/server application. To send an e-mail

ETHICS IN IT

Ethics: Politics Web 2.0 Style

The Internet and Web 2.0 technologies were leveraged for political campaigning in the recent 2008 presidential election more than in any other campaign in recent history. Twenty-first century politicians have realized the best way to reach the voting public is through the Internet. Hillary Clinton, for example, announced her campaign with a YouTube video, and several candidates created MySpace profiles, YouTube videos, and Second Life avatars. Pictures of candidates on the campaign trail appeared on Flickr. In fact, these Web sites created dedicated areas for politics. The Internet has become the new "town meeting" location.

The insurgence of Web 2.0 technologies also allowed Internet users to create and modify Internet content through videos, blogs, and podcasts—and it also changed how the voting public responded to political campaigns. Voter-generated content such as the "Vote Different" YouTube video ad that appeared in the beginning of the 2008 presidential campaign is a good example of the use of 2.0 technologies. That YouTube video is a remake of the classic 1984 Mac ad, and features voice-over comments made by Hillary Clinton in her candidacy announcement video and ends with an Obama 2008 endorsement. The Obama campaign did not create the ad and neither the Clinton nor Obama campaigns knew who did until a "citizen"—Phil de Vellis—admitted he had created the ad to illustrate how voters can voice and broadcast their personal opinions for all to hear and see. As de Vellis said, "This shows that the future of American politics rests in the hands of ordinary citizens."

Tech President, a blog site created specifically for the 2008 presidential campaign, tracked how the candidates used the Web and also how voter content affected the campaign by showing the current number of MySpace friends and YouTube views each candidate had. Tech President had its own blog content and linked to other blog content related to the 2008 campaign.

Being able to express personal opinions and reach a mass majority of American voters is truly a benefit of the Internet. However, the medium also poses some concerns and should require us to pause for thought. As with any publicly generated content, how much can we trust to be true and valid? Internet content has always had problems when determining authenticity, currency, relevance, and bias. When the main distribution of political information is transferred to the general public without review or validation, should issues be anticipated?

Almost anyone can upload video, image, or text content to the Web, but there is no governing authority to check for content validity. At least with public information generated by 20th-century media—TV, radio, and print (newspapers and magazines)—there were some standards of authentication because information had to go through some form of editorial review. Although we needed to be prepared to look for the other side of a story or determine personal opinion or editorial bias, the factual content in traditional media could reasonably be determined. There are no editorial boards through which Internet content must pass. On the other hand, as with wiki pages, can we be our own editorial board? Is there enough knowledge and participation that we will act to review and censor our own public content? Because this is just the beginning of politics Web 2.0 style, only time will tell. What do you think?

message, some form of e-mail software is necessary to compose the document and possibly include an attachment such as a spreadsheet or photograph. Popular software that needs to be installed on your computer includes Microsoft Outlook and Thunderbird, as well as Web-based e-mail software such as the increasingly popular Yahoo!, Hotmail, and Gmail.

As you read in Chapter 3, client-based software is installed on your computer, and all functions are supported and run from your computer. Web-based software is launched from a Web site; the programs and features are stored on the Web and are accessible anywhere you have access to an Internet connection. No matter which type of client software you use, on the way to its destination your mail will pass through **e-mail servers**—specialized servers whose sole function is to store, process, and send e-mail.

Where are e-mail servers located? If your ISP provides you with an e-mail account, it runs an e-mail server that uses SMTP. For example, as shown in Figure 13.18, say you are sending an e-mail message to your friend Cheyenne. Cheyenne uses Juno.com as her ISP. Therefore, your e-mail to her is addressed to Cheyenne@juno.com.

When you send the e-mail message, your ISP's Web server receives it and passes it to your ISP's e-mail server. The e-mail server reads the domain name (juno.com) and communicates with a DNS server to determine the location of juno.com. Once the address is located, the e-mail message is forwarded to juno.com through the Internet and arrives at a mail server maintained by Cheyenne's ISP. The e-mail is then stored on Cheyenne's ISP's e-mail server. The next time Cheyenne logs on to her ISP and checks her mail, she will receive your message.

If e-mail was designed for text messages, why are we able to send files as attachments? SMTP was designed to handle text messages. When the need arose to send files by using e-mail (in the early 1970s), a program had to be created to convert binary files to text. The text that represented the file was appended to the end of the e-mail message. When the e-mail arrived at its destination, the recipient had to run another program to translate the text back into a binary file. Uuencode and uudecode were the two most popular programs used for encoding and decoding binary files.

BITS AND BYTES

Are Old Web Pages Really Gone Forever?

Have you ever tried to find a site you've visited on the Web only to find it no longer exists? Or have you ever discovered that information you want to access has been removed from a site? Is the information lost forever? Groups such as the Internet Archive (**www.archive.org**) are trying to prevent the loss of information on the Internet as a result of Web site updates or the discontinuance of a site. Since 1996, the Internet Archive has been collecting information from the Web and preserving it. Visit the Internet Archive site, and use the "Wayback Machine" to visit archived versions of Web sites from times past. Want to see how Yahoo! has changed since 1996? Just type the URL into the Wayback Machine engine and you'll see links to snapshots of Yahoo! at various points in time. So next time you try to access a site that is no longer there, check the Wayback Machine—all may not be lost.

This was fine in the early days of the Internet when users were mostly computer scientists. However, when the Internet started to become popular in the early 1990s, it became apparent that a simpler methodology was needed for sending and receiving files. The **multipurpose Internet mail extensions (MIME)** specification was introduced in 1991 to simplify attachments to e-mail messages. All e-mail client software now uses this protocol to attach files.

E-mail is still being sent as text, but the e-mail client using the MIME protocol now handles the encoding and decoding for the users. For instance, in Yahoo! mail, on the Attach Files screen you merely browse to the file you want to attach (located somewhere on your hard drive), select the file, and click the Attach Files button. Unbeknownst to you, the Yahoo! e-mail client encodes and decodes the file for transmission and receipt.

E-MAIL SECURITY: ENCRYPTION AND SPECIALIZED SOFTWARE

If e-mail is sent in regular text, can other people read my mail? E-mail is highly susceptible to being read by unintended parties because it's sent in plain text. Also, copies of your e-mail message may exist (temporarily or permanently) on numerous servers as it makes its way through the

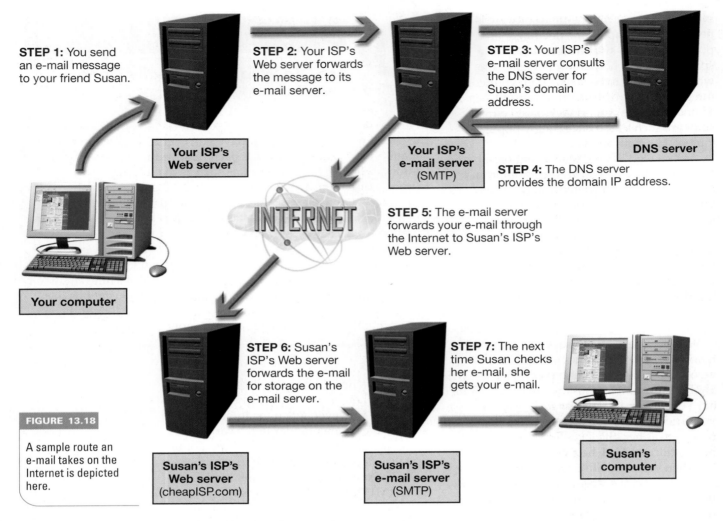

STEP 1: You send an e-mail message to your friend Susan.

STEP 2: Your ISP's Web server forwards the message to its e-mail server.

STEP 3: Your ISP's e-mail server consults the DNS server for Susan's domain address.

Your ISP's Web server

Your ISP's e-mail server (SMTP)

DNS server

STEP 4: The DNS server provides the domain IP address.

INTERNET

STEP 5: The e-mail server forwards your e-mail through the Internet to Susan's ISP's Web server.

Your computer

STEP 6: Susan's ISP's Web server forwards the e-mail for storage on the e-mail server.

STEP 7: The next time Susan checks her e-mail, she gets your e-mail.

Susan's computer

FIGURE 13.18

A sample route an e-mail takes on the Internet is depicted here.

Susan's ISP's Web server (cheapISP.com)

Susan's ISP's e-mail server (SMTP)

Internet. To protect your sensitive e-mail messages, encryption practices are used.

How do I encrypt my e-mail?
Encryption refers to the process of coding your e-mail so that only the person with the key to the code (the intended recipient) can decode (or decipher) and read the message. Secret codes for messages can be traced almost to the dawn of written language. The military and government espionage agents are big users of codes and ciphers. The trick is making the coding system easy enough to use so that everyone who needs to communicate with you can.

There are two basic types of encryption: private key and public key. In **private-key encryption**, only the two parties involved in sending the message have the code. This could be a simple shift code where letters of the alphabet are shifted to a new position (see Figure 13.19). For example, in a two-position right-shift code, the letter *a* becomes *c*, *b* becomes *d*, and so on. Or it could be a more complex substitution code

(*a* = *h*, *b* = *r*, *c* = *g*, etc.). The main problem with private-key encryption is key security. If someone steals a copy of the code or is savvy about decoding, the code is broken.

In **public-key encryption**, two keys, known as a **key pair**, are created. You use one key for coding and the other for decoding. The key for coding is generally distributed as a **public key**. You can place this key on your Web site, for instance. Anyone wishing to send you a message codes it using your public key.

When you receive the message, you use your **private key** to decode it. You are the only one who ever possesses the private key, and therefore it is highly secure. The keys are generated in such a way that they can work only with each other. The private key is generated first. The public key is then generated using a complex mathematical formula, often using values from the private key. The computations are so complex that they are considered unbreakable. Both keys are necessary to decode a message; if one key is lost, the other key cannot be used by itself.

What type of encryption is used on the Internet? Public-key encryption is the most commonly used encryption on the Internet. Tried-and-true public-key packages such as **Pretty Good Privacy (PGP)** are available for download at sites such as **www. download.com**, and you can usually use them free of charge (although there are now commercial versions of PGP). After obtaining the PGP software, you can generate key pairs to provide a private key for you and a public key for the rest of the world.

What does a key look like? A key is a binary number. Keys vary in length, depending on how secure they need to be. A 10-bit key has 10 positions and might look like this:

1001101011

Longer keys are more secure because they have more possible values. A 10-bit key provides 1,024 different possible keys, whereas a 40-bit key allows for 1,099,511,627,776 possible values. The key and the message are run through a complex algorithm in the encryption program (such as PGP) that converts the message into unrecognizable code. Each key turns the message into a different code.

Is my private key really secure? Because of the complexity of the algorithms used to generate key pairs, it is impossible to deduce the private key from the public key. However, that doesn't mean your coded message can't be cracked. As you learned in Chapter 12, a brute force attack occurs when hackers try every possible key combination to decode a message. This type of attack can enable hackers to deduce the key and decode the message.

What is considered a safe key then? In the early 1990s, 40-bit keys were thought to be totally resistant to brute force attacks and were the norm for encryption. But in 1995, a French programmer used a unique algorithm of his own and 120 workstations simultaneously to attempt to break a 40-bit key. He succeeded in just eight days. Since then, 128-bit keys have become the standard. Even using supercomputers, no one has yet cracked a 128-bit key. It is believed that even with the most powerful computers in use today, it would take hundreds of billions of years to crack a 128-bit key.

How do businesses protect e-mail? Using encryption doesn't always solve the

A = C	N = P
B = D	O = Q
C = E	P = R
D = F	Q = S
E = G	R = T
F = H	S = U
G = I	T = V
H = J	U = W
I = K	V = X
J = L	W = Y
K = M	X = Z
L = N	Y = A
M = O	Z = B

The word **C O M P U T E R** using the two-position code at the left now becomes:

E Q O R W V G T

This is difficult to interpret without the code key at the left.

FIGURE 13.19

The Word "COMPUTER" Using a Two-Position Right-Shift Encryption Code

other problems associated with e-mail. Messages leave a trail as they travel over the Internet, and copies of messages can exist on servers for long periods of time. In addition, immediate reading of sensitive documents is often essential, but encryption software doesn't provide a means for confirming that your messages have been delivered. To combat these issues, companies such as Securus Systems Ltd. (**www.safemessage.com**) have developed secure data transmission software (called SafeMessage) that works outside of the conventional SMTP mail servers.

How is SafeMessage software used? Both parties who wish to send secure messages install the SafeMessage software. When messages are to be sent, a secure point-to-point connection is established between the sender's and the recipient's e-mail boxes. Proprietary protocols with encryption, not SMTP, are used to send the messages. Additional options are provided such as delivery confirmation, message shredding (destruction of messages on command), and the ability to have messages erase themselves after a set period of time. Although this type of software is not free, it is catching on in those sections of the business community where fear of industrial espionage is high.

INSTANT MESSAGING

What do I need to run instant messaging? As was presented in Chapter 3, instant messaging is the act of communicating between two or more people over the Internet in real time. It differs from e-mail in that conversations are able to

ACTIVE HELPDESK

Keeping E-Mail Secure

In this Active Helpdesk call, you'll play the role of a helpdesk staffer, fielding calls about how e-mail works and how messages are kept secure.

Emerging Technologies: The Evolving Internet

The Internet and the ways you use it are constantly evolving. In the 1990s, most home users connected to the Internet with a dial-up modem. Today, DSL, cable, and satellite provide faster connections. Now fiber-optics, once available only for corporate and urban America, is beginning to reach homes in suburban and rural areas. This technology not only enables the transmission of data at close to the speed of light but also provides an uninterrupted data pathway that makes the delivery of communications more reliable.

Perhaps You Would Prefer to Use Your Wall Outlet?

There is more on the horizon than just increased fiber-optic reach. Many companies are exploring a technology that sends data, voice, and video signals over normal electrical power lines. That's right: Someday, you may be able to connect to the Internet through your normal wall outlet. Called *broadband over power line* (BPL), this technology is being tested in Europe, Australia, and by Duke Power in the pilot cities of Charlotte, North Carolina, and Cincinnati, Ohio. Although the current connectivity speeds of BPL are not quite as fast as cable or DSL broadband alternatives, the prospect is that with a power-line Internet connection, you could one day transfer *exobits* of data—that's 1 with 18 zeros after it—per second through power lines. Now that's *fast*.

How About WiMAX?

With the rise in portable computing devices, people want Internet access wherever they go. An up-and-coming wireless alternative to standard WiFi connections is WiMAX (short for worldwide interoperability for microwave access). Instead of the 300 feet of connectivity that WiFi offers, WiMAX has a range of as far as

31 miles, and its transmission speeds run in the 5 to 10 Mbps range, making it faster than cable or DSL. Plans are in place to provide WiMAX to approximately 133 million users by 2012. Sprint Xohm is currently being rolled out in major metropolitan areas such as Chicago, Baltimore, and Washington, D.C.

Or Blimps?

Most people are unaware that the high altitude of satellites currently used to provide wireless Internet access actually poses barriers to high-speed data communications. One solution currently being developed is deploying communications platforms at lower altitudes by using airships, or blimps. The company GlobeTel Communications has developed the Sanswire Stratellite (see Figure 13.20), a 245-foot-long unmanned airship that is designed to sail 13 miles above the Earth's surface. One such airship could provide communications coverage for an area as large as the state of Texas—that's 268,581 square miles! Aside from wireless Internet access, this technology could also serve as an alternative to satellites for cellular telephony.

FIGURE 13.20

Airships such as the Sanswire Stratellite will help break down barriers to high-speed wireless access.

happen at the same time rather than lagging by minutes or hours. Instant messaging requires the use of a client program that connects to an instant messaging service. AOL Instant Messenger (AIM), ICQ, Yahoo! Messenger, and Windows Live Messenger are the top four instant messaging services in use today. No matter which one you choose, you need to run the appropriate client software on your computer.

Looking for a Hot Spot?

Computing devices will continue to get smaller in the future, so **hot spots**—places where users can connect to the Internet wirelessly—will continue to abound. If you're looking for a hot spot, portable wireless network detectors, such as the WiFi Finder from Kensington, make it easy to detect wireless networks wherever you are. And if you know where you'll be in advance, you can use **www.wififreespot.com** or use Google maps by just typing "wifi hotspots" and your location in the search bar. Google maps will produce a map with locations highlighted and exact addresses in the margin (see Figure 13.21). Of course, just because you can locate a hot spot doesn't always mean it will be accessible when you find it!

Want a Safer Internet?

More research is needed to anticipate and defend against future cyberterror attacks. To this end, the NSF has issued a $5.46 million grant to the University of California, Berkeley, and the University of Southern California Information Sciences Institute in Cyber Defense Technology Experimental Research (DETER) Network. The money will be used to construct a cyber-security testbed that will simulate the real Internet. All types of cyberattacks (from worms to denial-of-service attacks) will be launched on the testbed's infrastructure. The testbed will provide researchers with a tool to learn how to better detect and deter cyberattacks that could potentially cripple the Internet.

Look for these and other Internet-related technologies coming soon to computers near you.

FIGURE 13.21

Google Maps provides you with a list of hot spots where you can go to connect to the Internet.

How does instant messaging work? The client software running on your computer makes a connection with the chat server using your Internet connection, as shown in Figure 13.22. Once contact is established, you can log in to the server with your name and password (you can sign up for a free account the first time you connect). The client software provides the server with connection information (such as the IP address)

BITS AND BYTES

Random Numbers: The Lifeblood of Encryption

E-mail encryption, SSL encryption, and just about anything we do to achieve privacy on the Internet requires random numbers. Encryption is accomplished using random number sequences, which are sequences of numbers in which no patterns can be recognized. Even for an e-commerce transaction (say, buying a book from Amazon.com) that uses SSL encryption to encode your credit card number, as many as 368 bits of random data might be needed. Only 128 bits are needed for the encryption key, but other random data is needed to create authentication codes and to prevent replay attacks. Replay attacks occur when hackers attempt to copy packets traveling across the Internet and extract data from them (such as encryption codes) to reuse (replay) them to gain access to networks or transactions. So where do all these random numbers come from?

Generating true random sequences is more difficult than it sounds. But in 1996, Landon Noll and two colleagues came up with a system called *LavaRnd* that used Lava Lite lamps (you read that right) to generate random numbers. The lamps have since been replaced with another random source: a webcam with the lens cap still on. The webcam emits "thermal noise," which is then digitized and run through a mathematical algorithm that generates the number set and strips out any sections that are predictable. This service is open source, unpatented, and license-free, so anyone can set up a server and generate much-needed random numbers. For more information, check out **www.lavarnd.org**.

for your computer. The server then consults the list of contacts ("Buddies" or friends) that you have previously established in your account and checks to see if any of your contacts are online. If any are, the server sends a message back to your client providing the necessary connection information (the IP addresses) for your friends. You can now click your friends' names to establish a chat session with them.

Because both your computer and your friend's computer have the connection information (the IP addresses) for each other, the server isn't involved in the chat session. Chatting takes place directly between the two computers over the Internet.

Is sending an instant message secure? Most instant messaging services do not use a high level of encryption for their messages—if they bother to use encryption at all. In addition to viruses, worms, and hacking threats, instant messaging systems are vulnerable to eavesdropping in which someone using a packet sniffer "listens in" on IM conversations. Although several measures are underway to increase the security of this method of real-time communication, major vulnerabilities still exist. Therefore, it is not a good idea to send sensitive information using instant messaging because it is susceptible to interception and possible misuse by hackers.

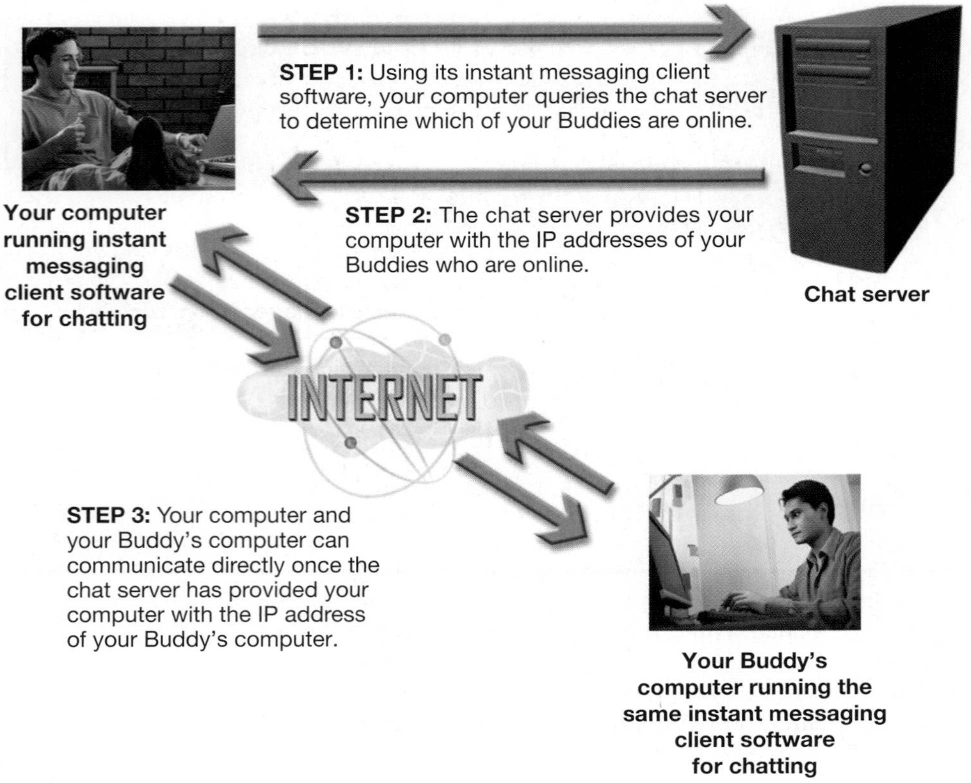

Your computer running instant messaging client software for chatting

STEP 1: Using its instant messaging client software, your computer queries the chat server to determine which of your Buddies are online.

STEP 2: The chat server provides your computer with the IP addresses of your Buddies who are online.

Chat server

STEP 3: Your computer and your Buddy's computer can communicate directly once the chat server has provided your computer with the IP address of your Buddy's computer.

Your Buddy's computer running the same instant messaging client software for chatting

VOICE OVER INTERNET PROTOCOL (VoIP)

What's so good about VoIP?

Voice over Internet Protocol turns a standard Internet connection into a way to make free long-distance phone calls. If you have friends and relatives that live a long-distance phone call away from you, then you need to know more about VoIP. From a user's perspective, the true advantage (at least right now) is that the service is free. Even some cell phones are VoIP-enabled.

FIGURE 13.22

How an Instant Messaging Program Works

T-Mobile's HotSpot@Home service allows customers to make cell phone calls over a VoIP network as long as the device can connect to a WiFi signal. When a WiFi signal is not detected, the cell phone makes the call through your usual cellular network.

How does VoIP work? From a user's perspective, there is little difference between VoIP and traditional phone service (see Figure 13.23), although the technology behind the wires and devices is a bit different. As explained in Chapter 3, VoIP is a method of taking analog voice signals that normally travel telephone wires and turning them into digital data that can be transmitted over the Internet. Like e-mail, VoIP uses packet switching as the method of transferring data. Unlike circuit switching (the method used with traditional phone calls), when a VoIP call is made, the transmission lines are only used when the two computers are communicating, thus allowing the computers to accept and process other information. Because digital data is far more efficient than analog data with respect to size, transmission speed, and compression capabilities, VoIP's long-term advantage is that it will be able to handle more phone calls at the same time. Although today's traditional phone calls have increased efficiency and reduced costs since they were first invented, there is considerable room for improvement compared to how digital data (such as e-mail) is transmitted.

How are VoIP security issues being handled? Since VoIP technology is similar to that of e-mail, VoIP is vulnerable to some of the same threats. However, the use of encryption methodologies, updated antivirus software, firewalls, and antispam tools helps cut down on VoIP's security vulnerabilities. With increasing growth of Internet capabilities, our dependency on the Internet also increases.

Security measures for all forms of communication technologies are constantly being evaluated. It is important for all users of Internet technologies to understand that threats to our security and privacy are real but controllable with the proper precautions.

FIGURE 13.23 Comparison of a Typical Call and a VoIP Call

Typical Telephone Call	VoIP Telephone Call
1. Pick up the phone and wait for dial tone to signal that you are connected to the local office of your telephone carrier.	1. Pick up the phone, which sends a signal to the computer or telephone adapter. The computer sends a dial tone indicating that you have a connection to the Internet.
2. Dial the number of your friend's phone.	2. Dial the number of your friend's phone. The tones are converted into digital data.
3. The call is routed through the switch at your local carrier through several switches along the way.	3. Assuming the phone number is in a valid format, your VoIP company translates the phone number into an IP address and then connects to the receiving device.
4. The phone at the other end rings, and your friend answers the call.	4. The signal "asks" the receiving device to ring, and your friend answers the call.
5. When the call is answered, a circuit is opened.	5. When your friend picks up the phone, each computer knows to expect packets of data from the other computer.
6. As you talk, the circuit remains open. No other data can be transmitted over the phone line during this time (a busy signal occurs if someone else tries to call).	6. As you talk, the packets of data are sent over the same Internet infrastructure as e-mail or a Web page. The digital data is translated into analog audio signals so that you and your friend can understand each other.
7. When you hang up, the circuit is closed, enabling another call to come in.	7. When you hang up, the session is terminated.

1. Who owns, manages, and pays for the Internet?

Management of the Internet is carried out by several nonprofit organizations and user groups such as the Internet Society (ISOC), the Internet Engineering Task Force (IETF), the Internet Architecture Board (IAB), the Internet Corporation for Assigned Names and Numbers (ICANN), and the World Wide Web Consortium (W3C). Each group has different responsibilities and tasks. Currently, the U.S. government (and subsequently the U.S. taxpayer) funds a majority of the Internet costs.

2. How do the Internet's networking components interact?

Individual computers or networks connect to the Internet using Internet service providers (ISPs). These providers vary in size and can be compared to the highway system. The largest paths along which data travels the most efficiently and quickly make up the Internet backbone, to which regional and local connections are made. Homes and all but the largest businesses connect to the Internet through regional or local connections, which then connect to the Internet through the companies that make up the Internet backbone. The largest businesses, educational centers, and some government agencies such as NASA make up the Internet backbone.

3. What data transmissions and protocols does the Internet use?

Data is transmitted along the Internet using packet switching. Data is broken up into discrete units known as *packets*, which can take independent routes to the destination before being reassembled. Although many protocols are available on the Internet, the main suite of protocols used to move information over the Internet is TCP/IP. The suite is named after the original two protocols that were developed for the Internet: the Transmission Control Protocol (TCP) and the Internet Protocol (IP). Whereas TCP is responsible for preparing data for transmission, IP actually sends data between computers on the Internet.

4. Why are IP addresses and domain names important for Internet communications?

An IP address is a unique number assigned to all computers connected to the Internet. The IP address is necessary so that packets of data can be sent to a particular location (computer) on the Internet. A domain name is merely a name that stands for a certain IP address and makes it easier for people to remember it. For example, MyWebPage.com is a domain name and is much easier to remember than the IP address 124.53.111.14. DNS servers act as the phone books of the Internet. They enable your computer to find out the IP address of a domain by looking up its corresponding domain name (which you typed into your browser).

5. What are FTP and Telnet, and how do I use them?

The File Transfer Protocol (FTP) enables users to share files that reside on local computers with remote computers. Current versions of browsers enable you to connect to FTP sites on the Internet to facilitate downloading or uploading files to and from FTP sites. Telnet is both a protocol for connecting to a remote computer and a TCP/IP service that would run on a remote computer to make it accessible to other computers. Telnet enables you to take control of a remote computer (the server) with your computer (the client) and manipulate files and data on the server as if you were sitting in front of that server.

6. What are HTML/XHTML and XML used for?

The HyperText Markup Language (HTML) is a set of rules for marking up blocks of text so that a browser knows how to display them. Most Web pages are generated with at least some HTML code. Blocks of text in HTML documents are surrounded by a pair of tags (such as <b> and </b> to indicate bolding). These tags and the text between them are referred to as *elements*. By examining the elements, your browser determines how to display them on your computer screen. Because HTML was not designed for information exchange, eXtensible Markup Language (XML) was created. Instead of being locked into standard tags and formats for data, XML enables users to create their own markup languages to accommodate particular data formats and needs. XML is used extensively in e-commerce for exchanging data between corporations.

7. How do e-mail, instant messaging, and Voice over Internet Protocol work, and how is information using these technologies kept secure?

Simple Mail Transfer Protocol (SMTP) is the protocol responsible for sending e-mail over the Internet. As in most other Internet applications, e-mail is a client/server application. E-mail passes through e-mail servers whose functions are to store, process, and send e-mail to its ultimate destination. ISPs and portals such as Yahoo! maintain e-mail servers to provide e-mail functionality to their customers. Your ISP's e-mail server uses DNS servers to locate the IP addresses for the recipients of the e-mail you send. Encryption software, such as Pretty Good Privacy (PGP), is used to code messages so that they can be decoded only by the authorized recipients.

Buzzwords

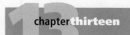

Word Bank

- applet
- backbone
- circuit switching
- DNS
- FTP
- HTML

- HTTP
- ICANN
- IP address
- OC line
- packet switching
- PGP

- point of presence
- public-key encryption
- SMTP
- SSL
- TCP/IP
- XML

Instructions: Fill in the blanks using the words from the Word Bank above.

As a network administrator, Patricia knows that she can count on the organization (1) _____ to ensure that she has an appropriate range of IP addresses for her work site. Her high-speed connection to her company's ISP was vital to providing the connectivity her employees need to get their jobs done. Recently, the company moved up from a DSL connection to a(n) (2) _____ line because of the high volume of Internet traffic it was generating. Hopefully, Patricia thinks, the government will continue to fund projects to continue research to improve the Internet (3) _____, the main highway to the Internet, and other vital technologies.

But Patricia has indulged in enough daydreaming. It is time to ensure that the Internet connection to the bank of modems, or (4) _____ provided by the ISP her company is using, is fully functional before the majority of the employees arrive for work. Because Patricia's company sends a tremendous amount of e-mail, old-fashioned (5) _____ technology would never have sufficed for sending messages. Fortunately, the Internet employs (6) _____ to enable messages to be sent over widely varying routes. Of course, she knows that the main suite of protocols that controls Internet data traffic is called (7) _____.

After ensuring that all is functional, Patricia begins to assist the Web development team with Web page creation. To provide robust interaction with company databases, (8) _____ is being used to code Web pages for the corporate Web site instead of (9) _____, which requires developers to use a standard set of tags. Unsure of her instructions, she e-mails the director of Web development for clarification, knowing that the (10) _____ protocol will ensure that the e-mail is delivered to the director at the company's office in the United Kingdom. Requiring secure communications, she encrypts the e-mail using a(n) (11) _____ algorithm, knowing that the director can retrieve Patricia's key from her personal Web site.

After reading the director's response to her e-mail, she quickly writes a Java (12) _____ to produce an interactive form to collect customer information. Using the (13) _____ protocol, Patricia posts her Web page to the corporate site. Of course, users will view the Web page using the (14) _____ protocol. And because the Web page contains potentially sensitive information, Patricia makes sure to use the (15) _____ protocol to provide added security for the data.

Becoming Computer Literate

While attending college, you are working at MultiSteel, Inc., which is a small manufacturer of specialty steel products. The new CEO has charged your supervisor with bringing the company into the 21st century by connecting it to the Internet and developing a company Web site. Your supervisor has asked you to help draft a memo to the CEO that lays out the benefits of having an Internet presence.

Instructions: Draft a memo for your boss that details the benefits of connecting the company to the Internet. Make sure to suggest which types of Internet connections will be appropriate and which type of ISP will be needed. Using as many of the keywords from the chapter as you can, ensure that the report can be presented to managers who may be unfamiliar with computers or the Internet.

Instructions: Answer the multiple-choice and true–false questions below for more practice with key terms and concepts from this chapter.

MULTIPLE CHOICE

1. So that all computers on the Internet can communicate with each other, they must use common rules called *protocols*. Which is not a common protocol used on the Internet?
a. FTP
b. TCP
c. Telnet
d. S-HTTP

2. Which is NOT a common server found on the Internet?
a. Commerce server
b. Web server
c. File server
d. Application server

3. Data is sent over the Internet in small chunks called
a. pockets.
b. packets.
c. pieces.
d. switches.

4. A typical IP address is expressed as
a. a dotted decimal number.
b. four octets.
c. 32-bit numbers.
d. All of the above.

5. IP addresses that are NOT assigned from an available pool of IP addresses are
a. called *dynamic*.
b. more secure.
c. temporary.
d. called *static*.

6. Which of the following is a set of formatting technologies used on the Internet to add interactivity?
a. HTML
b. XHTML
c. XML
d. DHTML

7. SMTP is the protocol to do what over the Internet?
a. Send e-mail
b. Communicate via instant messaging
c. Upload files to another computer
d. None of the above

8. Internet exchange points are:
a. the way individuals connect to the Internet.
b. the points of connection between ISPs.
c. the connection points between Internet tiers.
d. the routes taken by e-mail pieces as they are sent over the Internet.

9. Which is the most commonly used type of encryption on the Internet?
a. private key encryption
b. public key encryption
c. perfectly good privacy
d. primary key encryption

10. SSL is the protocol used to
a. create a secure connection between client and server.
b. transmit individual messages securely.
c. encrypt e-mail messages.
d. All of the above.

TRUE–FALSE

____ 1. The costs associated with running the Internet are paid through the collection of sales taxes charged on purchases made over the Internet.

____ 2. VoIP uses packet-switching technology that is similar to e-mail.

____ 3. A computer needs both the URL and the IP address to accurately locate a Web page.

____ 4. The main suite of protocols used on the Internet is TCP/IP.

____ 5. E-mail messages are secure because they are always encrypted.

Making the Transition to...
Next Semester

1. Creating a Web Site: Issues

Your American history instructor has asked your group to design a Web site about the battle of Gettysburg. The site will include textual and graphical information on the battle as well as an interactive quiz. Users will be encouraged to post college term papers on the site as a resource for other students. The following issues need to be addressed:

a. In which domain should you register the site? Why do you think this is appropriate?
b. What is an easy to remember domain name or Web site? Is this name already registered? Be sure to check in the appropriate domain and provide proof that the name isn't already registered.
c. How would you ensure that people are able to find the site once it's on the Web?
d. What Internet protocols will users need to access the site?
e. What browsers or plug-ins may be required to access the site?

2. Creating a Web Site: Issues 2

As president of your school's Future Business Leaders of America club, you would like to build a mailing list for your quarterly newsletter. You also would like to ensure that the newsletter is available on the college's Web site. When you visit the college Web developer, she asks you to provide the following information:

a. What data will you require all online subscribers to provide?
b. What optional data would you like subscribers to provide?
c. Will an e-mail address be provided to potential subscribers if they wish to make inquiries? If so, who will be reviewing and responding to these e-mails? What time frame will you guarantee for an answer to e-mails?

3. Creating a Web Site: Issues 3

You have been asked to create a Web page to promote a campus club to which you belong. Investigate the following and explain which ISP you will recommend and why:

a. Most schools will provide Web pages for sanctioned clubs on their Web server. Does your school place any content restrictions on club Web sites? How much storage space is provided for club Web pages? Can club Web pages gather data from prospective members (such as contact information) for storage in a database?
b. Assume your club is unsanctioned and your school will not provide space for a Web page. Using Web sites such as **www.ispfinder.com** and **www.findanisp.com**, find three ISPs where you could potentially host the Web site and prepare a chart comparing the following for each ISP:
   - Cost per month for hosting
   - Number and type of e-mail accounts
   - Level of technical support
   - Amount of disk storage space
   - Throughput allowed per month

4. Searching for Employment on the Web

With tuition costs rising, you feel it would be appropriate to find a part-time job next semester. Visit some popular employment sites such as **www.monster.com** and **www.careerbuilder.com** or your school's online career center Web site and complete the following tasks:

a. Search for a part-time job or internship opportunity in your field of study. Provide a listing of opportunities you think would be appropriate for you and briefly describe why they would be appropriate.
b. Search for full-time jobs for which you might apply when you graduate.
   - What are the average starting salaries?
   - Do the starting salaries vary by geographic location, or are they reasonably similar?
   - What are the educational and previous experience requirements for the job?
   - What gaps in your background, if any, would you need to fill to pursue this job?

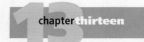

Making the Transition to... the Workplace

1. Web Site Security Issues

Your employer, a distributor of specialty stereo equipment, offers high-speed Internet access at the office where you work. Thirty-five workstations are connected to the Internet and are used by employees to send e-mail and conduct research. Recently, company trade secrets (traced to an employee e-mail) were printed in the local press. The company president has enlisted your help in determining preventive measures to avoid such security breaches in the future. Draft a memo that includes the following:

a. An employee e-mail policy that requires the use of encryption technologies.
b. Benefits and drawbacks to programs that monitor employee e-mails.
c. Policies on instant messaging in the workplace, including whether or not instant messaging should be banned.

2. Posting a Résumé Online

The director of your college placement office has suggested that you prepare a résumé that can be posted on the new college-graduate employment site that the university is developing. It must be in HTML format and include a picture of yourself. Consider the following:

a. What software would you use to develop the résumé?
b. Would straight HTML be sufficient or would you need to use JavaScript to display the picture?
c. Aside from your college's Web site, find at least three other Web sites where you could post your résumé so employers could see it.

3. "Googling"

At your company, someone was just fired because sensitive information related to a company product was associated with the person's name on the Internet. Discretion being the better part of valor, you decide to do a search for your name on the Web (in a search engine such as **www.google.com**) just to see what is out there. Prepare a report on what you found by exploring the following:

a. Did you find any accurate information about yourself (such as your homepage, résumé, etc.)? Did you find any erroneous information that you need to correct?
b. Did you find Web sites or information about other people with the same name as you? Could any of that information be damaging to your reputation if someone thought the other person was you? If so, provide examples.
c. Is there information that you found about yourself or others that you think should never be available on the Internet? Provide examples and an explanation of why you feel certain information should not be available.
d. Is there any information found at social network sites (such as **www.myspace.com** or **www.facebook.com**) that could be damaging to an individual if an employer or school administrator were to see it?

Critical Thinking Questions

Instructions: Albert Einstein used *Gedanken experiments,* or critical thinking questions, to develop his theory of relativity. Some ideas are best understood by experimenting with them in our own minds. The following critical thinking questions are designed to demand your full attention but require only a comfortable chair—no technology.

1. **Domain Names**

   Domain names often spark fierce controversy between competing companies. Legal wrangling over the rights to attractive names such as Buynow.com and Lowprices.com can generate large fees for attorneys. Meanwhile, some famous individuals such as Julia Roberts have had to fight for the right to own domains based on their own names.

   a. Should everyone be entitled to a Web site in a certain domain (say, .com) that contains their own name? How would you handle disputes by people who have the exact same name (say, two people named John Smith)?

   b. Is it ethical to register a domain name (say, Coke.net) just for the purpose of selling it to the organization that may benefit from it the most (such as the Coca-Cola Company)? Why or why not?

   c. Aside from the domains currently approved (such as .com and .org), what domain names do you think would have commercial appeal? For which types of Web sites would these domains be used?

2. **Network Security**

   Ensuring that computer-based information is secure is a key objective of many companies today.

   a. How would you prepare for a job as a network security specialist?

   b. Aside from computer-based security measures, what physical precautions should be taken to enhance computer data security?

3. **Encryption**

   Encryption programs built on 128-bit encryption algorithms are currently considered unbreakable.

   a. Because strong encryption programs using 128-bit encryption or better are considered unbreakable, the U.S. government places restrictions on exports of these encryption products. The government is also considering a requirement that all encryption products should have a "backdoor" code that would enable government agencies (such as the CIA and FBI) to read encrypted messages. Do you think this should be implemented? Why or why not?

   b. Assuming you figure out how to break 128-bit encryption, should you post that information on the Internet for anyone to use? Why or why not?

Problem:

As Web usage increases exponentially, demands are constantly placed on the Internet's infrastructure. Development groups such as the Internet2 consortium are designed to foster the innovation of new technologies to improve delivery of Internet services. In this Team Time, you'll research up-and-coming technologies and consider their impact on the Internet.

Task:

Your group has just received an invitation to speak at a technology conference being held at your school. Your topic is cutting-edge Internet technologies. You will be given 20 minutes at the conference to deliver a presentation to a group of approximately 250 students and educators, all of whom are interested in (but not necessarily familiar with) technology.

Process:

Break the class into small teams of three or four students. Each team should prepare a report as follows:

1. Explore sites such as **www.howstuffworks.com**, **www.internet2.edu**, and **www.wired.com** to investigate new technologies. Prepare a list of current innovations that are being developed.

2. Briefly present your group's findings to the class for debate and discussion. Are any ideas a replacement for the Internet as opposed to an extension of its capabilities? Your objective is to determine which topic would be of most interest to your class for a presentation.

3. Develop a PowerPoint presentation on the most popular topic. If the technology you choose seems futuristic or unbelievable, make sure you convey to the class why this will be achievable in the next 50 years.

Conclusion:

Don't be afraid to envision communications media that go beyond the current confines of the Internet. Great inventors such as Thomas Edison, Bill Gates, and Vint Cerf forced themselves to think outside the box instead of being trapped by current technology and engineering limitations. Encourage your friends to daydream about the future of data communications. After all, the next communications revolution may start with you!

Multimedia

 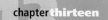

In addition to the review materials presented here, you'll find additional materials featured with the book's multimedia, including the *Technology in Action* Student Resource CD and the Companion Website (**www.prenhall.com/techinaction**), which will help reinforce your understanding of the chapter content. These materials include the following:

ACTIVE HELPDESK

In Active Helpdesk calls, you'll assume the role of helpdesk operator taking calls about the concepts you've learned in this chapter. You'll apply what you've learned and receive feedback from a supervisor to review and reinforce those concepts. The Active Helpdesk calls for this chapter are listed below and can be found on your Student Resource CD:

- Understanding IP Addresses, Domain Names, and Protocols
- Keeping E-Mail Secure

SOUND BYTES

Sound Bytes are dynamic multimedia tutorials that help demystify even the most complex topics. You'll view video clips and animations that illustrate computer concepts, and then apply what you've learned by reviewing with the Sound Byte Labs, which include quizzes and activities specifically tailored to each Sound Byte. The Sound Bytes for this chapter are listed here and can be found on your Student Resource CD:

- Creating Web Pages with HTML

COMPANION WEBSITE

The *Technology in Action* Companion Website includes a variety of additional materials to help you review and learn more about the topics in this chapter. The resources available at **www.prenhall.com/techinaction** include:

- **Online Study Guide.** Each chapter features an online true–false and multiple-choice quiz. You can take these quizzes, automatically check the results, and e-mail the results to your instructor.

- **Web Research Projects.** Each chapter features a number of Web research projects that ask you to search the Web for information on computer-related careers, milestones in computer history, important people and companies, emerging technologies, and the applications and implications of different technologies.

Glossary

3D sound card An expansion card that enables a computer to produce sounds that are omnidirectional or three-dimensional.

802.11 standard A wireless standard established in 1997 by the Institute of Electrical and Electronics Engineers; also known as WiFi (short for Wireless Fidelity), it enables wireless network devices to work seamlessly with other networks and devices.

A

Accelerated Graphics Port (AGP) bus A bus design that was designed to help move three-dimensional graphics data quickly; AGP buses establish a direct pathway between the graphics card and main memory so that data does not have to travel on the Peripheral Component Interconnect (PCI) bus.

access card reader A device that reads information from a magnetic strip on the back of a credit card–like access card (such as a student ID card); card readers are easily programmed by adding authorized ID card numbers, Social Security numbers, and so on.

access method A program or hardware mechanism that controls which computer is allowed to use the transmission media in a network at a certain time.

access time The time it takes a storage device to locate its stored data.

accounting software An application program that helps business owners manage their finances more efficiently by providing tools for tracking accounting transactions such as sales, accounts receivable, inventory purchases, and accounts payable.

ACK See *positive acknowledgment*.

active-matrix display An LCD monitor that uses active-matrix technology to charge each pixel individually as needed; the result is a clearer, brighter image than shown with a passive-matrix display.

Active Server Pages (ASP) A scripting environment in which users combine HyperText Markup Language (HTML), scripts, and reusable Microsoft ActiveX server components to create dynamically generated Web pages.

active topology A network topology in which each node on the network is responsible for retransmitting the token, or the data, to other nodes.

adapter card See *expansion card*.

adware A program that downloads on your computer when you install a freeware program, game, or utility. Generally, adware enables sponsored advertisements to appear in a section of your browser window or as a pop-up ad box.

affective computing A type of computing that relates to emotion or deliberately tries to influence emotion.

aggregator A software program that goes out and grabs the latest update of Web material (usually podcasts) according to your specifications.

AGP See *Accelerated Graphics Port (AGP) bus*.

AI See *artificial intelligence*.

aircard A device that enables users to have wireless Internet access with such mobile devices as PDAs and notebooks.

algorithm A set of specific, sequential steps that describe in natural language exactly what a computer program must do to complete its task.

all-in-one computer A desktop system unit that houses the computer's processor, memory, and monitor in a single unit.

all-in-one printer See *multifunction printer*.

alphabetic check Confirms that only textual characters are entered in a database field.

Alt key One of the keys on a standard PC computer keyboard that is used in conjunction with other keys to perform additional shortcuts and special tasks.

ALU See *arithmetic logic unit*.

American Standard Code for Information Interchange (ASCII) A format for representing each letter or character as an 8-bit (or 1-byte) binary code.

analog-to-digital converter chip Converts analog signals into digital signals.

analytical data See *structured (analytical) data*.

antivirus software Software that is specifically designed to detect viruses and protect a computer and files from harm.

applet A small program designed to be run from within another application. Java applets are often run on your computer by your browser through the Java Virtual Machine (an application built into current browsers).

application programming interface (API) A block of code in the operating system that software applications need to interact with.

application server A server that acts as a repository for application software.

application software The set of programs on a computer that helps a user carry out tasks such as word processing, sending e-mail, balancing a budget, creating presentations, editing photos, taking an online course, and playing games.

arithmetic logic unit (ALU) The part of the central processing unit (CPU) that is designed to perform mathematical operations such as addition, subtraction, multiplication, and division, and comparison operations, such as greater than, less than, and equal to.

arrow keys See *cursor control keys*.

artificial intelligence (AI) The science that attempts to produce computers that display the same type of reasoning and intelligence that humans do.

ASCII See *American Standard Code for Information Interchange*.

ASP See *Active Server Pages*.

assembly language A language that enables programmers to write their programs using a set of short, English-like commands that speak directly to the central processing unit (CPU) and give the programmer very direct control of hardware resources.

audio editing software Programs that perform basic editing tasks on audio files such as cutting dead air space from the beginning or end of the song or cutting a portion from the middle.

authentication The process of identifying a computer user, based on a login or username and password. The computer system determines whether the computer user is authorized and what level of access is to be granted on the network.

authentication server A server that keeps track of who is logging on to the network

and which services on the network are available to each user.

Automatic Backup utility A utility in the operating system that creates a duplicate copy of the data on your hard drive.

B

B2B See *business-to-business*.

B2C See *business-to-consumer*.

backdoor program A program that enables a hacker to take complete control of a computer without the legitimate user's knowledge or permission.

backup utility A software application that creates a duplicate copy of selected data on the hard disk and copies it to another storage device.

bandwidth (data transfer rate) The maximum speed at which data can be transmitted between two nodes on a network, usually measured in megabits per second (Mbps).

base 2 number system See *binary number system*.

base 10 number system (decimal notation) A number system that uses 10 digits, 0 through 9, to represent any value.

base class The original object class from which other classes are derived.

base transceiver station A large communications tower with antennas, amplifiers, and receivers/transmitters.

basic input/output system (BIOS) A program that manages the data between the operating system and all the input and output devices attached to the computer system; also responsible for loading the operating system (OS) from its permanent location on the hard drive to random access memory (RAM).

bastion host A heavily secured server located on a special perimeter network between the company's secure internal network and the firewall.

batch processing The process of accumulating transaction data until a certain point is reached, then processing those transactions all at once.

BD-ROM disc BD-ROM is defined as BluRay Disc Read Only Memory. BD-ROM is an optical disc storage media format for high-definition video and data storage.

behavior See *method*.

benchmarking A process used to measure performance in which two devices or systems run the same task and the times are compared.

beta version An early version of a software program that is still under development; usually provided free of charge in return for user feedback.

binary decision A decision point that can be answered in one of only two ways: yes (true) or no (false).

binary digit (bit) A digit that corresponds to the on and off states of a computer's switches. A bit contains a value of either 0 or 1.

binary language The language computers use to process data into information, consisting of only the values 0 and 1.

binary large object (BLOB) In databases, a type of object that holds extremely large chunks of data in binary form, which are usually video clips, pictures, or audio clips.

binary number system The number system used by computers to represent all data. Because it includes only two digits (0 and 1), the binary number system is also referred to as the *base 2 number system*.

biometric authentication device A device that uses some unique characteristic of human biology to identify authorized users.

bit See *binary digit*.

bit depth The number of bits the video card uses to store data about each pixel on the monitor.

black-hat hacker A hacker who uses his knowledge to destroy information or for illegal gain.

BLOB See *binary large object*.

blog See *Weblog*.

Blu-ray A format for optical storage devices that uses a disc similar in size and shape to a DVD and can hold up to 50 GB of data, or 4.5 hours of high-definition video.

Blu-ray disc A method of optical storage for digital data, developed for storing high-definition media. It has the largest storage capacity of all optical storage options.

Bluetooth technology A type of wireless technology that uses radio waves to transmit data over short distances. Often used to connect peripherals such as printers and keyboards to computers or headsets to cell phones.

bomb software Software that destroys data on a computing device if someone continually tries to access information by guessing the password.

Bookmark A feature in some browsers that places a marker of a Web site's Uniform Resource Locator (URL) in an easily retrievable list (called Favorites in Microsoft Internet Explorer).

Boolean operator A word used to refine logical searches. For Internet searches, these words—AND, NOT, and OR—describe the relationships between keywords in the search.

boot process (start-up process) The process for loading the operating system (OS) into random access memory (RAM) when the computer is turned on.

boot-sector virus A virus that replicates itself into the master boot record of a flash drive or hard drive.

breadcrumb list A list that shows the hierarchy of previously viewed Web pages within the Web site that you are currently visiting. Shown at the top of some Web pages, it aids Web site navigation.

bridge A network device that is used to send data between two different local area networks (LANs) or two segments of the same LAN.

brightness A measure of the greatest amount of light showing when the monitor is displaying pure white; measured as candelas per square meter (cd/m^2) or nits.

broadband connection A high-speed Internet connection such as cable, satellite, or digital subscriber line (DSL).

browser See *Web browser*.

browsing (1) The process of viewing database records. (2) The process of "surfing" the Web.

brute force attack An attack delivered by specialized hacking software that tries many combinations of letters, numbers, and pieces of a user ID in an attempt to discover a user password.

buddy list A list of contacts set up in an instant messaging program.

bus Inside a computer, a group of electrical pathways that provides communications between various parts of a computer, the central processing unit (CPU), and main memory.

bus (linear bus) topology A system of networking connections in which all devices are connected to a central cable called the bus (or backbone).

bus width The number of bits of data that can be transferred along a data pathway at one time.

business-to-business (B2B) E-commerce transactions between businesses.

business-to-consumer (B2C) E-commerce transactions between businesses and consumers.

byte Eight binary digits (bits).

C The predecessor language of C++ developed originally for system programmers by Brian Kernighan and Dennis Ritchie of AT&T Bell Laboratories in 1978. It provides higher-level programming language features (such as if statements and for loops) but still allows programmers to manipulate the system memory and central processing unit (CPU) registers directly.

C++ The successor language to C developed by Bjarne Stroustrup. It uses all of the same symbols and keywords as C but extends the language with additional keywords, better security, and more support for the reuse of existing code through object-oriented design.

C2C See *consumer-to-consumer.*

cable Internet connection A data transmission line that transmits data at high speeds along coaxial or fiber-optic cable.

cable modem A device that enables a computer to send data over cable lines. A modem modulates and demodulates the signal into digital data and back again.

cache memory Small blocks of memory located directly on and next to the central processing unit (CPU) chip that act as holding places for recently or frequently used instructions or data that the CPU

accesses the most. When these instructions or data are stored in cache memory, the CPU can more quickly retrieve them than if it had to access the instructions or data from random access memory (RAM).

CAD See *computer-aided design.*

cascading style sheets (CSS) A list of statements (also known as rules) that define in one single location how HTML/XHTML elements are to be displayed.

cathode ray tube (CRT) monitor A type of monitor that was based on the original design of the television set and features a picture tube device and screen made up of millions of pixels, or tiny dots. These monitors have been largely replaced by LCD monitors.

CD See *compact disc.*

CD-ROM disc A compact disc format that is read-only.

CD-ROM drive A drive that reads compact discs (CDs).

CD-RW drive A drive that can both read data from and write data to CDs.

cellular phone (cell phone) A telephone that operates over a wireless network. Cell phones can also offer Internet access, text messaging, personal information management (PIM) features, and more.

central processing unit (CPU or processor) The part of the system unit of a computer that is responsible for data processing (or the "brains" of the computer); it is the largest and most important chip in the computer. The CPU controls all the functions performed by the computer's other components and processes all the commands issued to it by software instructions.

centralized A type of network design in which users are responsible neither for creating their own data backups nor for providing security for their computers; instead, those tasks are handled by a centralized server, software, and a system administrator.

CGI See *Common Gateway Interface.*

CGI script A computer program that conforms to the Common Gateway Interface (CGI) specification, which provides a method for sending data between end users (using browsers) and Web servers.

cgi-bin A directory where Common Gateway Interface (CGI) scripts are normally placed.

chat room An area on the Web where people come together to communicate online. The conversations are in real time and are visible to everyone in the chat room.

chip See *integrated circuit.*

CIDR See *classless inter-domain routing.*

circuit switching A method of communication in which a dedicated connection is formed between two points (such as two people on telephones) and the connection remains active for the duration of the transmission.

class A collection of descriptive variables and active functions that together define a set of common properties. Actual examples of the class are known as objects.

classless inter-domain routing (CIDR) An addressing scheme that allows a single IP address to represent several unique IP addresses by adding a network prefix to the end of the last octet.

clickstream data Information captured about each click that users make as they navigate a Web site.

client A computer that requests information from a server in a client/server network (such as your computer when you are connected to the Internet).

client/server model A way of describing typical network functions. Client computers (desktop PCs) request services, and servers provide (or serve up) those services to the clients.

client/server network A network that consists of client and server computers, in which the clients make requests of the server and the server returns the response.

client-side program A computer program that runs on the client computer and requires no interaction with a Web server.

clock cycle The "ticks," or base time unit, of the system clock; one cycle equals one "tick."

clock speed The steady and constant pace at which a computer goes through machine cycles, measured in hertz (Hz).

coaxial cable A single copper wire surrounded by layers of plastic insulation and sheathing used mainly in cable television and cable Internet service.

code editing The step in which programmers actually type the code into the computer.

coding The process of translating an algorithm into a programming language.

cold boot The process of starting a computer from a powered down or off state.

collaboration tool A product that allows you to connect easily with other individuals, often in remote locations, for the purposes of communicating or working together on a project.

command-driven interface The interface between user and computer in which the user enters commands to communicate with the computer system.

comment (remark) A plain English notation inserted into program code for documentation. The comment is never seen by the compiler.

commerce server A computer that hosts software that enables consumers to purchase goods and services over the Web. These servers generally use special security protocols to protect sensitive information (such as credit card numbers) from being intercepted.

Common Gateway Interface (CGI) Provides a methodology by which a browser can request that a program file be executed (or run) instead of just being delivered to the browser.

communications server A server that handles all communications between the network and other networks, including managing Internet connectivity.

compact disc (CD) A method of optical storage for digital data; originally developed for storing digital audio.

compilation The process by which code is converted into machine language, or the language the central processing unit (CPU) can understand.

compiler The program that understands both the syntax of the programming language and the exact structure of the central processing unit (CPU) and its machine language. It can "read" the source code and translate the source code directly into machine language.

completeness check A process that ensures that all database fields defined as "required" have data entered into them.

computational field (computed field) A numeric field in a database that is filled as the result of a computation.

computed field See *computational field.*

computer A data-processing device that gathers, processes, outputs, and stores data and information.

computer-aided design (CAD) A 3D modeling program used to create automated designs, technical drawings, and model visualizations.

computer forensics The application of computer systems and techniques to gather potential legal evidence; a law enforcement specialty used to fight high-tech crime.

computer literate Being familiar enough with computers that you understand their capabilities and limitations and know how to use them.

computer protocol A set of rules for accomplishing electronic information exchange. If the Internet is the information superhighway, then protocols are the driving rules.

connection-oriented protocol A protocol that requires two computers to exchange control packets, which set up the parameters of the data exchange session, before sending packets that contain data.

connectionless protocol A protocol that a host computer can use to send data over the network without establishing a direct connection with any specific recipient computer.

connectivity port A port that enables the computer (or other device) to be connected to other devices or systems such as networks, modems, and the Internet.

consistency check The process of comparing the value of data in a database field against established parameters to determine whether the value is reasonable.

consumer-to-consumer (C2C) E-commerce transactions between consumers through online sites such as eBay.com.

contrast ratio A measure of the difference in light intensity between the brightest white and the darkest black colors that a monitor can produce. If the contrast ratio is too low, colors tend to fade when the brightness is adjusted to a high or low setting.

Control (Ctrl) key One of the keys on a standard PC computer keyboard that is used in combination with other keys to perform shortcuts and special tasks.

control structure The general term used for keywords in a programming language that allow the programmer to control, or redirect, the flow of the program based on a decision.

control unit A component that controls the switches inside the central processing unit (CPU).

convergence The bringing together of a combination of features into one device.

cookie A small text file that some Web sites automatically store on a client computer's hard drive when a user visits the site.

course management software A program that provides traditional classroom tools over the Internet such as calendars and grade books, as well as areas for students to exchange ideas and information in chat rooms, discussion forums, and e-mail.

CPU See *central processing unit.*

CPU usage The percentage of time a central processing unit (CPU) is working.

cradle Connects a personal digital assistant (PDA) to a computer using either a universal serial bus (USB) port or a serial port.

CRM software See *customer relationship management (CRM) software.*

CRT See *cathode ray tube (CRT) monitor.*

CSMA/CD A method of data collision detection in which a node connected to the network listens (that is, has carrier sense) to determine that no other nodes are currently transmitting data signals; short for Carrier Sense Multiple Access with Collision Detection.

CSS See *cascading style sheets.*

Ctrl key See *Control (Ctrl) key.*

cursor The flashing | symbol on a computer monitor that indicates where the next character will be inserted.

cursor control keys (arrow keys) The set of special keys on a keyboard, generally marked by arrows, that move the cursor one space at a time, either up or down or left or right. Other cursor control keys move the cursor up or down

one full page or to the beginning or end of a line.

custom installation The process of installing only those features of a software program that a user wants on the hard drive.

customer relationship management (CRM) software A business program used for storing sales and client contact information in one central database.

cybercrime Any criminal action perpetrated primarily through the use of a computer.

cybercriminal An individual who uses computers, networks, and the Internet to perpetrate crime.

D

data Numbers, words, pictures, or sounds that represent facts, figures, or ideas.

data centralization Having all data in one central location (usually a database). Data centralization helps ensure data integrity by requiring data to be updated only in one place if the data changes.

data collision When two computers send data at the same time and the sets of data collide somewhere in the media.

data dictionary (database schema) A file that defines the name, data type, and length of each field in the database.

data files Files that contain stored data.

data inconsistency Any difference in data in lists caused when data exists in multiple lists and not all lists are updated when a piece of data changes.

data integrity The process of ensuring that data contained in a database is accurate and reliable.

data line surge suppressor A device that protects lines carrying data (such as phone or cable modem lines) from power surges.

data mart Small slices of a data warehouse.

data mining The process by which great amounts of data are analyzed and investigated to spot significant patterns or trends within the data that would otherwise not be obvious.

data packet See *packet*.

data plan A connectivity plan or text messaging plan in which data charges are separate from cell phone calling charges and are provided at rates different from voice calls.

data projector A device that is used to project images from a computer onto a wall or viewing screen.

data redundancy When the same data exists in more than one place in a database.

data staging A three-step process: extracting data from source databases, transforming (reformatting) the data, and storing the data in a data warehouse.

data transfer rate See *bandwidth*.

data type (field type) An attribute of a data field that determines what type of data can be stored in the database field or memory location.

data warehouse A large-scale electronic repository of data that contains and organizes in one place all the data related to an organization.

database administrator (database designer) An individual trained in the design, construction, and maintenance of databases.

database designer See *database administrator*.

database management system (DBMS) A type of specially designed application software (such as Oracle or Microsoft Access) that interacts with the user, other applications, and the database to capture and analyze data.

database query An inquiry the user poses to the database to extract a meaningful subset of data.

database schema See *data dictionary*.

database server A server that provides client computers with access to information stored in a database.

database software An electronic filing system best used for larger and more complicated groups of data that require more than one table and, where necessary, to group, sort, and retrieve data and generate reports.

date field A field in a database that holds date data such as birthdays and due dates.

DBMS See *database management system*.

DDoS attack See *distributed denial of service (DDoS) attack*.

debugger A tool that helps programmers step through a program as it runs to locate errors.

debugging The process of repeatedly running a program to find errors and to make sure the program behaves in the way it should.

decentralized A type of network in which users are responsible for creating their own data backups and for providing security for their computers.

decimal notation See *base 10 number system*.

decision point A point at which a computer program must choose from a set of different actions based on the value of its current inputs.

decision support system (DSS) A system designed to help managers develop solutions for specific problems.

decode To translate the program's instructions into commands the CPU can understand.

dedicated server A server used to fulfill one specific function (such as handling e-mail).

default value The value a database will use for fields unless the user enters another value.

denial of service (DoS) attack An attack that occurs when legitimate users are denied access to a computer system because a hacker is repeatedly making requests of that computer system to tie up its resources and deny legitimate users access.

derived class A class created on the basis of a previously existing class (i.e., base class). Derived classes inherit all of the member variables and methods of the base class from which they are derived.

desktop As its name implies, the computer's desktop puts at your fingertips all of the elements necessary for a productive work session and that are typically found on or near the top of a traditional desk, such as files and folders.

desktop publishing (DTP) software Programs for incorporating and arranging graphics and text to produce creative documents.

detail report A report generated with data from a database that shows the individual transactions that occurred during a certain time period.

device driver Software that facilitates the communication between a device and the operating system.

Device Manager A feature in the operating system (OS) that lets individuals view and change the properties of all devices attached to the computer.

DHCP See *Dynamic Host Configuration Protocol*.

DHTML See *Dynamic HyperText Markup Language*.

dial-up connection A connection to the Internet using a standard telephone line.

dial-up modem A device that converts (modulates) the digital signals the computer understands to the analog signals that can travel over phone lines. In turn, the computer on the other end also must have a modem to translate (demodulate) the received analog signal back to a digital signal that the receiving computer can understand.

digital divide The discrepancy between those who have access to the opportunities and knowledge computers and the Internet offers and those who do not.

digital home A home that has a computer(s) and other digital devices that are all connected to a home network.

digital ink An extension of the text-entry systems used on many mobile devices.

digital signal processor A specialized chip that processes digital information and transmits signals very quickly.

digital subscriber line (DSL) A type of connection that uses telephone lines to connect to the Internet and that allows both phone and data transmissions to share the same line.

digital subscriber line (DSL) modem A device that connects the computer data to the DSL line and then separates the types of signals into voice and data signals.

digital video disc (DVD) A method of optical storage for digital data that has greater storage capacity than compact discs.

digital video editing software A program for editing digital video.

directory A hierarchical structure that include files, folders, and drives used to create a more organized and efficient computer.

Disk Cleanup A Windows utility that removes unnecessary files from the hard drive.

disk defragmenter A utility that regroups related pieces of files on the hard disk, enabling faster retrieval of the data.

display screen See *monitor*.

distributed denial of service (DDoS) attack An automated attack that is launched from more than one zombie computer at the same time.

DNS server See *Domain Name System (DNS) server*.

docking station Hardware for connecting a portable computing device to printers, scanners, full-size monitors, mice, and other peripherals.

Document Object Model (DOM) A means to organize objects and page elements in a Web page. DOM defines every item on a Web page such as graphics, tables, and headers as an object.

documentation A description of the development and technical details of a computer program, including how the code works and how the user interacts with the program.

DOM See *Document Object Model*.

domain name A part of a Uniform Resource Locator (URL). Domain names consist of two parts: the site's host and a suffix that indicates the type of organization. (Example: popsci.com)

Domain Name System (DNS) server A server that contains location information for domains on the Internet and functions like a phone book for the Internet.

DoS attack See *denial of service (DoS) attack*.

dotted decimal number (dotted quad) One of the numbers in an Internet Protocol (IP) address.

DRAM See *dynamic RAM*.

drawing software (illustration software) Programs for creating or editing two-dimensional line-based drawings.

drive bay A special shelf inside of a computer that is designed to hold storage devices.

DSL See *digital subscriber line (DSL)*.

DSL/cable router A router that is specifically designed to connect to digital subscriber line (DSL) or cable modems.

DSL modem See *digital subscriber line (DSL) modem*.

DSS See *decision support system*.

DTP software See *desktop publishing software*.

dual-processor design A design that has two separate central processing unit (CPU) chips installed on the same system.

DVD drive A drive that enables the computer to read (play) digital video discs (DVDs) and compact discs (CDs).

DVD-RAM One of three competing technologies for rewritable DVDs.

DVD-ROM disc DVD format in which data can only be read and not written.

DVD+R/RW One of two recognized DVD formats that enables you to both read and rewrite data on the disc.

DVD-R/RW One of two recognized DVD formats that enables you to both read and rewrite data on the disc.

DVD ± RW drive A drive that enables the computer to read and write to DVDs.

Dvorak keyboard A leading alternative keyboard that puts the most commonly used letters in the English language on "home keys," the keys in the middle row of the keyboard. It is designed to reduce the distance your fingers travel for most keystrokes, increasing typing speed.

dynamic addressing The process of assigning Internet Protocol (IP) addresses when users log on using their Internet service provider (ISP). The computer is assigned an address from an available pool of IP addresses.

dynamic decision making A mechanism that allows a Web page to decide how to display itself, based on the choices the reader makes as he or she looks at the page.

Dynamic Host Configuration Protocol (DHCP) The protocol that handles dynamic addressing. Part of the Transmission Control Protocol/Internet Protocol (TCP/IP) protocol suite, DHCP takes a pool of IP addresses and shares them with hosts on the network on an as-needed basis.

Dynamic HyperText Markup Language (DHTML) A combination of Web development technologies including HTML, cascading style sheets, and a scripting language that are used to add interactivity to a Web site after the Web site has been loaded onto the client computer.

dynamic RAM (DRAM) The most basic type of random access memory (RAM); used in older systems or in systems for which cost is an important factor. DRAM offers access times on the order of 60 nanoseconds.

E

e-commerce (electronic commerce) The process of conducting business online for purposes ranging from fund-raising to advertising to selling products.

e-mail (electronic mail) Internet-based communication in which senders and recipients correspond.

e-mail client A software program that runs on the computer and is used to send and receive e-mail through the ISP's server.

e-mail server A server that processes and delivers incoming and outgoing e-mail.

e-mail virus A virus transmitted by e-mail that often uses the address book in the victim's e-mail system to distribute itself.

editor A tool that helps programmers as they enter code, highlighting keywords and alerting the programmers to typos.

EISA bus See *Extended Industry Standard Architecture (EISA) bus.*

electrical switch A device inside the computer that can be flipped between two states: 1 or 0, on or off.

electronic commerce See *e-commerce.*

electronic mail See *e-mail.*

element In HyperText Markup Language (HTML), elements are the tags and the text between the tags.

embedded computer A specially designed computer chip that resides inside other devices such as your car. These self-contained computer devices have their own programming and typically neither receive input from users nor interact with other systems.

encryption The process of encoding data (ciphering) so that only the person with a corresponding decryption key (the intended recipient) can decode (or decipher) and read the message.

encryption virus A malicious program that searches for common data files and compresses them into a file using a complex encryption key, rendering the files unusable.

Enterprise Resource Planning (ERP) system A large-scale software system that accumulates data from all parts of an organization for the purpose of providing key information as needed to efficiently manage all key business operations.

entertainment software Programs designed to provide users with entertainment; computer games make up the vast majority of entertainment software.

Entertainment Software Rating Board (ESRB) A self-regulatory body established in 1994 by the Entertainment Software Association that rates computer and video games according to the age appropriateness of content.

ergonomics How a user sets up his or her computer and other equipment to minimize risk of injury or discomfort.

ERP system See *Enterprise Resource Planning (ERP) system.*

error handling In programming, the instructions that the program runs if the input data is incorrect or another error is encountered.

Error-Checking A Windows utility that checks for lost files and fragments as well as physical errors on a hard drive.

ESRB See *Entertainment Software Rating Board.*

Ethernet network A network that uses the Ethernet protocol as the means (or standard) by which the nodes on the network communicate.

Ethernet port A port that is slightly larger than a standard phone jack and transfers data at speeds of up to 10,000 Mbps; used to connect a computer to a DSL/cable modem or a network.

event Every keystroke, every mouse click, and each signal to the printer creates an action, or event, in the respective device (keyboard, mouse, or printer) to which the operating system responds.

exception report A report that shows conditions that are unusual or that need attention by users of a system.

executable program The binary sequence (code) that instructs the central processing unit (CPU) to perform certain calculations.

expansion bus An electrical pathway that expands the capabilities of a computer by enabling a range of different expansion cards, such as video cards and sound cards, to communicate with the motherboard.

expansion card (adapter card) A circuit board with specific functions that augment the computer's basic functions and provide connections to other devices; examples include the sound card and video card.

expansion hub A device that connects to one port, such as a universal serial bus (USB) port, to provide additional new ports; similar to a multiplug extension cord for electrical appliances.

expert system A system designed to replicate the decision-making processes of human experts to solve specific problems.

export The process of putting data into an electronic file in a format that another application can understand.

ExpressCard An electronic card that when plugged into notebook computers provides functionality such as wireless network connections, USB ports, or FireWire ports.

Extended Industry Standard Architecture (EISA) bus An older, legacy expansion bus for connecting devices such as a mouse, modem, and sound cards.

Extensible HyperText Markup Language (XHTML) A standard established by the World Wide Web Consortium (W3C) that combines elements from both Extensible Markup Language (XML) and HyperText Markup Language (HTML). XHTML has much more stringent rules than HTML does regarding tagging.

Extensible Markup Language (XML) A language that enables designers to define their own tags, making it much easier to transfer data between Web sites and Web servers.

extension (file type) In a filename, the letters that follow the user-supplied filename after the dot (.); the extension identifies what kind of family of files the file belongs to or which application should be used to read the file.

external data source Any source not owned by the company that owns a decision support system such as customer demographic data purchased from third parties.

external hard drive An internal hard drive that is enclosed in a protective case to make it portable; the drive is connected to the computer with a data transfer cable and is often used to back up data.

extranet A portion of a company's intranet that is used to share business information with business partners such as vendors, suppliers, and customers.

F

FAQ See *frequently asked questions.*

FAT See *file allocation table.*

Favorites A feature in Microsoft Internet Explorer that places a marker of a Web site's Uniform Resource Locator (URL) in an easily retrievable list in the browser's toolbar. (Called Bookmarks in some browsers.)

fiber-optic cable A cable that transmits data at close to the speed of light along glass or plastic fibers.

Fiber-Optic Service (FiOS) Internet access that is done by transmitting data at the speed of light through glass or plastic fibers.

field A place where a category of information in a database is stored. Fields are displayed in columns.

field constraint Any property that must be satisfied for an entry to be accepted into the database field.

field name An identifying name assigned to each field in a database.

field size The maximum number of characters (or numbers) that a field in a database can contain.

field type See *data type.*

fifth-generation language (5GL) A computer language that uses natural language processing or expert systems to make the programming experience better matched to human thinking processes.

file A collection of related pieces of information stored together for easy reference; see also *table.*

file allocation table (FAT) An index of all sector numbers that the hard drive stores in a table to keep track of which sectors hold which files.

file compression utility A program that takes out redundancies in a file to reduce the file size.

file management The process by which humans or computer software provides organizational structure to a computer's contents.

file path The exact location of a file, starting with the drive in which the file is located, and including all folders, subfolders (if any), the filename, and extension. (Example: C:\Users\username\Documents\Illustrations\EBronte.jpg)

file server A computer deployed to provide remote storage space or to act as a repository for files that users can access.

File Transfer Protocol (FTP) A protocol used to upload and download files from one computer to another over the Internet.

filename The first part of the label applied to a file, similar to our first names; it is generally the name a user assigns to the file when saving it.

financial planning software Programs for managing finances, such as Intuit's Quicken and Microsoft Money, that include electronic checkbook registers and automatic bill payment tools.

FiOS See *Fiber-Optic Service.*

firewall A software program or hardware device designed to prevent unauthorized access to computers or networks.

FireWire (previously called IEEE 1394) An interface based on a standard developed by the Institute of Electrical and Electronics Engineers (IEEE) with a transfer rates of 400 megabits per second (Mbps) or 800 megabits per second (Mbps). Today, it is most commonly used to connect digital video devices such as digital cameras to the computer.

FireWire 400 (IEEE 1394) An interface port that transfers data at 400 Mbps.

FireWire 800 One of the fastest ports available, moving data at 800 Mbps.

first-generation language (1GL) The actual machine language of a central processing unit (CPU); the sequence

of bits—1s and 0s—that the CPU understands.

Flash A software product from Adobe for developing Web-based multimedia.

flash drive A drive that plugs into a universal serial bus (USB) port on a computer and stores data digitally. Also called *USB drive, jump drive,* or *thumb drive.*

flash memory Portable, nonvolatile memory.

flash memory card A form of portable storage; this removable memory card is often used in digital cameras, PMP players, and PDA/smartphones.

flat-panel (LCD) monitor A type of monitor that is lighter and more energy-efficient than a CRT monitor; often used with portable computers such as notebooks.

floppy disk drive A drive that reads and writes floppy disks; these drives have become legacy technology.

flowchart A visual representation of the patterns an algorithm comprises.

folder A collection of files stored on a computer.

footprint The amount of physical space on a surface that a computer takes up.

For Keyword in Visual Basic used with the Next keyword to implement a loop.

foreign key The primary key of another database table that is included for purposes of establishing relationships with another table.

fourth-generation language (4GL) A sophisticated level of programming language like a report generator or database query language.

frame A container designed to hold multiple data packets.

freeware Any copyrighted software that can be used for free.

frequently asked questions (FAQ) A list of answers to the most common questions.

front side bus (FSB) See *local bus.*

FTP See *File Transfer Protocol.*

full installation The process of installing all the files and programs from the distribution CD/DVD to the computer's hard drive.

function keys Shortcut keys that perform special tasks; they are sometimes referred to

as the "F" keys because they start with the letter F followed by a number, such as F1.

fuzzy logic A type of logic that allows the interjection of experiential learning into an equation by considering probabilities.

Gadget A mini-application that runs on the desktop, offering easy access to a frequently used tool such as weather or a calendar item.

gaming keyboard A type of keyboard that is optimized for playing specific video games and has special keys that perform special functions.

gateway See *wireless router*.

GHz See *gigahertz*.

gigabyte (GB) About a billion bytes.

gigahertz (GHz) One billion hertz.

Global Positioning System (GPS) A system of 21 satellites (plus three working spares), built and operated by the U.S. military, that constantly orbit the earth. They provide information to GPS-capable devices to pinpoint locations on the earth.

graphical user interface (GUI) Unlike the command- and menu-driven interfaces used earlier, GUIs display graphics and use the point-and-click technology of the mouse and cursor, making them much more user-friendly.

graphics processing unit (GPU) A specialized logic chip that is dedicated to quickly displaying and calculating visual data such as shadows, textures, and luminosity.

grayware Computer programs such as adware and spyware that are not destructive but are primarily intrusive, annoying, or objectional and download on your computer when you install or use other online content such as a freeware program, game, or utility.

hacker Anyone who unlawfully breaks into a computer system (whether an individual computer or a network).

handshaking The process of two computers exchanging control packets that set up the parameters of a data exchange.

hard drive A device that permanently stores programs and data. Hard drives can be located inside the system unit or can be attached to the system unit via a data port.

hardware Any part of the computer (or peripherals) you can physically touch.

head crash Impact of read/write head with magnetic platter of the hard drive that often results in data loss.

hexadecimal notation A number system that uses 16 digits to represent numbers; also called a base 16 number system.

hibernation mode A power-saving mode that puts the computer in a state of deep sleep. Pushing the power button awakens the computer from hibernation, at which time the computer reloads everything to the desktop exactly as it was before it went into hibernation.

historical data Data that illustrates trends over time.

History list A feature on a browser's toolbar that shows all the Web sites and pages visited over a certain period of time.

hits A list of sites (or results) that match an Internet search.

home page The main or opening page of a Web site.

hot spot A place where users can connect to the Internet wirelessly.

HTML See *HyperText Markup Language*.

HTML tag The bracketed information that surrounds elements of a Web page in order to convey information about them and define how their content is to be displayed.

HTML/XHTML embedded scripting language A client-side method of embedding programming language code directly within the HTML/XHTML code of a Web page.

HTTP See *HyperText Transfer Protocol*.

hub A simple amplification device that receives data packets and retransmits them to all nodes on the same network (not between different networks).

hybrid topology A topology comprised of several topologies and combined into one network.

hyperlink A type of specially coded text that, when clicked, enables a user to jump from one location, or Web page, to another

within a Web site or to another Web site altogether.

hyperlink field A field in a database that stores hyperlinks to Web pages.

hypertext Text that is linked to other documents or media (such as video clips, pictures, and so on).

HyperText Markup Language (HTML) A set of rules for marking up blocks of text so that a Web browser knows how to display them. It uses a series of tags that define the display of text on a Web page.

HyperText Transfer Protocol (HTTP) The protocol that allows files to be transferred from a Web server so that you can see them on your computer by using a browser.

I

ICANN See *Internet Corporation for Assigned Names and Numbers*.

icon A picture on a computer display that represents an object such as a software application or a file or folder.

IDE See *integrated development environment*.

identity theft The process by which someone uses personal information about someone else (such as the victim's name, address, and Social Security number) to assume the victim's identity for the purpose of defrauding others.

IE See *Internet Explorer*.

IEEE 1394 See *FireWire 400*.

if Keyword used in many programming languages (such as C and Java) for binary decisions.

illustration software See *drawing software*.

IM See *instant messaging*.

image editing software (photo editing software) Programs for editing photographs and other images.

impact printer A printer that has tiny hammer-like keys that strike the paper through an inked ribbon, thus making a mark on the paper; the most common impact printer is the dot-matrix printer.

imported Data that is brought into one program from another program or data source.

index See *sort.*

Industry Standard Architecture (ISA) bus An older, legacy expansion bus used for connecting devices such as the mouse, modem, and sound cards.

information Data that has been organized or presented in a meaningful fashion.

information assurance As defined by the NAS, "the set of measures intended to protect and defend information and information systems by ensuring their availability, integrity, authentication, confidentiality, and non-repudiation."

information system A system that includes data, people, procedures, hardware, and software and is used to gather and analyze information.

information technology (IT) The set of techniques used in processing and retrieving information.

inheritance The ability of a new class of objects to automatically pick up all of the data and methods of an existing class and then extend and customize those to fit its own specific needs.

initial value A beginning point in a loop.

inkjet printer A nonimpact printer that sprays tiny drops of ink onto paper.

inoculation A process used by antivirus software; compares old and current qualities of files to detect viral activity.

input device A hardware device used to enter, or input, data (text, images, and sounds) and instructions (user responses and commands) into a computer; input devices include keyboards and mice.

input form A form that provides a view of the data fields to be filled in a database, with appropriate labels to assist database users in populating the database.

instant messaging (IM) A program that enables users to communicate online in real time with others who are also online.

instruction set The collection of commands a specific central processing unit (CPU) can run.

integrated circuit (chip) A tiny region of semiconductor material such as silicon that supports a huge number of transistors.

integrated development environment (IDE) A development tool that helps programmers write, compile, and test their programs.

integrated help Documentation for a software product that is built directly into the software.

integrated software application A single software program that incorporates the most commonly used tools of many productivity software programs into one integrated stand-alone program.

internal hard drive A hard drive that is installed inside the system unit.

Internet A network of networks and the largest network in the world, connecting millions of computers from more than 100 countries.

Internet2 An ongoing project sponsored by hundreds of universities (supported by government and industry partners) to develop new Internet technologies and disseminate them as rapidly as possible to the rest of the Internet community. The Internet2 backbone supports extremely high-speed communications.

Internet backbone The main pathway of high-speed communications lines over which all Internet traffic flows.

Internet cache A section of your hard drive that stores information that you may need again for surfing (such as IP addresses and frequently accessed Web pages).

Internet Corporation for Assigned Names and Numbers (ICANN) The organization responsible for allocating IP addresses to network administrators to ensure they are unique and have not been assigned to other users.

Internet exchange point A device that allows different Internet service providers to exchange information between networks.

Internet Explorer (IE) A popular graphical browser from Microsoft Corporation for displaying different Web sites, or locations, on the Web; it can display pictures (graphics) in addition to text, as well as other forms of multimedia such as sound and video.

Internet hoax An e-mail message or Web site that contains information that is untrue with the purpose of deceiving others. A hoax can be harmlessly annoying, or it could be part of a fraudulent scam.

Internet Protocol (IP) A protocol for sending data between computers on the Internet.

Internet Protocol address (IP address) The means by which all computers connected to the Internet identify each other. It consists of a unique set of four numbers separated by dots such as 123.45.178.91.

Internet Protocol version 4 (IPv4) The original IP addressing scheme.

Internet Protocol version 6 (IPv6) A proposed IP addressing scheme that makes IP addresses longer, thereby providing more available IP addresses. It uses eight groups of 16-bit numbers.

Internet service provider (ISP) A company that connects individuals, groups, and other companies to the Internet.

interpreter A software program that translates source code into an intermediate form line by line. Each line is then executed as it is translated.

interrupt A signal that tells the operating system that either software or hardware is in need of immediate attention.

intranet A private corporate network that is used exclusively by company employees to facilitate information sharing, database access, group scheduling, videoconferencing, and other employee and customer collaborations.

IP address See *Internet Protocol address.*

ISA bus See *Industry Standard Architecture (ISA) bus.*

ISP See *Internet service provider.*

IT See *information technology.*

J

jam signal A special signal sent to all network nodes, alerting them that a data collision has occurred.

Java A platform-independent programming language that Sun Microsystems introduced in the early 1990s. It quickly became popular because its object-oriented model enables Java programmers to benefit from its set of existing classes.

Java applet A small Java-based program.

Java Server Pages (JSP) An extension of the Java servlet technology with dynamic scripting capability.

JavaScript A scripting language often used to add interactivity to Web pages. JavaScript is not as fully featured as Java, but its syntax, keywords, data types, and operators are a subset of Java's.

join query A database query that links (or joins) two database tables using a common field in both tables and extracts the relevant data from each.

JSP See *Java Server Pages*.

jump drive See *flash drive*.

kB See *kilobyte*.

kernel (supervisor program) The essential component of the operating system that is responsible for managing the processor and all other components of the computer system. Because it stays in random access memory (RAM) the entire time the computer is powered on, the kernel is called *memory resident*.

kernel memory The memory that the computer's operating system uses.

key field See *primary key field*.

key pair A public and a private key used for coding and decoding encrypted messages.

keyboard A hardware device used to enter typed data and commands into a computer.

keyword (1) A specific word a user wishes to query (or look for) in an Internet search. (2) A specific word that has a predefined meaning for a particular programming language.

kilobyte (kB) A unit of computer storage equal to approximately 1,000 bytes.

knowledge-based system A support system that provides additional intelligence that supplements the user's own intellect and makes a decision support system (DSS) more effective.

L

LAN See *local area network*.

laptop computer See *notebook computer*.

large scale networking (LSN) A program created by the U.S. government, the objective of which is to fund the research and development of cutting-edge networking

technologies. Major goals of the program are the development of enhanced wireless technologies and increased network throughput.

laser printer A nonimpact printer known for quick and quiet production and high-quality printouts.

Last Known Good Configuration A Windows feature that starts the computer by using the registry information that was saved during the last shutdown.

latency The process that occurs after the read/write head of the hard drive locates the correct track, then waits for the correct sector to spin to the read/write head.

LCD See *liquid crystal display*.

LCD monitor See *flat-panel monitor*.

legacy technology Comprises computing devices, software, and peripherals that use techniques, parts, and methods from an earlier time that are no longer popular.

Level 1 cache A block of memory that is built onto the central processing unit (CPU) chip for the storage of data or commands that have just been used.

Level 2 cache A block of memory that is located either on the central processing unit (CPU) chip or on a separate chip near the CPU. It takes somewhat longer to access than the CPU registers. Level 2 cache contains more storage area than Level 1 cache.

Level 3 cache On computers with Level 3 cache, the central processing unit (CPU) checks this area for instructions and data after it looks in Level 1 and Level 2 caches, but before it looks in random access memory (RAM); often designed to hold between 2 megabytes (MB) and 4 MB of data.

linear bus topology See *bus (linear bus) topology*.

Linux An open source operating system based on UNIX. Because of the stable nature of this operating system, it is often used on Web servers.

liquid crystal display (LCD) The technology used in flat-panel computer monitors.

listserv An electronic mailing list of e-mail addresses of people who are interested in a certain topic or area of interest.

live bookmark A bookmark that delivers updates to you as soon as they become

available using Really Simple Syndication (RSS).

local area network (LAN) A network in which the nodes are located within a small geographic area.

local bus (front side bus or FSB) Located on the motherboard, this bus runs between the central processing unit (CPU) and the main system memory.

logic bomb A computer virus that runs when a certain set of conditions is met such as when a specific date is reached on the computer's internal clock.

logical error A mistake in the design and planning of the algorithm itself rather than in the use of syntax in the coding.

logical port A virtual communications gateway or path that enables a computer to organize requests for information (such as Web page downloads and e-mail routing) from other networks or computers.

logical port blocking A condition in which a firewall is configured to ignore all incoming packets that request access to a certain port so that no unwanted requests will get through to the computer.

loop An algorithm that performs a repeating set of actions. A logical yes/no expression is evaluated. As long as the expression evaluates to TRUE (yes), the algorithm will perform the same set of actions and continue to loop around. When the answer to the question is no, the algorithm breaks free of the looping structure and moves on to the next step.

loop topology See *ring (loop) topology*.

LSN See *large scale networking*.

MAC address See *media access control (MAC) address*.

Mac OS Apple Inc.'s operating system. In 1984, Mac OS became the first operating system to incorporate the user-friendly point-and-click technology in a commercially affordable computer; based on the UNIX operating system.

machine cycle (processing cycle) The time it takes to fetch and execute a single machine-level instruction by the central processing unit (CPU).

machine language A set of instructions executed directly by the central processing unit (CPU).

macro A small computer program that executes a series of commands as if they were a single command.

macro virus A virus that is distributed by hiding it inside a macro.

magnetically shielded microphone A computer microphone that is designed to reduce interference from external sources and that usually plugs into a port on the sound card of the computer.

mainframe A large, expensive computer that support hundreds or thousands of users simultaneously and executes many different programs at the same time.

malware Software that is intended to render a system temporarily or permanently useless or to penetrate a computer system completely for purposes of information gathering. Examples include spyware, viruses, worms, and Trojan horses.

MAN See *metropolitan area network*.

management information system (MIS) A system that provides timely and accurate information that enables managers to make critical business decisions.

many-to-many relationship A database relationship in which one record in a database table (A) can have many related records in another table (B). And any record in table B can have many related records in table A.

mapping program Software that provides street maps and written directions to locations.

master boot record (MBR) A small program that runs whenever a computer boots up.

MB See *megabyte*.

MBR See *master boot record*.

media access control (MAC) address A physical address similar to a serial number on an appliance that is assigned to each network adapter; it is made up of six 2-digit numbers such as 01:40:87:44:79:A5.

megabyte (MB) A unit of computer storage equal to approximately 1 million bytes.

megahertz (MHz) A measure of processing speed equal to 1 million hertz.

memo field A text field in a database that is used to hold long pieces of text.

memory bound A system that is limited in how fast it can send data to the central processing unit (CPU) because there's not enough random access memory (RAM) installed.

memory card See *memory module*.

memory effect The result of a notebook battery needing to be completely used up before it is recharged or it won't hold as much charge as it originally did.

memory module (memory card) A small circuit board that holds a series of random access memory (RAM) chips.

menu A list of commands that displays on the screen.

menu-driven interface A user interface in which the user chooses a command from menus displayed on the screen.

meta search engine A search engine that searches other search engines rather than individual Web sites.

metadata Data that describes other data.

method (behavior) An action associated with a class of objects.

metropolitan area network (MAN) A wide area network (WAN) that links users in a specific geographic area (such as within a city or county).

MHz See *megahertz*.

microbrowser Software that makes it possible to access the Internet from a PDA/smartphone.

microphone (mic) A device that allows you to capture sound waves, such as those created by your voice, and transfer them to digital format on your computer

microprocessor A chip that contains a central processing unit (CPU).

Microsoft Disk Operating System (MS-DOS) A single-user, single-task operating system created by Microsoft. MS-DOS was the first widely installed operating system in personal computers.

Microsoft Visual Basic (VB) A powerful programming language used to build a wide range of Windows applications. VB's strengths include a simple, quick interface that is easy for a programmer to learn and use. It has grown from its roots in the language BASIC to become a sophisticated and full-featured object-oriented language.

Microsoft Windows A proprietary operating system (OS) developed by Microsoft

that is based on a visual interface. Windows is the most popular operating system (OS) for desktop computers.

MIME See *multipurpose Internet mail extensions*.

MIS See *management information system*.

MMS See *multimedia message service*.

mobile computing device A portable electronic tool such as a cell phone, personal digital assistant (PDA), or notebook.

mobile switching center A central location that receives cell phone requests for service from a base station.

model management system A type of software that assists in building management models in decision support systems (DSSs).

modem card An expansion card that provides the computer with a connection to the Internet via conventional phone lines.

modem port A port that uses a traditional telephone signal to connect a computer to the Internet.

monitor (display screen) A common output device that displays text, graphics, and video as soft copies (copies that can be seen only on-screen).

Moore's Law A prediction, named after Gordon Moore, the cofounder of Intel; states that the number of transistors on a CPU chip will double every two years.

motherboard A special circuit board in the system unit that contains the central processing unit (CPU), the memory (RAM) chips, and the slots available for expansion cards; all of the other boards (video cards, sound cards, and so on) connect to it to receive power and to communicate.

mouse A hardware device used to enter user responses and commands into a computer.

multi-core technology When a chip uses two or more processors on the same chip to enable the execution of two sets of instructions at the exact same time.

multidimensional database A database that stores data in multiple dimensions and is organized in a cube format.

multifunction printer (all-in-one printer) A device that combines the functions of a printer, scanner, fax machine, and copier into one machine.

multimedia Anything that involves one or more forms of media plus text.

multimedia message service (MMS) An extension of short message service (SMS) that enables messages that include text, sound, images, and video clips to be sent from a cell phone or PDA to other phones or e-mail addresses.

multimedia software Programs that include image, video, and audio editing software, animation software, and other specialty software required to produce computer games, animations, and movies.

multipartite virus Literally meaning "multipart" virus; a type of computer virus that attempts to infect both the boot sector and executable files at the same time.

multiplayer online game An online game in which play occurs among hundreds or thousands of other players over the Internet in a persistent or ever-on game environment. In some games, players can interact with other players through trading, chatting, or playing cooperative or combative mini-games.

multipurpose Internet mail extensions (MIME) A specification that was introduced in 1991 to simplify attachments to e-mail messages. All e-mail client software now uses this protocol for attaching files.

multitasking The capability of the operating system to allow a user to perform more than one task at a time.

multiuser operating system (network operating system) An operating system (OS) that enables more than one user to access the computer system at one time by efficiently juggling all the requests from multiple users.

N

NAK See *negative acknowledgment.*

nanoscience The study of molecules and nanostructures whose size ranges from 1 to 100 nanometers (one billionth of a meter).

nanotechnology The science revolving around the use of nanostructures to build devices on an extremely small scale.

NAS device See *network attached storage (NAS) device.*

NAT See *network address translation.*

natural language processing (NLP) system A system that enables users to communicate with computer systems using a natural spoken or written language as opposed to using computer programming languages.

negative acknowledgment (NAK) What computer Y sends to computer X if a packet is unreadable, indicating the packet was not received in understandable form.

netiquette The general rules of etiquette for Internet chat rooms and other online communication.

network A group of two or more computers (or nodes) that are configured to share information and resources such as printers, files, and databases.

network adapter A device that enables the computer (or peripheral) to communicate with the network using a common data communication language, or protocol.

network address translation (NAT) A process that firewalls use to assign internal Internet Protocol (IP) addresses on a network.

network administrator Someone who has training in computer and peripheral maintenance and repair, network design, and the installation of network software; installs new equipment, configures computers for users, repairs equipment, and assigns network access to users.

network architecture The design of a computer network, which includes both physical and logical design.

network attached storage (NAS) device A specialized device attached to a network whose sole function is to store and disseminate data.

network interface card (NIC) An expansion card that enables a computer to connect other computers or to a cable modem to facilitate a high-speed Internet connection.

network navigation device A device on a network such as a router, hub, and switch that moves data signals around the network.

network operating system (NOS) Software that handles requests for information, Internet access, and the use of peripherals for the rest of the network nodes.

network prefix The part of a network address under the CIDR IP addressing scheme. It consists of a slash and a number

added to the end of the last octet in an IP address.

network-ready device A device (such as a printer or external hard drive) that can be attached directly to a network instead of needing to attach to a computer on the network.

network topology The layout and structure of the network.

newsgroup A method of communication, similar to a discussion group or forum, in which people create threads, or conversations. In a thread, a newsgroup member will post messages and read and reply to messages from other members of the newsgroup.

NIC See *network interface card.*

NLP See *natural language processing (NLP) system.*

node A device connected to a network such as a computer, a peripheral (such as a printer), or a communications device (such as a modem).

nonimpact printer A printer that sprays ink or uses laser beams to make marks on the paper; the most common nonimpact printers are inkjet and laser printers.

nonvolatile storage Permanent storage, as in read-only memory (ROM).

normalization The processing of designing a database to reduce data redundancy.

NOS See *network operating system.*

notebook computer (laptop computer) A powerful mobile computing solution that offers a large display and all of the computing power of a full desktop system.

number system A set of rules for representing integer numbers with symbols.

numeric check A data validation routine that confirms only numbers are entered in a database field.

numeric field A field in a database that stores numbers.

numeric keypad The section of a keyboard that enables a user to enter numbers quickly.

O

object A variable in a program that is an example of a class. Each object in a specific

class is constructed from similar data and methods.

object field A field in a database that holds objects such as pictures, video clips, or entire documents.

object-oriented analysis An approach to software design that differs from the traditional "top-down" design. In OO analysis, programmers first identify all of the classes (collections of data and methods) that are required to completely describe the problem the program is trying to solve.

object-oriented database A database that stores data in objects, not in tables.

object query language (OQL) A query language that is used to extract information from an object-oriented database.

OC (optical carrier) line A transmission channel consisting of high-speed fiber optic lines.

octet Eight bits. For example, each of the four numbers in the dotted decimal notation of an Internet Protocol (IP) address is represented with an octet.

office support system (OSS) A system (such as Microsoft Office) designed to assist employees in accomplishing their day-to-day tasks and to improve communications.

offshore The practice of relocating technical work to countries outside the United States.

OLTP See *online transaction processing*.

omnidirectional microphone A microphone that picks up sounds from all directions at once; best for recording more than one voice.

one-to-many relationship A database relationship in which one record in a data table can have many related records in another data table.

one-to-one relationship A database relationship in which one record in a data table has only one related record in another data table.

online transaction processing (OLTP) The immediate processing of user requests or transactions.

open source software Program code made publicly available for free; it can be copied, distributed, or changed without the stringent copyright protections of proprietary software products.

open system A system whose designs are public, enabling access by any interested party.

operating system (OS) The system software that controls the way in which a computer system functions, including the management of hardware, peripherals, and software.

operator Any of the coding symbols that represents the fundamental actions of a computer language.

optical carrier line See *OC (optical carrier) line*.

optical media Portable storage devices that use a laser to read and write data such as CDs, DVDs, and Blu-ray discs.

optical mouse A mouse that uses an internal sensor or laser to control the mouse's movement. The sensor sends signals to the computer, telling it where to move the pointer on the screen.

OQL See *object query language*.

OS See *operating system*.

OSS See *office support system*.

output device A device that sends processed data and information out of a computer in the form of text, pictures (graphics), sounds (audio), or video.

P

P2P network See *peer-to-peer (P2P) network*.

P2P sharing See *peer-to-peer (P2P) sharing*.

packet (data packet) A small segment of data that is bundled to be sent over transmission media. Each packet contains the address of the computer or peripheral device to which it is being sent.

packet screening A process that involves examining incoming data packets to ensure they originated from or are authorized by valid users on the internal network.

packet sniffer A program that looks at (or sniffs) each data packet as it travels on the Internet.

packet switching A communications methodology in which data is broken into small chunks (called *packets*) and sent over

various routes at the same time. When the packets reach their destination, they are reassembled by the receiving computer.

page file The file the operating system builds on the hard drive when it is using virtual memory to enable processing to continue.

paging The process of swapping data or instructions between main memory (RAM) and auxiliary memory on the hard drive.

Palm OS An operating system, manufactured by Palm, for PDA/smartphones.

PAN See *personal area network*.

parallel port A port that sends data between devices in groups of bits at speeds of 92 kilobits per second (Kbps); this legacy technology was commonly used to connect printers to computers.

parallel processing A network computer environment in which each computer works on a portion of the same problem simultaneously.

Pascal The only modern computer language that was specifically designed as a teaching language; it is seldom taught now at the college level.

passive-matrix display A screen that uses computer monitor technology in which electrical current passes through a liquid crystal solution and charges groups of pixels, either in a row or a column, causing the screen to brighten with each pass of electrical current and subsequently to fade.

passive topology When data merely travels the entire length of the communications medium and is received by all network devices.

path (subdirectory) The information following the slash or colon in a Uniform Resource Locator (URL).

path separator The backslash mark (\) used by Microsoft Windows and DOS in filenames. Mac files use a colon (:), and UNIX and Linux use the forward slash (/) as the path separator.

patient simulator A computer-controlled mannequin that simulates human body functions and reactions. Patient simulators are used in training doctors, nurses, and emergency services personnel by simulating dangerous situations that would normally put live patients at risk.

PC card (or PCMCIA, short for Personal Computer Memory Card International Association) A credit card–sized card that enables users to add fax modems, network connections, wireless adapters, USB 2.0 and FireWire ports, and other capabilities primarily to notebook computers.

PCI bus See *Peripheral Component Interconnect (PCI) bus.*

PCMCIA See *PC card.*

PDA See *personal digital assistant.*

PDA/smartphone A mobile phone with advanced capabilities as a result of a convergence (or combination) of features such as camera, PMP, and PC-like features.

PDLC See *program development life cycle.*

peer-to-peer (P2P) network A network in which each node connected to the network can communicate directly with every other node on the network.

peer-to-peer (P2P) sharing The process of transferring files between computers.

Peripheral Component Interconnect (PCI) bus An expansion bus that connects directly to the central processing unit (CPU) and supports such devices as network cards and sound cards. This has been the standard bus for much of the past decade and continues to be redesigned to increase its performance.

peripheral device A device such as a monitor, printer, or keyboard that connects to the system unit through ports.

personal area network (PAN) A network used to connect wireless devices (such as Bluetooth-enabled devices) in close proximity to each other.

Personal Computer Memory Card International Association See *PC card.*

personal digital assistant (PDA) A small device that enables a user to carry digital information. Often called *palm computers* or *handhelds,* PDAs are about the size of a hand and usually weigh less than 5 ounces.

personal firewall A firewall specifically designed for home networks.

personal information manager (PIM) software Programs such as Microsoft Outlook or Lotus Organizer that strive to replace the various management tools

found on a traditional desk such as a calendar, address book, notepad, and to-do lists.

PGP See *Pretty Good Privacy.*

phishing The process of sending e-mail messages to lure Internet users into revealing personal information such as credit card or Social Security numbers or other sensitive information that could lead to identity theft.

photo editing software See *image editing software.*

physical memory The amount of random access memory (RAM) that is installed in a computer.

piggybacking The process of connecting to a wireless network without the permission of the owner of the network.

PIM software See *personal information manager (PIM) software.*

pipelining A technique that enables the central processing unit (CPU) to work on more than one instruction (or stage of processing) at a time, thereby boosting CPU performance.

pixel A single point that creates the images on a computer monitor. Pixels are illuminated by an electron beam that passes rapidly back and forth across the back of the screen so that the pixels appear to glow continuously.

platform The combination of a computer's operating system and processor. The two most common platform types are the PC and the Apple Macintosh.

platter A thin, round, metallic storage plate stacked onto the hard drive spindle.

player See *plug-in.*

plotter A large printer that uses a computer-controlled pen to produce oversize pictures that require precise continuous lines to be drawn such as those required in maps and architectural plans.

Plug and Play (PnP) The technology that enables the operating system, once it is booted up, to recognize automatically any new peripherals and configure them to work with the system.

plug-in (player) A small software program that "plugs in" to a Web browser to enable a specific function—for example,

to view and hear certain multimedia files on the Web.

PMP See *portable media player.*

PnP See *Plug and Play.*

podcast A clip of audio or video content that is broadcast over the Internet using compressed audio or video files in formats such as MP3s.

point of presence (POP) A bank of modems through which many users can connect to an Internet service provider (ISP) simultaneously.

polymorphic virus A virus that changes its virus signature (the binary pattern that makes the virus identifiable) every time it infects a new file. This makes it more difficult for antivirus programs to detect the virus.

POP See *point of presence.*

port An interface through which external devices are connected to the computer.

portability The capability to move a completed solution easily from one type of computer to another.

portable media player (PMP) A small portable device (such as an iPod) that enables you to carry your MP3 or other media files around with you.

portal A subject directory on the Internet that is part of a larger Web site that focuses on offering its visitors a variety of information such as the weather, news, sports, and shopping guides.

positive acknowledgment (ACK) What computer Y sends when it receives a data packet that it can read from computer X.

possessed object Any object that a user carries to identify himself and that grants him access to a computer system or computer facility.

power-line network A network that uses the electrical wiring in a building to connect the nodes in the network.

power-on self-test (POST) The first job the basic input/output system (BIOS) performs, ensuring that essential peripheral devices are attached and operational. This process consists of a test on the video card and video memory, a BIOS identification process (during which the BIOS version, manufacturer, and data are displayed on the monitor), and a

memory test to ensure memory chips are working properly.

power supply A power supply regulates the wall voltage to the voltages required by computer chips; it is housed inside the system unit.

preemptive multitasking When the operating system processes the task assigned a higher priority before processing a task that has been assigned a lower priority.

presentation software An application program for creating dynamic slide shows such as Microsoft PowerPoint or Apple Keynote.

pretexting The act of creating an invented scenario (the pretext) to convince someone to divulge information.

Pretty Good Privacy (PGP) A popular public-key encryption package.

primary key field (key field) The unique field that each database record in a table must have.

print server A server that manages all client-requested printing jobs for all printers on the network.

printer A common output device that creates tangible or hard copies of text and graphics.

private key One-half of a pair of binary files that is needed to decrypt an encrypted message. The private key is kept only by the individual who created the key pair and is never distributed to anyone else. The private key is used to decrypt messages created with the corresponding public key.

private-key encryption A procedure in which only the two parties involved in sending a message have the code. This could be a simple shift code where letters of the alphabet are shifted to a new position.

private system See *proprietary (private) system*.

problem statement A clear description of which tasks the computer program must accomplish and how the program will execute these tasks and respond to unusual situations. It is the starting point of programming work.

processing Manipulating or organizing data into information.

processing cycle See *machine cycle*.

processor See *central processing unit*.

processor speed The number of operations (or cycles) the processor completes each second, measured in hertz (Hz).

productivity software Programs that enable a user to perform various tasks generally required in home, school, and business. Examples include word processing, spreadsheet, presentation, personal information management (PIM), and database programs.

program A series of instructions to be followed by a computer to accomplish a task.

program development life cycle (PDLC) A number of stages, from conception to final deployment, a programming project follows.

program file A file that is used in the running of software programs and does not store data.

programming The process of translating a task into a series of commands a computer will use to perform that task.

programming language A kind of "code" for the set of instructions the central processing unit (CPU) knows how to perform.

project management software An application program such as Microsoft Project that helps project managers generate charts and tables used to manage aspects of a project.

proprietary (private) system A system whose design is not made available for public access.

protocol (1) A set of rules for exchanging data and communication. (2) The first part of the Uniform Resource Locator (URL) indicating the set of rules used to retrieve the specified document. The protocol is generally followed by a colon, two forward slashes, www (indicating World Wide Web), and then the domain name.

prototype A small model of a computer program, often built at the beginning of a large project.

proxy server Acts as a go-between for computers on the internal network and the external network (the Internet).

pseudocode A text-based approach to documenting an algorithm.

public domain The status of software (or other created works) that are not protected by copyright.

public key One-half of a pair of binary files that is needed to decrypt an encrypted message. After creating the keys, the user distributes the public key to anyone he wishes to send him encrypted messages. A message encrypted with a public key can be unencrypted only using the corresponding private key.

public-key encryption A procedure in which the key for coding is generally distributed as a public key that may be placed on a Web site. Anyone wishing to send a message codes it using the public key. The recipient decodes the message with a private key.

Q

quarantining The placing of a computer virus by antivirus software in a secure area on the hard drive so that it won't spread infection to other files.

query The process of requesting information from a database.

query language A language used to retrieve and display records. A query language consists of its own vocabulary and sentence structure, used to frame the requests.

QWERTY keyboard A keyboard that gets its name from the first six letters on the top-left row of alphabetic keys on the keyboard.

R

RAD See *rapid application development*.

radio frequency identification tag (RFID tag) A tag that looks like a sticker or label, is attached to a batch of merchandise, and contains a microchip that holds a unique sequence of numbers used to identify the product to which it is attached.

random access memory (RAM) The computer's temporary storage space or short-term memory. It is located as a set of chips on the system unit's motherboard, and its capacity is measured in megabytes or gigabytes.

range check A type of data validation used in databases to ensure that a value entered falls within a specified range (such

as requiring a person's age to fall in a range of between 1 and 120).

rapid application development (RAD) A method of system development in which developers create a prototype first and generate system documents as they use and remodel the product.

read-only memory (ROM) A set of memory chips located on the motherboard that stores data and instructions that cannot be changed or erased; it holds all the instructions the computer needs to start up.

read/write head The mechanism that retrieves (reads) and records (writes) the magnetic data to and from a data disk. They move from the outer edge of the spinning platters to the center, up to 50 times per second.

real-time operating system (RTOS) A program with a specific purpose that must guarantee certain response times for particular computing tasks, or the machine's application is useless. Real-time operating systems are found in many types of robotic equipment.

real-time processing The process of updating a database (or information system) immediately as changes are made.

Really Simple Syndication (RSS) technology An XML-based format that allows frequent updates of content on the World Wide Web.

record A collection of related fields in a database.

Recycle Bin A folder on a Windows desktop in which deleted files from the hard drive are held until permanently purged from the system.

referential integrity For each value in the foreign key of one table, there is a corresponding value in the primary key of the related table.

register A special memory storage area built into the central processing unit (CPU).

registry A portion of the hard drive containing all the different configurations (settings) used by the Windows operating system (OS) as well as by other applications.

relation A database table that contains related data.

relational algebra The use of English-like expressions that have variables and operations, much like algebraic equations.

relational database A database that organizes data in table format by logically grouping similar data into relations (or tables) that contain related data.

relationship In relational databases, the link between tables that defines how the data are related.

remark See *comment*.

repeater A device that is installed on a long cable run to amplify a signal.

resolution The clearness or sharpness of an image, which is controlled by the number of pixels displayed on the screen.

response time The measurement (in milliseconds) of the time it takes for a pixel to change color; the lower the response time, the smoother moving images will appear on the monitor.

restore point The snapshot of the entire system's settings that Windows creates every time the computer is started, or when a new application or driver is installed.

reusability The ability to reuse existing classes of objects from other projects, enabling programmers to produce new code quickly.

RFID tag See *radio frequency identification tag*.

ribbon A group of icons collected for easy access.

ring (loop) topology A group of networked computers and peripherals that are laid out in a logical circle. Data flows around the circle from device to device in one direction only.

ROM See *read-only memory*.

root directory The top level of the filing structure in a computer system. In Windows computers, the root directory of the hard drive is represented as C:\.

root DNS server A group of servers maintained throughout the Internet to which ISP Web servers connect to locate the master listings for an entire top-level domain.

router A device that routes packets of data between two or more networks.

RSS See *Really Simple Syndication (RSS) technology*.

RTOS See *real-time operating system*.

runtime error An error in the problem logic that is only caught when the program executes.

S

S-HTTP See *Secure HyperText Transfer Protocol*.

Safe mode A special diagnostic mode designed for troubleshooting errors that occur during the boot process.

sampling rate The number of times per second a signal is measured and converted to a digital value. Sampling rates are measured in kilobits per second.

SAN See *storage area network*.

satellite Internet A way to connect to the Internet using a small satellite dish, which is placed outside the home and connects to a computer with coaxial cable. The satellite company then sends the data to a satellite orbiting the Earth. The satellite, in turn, sends the data back to the satellite dish and to the computer.

scalable network A type of network that enables the easy addition of users without affecting the performance of the other network nodes (computers or peripherals).

screen saver An animated image that appears on a computer monitor when no user activity has been sensed for a certain time.

script A list of commands (mini-programs or macros) that can be executed on a computer without user interaction.

script kiddy An amateur hacker who lacks sophisticated computer skills—typically teenagers, who don't create programs used to hack into computer systems but instead use tools created by skilled hackers that enable unskilled novices to wreak the same havoc as professional hackers.

scripting language A simple programming language that is limited to performing a specific set of specialized tasks.

scrollbar On the desktop, the bar that appears at the side or bottom of the window and controls which part of the information is displayed on the screen.

SDLC See *system development life cycle*.

search engine A set of programs that searches the Web for specific words (or keywords) you wish to query (or look for)

and then returns a list of the Web sites on which those keywords are found.

second-generation language (2GL) Also known as an assembly language. 2GLs deal directly with system hardware but provide acronyms that are easier for human programmers to work with.

second-level domain A domain that falls within top-level domains of the Internet. Each second-level domain needs to be unique within that particular domain but not necessarily unique to all top-level domains.

sector A section of a hard drive platter, wedge-shaped from the center of the platter to the edge.

Secure HyperText Transfer Protocol (S-HTTP) An extension to the HTTP protocol that supports sending data securely over the Web.

Secure Sockets Layer (SSL) A protocol that provides for the encryption of data transmitted using the Internet. The current versions of all major Web browsers support SSL.

seek time The time it takes for the hard drive's read/write heads to move over the surface of the disk, between tracks, to the correct track.

select query A query that displays a subset of data from a table based on the criteria the user specifies.

semiconductor Any material that can be controlled to either conduct electricity or act as an insulator (not allowing electricity to pass through).

serial port A port that enables the transfer of data, one bit at a time, over a single wire at speeds of up to 56 kilobits per second (Kbps); this legacy technology was used to connect external modems to the computer.

server A computer that provides resources to other computers on a network.

server-side program A program that is run on a Web server as opposed to inside a Web browser.

service pack See *software update.*

shareware Software that enables users to "test" the software by running it for a limited time free of charge.

shielded twisted pair (STP) cable Twisted pair cable that contains a layer of foil shielding to reduce interference.

short message service (SMS) Technology that enables short text messages (up to 160 characters) to be sent over mobile networks.

Sidebar In Windows Vista, the pane on the right side of the desktop that organizes gadgets for easy access.

sign bit In the binary (base 2) system, the representation of a negative number; usually the left-most bit.

simple mail transfer protocol (SMTP) A protocol for sending e-mail along the Internet to its destination.

simulation software Software often used for training purposes and that allows the user to experience or control an event as if it is reality.

single-user, multitask operating system An operating system that allows only one person to work on a computer at a time, but the system can perform a variety of tasks simultaneously.

single-user, single-task operating system An operating system that allows only one user to work on a computer at a time to perform just one task at a time.

sleep mode A low-power mode for electronic devices that reduces power consumption while the device is not in use and allows the user to resume working without rebooting.

smartphone A device that combines the functionality of a cell phone, a PMP, and a PDA into one unit.

SMS See *short message service.*

SMTP See *simple mail transfer protocol.*

social networking site A system of personal networks where individuals are invited or allowed to join and that are supported by electronic tools such as e-mail, instant messaging, and file transfer. Members create personal profiles, exchange information, and find others with similar interests.

software The set of computer programs or instructions that tells the computer what to do and enables it to perform different tasks.

software license An agreement between the user and the software developer that must be accepted before installing the software on a computer.

software piracy Violating a software license agreement by copying an application onto more computers than the license agreement permits.

software suite A collection of software programs that have been bundled together as a package.

software update (service pack) A downloadable software module that repairs errors identified in commercial program code.

sort (index) The process of organizing a database into a particular order.

sound card An expansion card that attaches to the motherboard inside the system unit and that enables the computer to produce sounds by providing a connection for the speakers and microphone.

source code The instructions programmers write in a higher-level language.

spam Unwanted or junk e-mail.

spam filter An option you can select in your e-mail account that places known or suspected spam messages into a folder other than your inbox.

speaker An output device for sound.

speech-recognition software (voice-recognition software) Software that translates spoken words into typed text.

spider A program that constantly collects information on the Web, following links in Web sites and reading Web pages. Spiders get their name because they crawl over the Web using multiple "legs" to visit many sites simultaneously.

spooler A program that helps coordinate all print jobs being sent to the printer at the same time.

spreadsheet software An application program such as Microsoft Excel or Lotus 1-2-3 that enables a user to do calculations and numerical analyses easily.

spyware An unwanted piggyback program that downloads with the software you want to install from the Internet and then runs in the background of your system.

SQL See *structured query language.*

SRAM See *static RAM.*

SSL See *Secure Sockets Layer.*

star topology An active (data is retransmitted) topology in which the nodes connect to a central communications device called a *switch*. The switch receives a signal from the sending node and retransmits it to the node that should receive it.

statement A sentence in programming code.

static addressing A means of assigning an Internet Protocol (IP) address that never changes and is most likely assigned manually by a network administrator.

static RAM (SRAM) A type of random access memory that is faster than DRAM. In SRAM, more transistors are used to store a single bit, but no capacitor is needed.

stealth virus A virus that temporarily erases its code from the files where it resides and hides in the active memory of the computer.

storage area network (SAN) A network specifically designed to store and disseminate large amounts of data to client computers or servers.

streaming audio Technology that enables audio files to be fed to a browser continuously. This lets users avoid having to download an entire file before listening.

streaming video Technology that enables video files to be fed to a browser continuously. This lets users avoid having to download the entire file before viewing.

structured (analytical) data Data that can be identified and classified as discrete bits of information (such as a name or phone number).

structured query language (SQL) The most popular database query language today.

stylus A pen-shaped device used to tap or write on touch-sensitive screens.

subdirectory See *path*.

subject directory A structured outline of Web sites organized by topics and subtopics.

subnotebook See *ultraportable*.

subwoofer A special type of speaker designed to more faithfully reproduce low-frequency sounds.

summary report A report that summarizes data in some fashion (such as a total of the day's concession sales at an amusement park). Also known as a *summary data report*.

supercomputer A specially designed computer that can perform complex calculations extremely rapidly; used in situations in which complex models requiring intensive mathematical calculations are needed (such as weather forecasting or atomic energy research).

surge protector A device that protects computers and other electronic devices from power surges.

surround (cage) A device that encloses the system unit of a computer and makes it difficult to access or steal.

surround sound speakers Speaker systems set up in such a way that they surround an entire area (and the people in it) with sound.

swap file (page file) A temporary storage area on the hard drive where the operating system "swaps out" or moves the data or instructions from random access memory (RAM) that have not recently been used. This process takes place when more RAM space is needed.

switch A device for transmitting data on a network. A switch makes decisions, based on the media access control (MAC) address of the data, as to where the data is to be sent.

Symbian OS An operating system for full-featured cell phones.

synchronizing The process of updating data so that the files on different systems are the same.

syntax An agreed-upon set of rules defining how a programming language must be structured.

syntax error An error that violates the strict, precise set of rules that defines a programming language.

system clock The computer's internal clock.

system development life cycle (SDLC) An organized process (or set of steps) for developing an information processing system.

system evaluation The process of looking at a computer's subsystems, what they do, and how they perform to determine whether the computer system has the right hardware components to do what the user ultimately wants it to do.

system file Any of the main files of an operating system.

system requirements The set of minimum storage, memory capacity, and processing standards recommended by the software manufacturer to ensure proper operation of a software application.

System Restore A utility in Windows that restores system settings to a specific previous date when everything was working properly.

system software The set of programs that enables a computer's hardware devices and application software to work together; it includes the operating system and utility programs.

system unit The metal or plastic case that holds all the physical parts of the computer together, including the computer's processor (its brains), its memory, and the many circuit boards that help the computer function.

T

T line A high-speed fiber-optic communications line that is designed to provide much higher throughput than conventional voice (telephone) and data (DSL or cable) lines.

table (file) In database terminology, a group of related records.

Tablet PC A notebook computer designed specifically to work with handwriting recognition technology.

tag A keyword or label that you use to categorize your favorite Web sites.

Task Manager utility A Windows utility that shows programs currently running and permits you to exit nonresponsive programs when you click End Task.

Task Scheduler utility A Windows utility that enables you to schedule tasks to run automatically at predetermined times with no interaction necessary on your part.

tax preparation software An application program such as Intuit's TurboTax and H&R Block's TaxCut for preparing state and federal taxes. Each program offers a complete set of tax forms and instructions as well as expert advice on how to complete each form.

TCP See *Transmission Control Protocol*.

TCP/IP See *Transmission Control Protocol/Internet Protocol*.

Telnet Both a protocol for connecting to a remote computer and a TCP/IP service that runs on a remote computer to make it accessible to other computers.

template A form included in many productivity applications that provides the basic structure for a particular kind of document, spreadsheet, or presentation.

terabyte 1,099,511,627,776 bytes or 2^{40} bytes.

terminator A device that absorbs a signal so that it is not reflected back onto parts of the network that have already received it.

test condition A check to see whether a loop is completed.

testing plan In the problem statement, a plan that lists specific input numbers that the program would typically expect the user to enter. It then lists the precise output values that a perfect program would return for those input values.

text field A database field that can hold any combination of alphanumeric data (letters or numbers) and is most often used to hold text.

thermal printer A printer that works either by melting wax-based ink onto ordinary paper (in a process called *thermal wax transfer printing*) or by burning dots onto specially coated paper (in a process called *direct thermal printing*).

third-generation language (3GL, or high-level language) A computer language that uses symbols and commands to help programmers tell the computer what to do.

thrashing A condition of excessive paging in which the operating system becomes sluggish.

three-way handshake A process used by the Transmission Control Protocol (TCP) to establish a connection.

throughput The actual speed of data transfer that is achieved. It is usually less than the data transfer rate and is measured in megabits per second (Mbps).

thumb drive See *flash drive*.

time bomb A virus that is triggered by the passage of time or on a certain date.

time-variant data Data that doesn't all pertain to one period in time—for example, data in a data warehouse.

TLD See *top-level domain*.

toggle key A keyboard key whose function changes each time it's pressed; usually it "toggles," or switches, between two (but sometimes more) functions.

token A special data packet used to pass data in a token-ring network.

token method The access method that ring networks use to avoid data collisions.

token-ring topology A network layout in which data is passed using a special data packet called a *token*.

toolbar A group of icons collected for easy access.

top-down design A systematic approach in which a programming problem is broken down into a series of high-level tasks.

top-level domain (TLD) The suffix, often of three letters, in the domain name (such as .com or .edu) that indicates the kind of organization the host is.

touch-screen monitor A type of monitor (or display in a notebook or PDA) that accepts input from a user touching the screen.

touchpad A small, touch-sensitive screen at the base of a notebook keyboard. To use the touchpad, you simply move your finger across the pad to direct the cursor.

TPS See *transaction processing system*.

track A concentric circle that serves as a storage area on a hard disk drive platter.

trackball mouse A mouse with a rollerball on top instead of on the bottom. Because you move the trackball with your fingers, it doesn't require much wrist motion, so it's considered healthier for your wrists than a traditional mouse.

trackpoint device A small, joystick-like nub that enables you to move the cursor with the tip of your finger.

transaction processing system (TPS) A system used to keep track of everyday business activities (such as sales of products).

transceiver In a wireless network, a device that translates the electronic data that needs to be sent along the network into radio waves and then broadcasts these radio waves to other network nodes.

transistor An electrical switch that is built out of layers of a special type of material called a *semiconductor*.

Transmission Control Protocol/Internet Protocol (TCP/IP) The main suite of protocols used on the Internet.

Transmission Control Protocol (TCP) A protocol that prepares data for transmission and provides for error checking and resending lost data.

transmission media The radio waves or cable that transport data on a network.

Trojan horse A computer program that appears to be something useful or desirable (such as a game or a screen saver), but at the same time does something malicious in the background without the user's knowledge.

twisted pair cable Cables made of copper wires that are twisted around each other and are surrounded by a plastic jacket (such as traditional home phone wire).

U

UDP See *User Datagram Protocol*.

ultraportable (ultramobile or subnotebook) A category of computers consisting of notebooks that weigh 2 pounds or less.

Unicode An encoding scheme that uses 16 bits instead of the 8 bits used in ASCII. Unicode can represent more than 65,000 unique character symbols, enabling it to represent the alphabets of all modern languages and all historic languages and notational systems.

unidirectional microphone A microphone that picks up sound from only one direction; best for recording podcasts with a single voice or making phone calls over the Internet.

Uniform Resource Locator (URL) A Web site's unique address such as www.microsoft.com.

uninterruptible power supply (UPS) A device designed to power a computer from large batteries for a brief period during a loss of electrical power.

universal serial bus (USB) port A port that can connect a wide variety of peripheral devices to the computer, including keyboards, printers, mice, smartphones, PDAs, flash drives, and digital cameras.

UNIX An operating system originally conceived in 1969 by Ken Thompson and Dennis Ritchie of AT&T's Bell Labs. In 1974, the UNIX code was rewritten in the standard programming language C. Today there are various commercial versions of UNIX.

unshielded twisted pair (UTP) cable The most popular transmission media option for Ethernet networks. UTP cable is composed of four pairs of wires that are twisted around each other to reduce electrical interference.

unstructured data Nontraditional data such as audio clips (including MP3 files), video clips, pictures, and extremely large documents. Unstructured data is also known as a *binary large object* (BLOB) because it is actually encoded in binary form.

UPS See *uninterruptible power supply*.

URL See *Uniform Resource Locator*.

USB 2.0 port An external bus that supports a data throughput of 480 Mbps; these buses are backward-compatible with buses using the original universal serial bus (USB) standard.

USB drive See *flash drive*.

USB port See *universal serial bus (USB) port*.

User Datagram Protocol (UDP) A protocol that prepares data for transmission but has no re-sending capabilities.

user interface Part of the operating system that enables individuals to interact with the computer.

utility program A small program that performs many of the general housekeeping tasks for the computer such as system maintenance and file compression.

UTP cable See *unshielded twisted pair (UTP) cable*.

V

vacuum tube Used in early computers, a vacuum tube acts as a computer switch by allowing or blocking the flow of electrical current.

validation The process of ensuring that data entered into a database is correct (or at least reasonable) and complete.

validation rule A rule that is set up in a database to alert the user to possible wrong entries.

variable A name or symbol that stands for a value.

variable declaration A line of programming code that alerts the operating system that the program needs to allocate storage space in random access memory (RAM) for the variable.

VB See *Microsoft Visual Basic*.

VBScript A subset of Visual Basic; also used to introduce interactivity to Web pages.

vertical market software Software that is developed for and customized to a specific industry's needs (such as a wood inventory system for a sawmill) as opposed to software that is useful across a range of industries (such as word-processing software).

video adapter See *video card*.

video blog See *video log*.

video card (video adapter) An expansion card that is installed inside a system unit to translate binary data (the 1s and 0s the computer uses) into the images viewed on the monitor.

video log (vlog or video blog) A personal online journal that uses video as the primary content in addition to text, images, and audio.

video memory RAM that is included as part of a video card.

viewing angle The distance you can move to the side of (or above or below) the monitor before the image quality degrades to unacceptable levels.

virtual memory The space on the hard drive where the operating system stores data if there isn't enough random access memory (RAM) to hold all of the programs you're currently trying to run.

virtual private network (VPN) A network that uses public communication pathways (usually the Internet) to provide branch offices or employees who are not at the office with secure access to the company network. VPNs maintain privacy by using secure data communication protocols.

virtual reality program Software that turns an artificial environment into a realistic experience.

virus A computer program that attaches itself to another computer program

(known as the host program) and attempts to spread itself to other computers when files are exchanged.

virus signature A portion of the virus code that is unique to a particular computer virus and makes it identifiable by antivirus software.

visual programming A technique for automatically writing code when the programmer says the layout is complete. It helps programmers produce a final application much more quickly.

vlog See *video log*.

Voice over Internet Protocol (VoIP) The transmission of phone calls over the same data lines and networks that make up the Internet. Also called *Internet telephony*.

voice-recognition software See *speech-recognition software*.

VoIP See *Voice over Internet Protocol*.

volatile storage Temporary storage such as in random access memory (RAM); when the power is off, the data in volatile storage is cleared out.

VPN See *virtual private network*.

W

WAN See *wide area network*.

WAP See *wireless access point*; *Wireless Application Protocol*.

warm boot The process of restarting the system while it's powered on.

Web See *World Wide Web*.

Web 2.0 Tools and Web-based services that emphasize online collaboration and sharing among users.

Web-based application software A program that is hosted on a Web site and does not require installation on the computer.

Web browser (browser) Software installed on a computer system that allows individuals to locate, view, and navigate the Web.

Web-enabled The capability of a device such as a desktop computer, notebook, or mobile device to access the Internet.

Web page authoring software Programs you can use to design interactive Web

pages without knowing any HyperText Markup Language (HTML) code.

Web server A computer running a specialized operating system that enables it to host Web pages (and other information) and provide requested Web pages to clients.

Web service A program used by a Web site to make information available to other Web sites.

Web site A location on the Web.

webcam A small camera that usually sits on top of a computer monitor (connected to the computer by a cable) or is built into a notebook computer and is usually used to transfer live video.

webcast The broadcast of audio or video content over the Internet. Unlike a podcast, a webcast is not updated automatically.

Weblog A personal log, or collection of journal entries, that is posted on the Web.

white-hat hacker A hacker who breaks into systems just for the challenge of it (and who doesn't wish to steal or wreak havoc on the systems). Such hackers tout themselves as experts who are performing a needed service for society by helping companies realize the vulnerabilities that exist in their systems.

whole-house surge protector A surge protector that is installed on (or near) the breaker panel of a home and protects all electronic devices in the home from power surges.

wide area network (WAN) A network made up of local area networks (LANs) connected over long distances.

WiFi (Wireless Fidelity) The 802.11 standard for wireless data transmissions established by the Institute of Electrical and Electronics Engineers (IEEE).

wiki A type of Web site that allows anyone visiting the site to change its content by adding, removing, or editing the content.

wildcard A symbol used in an Internet search when the user is unsure of the keyword's spelling or when a word can be spelled in different ways or can contain

different endings. The asterisk (*) is used to replace a series of letters and the percent sign (%) to replace a single letter in a word.

window In a graphical user interface, a rectangular box that contains programs displayed on the screen.

Windows Explorer The main tool for finding, viewing, and managing the contents of your computer by showing the location and contents of every drive, folder, and file.

Windows key A key specific to the Windows operating system. Used alone, it opens the Start menu; however, it's used most often in combination with other keys to perform shortcuts.

Windows Mobile An operating system for PDA/smartphones.

wireless access point (WAP) A device similar to a switch in an Ethernet network. It takes the place of a wireless network adapter and helps relay data between network nodes.

Wireless Application Protocol (WAP) The standard that dictates how handheld devices will access information on the Internet.

Wireless Internet service provider (wireless ISP) An ISP that provides service to wireless devices such as PDA/smartphones.

Wireless Markup Language (WML) A format for writing content viewed on a cellular phone or personal digital assistant (PDA) that is text-based and contains no graphics.

wireless media Communications media that do not use cables but instead rely on radio waves to communicate.

wireless network A network that uses radio waves instead of wires or cable as its transmission medium.

wireless network adapter A device that is required for each node on a wireless network for the node to be able to communicate with other nodes on the network.

wireless network interface card (wireless NIC) A card installed in a system that connects with wireless access points on the network.

wireless router (gateway) A device that combines the capabilities of a wired router with the ability to receive wireless signals.

wizard A step-by-step guide that walks you through the necessary steps to complete a complicated task.

WML See *Wireless Markup Language*.

word-processing software Programs used to create and edit written documents such as papers, letters, and résumés.

word size The number of bits a computer can work with at a time.

World Wide Web (WWW or Web) The part of the Internet used the most. What distinguishes the Web from the rest of the Internet is (1) its use of common communication protocols (such as Transmission Control Protocol/Internet Protocol, or TCP/IP) and special languages (such as the HyperText Markup Language, or HTML) that enable different computers to talk to each other and display information in compatible formats, and (2) its use of special links (called hyperlinks) that enable users to jump from one place to another in the Web.

worm A program that attempts to travel between systems through network connections to spread infections. Worms can run independently of host file execution and are active in spreading themselves.

WWW See *World Wide Web*.

X

XHTML See *Extensible HyperText Markup Language*.

XML See *Extensible Markup Language*.

Z

Zip disk A disk that resembles a floppy disk but is slightly wider and thicker; these disks are becoming legacy technology.

zombie A computer that is controlled by a hacker who uses it to launch attacks on other computer systems.

Index

Credits

Chapter 1

Chapter opener	Todd Davidson/Getty Images/Stock Illustration Source
Figure 1.1	www.CartoonStock.com
Figure 1.2	David Young-Wolff/PhotoEdit Inc.
Figure 1.3a	PRNewsFoto/D-Link Systems/AP Wide World Photos
Figure 1.3b	SanDisk Corporation
Figure 1.3c	Handout/MCT/Newscom
Figure 1.3d	Apple/Splash News/Newscom
Figure 1.3e	Reprinted with permission from Microsoft Corporation
Figure 1.3f	Belkin International, Inc.
Figure 1.4a	Photodisc/Getty Images
Figure 1.4b	Photo by Jim and Mary Whitmer
Figure 1.4c	Mary Kate Denny/PhotoEdit Inc.
Figure 1.5	Courtesy of Michael Koratich
Figure 1.6	Yoshikazu Tsuno/Agence France Presse/Getty Images
Figure 1.7a	Camille Utterback, "Untitled 5", from the "External Measures" series
Figure 1.7b	Camille Utterback, "Untitled 5", from the "External Measures" series
Figure 1.7c	Camille Utterback, "Untitled 5", from the "External Measures" series
Figure 1.8	Take 2 Games
Figure 1.10a	toy Alan King/Alamy Images
Figure 1.10b	Panasonic Corporation of North America
Figure 1.10c	Philips Consumer Electronics
Figure 1.12	Sara Krulwich/The New York Times
Figure 1.13a	©Digital Art/CORBIS All Rights Reserved
Figure 1.13b	Polhemus/Fast Scan
Figure 1.14a	Bill Pugliano/Getty Images, Inc.
Figure 1.14b	Olaf Doering/Alamy Images
Figure 1.15 a, b, c, d	Ninth Judicial Circuit Court of Florida
Figure 1.16	ColorBlind Images/Blend Images, LLC
Figure 1.18	Photo courtesy of METI ©METI
Figure 1.19	Ralph Hutchings/Getty Images Inc. Visuals Unlimited
Figure 1.20a	©2008 Intuitive Surgical, Inc.
Figure 1.20b	©2008 Intuitive Surgical, Inc.
Figure 1.21	Courtesy of Dr. Peter Fromherz/Max Planck Insitute of Biochemistry
Figure 1.22	Reuters/Eriko Sugita/Landov Media
Figure 1.23	Courtesy of Ilia Iankov Roussev, Ph.D.
Figure 1.24	Crew Creative
Figure 1.25	Interactive Sports Technologies
Figure 1.26	Science VU/NASA/ARC/Visuals Unlimited
Figure 1.27	©Y. Shirai, Rice University
Figure 1.28	Toshiyuki Aizawa/Corbis/Reuters America LLC
Figure 1.29	SparkFun Electronics
Figure 1.30	Gerald Herbert/AP Wide World Photos
Figure 1.31	Hugh Sitton/Corbis Zefa Collection

Technology in Focus: The History of the PC

Figure 1	Heinz Nixdorf Museums Forum/AP Wide World Photos
Figure 2a	Diana Walker/Getty Images, Inc. - Getty News
Figure 2b	©Roger Ressmeyer/CORBIS All Rights Reserved
Figure 3	SSPL/The Image Works
Figure 4	Roger Ressmeyer/Corbis
Figure 6	Jerry Mason/SPL/Photo Researchers, Inc.
Figure 7	Photo Courtesy of The Computer History Museum
Figure 8	Photo Courtesy of The Computer History Museum
Figure 9	Roberto Brosan/Getty Images/Time Life Pictures

Figure 10	©Doug Wilson/CORBIS All Rights Reserved
Figure 11	Daniel Bricklin
Figure 13	Photo Courtesy of The Computer History Museum
Figure 14	SSPL/The Image Works
Figure 15	©Historical Picture Archive/CORBIS
Figure 16	Photo Courtesy of The Computer History Museum
Figure 17	Photo Courtesy of The Computer History Museum
Figure 18	Ames Laboratory
Figure 19	U.S. Naval Historical Center Photography
Figure 20	Photo Courtesy of The Computer History Museum
Figure 21	Intel Corporation Pressroom Photo Archives

Chapter 2

Chapter opener	B2M Productions/Getty Images-Digital Vision
Figure 2.1	©Chuck Savage/CORBIS All Rights Reserved
Figure 2.4c	Ergodex
Figure 2.5	Martin Meissner/AP Wide World Photos
Figure 2.7	Paul Sakuma/AP Wide World Photos
Figure 2.11	©2008 Logitech. All rights reserved. Image used with permission from Logitech
Figure 2.12	EPOS
Figure 2.13	Logitech Inc.
Figure 2.14	Mtech Marketing Communications
Figure 2.15	Bennet/The Christian Science Publishing Society
Figure 2.17	P-59 Photos/Alamy Images
Figure 2.18	Judith Collins/Alamy Images
Figure 2.19a	Cherry Blossom Bonsai
Figure 2.19b	Canon U.S.A., Inc.

Figure 2.20	Courtesy Xerox Corporation
Figure 2.21	Newscom
Figure 2.22	Photo courtesy of XEROX Corporate Public Relations
Figure 2.26a	Dell, Inc.
Figure 2.26b	Apple Computer, Inc.
Figure 2.28	Microsoft product screen shot(s) reprinted with permission from Microsoft Corporation
Figure 2.29	Microsoft product screen shot(s) reprinted with permission from Microsoft Corporation
Figure 2.30b	Seagate Technology, Inc.
Figure 2.31a	SanDisk Corporation
Figure 2.31b	Manic Photos/Alamy Images
Figure 2.30e	Sony Electronics, Inc./Newscom
Figure 2.33	Courtesy of International Business Machines Corporation. Unauthorized use not permitted
Figure 2.35	Courtesy of International Business Machines Corporation. Unauthorized use not permitted
Figure 2.38	Courtesy of Grahl IndustriesInc.
Figure 2.39a	PhotoDisc/Getty Images, Inc. - PhotoDisc
Figure 2.39b	3M Corporation
Figure 2.41	Universal Display Corporation
Figure 2.42	Myvu Corporation

Chapter 3

Chapter opener	OPTE Project
Figure 3.1a	Apple Computer, Inc.
Figure 3.1b	Courtesy Park City Mountain Resort
Figure 3.1c	ebay.com
Figure 3.1d	Microsoft product screen shot(s) reprinted with permission from Microsoft Corporation
Figure 3.1e	Microsoft product screen shot(s) reprinted with permission from Microsoft Corporation

Figure 3.2	CarolinaAdvertising.com
Figure 3.4	Podcast.com
Figure 3.5	Gizmodo.com
Figure 3.6	Google.com
Figure 3.7a	Myrleen Ferguson Cate/PhotoEdit Inc.
Figure 3.7b	Dwayne Newton/PhotoEdit Inc.
Figure 3.7c	David Young-Wolff/PhotoEdit Inc.
Figure 3.8a	Getty Images
Figure 3.8b	Getty Images
Figure 3.9	Microsoft product screen shot(s) reprinted with permission from Microsoft Corporation
Figure 3.11	©Childnet International. All rights reserved
Figure 3.12 a, b, c	adobe.com
Figure 3.12d	Apple Corporation, Inc.
Figure 3.12e	Real.com
Figure 3.12f	adobe.com
Figure 3.12g	Microsoft product screen shot(s) reprinted with permission from Microsoft Corporation
Figure 3.13a	MySpace.com
Figure 3.13b	Facebook.com
Figure 3.13c	Friendster.com
Figure 3.14	Harleysville Savings Bank
Figure 3.15	Yahoo.com
Figure 3.16	Microsoft product screen shot(s) reprinted with permission from Microsoft Corporation
Figure 3.17	Microsoft product screen shot(s) reprinted with permission from Microsoft Corporation
Figure 3.18	AdAware/Lavasoft.com
Figure 3.19	Google Inc.
Figure 3.23	Yahoo.com
Figure 3.24	BusinessWeek.com
Figure 3.26	www.lli.org. All material copyright Librarian's Internet Index

Figure 3.29	Google Inc.
Figure 3.30	Hemera Technologies/AbleStock.com/ Jupiter Images Royalty Free
Figure 3.31	Courtesy of www.istockphoto.com
Figure 3.32	Sierra Wireless, Inc.

Technology in Focus: Ethics

Chapter opener 1	Jack Hollingsworth/PhotoDisc/Getty Images
Chapter opener 2	Image Source Pink/Alamy Images Royalty Free
Chapter opener 3	©Wojtek Wojtowicz/Courtesy of www.istockphoto.com
Chapter opener 4	©Kasia Biel/Courtesy of www.istockphoto.com
Chapter opener 5	Thinkstock/Corbis Royalty Free
Figure 2	©Anton Seleznev/Courtesy of www.istockphoto.com
Figure 3a	©Ryan McVay/PhotoDisc, Inc.
Figure 3b	Henning Christoph/DAS FOTOARCHIV/Peter Arnold, Inc.
Figure 3c	Jonathan Kirn/Stock Connection
Figure 3d	Sharie Kennedy/CORBIS- NY
Figure 5	©Neal Aspinall/Images.com
Figure 8b	istockphoto.com
Figure 10	Courtesy of www.istockphoto.com
Figure 12	Courtesy of www.istockphoto.com

Chapter 4

Chapter opener	©Digital Art/CORBIS All Rights Reserved
Figure 4.6a	Microsoft product screen shot(s) reprinted with permission from Microsoft Corporation
Figure 4.6b	OpenOffice
Figure 4.6c	Zoho.com
Figure 4.9a, b, c	Apple Computer, Inc.

Figure 4.10a	©2004 with express permission from Adobe Systems Incorporated
Figure 4.10b	Avanquest
Figure 4.10c	Reprinted with permission from Microsoft Corporation
Figure 4.10d	Corel
Figure 4.10e	Sun Microsystems, Inc.
Figure 4.10f	Courtesy of International Business Machines Corporation. Unauthorized use not permitted
Figure 4.12	Intuit Turbox Tax
Figure 4.13a	©Michael Keller/CORBIS All Rights Reserved
Figure 4.14	Wesabe.com
Figure 4.16	BLUE Images/Alamy Images
Figure 4.17	Adobe Photshop Elements
Figure 4.18	Apple Corporation, Inc.
Figure 4.19	Apple Corporation, Inc.
Figure 4.20	Colin Young-Wolff/PhotoEdit Inc.
Figure 4.21	Blackboard, Inc.
Figure 4.22	Microsoft product screen shot(s) reprinted with permission from Microsoft Corporation
Figure 4.25a - c	Lewis-Global Public Relations
Figure 4.27	Alamy Images
Figure 4.28	Tucows.com

Chapter 5

Chapter opener	Creatas Images/Jupiter Images Royalty Free
Figure 5.2a	Hugh Threlfall/Alamy Images
Figure 5.2b	NASA/John F. Kennedy Space Center
Figure 5.2c	Henny Ray Abrams/Corbis/Reuters America LLC
Figure 5.2d	White Box Robotics
Figure 5.3	AP Wide World Photos
Figure 5.6	Linspire.com
Figure 5.7	©2009 with express permission from Adobe Systems Incorporated

Figure 5.9	Yahoo.com
Figure 5.10	Fuse Project
Figure 5.11	Racepoint Group for One Laptop Per Child
Figure 5.12	Microsoft product box shot(s) reprinted with permission from Microsoft Corporation
Figure 5.18	Microsoft product screen shot(s) reprinted with permission from Microsoft Corporation

Technology in Focus: Computing Alternatives

Figure 3a	Marilyn Conway/Photographer's Choice/Getty Images
Figure 11a	Apple Computer, Inc.
Figure 11b	Hugh Threlfall/Alamy Images
Figure 11c	Roy McMahon/Corbis Royalty Free
Figure Inset	Marilyn Conway/Photographer's Choice/Getty Images

Chapter 6

Chapter opener	Corbis Royalty Free
Figure 6.1	Intel.com
Figure 6.4	Intel Corporation Pressroom Photo Archives
Figure 6.6	Dell, Inc.
Figure 6.8	Microsoft product screen shot(s) reprinted with permission from Microsoft Corporation
Figure 6.10	Microsoft product screen shot(s) reprinted with permission from Microsoft Corporation
Figure 6.13a	Tony Freeman/PhotoEdit Inc.
Figure 6.13b	PhotoEdit Inc.
Figure 6.14	Daisy Images/Alamy Images Royalty Free
Figure 6.15	Microsoft product screen shot(s) reprinted with permission from Microsoft Corporation

Figure 6.19a	Swiss Army Brands, Inc.
Figure 6.19b	EdgeTech Corp
Figure 6.19d	EdgeTech Corp
Figure 6.19e	MXI Security
Figure 6.19f	Lexar Media, USA
Figure 6.23	Seagate Technology, Inc.
Figure 6.24	PRNewsFoto/NVIDIA Corporation/AP Wide World Photos
Figure 6.27	Mac's Time Machine/YouTube.com
Figure 6.29	Creative Labs, Inc.
Figure 6.31a	PhotoEdit Inc.
Figure 6.31b	P-59 Photos/Alamy Images
Figure 6.31c	PhotoEdit Inc.
Figure 6.31d	Twilight Images/Alamy Images Royalty Free
Figure 6.31e	Manic Photos/Alamy Images
Figure 6.31f	Twilight Images/Alamy Images
Figure 6.32	Digital Vision/Robert Harding World Imagery
Figure 6.34	Saitek Industries
Figure 6.35	Look Twice/Alamy Images
Figure 6.36	Apple Corporation, Inc.

Chapter 7

Chapter opener	Corbis Royalty Free
Figure 7.2	Microsoft product screen shot(s) reprinted with permission from Microsoft Corporation
Figure 7.10a	Courtesy Western Digital Corporation
Figure 7.10b	Courtesy Western Digital Corporation
Figure 7.14a	Twilight Images/Alamy Images
Figure 7.14b	Twilight Images/Alamy Images
Figure 7.16	Microsoft product screen shot(s) reprinted with permission from Microsoft Corporation
Figure 7.17	Microsoft product screen shot(s) reprinted with permission from Microsoft Corporation

Figure 7.18	Netgear.com
Figure 7.19	Kevin Siers. ©2000 The Charlotte Observer. KING FEATURES SYNDI-CATE
Figure 7.29	Symantec-Norton
Figure 7.30	Symantec-Norton
Figure 7.31	Microsoft product screen shot(s) reprinted with permission from Microsoft Corporation

Technology in Focus: Protecting Your Computer and Backing Up Your Data

Figure 3	American Power Conversion Corporation
Figure 4	American Power Conversion Corporation
Figure 10	Mozilla.com
Figure 11	Ironkey
Figure 14a	SecuGen Corporation
Figure 14b	American Power Conversion Corporation

Chapter 8

Chapter opener	©Donna Day/CORBIS All Rights Reserved
Figure 8.1a	Dell, Inc.
Figure 8.1b	Motorola
Figure 8.1c	Apple Computer, Inc.
Figure 8.5	OpenMoko, Inc.
Figure 8.6c	©Rolf Bruderer/CORBIS All Rights Reserved
Figure 8.6a	Courtesy of AT&T Archives and History Center, Warren, NJ
Figure 8.6b	Helio Ocean by Virgin Mobile
Figure 8.7	Reuters/Steve Marcus/Landov Media
Figure 8.9	Alex Segre/Alamy Images
Figure 8.10a	Creative Labs, Inc.

Technology in Focus: Digital Entertainment

Chapter 9

Technology in Focus: Careers in IT

Figure 5d	©Gabe Palmer/CORBIS All Rights Reserved
Figure 5e	©Mark A. Johnson/CORBIS All Rights Reserved
Figure 11	Corbis Royalty Free

Chapter 10

Chapter opener	©Tomek Olbinski/Images.com / Corbis
Figure 10.3	PHOTOTAKE Inc./Alamy Images
Figure 10.20	Getty Images - Stockbyte, Royalty Free
Figure 10.20a	Apple Computer, Inc.
Figure 10.22	©Roger Ressmeyer/CORBIS All Rights Reserved
Figure 10.28	Luis Guillermo Restrepo Rivas
Figure 10.29	Crystal XP.net

Chapter 11

Chapter opener	Matthias Kulka/Corbis Zefa Collection
Figure 11.3a	Corbis Royalty Free
Figure 11.3b	©John Henley Photography/CORBIS All Rights Reserved
Figure 11.3c	©Jon Feingersh/CORBIS All Rights Reserved
Figure 11.3d	©Jose Luis Palaez, Inc./CORBIS All Rights Reserved
Figure 11.10	Yahoo
Figure 11.18	FBI Office of Public Affairs
Figure 11.22	State of Pennsylvania: tre.state.pa.us
Figure 11.26	Oracle.com
Figure 11.29a	©Reed Kaestner/CORBIS All Rights Reserved

Figure 11.29b	©LWA-JDC/CORBIS All Rights Reserved
Figure 11.30a	©Waren Morgan/CORBIS All Rights Reserved
Figure 11.30b	©Warren Morgan/CORBIS All Rights Reserved
Figure 11.30c	©Paul Buron/CORBIS All Rights Reserved
Figure 11.30d	©Tom & Dee Ann McCarthy/CORBIS All Rights Reserved
Figure 11.31a	©Norbert Schaefer/CORBIS All Rights Reserved
Figure 11.31b	Corbis Royalty Free
Figure 11.31c	Corbis Royalty Free
Figure 11.31d	©CORBIS All Rights Reserved
Figure 11.34	Clay Bennett/The Christian Science Publishing Society

Chapter 12

Chapter opener	©Cameron Beck/Images.com/Corbis
Figure 12.25	Google Inc.

Chapter 13

Chapter opener	CORBIS Images.com
Figure 13.2	Doug Armand/Stone/Getty Images
Figure 13.10a	Corbis/Bettmann
Figure 13.10b1	Tan Kian Khoon/Shutterstock
Figure 13.16	BLUE Images/Alamy Images
Figure 13.21a	©Paul Buron/CORBIS All Rights Reserved
Figure 13.20	©Brendan McDermid/epa/CORBIS All Rights Reserved

SINGLE PC LICENSE AGREEMENT AND LIMITED WARRANTY

READ THIS LICENSE CAREFULLY BEFORE OPENING THIS PACKAGE. BY OPENING THIS PACKAGE, YOU ARE AGREEING TO THE TERMS AND CONDITIONS OF THIS LICENSE. IF YOU DO NOT AGREE, DO NOT OPEN THE PACKAGE. PROMPTLY RETURN THE UNOPENED PACKAGE AND ALL ACCOMPANYING ITEMS TO THE PLACE YOU OBTAINED THEM. *THESE TERMS APPLY TO ALL LICENSED SOFTWARE ON THE DISK EXCEPT THAT THE TERMS FOR USE OF ANY SHAREWARE OR FREEWARE ON THE DISKETTES ARE AS SET FORTH IN THE ELECTRONIC LICENSE LOCATED ON THE DISK:*

1. GRANT OF LICENSE and OWNERSHIP: The enclosed computer programs ("Software") are licensed, not sold, to you by Prentice-Hall, Inc. ("We" or the "Company") and in consideration of your purchase or adoption of the accompanying Company textbooks and/or other materials, and your agreement to these terms. We reserve any rights not granted to you. You own only the disk(s) but we and/or our licensors own the Software itself. This license allows you to use and display your copy of the Software on a single computer (i.e., with a single CPU) at a single location for academic use only, so long as you comply with the terms of this Agreement. You may make one copy for back up, or transfer your copy to another CPU, provided that the Software is usable on only one computer.

2. RESTRICTIONS: You may not transfer or distribute the Software or documentation to anyone else. Except for backup, you may not copy the documentation or the Software. You may not network the Software or otherwise use it on more than one computer or computer terminal at the same time. You may not reverse engineer, disassemble, decompile, modify, adapt, translate, or create derivative works based on the Software or the Documentation. You may be held legally responsible for any copying or copyright infringement which is caused by your failure to abide by the terms of these restrictions.

3. TERMINATION: This license is effective until terminated. This license will terminate automatically without notice from the Company if you fail to comply with any provisions or limitations of this license. Upon termination, you shall destroy the Documentation and all copies of the Software. All provisions of this Agreement as to limitation and disclaimer of warranties, limitation of liability, remedies or damages, and our ownership rights shall survive termination.

4. DISCLAIMER OF WARRANTY: THE COMPANY AND ITS LICENSORS MAKE NO WARRANTIES ABOUT THE SOFTWARE, WHICH IS PROVIDED "AS-IS." IF THE DISK IS DEFECTIVE IN MATERIALS OR WORKMANSHIP, YOUR ONLY REMEDY IS TO RETURN IT TO THE COMPANY WITHIN 30 DAYS FOR REPLACEMENT UNLESS THE COMPANY DETERMINES IN GOOD FAITH THAT THE DISK HAS BEEN MISUSED OR IMPROPERLY INSTALLED, REPAIRED, ALTERED OR DAMAGED. THE COMPANY DISCLAIMS ALL WARRANTIES, EXPRESS OR IMPLIED, INCLUDING WITHOUT LIMITATION, THE IMPLIED WARRANTIES OF MERCHANTABILITY AND FITNESS FOR A PARTICULAR PURPOSE. THE COMPANY DOES NOT WARRANT, GUARANTEE OR MAKE ANY REPRESENTATION REGARDING THE ACCURACY, RELIABILITY, CURRENTNESS, USE, OR RESULTS OF USE, OF THE SOFTWARE.

5. LIMITATION OF REMEDIES AND DAMAGES: IN NO EVENT, SHALL THE COMPANY OR ITS EMPLOYEES, AGENTS, LICENSORS OR CONTRACTORS BE LIABLE FOR ANY INCIDENTAL, INDIRECT, SPECIAL OR CONSEQUENTIAL DAMAGES ARISING OUT OF OR IN CONNECTION WITH THIS LICENSE OR THE SOFTWARE, INCLUDING, WITHOUT LIMITATION, LOSS OF USE, LOSS OF DATA, LOSS OF INCOME OR PROFIT, OR OTHER LOSSES SUSTAINED AS A RESULT OF INJURY TO ANY PERSON, OR LOSS OF OR DAMAGE TO PROPERTY, OR CLAIMS OF THIRD PARTIES, EVEN IF THE COMPANY OR AN AUTHORIZED REPRESENTATIVE OF THE COMPANY HAS BEEN ADVISED OF THE POSSIBILITY OF SUCH DAMAGES. SOME JURISDICTIONS DO NOT ALLOW THE LIMITATION OF DAMAGES IN CERTAIN CIRCUMSTANCES, SO THE ABOVE LIMITATIONS MAY NOT ALWAYS APPLY.

6. GENERAL: THIS AGREEMENT SHALL BE CONSTRUED IN ACCORDANCE WITH THE LAWS OF THE UNITED STATES OF AMERICA AND THE STATE OF NEW YORK, APPLICABLE TO CONTRACTS MADE IN NEW YORK, AND SHALL BENEFIT THE COMPANY, ITS AFFILIATES AND ASSIGNEES. This Agreement is the complete and exclusive statement of the agreement between you and the Company and supersedes all proposals, prior agreements, oral or written, and any other communications between you and the company or any of its representatives relating to the subject matter. If you are a U.S. Government user, this Software is licensed with "restricted rights" as set forth in subparagraphs (a)-(d) of the Commercial Computer-Restricted Rights clause at FAR 52.227-19 or in subparagraphs (c)(1)(ii) of the Rights in Technical Data and Computer Software clause at DFARS 252.227-7013, and similar clauses, as applicable.

Should you have any questions concerning this agreement or if you wish to contact the Company for any reason, please contact in writing:

Multimedia Production
Higher Education Division
Prentice-Hall, Inc.
1 Lake Street
Upper Saddle River NJ 07458